INSTRUCTOR'S WRAPAROUND EDITION

PRINCIPLES OF BUSINESS

9e

Les R. Dlabay

James L. Burrow

Brad A. Kleindl

SOUTH-WESTERN
CENGAGE Learning

Australia • Brazil • Japan • Korea • Mexico • Singapore • Spain • United Kingdom • United States

SOUTH-WESTERN
CENGAGE Learning™

Instructor's Wraparound Edition
Principles of Business, Ninth Edition

Les R. Dlabay, James L. Burrow, Brad A. Kleindl

SVP, GM Skills & Global Product Management: Dawn Gerrain

Product Director: Matthew Seeley

Senior Director, Development: Marah Bellegarde

Product Manager: Nicole Robinson

Product Development Manager: Juliet Steiner

Sr. Content Developer: Karen Caldwell

Consulting Editor: Hyde Park Publishing Services

Product Marketing Manager: Kelsey Hagan

Sr. Content Project Manager: Martha Conway

Manufacturing Planner: Kevin Kluck

Production Service/Compositor: SPi Global

Sr. Art Director: Michelle Kunkler

Cover and Internal Designer: Tippy McIntosh

Cover Image: iStock/alphaspirit

Design Images: Unit & Part openers blue and yellow graphic: Thaiview/Shutterstock.com; Camera lens: ildogesto/Shutterstock.com; Net Knowledge web search bar: mileswork/Fotolia LLC; Work as a Team: sellingpix/Shutterstock.com; Business Insights: Rawpixel/Shutterstock.com; FYI: Oleksiy Mark/Shutterstock.com; Life/Work Skills: michaeljung/Shutterstock.com; Assessments graphics: Thaiview/Shutterstock.com; Doing Business In: Art Painter/Shutterstock.com; Question of Ethics: Rawpixel/Shutterstock.com

Intellectual Property Analyst: Kyle Cooper

Intellectual Property Project Manager: Lisa Brown

Photo Researcher: Darren Wright

Instructor's Edition ISBN: 978-1-305-65305-4
Student Edition ISBN: 978-1-305-65303-0

Cengage Learning
20 Channel Center Street
Boston, MA 02210
USA

Cengage Learning is a leading provider of customized learning solutions with employees residing in nearly 40 different countries and sales in more than 125 countries around the world. Find your local representative at **www.cengage.com.**

Cengage Learning products are represented in Canada by Nelson Education, Ltd.

For your course and learning solutions, visit **ngl.cengage.com.**

Visit our company website at **www.cengage.com**

Printed in the United States of America
Print Number: 01 Print Year: 2015

ABOUT the AUTHORS

Les R. Dlabay

Les R. Dlabay, EdD, is a Professor of Business in the Department of Economics, Business, and Finance at Lake Forest College in Illinois. He has taught more than 30 different business courses in high school, community college, university, teacher preparation, and adult education programs. Dr. Dlabay has presented more than 300 teacher workshops and seminars emphasizing interactive learning strategies, including team projects and field research activities. His hobbies include collecting cereal packages from more than 100 countries and banknotes from 200 countries. He uses these collections to teach economic, cultural, and political aspects of global business. In an effort to prepare students to do business in varied economic settings, Professor Dlabay makes extensive use of class assignments related to business development and microfinance for poverty alleviation. He serves on the boards of Bright Hope International, an organization which emphasizes microenterprise development through microfinance programs, and Andean Aid, which provides tutoring and educational services to school-age children in Colombia and Venezuela. His research includes alternative financial services in informal economic settings for youth enterprise and women empowerment.

James L. Burrow

James L. Burrow, PhD, has a background in marketing and human resource development. During his career he was a university faculty member in Iowa, Wisconsin, Nebraska, and North Carolina teaching marketing, marketing education, and human resource development. In addition, he worked with businesses and other organizations as a consultant on marketing and performance-improvement strategies. He recently retired from the faculty of North Carolina State University. Dr. Burrow holds a BA and MA from the University of Northern Iowa and a PhD from the University of Nebraska.

Brad A. Kleindl

Brad A. Kleindl, PhD, is dean of the School of Business at Park University in Kansas City, Missouri. He previously served as dean and professor of marketing of The Robert W. Plaster College of Business Administration at Missouri Southern State University. He has authored and co-authored six books and more than 60 articles and conference papers. His books have been translated into both Chinese and Russian. Dr. Kleindl has served twice as a Senior Fulbright Scholar, during 2007 in Austria and 2003 in South Africa. He has taught courses in consumer behavior, marketing research, principles of marketing, Internet marketing, international marketing, and has presented at conferences and industry meetings across the United States, Europe, Africa, and Asia.

BRIEF CONTENTS

CONTENTS

CHAPTER 7

Management and Leadership 146

Features

Assessment and Review

CHAPTER 8

Human Resources, Culture, and Diversity 170

Features

Assessment and Review

CHAPTER 11
Business and Technology 260

Features

Assessment and Review

CHAPTER 12
Financial Management 286

Features

Assessment and Review

RENA

SOLD
FOR
SAL

CHAPTER 17

Banking and Financial Services 424

CHAPTER 18

Consumer Credit 452

CHAPTER 19

CHAPTER 20

A Strong Foundation for Business Success!

Principles of Business, 9e

This comprehensive introductory business text provides complete instruction in business concepts and skills students need in today's competitive environment. This market-leading text offers extensive coverage in major business concepts in the areas of Finance, Marketing, Operations, and Management. Students will gain valuable information and skills for the workplace, as well as preparation for success in competitive events.

Principles of Business is the foundation course for the following Career Clusters pathways:

- Business, Management & Administration
- Finance
- Marketing

THE MOST COMPREHENSIVE

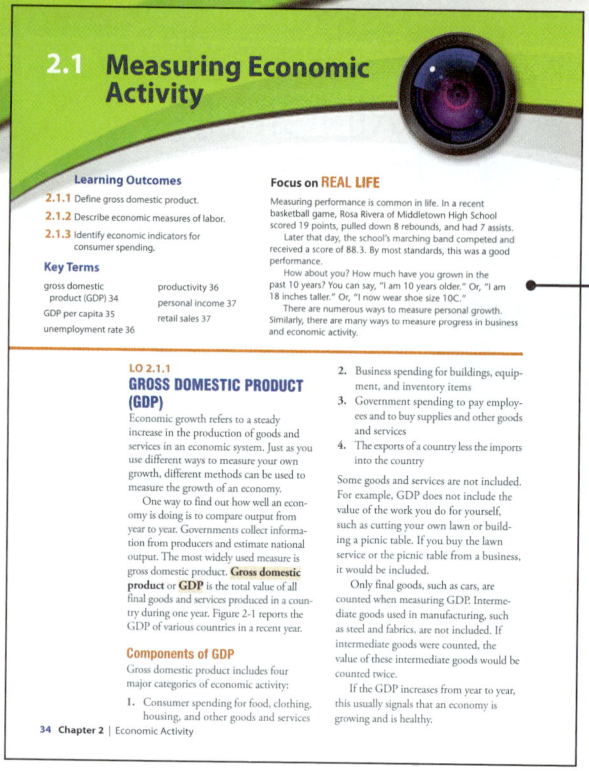

2.1 Measuring Economic Activity

Learning Outcomes

2.1.1 Define gross domestic product.
2.1.2 Describe economic measures of labor.
2.1.3 Identify economic indicators for consumer spending.

Key Terms

gross domestic product (GDP) 34
GDP per capita 35
unemployment rate 36
productivity 36
personal income 37
retail sales 37

Focus on REAL LIFE

Measuring performance is common in life. In a recent basketball game, Rosa Rivera of Middletown High School scored 19 points, pulled down 8 rebounds, and had 7 assists.

Later that day, the school's marching band competed and received a score of 88.3. By most standards, this was a good performance.

How about you? How much have you grown in the past 10 years? You can say, "I am 10 years older." Or, "I am 18 inches taller." Or, "I now wear shoe size 10C."

There are numerous ways to measure personal growth. Similarly, there are many ways to measure progress in business and economic activity.

LO 2.1.1

GROSS DOMESTIC PRODUCT (GDP)

Economic growth refers to a steady increase in the production of goods and services in an economic system. Just as you use different ways to measure your own growth, different methods can be used to measure the growth of an economy.

One way to find out how well an economy is doing is to compare output from year to year. Governments collect information from producers and estimate national output. The most widely used measure is gross domestic product. **Gross domestic product** or **GDP** is the total value of all final goods and services produced in a country during one year. Figure 2-1 reports the GDP of various countries in a recent year.

Components of GDP

Gross domestic product includes four major categories of economic activity:

1. Consumer spending for food, clothing, housing, and other goods and services
2. Business spending for buildings, equipment, and inventory items
3. Government spending to pay employees and to buy supplies and other goods and services
4. The exports of a country less the imports into the country

Some goods and services are not included. For example, GDP does not include the value of the work you do for yourself, such as cutting your own lawn or building a picnic table. If you buy the lawn service or the picnic table from a business, it would be included.

Only final goods, such as cars, are counted when measuring GDP. Intermediate goods used in manufacturing, such as steel and fabrics, are not included. If intermediate goods were counted, the value of these intermediate goods would be counted twice.

If the GDP increases from year to year, this usually signals that an economy is growing and is healthy.

34 Chapter 2 | Economic Activity

Business Insight

Cleantech: Energy Alternatives and Environmentally Friendly Products

The phrase *cleantech* refers to goods and services that are environmentally friendly. It is also part of the name of an organization that promotes clean technology among investors, entrepreneurs, and service providers.

The Cleantech Group provides a network of information, online services, and educational events to promote innovations that do not harm the environment. The group's emphasis is on balancing profit-making and environment-friendly business activities. Cleantech is not just interested in being socially responsible. It also recognizes the need for financial success.

Cleantech attempts to encourage and publicize investment and development for various *clean*, or environment-friendly, technologies. The companies in the Cleantech network are involved in a wide range of products, services, and processes designed to provide superior performance at lower costs. At the same time, these business activities must reduce or eliminate environmental concerns in an effort to improve the quality of life.

A concern for both companies and investors is that the "cleantech" label is often used for products and services that do meet the standards of the Cleantech Group.

Many organizations attempt to attract investors by calling their enterprise "cleantech" even though their business activities are not improving the environment.

Think Critically

1. How do consumers, businesses, and the economy benefit from cleantech activities?
2. What concerns might be associated with cleantech companies?
3. Conduct library or Internet research to obtain examples of various environment-friendly products and services.

Focus on Real Life

relates to student life to get them thinking about the topics in the lesson.

Business Insight

focuses on current technology and e-commerce issues in the business world.

PLANNING A CAREER IN . . .

BUSINESS DEVELOPMENT

The desire to provide food, water, health care, education, and financial services to the billions of people in need around the world is one reason to choose a career in business and economic development. A career in this field could involve a variety of employment opportunities—some close to home and some far away. If you have the interest and obtain the required training, you could be an organization executive, a government research director, or a field training consultant. Each of these jobs contributes to economic growth.

As you study various business topics, your awareness of economic activities will expand. Many business development positions are related to employment in government, technology, research, engineering, health care, nutrition, marketing, and financial planning.

Every country in the world can benefit from efforts to enhance its economic development and improve the quality of life for its citizens. Your decision to pursue a career in business development will empower you to help people plan, start, and operate small business enterprises in communities in your neighborhood and around the world.

Related Job Titles

- Economist
- Transportation Engineer
- Urban and Regional Planner
- Field Researcher
- Statistician
- Budget Analyst
- Microloan Officer

Analyze Career Opportunities in . . .
BUSINESS DEVELOPMENT

Use library and Internet resources to learn more about careers in business and economic development. Choose one of the job titles listed in the box above and answer the following questions.

1. What is the employment outlook for careers in this field?
2. Is this a career that interests you? What can you do now to help prepare yourself for this career?

What it's like to work as a . . . Field Business Consultant

As the sun rises over the mountains, hundreds of farmers are already on the job. Their goal is to harvest enough crops to generate income to provide for the basic needs of their families. They use traditional farming methods that they learned from their ancestors.

In a nearby village, an international organization helps some of the people obtain oxen and farm equipment. These items allow the workers to double and triple their daily harvests.

Many government and private agencies work to help people improve their labor productivity. The use of new growing methods, machinery, and other agricultural techniques can provide families with more money for food, housing, clothing, school fees, and health care.

Funding for these improvements is often uncertain. Money may come from private investors or government grants and loans. Many organizations now offer microloans to poor people throughout the world. These loans allow people to start and expand their own businesses.

What about you? What aspects of working in business development interest you?

Planning a Career in...

features correlate to the 16 Career Clusters and present the education, training, work experience, and industry opportunities for a variety of business-related career paths.

CHECKPOINT

What are the four phases of the business cycle?

Checkpoint

allows students to assess their understanding at key points in each lesson.

BUSINESS COVERAGE AVAILABLE

A QUESTION OF ETHICS

Ethical Analysis Guidelines

Most business decisions are viewed in various ways. In some countries, people expect family members to be given jobs in a company before others. In other places, payments or gifts are expected before you are able to do business.

These and many other situations create ethical problems. *Ethics* are principles of right and wrong that guide personal and business decisions. When contemplating the ethics of business situations, consider using these three guidelines:

1. **Is the action legal?** Laws vary among states and in different countries. Most companies base international decisions on the laws in their home countries. When a conflict occurs, managers usually consider other factors, such as professional standards and the effect of the action on society.
2. **Does the action violate professional or company standards?** Professional or company standards will frequently exceed those required by the law. This helps to ensure that decisions will be in the best interest of both the company and the society in which it operates.
3. **Who is affected by the action and how?** An action may be legal and within professional or company standards. However, decision makers should also think about possible effects on employees, consumers, competitors, and the environment.

Think Critically

1. What are some examples of situations faced by workers and consumers that require ethical decisions?
2. Describe the effect on business activities if no ethical guidelines existed.
3. Research recent ethical situations that have been reported in the news. How have these situations affected workers, investors, and others?

A Question of Ethics provides a link between theory and the real world of business for various moral dilemmas.

Net Knowledge encourages students to use the Internet for business-related research.

NET KNOWLEDGE

Most businesses today recognize the importance of ethics and have developed a code of ethics for their employees. Those codes are often available on the company's website. Use the Internet to access and review several company codes of ethics. In your view, which codes provide effective guidance to employees and which do not? Use your review to aid in developing a sample code of ethics for a business that contains 8 to 10 statements.

DOING BUSINESS IN... SOUTH AFRICA

In 1994, South Africa celebrated the arrival of democracy. After decades of apartheid, the government policy that segregated blacks and other non-whites from the dominant whites, voting rights were extended to all citizens. Today, the country is often seen as a model for developing economies and emerging markets. South Africa is now one of the most multicultural countries in the world.

South Africa has the largest economy on the African continent. Its growth has been driven primarily by a strong financial and banking industry, as well as manufacturing. An historic focus on mining is subject to reforms due to outdated management and labor practices.

In 2010 South Africa joined BRICS, an association of five major growing economies—Brazil, Russia, India, China, and South Africa. Combined, the five BRICS nations make up about 40 percent of the world's population and 20 percent of all goods and services produced.

With an abundance of natural resources and a more progressive government, South Africa has become a prime location for foreign investment and trade. However, the government is under growing pressure to extend basic services, improve education, and offer more job opportunities to all of its citizens. About half the population lives below the poverty rate and unemployment remains above 25 percent. The Industrial Policy Action Plan has been instituted to overcome continuing inequalities in employment, business management, and business ownership. It has a goal of reducing poverty and increasing opportunities for a broader group of citizens. Government investments will provide additional social services, education, and new job creation. The goal is to add 5 million new jobs across a variety of industries by 2020. Since 2000, the illiteracy rate across the country has been reduced from more than 30 percent of the population to less than 20 percent.

South Africa has two economies. The major economy is concentrated in large cities and is dominated by large international businesses. It primarily benefits the educated and wealthy citizens. The second economy is the cash economy operated by small traders who serve middle- and low-income South Africans.

South Africa has 11 official languages reflecting many cultures. English is most widely used in business. Business and social interactions can vary dramatically based on the cultural heritage of the participants as well as rural/urban differences across the country.

South African foods are influenced by the many local, European, and Asian cultures that are part of the country's heritage. *Bredie* is traditional stew of vegetables and mutton. *Frikkadels* are little nutmeg-flavored hamburgers wrapped in cabbage and served with yellow rice.

Think Critically

1. What makes South Africa an attractive location for foreign investment?
2. How might the two different economies affect business?
3. Use library or Internet resources to obtain additional information about the history and current economic and social conditions of South Africa.

What do you see in this photograph that illustrates changes that have occurred in South Africa's economy and culture?

153

Doing Business in... highlights various countries and provides a basic knowledge of international business activities that are vital for living and working in the global economy.

ENGAGE STUDENT INTEREST

LIFE/WORK SKILLS

INFORMATION LITERACY

Research Skills

Your abilities are more than just the sum of your experiences. Whether the goal is to improve a business or your own performance, you need to make sound decisions based on the best information available. Research skills are needed to improve decision making.

Research is a systematic, objective study to establish facts and principles. The research process begins with a question or problem and results in a possible answer that can become the basis for further research.

Here are the steps to follow when conducting research.

Formulate a question. What is the problem you are facing or what is the issue you are trying to resolve? The question should be as specific as possible and relate to an important personal or business issue.

Gather and review information related to the question. Determine if others have studied the same problem and if they have reported on the results of their study. This step usually involves a careful search of library information, including books, magazines, and documents.

Separate fact from opinion. Effective research relies on objective data. The opinions of others may provide interesting ideas to consider but should not be relied on for answers to your question. Consider if the sources of information are credible and if the information provided is factual.

Ditty_about_summer/Shutterstock.com

Even with Internet access, why is it often necessary to use library resources to gather and review information related to your research question?

Propose a hypothesis. A hypothesis is a prediction about the answer to your research question. The hypothesis can be based on the information gathered, your experience, or your beliefs. You will conduct a study to gather information that will either support the hypothesis or determine that it is wrong.

Collect data to test the hypothesis. Researchers carefully design studies to gather information related to the question and hypothesis. The common methods of collecting data are surveys, observations, and experiments.

Analyze the data. After data has been collected, it is organized and then analyzed using statistical procedures. Careful review of the results of the data analysis will provide evidence to support or disprove the hypothesis.

Report the results. It is important that researchers document and report the results of their research. A well-organized and carefully written report will help others understand the research and repeat it or improve upon it. It will also provide evidence that the research was objective.

Put the research results into practice. You began the research process to answer a question or solve a problem. You need to apply what you learned and determine if what you learned makes a difference. No matter the results, you will want to continue to conduct research and study the research of others. It will help you make sound decisions and have confidence in your knowledge and abilities.

Think Critically

1. Why should you try to avoid basing your actions on opinions rather than facts?
2. Do you believe some questions can be answered by just gathering and reviewing existing information rather than collecting new data? Why or why not?

Work as a TEAM

Do you believe your needs are very similar to or quite different from those that your parents had when they were your age? As a team, prepare a list of five needs that you agree would be similar to those of your parents when they were young and a list of five needs that you agree would likely be different. Justify why your selections are needs rather than wants.

Work as a Team allows students to experience dynamics that enhance the learning process and learn the benefits and concerns of shared decision making.

Life/Work Skills exposes students to important, transferable soft skills used in nearly every business setting.

a. Visit the website of a company that produces a popular American product and locate information about its international operations. Obtain information about a product sold in several countries. Describe to the class how the company adapted the product or packaging in another country. Illustrate your talk with images from the website.

b. Locate a website with information about the culture of a country. Write a paragraph describing an element of the culture that the company might need to consider when doing business in that country.

c. Share the information you discovered in your research with a family member or friend. Ask the person for reactions about the company's global business activities.

Emerging Business Issues Event

FBLA-PBL · DECA · WinningEdge

One of the most striking changes in U.S. food and retailing over the past two decades has been the rise of private labels, also known as store brands. The term *private label* describes products manufactured for sale under a specific retailer's brand. They are often designed to compete against branded products, offering consumers a cheaper alternative to national brands. Though they were once considered knock-offs of name brands or even generic "no-name brands," private labels have become increasingly accepted by the public. Many consumers now consider private labels as acceptable alternatives to national brands. Private labels offer many benefits to both retailers and customers, driving the segment's rising popularity.

Each team of two or three members must conduct research to gather facts regarding private labels and the impact they have on retailers and consumers. Students should brainstorm the benefits and drawbacks of private labels to both retailers and customers.

Teams also should give examples of the most successful private label brands. Teams will be permitted to bring prepared materials, written or printed, on white 8 ½" by 11" paper or note cards. One 4" by 6" index card will be given to each participant and may be used during the preparation and presentation.

Each presentation may last no more than five minutes. Following each oral presentation, judges may conduct a five minute question and answer period during which the presenters should be prepared to defend their research.

Performance Indicators Evaluated

- Demonstrate sound research with the information gathered.
- Present the rationale in a clear and logical manner.
- Provide supporting information for each point made.
- Choose examples that are relevant to the audience.

You Will Be Evaluated on

- Organization of your oral presentation.
- Rationale of your presentation.
- Speaker responded to questions fully, knowledgeably, and without hesitation.

For more detailed information about performance indicators, go to the FBLA website.

Think Critically

1. What can name brands do to compete with private labels?
2. How do private labels differentiate themselves from national brands?

www.fbla-pbl.org

Winning Edge activities prepare students for DECA, FBLA, and BPA competitive events.

ASSESS STUDENT LEARNING

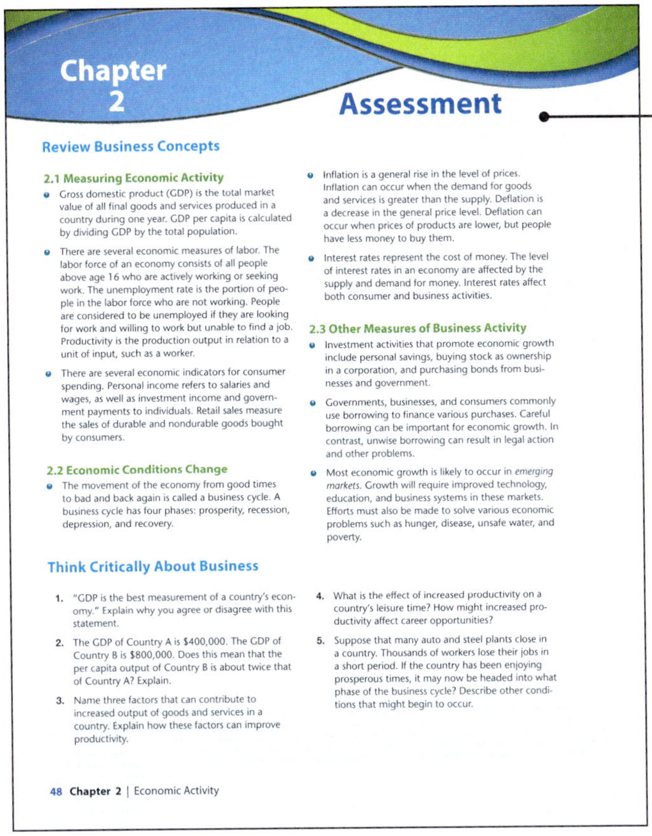

Chapter 2 Assessment

Review Business Concepts

2.1 Measuring Economic Activity

- Gross domestic product (GDP) is the total market value of all final goods and services produced in a country during one year. GDP per capita is calculated by dividing GDP by the total population.
- There are several economic measures of labor. The labor force of an economy consists of all people above age 16 who are actively working or seeking work. The unemployment rate is the portion of people in the labor force who are not working. People are considered to be unemployed if they are looking for work and willing to work but unable to find a job. Productivity is the production output in relation to a unit of input, such as a worker.
- There are several economic indicators for consumer spending. Personal income refers to salaries and wages, as well as investment income and government payments to individuals. Retail sales measure the sales of durable and nondurable goods bought by consumers.

2.2 Economic Conditions Change

- The movement of the economy from good times to bad and back again is called a business cycle. A business cycle has four phases: prosperity, recession, depression, and recovery.
- Inflation is a general rise in the level of prices. Inflation can occur when the demand for goods and services is greater than the supply. Deflation is a decrease in the general price level. Deflation can occur when prices of products are lower, but people have less money to buy them.
- Interest rates represent the cost of money. The level of interest rates in an economy are affected by the supply and demand for money. Interest rates affect both consumer and business activities.

2.3 Other Measures of Business Activity

- Investment activities that promote economic growth include personal savings, buying stock as ownership in a corporation, and purchasing bonds from businesses and government.
- Governments, businesses, and consumers commonly use borrowing to finance various purchases. Careful borrowing can be important for economic growth. In contrast, unwise borrowing can result in legal action and other problems.
- Most economic growth is likely to occur in *emerging markets*. Growth will require improved technology, education, and business systems in these markets. Efforts must also be made to solve various economic problems such as hunger, disease, unsafe water, and poverty.

Think Critically About Business

1. "GDP is the best measurement of a country's economy." Explain why you agree or disagree with this statement.
2. The GDP of Country A is $400,000. The GDP of Country B is $800,000. Does this mean that the per capita output of Country B is about twice that of Country A? Explain.
3. Name three factors that can contribute to increased output of goods and services in a country. Explain how these factors can improve productivity.
4. What is the effect of increased productivity on a country's leisure time? How might increased productivity affect career opportunities?
5. Suppose that many auto and steel plants close in a country. Thousands of workers lose their jobs in a short period. If the country has been enjoying prosperous times, it may now be headed into what phase of the business cycle? Describe other conditions that might begin to occur.

48 **Chapter 2** | Economic Activity

Review Business Concepts

reinforces business concepts.

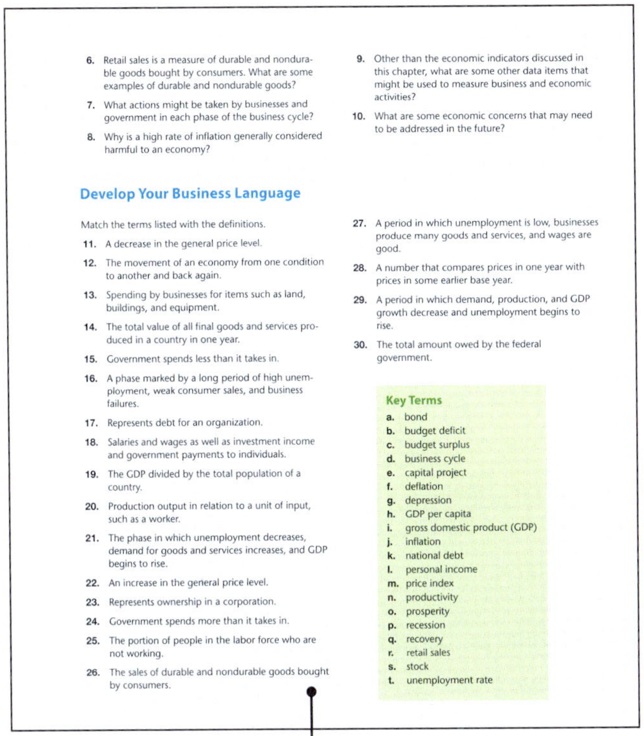

6. Retail sales is a measure of durable and nondurable goods bought by consumers. What are some examples of durable and nondurable goods?
7. What actions might be taken by businesses and government in each phase of the business cycle?
8. Why is a high rate of inflation generally considered harmful to an economy?
9. Other than the economic indicators discussed in this chapter, what are some other data items that might be used to measure business and economic activities?
10. What are some economic concerns that may need to be addressed in the future?

Develop Your Business Language

Match the terms listed with the definitions.

11. A decrease in the general price level.
12. The movement of an economy from one condition to another and back again.
13. Spending by businesses for items such as land, buildings, and equipment.
14. The total value of all final goods and services produced in a country in one year.
15. Government spends less than it takes in.
16. A phase marked by a long period of high unemployment, weak consumer sales, and business failures.
17. Represents debt for an organization.
18. Salaries and wages as well as investment income and government payments to individuals.
19. The GDP divided by the total population of a country.
20. Production output in relation to a unit of input, such as a worker.
21. The phase in which unemployment decreases, demand for goods and services increases, and GDP begins to rise.
22. An increase in the general price level.
23. Represents ownership in a corporation.
24. Government spends more than it takes in.
25. The portion of people in the labor force who are not working.
26. The sales of durable and nondurable goods bought by consumers.
27. A period in which unemployment is low, businesses produce many goods and services, and wages are good.
28. A number that compares prices in one year with prices in some earlier base year.
29. A period in which demand, production, and GDP growth decrease and unemployment begins to rise.
30. The total amount owed by the federal government.

Key Terms

a. bond
b. budget deficit
c. budget surplus
d. business cycle
e. capital project
f. deflation
g. depression
h. GDP per capita
i. gross domestic product (GDP)
j. inflation
k. national debt
l. personal income
m. price index
n. productivity
o. prosperity
p. recession
q. recovery
r. retail sales
s. stock
t. unemployment rate

Develop Your Business Language

offers a review of key terms to help students build a strong business vocabulary.

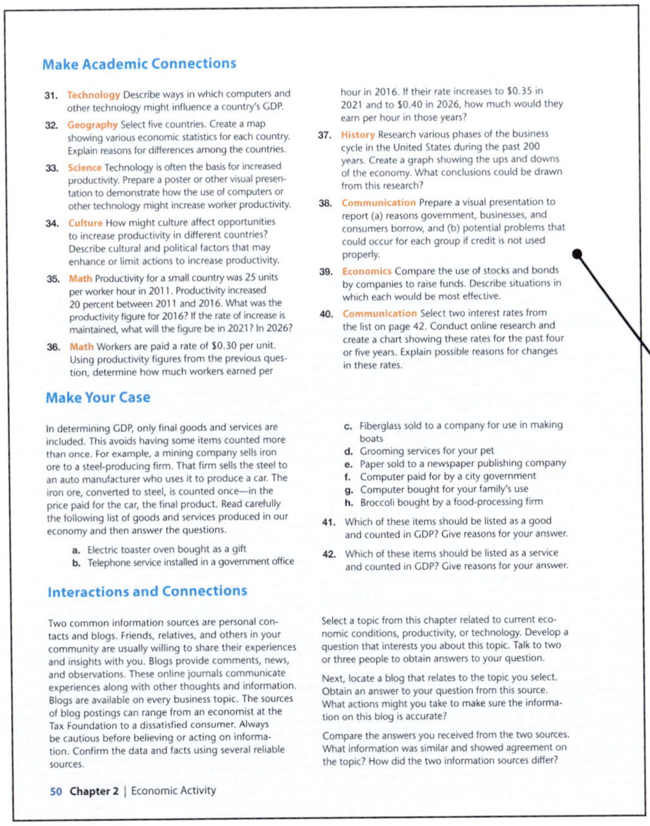

Make Academic Connections

31. **Technology** Describe ways in which computers and other technology might influence a country's GDP.
32. **Geography** Select five countries. Create a map showing various economic statistics for each country. Explain reasons for differences among the countries.
33. **Science** Technology is often the basis for increased productivity. Prepare a poster or other visual presentation to demonstrate how the use of computers or other technology might increase worker productivity.
34. **Culture** How might culture affect opportunities to increase productivity in different countries? Describe cultural and political factors that may enhance or limit actions to increase productivity.
35. **Math** Productivity for a small country was 25 units per worker hour in 2011. Productivity increased 20 percent between 2011 and 2016. What was the productivity figure for 2016? If the rate of increase is maintained, what will the figure be in 2021? In 2026?
36. **Math** Workers are paid a rate of $0.30 per unit. Using productivity figures from the previous question, determine how much workers earned per hour in 2016. If their rate increases to $0.35 in 2021 and to $0.40 in 2026, how much would they earn per hour in those years?
37. **History** Research various phases of the business cycle in the United States during the past 200 years. Create a graph showing the ups and downs of the economy. What conclusions could be drawn from this research?
38. **Communication** Prepare a visual presentation to report (a) reasons government, businesses, and consumers borrow, and (b) potential problems that could occur for each group if credit is not used properly.
39. **Economics** Compare the use of stocks and bonds by companies to raise funds. Describe situations in which each would be most effective.
40. **Communication** Select two interest rates from the list on page 42. Conduct online research and create a chart showing these rates for the past four or five years. Explain possible reasons for changes in these rates.

Make Your Case

In determining GDP, only final goods and services are included. This avoids having some items counted more than once. For example, a mining company sells iron ore to a steel-producing firm. That firm sells the steel to an auto manufacturer who uses it to produce a car. The iron ore, converted to steel, is counted once—in the price paid for the car, the final product. Read carefully the following list of goods and services produced in our economy and then answer the questions.

a. Electric toaster oven bought as a gift
b. Telephone service installed in a government office
c. Fiberglass sold to a company for use in making boats
d. Grooming services for your pet
e. Paper sold to a newspaper publishing company
f. Computer paid for by a city government
g. Computer bought for your family's use
h. Broccoli bought by a food-processing firm

41. Which of these items should be listed as a good and counted in GDP? Give reasons for your answer.
42. Which of these items should be listed as a service and counted in GDP? Give reasons for your answer.

Interactions and Connections

Two common information sources are personal contacts and blogs. Friends, relatives, and others in your community are usually willing to share their experiences and insights with you. Blogs provide comments, news, and observations. These online journals communicate experiences along with other thoughts and information. Blogs are available on every business topic. The sources of blog postings can range from an economist at the Tax Foundation to a dissatisfied consumer. Always be cautious before believing or acting on information. Confirm the data and facts using several reliable sources.

Select a topic from this chapter related to current economic conditions, productivity, or technology. Develop a question that interests you about this topic. Talk to two or three people to obtain answers to your question.

Next, locate a blog that relates to the topic you select. Obtain an answer to your question from this source. What actions might you take to make sure the information on this blog is accurate?

Compare the answers you received from the two sources. What information was similar and showed agreement on the topic? How did the two information sources differ?

50 **Chapter 2** | Economic Activity

Make Academic Connections

connects business concepts with core academic areas to support integrated learning.

Integrated Technology Tools

Instructor's Resource CD includes:

- Activities & Study Guide, Instructor's Edition
- Chapter & Unit Tests, Instructor's Edition
- Competitive Events Guide
- Global Business Project
- Lesson Plans
- Portfolio Activities
- Portfolio Forms
- PowerPoint Presentations
- Spanish Resources

cognero®

Cengage Learning Testing by Cognero is a flexible, online system that allows instructors to author, edit, and manage test bank content from multiple Cengage Learning solutions, create multiple test versions in an instant, and deliver tests from your learning management system or classroom.

NEW! MindTap for Principles of Business, 9e

MindTap®

- A highly personalized, cloud-based solution
- Unique digital platform with readings, application activities, multimedia, and assessments all in one singular Learning Path
- Automatic grading allows students to receive immediate feedback
- Instructors can monitor student engagement and progress in real time
- Customization options for coursework configuration and adding additional content

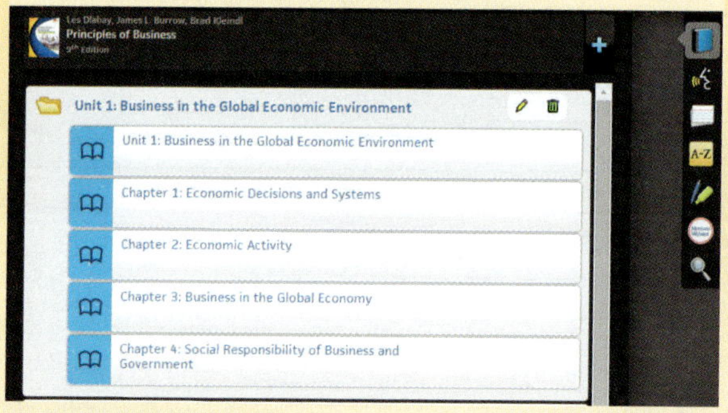

MindTap Learning Path

- Reading Activities
- Lesson Reviews
- PowerPoint Presentations
- Chapter Reviews
- Chapter Quizzes
- Chapter Tests
- Unit Tests
- Case Studies

Product website www.cengage.com/swep/pob9e

PRINCIPLES OF BUSINESS

9e

Focus on REAL LIFE

Ask students if they have spent time thinking about their future. Ask if anyone has written out a plan. Invite students to discuss how creating a plan might help them focus on their own life.

TEACH

Point out that there are three parts to the Life-Span Plan Project. The first part is reading, discussing, and understanding the content presented in this six-page introduction. The second part is completing the Life-Span Plan activities that appear throughout the book. The final part is actually creating a personal life-span plan.

THINK CRITICALLY THROUGH VISUALS

Answers will vary. Any goal that can be achieved within a year is a short-term goal. Possible answers include getting a driver's license, making a team, finding a part-time job, or saving money for a class trip.

Life-Span Plan Project

Learning Outcomes

Explain how personal goals impact a life-span plan.

Name six areas of your life that should be part of your life-span plan.

Identify three life-span goals that can be used as the foundation for your own life-span plan.

Key Terms

personal goals xxii

life span xxiii

life-span goals xxiv

life-span plan xxiv

Focus on REAL LIFE

"What are you doing? It looks like homework," Emilee asked her older sister.

Kelly looked up and smiled, "I'm planning my life. See, this is my life-span plan."

"How can you be planning your life? You haven't even finished high school. You are planning to finish high school aren't you?"

"Of course, but now's the time to think about what I want to do in the future—get a job, maybe own my own business, travel. I need to set some goals and figure out how I'm going to achieve them."

Emilee sat down and said, "I'm only two years behind you. I should probably be thinking about my future, too. Maybe you should tell me more about your life-span plan."

LIFE-SPAN PLANNING

The Life-Span Plan Project will help you see how you can start planning for the rest of your life. The project consists of this six-page introduction, 33 activities that appear throughout this book, and creating your own life-span plan. Completing the project will help you develop skills you can use to make better decisions throughout your life.

Photodisc/Getty Images

Besides graduating from high school, what is another one of your short-term goals?

Your Personal Goals

Personal goals are the things that people want most to achieve in their lives. They are the things that hold the greatest value to them. Most people have set a wide range of goals for themselves. Some are *short-term goals* that they hope to achieve within a year. Others are *long-term goals* that will take many years to attain. Individuals' goals are likely to involve family, living conditions, education, careers, community, and many other aspects of their lives. The goals you set for yourself are based on your personal values, your hopes, and your dreams. Although many people share common goals, most people also have unique goals that set them apart from others.

There is no way to judge most goals as right or wrong, or better or worse. Your most important goal may be to study law and become a judge while your best friend might want to own a farm and grow tomatoes. Your brother may want to start a family at a young age while you prefer to put off marriage and family responsibilities until well into the future. As long as a person's goals are based on what she or he really wants from life, there is no reason for them to be the same as other people's goals.

Photodisc/Getty Images

Although you might want to own a house in the future, what is your most important goal today?

Almost every important goal you could set for yourself involves topics you will learn about while studying this textbook. Suppose, for example, your most important personal goal is to have a happy and secure family life. You might think that this goal has little to do with what you will learn about businesses during this course. But, if what you learn about businesses helps you make a better career choice, then you may be able to earn a greater income and be more satisfied with your life. This will also allow you to provide a better standard of living for a family. The same is true for almost any other personal goal you might set.

A Life-Span Plan

As you grow older you should expect the things you want most in your life to change. Today you might believe that owning a nice car is your most important goal. In 10 years you may be more concerned with having a rewarding career, buying a home, or saving for your children's education. Even later you will want to have a satisfying retirement. Important events in your life, such as preparing for a career, raising a family, or enjoying retirement, are parts of your *life cycle*.

Your **life span** is the time from your birth to your death. It includes the events that make up your life cycle. When you are young, you will set long-term goals that you want to achieve over a period of years during your life span. Think of your life span as a straight line that contains the events of your life cycle.

The *life-span timeline* on the following page can help you understand the relationship between a life span and events in a person's life cycle. It shows a life span as a straight line along the top of the figure. Examples of events in the life cycle appear beneath the time in a person's life when they might happen. If you construct a figure like this for yourself, it is likely to have different events taking place at different times because your life will not be exactly the same as anyone else's.

TEACH

Discuss how the things people want most in life change over time. Ask students to think about what kinds of toys and games they wanted when they were younger. Ask them to think about things that are important to people who are in their twenties, forties, and sixties.

THINK CRITICALLY THROUGH VISUALS

Answers will vary. Possible answers include getting a driver's license, finding a job, graduating from high school, and owning a car. Other answers might focus on more immediate goals related to academic, athletic, and personal achievement.

TEACH

Introduce the idea of a person's life span as the time from birth to death. Refer to the figure on the top of the next page and point out that the life span is illustrated by the straight line at the top. Explain that the events of a person's life cycle are also illustrated.

▶ **Figure 1 *ANSWER***

High school students are teens or young adults.

ONGOING ASSESSMENT

CHECKPOINT ✓*ANSWER*

Answers will vary. You need to choose a career that will allow you to meet your personal goals.

TEACH

Introduce Kelly and point out that her life-span plan is being used as an example. Remind students that each person's life-span plan is unique.

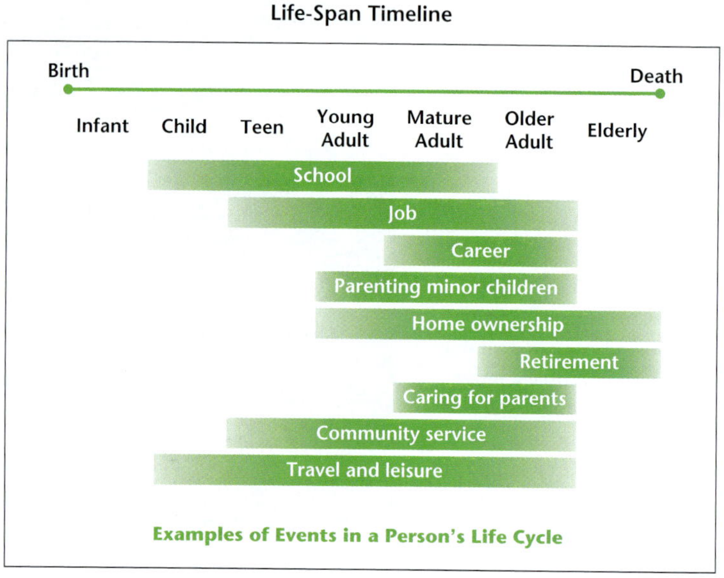

FIGURE 1
Where are you in on the life-span timeline?

Life-span goals are long-term goals that you want most to reach during your life. They shape many of the most important decisions you will make. Examples of life-span goals include earning a college degree, owning a business, raising a family, or achieving financial security. For most people, life-span goals don't just happen. Successful people create long-term plans for how they can achieve their life-span goals. These plans are called **life-span plans**.

CHECKPOINT ✓
How do personal goals impact your career choice?

A LIFE-SPAN PLAN FOR KELLY

To help you prepare your own life-span plan, consider the example of Kelly. She is fifteen years old and a high school sophomore. Like most people her age, she is busy with school and social activities. However, she does think about her future including going to college, getting a job and living on her own. She hopes to have a career, a family, and a comfortable home.

Kelly's favorite subject in school is art. She has signed up for every art class that she could fit into her schedule. Kelly wants a career in the art world, but not as an artist. She likes the idea of working in an art museum or gallery, but she also thinks of herself as an entrepreneur. Kelly dreams of owning a gallery where she will showcase and sell the works of local artists.

In addition to continuing to develop her skills as an artist, Kelly knows that she will need to learn how to run a business. She also knows she needs to set short- and long-term goals. She needs a plan—a life-span plan.

First Things First

To begin her life-span plan, Kelly looked at six areas of her life: education, career, family, finances, community, and retirement. She then identified six central life-span goals that she most wants to achieve over the next 50 years. These goals fit in well with her values, interests, and personality.

1. Gain training and education needed to work in a retail art gallery.
2. Own and operate a successful retail art gallery.
3. Get married, have children, and own a house and a car.
4. Become financially secure.
5. Be active in community, church, and local government.
6. Be able to retire and take up other interests by the age of 65.

Kelly realizes that achieving these life-span goals will involve careful planning and many trade-offs. Almost all life-span goals people set require money. To pay for her education, a business of her own, a home, and a secure retirement, she will need to save and invest part of the income she receives during her working life. At times, she may need to borrow funds from others. She will need to construct and follow a budget that allows her to do this. At the present, Kelly may decide to limit the amount she spends on eating out, clothing, and entertainment so she can save more now to pay for college tuition later. Kelly will also need to identify related short-term goals that can help her achieve her more-important life-span goals in the future.

Photodisc/Getty Images

How does Kelly's interest in art relate to her life-span plan?

Related Goals

Kelly's central life-span goals are related to each other. Saving and investing to achieve financial security, for example, will help her pay for training and later to start a business. If her business is successful, she will be able to afford the house she wants to own. Financial security will also allow Kelly to enjoy a few luxuries. For example, Kelly would like to visit Ireland and see where her ancestors lived. If her business is a success, she will be able to take this trip.

Kelly wants to achieve many short- and long-term goals that are not central goals in her life. These include buying cars, furniture, and owning a sailboat. Although these goals are important, they aren't among the things Kelly cares most about in life, and so they are not listed in her life-span plan. In preparing her life-span plan, Kelly listed and evaluated her goals to decide which ones were the most important. The most important goals are part of her life-span plan.

Organizing Goals

Kelly organized her life-span goals in a table as shown below. Across the top she placed six categories to represent her six central life-span goals. On the left side she placed periods of time. These started with the next 2 years at the top and went

THINK CRITICALLY THROUGH VISUALS

Answers will vary. Kelly's interest in art has a significant influence on her career plans. She is planning to study art in college and she wants a career related to art. She is also interested in using art as the basis for volunteer activities.

TEACH

Explain that every goal is not a part of a life-span plan. Only the most important goals are included.

TEACH

Point out that organizing goals by using a table or spreadsheet helps during planning. It also makes it easier to track progress and refine the plan.

Use Figure 2 to illustrate how Kelly's goals are organized. Point out that the first column identifies time intervals in Kelly's life. The column headings are used to divide Kelly's activities into different areas of life.

▶ **Figure 2** ***ANSWER***

Kelly plans to buy life insurance when she is twenty-five.

50 years into the future at the bottom. She then placed her goals according to when she would like to achieve them and how they contribute to her central life-span goals. In this way, she created a life-span plan that she believes will help her accomplish what she wants most in life.

Kelly feels a sense of satisfaction with her plan. She knows that she will almost surely revise it in the future, but she has a foundation on which to build. She can use her plan to help make decisions now. When she makes her class schedule for next year she will sign up for accounting, business management, and more art classes. She knows what type of work to look for and how to spend and save her income. Because she has definite goals, she is better able to make good spending decisions. Having goals makes it easier not to spend money for things she doesn't really need.

Kelly's life-span plan is right for her. It fits her values, personality, and family situation. Her plan, however, would not be right for most students, including you. You aren't Kelly. You have other values, abilities, and interests. Her personality is

KELLY'S LIFE-SPAN PLAN

TIME	EDUCATION	CAREER	FAMILY	FINANCES	COMMUNITY	RETIREMENT
Next 2 years	Complete high school. Apply to college.	Find a part-time job in an art gallery or museum.	Help parents with younger children.	Save $2,500 each year to help pay tuition.	Be an active member of my community.	No action is required at this time.
5 years from now	Graduate from college.	Work full time in an art gallery or museum.	Find a nice apartment in a good location.	Save and invest income to buy a home.	Teach art at the community center.	Open a retirement account.
10 years from now	Take classes in small business management.	Accept a managerial position at an art gallery.	Get married and buy a small home. Have one child.	Save and invest to buy an art gallery.	Continue teaching art classes.	Buy life insurance.
20 years from now	Travel to Ireland to see local artists' work.	Buy or start an art gallery.	Buy a larger house. Have another child.	Start a fund for children's education.	Continue teaching art classes.	Continue saving in retirement account.
35 years from now	Mentor young artists.	Build a successful business and look for a person to help run it.	Buy a vacation home at the beach.	Increase saving and investments now that children have moved out.	Run for town council or participate in government in some other way.	Investigate volunteer work I might enjoy.
50 years from now	Take classes in Irish cooking and history.	Sell business. Take part-time job in art store.	Buy a retirement home in a warm climate.	Manage investments carefully.	Volunteer to advise people who have small businesses.	Take at least one long trip each year and visit grandchildren.

FIGURE 2
How old will Kelly be when she plans to buy life insurance?

not your personality. Her family is not your family. You need to make your own life-span plan.

CHECKPOINT
What are the six areas of life that you should consider as you develop a life-span plan?

YOUR OWN LIFE-SPAN PLAN

Near the end of this class you will be asked to prepare a life-span plan for yourself. To do this, you should reflect on what you've learned throughout this course. You will study numerous topics and finish many activities that you can use to help you complete this assignment.

The table on this page shows the locations of Life-Span Plan activities throughout this text. Look for the Life-Span Plan icon on these pages.

You will also want to consider things about yourself that were not directly covered in this course. The type and size of family you want to have is important, but will not be discussed in this course. The same is true of where you want to live and the role you wish to play in your community. Preparing your life-span plan will require you to consider all of your values and goals, not just those that are related to businesses and your career choice.

After you accumulate as many useful resources as you can, use these materials as references while you write a list of your goals. Base your goals on what you want from life for yourself, your family, and your community. Sort them according to whether they are short- or long-term goals, and then classify them into overall life-span goals. Place your goals on a grid similar to Kelly's to construct your life-span plan.

When you have finished your life-span plan, it would be helpful to ask an experienced person to review your plan with you. A teacher, guidance counselor, or other adult you respect would be a good choice. Discuss your choices and the feasibility of your plan. This person can offer advice and encouragement for achieving your goals.

Making a life-span plan is an important first step. But, it is only a first step. Putting your life-span plan into action can make the difference between just thinking about your future and actually achieving the lifespan goals that are most important to you. If you fail to act on your life-span plan, it will only be a piece of paper.

LIFE-SPAN PLAN ACTIVITIES

Chapter 1	p. 14	**Chapter 11**	pp. 263, 275
Chapter 2	p. 44	**Chapter 12**	pp. 295, 305
Chapter 3	p. 55	**Chapter 13**	p. 323
Chapter 4	pp. 77, 80, 90	**Chapter 14**	p. 348
Chapter 5	p. 106	**Chapter 15**	p. 373
Chapter 6	pp. 124, 136	**Chapter 16**	pp. 400, 413
Chapter 7	pp. 155, 163	**Chapter 17**	p. 426
Chapter 8	pp. 175, 187	**Chapter 18**	pp. 456, 463
Chapter 9	pp. 200, 208, 215	**Chapter 19**	pp. 487, 492, 502
Chapter 10	p. 249	**Chapter 20**	pp. 526, 531

CHECKPOINT
What three life-span goals can be used as the foundation for your own life-span plan?

ONGOING ASSESSMENT

CHECKPOINT ✓ANSWER

The six areas of life are education, career, family, finances, community, and retirement.

TEACH

Encourage students to begin to create their own life-span plan.

Suggest that students use the table on this page to find and explore some of the Life-Span Plan activities that appear in the textbook.

ONGOING ASSESSMENT

CHECKPOINT ✓ANSWER

Answers will vary. Possible answers include finishing high school, choosing a career, and opening a retirement account.

CLOSE

Discuss any specifics about the way you expect students to complete individual Life-Span Plan activities. For example, you might ask students to keep a journal with entries for each activity.

Outline any long-term assignments related to the Life-Span Plan Project. For example, you might ask students to create a table similar to Figure 2. This could be a one-time assignment, or you could ask students to update their plan at specific intervals.

UNIT 1
Business in the Global Economic Environment

This unit introduces principles of economics and examines how economic decisions affect individual consumers, businesses, countries, and international competition.

Chapter 1 Economic Decisions and Systems This chapter describes how wants and needs affect economic decisions of consumers and businesses and the difference between goods and services.

Chapter 2 Economic Activity This chapter discusses the types of measures used to gauge economic activity and business conditions in our society.

Chapter 3 Business in the Global Economy This chapter examines the role economics plays in the development of international business.

Chapter 4 Social Responsibility of Business and Government This chapter describes how businesses can make socially responsible decisions and the role government plays in regulating business activities.

UNIT 1

Business in the Global Economic Environment

Nikolay Litov/Shutterstock.com

2

Unit 1 Global Business Project

Suggest that students read the chapter and lesson titles for this unit to get acquainted with business in the global economic environment. Introduce the Global Business Project for this unit: **Identify International Business Opportunities**.

Ask students to read the project assignment and plan to work on it as they progress through the unit. The project can be found on the website: www.cengage.com/swep/pob9e

Business Vision

The U.S. economy is the envy of people around the world. Americans have access to the latest products and services. Many families have the resources to purchase the products and services they need to maintain a good quality of life. Yes, the U.S. economy takes downturns from time to time, people have a hard time finding jobs, businesses struggle and may even fail, and governments raise taxes to pay for the public services people demand. But year after year, the U.S. economy continues to grow, offering people opportunities and advantages not seen in other countries.

In this unit you will learn about the U.S. economic system, how it compares to other economies, and how economic decisions are made. The United States operates in a global economy and so is affected by economic decisions made around the world. Decisions made by U.S. businesses can affect citizens of every other country as well as Americans. Businesses, consumers, and governments have responsibilities to make sure economic decisions are effective, fair, and contribute to the well-being of individuals and the environment.

Making a Dent in World Hunger

Throughout the world, people go hungry or starve while available fresh food is wasted. Inefficient distribution systems, lack of refrigeration, and a short window to distribute fresh food before it spoils means that more than one-third of all food produced today never reaches the consumer.

An Israeli agriculture technology company has created a product that could significantly reduce world hunger. If it's widely adopted, farmers, food packagers, and distributors could save millions of dollars that are presently lost to the rot, spoilage, and fungus associated with slow distribution.

Ample research by Pimi Agro's scientists has led to an all-natural, eco-friendly preservative called CleanTech. When applied to fresh produce, CleanTech helps retain the product's freshness for up to 10 weeks and gradually decomposes into oxygen and water. Many countries are currently testing the product and introducing it into their agricultural production processes. Sun Pacific (the large California-based food producer), Wal-Mart, Frito Lay, and PepsiCo are interested in how the product will help them with worldwide food distribution.

Nimrod Ben-Yehuda, Pimi Agro co-founder, says the company's goals are not limited to simply making a profit. "More produce means more food to feed hungry people, and our methods don't require the deployment of dangerous chemicals or expensive and questionable genetic reformulations of fruits and vegetables. With our products, we believe there will be enough to go around to make a real dent in world hunger."

Think Critically

Should corporations such as Pimi Agro be responsible for solving global problems such as hunger, poverty, and environmental damage? If they try, should profit still be their first concern? Why or why not?

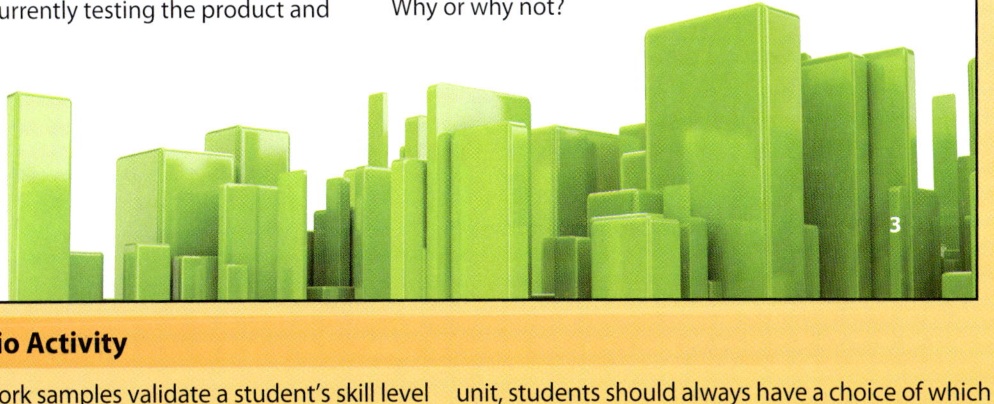

3

Business Vision

Encourage students to read the introduction to Unit 1. Suggest that students read the chapter and lesson titles for this unit to get acquainted with business in the global economic environment.

Making a Dent in World Hunger

Remind students that an innovation designed to make a positive impact on the world can also make a positive impact on a corporation's balance sheet. Draw attention to the slower spoilage rate of CleanTech-treated produce and ask students how this might affect the global price of produce.

Think Critically *Answers*

Students may offer various opinions. Some will feel corporations have no responsibility to the world and its inhabitants, some will say that corporations should try to solve the world's problems as long as efforts don't interfere with the bottom line, and some will state that profits should be secondary to the well-being of the planet and its people.

Portfolio Activity

Portfolio work samples validate a student's skill level and ability to accomplish tasks frequently performed on the job. The most important reason for including samples in a portfolio is to demonstrate a student's abilities and skills. In selecting work samples for each unit, students should always have a choice of which activities to include. Students might be encouraged to include samples from the end-of-chapter activities, particularly Think Critically About Business, Make Academic Connections, Make Your Case, and Interactions and Connections.

CHAPTER OVERVIEW

This chapter introduces the important economic concepts that determine the products and services available for consumers and how economic systems are structured.

1.1 Satisfying Needs and Wants

In this lesson, students learn to distinguish between wants and needs and between goods and services.

1.2 Economic Choices

This lesson presents the basic economic problem facing consumers and businesses and the steps in making effective decisions.

1.3 Economic Systems

In this lesson, students learn how the main types of economic systems answer three economic questions.

1.4 Supply and Demand

This lesson discusses supply and demand and how they affect the prices of goods and services offered for sale.

Chapter 1 Economic Decisions and Systems

iStockphoto.com/Anna Bryukhanova

Instructor Resources

- Activities and Study Guide IE
- Chapter and Unit Tests IE
- Lesson Plans
- PowerPoint Presentation
- Cognero Test, Ch. 1

Student Resources

Activities and Study Guide
www.cengage.com/swep/pob9e
- Portfolio Activity

Business, Management & Administration

PLANNING A CAREER IN...
CORPORATE ECONOMICS

Economists play an important role in the business world. They often seem to be fortunetellers for the future of the economy. Economists gather and analyze information to try to anticipate what economic changes are coming. This is a very important task, as businesses and government officials and even consumers use these predictions to make decisions. Most economists work in government agencies, for businesses and business associations, or as researchers and professors in colleges and universities.

Economists working for corporations forecast the size of markets, changes in consumer demand, and changes in sales and costs the businesses are likely to face. They analyze competitors' growth and market share and advise their company on how to plan. Economists pay attention to the international economy and the economic conditions in countries where the company currently operates or plans to expand.

Related Job Titles

- Actuary
- Regional/Urban Planner
- Budget Analyst
- Economics Journalist
- Economics Teacher or Professor
- Forecasting Assistant
- Investment Analyst
- Business Development Advisor

Analyze Career Opportunities in . . .
CORPORATE ECONOMICS

Use library and Internet resources to learn more about careers in corporate economics. Choose one of the job titles listed in the box above and answer the following questions.

1. Identify the minimum educational requirements for the job. Explain other training or education that might be needed for advancement.
2. Is this a career that interests you? Describe how you might use your talents, abilities, and skills in this career.

What it's like to work as a . . . Corporate Economist

Pierre Latrobe is on his way to the office at 4 A.M. each morning. As an associate analyst, he helps prepare a morning briefing. He is responsible for tracking changes in the European economy.

Heading into the city on the commuter train, Pierre checks the Internet to get the latest information from the major stock markets. Then he checks the international news services for important stories that might affect the European economy. He updates forecast charts and enters notes so he will be ready for the team meeting as soon as he arrives at the office. His office work is usually finished by 2 P.M. each day, but he continues to check economic information even as he works out at the gym or completes other leisure activities.

What about you? What do you like and dislike about Pierre Latrobe's schedule and activities? What do you think happens in the team meetings as Pierre and his colleagues prepare the morning briefing?

PLANNING A CAREER IN . . .
CORPORATE ECONOMICS

Ask students to take a moment and quickly write down two careers they are considering. Allow no more than 60 seconds for students to answer and then ask if anyone wrote down *economist*. Point out that economics is not a common career interest for most students, yet, economists help to make some of the most important decisions that affect the lives of consumers. Ask students: In what ways might the health of the U.S. and global economies affect you, your family, and your community? How might it help to understand the economy and how it works?

What about You?
Answers

Student answers will require thinking beyond what is presented as they formulate their own reactions. The following are possible answers:

1. Students will have varying responses to the early start time of Pierre Latrobe's day and the continuing responsibilities after his work day ends.

2. The morning team meeting likely includes a great deal of information covered rapidly, with the senior economist requiring team members to quickly explain their parts of the daily report.

Analyze Career Opportunities *Answers*
Student answers will vary depending on when the assignment is completed and individual interests.

Additional Career Information

Encourage students to investigate careers they find interesting and explore unfamiliar careers. Two resources for additional career information are the *Occupational Outlook Handbook*, an online publication (www.bls.gov/oco) of the U.S. Bureau of Labor Statistics, and the O*NET Resource Center (www.onetcenter.org) developed by the U.S. Department of Labor. Information about specific careers and jobs can be used to demonstrate the relevance of skills learned in this course.

Focus on REAL LIFE

Remind students that it is not always easy to determine the appropriate price for a new product. Ask whether they are ever inspired to pay more than they planned when they see a new product's features or realize that as it is new, few others yet own it.

TEACH

Before students read the information, ask them whether they believe there is a difference between a need and a want. Students should justify their decision and then compare their ideas with those presented in the lesson.

THINK CRITICALLY THROUGH VISUALS

The ease of meeting basic needs will vary among people and in different communities. However, meeting one's basic needs is generally easier in the United States than in many other countries of the world that are less developed or have different economic systems.

1.1 Satisfying Needs and Wants

Learning Outcomes

1.1.1 Compare and contrast needs and wants

1.1.2 Distinguish between goods and services

1.1.3 Describe the types of economic resources

Key Terms

needs 6
wants 7
goods 7
services 7
economic resources 9

Focus on REAL LIFE

Blake was contemplating a tablet purchase, so he and Lexi stopped by the electronics store on the way home from school to check out the latest offerings. Lexi quickly located the newest flagship model.

"Hey Blake," she said, "this one's got the biggest screen to date and the processor is as fast as they come!"

Blake was enthused until he noticed the price tag. "Lexi, it's nearly $700! I could go online and buy a used tablet for $100."

"But this is a top-of-the-line model. You have to pay for quality," Lexi said.

Blake thought for a moment and said, "also, I bet if I just waited a few months, I could get this one for significantly less. Do I really need a new tablet today?"

Blake's decision is one you often face. You see advertisements for exciting new products, but you do not need and cannot afford all of them. How do you decide which ones you should buy and how much to pay?

LO 1.1.1

NEEDS AND WANTS

Hardly a day goes by that you don't see products or services that you would like to have. You see them at the shopping mall, the grocery store, and school. Store displays and advertisements on television, radio, and the Internet attempt to convince you that you need whatever is new. How do you decide what to buy or even if you need to buy at all?

Needs Are Essential

You want many things, but do you really need them? Determining what is a need and what is a want is an important part of making good decisions.

Needs are things that are required in order to live. Everyone needs food, water, clean air, clothing, and shelter. Other needs in today's economy are a good education, a good job, and safety. Most people need transportation to and from school and work. To maintain healthy lives, people need access to effective health care.

Photodisc/Getty Images

How easy is it for you to meet your basic needs?

Different Learning Styles

Visual Learner Provide students with copies of catalogs from a variety of retail businesses. Students should page through the catalogs and identify products they believe satisfy needs and those that appeal to wants.

Wants Add to the Quality of Life

Wants are things that add comfort and pleasure to your life. You may believe you can't live without name-brand jeans and the latest smartphone upgrade, but you can, and many people do. A small apartment provides needed shelter, but many people want a large apartment or a house. Public transportation is available in many cities, but a late-model luxury car might provide a driver with an image of success.

It is not always easy to determine which products and services satisfy needs and which ones satisfy wants. The country in which you live, the economic status and lifestyle of your family, and the work you do help determine whether something is really necessary or not. Most purchases you make do more than meet your needs. They make your life easier and more comfortable.

Needs and Wants Are Unlimited

Your needs and wants never end. Satisfying them is limited only by your imagination and by what businesses make available for sale. A new style convinces you your current backpack is no longer adequate. One purchase often leads to another. You purchase the latest video game console and now you need new games. Purchasing a new pair of shoes may mean you will want matching accessories.

Your wants can go on and on, and they change from day to day. A product you thought you couldn't live without two weeks ago doesn't seem as important now and is replaced by a new want. Everyone has unlimited wants, but those wants will not be the same for each person.

CHECKPOINT ✓
What is the main difference between a need and a want?

Work as a TEAM

Do you believe your needs are very similar to or quite different from those that your parents had when they were your age? As a team, prepare a list of five needs that you agree would be similar to those of your parents when they were young and a list of five needs that you agree would likely be different. Justify why your selections are needs rather than wants.

LO 1.1.2

GOODS AND SERVICES

You satisfy your needs and wants by purchasing and consuming goods and services. **Goods** are things that you can see and touch. They are the products you can purchase to meet your wants and needs. **Services** are activities provided for the satisfaction of others that are consumed at the same time they are produced. You purchase and use services to satisfy your wants and needs, but unlike goods, businesses must create and provide services to you at the time you want to consume them.

Aliaksei Smalenski/Shutterstock.com

Do service businesses satisfy more of your needs or your wants?

Work as a TEAM

After students have identified similar and different needs, ask them to determine what products their parents might have used to satisfy their needs. Encourage them to ask their parents about those products or use the Internet to determine products that were sold when their parents were younger.

ONGOING ASSESSMENT

CHECKPOINT ✓ANSWER

Needs are those things required to live, such as food, clothing, and shelter. Wants are things that add comfort and pleasure to our lives.

TEACH

Tell students that the words "products" and "goods" mean essentially the same thing. Thousands of goods and services are produced and provided by businesses to meet the needs and wants of consumers. Ask students why more and more services are being developed by businesses today.

THINK CRITICALLY THROUGH VISUALS

Service businesses generally address wants more than they do needs, but there are important service businesses that satisfy needs. Examples include hospitals, schools, and government agencies such as police and fire departments.

Different Learning Styles

Auditory Learner Encourage auditory learners to repeat the definitions of goods and services aloud until they are certain of the meanings and differences.

Teaching Strategies

Expand Beyond the Classroom Ask students locate and bring to class a picture or description of a product that typically is purchased to satisfy a need and another one that most people would purchase to satisfy a want.

THINK CRITICALLY THROUGH VISUALS

Answers will vary. Some goods that are represented are furniture, floor coverings, electronics, and home accessories. Services are not directly shown, but some implied services are furniture delivery and home decorating service.

ONGOING ASSESSMENT

CHECKPOINT ✓ANSWER

Goods are physical products. Services are activities that are consumed at the same time they are produced.

TEACH

Explain to students that the more economic resources a country has, the better it will be able to meet the wants and needs of its citizens.

Thomas Barwick/Getty Images

What goods and services are represented in this photo?

Goods and Services for Businesses and Consumers

Goods and services are purchased by businesses as well as by individual consumers. Some goods and services are unique for business or consumer use. Others are similar but meet different needs and wants.

A business needs steel, plastic, gasoline, and computers in order to operate. It must have a constant supply of electricity, security for buildings and equipment, and accountants who maintain records and file tax returns.

Consumers buy furniture, televisions, smartphones, and books. They eat at restaurants, go on vacations, and take their car to service centers for maintenance and repairs. Businesses provide the goods and services that meet business and consumer needs and wants.

The U.S. Economy

The United States is the largest producer of goods and services in the world. In 2013 it produced more than the next two largest producers, China and Japan, combined. The United States is also the world's largest consumer. For example, the United States ranks first in oil consumption. In 2013, it consumed almost 19 million barrels per day, which was more than the combined consumption of the next three countries—China, Japan, and India.

America was the world leader in consuming goods and services throughout the twentieth century. While the economies of other countries are growing at a faster rate, the United States continues to be the world's largest consumer. The shift from an economy based on agriculture to an industrialized economy results in higher incomes and more choices of products and services for consumers. With more money to spend and more ways to spend it, consumer spending increases.

Increased consumer spending in a country results in more jobs and a higher standard of living. However, as consumption within a country increases, new challenges emerge for consumers. The ready availability of many products and services, combined with higher incomes, encourages consumers to buy things they may not need. With careful buying decisions, people can meet their basic needs, satisfy some of their wants, and still save and invest for the future.

Increased consumption also creates challenges for countries. Controlling pollution, preserving natural resources, and managing waste are all growing concerns worldwide. In addition to being the world's largest producer of goods and services, the United States is tops in another area—Americans produce more garbage per person per year than the residents of any other country.

CHECKPOINT ✓

What is the difference between a good and a service?

LO 1.1.3

ECONOMIC RESOURCES

How are the goods and services you need and want produced? Individuals no longer create most of the products and services they consume, as people once did. Businesses produce goods and services

Applied Skills

Communication Instruct students to develop an advertisement that might appear in a national magazine that highlights your state's natural resources.

Different Learning Abilities

English Language Learners (ELL) Obtain translations of the types of economic resources to help students with other dominant languages understand their meaning.

using economic resources. **Economic resources** are the things available to be used to produce goods and services. Economic resources are also known as *factors of production*. The three types of economic resources are natural resources, human resources, and capital resources. Businesses and individuals must be able to obtain the needed economic resources to produce goods and services.

Natural Resources

Raw materials supplied by nature are *natural resources*. The earth contains oil, minerals, and the nutrients needed to grow crops and forests and to feed animals. Rivers, lakes, and oceans are the sources of both food and water. The air you breathe comes from the atmosphere that surrounds you. All products you consume begin with one or more natural resources.

Consider something as simple as a can of vegetable soup. What natural resources were used in its production? The vegetables and spices are produced using resources grown on farms. The water comes from wells or reservoirs that were filled by rain. Iron was extracted from the ground and combined with other resources to produce the steel container.

While there is an abundance of many natural resources around the world, their supply is limited in many areas. Increased consumption and damage to the environment threatens the availability of many natural resources. Recycling and conservation practices, as well as the design of more efficient products, help to preserve resources.

Human Resources

The people who produce goods and services are known as *human resources*. In the example of the vegetable soup, many people are needed to complete the work required to produce that product. Farmers plant and harvest the vegetables and other ingredients. Factory workers and managers use equipment designed by engineers and manufactured by the employees of other businesses to process the food. Truck drivers, salespeople, advertisers, and supermarket employees are also involved in making the soup available to consumers for purchase.

One type of human resource is an entrepreneur. An *entrepreneur* is the risk taker who uses resources to create a new product or service. Without the creative ideas of entrepreneurs and their belief that they can develop a successful business, there would be fewer choices of goods and services and fewer employment opportunities.

FYI Even water, one of the most common substances on the planet, is a scarce natural resource, especially in the western United States. Disputes among southwestern states over water rights and access to the major riverways result in frequent political debate and court actions. Water will likely become an even more important natural resource in the future.

Lindsay Douglas/Shutterstock.com

In what ways does water contribute to the U.S. economy?

FYI

Start a discussion about the problems that can occur for individuals and businesses when there is a long-term water shortage. Encourage students to consider alternative solutions to legal actions. Examples might include new technology, lifestyles, and conservation practices.

TEACH

As each type of economic resource is introduced, ask students to name examples of the resources that are used by businesses in your community—natural resources such as water, lumber, and minerals; human resources such as the owners, managers, and employees of a business; and capital resources including money from investors, buildings, and equipment.

Discuss ways the demand for human resources has changed in businesses in the past decade. Examples might be the need for more education and higher skill levels, demand for more service employees, and businesses using more workers in other countries to produce goods and services.

THINK CRITICALLY THROUGH VISUALS

Water contributes to the U.S. economy in the following ways: as an energy source, in growing crops and raising livestock, in many manufacturing processes, as a method of transportation, and as a commodity sold to consumers for their personal consumption.

Teaching Strategies

Expand Beyond the Classroom Point out the relationship between the FYI and photo on this page. Ask students to research a current issue related to the reduced supply of natural resources such as rainforest destruction, ozone layer depletion, pollution, or increased worldwide oil consumption. Instruct students to prepare a written and/or oral report that includes possible causes, long-term economic consequences, and possible solutions.

TEACH

Tell students to imagine that they are entrepreneurs starting a new business. Ask them what type of capital resources they would need. Follow up by asking them to identify possible sources of the needed capital.

THINK CRITICALLY THROUGH VISUALS

Economic resources that go into the construction of a house could include natural resources, such as wood and minerals; human resources, such as the architect, builder, and construction workers; and capital resources, such as the tools and machinery used by the builder and the money loaned by the bank for the home construction.

Business Insight

New digital and video content is being developed every day. The individuals and businesses developing the content and the consumers who want to purchase it must have an easy and safe way to complete low-cost transactions known as micropayments.

Think Critically *Answers*

1. When consumers use the Internet to conveniently access products and services at a reasonable cost, they will be comfortable paying for it if the payment process is safe and easy.

2. Ask students to give oral presentations on the information they find on past and current micropayment systems.

Capital Resources

People must have access to tools and equipment in order to convert natural resources into products. The products and money used in the production of goods and services are *capital resources*. Capital resources include buildings, equipment, and supplies. They also include the money needed to build a factory, buy or lease vehicles, pay employees, or purchase goods and services required to manufacture and distribute other products.

Some people invest money in businesses so the business will have the capital needed to operate. Those people expect they will make money from the profits earned by the business. Other people

Ryan McVay/Getty Images

What economic resources are needed for the construction of a house?

Business Insight

Online Micropayments

The popularity of the Internet has ushered in new challenges for both businesses and consumers. Many consumers no longer buy and listen to entire music albums, purchase newspaper subscriptions, or care to own movies on DVD. Instead, these consumers download their favorite songs or listen to albums on a streaming service. To keep up with the latest news, busy people read a few current newspaper or magazine articles online. They download a favorite TV show or stream a movie whenever it is convenient.

In the past, most consumers believed everything on the Internet should be free. However, many are now willing to pay for desired content if the price is fair and payment is convenient and secure. A fair price may be a dollar for a song, less than four dollars for an online book or a movie, and five to ten cents for a magazine article. These small payments are difficult to make and collect. Businesses, banks, or credit card companies incur significant expenses to process these payments.

Low-value payments, typically less than five dollars and frequently less than one dollar, are known as micropayments. Credit card companies often charge 3 to 5 percent of the sale price plus an additional fee of 20 to 50 cents to process a transaction. With such large margins of their revenue positioned to go straight to credit card companies, online merchants have a clear incentive to find alternative ways to sell their products.

Businesses such as Starbucks and Microsoft have approached the problem by selling customers prepaid cards or creating accounts from which the cost of small purchases is then subtracted. A few credit card companies have allowed businesses to bundle a number of low-value sales together and process them as one purchase to reduce processing fees. However, until a better system to process micropayments is developed, the full potential of selling low-value products and services on the Internet will not be realized.

Think Critically

1. Why have many consumers changed their views about the value of online content so they are now willing to pay small fees?
2. Research micropayments and identify unique methods being used by companies to accept and process these small payments.

Different Learning Abilities

Hearing Impaired Be certain to face the student so lip reading will be possible. Utilize printed materials and visuals. Work with individual students to determine their specific needs.

receive income by selling their knowledge and skills to businesses in the form of labor. Those with special skills or knowledge of important business processes often command higher incomes than those with knowledge and skills that are more common or in less demand.

Resources Are Limited

All economic resources have a limited supply. Most resources can be used to produce several different products and services. If resources are used to produce one type of product, they will not be available for the production of something else.

Individuals, businesses, and even countries compete for access to and ownership of economic resources. Those resources that are in very high demand or that have a limited supply will command high prices. Because there is a limited amount of economic resources, there will also be a limit to the amount of goods and services that can be produced.

CHECKPOINT
What are the three types of economic resources? Give an example of each type of resource.

iStockphoto.com/Sculpies

How can a country plan for future limits on its natural resources?

1.1 ASSESSMENT

Key Concepts

Determine the best answer.

1. True or False. It is not always easy to determine the products and services that satisfy needs and those that satisfy wants.
2. Which of the following would an economist most likely classify as a need?
   a. gasoline for a florist's delivery truck
   b. a battery-powered automobile
   c. a flat-screen television
   d. a part-time job to earn extra money
3. An example of a natural resource is
   a. sunlight
   b. a computer programmer
   c. a fishing net
   d. money

Make Academic Connections

4. **Economics** List the three types of economic resources. Choose a product and describe how each type of economic resource is needed and used in its production. (Hint: refer to the vegetable soup example in the lesson.)
5. **Writing** Locate an article from a business publication or newspaper that illustrates the concepts of unlimited wants and needs and limited resources. Write a two-paragraph summary of the article that incorporates several of the key terms from the lesson.

RETEACH Ask students what they think is the most important concept in the lesson.

ENRICH Have students choose a business and identify its most important economic resource.

CLOSE Ask students to describe why the different economic resources are important for businesses.

TEACH

Ask students to provide examples of how a resource being used for one product results in a limited supply of another. For example, the production of fuel oil for winter heating may reduce the supply of gasoline for automobiles.

ONGOING ASSESSMENT

CHECKPOINT ✓ANSWER

Natural: water, land, trees, animals, and minerals. Human: labor (people who work on farms and in factories, transport goods, provide services, or manage businesses). Capital: money, land, buildings, tools, and equipment.

THINK CRITICALLY THROUGH VISUALS

A country can plan for future limits on natural resources by implementing conservation procedures and developing new products and production processes.

ASSESS

Key Concepts *Answers*

1. True. People and businesses have different uses for products and services.
2. a. gasoline for a florist's delivery truck
3. a. sunlight

Make Academic Connections *Answers*

4. The three economic resources are natural, human, and capital. Examples will vary based on the product chosen.
5. Summaries should demonstrate an understanding of the material presented in this lesson and key terms should be used properly.

Focus on REAL LIFE

Ask students to consider a real-life choice they faced that was similar to the one faced by Tom. Why is it so difficult to make that type of decision?

TEACH

Write "unlimited wants" and "limited resources" on the board. Ask students what problems people face because they have unlimited wants and limited resources.

THINK CRITICALLY THROUGH VISUALS

Answers will vary and will likely include a discussion about difference between wants and needs. Students should understand that scarcity forces people to make choices. People usually try to satisfy important needs first. When those needs are met, people may choose the things they want most and can afford.

1.2 Economic Choices

Learning Outcomes

1.2.1 Describe the basic economic problem.

1.2.2 Explain the steps in the decision-making process.

Key Terms

- scarcity 12
- economic decision making 13
- trade-off 13
- opportunity cost 13

Focus on REAL LIFE

As soon as Tom answers the phone, Jacques says, "Tom, I just won two tickets to the concert and I want you to go with me. It's tomorrow at eight so we need to leave by five-thirty."

"Oh no!" Tom said. "My Dad's birthday is tomorrow and my family expects me to go out to dinner to celebrate tomorrow night."

Tom really wants to go to the concert but doesn't want to cause hard feelings with his family. What advice would you give Tom to help him resolve the dilemma he is facing?

LO 1.2.1

THE BASIC ECONOMIC PROBLEM

Individuals and businesses have unlimited wants and needs. However, the economic resources that can be used to meet their needs are limited. The mismatch of unlimited wants and needs and limited economic resources is known as *the basic economic problem*. You may have identified several products you want to buy but you don't have enough money for all of them. Your school may be facing cutbacks on certain classes or extracurricular activities because operating costs are increasing faster than the annual budget. A business may want to expand in order to produce more products but does not have access to adequate land for a new larger building. A country may not be able to provide adequate health care for all of its citizens because it does not have enough doctors or hospitals.

The basic economic problem results from scarcity. **Scarcity** means not having enough resources to satisfy every need. Scarcity affects everyone, but some people are more affected than others. People with limited incomes have to carefully choose the best way to spend their money just to meet their basic needs. Countries with few natural resources or a poor education system may not be able to produce enough

Dora Zett/Shutterstock.com

How do you make personal choices between satisfying your wants and your needs?

Different Learning Styles

Visual Learner Ask students to sketch situations that illustrate scarcity. This will help them remember the basic economic problem. Invite students to share their sketches with classmates.

products and services for their citizens. If roads, bridges, and railways are not well maintained, people may not be able to easily obtain the variety of products and services found in other areas.

Choices

Everyone has to make financial decisions based on scarcity. Individuals and families must decide how to spread their income among all of the things they want and need. City, state, and national governments must cope with the problem of providing the many services citizens demand using the tax dollars they collect. In each case, someone has to make the difficult choices.

Scarcity forces you to make *choices* or decisions among the alternatives. How do you decide which option is best? You usually choose the things you want the most or can afford. Suppose you earn $75 a week from a part-time job. If you spend the money you earned this week on a new pair of shoes, you will not have enough left over to spend on a movie and pizza with your friends on Saturday night. Due to the limited resources or amount of money you have, you cannot afford everything at the same time. You must make a choice by deciding which of your wants—the shoes or pizza and movie—you want the most. How do you determine which of these two options will satisfy you the most?

Following a logical process can help you make better decisions. It is a proven way to make many decisions, but is especially useful for making important economic decisions. **Economic decision making** is the process of choosing which needs and wants will be satisfied. Once you learn the process, your decision making will be easier and the process may lead to better choices.

Trade-offs and Opportunity Costs

Most of the choices you make result from considering a number of alternatives. When you decide on one alternative, you give up on the other alternatives you might have chosen. When you give up something to have something else, you are making a **trade-off**. You aren't able to buy a pair of shoes because you decided to spend your money on a movie and pizza with your friends.

The decision-making process helps you select the best and most satisfying alternative from among a set of choices. Economists recommend that you evaluate an alternative by considering the opportunity cost of the decision. The **opportunity cost** is the value of the next-best alternative that you were not able to choose. In making a decision, part of your choice will be what you are giving up by the choice you make. The benefit you get from your choice should be greater than the benefit from the next-best choice.

Businesses carefully calculate the opportunity costs of decisions before they make a decision about how they will invest their money. If they use money to purchase land for a new building, what choices must they give up? Would there be a greater value if they spent the money to purchase new equipment that is faster and more reliable? Part of the cost of the land is the missed opportunity to have better equipment.

NET KNOWLEDGE

Knowledge makes you a better consumer. If you have the ability to compare quality and prices of products and services, this allows you to make the best use of your money when you make decisions about what to buy. Go online to identify three websites that help consumers compare and contrast various competing products and services. After studying each site, prepare a table that analyzes the sites on at least four factors you believe are important in making the best decision. Share your table with other students and discuss whether you believe the websites can improve consumer decisions.

CHECKPOINT
What is the basic economic problem?

NET KNOWLEDGE

Students should share their tables with other students. Discuss how gathering information about product choices prior to making a purchase can lead to better decisions about the best use of resources.

TEACH

Tell students to think of an important need or want and three possible products or services that would satisfy that need or want. Then ask them to describe how the concepts of "trade-off" and "opportunity cost" can be used as a part of the choice of how best to satisfy the need or want.

ONGOING ASSESSMENT

CHECKPOINT ANSWER

The mismatch of unlimited wants and needs and limited economic resources is the basic economic problem.

Applied Skills

Mathematics Challenge students to determine the opportunity cost of purchasing a new car versus a three-year-old used car of the same model. Ask them to use the Internet to determine the price of each choice, calculate the opportunity cost, and decide what they would have to give up to choose the new car.

TEACH

Use Figure 1-1, The Decision-Making Process, to review the steps in the process. Assign one student to explain each step and give an example from their own experiences in making economic decisions. Then select a local issue that requires a decision, such as making improvements to a rundown neighborhood or building a new elementary school. Guide the class through the steps in the decision-making process with consideration to the many factors that must be taken into account. Point out that the process leads to better choices because it forces you to think about the steps as you make them and to learn from each decision you make. Review and use the steps in the decision-making process throughout the course.

▶ **Figure 1-1** ***ANSWER***

The decision-making process helps you to carefully consider each step rather than rushing to a decision without adequate information.

Life-Span Plan *Answer*

Answers will vary. Essays should demonstrate students' understanding of how the decision-making process could be used to choose classes or make other important decisions about their future.

LO 1.2.2

THE DECISION-MAKING PROCESS

You make better decisions when you use a thoughtful process rather than letting your emotions lead you to a quick choice. An effective decision-making process involves six steps. You will be asked to use the process shown in Figure 1-1 many times as you proceed through the chapters in this book. You can also use it when making everyday decisions. Businesspeople and individuals use the process as they choose the best uses for their limited resources.

THE DECISION-MAKING PROCESS	
1.	Define the problem.
2.	Identify the choices.
3.	Evaluate the advantages and disadvantages of each choice.
4.	Choose the best alternative.
5.	Act on your choice.
6.	Review your decision.

FIGURE 1-1
How does the decision-making process lead to better choices?

Define the Problem

For every decision, the problem must be clearly defined in order to make a decision that will lead to a satisfying solution. If you only have two hours available to study for three tests, your problem is how to best use the limited amount of time to prepare for the tests.

Identify the Choices

It is common for you to face choices with many alternatives. Earlier we identified a problem deciding on the best use of $75. Along with spending money on shoes or the movies and pizza, some other choices you might face are covering your normal daily expenses and the need to save money for college. In fact, there are many ways you might choose to spend or save your $75. It is important to identify and then consider all of the alternatives when making a decision.

Evaluate the Advantages and Disadvantages of Each Choice

You might find it helpful to write down your choices and then list the advantages and disadvantages of each. If you buy the shoes, you will be able to wear them many times. It means you will miss the fun of pizza and a movie with friends on the weekend. If you choose to save some of the money, you may be able to make a larger purchase later. You and your friends may determine a less expensive way to spend your time on the weekend.

Choose the Best Alternative

Select the choice that you believe will be the best for you at this particular time. Even if you have done a good job with the first three steps, this is often a difficult step. Realize that choices have consequences both now and in the future. Remember that opportunity costs affect your decision.

Act on Your Choice

Once you have made what you believe is the best decision, do whatever you have chosen. If you have decided to spend your money on a movie and pizza with your friends, go and enjoy yourself. Try not to worry about the choices you have decided against. Rethinking your choices or regretting your decision after it is made can take away from the activity you decided upon. Life is full of choices. No matter what you do, there will be times when you will regret a decision even if you carefully considered the

Life-Span Plan

Write an essay that describes how you could use the decision-making process to select classes for next year that will help you achieve your life-span goals. In what other ways will the decision-making process benefit you in the future?

Different Learning Abilities

At-Risk Ask students to identify a personal choice they are facing. Ask them to list each step of the decision-making process and describe how they would use that step to help them make the best choice.

For this activity, suggest that they focus on a decision that they feel comfortable sharing with you and their classmates. Point out that they can use the process for a variety of personal decisions.

alternatives. The next step will help you deal with those situations.

Review Your Decision

After you have had a chance to experience the results of your choice, it is important to review your decision. On a scale of one to ten, how would you rank your choice in terms of the level of satisfaction it provided? What was good and not so good about it? If you had to do it over again, would you make the same choice? Given what you know now, do you think there was a better alternative? Were there consequences you hadn't identified?

Based on your review of the decision, how well did you follow the steps of the decision-making process? This step gives you an opportunity to think about your decision and learn from it. The next time you face a similar decision, you may be more comfortable with your choices or make a different decision based on what you learned.

Some decisions have to be made quickly and some with very little information available. But even in those situations, following the decision-making process will help you make wiser choices.

Work as a TEAM

You and some friends are meeting with city council members to ask them to build a skateboarding park that would cost $30,000. They ask you to identify the opportunity costs of other recreation alternatives for teenagers. As a team, identify two other alternatives for the city and discuss how you would determine the opportunity cost of each.

CHECKPOINT

What are the six steps in the decision-making process?

1.2 ASSESSMENT

Key Concepts

Determine the best answer.

1. True or False. The basic economic problem is that consumers have too many products and services to choose from.
2. The decision-making process is best to use when
   - a. you already know the choice you will make
   - b. you are facing a decision with several good alternatives
   - c. groups rather than individuals are making a choice
   - d. you don't have enough money to pay for any of the choices
3. John has two hours before having to go to his part-time job. He is deciding between studying for a math exam and taking a nap. If John chooses to take a nap, the opportunity cost of his decision is
   - a. the rest he is getting
   - b. the score he will earn on the math exam
   - c. the wages from his part-time job
   - d. all of the above
4. The first step in the decision-making process involves
   - a. defining the problem
   - b. setting a goal
   - c. identifying the choices
   - d. evaluating alternatives

Make Academic Connections

5. **Writing** Write a one-page essay about a decision you made recently. Describe how you did or did not use the steps of the decision-making process. Discuss the outcome of your decision.
6. **Economics** Locate and read a news report describing a decision made by a business. Describe what you believe could be the opportunity cost of its choice. Justify your answer.

RETEACH Instruct students to locate the vocabulary terms from the lesson and write the definition of each in their own words. Then compare the written definitions with those in the lesson.

ENRICH Engage students in the use of the decision-making process to choose between participating in an after-school activity and holding a part-time job.

Work as a TEAM

Encourage students to brainstorm for possible alternatives. Then ask them to discuss each one to come up with the two that the team will evaluate for the city council. Ask students to describe how opportunity costs were used in their analysis.

ONGOING ASSESSMENT

CHECKPOINT ✓ANSWER

1. Define the problem.
2. Identify the choices.
3. Evaluate the advantages and disadvantages of each alternative.
4. Choose the best alternative.
5. Act on your choice.
6. Review your decision.

ASSESS

Key Concepts *Answers*

1. False. The basic economic problem is satisfying unlimited wants and needs with limited resources.
2. b. you are facing a decision with several good alternatives.
3. b. the score he will earn on the math exam
4. a. defining the problem

Make Academic Connections *Answers*

5. Essays will vary. Ask volunteers to share their thoughts with the class.
6. Offer suggestions for how students should report their findings. Consider allowing students to work in pairs.

CLOSE Direct students to state the basic economic problem and provide one example of how it has affected them.

LIFE/WORK SKILLS

Students can't make effective decisions without access to (and use of) information. Research skills will help them gather the information they need to make better decisions. Effective research skills will aid students in their current classes and in their future education and careers, as well as in their personal life.

THINK CRITICALLY THROUGH VISUALS

Answers will vary. Library resources, including librarians, can help you find additional authoritative sources. These resources also allow you to narrow your search for information related to your research question.

Think Critically *Answers*

1. Opinions vary and are often not objective. They are formed by a variety of factors and may or may not be reliable. True data, or facts, are generally objective.

2. Some questions may be answered this way, but in order to formulate the best possible decision, it is usually wise to include your own specific observations and data. Other information sources may not be entirely accurate, current, complete, or relevant to your question.

LIFE/WORK SKILLS

INFORMATION LITERACY

Research Skills

Your abilities are more than just the sum of your experiences. Whether the goal is to improve a business or your own performance, you need to make sound decisions based on the best information available. Research skills are needed to improve decision making.

Research is a systematic, objective study to establish facts and principles. The research process begins with a question or problem and results in a possible answer that can become the basis for further research.

Here are the steps to follow when conducting research.

Formulate a question. What is the problem you are facing or what is the issue you are trying to resolve? The question should be as specific as possible and relate to an important personal or business issue.

Gather and review information related to the question. Determine if others have studied the same problem and if they have reported on the results of their study. This step usually involves a careful search of library information, including books, magazines, and documents.

Separate fact from opinion. Effective research relies on objective data. The opinions of others may provide interesting ideas to consider but should not be relied on for answers to your question. Consider if the sources of information are credible and if the information provided is factual.

Propose a hypothesis. A hypothesis is a prediction about the answer to your research question. The hypothesis can be based on the information gathered, your experience, or your beliefs. You will conduct a study to gather information that will either support the hypothesis or determine that it is wrong.

Collect data to test the hypothesis. Researchers carefully design studies to gather information related to the question and hypothesis. The common methods of collecting data are surveys, observations, and experiments.

Analyze the data. After data has been collected, it is organized and then analyzed using statistical procedures. Careful review of the results of the data analysis will provide evidence to support or disprove the hypothesis.

Report the results. It is important that researchers document and report the results of their research. A well-organized and carefully written report will help others understand the research and repeat it or improve upon it. It will also provide evidence that the research was objective.

Put the research results into practice. You began the research process to answer a question or solve a problem. You need to apply what you learned and determine if what you learned makes a difference. No matter the results, you will want to continue to conduct research and study the research of others. It will help you make sound decisions and have confidence in your knowledge and abilities.

Ditty_about_summer/Shutterstock.com

Even with Internet access, why is it often necessary to use library resources to gather and review information related to your research question?

Think Critically

1. Why should you try to avoid basing your actions on opinions rather than facts?
2. Do you believe some questions can be answered by just gathering and reviewing existing information rather than collecting new data? Why or why not?

Applied Skills

Writing Across the Curriculum Instruct students to write a few paragraphs illustrating how they can use the research process presented on this page in one of their other classes. Ask them to use a specific example based on a past or current assignment.

1.3 Economic Systems

Learning Outcomes

1.3.1 Identify the three economic questions.

1.3.2 Differentiate among the main types of economic systems.

1.3.3 Describe the economic system of the United States.

Key Terms

economic system 19
command economy 19
market economy 19
traditional economy 20
mixed economy 20
capitalism 21

Focus on REAL LIFE

Jiang Liang is a resident of modern-day China, but he knows what it was like to grow up in a farming community in the Yangtze valley.

"The farmers still work the land with the same tools and methods they have used for generations, and the government tells them what they can and cannot grow," Liang explains to a colleague.

His colleague asks, "What does your family think about you living in Hong Kong and working for a multinational company?"

Liang smiles and responds, "My parents were surprised when I told them that the company decides how many of each of our products we will produce each year and then sets the selling price for each of our markets."

Liang has experienced two very different economic systems. Which system seems most familiar to you?

LO 1.3.1

THE THREE ECONOMIC QUESTIONS

Every country in the world must deal with the basic economic problem. No country has unlimited resources and each one has citizens with important basic needs for food, housing, education, and health care. As economies develop, people have a growing set of wants as well.

In order to determine how available resources will be used to meet needs and wants, each country must answer three economic questions.

1. What goods and services will be produced?
2. How will the goods and services be produced?
3. What needs and wants will be satisfied with the goods and services produced?

How the questions are answered indicates the type of economic system that exists in each country.

What to Produce?

Countries have differing types and amounts of resources just as individuals differ in their skills and abilities. Some have rich soil and regular rains that yield large food supplies. Other nations have desert climates or long, cold winters that make farming difficult. Some countries have abundant supplies of oil, coal, and other energy

Tish1/Shutterstock Images

What resources are necessary for farmers to obtain large yields of their crops?

Focus on REAL LIFE

Ask any students who have lived in or visited another country for a length of time if they noticed any differences in the economic system of the country compared with the U.S. system. Suggest that international business makes those differences more apparent to people.

TEACH

Ask students how they would answer the three economic questions. Ask if they think the answers would change if they lived in a different country.

THINK CRITICALLY THROUGH VISUALS

Resources necessary for large farm yields include efficient labor, access to financing, high-quality seeds and fertilizers, adequate water supplies, and appropriate equipment.

Portfolio Activity

Assign the Portfolio Activity for Chapter, located on the product website.

COLLECT Offer suggestions to help students locate an example that illustrates an economic principle or concept from this chapter.

CREATE Remind students that they are to illustrate how the three economic decisions are made in the U.S. economic system.

CONNECT Point out that students need to connect their example to the visual they created.

FYI

Ask students to describe both the benefits and disadvantages that accrue from technology. Students should identify the benefits to lifestyles and work. They should also identify negative effects such as fewer jobs and changing lifestyles.

TEACH

Ask students how a country's resources might change over time. How might major changes in resources affect the way a country answers the three economic questions?

ONGOING ASSESSMENT

CHECKPOINT ✓ANSWER

The three economic questions are

1. What goods and services will be produced?
2. How will the goods and services be produced?
3. What needs and wants will be satisfied with the goods and services produced?

FYI Technology continues to change the way work is done. Today's jobs require less than 1 percent of the total muscle power used before the Industrial Revolution but much greater levels of education and skill.

sources, while many countries have only a meager supply. The resources of a country are very important in determining what goods can be produced. A country can decide to trade some of its resources with other countries to obtain those it needs.

Just as nations differ in the type and amount of resources, they also differ in what they determine to be their important needs and wants. One country may focus on manufacturing a variety of consumer products while another country emphasizes building roads and bridges. Some economies focus on improving agriculture while others develop industrial jobs. Some nations have excellent schools and health care while others build imposing military forces.

Deciding how to use resources and what to produce is never an easy decision. If a country spends too much in one area or on one group of people, there may not be enough resources to meet other needs. If most resources are used to produce consumer products, not enough attention may be paid to a country's infrastructure of roads, energy, and water systems.

How to Produce?

Countries must decide the best ways to use their resources to produce what is needed. As a country develops, tasks that were traditionally performed using human labor, such as farming and mining, are now performed with more efficient tools and equipment. Two centuries ago, more than 80 percent of U.S. citizens were involved in agriculture. Today, less than 3 percent of the U.S. population produces the food the country consumes. The labor needs of the U.S. economy have changed. Today's complex economy requires highly specialized healthcare professionals, financial managers, and computer specialists, as well as a rapidly growing number of skilled and unskilled service workers.

Each country decides how to use its resources to produce the goods and services it needs. It may rely on unskilled or skilled labor, on advanced or simple technology, on its own resources or on those it obtains from other countries. Privately owned businesses may be responsible for production or the government may own and manage the resources and businesses.

What Needs and Wants to Satisfy?

Because wants and needs are unlimited, many will remain unmet no matter what goods and services a country decides to produce. Decision makers must determine which needs and wants are the most critical when deciding what to produce. Some countries may decide to invest in capital goods, while others produce more consumer goods. Some countries devote more resources to producing the goods and services important to government activities. Other economies respond to those citizens who have the most money or the most political power.

In the United States, goods and services are plentiful and many decisions are left to individual consumers. What wants and needs you satisfy largely depends on how much money you have and how you choose to spend or save it. The amount of money you have available to spend depends a great deal on your education and abilities as well as how you decide to use them to earn income.

CHECKPOINT ✓
What are the three economic questions?

Applied Skills

Technology Instruct students to use the Internet to compare the number of U.S. businesses involved in farming and manufacturing today compared with 100 years and then 50 years ago. Encourage students to create a chart or graph to display the results.

Often, consumers found it difficult to find basic products such as bread or a hammer.

During the past decade, several of the Eastern European nations that had used a command economy have made major progress in converting to a mixed economy. Some of these countries made such economic progress that they were granted membership into the European Union.

Nearly 1.4 billion Chinese citizens live under a communist government that controls most of the resources and economic decisions. The economy of China is adopting elements of a market system for a growing number of economic decisions. Entire regions of the country, particularly the eastern cities bordering the ocean, are enjoying a rapidly growing consumer economy based on greater individual freedom of choice. For many years, China has been a world leader in goods and services produced. The country's developing education system is producing many skilled workers who are earning money to pay for the goods and services they want.

As many countries with traditional economies develop, they often adopt mixed economies. The government makes many of the decisions about how the country's resources will be used to develop schools, hospitals, roads, and utilities. As people become educated and develop new skills, they are able to obtain better jobs and earn more money. They then have the resources to purchase more goods and services. Often businesses from other countries will begin to sell products and services in the developing country or even open a business there, offering jobs and locally produced products to the citizens.

CHECKPOINT ✓
What are the main difference among the three economic systems?

LO 1.3.3

THE U.S. ECONOMIC SYSTEM

From the descriptions provided, can you identify the economic system of the United States? Because individual businesses and consumers make most of the decisions about what will be produced and consumed, the U.S. system best fits the definition of the market economy.

Another name for the U.S. economic system is capitalism. **Capitalism** refers to the private ownership of economic resources by individuals, rather than by the government. Individual owners are free to decide what to produce with the resources they own. Individual consumers are also free to decide how they want to use their money to purchase products and services. This economic freedom lends itself to other names often associated with the U.S. economy—*free enterprise* or *private enterprise*. Individual choices and decisions are vital to the success of the U.S. economy.

The U.S. economic system is based on four important principles. They are private property, freedom of choice, profit, and competition.

Private Property

The right of *private property* means you can own, use, or dispose of things of value. In the United States, provided you have the resources, you can own anything you want and decide what you want to do with it, as long as it does not violate the law. If you invent something of value, you are protected from others taking your idea.

Freedom of Choice

Freedom of choice means that you can make economic decisions independently and must accept the consequences of those decisions. Business owners can decide where to open a business, what to sell, and how to operate the company. Consumers can decide where to shop,

ONGOING ASSESSMENT

CHECKPOINT ✓ANSWER

The main differences between the economic systems are found in the ways in which the three economic questions are answered. In a command economy, the government decides what goods and services will be produced, how they will be produced, and so forth. In a market economy, the decisions are made by individual consumers and businesses. In a traditional system, decisions are based on custom or the way things have always been done. Command and traditional economies tend to limit personal economic control, whereas a market economy relies on personal economic choice.

TEACH

Ask students to identify terms they have heard people use to describe the U.S. economic system. Call on volunteers and write their answers on the board. Possible answers include "market economy," "free enterprise," "capitalism," and "private enterprise."

As each principle of the U.S. economic system is introduced, prompt students to identify the advantages and disadvantages of each one for consumers and businesses.

Applied Skills

Building Study Skills After students have read and discussed the principles of the U.S. economic system, assign them to prepare a one-paragraph summary that describes what they have learned. Suggest that students work in pairs to review and refine their summaries.

TEACH

Write on the board, "Profit is at the heart of the private enterprise system." Ask students why profit is necessary for the economy to work effectively and whether they can see any benefits to consumers when a business makes a profit.

ONGOING ASSESSMENT

CHECKPOINT ✓ANSWER

The four principles are private property, freedom of choice, profit, and competition.

ASSESS

Key Concepts *Answers*

1. b. requiring individuals to complete specific types of work
2. d. command
3. a. make a profit

Make Academic Connections *Answers*

4. Provide guidance regarding the acceptable length of reports and the preferred style for reference citations.

5. Journal entries will vary. Examples of how the type of economy affects daily life will vary, but should reflect differences in the two types of economic systems described in the lesson.

CLOSE Assign students to list the three main types of economic systems and identify their main differences.

what to buy, and what they want to spend. Only when individual decisions unfairly harm others will there be restrictions on freedom of choice.

Profit

Businesses invest resources and take risks for one primary purpose—to earn a profit. *Profit* is the money left from sales after all of the costs of operating a business have been paid. Because businesses are not guaranteed a profit, investors may lose the money they have put into a business. Businesses are challenged to plan carefully, invest wisely, and produce goods and services that customers want in order to make a profit.

While earning a profit is at the heart of the private enterprise system, it is not the only reason for investing money and operating a business. People enjoy the challenge and freedom of business ownership, as well as the satisfaction of providing goods and services that other people want.

Competition

The rivalry among businesses to sell their goods and services is known as *competition*. Consumers have many choices of products and services and will select the ones they believe will provide the greatest satisfaction for the money they must spend. Businesses work to improve their products and control their costs. If customers are not satisfied with one company's offerings, they will look for another choice. Competition encourages businesses to improve products, keep prices low, provide effective customer service, and improve business practices.

CHECKPOINT ✓

Name the four principles on which the U.S. economic system is based.

1.3 ASSESSMENT

Key Concepts

Determine the best answer.

1. Which of the following addresses the economic question of how to produce?
   - a. growing corn instead of potatoes
   - b. requiring individuals to complete specific types of work
   - c. producing more capital goods and fewer consumer products
   - d. selling natural resources to other countries
2. In which of the following economic systems is the government's role greatest?
   - a. mixed
   - b. traditional
   - c. market
   - d. command
3. The primary reason business owners make investments and take risks in a private enterprise economy is to
   - a. make a profit
   - b. satisfy customer needs
   - c. develop new products
   - d. meet government requirements

Make Academic Connections

4. **Research** Choose one of the following 10 countries. Research that country and write a report describing its current economic system. Determine if the economic system has changed during the last 100 years and include your findings in the report.

Botswana	Hong Kong
Chile	Kazakhstan
Costa Rica	Latvia
Germany	Singapore
Greece	United Arab Emirates

5. **Writing** Write a journal entry describing a typical school day in your life. Start with waking up in the morning and end at bed time. Include specific information about food, clothing, transportation, school, and activities. Write a second entry describing what you believe would be a typical day for someone your age living in a country with a traditional economy. Compare the journal entries and provide three examples of how the type of economy affects daily life.

RETEACH Ask students to individually list the three economic questions. As a group, check the answers and discuss why these answers are important to consumers and businesses.

ENRICH Assign students to prepare a three-paragraph writing exercise in response to the question, "How would you improve the U.S. private enterprise economy?"

1.4 Supply and Demand

Learning Outcomes

1.4.1 Describe supply and demand orally and with graphs.

1.4.2 Discuss how supply and demand affect prices of products and services.

Key Terms

consumer 23
producers 23
demand 24
supply 24
market price 26

Focus on REAL LIFE

Anna and Carlos are both in the mood for Italian food. Their town has two Italian restaurants, Ristorante Italia and Mamma's Pizzeria. Both Anna and Carlos are on a limited budget, so they are always careful about how they spend their money. Mamma's Pizzeria is famous for its delicious pizza and has excellent service. Ristorante Italia has a broader menu including pizza, pasta, salads, and sandwiches. Anna and Carlos both feel the food is good but doesn't have that authentic Italian flavor. Often, the restaurant is crowded and the service is slow. Because Momma's is known for the best pizza in town, the pizza prices are quite a bit higher than those at Ristorante Italia.

If you were going to eat with Anna and Carlos, how would you decide which restaurant to choose?

LO 1.4.1

PARTICIPATING IN A MARKET ECONOMY

In a market economy, buyers and sellers use the marketplace to make economic decisions. Buying decisions are made by consumers—including individuals, businesses, and government. A **consumer** is a person who buys and uses goods and services. The individual buying decisions of consumers have a tremendous influence in a market economy. Consumers decide what to buy, where to buy, from whom to buy, and what price they are willing to pay.

To be successful, producers must pay close attention to the needs and experiences of consumers. **Producers** are individuals and organizations that determine what products and services will be available for sale. Producers invest resources and take risks in order to make a profit. They determine what products and services will be available in the economy, what needs and wants they will try to satisfy, and the prices they will charge.

It may seem that the economy is a big, unorganized system in which everyone pursues his or her own self-interest. You may wonder how the system can work when each business makes its own decisions about what to produce and charge, while each consumer makes a decision about what and where to buy and how much to pay. The system does

Syda Productions/Shutterstock.com

What are the advantages of being a consumer in a market economy?

Focus on REAL LIFE

Ask students to suggest ways that each of the restaurants can attract new customers and make sure the customers are happy with their experience. Ask students if they think the two restaurants compete directly with each other for the same customers.

TEACH

Explain to students that, in order for a market economy to work well, consumers must be able to satisfy their needs and businesses must be able to make a profit. Ask what would happen to an economy when one of those results is not achieved.

THINK CRITICALLY THROUGH VISUALS

A consumer in a market economy has the freedom to choose what to buy, where to buy, from whom to buy, and what price to pay. These choices give consumers a great deal of influence on the market.

Different Learning Styles

Kinesthetic Learner Ask students to create a diagram or picture of how consumers and producers make independent decisions yet interact in a market economy. Students should explain the information included in their diagram.

TEACH

Tell students that estimating supply and demand is very important for businesses. Economists study competitors and consumers to help businesses determine how many products to produce and what prices they can charge.

Ask students to use their own words to define the terms "demand" and "supply." Then ask them to describe an experience they have had as a consumer that illustrates each term.

work—and works well—due to the economic principles of supply and demand.

Consumers Set Demand

When consumers make decisions about what they will purchase, they determine the demand for goods and services. **Demand** is the quantity of a good or service that consumers are willing and able to buy. A business depends on demand for their products and services in order to make a profit. For example, if a new restaurant opens in your town, but the service is slow, the quality of the food is poor, and the prices are high, will consumers continue to eat there? It is not likely. Suppose another restaurant opens with terrific food as well as fast and friendly service. It will soon be packed with people who prefer it to the first establishment.

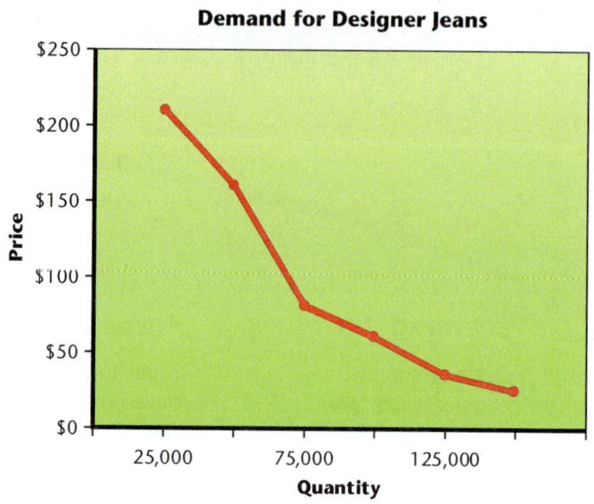

FIGURE 1-2
The quantity of a product or service customers are willing to purchase at various prices can be illustrated with a graph known as a demand curve.

A Graphic View

Demand and supply for a product or service can be illustrated using graphs known as demand curves and supply curves. The *demand curve* illustrates the relationship between the price of a product or service and the quantity demanded by consumers.

Producers Establish Supply

Understanding consumer demand helps businesses to determine what types and quantities of products to supply. **Supply** is the quantity of a good or service that businesses are willing and able to provide. If consumers want a popular product and are willing to pay a price that allows a business to make a profit, businesses will be willing to provide the product to meet the demand. On the other hand, if there is a greater supply of a product than consumers want or if customers are tiring of an older or poor-quality product, businesses are less likely to continue to offer the product for sale.

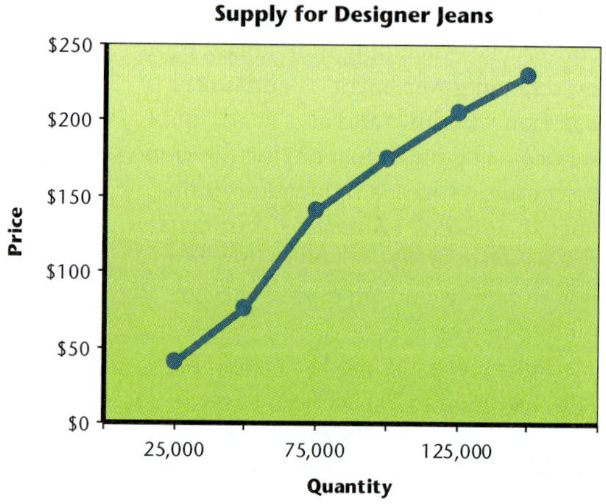

FIGURE 1-3
The quantity of a product or service businesses are willing to supply at various prices can be illustrated with a graph known as a supply curve.

Different Learning Styles

Visual Learner Draw a graph on the board to help demonstrate the relationship of supply and demand. Using Figure 1-4 on page 26 for guidance, draw and label the *x*-axis, *Quantity*. Draw and label the *y*-axis, *Price*. Demonstrate how the demand curve is created by identifying several quantity/price points on the graph and then connecting the dots. Repeat for the supply curve.

As the price decreases, the number of consumers willing and able to purchase the product and the quantity they will purchase increases. Figure 1-2 illustrates the possible customer demand for designer jeans at various prices in a specific market.

In the same way, the *supply curve* illustrates the relationship between the price of a product and the quantity businesses are willing to supply. At higher prices, businesses will be willing to supply larger quantities of the product or service. Figure 1-3 illustrates the possible supply of designer jeans manufacturers are willing to provide to a market at various prices.

CHECKPOINT
How does the price of a product affect demand and supply?

LO 1.4.2

DETERMINING PRICE

Why is the price of a hotel room in Phoenix, Arizona, higher in winter than summer? Why do the prices of many of the products sold by farmers remain quite low? Prices are affected by the relationship between supply and demand, plus other factors.

Factors Influencing Demand

If many consumers want (or demand) a particular good or service, its price will tend to go up. More people vacation in Phoenix in the winter than in the summer, so demand and prices for hotel rooms rise. When fewer people visit that area during the hot summer, the supply of hotel rooms is greater than the demand. Therefore, prices will decline.

When customers see a number of products that they believe will satisfy a particular want or need, demand for any one of those products will not be as high. Customers will be willing to switch from one product to another if the price of one is much higher than the others. When customers cannot find a good substitute for a product they want, demand for that product will be high. Even if the price increases, they will be willing to pay the higher price because they are unwilling or unable to switch to another choice.

Factors Influencing Supply

The supply of a product can also affect the price. Due to the immense supply of many of the crops and livestock raised on farms, prices remain low. If a drought cuts the quantity of corn grown by Midwest farmers, the price of corn will increase.

Competitors are businesses offering very similar products to the same customers. As the number of competitors increases, so does supply. A business will not be able to easily raise its prices. It will have to be much more sensitive to the prices charged by its competitors.

When competition is limited, consumers cannot find good alternatives. If you live in a part of town where there is only one supermarket, the prices at that store will often be high due to a lack of competition. The prices of products featuring new technology will often be high because the company offering the new product seldom has direct competition.

Sometimes a natural disaster or other unforeseen circumstance affects supply. If the supply of oil, gasoline, or water is disrupted, the price of the affected resource will increase. The supply of other products that use those resources in production may also be affected and their prices can increase as well. Sometimes businesses will

Work as a TEAM
The prices of some products change a great deal in a short time, while the prices for other products remain quite stable. Work as a team to identify several products that experience regular price changes and several that do not. List the products and then discuss how supply and demand appear to affect the prices of each of the products.

ONGOING ASSESSMENT

CHECKPOINT *ANSWER*
As prices decrease, the number of consumers willing and able to purchase the product and the quantity they are willing to buy (demand) will increase. As prices increase, businesses will be willing to supply larger quantities of the product.

TEACH

Ask students to identify products they have purchased in the past in which their demand for that product has changed. Ask them whether their demand increased or decreased and the reasons for the change.

Work as a TEAM

Encourage students to discuss differences in products that seem to have more stable prices and those for which prices tend to change frequently or a great deal. If they were business owners would they rather sell products that had stable or volatile prices?

Different Learning Abilities

English Language Learners (ELL) Ask students whose dominant language is not English to prepare a table listing the following words both in English and in their primary language: *supply, demand, price,* and *competitor.*

ONGOING ASSESSMENT

CHECKPOINT ✓ANSWER

Supply, demand, and competition determine the market price for a product or service. The market price is the point at which supply and demand are equal.

ASSESS

Key Concepts *Answers*

1. True
2. False. Supply refers to the quantity of goods or services that businesses are willing and able to provide.
3. c. usually will decrease

Make Academic Connections *Answers*

4. $20.00 × 8,500 = $170,000

$22.50 × 7,800 = $175,500

$25.00 × 6,200 = $155,000

$27.50 × 5,900 = $162,250

$30.00 × 4,300 = $129,000

5. Memos will vary, but should reflect an understanding of the material presented in this lesson.

CLOSE Review the roles of consumers and producers in determining the price of a product in a market economy. Summarize for students how each role affects the decisions of the other role.

try to restrict supply of products in order to obtain a higher price. That will only work if customer demand is high and if there are no good substitutes for the product.

Determining Market Price

Supply, demand, and competition determine the market price for a product or service. The **market price** is the point where supply and demand are equal. Figure 1-4 shows the market price for designer jeans in a specific market. Look at the point where the demand curve and the supply curve intersect. This illustrates that consumers are willing to purchase nearly 65,000 pairs of jeans and businesses are willing to supply that same quantity if the retail price is about $110 per pair.

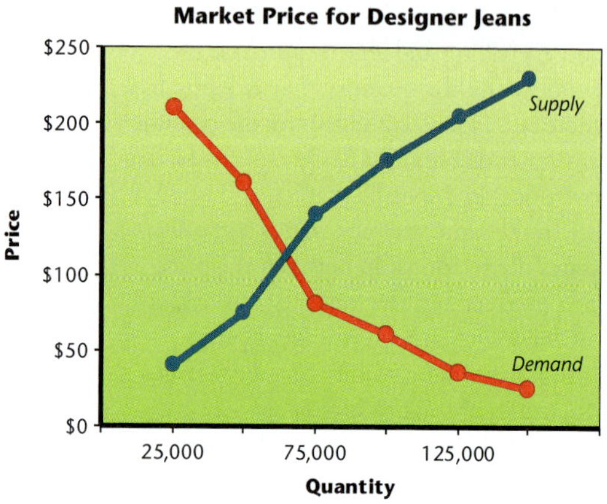

FIGURE 1-4

The market price for a product is the point where supply and demand are equal.

> **CHECKPOINT** ✓
> How is the market price for a product determined?

1.4 ASSESSMENT

Key Concepts

Determine the best answer.

1. True or False. Both individuals and organizations can be producers.
2. True or False. Supply is the quantity of a good or service that a consumer is willing and able to buy at a particular price.
3. As competition increases, prices
   - **a.** usually increase as well
   - **b.** are not affected so will usually not change
   - **c.** usually will decrease
   - **d.** There is no way to predict what will happen to prices due to competition.

Make Academic Connections

4. **Math** Calculate the total value of sales at each possible price for a product with the consumer demand shown

Price	Quantity demanded
$20.00	8,500
$22.50	7,800
$25.00	6,200
$27.50	5,900
$30.00	4,300

5. **Writing** Write an article for an online newsletter or blog about the importance of supply and demand in determining the prices to charge when opening a new restaurant. Be sure to include an explanation of how supply relates to competitors and demand relates to customers.

RETEACH Instruct students to use the Internet to locate examples of supply and demand curves. Ask students to show the graphs and explain the concepts of supply, demand, and market price using the information on the graphs.

ENRICH Explain that determining supply, demand, and market price is an area where mathematics is important to businesspeople. Ask students to make a list of other business activities in which mathematical skills are important.

BUSINESS IMPROVING SOCIETY

HEIFER INTERNATIONAL

How might a family in Tanzania, where this young boy lives, benefit from having a cow?

Ending hunger and poverty around the world! It sounds like such a big dream that no one would undertake it. Nevertheless, since 1944, Heifer International has had that dream as its goal. Through a unique program of giving communities a source of food rather than just distributing food, the organization has reached millions of families in more than 115 countries.

Dan West was a midwestern farmer serving as a relief worker during the Spanish Civil War. With a limited supply of milk and food, he had to decide who would receive the rations and who would not.

As a farmer, West realized that if people had livestock, farming tools, and some assistance in learning effective farming practices, they would have the capability to raise food for themselves and their families for a lifetime.

He returned to the United States and formed Heifers for Relief. He asked other farmers to donate a heifer. Dan delivered the first shipment of 17 heifers to Puerto Rico, giving them to families with malnourished children who had never tasted milk before. Why heifers? The young cows would give birth to a new calf. Each family that received a heifer and training in how to raise and maintain dairy animals was asked to "pass on the gift" by donating a calf to another family.

For more than 65 years, Heifer International has been developing new projects around the world. Their mission is to work with communities to end hunger and poverty and to care for the earth. They envision a world of communities living together in peace and sharing the resources of a healthy planet. Today, hundreds of thousands of people continue to donate heifers, rabbits, goats, and chickens. Others make cash contributions to purchase livestock and supplies. Many people volunteer their time to travel to the rural communities with the animals to provide training and assistance so that the livestock will remain healthy, grow, and multiply for further distribution.

Recent projects of Heifer International include:

- Sending five rural veterinarians to Mongolia to work with animal herders to teach them improved animal management. These herders will then work with 500 additional herding families.
- Mobilizing experts to help slow the spread of coffee leaf rust on small coffee farms in Latin America. Coffee leaf rust threatens the farmers' sole source of income. Experts also are helping to diversify the crops grown by introducing the farmers to bananas and avocados.
- Placing 500 hives of bees in five Adaklu communities in Ghana, Africa. The communities will be taught eco-friendly hive management and honey harvesting techniques. Honey is a major source of nutrition in an area that contends with a high child mortality rate.

Think Critically

1. How does this approach to solving world hunger differ from other relief efforts that distribute food, milk, clothing, and health supplies?
2. Use the Internet to locate examples of other organizations that are working to reduce hunger and increase economic opportunities around the world. How are they similar to or different from Heifer International?

BUSINESS IMPROVING SOCIETY

Heifer International has a long history of helping improve the economic well-being of families. The organization's projects also strengthen the traditional economies of the countries and regions in which they work.

THINK CRITICALLY THROUGH VISUALS

The family might benefit by drinking milk, learning how to raise dairy animals, and possibly passing on the gift by donating a calf to another family.

Think Critically *Answers*

1. Answers will vary, but should reflect an understanding that providing a one-time supply of food will not meet long-term needs. Creating self-sufficiency through programs such as Heifer International enables communities to address the unlimited need for food.

2. Answers will vary. Encourage interested students to give short presentations about one of the organizations they discover.

Applied Skills

Communication Instruct students to compose an essay on the ways that the work of Heifer International improves relationships between people from the United States and those from other countries around the world.

Think Critically About Business *Answers*

1. Examples will vary, but should demonstrate an understanding that both needs and wants may be satisfied at the same time and that wants for some people may be needs for others. A professional football player may be required to wear a team jersey in order to receive payment for doing his job, making it a need, but the same jersey becomes a want for a fan of the team.

2. Answers will vary, but should demonstrate an understanding of how natural, human, and capital resources are used in the business.

3. Answers will vary.

4. Answers will vary.

5a. Trying out for a team might be time lost from another important activity.

5b. Accepting a part-time job might mean time away from friends.

5c. Studying for an important exam might be time lost from sleep.

5d. Saving money for a car might be the amount of money you would otherwise spend on a hobby or other interest.

6. Student answers are to be in table format and should reflect accurate information about each economic system.

What goods and services will be produced?

Command: The government decides what goods and services will be produced or offered.

Market: The choices of consumers and producers determine which products and services are offered. Competition drives producers to provide new and better products and services based on buying trends.

Traditional: The same products and services that have always been produced continue to be produced whenever possible.

How will the goods and services be produced?

Command: The government decides on production methods and who will be involved in that work.

Market: Individual businesses decide how production will occur but competition drives businesses to find the most efficient ways of doing things.

Traditional: Things are done in much the same way they have always been done, often regardless of their effectiveness.

Chapter 1 Assessment

Review Business Concepts

1.1 Satisfying Needs and Wants

- Things that are necessary in order to live are needs. Things that add comfort and pleasure to life are wants.
- Goods are things that you can see and touch. Services are activities provided for others that are consumed at the same time they are provided.
- Economic resources are the things available to be used to produce goods and services. Economic resources are also known as factors of production. The three kinds of economic resources are natural resources, human resources, and capital resources.

1.2 Economic Choices

- Most choices result from considering a number of alternatives. When you give up something to have something else, you are making a trade-off. The opportunity cost is the value of the next best choice.
- The six steps in the decision-making process are: define the problem, identify the choices, evaluate each choice, choose the best alternative, act on the choice, and review your decision.

1.3 Economic Systems

- All economies must answer three economic questions: What goods and services will be produced? How will the goods and services be produced? What needs and wants will be satisfied with the goods and services produced?
- A nation's plan for answering the three economic questions is its economic system. In a command economy, most resources are owned and controlled by the government. In a market economy, resources are owned and controlled by the people of the country. In a traditional economy, goods and services are produced the way it has always been done. A mixed economy combines elements of command and market economies.
- Capitalism refers to the private ownership of resources by individuals rather than by the government. The U.S. economic system is based on the principles of private property, freedom of choice, profit, and competition.

1.4 Supply and Demand

- In a market economy, individual buyers and sellers use the marketplace to make economic decisions. Demand is the quantity of a good or service that consumers are willing and able to buy. Supply is the quantity of a good or service that businesses are willing and able to provide.
- If many consumers demand a particular good or service, its price will go up. If competition increases and therefore customers have more choices, businesses will not be able to easily raise their prices. The market price for a product or service is the point where supply and demand are equal.

Think Critically About Business

1. Identify five products or services that could be either a need or a want. Provide an example for each that illustrates when it would be considered a need and when it would be considered a want.
2. Select a business with which you are familiar. Describe factors of production used by the business that fit within each of the three kinds of economic resources.
3. Find a newspaper, magazine, or Internet article that deals with scarcity of a product, service, or natural resource. Write a summary of the article in which you identify who is affected by the scarcity and the effect it is having on businesses and consumers.
4. Identify an important decision you will need to make in the near future, such as selecting a college or career or making a major purchase. Prepare a visual to illustrate how you would complete each step in the decision-making process for the problem.

5. Identify a possible opportunity cost for each of the following:
   a. Trying out for an athletic team
   b. Accepting a part-time job
   c. Studying for an important exam
   d. Saving money to buy a used car
6. Develop a table that compares the answers to the three economic questions for a command economy, a market economy, and a traditional economy.
7. Explain how freedom of choice can affect the availability of products and services for consumers. Now explain how it can also affect the profit a business might make on the products and services it sells.
8. Do you agree that the term "private enterprise" is a good description of the U.S. economy? Why or why not?
9. Select a product that is a regular purchase of many consumers. Use a graphing program to develop an illustration of a supply and demand curve for the product. Prepare a brief oral description of the illustration.
10. Review recent news reports of products and services where the price has been affected by supply and demand factors. Write a report using those examples that discusses the effect of supply and demand on prices.

Develop Your Business Language

Match the terms listed with the definitions.

11. Process of choosing which needs and wants will be satisfied.
12. Individuals and organizations that determine what products and services will be available for sale.
13. The method a country uses to answer the three economic questions.
14. Things available to be used to produce goods and services.
15. Things that are required in order to live.
16. Not having enough resources to satisfy every need.
17. Quantity of a good or service that businesses are willing and able to provide.
18. Person who buys and uses goods and services.
19. Economy in which resources are owned and controlled by the government.
20. Things that you can see and touch.
21. Private ownership of resources by individuals rather than by the government.
22. Economy in which goods and services are produced the way it has always been done.
23. Economy that combines elements of the command and market economies.
24. Quantity of a good or service that consumers are willing and able to buy.
25. Point where supply and demand are equal.
26. Things that add comfort and pleasure to your life.
27. Activities provided for the satisfaction of others that are consumed at the same time they are produced.
28. Giving up on something to have something else.
29. Value of the next-best alternative that you were not able to choose.
30. Economy in which the resources are owned and controlled by the people of the country.

Key Terms

a. capitalism
b. command economy
c. consumer
d. demand
e. economic decision making
f. economic resources
g. economic system
h. goods
i. market economy
j. market price
k. mixed economy
l. needs
m. opportunity cost
n. producers
o. scarcity
p. services
q. supply
r. trade-off
s. traditional economy
t. wants

What needs and wants will be satisfied with the goods and services produced?

Command: The government decides which needs and wants will take priority and which people or businesses will benefit in the economy.

Market: Individual consumers and businesses make decisions based on their own self-interest. Consumers try to satisfy their needs and wants with the resources they have available. Businesses choose to produce and sell products and services that will result in a profit.

Traditional: The focus of traditional economies is usually placed on the most basic needs of the families and communities.

7. Freedom of choice produces a greater variety of customer wants and needs, along with greater business competition with products and services to meet those needs. More competition encourages product improvements and better prices for customers. Businesses can use this to their advantage by trying to satisfy customers better than competitors resulting in more sales and profits.

8. Private enterprise does describe the U.S. economy in that we each have a great deal of individual choice as consumers and businesses. Not everything is private, however, as government provides many products and services and many consumers and businesses look out for the needs of others rather than just their own self-interest.

9. Answers will vary.

10. Answers will vary.

Develop Your Business Language *Answers*

11. e. economic decision making
12. n. producers
13. g. economic system
14. f. economic resources
15. l. needs
16. o. scarcity
17. q. supply
18. c. consumer
19. b. command economy
20. h. goods
21. a. capitalism
22. s. traditional economy
23. k. mixed economy
24. d. demand

25. j. market price

26. t. wants

27. p. services

28. r. trade-off

29. m. opportunity cost

30. i. market economy

Make Academic Connections *Answers*

31. Answers will vary.

32. Answers will vary.

33a. (53.5 – 18.6) × 4 = 139.6 hr.; (53.5 – 24.7) × 4 = 115.2 hr.

33b. Country 1: 65.0 ÷ 8 = 8.125 days
Country 2: 132.0 ÷ 8 = 16.5 days
Country 3: 701.0 ÷ 8 = 87.625 days

33c. Country 1: 0.28 + 65.0 + 0.27 + 0.12 + 8.0 + 18.6 = 97.27 hr
Country 2: 0.48 + 132.0 + 0.22 + 0.18 + 7.0 + 24.7 = 164.6 hr
Country 3: 0.93 + 701.0 + 0.45 + 0.05 + 25.0 + 53.5 = 780.93 hr

Make Your Case *Answers*

34a. 29,970,000

34b. market economy

34c. seven times more productive

Make Academic Connections

31. Research Wise consumers make informed purchases. Are there better alternatives for the products you buy? Pick three brand-name products you use on a regular basis. Use the Internet to find two comparable products for each of these products. Prepare a table that compares price, consumer ratings, and product differences among each of the product categories. Write a short summary of your findings and note whether the information will change your purchasing habits or not.

32. Communication Your community has received a gift of 100 acres of land from a long-time citizen. A community group is encouraging the city council to use the land to develop a park. Another group would prefer that it be developed as an area for new small businesses. Prepare a one-page report for the city council comparing the two choices based on the opportunity costs of each.

33. Math The table below shows the average number of working hours it takes a worker in three cities in different countries to earn enough money to purchase several products and services. Use the information to answer the following questions:

a. How much longer than a worker in Country 1 must a worker in Country 3 work to earn enough to buy food for a family of four for a total of four weeks? Than a worker in Country 2?

b. How many eight-hour days would a worker in each country have to work to buy a large-screen TV?

c. What is the total amount of time a worker in each country would have to work to purchase all of the products and services listed?

	COUNTRY 1	COUNTRY 2	COUNTRY 3
1 lb. of ground beef	17.0 min.	29.0 min.	56.0 min.
Large-screen TV	65.0 hr.	132.0 hr.	701.0 hr.
1 tube of toothpaste	16.0 min.	13.0 min.	27.0 min.
City bus fare	7.0 min.	11.0 min.	3.0 min.
1 pair of men's shoes	8.0 hr.	7.0 hr.	25.0 hr.
1 week of food for a family of 4	18.6 hr.	24.7 hr.	53.5 hr.

Make Your Case

34. Countries that use modern technology and equipment can produce more with fewer people in a shorter time than countries in which many workers perform the work by manual labor. Study the figures below for farm workers and their yearly output in two different kinds of economic systems, and then answer the questions that follow.

a. How many more people were working in agricultural jobs in the traditional economy than in the market economy?

b. In which system was each farm worker more productive?

c. In terms of people supplied from the output of each farm worker, how much more productive was the worker in (b)?

	TRADITIONAL ECONOMY	MARKET ECONOMY
Size of the agriculture labor force	34,350,000	4,380,000
Number of people supplied with food from the labor of each agriculture worker	7	49

Interactions and Connections

35. Study businesses in your local community to learn more about how supply and demand work to establish the market price for products and services. Find one example of a type of business where there appears to be evidence of high consumer demand, another with evidence of a great deal of competition among businesses, and a third where other factors seem to be influencing the

Interactions and Connections

35. Ask students to present their reports to the class.

market price of a product or service. Gather information through reading, talking with community members, and observations to aid in your understanding. Prepare an oral report to describe what you learned about supply, demand, and price to other students in your class.

36. The U.S. government collects and reports information about the U.S. economy that is useful to businesses and individuals. The U.S. Census Bureau features economic data on its website, including economic indicators that provide important information about changes in the U.S. economy. Use your web browser to access the Census Bureau's website and locate the link to "Economic Indicators." Select one of the indicators and investigate how it has changed from the beginning of the century until now.

37. Prepare a table to present the economic information you found. Summarize the data in your table with a chart or graph.

38. Next, write a brief description of your findings. Explain how the economic indicator helps people understand the U.S. economy and how the information might be used by businesses or consumers.

American Enterprise Project

The American enterprise system encourages individuals to take the risk of starting a business. Consumers play an important role in the American enterprise system because their demand for goods and services influences which businesses will be successful. Business success depends upon paying attention to consumer demand.

Your team of three has been challenged to design a presentation for middle school students that explains the power of consumers, the role of entrepreneurs, and the role of government in the American enterprise system. Your presentation should include an example of a real business, describe key elements of the free enterprise system, and define important terms. Your team is also responsible for developing a quiz based on your classroom presentation which will determine what the middle school students learn about the American enterprise system.

You will create a business report with supporting statements. Creativity through design and use of meaningful graphics is encouraged. The report should be a clear presentation about the American enterprise system and your strategy for teaching middle school students key concepts. The report should include the following parts:

- purpose of project
- research to determine business needs of selected example
- description of project
- uniqueness of project
- evaluation and results

The format of your report will be evaluated for its clear, concise and logical presentation, creativity, correct use of grammar, punctuation, and spelling, and acceptable business style.

Performance Indicators Evaluated

- Understand the major concepts about the American enterprise system.
- Deliver an effective presentation to middle school students.
- Highlight measurable results through the use of a quiz about the American enterprise system.
- Strengthen middle school students' understanding of the American enterprise system.

For more detailed information about performance indicators, go to the FBLA website.

Think Critically

1. Why is it important for young Americans to understand the American enterprise system?
2. List two strategies to use during the presentation that will hold the attention of middle school students.
3. List five major concepts that middle school students should understand about the American enterprise system.
4. Describe a joint project between FBLA members and middle school students that could be used to strengthen understanding about the American enterprise system.

www.fbla-pbl.org

36. Encourage students to use a computer spreadsheet to organize their data and prepare a chart or graph.

37. Students should understand that businesses make plans to expand or reduce operations based on changes in the economy. Individuals need to understand how the economy is changing to make choices about how to use their resources. A growing economy increases business and consumer confidence, whereas a shrinking economy usually causes concerns.

38. Answers will vary.

WINNING EDGE American Enterprise Project

This activity gives FBLA members the experience of presenting to a challenging younger audience. The presenters will determine the effectiveness of their presentation from the results of the quiz given to the middle school students.

Think Critically *Answers*

1. America's economy is based on the principles of private enterprise. Much of the strength of the economy is directly related to the market economy and the incentives it provides to consumers and business owners.

2. Answers will vary. Some strategies that might be used include music, the use of visual aids, audience participation, and giving small prizes to students who answer questions correctly.

3. Answers will vary but might include ownership, supply, demand, consumerism, and profit.

4. Answers will vary. Some possible ideas include designing a billboard that emphasizes the American enterprise system, shadowing a local businessperson, or designing a newspaper advertisement that thanks community entrepreneurs and recognizes their spirit of free enterprise. High schools that operate a school store or other type of business could allow middle school students to "work" in the store and learn about the free enterprise system.

CHAPTER OVERVIEW

This chapter provides students with an understanding of measurements commonly used to gauge economic activity and business conditions in our society.

2.1 Measuring Economic Activity

This lesson provides information about fundamental economic data used in our society.

2.2 Economic Conditions Change

In this lesson, students will learn about business cycles, consumer prices, and interest rates.

2.3 Other Measures of Business Activity

Investing, borrowing, and various economic challenges are addressed in this lesson.

Chapter 2 Economic Activity

FotograFFF/Shutterstock.com

Instructor Resources

- Activities and Study Guide IE
- Chapter and Unit Tests IE
- Lesson Plans
- PowerPoint Presentation
- Cognero Test, Ch. 2

Student Resources

Activities and Study Guide
www.cengage.com/swep/pob9e
- Portfolio Activity

PLANNING A CAREER IN . . .
BUSINESS DEVELOPMENT

Business, Management & Administration

The desire to provide food, water, health care, education, and financial services to the billions of people in need around the world is one reason to choose a career in business and economic development. A career in this field could involve a variety of employment opportunities—some close to home and some far away. If you have the interest and obtain the required training, you could be an organization executive, a government research director, or a field training consultant. Each of these jobs contributes to economic growth.

As you study various business topics, your awareness of economic activities will expand. Many business development positions are related to employment in government, technology, research, engineering, health care, nutrition, marketing, and financial planning.

Every country in the world can benefit from efforts to enhance its economic development and improve the quality of life for its citizens. Your decision to pursue a career in business development will empower you to help people plan, start, and operate small business enterprises in communities in your neighborhood and around the world.

Related Job Titles

- Economist
- Transportation Engineer
- Urban and Regional Planner
- Field Researcher
- Statistician
- Budget Analyst
- Microloan Officer

Analyze Career Opportunities in . . . BUSINESS DEVELOPMENT

Use library and Internet resources to learn more about careers in business and economic development. Choose one of the job titles listed in the box above and answer the following questions.

1. What is the employment outlook for careers in this field?
2. Is this a career that interests you? What can you do now to help prepare yourself for this career?

What it's like to work as a . . . Field Business Consultant

As the sun rises over the mountains, hundreds of farmers are already on the job. Their goal is to harvest enough crops to generate income to provide for the basic needs of their families. They use traditional farming methods that they learned from their ancestors.

In a nearby village, an international organization helps some of the people obtain oxen and farm equipment. These items allow the workers to double and triple their daily harvests.

Many government and private agencies work to help people improve their labor productivity. The use of new growing methods, machinery, and other agricultural techniques can provide families with more money for food, housing, clothing, school fees, and health care.

Funding for these improvements is often uncertain. Money may come from private investors or government grants and loans. Many organizations now offer microloans to poor people throughout the world. These loans allow people to start and expand their own businesses.

What about you? What aspects of working in business development interest you?

PLANNING A CAREER IN . . .
BUSINESS DEVELOPMENT

Creation of jobs and improved educational systems provide the foundation of business and economic development. Students should be made aware of the importance of these efforts in relation to improved quality of life for countries around the world. Ask students: In what ways are you affected by people around the world who live in difficult economic conditions? Students might point out that raw materials and products used in the United States come from many different countries. Also, disease and hunger can cause health concerns and political unrest that affect people in the United States.

What About You? *Answers*

Student answers will require thinking beyond what is presented and formulating their own reactions. Students might be intrigued to learn that it is possible to have a career in improving living conditions and quality of life around the world. They may have thought that such opportunities only existed for volunteer work.

Analyze Career Opportunities *Answers*

Student answers will vary depending on when the assignment is completed and individual interests.

Additional Career Information

Encourage students to investigate careers they find interesting and explore unfamiliar careers. Two resources for additional career information are the *Occupational Outlook Handbook*, an online publication (www.bls.gov/oco) of the U.S. Bureau of Labor Statistics, and the O*NET Resource Center (www.onetcenter.org) developed by the U.S. Department of Labor. Information about specific careers and jobs can be used to demonstrate the relevance of skills learned in this course.

Focus on REAL LIFE

Remind students that measurements are important in many aspects of their lives. Ask students to name situations (that aren't sports- or business-related) in which measurements are used. Students might suggest school grades, test scores, the monetary value of collectibles, and population trends.

TEACH

Ask students to name items they use that would be included in the GDP.

Highlight the four main components of GDP on page 35.

▶ **Figure 2-1** ***ANSWER***

For the countries listed in the figure, the United States has the highest total GDP and Bolivia has the lowest. The United States also has the highest GDP per capita. Nigeria has the lowest GDP per capita. Point out some of the differences between the countries listed in Figure 2-1. Location, educational system, natural resources, and political environment can affect economic activities and GDP.

2.1 Measuring Economic Activity

Learning Outcomes

2.1.1 Define gross domestic product.

2.1.2 Describe economic measures of labor.

2.1.3 Identify economic indicators for consumer spending.

Key Terms

gross domestic product (GDP) 34
GDP per capita 35
unemployment rate 36
productivity 36
personal income 37
retail sales 37

Focus on REAL LIFE

Measuring performance is common in life. In a recent basketball game, Rosa Rivera of Middletown High School scored 19 points, pulled down 8 rebounds, and had 7 assists.

Later that day, the school's marching band competed and received a score of 88.3. By most standards, this was a good performance.

How about you? How much have you grown in the past 10 years? You can say, "I am 10 years older." Or, "I am 18 inches taller." Or, "I now wear shoe size 10C."

There are numerous ways to measure personal growth. Similarly, there are many ways to measure progress in business and economic activity.

LO 2.1.1

GROSS DOMESTIC PRODUCT (GDP)

Economic growth refers to a steady increase in the production of goods and services in an economic system. Just as you use different ways to measure your own growth, different methods can be used to measure the growth of an economy.

One way to find out how well an economy is doing is to compare output from year to year. Governments collect information from producers and estimate national output. The most widely used measure is gross domestic product. **Gross domestic product** or **GDP** is the total value of all final goods and services produced in a country during one year. Figure 2-1 reports the GDP of various countries in a recent year.

Components of GDP

Gross domestic product includes four major categories of economic activity:

1. Consumer spending for food, clothing, housing, and other goods and services
2. Business spending for buildings, equipment, and inventory items
3. Government spending to pay employees and to buy supplies and other goods and services
4. The exports of a country less the imports into the country

Some goods and services are not included. For example, GDP does not include the value of the work you do for yourself, such as cutting your own lawn or building a picnic table. If you buy the lawn service or the picnic table from a business, it would be included.

Only final goods, such as cars, are counted when measuring GDP. Intermediate goods used in manufacturing, such as steel and fabrics, are not included. If intermediate goods were counted, the value of these intermediate goods would be counted twice.

If the GDP increases from year to year, this usually signals that an economy is growing and is healthy.

Different Learning Styles

Visual Learner Use a large map or project a map from the Internet to show students the location of the various countries listed in Figure 2-1. Ask students why the countries have differences in GDP. Additionally, students could be asked to replicate Figure 2-1 with data from different countries.

COMPARISON OF GDP IN SELECTED COUNTRIES		
COUNTRY	TOTAL GDP (U.S. $)	GDP PER CAPITA (U.S. $)
United States	$16.72 trillion	$52,800
China	$13.39 trillion	$9,800
India	$4.99 trillion	$4,000
Japan	$4.729 trillion	$37,100
Germany	$3.227 trillion	$39,500
Brazil	$2.416 trillion	$12,100
Mexico	$1.845 trillion	$15,600
Canada	$1.518 trillion	$43,100
Saudi Arabia	$928 billion	$31,300
Poland	$814 billion	$21,100
South Africa	$596 billion	$11,500
Nigeria	$479 billion	$2,800
Vietnam	$359 billion	$4,000
Bolivia	$59 billion	$5,500

Note: GDP is reported at purchasing power parity (PPP), which values the goods and services produced based on current prices in the United States.

Source: CIA World Factbook

FIGURE 2-1

Which country has the highest GDP per capita? The lowest?

Comparing GDP

The more goods and services that are produced, the healthier an economy is considered to be. Just referring to the total monetary value of GDP as a measure of economic growth does not tell the whole story.

Another way to measure economic-growth is **GDP per capita**, or output per person. GDP per capita is calculated by

Work as a TEAM

The GDP of a country presents information about the economic output of that country. Work as a team to prepare a list of drawbacks resulting from only looking at GDP when evaluating the economic progress of a nation. What aspects of economic growth may not be reflected in the GDP of a country?

COMPARING GROSS DOMESTIC PRODUCT			
	CANADA	UNITED STATES	CHINA

Area (sq. km.)	9,984,670	9,826,675	9,596,961
Population	34,834,841	318,892,103	1,355,692,576
GDP (US $)	1,518,000,000,000	16,720,000,000,000	13,390,000,000,000
GDP per capita (US $)	43,500	52,400	9,880

Source: CIA World Factbook

FIGURE 2-2

How does this figure help you see how per capita output is measured?

Work as a TEAM

This activity will allow students to interact on the basic aspects of the GDP. Encourage students to create a list that considers other economic indicators of a society. Ask them to name actions not measured by GDP, such as home chores and volunteering.

TEACH

Emphasize that many actions that benefit a society are not included in the GDP.

Explain the need to compare GDP and other economic activities among various countries. Point out that these comparisons can assist when business and government are making decisions regarding investing and spending.

▸ **Figure 2-2** ***ANSWER***

Use this figure to point out the process for calculating the GDP per capita. Refer students to Figure 2-1 to view the GDP per capita for various countries.

Applied Skills

Visual Communication Instruct students to pick three countries not listed in Figure 2-1. Tell students to use Internet sources to find the most current GDP and population figures available for these countries and remind them how GDP per capita can be calculated from these figures. Assign students to utilize computer software to create a bar graph comparing GDP and GDP per capita among the three countries of their choosing.

ONGOING ASSESSMENT

CHECKPOINT ✓ANSWER

GDP only applies to reported final goods and services. Money earned for goods or services that are not reported would not be included. Goods and services used in the manufacture of other products are only counted once—in the final product.

TEACH

Explain that the unemployment rate does not include all people out of work, but only those who are "looking for work and willing to work."

Ask students why they think unemployment rates vary throughout different regions of the country. Ideas may include differences in wages, changing economic conditions, and the skills of available workers.

Describe ways in which productivity is measured, such as manufacturing output, the number of customers served, and reduced production costs per unit.

Ask students to name actions that might be taken to increase productivity in a society.

Discuss problems that can occur from actions to increase productivity. Problems may include technology causing unemployment or increased workplace accidents as workers attempt to do their jobs faster.

THINK CRITICALLY THROUGH VISUALS

Answers will vary. Students might suggest that money or personal satisfaction motivates them to work harder and faster.

dividing GDP by the total population (see Figures 2-1 and 2-2). For example, suppose that there is no change in GDP this year compared to last year. Suppose, also, that the population increases. The same output would have to be divided among more people.

An increase in GDP per capita means that an economy is growing. A decrease usually means that an economy is struggling.

CHECKPOINT ✓
What types of economic activities are not included in GDP?

LO 2.1.2

LABOR ACTIVITIES

The workers of a country contribute to the economy in several ways. First, their labor activities create needed goods and services. Additionally, the wages earned by workers are then spent, creating a demand for various products.

Employment

Today, more than 158 million people work in the United States. These members of the *labor force* are employed in thousands of different jobs. They produce thousands of different products and services. The labor force consists of all people above age 16 who are actively working or seeking work. Students, retired people, and others who cannot or do not wish to work are not part of the labor force.

One economic statistic of concern is the **unemployment rate**. The unemployment rate is the portion of people in the labor force who are not working. People are considered to be "unemployed" if they are looking for work and willing to work but unable to find a job.

Unemployment rates vary from year to year and in different areas of the country. The main cause of unemployment is reduced demand for the goods and services provided by various workers. If fewer people eat fast food, for example, fast-food chains will need fewer workers.

Spotmatik Ltd/Shutterstock.com

What motivates you to work harder and faster?

Productivity

A vital source of economic growth is an increase in output per worker. **Productivity** is the production output in relation to a unit of input, such as a worker. Improvements in capital resources (equipment and technology), worker training, and management techniques can result in more output per worker.

Over time, the rate of growth in labor productivity has ups and downs. While increases in productivity occur in many years, the amount of the increase often becomes smaller. Sometimes, productivity may actually decrease.

If wages increase faster than gains in productivity, the cost of producing goods increases and prices rise. Even though workers earn more money, they are not able to improve their standard of living because of rising prices. Higher productivity is vital for an economy. When productivity increases, workers improve the standard of living in a nation while improving their life situation.

An ability to produce more goods and services makes it possible to reduce the number of hours in a workweek. In the 1890s, the average worker in the United States put in about 60 hours a week. Today, the average workweek for many factory and union-contracted jobs has decreased to less than 40 hours.

Increased leisure time for many workers is the result of ever-improving

Portfolio Activity

Assign the Portfolio Activity for Chapter 2 available on the website for this textbook.

COLLECT Help students locate current data for economic indicators discussed in this chapter.

CREATE Remind students to choose the most appropriate type of graph for the data.

CONNECT Be sure students connect graphs to a concept related to this or another class.

technology and ever-increasing efficiency. *Specialization of labor* is the training of workers to do a specific task. This strategy allows for *division of labor*, in which workers are assigned specific elements of a manufacturing process to improve efficiency and productivity.

CHECKPOINT
How can productivity be increased?

LO 2.1.3
CONSUMER SPENDING

The money you earn and spend is one of the most important factors for economic growth.

Personal Income

Each day, many people receive money from their participation in production. **Personal income** refers to salaries and wages as well as investment income and government payments to individuals.

These funds provide the foundation for buying needed goods and services.

FYI In many countries, an accurate measurement of the labor force is difficult to obtain. Poor economic conditions may require family members of all ages to work on farms or in home factories to provide an income to cover basic living expenses.

Retail Sales

On a monthly basis, the U.S. Department of Commerce measures **retail sales**, or the sales of durable and nondurable goods bought by consumers. These retail sales are an indicator of general consumer spending patterns in the economy. Increasing retail sales usually points toward economic growth.

The main items whose sales are measured for estimating retail sales include automobiles, building materials, furniture, gasoline, and clothing, as well as purchases from restaurants, department stores, food stores, and drug stores.

CHECKPOINT
What are the main sources of personal income?

2.1 ASSESSMENT

Key Concepts

Determine the best answer.

1. Which of the following would not be included in GDP?
   - **a.** exports to other countries
   - **b.** purchases of computers by government
   - **c.** automobiles purchased
   - **d.** dinner preparation for your family
2. Productivity would likely increase as a result of
   - **a.** higher taxes
   - **b.** expanded production technology
   - **c.** decreased training programs
   - **d.** lower interest rates
3. Retail sales include
   - **a.** taxes collected
   - **b.** companies buying new equipment
   - **c.** borrowing by business
   - **d.** school supplies bought by students

Make Academic Connections

4. **Technology** Using the data in Figure 2-1, create a graph with a spreadsheet program to compare the total GDP and GDP per capita for five countries you select.
5. **Visual Art** Create a collage or photo essay to illustrate how specialization of labor and division of labor can increase productivity.

RETEACH Prepare a one-sentence summary of each of the economic indicators in this lesson.

ENRICH Have students find current data for one or more economic data items in the lesson.

CLOSE Ask students to choose one of the economic indicators mentioned in this lesson and explain why it is important that people understand it.

ONGOING ASSESSMENT

CHECKPOINT ✓ANSWER
Productivity may be increased by improvements in capital resources (equipment and technology), worker training, and management techniques.

TEACH

Ask students to explain how personal income and retail sales affect economic activity in a country.

Point out that measurement of labor force and other business activities in other countries may be affected by economic, cultural, and political influences.

ONGOING ASSESSMENT

CHECKPOINT ✓ANSWER
Sources of personal income include wages, salaries, investment income, and government payments.

ASSESS

Key Concepts *Answers*

1. d. dinner preparation for your family
2. b. expanded production technology
3. d. school supplies bought by students

Make Academic Connections *Answers*

4. Graphs should accurately illustrate the data students select from Figure 2-1. A column graph showing a pair of columns for each country is appropriate for this kind of data. Line graphs and pie charts should not be used.
5. Collages and photo essays will vary, but should clearly depict one or more ideas related to this lesson.

Focus on REAL LIFE

Ask students to name situations they have observed that reflect changes in the economy and business activity.

TEACH

Provide an overview of the four phases of the business cycle.

Explain the prosperity phase of the business cycle.

Ask students to suggest reasons why an economy does not stay in the prosperity phase. Students should understand that when people have an adequate amount of a product, demand will decline and the economy will slow down.

THINK CRITICALLY THROUGH VISUALS

Answers will vary, but will likely include a discussion of how a small business owner might have difficulty during a period of low consumer spending, especially if the business fulfills wants rather than needs.

2.2 Economic Conditions Change

Learning Outcomes

2.2.1 Describe the four phases of the business cycle.

2.2.2 Explain causes of inflation and deflation.

2.2.3 Identify the importance of interest rates.

Key Terms

business cycle 38	recovery 40
prosperity 38	inflation 40
recession 39	price index 41
depression 39	deflation 41

Focus on REAL LIFE

Do you have more knowledge than you had five years ago? Are you able to play a sport better than you did 10 years ago? As your skills and abilities increase, you will depend less on your family and begin to plan for your future. You might be concerned about earning and saving money. You will likely think about how your grades will affect plans for continuing your education. Various elements of your life change—both up and down. Your grades are likely to vary based on study habits and class efforts. The size of your savings account changes based on earning, saving, and spending.

Just as you change, the economy changes, too. Ups and downs occur for business activities. As economic conditions improve, quality of life in a country improves. In contrast, downward economic trends result in difficulties for workers and consumers.

LO 2.2.1

THE BUSINESS CYCLE

Economic and business activity tends to move in cycles. All nations experience economic good times and bad times. Fortunately, over time, bad conditions disappear and improved conditions return.

Looking at the economic changes during the history of the United States shows a pattern of good times to bad times and back to good times. This movement of the economy from one condition to another and back again is called a **business cycle**.

Business cycles are the recurring ups and downs of GDP. Business cycles have four phases: prosperity, recession, depression, and recovery.

Prosperity

At the peak of the business cycle is prosperity. **Prosperity** is a period in which most people who want to work are working, businesses produce goods and services in record numbers, wages are good, and the rate of GDP growth increases.

The demand for goods and services is high. This period is usually the high point of the business cycle. Prosperity, though, does not go on forever. The economy eventually cools off and activity slows down.

Blulz60/Shutterstock.com

Think of ways in which spending habits change during a dramatic economic shift. How might this affect a small business owner?

Different Learning Styles

Auditory Learner Ask students to say and repeat each of the phases of the business cycle. Then, describe a phase of the cycle and ask students to say the name for that phase.

Recession

When the economy slows down, a phase of the business cycle known as recession occurs. **Recession** is a period in which demand begins to decrease, businesses lower production, unemployment begins to rise, and GDP growth slows for two or more quarters of the calendar year.

This phase may not be too serious or last very long, but it often signals trouble for workers in related businesses. For example, if people buy fewer cars, a number of workers who make batteries, tires, and other parts may lose their jobs. This drop in related businesses is called the ripple effect.

Eventually, production weakens throughout the economy, and total output declines in the next quarter. Some recessions last for long periods as fewer factors of production are used and total demand falls.

NET KNOWLEDGE

The Bureau of Labor Statistics (BLS) provides data on a variety of economic activities. Conduct an online search for the BLS and select a topic on the BLS website. Inflation, unemployment, or productivity are some possibilities. Obtain recent information for this economic statistic. Prepare a brief written summary of your findings and describe how this information might affect consumers or businesses in your community.

Depression

If a recession deepens and spreads throughout the entire economy, the nation may move into the third phase, depression. **Depression** is a long period of high unemployment, weak consumer sales, and business failures.

A QUESTION OF ETHICS

Ethical Analysis Guidelines

Most business decisions are viewed in various ways. In some countries, people expect family members to be given jobs in a company before others. In other places, payments or gifts are expected before you are able to do business.

These and many other situations create ethical problems. *Ethics* are principles of right and wrong that guide personal and business decisions. When contemplating the ethics of business situations, consider using these three guidelines:

1. **Is the action legal?** Laws vary among states and in different countries. Most companies base international decisions on the laws in their home countries. When a conflict occurs, managers usually consider other factors, such as professional standards and the effect of the action on society.
2. **Does the action violate professional or company standards?** Professional or company standards will frequently exceed those required by the law. This helps to ensure that decisions will be in the best interest of both the company and the society in which it operates.
3. **Who is affected by the action and how?** An action may be legal and within professional or company standards. However, decision makers should also think about possible effects on employees, consumers, competitors, and the environment.

Think Critically

1. What are some examples of situations faced by workers and consumers that require ethical decisions?
2. Describe the effect on business activities if no ethical guidelines existed.
3. Research recent ethical situations that have been reported in the news. How have these situations affected workers, investors, and others?

Different Learning Styles

Tactile Learner Use various items to represent economic indicators. A brick could represent business spending for new facilities or a price tag might represent retail sales. Ask students to suggest items that represent each economic indicator. Create a display or use the items as a review tool.

NET KNOWLEDGE

Students should learn about the data gathered by the Bureau of Labor Statistics. Point out the various categories of economic data reported on this website. Discussion should indicate that students understand the concepts and how they relate to economic trends.

TEACH

Point out the characteristics of a recession.

Explain that the difference between recession and depression is the severity of economic difficulties.

A Question of Ethics

The three guidelines provided in this feature can be used throughout the course as a framework for the analysis and discussion of various ethical situations.

Think Critically *Answers*

1. Answers will vary, but might include situations involving race and gender bias, sexual harassment, theft, falsifying information, and breaking confidentiality.
2. Answers will vary, but should reflect an understanding of the effect on a company's reputation, employee morale, productivity, and profit.
3. Offer suggestions for how students should report their findings—oral presentation, role-playing, one-page report, etc. Consider allowing students to work in pairs.

FYI

Explain the main causes of inflation. Point out the difficulties that inflation can cause.

TEACH

Explain the recovery phase of the business cycle.

ONGOING ASSESSMENT

CHECKPOINT ✓ANSWER

The four phases of the business cycle are prosperity, recession, depression, and recovery.

TEACH

Ask students for the prices of various common items. Ask them whether they remember when these prices were different.

THINK CRITICALLY THROUGH VISUALS

Answers will vary, but could include the size of food containers, such as cans and jars, or personal items, such as shampoo or toothpaste. Higher prices on such items should prompt consumers to shop for bargains.

FYI During the 1980s and 1990s, some South American countries had an annual inflation rate as high as 300 to 400 percent. This is known as hyperinflation. In 1985, Bolivia had an annual inflation rate of more than 12,000 percent. More recently, the African nation of Zimbabwe experienced an annual inflation rate exceeding 230 million percent.

GDP falls rapidly during a depression. Fortunately, our economy has not had a depression for more than 70 years. The period from 1930 to 1940 in U.S. history is referred to as the Great Depression. Approximately 25 percent of the U.S. labor force was unemployed. Many people could not afford to satisfy even their basic needs.

Recovery

Economic downturns do not go on forever. A welcome phase of the business cycle, known as recovery, begins to appear. **Recovery** is the phase in which unemployment begins to decrease, demand for goods and services increases, and GDP begins to rise again.

People gain employment. Consumers regain confidence about their futures and begin buying again. Recovery may be slow or fast. As it continues, the nation moves back into prosperity.

CHECKPOINT ✓
What are the four phases of the business cycle?

LO 2.2.2

CONSUMER PRICES

Have you ever noticed that packages of some items get smaller while the price stays the same? Have you bought new technology products that are less expensive than earlier ones? These are examples of changes in the buying power of your money.

Inflation

Most nations must contend with the problem of inflation. **Inflation** is an increase in the general level of prices. In times of inflation, buying power decreases. For example, if prices increased 5 percent during the last year, items that cost $100 then would now cost $105. This means it now takes more money to buy the same amount of goods and services.

Inflation is most harmful to people living on fixed incomes. Due to inflation, retired people and others whose incomes do not change are able to afford fewer goods and services.

Causes of Inflation

One type of inflation occurs when the demand for goods and services is greater than the supply. When a large supply of money, earned or borrowed, is spent for goods that are in short supply, prices increase.

Even though wages (the price paid for labor) tend to increase during inflation, prices of goods and services usually rise so fast that the wage earner never seems to catch up.

Most people think inflation is harmful. Consumers have to pay higher prices for the things they buy. Therefore, as workers, they have to earn more money to maintain

Monkey Business Images/Shutterstock.com

Name something you regularly buy that has increased in price while its package and amount have decreased in size. How does this affect your decision to purchase the item?

Different Learning Abilities

At-Risk Encourage students to understand the connection among prices for items, wages they will receive on the job to buy needed items, and their education. Ask them to describe this relationship. Point out the importance of school and training for various job skills.

the same standard of living. Producers may receive higher prices for the goods and services they sell. If wages go up faster than prices, businesses tend to hire fewer workers, so unemployment worsens.

Measuring Inflation

Inflation rates vary. During the late 1950s and early 1960s, the annual inflation rate in the United States was in the 1 to 3 percent range. During the late 1970s and early 1980s, the cost of living increased 10 to 12 percent annually.

Mild inflation (perhaps 2 or 3 percent a year) can actually stimulate economic growth. During a mildly inflationary period, wages often rise more slowly than the prices of products. The prices of the products sold are high in relation to the cost of labor. Producers make higher profits and tend to expand production and hire more people. The newly employed workers increase spending, and the total demand in an economy increases.

In the United States, one of the most watched measures of inflation is called the Consumer Price Index (CPI). A **price index** is a number that compares prices in one year with prices in some earlier base year. There are different types of price indexes.

Inflation rates can be deceptive because the Consumer Price Index is based on a group of selected items. Many people face hidden inflation because they do not buy the exact items used to calculate the index. The cost of necessities (food, gas, health care) may increase faster than that of nonessential items, which could be dropping. This results in a reported inflation rate much lower than the actual cost-of-living increase that consumers experience.

Deflation

The opposite of inflation is called deflation. **Deflation** means a decrease in the general level of prices. It usually occurs in periods of recession and depression. Prices of products are lower, but people have less money to buy them.

Significant deflation occurred in the United States during the Great Depression of the 1930s. For example, between 1929 and 1933, prices declined about 25 percent. Deflation may occur for specific products. In recent years, the cost of computers and many other electronic products have declined mainly due to improved technology.

CHECKPOINT
What causes inflation?

LO 2.2.3

INTEREST RATES

In simple terms, interest rates represent the cost of money. Like everything else, money has a price. Interest rates have a strong influence on business activities. Companies and governments that borrow money are affected by interest rates. Higher interest rates mean higher business costs.

As a consumer, you are affected by interest rates. The earnings you receive as a

Emanuele Taroni/Stockbyte/Getty Images

How do interest rates affect you and other consumers?

TEACH

Explain how the Consumer Price Index (CPI) is calculated and how it is used by businesses and government.

Ask students to explain deflation.

Compare the dangers of deflation and inflation.

ONGOING ASSESSMENT

CHECKPOINT ANSWER

Inflation occurs when demand for goods and services is greater than supply.

TEACH

Explain that interest rates represent the cost of using money.

Ask students to describe situations in which they are affected by interest rates.

THINK CRITICALLY THROUGH VISUALS

Answers will vary. Students might wish that they could earn more interest on their savings. They might mention that higher interest rates cause higher business costs that often mean higher retail costs for products and services they purchase. Students might suggest that low mortgage interest rates make it easier for people to buy homes and high credit card interest rates make it hard for people to pay off their debts.

Different Learning Abilities

Gifted Instruct students to create a visual (poster or computer presentation) that shows how employment and consumer prices change in each phase of the business cycle. Ask them to explain actions that businesses and government might take in each phase.

Work as a TEAM

This activity will allow students to better understand the various types of interest rates. Encourage students to share answers with the class.

TEACH

Provide an overview of the seven types of interest rates. Explain that many types of interest rates exist for various borrowing and saving situations of consumers, businesses, and government.

Describe how the supply and demand for money are the main forces affecting interest rates.

ONGOING ASSESSMENT

CHECKPOINT ✓ANSWER

Interest rates can encourage or discourage borrowing and spending. Lower interest rates allow consumers greater spending power, which increases demand, productivity, and employment. Businesses will likely pass on the cost of higher interest rates to consumers.

ASSESS

Key Concepts *Answers*

1. False. Deflation is the general decrease of prices.

2. False. Interest rates go up due to higher demand for money.

3. d. depression

Make Academic Connections *Answers*

4. Offer suggestions for how you would like students to report their findings.

5. Suggest that students use the FYI feature on page 40 as a starting point for their research.

6. About a 39 percent decline. (4.6 – 2.8) ÷ 4.6

Work as a TEAM

Interest rates influence many aspects of our economy. Work as a team to examine the seven "Types of Interest Rates" discussed. Then, prepare a description of who in our economy would be most likely affected by each of these types of interest rates.

saver or an investor reflect current interest rates. Consumers also borrow. People with poor credit ratings pay a higher interest rate than people with good credit ratings.

Types of Interest Rates

Many types of interest rates exist in every economy. These rates represent the cost of money for different groups in different settings. Some of the types of interest rates include the following:

- The *prime rate* is the rate banks make available to their best business customers, such as large corporations.
- The *discount rate* is the rate financial institutions are charged to borrow funds from Federal Reserve banks.
- The *T-bill rate* is the yield on short-term (13-week) U.S. government debt obligations.
- The *treasury bond rate* is the yield on long-term U.S. government debt obligations of up to 30 years.
- The *mortgage rate* is the amount individuals pay to borrow for the purchase of a new home.
- The *corporate bond rate* is the cost of borrowing for large U.S. corporations.
- The *certificate of deposit rate* is the rate for time deposits at savings institutions.

Changing Interest Rates

Each day, the cost of money (interest) changes because of various factors. The supply and demand for money is the major influence on the level of interest rates. As amounts saved increase, interest rates tend to decline. This occurs because more funds are available. When borrowing by consumers, businesses, and government increases, interest rates are likely to rise.

CHECKPOINT ✓

How do interest rates affect business activities in our economy?

2.2 ASSESSMENT

Key Concepts

Determine the best answer.

1. True or False. Deflation results in lower buying power of money.

2. True or False. When consumers increase their borrowing, interest rates tend to decline.

3. The phase of the business cycle in which unemployment is highest is
   a. recession
   b. recovery
   c. prosperity
   d. depression

Make Academic Connections

4. Geography Obtain information about business cycles in other countries. Do these other economies face similar changes in economic activities?

5. History Conduct research about *hyperinflation*. What caused high inflation in various countries? What actions were taken to solve this problem?

6. Math Over time, interest rates increase and decline. If the rate being paid on a savings account was previously 4.6 percent and is now 2.8 percent, what is the percentage of change for that interest rate?

RETEACH Divide the class into four groups. Ask each group to prepare a short drama to help classmates better understand one phase of the business cycle.

ENRICH Ask students to describe how inflation and interest rates are connected.

CLOSE Ask students to name an action that might reduce inflation or encourage lower interest rates.

DOING BUSINESS IN... ECUADOR

How much can a dollar buy? That question might be asked in both the United States and Ecuador. In 2000, Ecuador adopted the U.S. dollar as its official currency. So today in Ecuador for just one U.S. dollar, you might be able to buy 20 fresh bananas, four cups of coffee, or a handmade bracelet.

In the late 1990s, Ecuador faced many economic difficulties, including high inflation, increased poverty, and a declining value of the sucre (its previous currency). Actions to address these concerns included adoption of the U.S. dollar. Dollarization generally helps control inflation and makes the country more attractive to investors.

When doing business in Ecuador, you will be expected to wear conservative clothing for business settings. You are likely to greet others with a handshake. As you get to know your business contacts, you'll begin to embrace when meeting; women may give "air" kisses on both cheeks.

Business meetings often start with an exchange of pleasantries. The importance of family in Ecuador is frequently emphasized in these conversations. Avoid discussion of politics and the country's relations with Peru.

You will be expected to be on time for a business meeting, but don't expect it to start on time. For social gatherings, plan to arrive approximately 30 minutes after the appointed time. Lunch is usually taken between 1 and 2 P.M. For dinner invitations, prepare to eat as late as 11 P.M.

A local agent for selling goods and services is vital. This representative is necessary to do business with the Ecuadorian government. The use of a local attorney will ease the difficulty of navigating the country's complex legal system.

Think Critically

1. What are the benefits and possible disadvantages of a country using the U.S. dollar as its official currency?
2. How do business customs in Ecuador differ from others with which you are familiar?
3. Conduct library or Internet research to obtain additional information about business and economic activities in Ecuador. Briefly outline what you learned.

What currency are shoppers at this open-air market in Ecuador most likely using?

Holger Mette/Shutterstock.com

Applied Skills

Language Arts Ask students who speak different languages to explain how some words may change meaning when translated. Point out the importance of language skills when doing business in the United States and other countries.

Doing Business in . . . ECUADOR

This feature will provide students with a better understanding of business activities in other countries and different cultures.

Encourage students who lived in or visited other countries to describe their observations and experiences.

Ask students: What are the educational and economic benefits of understanding other cultures?

THINK CRITICALLY THROUGH VISUALS

Shoppers are most likely using U.S. dollars, the official currency of Ecuador.

Think Critically *Answers*

1. Another country could benefit from using the U.S. dollar because its global acceptance helps to create stronger trade relations. Disadvantages could be that a country using the dollar is also subject to fluctuations in its value. Also, the country may lose some of its national identity without its own currency.

2. Differences in business practices in Ecuador include embracing when meeting; referring to family in business meetings, which is not as common in formal U.S. meetings; starting meetings late; eating later; and the use of agents, which is more common in Ecuador than in the United States.

3. Suggest topics such as the country's natural resources, recent economic conditions, cultural influences on business, and political activities.

Focus on REAL LIFE

Ask students to suggest actions that individuals, businesses, and governments might take when considering the purchase of expensive items.

TEACH

Ask students to name examples of capital projects in your community and around the world.

Explain how savings makes it possible for economic growth to occur.

THINK CRITICALLY THROUGH VISUALS

Possible long-term goals might include an education, car, apartment, buying big ticket items, or travel.

Life-Span Plan Answers

Answers will vary. Check to see that students correctly calculated their saving rates. Their explanations should demonstrate an understanding of how short-term saving goals that they set now can contribute to their ability to achieve their life-span goals in the future.

2.3 Other Measures of Business Activity

Learning Outcomes

2.3.1 Discuss investment activities that promote economic growth.

2.3.2 Explain borrowing activities by government, business, and consumers.

2.3.3 Describe future concerns of economic growth.

Key Terms

- capital projects 44
- stock 45
- bond 45
- budget surplus 46
- budget deficit 46
- national debt 46

Focus on REAL LIFE

"Eddie, are those new boots?" asked Fritz.

"Yep," responded Eddie, "do you like them?"

"They're great, but I thought you were trying to save money to buy a car."

You can't expect to have enough money to buy a car in the future if you always spend everything you receive. Today's savings makes your future purchase possible. In a similar way, saving and investing is the foundation of a country's economic growth.

Governments, businesses, and consumers must save and invest for their futures. Government must have funds available for needed services desired by citizens. Companies must obtain equipment and other productive resources for a profitable future. Individuals must make choices that balance current spending with future financial security.

LO 2.3.1

INVESTMENT ACTIVITIES

Investing for the future takes many different forms. Your time in school is an investment for your future. When companies buy buildings and equipment, they are also investing in their future.

Capital spending refers to money spent by a business for an item that will be used over a long period. **Capital projects** involve spending by businesses for items such as land, buildings, equipment, and new product development. The money for capital projects comes from three main sources: personal savings, stock investments, and bonds.

Personal Savings

A major source of investment funds is personal savings. Companies use money you deposit in a bank or other financial institution. These funds provide the money necessary for buying expensive equipment or creating new products. In return,

Anne Kitzman/Shutterstock.com

Name some long-term goals you might set for your savings account.

Life-Span Plan

Calculate your savings rate (percent of your current income that you save). Do you believe you save enough of your income? Explain how saving is related to people achieving their life-span goals. Set a short-term saving goal that you could achieve now to help you eventually reach future life-span goals.

Different Learning Abilities

Hearing Impaired Speak clearly, and be certain that you face the student so lip reading will be possible. Also make use of printed materials and visuals.

Ask students if there are specific things they find particularly helpful, and try to accommodate their requests.

savers are paid interest on the money they deposit.

The *savings rate* of a country is an important factor for economic growth. A low savings rate for a country, for example less than five percent, can cause economic concerns for the future.

The Stock Market

Corporations are a major type of business organization. Many people invest by becoming part owners of a corporation. **Stock** represents ownership in a corporation. Stock ownership is commonly called *equity*. This term means "ownership."

The value of shares of stock is affected by many factors. Once again, supply and demand are the major influences. If a company has higher earnings, more people will want to buy its stock. This causes the value to increase.

The Bond Market

Another investment activity involves the sale of bonds. A **bond** represents debt for an organization.

If you purchase a corporate or government bond, you are a *creditor*. This means you have lent money to the organization. In return, bondholders are paid interest for the use of their money.

CHECKPOINT
Name some examples of capital projects.

LO 2.3.2

BORROWING

"Buy now, pay later" commonly occurs in most economies of the world. Borrowing by governments, businesses, and consumers can have an important economic influence.

Business Insight

Cleantech: Energy Alternatives and Environmentally Friendly Products

The phrase *cleantech* refers to goods and services that are environmentally friendly. It is also part of the name of an organization that promotes clean technology among investors, entrepreneurs, and service providers.

The Cleantech Group provides a network of information, online services, and educational events to promote innovations that do not harm the environment. The group's emphasis is on balancing profit-making and environment-friendly business activities. Cleantech is not just interested in being socially responsible. It also recognizes the need for financial success.

Cleantech attempts to encourage and publicize investment and development for various *clean*, or environment-friendly, technologies. The companies in the Cleantech network are involved in a wide range of products, services, and processes designed to provide superior performance at lower costs. At the same time, these business activities must reduce or eliminate environmental concerns in an effort to improve the quality of life.

A concern for both companies and investors is that the "cleantech" label is often used for products and services that do meet the standards of the Cleantech Group.

Many organizations attempt to attract investors by calling their enterprise "cleantech" even though their business activities are not improving the environment.

Think Critically

1. How do consumers, businesses, and the economy benefit from cleantech activities?
2. What concerns might be associated with cleantech companies?
3. Conduct library or Internet research to obtain examples of various environment-friendly products and services.

TEACH

Point out the difference between stocks and bonds.

Ask students to tell you what they know about the "stock market."

ONGOING ASSESSMENT

CHECKPOINT ✓ANSWER

Capital projects include the purchase of any item a business will use over an extended period of time. Examples include land, buildings, and equipment.

TEACH

Explain various borrowing methods used by government, businesses, and consumers.

Business Insight

Point out that businesses can be both financially successful and socially responsible. Remind students that protecting the environment is only one aspect of corporate social responsibility.

Think Critically *Answers*

1. Benefits of cleantech activities include reduced pollution, improved use of technology, increased opportunities for business profits, and expanded social responsibility.
2. Companies that do not meet the necessary environmental standards may still promote themselves as a "cleantech" company. Also, companies may attempt to use technology that may not be completely appropriate for the organization.
3. Ask students to share their findings in a brief written or oral summary.

Applied Skills

Technology Technology can be part of the problem or part of the solution where the environment is concerned. Technology is used in many ways in various business settings such as banking, health care, manufacturing, financial services, and education. Ask students to identify some business activities where the use of technology benefits the environment and other activities where technology hurts the environment.

Work as a TEAM

Many economic and social concerns are present in the world. Encourage students to recommend specific actions to address the issue they discuss.

TEACH

Point out the difference between a budget surplus and a budget deficit.

Explain what factors cause the national debt to increase.

Ask students why debt can be important for businesses and consumers.

ONGOING ASSESSMENT

CHECKPOINT ✓ANSWER

A budget deficit occurs when a government or organization spends more than it takes in.

TEACH

Ask students to name causes for various economic problems.

THINK CRITICALLY THROUGH VISUALS

A small business may use more credit than it can afford. For example, payments on the debt might exceed the revenue being generated. Even if revenue exceeds the amount needed to repay a loan, there might not be enough money to pay employees, buy merchandise, or make improvements to keep up with competition. The company may eventually be forced out of business.

Work as a TEAM

Citizens can play a vital role in society by engaging with economic and social issues. Working as a team, select a current topic that needs attention. Prepare a list of actions that governments, businesses, and consumers might take to address this concern.

Government Debt

People expect services from federal, state, and local governments. Those services cost money. Often, government uses borrowing to finance various projects. New schools, public buildings, highways, and parks are often financed by borrowing.

A government may spend less than it takes in. When this occurs, a **budget surplus** is the result. If a surplus exists, government may reduce taxes or increase spending on various programs.

In contrast, a government may spend more than it takes in. This situation is called a **budget deficit**. Over time, deficits build up. The total amount owed by the federal government is called the **national debt**.

Business Debt

Loans, bonds, and mortgages are common borrowing methods used by businesses. Most companies, large and small, carry debt at some time.

Photodisc/Getty Images

What are some of the risks involved when a small business uses credit?

Efficient use of borrowing can be helpful to companies. Using the funds of others can help expand sales and profits. Sometimes, when poor decisions are made, debt creates problems. Poor debt management can result in a company going out of business.

Consumer Debt

People commonly use credit cards, auto loans, and home mortgages to finance their purchases. The use of credit can be convenient. The overuse of credit, however, often results in financial difficulties for individuals and families.

Careful use of credit can be important for economic growth. In contrast, unwise borrowing can result in legal action and other trouble.

CHECKPOINT ✓
What is the cause of a budget deficit?

LO 2.3.3

ECONOMIC CHALLENGES AND ADAPTING TO NEW MARKETS

Expanded economic output results in more goods and services. Global business growth happens in *emerging markets*, places where consumer incomes and buying power are increasing because of economic expansion. With more jobs and more income for workers, quality of life improves.

However, many countries lack the technology, education, and business systems needed for economic success. Today there are businesses and other organizations devoted to improving weak economies throughout the world. By providing training, technology, loans, and other assistance, these organizations create innovative solutions for various

---

Applied Skills

Communication Instruct students to create a visual presentation to communicate various uses of debt by families, businesses, and governments. Ask students to explain potential benefits and drawbacks in these various situations.

economic problems such as hunger, disease, unsafe water, and poverty.

In order to adapt to various market needs, companies must be aware of consumer preferences and behaviors. Researching the culture, economic conditions, and political environment is the foundation for successful business activities. No one can predict the economy's future with certainty. To maintain or increase a country's standard of living and to prevent unemployment, government, businesses, workers, and consumers must coordinate their efforts. This cooperation can result in creating jobs and providing for the needs and wants of people.

Donatas Dabravolskas/Shutterstock.com

How can business activities be used to solve various economic problems?

CHECKPOINT ✓
What economic challenges will countries face in the future?

2.3 ASSESSMENT

Key Concepts

Determine the best answer.

1. Equity refers to
   a. reduced spending by government
   b. ownership in a company
   c. borrowing to finance a capital project
   d. increased government taxes
2. Which of the following would most likely cause a budget surplus for government?
   a. higher spending
   b. lower spending
   c. higher borrowing
   d. lower taxes
3. In emerging markets, consumer incomes and buying power are
   a. decreasing
   b. fluctuating
   c. increasing
   d. stable

Make Academic Connections

4. **Economics** Taxes are a necessity. They provide necessary money for government services. What types of taxes do you believe would be best for a society?
5. **Social Studies** How might the future economic concerns of other countries differ from those of the United States?

RETEACH Explain possible causes for various economic problems in our society and around the world.

ENRICH Instruct students to research the advantages and disadvantages of stocks and bonds. Have them write a paper to describe their findings.

CLOSE Instruct students to develop a list of economic benefits of higher savings by consumers.

TEACH

Ask students to suggest actions that might be taken to solve various economic problems around the world.

ONGOING ASSESSMENT

CHECKPOINT ✓ANSWER

Future economic concerns for any country include the ability to increase its output and provide a means for its citizens to meet the basic needs of food and shelter, adequate health care, education, transportation, employment, and safety.

THINK CRITICALLY THROUGH VISUALS

Answers will vary, but could include education, business training, job creation, and technology and innovation related to water, food, health care, housing, and transportation.

ASSESS

Key Concepts *Answers*

1. b. ownership in a company or other asset
2. b. lower spending
3. c. increasing

Make Academic Connections *Answers*

4. Answers will vary, but might include income taxes, sales taxes, and property taxes.
5. Answers will vary, but should reflect an understanding of various levels of economic development. Some countries are similar to the United States in their need to continue increasing production, while others will be focused on building infrastructure, literacy, and political stability.

Think Critically About Business *Answers*

1. GDP may not be entirely accurate in reflecting the economic standing of a country. GDP per capita is a more accurate measure of the production of a country, and "real" GDP will allow for variations in prices. Other indicators of a healthy economy for developing countries include new businesses, technology, and rising literacy rates.

2. No, not unless Country B had the same population as Country A, which would be unlikely. GDP per capita is determined by dividing GDP by the total population. In the example, if Country B had twice the population of Country A, the per capita output would be about the same in both countries. In order for Country B to have twice the per capita output of Country A, the population would have to be the same in both countries.

3. Improvements in capital resources (equipment and technology), worker training, and management techniques can each result in more output per worker (productivity).

4. Increased productivity means that workers are able to work fewer hours to produce the same amount or more products, leaving leisure time. Increased productivity usually indicates an increased demand for skilled workers, including those hired for production, as well as marketing and management personnel.

Chapter 2 Assessment

Review Business Concepts

2.1 Measuring Economic Activity

- Gross domestic product (GDP) is the total market value of all final goods and services produced in a country during one year. GDP per capita is calculated by dividing GDP by the total population.
- There are several economic measures of labor. The labor force of an economy consists of all people above age 16 who are actively working or seeking work. The unemployment rate is the portion of people in the labor force who are not working. People are considered to be unemployed if they are looking for work and willing to work but unable to find a job. Productivity is the production output in relation to a unit of input, such as a worker.
- There are several economic indicators for consumer spending. Personal income refers to salaries and wages, as well as investment income and government payments to individuals. Retail sales measure the sales of durable and nondurable goods bought by consumers.

2.2 Economic Conditions Change

- The movement of the economy from good times to bad and back again is called a business cycle. A business cycle has four phases: prosperity, recession, depression, and recovery.
- Inflation is a general rise in the level of prices. Inflation can occur when the demand for goods and services is greater than the supply. Deflation is a decrease in the general price level. Deflation can occur when prices of products are lower, but people have less money to buy them.
- Interest rates represent the cost of money. The level of interest rates in an economy are affected by the supply and demand for money. Interest rates affect both consumer and business activities.

2.3 Other Measures of Business Activity

- Investment activities that promote economic growth include personal savings, buying stock as ownership in a corporation, and purchasing bonds from businesses and government.
- Governments, businesses, and consumers commonly use borrowing to finance various purchases. Careful borrowing can be important for economic growth. In contrast, unwise borrowing can result in legal action and other problems.
- Most economic growth is likely to occur in *emerging markets*. Growth will require improved technology, education, and business systems in these markets. Efforts must also be made to solve various economic problems such as hunger, disease, unsafe water, and poverty.

Think Critically About Business

1. "GDP is the best measurement of a country's economy." Explain why you agree or disagree with this statement.
2. The GDP of Country A is $400,000. The GDP of Country B is $800,000. Does this mean that the per capita output of Country B is about twice that of Country A? Explain.
3. Name three factors that can contribute to increased output of goods and services in a country. Explain how these factors can improve productivity.
4. What is the effect of increased productivity on a country's leisure time? How might increased productivity affect career opportunities?
5. Suppose that many auto and steel plants close in a country. Thousands of workers lose their jobs in a short period. If the country has been enjoying prosperous times, it may now be headed into what phase of the business cycle? Describe other conditions that might begin to occur.

5. The country might be headed into a recession. If so, the auto and steel workers who have lost their jobs will reduce their demand for other goods and services, causing other businesses to lose business and perhaps lay off more workers. This lowered demand, lowered production, and increasing unemployment might spread throughout the economy.

6. Retail sales is a measure of durable and nondurable goods bought by consumers. What are some examples of durable and nondurable goods?

7. What actions might be taken by businesses and government in each phase of the business cycle?

8. Why is a high rate of inflation generally considered harmful to an economy?

9. Other than the economic indicators discussed in this chapter, what are some other data items that might be used to measure business and economic activities?

10. What are some economic concerns that may need to be addressed in the future?

Develop Your Business Language

Match the terms listed with the definitions.

11. A decrease in the general price level.

12. The movement of an economy from one condition to another and back again.

13. Spending by businesses for items such as land, buildings, and equipment.

14. The total value of all final goods and services produced in a country in one year.

15. Government spends less than it takes in.

16. A phase marked by a long period of high unemployment, weak consumer sales, and business failures.

17. Represents debt for an organization.

18. Salaries and wages as well as investment income and government payments to individuals.

19. The GDP divided by the total population of a country.

20. Production output in relation to a unit of input, such as a worker.

21. The phase in which unemployment decreases, demand for goods and services increases, and GDP begins to rise.

22. An increase in the general price level.

23. Represents ownership in a corporation.

24. Government spends more than it takes in.

25. The portion of people in the labor force who are not working.

26. The sales of durable and nondurable goods bought by consumers.

27. A period in which unemployment is low, businesses produce many goods and services, and wages are good.

28. A number that compares prices in one year with prices in some earlier base year.

29. A period in which demand, production, and GDP growth decrease and unemployment begins to rise.

30. The total amount owed by the federal government.

Key Terms

a. bond
b. budget deficit
c. budget surplus
d. business cycle
e. capital project
f. deflation
g. depression
h. GDP per capita
i. gross domestic product (GDP)
j. inflation
k. national debt
l. personal income
m. price index
n. productivity
o. prosperity
p. recession
q. recovery
r. retail sales
s. stock
t. unemployment rate

6. Durable products are those that will not have to be repeatedly replaced within a short amount of time. Examples include furniture, appliances, vehicles, and office equipment. Non-durable products include food, electricity, and gasoline.

7. In prosperity, businesses hope to continue their profits; government will try to control any inflation. During a recession, businesses hope to stimulate demand; government may cut interest rates to stimulate demand. During a depression, businesses hope to avoid going out of business; government may increase spending to stimulate job creation. During recovery, businesses will likely expand hiring; government may encourage business expansion with tax incentives.

8. Inflation makes it difficult for businesses and consumers to plan for the future. It also slows economic growth.

9. New businesses, new types of business, new technology, home buying, and interest rates are all indicators of business and economic activity. Improved health care, housing, transportation, and an increase in literacy and skilled labor could also indicate increased economic activity.

10. Some people in our country—not to mention millions more throughout the world—still do not have enough food, proper housing, and medical care. We need to develop ways and means to satisfy the basic human needs of all of our citizens. Other possible answers are up to the imagination of students.

Develop Your Business Language *Answers*

11. f. deflation
12. d. business cycle
13. e. capital project
14. i. GDP
15. c. budget surplus
16. g. depression
17. a. bond
18. l. personal income
19. h. GDP per capita
20. n. productivity
21. q. recovery
22. j. inflation
23. s. stock
24. b. budget deficit
25. t. unemployment rate
26. r. retail sales
27. o. prosperity
28. m. price index
29. p. recession
30. k. national debt

Make Academic Connections *Answers*

31. Technology would likely have a positive effect on a country's GDP by increasing productivity and broadening job opportunities.

32. Maps and explanations will vary.

33. Posters or other visuals should illustrate how the use of computers or other technology can improve productivity.

34. Answers will vary, but should include a discussion of how some cultures value and encourage hard work and high productivity, while the political climate in other cultures might discourage initiative and productivity.

35. 2016: 30 (25 + (0.2 × 25)) 2021: 36 (30 + (0.2 × 30)) 2026: 43.2 (36 + (0.2 × 36))

36. 2016: $9.00 (30 × 0.30) 2021: $12.60 (36 × 0.35) 2026: $17.28 (43.2 × 0.40)

37. Graphs should depict the phases of the business cycle during the past 200 years.

38. Visual presentations will vary. They should illustrate reasons government, businesses, and consumers borrow and the problems that could occur if credit is used unwisely.

39. Stocks represent ownership in the company and are more effective if a company has high earnings. Bonds, representing debt, are sold to bondholders who must be paid interest for the use of their money.

40. Students are to select two interest rates, create a chart showing how the rates changed over the past four or five years, and explain possible reasons for the changes in rates.

Make Academic Connections

31. **Technology** Describe ways in which computers and other technology might influence a country's GDP.

32. **Geography** Select five countries. Create a map showing various economic statistics for each country. Explain reasons for differences among the countries.

33. **Science** Technology is often the basis for increased productivity. Prepare a poster or other visual presentation to demonstrate how the use of computers or other technology might increase worker productivity.

34. **Culture** How might culture affect opportunities to increase productivity in different countries? Describe cultural and political factors that may enhance or limit actions to increase productivity.

35. **Math** Productivity for a small country was 25 units per worker hour in 2011. Productivity increased 20 percent between 2011 and 2016. What was the productivity figure for 2016? If the rate of increase is maintained, what will the figure be in 2021? In 2026?

36. **Math** Workers are paid a rate of $0.30 per unit. Using productivity figures from the previous question, determine how much workers earned per hour in 2016. If their rate increases to $0.35 in 2021 and to $0.40 in 2026, how much would they earn per hour in those years?

37. **History** Research various phases of the business cycle in the United States during the past 200 years. Create a graph showing the ups and downs of the economy. What conclusions could be drawn from this research?

38. **Communication** Prepare a visual presentation to report (a) reasons government, businesses, and consumers borrow, and (b) potential problems that could occur for each group if credit is not used properly.

39. **Economics** Compare the use of stocks and bonds by companies to raise funds. Describe situations in which each would be most effective.

40. **Communication** Select two interest rates from the list on page 42. Conduct online research and create a chart showing these rates for the past four or five years. Explain possible reasons for changes in these rates.

Make Your Case

In determining GDP, only final goods and services are included. This avoids having some items counted more than once. For example, a mining company sells iron ore to a steel-producing firm. That firm sells the steel to an auto manufacturer who uses it to produce a car. The iron ore, converted to steel, is counted once—in the price paid for the car, the final product. Read carefully the following list of goods and services produced in our economy and then answer the questions.

a. Electric toaster oven bought as a gift
b. Telephone service installed in a government office
c. Fiberglass sold to a company for use in making boats
d. Grooming services for your pet
e. Paper sold to a newspaper publishing company
f. Computer paid for by a city government
g. Computer bought for your family's use
h. Broccoli bought by a food-processing firm

41. Which of these items should be listed as a good and counted in GDP? Give reasons for your answer.

42. Which of these items should be listed as a service and counted in GDP? Give reasons for your answer.

Interactions and Connections

Two common information sources are personal contacts and blogs. Friends, relatives, and others in your community are usually willing to share their experiences and insights with you. Blogs provide comments, news, and observations. These online journals communicate experiences along with other thoughts and information. Blogs are available on every business topic. The sources of blog postings can range from an economist at the Tax Foundation to a dissatisfied consumer. Always be cautious before believing or acting on information. Confirm the data and facts using several reliable sources.

Select a topic from this chapter related to current economic conditions, productivity, or technology. Develop a question that interests you about this topic. Talk to two or three people to obtain answers to your question.

Next, locate a blog that relates to the topic you select. Obtain an answer to your question from this source. What actions might you take to make sure the information on this blog is accurate?

Compare the answers you received from the two sources. What information was similar and showed agreement on the topic? How did the two information sources differ?

Make Your Case *Answers*

41. (a) It is a good and is purchased at a store; (f) it is a good that is being purchased for use by the government; (g) it is a good and is purchased at a store.

42. (b) The telephone service will be used by the government office employees; (d) the grooming service is performed and paid for.

Quick-Serve Restaurant Management Series Event Role Play

The DECA Series Event challenges participants to develop a plan of action for a business role play. You will have 10 minutes to develop a solution that covers the performance indicators associated with the role play. Participants have five minutes to explain their plan of action to the judge. The judge has an additional two minutes to ask questions about the plan of action.

Pearl's is a diner that has been in operation for five years. It is located along a major highway in a community that has a population of 5,000 people. The restaurant was built during an economic boom and business has grown steadily during the first five years of operation. The current economic recession has dramatically changed the business environment. Unemployment has grown to 12 percent and business for Pearl's is down 25 percent from last year. The prices of menu items at the diner range from $3.50 to $8.00; the restaurant accepts cash and local checks for payment. Pearl's has advertised in the local newspaper and counted heavily on word-of-mouth advertising. The diner is open daily from 7 A.M. until 9 P.M. You have been hired as a consultant to help Pearl's increase business during the recession. You are challenged to describe the marketing strategy for the restaurant considering its location, menu items and prices, hours of operation, and promotion. Your plan must cover all performance indicators.

Performance Indicators Evaluated

- Describe the economic impact of a recession on business.
- Explain customer buying behavior.
- Identify a company's unique selling proposition.
- Identify product opportunities.
- Explain the types of promotion.

For more detailed information about performance indicators, go to the DECA website.

Think Critically

1. How does a recession affect the spending habits of consumers?
2. How can the location of Pearl's be used to increase business beyond the town's population?
3. What promotional activities might bring more customers to Pearl's during the recession?
4. What are some advertising strategies that Pearl's should consider to increase business?

www.deca.org

WINNING EDGE

Quick-Serve Restaurant Management Series Event Role Play

Students must understand how businesses are challenged by economic conditions. Small businesses feel the impact of a recession. Students must explain a marketing strategy to help a restaurant stay in business during a recession. Students must consider the product, price, place, and promotion for the restaurant.

Think Critically *Answers*

1. Most consumers will spend less money during a recession. Consumers eat more meals at home and go to restaurants less often.

2. The potential customer base of Pearl's is much larger than the population of the town where it is located. The restaurant should have signage to attract the attention of travelers on the busy highway.

3. Answers will vary. Pearl's could consider offering different specials each day of the week. Family specials, coupons for food discounts, and other promotions should encourage more business for the restaurant.

4. Answers will vary. Students might suggest that Pearl's continue advertising in the local newspaper and include coupons to encourage customers to visit the restaurant. Pearl's should have good signage along the highway to attract business and should consider using social media to attract customers.

Interactions and Connections

This activity allows students to assess and compare the value of different information sources. Encourage students to carefully compare information received from personal contacts with blog posts.

Student questions, responses, actions, and comments will vary. Encourage students to carefully prepare a question that requires a thoughtful response. Consider asking students to share their activities with the class.

CHAPTER OVERVIEW

This chapter provides students with a foundation for understanding business in the global economy. It focuses on exporting, international trade, and global business activities.

3.1 International Business Basics
Importing, exporting, trade relations, and global currencies are covered in this lesson.

3.2 The Global Marketplace
Geographic, economic, cultural, and political aspects of international business, along with trade relations, are the focus of this lesson.

3.3 International Business Organizations
Methods of organizing international business activities, such as joint ventures and multinational corporations, are the basis for this lesson.

Chapter 3 Business in the Global Economy

EvrenKalinbacak/Shutterstock.com

3.1 International Business Basics
3.2 The Global Marketplace
3.3 International Business Organizations

Instructor Resources

- Activities and Study Guide IE
- Chapter and Unit Tests IE
- Lesson Plans
- PowerPoint Presentation
- Cognero Test, Ch. 3

Student Resources

Activities and Study Guide www.cengage.com/swep/pob9e
- Portfolio Activity

PLANNING A CAREER IN . . .

INTERNATIONAL BUSINESS

Transportation, Distribution & Logistics

Global business activities create many employment opportunities. People working in international business direct foreign sales, negotiate with foreign distribution centers, arrange shipping, and plan conversion of products from American to foreign specifications. While the international business skills necessary to perform these tasks are increasingly important, job titles may not reflect them directly because workers often have other duties unrelated to importing and exporting. Transportation managers, for example, oversee both foreign and domestic shipping, including settlements between shippers. U.S. Customs Service agents investigate persons, common carriers, and merchandise arriving in or departing from the United States to prevent prohibited importing or exporting.

Related Job Titles

- Customs Inspector
- Interpreter or Translator
- Global Purchasing Manager
- Freight Inspector
- Cross-Cultural Trainer
- International Sales Representative
- International Marketing Manager
- Import-Export Coordinator

Analyze Career Opportunities in . . .

INTERNATIONAL BUSINESS

Use library and Internet resources to learn more about careers in international business. Choose one of the job titles listed in the box and answer the following questions.

1. How would you describe the earnings potential for this field?
2. Is this a career that interests you? Describe a few things you could do to learn more about this career.

What it's like to work as a . . . Freight Forwarder

"I'm sorry, your shipment is being held at the Port of Hong Kong until the proper documentation is prepared."

These are words no exporter wants to hear. To avoid this type of situation, exporters turn to freight forwarding companies to help them ship their products around the world.

Freight forwarders specialize in shipping goods to customers in other countries. These global intermediaries also help businesses around the world with other services. Areas of expertise include export regulations, costs for various shipping methods, and the customs process.

Most freight forwarders also serve as customs brokers, helping international companies pass inspections when goods enter another country. Customs brokers prepare needed documents and make sure the required tariffs are paid.

What about you? Are you interested in any aspects of international business? Which ones and why?

PLANNING A CAREER IN . . .

INTERNATIONAL BUSINESS

International career opportunities exist in many settings. Use the career feature to point out how most careers are directly or indirectly related to global business activities. Ask students to name some skills and competencies that might be important when working in an international career. You could also use the "What About You?" question that follows this feature as the basis for a class discussion.

What About You? ***Answer***

Student answers will require thinking beyond what is presented and formulating their own reactions. You may want to develop a class list of the interesting aspects of international business such as opportunity for travel and proficiency in multiple languages, job security and varied career opportunities, and intimate knowledge of other cultures and ways of life.

Analyze Career Opportunities *Answers*

Student answers will vary depending on when the assignment is completed and individual interests.

Additional Career Information

Encourage students to investigate careers they find interesting and explore unfamiliar careers. Two resources for additional career information are the *Occupational Outlook Handbook*, an online publication (www.bls.gov/oco) of the U.S. Bureau of Labor Statistics, and the O*NET Resource Center (www.onetcenter.org) developed by the U.S. Department of Labor. Information about specific careers and jobs can be used to demonstrate the relevance of skills learned in this course.

Focus on REAL LIFE

This feature can provide a foundation for the importance of international business activities.

TEACH

Ask students to suggest positive and negative aspects of international business activities.

Point out factors (technology, improved political relations) that have resulted in increased global business.

THINK CRITICALLY THROUGH VISUALS

International trade allows consumers to access a wider variety of products at lower costs. Disadvantages of international trade include stiffer competition for domestic companies and jobs lost to lower-paid workers in other countries.

3.1 International Business Basics

Learning Outcomes

3.1.1 Describe importing and exporting activities.

3.1.2 Compare balance of trade and balance of payments.

3.1.3 List factors that affect the value of global currencies.

Key Terms

- imports 55
- exports 55
- balance of trade 56
- balance of payments 57
- exchange rate 58

Focus on REAL LIFE

What did you and your family have for breakfast this morning? Coffee, cereal, and sliced bananas, perhaps? If it were not for trading with Brazil for coffee and with Honduras for bananas, you might have had only cereal. The sugar on your table may have come from the Philippines. The textbook you are reading to get ready for class was printed on paper that may have come from Canada.

As you look around your home, you will find many products made in other countries. For example, you may find a TV made in Japan or Korea, a music player made in Taiwan or China, clothing made in the Philippines or Honduras, kitchen appliances made in Hong Kong or Malaysia, and cocoa from Brazil or Colombia. Look around your classroom. Can you identify products made in other countries?

LO 3.1.1

TRADE AMONG NATIONS

Most business activities occur within a country's own borders. *Domestic business* is the making, buying, and selling of goods and services within a country. *International business* refers to business activities needed for creating, shipping, and selling goods and services across national borders. International business is frequently referred to as *foreign* or *world trade*. Evidence of foreign trade is everywhere.

T Photography/Shutterstock.com

What are some of the advantages and disadvantages of international trade?

Although the United States has many natural resources, a skilled labor force, and modern production facilities, American companies and consumers purchase goods and services created throughout the world. The United States conducts trade with more than 180 countries.

In the past, economies were viewed in terms of national borders. With international trade expanding every day, economies cannot be defined solely by borders. Countries are interdependent and so are their economies. Consumers have come to expect goods and services from around the world.

Absolute Advantage

Two economic principles define buying and selling among companies in different countries. *Absolute advantage* exists when

Different Learning Abilities

Specific Learning Disability (SLD) Ask students who are passive or who may lack confidence to name or bring in examples of products they use made in other countries. Consider asking students to work in pairs to create a display of some of the products.

a country can produce a good or service at a lower cost than other countries. This may result from an abundance of natural resources or raw materials in a country. For example, some South American countries have an absolute advantage in coffee production, and Saudi Arabia has an absolute advantage in oil production.

Comparative Advantage

A country may have an advantage in more than one area. If so, it must decide how to maximize its economic wealth. A country may be able to produce both smartphones and clothing better than other countries. The world market for smartphones might be stronger than the market for clothing. This means it would be better for the country to produce smartphones but to buy clothing from other countries. *Comparative advantage* is a situation in which a country specializes in the production of a good or service at which it is relatively more efficient.

Importing

Imports are items bought from other countries. Did you know that imports account for the total supply of bananas, coffee, cocoa, certain spices, tea, silk, and crude rubber in the United States? The United States buys about half of its crude oil and fish from other countries. Imports also account for 20 to 50 percent of the supply of carpets, sugar, leather gloves, dishes, and sewing machines. U.S. companies must import tin, chromium, manganese, nickel, copper, zinc, and other metals to manufacture certain goods. Figure 3-1 shows how dependent the United States is on imported raw materials.

Without foreign trade, many things you buy would cost more or not be available. Other countries can produce some goods at a lower cost because they have the needed raw materials or have lower labor costs. Some consumers purchase foreign goods, even at higher prices, if they perceive the quality to be better than domestic goods. They may simply enjoy products made in other countries. French perfumes, Norwegian sweaters, and Swiss watches are examples.

Life-Span Plan

Identify your special aptitudes or abilities that you believe could help you achieve your life-span goals. Explain how these aptitudes or abilities are similar to absolute or comparative advantage among nations in production and trade.

Exporting

Goods and services sold to other countries are called **exports**. Just as imports benefit you, exports benefit consumers in other countries. Workers throughout the world

U.S. Import Reliance for Selected Raw Materials

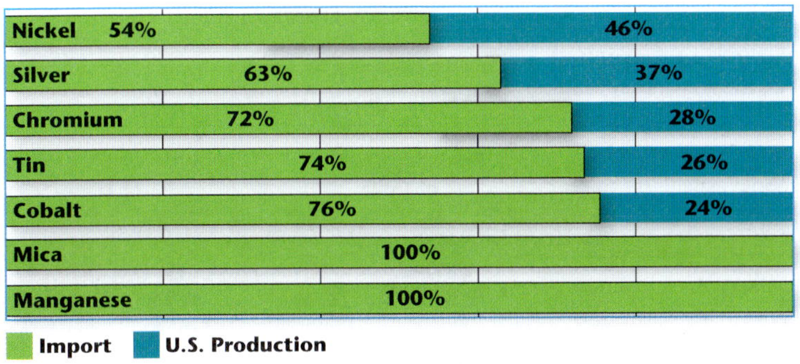

Source: U.S. Department of the Interior, U.S. Geological Survey, Mineral Commodity Summaries

FIGURE 3-1
How would U.S. manufacturing be affected if these imports were not available?

TEACH

Explain the difference between an absolute advantage and a comparative advantage.

Ask students to list benefits and concerns associated with importing.

Name various problems that can result from extensive importing.

Life-Span Plan Answer

Answers will vary. Students should identify aptitudes or abilities they possess and logically explain how these may contribute to them achieving their life-span goals.

▶ Figure 3-1 *ANSWER*

The graph in Figure 3-1 indicates that without imports, there would be shortages of these raw materials used in U.S. manufacturing.

Applied Skills

Building Study Skills Assign students to develop a summary of various international business concepts such as absolute advantage, comparative advantage, importing, and exporting. Encourage students to include visuals such as photos and personal drawings.

TEACH

Contrast importing with exporting.

Describe various activities needed for exporting such as labeling, financing, shipping, and inspections.

▸ **Figure 3-2** ***ANSWER***

Figure 3-2 reveals that China has the largest trade imbalance with the United States.

ONGOING ASSESSMENT

CHECKPOINT ✓*ANSWER*

Importing is bringing items from other countries into a country. Exporting is selling goods and services to other countries.

TEACH

Explain how *balance of trade* is calculated.

Ask students to suggest actions that might be taken to improve a country's balance of trade.

Explain how *balance of payments* is calculated. Describe how balance of payments differs from balance of trade.

▸ **Figure 3-3** ***ANSWER***

It is better for a country to export more than it imports so that it will not be too dependent on other countries. A favorable balance of trade also means money will be flowing into a country rather than out of it. An unfavorable balance of trade causes a trade deficit.

use factory and farm machinery made in the United States. They eat food made from U.S. agricultural products and use chemicals, fertilizers, medicines, and plastics from the United States. People in other countries like to view U.S. movies. They also watch CNN and ESPN. They read books, magazines, and newspapers published by U.S. companies. The goods and services exported by the United States create many jobs. One of every six jobs in the United States depends on international business. Figure 3-2 shows U.S. balance of trade with its top trading partners.

U.S. TRADE BALANCES

COUNTRY	GOODS EXPORTED (IN BILLIONS)	GOODS IMPORTED (IN BILLIONS)	U.S. TRADE BALANCE
All Countries	1,623.2	2,344.8	−721.6
Canada	312.0	346.0	−34.0
Mexico	240.3	294.1	−53.8
Japan	67.0	134.0	−67.0
Netherlands	43.7	20.8	+22.9
Australia	26.7	10.7	+16.0
Brazil	42.4	30.3	+12.1
Taiwan	26.8	40.5	−13.7
China	124.0	466.6	−342.6
European Union	276.7	417.8	−141.1

Source: U.S. Census Bureau

FIGURE 3-2
Which country has the largest trade imbalance with the United States?

CHECKPOINT ✓
How does importing differ from exporting?

LO 3.1.2

MEASURING TRADE RELATIONS

A major reason people work is to earn money to buy things. First, they sell their labor for wages. They then spend the major part of those wages on goods and services. People usually try to keep their income and spending in balance. They know that if they spend more than they earn, they can experience financial problems. Nations are also concerned about balancing income with expenditures. When people buy more than their income allows, they go into debt. In the same way, when a country has an unfavorable balance of trade, it owes money to others. *Foreign debt* is the amount a country owes to other countries.

Balance of Trade

The difference between a country's total exports and total imports is called the **balance of trade**. If a country exports (sells) more than it imports (buys), it has a *trade surplus*. Its trade position is said to be favorable. If it imports more than it exports, it has a *trade deficit* and its trade position is unfavorable.

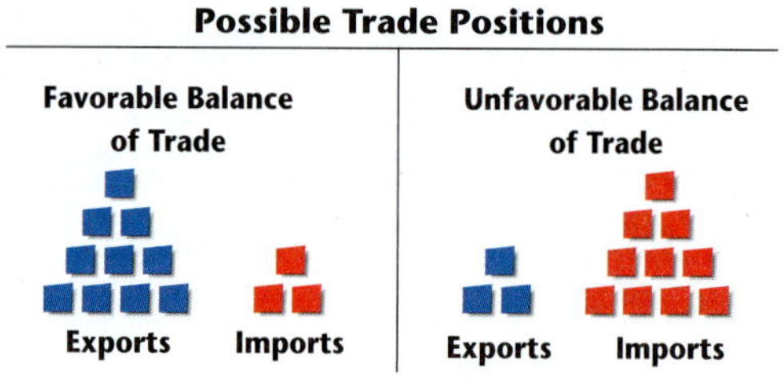

FIGURE 3-3
Why is it better for a country to export more than it imports?

Applied Skills

Communication Instruct students to create an advertisement to promote exporting by U.S. businesses. Be sure students communicate the benefits of exporting to business, workers, and our society. Consider allowing students to work in pairs or small groups.

A country can have a trade surplus with one country and a trade deficit with another. Countries should strive to keep their international trade in balance. Figure 3-3 shows the two possible trade positions. After a long history of a favorable balance of trade, the United States has had a trade deficit in recent years.

Balance of Payments

In addition to exporting and importing goods and services, nations participate in other forms of exchange. Money passes from one country to another through investments and tourism. A citizen of one country might invest in a corporation in another country. A business may invest in a factory in another country. One government might give financial assistance or military aid to another nation. Banks may deposit funds in foreign banks.

When tourists travel, they add to the flow of money from their country to the country they are visiting. Some countries limit the amount of money their citizens can take out of the country when they travel.

The **balance of payments** is the difference between the amount of money that comes into a country and the amount that goes out of it. A *positive* or *favorable* balance of payments occurs when a nation receives more money in a year than it pays out. A *negative* balance of payments is *unfavorable*. It is the result of a country sending more money out than it brings in.

Work as a TEAM

Countries attempt to establish or maintain a favorable balance of payments. Create a list of actions a nation might take to improve its trade relations with other countries.

CHECKPOINT

How does balance of trade differ from balance of payments?

A QUESTION OF ETHICS

Bribery and Gift Giving

In the United States, it is considered unethical for a businessperson to pay bribes to government officials or to other businesspersons in exchange for favorable treatment, such as the awarding of well-paid contracts. In fact, it is against the law, whether the recipient is an American or someone in another country. The Foreign Corrupt Business Practices Act of 1977 outlawed the payment of bribes by Americans to foreign officials, companies, or individuals. At times, the inability to bribe may put U.S. businesses at a competitive disadvantage. In some countries, paying and accepting bribes of various sorts is common, even expected. As more countries recognize how harmful bribes are to economic progress, bribery is decreasing.

While it is relatively easy to outlaw bribes, it is much harder to define and identify what is a bribe and what is a gift given as a token of appreciation. Gift giving among businesspeople is relatively limited and infrequent in the United States and Canada. In other cultures, it is very common and regarded as entirely appropriate. Many organizations have policies that limit the monetary value and type of gifts that are acceptable. Policing intent is much more difficult because it is highly subjective. A social dinner invitation is usually meant to influence the recipient's behavior, even if in a subtle way.

Think Critically

1. How can U.S. businesspeople handle situations in foreign countries where officials expect bribes to be paid as a condition for doing business there?
2. Suppose you work for a manufacturing company. A plastics supplier who is trying to get more business sends you a case of golf balls made with one of its high-tech composite materials. What would you do?

Work as a TEAM

In this activity, students are asked to list actions to improve a nation's trade relations. Encourage students to think of actions that might be taken by businesses, government, workers, consumers, schools, and others.

ONGOING ASSESSMENT

CHECKPOINT ✓ANSWER

Balance of trade is the difference between a country's total exports and total imports. Balance of payments is the difference between the amount of money that comes into a country and the amount that goes out of it. Trade is not the only thing influencing the balance of payments. For example, money can enter or leave a country through investments, tourism, financial aid, and bank deposits.

A Question of Ethics

This feature provides an example of the influence of culture on global business.

Think Critically Answers

1. Businesspeople could politely explain that the United States does not follow the custom of showing appreciation in this way and that U.S. laws forbid such practices. Businesspeople could emphasize the superiority of their products or services as compensation for not participating in the gift-giving custom.

2. The employee at the manufacturing company who received the case of golf balls could send the balls to the company's technical department for evaluation and send the plastics supplier a letter of thanks for allowing the company to test the product. To further emphasize that this was not accepted as a personal gift, the letter could mention that the leftover balls will be donated to a local youth golf team.

TEACH

Ask students to describe factors that could affect the value of a country's currency.

Assign students to conduct an online search to find photos of currencies from various countries. Point out that images on currencies reflect the history, culture, geography, and economic activities of a country.

THINK CRITICALLY THROUGH VISUALS

Unique currencies contribute to countries' identities. Changing values can cause foreign trade difficulties.

▶ Figure 3-4 *ANSWER*

Figure 3-4 shows that Britain's pound is worth the most in terms of U.S. dollars. Point out that these values change on a daily basis. Encourage students to find a website that gives the current value of these currencies.

LO 3.1.3

INTERNATIONAL CURRENCY

In every economy, money serves three functions: (1) a *store of value* for future buying; (2) a *medium of exchange* for business transactions; and (3) a *unit of measure* to value goods and services. One challenge of international trade is the various currencies used around the world. For instance, Russia uses the *ruble*; the European Union, the *euro*; Brazil, the *real*; India, the *rupee*; and Saudi Arabia, the *riyal.*

Michael Dechev/Shutterstock.com

What are the benefits and concerns associated with having many different currencies around the world?

Foreign Exchange Rates

The process of exchanging one currency for another occurs in the *foreign exchange market*, which consists of banks that buy and sell different currencies. Most large banks provide currency services for businesses and consumers. The **exchange rate** is the value of a currency in one country compared with the value in another. Supply and demand affect the value of currency. The approximate values of various currencies on a recent date in relation to the U.S. dollar (USD) are listed in Figure 3-4.

Travelers and businesspeople must deal with currency exchanges as they go from one country to another. Travelers in another country can go to a currency exchange and buy the local currency. The amount of local currency they receive depends on the value of the two currencies at that time. Current rates are available online and at exchange windows. Currency exchange operators charge a fee. They are located at airports, train stations, hotels, and banks. Foreign currencies may also be purchased online.

Factors Affecting Currency Values

Three main factors affect currency exchange rates among countries: the country's balance of payments, economic conditions, and political stability.

Balance of Payments When a country has a favorable balance of payments, the value of its currency is usually constant or rising. An increased demand for both the nation's products and its currency

RECENT VALUES OF CURRENCIES

COUNTRY	CURRENCY	UNITS PER USD *	VALUE IN USD *
Britain	pound	0.67	1.49
Brazil	real	3.23	0.31
Canada	dollar	1.26	0.795
European Union	euro	0.924	1.08
Japan	yen	120	0.0083
Saudi Arabia	riyal	3.75	0.27
South Africa	rand	12.04	0.083
South Korea	won	1113.4	0.0009
Venezuela	bolivar	6.29	0.159

*United States Dollar

FIGURE 3-4

Which currency is worth the most in terms of U.S. dollars?

Different Learning Styles

Print Learner Use text and visuals on pages 58–59 to present and reinforce various factors that affect the value of a country's currency.

Tactile Learner Set up a foreign exchange window in your classroom using "play" money from several of the countries listed in Figure 3-4.

influences this situation. When a nation has an unfavorable balance of payments, its currency usually declines in value.

Economic Conditions When prices increase and the buying power of the country's money declines, its currency is not as appealing. Inflation reduces the buying power of a currency. High inflation in Brazil, for example, would reduce the demand for the real.

Interest rates are the cost of using someone else's money. These rates can affect the value of a country's currency. Higher interest rates usually create lower consumer demand. This usually results in a reduced demand for a nation's currency, causing a decline in its value.

Political Stability Companies and individuals want to avoid risk when they do business in other nations. If a government changes suddenly, this may create an unfriendly setting for foreign business. A company could lose its buildings, equipment, or money on deposit in banks.

Political instability may also occur when new laws are created. These laws may not allow foreign businesses to operate as freely as they did under the old laws. Uncertainty in a country reduces the confidence that businesspeople have in its currency.

FYI The U.S. dollar is the official currency of Ecuador, El Salvador, and Panama. A country may adopt a "dollarization" policy in an attempt to reduce economic troubles and enhance trade with other nations. The dollar is also the unofficial monetary unit for tourist transactions in countries such as the Bahamas and Haiti.

CHECKPOINT ✓
What factors affect the value of a country's currency?

3.1 ASSESSMENT

Key Concepts

Determine the best answer.

1. Which of the following would be an example of international business?
   a. A farmer in Iowa using equipment made in Indiana
   b. A sales staff in South Carolina representing a foreign producer
   c. A restaurant in Chicago offering Asian menu items
   d. A retail store in Oregon selling craft items from local artists
2. When a country's imports exceed its exports, there is a trade
   a. surplus
   b. deficit
   c. exchange
   d. balance
3. The value of a country's currency is likely to decline as a result of
   a. higher inflation
   b. lower interest rates
   c. a trade surplus
   d. a favorable balance of payments

Make Academic Connections

4. **Culture** While business knowledge is important, often cultural awareness in foreign markets is even more important. Interview someone who has lived in or visited another country about cultural factors that affect business activities in that country.
5. **History** Conduct research to identify various items that have been used as money in the past. Obtain photos online of the different forms of money. Explain how these items served as medium of exchange, store of value, and unit of measure.

FYI

Describe how countries can grow interrelated through their currencies.

ONGOING ASSESSMENT

CHECKPOINT ✓ANSWER

The three main factors affecting the value of a country's currency are the country's balance of payments, economic conditions, and political stability.

ASSESS

Key Concepts *Answers*

1. b. A sales staff in South Carolina representing a foreign producer
2. b. deficit
3. a. higher inflation

Make Academic Connections *Answers*

4. Consider allowing students to choose how they would like to report their findings. For example, students might prepare an oral report that includes a short video clip from their actual interview. This assignment is appropriate for pairs or small groups.
5. Students should identify items such as gold, silver, and various agricultural products that have served as money in the past. While these items were accepted as money in various settings, they often had limitations related to their acceptability, perishability, and transportability.

RETEACH List the main ideas on the board. Ask students to describe each concept.

CLOSE Ask students to list the main reasons why international business activities continue to expand.

ENRICH Instruct students to research what their state (or a neighboring state) is doing to encourage international trade. Most states have an exporting program in their state department of commerce.

Focus on REAL LIFE

After reading the feature, ask students if they can think of other possible benefits of trade among countries. Point out that trade spurs economic growth, creates jobs, increases standard of living, and makes goods and services more affordable.

TEACH

Ask students to list factors that would create differences when doing business in other countries.

Use Figure 3-5 (on page 61) to provide an overview of the four main elements of the international business environment.

Point out examples of how geography, culture, and economic factors might affect global business activities.

3.2 The Global Marketplace

Learning Outcomes

3.2.1 Describe the components of the international business environment.

3.2.2 Identify examples of formal trade barriers.

3.2.3 Explain actions to encourage international trade.

Key Terms

infrastructure 61	tariff 62
trade barriers 62	embargo 63
quota 62	

Focus on REAL LIFE

"Look, this shirt was made in El Salvador," Ross announced as he put the hanger back on the rack. "I want shirts made in the U.S.A."

Calinda touched the shirt and asked, "What's wrong with shirts from El Salvador?"

"I don't know, but wouldn't it be better if we bought things made here rather than giving our money to other countries?"

"Actually, trading with other countries can be good for us," Calinda explained. "When we buy goods from El Salvador it helps that country's economy and makes it possible for Salvadorans to buy goods and services from U.S. companies."

Ross picked up the shirt and said, "In that case, I'll buy this one."

LO 3.2.1

INTERNATIONAL BUSINESS ENVIRONMENT

Doing business in other countries requires knowledge of the differences that exist among people and places. As shown in Figure 3-5, businesses must consider four main factors—geography, cultural influences, economic development, and political and legal restrictions.

Geography

The location, climate, terrain, seaports, and natural resources of a country influence business activity. Very hot weather will limit the types of crops that can be grown. A nation with many rivers or ocean seaports can easily ship products for foreign trade. Countries with few natural resources must depend on imports.

Cultural Influences

In some societies, hugging is an appropriate business greeting. In other societies, a handshake is the custom. These differences represent different cultures. *Culture* is the accepted behaviors, customs, and values of a society. A society's culture has a strong influence on business activities. In Mexico, many businesses close for a few hours in the afternoon while people enjoy lunch and a siesta (relaxing rest period).

The main cultural and social factors that affect international business are language, religion, values, customs, and social relationships. These relationships include interactions among families, labor unions, and other organizations.

Economic Development

Countries and individuals face the problem of limited resources to satisfy needs and wants. You continually make decisions about the use of your time, money, and energy. In a similar way, every country plans the use of its land, natural resources, workers, and wealth to best serve the needs of its people.

In some countries, people travel on a high-speed bullet train to manage a computer network in a high-rise building.

Different Learning Abilities

Visually Impaired Use five pieces of colored paper to create a large display of the information presented in Figure 3-5 to assist students who might need this type of visual assistance.

Use the display to help all students understand the components of the international business environment.

In other countries, people go by oxcart to a grass hut to operate a hand loom to make cloth for people in their village. These differences in living and work environments reflect the level of economic development. The key factors that affect a country's level of economic development are:

- **Literacy Level** Countries with better education systems usually provide more and better goods and services for their citizens.
- **Technology** Automated production, distribution, and communications systems allow companies to create and deliver goods, services, and ideas quickly.
- **Agricultural Dependency** An economy where most workers are involved in agriculture does not have the manufacturing base to provide citizens with great quantity and high quality of a product.

Another factor that supports international trade in industrialized countries is **infrastructure**. Infrastructure refers to a nation's transportation, communication, and utility systems. A country such as Germany—with its efficient rail system, high-speed highways, and computers—is better prepared for international business activities than other nations with a weaker infrastructure.

Political and Legal Restrictions

Each day you encounter examples of government influence on business. Governments regulate fair advertising and enforce contracts. They require safety inspections of foods and medications. People in the United States have a great deal of freedom in their business activities. This is not true in all countries. In many places, the activities of consumers and business operators are restricted. The most common political and legal factors that affect international business activities include the type of government, the stability of the government, and government policies toward business.

Work as a TEAM

Knowledge of the international business environment is important for all global activities. As a team, create a list of items for each of the following categories: geography, cultural influences, economic development, and political/legal concerns. Explain how these items could affect a company when doing business in another country.

CHECKPOINT

List the four main elements of the international business environment.

GEOGRAPHIC FACTORS
- Location
- Climate
- Terrain
- Waterways
- Natural resources

ECONOMIC FACTORS
- Technology
- Education
- Inflation
- Exchange rate
- Infrastructure

INTERNATIONAL BUSINESS ENVIRONMENT

CULTURAL FACTORS
- Language
- Family
- Religion
- Customs
- Traditions
- Food

POLITICAL AND LEGAL FACTORS
- Government system
- Political stability
- Trade barriers
- Business regulations

FIGURE 3-5
What are some specific examples of the four main factors of the international business environment?

Work as a TEAM

This activity will help students better understand the international business environment.

TEACH

Describe the three main factors that affect the economic development of a country.

Explain the importance of infrastructure for business activities.

Point out that a country also has a *natural infrastructure* (including climate, natural resources, terrain, and waterways), which can enhance or deter business activities.

ONGOING ASSESSMENT

CHECKPOINT ✓ANSWER

The four main elements of the international business environment are geography, cultural influences, economic development, and political and legal concerns.

▶ Figure 3-5 ANSWER

Answers will vary. Students might mention rivers and canals as examples of waterways. Celebrations of various holidays are examples of religion, customs, and traditions. High-speed rail service and public wi-fi are examples of economic factors. Taxes and workplace safety rules are examples of political and legal factors.

Different Learning Styles

Kinesthetic Learner Organize students into three or four groups and ask them to develop a game that their classmates could play to help them remember and understand the elements of the international business environment. Suggest that students adapt a familiar board game or party game. Allow time for students to actually play some of the games.

TEACH

Explain the difference between formal and informal trade barriers.

Describe examples of quotas that might be used by a country.

Explain the purpose of a tariff in international trade relations.

THINK CRITICALLY THROUGH VISUALS

Tariffs on imported goods do not help consumers because they lead to higher prices, lower quantities of products, and less competition among manufacturers.

LO 3.2.2

INTERNATIONAL TRADE BARRIERS

Government actions can create **trade barriers**, which are restrictions to free trade. These political actions are *formal* trade barriers. Three common formal trade barriers are quotas, tariffs, and embargoes.

The culture, traditions, and religion of a country can create *informal* trade barriers. These situations are not related to formal government actions but they can still restrict trade.

Quotas

To regulate international trade, governments set a limit on the quantity of a product that may be imported or exported within a given period. This limit is called a **quota**.

George Doyle/Stockbyte/Getty Images

Do tariffs on imported consumer goods help consumers or hurt them?

Quotas may be set for many reasons. Countries that export oil may put quotas on crude oil so that the supply will remain low and prices will stay at a certain level. Quotas may be set on imports from another country to express displeasure at the policies of that country.

Quotas can also be set by a country to protect one of its industries from too much competition from abroad. This often is done by a nation to shield its "infant industries," which need protection to get started. In the past, the U.S. government has imposed quotas on sugar, cattle, dairy products, and textiles.

Tariffs

Another device that governments use to control international trade is the tariff. A **tariff** is a tax that a government places on certain imported products. Suppose you want to buy an imported bicycle. The producer charges $140, but the government collects a 20 percent tariff ($28) on the bicycle when it is imported. Therefore, you will have to pay $168 plus shipping charges for the bike. The increased price may cause you to decide to buy a bike manufactured in the United States at a lower price.

Some tariffs are a set amount per pound, gallon, or other unit, while others are figured on the value of the good, as in the example of the bicycle. A tariff increases the price for an imported product. A high tariff tends to lower the demand for the product and reduce the quantity of that import. Many people believe that tariffs should be used to protect U.S. jobs from foreign competition.

Applied Skills

Mathematics Assign students to calculate different tariff amounts. Ask them to explain the benefits and drawbacks of tariffs for countries, companies, and consumers. Remind students that Appendix A: Using a Calculator and Computer Keypad is available at the back of this textbook. See page 546.

Embargoes

If a government wishes to do so, it can stop the export or import of a product completely. This action is called an **embargo**. Governments may impose an embargo for many reasons. They may wish to offer more protection from international competition for their own industries than either the quota or the tariff will provide. The government may wish to prevent sensitive products, especially those vital to the nation's defense, from falling into the hands of unfriendly groups or nations. A government sometimes imposes an embargo to express its disapproval of the actions or policies of another country.

CHECKPOINT ✓
What are three formal trade barriers?

LO 3.2.3

ENCOURAGING INTERNATIONAL TRADE

Specific actions by governments can promote international business activities. Governments view exporting as an effective way to create jobs and foster economic prosperity. Common efforts to encourage international trade include free-trade zones, free-trade agreements, and common markets.

Free-Trade Zones

To promote international business, governments often create free-trade zones in their countries. A *free-trade zone* is a selected area where products can be imported duty-free and then stored, assembled, and/or used in manufacturing. A free-trade zone is often located around a seaport or airport. The importer pays duty only when the product leaves the zone.

Business Insight

Mobile Phone Financial Services in Developing Economies

In many rural areas of Africa, smartphones are changing the way farmers do business and improving economic development. From Senegal to Kenya, smartphones provide access to financial services such as savings accounts, payment accounts, and loans. These services are especially needed in rural areas because banks are rare. Farmers can use smartphones to pay for livestock, agricultural equipment, seeds for crops, and other business expenses.

Organizations such as the Grameen Bank and Opportunity International have created mobile banking systems to serve farmers, business owners, and entrepreneurs in Africa and Asia. Customers use their phones to check account balances, pay bills, maintain savings accounts with debit cards, and obtain small loans. These loans are often used to start a community-based business.

In some cases the banks lease smartphones to help people set up a grocery shop, open a café, or start a weaving business. The loan funds are accessed by phone to pay workers and other business expenses. As farmers and entrepreneurs achieve business success, they create jobs which provide money to families for food, clean water, health care, and education.

Think Critically

1. What are the benefits of mobile banking services for people in poor and rural areas?
2. Conduct an online search to locate additional information about mobile banking in developing economies.

TEACH

Describe how a country might use an embargo.

ONGOING ASSESSMENT

CHECKPOINT ✓*ANSWER*

Three formal trade barriers are quotas, tariffs, and embargoes.

TEACH

Provide an overview of actions that might be used to encourage international business trade activities.

Explain the purpose of a free-trade zone.

Describe the benefits of free-trade agreements.

Ask students to point out some concerns of free-trade agreements.

Explain how common markets differ from free-trade agreements.

Business Insight

Mobile banking in developing economies is improving the economic situation for millions of people who previously had no access to financial services.

Think Critically *Answers*

1. Mobile banking service allows business owners to save, make payments, and take out loans. This creates jobs, which in turn improves economic and social conditions.
2. Findings will vary depending on the websites visited.

Portfolio Activity

Assign the Portfolio Activity for Chapter 3, available on the website for this textbook.

COLLECT Offer suggestions for locating packaging from a food item from another country.

CREATE Remind students to include all of the required components in their visual.

CONNECT Point out that students need to connect visuals to something already in their portfolio.

THINK CRITICALLY THROUGH VISUALS

U.S. businesses are interested in exporting because it provides an opportunity to expand sales of goods and services.

ONGOING ASSESSMENT

CHECKPOINT ✓ *ANSWER*

Actions that could be taken to encourage international trade include free-trade zones, free-trade agreements, and common markets.

ASSESS

Key Concepts *Answers*

1. True. Infrastructure has a profound effect on a country's development.

2. False. Government actions create formal, not informal, trade barriers.

3. c. cultural

4. b. a common market

Make Academic Connections *Answers*

5. Consider helping students identify specific areas of law to investigate, such as voting age, compulsory school attendance, and family leave.

6. Consider coordinating students' selection of regions to minimize repetition in the presentations.

7. Answers will vary. Students should identify the group, its members, and its history. They should also describe how the union has benefited member countries.

CLOSE Prepare a list of actions that can enhance and deter international trade activities.

Orientaly/Shutterstock.com

Why do you think U.S. businesses would be interested in exporting?

Free-Trade Agreements

Many countries set up free-trade agreements with other nations. Under a *free-trade agreement*, member countries agree to remove duties, also called import taxes, and trade barriers on products traded among them. This results in increased trade between the members. For example, the United States, Canada, and Mexico began implementing the North American Free Trade Agreement (NAFTA) in 1994. This pact does away with tariffs on goods traded among the three countries and eases the movement of goods. NAFTA is designed to enlarge the markets and economic bases of the countries involved.

Common Markets

In a *common market*, members do away with duties and other trade barriers. They allow companies to invest freely in each member's country. They allow workers to move freely across borders. A common market is also called an *economic community*. Common market members have a common external duty on products being imported from nonmember countries. Examples of common markets include the European Union (EU) and the Latin American Integration Association (LAIA). The goals are to expand trade among member nations and promote regional economic integration.

CHECKPOINT ✓
What actions could be taken to encourage international trade?

3.2 ASSESSMENT

Key Concepts

Determine the best answer.

1. True or False. Infrastructure is a significant factor that affects the economic development of a country.
2. True or False. An informal trade barrier is created by government actions.
3. Religion is an element of the ___ component of the international business environment.
   a. geographic **b.** economic
   c. cultural **d.** political
4. A country that wishes to enhance international trade activities would most likely use
   a. a tariff **b.** a common market
   c. an embargo **d.** a quota

Make Academic Connections

5. **Law** Use the Internet to locate information about laws in foreign countries that are different from those in the United States.
6. **Geography** Using library resources or the Internet, obtain copies of maps for various geographic regions. On your map, indicate how the terrain, climate, and waterways might influence international trade activities. Present a one- to two-minute summary of your findings.
7. **History** Conduct research on the history of a common market such as the EU or the LAIA. Describe some of the benefits the community provides to its member nations.

RETEACH Provide examples for each component of the international business environment and the various actions to encourage or discourage trade activities.

ENRICH Ask students to debate various types of actions that countries might take to encourage or discourage international trade.

3.3 International Business Organizations

Learning Outcomes

3.3.1 Discuss activities of multinational organizations.

3.3.2 Explain common international business entry modes.

3.3.3 Describe activities of international trade organizations and agencies.

Key Terms

multinational company (MNC) 65
joint venture 67

Focus on REAL LIFE

"How was Italy?" Cory asked as he settled into a chair across from a colleague who had just returned from a six-month assignment.

"I worked really hard, but I found time to enjoy some Italian culture and eat some great food. Living and working in another country was a good experience and I would do it again. However, I must admit that I'm glad to be home," responded Duncan as he put a straw in his soft drink.

"What did you miss the most?"

Duncan held up his cup and said, "American soft drinks. It was easy to find my favorite brands, but they just weren't quite the same."

LO 3.3.1

MULTINATIONAL COMPANIES

A **multinational company (MNC)** is an organization that does business in several countries. MNCs usually consist of a parent company in a *home country* and divisions or separate companies in one or more other countries. The different country in which the MNC conducts business activities is called the *host country*.

MNC Strategies

Multinational corporations can use either a global or multinational strategy. A *global strategy* uses the same product and marketing strategy worldwide. The same, or a very similar, product is sold throughout the world. For example, Coca-Cola tends to use a global strategy with slight variations.

A *multinational strategy* treats each country market differently. Firms develop products and marketing strategies that adapt to the customs, tastes, and buying habits of a distinct national market.

Many restaurant chains use a multinational strategy when they modify their menus to local tastes.

MNC Benefits

Several benefits are associated with international business. Consumers have a large amount of goods available. Often, these goods are sold at lower prices than goods made domestically. Career opportunities

paul prescott/Shutterstock.com

What are the advantages of a multinational strategy?

Focus on REAL LIFE

Discuss the situation presented. Ask students to name other differences they might encounter when living or working in another country.

TEACH

Ask students to name reasons for the expansion of multinational companies.

Explain the difference between a "global" (standardized) strategy and a "multinational" (adapted) strategy.

THINK CRITICALLY THROUGH VISUALS

A multinational strategy allows businesses to sell their goods and services to customers in various markets and expand their product lines to meet the needs and wants of different cultures. Businesses are better equipped to absorb losses in one market when they have diversified interests elsewhere.

Different Learning Abilities

Attention Deficit Disorder Clearly explain global and multinational strategies so students can write a definition and examples. Slowly present these items to allow students to focus.

TEACH

Highlight the benefits and drawbacks of multinational companies.

THINK CRITICALLY THROUGH VISUALS

Good prices and expanded consumer choice are two advantages of international business.

ONGOING ASSESSMENT

CHECKPOINT ✓ ANSWER

Two strategies commonly used by multinational companies are a global strategy (offering the same product the same way everywhere) and a multinational strategy (approaching each country's market differently).

TEACH

Provide an overview of the various global market entry modes used when doing business around the world.

Explain the difference between licensing and franchising.

Work as a TEAM

This exercise will help students better understand the importance of using partners when doing business around the world.

---

also expand as a company does business in a variety of countries.

Global business activities may also foster understanding, communication, and respect among people of different nations. Nations that are business partners usually try to maintain friendly relations for economic reasons.

Drawbacks of Multinational Companies

An MNC can become a major economic power in a host country. The workers of the host country may depend on the MNC for jobs. Consumers become dependent upon it for goods and services. The MNC may actually influence or control the political power of the country.

Sakonboon Sansri/Shutterstock.com

What are some advantages of international business?

CHECKPOINT ✓

What are two strategies commonly used by multinational companies?

LO 3.3.2

GLOBAL MARKET ENTRY MODES

As companies expand into other countries, several methods are available for their use.

Licensing

Some companies want to produce items in other countries without being actively involved. They may allow a foreign company to use a procedure they own. *Licensing* is selling the right to use some intangible property (production process, trademark, or brand name) for a fee or royalty.

The Gerber Company started selling its baby food products in Japan by means of licensing. The use of movie characters or sports team logos on hats, shirts, jackets, notebooks, luggage, and other items also involves a licensing agreement. Licensing has a low financial investment, so the potential financial return is often low. The risk for the company is also low.

Franchising

Another method often used to expand into other countries is the *franchise*. A franchise is the right to use a company name or business process in a specific way. Organizations enter into contracts with people in other countries to set up a business that looks and runs like the parent company. The company obtaining the franchise will usually adapt a

Work as a TEAM

International business success often increases when a company works with a local business partner in another country. Choose a company or product that could be sold in other countries. Identify the types of companies that you might consider as a partner in other countries. Then identify information sources that you might contact to make sure these potential partners would be suitable companies with which to do business.

Applied Skills

Writing Across the Curriculum Assign students to write a paragraph comparing the benefits and drawbacks of multinational companies. Encourage students to relate their discussion to something learned from another class.

range of business elements. Marketing elements such as food products, packaging, and advertising messages must meet both cultural sensitivities and legal requirements.

Both franchising and licensing involve a royalty payment for the right to use a process or company name. Licensing usually involves a manufacturing process. Franchising commonly involves selling a product or service. Franchise agreements are popular with fast-food companies. McDonald's, Burger King, Wendy's, KFC, and Pizza Hut all have used franchising to increase their presence in foreign markets.

Joint Venture

Business partnerships can provide benefits to all parties involved. One type of global partnership is the joint venture. A **joint venture** is an agreement between two or more companies to share a business project.

The main benefit of a joint venture is the sharing of raw materials, shipping facilities, management activities, or production facilities. Concerns about this type of partnership include sharing of profits and not as much control because several companies are involved.

This arrangement is very popular for manufacturing. Joint ventures between Japanese and U.S. automobile manufacturers have been common. For example, the Ford Motor Company entered a joint venture with Mazda Motor Corporation. Ford used Mazda-produced parts for several of its cars. Mazda set up assembly plants for Ford vehicles.

CHECKPOINT ✓
How does licensing differ from a franchise?

FYI
Cereal Partners Worldwide (CPW) is a joint venture between General Mills and Nestlé to sell cereal in Latin America, Europe, the Middle East, and other areas of the world. General Mills brought popular products, such as Cheerios, Lucky Charms, and Trix, into the partnership. Nestlé, well known all over the world, has a broad distribution system and is a popular brand in most foreign countries.

LO 3.3.3

INTERNATIONAL TRADE ORGANIZATIONS

International business activities can be very complex. As a result, several organizations have been created to help companies with global trade activities.

World Trade Organization

The World Trade Organization (WTO) was created in 1995 to promote trade around the world. With 160 member countries representing 95 percent of world trade, WTO settles trade disputes and enforces free-trade agreements between its members. Other goals of WTO include the following.

- Lowering tariffs that discourage free trade
- Eliminating import quotas
- Reducing barriers for banks, insurance companies, and other financial services
- Assisting poor countries with economic growth

International Monetary Fund

The International Monetary Fund (IMF), with more than 180 member nations, helps to promote economic cooperation. It maintains an orderly system of world trade and exchange rates. The IMF was established in 1946 when the economic interdependence among nations was growing at a greater pace than ever before in history.

FYI
Explain how companies use joint ventures. Instruct students to conduct online research for more examples of joint ventures.

ONGOING ASSESSMENT

CHECKPOINT ✓ANSWER

Licensing does not require as much financial investment or risk as franchising. Both licensing and franchising involve royalty payments, but licensing usually involves a manufacturing process, while franchising commonly involves selling a product or service.

TEACH

Explain the activities of the World Trade Organization (WTO).

Describe methods used in the International Monetary Fund (IMF) to assist countries.

Different Learning Styles

Auditory Learner Encourage auditory learners to repeat the names of the international trade organizations discussed on pages 67 and 68. Ask them to describe one activity of each organization.

NET KNOWLEDGE

Students should locate a website with information sources for exporters. Students should be able to describe how the information they access could help companies that are starting or expanding their exporting activities.

TEACH

Describe services provided by the World Bank.

ONGOING ASSESSMENT

CHECKPOINT ✓ ANSWER

The International Monetary Fund assists countries by promoting economic cooperation and maintaining an orderly system of world trade and exchange rates. This cooperation makes harmful trade wars among IMF nations less likely.

ASSESS

Key Concepts *Answers*

1. d. licensing agreement
2. a. WTO

Make Academic Connections *Answers*

3. Students are to list information they find that indicates a licensing agreement.
4. Invite students to share their presentations with the class.
5. Answers will vary depending on the article selected. Provide guidance regarding the format for the citation.

CLOSE Ask students to name the three international organizations that promote international trade.

NET KNOWLEDGE

The U.S. Department of Commerce and other federal government agencies provide extensive help to companies involved in exporting. Locate a website that provides export assistance. Describe how the information available could be useful to companies that are starting or expanding their exporting activities.

Before the International Monetary Fund was instituted, a country could change the value of its currency to attract more foreign customers. As other countries lose business, they may impose trade restrictions or lower the value of their currency. As one nation tries to outdo another, a trade war may result. Today, cooperation among IMF nations makes trade wars less likely.

World Bank

The International Bank for Reconstruction and Development is commonly called the *World Bank*. It was created in 1944 to provide loans for rebuilding after World War II. Today, the bank's key function is to give economic aid to less-developed countries. These funds build communications systems, transportation networks, and energy plants.

The World Bank, with nearly 190 member countries, has two main divisions: the International Development Association and the International Finance Corporation. The International Development Association (IDA) makes loans to help developing countries. The International Finance Corporation (IFC) provides capital and technical help to private businesses in nations with limited resources. The IFC promotes joint ventures between foreign companies and local companies to further capital investment in developing nations.

CHECKPOINT ✓
How does the International Monetary Fund assist countries?

3.3 ASSESSMENT

Key Concepts

Determine the best answer.

1. A company is planning to sell the rights to its brand name for use in other countries. This is an example of a
   - **a.** joint venture
   - **b.** trade agreement
   - **c.** franchise
   - **d.** licensing agreement
2. The international organization that settles trade disagreements and enforces free-trade agreements is the
   - **a.** WTO
   - **b.** United Nations
   - **c.** IMF
   - **d.** World Bank

Make Academic Connections

3. **Economics** Visit a store or online business that sells toys, sporting goods, or other merchandise printed with logos or images belonging to other companies. List the information given that indicates a licensing agreement.
4. **Communication** Create a visual presentation (using software, photos, or a poster) that communicates the purpose of the International Monetary Fund or the World Bank.
5. **Read** Find a news article that relates to a topic addressed in this lesson. Read the article and write a one-sentence summary of the main idea. Include a properly formatted citation for your source.

RETEACH Assign students to create an example or expanded explanation for one of the points in this chapter summary by utilizing the Review Business Concepts segment at the end of the chapter.

ENRICH Assign students to small groups and ask each group to prepare a brief drama to communicate one of the points in the Review Business Concepts (chapter summary) on page 70.

BUSINESS IMPROVING SOCIETY

THE SAFE WATER TEAM

Africa924/Shutterstock.com

What actions can people take to help provide clean water in local and global settings?

Over 800,000 people die each year due to a lack of safe drinking water. The Safe Water Team (SWT) is taking action to attack this leading cause of death in Africa and other regions. They are committed to connecting organizations concerned with the growing dangers of unsafe water and sanitation issues around the world. SWT provides simple and sustainable water filtration units. These units use the Hydraid filter, a slow sand method. The device uses natural materials to filter out impurities in the water. The simplicity of this system makes maintenance and repairs unnecessary.

The Safe Water Team uses a corporate social responsibility (CSR) approach to partner with various groups for its work in the Dominican Republic, Ghana, Honduras, Haiti, Kenya, and Nigeria. Financial support and participation comes from corporate partners, individuals, churches, aid organizations, and governments. SWT has created a sustainable safe water delivery system that costs pennies per day.

To implement its business model, SWT first selects a community and appoints a village leader as project manager. This person recruits a community member to educate and train others about the filter operating system. All village residents are invited to learn about the system. To qualify to receive a filter, a member of the household must be educated on filter use and hygiene. This ensures local involvement and a community commitment to continually provide clean water to families.

In Kenya, the Safe Water Team distribution center is used to store the filter equipment. This facility is also used to process sand and gravel for the filtration systems. Fortunately, the SWT center in Kenya is located near Lake Victoria, which has a natural supply of quality sand and gravel that are just right for use in the filters.

The Safe Water Team places an emphasis on entrepreneurship among the people they serve. As water-related illnesses are reduced, healthy people are able to pursue economic opportunities. Entrepreneurial activity empowers people to start businesses and to better provide for the educational, health, and household needs of their families and community.

Think Critically

1. Locate another website that promotes awareness and attempts to solve a social issue or concern. Write a brief description of the website, the issue, and the goals of the organization. Discuss your opinion about the likelihood of success.
2. Identify a social issue or economic concern of interest to you and plan a website that might raise awareness of the situation.

BUSINESS IMPROVING SOCIETY

Use this feature to point out how the actions of businesses and other organizations can help to solve various social and economic problems.

THINK CRITICALLY THROUGH VISUALS

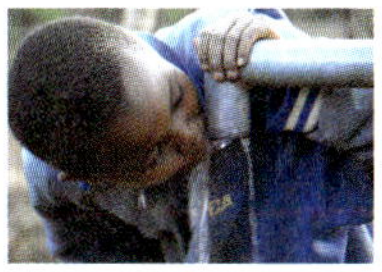

Donations to various international development organizations can help provide clean water. Also, training people to dig and maintain wells and water filtration systems can ensure an ongoing supply of clean water.

Think Critically *Answers*

1. Student answers will vary depending on the sites they locate. Students should give reasons why they think the sites will succeed or fail.

2. Ask students to share their website plans with the class. Invite class members to evaluate the proposed websites and predict whether the sites will be successful.

Different Learning Styles

Kinesthetic Learner Ask students to create a visual that might be used on a website to encourage people to donate or volunteer their time for a community service group or a world relief organization. Encourage students to communicate using various visuals and messages that motivate people to take action.

Think Critically About Business *Answers*

1. Examples will vary, but should incorporate the idea that having an absolute advantage in a product means that the country will experience strong demand for the good. It can sell its good abroad at a profit, allowing the country to import items in which it does not have an advantage.

2. Most communities and nations will not have all the raw materials and resources necessary to supply all the wants and needs of their people.

3. International business allows countries to export the items that they can produce most efficiently and cheaply while importing items they cannot produce as efficiently as other countries. Free trade allows these items to flow to consumers around the world, giving them the lowest prices possible. When markets are open across international borders, consumers have many products from which to choose. International trade also brings jobs, giving workers more purchasing power and thus a higher standard of living.

4. The perception that the foreign-based company is taking jobs away from U.S. workers could make it difficult for the company to gain loyal customers. The foreign-based company's products may be perceived as inferior. Foreign-based companies may not understand the cultural preferences of U.S. consumers or common U.S. business practices or U.S. laws regulating businesses.

Chapter 3 Assessment

Review Business Concepts

3.1 International Business Basics

- Domestic business is the making, buying, and selling of goods and services within a country. International business refers to the business activities needed for creating, shipping, and selling goods and services across national borders.
- A country is said to have an absolute advantage when it can produce a good or service at a lower cost than other countries. If a country specializes in the production of a good or service at which it is more efficient, it is said to have a comparative advantage.
- Imports are items bought from other countries. Exports are goods and services sold to other countries. Nations do business with each other to increase the variety of goods and services available to their consumers.
- Balance of trade is the difference between a country's exports and imports. The difference between a country's total payments to other countries and its total receipts from other countries is the balance of payments.
- The exchange rate is the value of a currency in one country compared with the value of a currency in another country.
- The value of global currencies is affected by three main factors: balance of payments, economic conditions, and political stability.

3.2 The Global Marketplace

- The international business environment involves four main components: geography, cultural influences, economic development, and political and legal concerns.
- Three formal barriers to international trade are quotas, tariffs, and embargoes. A quota is a limit set on the quantity of a product that may be imported or exported within a given period. A tariff is a tax placed on certain imported products. An embargo stops the import or export of a product completely.
- Actions to encourage international trade include free-trade zones, free-trade agreements, and common markets.

3.3 International Business Organizations

- Multinational companies conduct business activities in several countries and have management capable of doing business worldwide.
- Common methods used for global business include licensing, franchising, and joint ventures.
- The World Trade Organization was created to promote trade around the world. The International Monetary Fund helps to promote economic cooperation by maintaining a system of world trade and exchange rates. The World Bank provides economic assistance to less-developed countries.

Think Critically About Business

1. Describe how an absolute advantage might affect a country's imports and exports.
2. Explain why it is difficult for a community or a nation to be completely independent.
3. How does international business contribute to a better standard of living for many people in various countries?
4. What are some attitudes and behaviors that might make it difficult for a foreign-based company to do business in the United States?
5. For the following situations, decide whether this is an example of an *informal* or *formal* trade barrier.
   - **a.** Law requiring that stores be closed on Sunday
   - **b.** Beliefs about not eating certain foods
   - **c.** Special tax on the sale of books
   - **d.** Required nutritional information on food packaging
   - **e.** Hiring family members when jobs are available in an organization

6. Describe situations in which a joint venture would benefit a company involved in international business.
7. A country sometimes uses high tariffs to protect its new and developing industries. What are two examples of new and developing industries either in the United States or in other countries? Do you think that such industries should be protected by high tariffs? If so, how long should they be protected?
8. Some people believe that the United States should place stiff controls on imports of goods that compete with U.S. businesses to prevent the "exporting of American jobs" to other countries. Give arguments for and against such a position.

Develop Your Business Language

Match the terms listed with the definitions.

9. Goods and services sold to another country.
10. A limit on the quantity of a product that may be imported and exported within a given period.
11. Government restrictions to reduce free trade.
12. An organization that conducts business in several countries.
13. The value of money of one country expressed in terms of the money of another country.
14. Goods and services bought from another country.
15. Stopping the importing or exporting of a certain product or service.
16. An agreement between two or more companies from different countries to share a business project.
17. The difference between a country's total exports and total imports of goods.
18. A tax that a government places on certain imported products.
19. The difference between a country's total payments to other countries and its total receipts from other countries.
20. A nation's transportation, communication, and utility systems.

Key Terms

- **a.** balance of payments
- **b.** balance of trade
- **c.** embargo
- **d.** exchange rate
- **e.** exports
- **f.** imports
- **g.** infrastructure
- **h.** joint venture
- **i.** multinational company (MNC)
- **j.** quota
- **k.** tariff
- **l.** trade barriers

5a. formal trade barrier

5b. informal trade barrier

5c. formal trade barrier

5d. formal trade barrier

5e. informal trade barrier

6. Answers may vary, but a joint venture will be especially helpful when a company is introducing a product or service that is new to a particular country. The joint venture partner brings insight into the country's culture and business climate and appropriate ways to manufacture and market the product.

7. Answers will vary. Make sure students have reasons to support their opinions as to whether a particular developing industry should be protected by tariffs and how long that protection should last. Remind them to consider the tariff's potential effect on consumers.

8. The argument for stiff controls on imports of goods that compete with U.S. products is to protect jobs held by U.S. workers. The argument against such controls is fear of retaliation against U.S. exports and higher prices and less selection for U.S. consumers.

Develop Your Business Language *Answers*

9. e. exports
10. j. quota
11. l. trade barriers
12. i. multinational company (MNC)
13. d. exchange rate
14. f. imports
15. c. embargo
16. h. joint venture
17. b. balance of trade
18. k. tariff
19. a. balance of payments
20. g. infrastructure

Make Academic Connections *Answers*

21. Maps will vary.

22. Answers will vary. Encourage students to obtain information about the European Union, NAFTA, Mercosur, ASEAN, CARICOM, or other regional trade agreements.

23. Examples will vary. Encourage students to share their findings.

24. Answers will vary. You may want to invite students to play examples of music from other countries using instruments or recordings. Students are to describe distinctive features of the music from a particular country.

25a. One quart equals 0.95 liter; 1 liter bottle.

25b. A 50-yard bolt of fabric equals about 45 meters (50×0.9).

25c. The automobile engine would be measured in cubic centimeters.

25d. A 12-inch ruler would be about 30 centimeters (12×2.5).

25e. The bathroom scale would measure in kilograms.

26. Students will prepare a table and graph to record the changing value of the U.S. dollar compared with the currencies of three other countries. Answers will vary depending on the countries and timeframes chosen.

27a. \$9.96 ($1{,}200 \times 0.0083$)

27b. \$3.98 (5×0.795)

27c. \$40.50 (150×0.27)

28. Ask students to briefly present to the class the most interesting aspects of the legal agreements they investigated.

Make Academic Connections

21. **Geography** Locate examples of multinational companies in different countries. Create a map showing where the companies are based and the other nations in which the companies operate.

22. **Economics** Go to the website of an economic community (common market) or a regional trade organization. Make a list of the countries involved and describe some of the organization's activities.

23. **History** Conduct research on the history of money systems that have been used in other countries. Find examples of the use of a country's currency in another country.

24. **Music** Very often, the music of a country reflects its history, culture, and religion. Find examples of music from other nations that reflect the past and current culture. What aspects of the music are distinctive to that country?

25. **Math** To make their exports suitable for use in other countries, U.S. manufacturers must produce goods that are measured in the metric system. For example, if a manufacturer wanted to export paint, which is sold in gallons in this country, it would probably export the paint in 4-liter cans (about 1.4 gallons). To what sizes would the items listed be converted for export to countries using the metric system? (See Appendix D.)

- **a.** A quart bottle of liquid detergent
- **b.** A 50-yard bolt of fabric
- **c.** An automobile engine measured in cubic inches
- **d.** A 12-inch ruler
- **e.** A bathroom scale that measures in pounds

26. **Technology** Using a spreadsheet program, create a table and graph to report the changing value of the U.S. dollar compared with currencies of three other countries.

27. **Math** Using the information in Figure 3-4, determine how many U.S. dollars someone could buy for these amounts of currencies from other countries.

- **a.** In Japan, 1,200 yen
- **b.** In Canada, 5 Canadian dollars
- **c.** In Saudi Arabia, 150 riyals

28. **Career Planning** Investigate what types of legal agreements a person might encounter when applying for a job to work for a multinational company in another country.

Make Your Case

Assume you have started a business that manufactures electric toasters that you want to sell to the people of China.

29. What are some potential difficulties that you might encounter when doing business in the Chinese market?

30. What actions could your company take to help improve your opportunities for success?

Interactions and Connections

31. Examine the labels of 10 clothing items you own to collect the following information for each item: description of garment, fiber content, and country of origin. Use the data to prepare a list or table of your findings. Be prepared to discuss these questions: Which countries appear most often on your list? Are there several countries from the same geographic region? What are some possible similarities among these countries? What are the economic advantages of these countries being involved in clothing manufacturing?

32. The products of Coca-Cola, Kellogg's, General Mills, and other companies are sold in many countries. These businesses often use brand names, logos, or other visuals that are recognized around the world. At the same time, the product or package might need to be adapted to address cultural differences in different countries.

Make Your Cases *Answers*

29. The Chinese people may not eat bread or other items that fit into toasters. Domestically produced toasters might be cheaper or more durable. The supply of electricity in rural areas of China might not be reliable enough for consumers to desire electrical products. Your company might not understand Chinese businesses or laws.

a. Visit the website of a company that produces a popular American product and locate information about its international operations. Obtain information about a product sold in several countries. Describe to the class how the company adapted the product or packaging in another country. Illustrate your talk with images from the website.

b. Locate a website with information about the culture of a country. Write a paragraph describing an element of the culture that the company might need to consider when doing business in that country.

c. Share the information you discovered in your research with a family member or friend. Ask the person for reactions about the company's global business activities.

Emerging Business Issues Event

One of the most striking changes in U.S. food and retailing over the past two decades has been the rise of private labels, also known as store brands. The term *private label* describes products manufactured for sale under a specific retailer's brand. They are often designed to compete against branded products, offering consumers a cheaper alternative to national brands. Though they were once considered knock-offs of name brands or even generic "no-name brands," private labels have become increasingly accepted by the public. Many consumers now consider private labels as acceptable alternatives to national brands. Private labels offer many benefits to both retailers and customers, driving the segment's rising popularity.

Each team of two or three members must conduct research to gather facts regarding private labels and the impact they have on retailers and consumers. Students should brainstorm the benefits and drawbacks of private labels to both retailers and customers.

Teams also should give examples of the most successful private label brands. Teams will be permitted to bring prepared materials, written or printed, on white 8 ½" by 11" paper or note cards. One 4" by 6" index card will be given to each participant and may be used during the preparation and presentation.

Each presentation may last no more than five minutes. Following each oral presentation, judges may conduct a five minute question and answer period during which the presenters should be prepared to defend their research.

Performance Indicators Evaluated

- Demonstrate sound research with the information gathered.
- Present the rationale in a clear and logical manner.
- Provide supporting information for each point made.
- Choose examples that are relevant to the audience.

You Will Be Evaluated on

- Organization of your oral presentation.
- Rationale of your presentation.
- Speaker responded to questions fully, knowledgeably, and without hesitation.

For more detailed information about performance indicators, go to the FBLA website.

Think Critically

1. What can name brands do to compete with private labels?
2. How do private labels differentiate themselves from national brands?

www.fbla-pbl.org

30. Start by conducting research about the market situation. Next, you could enter into a joint venture with a manufacturing company already established in China. Alternatively, your company could hire Chinese nationals who are knowledgeable about the Chinese business scene.

Interactions and Connections *Answers*

31. Lists and tables will vary. Similarities among countries could include abundance of natural fibers, such as cotton or silk; workers who will work for lower wages; and a large pool of highly skilled garment workers. These can also be possible economic advantages for these countries.

32. Reports will vary based on products and cultures chosen, as well as students opinions.

WINNING EDGE

Emerging Business Issues Event

Think Critically *Answers*

1. To compete with private labels, manufacturers must adopt a collaborative mindset and help retailers win with both private brands and brands across the total store. Manufacturers might consider joint promotional opportunities. They also could look for retailers who don't offer private labels and discuss placement options with them.

2. Manufacturers of private labels differentiate by lower pricing, improved quality over private label products, innovative products, and the development of premium private label brands.

CHAPTER OVERVIEW

This chapter offers a basic understanding of social responsibility along with discussion of the various roles of government in relation to business.

4.1 Social Responsibility and Business Ethics

Various actions that businesses take to improve society are covered in this lesson.

4.2 Government Protection Activities

This lesson addresses actions by government to protect workers, consumers, and business activities.

4.3 Government Regulation and Assistance

Regulation of utilities, unfair business practices, and government spending and borrowing are the main focus of this lesson.

Chapter 4 Social Responsibility of Business and Government

Calin Tatu/Shutterstock.com

4.1 Social Responsibility and Business Ethics

4.2 Government Protection Activities

4.3 Government Regulation and Assistance

Instructor Resources

- Activities and Study Guide IE
- Chapter and Unit Tests IE
- Lesson Plans
- PowerPoint Presentation
- Cognero Test, Ch. 4

Student Resources

Activities and Study Guide
www.cengage.com/swep/pob9e
- Portfolio Activity

PLANNING A CAREER IN . . .
GOVERMENT

Government & Public Administration

Accountants, interviewers, restaurant inspectors, and engineers are just a few of the many employment opportunities in government. Federal, state, and local agencies employ more than 21 million people. As you can see, government is a major employer in the U.S. economy.

About 60 percent of federal workers hold managerial, business, financial, and professional positions. While many business and government jobs require similar training, some government positions demand specialized training. Food production regulators and homeland security officials need academic and practical experiences related to their fields.

Increased job opportunity in some federal agencies is being offset by slow growth and declines in other federal sectors. Despite increased demand for services from state and local governments, employment levels are affected by economic conditions and the availability of tax revenues. Staffing of government positions is directly affected by budget levels approved by legislative bodies and local governing boards.

Related Job Titles
- Purchasing Agent
- Conservation Scientist
- Correctional Officer
- Firefighter
- Highway Maintenance Engineer
- Municipal Clerk
- Social Worker

Analyze Career Opportunities in . . . GOVERNMENT

Use library and Internet resources to learn more about careers in government. Choose one of the job titles listed in the box above and answer the following questions.

1. How would you describe the nature of the work? Include examples of things that might happen in a typical work day.
2. Is this a career that interests you? Explain how careers in this field match up with your goals and interests.

What it's like to work as a . . . Government Employee

Kathleen works for her local school district, but her job lasts all year. She is the assistant accountant for the district. Her accounting job is just like an accounting job at a nonpublic business.

Kathleen is responsible for collecting expense and payment records. She must make sure that incoming bills are correct and that payments are made in a timely manner. Kathleen also works with the school district's head accountant to develop expense reports and budgets. Throughout the year, Kathleen helps the head accountant present reports to the school board.

Kathleen uses computer software for accounting records, report writing, and presentations. She could use her accounting skills in the private sector and perhaps earn more money. Although a higher salary would be nice, Kathleen enjoys working for the school district and is happy with her career choice.

What about you? What are some government jobs that might interest you? How would your state's or city's financial situation impact your desire to work in those jobs?

PLANNING A CAREER IN . . . GOVERNMENT

A wide variety of government employment positions are available. Point out to students that most types of business jobs are also available with government agencies. After reading this career feature, ask students what they think about the position described. Do they know anyone who holds a similar job? At the conclusion of the discussion, direct students to answer the "What About You?" question that follows this feature.

What About You? *Answers*

Answers will vary, but could include discussion of the variety of government jobs; virtually all sectors of employment are found within federal, state, or local governments.

Analyze Career Opportunities *Answers*

Student answers will vary depending on when the assignment is completed and individual interests.

Additional Career Information

Encourage students to investigate careers they find interesting and explore unfamiliar careers. Two resources for additional career information are the *Occupational Outlook Handbook*, an online publication (www.bls.gov/ooh/) of the U.S. Bureau of Labor Statistics, and the O*NET Resource Center (www.onetcenter.org) developed by the U.S. Department of Labor. Information about specific careers and jobs can be used to demonstrate the relevance of skills learned in this course.

Focus on REAL LIFE

Use this feature to point out that most businesses are involved in various community activities. Ask students about the benefits of these types of actions.

TEACH

Ask students to name ways that businesses contribute to communities.

Describe some environmental concerns faced by businesses.

THINK CRITICALLY THROUGH VISUALS

By preserving the environment, businesses can protect the resources they will need in the future and protect the general well-being of the community. In addition, their efforts will be seen as socially responsible.

4.1 Social Responsibility and Business Ethics

Learning Outcomes

4.1.1 Describe social responsibility issues.

4.1.2 Identify benefits and costs of social responsibility.

4.1.3 Explain the purpose of a code of ethics.

Key Terms

- social responsibility 76
- nonrenewable resource 76
- ethics 79
- business ethics 79
- code of ethics 79

Focus on REAL LIFE

"At JA Custom Kitchens, we take social responsibility seriously," Jo Ann Keck told an audience of business students.

"As a business owner, I know that this is good for my business, my community, my employees, and for me as a person," she continued.

Later in her speech, Jo Ann said, "The company encourages employees to be active in community affairs and to volunteer with a variety of organizations. In some cases, the company provides paid time off for volunteer commitments during work hours. Workers are likely to be more satisfied with their job if they believe their company actively contributes to community life."

LO 4.1.1

SOCIAL RESPONSIBILITY ISSUES

Social responsibility refers to the duty of a business to contribute to the well-being of a community. In considering its responsibility to society, a business must weigh the interests and concerns of many groups. A broadened view of social responsibility of business calls for more attention to social concern. This includes protection of the environment, inclusion of minorities and women in the workplace, employment of physically challenged and older workers, and a healthy and safe work environment.

iStockphoto.com/amokly

How does preserving the environment benefit business?

Environmental Protection

Conservation is saving scarce natural resources. It is a goal of many companies. For example, lumber companies that consume trees have reforestation programs. Some natural resources cannot be replaced. A **nonrenewable resource** is a natural resource that cannot be replaced when used up. Examples are gas, oil, and minerals, such as copper and iron ore.

Pollution occurs when the environment is tainted with the by-products of human actions. Some production methods cause pollution of lakes, rivers, groundwater, and air. A socially responsible business takes action to improve or change operations that cause pollution. For example, engineers design new equipment for reducing pollution.

Applied Skills

Science Ask students to identify various health concerns associated with environmental issues in the United States and around the world. Point out that many industries in developing economies use older manufacturing methods and more polluting energy sources that can result in environmental damage.

The federal government has set measurable standards for water and air quality. The Environmental Protection Agency (EPA) monitors and enforces those standards. Businesses and the EPA work together to reduce pollution. They try to make the environment healthier.

Workplace Diversity

Businesses are sensitive to diversity and to the role of women, ethnic groups, and physically challenged and older workers. The workforce of a business should reflect the groups in a community. Members of these groups must have equal access to education, training, jobs, and career advancement. A major challenge facing businesses today involves learning how to manage a workforce made up of workers who represent the diverse cultures in society.

Another issue involves the removal of employment barriers for women. For example, employers are not allowed to exclude women applicants from a physically demanding job unless the business can prove the job requires physical skills that women do not have.

Employers also have taken steps to accommodate individuals who are physically challenged. Passage and enforcement of the Americans with Disabilities Act (ADA), along with other federal and state legislation, has resulted in major improvements in accommodating workers who are physically challenged. Buildings must have access for wheelchairs. People with sight or hearing limitations must be accommodated on the job.

Other laws have been passed to eliminate bias against older workers. The passage of the Age Discrimination in Employment Act bars employers from using age as a basis for employment decisions, including hiring, promotions, or termination from a job. The law protects persons aged 40 and older.

Life-Span Plan

Create a list of five social and environmental issues that might have an impact on your future. How well do you understand these issues? Explain how these issues might affect the life-span goals you set for yourself.

Job Safety

Having a safe place in which to work is important to all employees. They should be able to work in an office or factory free from risks that could cause accidents. The work environment should provide full protection from fire and other hazards. In addition to protection from physical harm, workers need to know how to manage the unexpected. Safety also involves employee training in how to work safely and what to do in case of an emergency.

To ensure the right to safety, most employers have put a variety of programs into practice to protect workers. Federal and state governments have also passed laws to make the workplace safer. Safety standards are regulated and enforced by agencies such as OSHA, the Occupational Safety and Health Administration.

Image Source/DigitalVision/Getty Images

How has the Americans with Disabilities Act increased employment opportunities for people who are physically challenged?

Life-Span Plan Answer

Answers will vary. Students should explain how environmental issues could alter their life-span goals and ability to achieve them.

TEACH

Explain the economic and social value of workplace diversity.

Ask students to describe situations that could be avoided by creating a safer workplace.

THINK CRITICALLY THROUGH VISUALS

The Americans with Disabilities Act has mandated workplaces to provide accommodation for physically challenged workers. Examples of accommodation include designated parking spaces, entrance ramps, automatic doors, elevators, wider doorways, and accessible restroom facilities.

Different Learning Abilities

Visually Impaired Work with students individually to determine what kinds of tools would be helpful. For example, you might use a large font to prepare a list of key points related to social responsibility. Providing enlarged photographs also might be useful for some students.

TEACH

Emphasize the importance of good health for individual workers, the company, and society.

Ask students to suggest additional methods to encourage good health among employees.

ONGOING ASSESSMENT

CHECKPOINT ✓ ANSWER

Four areas of social responsibility that may require the attention of business are environmental protection, workplace diversity, job safety, and employee wellness.

THINK CRITICALLY THROUGH VISUALS

Healthy employees benefit their employers because they are more productive and energetic and have fewer illnesses.

TEACH

Highlight the benefits and costs of social responsibility actions in various business settings.

ONGOING ASSESSMENT

CHECKPOINT ✓ ANSWER

The main benefits of social responsibility are expanded justice for groups of a society, enhanced company image, reduced need for government actions, improved quality of life in communities and around the world, and an increased awareness of social issues among workers, consumers, and others.

Employee Wellness

A healthy workforce is a productive workforce. Workers who have good physical health are valuable assets. Businesses today do a number of things to improve the health of their workforce. Among programs offered are stop-smoking seminars, counseling for employees with drug problems, and weight-loss sessions.

Your general well-being as an employee needs to be protected, too. Clauses that relate to employee well-being are often included in labor contracts and company policy manuals. These clauses are *conditions of work* that pertain to the health and safety of employees while on the job.

Many companies offer programs to promote good health. Seminars on eating a balanced diet, getting proper exercise, and maintaining a healthy lifestyle are a few examples. Some businesses sponsor sports teams and encourage employees to take part.

Blazej Lyjak/Shutterstock.com

How do employees who are healthy benefit their employers?

CHECKPOINT ✓

What are four areas of social responsibility that may require the attention of business?

LO 4.1.2

SOCIAL RESPONSIBILITY EVALUATION

Socially responsible actions can cause controversy. While a number of benefits exist, these actions also have various costs.

Benefits

Common benefits of socially responsible activities include the following:

- Expanded justice for groups of a society
- Enhanced company image
- Reduced need for government actions
- Improved quality of life in a community and around the world
- Increased awareness of social issues among workers, consumers, and others

Costs

There are costs involved when a business takes socially responsible actions. Money must be spent for new nonpolluting or safer equipment, for building repairs to remove risks, for wellness and rehabilitation programs, and for social projects sponsored by a company.

A business must make a profit to stay open. If a business does not earn a profit, the business will close and employees will lose their jobs. Spending on social programs must remain at a suitable level so a business can still earn a reasonable profit.

CHECKPOINT ✓

What are the main benefits of social responsibility?

Different Learning Styles

Tactile Learner Use samples of various items to represent social responsibility. These items can allow students to "touch" the chapter concepts. For example, you might use food package nutrition labels to start a discussion about social responsibility and food manufacturers. Consider asking students to help identify the items to be used.

LO 4.1.3

BUSINESS ETHICS

A socially responsible business engages in ethical business practices. **Ethics** are principles of morality or rules of conduct. **Business ethics** are rules about how businesses and their employees ought to behave. Ethical behavior involves conforming to these rules. Unethical behavior violates them. In dealing with business ethics, a code of ethics can help a business identify proper employee behavior.

Code of Ethics

A **code of ethics** is a set of rules for guiding the actions of employees or members of an organization. Codes of ethics address topics such as confidentiality of business information. Figure 4-1 lists topics to consider when developing a code of ethics. Once established, the code should be a guide for all employees within that company.

A code must be worded in terms of acceptable behavior rather than forbidden action. Even with a code of ethics, the choice of proper behavior can cause dilemmas for decision makers within a business. Here are some examples of ethical dilemmas.

- Should a company expand into a profitable market in a country where doing business requires giving expensive gifts to government officials?
- Should a company continue to produce a popular product after it discovers a minor defect in it?

Ethical Conduct Guidelines

The ethical conduct of a business is largely determined by its top management. Executives who show strong moral character and make ethical business decisions set the ethical standards for a business.

Companies concerned about the ethical behavior of their employees have set up educational programs on ethical conduct. These programs are designed to promote employee honesty and integrity. Program topics range from making personal phone calls during work hours to taking supplies for personal use. Employees are also trained on how to make ethical decisions on the job.

When considering the ethics of business situations, you could follow these guidelines.

1. Is the action legal?
2. Does the action violate professional or company standards?
3. Who is affected by the action and how?

Work as a TEAM

Using the three ethical conduct guidelines on this page, select a situation in a work setting that might be considered unethical. As a team, use these three questions to assess the ethical aspects of the situation.

GUIDELINES FOR WRITING A CODE OF ETHICS	
1.	Determine the purpose of the code.
2.	Tailor the code to the needs and values of the organization.
3.	Consider involving employees from all levels of the company in writing the code.
4.	Determine the rules or principles that all members of the organizations will be expected to adhere to.
5.	Include information about how the code will be enforced.
6.	Determine how the code will be implemented and where it will be published or posted.
7.	Determine how and when the code will be reviewed and revised.

FIGURE 4-1
Do you think a code of ethics can increase a business' profits? How?

Work as a TEAM

The situations used for this activity might include engaging in personal activities on company time, taking company items for personal use, or revising reports for personal gain.

TEACH

Ask students to describe a society in which laws and rules were not implemented consistently.

Describe various issues related to business ethics.

Explain the purpose of a code of ethics.

Highlight the three guidelines that could be used to assess various ethical issues.

Have students describe situations in which ethical concerns might arise.

▸ Figure 4-1 *ANSWER*

A code of ethics can increase business profits. Employees are encouraged to be honest on the job and the company is committed to providing excellent customer service, which will translate into increased profits.

Applied Skills

Language Arts Have students use the guidelines for writing a code of ethics presented in Figure 4-1 to develop a code of ethics for a business or organization in your community. Suggest that students look for examples of codes that they can use for additional guidance. Some companies and nonprofit organizations post their code of ethics on their website.

Life-Span Plan *Answer*

Answers will vary. Students should explain how their ethics might affect the life-span goals they set for themselves.

THINK CRITICALLY THROUGH VISUALS

Some costs to society of unethical business behavior include higher prices on products and services, substandard or defective products, and unfair benefits due to conflicts of interest.

ONGOING ASSESSMENT

CHECKPOINT ✓ *ANSWER*

The purpose of a code of ethics is to guide actions and decisions of employees or members of an organization.

ASSESS

Key Concepts *Answers*

1. b. gold

2. b. find ways to help workers who are physically challenged

3. c. provide guidelines for proper behavior

Make Academic Connections *Answers*

4. Examples will vary, but should include natural resources such as water, minerals, and land. Businesses might employ various methods such as recycling or replacement programs, following EPA standards, and changing methods and designs in order to reduce pollution.

5. Provide instructions for how you would like students to report their findings.

Life-Span Plan

Do you have a personal code of ethics? Even if you have never thought of it as a code of ethics, you have principles that guide your life. Consider spending some time thinking about your personal code of ethics and writing it down. Explain how your ethics might affect the life-span goals you set for yourself.

Leonid Ikan/Shutterstock.com

What are some costs to society of unethical behavior?

A common concern in ethical decision making involves a *conflict of interest*. This can occur when an action by a company or individual results in an unfair benefit. For example, it would be a conflict of interest if a person serving on a company's board pressured the company to buy items only from businesses that the board member owns or controls.

In addition to workplace codes of ethics, many employees, including accountants and engineers, adhere to codes of professional conduct established by their professional associations. They also participate in continuing education related to ethical issues specific to their professions.

CHECKPOINT ✓

What is the purpose of a code of ethics?

4.1 ASSESSMENT

Key Concepts

Determine the best answer.

1. An example of a nonrenewable resource would be
   - **a.** solar energy
   - **b.** gold
   - **c.** agricultural products
   - **d.** a library book
2. The Americans with Disabilities Act (ADA) requires that a company
   - **a.** provide training to people with disabilities
   - **b.** find ways to help workers who are physically challenged
   - **c.** hire a certain number of people with special needs
   - **d.** adapt products manufactured for special-needs customers
3. A code of ethics is designed to
   - **a.** meet government regulations
   - **b.** reduce operating costs of a company
   - **c.** provide guidelines for proper behavior
   - **d.** improve employee productivity

Make Academic Connections

4. **Science** List a variety of natural resources and agricultural products used in the production of goods and services. What actions might be taken by companies to improve the efficient use of these resources?
5. **Technology** Search the Internet to locate an example of a code of ethics. Describe the benefits of this code of ethics for the organization.

RETEACH Assign students to provide a unique example for each of the categories of social responsibility discussed in this chapter.

ENRICH Ask students to talk to relatives or friends about ethical situations they have seen in business.

CLOSE Have students list actions a company might take related to social responsibility.

LIFE/WORK SKILLS

COMMUNICATION AND COLLABORATION

Working in Teams

Each day, thousands of workers make decisions and apply business actions in team settings. The ability to work in a team is rated by most employers as one of the most important career skills. The combined skills of the people in a team are greater than that of individuals working alone. When working in a team in class or on the job, consider the following:

- Be prepared for minor conflicts in the first phase of a team project. Differences in opinions will surface. Be ready to adapt to the personalities, behaviors, and actions of others.
- Agree upon guidelines for project goals, meeting times, location, agenda, missed meetings, conflict resolution, and other procedures.
- Define leadership and other roles. Some team members will keep notes and bring needed materials. Others will conduct research or create visuals for a presentation.
- Determine methods for decision making. Usually this will be done based on agreement among team members after discussion of various issues and opposing points of view.
- Keep focused on your goals. Avoid being distracted by minor issues and personality conflicts. Maintain a team-oriented environment by saying "we, us, ours." Avoid using "I, me, my, mine."
- Be courteous to others. Respect differences in opinions, personalities, and decision-making styles.

Digital Vision/Getty Images

Why is it important to define roles when working in teams?

Working in teams is something you are likely to do throughout your life. These experiences can be enjoyable and productive. Members of an effective team take responsibility for its work and take pride in its accomplishments. Some team projects will be frustrating. It is important to maintain a positive attitude. Some of the best learning and most valuable experiences result from encounters with others with different backgrounds and diverse points of view.

Think Critically

1. What do you like about working in teams? Are there any aspects about working in teams that you dislike? Describe them.
2. Describe a problem that might occur when working in teams. Explain how this situation might be resolved.

LIFE/WORK SKILLS

Emphasize the importance of being able to successfully work in teams. Point out some of the situations in school, community organizations, and other settings in which students might obtain experience working in teams.

Ask students to point out some concerns associated with working in teams. What actions might be taken to reduce those problem areas?

THINK CRITICALLY THROUGH VISUALS

Answers will vary. When roles are defined, team members know what is expected of them and what they can expect from others.

Think Critically *Answers*

1. Answers will vary.
2. Answers will vary, but most conflicts can be avoided or resolved by following the guidelines listed.

Teaching Strategies

Expand Beyond the Classroom Cross-cultural teams are becoming more common in both domestic and international work settings. Remind students that cross-cultural teams can provide (1) improved cultural understanding, (2) increased creativity from diverse points of view, and (3) expanded global business effectiveness.

4.2 Government Protection Activities

Learning Outcomes

4.2.1 Identify the roles and levels of government.

4.2.2 Explain the role of government protection and the legal system in business.

4.2.3 Describe types of intellectual property.

Key Terms

contract 83	copyright 85
patent 84	trademark 85

Focus on REAL LIFE

Brenda Hiam was concerned about a deteriorating road on her commute to work. She believed that it was becoming dangerous and could lead to someone losing control.

Brenda wanted to contact a government agency to notify them of this potentially dangerous driving hazard. She asked her neighbor, Kevin, if he knew whether the city, county, state, or federal highway department was responsible for the road.

"I think we should contact the county highway department and ask that question," he answered. "The county highway office keeps records on roads in this area."

"Let's call." said Brenda. "If they can't help us, we can call our county commissioner."

LO 4.2.1

GOVERNMENT IN SOCIETY

Government plays a role in all economic systems. Your role as a citizen and voter has an effect on the decisions and actions taken by government. In a private enterprise system, government's role is much less extensive than in other economic systems. It is still a vital one. The role of government in the economy often changes as newly elected officials take office.

Roles of Government

As issues facing society change, so must government change. There are some basic roles of government.

Government is mainly concerned with these areas:

- Providing services for members of society
- Protecting citizens, consumers, businesses, and workers
- Regulating utilities and promoting competition
- Providing information and support to businesses
- Buying goods and services
- Hiring public employees
- Raising revenue

Each of these roles has either a direct or indirect impact on business expansion, consumer affairs, and economic growth in the economy.

Levels of Government

When it comes to commerce, the main goal of the federal government is to oversee activities that involve two or more states

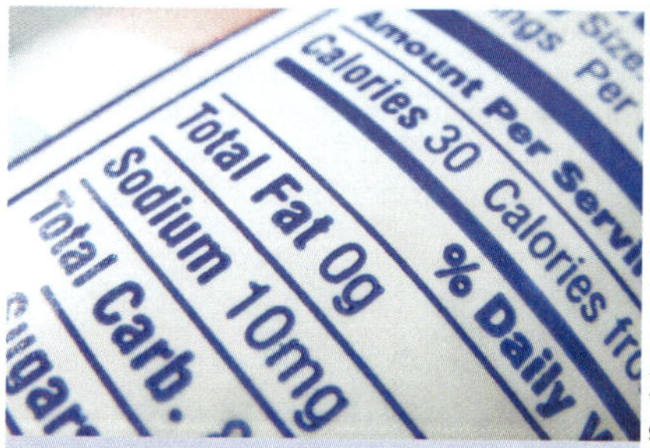

iStockphoto.com/jaminwell

Can governmental activities support both businesses and consumers?

Focus on REAL LIFE

Often, people face frustrations about services they believe government should provide more effectively. Ask students to comment on positive and negative aspects of government services they have observed.

TEACH

Provide an overview of the various roles of government. Ask students to give specific examples of each role.

THINK CRITICALLY THROUGH VISUALS

Governmental activities can support both businesses and consumers. These activities benefit both businesses and consumers by providing information and support, buying goods and services, hiring employees, providing regulation and protection, and promoting competition.

Different Learning Abilities

Specific Learning Disability (SLD) To motivate students, ask them to name various items and activities they observe in the community. Explain how most of these observations are related to government activities.

or other countries. In general, the Constitution gives the federal government the power to regulate foreign and interstate commerce.

Interstate commerce is any business conducted that involves companies in more than one state. The federal government would regulate a trucking company that ships products to several states.

State governments regulate business actions within their own borders. *Intrastate commerce* refers to business dealings involving companies that do business in only one state. For example, states set the speed limits for their highways. The federal government regulates truck design because trucks can and do travel between states.

All states have assigned some of their legislative power to local governments. Local governments include county boards and city or town councils. Local governments provide services needed for an orderly society, such as police and fire protection.

CHECKPOINT ✓
What are the three levels of government?

LO 4.2.2

GOVERNMENT PROTECTION ACTIVITIES

Government protects your rights in a number of ways. Citizens are protected through police and firefighting services. The armed forces provide for national defense. National security is a chief concern of the federal government.

Worker Protection

Laws have been established to help provide a safe work environment. As a worker, you have a basic right to safe working conditions. Safety standards for buildings, machines, and chemicals are

Scott J. Ferrell/Getty Images

How does government regulate commerce?

set by government agencies. Government inspection and regulation of work areas help reduce the number of job-related accidents.

More government regulations result from the need to protect the basic human rights of workers. For example, you cannot be denied work because of your race, religion, sex, or age. Selection of someone for a job must be based on job requirements, training, and experience. Prejudices and personal biases must not affect a hiring decision.

Contract Enforcement

Contracts are another example of government protection. A **contract** is an agreement to exchange goods or services for something of value, usually money. It is a basic part of doing business. A contract may be written or unwritten. Certain elements must be included for the contract to be enforceable. Figure 4-2 on page 84 highlights the main provisions of every enforceable contract.

FYI It is important to read and understand a contract before signing it. The court system does not protect you from your own lack of common sense.

TEACH

Explain the main activities of the three levels of government—federal, state, and local.

Ask students to name services commonly provided by each level of government.

THINK CRITICALLY THROUGH VISUALS

Government regulates commerce by overseeing and regulating business activities.

ONGOING ASSESSMENT

CHECKPOINT ✓ ANSWER

The three levels of government are local, state, and federal.

TEACH

Describe some of the services provided by government that protect workers.

Ask students to name some examples of contracts in our society.

FYI

Ask students to explain why it is important to read and understand a contract. Discuss the idea that the court system does not protect you from your own lack of common sense.

Applied Skills

Word Processing/Office Technology Use database software to categorize various types of government services and activities. Have students sort the items into three groups: local, state, and federal government.

▶ Figure 4-2 ANSWER

Examples of contracts include an apartment lease, a credit card agreement, and a wireless contract.

TEACH

Use Figure 4-2 to explain the four main elements of a contract.

Remind students of guidelines to follow before entering into a contract.

ONGOING ASSESSMENT

CHECKPOINT ✓ ANSWER

The main elements of a contract are agreement, competent parties, consideration, and legality.

TEACH

Explain what is meant by *intellectual property*. Provide an overview of patents, copyrights, and trademarks.

Describe situations in which a patent would be used.

Work as a TEAM

Students observe many examples of intellectual property each day. Encourage students to discuss the benefits and importance of protection for these items.

CONTRACT BASICS	
Valid, enforceable contracts must contain:	
Agreement	An offer must be made, and an acceptance must occur.
Competent Parties	Those entering into the contract must be of legal age and must be mentally competent.
Consideration	Something of measurable value must be exchanged by the parties involved.
Legality	The contract must be for a product or service that may be legally sold; also, no fraud or deception exists in the agreement.

FIGURE 4-2
Provide examples of contracts you might encounter in the future.

These four elements—agreement, competent parties, consideration, and legality—are the basis for many legal disputes. An item seen as having different values (*consideration*) by different people can result in a legal dispute. Examples of contracts include a lease to rent an apartment, a credit card agreement, and documents that state the terms of a purchase.

Both consumers and businesses benefit from government enforcement of contracts. If you agree to have repairs made on your car for $65, the business firm must do the work as agreed upon. You must pay for the work when it is finished. If work is not done correctly or if you fail to pay, legal action can be taken to force the work to be corrected or force you to pay.

Legal System

Without enforcement, dishonest consumers or business owners could refuse to honor their agreements. Daily business activities would be very difficult.

The legal system enforces laws and government regulations. There are typically two types of cases that move through our legal systems, criminal cases and civil cases.

A *criminal case* is brought for violations of criminal laws. A business could be involved in a criminal case if it pressed charges against a customer or employee engaged in shoplifting. If a business violates criminal or regulatory laws, it could be a defendant in a criminal case.

A *civil case* typically has a plaintiff who asks the court to take action against a defendant. Businesses can both sue and be sued for a breach, or violation, of contract. They may be liable for damage caused by someone's action or unauthorized use of copyrights, trademarks, or patents.

Unethical behavior can violate either criminal laws or government regulations. A business can be held responsible for products that cause harm, unsafe working conditions, or failure to pay taxes.

CHECKPOINT ✓
What are the main elements of a contract?

LO 4.2.3

PROTECTION OF INTELLECTUAL PROPERTY

Intellectual property is purely intangible, with no physical characteristics—a person cannot touch it. Intellectual property includes patents, copyrights, and trademarks.

Patents

When individuals or companies create new products, they may obtain a patent. A **patent** gives the inventor the sole right to make, use, or sell the item for 20 years. A company that creates a new means to

Work as a TEAM

Intellectual properties are also called intangible assets. As a team, prepare a list of various patents, copyrights, and trademarks owned by companies and nonprofit organizations. Explain how these assets contribute to the success of the organization. Why is protection of intellectual property important?

Different Learning Abilities

Gifted Encourage students to research additional information about the elements of a contract. Have them report their findings to the class. Challenge students to identify potential controversial areas in different contracts.

record programs from television could get a patent for this process. It would prevent other companies from making or selling recorders using this process.

Copyrights

A **copyright** protects the creative work of authors, composers, and artists. Copyright protection lasts for the life of the person receiving the copyright. It also extends for 70 years after the person's death. Examples of copyright statements can be found on the front pages of most books. A federally registered copyright is identified with the symbol©.

VGStockstudio/Shutterstock.com

What are some examples of creative work that can be copyrighted?

Trademarks

A **trademark** is a word, letter, or symbol linked with a specific company or product. Businesses register company names, team emblems, and label designs with the government. A trademark can be very valuable. Many trademarks are recognizable worldwide. Trademarks are often identified with a symbol, called a *logo*. A trademark is indicated with a TM. A federally registered trademark will have a®.

CHECKPOINT ✓
What are three types of intellectual property?

4.2 ASSESSMENT

Key Concepts

Determine the best answer.

1. True or False. International trade with other countries is the responsibility of state and local governments.
2. True or False. An oral contract can be legally binding.
3. Fire and police protection is the main responsibility of
   a. local government
   b. state government
   c. federal government
   d. all levels of government
4. A ________ would protect the composer's musical score.
   a. patent
   b. trademark
   c. copyright
   d. contract

Make Academic Connections

5. **Math** A city government spends $1,860,000 a month on public services. Of that amount, 46 percent is used for fire and police protection.
   a. How much is spent each month for fire and police protection?
   b. How much is spent by the city in a year for fire and police protection?
6. **Math** In a city in which there are 90,000 employed workers, 18,000 are public employees. Of this number, the federal government employs 6,000; the state, 8,000; and the city, 4,000.
   a. What percentage of all workers are public employees?
   b. What percentage of the public employees does the federal government employ?
7. **Law** Prepare a list of possible problems that could occur in a contract situation.

RETEACH Name various government activities. Ask whether each is a local, state, or federal government responsibility.

ENRICH Have students use the Internet to find examples of patents, copyrights, and trademarks.

CLOSE Name various items and ask if they would be protected by a patent, copyright, or trademark.

TEACH

Point out the importance of copyrights. Ask students to explain how technology has affected copyrights. Explain how businesses use trademarks.

THINK CRITICALLY THROUGH VISUALS

Answers will vary. Examples of works protected by copyright include paintings, music, lyrics, plays, wallpaper designs, and greeting cards.

ONGOING ASSESSMENT

CHECKPOINT ✓*ANSWER*

Patents, copyrights, and trademarks are types of intellectual property.

ASSESS

Key Concepts *Answers*

1. False. International trade is the responsibility of the federal government.
2. True.
3. a. local government
4. c. copyright

Make Academic Connections *Answers*

5. a. $1,860,000×46%= $855,560
   b. $855,600×12=$10,267,200
6. a. 18,000÷90,000= 0.20 or 20%
   b. 6,000÷18,000=0.33 or 33%
7. Answers will vary. Many contract problems are related to complying with contract agreements, such as completing work or making payments.

Doing Business in... VIETNAM

Many countries in Asia are increasing their market shares and emerging as powerful competitors in the world economy. Encourage students to develop an awareness of the economic, cultural, and political differences that exist in various countries in Asia and other regions of the world.

Ask students who have lived in or visited other countries to explain some of the cultural differences they have observed.

THINK CRITICALLY THROUGH VISUALS

Answers will vary. Customers traveling by motorcycle can visit stores outside their immediate neighborhood, but cannot carry much merchandise. Larger products might require delivery service.

Think Critically *Answers*

1. Answers will vary and might include age preferences, the value of family, and various rules of etiquette, including those pertaining to greeting one another, meals, and meeting procedures.

2. In order to conduct business in Vietnam, one must have approvals from various levels of government. Vietnam is also relatively new to capitalism. Proceedings move slowly, in contrast to the American tendency to get things done quickly.

DOING BUSINESS IN... VIETNAM

One minute you see peaceful villages with carts pulled by animals. A moment later, you see busy city streets in which seven of ten Vietnamese families use a motorcycle as their main method of transportation.

Vietnam is a country of contrasts, combining traditional production methods with modern business activities. The nation is transitioning from decades of strong central planning to a capitalist system.

Even as Vietnam emerges as a modern market economy, the Vietnamese people continue to place a high value on traditions and family relationships. Several generations may live together in the same home. Children show great respect for the elders of the family, even their older brothers and sisters.

Vietnam's business environment is rapidly evolving as it moves from a command system to a more capitalistic business environment. Vietnam is attempting to put in place rules and regulations that comply with the Word Trade Organization (WTO) and the U.S.–Vietnam Bilateral Trade Agreement (BTA). This should lead to more government transparency, stronger commercial laws, and lowered trade barriers.

At the start of a business meeting in Vietnam, the exchange of business cards occurs. Cards should be presented and received with both hands. If your card is printed in both English and Vietnamese, it is polite to have the Vietnamese side facing up. You may be asked how old you are. This classifies you as either older or younger than the Vietnamese person in order to determine the correct form of address.

The business meal is likely to include tea and perhaps some exotic foods. You may be served bat meat, stir-fried baby birds, or snake, as well as many types of seafood. It is polite to taste and drink small amounts of all items you are offered.

The conversation will slowly lead to business negotiations. Take care to not move too quickly through the agenda because this is considered rude. Use a low-pitched voice and low-key gestures. Do not allow your hosts to see the soles of your shoes.

Think Critically

1. What cultural factors affect business activities in Vietnam?
2. How do business activities in Vietnam differ from those in other countries?
3. Conduct library or Internet research to obtain additional information about business and economic activities in Vietnam.

What impact might the use of motorcycles in Vietnam have on a company's efforts to sell products to Vietnamese consumers?

3. Encourage students to locate authoritative sources such as *The World Factbook*, an online publication of the Central Intelligence Agency. Let students know how you would like them to report their findings. Consider allowing students to work in pairs.

Applied Skills

Geography Create a list of 15 to 20 countries. Using a blank sheet or an outline of a world map, ask students to identify the general location of each country.

4.3 Government Regulation and Assistance

Learning Outcomes

4.3.1 Explain actions by government to regulate business.

4.3.2 Discuss efforts of government to assist businesses.

4.3.3 Identify methods used by government to raise money.

Key Terms

public utility 87
antitrust laws 88
monopoly 88

Focus on REAL LIFE

The riverfront skateboard park is one of the most popular areas in the city. Kent Walling recently noticed that due to extensive use, the pipes, funboxes and rails are wearing out.

Kent mentioned the condition of the park to his dad and asked, "Why doesn't the city spend some money to improve the skate park?"

His dad responded, "The city has many financial needs. The skate park might not be a priority. Maybe the city should charge a fee for using the park."

Kent smiled and said: "Or they could raise your taxes, Dad!"

LO 4.3.1

REGULATORY ACTIVITIES

Business activity in the United States is structured as a private enterprise (or free market) system. Private organizations own the factors of production. They choose efficient methods of production in order to earn a profit. Price and output decisions are made not by the government, but by businesses and consumers acting under varying economic conditions.

Government, however, is involved in some areas of business activities. These include regulating utilities and preventing unfair business practices.

Regulation of Utilities

Most goods and services you use come from private businesses. These businesses are for the most part free of government regulation. A **public utility** is an organization that supplies a service or product vital to all people. These include companies that provide local telephone service, water, and electricity. A public utility is chosen to serve a community. If your city had six different electric companies, each might have its own utility poles, lines, and expensive equipment. The service you would get would be more

Photodisc/Getty Images

Is it better for consumers if utilities are offered by competing businesses?

Focus on REAL LIFE

This feature can be used to introduce students to the financial needs and funding methods used by governments. Ask students to identify government services they feel are important and those they think could be reduced or eliminated.

TEACH

Provide an overview of the various regulatory activities of government.

Explain the importance of public utilities for business operations and economic activities.

THINK CRITICALLY THROUGH VISUALS

It could be better for consumers if utilities compete for business because that keeps prices low; however, utilities are regulated so that their products are reliable and efficient.

Different Learning Styles

Visual Learner Encourage visual learners to create a drawing or sketch that depicts one or more public utilities in your community. Ask students to explain the services provided by these companies.

Different Learning Abilities

English Language Learners (ELL) Obtain translations of various government activities and services to reinforce these concepts in both English and other dominant languages used by students.

Work as a TEAM

There are many conceivable actions that may inhibit competition.

TEACH

Explain various types of monopolies that might exist in an economy.

Describe the purpose of antitrust laws.

NET KNOWLEDGE

Students should access the website and select a topic area of interest to them. Students should be able to describe information that could be of value to consumers or businesses.

ONGOING ASSESSMENT

CHECKPOINT ✓ ANSWER

Reasons for government regulation of utilities might include to assure fair prices, to conserve resources, and to avoid overcrowding of utility poles and other facilities, such as power plants.

TEACH

Point out ways in which government interacts with businesses.

Work as a TEAM

Companies can take actions that reduce competition and give consumers fewer choices. Describe some advertising, pricing, or branding actions that could result in unfair competition.

expensive and less efficient. The extra poles and wires would create an unattractive environment.

While many utility companies are privately owned, usually government closely regulates them. The rates they can charge for things such as electricity, water, or natural gas have to be approved by government agencies. In recent years, there has been a trend toward deregulation of prices where competition can be introduced.

Prevent Unfair Business Practices

Most businesspeople are fair and honest. A few may try to take advantage of their customers or competitors. Government attempts to promote fair competition. If a company charges different prices to different people for the same product, it is treating its customers unfairly. If one business receives lower rates for the same quality and quantity of supplies than other businesses receive, it has an advantage. Such action may result in unfair competition.

A **monopoly** exists when a business has control of the market for a product or service. A public utility monopoly may benefit consumers by making sure they receive a needed service at a fair price. Other monopolies may not be good for the economy. If the same company owned all food stores in your city, consumers might not be treated fairly. This business could charge high prices and sell poor-quality products. When competition is present, consumers get the best values at the fairest prices.

One government action meant to promote competition and fairness and to avoid monopolies was the passage of **antitrust laws**. Antitrust laws prevent other unfair business practices such as false advertising, deceptive pricing, and misleading labeling. Each of these unfair practices hurts competition and reduces consumer choice.

NET KNOWLEDGE

With hundreds of agencies, the U.S. federal government has created a website, www.usa.gov, to assist citizens. This website offers information about everything from Amtrak to zoos. Access the website. Select a topic area of interest to you. Obtain information on the topic and prepare a written summary of how this information might be used by consumers or businesses.

CHECKPOINT ✓

Why does government regulate utilities?

LO 4.3.2

GOVERNMENT ASSISTS BUSINESS

Government helps businesses by collecting and reporting valuable information. Data gathered by the government can help with planning. Information about incomes, prices, worker availability, and business failures can help a businessperson make wiser choices. For example, census information can help a business decide where a majority of potential customers live. The Bureau of Labor Statistics, the Department of Agriculture, and the Department of Commerce are a few of the government agencies that provide information.

The federal government, through the Small Business Administration (SBA), helps new businesses get started by guaranteeing private bank loans. The new

Applied Skills

Communication Ask students to locate an advertisement with wording that may not be completely clear. Ask them to explain how this creates an unfair business practice that could be deceptive to consumers.

businesses must develop an acceptable business plan. Farmers and others may receive financial help in times of great hardship, such as during a drought, flooding, or other natural disasters. Destruction of home and property by a tornado may make a person eligible for a low-interest government loan. These programs are designed to promote the financial well-being of society.

Government Buys Goods and Services

Government spends a great deal of money each day to buy an array of products and services. Around 32 percent of all goods and services bought in the United States are purchased by state, local and federal governments.

Governments buy everything from file cabinets to buildings to military jet aircraft. In this role, government is a key economic force. Many businesses depend on government contracts for their survival. For instance, government pays businesses to construct highways and build schools.

Government Employs Workers

Government is the single largest employer in the U.S. economy. About 16 percent of workers are public employees. Most people think only of police officers, firefighters, and sanitation workers as government workers. Government also employs the same types of workers as private businesses. Administrative assistants, lawyers, teachers, meat inspectors, and data analysts are all employed by government. Although the number of employees has grown slowly in recent years, good employment opportunities in government continue—in spite of efforts to eliminate or reduce the size of some agencies.

CHECKPOINT
How does government assist business?

Stockbyte/Getty Images

Why do you think a company would want to perform work for the government?

LO 4.3.3

GOVERNMENT RAISES MONEY

Government must have a way to raise money to fund operations and pay wages to workers. Government income is called *revenue*. Governments can obtain revenue through taxes and borrowing. In addition, governments can raise revenue in other ways. Fines for traffic violations and other violations of the law provide revenue for government. Fees and licenses are a source of income. Certain types of ventures require a business license. For example, insurance and real estate agents pay a fee for the privilege of running a business. Governments also charge fees for such things as driver's licenses and fishing privileges.

THINK CRITICALLY THROUGH VISUALS

Companies might want to work for the government because governmental purchases and contracts are often for large and ongoing projects.

TEACH

Highlight methods in which government assists businesses.

Ask students to name various goods and services commonly purchased by governments.

ONGOING ASSESSMENT

CHECKPOINT ANSWER

Government assists businesses in a variety of ways, including providing demographic data, buying goods and services, and employing workers who then have the means to buy goods and services.

TEACH

Ask students to name items for which government needs money.

Explain the various types of taxes used by government to raise funds.

Teaching Strategies

Expand Beyond the Classroom Ask a local government employee to speak to your class about various career opportunities in government. As an alternative, assign students to interview a person who is employed by the government. Ask students to report their findings to the class.

Life-Span Plan Answers

Answers will vary. Students should explain how taxes could impact their ability to accumulate the funds they need to achieve their life-span goals.

Business Insight

Explain to students that government agencies and offices often cite two reasons for their increased use of the Internet—savings in the cost of offering the services and time savings for citizens. Yet these services are often very complex, and not all citizens want to use or have easy access to the Internet.

Think Critically *Answers*

1. Answers will vary depending on the websites visited. Consider asking volunteers to showcase examples of websites that fit into the various stages.

2. To overcome privacy and security barriers, governments can utilize strong encryption on their sites. Access and help with computer skills can be provided in government agency locations and in libraries.

Life-Span Plan

Think about the role of government services for you and for businesses today and in the future. Explain how these government services, and the associated taxes, could affect the life-span goals you set for yourself. Describe how government programs and spending might impact your ability to achieve your goals.

Taxes

A government creates tax policies to pay for the services it provides. Taxes are levied on earnings, the value of property, and on the sale price of goods and services. Your earnings as an individual are subject to an income tax. *Income taxes* are levied on the income of individuals. The individual income tax is the largest source of revenue for the federal government. Corporate income taxes also provide government revenue. The corporate income tax is based on business profits.

A major source of revenue for local governments is the real estate *property tax*. This tax is based on the value of land and buildings. Most property tax revenue is used to pay for schools and other local

Business Insight

Supporting E-Government

Computers have a major impact on the way government operates. More than 80 percent of adults who use the Internet have been to a government website within the last 12 months. Rather than going to a government office to pick up a form, apply for a license, or make a payment, people can complete many of these activities online.

In a study of the development of e-government services around the world, the United Nations has identified the following five stages:

- ***Emerging*** Official government online presence established
- ***Enhanced*** Number of sites increases; sites become more interesting and useful
- ***Interactive*** Users can download forms, e-mail officials, and interact through the Internet
- ***Transactional*** Users can complete transactions and pay for services online
- ***Connected*** Responds to the needs of its citizens by developing integrated back-office operations

The U.S. government has an online portal to all of the information and services offered online. USA.gov links to more than 10,000 federal, state, and local web pages. The site receives over 4 million hits per month. In addition to computer-based access, smartphone apps are opening new avenues for contact.

The federal government spends more than $80 billion per year for information technology services. Moving government services online saves more than 1 billion dollars each year.

Two major barriers stand in the way of e-government expansion. Most important is the privacy and security of the personal information contained in government records and submitted by citizens. That information includes tax records and personal information such as driver's license and social security numbers. The second barrier is the unequal access to technology. Thousands of citizens do not have secure high-speed Internet connections. Others do not have the literacy or computer skills to use online government services.

Think Critically

1. Search the Internet and identify government services provided by your local and state governments. What stage of development is demonstrated by the websites you visited?
2. What can governments do to reduce the barriers of privacy, security, and citizen access to e-government services?

Portfolio Activity

Assign the Portfolio Activity for Chapter 4, available on the website for this textbook.
COLLECT Offer suggestions to help students locate an example of a government regulation.
CREATE Remind students that the visual needs to illustrate a government regulation; it does not have to be a literal symbol of the regulation.
CONNECT Point out that students should use their visuals to illustrate their presentation.

government services, such as police protection and community parks. Businesses also pay a property tax.

The cost of buying things is increased by a sales tax. A *sales tax* is a state or local tax on goods and services that is collected by the seller. If you buy a can of paint for $15.00 and the state sales tax is 6 percent, the seller collects $15.90 from you. The seller then will pay 90 cents to the state. You were the one who provided the money for the tax.

Paying taxes is a duty of citizens and businesses. You should pay your taxes, but not more than your share. Tax laws and policies are set to help make the paying of taxes fair. Whether a particular tax or tax policy is fair is always subject to debate. Businesses, in spite of public misconceptions, pay a lot of taxes to all levels of government.

Borrowing

Government income from taxes and other sources may not always be enough to cover the costs of providing services. Borrowing is another activity of government. When a government wants to construct a building, such as a new courthouse or convention center, the funds needed are often raised through borrowing.

Government borrows money by selling bonds. When you buy a government bond, you are helping to fund the services provided by government. Banks, insurance companies, and other financial institutions help finance governments by purchasing bonds in large numbers.

By borrowing money, the government becomes a debtor and must pay interest on its debt. Bonds issued by the U.S. government are backed by the "full faith and credit" of the federal government. Bonds issued by the federal government are considered the least risky of all debt.

CHECKPOINT ✓
What is the difference between tax revenue and borrowing by government?

4.3 ASSESSMENT

Key Concepts

Determine the best answer.

1. Antitrust laws are designed to
   a. reduce utility rates
   b. lower taxes
   c. create more jobs
   d. maintain competition

2. A(n) ________ tax is a common source of revenue for state and local governments.
   a. sales
   b. import
   c. gift
   d. unemployment

3. True or False. A monopoly is never a benefit to consumers.

Make Academic Connections

4. **History** Conduct research about various antitrust laws. What situations caused the creation of these laws?

5. **Communication** Conduct a survey of people to obtain their opinions about which types of taxes are most appropriate to raise government revenue. Prepare a summary data table with your findings.

6. **Economics** Describe government actions to raise money that might have a positive or negative influence on business activities.

TEACH

Explain the effect sales tax can have on various people. Describe borrowing actions commonly taken by government.

ONGOING ASSESSMENT

CHECKPOINT ✓ANSWER

Tax revenue is money the government collects to cover the costs of services. This is money that the government is not required to pay back. The government is required to pay back borrowed money.

ASSESS

Key Concepts *Answers*

1. d. maintain competition
2. a. sales
3. False. A monopoly can be beneficial to consumers. Without competition, some companies, such as utilities, may keep costs and therefore prices low.

Make Academic Connections *Answers*

4. Offer suggestions for how students should present their findings.
5. Data tables will vary.
6. Answers will vary. Some positives might include sale of bonds to earn interest and providing funds for buying goods and services. Negatives include the cost of property tax on buildings that a business owns; income taxes decrease the consumer's ability to pay for goods and services.

RETEACH Describe the types of taxes and borrowing activities of local, state, and federal governments.

ENRICH Assign students to research various types of government bonds that might be considered by an investor.

CLOSE Instruct students to explain various ways government assists businesses.

Think Critically About Business *Answers*

1. Examples of natural resources used every day include water, natural gas, gasoline, tin, and other minerals. All of these resources need to be protected. Strategies to avoid depleting natural resources include avoiding the waste of water, recycling cans and bottles, driving only when necessary, and minimizing the use of electricity.

2. Examples will vary, but might include following all manufacturing procedures accurately, keeping electrical cords secured and walkways clear of objects, maintaining adequate lighting, keeping first aid and emergency exits posted, and providing security in areas where needed.

3. Answers will vary. The term "discrimination" could mean an individual is denied a chance for employment or a promotion because of gender, race, or age. The term could also mean evaluating someone differently than others based on gender, race, or age. Examples of discrimination will vary.

4. Healthy employees are generally more productive employees. The cost of health care insurance is also a concern to employers.

5. The list may include water, sanitation, electric, gas, and cable television.

These utilities provide things that make life healthier and more convenient. We have water purification sites, waste removal, and electricity for our homes, schools, hospitals, and businesses.

Some resources, and the resources used to process them, would have a greater demand put upon them if they were privatized and could become scarce. As private companies would compete for the same source and would have to pay for their own equipment, these types of utilities would become more expensive for the provider as well as the consumer. Competition might improve the quality of some services and could reduce costs.

Chapter 4 Assessment

Review Business Concepts

4.1 Social Responsibility and Business Ethics

- Socially responsible businesses care about their communities. They help make them better places in which to live. Social responsibility concerns relate to environmental protection, workplace diversity, safety on the job, and employee wellness.
- Benefits of social responsibility include expanded justice for societal groups, enhanced company image, reduced need for government action, improved quality of life, and increased awareness of social issues. Costs of social responsibility are that money must be spent for new or safer equipment, for building renovations to remove hazards, for wellness and rehabilitation programs, and for social projects sponsored by a company. These costs must be balanced with profits to make sure the business stays viable.
- A code of business ethics is a guide for behavior within an organization.

4.2 Government Protection Activities

- The primary roles of government are to provide services to society; protect citizens, consumers, businesses, and workers; regulate utilities and promote competition; provide information and help to businesses; buy goods and services; hire public employees; and raise revenue. The levels of government are federal, state, and local.
- Government protects citizens through police and fire services, protects consumers and business owners by enforcing contracts and intellectual property rights, and protects workers through laws that require safe working conditions.
- The three types of intellectual property are patents, copyrights, and trademarks.

4.3 Government Regulation and Assistance

- Government regulates utilities and prevents unfair business practices.
- Government buys a wide range of goods and services. Many workers are employed by government. Governments also collect and report valuable information and provide loans to help businesses get started or overcome natural disasters.
- Governments raise needed funds through taxes and borrowing.

Think Critically About Business

1. What are some natural resources that you use every day? Which of those natural resources need to be protected? What can you as an individual do to avoid using up nonrenewable resources?
2. Safety is often a matter of individuals being careful about where they place things and how they conduct their own business. Name some ways in which you and others can help make a workplace safe.
3. What does the term "discrimination" mean to you? What examples of discrimination in the workplace are you aware of?
4. Why do you think employers are willing to spend money to help employees improve their general health? Be specific about how a company might benefit.
5. Make a list of public utilities that serve your community. What services do they provide? Do you think it would be better for these services to be offered by several competing businesses? Explain your answer.
6. Here is a list of some of the public services provided by government. For each item, tell whether the federal, state, or local government would most likely have the responsibility for the service. (Some services may be provided by more than one level of government.)
   - **a.** Fire protection
   - **b.** Education
   - **c.** Parks and recreation
   - **d.** Water supply

e. Highways between cities
f. Assistance to low-income families
g. Sewage and trash disposal
h. Public buses
i. Police protection
j. Public libraries
k. Street maintenance
l. National defense

7. Each day people enter into many contracts, both written and unwritten.
   a. Give examples of contracts between a consumer and a business, between two businesses, and between a worker and a business.
   b. What services does government provide to enforce contracts?

8. Two students are discussing the topic "Government Is Our Biggest Business." Dan believes that some government activities are in direct competition with private businesses. He thinks that this is unfair. He believes that government should limit its activities to those that private businesses cannot or will not take on. Brian thinks that government should undertake any business activities that it can perform better or at a lower cost than private business. What do you think? Give some examples of business activities undertaken by both private businesses and by government.

9. Why do you suppose government raises revenue through bonds that create debt and require interest payments when government could raise the revenue through an increase in taxes?

Develop Your Business Language

Match the terms listed with the definitions.

10. Principles of morality or rules of conduct.
11. The obligation of a business to contribute to the well-being of a community.
12. Rules about how businesses and their employees ought to behave.
13. A natural resource, such as gas, coal, copper, or iron ore, that cannot be replaced once it is used up.
14. A statement of values and rules that guides the behavior of employees or members of an organization.
15. A business that supplies a service or product vital to all people; the price charged for the service (or product) is determined by government regulation rather than by competition.
16. Laws designed to promote competition and fairness and to prevent monopolies.
17. Protection of the work of authors, composers, and artists.
18. An agreement to exchange goods or services for something of value.
19. The exclusive right given to a person to make, use, or sell an invention for a period of 20 years.
20. A word, letter, or symbol associated with a specific product or company.
21. A business that has complete control of the market for a product or service.

Key Terms

a. antitrust laws
b. business ethics
c. code of ethics
d. contract
e. copyright
f. ethics
g. monopoly
h. nonrenewable resource
i. patent
j. public utility
k. social responsibility
l. trademark

Develop Your Business Language *Answers*

10. f. ethics
11. k. social responsibility
12. b. business ethics
13. h. nonrenewable resource
14. c. code of ethics
15. j. public utility
16. a. antitrust laws
17. e. copyright
18. d. contract
19. i. patent
20. l. trademark
21. g. monopoly

6a. Fire protection, local

6b. Education, local and state

6c. Parks and recreation, local, state, and federal

6d. Water supply, local

6e. Highways between cities, state and federal

6f. Assistance to low-income families, state and federal

6g. Sewage and trash disposal, local

6h. Public buses, local

6i. Police protection, local and state

6j. Public libraries, local

6k. Street maintenance, local

6l. National defense, federal

7a. A contract between a homeowner and an electrician, a contract between an advertising agency and a soap manufacturer, and a work-for-hire agreement are examples of these types of contracts.

7b. The government has established laws regarding the definition of contracts and their enforcement. Court systems exist to settle disputes. Other forms of government protection, such as the protection of workers and intellectual property, often contribute to the regulation of many contracts.

8. Answers will vary. Education, transportation, and health care are all examples of services that can be both public and private.

9. Taxes reduce the consumer's ability to buy goods and services, which weakens the economy as a whole. By providing bonds, governments can increase the consumer's ability to contribute to the flow of the economy, while covering its cost for public services.

Make Academic Connections *Answers*

22. Reports will vary. Several definitions and examples should be included.

23a. pollution control: \$37,500÷\$750,000=5%; community projects: \$22,500÷\$750,000=3%; employee fitness: \$7,500÷\$750,000=1%; total spent: \$37,500+\$22,500+\$7,500=\$67,500

23b. pollution control: \$37,500×1.15=\$43,125; community projects: \$22,500×1.15=\$25,875; employee fitness: \$7,500×1.15=\$8,625; total spent: \$43,125+\$25,875+\$8,625=\$77,625

24. The electronic transmission and duplication of data are easy and fast, and it is more difficult to regulate the use and sale of products.

25. Students find examples of U.S. and foreign logos and trademarks and design a brand name or trademark that they think would be effective in countries around the world.

26. Students are to research different systems of government and explain how history and culture affect business regulations in various countries.

27. Reports will vary depending on the product selected. Reports should identify the product, the inventor, the year of the patent, and the product function. Students then prepare a summary report.

28. Students are to investigate various legal restrictions they might encounter when applying for a job.

Make Academic Connections

22. **Communication** Interview various people to ask them for a definition and an example of "conflict of interest." Prepare a summary report of two to three paragraphs.

23. **Math** The Johnson Manufacturing Co. has an annual operating budget of \$750,000. Each year it budgets for the following expenses: pollution control equipment, \$37,500; contributions to community projects, \$22,500; employee fitness/sports programs, \$7,500.

- **a.** What percentage of the annual budget is allocated to each socially responsible action (pollution control, community projects, fitness/sports)? What is the total spent?
- **b.** What will be the amount budgeted for each expense category next year if there is a 15 percent increase? What will be the total spent?

24. **Technology** Explain how new technology is making it more difficult to protect intellectual property rights.

25. **Visual Art** Look for examples of trademarks and logos of products from companies based inside and outside of the United States. Design a brand name or trademark that might be effective in several countries around the world.

26. **Culture** Research different systems of government. Explain how history and culture can affect business regulations in various countries.

27. **Science** Research a patent on a product. Identify the inventor, the year the patent was granted, and the product's function. Prepare a summary report of your findings.

28. **Career Planning** Investigate various legal restrictions that might be encountered when applying for a job position.

Make Your Case

Centerville wants to build a new sports complex near the center of town. The complex will cost \$250,000. There are two financing proposals:

Proposal A Issue \$250,000 worth of bonds at an interest rate of 4 percent. The town will pay \$10,000 per year in interest for 15 years. The total interest would be \$150,000. The amount borrowed (\$250,000) would have to be paid off in 15 years. Fees charged to users of the complex would pay the interest each year and the amount due bondholders (\$250,000). Construction could begin right away.

Proposal B Establish a 1/4 percent city sales tax on all purchases. The revenue needed could be raised in about five years. There would be no user fee charged to residents of Centerville. Construction would be delayed for a few years.

29. What are the advantages and disadvantages of the two proposals?

30. Which proposal do you favor, and why?

Global warming is a hot topic. There is strong consensus that the world is getting warmer. Eleven of the last 12 years have been the warmest on record.

Although the warming trend is well documented, there is considerable debate about the cause. Could it be part of a natural cycle? Or, is it due to human activity? Scientists, environmentalists, and policymakers who believe that human activity is the cause of global warming point to the reduction of carbon emissions as part of the solution.

31. Use the Internet to learn more about global warming and get some different perspectives on the issue. Visit at least one website for each of the following categories: government agency, environmental advocacy organization, large manufacturer, and energy company. In a short report, summarize what you find and offer an opinion about what should be done to combat global warming.

32. Use the Internet to identify actions and strategies that businesses, governments, and individuals could adopt to limit greenhouse gases. Report your findings in a table.

33. Choose three actions or strategies that could help reduce greenhouse gases and write a short explanation of how they might impact business practices.

Make Your Case *Answers*

29. A: Construction begins right away and user fees pay for the complex. B: Construction is delayed and all consumers pay the sales tax, but residents do not pay to use complex.

30. Answers will vary.

31. Reports will vary. Students should summarize their findings and offer their opinion about what should be done to combat global warming.

32. Tables will vary. For example students might suggest that businesses could use energy-saving equipment, governments could offer tax incentives

Interactions and Connections

Interview someone in your community who owns a business or works for a large company or organization. Obtain information about actions that need to be considered when hiring people, designing products, and making other business decisions. Ask them how ethics might affect their daily lives and the lives of others. Based on their answers, create a short code of ethics that might be used to guide the decisions made by managers and employees in a company.

Prepared Speech Event

Every day, in companies around the world, employees are spending part of their workday making personal phone calls and using their work computers for shopping online, playing games, sending personal e-mails, and visiting social networking sites. This unethical behavior results in decreased productivity. Today's focus on technology has many people thinking about personal interests over dedication to their employer. Business leaders are challenged to monitor employees in the workplace for ethical use of their time.

You will prepare a speech that identifies current ethical challenges and offers strategies to encourage respect and ethical conduct in the workplace. Your speech must emphasize the expectation of employee productivity in the work world and how attention must be shifted from personal interests of employees to customer service and ethical use of work time.

You will have three to five minutes to present your plan to improve ethical conduct in the workplace. Audiovisual equipment and visual aids may be used in this presentation.

Performance Indicators Evaluated

- Define ethical conduct in the workplace.
- Explain the relationship between the employee's commitment to the workplace and productivity.
- Describe strategies to improve ethical conduct in the workplace.
- Explain how ethical standards will be implemented and monitored in the workplace.
- Describe a work environment that requires and rewards sound ethical behavior.

You will be evaluated for your

- Knowledge of the topic
- Organization of the presentation
- Confidence, quality of voice, and eye contact
- Presentation of the business strategy

For more detailed information about performance indicators, go to the BPA website.

Think Critically

1. Why must businesses have standards and rules for employees?
2. Why are many ethical issues associated with technology in the workplace?
3. How can businesses increase employee dedication?
4. What has contributed to the lack of productivity in the workplace?
5. What should happen to employees who have demonstrated unethical behavior in the workplace?

www.bpa.org

to businesses to encourage green business practices, and consumers could plant a tree.

33. Explanations will vary depending on the actions or strategies selected.

Interactions and Connections

Answers will vary. Students are to talk to people about ethics in business and in daily life, and then create a code of ethics for a company.

WINNING EDGE

Prepared Speech Event

The Prepared Speech Event challenges students to research an issue that businesses are facing and then develop strategies to overcome it. This event focuses attention on the problem of decreased productivity due to a lack of employee work ethic.

Think Critically

Answers

1. Rules and standards serve as guidelines for behavior at work. They dictate how employees and employers should behave while on the job.

2. Individuals have become addicted to the latest technology. Smartphones, the Internet, and other electronic devices have led to distractions at home, the workplace, and the roadways. Most employees use office computers and are tempted to surf the Internet. Smartphones are hard to regulate in the workplace. Text messaging is a distraction for many people.

3. Businesses can monitor employees' contribution to company goals, reward individuals for superior work and ethical behavior, and recognize individuals who meet or exceed these expectations.

4. Answers will vary. The lack of productivity in the workplace can be attributed to employees using technology for their personal use or layoffs and downsizing decreasing motivation.

5. Employees who are demonstrating unethical behavior should be reprimanded according to company policy with no exceptions.

UNIT 2
Business Organization and Management

The chapters in this unit describe various forms of business ownership and organization, the role and work of management, and how to undertake career planning.

Chapter 5 Business Organization This chapter focuses on the major forms of business ownership in the United States and the role each plays in the economy.

Chapter 6 Entrepreneurship and Small Business Management The chapter helps students develop an understanding of the steps in starting a new business and the characteristics of entrepreneurs.

Chapter 7 Management and Leadership The chapter presents information on the major activities common to all managers and how to be an effective leader.

Chapter 8 Human Resources, Culture, and Diversity This chapter describes the important role of human resources in businesses and ways to build a positive and diverse work environment.

Chapter 9 Career Planning and Development In this chapter students study the variety of career opportunities in business and learn how to prepare a career plan and apply for and secure a job.

UNIT 2

Business Organization and Management

Unit 2 Global Business Project

Suggest that students read the chapter and lesson titles for this unit to get acquainted with business organization and management. Introduce the Global Business Project for this unit: **Organize International Business Activities**.

Ask students to read the project assignment and plan to work on it as they progress through the unit. The project can be found on the website: www.cengage.com/swep/pob9e

Business Vision

There are three factors of production: economic resources, natural resources, and human resources. This unit looks at how a business organizes and manages human resources.

Each chapter in this unit includes some aspect of organizing and managing a business. These include different forms of ownership. Some businesses are entrepreneurial start-ups; others are large corporations. Some small businesses need to manage only a few workers; others may have thousands of employees. In all cases, businesses are challenged with finding qualified human resources.

From Start-up to Global Dominance

In the late 1960s, two friends had a hobby of writing software. In 1975 they wrote a BASIC programming language for the first personal computer, the Altair 8800. The entrepreneurs, Bill Gates and Paul Allen, named their new partnership Micro-Soft. Revenue for the first year in business was $16,000.

In 1980, the computer company IBM introduced a new personal computer and needed an operating system. They chose Microsoft's MS-DOS. Microsoft grew as its DOS became the standard for all PC manufacturers. Microsoft incorporated in 1981 to become Microsoft, Inc.

In 1986, Microsoft moved to Redmond, Washington. The company built a 40-acre campus for its employees. Buildings were designed in an X pattern to allow workers to have offices with windows. The goal was to develop a culture where Microsoft employees could sit and think. Microsoft tried to hire the "smartest" people and then give them the freedom to think and develop products. By 1995, Microsoft's revenue exceeded $6 billion and it had more than 17,000 employees.

Perhaps Microsoft's greatest challenge was underestimating how the World Wide Web could replace Microsoft's software dominance. Microsoft was able to tap into its human resources to turn the company around. Microsoft employees camped out by sleeping at their headquarters to change the design of their products to support the Internet.

By 2015 Microsoft's revenue was more than $86 billion and it had grown to 118,000 employees. Today, some people think that Microsoft has become too large and less entrepreneurial. Microsoft is facing competition from a number of start-up companies. One was started by two friends, Larry Page and Sergey Brin. This company is called Google.

Think Critically

Explain why Microsoft's growth over time would affect how it was organized and how it would manage employees.

97

Business Vision

Encourage students to read the introduction to Unit 2. Suggest that students read the chapter and lesson titles for this unit to get acquainted with business organization and management.

From Start-up to Global Dominance

In less than 40 years, Microsoft grew from a hobby business to world dominance. Ask students to give examples of other technology businesses that have had a major impact on the world over the last few decades. Answers could include Apple, Yahoo, Google, Twitter, and Facebook.

At the conclusion of the discussion, direct students to answer the Think Critically question that follows the feature.

Think Critically

Answers

Answers will vary. For example, students might point out that when a business is small and growing all employees can know each other. When a business has 17,000 employees, stronger lines of control may be needed.

Portfolio Activity

Portfolio work samples validate skill level and a student's ability to accomplish tasks frequently performed on the job. The most important reason for including samples in a portfolio is to demonstrate a student's abilities and skills. In selecting work samples for each unit, students should always have a choice of which activities to include. Students might be encouraged to include samples from the end-of-chapter activities.

CHAPTER OVERVIEW

The chapter examines the forms of business ownership and the role of each in the U.S. economy.

5.1 Business in the U.S. Economy

This lesson describes changes that have occurred in U.S. employment and changes in the types and numbers of businesses.

5.2 Forms of Business Ownership

This lesson introduces the major forms of business ownership and outlines the strengths and limitations of each.

5.3 Organizational Structure for Businesses

The lesson provides information on how to organize effective businesses and alternative structures for businesses.

Chapter 5 Business Organization

Pressmaster/Shutterstock.com

Instructor Resources

- Activities and Study Guide IE
- Chapter and Unit Tests IE
- Lesson Plans
- PowerPoint Presentation
- Cognero Test, Ch. 5

Student Resources

Activities and Study Guide
www.cengage.com/swep/pob9e
- Portfolio Activity

Business, Management & Administration

PLANNING A CAREER IN . . .
CORPORATE LEADERSHIP

Rising to the top of one of the world's largest corporations seems like the dream job in business. The chief executive officer (CEO) of a corporation may make several million dollars a year in salary and bonuses, have a large office with dozens of support staff, travel worldwide on a corporate jet, and make daily decisions that directly influence the success of the company. Corporate executives also work long hours and face the competing expectations of stockholders, the board of directors, employees, and customers. While CEOs receive many perks and benefits, their success or failure may be determined more by economic conditions, government regulations, and the stock market than their own decisions and abilities.

Related Job Titles

- **Chief Executive Officer**
- **Chief Operating Officer**
- **President**

A corporation's goals and policies are established by the top executives. The executives meet frequently to set direction, review company performance, and establish policy. They then delegate work to the organization's managers and employees. They know that they are ultimately responsible and accountable for the performance of the company.

Analyze Career Opportunities in . . .
CORPORATE LEADERSHIP

Use library and Internet resources to learn more about careers in corporate leadership. Choose one of the job titles listed in the box above and answer the following questions.

1. How would you describe the physical work environment for jobs in this field?
2. Is this a career that interests you? Describe how you might use your talents, abilities, and skills in this career.

What it's like to work as a . . . Corporate Executive

Most days, a CEO's schedule is packed. It may start with an hour of reading before attending a conference with the heads of other companies and government officials. Lunch is eaten with the management team to review the company's financial performance, followed by a press conference. Two hours are spent on the telephone talking to a senator about a telecommunications law, discussing labor contract negotiations with the vice president of human resources, and speaking with a manufacturer in Japan about a proposed joint venture. After a workout at the executive gym and a quick dinner, it is off to the airport for a flight to Brazil to oversee the opening of a new manufacturing facility. The flight is spent studying reports, completing correspondence, and watching a video briefing on Brazil's economy.

What about you? How would you prepare for the stress of being a corporate executive? Do you believe that the work justifies the high salary and benefits?

PLANNING A CAREER IN . . .
CORPORATE LEADERSHIP

The life of a corporate executive can seem glamorous and exciting. Along with the glamour comes immense responsibilities and challenges, as well as long hours and varied duties. It takes both education and years of experience to become the top leader of a business.

What About You? ***Answers***

Answers will vary, but could include discussion of the need for a broad range of experience and years spent at lower levels in an organization.

Analyze Career Opportunities *Answers*

Student answers will vary depending on when the assignment is completed and individual interests.

Additional Career Information

Encourage students to investigate careers they find interesting and explore unfamiliar careers. Two resources for additional career information are the *Occupational Outlook Handbook*, an online publication (www.bls.gov/) of the U.S. Bureau of Labor Statistics, and the O*NET Resource Center (www.onetcenter.org) developed by the U.S. Department of Labor. Information about specific careers and jobs can be used to demonstrate the relevance of skills learned in this course.

Focus on REAL LIFE

Ask students to consider how hobbies and interests might lead to a career and even the opportunity to start their own business. Combining personal interests and a career can be a very satisfying choice.

TEACH

Ask students whether they believe the jobs that interest them today will be available in 10 years. As young people begin career planning, they need to pay attention to the types of jobs that are increasing and declining.

Ask students to identify any information that surprises them in the section on employment data. Lead a discussion about how employment changes have affected employers.

THINK CRITICALLY THROUGH VISUALS

Over the next decade, the average age of U.S. workers will increase, and there will be a mini-boom of younger workers aged 20–30. Also, the percentage of white workers will decrease, and the percentage of women in the workforce will increase.

5.1 Business in the U.S. Economy

Learning Outcomes

5.1.1 Describe the changing status of U.S. employment.

5.1.2 Discuss the role of business in the U.S. economy.

5.1.3 Describe three major types of businesses.

Key Terms

contingent worker 101

intermediaries 105

service business 105

Focus on REAL LIFE

Sami Rehm loves digital photography. Last year she turned her hobby into a professional photography business. She uses photo editing software to produce digital images. Sami has started to wonder if she might be able to expand her business. Sami has a friend who can help sell the images to newspapers, magazines, advertising agencies, and other businesses.

Sami isn't sure if her friend should be an employee or a partner. To expand, the business will need to purchase new equipment and develop sales brochures.

Sami expressed her feelings to her mother. "I love my photography business. Would I like it as much if I had to share control with a partner? I wonder if I can afford to purchase new equipment by myself?"

LO 5.1.1

THE CHANGING U.S. JOB MARKET

In the first decades of the twenty-first century, the United States has experienced a cycle of employment growth and decline. Part of this change is due to careers shifting from manufacturing and agriculture work to service jobs. Employment also declines during recessions and grows during recoveries.

Employment Data

Following the 9/11/2001 terrorist attacks, a recession resulted in job losses that peaked in 2003. From 2003 to 2007, total employment grew by nearly 6 percent. The Great Recession from 2007 through 2009 resulted in a loss of more than 8.7 million jobs. The same number of jobs had returned by 2014.

A wave of retirements started in 2011 as the first group of *baby boomers*, the people born between 1946 and 1964, turned 65. Although retirements will continue, the average age of U.S. workers in 2020 will be higher than 50. At the same time, a mini-boom of younger workers will cause the 20- to 30-year-old age group to grow faster than the overall labor force for the first time in

Monkey Business Images/Shutterstock.com

How will the demographics of U.S. workers change over the next decade?

Different Learning Styles

Visual Learner Instruct students to search through magazines and newspapers to locate photographs that illustrate the changes in the workforce described in the chapter. If possible, they should clip or copy the picture and create a photo essay, poster, or collage that visually illustrates the changes.

25 years. Other groups that will go through higher employment growth rates are Asian-, Hispanic-, and African-American workers. Currently, white non-Hispanic workers make up 68 percent of the labor force. That number will drop to 62 percent by 2020. Over the last 50 years, one of the most striking trends in employment has been the participation of women. In the early 1960s, 35 percent of women were working outside the home. The number of working women doubled by 2000. By 2020 nearly one half of all jobs (47 percent) in the United States will be held by women.

Pressures on Employees

At one time, it was assumed that technology would allow people to work fewer hours. This has not occurred. Economic stress has led to downsizing of the number of people employed by many companies. Companies streamlined production and implemented other cost-cutting procedures. Businesses required employees to take on new tasks and work extra hours. Some full-time jobs were reduced to part-time. Wage rates decreased. Many people were forced to find second jobs to meet their economic needs.

A recent survey reported that 7 of 10 parents felt they were not able to spend enough time with their children. At the same time, children see their parents changing jobs, taking on more responsibility, completing additional education to improve career opportunities, and making important decisions to balance work and family life. Those experiences will likely shape the career and family decisions of the next generation.

Economic pressures also resulted in the increased use of contingent workers. A **contingent worker** is one who has no explicit or implicit contract for long-term employment. About 5 percent of the U.S. workforce (nearly 6 million people) is made up of contingent workers. Some estimates predict that number will double in 10 years. Many people take contingent work because they cannot find permanent employment. Others choose contingent work because they like the flexibility it offers.

NET KNOWLEDGE

The U.S. Bureau of Labor Statistics collects and reports detailed information on the status of the work force nationwide. Access the www.bls.gov website. Locate the Economic and Employment Projections. Identify and study tables that describe how employment is projected to change for people of your age and race and for an industry in which you might be interested in working. How can you use that information to help you make education and career decisions in the next several years?

CHECKPOINT

List several groups that will increase as a percentage of the total U.S. workforce in the next decade.

LO 5.1.2

BUSINESS AND THE ECONOMY

Businesses make the goods and services you use each day. That includes the products and services used by other businesses as well as those needed by individual consumers. In 2014, all businesses worldwide produced more than $77.6 trillion of goods and services. U.S. businesses were responsible for almost 20 percent of that production. Nearly 27 million full- and part-time businesses produce those goods and services.

Size of U.S. Businesses

Most U.S. businesses are quite small. The largest category, with nearly 21.7 million businesses, is businesses with no employees other than the owner. About 5.8 million companies employ fewer than 20 people. Just over 526,000 employ 20–99 people. About 109,000 large U.S. businesses employ 100 or more workers. Of those large companies, 981 employ more than 10,000 people. Figure 5-1 shows the distribution of U.S. businesses by employment size.

NET KNOWLEDGE

Tell students that the U.S. Bureau of Labor Statistics provides many resources that are helpful in career planning. Ask them whether they are aware of any other career resources available on the Web.

TEACH

Ask students whether they believe today's workers have more or fewer pressures on them than workers in the past. Ask them to identify the work, family, and personal pressures that can affect employees.

ONGOING ASSESSMENT

CHECKPOINT ANSWER

Younger workers (16–24 years of age); Asian-, Hispanic-, African-American groups; and women will compose larger percentages of the workforce in the next decade.

TEACH

Before students read the information, ask them whether they believe that most U.S. businesses are large or small. Ask them to guess the average number of employees that work for most businesses. Then instruct students to read the paragraph and ask for their reactions.

Different Learning Styles

Kinesthetic Learner Ask students to write $70 trillion numerically on the board or a piece of paper. Then ask them to determine what 20 percent of that amount is and write that number, describing the total of U.S. business production.

When written out, $70 trillion contains 13 zeros: $70,000,000,000,000. Twenty percent of $70 trillion is $14 trillion. When written out, there are 12 zeros: $14,000,000,000,000.

TEACH

Ask students whether they agree with the statement, "The most important role of businesses is to make and distribute products and services needed by consumers, government, and other businesses." If students disagree, ask them to identify what they believe to be the most important role.

Write "How Businesses Help" on the board. Below that heading, write "the community" and "individuals." Ask students to brainstorm the benefits of businesses and write them under the appropriate heading when they are identified.

▸ **Figure 5-1** ***ANSWER***

Answers will vary. Students should identify the ideal size of a business in which they would prefer to work.

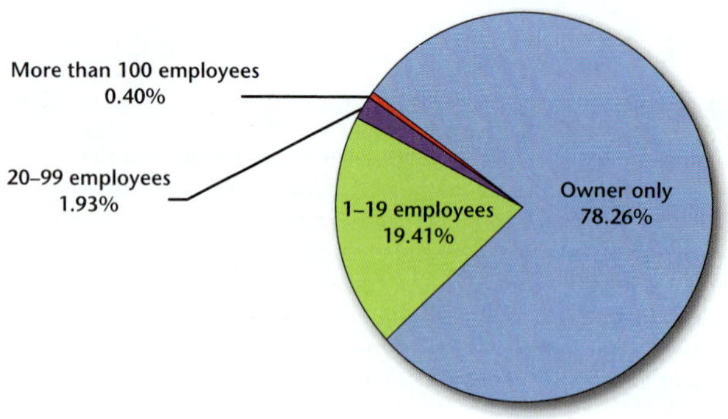

FIGURE 5-1
Would you prefer to work in a large or small business? Explain your answer.

Roles of Business

Businesses play several key roles in the U.S. economy. The most important role of businesses is to make and distribute products and services needed by consumers, government, and other businesses. Businesses make the clothing, movies, music, food, and other items you use every day.

Businesses provide employment for millions of people. Employee wages are used to purchase goods and services. Profits earned by businesses are used to compensate owners and investors. Most businesses pay taxes to federal, state, and local governments. Governments spend these taxes to provide services such as clean water, well-maintained streets, police and fire protection, hospitals, and schools.

Impact on a Community

A business can have an important impact on the community in which it operates. When a new business opens, it pays wages to its workers. It also buys goods and services from other businesses in the area. This results in additional money being introduced into the community. Employees and businesses in turn spend much of the money to purchase things they need.

The money spent may result in the need for more employees in the community. They will need housing, automobiles, food, and entertainment. They will pay taxes to the community to support needed community services.

When a large business opens in an area, other businesses will often locate there to support the larger business. Small businesses may be started to meet the needs of the residents and other businesses. Successful businesses contribute to more jobs, more income, and a thriving economy in the communities where they operate.

Business Activities

Businesses may be large or small, simple or complex. A business might operate in only one community. It may have many locations across the nation or around the world. Although there are many types and sizes of businesses, all firms perform six basic activities.

Generating Ideas A business begins with a new idea. Someone must have an idea for a new product or service or a new way to carry out a business process. A business must continue to improve and develop new ideas in order to remain successful. Businesses must remain competitive with other firms that sell similar goods and services. Many companies have research and development departments that works full-time to discover new product, service, and operating ideas.

Raising Capital Businesses need financial resources to operate. They use these financial resources to buy buildings and equipment, hire and train workers, and complete day-to-day business operations. A large amount of capital is needed to start most businesses. Some capital comes from owners. Most is obtained through loans from financial institutions or from investors.

A business needs more capital as it develops and grows. Some of that capital will come from reinvested profits. A business will need to continue to borrow

Teaching Strategies

Collaborative Learning Divide the class into several three- to four-person teams. Ask each team to identify an industry that they would like to study. Teams should use the Internet to identify the five largest U.S. and international businesses in their industry based on the number of employees and develop a chart to present their findings.

from banks and attract additional investors to have enough money for ongoing operations.

Employing and Training Personnel Businesses need human resources. Even businesses that begin with no employees other than the owner will add part- and full-time employees as they grow. Businesses have procedures for recruiting, hiring, and training employees. They pay wages, benefits, and employment taxes. New employees receive training in order to perform their jobs correctly. Further training will be necessary when procedures change, new tasks are added, or technology is introduced.

Buying Goods and Services All businesses buy goods and services. Businesses use many of the purchases for their own operations. Other purchases are resold. Manufacturers of automobiles must buy steel, aluminum, and plastics to be used to form the frame and body of new cars. They will also purchase tires, batteries, airbags, and air conditioning units that will be installed on the production line.

Work as a TEAM

If you own a business, would you rather raise capital by obtaining a loan from a financial institution or by offering partial ownership to other investors? As a team, create a list of advantages and disadvantages of each method of raising capital.

Business Insight

Digitization

Today it seems that everything is digital. The digits are the binary 0 and 1 codes used by computers to represent data. The idea of binary code originated in the 17th century, but its use in computers started in 1946 with ENIAC, the Electronic Numerical Integrator and Calculator. The digitization revolution brings products and services directly to devices. Expanding digital bandwidth allows for more parts of our lives to be digitized and delivered.

Generations born before 1985 have witnessed this digital transformation. At one time music was primarily played over a radio or cut into tracks on vinyl records. By the early 1980s, music was digitized and placed on CDs that contained 10 to 15 "tracks." Today, you can choose the songs you want and load them on your digital device or receive a streaming digital music service. Newspapers, books, and magazines used to be the primary source of reading material. Now these information sources have become digitized and are available on any Web-connected device for immediate download and use. The digitization of video has had an impact beyond talking to friends or streaming movies and television shows. Doctors engage in telemedicine, teachers digitize lectures and courses, and businesses save money by teleconferencing.

Digitization allows information to travel from device to device over the Internet. As the power and speed of computers continues to grow, we will see more parts of our lives become digitized. We'll ask our phones to answer our questions about digitization.

Think Critically

1. Identify a product or service that is accessed digitally through a device. Research how this product or service was accessed before it was digitized. How does digitization change the delivery of this product or service?
2. Describe a product or service that you believe will be digitized in the future. Explain how users will benefit from this change.

Work as a TEAM

After students have discussed the question and developed their lists, ask them whether their decision might be different based on the type of business or whether the business was new or well established.

TEACH

List the six basic business activities on the board. As you introduce each one, ask students to think about two questions: How does the activity contribute to business success? If the activity is not done well, what problems might result? Discuss students' answers to the questions.

Business Insight

Technology allows companies to serve individual needs and wants in a cost-efficient manner. Ask students to suggest benefits and potential drawbacks of digitization.

Think Critically *Answers*

1. Answers will vary. Students should provide specific examples of products or services and explain how these were formerly accessed and how they are now delivered digitally.

2. Answers will vary. Students should describe specific ideas for how products or services will be delivered and how users will benefit.

Different Learning Abilities

Visually Impaired Help students to locate government websites and services that have been developed to effectively accommodate citizens with visual impairments. Assign students to write a brief report on the accommodations that have been made and any ways they believe further accommodation could be provided.

ONGOING ASSESSMENT

CHECKPOINT ✓ ANSWER

The six basic activities completed by all businesses are generating ideas, raising capital, employing and training personnel, buying goods and services, marketing goods and services, and maintaining business records.

TEACH

For each of the three major categories of businesses, instruct students to identify some local businesses that fit into the category. Ask students whether they believe the community has more businesses that are producers, intermediaries, or service businesses.

THINK CRITICALLY THROUGH VISUALS

Effective marketing can provide consumers with the information they need to make the decision to purchase products and services, plus the information to obtain easy access to them.

A retailer buys an assortment of products to sell to customers. It must also buy the display equipment, computers, and cleaning supplies used to operate the business. Businesses purchase an array of services from other companies. These include advertising, legal and accounting services, lawn care and building maintenance, and security.

Marketing Goods and Services Marketing refers to the activities directed at providing the goods and services wanted by a business's customers. Without marketing, even the best products and services may remain unsold. Businesses need to understand and perform many marketing activities. They must satisfy customers who usually can choose to buy from competitors offering similar products and services.

Maintaining Business Records All businesses must have some type of record-keeping system. Owners and managers need records to track performance and make decisions. Customers need information about orders and payments. Businesses are required by government to keep records and submit information. Today, technology helps make record keeping easy and accurate. With computer technology, business owners and employees can quickly access information needed to understand business performance and solve problems.

> **CHECKPOINT ✓**
> What are the six basic activities completed by all businesses?

LO 5.1.3

TYPES OF BUSINESSES

You use a variety of businesses to buy the things you want and need. You recognize other businesses but never use them. You don't even know about many others. There are three major categories of businesses—producers, intermediaries, and service businesses.

Producers

Producers create the products and services used by individuals and other businesses. They are responsible for using resources to make something that is needed by others. Businesses that take resources from nature for direct consumption or for use in developing other products are *extractors*. Extractors pump oil, mine coal, or cut timber. *Farmers* cultivate land and use other natural resources to grow crops and raise livestock for consumption. *Manufacturers* get supplies from other producers and convert them into products. They sell their products to consumers and other businesses.

Business activities start with producers. A builder obtains lumber, cement, shingles, carpet, and paint to construct a house, factory, or office building. A cereal manufacturer buys wheat and oats, sugar, and dried fruit as well as cardboard, glue, and ink to process and package your favorite breakfast food.

Sean Pavone/Shutterstock.com

How does marketing affect a consumer's decision to purchase a product?

Different Learning Abilities

At-Risk Ask students to write a short paragraph identifying and explaining which type of business they would rather own—production, intermediary, or service business. Encourage students to give examples and illustrate their work.

Intermediaries

Intermediaries are businesses involved in selling the goods and services of producers to consumers and other businesses. The most common types of intermediaries are retailers and wholesalers. Many other businesses focus on one or a few activities that assist in distributing and selling products and services. Specialized intermediaries include transportation companies, advertising agencies, storage centers, sales offices, and data-processing centers.

Service Businesses

Many businesses do not make products. They offer something that is intangible, meaning it has no physical qualities. A **service business** carries out activities that are consumed by its customers. It does not offer products for sale. Service businesses include dentists, physicians, and lawyers as well as pet sitters, painters, and furniture movers. New types of service businesses are Internet service providers, web designers, and online travel agents. Businesses as well as final consumers use services. A business might contact an international trade specialist to help it set up a sale to a new customer in Africa. A communications firm could design and install a new phone system for large telemarketing businesses.

Service businesses are the fastest-growing part of the economy. More than 60 percent of all U.S. employment is now in service-producing businesses. While you often hear about low-pay and low-skill service jobs, there are many new businesses offering professional and technical services requiring highly educated employees.

CHECKPOINT ✓
How does a manufacturer differ from an extractor?

5.1 ASSESSMENT

Key Concepts

Determine the best answer.

1. The largest number of U.S. businesses employ
   - **a.** more than 100 people
   - **b.** between 50 and 100 people
   - **c.** between 10 and 20 people
   - **d.** no employees other than the owner
2. Which of the following is not one of the common activities of all businesses?
   - **a.** producing goods and services
   - **b.** employing and training personnel
   - **c.** marketing goods and services
   - **d.** maintaining business records
3. A retailer is an example of a(n)
   - **a.** extractor
   - **b.** producer
   - **c.** intermediary
   - **d.** service business

Make Academic Connections

4. **Math** If 42 percent of all people working in the United States are baby boomers, how many were working in 2016? If 15 percent of the baby boomers retire within 10 years, how many jobs will this represent from 2016 employment? Use an employment figure of 155 million to make the calculations.
5. **Visual Arts** Select a product that involves all of the types of businesses in its production and marketing. Draw an illustration that shows each business and its role in the successful production and sale of the product. Title your illustration and label the component parts.

RETEACH Ask students to write two ideas they learned from the lesson that help to describe the role of businesses in the U.S. economy. Instruct each student to read his or her ideas. Discuss and clarify the ideas to ensure understanding.

ENRICH Assign students to contact and interview the human resources director for a major company in your community. The interview should focus on the changes and challenges in employment facing the company.

TEACH

Ask students to identify service businesses with which they are familiar. Encourage them to think about businesses that offer professional and technical services and employ a number of highly educated employees.

ONGOING ASSESSMENT

CHECKPOINT ✓ANSWER

An extractor takes natural resources, such as oil or timber, for direct consumption or for use in developing other products. A manufacturer takes resources supplied by others and converts them into useable products.

ASSESS

Key Concepts *Answers*

1. d. no employees other than the owner

2. a. producing goods and services

3. c. intermediary

Make Academic Connections *Answers*

4. In 2008: 155,000,000 × 42% = 65,100,000

65,100,000 × 15% = 9,765,000

5. Answers will vary depending on the product selected. Illustrations should depict the business and its role in the production and sale of the product.

CLOSE Remind students that the business world and employment opportunities have changed a great deal in the lifetimes of their parents and grandparents. Ask them what changes they predict will occur in their lifetimes.

Focus on REAL LIFE

Point out that owning a company's stock makes you a business owner. Ask students how stockholders can influence the success of a company.

TEACH

Ask each student to indicate whether they would like to own their own business or not. Ask volunteers to explain why they are interested or not interested in owning their own business.

THINK CRITICALLY THROUGH VISUALS

Advantages of owning your own business include being in control, making your own decisions, and investing your money to make a profit. Disadvantages include having sole responsibility for the success of the business, having to satisfy creditors, and making a profit.

Life-Span Plan Answer

Answers will vary. Students who have a goal of owning a business should describe a logical series of steps they could take to achieve their goal.

5.2 Forms of Business Ownership

Learning Outcomes

5.2.1 Understand the three major forms of business ownership.

5.2.2 Determine when each form of business ownership is most appropriate.

5.2.3 Recognize other specialized business ownership forms.

Key Terms

proprietorship 106	partnership agreement 108
partnership 107	articles of incorporation 109
corporation 107	franchise 111

Focus on REAL LIFE

Jaden keyed in the ticker symbol APPL at his favorite financial website. He was checking the listing of the stock he owned—Apple.

Jaden's grandparents had given him five shares of stock in Apple when he was born. He didn't get interested in it until recently when he learned more about the stock market. Now he knew he was an owner of the technology company. The success of the company determined the value of his ownership. While the stock price had gone up and down, it was now at its highest point since he began following it.

LO 5.2.1

BUSINESS OWNERSHIP FORMS

Many people think they would like to own a business. The chance to be in control, make decisions, and invest money to make a profit is challenging and exciting. Thousands of people are business owners. The amount of control they have, how decisions are made, the sources of money for the business, and control over profits is not the same for every business owner. The form of ownership affects each of those aspects of the business.

There are three major forms of business ownership—proprietorship, partnership, and corporation. There are also several other specialized forms of ownership.

Life-Span Plan

Is owning a business something you might want to explore as you plan your future? What kind of businesses might you consider? What steps do you need to take now to make owning a business part of your life-span plan?

Proprietorship

A **proprietorship** is a business owned and run by just one person. It is the easiest form of business to start and end. There

Kali Nine LLC/Shutterstock.com

What are the advantages and disadvantages of owning your own business?

Applied Skills

Writing Across the Curriculum Assign students to prepare a paragraph that shows the connection between successful business ownership and what they are learning in another class they are currently taking.

U.S. BUSINESS COMPARISON BY FORM OF OWNERSHIP				
	NUMBER OF BUSINESSES (2008)	TOTAL REVENUE (THOUSANDS)	PERCENT OF ALL BUSINESSES	PERCENT OF TOTAL REVENUE
Proprietorship	22,614,483	1,317,443,005	71.55%	3.93%
Corporation	5,847,000	27,266,000,000	18.50%	81.28%
Partnership	3,146,000	4,963,000,000	9.95%	14.79%
TOTAL	31,607,483	33,546,443,005	100.00%	100%

Source: U.S. Census

FIGURE 5-2
Why are there so many proprietorships?

are very few legal requirements regarding the business ownership or capital needs that must be met.

Many individuals favor the proprietorship form of ownership. It gives them sole control over all business decisions. The owner receives all profits made by the business. He or she can determine how those profits are used. The owner is also responsible for all debts of the business. If the business fails, the owner has almost no shelter from creditors. Any money and other assets owned by the proprietor, whether used in the business or not, can be claimed by creditors to pay the business debts.

Partnership

A **partnership** is a business owned and controlled by two or more people who have entered into an agreement. A partnership is very similar to a proprietorship in several ways. It is quite easy to start. The owners are both responsible for key business decisions and functions. The partners share both investments and profits based on the terms of the partnership agreement. Each partner is liable for all of the debts of the business should it fail.

Corporation

A **corporation** is a separate legal entity formed by documents filed with a state. It is owned by one or more shareholders and managed by a board of directors. Most corporations have several owners who invest in the business by purchasing shares of stock. Corporations are more difficult to form than either proprietorships or partnerships. They must also meet more legal requirements. Not all owners have direct involvement in decision making about business functions. They will not have access to profits unless the board of directors approves it. Corporations protect the liability of stockholders to only the amount of money they have invested.

Most U.S. businesses are organized as proprietorships. However, as shown in Figure 5-2, proprietorships have a very small percentage of business revenues.

CHECKPOINT ✓
What are the differences between the three main forms of business ownership?

LO 5.2.2

CHOOSING A FORM OF BUSINESS OWNERSHIP

When a new business is started, the owner should carefully consider the form of ownership. While it is possible to change the form of ownership for an existing business, it is best to decide which form to use both for the long-term future of the business as well as for its first few years.

Different Learning Styles

Visual Learner Instruct students to create a chart or poster to illustrate the major differences among the three types of business ownership. Encourage students to use words, numbers, and pictures as they work on their chart or poster.

▸ **Figure 5-2** ***ANSWER***
Several answers are possible. Proprietorships may be so prevalent because they are so easy to form.

TEACH

Tell students that effective partners often complement each other in that one offers skills and abilities the other does not possess. Ask each student to identify skills and abilities they might look for in a partner that would complement those that they possess.

ONGOING ASSESSMENT

CHECKPOINT ✓***ANSWER***
Business forms differ in the ways in which decision making and investments are made and to whom liabilities are distributed. A sole proprietorship is owned by one person. One person is responsible for all decisions and financial liability and that person solely benefits from all profits. A partnership is owned and controlled by two or more partners who share investments, decisions, liability, and profits. A corporation is owned by shareholders and managed by a board of directors. Not all owners share decisions. Their liability is limited to the amount they invest. They only share profits as the board approves.

TEACH

Ask students to identify problems a business can face if it attempts to change the form of business ownership.

Work as a TEAM

After students have identified possible businesses, they should create a name for the business that identifies the uniqueness of each partner.

TEACH

Tell students that, because starting a proprietorship is so easy, it often leads to business failure. Without careful thought and planning, the proprietor may not be well prepared for the challenges he or she will likely face.

THINK CRITICALLY THROUGH VISUALS

A partnership might be more advantageous than a proprietorship because two owners can share the responsibilities and costs of the business, as well as combining their expertise.

Work as a TEAM

Businesses achieve goals through teamwork. Think of teammates you would like to work with. Compare the unique interests and skills of each member of your team. Identify possible businesses that could be formed as a partnership by combining the talents of two or more team members.

Choosing a Proprietorship

Most businesses begin as a proprietorship. They remain in that form as long as the sole owner operates the business. Often people choose to start a business because they prefer the freedom of working for themselves rather than for another person. They want to be in total control of the business. Many new business owners have limited knowledge of the forms of ownership and want to start their businesses in the simplest way. Some people form a business from a hobby or operate a business on a part-time basis. They may expand the business over a few years while spending little time thinking about other ways the business could be organized.

Starting a proprietorship is easy. You just have to begin buying and selling as a business. You don't even need a business name. You do need to obtain any required government licenses and permits. You will need to account for income and expenses and pay taxes on the profits of the business. If operating the business for several years will be your primary job, it is best to choose a name for the business. You will need to register the name with local, state, and federal governments.

A proprietorship provides a tax advantage for the owner. All income is taxed as a part of your personal income. Many business expenses can be used to reduce the income. That benefit also carries the most significant disadvantage of a proprietorship. In the eyes of the law, the owner is the same as the business. Any debts of the business are the responsibility of the owner. Personal assets not connected to the business will be seized to pay business debts if business assets are not adequate to cover those debts. As a result, a failed business may cause its owner to lose almost everything.

For people who want total independence, do not want to be exposed to significant government regulation, want to be in control of all business decisions, and are willing to take on the entire risk of a business, the proprietorship offers an effective form of ownership. For a person who wants to expand the business, is willing to share control and decision-making in return for additional resources and reduced risk, and wants some protection for money invested, other forms of ownership are better.

Choosing a Partnership

A partnership is a bit more complex and formal than a proprietorship. In many states, a partnership can be formed by the verbal agreement of two or more people. It is usually better to have a written partnership agreement. The **partnership agreement** is a written agreement among

iStockphoto.com/Susan Chiang

How might a partnership be more advantageous than a proprietorship?

Different Learning Abilities

Gifted Assign students to meet with an accountant or other tax specialist to learn more about how the income of proprietorships, partnerships, and corporations are taxed differently. Assign students to report their findings to the class.

Specific Learning Disability (SLD) Give students a business or telephone directory. Ask them to locate a business that is clearly a partnership and another that is clearly a corporation. Students should explain why each fits the category.

all owners. It details the rules and procedures that guide ownership and operations. It typically identifies the business name, the investments, and other contributions of each partner. The agreement shows how profits and losses will be divided among the partners. It defines the authority and responsibilities granted to each person and how the partnership can be dissolved. Most states require that partnerships register a business name as well as the name of each person in the partnership.

The advantage of a partnership is that two or more people can contribute to the investment needed to start a business and provide the expertise required to run it. At the same time, each partner is responsible for decisions made by all other partners. There is no protection for the personal assets of any partner. If the business fails, each person can lose much more than the amount of the original investment. If a partner chooses to leave the partnership or dies, the partnership normally must be dissolved.

A partnership is a good ownership form for people who share an idea for a business. They want to cooperate in managing and investing in the business. It is the easiest form for people who work well together and want to share the risks and rewards of the business. It has the same liability of a proprietorship and presents problems if other people want to join the partnership or if it needs to be dissolved.

Choosing a Corporation

Most people think of corporations as very large businesses. Indeed, corporations are the most popular form of ownership for large businesses. Incorporation is an increasingly popular option for new and small businesses as well. Corporations are subject to many more laws and are more difficult to form than either proprietorships or partnerships. They offer a number of advantages to the owners as well.

FYI Proprietors must pay self-employment taxes in addition to their income tax. Self-employment taxes are contributions to Medicare and Social Security. People employed by another business have those payments deducted from their paychecks, and employers contribute half of the required payments.

A corporation is treated as though it were an "individual" by governments. It must follow the laws of the state in which it is organized. To form a corporation, you must file articles of incorporation with the appropriate state government office. The **articles of incorporation** is a written legal document that defines ownership and operating procedures and conditions for the business. Each state has specific information that must be included. States usually provide a form for this purpose. The business must create *corporate bylaws*, or the operating procedures for the corporation. It must name a *board of directors*, the people who will make the major policy and financial decisions for the business. The corporation also issues shares of stock to investors and determines whether future stock shares will be distributed or sold.

Even though a corporation is more difficult to form and is subject to more government rules, it offers several advantages to owners. The liability of any owner is limited to the amount of money invested. The amount of debt of the business does not matter. People can invest in the business and receive some of the profit without having to take part in the day-to-day management and operations. It is easy for a corporation to expand. Ownership can change with the sale of stock.

Disadvantages of corporate ownership are that decision making is shared among managers, the board of directors, and shareholders. Many more records are

FYI

Explain to students that because proprietors pay all their Medicare and Social Security tax and employees only pay half, proprietors face a greater tax burden.

TEACH

Most states have a relatively simple form that a small business can use to prepare the articles of incorporation for their business. Locate a copy from your state or an adjoining state and let students examine it to observe that it does not have to be a complex document.

Portfolio Activity

Assign the Portfolio Activity for Chapter 5, located on the product website.

COLLECT Point out that students can use the list of key terms in Lesson 5.2 for the business categories.

CREATE Encourage students to explore their options before settling on a visual medium.

CONNECT Remind students that they should incorporate their visuals in their presentations.

ONGOING ASSESSMENT

CHECKPOINT ✓ ANSWER

The corporation is more complex to begin than other business forms. Forming a corporation requires much more bureaucracy, is more subject to government regulations, requires the organization of a board, and necessitates the establishment of clearly defined bylaws.

TEACH

For each of the specialized forms of business ownership, ask students to identify why they believe it could be preferable to one of the traditional forms of ownership.

THINK CRITICALLY THROUGH VISUALS

Answers will vary. Encourage students to think about the businesses they frequent, organizations they have heard about, and services they use. Encourage volunteers to share their answers and create a master list on the board.

required and more laws regulate operations than for other forms of ownership. Because corporations are treated as individuals by governments, they must pay corporate taxes on profits earned. Then the investors also pay taxes on their individual earnings from the business.

CHECKPOINT ✓

Which form of business ownership is the most complex and difficult to form?

LO 5.2.3

OTHER FORMS OF OWNERSHIP

Most businesses are organized as one of the three common forms just discussed. However, there are other choices of ownership. Some are specialized forms of partnerships and corporations. Others are totally unique forms.

Specialized Partnerships and Corporations

In a general partnership, all partners take part in ownership and operation of the business. A *limited liability partnership* identifies some investors who cannot lose more than the amount of their investment, but they are not allowed to participate in the day-to-day management of the business. This type of partnership is difficult and costly to establish. A *joint venture* is a unique business organized by two or more other businesses to operate for a limited time and for a specific project. It is a type of partnership.

A corporate form that is favored by many small businesses is the S corporation. An *S corporation* offers the limited liability of a corporation. All income is passed through to the owners based on their investment and is taxed on their individual tax returns. A newer ownership form is the limited liability company (LLC). It combines the best features of a partnership and a corporation. A *limited liability company* provides liability protection for owners. It has a simpler set of organizing and operating requirements than a corporation. No articles of incorporation or bylaws are needed. A simple document much like a partnership agreement must be developed.

A *nonprofit corporation* is a group of people who join to do some activity that benefits the public. They work in areas such as education, health care, charity, or the arts. Nonprofit corporations are free from corporate income taxes. They can raise funds by receiving grants and donations from individuals and businesses. As with other corporations, they must organize as a corporation. The government must approve their purpose and operations.

Cooperatives and Franchises

Sometimes a group of people forms a cooperative to provide goods and services that they all need. A *cooperative* is owned by members, serves their needs, and is managed in their interest. Members form a consumer cooperative

iStockphoto.com/leezsnow

What forms of corporate business ownership exist in your community?

Applied Skills

Building Study Skills Assign students to prepare an outline with each of the common and specialized forms of business ownership as a major heading. Ask them to prepare a study guide by listing the major features of each form under the appropriate heading. Consider allowing students to work in pairs.

so that they can purchase goods and services more cheaply as a group than they could individually. A business cooperative forms to market the products produced by members or to purchase products needed by the members. Large numbers of small businesses will have greater bargaining power than the individual businesses.

A **franchise** is a written contract granting permission to operate a business to sell products and services in a set way. The company that owns the product or service and grants the rights to another business is known as the *franchiser*. The company or person purchasing the rights to run the business is the *franchisee*. A franchise is a way to expand a business using the investments of others while maintaining control over the name, product quality, and operating procedures.

The franchisee maintains day-to-day operations and receives the profits of the business. It pays a fee and percentage of the profits to the franchiser in return for operating assistance. Some popular and successful franchises include Jiffy Lube, Century 21 real estate offices, Mail Boxes Etc., 7-Eleven, Merry Maids, Dunkin' Donuts, Anytime Fitness, and Subway.

CHECKPOINT ✓
What are the other specialized forms of business ownership?

5.2 ASSESSMENT

Key Concepts

Determine the best answer.

1. The form of ownership that gives one person sole control over all business decisions is the
   a. proprietorship
   b. partnership
   c. corporation
   d. franchise
2. True or False. All investors in a general partnership have full liability for the debts of the business.
3. The people who make the major policy and financial decisions in a corporation are the
   a. investors
   b. board of directors
   c. managers
   d. owners
4. A special form of business organization that combines advantages of a corporation and a partnership is a
   a. franchise
   b. nonprofit corporation
   c. cooperative
   d. limited liability company

Make Academic Connections

5. **Communication** Two friends who want to open a store to sell the work of local artists ask you to explain the advantages and disadvantages of the three common forms of business ownership. Write a memo outlining the advantages and disadvantages. Include a list of questions that might help your friends make a decision.
6. **Research** Go online to find information on a franchise opportunity related to a current career interest. Prepare a table that describes the franchise, the products or services, the investment requirements, and the benefits of becoming a franchisee.
7. **Read** Find a news article about cooperatives or a specific cooperative. Read the article and write a reaction. Respond as if you were posting an online comment for other readers to see. Prepare a properly formatted citation for the article. Possible sources include printed and online versions of newspapers or magazines. You should also consider independent online sources that produce original content.

TEACH

Ask students to use the telephone directory to identify any business and consumer cooperatives that operate in your community.

ONGOING ASSESSMENT

CHECKPOINT ✓ANSWER

Specialized forms of business ownership include limited liability partnerships, joint ventures, S corporations, limited liability companies (LLC), and nonprofit corporations. Cooperatives and franchises could also be discussed here.

ASSESS

Key Concepts *Answers*

1. a. proprietorship
2. True
3. b. board of directors
4. d. limited liability company

Make Academic Connections *Answers*

5. Memos will vary but should include the advantages and disadvantages mentioned in this lesson. The questions should reflect an understanding of how the forms of ownership differ.
6. Tables will vary depending on the franchise selected. Charts should include all the information listed in the instructions.
7. Answers will vary depending on the article selected.

CLOSE Ask students to write a brief description of the three common forms of business ownership without referring to the lesson or their notes. Have students read their answers aloud and compare them with those of other students.

RETEACH Working in teams of three, ask each team member to assume the role of a proprietor, partner, or corporate stockholder. Members should the explain the pros and cons of their ownership form to the team.

ENRICH Instruct students to go online to determine the percentage of businesses in one state by the number of employees. Ask them to prepare a chart of the results and present the information to other students.

LIFE/WORK SKILLS

Many people of all ages own shares of stock in companies. For those who do not, it is often because they do not understand how to evaluate and compare stocks. If you are comfortable with reading stock data, you are more likely to purchase stock.

Think Critically *Answers*

1. Answers will vary. A stock owner would likely find the Dividend Yield and the Closing Price to be the most important and the 52 Week Hi-Lo to be the least important.

2. Stock data provides the Yield of the Dividend Paid information, which makes it easier to compare stocks that have different prices.

LIFE/WORK SKILLS

CRITICAL THINKING AND PROBLEM SOLVING

Knowing how to understand financial stock data is an important life skill. People who own stock or are interested in buying stock must be able to evaluate those stocks. Historically, stock data was found in stock tables available in most daily newspapers. Websites are now the primary sources of stock data. Websites can track the daily performance of the stocks and provide historical trends. To determine how well a company is performing, investors must track more than just the stock price over time.

Investors need to decide whether to maintain their investment, buy additional stock, or sell and move their money to another investment. To make these decisions, investors will look at the following stock data.

Symbol (SYM) is the company symbol or abbreviation that identifies the firm issuing the stock. The symbol is an abbreviation for a longer company name. For example, the symbol for International Business Machines Corporation is IBM. In this example, the symbol is XMPL.

Dividends are the amount of money approved by the board of directors of the company to be paid to stockholders. Dividends may be indicated as DIV in a table or D on a chart. Dividends are another way that stockholders earn a return on their investment in addition to gains in the value of the stock. High growth stocks may pay low dividends. Utility stocks may not have high growth, but they often pay steady dividends.

Yield (YLD) is the current rate of return on all capital invested in the company. This allows easier comparison of the performance of companies with different stock prices. The yield is calculated by dividing the total annual dividends by the stock price.

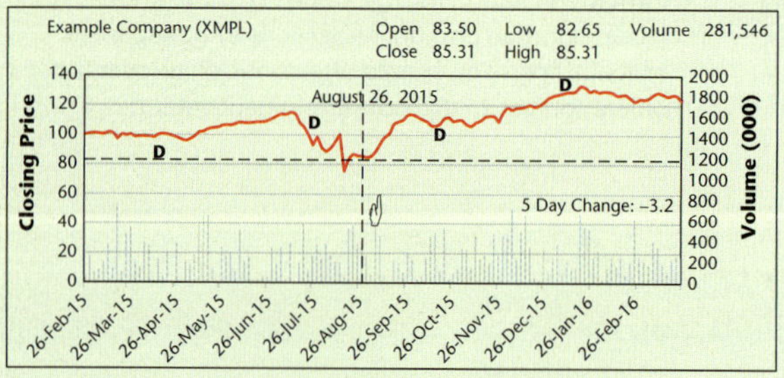

$$\frac{\text{Dividends}}{\text{Price}} = \frac{\$5.82}{\$127.00} = 4.58\%\ \text{yield}$$

Price to Earnings (PE) Ratio is the comparison of the price per share to the earnings per share. It shows how much an investor is willing to pay for $1 of current earnings by one share of stock. The ratio is calculated by dividing the price by the earnings per share (EPS). In the example, XMPL stock is selling for more than 10 times the current earnings.

$$\frac{\text{Price}}{\text{EPS}} = \frac{\$127.00}{\$12.06} = 10.53\ \text{PE}$$

Many websites allow for stock charting. These charts can provide daily or historical data. Many charts can show historic data by placing a cursor over the stock price line. In this example, the cursor is over August 16, 2015. The display may show the **HI-LO** data representing the highest and lowest prices of all trades made during the time period such as daily HI-LO or 52 week HI-LO. Some charts will feature daily bars showing highs and lows. Charts can show opening (O) and the last price at which a trade was made during the trading day or closing (C) price. In the XMPL example, $85.31 is the closing price.

Percent Change is the percent difference between the current closing price and a previous closing price. The stock price five days ago was $127.97 and today's closing price is $124, the percent change listed shows a negative 3.2%.

Volume shows the volume of shares traded at the date in the chart. Volume gives information on the change in demand for the company's shares. In the example, 281,546 shares of XMPL were traded.

Think Critically

1. What information from the stock data do you think is most important for a stock owner to watch on a regular basis? What is the least important?
2. How does stock data help in comparing the performance of two stocks with very different prices?

Applied Skills

Technology Assign students to select and track a stock for one week. Students should use a spreadsheet program to prepare a stock table example, as shown in the Life/Work Skills example. The table should show information for each of the five days in the business week.

5.3 Organizational Structure for Businesses

Learning Outcomes

5.3.1 Understand important principles in designing an effective organization.

5.3.2 Compare alternative organizational structures for businesses.

Key Terms

mission statement 113
goal 113
policies 114
procedures 114
organization chart 115

Focus on REAL LIFE

Mary Jo's company has just approved a policy that allows some employees to telecommute. This means employees can work from home and complete their work using a computer and other technology. Mary Jo is interested in the idea but isn't sure if she should apply.

She is afraid she might not be as motivated to complete her work every day if she doesn't have to go to the office and keep a regular schedule. She also is concerned that it may be much more difficult to communicate with coworkers and get feedback from her manager using the technology. Mary Jo also wonders if she will be viewed as a productive and valued employee if people don't see her at work every day.

LO 5.3.1

DESIGNING AN EFFECTIVE BUSINESS ORGANIZATION

It is not easy to create a successful business. Many new businesses fail in the first few years. Few businesses maintain their success for the lifetime of the owner. Successful businesses need more than a good product or service. Skilled managers, well-prepared and motivated employees, adequate resources, and effective procedures all contribute to business success. A business needs to be well organized to help people do their work properly. An effective business begins with a clear purpose and the application of key principles for organizing work.

Setting Direction

The direction for a business comes from its **mission statement**. A mission statement is a short, specific written statement of the reason a business exists and what it wants to achieve. Here is an example from Starbucks: *To inspire and nurture the human spirit—one person, one cup and one neighborhood at a time.*

After a mission statement is developed, the business sets goals. A **goal** is a precise statement of results the business

How does effective organization help a business "hit the mark"?

Photodisc/Getty Images

Focus on REAL LIFE

Ask students to define telecommuting. Ask them whether they believe it will become more popular in the future or whether employees will prefer to work face to face with their colleagues.

TEACH

Ask students to brainstorm a list of factors that would suggest an organization is effective and then do the same for factors that would suggest an organization is ineffective. Ask them to review the lists and discuss why some organizations are effective while others are not.

THINK CRITICALLY THROUGH VISUALS

Effective organization provides a business with a clear purpose and key principles to follow that help employees and managers do their work well.

Applied Skills

Language Arts Ask students to imagine that they are the owner of a fitness center. Students should write a two-sentence mission statement for their business that describes the reason the business exists and what they want the business to achieve. Consider allowing students to work in pairs.

FYI

Explain to students that while a proprietorship offers the security of continued involvement in the enterprise, established businesses are much more likely to keep their doors open.

TEACH

Discuss with students what will happen if an employee has authority for an activity, but does not take responsibility for it. Then discuss the effect of giving an employee an important responsibility, but no authority to get it done. How can businesses make sure employees have both the needed authority and responsibility for their work?

THINK CRITICALLY THROUGH VISUALS

Answers will vary. Some organizational roles that students might mention include manager, worker, supervisor, coach, player, captain, and director. Encourage students to think of a specific organization as they describe roles.

FYI In a recent Junior Achievement survey, 41 percent of teens believe starting and operating their own business will offer greater job security than being an employee in another company. Nearly 75 percent of the teens indicated they would like to start their own business someday.

expects to achieve. Goals are used to define what needs to be accomplished and to determine if the business is successful. An example of a goal for an automobile manufacturer is "to produce the top-rated brand for quality and customer satisfaction."

Finally, the business sets policies and procedures for the organization. **Policies** are guidelines used in making consistent decisions. **Procedures** are descriptions of the way work is to be done. Effective policies and procedures provide guidance and direction to people working in the organization.

Principles of Effective Organization

When several people work together, their work needs to be organized so they work together well and achieve their tasks. Several principles guide the effective organization of work.

Responsibility, Authority, and Accountability *Responsibility* is the obligation to complete specific work. *Authority* is the right to make decisions about how responsibilities should be accomplished. *Accountability* is taking responsibility for the results achieved. In an effective organization, all managers and employees have a set of responsibilities as a part of their jobs. With every job assignment, they know they have the authority to make the decisions and obtain the resources needed to complete the assignment. They know they will be recognized and rewarded if they are successful. They will be held accountable if the work is not completed well.

Matthew Jacques/Shutterstock.com

In an organization, every member has a specific role to fill. Describe some roles.

Different Learning Abilities

Attention Deficit Disorder Tell students to think of a specific task they complete regularly, such as brushing their teeth or using an ATM. Ask them to carefully review how they complete the task and list at least four procedures they use in the correct order necessary for completion.

Unity of Command A key organizing principle is unity of command. *Unity of command* means there is a clear reporting relationship for all staff of a business. If there is confusion in assignments and unclear relationships among people who are working together, it will be hard for people to know what to do or where to go for help. For each work assignment, people need to know who is the leader and how decisions will be made.

Span of Control The last organizing principle is span of control. *Span of control* is the number of employees who are assigned to a particular work task and manager. A large number of people working with little support from their manager cannot be effective. In the same way, a manager with only a very small number of people may provide too much control. Organizations need to make sure that workers have a balance of supervision and freedom to do their work. The span of control for well-trained, experienced, and motivated employees can be much greater than the span of control for new and inexperienced employees who are not enthused about their work.

CHECKPOINT ✓
What is the difference between a mission statement and a goal?

LO 5.3.2

TYPES OF ORGANIZATIONAL STRUCTURES

When only one person works in a business, there is little need for an organizational structure. The sole employee is responsible for all of the work. When more people are hired, there will need to be an agreement on what work each person will do and if one person has authority over the work of others. An **organization chart** is a diagram that shows the structure of an organization, classifications of work and jobs, and the relationships among those classifications. You can see a simple organization chart for a business in Figure 5-3.

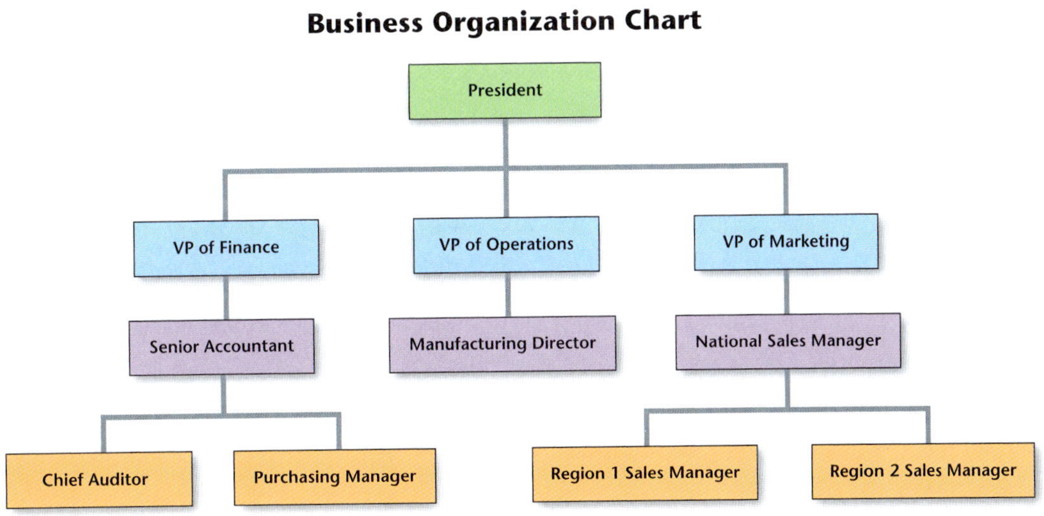

FIGURE 5-3
Why is it important for employees to understand the structure of the company where they work?

TEACH

Ask students how they would know if there is unity of command in a business. Suggest that no one would report to more than one person, and there would be no confusion about what work is to be done and who is responsible.

ONGOING ASSESSMENT

CHECKPOINT ✓ANSWER

A mission statement communicates the purpose of existence for a business and what it hopes to achieve. A goal is a more specific statement of what a business expects to achieve and may be used to measure a business's success.

TEACH

Locate several different organization charts representing different types and sizes of businesses. Show the charts to students, and then ask them to identify what the organizations have in common and what is different in the way they are organized.

▶ **Figure 5-3 *ANSWER***

Employees need to understand the structure of their company so that they know who has authority in different areas and who is responsible for different organizational functions. They will also know how activities are related and what types of activities occur in the company.

Applied Skills

Technology Instruct students to work together to design a sample organizational chart for a movie theater. Encourage students to use a computer, along with a drawing program or other software, to complete this assignment. Organization charts can be created using word processing or presentation software.

Work as a TEAM

Ask students why the goal listed is important in identifying the tasks and establishing the organization of the team.

TEACH

Ask students to compare the functional organization and the matrix organization from the viewpoints of a manager and an employee. Would one or the other usually be better, or would it depend on the individual who is the manager or the employee?

ONGOING ASSESSMENT

CHECKPOINT ✓ ANSWER

Employees in a functional organizational structure may tend to lose sight of overall corporate goals. Workers tend to be limited to specific duties and may not see their relationship to the organization as a whole. This can result in lack of interest and motivation over time.

ASSESS

Key Concepts *Answers*

1. True
2. a. responsibility
3. c. job descriptions

Make Academic Connections *Answers*

4. Answers will vary depending on the mission statements selected. Ratings should demonstrate an understanding of the purpose of a mission statement.

5. Although charts will vary depending on the school, they should show an organization structured around specific projects, products, or customer groups.

Work as a TEAM

Your class is responsible for selling advertising for the school's yearbook. Work as a team to identify the tasks that will need to be completed to sell 50 ads in the next three weeks. Describe how a project team can be organized to achieve that goal.

Functional Organization Structure Most businesses use a *functional organizational structure*. In this type of organization, work is arranged within main business functions such as production, operations, marketing, and human resources. All of the people with jobs related to one of the functions will work together. They report to managers who are responsible for that function. The advantage of a functional organization is that people work with others who have the same skills. A drawback is that people become more focused on their specific function than on the success of the whole business. Often, people working in one function have little interaction with people in other parts of the business.

Matrix Organizational Structure A newer organizational structure designed to overcome the drawbacks of the functional structure is the matrix organization. In a *matrix organizational structure*, work is structured around specific projects, products, or customer groups. People with varied backgrounds are assigned together because their expertise is required for the project or to serve the customer. The assignment may be temporary or long term.

A matrix organization can be interesting and motivating to employees. They work with many different people. They are focused on a specific project or task. However, it can be confusing and inefficient without effective leadership and communication.

CHECKPOINT ✓

What problems can result from the use of a functional organizational structure?

5.3 ASSESSMENT

Key Concepts

Determine the best answer.

1. True or False. Policies and procedures help provide direction for a business.
2. The obligation to complete specific work is
   a. responsibility
   b. authority
   c. accountability
   d. recognition
3. Which of the following is not shown on an organizational chart?
   a. the structure of an organization
   b. work relationships
   c. job descriptions
   d. classifications of jobs

Make Academic Connections

4. **Technology** Use the Internet to collect examples of the mission statements of five businesses. Rate each mission statement in terms of how effectively it communicates the purpose and direction of the company.
5. **Critical Thinking** Many schools are organized using a functional organizational structure. Teachers are organized into departments such as English, Mathematics, Science, and Business. How could a school be organized using a matrix structure? Design an organizational chart that illustrates a matrix structure for your school. Describe the advantages and disadvantages of the matrix structure as applied to a school.

RETEACH Working in teams, have students review the lesson and write two quiz questions for each learning outcome. Teams should exchange questions and answer without looking at the text or their notes.

ENRICH Students can search online for sample organizational charts to share with the class.

CLOSE Ask students to list the things they believe will contribute the most to an effective organization.

BUSINESS IMPROVING SOCIETY

ELECTRICITY WHERE THERE WAS NONE

More than 25 percent of the world's population does not have electricity. No electricity means no water pumps, no lights, no refrigerators, and no real chance for a better life. Knowing that electricity is crucial to improving the standard of living, some young innovators have devised strategies to help bring electricity to their communities.

At 22 years old, Fabio Rosa was named secretary of agriculture in Palmeras, a city in rural Brazil. He faced a challenge. People were leaving their farms and moving to Palmeras because it was hard to earn a living in agriculture without electricity. This population shift put stress on city services and threatened the future of area farms.

Fabio had an idea. He thought a dependable supply of low-cost solar energy would result in higher levels of food production. At the same time, improved health and education services could be provided, pollution levels would be reduced, and people could go back to their farms. He envisioned small business communities powered by solar energy springing up to serve the local farmers.

Photo courtesy of Paul McKay

How did Fabio Rosa's ideas about a dependable supply of low-cost solar energy change rural Brazil while allowing some things to remain the same?

Fabio knew that farm families spent at least $11 per month on kerosene, candles, and batteries. This was about the same amount that would be needed to rent a simple solar energy system that would provide enough electricity for one farm. With that knowledge, he set out to electrify the rural areas of his country with solar energy kits. These kits came in three sizes. The smallest one rented for $10 per month. It came complete with a 60-watt solar panel, high-performance battery, all the wiring, plus a number of 12-volt fluorescent lights and electrical outlets for appliances. The system provided, on average per day, six to seven hours of light and several hours for running appliances, equipment, and a water pump. Two larger kits rented for $16 and $24 per month, respectively, and came with more lights, outlets, and wattage. The installation cost for a kit, about $150, could be paid off over 12 months. When Rosa distributed the solar kits to farmers, he included materials about how to develop an irrigation system and build electric fences to protect farm animals as well as information on modern farming practices. Before long, power tools and appliances were humming and people were enjoying warm showers.

Around the same time Fabio was working to improve life in Brazil, William Kamkwamba also had a powerful idea. He was 14 when he decided to make a windmill to help grow crops in his village in Malawi, Africa. During a famine in 2002, William was forced to drop out of school, but he continued to read and study windmill construction. He collected scrap metal and tractor parts; he built wind blades by heating and hammering PVC pipe. His first working windmill created enough electricity to power four light bulbs and two radios for his family. His next accomplishment was building a solar-powered water pump to supply the first drinking water from a well in his village.

Collaborating with journalist Bryan Mealer, William wrote a book about his life. *The Boy Who Harnessed the Wind* was published in 2009. William also inspired the Moving Windmills Project, a not-for-profit organization that raises money for windmills, books for libraries, and other support activities for Malawi.

Think Critically

1. In what ways might the standard of living improve when people have access to electricity?
2. Locate additional information about the work of Fabio Rosa or William Kamkwamba.

BUSINESS IMPROVING SOCIETY

Lack of electricity in rural areas is one of the reasons that people migrate to cities. They are looking for a better way of life and a higher standard of living.

Fabio Rosa and William Kamkwamba are two examples of how innovation and technology can improve society.

THINK CRITICALLY THROUGH VISUALS

A dependable supply of low-cost solar energy allowed people to continue farming in rural Brazil while allowing them to make more money and enjoy a better standard of living.

Think Critically *Answers*

1. Answers will vary. Some possible answers include indoor and outdoor lighting and ability to use appliances, hot water heaters, power tools, water pumps, and electric fences for easier farming.

2. Offer suggestions for how students are to report their findings.

Teaching Strategies

Expand Beyond the Classroom Ask students to review local newspapers, business magazines, and other information sources to identify local businesses or nonprofit organizations that offer services and support to help low-income individuals and families improve their standard of living.

Think Critically About Business *Answers*

1. Rapidly growing employment opportunities include those in service industries, communications, technology, and health care. Jobs declining in numbers include those in manufacturing and agriculture. Answers to the question about how to predict the growth or decline of job categories will vary.

2. Sole proprietorships make up the majority of businesses. Some proprietors may make their entire income from these businesses, as many leave little time for other employment. Others may depend on other sources of income when first starting a business until it becomes profitable.

3. Answers will vary.

4. Answers will vary.

5. Julie may want to consider a partnership, a limited liability partnership, or limited liability company. Each would allow her control over decisions, as well as the benefit of having other investors.

Chapter 5 Assessment

Review Business Concepts

5.1 Business in the U.S. Economy

- The employment status of the United States is changing. Recessions have resulted in periods of lower employment. The labor pool is currently getting older, but that will begin to change as baby boomers retire. Minority groups make up a larger percentage of the workforce.
- Businesses play several key roles in the U.S. economy. They make and distribute products and services needed by consumers, government, and businesses. They provide employment for millions of people. They compensate owners and investors. They pay taxes to federal, state, and local governments.
- The three major categories of businesses are producers, intermediaries, and service businesses. Producers create the products and services used by individuals and other businesses. Intermediaries sell goods and services. A service business carries out activities that are consumed by its customers.

5.2 Forms of Business Ownership

- Most businesses are organized as proprietorships, partnerships, or corporations. A proprietorship is a business owned and run by one person. A partnership is a business owned and controlled by two or more people. A corporation is a separate legal entity owned by one or more shareholders and managed by a board of directors.
- For people who want to work and make decisions independently, do not want to be exposed to significant regulation, and are willing to take on the risk of a business, the proprietorship is an effective form of ownership. A partnership is good for people who share an idea for a business, want to cooperate in managing and investing, and want to share the risks and rewards of the business. A corporation is more difficult to form and is subject to more regulations. Investors' liability is limited to the amount invested, and they can invest without taking part in the day-to-day management of the business.
- Other forms of ownership include limited liability partnership, joint venture, S corporation, limited liability company, nonprofit corporation, cooperative, and franchise.

5.3 Organizational Structure for Businesses

- Successful businesses have an effective organizational structure. A mission statement, goals, policies, and procedures guide them.
- The specific structure of a business can be illustrated with an organizational chart. Traditionally, businesses have used a functional structure but now many use a matrix organizational structure.

Think Critically About Business

1. What are some rapidly growing employment opportunities? What types of jobs are declining in numbers? How can you predict what job categories may grow or decline in the future?
2. Why do most businesses have no employees other than the owner? Do you believe most of those business owners earn their entire income from that business? Why or why not?
3. Identify several businesses from your community that fit within each of the three categories of businesses listed in Lesson 5-1. Do you believe your community has more producers, intermediaries, or service businesses? Justify your answer.
4. Would you like to start and own your own business? Why or why not? What do you believe are the risks and benefits you would face if you decided to start a business?
5. Julie states that she wants to be her own boss. If she starts a business, it will be a proprietorship rather than a partnership or corporation. Explain to Julie why she might want to consider another ownership form. Is it possible for her to be her own boss and yet not use the proprietorship form of ownership?

6. Use a business directory to identify several non-profit corporations in your area. What public service is each providing? Why do you think each is a public rather than a private corporation?

7. "An effective organizational structure is as important to a business as the quality of its products and services." Do you agree or disagree with that statement? Discuss your beliefs with another student who has the opposing view.

8. You are starting a shopping service for elderly people in your community who cannot leave their homes. Write a mission statement that clearly communicates the purpose of your business.

9. How will the appearance of an organizational chart for a business using a functional organizational structure be different from one using a matrix organizational structure? What should you be able to learn about a business by studying its organizational chart?

Develop Your Business Language

Match the terms listed with the definitions.

10. A business owned and controlled by two or more people who have entered into a written agreement.
11. A short, specific written statement of the reason a business exists and what it wants to accomplish.
12. One who has no explicit or implicit contract for long-term employment.
13. Descriptions of the way work is to be done.
14. A specific statement of results the business expects to achieve.
15. A written legal document that identifies ownership and operating procedures and conditions for the business.
16. Businesses involved in selling the goods and services of producers to consumers and other businesses.
17. A separate legal entity, formed by documents filed with the state, which is owned by one or more shareholders and managed by a board of directors.
18. A written contract granting permission to operate a business to sell products and services in a prescribed way.
19. A business that completes activities that are consumed by customers rather than offers products for sale.
20. A business owned and controlled by just one person.
21. A written agreement among all owners that specifies the rules and procedures that guide ownership and operations.
22. Guidelines used in making consistent decisions.
23. A diagram that shows the structure of an organization, classifications of jobs, and the relationships among those classifications.

Key Terms

- **a.** articles of incorporation
- **b.** contingent worker
- **c.** corporation
- **d.** franchise
- **e.** goal
- **f.** intermediaries
- **g.** mission statement
- **h.** organization chart
- **i.** partnership
- **j.** partnership agreement
- **k.** proprietorship
- **l.** policies
- **m.** procedures
- **n.** service business

6. Answers will vary.

7. Answers will vary.

8. Answers will vary.

9. A functional chart would consist of a list of groups of people, arranged under various functions of the business. A matrix organizational chart will arrange teams under their respective projects, with functions appearing across each project. By studying an organizational chart, one can learn how a company organizes its work load, how it views the significance of each of its employees and their respective roles, and what type of goal setting it uses to motivate them.

Develop Your Business Language *Answers*

10. i. partnership
11. g. mission statement
12. b. contingent worker
13. m. procedures
14. e. goal
15. a. articles of incorporation
16. f. intermediaries
17. c. corporation
18. d. franchise
19. n. service business
20. k. proprietorship
21. j. partnership agreement
22. l. policies
23. h. organization chart

Make Academic Connections *Answers*

24a. Total property taxes: $15,825,500 ÷ $1000 = $15,825.5 × $0.78 = $12,343.89

Total payroll taxes: $36,000 × 1% = $360; $360 × 328 = $118,080

Total taxes: $12,343.89 + $118,080 = $130,423.89

24b. Additional benefits might include more employment, new customers for existing businesses, or population increase.

25. Charts and graphs will vary. Students should choose a type of graph or chart that accurately depicts their data.

26. Mission statements should be short and clearly identify the reason the business exists. Goals should be precise and achievable. Policies should offer guidelines for making consistent decisions.

27. Answers will vary. For example, coal is used to produce electricity and Wyoming leads the nation in coal production. Alaskan mines produce the most gold and silver, which are both used in jewelry and dentistry. Silver is also used in radio frequency identification devices (RFIDs).

28. Provide information about how students should report their findings.

Make Your Case *Answers*

29. By combining their businesses, they are offering a complete landscape service with customized plans to meet client needs. They might also consider seeding, fertilizing, and tree care.

Make Academic Connections

24. **Math** To provide additional employment and add to its tax base from businesses, Yorketowne's city council opened a business park on the edge of the city. After five years, they had attracted two new manufacturers and four supporting service businesses to the park. The total value of the property of all six businesses was $15,825,500. The companies paid $0.78 per $1,000 of property value each year as property tax. In addition, the businesses employed 328 people at an average salary of $36,000. Each person paid a 1 percent city income tax each year.

- **a.** What is the total amount of taxes the city collected as a result of opening the business park?
- **b.** In addition to the tax dollars, what other benefits might the city receive from opening the business park?

25. **Technology** Use a spreadsheet and graphics program to make a chart or graph showing one of the following sets of data: (a) the five largest employers in the world and the number of employees for each, (b) the composition of the U.S. workforce by the age of employees, (c) the average size of U.S. business by annual sales revenues.

26. **Communication** The DECA chapter in your school is planning to open a school store to sell school supplies, school-related apparel, and spirit items before and after school. Prepare a mission statement for the store. Write one goal that identifies a specific result the store should achieve. Write a policy statement for accepting returns of merchandise purchased by customers.

27. **Science** Identify five types of natural resources that are extracted in the United States for use in manufacturing. For each, identify the leading states where the natural resources are extracted and important products for which the natural resource is needed.

28. **Public Service** Most communities have nonprofit corporations that support education. Find out if one or more organizations is working to support your school. If so, contact a leader of the organization. Determine how the organization is structured, if it is has articles of incorporation and bylaws, and its purpose. Find out how students in your school can support the organization through volunteer activities.

Make Your Case

Sonja Bartholomew started a lawn mowing service. She could not charge as much as she needed to make the profit she desired. Her competitors only charged $15 per lawn while she charged $20, but she did a superior job cutting lawns. Still, potential customers did not want to pay the extra $5.

A friend, Eduardo Guadalupe, suggested that they work together. He was good at trimming shrubs and had ideas for improving landscapes with flowers and lawn ornaments. They would offer a unique service when they combined their businesses. They could charge an amount that would result in a good profit for both of them. They would seek out homes in neighborhoods with above-average income levels.

29. What will be special about the services that Sonja and Eduardo can offer together? What other services might they include?

30. Why would they target above-average income levels?

31. Should Sonja continue to run her business as a proprietorship and hire Eduardo as an employee? If not, what other form of business ownership would you recommend? Justify your choice.

Interactions and Connections

Interview a stockbroker or financial advisor in your community about the process of selecting and purchasing stock. Ask the professional to share information about how people decide which stock to purchase and how a stockholder can track the stock's performance. Ask the broker or advisor if he or she has any general advice for young investors.

The U.S. government provides support to small businesses through the Small Business Administration (SBA). Visit the SBA website to learn more about this resource. Browse or search for information about forms of ownership that small businesses might consider. Be sure to read the advantages and disadvantages of each form or ownership.

Interactions and Connections

Students should make notes on what the stock advisor believes is important in choosing to invest in a company. They should also create a list of the reasons young people should invest. Students should compare their notes to see what is common across all interviews.

32. Use information from your textbook and the SBA website to identify and make a list of factors that influence the form of ownership choice.

33. Provide an example of a business that might benefit from choosing the proprietorship form of ownership. Provide an example for each of these other types of ownership: partnership and corporation.

34. Based on one of your examples from above, write a short scenario describing the advantages and disadvantages of the chosen form of ownership. Describe how the business plans to use the form of ownership to its advantage and how it plans to deal with the disadvantages.

Small Business Management Team Event

Starting a business involves financial investment and risk. Individuals must decide the best form of business ownership for the business that they want to open. Your team has expertise in working at quick-serve and full-serve restaurants. Team members have college degrees in finance, hospitality marketing, and culinary arts. Your team is very excited about opening an Italian restaurant in a growing city with a population of 75,000 people. Currently there are two Italian restaurants associated with national franchises located in the community. Your team must describe the advantages associated with operating the restaurant as a sole proprietorship, partnership, corporation, and franchise. Then your team must decide upon the best type of ownership for your proposed restaurant and explain the rationale for your decision.

The Small Business Management Team Event involves a 90-minute test and a 10-minute oral presentation followed by a five-minute question and answer session with the judges. A team of two to four members must present a solution for a Management Case Study. Your team may use one laptop/notebook computer, posters, flip charts, or graphs for the presentation.

Performance Indicators Evaluated

- Evaluate, prioritize, interpret, and communicate analysis of data.
- Negotiate business solutions with the team.
- Organize ideas and communicate orally in a group presentation.
- Apply an understanding of forms of business ownership.

Your team will be evaluated for

- Equality of responsibilities among team members of required tasks
- Demonstration of teamwork skills needed to function in a business setting
- Demonstration of self-esteem, self- and team-management, and integrity
- Demonstration of a working knowledge of business management/ownership concepts
- Demonstration of critical thinking skills to make decisions and solve problems

For more detailed information about performance indicators, go to the BPA website.

Think Critically

1. What advantages are offered by choosing to operate the restaurant as a partnership?
2. What advantages are offered by choosing the franchise form of business?
3. Why should tax laws be considered when deciding on the form of business ownership?

www.bpa.org

30. Above-average income homeowners are more likely to pay someone to care for their lawns and can afford to pay higher rates for special services.

31. Answers will vary. A partnership would allow each to participate in the decision making and bring their existing assets to the combined business. This would also allow Sonja to share liability with Eduardo. They might also consider an LLC.

WINNING EDGE

Small Business Management Team Event

Each form of business ownership has different legal implications and financial commitments. Students must make a major decision after thoroughly considering the pros and cons of the different forms of business ownership.

Think Critically *Answers*

1. The combined expertise and degrees of the team members could be combined successfully in a partnership. Also the initial investment and profits can be shared among the members of the partnership.

2. The franchise might take away some of the financial burden for new business owners. The franchise provides a proven business strategy, advertising, commitment, and expertise.

3. Each form of business ownership is taxed differently. A large amount of money can be saved by choosing the best form of business ownership.

32. Answers will vary. Students should consider costs, liability, sources of financing, and tax issues.

33. Examples will vary. Many small businesses are proprietorships. Professionals such as doctors and accountants often form partnerships. Most large businesses are corporations.

34. Answers will vary. Students should match the business type to the issues outlined in the answer to the first question.

CHAPTER OVERVIEW

This chapter describes the role that small business plays in the U.S. economy and how to start and manage a small business.

6.1 Becoming an Entrepreneur

In this lesson, students will learn about the characteristics of today's entrepreneurs and what it takes to start their own business.

6.2 Small Business Basics

This lesson presents information on the advantages and disadvantages of small business ownership and resources available to small business owners.

6.3 Starting a Small Business

This lesson introduces students to the elements of a business plan and the sources of financing for a new business.

Chapter 6 Entrepreneurship and Small Business Management

istockphoto.com/LifesizeImages

6.1 Becoming an Entrepreneur

6.2 Small Business Basics

6.3 Starting a Small Business

Instructor Resources

- Activities and Study Guide IE
- Chapter and Unit Tests IE
- Lesson Plans
- PowerPoint Presentation
- Cognero Test, Ch. 6

Student Resources

Activities and Study Guide
www.cengage.com/swep/pob9e
- Portfolio Activity

Business, Management & Administration

PLANNING A CAREER IN . . .
CONSULTING

When businesses face unique problems or undertake major changes, they often turn to consultants for advice and help. Consultants are not long-term employees of a company. They are hired to complete a specific task or to focus on an important challenge facing the business. Consultants may be self-employed and work independently, or they may be part of a large consulting business that employs many specialists. Large companies often form teams of specialists to work with a client.

Consultants provide a level of expertise to a business that may not be present among its employees and that would be difficult to develop quickly enough to solve a current problem. Consultants also may be more objective about the business than people who are working there. The primary work of consultants is to conduct research and complete other types of analysis that help businesses address important challenges they are facing. Consultants often prepare written reports and plans, provide advice to decision makers, and may even offer help in reorganizing the company and redirecting its efforts.

Related Job Titles

- **Business Analyst**
- **Management Consultant**
- **Performance Consultant**
- **Quality Control Consultant**
- **Security Consultant**
- **Training Consultant**

Analyze Career Opportunities in . . . CONSULTING

Use library and Internet resources to learn more about careers in consulting. Choose one of the job titles listed in the box and answer the following questions.

1. Identify the minimum educational requirements for the job. Explain other training or education that might be needed for advancement.
2. Is this a career that interests you? What can you do now to help prepare yourself for this career?

What it's like to work as a . . . Consultant

Erin Gerrard works as a small business consultant for Security Savings Bank. The bank is committed to strengthening its services to small businesses. Security employs a 10-person team to support its small business customers.

Erin earned a degree in accounting, worked five years for a major accounting business, and then operated her own accounting service for five years. The bank hired her as a small business consultant because of her accounting expertise and reputation in the community. She decided the consulting opportunity would be an interesting challenge.

This morning, Erin is meeting with Dawn Perrot, who is planning to open a florist shop. Dawn has submitted a business plan, but the financial plan is incomplete. Erin is looking forward to helping Dawn gather information and develop a complete picture of the financial needs of her business.

What about you? How do you believe Erin's work as a consultant is similar to and different from the work she did as the owner of a small accounting business?

PLANNING A CAREER IN . . . CONSULTING

Consultants work for a number of businesses on a variety of activities. When businesses need help on a new project or expertise that the owners do not have, they will often work with a business consultant.

What About You? *Answer*

Student answers will require thinking beyond what is presented and formulating their own reactions. As a consultant, Erin probably does less hands-on accounting and more research and advising. She uses both her accounting expertise and her experience as a small business owner to provide advice and support to her clients.

Analyze Career Opportunities *Answers*

Student answers will vary depending on when the assignment is completed and individual interests.

Additional Career Information

Encourage students to investigate careers they find interesting and explore unfamiliar careers. Two resources for additional career information are the *Occupational Outlook Handbook*, an online publication (www.bls.gov) of the U.S. Bureau of Labor Statistics, and the O*NET Resource Center (www.onetcenter.org) developed by the U.S. Department of Labor. Information about specific careers and jobs can be used to demonstrate the relevance of skills learned in this course.

Focus on REAL LIFE

Hobbies and interests often form the idea for a new business. Tell students that if they already have an interest and have developed unique skills in that area of interest, they may want to consider turning it into a small business idea.

TEACH

Tell students that entrepreneurs are very important to consumer satisfaction and economic growth. Entrepreneurs create new product ideas and new businesses. Their ideas often respond to customer needs that are not being satisfied by current businesses. If entrepreneurs are successful, their businesses will be profitable and will usually grow, offering employment opportunities and paying taxes. Point out that 42 percent of entrepreneurs launched businesses during their childhood. Sixty-nine percent had businesses in their teens.

Ask students to identify as many current and historical entrepreneurs as they can. When each is named, ask other students to try to identify the product or business associated with the entrepreneur.

Life-Span Plan Answers

Answers will vary. Students should identify personal characteristics and explain how these might affect their ability to achieve their life-span goals.

6.1 Becoming an Entrepreneur

Learning Outcomes

6.1.1 Identify characteristics of successful entrepreneurs.

6.1.2 Recognize the importance of entrepreneurship in the economy.

6.1.3 Describe opportunities and risks of entrepreneurship.

Key Terms

entrepreneur 124
entrepreneurship 124
venture capital 127
innovation 128
improvement 128

Focus on REAL LIFE

Jerelyn Frank has been working as an aerobics instructor for the Phase 4 Fitness Center for the past six years. Jerelyn enjoys her work because she has always been active and athletic. Since high school, she has taken wellness, first aid, and nutrition classes at the local adult education center. She has completed a number of certification courses in aerobics instruction and yoga. In her spare time, she has developed fitness programs for some of her friends and members of the fitness center where she works.

Jerelyn is seriously thinking about starting a personal fitness service. She wants to go to people's homes and offices to help them plan and maintain a fitness schedule and offer half-hour to one-hour workouts. She already has a number of contacts to help her get underway. Jerelyn has no family responsibilities or debts. She has been able to save more than $15,000 in her bank account.

Jerelyn decides to go forward with the plan, just as thousands of other entrepreneurs do each year. Those that become new business owners are willing to contribute a great deal of time and energy and risk personal economic resources for their venture. They hold the hope of a successful business and a reasonable profit.

LO 6.1.1

CHARACTERISTICS OF ENTREPRENEURS

An **entrepreneur** is someone who takes a risk by starting a business to try to earn a profit. Some key factors in starting your own business are having a real desire to be your own boss and developing a good initial plan. Possessing special skills and abilities and developing innovative ideas are also important.

Life-Span Plan

What personal characteristics do you have that could help you become a successful entrepreneur? What characteristics would you need to develop to be a successful entrepreneur? Describe how these characteristics may affect the life-span goals you set for your future.

Can you think of some service or product that is not being offered at this time but might be popular with consumers? Is there some service or product that you could offer more efficiently than others are doing now? Is there some special talent you have that could become the starting point for a business of your own? If so, you have the basis for a new business enterprise. There are good opportunities for entrepreneurship through small business ownership. **Entrepreneurship** is the process of starting, organizing, managing, and assuming the responsibility for a business. Here are some real-life examples of young entrepreneurs.

Entrepreneurs in Action

Joshua Moore was a high school student and brother to four-year-old Sophie when he developed an idea for a baby stroller

Different Learning Abilities

English Language Learners (ELL) Instruct students to translate the word "entrepreneur" into as many different languages as possible. Students with proficiency in other languages should offer suggestions. Other students can use translation dictionaries or the Internet to identify appropriate words. Ask students to write the new words on the board.

braking system. To fund work on his invention, Joshua started Personal Affections, selling key chains, picture frames, mirrors, and personalized stickers at his Walhalla, South Carolina, high school. He received an Entrepreneur of the Year award for an operational business from the National Foundation for Teaching Entrepreneurship. At age 15, he was on his way to his dream of becoming an inventor and business owner.

Ben Cathers of Long Island, New York, was not a typical student. At age 12 he started a web marketing and advertising business. His business grew to 10 employees and a network of more than 300 million advertisements per month. By age 17, Ben started a syndicated radio show called Teen America. Not content with just his own entrepreneurship, at age 19 Ben wrote *Conversations with Teen Entrepreneurs*. By 19, he co-founded Search Rate Technologies and Klick-TV. By the age of 25, Ben had turned his talent to working with the next generation of young entrepreneurs.

Rich Stachowski of Moraga, California, is an avid scuba diver. While enjoying his hobby, he recognized that he was unable to talk to others who were snorkeling with him. He put his imagination to work and invented Water Talkies™ at the age of 11. These walkie-talkies can be used under water. Rich worked with a family friend who developed the manufacturing process. He then opened a business to make and sell his product before he was even a teenager. Rich moved on to invent and patent seven more products, including underwater binoculars and an underwater periscope.

Sometimes ideas for new products come from problems in daily life. Abbey Fleck was watching her father use a microwave oven to cook bacon one morning in their White Bear Lake, Minnesota, home. The bacon came out soaked in grease. Abbey had an idea to develop a pan that would cook the bacon while letting the grease drain out below. She and her father tested several designs that resulted in the Makin Bacon® microwave bacon tray. They were able to convince the producers of Armour brand bacon to promote the tray with an advertisement and order form printed on each package of bacon. The product was an instant hit. Abbey's company currently sells Makin Bacon® trays on its website, on Amazon, and at Wal-Mart.

istockphoto.com/PeopleImages

Do you have ideas or skills that you could use to start a small business?

These entrepreneurs are examples of the thousands of young people who have creative ideas and turn them into businesses each year. Not all ideas lead to successful businesses, but each provides evidence of the opportunities that exist for people who believe they can turn their idea into a profitable business.

What Does It Take?

Not all people who own or manage a business are entrepreneurs. It takes unique skills and personal characteristics to develop a new idea for a product or service. A person must also have both the confidence and capability to turn an idea into a business.

TEACH

Ask students why they believe that people their age and even younger have been successful in starting their own businesses. Discuss what they think it would take for a young person to actually go ahead with an idea and turn it into a business.

THINK CRITICALLY THROUGH VISUALS

Answers will vary, but could include discussion of hobbies and interests as well as skills.

Different Learning Styles

Visual Learner Ask students to sketch an illustration of a new product or the front of the building for a new business idea they have. Ask students to show their sketches to other students and describe why the idea interests them. Consider allowing students to work in pairs.

THINK CRITICALLY THROUGH VISUALS

Some advantages of turning a hobby into a business are that the knowledge and expertise for the activity are already there. Disadvantages are that the hobby might not be a good basis for a business and that it might not be as enjoyable if it becomes a business.

TEACH

Ask students why they believe that young entrepreneurs today are more evenly divided between men and women even though most business owners are male. Some entrepreneurs have not completed any formal education beyond high school. Ask students how these entrepreneurs are able to compensate for having less education than college-educated managers of competing businesses.

ONGOING ASSESSMENT

CHECKPOINT ✓ANSWER

Any characteristics listed in Figure 6-1 are acceptable, such as persistence, inquisitiveness, self-confidence, creativity, and so forth.

▸ Figure 6-1 ANSWER

Answers will vary. Ask volunteers to share their answers with the class.

Creatas/Getty Images Plus/Getty Images

What are some advantages and disadvantages of turning a hobby into a business?

It is important to have an understanding of business operations and management. This understanding does not always come from getting a business degree in college. People learn how to run a business in many ways. They may work in a business or ask for help and advice from an experienced business owner. They may read and study on their own as well as in school.

There are personal traits that are common to successful entrepreneurs, as shown in Figure 6-1. While some people already have many of these qualities, others do not. If you have a desire to become an entrepreneur, you can work to develop these characteristics.

Entrepreneurs come from all age categories and racial and ethnic groups. They represent both genders as well as varied amounts and types of education. Many entrepreneurs own their first business while in their teens. Others do not take the step until retirement. More business owners are male, but young entrepreneurs are more equally divided between male and female.

CHECKPOINT ✓

What personal characteristics are common to most successful entrepreneurs?

PERSONAL CHARACTERISTICS OF SUCCESSFUL ENTREPRENEURS

ENTREPRENEURS ARE	ENTREPRENEURS HAVE
• competitive	• ability to partner
• creative	• ability to secure resources
• energetic	• ability to spot opportunity
• goal-oriented	• capability to learn from failure
• independent	• personal initiative
• inquisitive	• problem-solving skills
• persistent	• strong integrity
• reliable	• tolerance for ambiguity
• self-confident	• willingness to work hard

FIGURE 6-1
Which characteristics of successful entrepreneurs do you possess? Which ones would you like to develop?

Applied Skills

Communication Assign students to create an advertisement or brochure that showcases the personal characteristics of an effective entrepreneur. Encourage students to use a computer to complete this assignment.

LO 6.1.2

ENTREPRENEURSHIP AND THE ECONOMY

Entrepreneurship is a key part of the U.S. economy. Nearly 13 percent all Americans 18–64 years old is involved in some type of entrepreneurship activity. More than 500,000 new businesses are created annually. Entrepreneurship is also risky. Nearly as many small businesses close as begin each year.

Employment

Small businesses are responsible for most new employment. Figure 6-2 shows employment growth by firm size between 1990 and 2009. Over 82 percent of new jobs were created by businesses with fewer than 500 employees.

Financing

Most new businesses start on $10,000 or less. High-tech firms are more likely to obtain funding from outside sources. Research data shows that start-up capital comes from owner and family savings (13%), personal and business loans (32%), and credit card debt (11%). Funding also comes from the entrepreneur's family and friends. One in ten Americans has invested in a business of someone they know well. Obtaining funding from family and friends can be risky for both the entrepreneur and the investors. If the business fails and the investment is lost, hurt feelings and resentment are common.

Another source of money for some new businesses is venture capital. **Venture capital** is money provided by large investors to finance new products and new businesses that have a good chance to be very profitable. In the late 1990s, many venture capital companies were formed. They supplied more than $100 billion each year to new businesses. Many of the businesses receiving those funds were e-commerce and high-tech start-ups. When many of those businesses failed, the amount of venture capital declined to less than $16 billion in 2009. By 2014, the venture capital market grew to $48 billion, with more than 4,300 agreements. This indicates that many people think new businesses provide good investment opportunities. The other sources of financing for new businesses are loans from banks and financial institutions and credit given by businesses that sell products and services to the new business.

Employment Growth by Business Size 1990–2009

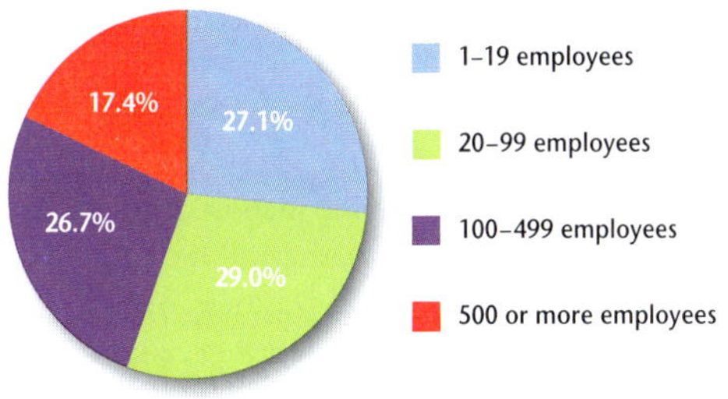

Source: U.S. Bureau of Labor Statistics

FIGURE 6-2

What percentage of job growth came from businesses with fewer than 100 employees?

Productivity

New and small businesses produce a large volume of goods and services for the economy. Businesses with just a single owner and no staff account for more than $990 billion in sales annually. Small businesses are responsible for more than half of the U.S. gross domestic product each year. They account for more than half of all innovative products and services developed.

CHECKPOINT

What are the sources of financing that entrepreneurs use for their new businesses?

▶ **Figure 6-2** ***ANSWER***

Businesses with fewer than 100 employees created 56.1 percent of new jobs. The answer is the result of adding 27.1 percent and 29 percent.

TEACH

Ask students to consider ways that people can be involved in an entrepreneurship activity without actually being the entrepreneur. Possible answers are by lending money, working with the entrepreneur to plan the business, and being an employee.

Explain to students that most new entrepreneurs have difficulty obtaining enough financing to start their business, so they often turn to family and friends. Businesses will usually fail without adequate financing.

ONGOING ASSESSMENT

CHECKPOINT ✓*ANSWER*

Sources of financing for entrepreneurs include personal savings, friends and family, venture capital, and bank loans.

Different Learning Abilities

Gifted Assign students to research and prepare a report on the dot-com bust of the late 1990s. Ask them to present a summary that highlights the major reasons for the large number of start-up business failures.

Dyslexia Encourage students to read each paragraph carefully. After reading each paragraph, ask students to write a few words or a short sentence that summarizes the information.

TEACH

Ask students to identify the difference between an opportunity and a risk. Do they believe all opportunities have risks? Can an opportunity that is not very risky result in a profitable business?

Explain to students that most new businesses offer improvements to existing products or current business operations rather than offering innovations. Ask them whether they believe the process to develop an innovation is different from the process to design a major improvement to an existing product.

THINK CRITICALLY THROUGH VISUALS

Entrepreneurship opportunities emerge from innovation, invention, and improvement.

Work as a TEAM

When students have completed their lists, ask them to rank the questions in order from most important to least important to help determine whether to invest in the business or not.

LO 6.1.3

OPPORTUNITIES AND RISKS

When Jerelyn Frank was deciding whether she would open her own personal fitness business, she had to think about both the opportunities and the risks. Giving up a regular job and stable income is a difficult choice. As a reward, she will have personal control over her own business. She can take personal satisfaction if her idea develops into a successful, profitable company.

hopsalka/Shutterstock.com

What do innovation, invention, and improvement have to do with entrepreneurship opportunities?

New Business Opportunities

The American private enterprise economy promotes innovation and new business development. Individuals are able to take the risk to start a new business. They can compete with other businesses to sell their products and services and make a profit. Consumers are always looking for new and better choices to meet their wants and needs.

Many opportunities are open to prospective entrepreneurs. The opportunities begin with the creation of new or improved products and services. An **innovation** is an invention or creation that is brand new. An **improvement** is a designed change that increases the usefulness of a product, service, or process.

Inventors often develop innovations. Those inventions may become the basis for a new business. The inventor may sell them to another company for development and sale. Examples of well-known innovations include the Apple personal computer developed by Steve Jobs and Stephen Wozniak and Post-it Notes created by Arthur Fry and Spencer Silver. Recent innovations that may become successful products include miniaturized personal drones, self-driving cars, and 3-D printers that allow individuals and small businesses to create products without a manufacturing process.

In addition to inventions, innovators create new services that become the basis for a business. Frederick Smith envisioned an economical worldwide system for quickly and efficiently shipping packages. The creation of FedEx was the result. Mary Kay Ash founded Mary Kay Cosmetics and has helped more than 1.8 million businesspeople worldwide. When the Internal Revenue Service no longer prepared individual tax returns for free, two brothers, Henry and Richard Bloch, created the H & R Block Company. They trained people to provide efficient, low-cost tax preparation services to individual taxpayers.

Not all entrepreneurship opportunities emerge from those types of inventions and innovations. Many come from an improved design, more effective procedures, or greater attention to quality. Entrepreneurs are creative problem solvers. Those traits lead to ideas for improved products and services.

Work as a TEAM

New businesses usually need investments from other people. As a team, develop a list of questions you would ask an entrepreneur to determine if the new business would be one in which you would want to invest some of your money.

Portfolio Activity

Assign the Portfolio Activity for Chapter 6, located on the product website.
COLLECT Offer suggestions to help students locate data.
CREATE Remind students that their visuals should illustrate the contributions of small businesses.
CONNECT Point out students need to connect visuals to something in their portfolio.

Recognizing Risks

Many successful entrepreneurs and their businesses are well known. Their success encourages others to think about starting a new business. Developing a successful new business is not easy. Many more new businesses fail than succeed. The time and energy required of new business owners is much higher than most people expect.

The National Federation of Independent Business reports that of all new businesses, about one-third are profitable, one-third do not make a profit but continue to operate, and the remaining third lose money. Over a 10-year period, more than 50 percent of all new businesses are discontinued. The primary reasons that businesses started by entrepreneurs close are

- Lack of adequate capital
- Low sales
- Higher than expected expenses
- Competitive pressure
- An owner unprepared to manage a growing business
- Operations requiring more time than the owner is willing to commit

Entrepreneurs need to be aware of the many risks they may face and prepare for them. Most entrepreneurs are willing to take risks. They will work hard to make their businesses succeed. However, many entrepreneurs have seen one or more of their business ideas fail before they were able to grow a successful company.

CHECKPOINT
Where do entrepreneurship opportunities begin?

6.1 ASSESSMENT

Key Concepts

Determine the best answer.

1. True or False. Everyone who owns or manages a business is an entrepreneur.
2. Which of the following is *not* a characteristic of entrepreneurship in the United States?
   a. About 3 percent of people aged 18–64 are involved in entrepreneurship activity.
   b. About 500,000 new businesses are created each year.
   c. About 27 percent of job growth comes from businesses with less than 20 employees.
   d. One in every ten Americans has invested in a business of someone who they know well.
3. Money provided by large investors to finance new products and new businesses that have a good chance to be very profitable is known as
   a. a loan
   b. credit
   c. venture capital
   d. start-up funding

Make Academic Connections

4. **Math** Ronaldo Jacarda is opening a manufacturing business. It will produce a new type of USB flash storage card for smartphones and digital cameras. He has several sources for the money needed to start his business. Those sources and amounts are personal savings, $56,500; loans from family and friends, $38,000; venture capital investment, $128,000; bank loan, $22,500. Determine the total amount of capital he has accumulated and the percentage of that total from each of the sources. Prepare a pie chart that illustrates the answers.
5. **History** Use the Internet to identify important inventions and innovations developed in the past 50 years. Select the five you believe have had the greatest business success. Now select the five you believe have been most important in improving society. Prepare a short report in which you identify and briefly describe each of the inventions and innovations you selected and justifications for your choices.

TEACH

List each of the reasons that entrepreneur's businesses fail on the board. Ask students why each reason has a negative effect on the business.

ONGOING ASSESSMENT

CHECKPOINT ANSWER

Opportunities begin with innovations (ideas about new products and services) or improvements (ideas for changes to existing products, services, or processes).

ASSESS

Key Concepts *Answers*

1. False. Not everyone who owns or manages a business is an entrepreneur.
2. a. About three percent of people aged 18–64 are involved in entrepreneurship activity.
3. c. venture capital

Make Academic Connections *Answers*

4. Total: 56,500 + 38,000 + 128,000 + 22,500 = 245,000
Personal savings: 56,500 ÷ 245,000 = 23%
Family and friends: 38,000 ÷ 245,000 = 16%
Capital investment: 128,000 ÷ 245,000 = 52%
Bank loan: 22,500 ÷ 245,000 = 9%
5. Reports will vary. Offer suggestions regarding an acceptable format for reports.

CLOSE Ask students to discuss their feelings about becoming an entrepreneur.

RETEACH Ask students to review the learning outcomes and write a sentence about each.

ENRICH Ask students to identify their favorite interest, hobby, or activity. Then instruct them to use a telephone directory or the Internet and identify small businesses that offer related products or services.

Focus on REAL LIFE

Ask students whether any of them have family members who used to own a small business, but no longer do. Discuss reasons why people might enjoy owning a business but decide to sell it.

TEACH

Students are usually surprised to learn that the federal government defines small businesses as those with fewer than 500 employees. Before disclosing that information, ask students how many employees they believe a business must have before it is no longer considered small.

Write the following phrase on the board: 21 million businesses. Ask students what they believe makes that many U.S. businesses alike. After they have guessed, ask them to read the statement in the text that identifies that those businesses have no employees; the owner is the only person who works in the business. Ask them to think of businesses in their community that might fit into that category.

6.2 Small Business Basics

Learning Outcomes

6.2.1 Identify important characteristics of small businesses.

6.2.2 Recognize the competitive advantages of small businesses.

6.2.3 Identify problems faced by many small businesses.

Key Terms

small business 130

Small Business Administration (SBA) 134

Focus on REAL LIFE

During dinner, Jasmine excitedly told her family what happened in her Principles of Business class. The class had spent the time thinking about opportunities for owning a small business. Jasmine knew that is what she wanted to do.

Jasmine's grandfather said, "Did you know I ran a small business for almost 10 years when I was young? I was as excited as you are about starting a business when I graduated from high school. I went to work for the owner of a small hardware store. I hoped that I could save enough money to open my own store. Luckily, after eight years, he decided to retire. We worked out an arrangement where I could buy the store from him over a number of years."

"What happened to the business?" Jasmine asked.

"Being a small business owner is exciting, but it is a difficult life," explained her grandfather. "As the bigger stores moved in, I found it more and more difficult to attract customers. I decided to sell the business. I'm excited for you, but I want you to know that achieving your goals will be challenging."

LO 6.2.1

SMALL BUSINESS OWNERSHIP

When people think about business, they often picture very large corporations. These companies employ thousands of people with locations all over the country and the world. That is not the true picture of most businesses. Small businesses account for the vast majority of businesses in the the United States. They employ more than 50 percent of all private sector employees.

You may be surprised by the definition of small business used by the federal government. According to the Small Business Administration (SBA), a **small business** is an independent business with fewer than 500 employees. Using that standard, 96 percent of the roughly 29 million U.S. businesses are small businesses.

A more specific description of a small business includes the following points.

- The owner is usually the manager.
- It operates in one or very few locations.
- It typically serves a small market.
- It is not dominant in its field.

Most people would probably not consider businesses with 500 employees to be small. Even if you use a standard of fewer than 100 employees, 27 million businesses fit that description. More than 21 million businesses have no staff other than the owner. Many of those businesses are run on a part-time basis from the owner's home. Twenty-two million businesses are set up as proprietorships. No matter how

Different Learning Abilities

Attention Deficit Disorder Ask the student to be the recorder at the board. As other students read the information on page 130 aloud, the recorder should write the numbers on the board that describe small business ownership in the United States.

you identify small businesses, they are by far the greatest number of businesses operating today.

Small Business Employment

On average, small businesses are responsible for creating 82 percent of all new jobs. Figure 6-3 shows some of the common types of small business. It is not surprising that there are a large number of service businesses. Many small business services are professional and technical. Many construction companies operate as small businesses.

Ownership Diversity

Women own more than one-third of all small businesses. More than 14 percent of small businesses have African-American, Asian-American, or Hispanic-American ownership. The majority of small business owners are over 50 years old, but nearly 15.9 percent are under 35. Today, almost all people starting small businesses have at least a high school diploma. Nearly 62 percent have finished some college work.

Half of all small businesses are home-based businesses. Because many businesses are part-time ventures or service businesses, the owners report that on average they needed $5,000 or less to start that type of business. Full-time businesses with buildings, equipment, and employees may require more than $100,000 of initial capital.

FYI Small business owners report that the Internet is having a positive impact on their companies. In a recent survey, 51 percent said the Internet helped increase their profits and 49 percent said its use resulted in reduced operating costs.

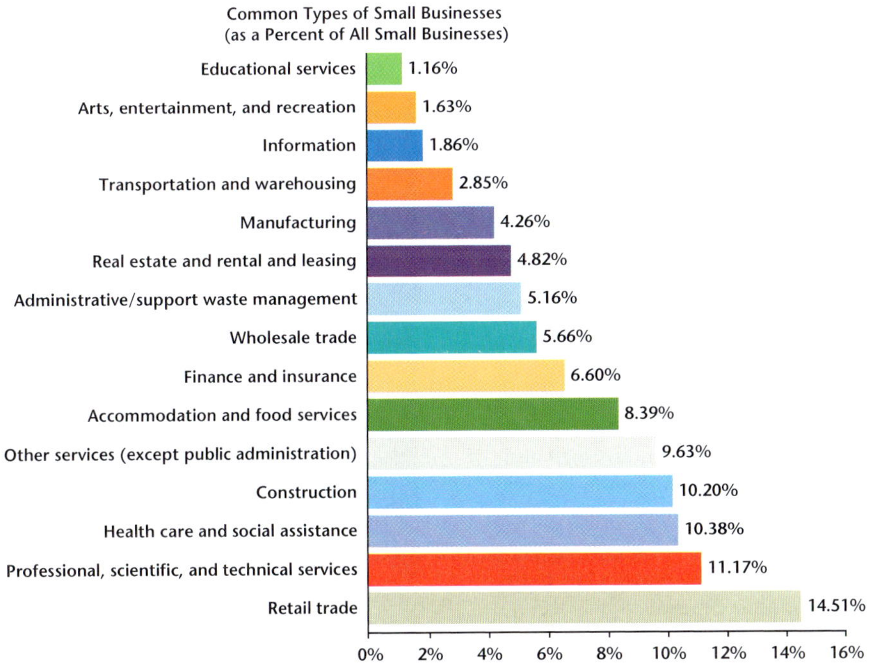

Source: U.S. Census Bureau

FIGURE 6-3
Why are so many small businesses in services and retailing?

TEACH

Ask students how many of them have family members who work in small businesses. Remind students that small businesses employ fewer than 500 people. Ask those students to stand and then instruct the class to calculate the percentage of students who have family members employed in small businesses.

FYI

Ask students to suggest reasons why the use of the Internet can save money and increase profits for small businesses.

TEACH

Instruct students to use the Internet to determine what percentage of the U.S. population is female and what percentage is African-American, Asian-American, and Hispanic-American. Compare those percentages to the percentage of small business ownership listed for each group. Discuss the findings.

▶ **Figure 6-3** ***ANSWER***

Services and retailing are two categories in which small businesses can get a start and provide customer service and customization that large businesses may not be able to match.

Applied Skills

Mathematics Instruct students to determine the total number of small businesses in the United States as listed in the lesson. Using the information in Figure 6-3, then ask students to calculate the number of businesses for each of the categories listed in the figure. Students should show the results in a table.

ONGOING ASSESSMENT

CHECKPOINT ✓ ANSWER

The following points can be used to describe a small business: the owner is usually the manager; it operates in one or very few locations; it typically serves a small market; and it is not dominant in its field.

TEACH

Ask students why small service businesses may be able to respond to customer needs better than small businesses that sell products. After students present their ideas, instruct them to read the information on pages 132 and 133 to see whether their ideas are similar or different.

THINK CRITICALLY THROUGH VISUALS

Small businesses can provide more personalized service and satisfy customers' unique needs. They are able to work more directly with fewer customers than larger businesses.

CHECKPOINT ✓

Beyond the formal definition of a small business, what four points can be used to describe a small business?

LO 6.2.2

SMALL BUSINESS ADVANTAGES

You need someone to mow your lawn, make a gourmet meal in your home for a few close friends, build a custom display case for a model train, or repair hardware on your home computer. Where would you turn for help? It's not likely that you will find a large business for any of those services.

Meeting Customer Needs

Small businesses play a vital role in the economy. They often serve customers where the number of products and services needed is small or the requirements are too specialized for large businesses to make a profit. It is easier for a small business to meet the precise needs of customers than a large business. Even though a large business has more resources, to operate efficiently it must focus on products and services that meet the needs of a large group of customers. That makes it harder to satisfy the unique needs of single customers.

Small businesses often are not able to match the lower operating costs of larger businesses. They can compete by paying attention to their customers. Small businesses serve fewer customers and usually have more frequent contact with those customers than large businesses. They are more likely to be located close to the customer. They depend less on other businesses to distribute or service their products.

Large businesses often rely on consumer research to gather information. Small businesses usually get direct information from their customers about what they like and dislike.

Providing Unique Services

Small businesses are especially suited to provide unique services for customers. They may plan a wedding or design a customized sound system for your home. Providing those types of services means that business representatives must take a special interest in the customer. They spend time determining needs and discussing alternatives. They have the expertise to plan and deliver the services that satisfy the customer. Large businesses may not find it profitable to spend that much time with each customer. Each employee that works with customers may not have the expertise to design the needed service.

Big business has a clear advantage when a large number of customers are willing to buy standard products and prefer low cost

Christina Richards/Shutterstock.com

How do small businesses provide unique services that large businesses cannot?

Applied Skills

Word Processing/Office Technology Organize students into small teams. Instruct each team to prepare a visual slide presentation using computer software that describes the competitive advantages and disadvantages of small businesses.

and efficient delivery. Small businesses gain an advantage when customers have unique needs, want more individual attention, and are willing to pay a bit more for the product or service to obtain what they really want. When asked, "What businesses do you believe are most concerned about you as a customer?" the majority of consumers identify small businesses.

Work as a TEAM

Identify two or three small businesses in your community that have been successful for many years. As a team, discuss what you think these businesses do that allows them to compete successfully with other small and large businesses.

CHECKPOINT

How can small businesses compete successfully with larger businesses?

LO 6.2.3

COMMON SMALL BUSINESS PROBLEMS

Not all small businesses succeed. In fact, their failure rate is much higher than larger businesses. Many failures result from the inability to pay expenses. The business is then forced to close. Some companies quietly go out of business when the owner believes that he or she is not doing well enough to continue. The owner may also get tired of the long hours and hard work.

Reasons for Failure

The following are the most common reasons for small business failure:

- Not keeping adequate records
- Not having enough start-up money
- Lack of management experience
- Lack of experience with the type of business
- Not controlling operating expenses
- Poor location for the business
- Failure to manage credit offered to customers

Small Business Assistance

With the right kind of assistance, small businesses can overcome each of the causes of failure listed above. Small business owners can get help from a number of sources. Universities and colleges often have faculty members who can give advice and support to people who are starting or have started their own businesses. Local groups of business people, such as chambers of commerce, have members who can help others with business problems.

The **Small Business Administration (SBA)** is a government agency that helps small business owners develop business plans and obtain financing and other support for their companies. Information about the SBA and its services can be obtained by visiting www.sba.gov.

rSnapshotPhotos/Shutterstock.com

Where can small businesses find assistance?

Work as a TEAM

Ask students whether the team members were in agreement on the success factors for the businesses they identified. Did their opinions change if they were customers of the business or not?

ONGOING ASSESSMENT

CHECKPOINT ANSWER

Smaller businesses are able to provide more personalized products and services to their customers. They are able to provide products and services where smaller orders and projects are required and tend to fill unique customer needs, which larger companies do not provide.

TEACH

List the reasons for small business failure on the board. Ask students to describe things that people who are considering starting a small business could do to avoid most of the problems.

THINK CRITICALLY THROUGH VISUALS

Small business assistance is available through the SBA, universities and colleges, and local business groups.

Different Learning Styles

Kinesthetic Learner Ask students to write each of the reasons for small business failure on a strip of paper. Then instruct them to select a strip, hold it, and read the reason aloud.

TEACH

Point out the advantages of seeking help to avoid failure.

NET KNOWLEDGE

The U.S. government, as well as state and local governments, offer support to entrepreneurs. They particularly encourage people who have not had opportunities in business, such as women and racial minorities. Most government agencies and other organizations have developed websites to make it easier for entrepreneurs to access information.

ONGOING ASSESSMENT

CHECKPOINT ✓ *ANSWER*

Common reasons for failure include not keeping adequate records, insufficient start-up money, lack of management experience, lack of experience with the type of business, not controlling operating expenses, poor location, and failure to manage credit.

ASSESS

Key Concepts *Answers*

1. d. 500
2. d. attention to unique customer needs
3. d. not enough employees to do the work

Make Academic Connections *Answers*

4. Answers will vary. Small businesses might use eBay to reach a wider audience, help control customer credit, and keep down costs by not having a brick-and-mortar location.
5. Presentations will vary.
6. Tables and charts will vary. Invite volunteers to summarize all the data collected in a single table or chart.

NET KNOWLEDGE

The U.S. government Small Business Administration, or SBA, provides a variety of services and programs for individuals who own their own businesses. The SBA is dedicated to providing information for small businesses and entrepreneurs. The site has information about starting a business, women-owned businesses, and many other aspects of running a small business. Surf the Web to find the Small Business Administration website. Review the types of resources that can be accessed through the website. Choose one of the options and write a short summary about the information available.

The SBA offers information, publications, counseling, and many other forms of support. The SBA sponsors the Service Corps of Retired Executives (SCORE). Members of SCORE are retired local businesspeople who volunteer their services to counsel and mentor new business owners.

CHECKPOINT ✓

List common reasons for small business failure.

6.2 ASSESSMENT

Key Concepts

Determine the best answer.

1. The Small Business Administration considers a business small if it employs fewer than _______ employees.
   a. 5
   b. 20
   c. 100
   d. 500
2. A competitive advantage that small businesses have over larger businesses is
   a. lower costs
   b. more consumer research
   c. lower prices
   d. attention to unique customer needs
3. Which of the following is not one of the reasons small business fail?
   a. poor customer credit practices
   b. the owner does not have adequate experience
   c. a poor business location
   d. not enough employees to do the work

Make Academic Connections

4. **Technology** eBay has become the home of many small businesses. Thousands of small business owners earn an excellent income by selling their products using the online auction services provided by eBay. Visit the eBay website and identify three ways a small business can use the website to support its operations.
5. **Communication** Interview a small business owner who has operated his or her business for at least three years. Determine the factors that have contributed to success as well as the major challenges that have been faced. Prepare an audio or video presentation based on your interview.
6. **Research** Interview 10 people who have recently purchased products or services from a small business. Ask them to list the top three reasons they made the purchase from a small business rather than a large business. Summarize the results from your interviews and present your findings in a table or chart.

RETEACH Instruct students to review the lesson goals and write two quiz questions for each goal.

CLOSE Ask students to list advantages and disadvantages to owning a small business.

ENRICH Assign students to search the Internet to find information on a successful small business owner, and then write a brief report on the reasons the business has been successful.

LIFE/WORK SKILLS

INFORMATION, COMMUNICATIONS, AND TECHNOLOGY LITERACY

Today's technology allows written communication to be exchanged at a much faster pace. Traditional forms of written communication, including letters, reports, and brochures, have not changed. However, when composed and completed, they can be sent to recipients in minutes using the Internet.

Many uses of traditional written communication have been replaced by instantaneous informal communications including e-mail, texting, and other new media. The immediate nature of the technology as well as the informal approach to composing those messages often results in poor communication or even miscommunication. When you use technology for written communication, especially in business, a few basic rules will demonstrate to your recipients that they are important and you want to communicate effectively.

The two primary types of communication used in business are memos and e-mail messages. Memos are formal and are used to convey more complex information. A memo can be sent by mail or attached to an e-mail when there is a need for a more permanent record of correspondence. When there is a need for formal language, or if the information included would make an e-mail too long, a memo is appropriate. E-mail is more informal and used for direct and brief communication. Here are some important guidelines.

When Composing a Memo

1. ***Know your audience***. Direct your memo to one person or a small group of people. Who needs the information? What do they need to know?
2. ***Focus on one specific subject***. Make sure the subject is important to the audience. Specifically identify the subject of the memo. Do not stray into other topics.
3. ***Select your words carefully***. Use language appropriate for the organization and understandable to your audience. Be clear, direct, and objective.
4. ***Start strong***. Begin with an attention-getting first sentence. Focus the attention of the reader and get to the point.
5. ***Provide only needed information***. Keep the memo brief, usually no more than one page, so it can be read in a few minutes. Before you end, be sure the information is complete.
6. ***End effectively***. Identify any action needed and emphasize the importance of the information.

When Composing an E-mail Message

1. ***Send only to the people who need the information***. Do not "reply to all" or use a mass e-mail list. Use e-mail for more individualized and specific messages.
2. ***Use a specific subject line***. People get many e-mails. They can read and respond more efficiently if they can identify a clear subject.
3. ***Provide a context***. If you are responding to an e-mail, briefly identify the information to which you are responding. Provide any information needed by the reader to understand your message.
4. ***Don't get caught up in the technology***. Avoid "flaming" with all caps or inserting emoticons, flashing text, or other gimmicks that detract from the information.
5. ***Keep the message short***. An e-mail should be read in about a minute. If the message is longer, send it in a different format or add an attachment or link.
6. ***Don't write in haste***. You may regret an emotional message sent in haste. Consider the effect your message may have on the recipient.
7. ***Even when writing informally, use effective writing skills***. Write in complete, active sentences, organize using paragraphs, and check your spelling.
8. ***Use e-mail to create a record***. E-mail servers hold records of your files, even after you think they are deleted. If you need a record of a memo, use e-mail.

Think Critically

1. When should you send a memo rather than an e-mail?
2. What are the communication problems that are most likely to occur when using instant communication methods?

LIFE/WORK SKILLS

Explain to students that technology may make communications faster and easier, but may also result in less effective communications. It is important to use technology correctly when preparing business communications.

Think Critically *Answers*

1. Send a memo when there is a need for a more permanent record of your correspondence, a need for formal language, or if the information included would make an e-mail too long.

2. Misinterpretation is a common problem because e-mail writers tend to write in a brief, casual style. Instant messaging is also more immediate and therefore invites emotional responses that might otherwise be tempered in a more formal letter or printed memo.

E-mails can also be disregarded as "spam" if the sender does not use an appropriate subject line or may not be read in their entirety if they are too long.

Applied Skills

Communication Assign each student to prepare an e-mail message and a two-paragraph memo using the guidelines provided. The communications should relate to a topic from the current lesson and should be directed to other students in the class.

Focus on REAL LIFE

Explain to students that budgets are very important for businesses because they can alert the business owner to problems before they become too big to solve. Budgets may have to be adjusted if changes occur in the economy or in business operations.

TEACH

List the lesson subheadings on the board. Explain to students that there are several important factors that contribute to the success of a new business. As you disclose each of the factors, ask students to give reasons why each factor can affect the success or failure of the business.

Life-Span Plan Answer

Answers will vary. Students should identify hobbies, interests, and experiences and describe steps they can take to expand their experiences and opportunities to help them achieve their life-span goals.

6.3 Starting a Small Business

Learning Outcomes

6.3.1 Recognize important factors to be considered when starting a business.

6.3.2 Describe the elements of a business plan.

6.3.3 Identify types and sources of financing for a small business.

Key Terms

business plan 138
start-up financing 139
short-term financing 140
long-term financing 140

Focus on REAL LIFE

Quinn turned his baseball card hobby into a business. He had a small store where he bought and sold baseball cards and memorabilia. Quinn began his business with a small bank loan and money saved from working while in college.

The business grew steadily and Quinn prepared a specific budget at the start of each year. He was able to spend his money on inventory, advertising, and improvements to his store.

This year he used the same budgeting process that he had for the past four years. Based on last year's results, he estimated a sales increase of 8 percent. Even with the increased expenses, the budget projected another nice profit.

The first two months of the year went well. Then the economy faltered and customers cut back on spending. Quinn's sales declined while his expenses continued to increase. Quinn studied his budget to determine why he had problems in the fifth year when his planning had been so successful in the past.

LO 6.3.1

THE BUSINESS DECISION

Many people think about starting a business. Few actually do. The procedures followed to start a business often determine whether it will be successful. The process begins with an idea and concludes with a careful study of information to establish whether the idea can be successful.

An Idea Plus Experience

Business ideas come from many sources. Hobbies, interests, and business experiences often give people ideas for new businesses. Books and magazines suggest new business opportunities, including available franchises. Few people should think about starting a business without working for some time in a small business. Several years of training in a range of business operations will prepare you for the role of owner. Having responsibility for decisions and opportunities to manage people is a key part of that experience.

Life-Span Plan

What hobbies, interests, and experiences do you have that could help you achieve your life-span goals? Describe steps you could take now that would expand your experiences and opportunities for achieving your life-span goals.

Right Place and Time

Putting your business idea into action means finding the right place to open the business. Most retail businesses need good customer traffic. If the business is not easy to find or requires a great deal of travel time, many potential customers will stay away. A wholesaler needs easy access to manufacturers where products

Different Learning Styles

Kinesthetic Learner As students study the factors to consider when starting a business, encourage them to draw a picture or graphic that illustrates each factor. They can use the illustrations as reminders of the important factors.

are obtained for resale to other businesses. Manufacturers must be located in an area with access to the raw materials used in manufacturing. Transportation systems must also be easy to reach for distributing finished products. Timing is another key factor in starting a business. Most successful businesses start during a period when customer demand for their products or services is high.

Work as a TEAM

You are planning to open a small business that will rent bicycles, rollerblades, push scooters, and electric scooters by the hour for people to use for relaxation and exercise. As a team, identify three possible business locations in your community and discuss which location would be best for the business. Prepare a presentation that compares and contrasts the locations. Use visuals such as maps, photos, and drawings to help illustrate your presentation.

Team Approach

Many small business owners are quite independent. They started their businesses because they do not want to take direction from other people. A business is not easy to run without the help of others. Even the smallest businesses need a few full- or part-time employees to grow or cover extended hours. The employees must be chosen carefully for their ability to work as a team. Choosing the "team" members becomes one of the most important initial business decisions.

In addition to employees, small business owners will need assistance from people with specialized business knowledge. These include bankers, lawyers, and accountants. If possible, the new owner should identify business professionals who focus on working with small businesses.

Preparation and Research

The most important step in starting a business is preparation. Preparation includes having enough information to make good decisions about the business. Time spent gathering and studying information before the business is started will save time and avoid later problems.

Information is needed about customers, competitors, important operations, government regulations, and many other topics. This information is available through the Internet, libraries, colleges or universities, and small business assistance centers. At times, the new business owner will have to do further research to gather more current data. Information will help to make sure that decisions are made objectively.

PhotoDisc/Getty Images

Is there a small business assistance center in your neighborhood? What resources can you use to locate the closest center?

Work as a TEAM

Students should identify locations that will attract a large number of people who are interested in the products and also determine where there is a safe and pleasant area to use them nearby.

TEACH

Remind students that many entrepreneurs are independent and not always good team players. Lead a discussion about how an independent-minded entrepreneur can result in problems for a business and why working with a team can benefit a new small business owner.

THINK CRITICALLY THROUGH VISUALS

Answers will vary. Students can determine the answer by searching the local telephone directory.

Applied Skills

Language Arts Ask students to write a memo to a friend who is considering starting a new business. In the memo, the student should offer advice on issues the friend should consider carefully before making a final decision.

ONGOING ASSESSMENT

CHECKPOINT ✓ ANSWER

A team approach allows employees to feel valued and motivated to take personal responsibility for the benefit of the business. Owners cannot expect to be able to do everything alone. Building a team will allow the business to increase productivity and, ultimately, profits.

TEACH

Locate an example of a business plan for a small business in your community or find one online. Allow students to examine the plan so they have a visual image of the length, format, and content of the business plan. Tell them that all business plans are not alike, but most include information on a common set of elements.

▸ Figure 6-4 ANSWER

The elements in Figure 6-4 are important when planning a new business because they force the owners to think about and plan all major business activities and how they will be carried out.

CHECKPOINT ✓

Why is it important to use a team approach when starting a new business?

LO 6.3.2

DEVELOPING A BUSINESS PLAN

When successful businesses are compared with those that fail, one factor stands out as the most important difference. The owners of successful businesses develop and follow a business plan. The owners of businesses that fail often do not have a business plan.

ELEMENTS OF A BUSINESS PLAN
Description of the Business • the business idea • major products and services • ownership structure • strengths/weaknesses • long- and short-term goals
Customer Analysis • description of customers • location, number, and resources of customers • sales forecasts
Operations Plan • organization of the company • description of major operations • analysis of resources needed • human resource plans
Marketing Plan • description of major marketing activities • description of resources needed • schedule of marketing activities
Financial Plans • start-up costs • short- and long-term financial needs • sources of financing • budgets and financial statements

FIGURE 6-4

Why are each of these elements important when planning a new business?

What Is a Business Plan?

A **business plan** is a written description of a business idea and how it will be carried out, including all major business activities. Key features of a business plan are a general description of the company, the credentials of the owner(s), a description of the product or service, an analysis of the market (demand, customers, and competition), and a financial plan. Most business plans are developed for one year and then updated for the next year. If the business owner needs help from others, especially for financing the new business, a business plan will usually be required. Figure 6-4 is an outline of the sections of a business plan.

Even if help is not needed, a business plan should be developed. By developing a plan, the owner is forced to think about important activities, the amount of time they will take, and their cost. This process may identify potential problems. The plan also serves as a guide to keep the business on track.

Steps in Developing the Business Plan

The business owner is in charge of developing the business plan. The most popular use of business plans is to persuade lenders and investors to finance the venture. A well-developed plan will lay out an idea and will require an owner to analyze his or her concept and make decisions about key business activities such as production, marketing, staffing, and financing.

Some owners hire someone to write the plan. Others get help from a bank or a local office of the Small Business Administration. Even if others are involved in developing the plan, the owner must be familiar with all of the information and make the major decisions for the plan.

The first step in developing the business plan is to gather and review information. If possible, the owner should review other business plans and study information

Different Learning Abilities

Visually Impaired Reproduce Figure 6-4 and increase the font size so each section of the business plan is on a separate sheet of paper. This visual aid can be used to highlight the kind of information that should be included in each element of a business plan.

Digital Vision/Getty Images

Where can the entrepreneur find help in creating a business plan?

on the activities and financial performance of similar businesses, especially potential competitors.

Next, the owner should develop strategic alternatives. Alternative plans for production, marketing, staffing, and financing should be studied and identified. The owner can select the best choices from the alternatives.

Finally, each section of the business plan should be written. A plan devotes several sections to a general description of the business. These sections include the basic legal form of the organization and major products or services. Other sections detail the competition, potential customers, operations, marketing, and finances. Before the plan is completed, the owner should have business experts review the plan and offer their advice about its strengths and weaknesses.

CHECKPOINT ✓

What are "strategic alternatives" in a business plan?

LO 6.3.3

FINANCING THE SMALL BUSINESS

A new business with a good product or service may run out of money before it can become profitable. Several years of operation are required before most new businesses earn a profit. Finding adequate financing is a key step in starting and running a new business.

Types of Financing

Three types of financing must be considered. **Start-up financing** is the amount of money needed to open the business.

TEACH

Engage the class in a debate centering around this question: Should a new business owner write the business plan or hire someone else to write it? Record the major points made for each side of the issue on the board.

ONGOING ASSESSMENT

CHECKPOINT ✓ANSWER

Strategic alternatives are alternative plans for production, staffing, financing, and so on. Even the best business plan cannot predict every possible circumstance. An alternate plan allows a business to be prepared for the unforeseeable.

THINK CRITICALLY THROUGH VISUALS

An entrepreneur can find help creating a business plan by consulting business experts and using the support provided by the Small Business Administration and other business support groups.

Applied Skills

Writing Across the Curriculum Assign students to prepare a paragraph that compares planning and writing a business plan to writing assignments they have had in other classes, such as a research report in a science class.

FYI

As a class, discuss what lenders look for in each part of the business plan.

TEACH

Assign students to prepare an outline that lists the three major types of financing as headings. Then, as each type is discussed, students should list examples of each type of financing under the appropriate heading.

Business Insight

Think Critically
Answers

1. Answers will vary. Students should indicate that earning a profit is the main motivation. They might also mention the need to compete against local and regional businesses.

2. Presentations will vary. Students might report on Coca-Cola's sustainability efforts to reduce water use, recycle packaging, reduce greenhouse gasses, and achieve balance in their communities and in nature. Another example is Boeing's commitment to produce aircraft that weigh less. This means more fuel efficiency and less pollution.

3. Summaries will vary. Students should be able to locate McDonald's values on its website. Some of the programs mentioned include sustainability, green efforts, recycling, and animal welfare.

FYI Bankers and other lenders want to see a written business plan before considering making a loan. Looking at the business plan can help a potential lender determine if the owner really understands the business and is committed to its success.

It includes the cost of buildings, equipment, *inventory* (products or raw materials on hand), supplies, licenses, and the like. **Short-term financing** is the money needed to pay for the current operating activities of a business. Short-term financing is obtained for a period of less than a year and often for one or two months. **Long-term financing** is money needed for the main resources of a business (such as land, buildings, and equipment) that will last for many years. These resources usually require large amounts of money and will be paid over many years.

Sources of Financing

Finding the needed money may be the most difficult part of starting a business. The money required to start and operate a new business usually comes from a mixture of owner-supplied and borrowed funds.

The source of owner-supplied money depends on the ownership structure. In a proprietorship, one person will supply the money. In most partnerships, each

Business Insight

Global Social Responsibility

Many Europeans are concerned about their personal health and the health of their environment. In part, this concern is based on Europe's high population density. There are 3.6 times as many people per square mile in Europe as there are in the United States. Europe's high population density has led to concerns about waste disposal, air quality, and the availability of natural resources such as fresh water.

Some businesses based in the United States and doing business in Europe are working hard to address the concerns of European customers and governments, including that of the European Union. McDonald's wants to be seen as a socially responsible company and has policies and practices to address concerns about the nutritional value of its products and the impact of its operations on the environment.

Throughout Europe, McDonald's prints nutrition information directly on food containers and wrappers. This means consumers can see information about calories, fat, and sodium as they pluck fries out of a cardboard pouch.

McDonald's started an environmental initiative in England to convert more than 90% of its used cooking oil into products including biodiesel. The fuel is used to power the company's delivery vehicles. This program removes cooking oil from the waste stream and reduces the consumption of gasoline.

Think Critically

1. What motivates U.S. companies to tailor their policies and practices to address the social concerns of global customers?
2. Research another company's efforts to be socially responsible and address social concerns around the world. Develop a short presentation about your findings.
3. Use the Internet to locate McDonald's Worldwide Corporate Values in Action website. Write a summary of one of the programs mentioned on the website.

Different Learning Abilities

Specific Learning Disability (SLD) Provide students with a local business directory or business listings in a telephone directory and ask them to locate the names of three banks that offer financing and other services to small businesses. Students should record the name of the bank, the address, main telephone number, and the URL for the bank's website if available.

partner will be expected to contribute. A corporation is owned and financed by the shareholders.

Borrowed funds are obtained through loans from banks and other financial institutions or through funding provided by other people, such as family and friends. Often companies that sell equipment, materials, or inventory to a business will offer credit if the business does not have financial problems. A new business owner should be careful about accepting credit. The owner must take into account the cost of the credit and when payments are due.

Pressmaster/Shutterstock.com

Why would a lending institution insist that the money required for starting a business be a mixture of owner-supplied and borrowed funds?

CHECKPOINT
In addition to owner-supplied capital, what are several other sources of financing for a small business?

6.3 ASSESSMENT

Key Concepts

Determine the best answer.

1. Every business begins with a(n)
   a. customer
   b. profit
   c. idea
   d. invention
2. True or False. Most small business owners enjoy being part of a team.
3. True or False. A business plan does not have to be written because the business owner is well aware of the information in the plan.
4. Money needed for the important resources of a business (such as land, buildings, and equipment) that will last for many years is called
   a. start-up financing
   b. short-term financing
   c. long-term financing
   d. credit

Make Academic Connections

5. **Technology** Locate an outline for a business plan on the Internet. Compare the sections of the plan you found with those in Figure 6-4. Develop a final outline using both resources. Write a two-sentence statement for each section of the outline describing why that section is important to a successful small business.
6. **Math** Gwen Osterhaus and Portia Juarez have formed a partnership to open a garden coffee cafe in Central Park. Gwen invests $23,000 and Portia invests $31,000. They get a micro loan from the Small Business Administration for $18,500. They have $9,000 of credit from the Bean Machine Company that sold them some of their equipment. Calculate the total amount of start-up financing available to the partnership. Make a pie chart that shows the percentage of total financing that is provided from each source. How much of the financing is owner supplied and how much is borrowed?

THINK CRITICALLY THROUGH VISUALS

A lending institution is more willing to loan money if the owners of the business are willing to invest their own savings in the business because they are more likely to repay their loans than people who do not invest their own money.

ONGOING ASSESSMENT

CHECKPOINT ANSWER

Borrowed money may come from banks, finance companies, or other individuals, such as friends and family. Some suppliers may also be willing to extend credit.

ASSESS

Key Concepts *Answers*

1. c. idea
2. False. Most small business owners are very independent and prefer to work alone.
3. False. A business plan should be written.
4. c. long-term financing

Make Academic Connections *Answers*

5. Answers will vary. The outlines should show evidence of two sources and should be presented in a logical order.
6. Total financing: $81,500
Pie chart slices: Gwen, 28%; Portia, 38%, Loan, 23%, and Credit, 11%
Owner supplied: $54,000 (66%)
Borrowed: $27,500 (34%).

CLOSE Ask each student to describe one activity or type of information that is important to a small business owner when planning a new business.

RETEACH Display Figure 6-4. Ask students to describe the importance of the business plan and explain the reason for having strategic alternatives for each section of the business plan.

ENRICH Ask a successful small business owner to speak to the class and discuss the advantages and disadvantages of being a small business owner. Students should prepare questions in advance.

Think Critically About Business *Answers*

1. Answers will vary depending on students' interests, hobbies, and skills.

2. Small businesses contribute more new jobs because new businesses start frequently. Larger, established businesses have often reached growth limits and have fewer opportunities to offer.

3. Personality plays a key role in the success of many small business owners, a fact well demonstrated. The young entrepreneurs each had marketable skills and good ideas, but their skills and ideas could not sell themselves. Through their persistence, initiative, and ability to secure the help of others, they were able to turn ideas and skills into businesses.

4. By using the Internet, small businesses eliminate some overhead costs, increase the size of available markets, and increase the speed of communication. In doing so, many are able to compete with larger businesses.

5. Freddie can increase his chances for success by considering what type of business he is qualified to manage; how he will finance the start-up, short-term, and long-term goals of the business; how much time he can devote; how he will manage recordkeeping and competition; where he will locate; and who he will enlist for help. Preparing a written business plan will force him to consider each of these questions.

Chapter 6 Assessment

Review Business Concepts

6.1 Becoming an Entrepreneur

- Successful entrepreneurs have a real desire to be their own boss. They use special skills and abilities to come up with innovative ideas and then develop a good initial plan for a business. Entrepreneurs represent all age categories, racial and ethnic groups, and both genders, as well as varied educational levels.
- Entrepreneurship is a key part of the U.S. economy. Money needed to start a new business may come from the owner, family, friends, or venture capital. Other sources of financing are loans from banks and financial institutions and credit given by other businesses. Small businesses are responsible for nearly half of the U.S. gross domestic product each year and more than half of all innovative products and services developed.
- Opportunities open to entrepreneurs include the creation of new or improved products and services, an improved design, more effective procedures, or greater attention to quality. Risks include lack of adequate capital, low sales, higher than expected expenses, competitive pressure, an owner unprepared to manage a growing business, and operations that require more time than the owner is willing to commit.

6.2 Small Business Basics

- In a small business, the owner is usually the manager, it operates in one or very few locations, it typically serves a small market, and it is not dominant in its field of operation.
- Small businesses play an important role in the economy. They often serve customers where the number of products and services needed is small or the requirements are too specialized for large businesses to be profitable.
- The most common reasons for small business failure are not keeping adequate records, not having enough start-up money, lack of management experience, lack of experience with the type of business, not controlling operating expenses, poor location for the business, and failure to manage customer credit.

6.3 Starting a Small Business

- Factors that lead to a successful new business are an idea plus experience, the right time and place, a team approach, and preparation and research.
- By developing a written business plan, the owner will think about important activities, the amount of time they will take, and their cost. The plan also serves as a guide to keep the business on track.
- Obtaining adequate financing is an important step in starting and operating a new business. Three types of financing to be considered are start-up, short-term, and long-term financing. The money required to start and operate a new business usually comes from a mixture of owner-supplied and borrowed funds.

Think Critically About Business

1. What is a new product or service that could become the basis for a new business that fits your interests, hobbies, or special skills and abilities? What are some reasons you would be interested or not interested in becoming an entrepreneur?
2. Why do you believe that small businesses contribute more new jobs to the economy than large, established businesses?
3. What are factors that you believe contributed to the success of the young entrepreneurs described in Lesson 6-1? Do you believe the idea for their product or service was more or less important than their personal characteristics?
4. How is the Internet changing the characteristics of small businesses? Do you believe the Internet can make small businesses more competitive with large businesses? Why?

5. Freddie is thinking about starting a small business and has come to you for advice. Using the reasons why most small businesses fail as listed in Lesson 6-2, what would you tell Freddie that will help him increase his chances for being successful?

6. In most communities, there are several locations where retail businesses locate but soon fail. They are followed by other businesses that also fail. People say the pattern of failure is because of a poor location. Do you agree that the location is the most likely reason that the businesses fail? Why would a new business consider a location where a previous business has already failed?

7. Identify the three types of people you believe would be the most important to assist a new small business owner. Justify each of your choices.

8. If you were a banker reviewing a business plan to determine if you will provide financing, what information would be most important in determining if you would support the small business or not?

9. What are the advantages and disadvantages of hiring another, more experienced person to develop and write the business plan for the owner of a new business?

Develop Your Business Language

Match the terms listed with the definitions.

10. A government agency that helps small business owners develop business plans and obtain financing and other support for their companies.

11. Money provided by large investors to finance new products and new businesses that have a good chance to be very profitable.

12. The money needed to pay for the current operating activities of a business.

13. The amount of money needed to open the business.

14. An invention or creation that is brand new.

15. Someone who takes a risk in starting a business to earn a profit.

16. A written description of the business idea and how it will be carried out, including all major business activities.

17. Money needed for the important resources of a business (such as land, buildings, and equipment) that will last for many years.

18. An independent business with fewer than 500 employees.

19. A designed change that increases the usefulness of a product, service, or process.

20. The process of starting, organizing, managing, and assuming the responsibility for a business.

Key Terms

- **a.** business plan
- **b.** entrepreneur
- **c.** entrepreneurship
- **d.** improvement
- **e.** innovation
- **f.** long-term financing
- **g.** short-term financing
- **h.** small business
- **i.** Small Business Administration (SBA)
- **j.** start-up financing
- **k.** venture capital

6. This particular location is probably not well suited to retail business. It may not have enough traffic or the traffic may move by too quickly. It may not be visible, have adequate lighting, signage, or walk-by traffic to support a retail business. This does not mean, however, that this same location would not work for a service business for which these elements may not be as critical.

7. A lawyer, accountant, or consultant can assist with a business plan and the necessary legal forms for beginning a business. A loan officer or other finance specialist can assist with securing funds, as can friends and family. Mentors can provide encouragement and insight from their own experience.

8. A banker will want to know that a business owner has considered all aspects important to success. A thorough business plan will provide him or her with answers to critical questions about how well-informed and prepared the applicant is. This information will be the most important to consider.

9. The advantages of hiring someone to write a plan would be the insight he or she could offer. A consultant or experienced business owner would recognize any flaws in the plan and could assist the new owner in making needed improvements. The disadvantages might be that another person may not share the same enthusiasm or vision for the business that the prospective owner has.

Develop Your Business Language *Answers*

10. i. Small Business Administration (SBA)
11. k. venture capital
12. g. short-term financing
13. j. start-up financing
14. e. innovation
15. b. entrepreneur
16. a. business plan
17. f. long-term financing
18. h. small business
19. d. improvement
20. c. entrepreneurship

Make Academic Connections *Answers*

21. Letters and brochures will vary. The communications should be persuasive and include the benefits of investment.

22. Reports will vary depending on the agencies selected. Reports should describe each agency, the services provided, and how a new business can qualify for services.

23. Answers will vary depending on the county of residence. Answers should include the total number of businesses with one to four employees, the five industries with the most businesses employing fewer than five employees, and the total number of businesses in each of those industries.

24. Charts and graphs will vary. Consider asking students to include a source for their findings.

Make Your Case *Answers*

25a. A partner would provide the additional cash right away, but then David would not be the sole owner of his business.

25b. David would be able to buy the business himself, but he would have to wait seven years.

25c. He would be able to start his business right away, but he would owe a franchise fee each year that would reduce his profits.

26. Answers will vary.

Make Academic Connections

21. Communication Many small business owners obtain some of their start-up financing from family members and friends. Assume you are starting a small Internet business that will develop and maintain low-cost websites for local organizations, clubs, and nonprofit groups. You have $2,500 of your own money to invest and need to raise an additional $5,000. Develop a letter or one-page brochure that you can use to interest family and friends in investing $500 or more in your new business. Make sure it is persuasive and tells them what benefits they will receive from their investment.

22. Government The federal government and most state governments provide many resources as well as financial support for small businesses. Use the Internet to locate two agencies of the federal government that provide services developed specifically for small businesses. Then search the website for your state's government and locate one state agency that provides small business services. Prepare a three-paragraph report on each of the agencies you identified in which you describe the agency, the services provided, and how a new business can qualify for the services.

23. Economics The U.S. Census Bureau maintains information on the number of businesses and amount of business activity in every county of each state. Access the U.S. Census Bureau website and then search for "County Business Patterns." Choose your state and then choose the county where you live. Find data on the number of businesses with one to four employees in your county. List the total number of businesses of that size, the five industries with the most businesses employing fewer than five employees, and the total number of establishments in each of those industries.

24. Technology Use the Internet to identify the number of small business owners by age. Enter the information in a spreadsheet program and calculate the percentage of all small business owners represented by each age classification. Then use the graphing function to create a chart or graph illustrating the results.

Make Your Case

David Obolski completed a community college program in Small Business Management. He wanted to own his own floral business. He had worked for Flower-a-Bunda during high school and college. In addition, he was able to save almost $20,000 toward starting his own business. However, he knew that he would need more than $20,000 to buy a florist shop. He would need almost double that amount to qualify for the necessary loans to start up the business. David studied three ways he might start his business.

- **a.** He could find a partner to provide the additional cash.
- **b.** He could work for the owner of Flower-a-Bunda until she retired in seven years and buy the business with his accumulated savings.
- **c.** He could purchase a franchise for an investment of $20,000. However, David would have to pay a franchise fee of 6 percent of total sales each year to the franchisor.

25. What are the advantages and disadvantages of each route to small business ownership for David?

26. If you were David, which choice would you make? Why?

Interactions and Connections

27. Survey at least 10 people in your community about their experiences as consumers with small businesses and large businesses. Ask them to describe the reasons they prefer to buy from small businesses and the reasons they prefer to buy from large businesses. Then ask them to describe the disadvantages of each. Summarize the results of your discussions in a chart or short written report.

Interactions and Connections

27. Reports will vary. Consider allowing students to work in pairs.

28. The World Wide Web has opened a world of opportunities for teen entrepreneurship. Teen entrepreneurs can now easily reach customers with online games, products, social networking opportunities, or by supporting social causes. Often the businesses developed from teen entrepreneurs' ideas are purchased by larger companies, making young entrepreneurs millionaires.

a. Use the Internet to find information about teen entrepreneurs and how they used the World Wide Web to launch their business. Determine why these entrepreneurs' businesses were successful.

b. Identify an idea for a business that you would like to start using the World Wide Web. Develop a short business plan to determine if your idea would be feasible.

Desktop Publishing Event

You and a partner have been hired to create, design, and produce a business publication using desktop publishing software. You have two hours of class time to prepare a newsletter that focuses attention on entrepreneurship, small business management, time management tips, professional networking, and successful entrepreneurs. The target audience for your newsletter includes entrepreneurs, student business leaders, and community leaders. Content of the newsletter must be up-to-date and relevant. The newsletter should provide solid tips for successful entrepreneurs. Your team is allowed to use two computers, a scanner, and clip art. No other equipment may be used. The finished product may be submitted in black and white or in color on plain paper. Word division manuals and dictionaries may be used as reference materials. The second part of this competition includes a one-hour written objective test to determine your knowledge of desktop publishing. The score received on the test will equal 15 percent of the final event score.

Performance Indicators Evaluated

- Understand graphics, text creation, layout, creativity, and selection of appropriate fonts and type sizes for desktop publishing.
- Prepare an interesting newsletter about entrepreneurship and related concepts.
- Incorporate graphics and layout that are visually appealing.
- Use correct punctuation, grammar, and sentence structure.
- Demonstrate creativity throughout the publication.

For more detailed information about performance indicators, go to the FBLA website.

Think Critically

1. What characteristics make a great publication?
2. What can be done to make a publication reader-friendly?
3. Who should be considered when producing a publication?
4. Give two examples of items in a newsletter that might be distracting to readers.

www.fbla-pbl.org

WINNING EDGE

Desktop Publishing Event

Newsletters are competing with the latest technology and up-to-date forms of communication. Many individuals are not willing to spend time reading information that appears to be boring or irrelevant. Newsletters must contain information that the target market can use and encourage professional networking. Students must conduct research to include stories about successful entrepreneurs.

Think Critically *Answers*

1. A great publication has a balance between text and graphics. A great publication uses proper grammar and sentence structure, and clearly presents the major ideas.

2. Using easy-to-read fonts, bulleted lists, and a conversational writing style can make a publication more reader-friendly.

3. Consider the publication's target audience when planning the content and designing the layout.

4. Too many graphics, not enough white space, outdated or irrelevant topics, and long text passages with no visual breaks are examples of distracting items in a publication.

28a. Answers will vary depending on the entrepreneur.

28b. Business plans will vary and should include information about how the proposed business will gain a competitive advantage over competition.

CHAPTER OVERVIEW

In this chapter, students learn about the role and common functions of managers, how leadership differs from management, and the importance of ethical leadership.

7.1 Management Functions and Styles

This lesson introduces the five functions of management that are common to all levels of managers and the styles managers use to work with employees.

7.2 Leadership

While studying this lesson, students will compare leadership with management and learn about the characteristics of effective leaders. They will also review human relations skills and the ways leaders influence others.

7.3 Ethical Management

This lesson focuses on the importance of ethical management and how leaders can influence the behavior of others.

Chapter 7 Management and Leadership

Monkey Business Images/Shutterstock.com

Instructor Resources

- Activities and Study Guide IE
- Chapter and Unit Tests IE
- Lesson Plans
- PowerPoint Presentation
- Cognero Test, Ch. 7

Student Resources

Activities and Study Guide
www.cengage.com/swep/pob9e
- Portfolio Activity

PLANNING A CAREER IN . . .
MANAGEMENT

Business, Management & Administration

The career choice you make will likely be driven by your interests and abilities. People who are focused on a specific field such as accounting, sales, nursing, or biomedical engineering may or may not have aspirations to become managers. However, many people start their business careers with the goal of becoming a manager some day. They view the chance to demonstrate success as a manager and contribute to major decisions as a challenging goal.

Managers are an important key to the success of a company. Management opportunities exist in all companies and in every part of a business. Whether your interests are in finance, marketing, information management, engineering, or human resources, you can become a manager.

You can take the first step by accepting a role such as a team leader. You can then advance to a position as a supervisor or assistant manager after only a few years of experience. With additional experience, and perhaps some additional education, you can become a mid- or top-level manager. Your career advancement will be based on how well you perform management duties and your contribution to the overall success of the business.

Related Job Titles

- Administrator
- Assistant Manager
- Coordinator
- Department Head
- Project Manager
- Supervisor

Analyze Career Opportunities in . . .
MANAGEMENT

Use library and Internet resources to learn more about careers in management. Choose one of the job titles listed in the box and answer the following questions.

1. What is the employment outlook for careers in this field?
2. Is this a career that interests you? Describe a few things you could do to learn more about this career.

What it's like to work as a . . . Supervisor

Although Frank enjoys his job as the supervisor of a production line at the Emprex Corporation, today will be challenging. This morning, Frank needs to interview nine people to fill three full-time positions and one part-time position. This afternoon he is meeting with his team to talk about overtime and budgets.

Frank needs to let his work group know that they will have to work at least 10 hours of overtime each week for the next two months to meet their quota. Some team members will be happy about the extra money but others will complain about giving up their free time.

He also needs to talk to his group about the budget. He doesn't have full authority over the budget, but his manager has asked him to help find ways to reduce expenses.

Finally, Frank has to complete one of his least favorite duties—terminating an employee. A new employee has not been able to meet the job expectations and has to be let go. Frank has a meeting scheduled at 3 P.M. with the employee to break the news.

What about you? What would you find the most and least enjoyable about Frank's work?

PLANNING A CAREER IN . . .
MANAGEMENT

Tell students there are many opportunities in management for young people with limited business experience as well as older, more experienced businesspeople. Management combines knowledge of the entire business, specific business activities, and how to work effectively with others. At the conclusion of the discussion, direct students to answer the "What About You?" question that follows the feature.

What About You? ***Answers***

Answers will vary. Some students will find the manager's work exciting and varied, while others will think it seems too hectic and difficult. You may want to ask the class to list specific pros and cons of management careers and then compare different types of management jobs. Ask students how their existing ideas about the work of managers compare to the description of Frank's activities.

Analyze Career Opportunities *Answers*
Student answers will vary depending on when the assignment is completed and individual interests.

Additional Career information

Encourage students to investigate careers they find interesting and explore unfamiliar careers. Two resources for additional career information are the *Occupational Outlook Handbook*, an online publication (www.bls.gov/oco) of the U.S. Bureau of Labor Statistics, and the O*NET Resource Center (www.onetcenter.org) developed by the U.S. Department of Labor. Information about specific careers and jobs can be used to demonstrate the relevance of skills learned in this course.

Focus on REAL LIFE

Tell students that almost everyone is involved in the type of work managers complete, but most often it involves personal or family activities. However, the experience of planning, budgeting, decision making, and working with others can help people understand the skills that can be further developed as a business manager.

TEACH

Write the definition of "management" on the board. Instruct students to brainstorm activities that managers might complete to accomplish the goals of an organization. Ask students to rate the activities listed from the simplest to the most complex and justify their rankings.

Ask students whether they believe the job of a new supervisor responsible for the work of eight employees and that of the chief executive of an international corporation have anything in common. Explain that while their day-to-day work is quite different, there are five common functions that all managers perform.

7.1 Management Functions and Styles

Learning Outcomes

7.1.1 Define the five functions of management.

7.1.2 Describe the levels of management in businesses and organizations.

7.1.3 Discuss how and when to use the two management styles.

Key Terms

- management 148
- planning 148
- organizing 148
- staffing 149
- implementing 149
- controlling 149
- management style 151

Focus on REAL LIFE

Have you considered a career in management? Do you realize that you might already have experience with activities that are similar in some aspects to those of a manager's work? You manage your time and your money. You might be a leader of a team or an organization. Maybe you have taken a leadership role in a group activity. As a leader you probably took responsibility, gave directions, and solved problems.

While not the same as leading a business, these activities give you a taste of the work of managers. Consider what it would be like to be responsible for a million-dollar budget, directing the work of hundreds of people, or making sure an important project involving several parts of a business is completed on schedule.

Do you think you have what it takes to be a manager? Would you find working as a manager exciting as well as challenging? If so, what can you do now to begin to prepare for a management career?

LO 7.1.1

ROLE AND WORK OF MANAGERS

Managers are responsible for the success or failure of businesses and organizations. Managers receive recognition and other rewards when a business meets its goals. They also are held accountable when goals are not met. People who want to experience the risks and rewards of leading a business often become managers.

Who Is a Manager?

Management is the process of accomplishing the goals of an organization through the effective use of people and other resources. Managers make things happen in businesses. The entrepreneur who develops the idea for a new business is a manager. The top executive of a multimillion-dollar business who must make the final decision on a plan to enter a new international market is a manager. Supervisors with responsibility for the work of a small number of employees are managers, as are vice presidents with hundreds of employees reporting to them.

What Do Managers Do?

Every manager has specific job duties, but all managers must complete similar activities no matter what the size or type of organization. Managers' work can be organized within five functions: planning, organizing, staffing, implementing, and controlling.

- **Planning** involves analyzing information, setting goals, and making decisions about what needs to be done.
- **Organizing** means identifying and arranging the work and resources needed to achieve the goals that have been set.

Different Learning Abilities

English Language Learners (ELL) Provide students whose primary language is not English with a handout listing the terms and definitions from pages 148 and 149. Provide pronunciation guides for each term and make sure students understand the meaning of each term.

- **Staffing** includes all of the activities involved in obtaining, preparing, and compensating the people who work for a business.
- **Implementing** is the effort to direct and lead people to accomplish the planned work of the organization.
- **Controlling** determines to what extent the business is accomplishing the goals it set out to reach in the planning stage.

Large businesses and organizations have many managers. Responsibilities for specific management functions are assigned to each manager. Often, due to the size of a business, several managers may have responsibilities within just one of the functions. If a business is owned by more than one person, the management functions are usually divided among the owners based on the type of work each enjoys and does well. In a new small business, the owner usually is responsible for all of the management functions. As the business grows, other employees will be moved into management positions. They will be assigned one or more of the management functions to complete.

Managing a business or even a part of a business can be a very complex process. Managers must make decisions, solve problems, respond to competition, and develop new strategies. Decisions made to complete one management function often affect other functions. The efforts of each manager impact the work of others. Effective managers motivate employees to do their best work. They also use the money and other resources of the business wisely. Successful businesses must have managers who are able to complete each of the management functions well.

istockphoto.com/kzenon

Think of a business in your neighborhood. What levels of management do you think it has?

Work as a TEAM

Your class is responsible for picking up litter on a highway on the edge of your town. Your team has responsibility for managing that project. For each of the five management functions, identify two or three management activities that your team must complete in order for the project to be successful.

CHECKPOINT ✓

What are the five management functions?

LO 7.1.2

MANAGEMENT LEVELS

Unless a business is very small, there will be several managers with responsibilities for the success of the business. Every manager devotes some time to each of the management functions and has authority over other people and their work. Not every manager gives the same amount of attention and time to each of the functions. Most larger organizations have three levels of managers—executives, middle managers, and supervisors.

Different Learning Abilities

Attention Deficit Disorder Assign students to prepare flash cards with each management function on one side of a card and the definition of the function on the other side. Instruct students to work with the flash cards in teams of two to learn the terms and definitions.

Work as a TEAM

Ask students whether the task could be completed without one or more of the management functions being performed. Students should decide whether one of the functions is more important than others to the success of the task.

TEACH

Provide students with a handout that has a 3 × 5 table. List the five management functions in the left column. Then ask students to complete the middle column by listing activities they complete in their personal lives that fit the definition of each function. As a group, complete the final column by listing activities that managers complete in their businesses that fit the function's definition.

ONGOING ASSESSMENT

CHECKPOINT ✓ANSWER

The five management functions are (1) planning, (2) organizing, (3) staffing, (4) implementing, and (5) controlling.

THINK CRITICALLY THROUGH VISUALS

Answers will vary. Students may identify businesses that have all three levels of managers—executives, middle managers, and supervisors—as well as some smaller businesses that may have just one or two levels.

FYI

Assign students to use the Internet to identify current female CEOs of Fortune 500 companies. Ask students to select one individual and study the career path she followed to be selected as the corporate leader.

TEACH

Explain to students that, in traditional organizations in the past, there were often many levels of managers, each with responsibilities for small numbers of people and activities. Today, there are fewer management levels with greater responsibilities. Employees and employee teams have been given some responsibilities formerly held by managers.

ONGOING ASSESSMENT

CHECKPOINT ✓ANSWER

Top-level managers are executives with responsibilities for the direction and success of the entire business. Mid-level managers are specialists with responsibilities for specific parts of a company's operations. Supervisors are first-level managers who are responsible for the day-to-day work of a small group of employees.

FYI The glass ceiling for women in management persists at many of the largest U.S. businesses. While men still hold a disproportionate number of key management roles in large corporations, progress is evident. As of 2000, only four women headed Fortune 500 companies. By 2015, that number had grown to 25. Women are now found in many more executive jobs, so there are good choices to fill more of the top leadership positions in the near future.

Top Management

Executives are top-level managers with responsibilities for the direction and success of the entire business. They set long-term direction and plans. They are held accountable for the profitability and success of the business. Job titles of executives include chief executive officer, president, chief operating officer, and vice president.

Executives spend most of their time on planning and controlling activities. They study the economy and competition. They approve all major business decisions and expenditures. Executives are responsible for the work of all other managers and employees.

Middle Management

Middle managers are specialists with responsibilities for specific parts of a company's operations. Examples of middle management jobs are marketing manager, information technology manager, customer service manager, operations manager, and human resources manager. Middle managers work with the company's business plan once it has been approved by executives and develop specific plans for their part of the business. They must coordinate their work with other managers. Much of their time is devoted to the organizing, staffing, and implementing functions.

Supervisors

Supervisors are the first level of management in a business. They are responsible for the day-to-day work of a small group of employees. They help employees plan their work. Supervisors also monitor employee activities and results. They make sure that needed resources are available and used wisely. Supervisors must evaluate the quality of the work of their employees and help to solve problems that occur in their area. Supervisors spend most of their time implementing the plans of executives and middle managers. They may have non-management duties in addition to their management work.

Management by Others

Employees who are not managers may complete work that seems to be a part of one of the management functions. Employees plan and organize their work. They might take part in hiring and training new employees. They may evaluate the quality of the work they complete. However, managers are responsible for the work of others and have authority over those employees. Without that authority and responsibility, the work of an employee is not considered management.

Some experienced employees are asked to serve as leaders in their work group. They may lead a project or oversee the work of a new employee.

Many companies organize employees into work teams. Those teams have both authority and responsibility for much of their work. The team meets to make plans, determine how work will be completed, and divide the work among the team members. The team is responsible for meeting objectives and may even have some say about their budget. Work teams still report to a manager and can ask for assistance when needed.

Both work group leaders and employee teams complete a limited number of management activities. Both situations are effective ways for employees to develop experience with management activities. They are an effective way to develop skills needed by managers and increase employee interest and confidence in a management career.

Applied Skills

Building Study Skills Assign students to prepare a study guide to understand the three levels of management. In the study guide, students should identify the management functions that are most and least important to each management level.

CHECKPOINT
What are the differences among the three levels of management?

LO 7.1.3
MANAGEMENT STYLES

Managing a group of people can be a difficult job. Managers must encourage people with different backgrounds, personalities, and experience to work well together. Have you been a part of an athletic team or musical group? If so, you can remember how hard it was at first to coordinate the talents of each group member so the team or group performed well.

Managers approach the task of directing a group in different ways based on their management style. **Management style** is the way a manager works with and involves employees. Two very different styles often used by managers are tactical management and strategic management.

Sometimes a management style is chosen based on the characteristics of the employees being managed. At other times, the choice is based on the work assignment. Figure 7-1 describes situations where each style will be more effective. Experienced and effective managers can change their management style. It should be based on the urgency of the work to be done and the confidence the manager has in the employees.

Golden Pixels LLC/Shutterstock.com

As an employee, which management style would you prefer from your supervisor?

Tactical Management Sometimes managers are faced with a crisis. They feel they don't have time to let the group decide how to complete the task. In other situations, a manager may be working with a group of new employees or may have work in which the members have no previous experience. In those situations, the manager should use tactical management. *Tactical management* is a style in which the manager is more directive and

CHOOSING A MANAGEMENT STYLE

A MANAGER SHOULD USE TACTICAL MANAGEMENT WHEN	A MANAGER SHOULD USE STRATEGIC MANAGEMENT WHEN
• Working with part-time or temporary employees	• Employees are skilled and experienced
• Working with employees who lack motivation for a new task	• The work is routine with few new challenges
• Working under tight time pressures	• Employees are doing work they enjoy
• Assigning a new task for which employees are not experienced	• The manager wants to improve group relationships
• Employees prefer not to be involved in decision making	• Employees are willing to take responsibility for planning their work

FIGURE 7-1
Why is tactical management appropriate when assigning a new task that must be completed quickly?

TEACH

Ask students to think of a coach, teacher, or other leader with whom they particularly liked to work. Students should identify the approach the person used in working with people and describe why that approach seemed to be effective.

Work with students to prepare a list of several situations in an organization that would require management action, such as preparing a budget, handling a conflict among co-workers, or solving a production problem. Ask students to decide which management style would be most appropriate for each situation. Ask them to justify their decisions.

THINK CRITICALLY THROUGH VISUALS

Student answers will vary. Encourage students to give specific reasons why they find a particular management style most appealing.

▸ Figure 7-1 *ANSWER*

Tactical management allows the manager to move quickly with more control. There may be little time to discuss the new task, and employees may have limited understanding of what needs to be done in this situation.

Teaching Strategies

Expand Beyond the Classroom Ask students to talk with several people who have full-time jobs about the management styles of their bosses. Instruct students to ask each person to describe the management style his or her boss uses. They should also ask what the person likes and dislikes about the management style.

ONGOING ASSESSMENT

CHECKPOINT ✓ ANSWER

The tactical management style is more directive and controlling than the strategic management style. Using tactical management, the manager makes the major decisions and supervises employees closely to make sure the work is done well. In strategic management, managers are less directive and involve employees in decision making.

ASSESS

Key Concepts *Answers*

1. False. An entrepreneur who starts a new business must perform the five management functions.

2. c. producing

3. a. top management

4. False. Effective managers will use the management style best suited to the situation.

Make Academic Connections *Answers*

5. Reports will vary. Students will prepare a report on one top executive or entrepreneur.

6. Tables will vary. Students will create a table that lists the main duties (classified within the five management functions) of the management job listings they choose.

7. Answers will vary. Students should propose valid situations and should be able to defend their decisions.

CLOSE Ask students to discuss why the number of managers in organizations might have decreased in the past several years, while the number of management activities required have not changed.

controlling. The manager will make the major decisions and stay in close contact with employees while they work to make sure the work is done well.

Strategic Management When a group of employees is experienced and works well together, a manager does not have to be as directive and controlling. If there is enough time to bring a team together to help plan a work assignment, team members will often prefer being involved in the decision-making process. These are examples of the use of strategic management. *Strategic management* is a style in which managers are more collaborative and involve employees in decision making. A manager using a strategic style expects employees to work well without direct supervision and will seek their input on important decisions.

Mixed Management Which of the two management styles would you prefer if you were an employee? If you were a manager, which of the styles would you use? Everyone will not answer these two questions the same way. In the past, many managers believed they needed to use the tactical style of management. They believed they needed to be directive and controlling in order to make sure that work was completed. Some employees became frustrated when they felt their manager did not trust them. Some employees prefer that the manager make day-to-day decisions. Other employees are not experienced enough to work without close supervision. As a result, effective managers are prepared to use both styles. The combined use of tactical and strategic management is known as *mixed management.*

CHECKPOINT ✓
How is tactical management different from strategic management?

7.1 ASSESSMENT

Key Concepts

Determine the best answer.

1. True or False. An entrepreneur who starts a new business is not considered to be a manager.
2. Which of the following is not one of the five functions of management?
   a. planning
   b. implementing
   c. producing
   d. controlling
3. Which level of management spends most of its time completing planning and controlling activities?
   a. top management
   b. middle management
   c. supervisors
   d. team management
4. True or False. Effective managers should use strategic management rather than tactical management.

Make Academic Connections

5. **Research** Use the Internet or library to gather information on the top executive of a large corporation or an entrepreneur. Prepare a written report on the manager, describing the person's career path to his or her current position. Identify the important responsibilities of the executive in leading the company.
6. **Careers** Use an employment website to identify job listings for a top management position, a middle management position, and a supervisor position. Develop a table that lists the main duties the person in each position needs to perform. Classify those duties within the five management functions.
7. **Critical Thinking** Imagine you are managing a team of students that is running the concession stand at a basketball game to raise money for your school's student business association chapter. List two situations that could occur for which a tactical management style would be most appropriate and two other situations when a strategic style would be most appropriate. Discuss the situations with other students and see whether they agree with your decisions.

RETEACH List each of the vocabulary terms on the board. Tell students to write their own definition of each term without referring to the lesson. Then ask students to compare their own definitions with those in the lesson and make any corrections necessary.

ENRICH Instruct students to locate a magazine article on a successful young manager. Ask them to provide a summary of the article that describes the person's beliefs about management and the preferred management style.

DOING BUSINESS IN... SOUTH AFRICA

In 1994, South Africa celebrated the arrival of democracy. After decades of apartheid, the government policy that segregated blacks and other non-whites from the dominant whites, voting rights were extended to all citizens. Today, the country is often seen as a model for developing economies and emerging markets. South Africa is now one of the most multicultural countries in the world.

South Africa has the largest economy on the African continent. Its growth has been driven primarily by a strong financial and banking industry, as well as manufacturing. An historic focus on mining is subject to reforms due to outdated management and labor practices.

In 2010 South Africa joined BRICS, an association of five major growing economies—Brazil, Russia, India, China, and South Africa. Combined, the five BRICS nations make up about 40 percent of the world's population and 20 percent of all goods and services produced.

With an abundance of natural resources and a more progressive government, South Africa has become a prime location for foreign investment and trade. However, the government is under growing pressure to extend basic services, improve education, and offer more job opportunities to all of its citizens. About half the population lives below the poverty rate and unemployment remains above 25 percent. The Industrial Policy Action Plan has been instituted to overcome continuing inequalities in employment, business management, and business ownership. It has a goal of reducing poverty and increasing opportunities for a broader group of citizens. Government investments will provide additional social services, education, and new job creation. The goal is to add 5 million new jobs across a variety of industries by 2020. Since 2000, the illiteracy rate across the country has been reduced from more than 30 percent of the population to less than 20 percent.

South Africa has two economies. The major economy is concentrated in large cities and is dominated by large international businesses. It primarily benefits the educated and wealthy citizens. The second economy is the cash economy operated by small traders who serve middle- and low-income South Africans.

South Africa has 11 official languages reflecting many cultures. English is most widely used in business. Business and social interactions can vary dramatically based on the cultural heritage of the participants as well as rural/urban differences across the country.

South African foods are influenced by the many local, European, and Asian cultures that are part of the country's heritage. *Bredie* is traditional stew of vegetables and mutton. *Frikkadels* are little nutmeg-flavored hamburgers wrapped in cabbage and served with yellow rice.

Think Critically

1. What makes South Africa an attractive location for foreign investment?
2. How might the two different economies affect business?
3. Use library or Internet resources to obtain additional information about the history and current economic and social conditions of South Africa.

istockphoto.com/THEGIFT777

What do you see in this photograph that illustrates changes that have occurred in South Africa's economy and culture?

Doing Business in... SOUTH AFRICA

South Africa has adjusted to many political, economic, and social changes and has become an attractive country for international trade for many companies.

THINK CRITICALLY THROUGH VISUALS

This photo shows people of different races working together at a modern cafe. It demonstrates the demise of apartheid, the growing major economy, and the interaction of cultures.

Think Critically *Answers*

1. South Africa is an attractive location for foreign investment because it has abundant natural resources, a strong economy, and a progressive government.
2. It may be difficult for businesses to sell products and services in South Africa because many citizens use the cash economy. People may not be happy with two different economies when many of them are unemployed with a low standard of living. Businesses may have difficulty finding a skilled workforce.
3. Research results will vary depending on the sources used.

Different Learning Styles

Tactile Learner Provide students with a world map or globe and ask them to locate South Africa. Instruct students to review the features of the country displayed on the map or globe and identify major cities, rivers, and other geographic features.

Focus on REAL LIFE

People have different views about what makes an effective leader and how leaders contribute to the success of a business. Ask students to discuss each of the points of view in the Focus feature and decide whether they agree or disagree and the criteria they would suggest the committee should use.

TEACH

Ask students to consider a club or organization to which they belong. Ask them to identify and discuss what qualities they would look for in selecting a leader for that club or organization. At the end of the discussion, make a list of the qualities that most students agree are important for a leader.

THINK CRITICALLY THROUGH VISUALS

Answers will vary. Students should recognize that good leaders make large contributions to effective organizations.

7.2 Leadership

Learning Outcomes

7.2.1 Describe the need for leadership skills and the characteristics of an effective leader.

7.2.2 Identify the human relations skills needed by managers and leaders.

7.2.3 Recognize four types of leadership influence.

Key Terms

Focus on REAL LIFE

The Downtown Business Council's Leadership Award committee is meeting to identify possible nominees for the award.

Janice offered the first suggestion, "We should find out which businesses showed the greatest growth and profits during the past year and each company's top manager should be nominated."

"I think there is more to leadership than being the top manager of a profitable company. There are other things that demonstrate outstanding leadership," Franklin offered.

"We shouldn't limit it to the top manager. I believe the managers who work with employees every day are at least as responsible for a company's success as the top manager," Jack pointed out.

Felicia asked, "Does the award have to go to a manager? Many employees provide outstanding leadership within their organizations."

Janice looked around the table and said, "Before we go any further, it looks like we need to agree on what leadership is."

LO 7.2.1

WHAT IS LEADERSHIP?

A business uses many resources to accomplish its work and make a profit. Those resources include buildings, equipment, money, materials, supplies, and people. The ability to manage resources, including people, is critical to the success of any business. Some managers are effective at managing other resources but not as good at managing people. Because employees are so important, managers who can effectively manage people are in high demand.

Need for Leadership

Ideas about the effective management of people have changed in recent years. In the past, it was acceptable for managers to decide what needed to be done and how it was to be done without consulting the people who would be asked to do the work. Employees were expected to do what they were told. Although workers might have done what was asked of them, they might not have been doing their best.

Most businesses cannot afford to have employees who are not doing their best. The

Monkey Business Images/Shutterstock.com

Think of an organization or group in which you have been involved. Do you feel there was effective leadership? Why or why not?

Applied Skills

Language Arts Assign students to write a paragraph on what they believe makes a good leader. Then ask students to work with a partner to create a poem, poster, collage, or skit that illustrates the qualities and characteristics of a good leader.

cost of hiring, training, and paying employees is usually one of the largest expenses for a business. Employees who do not feel their contributions are valued may not perform well. They might not produce the quantity or quality of work that is required. Other employees who do not feel appreciated might look for other jobs. Companies pay a high cost for these kinds of problems.

Today, managers are expected to do more than just give orders. They are expected to find ways to meet employee needs as well as business needs. Managers must be effective leaders.

Leadership is the ability to motivate individuals and groups to accomplish important goals. When a manager can get individual employees and groups to work well together to accomplish objectives, she or he is an effective leader.

Leadership Characteristics

Leadership is much more than just being friendly with employees. It takes skill to get people with different characteristics, needs, and interests to work well together and do the work needed by the business. The characteristics of effective leaders are listed and described in Figure 7-2.

You may have heard, "Leaders are born and not made." Most leaders will say that they did not always have the characteristics needed for success. Rather, they worked hard over many years to develop them.

It is harder for some people to develop leadership skills. You may be shy and find it hard to assume leadership roles. You may prefer to let others make decisions while you work to make those decisions successful. You may believe other students seem to be natural leaders or already have mastered many of the leadership characteristics.

> **Life-Span Plan**
>
> Identify and evaluate your own leadership abilities. List things you have done and activities you have completed that you believe contribute to your leadership skills. Explain how your leadership skills may affect the life-span goals you set for yourself. Identify possible leadership roles in your school and community that can help you achieve your life-span goals.

CHARACTERISTICS OF EFFECTIVE LEADERS

CHARACTERISTIC	DESCRIPTION
Understanding	Respecting the feelings and needs of the people they work with.
Initiative	Having the ambition and motivation to get work done without being asked.
Dependability	Following through on commitments.
Judgment	Making decisions carefully.
Objectivity	Looking at all sides of an issue before making a decision.
Confidence	Being willing to make decisions and take responsibility for the results.
Stability	Not being too emotional or unpredictable.
Cooperation	Working well with others, recognizing others' strengths, and helping to develop effective group relationships.
Honesty	Being honest and sincere in decision making and treatment of others.
Courage	Willing to take reasonable risks and make unpopular decisions.
Communication	Able to listen, speak, and write effectively.
Intelligence	Having the knowledge and understanding needed to perform well.

FIGURE 7-2
Identify people who you believe have most of these leadership characteristics. How do they demonstrate their leadership?

TEACH

Instruct students to compare the leadership definition with the definition of management from the previous lesson. Ask them what is different and similar in the two definitions.

Life-Span Plan Answers

Answers will vary. Students should identify leadership abilities they possess and plan to develop. They should also explain how these characteristics may contribute to their ability to achieve their life-span goals.

▸ Figure 7-2 *ANSWER*

Answers will vary. Follow up by asking students to describe specific instances in which they have observed the leader they selected demonstrating characteristics listed in this figure.

Different Learning Styles

Visual Learner Assign students to prepare a simple drawing or find a picture to illustrate each of the characteristics of effective leaders. Ask students to organize the items to create a display or poster. Suggest that they label their drawings and pictures.

ONGOING ASSESSMENT

CHECKPOINT ✓ ANSWER

Leadership skills can be developed through studying leadership, participating in organizations and activities, practicing leadership at work, observing leaders, working with a mentor, and doing a self-analysis and asking for feedback.

TEACH

Instruct students to prepare a two-column table with the heading "My Plan to Become a Leader." They should label the first column "Things I Have Done" and the second column "Things I Plan to Do." As students review each of the ways to develop leadership skills, they can complete the two columns of the table.

THINK CRITICALLY THROUGH VISUALS

Answers will vary. Consider asking students to offer reasons for their choices and name specific steps they plan to take to develop leadership qualities.

TEACH

Ask students to review the definition of human relations. Then ask students to list ways that people demonstrate both good and poor human relations.

They are the ones who seem to be willing to accept a challenge, take a risk, or make a hard decision. Others look to them for direction and ideas.

Preparing to Be a Leader

You will have many opportunities to be a leader even if you are not a manager. Don't wait until you find yourself in a leadership role to develop leadership skills. There are several ways you can develop them right now, including:

- *Study leadership.* Books, videos, and blogs on the subject of leadership and leadership skills can help you understand what it takes to be a leader. You can also take courses to develop specific leadership skills.
- *Participate in organizations and activities.* Clubs, teams, and organizations need leaders and offer a variety of opportunities to develop leadership skills.
- *Practice leadership at work.* If you have a part-time job, you can develop leadership skills as you help customers, complete work assignments, take initiative to solve problems, and demonstrate dependability and honesty.
- *Observe leaders.* Every day you can observe people in leadership positions in your school and community. You also can see and read media reports about people in leadership positions in business and government. Some are effective, while others are not.
- *Work with a mentor.* An older sibling, a trusted adult, a teacher or coach, or your supervisor at work may be willing to help you learn more about leadership skills and offer guidance and feedback on your progress.
- *Do a self-analysis and ask for feedback.* Find opportunities to demonstrate leadership characteristics. Review the results to identify what you did well and what you can improve. Ask others for constructive feedback.

Monkey Business Images/Shutterstock.com

Which leadership qualities do you possess? Which qualities do you most need to develop? Are there others that you think you could develop?

CHECKPOINT ✓
What are several ways to develop leadership skills?

LO 7.2.2

IMPORTANCE OF HUMAN RELATIONS

Managers and leaders must be able to work well with other people. Most managers spend a majority of their time interacting with people. They work with employees, customers, people from other businesses, and other managers in their own organizations. The ability to get along with other people largely determines whether a manager is successful or not. **Human relations** is the way people get along with each other.

Human Relations Skills

Effective managers and leaders must develop and maintain effective relationships with all of the people with whom they work. In addition, they must help employees develop effective human relations skills. The important human relations skills needed by leaders and managers are (1) self-understanding, (2) understanding others, (3) communication, (4) team building, and (5) developing job satisfaction.

Portfolio Activity

Assign the Portfolio Activity for Chapter 7 available on the website for this textbook.
COLLECT Point out that students should collect information about people who have demonstrated effective leadership.
CREATE Encourage students to use headings and captions to illustrate the leadership characteristics.
CONNECT Remind students to connect visuals to something in their portfolio or from another class.

Self-Understanding To be able to meet the expectations of others, leaders must first understand their own strengths and weaknesses. A manager cannot always do exactly what employees would prefer or make decisions with which every employee agrees. In addition, a manager cannot be viewed as either unpredictable or unfair. To gain a better understanding of yourself, you can study how you get along with others. Try to recognize the ways you communicate and work with others individually and in groups. It is important to recognize how you make decisions. You must learn which decisions were effective and which were not so you can improve your decision-making ability over time.

Work as a TEAM

List the five human relations skills and rank them 1–5 in the order you believe is most important to effective leadership. Now compare your rankings with those of your team members. As a team, agree on a final ranking of the skills. When you are finished, discuss whether the process used to agree on rankings demonstrated effective human relations skills among team members or not.

Understanding Others Leaders recognize that people they work with often are more alike than different. Recognizing those

Business Insight

Assistive Technology In the Workplace

People with physical disabilities face special challenges when completing many personal and job functions. But companies benefit when they employ people with physical disabilities and provide modified tools and equipment that allow employees to complete their work tasks. Those modifications are known as assistive technologies. Assistive technologies make many tasks possible that previously were difficult or impossible to complete. *Assistive technology* is any unique equipment, modification, or special design used to increase, maintain, or improve the capabilities of persons with disabilities.

A number of assistive technologies are available to aid individuals with disabilities in the use of computers. For blind persons, software is available that gives audio signals for on-screen images such as windows, menus, icons, and cursor location. A computer can also become a translator for the blind by converting printed pages to speech. In the same way, a device can monitor computer sounds and alert a deaf computer user with light signals or convert speech to text.

Special applications have been designed for people with other physical disabilities. Low-pressure, touch-sensitive keyboards can make typing easier, and special seven-key keyboards are designed primarily for one-handed typists. Special keyboard designs can customize each key's size, position, and function. Touch-screen keyboards and menus allow computer use with almost any part of the body. In addition, joysticks, writing pads, and alternative pointing devices can facilitate the use of most computer software when the physical disability requires it. Technology allows accommodation for jobs that are not directly computer-related as well. Work spaces can be arranged to allow for wheelchairs or special equipment. Equipment can be modified so it can be used with hand or even foot controls. Pneumatics and hydraulics change the amount of strength or force required to lift or move heavy objects.

Think Critically

1. In what ways does a company benefit when it provides assistive technologies for employees with disabilities?
2. What other uses can you see for the technologies described in addition to benefiting physically disabled employees?

Different Learning Abilities

Gifted Instruct students to locate examples of the newest innovations in assistive technologies. Ask students to prepare a display showing the technology and the assistance it offers.

At-Risk Ask students to identify two things they can do at school and at home that will help them practice and improve one of the human relations skills needed by leaders and managers.

Work as a TEAM

As a class, compare the final team rankings. Note the items that have very similar and very different rankings. Discuss those items and the reasons for the rankings.

Business Insight

Advances in technology have provided many ways to help people with physical disabilities with their personal and work lives. However, some companies have been slow in adopting the technologies, while others have been leaders in providing assistive technologies for employees with those needs.

Think Critically *Answers*

1. A company benefits when it provides assistive technologies for employees with disabilities because it gains a larger pool of potential employees from which to select new hires. Such technologies allow employees with disabilities to be productive, often at the same level as nondisabled employees.
2. Answers will vary, but should reflect ways assistive technology can help nondisabled individuals. For example, low-pressure, touch-sensitive keyboards can help nondisabled employees avoid carpal tunnel syndrome. On-screen keyboards can be useful in work environments where there may not be room for a keyboard or where its use may be difficult. Modifications that make physical tasks easier may avoid back and muscle injuries.

THINK CRITICALLY THROUGH VISUALS

Answers will vary. Students should realize that many problems could occur and that the loss of technology services could disrupt business and result in loss of income. Specific examples of problems include customers not being able to place orders, managers not being able to contact employees, and employees not being able to access needed information or complete many work tasks.

TEACH

List each of the classifications of communication on the board. As you discuss each, instruct students to develop a picture or diagram that illustrates the differences within each classification.

Ask students to describe how each of the human relations skills listed contributes to a more effective business and better relationships between managers and employees.

Brand X Pictures/Getty Images

List some problems that might occur if a business lost communications, computer, and Internet services for a day.

similarities will help develop a stronger team. Differences can also improve a work team. If everyone thought and acted the same, there would seldom be new ideas or anyone to question a decision in order to improve it. An effective leader gets to know each person's skills and abilities as well as strengths and weaknesses. The leader will not treat everyone alike, but will attempt to involve each person in the way that is most beneficial to the business and that employee.

Communication Communication is an essential part of every business. Managers must have effective communication skills. Communication can be classified in several ways.

- *Formal or informal* Formal communications methods are the established and approved ways for information to move between managers, employees, customers, and others in the business. Informal communications are commonly used but unofficial ways that information moves in an organization.
- *Internal or external* Internal communications occur between managers, employees, and work groups. External communications occur between people inside the organization and people outside the organization such as customers, suppliers, and other businesses.
- *Vertical or horizontal* Vertical communications move up or down in an organization between management and employees. Horizontal communications move across the organization at the same level—employee to employee or manager to manager.
- *Oral or written* Oral communications are spoken directly or using technology. Written communications include notes, letters, reports, and text or graphics sent via technology.

Managers need to recognize and effectively use many methods of communication. The message must include specific words that are understandable and meaningful to the people receiving the communications. An effective communicator must be a good listener as well as skilled at providing information. Listening helps managers understand employees and demonstrate respect for their ideas.

Team Building Businesses are organized into groups and teams. The combined skills of the people in an effective team are greater than those of individuals working alone. On the other hand, if there are problems in the team and members cannot get along, the team will not be effective. Managers and leaders need team-building skills to help people understand each other and their responsibilities. A leader must be able to identify problems developing within the group and help resolve them quickly.

Developing Job Satisfaction Most people are more satisfied than dissatisfied with their work when they have jobs that use their skills and interests. Managers can influence how employees feel about their jobs on a daily basis. Sources of dissatisfaction include assignments employees do not like, difficult working conditions, ineffective communication, and lack of recognition or adequate rewards. A small concern that is unresolved can lead to long-term dissatisfaction. Employees appreciate it when

Applied Skills

Writing Across the Curriculum Ask students to prepare a paragraph that describes how another class they are taking contributes to developing or improving one or more of the human relations skills.

a manager pays attention to the needs and concerns of individual employees, even if problems cannot be immediately resolved.

CHECKPOINT ✓
Why do managers and leaders need effective human relations skills?

LO 7.2.3

INFLUENCING PEOPLE

Have you been a part of a group that often disagrees on how things should be done and takes a long time making decisions? It is interesting to see what the leader of a group does when the group is not working well. Some leaders will complain and criticize group members. Others will give up on the group and attempt to do the work themselves. Neither of those responses improves the group's effectiveness. Effective leaders must be able to influence team members and others in positive ways. **Influence** enables a person to affect the actions of others.

Kinds of Influence

There are several kinds of influence a leader may be able to use.

Position influence is the ability to get others to accomplish tasks because of the position the leader holds. If the leader is a manager with authority over an employee, it is likely that the employee will feel obligated to respond to the leader's requests.

Reward influence results from the leader's ability to give or withhold rewards. Rewards may be monetary, such as wages or job benefits. Rewards can also be non-monetary, such as recognition and praise. Rewards are usually positive. Negative rewards include requiring people to work overtime on short notice or criticizing rather than praising employees.

Expert influence exists when group members recognize and appreciate a leader's expertise in a specific area. For example, a group of inexperienced sales representatives with a manager who has years of successful selling experience will likely look to the manager for guidance.

Identity influence stems from the personal trust and respect members have for the leader. If the leader is well liked and appears to have the best interests of the group in mind, members are likely to support the leader.

The influence of leaders is not always positive. It may not be effective for a long period. If a manager is not viewed as an expert and is not well liked, he or she will have to rely on position and reward influence. It is not easy to continue to get people to do things for you just because you are their manager. They will probably do just enough to get by, get a reward, or avoid punishment. Effective leaders work to develop expert and identity influence to gain the respect and support of the group.

Formal and Informal Influence

Groups can be affected by both formal and informal influence. It depends on the person's role within the organization. Managers have formal influence. Others can have informal influence as a result of their personal characteristics rather than their role in the organization.

Goodluz/Shutterstock.com

Think of a manager, coach, or teacher you've enjoyed working with. What characteristics made it easy to follow his or her lead?

ONGOING ASSESSMENT

CHECKPOINT ✓ANSWER

Managers and leaders need effective human relations skills because much of their success depends on their ability to get along well with all of the people with whom they work and build effective work groups.

TEACH

List the following words on the board: home, school, work. As you discuss each of the four kinds of influence, ask students to describe an example of that type of influence being used in each of the three situations listed on the board.

THINK CRITICALLY THROUGH VISUALS

Answers will vary. Students should list specific characteristics of the good leader they have identified and why they were important.

Teaching Strategies

Collaborative Learning Divide students into small learning teams. Assign each of the teams one of the kinds of influence. The teams should prepare a role-play script in which a manager uses that kind of influence ineffectively and then effectively. The teams should present their role plays to the other students.

ONGOING ASSESSMENT

CHECKPOINT ✓ ANSWER

Formal influence results from a position that is a part of the organization's structure. Informal influence results from personal characteristics rather than a formal position in the organization.

ASSESS

Key Concepts *Answers*

1. d. leadership
2. False. Most leaders report that they worked hard over many years to develop those qualities.
3. a. human relations
4. d. informal influence

Make Academic Connections *Answers*

5. Students are to write a report that describes a project completed by a virtual team and discuss ways technology was used to support successful communication among team members.
6. Students will role-play a discussion between a supervisor and an employee who is reluctant to ask questions of more experienced employees. Students should be sure to keep the discussion positive and specific.
7. Students will use the data provided to prepare a chart showing types of influence used most often by their managers.

CLOSE Remind students that employees with effective leadership skills can be positive influences on their work group and will often have opportunities to move into management positions if they choose to do so.

What happens when your teacher assigns a group project and the team members get together for the first time? Often, one or two people emerge as leaders to help get the group focused and organized using informal influence. **Informal influence** is power resulting from the personal characteristics of a leader rather than the formal structure of an organization. Consider another situation where members of the student council meet for the first time. There are bylaws that call for the election of officers. The person elected president has formal influence. **Formal influence** is power based on a leader's position within the formal structure of an organization.

Often in organizations, both formal and informal influence will operate at the same time. One person will be the manager and have formal influence. There may be a well-liked and respected employee in the group who will have informal influence. If there is a conflict between the formal and informal influence, the group will probably not work effectively. Group members will have difficulty deciding whose influence to follow. Effective managers recognize informal influence and work closely with the informal leaders to gain their support and avoid conflicts.

CHECKPOINT ✓
What is the difference between formal and informal influence?

7.2 ASSESSMENT

Key Concepts

Determine the best answer.

1. The ability to motivate individuals and groups to accomplish important goals is
   a. influence
   b. power
   c. management
   d. leadership
2. True or False. Research has proven that effective leaders are born and not made.
3. The way people get along with each other is known as
   a. human relations
   b. influence
   c. management style
   d. communications
4. A person who is not a manager but is still able to get a group focused and organized is using
   a. tactical management
   b. strategic management
   c. formal influence
   d. informal influence

Make Academic Connections

5. **Technology** Virtual teams complete projects by communicating using technology rather than meeting face to face. Complete Internet research on virtual teams. Prepare a report that describes a business project completed by a virtual team. Discuss how technology was used to support communication among team members and achieve successful completion of the project.
6. **Communication** You are the supervisor of a new employee who is having difficulty completing some tasks. You believe the new employee may be reluctant to ask questions of experienced employees. You encourage your employees to help each other when asked. You want to meet with the new employee to discuss the situation and want the discussion to be positive and result in improved performance. Role-play the discussion with another student using effective oral communication.
7. **Math** A survey of one company's employees asked them to identify which type of influence their managers used most often. Seven hundred employees responded with the following results: Position influence, 305 responses; reward influence, 80 responses; expert influence, 120 responses; identity influence, 195 responses. Prepare a chart that illustrates the percentage of managers using each of the types of influence most frequently.

RETEACH Divide the class into three teams. Assign each team one of the learning outcomes in this lesson. The team should review the lesson information for its goal and prepare a handout that summarizes the important points.

ENRICH Invite a dynamic manager to speak to your class about the importance of human relations in business. Ask the speaker to describe specific situations he or she has encountered that require effective human relations.

7.3 Ethical Management

Learning Outcomes

7.3.1 Justify the need for ethical management.

7.3.2 Identify the role of leaders in increasing ethical behavior.

Key Terms

ethical business practices 162

core values 163

Focus on REAL LIFE

"Did you hear about the people who got fired for taking kickbacks from one of our suppliers?" Nadia asked as she walked to the parking lot with her co-workers.

"Yeah, I heard some of them got tickets to ball games and concerts, vacations, and even cash. What were they thinking?" Gilbert added.

"The employee handbook is pretty clear—no gifts worth more than $25. It's obvious that stuff costs more than 25 bucks!" Sandrine exclaimed.

"They were wrong to take the stuff, but how about the suppliers who offered it to them?" Nadia asked.

Most people, including corporate executives, employees, and consumers, are honest and behave ethically. Unfortunately, there are plenty of people who don't think the rules apply to them. This includes businesspeople who exaggerate the effectiveness of their products and job seekers who embellish their résumés. It also includes employees who spend time conducting personal business during work hours and students who plagiarize the work of others.

LO 7.3.1

IMPORTANCE OF ETHICAL BEHAVIOR

Would you copy a paper from the Internet and submit it to your teacher as your own work? Would you cheat on a test to ensure a higher grade? Is it okay for an employee to call in sick to justify a day off from work or to take office supplies from the company for use at home? Do you believe a manager should ever lie to an employee or ignore unsafe working conditions in order to save money or avoid a production delay?

Each of those situations describes an ethical decision you and others may face in your personal life and in business. Not everyone will have the same beliefs about what is ethical and what is not ethical. It is important for each business and those who work in the business to develop agreement on behaviors and decisions that are acceptable and unacceptable.

AVAVA/Shutterstock.com

What effect could the unethical behavior of one employee have on a work team?

Focus on REAL LIFE

Ask students whether they believe most businesspeople are ethical or unethical. Tell them that most businesspeople are ethical, but workplace pressures may tempt people to act unethically. Point out that acting ethically will result in better long-term outcomes as well as greater respect and confidence from others.

TEACH

Ask students to name a business activity that they believe almost everyone would recognize as unethical. Then ask them to name another activity that they believe some people would believe is ethical, while others would believe it is unethical. Discuss why there may be disagreement on what is unethical.

THINK CRITICALLY THROUGH VISUALS

Answers will vary. Students should discuss how the actions of one person can have a negative impact on co-worker attitudes, work relationships, and even the quality of others' work.

Different Learning Abilities

English Language Learners (ELL) Ask students whether they understand the meaning of the words "ethical" and "unethical." Instruct them to use a translation dictionary to determine words with similar meanings in their primary language.

NET KNOWLEDGE

Students will identify and study several business codes of ethics using company websites. They are to develop a sample code of ethics consisting of eight to ten statements.

TEACH

Ask students: "If an action of a manager or employee has a negative effect on others, is it always unethical?" Remind them that unethical behavior involves both the behavior and the results of that behavior.

Remind students that one of the consequences of unethical behavior is how family, friends, and others feel about you when they learn of your actions. Ask them to consider how they believe the families and friends of executives who have recently been in the news for illegal and unethical behavior felt when those actions were reported in the media.

THINK CRITICALLY THROUGH VISUALS

No, not all unethical activities are illegal, although many are. It is not possible for laws to cover every unethical activity that could be performed. On the other hand, all ethical behavior is lawful by definition.

NET KNOWLEDGE

Most businesses today recognize the importance of ethics and have developed a code of ethics for their employees. Those codes are often available on the company's website. Use the Internet to access and review several company codes of ethics. In your view, which codes provide effective guidance to employees and which do not? Use your review to aid in developing a sample code of ethics for a business that contains 8 to 10 statements.

Individuals and organizations develop reputations based on their actions and the decisions they make. You can identify people who you believe are not trustworthy and companies that do not seem to compete fairly. When an individual or a company develops that reputation, others will not trust them or want to work with them. Once a good reputation is lost, it is difficult to rebuild. It is important for an organization to develop and enforce a climate of acceptable and ethical business behavior for all employees.

What Is Ethical Behavior?

Ethics are the principles of conduct governing an individual or a group. **Ethical business practices** ensure that appropriate standards of conduct are maintained by everyone who is a part of the business and with anyone affected by the business. Ethical behavior is not just the responsibility of a company's executives and managers. It is expected for all decisions and actions of every employee.

Ethical behavior is made up of two parts: the decisions and actions of individuals and groups and the results of those actions. Ethical behavior meets several standards:

- It is lawful.
- It is consistent with company values and policies.
- It is not intended to harm some so that others can benefit.
- If the actions and results become public, it will not embarrass the company.

Ethical Management

Managers are ultimately responsible for the success of a business. Success or failure is not just determined by financial results, such as sales, profits, or losses. It is also determined by the actions and activities of the business. Are the actions legal, honest, and ethical? Are consumers, other companies, and other stakeholders, treated fairly? Does the work of the company improve the communities and countries in which it operates? Are resources used efficiently with consideration of the effects on people and the environment? In order to say "yes" to all of these questions, managers must make sure that the decisions and actions of employees are honest, responsible, and ethical.

istockphoto.com/jonya

Are all unethical activities illegal? Explain your answer.

Teaching Strategies

Expand Beyond the Classroom Tell students that unethical behavior often receives more attention than ethical behavior. Instruct students to find news reports about businesspeople who have demonstrated ethical behavior and share those reports with class members.

CHECKPOINT

What are the two parts of ethical behavior?

Life-Span Plan

Prepare a personal statement of core values. Develop one or more statements to guide your actions for each of the following situations: (1) relationships with family members, (2) interacting with peers, (3) commitment to school, (4) improving community, and (5) preparing for a career.

LO 7.3.2

INCREASING ETHICAL BEHAVIOR THROUGH LEADERSHIP

Most people want to do what is right. When they are under time pressures or facing a major problem, some workers act unethically. That unethical behavior usually ends up harming the business and its relationships with customers and the community. Leaders must take actions to prevent unethical behavior.

Preparing the Organization

It is easier for employees to make poor choices when they do not view ethics as important. The day-to-day atmosphere of a business will usually suggest to employees whether ethical behavior is important or not. If employees see managers cutting corners, overlooking improper employee behavior, and approving activities that may be illegal, they will soon recognize that ethical behavior is not a priority. On the other hand, managers can create an atmosphere in which all employees know they are expected to act ethically. Employees must know they will be supported when they make ethical choices. Leaders also must demonstrate that unethical behavior is unacceptable and will be punished if it occurs. Managers can take several steps to develop an ethical environment.

Most organizations have a mission statement. A *mission statement* describes the reason a business exists and what it wants to accomplish. To make ethical behavior a part of a company's mission, many businesses develop a statement of core values. **Core values** are the important principles that will guide decisions and actions in the company. Figure 7-3 shows the core values of Rite Aid Corporation. There is no standard form for communicating core values. Some companies use simple statements similar to Rite Aid's. Other companies convey their core values by using a list of single words such as integrity, leadership, passion, humility, and trust. In most cases, companies provide descriptions and examples to help employees see how the core values can be incorporated throughout the company. As a part of the planning process, managers should work with employees to develop and communicate core values that emphasize ethical behavior.

The staffing function offers another chance for managers to emphasize the importance of ethical behavior. The company's commitment to ethical behavior should be made clear when each new employee

RITE AID CORPORATION'S CORE VALUES
Passion for our customers
Encouragement for our associates
Winning through teamwork
Commitment to diversity and respect for the individual
Accountability for our actions and results
Integrity in all we do
Value for our shareholders
Caring neighbors

FIGURE 7-3
Can you think of other core values that are important to a business?

ONGOING ASSESSMENT

CHECKPOINT ANSWER

The two parts of ethical behavior are (1) the actions of individuals and groups and (2) the results of those actions.

TEACH

Ask students to read Rite Aid Corporation's core values in Figure 7-3. Ask them to describe activities that employees and managers could complete that would demonstrate each of the core values of the company. Ask students: How can managers make sure that everyone in the company supports the core values?

Life-Span Plan Answers

Answers will vary. Students should develop specific statements that represents a personal belief or value that can guide decisions and actions for each of the situations listed.

▸ Figure 7-3 ANSWER

Answers will vary. Most often core values identify a company's concern about its employees, its customers, and the communities in which it operates. Students can suggest other values not listed that might apply to Rite Aid or other companies.

Applied Skills

Word Processing/Technology Instruct students to use the Rite Aid core values from Figure 7-3 to develop a card, poster, or handout that could be distributed to company employees. Students should use a word-processing program and develop a format for the core values that is both engaging and memorable for readers. Instruct students to print a copy of their finished product to share with others.

Work as a TEAM

After students have agreed on their statements of core values, ask them to share the statements with other people in the school. Instruct students to ask those people what effect acceptance of the values would have on the school.

A Question of Ethics

Ask students if they believe some businesses place rules or requirements on customers that they themselves are not willing to meet. Suggest to students that businesses need to carefully consider how their own behaviors will be viewed by their customers and other businesses they work with.

Think Critically *Answers*

1. Answers will vary and could form the basis for a lively class discussion. Challenge students to determine why unethical activities could also be considered common and accepted practices in many companies.

2. Students will have different views regarding the need for a law. Point out that it could be difficult to write a law that would fit all situations and that it may be more effective for businesses to be straightforward with customers about how long it will take to process payments and refunds.

3. This is an opportunity to discuss the difficulties an employee might face in confronting unethical behavior. Ask students how they would approach their manager or an experienced co-worker about their concern.

Work as a TEAM

Work with your team members to develop four or five statements of core values for your school. The statements should be important principles that guide the actions of students, teachers, administrators, and other school employees. If your school already has a statement of values, compare them with the values statements developed by your team.

is hired. In employment interviews, prospective employees should be questioned about ethics and asked to describe how they would handle situations involving ethical behavior. New employee training should include information about the company's commitment to ethics and values.

In the day-to-day operations of the business, managers and supervisors should often stress the importance of ethics. They should look for situations that might encourage employees to act unethically and take preventive action before problems occur. Individual employees and work teams should be encouraged to develop ethical solutions to problems. Employees should also be encouraged to speak up when they become aware of any behavior or decision they believe may be unethical.

Ethical behavior should be a part of employee evaluations and promotions. Managers and supervisors should recognize and reward employees who display high

A QUESTION OF ETHICS

Making Timely Payments

Making timely payments is important to build and maintain a strong relationship between a business and its customers. When a business sends a customer an invoice for a purchase or a monthly bill, the expectation is that it will be paid no later than the due date. In most cases, consumers know they must pay their bills on time or they will be penalized with a late fee or an increased interest rate.

While most businesses and government agencies insist their customers pay accounts on time or suffer the consequences, not all of them are as conscientious about paying their own bills when they are due. When a large business knows that it is a major customer of a smaller business, it might be easy to hold a payment several weeks or months beyond the due date. The large business may delay the payment believing that because they are an important customer of the smaller business, that business will not choose to enforce collection of the account or add additional fees for a late payment. A utility company, cable service provider, or government agency may insist that customers pay on time or risk having services terminated or a significant late fee added to the customer's account. Yet, if the company or agency is required to make a refund or repayment to a customer, that payment may be delayed for days, weeks, or even months. They may blame it on a long processing time or the need to confirm the amount to be paid is correct. They may not even be concerned if customers complain about the amount of time it takes to receive the money due.

Some businesspeople justify the delayed payments by stating "it's a normal business practice" or "we really can't do anything about it." They may look at the bottom line and justify the decision on the basis of how the practice adds to profits. But the practice is unethical, if not illegal. An ethical company responds to its customers with the same policies and procedures it expects of them and will process payments and refunds quickly and efficiently.

Think Critically

1. Do you believe the practice of delaying payments to customers while penalizing them if their payments are late is unethical or just a normal business practice that customers should expect? Justify your answer.
2. Should it be illegal for companies to take a longer time to make payments than they require of their own customers? Why or why not?
3. If you worked in the accounting department and saw that your company regularly delayed making refunds and payments they owed, what would you do?

Applied Skills

Mathematics Instruct students to use the Internet to find information on how various categories of U.S. jobs have been affected by outsourcing. Students should use the information to prepare a graph or chart to illustrate what they have learned.

ethical standards. They also need to be quick to identify and correct ethical problems if they occur.

Modeling Ethical Behavior

The most important action leaders can take to emphasize the importance of ethical behavior in an organization is to always act ethically. If employees read the core values of a company but do not see managers living up to those values, it will be clear that ethics are not that important. On the other hand, if employees see their manager acting in ways that demonstrate the company's values, they will be encouraged to act ethically as well.

When managers show respect for each employee, it demonstrates that everyone in the organization is valued. When a manager forcefully rejects a decision that is illegal or damaging to the company's reputation even though it would be profitable, employees know that ethical behavior is a core value of the organization. Being an ethical role model inspires others to do the same.

arek_malang/Shutterstock.com

Think of a time when you were faced with an ethical dilemma. How did you handle it?

CHECKPOINT
What are the core values of an organization?

7.3 ASSESSMENT

Key Concepts

Determine the best answer.

1. Which of the following is *not* a standard of ethical behavior?
   - **a.** It should be lawful.
   - **b.** It should not harm some so others benefit.
   - **c.** It should not give the company a competitive advantage.
   - **d.** It should not result in embarrassment for the company.
2. True or False. Managers are responsible for the ethical actions of a business.
3. Important principles that guide decisions and actions in a company are known as
   - **a.** a mission statement
   - **b.** a business plan
   - **c.** ethical behavior
   - **d.** core values

Make Academic Connections

4. **Writing** Use the Internet to locate a news report on a business charged with unethical or illegal activities. Gather information to identify the unethical actions taken, the impact of those actions on individuals inside and outside of the company, and the effect of the actions on the image of the company. Prepare a written report on what you learned.
5. **Debate** Form two debate teams. Assign each team the pro or con position on the following statement: "Managers must be responsible for the ethical behavior of every employee." Each team will have five minutes to present their arguments and then two minutes of rebuttal time. At the end of the debate, class members can vote on which team made the most convincing argument.

RETEACH Ask students to review the lesson and prepare an outline of the important information about the need for ethical business practices and the role of leaders in increasing ethical behavior.

ENRICH Discuss ways that businesses could identify and reward ethical business practices by their managers and other employees.

THINK CRITICALLY THROUGH VISUALS

Answers will vary. Point out that ethical dilemmas can occur in settings other than employment situations, such as at home, in social settings, or as a member of a team or organization.

ONGOING ASSESSMENT

CHECKPOINT ✓ANSWER

An organization's core values are the principles that guide decisions and actions in the company.

ASSESS

Key Concepts *Answers*

1. c. It should not give the company a competitive advantage.
2. True
3. d. core values

Make Academic Connections *Answers*

4. Students prepare a written report on unethical actions taken by a business and the impact of those actions on individuals, as well as the effect of the unethical behavior on the company's image.
5. Students form two teams to debate the statement: "Managers must be responsible for the ethical behavior of every employee." Follow formal debate guidelines for a memorable class activity.

CLOSE Ask students whether they believe ethical business practices are increasing, decreasing, or remaining about the same in businesses today. Students representing each viewpoint should present reasons for their beliefs.

Think Critically About Business *Answers*

1. Answers will vary, but students should be able to identify similarities and differences between the managing activities of an entrepreneur starting a new business and that of a top executive. Both are involved in long-range planning and bear the responsibility for the direction and success of the business. Top-level managers work within an organizational structure that includes middle managers and supervisors who do much of the staffing and execution. A new entrepreneur likely has fewer employees, so she executes most of the management functions. Both must be skilled at human relations.

2. Student answers will vary, but should describe one activity specific to each of the five management functions: planning, organizing, staffing, implementing, and controlling.

3. Answers will vary. Some advantages of fewer levels of management include employees who are more responsible and empowered, more efficient vertical communication, and cost savings related to management salaries. Disadvantages include less control over individual employee, fewer opportunities for managers to gain experience, and no comparable compensation for employees who must assume more responsibility.

4. Answers will vary, but most students will probably prefer their supervisors to use a strategic management style rather than a tactical one because it allows more independence and less direct supervision. To be successful when working for a manager who uses the tactical management style, an employee would need to listen carefully and follow directions closely. Employees working for managers who use the strategic management style need to be self-motivated, responsible, and independent.

5. Answers will vary, but one of the first steps is to recognize informal leaders within the team and work closely with them to gain their support and reduce potential group conflict. An effective leader also gets to know each person's skills and abilities, as well as strengths and weaknesses, and will attempt to involve each person in the way most beneficial to the person and the team.

Chapter 7 Assessment

Review Business Concepts

7.1 Management Functions and Styles

- Managers' work can be organized within five functions: planning, organizing, staffing, implementing, and controlling. Not every manager devotes the same amount of attention and time to each of the functions.
- Most organizations have three levels of managers. Executives are top-level managers with responsibilities for the direction and success of the entire business. Middle managers are specialists with responsibilities for specific parts of a company's operations. Supervisors are the first level of management in a business and are responsible for the day-to-day work of a small group of employees.
- A manager might choose tactical management when working with employees who are inexperienced, unmotivated, or uncomfortable being involved in decision making. Tactical management might also be a good choice when operating under tight time pressures or assigning a new task. A manager should use strategic management when employees are skilled and experienced, the work is routine with few new challenges, employees are doing work they enjoy, the manager wants to improve group relationships, or employees are willing to take responsibility for the results of their work.

7.2 Leadership

- Strong leadership helps people with different backgrounds and personalities to work well together and do the work needed by the business. The characteristics of an effective leader are understanding, initiative, dependability, judgment, objectivity, confidence, stability, cooperation, honesty, courage, communication, and intelligence.
- The important human relations skills needed by leaders and managers are (1) self-understanding, (2) understanding others, (3) communication, (4) team building, and (5) developing job satisfaction.
- Position influence is the ability to get others to accomplish tasks because of the position the leader holds. Reward influence results from the leader's ability to give or withhold rewards. Expert influence arises when group members recognize a leader's expertise. Identity influence stems from the personal trust and respect members have for the leader.

7.3 Ethical Management

- When an individual or a company develops an unethical reputation, others will be reluctant to trust them or work with them. It is important for an organization to develop a clear view of what is acceptable business behavior and what is not.
- It is the responsibility of managers to establish an atmosphere in which all employees know they are expected to act ethically and believe they will be supported when they make the right decision. Managers demonstrate their commitment to ethical behavior with their actions.

Think Critically About Business

1. How are the managing activities of an entrepreneur starting a new business and the top executive of a large corporation similar and different? What are the most important management skills both types of managers need for their companies to be successful?
2. Describe one important management activity for each of the five management functions.
3. The number of middle managers has been declining in many businesses as companies cut personnel and give employees more responsibilities. In your opinion, what are the advantages and disadvantages of that change for businesses? How will the skills needed by employees change when there are fewer middle managers?
4. Which type of management style would you personally prefer a manager you work for to have? Why? What would you have to do to work effectively for a manager who used another style?

5. You have been assigned to be the team leader of a work group that must complete a very important project. What are the first things you would do to prepare and motivate the individuals to work well as a team to complete the assignment?

6. Review the list of leadership characteristics in Figure 7-2. Which three characteristics do you believe are the most important to managers? Which three do you believe are least important? Justify your choices. Compare your decisions with those of other students.

7. To demonstrate your self-understanding, what do you believe are your human relations strengths? What are your current weaknesses? Describe some examples of situations where you believe you demonstrated effective human relations.

8. In your school or another organization, identify four people that illustrate each of the four kinds of influence. Prepare an example of how each person uses his or her influence to accomplish the work of the organization.

9. Do you believe the ethical behavior that a person demonstrates in his or her personal life will be the same as the person's ethical behavior in business? Why or why not?

10. As an employee, what would you do if you saw the following individuals behaving unethically: a co-worker, a customer, a competitor, the top executive of your company?

Develop Your Business Language

Match the terms listed with the definitions.

11. Power based on a leader's position within the formal structure of an organization.
12. The important principles that will guide decisions and actions in the company.
13. The effort to direct and lead people to accomplish the planned work of the organization.
14. All of the activities involved in obtaining, preparing, and compensating the employees of a business.
15. Enables a person to affect the actions of others.
16. Ensures that appropriate standards of conduct are maintained by everyone who is a part of the business and with anyone affected by the business.
17. The process of accomplishing the goals of an organization through the effective use of people and other resources.
18. The way people get along with each other.
19. The ability to motivate individuals and groups to accomplish important goals.
20. Determines to what extent the business is accomplishing the goals it set out to reach in the planning stage.
21. Analyzing information, setting goals, and making decisions about what needs to be done.
22. The way a manager works with and involves employees.
23. Identifying and arranging the work and resources needed to achieve the goals that have been set.
24. Power resulting from the personal characteristics of a leader rather than the formal structure of an organization.

Key Terms

a. controlling
b. core values
c. ethical business practices
d. formal influence
e. human relations
f. implementing
g. influence
h. informal influence
i. leadership
j. management
k. management style
l. organizing
m. planning
n. staffing

6. Students will list what they consider to be the three most and three least important leadership characteristics from Figure 7-2. They should be able to justify their choices. You may want to create a chart to help students in the class compare their choices with those of their classmates.

7. Student answers will vary as they list their individual human relations strengths and weaknesses. They should reflect the skills described in the text: self-understanding, understanding others, communication, team building, and developing job satisfaction. You may want the class to brainstorm ways of improving skills in this vital area.

8. Students are to list the four kinds of influence (position, reward, expert, identity) and identify a person they have observed who illustrates each type, with an example of how each person uses his or her influence to achieve results in the organization.

9. Answers will vary. Students should justify their opinions as to whether individuals can have different levels of personal and business ethical behavior.

10. Answers will vary. Students should list their probable responses to unethical behavior by the four types of individuals mentioned. You may want to discuss why there might be differences in responses to each situation.

Develop Your Business Language *Answers*

11. d. formal influence
12. b. core values
13. f. implementing
14. n. staffing
15. g. influence
16. c. ethical business practices
17. j. management
18. e. human relations
19. i. leadership
20. a. controlling
21. m. planning
22. k. management style
23. l. organizing
24. h. informal influence

Make Academic Connections *Answers*

25. Speeches should emphasize the importance of behaving ethically and maintaining the company's reputation for being ethical.

26. Students create a three-column table based on the characteristics of effective leaders found in Figure 7-2. The table will help students explore their own leadership strengths and potential.

27. Reports will vary.

28. Graphs should indicate percentages for each level of management. Executives: 42%, 12%, 4%, 8%, 35%. Middle managers: 20%, 24%, 14% 28%, 14%. Supervisors: 12%, 19%, 7%, 48%, 14%.

Make Your Case *Answers*

29. Valencia was doing many things correctly. She was trying to work with Manny, who wielded informal influence. She was being sensitive to workers' concerns that she had heard expressed over the years. She chose a strategic management style because the employees were experienced. This style of management should have allowed her to improve group relationships.

30. Employees did not feel that Valencia was leading them. It appeared that she was transferring her responsibility to others. She did not take the time to develop expert power, so people recognized she understood management and supervision.

Make Academic Connections

25. Speech Managers are responsible for reinforcing the importance of ethical behavior in a business. You are the CEO of a company that has a reputation of being a very ethical business. Prepare a two-minute speech that you will give to a group of newly hired employees that focuses on the importance of that reputation and encourages each person to act ethically in all they do.

26. Personal Development The characteristics of effective leaders are shown in Figure 7-2. Create a three-column table. In the first column, list the characteristics from the figure. In the middle column, describe things you have done (hobbies, work, projects) that give evidence of each leadership characteristic. In the final column, list other things you can do in the next two years to further develop your capabilities as a leader.

27. Economics Some people believe that ethical behavior and a company's profitability do not go hand in hand. Use the Internet to locate research on the relationship between ethics and profits. Develop a one-page report on your findings. In the report, indicate whether you believe an ethical company can also be profitable.

28. Math The three levels of management spend different amounts of time on the five management functions. The records of one company show the average amount of time their managers spent on each function in a week. The results are shown in the table below. Calculate the total time spent per week by all levels of management for each of the five functions. Develop a graph that shows the percentage of the total hours each group devotes to each of the management functions during their workweek.

WEEKLY AVERAGE HOURS DEVOTED TO MANAGEMENT FUNCTIONS

	EXECUTIVES	MIDDLE MANAGERS	SUPERVISORS
Planning	22	10	5
Organizing	6	12	8
Staffing	2	7	3
Implementing	4	14	20
Controlling	18	7	6

Make Your Case

Valencia Price has just been promoted to a supervisor role in the Roxbury Manufacturing Company, where she has worked for 11 years. She had often heard employees complain that their supervisors were not interested in employees' ideas and did not involve them in decision making. As a result, Valencia felt it was important to avoid using position and reward influence and to try to adopt a strategic leadership style. From the first day of work as a supervisor, Valencia asked employees to discuss how the work could be improved. She knew that the other employees respected Manny, a long-time member of the work team. When Valencia wanted the team to make a decision, she would often ask Manny to lead the discussion so the employees would not think she was trying to influence them. After a month, Valencia started to hear that employees believed she could not make a decision on her own and wasted too much time in meetings. Several even suggested that maybe Manny should be the supervisor. They said that if Valencia had to ask Manny to run her meetings, she must not have any confidence in her own supervisory skills.

29. What principles of effective leadership was Valencia demonstrating as a supervisor?

30. Why were the employees not satisfied with the way Valencia was leading?

31. What would you recommend she do?

31. Valencia could adopt a mixed management style. She could make many of the day-to-day decisions and hold employee meetings for major new decisions or changes. She should continue to seek input from the informal leader, but she should lead the meetings.

Interactions and Connections

32. There are many opportunities in your community to develop skills that will help you become an effective business leader. Select five of the leadership characteristics shown in Figure 7-2 that you would like to develop. For each characteristic selected, identify a community activity in which you can participate that will help you develop the characteristic. List the community group or organization that offers the activity and the requirements to participate in the activity. Using the organization website or by making a direct contact, identify the procedures and requirements for volunteering at one of the groups or organizations.

33. Leadership and leadership development are important issues in business today. Many business executives maintain personal blogs to discuss their ideas, beliefs, and leadership experiences. Most of the leadership blogs encourage feedback and discussion of leadership from blog readers both inside and outside of the executive's company. Go online and locate a blog written by a business executive on the topic of leadership. Identify and write a brief description of one blog posting that discusses an aspect of leadership that you studied in this chapter. Identify and briefly describe another blog posting that provides information on leadership you did not study in the chapter. Describe how reading blogs of business executives can help develop your leadership skills.

Travel and Tourism Team Decision-Making Event

During the DECA Team Decision-Making Event, each team of two has 30 minutes to develop a plan of action for the specific situation described. Your team will present a 10-minute detailed strategy to the state director of economic development.

The economies of the states that border the Gulf of Mexico depend heavily on tourism dollars. Their semi-tropical climate and sandy beaches make them ideal vacation spots. Your team works for the governor and the director of travel and tourism for a Gulf Coast state. Your team is concerned about the negative economic impact of a recent natural disaster on travel and tourism. The national media has focused on the disaster and many tourists have changed their travel plans due to the images they have seen in the news.

Although your state has made great strides in repairing damage following the disaster, tourism is down 40 percent this year compared to last year. Your team must do the following:

- Develop a marketing campaign to counter the negative images in the media.
- Describe a plan to restore your state's image and increase travel and tourism.
- Describe a marketing campaign that generates more tourism dollars for your state.
- Include promotions and advertisements as part of the marketing campaign.

Performance Indicators Evaluated

- Demonstrate understanding of the economic impact of a natural disaster.
- Explain the impact that media has on consumer perception.
- Describe an advertising campaign to meet the challenge.
- Explain the best advertising media to communicate a message.
- Describe a promotional campaign to meet specific goals.
- Explain how to measure the effectiveness of an advertising campaign.

For more detailed information about performance indicators, go to the DECA website.

Think Critically

1. How are consumer decisions influenced by the media?
2. What are the best methods for promoting travel and tourism?
3. What are the drawbacks and benefits of mentioning the natural disaster in the advertising campaign?

www.deca.org

WINNING EDGE

Travel and Tourism Team Decision-Making Event

The event encourages students to work effectively as a team and emphasizes skills in communication, critical thinking, problem solving, production, teamwork, and time management. Students are also challenged to understand the leadership responsibilities of public officials and government leaders. Students must understand the economic impact of a natural disaster and the advertising campaign needed to regain lost tourism.

Think Critically *Answers*

1. Graphic stories presented by the media can have a negative impact on travel and tourism. Consumers may hesitate to visit a place that has been hit with a natural disaster if they have seen images of debris and damaged property.

2. Creative television commercials that highlight tourist attractions for a state are effective. Other forms of media might include printed advertisements, billboards, and the Internet.

3. Drawbacks: Mentioning the natural disaster may remind people of the images they saw following the disaster and might cause them to decide against visiting there. Benefits: People's concerns about the state of the area after the disaster and recovery can be directly addressed and appeased.

Interactions and Connections

32. Challenge students to follow through with one of the organizations they listed and develop the leadership characteristics they identified.

33. Descriptions of the postings will vary, but students should identify and discuss the leadership concept or principle for each posting.

Answers on the benefits of reading blogs will also vary. Students might point out the value of reading about real-world situations and being able to compare the ideas of several leaders.

CHAPTER OVERVIEW

In this chapter, students will learn about the role of human resources, effective human resource management skills, and the importance of an effective organizational culture.

8.1 Human Resources Basics

This lesson describes the changing workforce in today's businesses and introduces the work of human resources personnel.

8.2 Managing Human Resources

This lesson focuses on how to identify and hire employees, the types of compensation and benefits plans used in business, and the steps in employee performance management.

8.3 Organizational Culture and Workforce Diversity

This lesson discusses the benefits of diversity to a business, employees, customers, and society. The important factors leading to an effective organizational culture are presented.

Chapter 8 Human Resources, Culture, and Diversity

istockphoto.com/Susan Chiang

Instructor Resources

- Activities and Study Guide IE
- Chapter and Unit Tests IE
- Lesson Plans
- PowerPoint Presentation
- Cognero Test, Ch. 8

Student Resources

Activities and Study Guide
www.cengage.com/swep/pob9e
- Portfolio Activity

PLANNING A CAREER IN . . .
HUMAN RESOURCES

Businesses with a long history of success recognize the importance of their employees. A highly skilled, motivated workforce can provide a competitive edge. Companies often spend more money on their personnel than on any other resource. With so large an investment, companies need professional human resources personnel to recruit, train, motivate, and compensate employees.

The goal of human resources is to ensure that the right people are in the right jobs at the right time. This is accomplished by hiring the best people, maintaining a work environment that encourages productivity and satisfaction, and offering programs that allow employees to develop skills to meet rapidly changing job requirements.

Large human resources departments are made up of a number of specialists. They work closely with managers and employees to ensure that employees are available, capable, and willing to work. They also make sure employees are paid and recognized for their contributions.

Related Job Titles

- **Director of Human Resources**
- **Benefits Specialist**
- **Employment Recruiter**
- **Employee Relations Manager**
- **Organizational Development Consultant**
- **Training Specialist**
- **EEO/Affirmative Action Representative**
- **Labor Contracts Negotiator**
- **Job Analyst**

Analyze Career Opportunities in . . .
HUMAN RESOURCES

Use library and Internet resource to learn more about careers in human resources. Choose one of the job titles listed in the box and answer the following questions.

1. How would you describe the earnings potential for this field?
2. Is this a career that interests you? Explain how careers in this field match up with your goals and interests.

What it's like to work as a . . . Corporate Trainer

Emiko is a lead trainer for the Orbis Company. She has had an interesting career path, starting as a high school science teacher, followed by five years as a laboratory specialist at Orbis. Six months ago, she applied for a training position in the company. In this new job, Emiko combines her passions for teaching, science, and helping her co-workers.

As a lead trainer, Emiko meets with managers to identify training needs. Those needs might be helping new employees learn their jobs, preparing experienced employees for new processes, or developing a teamwork course. Emiko works with instructional designers and media specialists to prepare training materials. She must stay up to date with the latest educational technology in order to deliver training to employees located at sites all over the world.

What about you? What aspects of a career as a corporate trainer do you think you would find interesting?

PLANNING A CAREER IN . . .
HUMAN RESOURCES

Human resources is a very complex and important aspect of business, presenting many interesting career opportunities. Human resources personnel work with managers and employees in recruiting and hiring new employees, establishing pay systems and benefits programs, managing payroll and other records systems, and assisting with performance management and performance improvement.

What About You? ***Answers***

Interest in a career as a corporate trainer will vary. Some students might suggest that a career as a trainer combines many different interests and skills. Trainers get to work in many parts of the company with a variety of people. They are introduced to the latest types of technology and must keep current with new processes and procedures in order to train employees.

Analyze Career Opportunities *Answers*

Student answers will vary depending on when the assignment is completed and individual interests.

Additional Career Information

Encourage students to investigate careers they find interesting and explore unfamiliar careers. Two resources for additional career information are the *Occupational Outlook Handbook*, an online publication (www.bls.gov/oco) of the U.S. Bureau of Labor Statistics, and the O*NET Resource Center (www.onetcenter.org) developed by the U.S. Department of Labor. Information about specific careers and jobs can be used to demonstrate the relevance of skills learned in this course.

Focus on REAL LIFE

Employees have always been an important part of all businesses. That is not likely to change. While technology replaces some work and can do many tasks more efficiently, businesses need the energy, creativity, innovation, and unique skills of employees.

TEACH

Remind students that if they currently hold a job or are looking for one they are a part of the workforce. Most of them will remain in the workforce for the next 40 or 50 years. The types of jobs and even the nature of work will probably change dramatically during their work life.

If available, obtain a copy of the *Occupational Outlook Handbook* and show it to students so they can see the vast amount of information available about careers.

Encourage students to visit the OOH website. Point out that the website is a source of some of the most up-to-date information on the changing workforce. If possible, allow teams of students to browse the website to see how information is organized. Refer to the Teacher's Guide on the OOH website for tips on using the information with your students.

8.1 Human Resources Basics

Learning Outcomes

8.1.1 Describe the nature of today's workforce.

8.1.2 Identify important goals and activities of human resources.

Key Terms

workforce 172

downsizing 175

outsourcing 175

Focus on REAL LIFE

"Do you think we'll ever see the time when people don't have jobs because robots do all the work?" Indee asked Alex as they left the theater after enjoying the latest sci-fi thriller.

"It would be fun to think about never having to work but I think I'd get bored after awhile," replied Alex. "Besides, I want to be an industrial designer. That will require creativity and I don't think robots can be creative."

Indee laughed and said, "There are probably lots of things computers can't do. Plus, even if computers and robots are able to complete even more complex tasks in the future, people will still be responsible for planning and programming the work."

"The creativity, personalities, and skills of employees are what really make a business," Alex responded.

"So I guess we won't be replaced by robots," said Indee. "We'll just have to learn how to get along with them."

LO 8.1.1

THE CHANGING WORKFORCE

The **workforce** is made up of all the people 16 years and older who are employed or who are looking for a job. In 2015, the size of the U.S. workforce was more than 157 million people. That includes everyone holding a full- or part-time job and those seeking employment. It does not include the nearly 1.4 million people serving in the active military.

The days when you could get a full-time job if you had basic skills and a willingness to work hard are gone. Nearly two-thirds of U.S. jobs today require at least a high school education. For many jobs you need specialized training beyond high school or a college degree. Today's jobs offer a variety of working conditions and different wages and benefits. Some involve working mainly with machines and technology. Others deal mainly with people and information.

Types of Jobs

The business world consists of hundreds of thousands of companies offering a wide variety of jobs. The federal government and many state governments provide useful information about the jobs available to the workforce. The Bureau of Labor Statistics (BLS), part of the U.S. Department of Labor, researches thousands of different jobs. It offers up-to-date information about the U.S. workforce through publications and websites, including the *Occupational Outlook Handbook*.

There are two major types of industries analyzed in the *Occupational Outlook Handbook*. The *service-providing industries* include businesses that perform services that satisfy the needs of other businesses and consumers. Service companies include healthcare facilities, insurance companies, retail stores, transportation businesses, and many others. *Goods-producing industries*

Teaching Strategies

Expand Beyond the Classroom Instruct students to interview a family member or neighbor who has worked for more than 20 years. The student should ask about the changes the person has seen in the workforce in his or her lifetime, as well as the things that have not changed.

INDUSTRY CATEGORIES	
GOODS-PRODUCING INDUSTRIES	**SERVICE-PROVIDING INDUSTRIES**

Construction
Manufacturing
Natural Resources and Mining
  Agriculture, Forestry, Fishing and Hunting
  Mining, Quarrying, and Oil and Gas Extraction
	Education, Health Care, and Social Assistance Services
	Financial Activities
	  Finance and Insurance
	  Real Estate, Rental and Leasing
	Information Services
	Leisure and Hospitality
	  Arts, Entertainment, and Recreation
	  Accommodation and Food Services
	Professional and Business Services
	  Scientific and Technical Services
	  Management of Companies and Enterprises
	  Administrative and Support Services
	  Waste Management and Remediation
	Trade, Transportation, and Utilities
	  Wholesale Trade
	  Retail Trade
	  Transportation and Warehousing
	  Utilities

Source: U.S. Bureau of Labor Statistics

FIGURE 8-1
In your opinion, which category, service-providing or goods-producing, accounts for more jobs in your community?

include businesses that produce or manufacture products used by other businesses or purchased by final consumers. These companies are involved in construction, manufacturing, mining, and agriculture. Figure 8-1 highlights the industry categories from the *Occupational Outlook Handbook*.

The U.S. economy continues to evolve. It is shifting its emphasis from goods-providing businesses to service-providing ones. The BLS estimates that the economy will add nearly 16 million new jobs over the next 10 years. Almost all of that job growth will be in service-providing industries, with fewer than one million new jobs created in goods-producing industries. All job opportunities won't be in service businesses, though. Retiring workers and a growing economy will ensure that there are jobs in every category.

Another way of looking at the changing workforce is to think about groups of occupations. Occupations are affected by short- and long-term changes in industries, technology, and the overall economy. Figure 8-2 shows BLS estimates for future employment trends in selected occupational groups.

Traditionally, different occupations have been grouped into two broad categories: white-collar and blue-collar. A *white-collar worker* is one whose work is more mental than physical and involves the handling and processing of information. Most white-collar workers are employed in offices and stores. They include professional, managerial, and clerical workers. A *blue-collar worker* is one whose job involves more physical work, including the operation of machinery and equipment or other production activities. Blue-collar workers are employed in factories, on construction sites, on farms, and in the delivery of many basic services. With the growth of service industries, a new category of worker has emerged. *Service workers* produce intangible goods for businesses and consumers. Some service jobs require high levels of education and skill. Others do not.

▸ Figure 8-1 *ANSWER*

Students should consider the overall economic makeup of the community. Is there a large agriculture or manufacturing sector? If students live in agricultural or other rural areas, they may have a near balance of service-providing and goods-producing industries, but service-providing industries will most likely dominate in most communities.

TEACH

Ask students: "Even though more products are increasingly demanded and consumed by people in the United States and around the world, why has the U.S. economy moved from an emphasis on goods-producing businesses to an emphasis on service-providing businesses?" Suggest that many developing countries are increasing goods production and U.S. consumers are increasing their demand for services.

Different Learning Abilities

Visually Impaired Ask another student to describe the information in Figure 8-2 to a visually impaired student and discuss the information to make sure it is understood.

▶ **Figure 8-2** ***ANSWER***

Answers will vary. For example, students might suggest personal interests and skills, education and training required, wage and salary rates, the nature of the work, and other factors.

Work as a TEAM

Students should review their lists to see which items related directly to increasing monetary rewards and which were not directly related to compensating employees. Ask students to consider how their lists might be different if they were older with a busy family schedule.

THINK CRITICALLY THROUGH VISUALS

Answers will vary. For example, computerized machinery could generate more precision and less waste in manufacturing or packaging processes. Computers can keep track of inventories, making it less likely that a production facility would run short of needed parts. Employee performance can be evaluated using computers that track production output. Computer networks allow individuals in all parts of a large production facility to communicate. Also, computer technology can perform repetitive tasks with increased efficiency, leading to a decreased need for production workers.

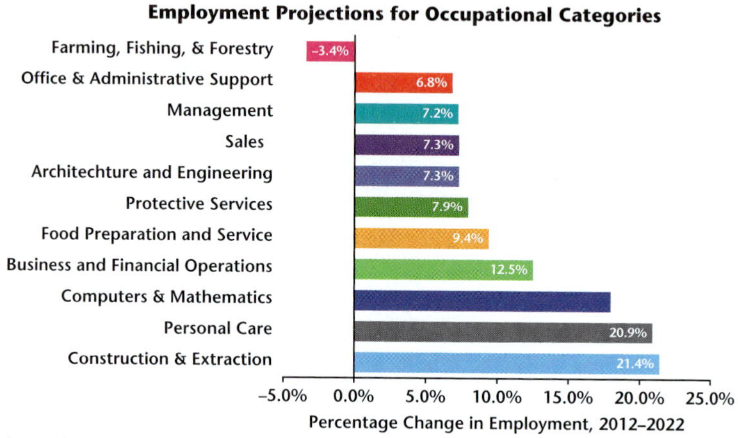

Source: U.S. Bureau of Labor Statistics

FIGURE 8-2

What factors other than the rate of employment growth would you consider when choosing an industry in which to work?

Work as a TEAM

Each year, *Fortune* magazine and the Great Place to Work Institute identify the "Best Companies to Work For." These rankings are based on surveys taken by the employees of many top companies. As a team, make a list of ten things a company can do that you believe would help it make it to the "Best Companies . . ." list.

Changing Job Requirements

White-collar, blue-collar, and service workers are all necessary in the workforce. Increased use of computers and information technology in factories, on farms, and in construction is changing the nature of many types of work. The changes call for higher levels of education and training. More than half of all new job openings in the next 10 years will require education beyond high school.

A variety of factors will require future jobs to change and some to be eliminated. The nature of jobs will continue to evolve. Many jobs will be eliminated or substantially modified. Some jobs, while performing the same function as always, will require different skills and training. A mix of factors will drive the evolution of work in the future. Among these factors are consumer preferences, economic conditions, new technology, and business competition.

Consumer Preferences Jobs are affected by consumer demand for a product or service. Sometimes new products entering the market make existing products obsolete. Workers making the old products may find that their jobs are changed or even eliminated. New jobs may be created by the demand for the new products.

Juice Images/SuperStock

Name ways in which computer technology changes the way manufacturing businesses operate.

Different Learning Abilities

Specific Learning Disability (SLD) Instruct students to use the *Occupational Outlook Handbook* to identify two white-collar, two blue-collar, and two service jobs that interest them. Suggest that students make lists of the requirements for each of the jobs.

Economic Cycles Changes in the economy affect job opportunities. When businesses expand because consumers buy more goods and services, new jobs are created to meet the growing demand. More workers are employed and earn more money. In turn, they are able to spend more on goods and services. All of this contributes to a growing economy.

Higher prices may cause consumers to decrease the amount they buy. When interest rates increase, both businesses and consumers find it difficult to borrow money. Demand for goods and services decreases. As a result, jobs may be eliminated or work hours may be reduced. Consumer spending and demand is decreased even more as the economy slows.

New Technologies *Technology* refers to the use of automated machinery, electronic equipment, and integrated computer systems to help increase the efficiency of producing goods and services. Technology is important in the workplace. It improves efficiency so that businesses may stay competitive. Computerized systems and robots have greatly reduced the need for production workers in many manufacturing industries. These include steel, autos, tires, and consumer electronics. Sophisticated computer and communications systems have also reduced the need for office employees such as bookkeepers and clerks. New technology continues to change the types of jobs in production and manufacturing. It has also changed how most office workers, service workers, and professionals perform their jobs.

Business Competition Companies must be competitive in order to stay in business. Costs are a major factor. The cost of running a business affects jobs and workers. When costs begin to increase, a business must look for ways to stay profitable. Installing new equipment and streamlining processes make workers more productive. Businesses may also decide to downsize. **Downsizing** is a planned reduction in the number of employees in order to cut costs and make a business more efficient. **Outsourcing** removes work from one company and sends it to another company that can complete it at a lower cost. Since 2000, U.S. businesses have outsourced more than 2.5 million manufacturing and professional jobs to other countries.

> **Life-Span Plan**
> Why might a young person be cautious about setting a life-span goal to become a printing press operator? Explain why it is necessary to understand changes that are taking place in the workplace when you set your life-span goals.

> **CHECKPOINT**
> What are several strong influences on changes in the workforce?

LO 8.1.2

HUMAN RESOURCES OVERVIEW

The work of every company is completed by the organization's employees. Employees who have the knowledge and

Mr. Green/Shutterstock.com

Think of the places you frequent regularly. What types of workers are visible? Are there "behind the scenes" employees?

Life-Span Plan Answers

Answers will vary. Students should explain that today there are few jobs for printing press operators because more media is delivered electronically. People need to consider future employment opportunities when they set life-span goals.

ONGOING ASSESSMENT

CHECKPOINT ✓ANSWER

Strong influences for change in the workforce include consumer preferences, economic conditions, new technology, and business competition.

TEACH

Point out to students that many companies have a hard time finding qualified employees even when the economy is not strong. Ask them to identify reasons why it may be difficult for some companies to find qualified employees while other companies can easily fill open positions.

THINK CRITICALLY THROUGH VISUALS

Answers will vary depending on what types of businesses students patronize regularly. Ask students to list some of the visible employees, as well as the types of work that would occur "behind the scenes."

Different Learning Abilities

At-Risk Ask students to list two or three ways that technology is affecting a job they are interested in as a career. Ask them to think about the technology skills they will likely need for that work. Work with students to identify ways they can develop these needed skills.

THINK CRITICALLY THROUGH VISUALS

Answers will vary. Some of the many challenges human resources managers might encounter include identifying qualified applicants for positions that need to be filled, the need to stay current with the many federal and state laws pertaining to human resources, meeting safety requirements for dangerous jobs, managing employee turnover, and keeping the necessary records for payroll and benefits.

TEACH

Divide students into teams and assign each team one or two of the major goals of human resources. Ask teams to suggest ways they can work with other managers in a company to successfully accomplish the goals they have been assigned.

iStockphoto.com/Aiden Franklin

Meeting the ongoing need for training and retraining employees is one of the many challenges a human resources manager might encounter. What are some others?

skills needed, who are motivated to work efficiently, and who complete their jobs with quality contribute to the success of the business. Companies that have difficulty finding qualified employees, have a poor work environment, and suffer from quality issues, waste, and employee errors will have difficulty remaining competitive or meeting customer needs.

Human resources are the people who work for a business. Human resources include management and employees, full-time and part-time workers. People hired to fill temporary positions as well as those who have worked for the company for many years are human resources. Managing human resources is one of the most important responsibilities of a business. Most medium- to large-sized businesses have a department devoted to human resources management and activities. The owner of a small business will be responsible for managing human resources or will hire others to complete the work.

Human Resources Goals

Human resources are different from almost every other resource needed by businesses. Each person is different. They bring varied knowledge, skills, experience, and motivation to their jobs. People are used in different ways in a company. Some will be required to do hard, physical labor. Others will operate complex equipment. Some employees will work in groups where they must have effective interpersonal skills and demonstrate teamwork. Others will work independently, relying on their own abilities. Managers will direct the work of others and make decisions and plans that can affect the entire company. New employees must be willing to follow directions and may have few decision-making responsibilities at first.

Human resources must be able to work with the differences and unique capabilities of each employee and develop a workforce that is productive and efficient. There are seven major human resources goals.

1. Identify the personnel needs of the company.
2. Maintain an adequate supply of people to fill those needs.
3. Match abilities and interests with specific jobs.
4. Provide training and development to prepare people for their jobs and to improve their capabilities as job requirements change.
5. Develop plans to compensate personnel for their work.
6. Protect the health and well-being of employees.
7. Maintain a productive and satisfying work environment.

Human Resources Activities

Managing human resources involves four broad categories of activities. The categories are planning and staffing, performance management, compensation and benefits, and employee relations. Specific human resources activities for each of the categories are listed in Figure 8-3.

Planning and staffing activities are directed at identifying and filling all of the jobs in the company with qualified

Applied Skills

Communication Instruct students to use the information from the lesson to develop an advertisement to recruit a manager of human resources in a business. The advertisement should include a description of the major duties as well as the preparation and experience expected of applicants. The ad should be prepared and printed in the format of a classified advertisement in a newspaper or an online job listing.

HUMAN RESOURCES ACTIVITIES			
PLANNING & STAFFING	PERFORMANCE MANAGEMENT	COMPENSATION & BENEFITS	EMPLOYEE RELATIONS
• Job analysis • Recruitment and selection • Job placement	• Performance assessment • Performance improvement • Managing promotions, transfers, and terminations	• Wage and salary planning • Benefits planning • Payroll, benefits, and personnel records management	• Health and safety planning • Labor relations • Employment law and policy enforcement • Organizational development

FIGURE 8-3
Which activities do you think are the most important to the success of the business? Explain your answer.

people. *Performance management* involves evaluating the work of employees and improving performance through training and development. *Compensation and benefits* concerns planning and managing payroll, personnel records, and benefits programs. *Employee relations* is responsible for maintaining a safe, healthy, and productive work environment for all employees.

CHECKPOINT ✓
What are the seven major goals of human resources?

8.1 ASSESSMENT

Key Concepts

Determine the best answer.

1. The U.S. workforce is made up of nearly ___ people.
   - **a.** 80 million
   - **b.** 110 million
   - **c.** 160 million
   - **d.** 260 million
2. The Bureau of Labor Statistics publication that provides detailed and up-to-date information about the U.S. workforce is the
   - **a.** *Occupational Outlook Handbook*
   - **b.** *IRS Publication 15*
   - **c.** *Congressional Record*
   - **d.** *Business Report*
3. A person whose work is more mental than physical and involves the handling and processing of information is a
   - **a.** blue-collar worker
   - **b.** human resources manager
   - **c.** white-collar worker
   - **d.** entrepreneur
4. Which of the following would *not* be a part of a company's human resources?
   - **a.** managers
   - **b.** full-time employees
   - **c.** temporary employees
   - **d.** All would be included as human resources.

Make Academic Connections

5. **Math** The population of the United States is approximately 324,500,000. If 167,000,000 people are not employed, what percentage of the total population is not currently working? What accounts for the difference in that percentage and the 4 percent unemployment rate that is considered full employment by the Bureau of Labor Statistics?
6. **Art** Create a collage on poster board that illustrates the many activities that are a part of human resources. Clip pictures from newspapers and magazines that represent the four broad categories of activities. Show your collage to other students and describe the activities you illustrated.

▶ **Figure 8-3** ***ANSWER***
Answers will vary, but reasons should be specific to the needs and goals of the business and to employee satisfaction and effectiveness.

ONGOING ASSESSMENT

CHECKPOINT ✓*ANSWER*
The seven major goals of human resources are listed on page 176.

ASSESS

Key Concepts *Answers*

1. c. 150 million
2. a. *Occupational Outlook Handbook*
3. c. white-collar worker
4. d. All would be included as human resources.

Make Academic Connections *Answers*

5. More than 50 percent of the population is not working: 167,000,000 ÷ 324,500,000 = 0.515 or 51.5%. The reported unemployment rate reflects only persons aged 16 and older who are actively seeking employment. Children, stay-at-home parents, active military, and the retired, for example, are not included when computing the unemployment rate.
6. Designate a location for displaying collages and allow time for students to discuss their work.

CLOSE Ask students to identify reasons why human resources is one of the fastest-growing career areas in business today.

RETEACH Ask students to use Figure 8-3 to discuss the role of human resources and the activities performed by human resources personnel.

ENRICH Instruct students to use Internet career information to identify five jobs that did not exist 20 years ago and five more that may not exist in the next 20 years.

Focus on REAL LIFE

Tell students that all sizes of businesses have human resources and need to address human resource issues. Small businesses are challenged to hire and keep well-qualified employees even though they may not be able to pay as much money or provide the same opportunities for advancement as larger businesses. Small businesses try to compete by offering a more personalized and flexible work environment, building positive working relationships, and giving employees greater responsibility and control over their work.

TEACH

Ask students whether they agree with the statement, "If human resources management does its job well, the company will have employees who do their jobs well." Students should justify their opinions.

Instruct students to prepare a table that compares the four types of employees described—permanent, temporary, full-time, and part-time.

8.2 Managing Human Resources

Learning Outcomes

8.2.1 Identify important planning and staffing activities.

8.2.2 Describe compensation and benefits plans.

8.2.3 Recognize the goals of performance management.

Key Terms

job analysis 179	incentive systems 181
compensation 181	promotion 183
salary and wages 181	transfer 184
benefits 181	termination 184

Focus on REAL LIFE

"How was your day?" Jacqueline asked her business partner as she dropped into a chair after a busy day.

"It was fine until Esme came to see me," Leo responded as he looked up from the report he was reading. "She is going to work for a competitor."

"That's a shame," said Jacqueline, "She is great with customers and her work is terrific. Did she say why she is leaving?"

"The usual reasons: better benefits and more opportunities for advancement," Leo replied.

"We need to look for a replacement right away," Jacqueline said. "I'll call the staffing agency tomorrow."

"Maybe we should take our time and think about our needs. It might be time to plan a better hiring strategy rather than just quickly replacing people when they leave," Leo said.

"Leo, you're right. We should turn this in to an opportunity for reviewing the way we manage our human resources. I bet there are things we can do to be more competitive. We especially need to focus on ways to retain our talented employees."

LO 8.2.1

HUMAN RESOURCES PLANNING AND STAFFING

Human resources management ensures that needed employees are available, productive, paid, and satisfied with their work. If human resources management does its job well, the company will have employees who do their jobs well. This contributes to a successful, profitable business.

Planning and Job Analysis

Human resources management begins by analyzing where the business currently is in terms of its personnel and where it wants to be. The decision to hire people must be made carefully. Once an employee is hired, the person's salary must be paid whether the company is profitable or not. An employee should be hired when the work of that employee will add more to the company's profitability than it will cost.

Classifying Employees The company must decide whether the person to be hired will be permanent or temporary. A *permanent employee* is one to whom the company makes a long-term commitment. It is expected that the employee will work for the business as long as the business is profitable and the employee's performance is satisfactory. A *temporary employee* is one hired for a specific time or to complete a specific assignment.

Because permanent employees feel that they are a part of the business, they are often more productive than temporary employees. On the other hand, there is more control over the company's resources when temporary employees are hired. The employee is paid only until the temporary assignment

Applied Skills

Mathematics A company currently has 2,550 employees. Eighty-five percent are permanent and 63 percent are full-time. Assign students to calculate the number of employees in all four employment categories and present the results in a chart or graph.

ends. Temporary employees are usually hired during a busy time for the business or when a special task needs to be done.

Whether permanent or temporary, employees can be hired full-time or part-time. A *full-time employee* regularly works a schedule of 30 or more hours a week. A *part-time employee* has a shorter work schedule with either fewer hours each day or fewer days each week.

Determining Job Requirements Before starting the hiring process, human resources staff studies the work that must be done in the job. Specific information about each job is needed in order to hire people with the right skills. That information is often collected by completing a job analysis. A **job analysis** is a specific study of a job to identify in detail the job duties and skill requirements.

First, human resources staff studies the current job in detail by observing the work and talking with employees and managers. They identify all important job duties, as well as the knowledge and skills required to successfully complete the job. Next, they add any new activities planned for that job to the analysis. The job analysis helps determine if the needs of the business can best be met with temporary, permanent, part-time, or full-time employees.

Monkey Business Images/Shutterstock.com

Why would a business choose not to advertise a job opening outside the company?

Recruiting and Hiring

Once the specific need and skill requirements are determined, prospective employees meeting the requirements must be located. If this search is not done carefully, an employer may spend a great deal of time and expense and an appropriate employee may still not be found. Several good sources of prospective employees exist and are identified in Figure 8-4. Businesses should use sources that will provide an adequate number of qualified candidates for the position. The candidates should have the skills required for the job and an interest in working for the business.

The Application Process Most companies ask prospective applicants to fill out an employment application. The application gathers personal information, information on education, and work experience history. It may also ask for specific skills related to the job and contact information for

EFFECTIVE SOURCES FOR RECRUITING PROSPECTIVE EMPLOYEES	
Company employment office	Job and career affairs
Company websites	Newspaper advertising, online and print
Employment agencies, public and private	Placement offices, school and college
Executive recruiters	Radio and television advertising
Industry publications	Referrals by employees
Job search and career websites	Social networking

FIGURE 8-4
Why do employers often use multiple sources when recruiting new employees?

THINK CRITICALLY THROUGH VISUALS

A business might choose not to advertise a job opening because of the unique type of work or a specific company policy. A business may already have a number of qualified candidates among its current employees and prefer to promote from within.

TEACH

Instruct students to find several job descriptions using the Internet. Ask them to compare the descriptions in terms of the amount of detail provided. Ask them how a job analysis helps companies prepare a detailed job description.

▶ Figure 8-4 *ANSWER*

Employers want to make sure they recruit the best possible group of prospective employees. A variety of sources will usually increase the number and type of people who are aware of the company's job openings.

Teaching Strategies

Collaborative Learning Group students into learning teams. Each team should review Figure 8-4 and use newspapers, magazines, the Internet, and other resources to identify an example of each of the employee recruitment sources listed.

TEACH

Locate several job application forms from local businesses and from the Internet. Distribute copies to students and instruct them to study the types of information collected. Lead a discussion on how businesses might use the information from the completed application forms to determine which applicants to reject and which to keep in the application process.

Business Insight

Think Critically *Answers*

1. The company does not have to pay benefits to the people hired. If the work is no longer needed, the company can easily end the employment. Recruiting costs are reduced as well if the temporary employee is later offered a full-time job.

2. Both companies and workers may prefer the greater flexibility. The number of workers can be increased or decreased quickly, allowing the company to respond to changing market conditions and competition. Workers can be more selective in the companies they work for and confident that they like the job and company before they commit to a permanent job.

people who can serve as references. For more advanced jobs, the applicant may be asked to submit an application letter and a résumé as well. Applications are used to eliminate people who are clearly not qualified for the job and to identify those who appear to be especially qualified.

Once applications have been reviewed, the remaining applicants are studied more carefully. Information is checked for accuracy. References are contacted. The employer selects a few applicants to interview. These applicants may be asked to complete special tests related to needed job knowledge and skills. During the interview, the applicant may be introduced to the work area, managers, and co-workers. The applicant will be given more detailed information about the company and the job. Finally, the applicant whose qualifications best match the job requirements will be offered the job.

New Employee Orientation The final step in the hiring process is to help the new employee get a good start in the company. As a part of the orientation, the new employee will meet with human resources specialists to complete all of the forms and documents needed to receive pay and benefits. This will also allow the company to develop a complete employee record. There will usually be several days of

Business Insight

Temp-To-Hire

Companies are continually challenged to maintain an effective workforce while controlling costs. Payroll expenses typically account for 30 to 50 percent of company expenses. Some companies spend much more. Human resources managers are challenged to find ways to hire qualified, productive personnel while keeping costs down.

In difficult economic times, the challenge is even greater. Companies must be cautious about hiring new employees when sales and profits are declining. On the other hand, companies must function in the present and be prepared when the economy improves.

Today, human resources managers often use hiring practices to help create a flexible workforce. Hiring temporary employees is a way to meet urgent, short-term needs. Temps are hired for a limited time, a specific project, or when a company does not want to risk committing to a new permanent employee. Another approach, known as temp-to-hire, adds the possibility of full-time employment for temporary employees. Sometimes called "try it before you buy it," the temporary employee is offered a trial period. If the temp and the company are good fits for one another, the temp may be offered a permanent position.

The American Staffing Association, a trade association, reported that in a recent year nearly 3 million people worked in temporary or nonemployee positions each week. Temp-to-hire is quite effective. The association found that nearly 41 percent of such workers were offered permanent positions. However, to place that many temporary employees, staffing companies had to recruit nearly 12 million prospective employees during the year.

Think Critically

1. How do the temporary employment options discussed help a company control costs if they are actually hiring people to do the work?
2. Why might temp-to-hire be used by companies in good economic times?

Applied Skills

Language Arts Assign students to write a paragraph about the importance of effective communication skills when completing the application process for a new job. Ask them to provide some specific examples of how good communication skills help the process and how poor communication skills hinder it.

training. The employee may be paired with an experienced co-worker, or mentor.

The mentor answers questions and helps the new employee solve problems and build confidence for the new job. The company may have a probationary period of several weeks to several months. During that time, the new employee is evaluated to ensure job performance is meeting the company's expectations.

CHECKPOINT
Why do human resources personnel need to study jobs before beginning the hiring process?

LO 8.2.2
COMPENSATION AND BENEFITS

One of the reasons people work is to earn money. **Compensation** is the amount of money paid to an employee for work performed. Compensation is made up of two parts. **Salary and wages** are direct payment of money to an employee for work completed. Compensation in forms other than direct payment is known as **benefits**. Examples of benefits are insurance, vacations, retirement plans, and health and fitness programs.

Compensation Methods

A *time wage* pays the employee a specific amount of money for each hour worked. A *straight salary* pays a specific amount of money for each week or month worked. Neither of these types of compensation are based directly on the amount or quality of work done, but are determined by the amount of time spent on the job. For that reason, it is a simple system to manage. The business just has to keep records on the amount of time each employee works.

Incentive systems connect the amount of compensation to the quality or quantity of an employee's performance. Some businesses pay a *commission* in which an employee is paid a percentage of sales for which he or she is responsible. Salespeople are often compensated with commissions. Another pay-for-performance plan is known as a *piece rate*. An employee receives a specific amount for each unit of work produced. Piece rates are commonly used in manufacturing, agriculture, and service centers. For example, workers might be paid a piece rate for each seam they sew, each pound of grapes they pick, each call they answer, or each claim they process.

Some companies use a *base plus incentive* compensation system. This system combines a wage or salary with an additional amount based on the employee's performance. One type of base plus incentive plan is profit sharing.

Work as a TEAM

Automobile dealerships have traditionally paid their salespeople with a straight commission. Some dealerships now pay each salesperson a salary and add a bonus based on customer satisfaction surveys. As a team, discuss how this change might affect the performance of the salespeople and why the dealerships may have chosen to make the change.

wavebreakmedia/Shutterstock.com

If you were a telemarketer, would you rather be paid commission on your sales or an hourly wage rate? Explain your answer.

ONGOING ASSESSMENT

CHECKPOINT ANSWER

Human resources personnel need to study jobs before beginning the hiring process to determine the job duties and the specific skills that are needed so that they can hire a person with the ability to successfully perform the job.

TEACH

Ask students to list each of the types of compensation methods, write a definition of each, and then develop an example of how the amount of money paid to an employee would be calculated using each method.

Work as a TEAM

Invite a representative of each team to summarize the team's findings. Ask students if the way salespeople are compensated may influence the qualifications a dealership would use to hire its salespeople.

THINK CRITICALLY THROUGH VISUALS

Answers will vary. Some students will prefer to be paid hourly in order to have a reliable income. Others will prefer to be paid on commission so they have the opportunity to earn more than the hourly rate based on their ability to make sales.

Different Learning Abilities

English Language Learners (ELL) Ask students to write each of the bold and italicized terms and then write the definition of each. Assign students to work in pairs to read each of the terms and its definition, working on correct spelling, punctuation, and comprehension of each definition.

FYI

Before they read the feature, ask students to predict the average hourly wage of U.S. workers and the additional amount employers spend for employee benefits. Then compare and discuss their answers with the information provided by the BLS.

TEACH

Ask students to review all employee benefits described in the lesson. Tell students to select the three benefits they would currently prefer if they were employed. Then ask them how they believe those preferences would change if they were raising children or nearing retirement.

THINK CRITICALLY THROUGH VISUALS

Answers will vary, but may include insurance, vacations, profit sharing, bonuses, on-site child care, fitness programs, personal or sick days, retirement savings plans, and flexible work schedules.

ONGOING ASSESSMENT

CHECKPOINT ✓ANSWER

Three types of incentive systems for employee compensation are pay-for-performance plans such as (1) commission or (2) piece rate and (3) base-plus-incentive systems, such as profit sharing.

FYI In a recent year, employers spent an average of $31.32 per hour worked on total employee compensation, according to the BLS. Hourly wages and salaries averaged $21.72 per hour and accounted for 69.4 percent of the costs. Benefits averaged $9.60, or 30.6 percent of the total.

With profit sharing, employees receive their regular compensation plus a share of the profits earned by a company. This system encourages commitment, teamwork, and effective job performance so that profits will be high.

Employee Benefits

Employee benefits can be an expensive addition to the cost of compensation. On average for all businesses, an additional 20 to 40 percent of an employee's wages is spent on benefits. If an employee earns $11.00 an hour, 30 percent added for benefits increases the hourly cost to $14.30. If the employee works 40 hours a week, the additional cost can be over $6,000 per year.

State and federal laws require some benefits. Most businesses must offer and pay the cost of these required benefits. Benefits include compensation for overtime hours worked, social security, Medicare, and contributions to funds to compensate injured employees and unemployed workers. Full-time employees may expect their employer to offer insurance plans such as health, life, dental, and disability insurance. Many companies, especially small businesses, cannot afford the cost of all of those types of insurance. The rapidly rising cost of health insurance has been particularly difficult for businesses to handle. As a result, many companies are reducing health insurance coverage or require employees to pay a larger part of insurance costs.

Time away for vacations is another popular benefit for employees. Paid vacations are a costly benefit because employees are paid for time when they are not working. On the other hand, the time off may result in a more satisfied and productive employee. Other benefits offered by businesses include retirement savings plans, health and wellness programs, personal or sick days, and flexible work schedules.

The costs of benefits programs continue to increase. Each employee may prefer different benefits. As a result, human resources departments have developed cafeteria plans. A *cafeteria plan* allocates a certain amount of money to each employee that can be spent on benefits. The employee selects the preferred benefits. If the cost of the benefits does not use all of the allocated money, the employee can receive the difference in additional pay. If the costs are higher, the employee has to pay the difference.

Steve Mason/Photodisc/Getty Images

What kinds of benefits are important to you?

CHECKPOINT ✓

List three types of incentive systems for employee compensation.

Applied Skills

Building Study Skills Assign students to prepare a study guide that outlines the types of compensation systems and employee benefits that employers frequently offer.

LO 8.2.3

PERFORMANCE MANAGEMENT

Managers work closely with their employees to make sure work goals are accomplished as planned. Every employee is expected to meet quality standards as well as work efficiently. In addition, employees must demonstrate effective working relationships with co-workers, managers, and customers. As jobs change, new equipment and procedures will be introduced. Employees must upgrade their skills to meet the changing job requirements. Most companies offer training and development programs to help employees perform their work well.

Employee Evaluation

Managers should evaluate the work of each of their employees on a regular basis. The human resources department is in charge of developing the evaluation procedures and forms. Managers are trained to complete objective evaluations and hold effective evaluation conferences with employees. Human resources maintains the records of employee evaluations in each employee's personnel file.

The Evaluation Process Performance evaluations focus on the specific job duties of each employee. They also review the important work qualities expected of all employees. Those qualities include factors such as communication, interpersonal relationships, quality and quantity of work, and ethical behavior.

Managers are given evaluation forms to complete. Evaluation decisions are based on observations of the employee's performance and review of the quantity and quality of the work. When teamwork is involved, co-workers may be asked to provide feedback as well. Using the evaluation form, the manager rates specific skills and identifies each employee's strengths and areas that need improvement.

The Evaluation Conference After the manager completes the evaluation form, a conference is scheduled with the employee. The purpose of the conference is to review and discuss the results of the evaluation and to plan for performance improvement. Both the manager and employee may have concerns about the conference. They might not be comfortable with a specific discussion of performance. Human resources personnel should help everyone understand and prepare for evaluation conferences. The conference should be meaningful and positive. It should result in reasonable agreement on the employee's performance, goals, and plans for the future. An important part of the conference is to identify the support the employee can expect from the manager and the company in order to improve performance.

Promotions, Transfers, and Terminations

Employees expect that if they work for a company for a long time and perform well, they should be rewarded with increased pay and the chance of promotion. A **promotion** is the advancement of an employee to a position with

iStockphoto.com/Neustockimages

Is earning a good wage or salary enough for you to be satisfied with your work? What else do you expect?

TEACH

Discuss with students the problems that can occur if an employee evaluation process is not planned and handled well by a manager and an employee. Ask students to brainstorm things managers and employees can do to improve the effectiveness of the employee evaluation and evaluation conference.

THINK CRITICALLY THROUGH VISUALS

Answers will vary. Some students will say that earning money is reason enough to work, although they may also expect benefits, such as health insurance and paid vacation. Others will want recognition of their contributions to the company's success, positive work relationships with managers and co-workers, and opportunities to improve their skills and advance in their careers.

Different Learning Styles

Kinesthetic Learners Organize students into teams of three. Instruct them to take turns role-playing an effective employee evaluation conference. One person should act as the employee, one as the manager, and one as an observer who identifies the strengths and weaknesses of the conference.

TEACH

Lead a discussion about the differences between a promotion and a transfer and between a discharge and a layoff.

ONGOING ASSESSMENT

CHECKPOINT ✓ ANSWER

The purpose is to review and discuss the results of the evaluation and plan for the future. This includes support for performance improvement.

ASSESS

Key Concepts *Answers*

1. c. permanent
2. False. A company should not waste time interviewing unqualified persons.
3. c. 20–40%
4. a. termination

Make Academic Connections *Answers*

5. Augusta's sales commission for the year is $3,724 ($186,200 × 0.02 = $3,724). Her salary is $37,200 ($3,100 × 12 = $37,200). Her annual total compensation is $45,424 ($3,724 + 37,200 + $4,500 bonus = $45,424).
6. Tables will vary depending on sources used.
7. Answers will vary. Students might recommend that an effective performance evaluation conference should (1) be meaningful, objective, and positive; (2) result in a reasonable agreement on the employee's performance, goals, and plans for the future; and (3) detail the support the employee can expect from the manager and the company in order to improve performance.

greater responsibility. Companies want to keep good employees. They want to place good employees in positions where they can provide the most benefit to the company. When possible, companies should fill open positions by promoting current employees. They are familiar with the company and will view the promotion as a reward. They should be motivated to stay with the company and continue to work effectively.

In some cases, a promotional opportunity may not exist, but employees want to change jobs. Some jobs in a company may be eliminated while others are being created. Employees may be able to accept a job transfer. A **transfer** is the assignment of an employee to another job in the company with a similar level of responsibility. A job transfer may provide a new challenge for an employee or offer a better match for a person's skills.

If performance does not meet the company's expectations or if jobs are being reduced, the company may have to terminate employees. A **termination** ends the employment relationship between a company and an employee. The termination may be a *discharge* that ends employment due to inappropriate work behavior. Another type of termination is a *layoff*, which is a temporary or permanent reduction in the number of employees due to changing business conditions. The company should complete all terminations carefully. The terminations must meet legal requirements and the company must be as helpful as possible to the employees who are asked to leave the business.

CHECKPOINT ✓

What is the purpose of an evaluation conference?

8.2 ASSESSMENT

Key Concepts

Determine the best answer.

1. An employee to whom a company makes a long-term commitment is considered to be
   a. full-time
   b. part-time
   c. permanent
   d. temporary
2. True or False. Companies should interview all prospective employees who apply for a job.
3. On average, the percentage of employees' compensation spent on benefits is
   a. less than 5%
   b. 10%–20%
   c. 20%–40%
   d. more than 50%
4. The employment relationship between a company and an employee is ended with a(n)
   a. termination
   b. interview
   c. evaluation
   d. lawsuit

Make Academic Connections

5. **Math** Augusta is paid $3,100 a month and a commission of 2 percent on all sales. She also is given a yearly bonus of $4,500. If Augusta's sales for the year are $186,200, what is her total compensation for the year?
6. **Research** Use the Internet to locate four different sources of current job opportunities. Develop a table that compares the sites in terms of their effectiveness in providing information about the job, the company, and the procedure applicants should follow in applying for a job.
7. **Critical Thinking** You are a human resources specialist giving advice to a new supervisor on how to conduct a performance evaluation conference with an employee. List three recommendations you would make to the supervisor that will contribute to an effective conference.

RETEACH Ask students to list all of the human resources activities discussed and add a brief description for each.

ENRICH Ask a human resources professional to speak about the use of technology in their work.

CLOSE Ask students to complete this sentence: "Human resources management activities are important to an organization because . . ."

8.3 Organizational Culture and Workforce Diversity

Learning Outcomes

8.3.1 Recognize factors that contribute to an effective organizational culture.

8.3.2 Describe the benefits of diversity to an organization, individuals, and society.

Key Terms

organizational culture 185
work environment 186
labor union 188
diversity 190
glass ceiling 191

Focus on REAL LIFE

Three years of related employment experience required. Josh, a recent graduate, reads this line in a job description and decides he is not qualified even though he has all the skills the job requires. Josh doesn't think the employer will recognize the skills he has developed through leadership activities and community service.

Must be energetic and eager. Madeline, who is 58, sees this phrase as she views job postings on a career website. She doesn't bother to apply for the job because she believes the employer must be looking for young people.

Requires heavy lifting. Kamala is surprised to see this requirement listed in a job description because her friend Ed, who told her about the job, said she might have to lift boxes occasionally, but never anything over 50 pounds. She wonders if this qualification was included in the job description to discourage women from applying.

Can employment advertisements intentionally or unintentionally discourage otherwise well-qualified people from applying? To build the best workforce, job recruitment should focus on the skills and abilities needed to do the work, not on the type of person the manager believes would be best for the job.

LO 8.3.1

DEVELOPING AN EFFECTIVE CULTURE

The ways businesses are organized and operated have changed a great deal in the past few decades. Some of the changes are obvious. Technology has reduced the need for low-skilled employees and demanded that current workers have much greater skills. The Internet has changed the way consumers and businesses communicate, share information, and buy and sell. Globalization of business has resulted in greater competition. It has also resulted in more opportunities for every business to reach many new customers.

Other changes are just as important but not as clear. The workforce is more diverse, with growth among both younger and older workers. Jobs are changing, with a larger temporary and part-time workforce and a rise in the number of successful small businesses. Jobs are being shifted to other countries in an effort by businesses to cut costs. The number of manufacturing jobs is declining while service jobs are growing at a rapid pace. Some of the service jobs require little skill. Others are complex jobs requiring technical knowledge, creativity, and decision-making skills.

Businesses have to respond to all of the changes and maintain a positive organizational culture. An **organizational culture** is the environment in which people work, made up of the atmosphere,

Focus on REAL LIFE

Show students an employment advertisement that is very general and one that is very specific. Ask them which would be most helpful in locating the most applicants. Which would be most helpful in locating the best-qualified applicants? Ask students to suggest ways to focus advertisements on the job requirements rather than types of people. Understanding the job duties and using specific language are important in developing employment ads.

TEACH

Write the term "organizational culture" and its definition on the board. Ask students to provide examples of each of the parts of the definition—atmosphere, behaviors, beliefs, and relationships. Discuss how those factors contribute to a positive or negative place to work.

Different Learning Styles

Visual Learner Ask students to locate pictures of different work settings in business—a factory, an office, a farm, a service business. Instruct them to use the pictures to point out factors that comprise the business's organizational culture.

FYI

Remind students that millennials are those born from 1980 to the early 2000s. Discuss each of the factors and why they might be important to that age group but less important for workers who are older or younger.

TEACH

Write "physical conditions" and "psychological atmosphere" on the board. Ask students to suggest characteristics of each that can contribute to both a negative work environment and a positive work environment.

THINK CRITICALLY THROUGH VISUALS

Answers will vary greatly depending on personal preferences. Discuss how those preferences will help students make decisions about their career plans.

FYI Millennials report that the top factors they consider in choosing an employer are: what the company does, sells, or produces; the work culture; the company's involvement with causes; the work environment; diversity; and HR awards. (Millennial Impact Report)

behaviors, beliefs, and relationships. An organizational culture shows people how they will be treated and how they are expected to treat others. It identifies what is acceptable behavior and what is not. If a company has a positive organizational culture, employees enjoy going to work. They have positive working relations with co-workers and managers. They believe the organization values them and their work. They are motivated to do a good job for the company.

Work Environment

The **work environment** is the physical conditions and the psychological atmosphere in which employees work. The physical conditions are the work area, offices, break rooms, storage areas, and all other spaces where employees spend time while at work. Tools and equipment, lighting, temperature, and air quality are also a part of the physical work environment. The physical conditions must be safe and healthy. That is certainly a legal requirement of businesses. It is also important in assuring employees that the company has their interests at heart. A business with a reputation for safety and health problems will have difficulty attracting and keeping employees.

In addition to the physical conditions, companies need to provide a positive psychological atmosphere. Employees do not want to work in a place where they feel they are mistreated or where their work and ideas are not valued. An atmosphere of mistrust or fear is likely to result in low employee morale and poor performance.

Not all jobs can be physically comfortable. Some require people to work outside in very hot or cold conditions. Other jobs require a great deal of physical effort or can be quite hazardous. Even in those jobs, the business needs to find ways to provide as much physical comfort and safety as possible. The business should offer protective clothing and equipment, allow needed breaks, and ensure that every employee receives adequate safety training.

Offering a positive psychological environment means that managers are trained in effective communications and interpersonal skills. They are honest, fair, and ethical in their treatment of each employee. Employees get important information from their managers rather than from rumors through the grapevine. They believe their work is important and valued. They are recognized and rewarded for their contributions to the company.

Work–Life Relationships

People seem to be working more days and longer days. Some people hold two or more jobs. There are many two-career

Brand X Pictures/Getty Images

Would you rather work inside or outside? Alone or in a group?

Different Learning Styles

Tactile Learner Allow students to walk around the classroom and point out physical conditions that contribute to making it a positive work environment. Continue this activity by asking them to point out physical conditions that contribute to making it a less-positive work environment.

families. Balancing work and personal life is a very important issue for most employees. Work–life surveys generally find that a majority of people would give up additional income from overtime work to be able to spend more time with their families.

A positive organizational culture is one that respects the pressures on employees from outside of the job. It offers ways for employees to meet those demands while also fulfilling the requirements of the job. Some of those ways include personal time, family leave, flextime, job sharing, and flexplace.

Many companies now offer personal time for employees to complete nonjob activities that can only be done during work time. It is hard to schedule a dental or medical appointment, visit a child's school, or renew a driver's license while working. *Personal time* is a few hours each month that can be scheduled for nonjob activities. Some companies even offer paid time for employees to volunteer at schools or other community organizations.

Family leave policies allow employees to take a leave from work for the birth or adoption of a child, to care for a sick family member, or for other personal emergencies. In 1993, the U.S. Congress passed the Family and Medical Leave Act. It requires companies employing 50 or more people to provide up to 12 weeks of unpaid leave annually for employees who face specific family or personal circumstances.

Flextime allows employees some choice in how their work days and work hours are arranged. Some employees may start and end their work day earlier or later than normal. They may be able to work a longer day and thereby work fewer days each week. *Job sharing* offers one job to two people. Each person works a part-time schedule. They share the work space and duties of the job. *Flexplace* means that some employees can complete part or all of their work away from the business site. Telecommuting is becoming increasingly popular. Employees who primarily use computers and other personal technologies may be able to work from home. They communicate with managers, co-workers, and customers using the Internet, telephone, and other technologies.

Some of the strategies for improving work–life relationships cost companies very little. Others do have a cost but often result in reduced absenteeism, lower employee turnover, and happier and more productive employees.

Life-Span Plan How important do you believe family leave policies, flextime, or job sharing would be to you in choosing a career? Explain why work–life relationships are important when people set their life-span goals.

Monkey Business Images/Shutterstock.com

Which work–life program might allow a parent to take time off to take a child to a medical appointment in the middle of the day?

TEACH

Ask students to describe why work–life relationships are important for a part-time employee who is also a college student, for a single mother with two children, for a middle-aged worker with elderly parents who are quite ill, and for a retired person who is working part-time.

As you discuss each of the ways employers are trying to meet employee work–life relationship needs, instruct students to write each method and its definition in their notes.

Life-Span Plan Answers

Answers will vary. Students might indicate that the importance of work–life relationships varies at different times in workers' lives.

THINK CRITICALLY THROUGH VISUALS

Personal time allows employees to take a few hours each month to schedule nonjob activities. Flextime and job sharing also allow employees the flexibility to make appointments during regular business hours.

Different Learning Abilities

Visually Impaired Type the name and definition for each of the strategies for improving work–life relationships on computer-generated slides so they can be projected on a screen in a size large enough for students to read.

NET KNOWLEDGE

Students will identify three different employment laws that apply to teens holding part-time jobs. They should briefly describe each law and explain how an employer or employee could comply with the law.

TEACH

Explain to students that businesses with poor employer–employee relations will have a difficult time being successful in the long run. People will work for the company only until they can find a better job and may not give their best effort. Even when many people are available to work for a company, the business should work to develop effective relationships with its employees.

THINK CRITICALLY THROUGH VISUALS

Employee input gives a manager many advantages. Insights from the people actually performing the job can help managers make better decisions. Employees are more likely to support management decisions if they feel their ideas and suggestions are valued.

NET KNOWLEDGE

Employer–employee relations are governed by a number of federal laws administered by the Department of Labor. Those laws relate to wages and salaries, benefits, employment age, health and safety, and many other issues. Locate the Department of Labor website and identify three different employment laws that would apply specifically to you and your classmates if you held a part-time job. Prepare a brief description of each law and what an employee or employer must do to comply with the law.

Employer–Employee Relations

Both managers and employees want their business to succeed. Unprofitable businesses have to reduce the number of employees they hire. They must limit salary and benefit increases. Working together to make the business successful should benefit everyone. Managers and employees do not always have the same immediate goals. Managers must make sure that a company makes a profit. They try to get more work done at a lower cost. Employees are more concerned about compensation, working conditions, job security, and nonwork issues.

Photodisc/Getty Images

What are the advantages a manager might experience by gaining employee input?

Many years ago, a boss made all of the important decisions and told employees what to do. Employees had little input as to what they did or how they did it. Each person was assigned a specific job. They often had little interaction with other employees while they worked.

That approach often left employees thinking that their ideas were not welcomed or appreciated. They believed they knew a great deal about their jobs and the business and could offer suggestions to improve the way work was done. Those differences led to disagreements and conflicts between many employers and their employees.

Even though there are differences between management and employees, there may be more things that are alike than different between the two groups. When managers and employees work together, they often can find ways to accomplish the goals of both the organization and the individuals who work for it. Managers who involve employees in decision making find that better decisions can result. Employees are more likely to support those decisions. Employees discover that when they cooperate with management, managers have a better understanding of their needs and expectations. Both groups, as well as the organization, benefit through cooperation.

Labor Unions

Early in the twentieth century, as industries were growing rapidly, many employers did not treat their employees well. Low wages, long hours, and unsafe working conditions caused employees to band together and form labor unions. A **labor union** is an organized group of employees who negotiate with employers about issues, such as wages and working conditions. Unions can be effective because they represent large numbers of employees. The popularity

Different Learning Abilities

Gifted Assign students to study several companies that have introduced programs to improve the health and fitness of employees in order to reduce healthcare costs. Ask students to report to other class members on several interesting programs and the benefits derived by the employer and its employees.

of labor unions peaked in the 1940s and 1950s when more than one-third of the U.S. labor force was unionized. Unions, particularly in the goods-producing industries, were successful in achieving higher wages and benefits. At the same time, federal and state governments were regulating unsafe working conditions. Beginning in the 1970s, the U.S. economy moved from a goods-producing to a service-providing economy. Employment in heavily-unionized industries has declined. The percentage of U.S. workers who belong to a union has been steadily declining during that same time and is now about 11 percent.

As union participation in traditional industries has declined, membership in service-providing industries has grown. Some of the largest unionized employment sectors today are government, education, public safety, health care, and hospitality.

Unions and management resolve issues through *collective bargaining*, which is formal negotiation between members of both groups. When agreement is reached, both groups sign a written labor contract. There are also federal and state laws that regulate the relationships of businesses and unions.

Relationships between many companies and unions are much more positive today than in the past. They work together on issues that affect the success of the business and the work life of employees. Examples include job training to keep employee skills up to date, employee assistance if a business site closes, and improving product quality to make businesses more competitive.

CHECKPOINT
What are some ways that companies help employees meet personal demands outside the job?

Monkey Business Images/Shutterstock.com

How might human resources managers help increase diversity in the workplace?

LO 8.3.2

WORKFORCE DIVERSITY

Imagine a world where everyone looked, thought, and acted alike. The world is diverse, and the United States is one of the most diverse countries in the world. That diversity continues to grow. Not all businesses reflect that diversity. Even in companies with a diverse workforce, that diversity is not always reflected in various job categories or in management positions.

A business that has a diverse workforce will be much more attractive to prospective employees and customers. When people with diverse backgrounds and characteristics are promoted into leadership and management positions, it will offer encouragement to others like them.

Applied Skills

Technology Instruct students to use the Internet to find information from companies that describes the methods and results of increasing diversity in their workforce. Students should write a one-page report on their findings.

TEACH

Ask students why they believe labor union membership declined in the last half of the 1900s. Discuss reasons why membership might change in the first half of the current century.

ONGOING ASSESSMENT

CHECKPOINT ANSWER

Companies can maintain a positive organizational culture that respects the demands on employees from outside of the job through personal time, family leave, flextime, job sharing, and flexplace policies.

THINK CRITICALLY THROUGH VISUALS

Answers will vary. Human resources managers can provide information and training to other managers and continually emphasize the benefits of diversity throughout the organization. Employee diversity can be increased by promoting diversity in the company, broadly advertising job openings, widening the locations for recruiting employees and managers, and ensuring the company's facilities are accessible to people with disabilities.

TEACH

Ask students how they would feel if they worked in a company and almost all management positions were filled by people of a different gender and race than they are. What would be their feelings if they were a customer and didn't see people like them working for a business?

TEACH

Discuss with students why many characteristics of employees beyond gender and race should be considered as businesses work to improve the diversity of their workforce. Ask them whether they believe focusing on many characteristics may reduce the importance of gender and race in that company.

▶ **Figure 8-5** ***ANSWER***

The federal laws regulating discrimination have increased employment opportunities for all Americans by prohibiting job discrimination based on race, color, religion, gender, and national origin; protecting individuals who are 40 years of age or older from age discrimination; and forbidding discrimination based on disabilities. Many Americans will belong to one or more of these groups during their working lives, so these laws protect everyone in the workforce.

Work as a TEAM

Ask students what a company can do in addition to developing a diversity statement to demonstrate its commitment to diversity.

Benefits of Diversity

"Workplace diversity" has many definitions. The basic definition of **diversity**, as it applies to the workplace, is the comprehensive inclusion of people with differences in personal characteristics and attributes. The federal government has recognized important personal characteristics in equal employment legislation. The key laws are identified in Figure 8-5. Today, businesses working to build a diverse workforce use a much broader view of diversity. They try to build a broad workforce that reflects the communities in which they operate and the markets they want to serve. Diversity includes race, ethnicity, gender, age, and disability. It also includes socio-economic status, culture, religion, and even personal interests, abilities, and values.

When people in an organization are more alike than different, there is often reduced creativity and innovation. There will be limited understanding of people who are different. Their attitudes, experiences, and needs won't be considered. It will be difficult to recognize and plan for those differences when developing products and services for customers who are different from the people in the company. Companies that build a diverse workforce see several benefits. The benefits can be classified as organizational, individual, and societal.

Organizational Benefits *Prospective employees and managers are drawn from the broadest possible employment pool.* The greatest increase in the labor force in the future will be women, ethnic and racial minorities, and older workers. If people from those groups are not considered, the company will have a much smaller pool from which to choose.

The company will have a broader base of knowledge and understanding when making decisions. People with different backgrounds, experiences, and even ways of thinking and planning will be a part of the organization. They will bring new ideas on how to design processes, plan products, work and communicate with others, and provide leadership.

Prospective customers will have a more positive image of the company. Customers with diverse characteristics will see a company that values diversity. They will have a greater level of respect and trust for the company and its products. They will see their own views and interests represented within the company.

The company will be better at serving diverse markets. The company will understand similarities and differences in needs,

FEDERAL LAWS REGULATING DISCRIMINATION
• The **Equal Pay Act of 1963** disallows pay discrimination based on gender for jobs requiring equal skill, effort, and responsibility.
• The **Civil Rights Act of 1964** prohibits job discrimination based on race, color, religion, gender, and national origin.
• The **Age Discrimination in Employment Act of 1967** protects individuals who are 40 years of age or older.
• The **Americans with Disabilities Act of 1990,** which was amended in 2008, prohibits discrimination against qualified disabled workers and requires employers to make reasonable work accommodations.

FIGURE 8-5
How have these laws increased employment opportunities for all Americans?

Work as a TEAM

Many companies and organizations have developed diversity statements to reflect their beliefs about the importance of diversity. As a team, use the Internet to identify and study examples of those statements from several companies. Select one that your team agrees is the best statement. Justify your choice.

Applied Skills

Communication Assign students to create an advertisement for a company that illustrates its commitment to diversity and the benefits to employees and customers. Consider allowing students to work in pairs or small groups to develop an ad for a magazine, newspaper, television, radio, or the Internet.

decision-making processes, and communication strategies among diverse customer groups. Traditional stereotypes that may have upset consumers in the past will no longer be used.

Global business strategies will improve. The United States is among the most diverse countries in the world. We are a nation of immigrants. This offers American businesses a unique advantage to recognize and understand global needs and differences. They have an advantage over companies from countries with limited diversity.

Individual Benefits *All employees will have the opportunity to develop to their full ability.* In the past, women and other minority employees have faced a glass ceiling. A **glass ceiling** is an artificial limit placed on minority groups moving into positions of authority and decision making. Businesses that value diversity work to remove those obstacles so everyone has an opportunity to advance based on ability and performance.

Individuals will feel they are respected and supported despite their differences. Employees who are different from the typical employee do not have to hide those differences. They do not have to be uncomfortable because they are different. Individual differences will be expected and viewed as a valuable part of the organization. Employees can comfortably represent their uniqueness when participating in planning and decision making.

Societal Benefits *Prejudice and discrimination will be reduced as a societal problem.* People involved in diverse organizations increasingly recognize and value diversity. This is true for neighborhoods, schools, and businesses alike. They lose their

iStockphoto.com/Chris Schmidt/track5

How does a new business benefit from an immediate commitment to diversity?

stereotypes and recognize the benefits that come from the acceptance and participation of every person.

The country has a more talented, experienced, economically successful workforce. Diversity opens more job opportunities for everyone. It allows people to develop and use all of their abilities. It increases access to higher-paying jobs for more people. Diversity in business leads to greater opportunities in society.

Developing a Diverse Organization

An organization's culture develops over many years. Employees and managers often become comfortable with the way things have always been done. It may be hard to recognize all of the ways that an organization makes it difficult for people from diverse backgrounds to be successful in the organization. The whole organization needs to be committed to diversity

THINK CRITICALLY THROUGH VISUALS

A new business needs to appeal to a broad base of customers. A commitment to diversity from the very beginning will help attract more customers, build better supplier relationships, and help with recruiting employees as the business grows.

TEACH

Ask students how they could determine whether a company has a "glass ceiling." How would they use data about a company's promotion record when making career choices?

Teaching Strategies

Expand Beyond the Classroom Facilitate a meeting between students and people who lead diversity training sessions in business. Students should learn more about the methods and activities they use to build understanding of and appreciation for individual differences.

TEACH

As each step used by companies to promote diversity is discussed, ask students to identify how they believe that activity contributes to a successful organization.

ONGOING ASSESSMENT

CHECKPOINT ✓ *ANSWER*

Organizations benefit from having a larger employment pool from which to select qualified applicants, the ability to project a positive image, and enhanced capability to serve diverse customers. Individuals benefit by having the opportunity to develop to their full potential and to feel respected and supported despite their differences. Society benefits by a reduction in the social problems related to prejudice and discrimination. The entire society benefits as diversity opens more job opportunities for everyone.

ASSESS

Key Concepts *Answers*

1. True
2. b. flexplace
3. d. inclusion

Make Academic Connections *Answers*

4. Actual reports, tables, and charts will vary. Encourage students to use the most current data they can find.
5. Bulletin boards, exhibits, and displays will vary. Consider making arrangements for the works to be displayed for several days.
6. Features will vary. You may want to ask students to use desktop publishing software to "publish" their reports.

in order for the necessary changes to occur.

The following steps have been used successfully in a number of businesses and other organizations to increase diversity.

1. **Develop a written commitment to diversity.** Prepare a mission statement that clearly communicates the company's values.
2. **Have the full support of top executives.** The top managers in the business must make diversity a priority in their written and oral communications and in their actions.
3. **Review evidence of diversity in the company.** Gather data on the diverse characteristics of all employees, managers, and customers. If any part of the organization does not reflect the diversity expectations, determine what is standing in the way and develop ways to make changes.
4. **Update policies and procedures.** Make sure that recruiting, hiring, performance evaluation, and promotion practices encourage diversity.
5. **Provide continuing diversity education.** Managers and employees benefit from increased understanding of inclusion and diversity. Participating in classes and workshops prepares employees to work more effectively in a diverse organization.
6. **Recognize and celebrate diversity.** Make diversity a part of the organization's culture. Have visible evidence of the variety of languages, music, art, celebrations, and customs of employees and customers.

CHECKPOINT ✓

Identify several organizational, individual, and societal benefits of diversity.

8.3 ASSESSMENT

Key Concepts

Determine the best answer.

1. True or False. There are greater numbers of both younger and older employees in the workforce today than there were in the past.
2. Some employees can complete part or all of their work away from the business site under
   a. flextime
   b. flexplace
   c. job sharing
   d. personal time
3. The term most closely related to diversity is
   a. affirmative action
   b. discrimination
   c. minority
   d. inclusion

Make Academic Connections

4. **Social Studies** Use the Internet to identify data that describe the changing characteristics of the U.S. population in terms of age, gender, race, religion, and immigration status. Develop a written report of your findings. Include at least three tables and charts to support your written report.
5. **Art** Working with other students in your class, create a bulletin board, exhibit, or display that illustrates the diversity in your school and community.
6. **Journalism** Select a business in your community and contact a company manager to schedule an interview. Prepare several questions on the steps the company has taken to increase diversity and the results of those steps. Record your interview. Use the information to prepare a 500–750 word feature for an online news service or business blog site.

RETEACH Instruct students to review the learning outcomes. Then have them prepare a summary of key information in the lesson.

ENRICH Ask students to discuss the diversity in their school, community, local businesses, and organizations. Assign students to prepare a creative visual representation of that diversity.

CLOSE Ask students to point out any personal experiences they have had that will help them in their career.

BUSINESS IMPROVING SOCIETY

COFFEE AND A CONSCIENCE

How do coffee companies benefit from paying small coffee growers a fair minimum price for their coffee beans?

In 1981, while on a skiing trip in Vermont, Robert Stiller stopped at a coffee shop for a cup of coffee. He liked the coffee so much that he decided to buy the business. Green Mountain Coffee Roasters is no longer a small-town coffee shop. It has expanded to become a major wholesaler of specialty coffees with a large direct-mail and Internet business. The company has been recognized by *Forbes* magazine as one of the best 200 small companies in America, by *Fortune*, appearing near the top of their Most Admired Companies list, and by *Corporate Responsibility* magazine as one of the 100 best corporate citizens.

Mr. Stiller was not only interested in developing a successful business. He had a belief that a company can be profitable and still have a social conscience. He wanted to operate a company that demonstrated a concern for the environment, for the people who grow and supply the coffee, and for the local and global community. Green Mountain Coffee is a partner and advocate in Businesses for Social Responsibility and the Fair Trade Partners.

Most coffee growers are small family farmers who are at the mercy of large coffee companies. Those companies had pushed the price paid for coffee beans to less than 70 cents a pound. The result was a drop in the income of small farmers to a level that didn't allow them to maintain their families' nutrition, health care, or education. Fair Trade Partners guarantee a minimum fair price when they purchase a farmer's coffee beans, as much as $1.40 per pound. In return, they ask the farmers to use farming practices that result in high-quality products and that protect the environment.

Another program supported by Green Mountain is Coffee Kids, a nonprofit international organization. It is committed to improving the lives of children and families in the small mountain towns of coffee-growing regions around the world. The organization offers health care, nutrition training, educational scholarships, and money for local schools to improve the lives of children living in poverty. Green Mountain and its employees have donated more than a million dollars to Coffee Kids.

Through the Community Action For Employees (CAFE) program, Green Mountain encourages employees to perform volunteer work while on company time. Every employee is allowed up to 52 hours each year in paid time off to volunteer for nonprofit organizations in their communities.

Social responsibility is an ongoing focus and commitment of the company. The following are examples of Green Mountain's principles.

Ethics Do the right thing. Integrity is the foundation of all our decisions, actions, and relationships.

Sustainability Pathway to our future. We use resources wisely and make decisions that take into account the well-being of people, profit, and the planet.

World Benefit Creating positive change. We are a force for good in the world. We celebrate and support the power of businesses and individuals to bring about positive changes, locally and globally.

Think Critically

1. Why would Green Mountain be willing to pay farmers almost twice as much for their coffee beans than the large coffee companies pay?
2. How do you believe social programs, such as those supported by Green Mountain Coffee, affect customers' views of the company? Do you believe it affects the sales of their products? Why or why not?

BUSINESS IMPROVING SOCIETY

Students should read about the personal experience of Robert Stiller and how he was able to accomplish his goals as an entrepreneur while holding to important personal values. Point out to students that businesspeople can maintain a strong social conscience and work to solve important world problems while operating a successful business.

THINK CRITICALLY THROUGH VISUALS

Paying a fair minimum price allows coffee companies to build trusting relationships with growers. This results in a steady supply of high-quality coffee beans.

Think Critically *Answers*

1. The practical reason for paying the farmers more is that Green Mountain can then influence the growers to use sustainable agricultural practices that result in high-quality products. Paying more than the market rate also allows the company to achieve its goal of creating positive change.
2. Answers will vary. Students might suggest that Green Mountain's support of social programs encourages customer goodwill and loyalty. Many people want to help solve the problems caused by poverty and to feel good about their consumer choices.

Portfolio Activity

Assign the Portfolio Activity for Chapter 8. Students can access the activity by going to the website for this textbook and choosing the link for Chapter 8.
COLLECT Offer suggestions to help students locate information about employment policies.
CREATE Suggest that students limit the focus of their visuals to one policy or practice.
CONNECT Point out that students need to connect visuals to something already in their portfolio or to a concept from another class.

Think Critically About Business *Answers*

1. New technology has made manufacturing more efficient so that fewer workers are needed. Many goods-producing industries have moved their operations to countries with lower labor costs. The large, aging baby boomer generation needs an ever-increasing number of services. Over the next 10 years, people will need more proficiency in technology, more specialized job training, and top-notch human relations skills.

2. Consumer preferences dictate which industries thrive and which decline. The decreased fashionability of hats caused many people who made expensive hats to lose their jobs. Another example of an industry that has lost jobs is newspaper publishing. Consumers have opted to obtain their news from the Internet. On the other hand, jobs related to video games, smartphones and tablets, Internet services, express delivery services, social media, security services, and a growing list of new products and services exist today because of consumer demand.

3. Small businesses can compete by offering more flexible work schedules, the opportunity to perform a wider variety of tasks, greater control over individual work, and a more creative and personable environment in which to work.

4. The first step is compliance with all local, state, and federal health and safety regulations. The physical layout of the workplace should be ergonomically correct. A well-designed work environment will also reduce stress that could lead to illnesses or careless injury. Breaks, nutritious food, and areas for relaxation and fitness training can be provided.

5. Part-time and temporary employees do not have to be maintained on the payroll if the amount of work decreases. Also, they usually do not receive as many benefits while they are employed. They may not understand or embrace the organization's values and they may not develop the level of skills of full-time employees.

6. Answers will vary. Students should prepare slides to introduce and justify their choices based on the needs of the community and the nature of

Chapter 8 Assessment

Review Business Concepts

8.1 Human Resources Basics

- There are more than 157 million people who have full-time or part-time jobs in the United States workforce. Changes in the economy may require employees to develop new skills and receive additional training. Consumer preferences, economic conditions, new technology, and business competition are strong influences on the workforce.
- Human resources are the people who work for a business. The major goals of human resources are to (1) identify the personnel needs, (2) maintain a supply of people to fill needs, (3) match abilities and interests with specific jobs, (4) provide training and development, (5) develop compensation plans, (6) protect the health and well-being of employees, and (7) maintain a satisfying work environment. The activities of human resources are planning and staffing, performance management, compensation and benefits, and employee relations.

8.2 Managing Human Resources

- Human resources management ensures that needed employees are available and that they are productive, paid, and satisfied with their work. If human resources management does its job well, the company will have productive and motivated employees who do their jobs well and contribute to a successful, profitable business.
- Compensation is the amount of money paid to an employee for work performed. Compensation is made up of two parts. Salary and wages are direct payment to an employee for work completed. Compensation in forms other than direct payment for work is known as benefits.
- The manager regularly evaluates the work of all employees. Performance evaluations focus on the specific job duties of each employee as well as the important work qualities expected of all employees.

8.3 Organizational Culture and Workforce Diversity

- An organizational culture is the environment in which people work. It is made up of the atmosphere, as well as the behaviors, beliefs, and relationships among people. An organizational culture shows people how they will be treated and how they are expected to treat others. A positive organizational culture respects the demands on employees from outside of the job.
- Prospective employees and customers are attracted to work and shop in businesses where people like them work. Companies that build a diverse workforce see several benefits. The benefits can be classified as organizational, individual, and societal.

Think Critically About Business

1. Why are service-providing industries growing more rapidly than goods-producing industries? What effect will this trend have on the skills people need for careers in the next 10 years?
2. Provide several examples of the effect of consumer preferences on employment. What are some jobs that have increased and decreased in importance due to consumer demands?
3. Small businesses usually cannot offer the same levels of wages and benefits to employees as large businesses. In what other ways can small businesses compete to hire and retain highly qualified employees?
4. In addition to offering insurance benefits, what types of activities should businesses undertake to protect and improve the health and safety of their employees?
5. What are the advantages and disadvantages for a company in hiring part-time and temporary employees rather than full-time and permanent employees?

6. You are the economic development director for your community. Identify three service-providing companies that you believe could be successful in your community and offer the potential for many new jobs. Develop a short computer slide presentation for your board of directors introducing your selections and justifying your choices.

7. You are the human resources manager for a company and want to hire an accountant. List three good recruiting sources and justify your choices. If you wanted to hire a web designer, would your sources change? Why or why not?

8. Make a list of three benefits you would personally like to see a company offer its employees. How do you believe your list might change as your life situation changes?

9. Do you believe the physical conditions or psychological atmosphere of a business are more important to maintaining an effective work environment? Justify your choice.

10. Why has union membership declined dramatically in the United States? What are some reasons why the decline may continue or that membership may begin to increase in some industries?

Develop Your Business Language

Match the terms listed with the definitions.

11. Ends the employment relationship between a company and an employee.

12. Removes work from one company and sends it to another company that can complete it at a lower cost.

13. Amount of money paid to an employee for work performed.

14. Environment in which people work, made up of the atmosphere, behaviors, beliefs, and relationships.

15. Compensation in forms other than direct payment for work.

16. The assignment of an employee to another job in the company with a similar level of responsibility.

17. The comprehensive inclusion of people with differences in personal characteristics and attributes.

18. An organized group of employees who negotiate with employers about issues, such as wages and working conditions.

19. All the people 16 years and older who are employed or who are looking for a job.

20. Physical conditions and psychological atmosphere in which employees work.

21. The advancement of an employee to a position with greater responsibility.

22. Connect the amount of compensation to the quality or quantity of an employee's performance.

23. Direct payment to an employee for work completed.

24. A planned reduction in the number of employees needed in a firm in order to reduce costs and make the business more efficient.

25. A study of a job to identify in detail the specific job duties and skill requirements.

26. An artificial limit placed on minority groups moving into positions of authority and decision making.

Key Terms

a. benefits
b. compensation
c. diversity
d. downsizing
e. glass ceiling
f. incentive systems
g. job analysis
h. labor union
i. organizational culture
j. outsourcing
k. promotion
l. salary and wages
m. termination
n. transfer
o. work environment
p. workforce

the business. Each business should have the potential of offering a number of new jobs in the community.

7. Answers will vary. Recruiting sources for an accountant might include college placement offices, classified advertising, employment agencies, Internet career services, and industry publications. Some of the same sources could be used for hiring a web designer, but the focus would need to shift from accounting to web design.

8. Students should give reasons for their recommendations. They should recognize that people need different benefits at different stages of their lives.

9. Answers will vary. Some students will say that employees want safe, healthy physical working conditions, so the psychological factors are less important. Others will believe that many jobs require a less-than-ideal physical work situation so the company needs to provide a positive psychological environment.

10. Students may offer several reasons for the decline, including a shift of employment from low-skill to high-skill jobs, growing employment in states and regions where union membership has never been strong, changing labor laws in some states, and others. Many traditional unionized job categories will likely continue to see declines in membership. Some service industry jobs and jobs where wage rates are very low or working conditions difficult may see increases in efforts to unionize employees.

Develop Your Business Language *Answers*

11. m. termination
12. j. outsourcing
13. b. compensation
14. i. organizational culture
15. a. benefits
16. n. transfer
17. c. diversity
18 h. labor union
19. p. workforce
20. o. work environment
21. k. promotion
22. f. incentive systems
23. l. salary and wages
24. d. downsizing
25. g. job analysis
26. e. glass ceiling

Make Academic Connections *Answers*

27a. Last year's total training cost was \$3,580 (6 × \$130 = \$780 plus 35 × \$80 = \$2,800).

27b. Around 22 percent of the cost of training was spent on new employees (780 ÷ 3,580 = 0.217 or 21.7%).

27c. It will cost \$143 to train a new employee and \$88 to train existing employees.

27d. The total cost of training for all employees will be \$4,180 (41 × \$88 = \$3,608 plus 4 × \$143 = \$572).

28. Answers will vary.

29. Answers will vary depending on the article selected. Provide guidance for the citation format you want students to use.

30. Answers will vary.

31a. Monday, \$64.70; Tuesday, \$40; Wednesday, \$51.40; Thursday, \$30; Friday, \$0; Saturday, \$91.

31b. \$260

31c. \$17.10

31d. \$277.10

Make Your Case *Answers*

32. Imposing an education requirement will likely provide better-qualified candidates, but it might eliminate some potentially excellent employees. Developing a training program for all employees would allow Mr. Malik to provide standard training for all employees, but it would be a new expense and might be a waste of time for community college grads.

33. Answers will vary. Students might suggest paying a higher wage to new employees with specific educational requirements and offering a lower wage to new employees who need more training.

Make Academic Connections

27. Math A small business budgets \$80 per employee per year for training costs. An additional \$50 is provided for the first year of training for each new employee. Last year the firm started with 35 employees and added 6 new employees. Both parts of the training budget have been increased by 10 percent for this year.

a. What was the total cost of training for last year?
b. What percentage of that amount was spent on new employee training?
c. With the proposed increase, how much will be spent for training each experienced employee and each new employee this year?
d. What will be the total cost of training for all employees if four new employees are hired this year?

28. Technology Use a spreadsheet and graphics program to make a chart or graph showing current data for the U.S. workforce using the following characteristics: (a) part-time versus full-time employees; (b) gender of employees; (c) racial classification of employees.

29. Read Companies participate in community activities to demonstrate that they value diversity. Find a news article that relates to a community activity or service project completed by a company in your state. Read the article and outline the major concepts presented in the article using bullet points. Include a properly formatted citation for your source. Possible sources include printed and online versions of newspapers, magazines, and business or organization websites.

30. Advertising Use the Internet or a newspaper to locate classified advertising for employment opportunities. Select a job of interest to you and find detailed listings from three different companies for that type of job. Develop a table that compares the three opportunities based on job duties, wages or salary and benefits, and work environment of the company.

31. Math Nicole works for a store that pays her an hourly wage of \$10 plus a commission of 2 percent on all sales over \$500 per day. Her hours worked and daily sales for the past week are shown in the table.

a. How much did Nicole earn in base salary and commission for each of the days she worked?
b. How much was the total of her base salary for the week?
c. How much was the total of her commissions for the week?
d. What were Nicole's total earnings for the week?

Monday	6 hrs	\$735 total sales
Tuesday	4 hrs	\$320 total sales
Wednesday	5 hrs	\$570 total sales
Thursday	3 hrs	\$450 total sales
Friday	0 hrs	\$0 total sales
Saturday	8 hrs	\$1,050 total sales

Make Your Case

Arte Malik has operated a lawn care business for many years. The business offers landscaping services including seeding and sodding lawns, applying chemicals and fertilizer, and regular lawn mowing. Mr. Malik has 25 employees. Many of them have worked for him for 5 to 10 years. He usually hires two or three new employees each year. In the past, Arte was not concerned about the skills of new employees. He prefers to find people who are interested in the work and want to learn. Yet the machinery he uses is getting more complex, and employees must know a great deal about safe handling of chemicals, detecting plant diseases, and effective lawn care. The local community college has a two-year degree program in lawn care management. Arte is deciding whether to continue his present hiring procedure of allowing new employees to learn on the job, develop a training program to be offered to all employees, or hire only people who have completed the community college program.

32. What are the advantages and disadvantages of each of the choices Mr. Malik is considering?

33. If you were Mr. Malik's human resources manager, what choice would you recommend? Why?

Interactions and Connections

34. Identify several people from your community who work full time. Ask them their views on the importance of maintaining a balance between their work life and their personal life. Ask them to identify ways they believe the company they work for supports or does not support a balance in work–life relationships. Based on your discussions, do you believe most of the companies are or are not sensitive to work–life relationships?

35. Each year *Fortune* magazine publishes a list of the "100 Best Companies to Work For." This is not the only list that ranks employers. Several organizations, magazines, and websites publish lists of outstanding employers in specific industries or for particular types of workers. Because each set of rankings is based on different criteria, the companies appearing on each list may be different.

Looking at the lists and the criteria used to rank employers can provide insight into these businesses for consumers, investors, and potential employees. They give particular insight into companies that appear to be working hard to develop and maintain a positive organizational climate and work environment.

Think about the criteria you might use to rank companies as the best places to work.

Locate the website of an organization or magazine that provides an annual ranking of the best places to work.

Choose a company from the list you found and visit the company's website. Locate information about organizational culture, work environment, and work–life relationships. Describe your findings and offer your opinion about this company as a great place to work based on the criteria that are most important to you.

International Business Plan Event

Opening a business in another part of the world presents a unique challenge that requires a detailed business plan. The business plan is used to convince potential investors to financially support the international business idea.

This event may be completed by one to three students. Participants will conduct research for a specific international location, determine a business/product/service needed for the selected country, and prepare a business plan to convince investors about the soundness of the international plan.

Participants will prepare a business plan limited to 30 pages that includes an introduction for the business plan, trade area and cultural analysis, planned operation, and planned financing for the international business. The body of the business plan must be typed following the sequence outlined. Participants may bring a copy of the written entry or note cards and appropriate visual aids to use during the presentation. Participants have 10 minutes to present their international business plan. Five additional minutes are allotted for the judges or audience members to ask questions about the business plan.

Performance Indicators Evaluated

- Demonstrate critical thinking and problem-solving skills associated with starting an international business.
- Work effectively as a team.
- Demonstrate an understanding of the basic steps involved in starting a business in an international setting.
- Analyze information to derive data necessary for a convincing business plan.
- Present facts that support the rationale for locating a business in another part of the world.

For more detailed information about performance indicators, go to the DECA website.

Think Critically

1. Why is it important to research the culture of the location for a potential international business?
2. Why is it more difficult to obtain domestic funding for an international business idea?
3. What demographics should be considered when locating a business in another part of the world?
4. What sources can be used to locate solid financial information when developing an international business?
5. Why might investors be reluctant to support an international business idea during a recession?

www.deca.org

Interactions and Connections

34. Answers will vary depending on the individuals interviewed. Encourage students to prepare for their interviews by re-reading the content about work–life relationships in Lesson 8.3 and reviewing their class notes.

35. Descriptions and opinions will vary based on the ranking source, the company studied, and the student's criteria for a great place to work. Invite students to share their findings with the class.

WINNING EDGE

International Business Plan Event

The International Business Plan Event challenges students to understand the global marketplace. Students must research another part of the world, understand the challenges of international business, and learn about the culture. Students are challenged to create a thorough business plan that results in the support of potential investors.

Think Critically *Answers*

1. To conduct business successfully in another country, you must study and understand its culture. Respecting local culture is the first step for conducting international business.

2. Economic stability is a major factor for potential investors. Businesses are less likely to be successful during bad economic conditions. International investments may carry additional risks associated with economic and political issues.

3. Demographic information that should be considered includes age, income, level of education, disposable income, and size of households.

4. Financial information for international business documents can be obtained from current businesses operating in other countries, the federal government, and trade offices representing different countries.

5. Investment resources can be limited during a recession. Investors must determine the best strategy with the least amount of risk for spending limited funds.

CHAPTER OVERVIEW

Students study the variety of career opportunities in business and learn how to prepare a career plan and apply for and secure a job.

9.1 Career Opportunities

This lesson presents an overview of career planning activities.

9.2 Planning Your Career

While studying this lesson, students will consider various personal factors, career experience, and information sources about jobs.

9.3 Applying for Employment

This lesson introduces employment application forms, résumés, and cover letters. Applying for employment online is also addressed.

9.4 Securing a Job

The interview process, factors to assess when accepting employment, and successful career attitudes provide the focus of this lesson.

Chapter 9 Career Planning and Development

iStockphoto.com/wdstock

Instructor Resources

- Activities and Study Guide IE
- Chapter and Unit Tests IE
- Lesson Plans
- PowerPoint Presentation
- Cognero Test, Ch. 9

Student Resources

Activities and Study Guide
www.cengage.com/swep/pob9e
- Study Tools
- Portfolio Activity

PLANNING A CAREER IN . . .

EMPLOYMENT ASSISTANCE

The field of employment assistance includes a variety of career development activities to help people obtain employment and guide them to advance in their careers. Some workers are employed by schools and companies to help people explore career options. Others assist people with preparing a résumé, writing a cover letter, or practicing interview skills.

Every state has an employment bureau to help workers who have lost their jobs or who require retraining if they are injured on the job. Employment assistance workers are available to help identify, encourage, and plan advanced training for persons who have jobs. In addition to schools, businesses, and government agencies, some career professionals provide fee-based services for individuals. The field of career counseling is especially important as employment opportunities change due to technology, global competition, and demographic trends.

Related Job Titles

- Career Counselor
- Career Placement Advisor
- Career Planning Instructor
- Career Coach
- Résumé Writer
- Interviewing Trainer
- Vocational Testing Center Manager

Analyze Career Opportunities in . . .

CAREER COUNSELING

Use library and Internet resources to learn more about careers in employment assistance. Choose one of the job titles listed in the box and answer the following questions.

1. How would you describe the nature of the work? Include examples of things that might happen in a typical work day.
2. Is this a career that interests you? Describe how you might use your talents, abilities, and skills in this career.

What it's like to work as a . . . Career Counselor

"You are very capable in science, mathematics, and computer technology. However, your interests seem to lie in working with people." Comments like this from a career counselor can help people better understand what they do well and what they enjoy doing.

In the next stage of the career search process, a career counselor will provide assistance with developing the content and format for a résumé. Then, sample interviews will take place to help the person present a confident and competent appearance.

The counselor's work doesn't end when a person obtains a job. A desire to advance in a career field can result in additional interaction with a counselor. Or, if someone desires a career change the counselor can direct them to needed resources for education and training.

What about you? Have you ever helped someone with finding a job or preparing for an interview? Is this something you enjoy?

PLANNING A CAREER IN . . .

EMPLOYMENT ASSISTANCE

As various economic and technological factors change the types of jobs that are available and the application process, many people seek assistance. The employment assistance field involves helping others to obtain or change jobs. A strong knowledge of career planning activities is required. Use this career feature to give students a more specific profile of work in this field. Use the follow-up questions to encourage further student discussion.

What About You? *Answers*

Answers will require students to think beyond what is presented and formulate their own reactions. Students who have some experience with job interviews will be able to provide opinions. Helping someone prepare for an interview with role-playing can be enjoyable.

Analyze Career Opportunities *Answers*

Student answers will vary depending on when the assignment is completed and individual interests.

Additional Career Information

Encourage students to investigate careers they find interesting and explore unfamiliar careers. Two resources for additional career information are the *Occupational Outlook Handbook*, an online publication (www.bls.gov/oco) of the U.S. Bureau of Labor Statistics, and the O*NET Resource Center (www.onetcenter.org) developed by the U.S. Department of Labor. Information about specific careers and jobs can be used to demonstrate the relevance of skills learned in this course.

Focus on REAL LIFE

This scenario can help students begin to think about employment opportunities for their futures and the career planning process.

TEACH

Contrast an *occupation* and a *career*. Ask students to provide examples of each.

Use Figure 9-1 to provide an overview of the career planning process.

THINK CRITICALLY THROUGH VISUALS

Advantages exist for both careers and occupations as defined in the text. Discussion might include the fact that a series of occupations generally precede a career—or a career choice.

Life-Span Plan Answer

Answers will vary. Students should describe a process that includes personal assessment, employment market analysis, application process, interview process, employment acceptance, and career development and advancement.

9.1 Career Opportunities

Learning Outcomes

9.1.1 Describe the steps in the career planning process.

9.1.2 Identify the main sources of career information.

9.1.3 Discuss career fields with the most growth potential.

Key Terms

career 200

informational interview 202

mobility 204

Focus on REAL LIFE

"How did Uncle Ted prepare for his job as a regional sales manager?" Dan asked his mother.

"You should talk to him about that," she responded. "Your Uncle Ted could give you some very helpful information for your career planning activities."

Later on the phone, Dan asked, "Uncle Ted, how did you become a regional sales manager? What experience and training was most important? What computer software do I need to know? What classes should I take in school to help me prepare for a similar job? How can I get some work experience while in school?"

"Wait a minute, one question at a time," Uncle Ted responded. "Let's start by talking about the classes that you find most interesting and those in which you receive high grades."

LO 9.1.1

THE CAREER PLANNING PROCESS

An *occupation* is a task or series of tasks that is performed to provide a good or service. People are hired to fill occupations, and they are paid for the work they perform.

A **career** is a goal for work that is fulfilled through an occupation or series of occupations. You actually have a career goal now: "to complete your schooling and get ready for your future."

Career planning is the process of studying careers, assessing yourself in terms of careers, and making decisions about a future career. As shown in Figure 9-1 on the next page, this process begins by carrying out a personal assessment. Your interests, values, talents, and abilities provide the basis for a career choice as you develop new interests and abilities.

Your search for the right career could continue for a long time. In the years ahead, some of your values and goals will change. You will develop new interests and abilities.

Life-Span Plan

Describe a career planning activity you might complete to help you achieve your life-span goals. Consider talking to people you know about their work activities and careers. You might also observe various work situations to determine if those jobs would be of interest to you.

iStockphoto.com/fatihhoca

Do you want a career or an occupation? Explain your answer.

Different Learning Abilities

Attention Deficit Disorder Instruct students to write down the difference between an occupation and a career based on your clear directions. Students should list examples of each based on their real-world observations.

Your Study of Careers

The study of careers is a continuous process. New career opportunities occur all the time. You do not just decide to study careers for one day or one week. It is important to view learning about careers as a lifelong activity. This process is something that continues even after you begin your career.

Your first decision will likely be a *tentative career decision*—a decision that is subject to change as new information is received. A tentative decision is much better than no decision at all. Your career decision will provide you with much-needed direction.

Making initial career decisions while you are in school has many advantages. One is that, in school, you have a lot of information readily on hand. More importantly, early career planning will help you choose the right courses of study. An early career decision can also encourage you to become involved with organizations such as Future Business Leaders of America (FBLA), DECA, and Business Professionals of America (BPA). These organizations teach you about business and careers.

THE CAREER PLANNING PROCESS

Step 1	**Personal Assessment** • Determine interests and values • Identify talents and abilities
Step 2	**Employment Market Analysis** • Geographic influences • Business and economic trends
Step 3	**Application Process** • Application form • Résumé and cover letter
Step 4	**Interview Process** • Prepare for interview • Follow-up activities
Step 5	**Employment Acceptance** • Salary and financial factors • Organizational environment
Step 6	**Career Development and Advancement** • Practice career success behaviors • Develop strong work relationships

FIGURE 9-1
What are some resources you can use in planning your career?

Career Training

Many careers require education and training beyond high school. These educational alternatives include:

- Two-year schools, often called community colleges or junior colleges, offer various training programs.
- Four-year colleges and universities, both public and private, provide education for many careers and professions.
- Private business schools and other institutions specialize in training students for specific occupations such as court reporter, computer technician, barber, or medical assistant.

Consider the cost for further schooling as an investment in your future that will help you earn higher wages and expand your potential. There are many available methods to help finance additional schooling. Most schools have financial aid programs that include scholarships, student loans, and work-study opportunities.

Some financial aid programs are based on your academic record. Others are based on financial need. You should assess these methods for financing an education as you continue your career planning and decision making.

How can you be sure that you are making the best career decision? There is no way to guarantee a perfect decision. However, those who follow the right steps generally make good decisions.

CHECKPOINT ✓
List the six steps in the career planning process.

TEACH

Emphasize the personal, social, and economic benefits of studying careers and effective career planning.

Use Figure 9-1 to discuss the various activities in the career planning process.

Provide an overview of the various benefits of different types of career training options.

▸ Figure 9-1 *ANSWER*

Answers will vary. Resources that can be used in planning a career include research tools on the Internet or in the library, organizations such as FBLA or BPA, school guidance counselors, and talking with people who work in various careers.

ONGOING ASSESSMENT

CHECKPOINT ✓*ANSWER*

The steps in the career planning process are: (1) personal assessment, (2) employment market analysis, (3) application process, (4) interview process, (5) employment acceptance, and (6) career development and advancement.

Different Learning Styles

Print Learner Use Figure 9-1 to teach and reinforce the various activities of the career planning process. Suggest that students copy the content and expand the figure to include examples for each bullet point.

NET KNOWLEDGE

Students are guided to the online career planning sources. Ask students to report their findings from the various sources they access. Class discussion should allow students to better understand various career planning activities.

TEACH

Discuss the main career planning sources. Remind students that many sources are available.

Explain the value of informational interviews. Discuss possible sources for these information-gathering sessions, such as other students, friends, relatives, and co-workers.

THINK CRITICALLY THROUGH VISUALS

Answers will vary. Students can obtain career information by library or Internet research, conducting informational interviews with people in careers that interest them, taking part-time jobs in various areas, and joining student organizations such as FBLA or BPA.

NET KNOWLEDGE

Many online sources offer information and links on career planning activities. Locate two websites for a career topic such as preparing a résumé, identifying job opportunities, networking, or effective interviewing. What are the similarities and differences between the advice presented on the two websites? How might the information be useful to you in the future?

LO 9.1.2

CAREER INFORMATION SOURCES

Many information sources for career planning are readily available. Your school may have a career resource center with magazines, books, videos, and other material related to careers. Some information covers careers in general.

Monkey Business Images/Shutterstock.com

What are some ways you can get career information?

Other sources provide specific coverage about occupations and careers in your area.

Media and Online Sources

The *Career Outlook* and other resources from the Bureau of Labor Statistics can be helpful. The *Occupational Outlook Handbook* gives in-depth information on hundreds of occupations. It includes job duties, working conditions, education and training requirements, advancement possibilities, employment outlook, and earnings. These resources are available online.

Online and print versions of newspapers are valuable career information sources. Articles about business trends, local companies, and career topics are published in the job and business sections. Ads for available employment positions provide insight into possible career opportunities. These ads also indicate the training and skills that are needed in the current job market.

Many websites are available to help you with career planning. These sites offer information about career opportunities, résumés, effective interviewing, and creating a career portfolio.

Informational Interviews

A very useful method to obtain career information is an informational interview. An **informational interview** is a planned discussion with a worker who is willing to answer questions and provide insight about their career, the preparation needed for that career, and the person's feelings about the career. Informational interviews will help you gain insight into what actually happens in a specific career area.

You will find that most workers like to talk about their career experiences.

Portfolio Activity

Assign the Portfolio Activity for Chapter 9, available on the website for this textbook.

COLLECT Offer suggestions to help students locate information about an organization that interests them.

CREATE Remind students to make two lists: one about the potential employer and the other about the potential employee.

CONNECT Remind students to show connections between the two lists.

Be sure to plan your questions for a career information interview. Some suggested questions might include:

- How did you get your current job?
- In what ways do you find your work most satisfying? What are your main frustrations?
- What tasks and activities are required in your work?
- What are the most important qualifications for working in this field?
- What advice would you give a young person who is thinking about this type of work?

Keep notes on what you learn in your informational interviews. The experiences of others can provide key career planning information.

If a specific career interests you, ask your teacher or guidance counselor about the possibility of becoming a *job shadow* at a company employing workers that share your career interest. Job shadowing allows you to spend time with a worker for a day or longer to learn about a certain occupation.

Work as a TEAM

Using Figure 9-2, select three of the career areas listed. For each career area: (1) create a list of additional jobs, and (2) describe various skills that would be necessary to work in this career area.

Business Contacts

The process of talking to other people about their jobs is called *networking*. The advantage of networking is that your contacts are not limited to the people you know personally. Every person you meet is a potential contact for career information. The contacts in your network can provide support when you start work as well throughout your career.

CHECKPOINT
What are the main sources of career information?

CAREER AREAS WITH GREATEST EMPLOYMENT POTENTIAL		
Business and management services • data analysts • employee benefits administrators • language translators • production and office supervisors	**Environmental services** • conservation biologists • environmental educators • environmental scientists • sustainability systems developers	**Hospitality and food service** • customer service representatives • food service managers • meeting planners • resort and hotel administrators
Computer technology • computer operators • service technicians • systems analysts • website developers	**Financial services** • actuaries • investment consultants • personal financial advisors • risk assessment managers	**Sales and retailing** • electronics marketing representatives • financial services representatives • medical products sales managers
Education • corporate trainers • college and vocational teachers • educational administrators • special education teachers	**Health care and biotechnology** • biological technicians • health care administrators • home health workers • physical therapists	**Social services** • child care workers • elder care supervisors • family counselors • social service agency administrators

FIGURE 9-2
Which of the career areas shown above interest you? Do you think you should limit your career exploration to these career areas?

TEACH

Explain the value of the suggested informational interview questions.

Use Figure 9-2 to provide an overview of the career areas with the most potential. Remind students that jobs will be available in every career area, and they should be encouraged to pursue their interests and abilities.

Describe how business contacts can assist in the career planning process.

Work as a TEAM

This activity will allow students to share their knowledge with others in the class.

▸ **Figure 9-2** ***ANSWER***

Answers will vary. Some students may be interested in a career that is not on the list—one without much growth potential. This could provide an interesting discussion on how to prepare for and succeed in a less common career. Point out that, while demand for a field may be low, a person's ability and perseverance can make a difference.

ONGOING ASSESSMENT

CHECKPOINT ***ANSWER***

Print media, online sources, informational interviews, and business contacts are the main sources of career information.

Different Learning Styles

Auditory Learner Assign students to work in pairs or small groups. Ask them to discuss the career areas and job titles in Figure 9-2. Ask students to (1) name other types of jobs in these fields and (2) suggest needed skills in these career areas.

TEACH

Explain how geographic factors can influence career opportunities.

Ask students to name recent social, economic and technological trends that could affect demand for various jobs.

ONGOING ASSESSMENT

CHECKPOINT ✓ANSWER

Future employment opportunities are influenced by geography and economic trends. Consumer demand, changing demographics, and new technology all affect employment trends.

ASSESS

Key Concepts *Answers*

1. c. determine your interests and abilities
2. a. obtain information about a career area
3. d. job shadowing

Make Academic Connections *Answers*

4. Answers will vary. Students should identify several areas with strong demand for various careers and draw logical conclusions about the factors that affect job opportunities in these geographic regions.
5. Answers will vary depending on when the assignment is completed and the scientific developments identified.
6. Before the closure, there were 13,750 workers (25,000 × 0.55) in town. Prior to closing, the business employed 25.5 percent of workers (3,500 ÷ 13,750) in town.

LO 9.1.3

GROWTH CAREER AREAS

The life work you choose could be affected by the careers available. Future employment opportunities are influenced by geography and business trends.

Geographic Influences

You may have to decide whether you want to work in the geographic area in which you now live or whether you are willing to move to where the job you really want is located. There may be reasons why you would prefer to live and work near your home. People who successfully pursue the careers of their choice often have mobility. **Mobility** is the willingness and ability of a person to move to where jobs are located.

The lack of mobility can lead to *locational unemployment*. This occurs when jobs are available in one place but go unfilled because those who are qualified to fill those jobs live elsewhere and are not willing to relocate.

Economic and Industry Trends

Career areas with the most potential are influenced by economic trends and current business activities. Consumer demand, changing demographic trends, and new technology are factors that often affect career opportunities. As shown in Figure 9-2 on the previous page, service industries are expected to have the greatest employment potential.

While these are fields with strong future demand, do not limit yourself. Every career area will need new employees. Think about your personal interests and abilities in addition to economic and business trends.

CHECKPOINT ✓

What factors affect the career areas that will be in demand in the future?

9.1 ASSESSMENT

Key Concepts

Determine the best answer.

1. The first step of the career planning process is to
   a. prepare a résumé and cover letter
   b. interview for a job
   c. determine your interests and abilities
   d. obtain career training
2. The purpose of an informational interview is to
   a. obtain information about a career area
   b. apply for a job with a nonprofit organization
   c. research salaries for starting employees
   d. gain career training experience
3. Spending time with a worker on the job to learn about a career is called
   a. networking
   b. personal assessment
   c. career training
   d. job shadowing

Make Academic Connections

4. **Geography** Conduct research to identify areas of the country with strong demand for various careers. What factors have affected job opportunities in these geographic regions?
5. **Science** Identify recent scientific developments. Explain how these discoveries might affect (a) the type of career opportunities available in the future and (b) how people work in organizations.
6. **Math** A small town has a population of 25,000 and 55 percent of its residents are employed. Due to a sudden lack of demand for its products, the town's largest employer closes and 3,500 townspeople are left without work. Before the business closed, what percentage of all the workers in town did it employ?

CLOSE Ask students to name the most important actions in the career planning process.

RETEACH Use Figure 9-1 to provide additional reinforcement of career planning activities.

ENRICH Based on Figure 9-2, assign students to prepare a summary of their plans to work in one or more of these fields.

DOING BUSINESS IN... UKRAINE

After the fall of the Soviet Union, an unusual situation developed in Ukraine with regards to currency. To prevent a shortage of money, the government issued coupons for redeeming some of the limited food and other products. While the coupons were not intended to become currency, their acceptance grew as the Russian ruble became less attractive. The people of Ukraine desired to separate themselves from their past as a Russian state. The coupons, called karbovantsy, were eventually replaced by an official currency, the hryvnia.

The hryvnia has served to reflect Ukrainian independence and encourage business investment from around the world. Ukraine's strategic location, between Europe and Asia, is attractive for business. Several hundred U.S. companies have business operations there. Ukraine's economy benefits from fertile farmland, rich natural resources, an industrial base, and a well-trained labor force.

Ukraine has an interesting and varied history. The country was the major political and cultural center in Eastern Europe until conquered in 1240. More recently, Ukraine was part of the Soviet Union for 70 years. It became independent in 1991 and has expressed interest in being considered for membership in the European Union. In recent years, a territorial dispute and military action resulted in the destruction of some of Ukraine's industrial facilities, which will probably take years to replace.

Visitors to the country often comment on the friendliness and generosity of the Ukrainian people. In business, however, be sure to use formal titles, such as Mr., Mrs., Miss, Ms., or Dr., until you are told to use a first name. When conducting business negotiations, don't accept the first "no." This initial "no" may be quick and automatic. Instead, be pleasant and ask again using a different phrasing. In addition, "final offers" may not be final. Be prepared to wait. Ukrainian businesspeople may walk out or shout. While responding in a similarly dramatic way might be useful, patience will usually be more effective.

Social events are important in the business process. As you develop trust, you will be accepted. Meetings will usually include highly sweetened coffee or tea along with chocolates or cookies. Some of the most popular foods of Ukraine include pork, chicken, seafood, potatoes, and many types of bread—white, brown, rolls, bagels, pita, and flat bread. A business lunch will most likely include borscht, a traditional Ukrainian beet soup.

Think Critically

1. How does Ukraine's history affect current business and economic activities?
2. What aspects of Ukrainian culture might create difficulties for international companies?
3. Conduct library or Internet research to obtain additional information about business and economic activities in Ukraine.

How would using a new currency help the Ukrainian people to separate themselves from their past as a Russian state?

Doing Business in... UKRAINE

Point out some of the difficulties that companies have encountered when Eastern European countries transitioned from state-controlled economies to free-market economies.

If any students have lived in or visited Eastern Europe, ask them to explain some of their experiences.

THINK CRITICALLY THROUGH VISUALS

Using a different currency would reflect economic independence from Russia and the Russian economy.

Think Critically *Answers*

1. As Ukraine distanced itself from Russia, its reputation in the global marketplace improved. Its history as a political and cultural center is testimony to its geographic advantages. Recent territorial differences created some uncertainty regarding future economic growth and international trade.
2. The Ukrainian reputation for corruption and unfriendliness is changing. However, some international groups may be slow in trusting Ukrainian business, and some may be too impatient for dealing with a slower negotiation process.
3. Students conduct research to learn more about business and economic activities in Ukraine.

Applied Skills

Geography Provide students with a current map of Europe and Asia and ask them to identify the location of Ukraine. Also ask them to locate Russia, Turkmenistan, China, and all the countries that are members of the European Union.

Focus on REAL LIFE

Explain to students that they already have many school and personal experiences that can serve as the basis for planning a career.

TEACH

Provide an overview of interests, values, talents, and abilities.

Explain how interests can be identified and enhanced.

Ask students to name some interests that could be the basis of future employment.

THINK CRITICALLY THROUGH VISUALS

Answers will vary. When students allow their own interests and values to influence their choices, it will likely result in a rewarding career. If students choose a career on the advice of someone else, their career might not be as fulfilling.

9.2 Planning Your Career

Learning Outcomes

9.2.1 Describe factors of a personal assessment for career planning.

9.2.2 Discuss methods for obtaining career experience.

9.2.3 Identify information sources for available jobs.

Key Terms

values 207

talent 207

ability 207

Focus on REAL LIFE

"Brianna, what things have you done to develop a better understanding of careers that you are considering?" asked the guidance counselor.

"I prepared a career study on becoming a corporate lawyer for one of my classes," Brianna responded. "I also interviewed two local lawyers. One of them works in private practice and the other one is legal counsel for a local company."

The counselor nodded and followed up by asking, "Anything else?"

"I took a marketing course last year and found it interesting." Brianna replied. "Then I got a part-time job as a marketing assistant last summer. It was a great experience. I learned tons about marketing activities. But the best part was getting to talk to sales and marketing people about their careers. Since then, I have decided to take more courses related to marketing."

"OK, let's review your class schedule."

LO 9.2.1

PERSONAL ASSESSMENT

How can you make sure you select a job you will enjoy and that fits your life situation? Your career planning activities should start with a self-assessment of your interests, values, and abilities. These three areas will help you better understand the careers that will be the best for you. With a thorough self-assessment, you will be more likely to have a satisfying and successful career.

Interests

Many resources are available in print and online to determine the activities that give you satisfaction. Your *interests* provide a basis for your employment goals and possible career paths.

People with strong social tendencies may be best suited for work interacting with people. If you enjoy investigating situations, a career in some type of research should be considered. What are some topics or activities that interest you?

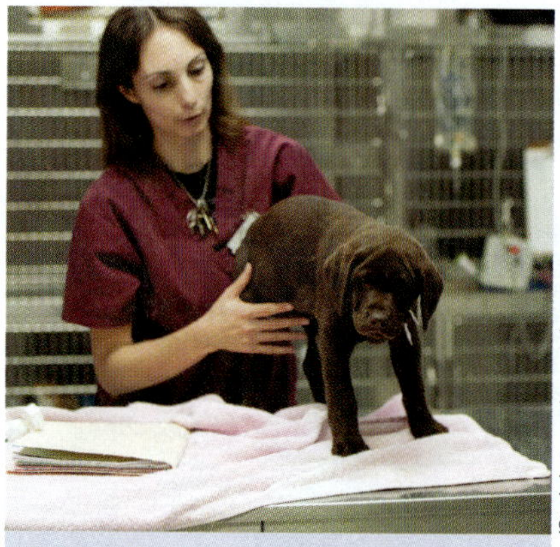

iStockphoto.com/aspenrock

What interests and values will influence your choice of career?

Different Learning Abilities

At-Risk Ask students which topics and activities are interesting to them. Help them name jobs related to these interest areas. Pair students and ask them to work together to learn more about these jobs and what education or training is required.

Values

Your **values** are things that are important to you. You can learn about your values with exercises or activities. These exercises show how you rank items such as prestige, money, power, achievement, independence, security, belonging, or serving others. Each of these may influence you, directly or indirectly, when you select your life's work.

You can begin to look at your values by answering some questions. Your answers will help you understand what you consider important. Examples of questions include:

- Is it important for me to earn a lot of money?
- Am I mainly interested in work that provides a service for others?
- Is it important for me to have an occupation that others think is important even if I do not really care for it?
- Do I want an occupation that is very challenging and may require additional schooling?
- Would I be willing to start in a job that pays a lower salary than another if that job was more challenging and offered better opportunities for future advancement?
- Do I consider investing money in education or occupational training as important as spending for other things?

Another question to better understand your values is: "What would you do if someone gave you a large sum of money to be used in any way you desire?" Would you start your own business? Would you charter a jet and travel around the world? Would you set up a foundation to support athletics for underprivileged children? Would you buy the trendiest wardrobe ever? Would you use the money to finance an expensive education? Your answers will reveal something about your personal values.

Work as a TEAM

Prepare a list of common values of people in our society. For each item on your list, describe career situations that would be appropriate for people with this value. Identify the career situations on your list that represent a type of work you might enjoy.

Talents and Abilities

Each of you has certain talents and abilities. A **talent** is a natural, inborn aptitude to do a certain thing. People often say someone has a "natural talent." **Ability** is the quality of being able to perform a mental or physical task. Your talents and abilities, along with your career goals and interests, are important in career planning.

You can learn about your abilities in a number of ways. Think about the courses you have taken and the grades you have received in school. What kinds of courses have you taken? In which ones have you done your best work? Which courses have been easiest for you? Which have been the most difficult? Which do you like the best?

michaeljung/Shutterstock.com

How can your natural abilities help you get a job?

TEACH

Explain the role of values when making career decisions and other choices in life.

Point out the importance of certain values for success in a career.

Ask students to describe some talents and abilities that are necessary for various types of careers.

Work as a TEAM

This activity will help students recognize the relationship between values and their future employment.

THINK CRITICALLY THROUGH VISUALS

Answers will vary, but could include discussion of the fact that talents are inborn aptitudes, while abilities can be developed and strengthened.

Applied Skills

Mathematics Point out various calculations that will be of importance in most job situations. Use Appendixes A, B, C, and D to highlight some of the math competencies needed by students.

Life-Span Plan Answers

Answers will vary. Students should complete personal assessments that identify their interests, values, talents, and abilities and explain how these are related to their life-span plans.

TEACH

Explain how various courses in high school and college can help people develop their abilities.

Point out the importance of various abilities (writing, researching, speaking, math, computer applications) for certain types of careers.

ONGOING ASSESSMENT

CHECKPOINT ✓ANSWER

One might have several areas of interest; talents, however, are inborn abilities that can assist in narrowing career interests.

A Question of Ethics

This feature will help students better understand some of the difficulties a person might face in the career planning process.

Ask students to offer examples of discriminatory practices that job seekers might encounter.

Think Critically *Answers*

1. Race, gender, age, and disabilities are areas in which discrimination can occur.

2. By staying focused on relevant career skills, training, and experience, both employers and potential employees can avoid unethical topics during the interview process.

Life-Span Plan

Complete a personal assessment of yourself. It should include lists of your interests, values, talents, and abilities. Explain how these lists may help you create your own life-span plan. Describe some work situations that reflect your current interests, values, talents, and abilities.

Answers to questions such as these will identify your talents and abilities.

Abilities can be developed, and that is important to keep in mind. If you are weak in a certain area, you may want to take courses that will improve that area. For instance, employers continually report that writing, reading, and technology skills are very important.

If you are not strong in preparing reports, take extra courses in English and business communication. If reading is a concern, get help in that area. If your computational skills are weak, more courses in math, including business math, would be desirable. Work to strengthen your weak areas *before* you go into full-time work. You can plan your courses and future activities to help you grow toward your chosen career.

CHECKPOINT ✓

What is the difference between an interest and a talent?

LO 9.2.2

EMPLOYMENT EXPERIENCE

Most people have more career skills than they realize. Your involvement in a range of school and community activities provides the basis for employment experiences. You can obtain further career-oriented abilities in four main ways: work-study programs, part-time employment, volunteering, and school activities.

A QUESTION OF ETHICS

Discriminatory Hiring Practices

Tomas Novak applied for a position as a regional sales manager for a technology company. Tomas was born and educated in Prague, located in what is now the Czech Republic. He has lived and worked in the United States for eight years and recently became an American citizen. He has more than 10 years of computer sales experience.

After the interview, Tomas was told that other applicants were more qualified. He did not receive a job offer. Tomas feels he was a victim of discrimination due to his slight Czech accent. He believes his ability and skills were comparable to others who were hired.

According to the Civil Rights Act and the Americans with Disabilities Act (ADA), it is illegal for employers to make hiring decisions based on personal characteristics such as age, marital status, ethnicity, race, and gender.

You can help reduce illegal hiring practices. Be cautious when deciding what kinds of personal information you include in a résumé or cover letter. Most potential employers do not want to see this personal information related to characteristics that might be a basis for hiring bias. Instead, only offer personal information that is related to the job and your career skills, such as hobbies, community activities, memberships, or personal interests.

Think Critically

1. Describe other situations in which a person might be discriminated against when applying for a job.
2. What actions can companies and workers take to eliminate discriminatory hiring practices?

Different Learning Abilities

English Language Learners (ELL) Obtain translations of various key terms and concepts in this lesson to reinforce these ideas in both English and other dominant languages used by students. Discuss how some career planning words may not translate exactly.

Work-Study Programs

Cooperative education combines school with work-related experience. These programs provide an opportunity to develop your on-the-job skills. You will not only learn about technical aspects of the job, but will also learn to interact in work settings.

In a similar way, *internships* involve work experience in organizations while learning about a career field. Internships for careers in accounting, finance, marketing, and communications are available with many companies and nonprofit organizations.

Applying for an internship is similar to applying for a job. First, identify potential positions. Then prepare a résumé and cover letter to communicate your background and interest in participating in an internship.

Brand X Pictures/Getty Images

Name some volunteer and part-time activities that could help in a career search.

Part-Time Employment

Summer and part-time work can provide valuable experience. In addition, these work situations will allow you the chance to see if you enjoy a particular career field. Your part-time work experience also helps you make contacts. These people will be able to guide you and offer support throughout your working life.

Volunteer Activities

Involvement in community service can result in gaining career experiences and improving work habits. Volunteering in community organizations also helps you develop organizational skills while making future career contacts.

School Activities

Class assignments can provide work-related experiences. For example, research and communication skills are developed when you prepare reports and oral presentations. Working on team projects offers you a chance to interact with others, a skill vital in every career.

School clubs and organizations can result in a range of valuable skills. Goal setting, planning, supervising, and delegating responsibility are activities needed in many employment settings.

CHECKPOINT ✓
What are methods for obtaining employment experience?

LO 9.2.3

SOURCES OF AVAILABLE JOBS

Finding available positions is a common concern for job hunters. Several sources are often used to obtain leads. Your ability to find job openings is a key part of career planning activities.

TEACH

Explain some of the ways in which people can obtain work skills and organizational experiences before getting their first job.

Explain various types of work-study programs. Describe the process for becoming involved in these programs.

Ask students to describe some of their experiences working part-time or in the summer. Relate these experiences to possible future careers.

Discuss the connection between volunteer activities and career choices.

Explain how various volunteer situations and school activities provide experiences that can later be used in work settings.

THINK CRITICALLY THROUGH VISUALS

Answers will vary, but could include service in the community, retail or service jobs that might provide management experience, or work in an area of interest or a hobby.

ONGOING ASSESSMENT

CHECKPOINT ✓ANSWER

Work-study programs, part-time employment, volunteering, and school activities are each ways of gaining work experience.

TEACH

Provide an overview of the sources of available jobs. Point out the limitations of the media for identifying available jobs.

Applied Skills

Technology Ask students to name computer and technology skills needed in most work settings. Ask them to describe actions that could be taken to develop these skills. Point out that basic computer and technology skills are often needed in order to learn job-specific technology skills.

FYI

Remind students about the importance of personal connections for obtaining employment.

TEACH

Explain the value of personal and business contacts in the job search process.

Describe the activities that might occur at a job fair. Explain that a person must be ready to answer a few brief questions. These screening questions can be the basis for a longer interview.

THINK CRITICALLY THROUGH VISUALS

Answers will vary. Job openings can be found in the media, by personal and business contacts, through career fairs, or by using employment agencies.

FYI Career experts estimate that more than 70 percent of available jobs are not advertised to the public. Talk to people you know, attend career fairs, and contact companies directly to identify possible job opportunities.

Media Sources

Some of the same sources that provide career planning information are also valuable for identifying potential employment positions. Advertisements with job positions are one starting point. These are offered on the websites and in the print editions of newspapers. Online job searches also can lead you to currently available positions. Be aware that most available positions are not advertised to the public. Therefore, other job search actions are very important.

Personal Contacts

You need to let as many people as possible know that you are looking for a job. Your school counselors and business teachers can be helpful. If your school has a placement office, be sure to register with that office. Your relatives, friends, neighbors, and others can be valuable sources of job leads.

iStockphoto.com/Steve Debenport

Name some ways you can find out about job openings.

Business Contacts

You should visit businesses and ask about their openings. Some businesses post signs at their business locations. Some retail businesses, including restaurants, accept applications continuously. They make it easy for prospective employees to pick up and turn in applications. Employment kiosks, where you can apply for a job online, may be available in large stores. Getting a job means going out and looking around. During a visit, you will be able to observe the types of activities performed by employees. You may also be able to make contacts for future career information.

Use online business directories and web searches to find names of organizations that may have unadvertised jobs. Communicating with these companies can produce business contacts that can result in current or future employment opportunities.

Career Fairs

Career fairs are often held at schools or community centers. These events allow a chance to contact several prospective employers in a short time. You will be asked a few questions to determine if you qualify for a longer interview.

Get ready for job fairs by being prepared to quickly communicate your potential contributions to an organization. Knowing something about the company will help set you apart from other applicants.

Government Employment Offices

Local and state government employment offices are another source for information about available jobs. These

Applied Skills

Communication Assign students to develop a visual presentation to communicate the main sources of job information. Encourage students to be creative with photos and other graphics.

tax-supported agencies help people find jobs and provide career information. They also work with employers to find qualified workers.

Employment offices can provide up-to-date information about the job market in your area. They can help you look for part-time, summer, or full-time work.

When seeking employment, use a variety of sources. Be sure to talk to as many people as possible about potential jobs and job search strategies. Use this information to create a plan that will make you a strong job candidate.

iStockphoto.com/Steve Debenport

What do you think would be the most reliable source of job information?

CHECKPOINT ✓

What are the main sources of information about available jobs?

9.2 ASSESSMENT

Key Concepts

Determine the best answer.

1. True or False. A person's values are also called natural talents.
2. True or False. Volunteering experience can result in obtaining career skills.
3. A desire to assist others in your job is an example of your
   - **a.** talents
   - **b.** interests
   - **c.** abilities
   - **d.** values
4. A(n) _____ is an event that allows a person to contact several prospective employers in a short time.
   - **a.** career fair
   - **b.** informational interview
   - **c.** network
   - **d.** career resource center

Make Academic Connections

5. **Research** Use library research or an online search to locate a career assessment tool. After answering the questions, describe what you learned about yourself in relation to potential future careers.
6. **Communication** Using online or newspapers job ads, locate three available positions that you might be interested in pursuing. Prepare a paragraph explaining actions a person might take to prepare for these jobs.
7. **Read** Locate an article that relates to obtaining employment experience or locating available job positions. Read the article and outline the major ideas presented in the article using bullet points. Include a properly formatted citation for your source. Possible sources include printed and online versions of newspapers or magazines. Also consider online sources that produce original content.

TEACH

Explain the value of government employment agencies in the job search process.

Remind students that some for-profit employment agencies may charge a fee.

THINK CRITICALLY THROUGH VISUALS

Answers will vary. Personal and business contacts are often considered to be the most reliable source of job information.

ONGOING ASSESSMENT

CHECKPOINT ✓ *ANSWER*

Business and personal contacts are the main sources of employment information. Others include newspapers and other publications, career fairs, employment agencies, and online sources.

ASSESS

Key Concepts *Answers*

1. False. Values are different from talents.
2. True
3. d. values
4. a. career fair

Make Academic Connections *Answers*

5. Results will vary. Ask volunteers to share their findings with the class.
6. Paragraphs will vary depending on the classified advertisements used.
7. Answers will vary depending on the article selected. Provide guidance for the citation format you want students to use.

CLOSE Ask students to compare values, interests, and abilities. Ask for opinions regarding which of these would most affect their career goals.

RETEACH Explain various actions that a person might take to obtain employment experience.

ENRICH Organize a debate among students about which source of job information would be most valuable to various groups. Possible examples are students, college graduates, and people looking to change careers.

LIFE/WORKSKILLS

Emphasize the importance of making effective presentations. Ask students to explain effective presentations from the perspective of the audience. When observing presentations, what are some actions that can make a talk memorable?

THINK CRITICALLY THROUGH VISUALS

You can see the other person's reaction to the presentation and the other person can provide feedback about the content and your presentation skills. You can then make improvements before actually delivering the presentation.

Think Critically *Answers*

1. Plan and practice your presentation. When making your presentation, speak openly rather than reading from your notes, project your voice without repetition, stand up straight, and make eye contact.

2. Answers will vary because the need to present ideas effectively is useful in a variety of professional and casual arenas. The classroom, sales calls, development meetings, professional trade conventions, and interviews are common areas in which presentations are used.

LIFE/WORK SKILLS

MEDIA LITERACY

Effective Presentations

"Please prepare a presentation about the recent changes in our product line for the executive committee meeting."

A request such as this illustrates the importance of developing oral presentation skills. Your ability to communicate orally is a vital skill that can be enhanced by performing these actions.

Plan Your Presentation

- Clearly define your purpose. Organize the main sections. Conduct research to get needed information.
- Plan a creative introduction. Use a story, quote, statistic, or involvement activity to get the audience's attention and to communicate your main theme.
- Consider using a handout with key ideas, graphs, tables, maps, or other visuals.
- Develop a clear conclusion. Summarize the main ideas and key findings.

Practice Your Presentation

- Prepare an outline of key ideas and main phrases. Do not memorize or read your entire presentation.
- Present your complete presentation several times. Record your presentation to determine areas for improvement.

Make Your Presentation

- Talk to the audience, don't read to them. Don't read from your visuals—posters, slides, or other items.
- Use effective voice projection, expression, and enthusiasm. Avoid repetitious phrases such as "OK," "you know," and "like."
- Look and talk professionally—dress appropriately and stand up straight.

You are likely to make many presentations throughout your life. At first it may seem difficult. As you prepare, practice, and present more talks, your ability and comfort level will increase.

Think Critically

1. What are the main suggestions you should follow for making an effective presentation?
2. Describe some situations in which you may make presentations during your life.

Dragon Images/shutterstock.com

How might you benefit from practicing a presentation in front of a colleague or classmate?

Teaching Strategies

Expand Beyond the Classroom Students should talk to people about making presentations as part of their job or in other settings. Instruct students to ask these people how they prepare for a presentation. Ask students to report their findings to the class.

9.3 Applying for Employment

Learning Outcomes

9.3.1 Prepare an application form and a résumé.

9.3.2 Identify the parts of an application cover letter.

9.3.3 Discuss the online application process.

Key Terms

application form 213

résumé 214

career portfolio 216

cover letter 216

Focus on REAL LIFE

"Congratulations, Fran!" said Maria as she hugged her niece. "What are you going to do now that you've graduated?"

"Get a job," responded Francisca. "My résumé is ready and I've already created profiles on some of the job search websites."

"What kind of job are you looking for?" asked Maria as they posed for a photo.

"I've got a plan, Aunt Maria. I'm looking for an accounting position where I can use the skills I learned in high school. In the fall, I want to take an accounting class at the community college. Eventually, I want to transfer to the university. For now, I want to earn some money and get some experience."

Maria smiled and said, "There might be an opening where I work. I'll check the website."

LO 9.3.1

APPLICATION ACTIVITIES

The application process may start in several ways. You might fill out an application form provided by the employer. This might be a printed form or an online application. You may also apply by submitting a résumé and cover letter by mail, e-mail, or posting to a website.

Personal Data Sheet

Before you fill out an application form, consider preparing a *personal data sheet*. A personal data sheet is a summary of your important job-related information. It should list your education and work experience, as well as your references. Preparing your personal data sheet will ensure you have all the necessary information to fill out the application form.

Application Form

An employer often has each applicant complete an application form. An **application form** asks for information related to employment. The form gives the employer standard information about each job applicant. The form will likely ask for your name, address, education,

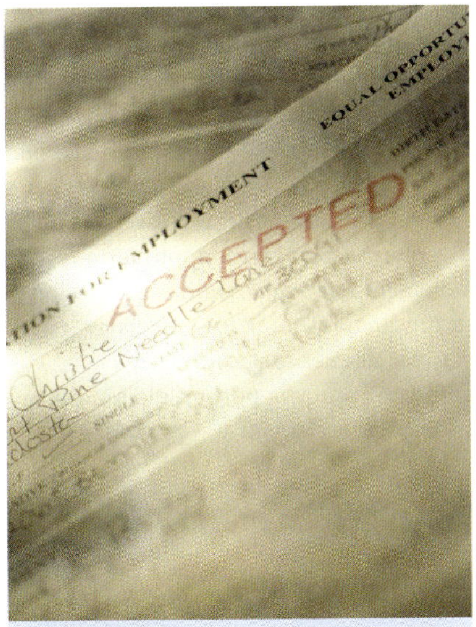

Photodisc/Getty Images

How can letters and forms provide insight into your personal attributes?

Different Learning Styles

Kinesthetic Learner Instruct students to create an employment application form they might use if they owned a small business. Ask them to explain why certain information is requested on the form they create.

Focus on REAL LIFE

Ask students to identify actions taken in this scenario that may be valuable to them in the future.

TEACH

Describe the purpose of a personal data sheet. Ask students to explain how it will be used when applying for a job.

Explain the role of the application form in a job search. Point out that application forms are used in some settings and not in others.

THINK CRITICALLY THROUGH VISUALS

Answers will vary. The high-quality forms and letters students produce show they are neat, orderly, and can follow directions—all positive attributes for any job.

TEACH

Use Figure 9-3 to explain the various sections of an application form. Ask students to relate their experiences with completing an application form.

Provide an overview of the purpose and main sections of a résumé.

▶ **Figure 9-3** ***ANSWER***

Answers will vary. If the requested items are answered fully with no spelling or other data entry errors, it reveals a person who does thorough work and pays attention to details.

Online Employment Application

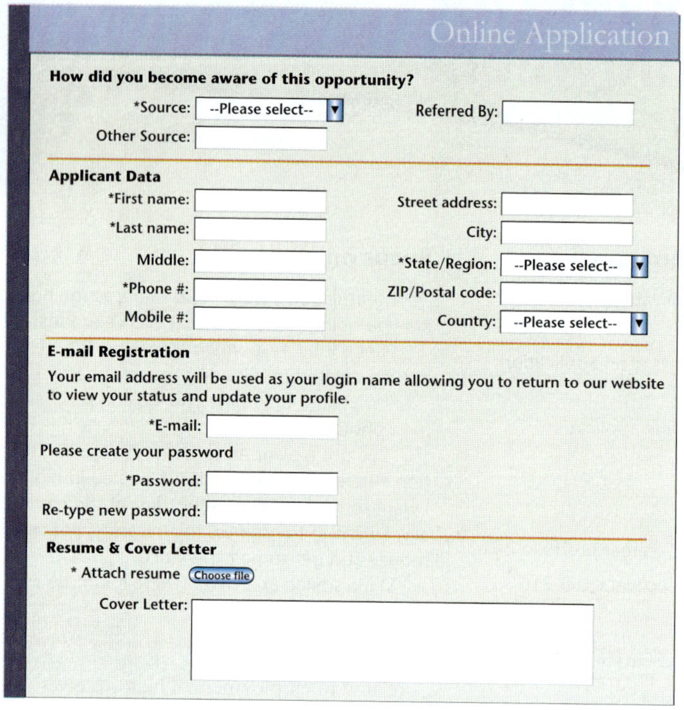
Online Application
How did you become aware of this opportunity?
*Source: --Please select--
Referred By:
Other Source:
Applicant Data
*First name:
*Last name:
Middle:
*Phone #:
Mobile #:
Street address:
City:
*State/Region: --Please select--
ZIP/Postal code:
Country: --Please select--
E-mail Registration
Your email address will be used as your login name allowing you to return to our website to view your status and update your profile.
*E-mail:
Please create your password
*Password:
Re-type new password:
Resume & Cover Letter
* Attach resume Choose file
Cover Letter:

FIGURE 9-3
How might your completion of an online application form reflect how you would approach your work?

work experience, the job for which you are applying, and references.

Filling out the application form should be viewed as your first job task. Follow directions carefully. Print answers neatly if you are using a paper application form. When completing an online application form, carefully enter accurate data. Answer all questions completely. Figure 9-3 shows a portion of an online application form.

Résumé

A **résumé** is a tool that provides information about you to a potential employer. Two of the most popular types of résumés are experience-based and qualifications-based. In an *experience-based résumé*, experiences are usually listed in order of work history. In a *qualifications-based résumé*, your abilities and experiences related to the job for which you are applying are highlighted.

As shown in Figure 9-4, a résumé usually includes the following sections:

- **Personal information** Name, address, phone, e-mail
- **Career objective** A focused, specific, personal employment goal
- **Education** Schools attended, dates, degrees, programs of study
- **Experience** Work and volunteer activities with dates and responsibilities
- **Career-related honors and other activities** Awards, school and community involvement

Different Learning Abilities

Dyslexia Prepare short written explanations of the various elements of an application form. Instruct students to carefully read each item and explain it in their own words.

Francisca Negalo

1602 Collegewood Drive
Madison, WI 53711-2821

(608) 555-0308

fnegalo@badgernet.com

CAREER OBJECTIVE

To use my accounting, computer, and business skills in an organization with an opportunity for advancement

EDUCATION

Four Lakes High School, Madison, Wisconsin

- Emphasis in Business Education
- Graduated June 10, 20xx

EXPERIENCE

Records Clerk, Tempest Tea Pot Company, Houghton, Wisconsin

- Created and updated database of customer contact information for promotional mailings
- Maintained sales records for online and mail order shipments
- Designed promotional materials for mailings and website content

General Clerk, City Assessor's Office, Cambridge, Wisconsin

- Updated Excel spreadsheets with listings of homeowners tax assessments
- Researched government programs to assist delinquent taxpayers

HONORS AND ACTIVITIES

- Markley Leadership Award, Four Lakes Alumni Association
- Honor Roll, Four Lakes High School
- Treasurer, Future Business Leaders of America
- Program Planning Committee, Dane County Youth Council
- Publicity Coordinator, Four Lakes Pep Club
- Co-captain, Lakeside Recreation Center swim team
- Volunteer, Lakeside Library Young Readers Club

FIGURE 9-4
How will the information in this résumé help an employer who wants to hire the best possible candidate?

Be sure your résumé is presented in a professional manner—clean, organized, and free of errors. Limit your résumé to one page. Use a format that highlights how your skills will contribute to the company's needs.

Remember that résumés are usually skimmed quickly. Some companies even use scanners to check for keywords. Be sure to connect your experiences to the requirements of the job, such as: fluent in Japanese, proficient with Adobe Illustrator, Cisco network certification,

Life-Span Plan

Complete a résumé for yourself. Identify steps you could take over the next year that would improve your résumé and increase your chances of being hired. Explain how these short-term steps might help you achieve your life-span goals.

TEACH

Use Figure 9-4 to explain the various sections of a résumé.

Point out that a career objective might not be included on the résumé. Instead, this information might be communicated in a cover letter.

Solicit student suggestions for various tips to follow when creating a résumé.

Ask students for suggestions that might improve the résumé presented in Figure 9-4.

▶ Figure 9-4 *ANSWER*

Answers will vary. The information in a résumé shows an employer whether the applicant's education, experience, activities, and interests would be a good fit for the job.

Life-Span Plan *Answer*

Résumés will vary and should include students' personal data, employment history, education, and personal references. Steps for improving a résumé should focus on things students can do to enhance their value to potential employers and how each relates to life-span goals.

Applied Skills

Word Processing/Office Technology Instruct students to use a résumé template in a word processing software program. Ask students to comment on the benefits and drawbacks of using this kind of preformatted document.

TEACH

Discuss some of the points to remember when preparing a résumé.

Ask students to share their experiences in preparing a résumé.

Use Figure 9-5 to point out the action verbs that can help students better communicate their experiences in a résumé or cover letter.

Explain that a career portfolio may be in a printed or digital format, or posted online.

▶ Figure 9-5 *ANSWER*

Answers will vary. Additional verbs may include *wrote*, *completed*, *engineered*, *maintained*, *determined*, *conducted*, *recommended*, *executed*, *provided*, and *authorized*.

ONGOING ASSESSMENT

CHECKPOINT ✓*ANSWER*

A typical résumé includes personal information, career objective, education, experience, career-related honors, and other activities.

TEACH

Explain the purpose of a cover letter.

Ask students to name some actions that might be taken before starting to write a cover letter.

research ability, team projects, leadership skills, overseas study, or international experience.

Use action words that demonstrate what you have achieved. See Figure 9-5 for examples of strong action words.

When preparing your résumé, be completely honest about your qualifications. Remember that employers check résumé information. Providing false information can cause you to lose a job. If false information is found after you have been hired, it can lead to your dismissal, as well as long-term career problems.

Many career experts suggest not including a career objective on your résumé. Often, a career objective is too vague or too general. Instead, this goal is better addressed in the cover letter when you connect your abilities to the organization's needs.

References are not usually included on the résumé. Have this information on hand when requested by a prospective employer. Prepare a list of people who can give a report about your character, education, and work habits. These individuals may be teachers, previous employers, supervisors, or co-workers. Be sure to obtain permission from the people you plan to use as references.

Career Portfolio

Some job applicants prepare a career portfolio. A **career portfolio** provides tangible evidence of your ability and skills. A career portfolio may include the following items:

- Résumé, cover letter, and answers to sample interview questions
- Sample reports, presentation materials, and research findings from school projects
- Website designs, creative works from school activities or previous employment such as ads, packages, and promotions
- News articles of community activities or other experiences in which you have participated
- Letters of recommendation

ACTION VERBS FOR RÉSUMÉS AND COVER LETTERS		
Achieved	Directed	Organized
Accomplished	Edited	Planned
Administered	Facilitated	Produced
Coordinated	Initiated	Researched
Created	Implemented	Supervised
Designed	Managed	Trained
Developed	Monitored	Updated

FIGURE 9-5

What are some other action verbs that might be used on a résumé or in a cover letter?

A career portfolio can show your abilities in a tangible manner to prospective employers. In addition, these materials will communicate your initiative and uniqueness.

CHECKPOINT ✓

What are the main sections of a résumé?

LO 9.3.2

APPLICATION COVER LETTER

The application **cover letter** expresses your interest in a specific job. Think of this as a sales letter for the purpose of obtaining an interview. Like any good sales letter, a cover letter should draw attention and interest. It should build a desire to meet you. Your letter should urge the reader to invite you to come for an interview. Figure 9-6 on the next page shows a cover letter that is carefully composed for an e-mail format. A carelessly written letter may cause the employer to think that you will be a careless worker. A cover letter usually involves three main sections: introduction, development, and conclusion.

Introduction

Your cover letter should start by getting the reader's attention. Next, indicate the reason for writing. Refer to the job or type

Different Learning Abilities

At-Risk Ask students to name some of their work experiences or school activities. Ask them to explain how these experiences might be described in a cover letter when applying for a job.

of employment in which you are interested. Give a brief summary of your experience and qualifications. If applicable, mention the name of the person who referred you to the organization.

Development

This section should highlight your background and experiences that specifically qualify you for the job. Refer the employer to your résumé for more details. At this point, summarize information about your experiences and training. Connect your skills and background to specific organizational needs.

6/25/201-
Francisca Negalo
Accounting Clerk Position
To David Haugen <d.haugen@lakeviewcol.edu>
Message Negalo résumé.docx

Dear Dr. Haugen

This is to express my interest in the accounting clerk position available with Lakeview College. My academic training and previous work experience quality me for this position.

While attending Four Lakes High School, I achieved a strong academic record and developed many business skills that would be valuable to your organization. My part-time employment experiences provide evidence of skills and competencies required for the available position.

In a work experience program during my senior year, I was employed ten hours a week at the Tempest Tea Pot Company. In that position, I participated in various recordkeeping and marketing activities. In addition, I worked on projects related to online sales and website development.

During my summer job in the city assessor's office, I was part of an office team responsible for maintaining spreadsheets and conducting research. The skills I developed in this position will allow me to effectively contribute to the needs of your organization.

Attached is my résumé with additional information about my experiences. Please contact me to set up an interview. My telephone number is 608.555.0308, and my email address is fnegalo@westmail.com. I look forward to the opportunity to meet with you to discuss my qualifications and learn more about the accounting clerk position.

Sincerely

Francisca Negalo

Francisca Negalo
1602 Collegewood Drive
Madison, WI 53711-2821

FIGURE 9-6
What aspects of this e-mail message would cause a reader to want to meet the applicant in person?

Conclusion

The final section is designed to request action—ask for the opportunity to discuss your qualifications in more detail. In other words, request an interview! Include your contact information, telephone numbers, and e-mail address. Make sure your e-mail address is professional. Close the letter with a summary of how you could benefit the organization. Create a personalized cover letter for each position for which you apply.

Targeted Letter

In recent years, some job applicants are using a *targeted application letter* instead of a résumé and cover letter. This letter provides a quick summary of your ability to meet the needs of an organization. A targeted letter includes a list of your skills and competencies as they relate to the available position. Your goal is to emphasize achievements and skills so you will be invited for an interview.

CHECKPOINT ✓
What is the purpose of a cover letter?

Work as a TEAM

Plan an online portfolio. Design a website that could serve as a career portfolio. Describe the format, elements, graphics, and links of this electronic portfolio. Talk about how an online portfolio could be used when applying for various types of careers.

TEACH

Discuss each section of a cover letter. Ask students to suggest specific information that might be included in each section.

Point out how a target cover letter can improve your opportunities for obtaining a job interview.

Use Figure 9-6 to provide an example of a cover letter. What items might be presented in a different manner?

▸ Figure 9-6 ANSWER

Answers will vary. A good cover letter makes the applicant sound interesting and gives enough information to make the reader want to know more about the applicant.

ONGOING ASSESSMENT

CHECKPOINT ✓ANSWER

The cover letter is used to express interest in a company and to invite interest in your résumé. Its ultimate goal is to solicit an interview.

Work as a TEAM

This activity can help students better understand the items that could be included in a portfolio.

Applied Skills

Writing Across the Curriculum Assign students to prepare a paragraph for a cover letter that shows the value of an activity or project in another class to a future career.

TEACH

Explain how computers and technology are changing the job search process. Highlight some of the examples mentioned in the textbook.

Describe how an online résumé might differ from a traditional one.

Ask students to suggest ways that career planning activities might be different in the future.

ONGOING ASSESSMENT

CHECKPOINT ✓ANSWER

Job seekers may learn job-seeking skills, post résumés, learn more about a company, and apply for jobs online. Employers may post positions, review résumés, and perform screening interviews online.

ASSESS

Key Concepts *Answers*

1. b. your references
2. a. request an interview.

Make Academic Connections *Answers*

3. Answers will vary. In general, employers cannot discriminate on the basis of age, race, religion, marital status, national origin, religion, or disability.
4. Answers will vary. Invite students to share their findings with classmates.
5. $58,320 ($54,000 × 1.08)

LO 9.3.3

ONLINE APPLICATION PROCESS

Many people use websites, social media, and apps for career planning activities. While researching potential employment is the most common activity, job seekers also apply and interview online. Because an Internet résumé is less personal, do not overlook other job search methods—phone calls, ads, job fairs, and personal contacts.

Online Applications and Résumés

Many organizations allow you to apply online. In addition to the basic application, you may also be asked some preliminary questions to determine your suitability for the position available. When posting your résumé online or sending it by e-mail, consider the following:

- Use a simple format. Avoid bold, underline, italics, and tabs.
- Do not attach files that may be difficult to open.

Résumés are also posted on various websites. They are scanned for keywords to identify candidates with the necessary job qualifications. The words and phrases that might make you an attractive job candidate vary depending on the company and the position. Companies often search for words such as *leadership*, *research experience*, *team project*, *foreign language skills*, and *software application ability* along with keywords from the job description.

Online Interviewing

Some organizations hold screening interviews using video conferencing. Others require that you post preliminary interview responses online. These online interviews may involve questions such as: "Would you rather have structure or flexibility in your work?" and "What approach do you use to solve difficult problems?"

Online interviewing may also be used to test a person's ability in job-related situations. For example, an applicant may be asked to respond to tasks such as those that a bank teller or retail clerk might encounter.

CHECKPOINT ✓
How is the Internet used in the job application process?

9.3 ASSESSMENT

Key Concepts

Determine the best answer.

1. The item *least* likely to be included on a résumé is
   - **a.** a school award
   - **b.** your references
   - **c.** schools attended
   - **d.** your work experience
2. The main purpose of a cover letter is to
   - **a.** request an interview
   - **b.** obtain career information
   - **c.** ask a person to be a reference
   - **d.** apply for a government job

Make Academic Connections

3. **Law** Conduct library or online research to obtain information on laws that protect people during the hiring process. What actions are illegal when selecting among various people for a job?
4. **Technology** Locate an online application form. What types of questions are asked? Are you prepared to answer these questions? How?
5. **Math** A person who makes $54,000 at work in a small city is considering taking a new job in a larger city that has an 8 percent higher cost of living. What would be a comparable salary in the new city?

CLOSE Ask students to name mistakes that might be made when preparing an application form, résumé, or cover letter.

RETEACH Use Figures 9-3, 9-4, 9-5, and 9-6 to highlight major ideas about application forms, résumés, and cover letters.

ENRICH Ask students to develop answers for interview questions that might be asked online.

9.4 Securing a Job

Learning Outcomes

9.4.1 Describe activities involved in the interview process.

9.4.2 Compare factors to consider when accepting a job offer.

9.4.3 Identify attitudes and actions for success on the job.

Key Terms

employment interview 219

mentor 222

exit interview 223

Focus on REAL LIFE

"Hello Barda, this is Mr. Yang from the Child Development Care Facility calling about the part-time job to assist our program director. Would you be available to come in for an interview at noon on Thursday?"

Barda is able to attend the interview as scheduled. As she gets ready, she asks her aunt, "How should I respond to the questions they might ask?"

"Be ready to tell them about your volunteer work with children at the park district, such as helping to coach soccer," her aunt reminded Barda. "Also, explain why you are interested in working with children."

"Finally," Barda's aunt added, "be ready to ask questions about the organization and your job responsibilities."

LO 9.4.1

THE INTERVIEW PROCESS

"We want to meet with you in person." This is your goal after submitting an application or résumé. An **employment interview** is a two-way conversation in which the interviewer learns about you and you learn about the job and the company.

Before You Interview

Prepare for an interview by obtaining more information about your prospective employer and the job for which you are applying. Prepare questions to ask in the interview. These might include:

- What training opportunities are available to employees?
- What qualities do your most successful employees possess?
- What new opportunities are your company considering in the next few years?

Successful interviewing requires practice. Record yourself so you will answer questions in a smooth and complete manner. Prepare concise answers for specific questions you might be asked. Ask friends to help you practice your interview skills. Attend workshops on interviewing skills. Work to organize your ideas. Speak clearly and calmly. Be sure to communicate enthusiasm.

iStockphoto.com/Michael DeLeon

What kinds of information can you learn about a position in an interview?

Focus on REAL LIFE

Use this feature to explain to students various activities involved with the interview process.

TEACH

Ask students to name some actions that might be taken when preparing for an interview.

THINK CRITICALLY THROUGH VISUALS

An interview can provide information on the responsibilities of the position, the pay and benefits, the opportunities for training and advancement, and the goals of the company.

Different Learning Abilities

Hearing Impaired Encourage students to seek out resources about successful interviewing of job applicants who are deaf or have a hearing impairment. Make sure to include all students in practice interviews and role-playing activities.

FYI

Remind students what an interviewer can and cannot ask an applicant. Ask students for some of their experiences when preparing for a job interview. Discuss some of the activities that might take place during an actual interview.

▸ Figure 9-7 *ANSWER*

Ask students to share their thoughts regarding possible answers for the various interview questions listed in the figure.

FYI

During job interviews, potential employers cannot ask you about your religion or where you were born. They can, however, ask you if you are authorized to work in the United States. Employers cannot ask your age, but they can ask for proof that you are over 18. Although employers cannot ask if you have any disabilities, it is appropriate for an employer to ask if you have the physical ability to perform the job for which you are applying. You cannot be asked about your marital status or family responsibilities, but an employer may ask if there are days or times when you are not available for work.

As part of your interview preparation you should plan to make a good first impression. It is important to arrive on time for your appointment and dress appropriately. Make sure you know how to get to the interview location and give yourself plenty of time to get there. You should go alone to the interview even if someone else is providing transportation. Wear the type of clothing that is appropriate for the company and the job for which you are applying.

During the Interview

The person who interviews you wants to find out about your personal qualities, communication skills, and abilities for the job. An interviewer may take a number of different approaches. Most interviewers will try to put you at ease when your interview begins. Interviews may include situations or questions to determine how you react under pressure. Answer clearly in a controlled manner. Use of *behavioral interviewing* is expanding to better evaluate an applicant's on-the-job potential. Questions typically begin with "describe" or "tell me about. . ." Some common interview questions are shown in Figure 9-7.

Some employers use pre-employment tests to screen applicants for skills and abilities needed on the job. Examples of pre-employment tests include keyboarding, word processing, calculating, and other skills. The interviewer may review your test results and discuss specific job requirements with you.

Avoid talking too much, but answer each question completely using good eye contact. Stay calm during the interview. Remember, you are being asked questions on a subject about which you are the world's expert—you! Finally, thank the interviewer for the opportunity to discuss the job and your qualifications.

After the Interview

Within a day or two, send a *follow-up letter* or e-mail to express your appreciation for the opportunity to interview. Even if you don't get the job, this thank-you letter will make a positive impression for future consideration.

COMMON INTERVIEW QUESTIONS

Education and Training Questions
- What qualifies you for this job?
- Why are you interested in this company?
- What activities have helped you to expand your interests and knowledge?

Work and Other Experience Questions
- In what situations have you done your best work?
- Describe the supervisors who motivated you most.
- Which of your past accomplishments are you most proud of?
- Describe people with whom you have found difficult to work.

Personal Qualities Questions
- What are your major strengths?
- What are your major weaknesses? What have you done to overcome these?
- What do you plan to be doing 5 or 10 years from now?
- Which individuals have had the greatest influence on you?

FIGURE 9-7
Think of answers to each question and write them down.

Applied Skills

Communication Ask students to prepare sample answers for the interview questions in Figure 9-7. Invite students to participate in a role-playing activity using the questions from the figure and their prepared answers. Consider organizing students into groups of three, with each student taking turns as an interviewer, a job applicant, and an observer.

Next, evaluate your interview performance. Try to remember questions that you were not expecting or not prepared to answer. Write notes about areas in which you need improvement. The more interviews you have, the better you will present yourself. More interviews will also increase the chance of being offered a job.

Be patient after the interview. It may take several weeks for the company to complete all of its interviews and make its selection.

CHECKPOINT
What actions should be taken when preparing for an employment interview?

LO 9.4.2

JOB OFFERS

"We'd like you to work for us." When you hear those words, remember to consider several factors before accepting or declining the position. The financial aspects of a job should be assessed along with some organizational factors.

Salary and Financial Factors

The type of work and your experience will affect your rate of pay. The position may include *employee benefits*. Insurance, vacation time, and retirement programs are examples of common employee benefits. Some companies offer free parking, on-site fitness centers, discount gym memberships, and other programs and services. Ask what benefits, services, and programs will be available to you and how much you will be expected to pay for them. Part-time and seasonal employees may or may not be offered benefits.

Organizational Environment

While the financial elements of a job are very important, also consider the working environment. Leadership style, dress code, the physical workspace, and the social atmosphere should be explored.

Advancement potential and training programs should be assessed. Some companies take pride in promoting from within and work hard to provide career and personal growth opportunities for workers.

Work as a TEAM

Work in teams of three to practice answering the common interview questions that appear in Figure 9-7. Take turns playing the roles of interviewer, job applicant, and observer. The team member acting as the interviewer should create follow-up questions based on responses from the job applicant. Both the interviewer and observer should comment on the strong aspects of answers and make suggestions for improvement.

CHECKPOINT
What factors should a person consider when accepting a job?

iStockphoto.com/Yuri_Arcurs

How would you describe a work environment that appeals to you?

TEACH

Explain some actions that might be taken after the interview.

ONGOING ASSESSMENT

CHECKPOINT ANSWER

An applicant should gather information about the organization, prepare questions, prepare answers to anticipated questions, arrive on time, and dress appropriately.

TEACH

Ask students to suggest factors to consider when deciding whether to accept a job offer. Discuss the financial and organizational factors that are commonly considered when evaluating a job offer.

Work as a TEAM

Students should take turns asking and answering questions. Remind the person asking questions to follow up on the respondent's answers.

ONGOING ASSESSMENT

CHECKPOINT ANSWER

In addition to salary, one should consider what types of benefits are offered, what kind of work environment is involved, and what opportunities for training and advancement exist.

THINK CRITICALLY THROUGH VISUALS

Answers will vary. Ask students to describe work environments that they may find both positive and negative.

Applied Skills

Building Study Skills Suggest the following activities to build study skills: (1) Develop a list of items to obtain when researching an organization for which a student might work. (2) Create sample questions that might be asked in an interview. (3) Prepare a summary of factors to consider when evaluating a job offer.

TEACH

Ask students to name attitudes or behaviors they have observed or experienced that can contribute to success on the job.

Highlight examples of the "Job Success Strategies" listed.

THINK CRITICALLY THROUGH VISUALS

Answers will vary, but one of the most often cited reasons for leaving a job is an inability to get along with co-workers. A congenial work atmosphere is one of the most important aspects contributing to employee satisfaction. Hours, pay, benefits, and opportunity for advancement are also important.

LO 9.4.3

ON-THE-JOB BEHAVIOR

Attitude can make a big difference in your career success. A positive attitude helps you learn and cooperate with others. Always think, speak, dress, and act in ways that project a positive image. Then, you will likely find your job more satisfying and enjoyable.

Job Success Strategies

As you prepare for your first day of work, remember the following:

- **Ask questions.** If you do not understand directions, have them repeated and listen carefully. You probably will make mistakes when learning your job. Be sure to learn from each mistake and avoid repeating it.
- **Avoid complaining.** If you seem to have more work to do than you can handle, talk with your supervisor.
- **Honor the time for breaks.** Don't abuse rest periods and lunch breaks by extending the time limit.
- **Consider your appearance.** Dress neatly and be well groomed. Employers often observe that sloppy appearance reflects sloppy work habits.
- **Be on time.** Arriving late or leaving early are poor practices.
- **Connect with all co-workers.** Respect your co-workers and learn to get along. Each person in an organization is important. Any co-worker may be of help to you in the future.
- **Show you are dependable.** Do quality work that is completed on time. Sloppy work or work turned in late affects others. You are part of a team—take pride in that. Pay attention to details. Return phone calls and e-mails promptly to show that you care about your work.

Monkey Business Images/Shutterstock.com

What aspect of a job do you think contributes the most to employee satisfaction?

Teaching Strategies

Expand Beyond the Classroom Ask students to interview several adults about job success strategies they have used or have witnessed other workers use. Invite students to share their findings. Make a list of the strategies mentioned and ask students to compare it to the strategies listed in the textbook.

- **Follow the rules.** If a rule seems unfair or unreasonable, discuss it with others and find out why it was created.

Many successful people get assistance from a person with more experience. A **mentor** is an experienced employee who serves as counselor to a person with less experience. Mentors frequently offer specific advice related to work assignments as well as general career guidance. For example, your mentor might help you develop skills needed in your current position and provide insight about future opportunities.

Stockbyte/Getty Images

Is it possible that your new job may bring you back in contact with a former employer?

Leaving a Job

When the time comes to leave a job, it is important to depart on good terms. The following tips can help you leave a job in an appropriate manner.

- Give at least a two-week notice. Write a short, polite letter of resignation; include the date of the last day you will be working.
- Try to finish all of your current projects. If they are not completed, leave a note explaining to the next person where to begin.
- If there is an **exit interview**, in which your employer asks questions about your work, be constructive and cooperative.
- Let co-workers know that you appreciated the opportunity to work with them.

Leaving on a positive note is good for you and for those you are leaving.

CHECKPOINT
What are some strategies that a person can use to maximize the chance of success on the job?

9.4 ASSESSMENT

Key Concepts

Determine the best answer.

1. A commonly suggested action to take after an interview is to
   a. contact the organization about the salary
   b. evaluate your performance in the interview
   c. revise your résumé
   d. estimate the cost of career training for the job
2. The ________ interview occurs when leaving a job.
   a. informational
   b. exit
   c. employment
   d. coaching

Make Academic Connections

3. **Communication** Work with another person to improve your interview skills. Ask each other some of the questions in Figure 9-7. Describe strengths and needed improvements to each other.
4. **Culture** Describe questions and actions that might occur in the interview process in different countries. How could body language be interpreted differently in various cultures?

RETEACH Highlight the main actions to take before, during, and after an interview.

ENRICH Ask students to describe a work environment that they might enjoy in the future.

CLOSE Ask students to name the most important actions that might be taken that could result in obtaining a job offer.

TEACH

Explain the role of a *mentor*. Describe actions that might be taken to identify a potential mentor.

Discuss appropriate actions to take when leaving a job. Ask students to describe their experiences when leaving a job.

THINK CRITICALLY THROUGH VISUALS

A new job might bring a person in contact with a former employer, so it makes sense to leave a job with a positive attitude.

ONGOING ASSESSMENT

CHECKPOINT ANSWER

Ask questions, avoid complaining, respect the company's time, look your best, connect with co-workers, demonstrate dependability, and follow the rules.

ASSESS

Key Concepts *Answers*

1. b. evaluate your performance in the interview
2. b. exit

Make Academic Connections *Answers*

3. Ask volunteers to share what they learned. Encourage them to describe strengths and areas that need improvement.
4. Answers will vary. For example, job applicants in other countries should be prepared for differences in the etiquette of greeting one another, in the duration of the interview process, and in the types of questions permitted.

Think Critically About Business *Answers*

1. Answers will vary. Students should consider family friends, relatives, and others.

2. Consumer trends tend to move toward new and improved products and services, creating career opportunities. Both an aging population and an increasingly younger workforce create demands for products and services that appeal to these groups, such as special services for senior citizens. As technology continues to advance, the demand for workers with technical training continues to grow.

3. Answers will vary. Encourage students to consider several of their abilities. Ask them to explain how these might lead to a career.

4. Research the career fair to learn which companies will be there and which will be giving on-site interviews, research each of these companies to learn which might have positions of interest, bring copies of your résumé in various formats specific to those positions, dress professionally, meet with recruiters, and follow up on any interviews.

5. Answers will vary. Encourage students to consider teachers, worker supervisors, and youth program leaders.

Chapter 9 Assessment

Review Business Concepts

9.1 Career Opportunities

- The career planning process involves a self-assessment, an analysis of the employment market, application activities, the interview process, a comparison of job offers, and career development activities.
- Important sources of career information include media sources, online sources, informational interviews, and business contacts.
- Career fields with the most growth potential include computer technology, health care, business services, social services, sales and retailing, education, hospitality and food service, financial services, management, and human resources. Service industries are expected to have the greatest employment potential in the future.

9.2 Planning Your Career

- Your interests, values, talents, and abilities should be assessed when making a career decision.
- Employment experience may be obtained through work-study programs, part-time employment, volunteer activities, and school activities.
- Information sources about available jobs include the media, personal contacts, business contacts, career fairs, and employment agencies.

9.3 Applying for Employment

- The application process may start with completing an application form or with the use of a résumé and cover letter.
- There are three main parts to an application letter. The introduction gets the reader's attention. The development highlights your background and the skills that qualify you for the job. The conclusion asks for an interview.
- Online application activities include the application process, résumé posting, and online interview questions.

9.4 Securing a Job

- The interview process involves preparing for the interview, participating in the interview, and follow-up activities.
- Factors to consider when accepting a job offer are salary, benefits, leadership style, dress code, social atmosphere, and advancement potential.
- A positive attitude is the foundation of success on the job. Other success strategies include asking questions, avoiding complaints, giving attention to your appearance, following the rules, and being on time, dependable, and friendly.

Think Critically About Business

1. Who are some people you know that you might consider for an informational interview?
2. Give examples of how consumer demand, changing demographic trends, and new technology might affect career opportunities.
3. Make a list of your talents and abilities. Specify whether you believe each one is strong or weak. Indicate how you might use your strengths in career planning. Also indicate what actions you might take to improve your weak areas.
4. What actions might a person take when preparing to attend a career fair?
5. Your personal data sheet should list several references. Application forms also ask references to be listed. Make a list of three or more references you could use right now. Then note the type of information each reference could give that would be of help to a potential employer.
6. Prepare a list of items that you might include in a career portfolio when applying for a job.
7. If you were in charge of hiring people, what information would you want to obtain from applicants? How would you go about getting this information? What are some specific questions you would ask if you were to interview the applicants?

8. Job applicants may encounter role-playing situations in an interview. What types of situations may be used to assess the skills and abilities of prospective employees?

9. Information has been received about three job openings in your community. Each is quite different. Assume that you are qualified for only one position. Create a list of qualifications you think you would like to present to a prospective employer. Then write a letter of application for the position.

   a. Reliable person is needed to handle a variety of responsibilities in a small business office. Must be able to work without supervision and communicate effectively with people who call for information. Word processing and other office skills are desirable. Salary is better than average in this community.

   b. Salespeople are needed for the auto parts and cosmetics departments of a large retail store. Applicants should have some familiarity and/or experience with selling. Hours are flexible, although some evening and weekend work will be required. Benefits are especially attractive; incentive bonus policy can provide a good income for the right person.

   c. Ours is a leading bank in this region. We are in need of capable people who want to begin a career in banking. Our training program starts at the bottom, but provides a great opportunity to learn about the banking industry. Salary is competitive.

10. What kinds of questions would you ask in an exit interview if you were the supervisor interviewing a sales clerk who is leaving?

Develop Your Business Language

Match the terms listed with the definitions.

11. A planned discussion with a worker to find out about the work that person does, the preparation necessary for the career, and the person's feelings about the career.
12. The willingness and ability of a person to move to where jobs are located.
13. The things that are important to you in life.
14. A natural, inborn aptitude to do certain things.
15. A goal in life that is fulfilled through a job or a series of occupations.
16. The quality of being able to perform mental or physical tasks.
17. A sales letter about an applicant written for the purpose of getting an interview.
18. A summary of job-related information about yourself.
19. An experienced employee who serves as counselor to a person with less experience.
20. A document used by employers that asks for information related to employment.
21. A two-way conversation in which the interviewer learns about you and you learn about the job and the company.
22. An interview in which an employer asks questions about how an employee liked his/her work and inquires about job improvements that might be made.
23. Tangible evidence of your ability and skills provided when applying for a job.

Key Terms

a. ability
b. application form
c. career
d. career portfolio
e. cover letter
f. employment interview
g. exit interview
h. informational interview
i. mentor
j. mobility
k. résumé
l. talent
m. values

6. A portfolio should contain a résumé, cover letter, answers to sample interview questions, sample reports, presentation materials, research interests, creative works from school activities or previous employment, evidence of community activities, and letters of recommendation.

7. Answers will vary, but should include typical résumé information; recruitment activities, such as advertising; and appropriate questions, such as those found in Figure 9-7.

8. Employers might utilize a variety of interview techniques including role-playing, behavioral interviewing, and skills assessments. Situations might include on-the-job activities or interactions with customers.

9. Answers will vary. Encourage students to connect their training and experiences to the specific needs of the position.

10. Answers will vary, but should express continued respect for the exiting employee. They could include questions about how the company might improve—specifically, what changes should be made to the job he or she is leaving?

Develop Your Business Language *Answers*

11. h. informational interview
12. j. mobility
13. m. values
14. l. talent
15. c. career
16. a. ability
17. e. cover letter
18. k. résumé
19. i. mentor
20. b. application form
21. f. employment interview
22. g. exit interview
23. d. career portfolio

Make Academic Connections

24. Economics The website for the Bureau of Labor Statistics presents a wide variety of data on employment and wages. Select a topic area and present a two-paragraph summary. Explain how this information could be useful in your career planning activities.

25. Culture Talk to someone who has worked in another country. Obtain information about the application process and hiring activities in a different culture.

26. Math Nancy's college tuition and fees come to $9,500 per year. She spends $1,200 each year on books and supplies. In addition, she has living expenses of $11,600 per year. She has three sources of income: financial aid of $3,500 per year, a scholarship that pays one-half of her tuition, and a work-study job from which she earns $5,300 per year.

a. How much income does Nancy receive each year from her three sources of income?
b. How much does it cost Nancy to go to this college each year?
c. What percentage of her annual college costs is covered by her three sources of income? (Round off your answer.)
d. How much money does Nancy need to borrow each year?

27. Communication Prepare an in-class presentation or video with examples of strong and weak interview behaviors.

28. Technology Visit a website that allows people to post their résumés. Prepare a summary of the procedure, cost (if any), and other information from the website.

29. Math Emilie Antoine is a personnel interviewer. On Monday, she interviewed seven job applicants; on Tuesday, six applicants; on Wednesday, nine applicants; on Thursday, five applicants; and on Friday, eight applicants.

a. How many applicants did Emilie interview that week? What was the average number per day?
b. On Wednesday, the first interview took 50 minutes; the next two each took 40 minutes; the next four took 35 minutes each; and the last two took 45 minutes each. How many total hours did Emilie spend in these interviews? What was the average length of the interviews?

30. Geography Obtain information about salaries in different geographic regions of the United States. What factors affect the differences that exist?

31. History Research a significant world event. Explain how this event affected the location and types of careers available around the world.

Make Your Case

Jeff Barbson is looking to his future and wondering what kind of career he should prepare for. His father is a civil engineer. His mother is a buyer for a department store. Both of his parents are successful and enjoy their careers. Both of them have talked with Jeff about their work. He has visited his father's office and has worked as a sales clerk in his mother's store. Jeff's favorite subjects are computer science, economics, and art. His least favorites are history, English, business law, and math. He earns his best grades in computer science and art. Jeff's father wants him to be an engineer because there is a need for engineers in their state. His mother wants him to go into retailing. Jeff would like to go to medical school and become a heart specialist.

32. Based on his school record, which of the three career areas do you think he should choose?

33. What advice would you give Jeff regarding career planning?

34. Describe how Jeff might use an online search and various websites to help with his career decision.

35. How might Jeff's situation be valuable to you in the future?

Make Academic Connections *Answers*

24. Paragraphs will vary. Students should summarize the topic and explain the value of the information in career planning activities.

25. Answers will vary and should include information about the application process and hiring activities in a different culture.

26a. $3,500 + ($9,500 ÷ 2) + $5,300 = $13,550

26b. $9,500 + $1,200 + $11,600 = $22,300

26c. $13,550 ÷ $22,300 = 0.605 or 61%

26d. $22,300 – $13,550 = $8,750

27. Presentations will vary and should include examples of strong and weak interview behaviors. Consider allowing students to work in pairs.

28. Answers will vary and should include information about the procedure, cost, and other information.

29a. Total: 7 + 6 + 9 + 5 + 8 = 35; Average: 35 ÷ 5 = 7

29b. Total: 50 + 40 + 40 + 35 + 35 + 35 + 35 + 45 + 45 = 360 minutes or 6 hours; Average: 360 ÷ 9 = 40 minutes.

30. Answers will vary. Answers could include the demand for various jobs in different areas, the cost of living, and the number of qualified applicants.

31. Explanations will vary depending on the world event selected.

Make Your Case *Answers*

32. Answers will vary. For example, students might suggest that Jeff should think about a career related to his interests and abilities.

33. If he is serious about medicine, Jeff should consider what steps he needs to take to improve his math skills; he should shadow a heart specialist or do an informational interview to learn more about what is involved. If he wants to use his abilities in computers and art, he might consider a career in graphic arts where he could illustrate medical publications, thus incorporating all of his interests.

34. Students should suggest key words or phrases that might be used for the search.

Interactions and Connections

Talk to two or three relatives, family friends, or other people in your community to obtain information about their job search and interviewing experiences. Use the following questions in your discussion with these people:

- What are some ways that you have learned about available jobs?
- What actions did you take to improve your chances of being selected for a job?
- How did you prepare for job interviews?

Prepare a one-page summary of your findings. Which of these ideas did you find most interesting and potentially useful in the future?

Job Interview Event

You are applying for an entry-level management position at ABC Corporation in Charlotte, North Carolina. Company benefits include paid holidays and vacations, sick leave, a retirement plan, and health insurance. Salary will be based upon experience and education. The event consists of three parts:

- Letter of application and résumé
- Job application form
- Interviews

You are required to prepare a one-page letter of application. Your résumé should not exceed two pages in length. The résumé, letter of application, and job application should be put together in a file folder with your name on the tab of the folder. You will be required to complete a job application form with the use of your résumé and a one-page reference sheet. No other reference materials may be used. Your initial interview with a member from the business community (representing ABC Corporation) will last 10 minutes. Finalists from the first round of interviews will have a 15-minute second interview. Total scores will be calculated for the letter of application, résumé, job application, and interview to determine which students will be hired.

Performance Indicators Evaluated

- Understand the importance of a professional portfolio that includes a résumé and letter of application.
- Demonstrate strong interviewing skills necessary to earn a job.
- Prepare a business résumé and letter of application that generate results.

You will be evaluated for

- Organization of your professional portfolio
- Performance during the interview
- Quality of participation in the interview

For more detailed information about performance indicators, go to the FBLA website.

Think Critically

1. Why is the letter of application important?
2. Why should you research a company before going on the interview?
3. Give two good examples of questions a candidate can ask the interviewer.
4. List the major sections of the résumé.

www.fbla-pbl.org

WINNING EDGE

Job Interview Event

Students must realize that applying for a job requires research about the company. Students who are equipped with information about the company are more likely to be hired. Students must also realize that the résumé and letter of application should be free of errors.

Think Critically *Answers*

1. The letter of application introduces the applicant to the prospective employer.

2. The more you know about the company, the more prepared you will be at the interview. You will be able to communicate more intelligently and ask better questions.

3. Answers will vary, but could include: What is the possibility for promotion of hard-working employees? What types of training do you offer employees?

4. Parts of a résumé include personal/contact information (name, address), objective, education, work experience, skills, extracurricular or community service activities, and references.

35. Answers will vary. Students should mention one possible career that interests them.

Interactions and Connections

Summaries will vary and should reflect responses to the three questions. Reactions to the information gathered during interviews also will vary.

UNIT 3 Business Operations and Technology

In this unit, students learn about specialized operations in business and how technology affects those operations.

Chapter 10 Marketing This chapter presents information on how goods and services are planned, promoted, distributed, and sold to customers.

Chapter 11 Business and Technology In this chapter, students will learn about computers and other technology applications in business.

Chapter 12 Financial Management This chapter focuses on financial planning and decision making and the financial records businesses use.

Chapter 13 Production and Business Operations Students will study the forms of production and how businesses complete production planning. They will also learn about tools and procedures for managing business operations.

Chapter 14 Risk Management In this chapter, students will learn about the types of risks that businesses encounter, how insurance helps protect against losses, and other ways businesses reduce and manage risks.

UNIT 3

Business Operations and Technology

Unit 3 Global Business Project

Suggest that students read the chapter and lesson titles for this unit to get acquainted with business operations and technology. Introduce the Global Business Project for this unit: **Implement International Business Operations.**

Ask students to read the project assignment and plan to work on it as they progress through the unit. The project can be found on the website: www.cengage.com/swep/pob9e

Business Vision

Businesses perform many functions to produce goods and services. Regardless of the size of the organization, similar business functions are carried out by extractors, manufacturers, wholesalers, retailers, service providers, government agencies, and nonprofit organizations. Businesses use marketing to communicate with and deliver value to customers. Financial planning and management ensure adequate resources are available and used efficiently. Computers and other technology increase the speed and accuracy of ever more complex business activities.

In this unit you will study some of the most important functions of business and the activities that managers and employees complete for each. Most medium- and large-sized businesses employ workers skilled in a particular type of work. Engineers, maintenance and service personnel, advertising and marketing specialists, accountants, computer technicians, and others complete the day-to-day operations of businesses. All parts of the business must operate effectively and in coordination with each other. Today's employees need to know how to do their specific work, how to use the technology that is a part of that work, and how their work interfaces with and supports the other activities in the business.

Keeping Them in the Air

The operation of a major airline is a complex business filled with unpredictable problems. A mechanical problem discovered shortly before takeoff has passengers waiting in Baltimore as a replacement aircraft is located. Thunderstorms in Dallas result in flight delays and missed connections. A security issue in Chicago means planes must be held at the gate. A flight delay, even a short one, can affect many other operations not only in the airport where the problem occurred but all across the country and possibly around the world. These problems affect almost all areas of airline operations: ground and gate personnel, flight crews, ticketing, and customer service. Rescheduling a flight and rebooking passengers costs thousands of dollars.

When a problem occurs, managers immediately involve other personnel in resolving the problem as quickly and effectively as possible. Dispatchers, customer service agents, and ground and flight crew managers are all called upon to contribute to solutions. Technology allows instant communication and access to complete information about aircraft, personnel, and costs. In order to resolve the problem, managers need to identify the problem, evaluate options, choose the best course of action, and resolve the issue. The goal is to keep customers happy and keep the planes in the air.

Think Critically

Why is it important for airlines to involve managers from so many areas of the company in resolving problems?

Business Vision

Encourage students to read the introduction to Unit 3. Suggest that students read the chapter and lesson titles for this unit to get acquainted with business operations and technology.

After students read the Unit Opener, ask them why many airlines have a poor reputation for customer service. Tell them that businesses have often operated in "silos" where people don't communicate well with those in other parts of the business. This leads to poor problem solving and less-effective operations.

Think Critically *Answer*

A problem in one part of an airline's operations will have an effect on other parts. Managers need to bring all of their expertise together to develop quick and effective solutions. They need to be well informed in order to communicate with frontline employees who are responsible for customer service.

Portfolio Activity

Portfolio work samples validate skill level and a student's ability to accomplish tasks frequently performed on the job. The most important reason for including samples in a portfolio is to demonstrate a student's abilities and skills. In selecting work samples for each unit, students should always have a choice of which activities to include. Students might be encouraged to include samples from the end-of-chapter activities, particularly Think Critically About Business, Make Academic Connections, Make Your Case, and Interactions and Connections.

CHAPTER OVERVIEW

Marketing is an increasingly important activity in all businesses. This chapter presents information on how marketing is planned and executed to satisfy customer needs at a profit.

10.1 Marketing Basics

Students will be introduced to basic marketing concepts, the importance of a marketing strategy, and how consumers make buying decisions.

10.2 Develop Effective Products and Services

This lesson describes the importance of marketing research in developing new products and services and how products and services are different.

10.3 Price and Distribute Products

Students will study how to determine an effective selling price and the characteristics of channels of distribution and retailing.

10.4 Plan Promotion

Students will learn about the importance of communication in marketing and the common types of promotion used by businesses and the role of merchandising for retailers.

Chapter 10 Marketing

Monkey Business Images/Shutterstock.com

Instructor Resources

- Activities and Study Guide IE
- Chapter and Unit Tests IE
- Lesson Plans
- PowerPoint Presentation
- Cognero Test, Ch. 10

Student Resources

Activities and Study Guide

www.cengage.com/swep/pob9e

- Portfolio Activity

PLANNING A CAREER IN . . .
MARKETING

Marketing, Sales & Service

Marketing is a career area that offers a great variety of job opportunities. Company positions range from entry level to top management and everything in between. There are career opportunities in all industries, including technology, health care, manufacturing, and entertainment. If you want to work in marketing, you might find a job in your hometown, in a different state, or halfway around the globe.

Related Job Titles

- **Sales Agent**
- **Merchant Wholesaler**
- **Marketing Consultant**
- **Manager of Corporate Brands**
- **Trade Show and Special Events Coordinator**
- **Marketing Database Manager**
- **Media Relations Specialist**

The work of marketers is diverse and exciting. A marketing researcher conducts focus group interviews in a mall or for a political candidate. A marketing team designs a multimillion dollar advertising campaign for a new product. An international sales representative for a pharmaceutical company travels the world to introduce a life-saving drug. A distribution center manager develops a plan to reduce shipping costs. Not only are marketing careers available to people with a wide range of interests, talents, and education, they also include some of the highest-paying business careers.

Analyze Career Opportunities in . . . MARKETING

Use library and Internet resources to learn more about careers in marketing. Choose one of the job titles listed in the box and answer the following questions.

1. How would you describe the physical work environment for jobs in this field?
2. Is this a career that interests you? What can you do now to help prepare yourself for this career?

What it's like to work as a . . . Sales Manager

Before Kerri Snodgrass boards a flight to Cairo, she returns a call to Ferris Joachum, one of her sales representatives. Kerri knows Ferris is in negotiations with a customer for a $1.5-million order of environmental monitoring equipment.

Ferris says, "If we can get the order shipped within two weeks and spread the payments over two years, I think I can make the sale."

Kerri calls her company's production manager and the loan officer of the international bank they use for customer financing. After several discussions, they get approval on the shipping date and are able to offer free financing for one year. As she gets off the plane, Kerri receives a text message—the sale has been completed and the order has been placed.

As a sales manager, Kerri needs to understand all aspects of her business, gather information, and make quick but effective decisions to support her salespeople and satisfy the customers. Salespeople and sales managers are the face of the company to its customers.

What about you? What skills and personal qualities do you believe make Kerri Snodgrass a successful sales manager?

PLANNING A CAREER IN . . .
MARKETING

Not all marketing careers are well known, but selling is one that most people recognize. Effective salespeople work to understand customers and sell them products and services they need. If they excel at understanding their customers' needs and make a profit for the company, they will be well compensated for their work.

What About You?
Answer

Answers will vary. Examples of skills and qualities include her understanding of the business and experience, her ability to make quick decisions, her trust in her employees, and her attention to customer service.

Analyze Career Opportunities *Answers*
Student answers will vary depending on when the assignment is completed and individual interests.

Additional Career Information

Encourage students to investigate careers they find interesting and explore unfamiliar careers. Two resources for additional career information are the *Occupational Outlook Handbook*, an online publication (www.bls.gov/ooh) of the U.S. Bureau of Labor Statistics, and the O*NET Resource Center (www.onetcenter.org) developed by the U.S. Department of Labor. Information about specific careers and jobs can be used to demonstrate the relevance of skills learned in this course.

Focus on REAL LIFE

Ask students to compare selling today with selling hundreds of years ago. How is it the same and how is it different? Ask the same question about advertising. Tell students that businesses continue to use things that work, but must adapt to changes in consumer needs and technology.

TEACH

Ask students to list as many words as they can think of that describe marketing. As a class, review the lists and help students determine which terms actually describe marketing or marketing activities. Explain that marketing is very important to businesses and involves a large number of activities.

Divide the class into small groups and assign a local business to each group. Ask each group to make a list of all activities the company needs to perform to sell its products and services to its customers. Encourage groups to compare their lists.

Reinforce to students that products are often called "goods," as in "goods and services." Marketers differentiate between tangible products (or goods) and intangible services.

10.1 Marketing Basics

Learning Outcomes

10.1.1 Define important marketing concepts.

10.1.2 Identify the steps in a marketing strategy.

10.1.3 Describe the consumer decision-making process.

Key Terms

- marketing 232
- marketing strategy 235
- target market 235
- marketing mix 235
- marketing orientation 236
- final consumers 237
- business consumers 237
- consumer decision-making process 237
- buying motives 238

Focus on REAL LIFE

"MJ Support Solutions provides two main services. We help small businesses clients communicate through targeted e-mail and we provide fulfillment services," Malcolm explains to a new employee.

"Okay, I understand targeted e-mail. I get e-mail ads from an online bookseller with recommendations based on what I have bought in the past. What do you mean by fulfillment services?" Janice asks.

Malcolm replies, "We develop distribution strategies. Online retailers contract with us to warehouse their products and ship them to customers as the orders come in. Some clients batch their orders and transfer the data to us electronically every night."

"Then why do you have such a big call center?"

"Well Janice, for other clients, we actually function as the customer service department."

"Exactly what kinds of products are we talking about?" inquires Janice.

"Come on, I'll show you the warehouse. You'll be surprised by how many products we have out there."

LO 10.1.1

UNDERSTAND MARKETING

Marketing may be the most visible set of business activities to consumers. Yet it may also be the most misunderstood business function. When asked to define marketing, people often use terms such as advertising or selling. While both of these are important, many other activities are a part of effective marketing.

The American Marketing Association's definition of marketing shows how complex it is: "**Marketing** is the activity, set of institutions, and processes for creating, communicating, delivering, and exchanging offerings that have value for customers, clients, partners, and society at large." These words describe a complex but key part of every business. Marketing includes a range of activities and a number of businesses in the U.S. economy.

Marketing Activities

As a consumer you are exposed to marketing activities all of the time. You take part in many of these activities. You see or hear advertisements for goods and services. You see the brand names on the packages of foods you eat and on the clothes that you and your friends wear. You read product descriptions on a company's website. You interact with salespeople in your favorite retail store. These are all examples of marketing.

There are less obvious but equally important marketing activities. These include storing products in warehouses and distribution centers and moving the products to the places where they will be sold or used. Establishing and accepting credit and arranging means of online payment are marketing activities. Businesses use marketing when they gather data on

Different Learning Styles

Visual Learner Prepare the background for a bulletin board and label it "The Many Faces of Marketing." Instruct students to use magazines, newspapers, advertisements, promotional materials, and the Internet to locate pictures of people completing a variety of marketing activities. Ask them to cut out the pictures and display them on the bulletin board.

consumer needs, use that information to improve products, and test new products before they are sold.

A great deal of marketing is not even aimed at final consumers. Businesses market products and services to other businesses. These businesses then use the products and services in their own business processes or sell them to final consumers. More time and money is spent in business-to-business marketing than in marketing products and services to final consumers.

Marketing Businesses

All businesses, including service businesses, must complete some marketing activities, even if marketing is not their focus. Many businesses are directly involved in marketing. Marketing businesses include advertising agencies and marketing research firms. Transportation companies in such industries as trucking, railroad, and air freight move products from producers to consumers. Shipping and delivery companies provide express pickup and delivery of documents and packages. Financial services companies issue and manage credit cards. They can also provide loans to businesses for purchasing raw materials and finished goods. Wholesalers and retailers participate in the distribution, storage, and sale of products to connect manufacturers and their customers. Marketing activities, marketing businesses, and marketing careers are an important part of the U.S. economy.

Marketing Functions

Marketing activities can be organized into seven functions, as shown in Figure 10-1. Each function occurs every time a product or service is developed and sold. Businesses provide many of the marketing functions. Consumers often take part in one or more of the marketing functions when they make purchases.

Work as a TEAM

A company in Ft. Lauderdale, Florida, meets fishing boats when they dock. They buy fresh fish caught that day. Each member of your team should identify a marketing activity that must be completed by the company to purchase and then resell the fish to restaurants and supermarkets.

Product and service management is designing, developing, maintaining, improving, and acquiring products and services that meet consumer needs. Producers and manufacturers develop new products. Other businesses are also involved in product/service management when they obtain products for resale. Services are created and provided by the employees of service businesses.

Distribution involves determining the best ways for customers to locate, obtain, and use the products and services of an organization. Careful shipping, handling, and storing of products are needed for effective distribution.

FIGURE 10-1
Why is each marketing function needed whenever a product or service is sold?

TEACH

Provide students with a local business directory or telephone directory and ask them to identify as many different types of companies as they can that are directly involved in marketing. Ask students to describe the primary activity of each company.

Work as a TEAM

After the team has completed its list, ask team members to match each activity with one of the marketing functions cited in Figure 10-1. If there are marketing functions with no activities, students should consider possible marketing activities for those functions.

▶ Figure 10-1 *ANSWER*

Each marketing function is needed because marketers include all of these concepts when designing a strategy. This creates a "total product" concept.

Different Learning Styles

Kinesthetic Learner Instruct students to use art supplies or a computer drawing program to re-create Figure 10-1. Ask them to try to fill in as many of the marketing functions as possible without referring to the figure in the lesson. Suggest that students add notes to the illustration and use it as a study aid.

Business Insight

Ask students to describe how they feel about their own experiences with marketers.

Think Critically *Answers*

1. Many people think marketers communicate unnecessarily, aren't truthful, and are only interested in making money.

2. Marketers deliver a standard of living by identifying new products and getting those products into customers' hands conveniently at low costs.

3. Ethical marketers must do no harm and adhere to all applicable laws and regulations. Marketers must make products that work and advertising should not be intentionally deceptive or misleading. Marketers must also be honest, responsible, fair, have respect, be open, and be good corporate citizens.

Selling is communicating directly with potential customers to determine and satisfy their needs. Selling can be face to face, such as when a customer visits a business or when a salesperson goes to the home or business of a potential customer. Selling is also performed using a telephone or other technology such as instant messaging or video conferencing to communicate directly with a customer.

Marketing-information management is obtaining, managing, and using market information to improve business decision-making and the performance of marketing activities. Marketing-information management includes marketing research and the development of databases with information about products, customers, and competitors.

Financial analysis is budgeting for marketing activities, obtaining the necessary funds needed for operations, and providing financial assistance to customers so they can purchase the business's products and services. Customers must have the resources and methods to pay for their purchases. Businesses must receive timely payments so they can continue to operate.

Pricing is setting and communicating the value of products and services. Customers must be able to easily identify the price of items that interest them or they will move on to another choice. Consumers want to know that they are getting a fair value for the money they are spending. Prices must be set low enough so that customers are willing to pay but high enough so that the business makes a profit.

Promotion is communicating information about products and services to potential customers. Advertising and other promotional methods are used to encourage consumers to buy. Advertising may appear in a variety of media—television, newspapers, magazines, radio, direct mail,

Business Insight

Marketing Ethics

Some people may think that the term "marketing ethics" is an oxymoron, or a contradiction in terms. Many people have a low opinion of marketers. Individuals receive unsolicited sales calls, junk mail, and spam. They watch advertisements that don't tell the whole story on products. They encounter salespeople who only seem to be interested in their own commissions.

Marketers, however, play a very important role in society. They deliver a standard of living. They identify new products. They find ways to get those products into customers' hands through convenient distribution and at low costs. If marketers did not work within a society, customers' choices would be very limited.

Ethical marketers abide by a set of standards outlined by the American Marketing Association. These standards require that marketers must do no harm and adhere to all applicable laws and regulations. Marketers must make products that work, and advertising should not be intentionally deceptive or misleading. Marketers also must be honest, responsible, fair, respectful, open, and good corporate citizens.

Think Critically

1. Describe why individuals may have a low opinion of marketers.
2. Explain why marketers play an important role in society.
3. Describe ethical standards that marketers should follow.

Different Learning Abilities

Visually Impaired Record the term and definition for each of the seven marketing functions on an audiotape. Ask students to listen to the definitions as many times as needed to remember the meaning of each. Make the recording available to all interested students.

and the Internet. Other methods include contests, product displays, sponsorships, and public relations activities.

CHECKPOINT
Define marketing and the seven marketing functions.

LO 10.1.2

MARKETING STRATEGY

Marketing is an important and costly part of business operations. Marketing activities often cost 50 percent or more of the selling price of a product or service. In order for a company to make a profit, marketing must be carefully planned. It must be done well, yet at a low cost. Consumers usually have many choices of products and services. If they are not satisfied with the offering of one company, they will look to a competitor to meet their needs. Careful marketing will aid a company in understanding and meeting customer needs. Successful marketing results in satisfying exchanges between businesses and consumers. Businesses offer products and services that satisfy their customers' needs. Customers pay for those products and services, providing the businesses with revenues and profit.

Marketing Planning

Marketing planning is aimed at satisfying customer needs better than competitors do, resulting in sales and profits. A company's plan that identifies how it will use marketing to achieve its goals is called a **marketing strategy**.

Developing a marketing strategy is a two-step process. The first step is to identify a target market. A **target market** is a specific group of consumers who have similar wants and needs. Many companies try to promote their products to a wide audience whose wants and needs are quite varied. It is not easy for the company to meet all of those needs. The result is that many people will not want the company's products or will be dissatisfied with them. Focusing on a target market makes it easier to develop products and services that specific groups of customers want.

The second step in developing a marketing strategy is to create a marketing mix. A **marketing mix** is the blend of four marketing elements—product, distribution, price, and promotion. A successful marketing mix satisfies the wants and needs of the target market. It also provides a profit for the company.

Develop a Successful Marketing Strategy

Many businesspeople believe they know what consumers want. They produce a product and then begin to plan how they will market it to consumers. This approach to marketing typically results in an emphasis on advertising and promotion in order to attract the attention of potential customers and convince them to buy the company's product. If the product does not appeal to consumers, the business will be forced to cut the price. Lower profits or even losses may be the result.

To increase the chances of developing a product or service that meets

Digital Vision/Photodisc/Getty Images

How would the elements of a marketing mix be used for a new apparel line?

ONGOING ASSESSMENT

CHECKPOINT ✓ANSWER

Marketing is the activity, set of institutions, and processes for creating, communicating, delivering, and exchanging offerings that have value for customers, clients, partners, and society at large. The seven marketing functions are product and service management, distribution, selling, marketing information management, financial analysis, pricing, and promotion.

TEACH

As you introduce the terms "target market" and "marketing mix" to the class, each student should draw an image of each of the terms on a sheet of paper. Invite students to share their illustrations with other class members and explain how they fit the definitions.

THINK CRITICALLY THROUGH VISUALS

A marketing mix for a new apparel line requires planning the product line designs, determining how the new line will be distributed, deciding how the line will be priced, and creating the promotional campaign.

Applied Skills

Language Arts Assign students to write a paragraph that begins, "Businesses should use a marketing orientation because. . ." Invite interested students to share their paragraphs with the class.

TEACH

Ask students why some businesses do not offer products and services that seem to satisfy customers. Ask them to suggest ways that these businesses could better understand customer needs in order to provide satisfying products and services. Explain that the process of considering customer needs when planning a marketing mix is known as a marketing orientation.

THINK CRITICALLY THROUGH VISUALS

Answers will vary, but could include costs, destinations, duration, dates, amenities, and activities.

ONGOING ASSESSMENT

CHECKPOINT ✓ANSWER

The two steps are identifying a target market and developing a marketing mix.

TEACH

Write the following sentence on the board, "Effective marketing begins with consumers." Ask students to discuss the meaning of the sentence.

Ask students to discuss the similarities and differences between final consumers and business consumers. Students should identify products and services that would appeal to both types of consumers and others that would appeal to one or the other type.

customer needs and can be sold at a profit, companies adopt a marketing orientation. A **marketing orientation** considers the needs of customers when developing a marketing mix. With a marketing orientation, businesspeople don't assume they know what customers want. They use research to study customers and their needs. The results of the research are used to plan a marketing mix designed to satisfy those needs.

A company that owns a fleet of cruise ships gathers information on people who might consider a cruise as a vacation choice. Families with young children, young singles, and retirement-age adults usually will want different kinds of vacation experiences. First-time cruisers will need different information than experienced cruisers. Menu items, entertainment, travel arrangements to and from the port, and payment options all must be planned to appeal to potential customers.

The company will first study possible customers and the similarities and differences in vacation wants and needs. Then it will select the target market that presents the best opportunity for planning a successful cruise. Using the information gathered about the target market, the company then develops the marketing mix. The product will be an exciting and relaxing cruise experience. There will be enjoyable onboard activities and interesting onshore excursions at cities on the ship's schedule. Distribution will include providing all of the documents needed by travelers, arranging customer travel to and from the port city, handling baggage, and ensuring effective customer service throughout the process. Pricing decisions provide an affordable cruise with payment options to meet the budgets of the target customers. Promotion offers information to interest prospective customers in the cruise and persuade them to decide it is the best vacation choice.

The cruise company will make each of these marketing mix decisions to meet the specific needs and expectations of their target market. The decisions will be different in many ways than if the cruise was planned for a different group of consumers.

Photodisc/Getty Images

What information would you need before you decide to purchase tickets for a cruise?

CHECKPOINT

What are the two steps in developing a marketing strategy?

LO 10.1.3

UNDERSTAND CONSUMERS

Effective marketing begins with consumers. Think of a recent product or service you purchased and why you made the choice you did. You likely had several products that would generally meet your needs. You considered those choices and selected the one that you believed would provide the most satisfaction for the money you had to pay.

Many new businesses fail because the owners have an idea for a product but fail to consider consumers and their needs. If a product appeals to a group of consumers with unsatisfied needs, it has a real chance to succeed. If consumers do not see a need

Different Learning Abilities

English Language Learners (ELL) Instruct students to write each marketing term and its definition in their notebook. Then ask students whose first language is English to work with ELL students to understand the correct pronunciation of each term and its definition.

for a product or believe they have other choices that are better or less costly, the product will likely not succeed.

Businesses can develop products for two types of consumers. **Final consumers** are persons who buy products and services mostly for their own use. **Business consumers** are persons, companies, and organizations that buy products for the operation of a business, for incorporation into other products and services, or for resale to their customers.

Consumer Decision Making

The specific sequence of steps consumers follow to make a purchase is known as the **consumer decision-making process**. Both the steps and the sequence of decisions are the same for all consumers. The length of time taken to complete the process and the information used to complete each step might be quite different from one consumer to the next. The five steps in the consumer decision-making process are shown in Figure 10-2.

Decision making begins with a need. You may be hungry or thirsty, or you may want to plan an evening's entertainment with friends. Maybe you need a summer job or are trying to choose a college to attend. If the need is urgent, you will try to satisfy it right away. If it is less important you may put it off or even ignore it. If the need is one that is familiar to you and you have satisfied it before, you will often use that past experience to help make a decision. If it is a new need, you may have a hard time deciding how to make the best choice because you have no similar experience.

People use information to make decisions. You may talk to friends or a trusted adult. An advertisement, magazine article, or Internet site may catch your attention because it provides information related to an important need. You choose sources that you trust and that provide information you understand. Using this information, you will select a very few products that seem to meet your needs. Once the choices are narrowed, you will compare them to determine if one appears to be a better choice or a greater value than the others.

Based on the information you have obtained and the urgency and importance of the need, you will make a decision. The decision is usually to buy the product you have decided is best for you. The decision may be not to buy because you have not found a satisfying choice or you do not have

STEPS IN THE CONSUMER DECISION-MAKING PROCESS
1. Recognize a need.
2. Gather information.
3. Select and evaluate alternatives.
4. Make a purchase decision.
5. Determine the effectiveness of the decision.

FIGURE 10-2
How might you use these steps to help you make your next consumer decision?

iStockphoto.com/Mark Bowden

How do you decide which products to purchase when you visit a supermarket?

TEACH

Ask students to recall their most recent purchase of a product they bought for the first time. Instruct student to list in order every activity they completed to identify the product they would buy and make the purchase. Then students should compare their lists with the five steps in the consumer decision-making process. After reviewing the five steps, ask students whether it represents the way they usually make purchase decisions.

▸ Figure 10-2 *ANSWER*

Answers will vary. Encourage discussion about using the process when making consumer decisions such as what clothes to buy, where to eat, or which concerts to attend.

THINK CRITICALLY THROUGH VISUALS

Answers will vary, but could include the price of the products, what is on the shopping list for that day, what looks attractive at the store, or nutritional content or ingredients.

Different Learning Abilities

Attention Deficit Disorder As each step of the consumer decision-making process is discussed, ask two students to present a short role-playing exercise of a consumer completing that step.

FYI

Ask students which companies they admire most and why.

TEACH

Divide the class into two groups. Assign one group to make a list of emotional buying motives and the second group to make a list of rational buying motives. Groups should exchange lists and identify one product that could be marketed using each of the motives.

ONGOING ASSESSMENT

CHECKPOINT ✓ANSWER

The steps in the consumer decision-making process are recognizing a need, gathering information, selecting and evaluating alternatives, making a purchase decision, and determining the effectiveness of the decision.

ASSESS

Key Concepts *Answers*

1. d. None of the above is correct.

2. b. identifying a target market and developing a marketing mix

3. c. economy

Make Academic Connections *Answers*

4. Answers will vary.

5. Charts and illustrations will vary.

CLOSE Now that they have been introduced to important marketing concepts, ask students how their new understanding of marketing is different from their ideas before beginning the lesson.

FYI From 2007 to 2015, only three companies have been able to place in the top 10 of Fortune magazine's list of Most Admired Companies each year. They are Apple, Berkshire Hathaway, and Google.

the money you need at the time. You may then go back to a previous step and look at other choices or gather more information.

If you decide to purchase a product, you will complete the purchase and use the product you chose. Based on that experience you will decide if you made a good choice. If you liked the product, you will probably make the same decision the next time you have the same need. You may also make the decision more quickly and easily. If the product was not what you expected, you will be unlikely to purchase that product again.

Buying Motives

Why do you shop in a certain store or choose one brand of a product over another? The reasons consumers decide what products and services to purchase are called **buying motives**. Understanding the motives of consumers helps businesses plan a marketing mix.

Some purchases are guided by emotions. *Emotional buying motives* are reasons to purchase based on feelings, beliefs, and attitudes. If you are concerned about protecting your family and possessions, you may decide to buy a home security system. Purchases of gifts and cards for holidays and occasions are triggered by feelings of love and affection.

Rational buying motives are guided by facts and logic. You may want the most cost-effective car, so you consider fuel use and repair costs of various models. When choosing a college to attend, you can compare the costs of tuition and the reputation of the college in the major you plan to study.

CHECKPOINT ✓
What are the steps in the consumer decision-making process?

10.1 ASSESSMENT

Key Concepts

Determine the best answer.

1. The best definition of marketing is
   a. promotion and selling
   b. producing and distributing products and services to customers
   c. finding customers and convincing them to buy your products
   d. None of the above is correct.
2. The two steps in a marketing strategy are
   a. developing a product and promoting it to consumers
   b. identifying a target market and developing a marketing mix
   c. conducting marketing research and planning production
   d. pricing a product and distributing it to customers
3. Which of the following is an example of a rational buying motive?
   a. love
   b. fear
   c. economy
   d. self-image

Make Academic Connections

4. **Marketing** List the seven marketing functions. Using a business directory, a telephone book, or the Internet, identify a business that specializes in providing each service for final consumers or other businesses. Briefly describe what the business does and the types of customers it serves.
5. **Technical Writing** Select one of your recent purchases. Using computer software, develop a chart or illustration that identifies the steps in the decision-making process and how you completed each step to make the purchase decision.

RETEACH Instruct students to write each of the marketing terms that appear in bold type in their notes. Then ask them to write a definition for the term in their own words before comparing their definition with the one provided in the lesson.

ENRICH Each student should select a product or service. Ask students to identify a target market and a marketing mix for the product they chose.

10.2 Develop Effective Products and Services

Learning Outcomes

10.2.1 Justify the importance of marketing research.

10.2.2 Identify the components of a product.

10.2.3 Describe how services differ from products.

Key Terms

- marketing research 239
- product 241
- services 242
- intangible 242
- inseparable 243
- perishable 243
- heterogeneous 243

Focus on REAL LIFE

Eli and Tedra wanted to start a new custom hat design store and sell their products online. They knew that they would have a lot of competition with other companies selling online.

"We need to decide what will make our products different from those offered by other companies," Tedra said. "I think we need to develop a brand name for our products."

Eli had his own thoughts, "I think we need to find differences in the way we design our products and the features we offer. We can also offer a number of options on our design."

"We don't want to make our ordering process too complex," Tedra replied. "We need to help consumers sort through their choices. We should offer additional services to help customers find a design that meets their needs. Maybe we should do some research on how customers make these choices."

LO 10.2.1

CREATE AND IMPROVE PRODUCTS

How do businesses develop new products? In many cases, products that are identified as new in a company's advertising are not new at all. Some type of change has been made in the product that may be a major improvement. The change may also be a minor one that provides little benefit to the customer. The business calls the product new to attract the attention of customers and encourage them to buy.

Totally new products that have never been seen before by customers are not often introduced. What new products can you recall having been introduced during your lifetime? The Internet, airbags in automobiles, scanning equipment used in retail stores, and artificial hearts did not have similar substitutes before they were introduced. They were the result of research by engineers and scientists seeking to find solutions to important problems. Most products you use today are minor or major improvements in existing products. New cell phone technologies that store and replay music, take pictures or video, and access the Internet are improved versions of older wireless telephones, MP3 players, and digital video cameras. These and many other product improvements occur through the development of new technology or redesign of current products.

Scientists and other researchers often develop product improvements. Many ideas for product improvements result from the ideas of consumers and from their experience in using current products. Finding solutions to problems through carefully designed studies involving consumers is known as **marketing research**.

Focus on REAL LIFE

Suggest to students that the products offered by most companies have competitors that are quite similar. Consumers may have difficulty deciding which of the choices will be best for them. Businesses must find ways to help consumers make good choices.

TEACH

Ask students to make a list of products that have been introduced in the last two or three years. Lead a discussion about which of the products were truly unique upon release, meaning there were no other products like them, and which were improvements on existing products. Are they familiar with any products that companies promoted as "new" when they did not appear to differ substantially from older products? Based on the discussion, ask students how they believe companies can come up with ideas for genuinely new products.

Different Learning Abilities

Gifted Instruct students to use the Internet to research technology and processes that are currently being studied by scientists and engineers that may result in new products several years in the future. Ask them to report on their findings and discuss with other class members whether they believe the new product ideas will be successful or not.

TEACH

Present students with the following marketing problem: A manufacturer of athletic shoes learns that its brand is ranked in the top three by people over 25 years old, but is not in the top five for people between the ages of 15 and 24. Students should use the five steps in marketing research to plan a way to improve the ranking with younger consumers.

▸ **Figure 10-3 *ANSWER***

Answers will vary. Point out that none of the other steps can be completed without first defining the problem.

TEACH

Explain that a company wants to test a new product to determine whether customers will buy it. Ask students to describe how each of the types of research studies can be used by the company to test the product.

NET KNOWLEDGE

Explain to students that the government and other organizations, such as professional associations, provide a great deal of useful information that businesses can use to make marketing decisions. The U.S. Census Bureau is an excellent resource to help people understand more about prospective customers.

ONGOING ASSESSMENT

CHECKPOINT ✓ *ANSWER*

The steps in marketing research are to define the marketing problem, study the situation, develop a data collection procedure, gather and analyze information, and propose a solution.

Plan Marketing Research

Many types of research procedures can be used to solve marketing problems. Each type of research follows the scientific problem-solving process outlined in Figure 10-3.

All marketing research studies involve gathering and analyzing information. A great deal of information about consumers and competitors is available to businesses without doing new studies. Analyzing existing information gathered for another purpose but used to solve a current problem is known as *secondary research*. Studies carried out to gather new information specifically directed at a current problem is *primary research*.

STEPS IN MARKETING RESEARCH
1. Define the marketing problem.
2. Study the situation.
3. Develop a data collection procedure.
4. Gather and analyze information.
5. Propose a solution.

FIGURE 10-3
Why is defining the problem the first step in marketing research?

Types of Research Studies

The most common type of marketing research study involves consumer surveys. *Surveys* gather information from people using a carefully planned set of questions. The surveys are often sent to consumers through the mail or using the Internet. They can also be conducted over the telephone.

Another less structured way of gathering the ideas, experiences, and opinions of consumers is through *focus groups*. In this research method, a small number of consumers take part in a group discussion. A focus group leader acts to identify areas of agreement and disagreement and to develop new ideas. Focus group members might discuss their experiences with a product, react to new product ideas, or make suggestions for product improvements.

Observations of consumers provide useful information for marketing researchers. An *observation* collects information by recording the actions of consumers rather than asking them questions. A store may be interested in how customers study and choose products in a display case or the routes they take through a store when shopping. A product design team may observe any problems consumers have using a product in order to make design improvements.

A final method of marketing research is conducting experiments. An *experiment* presents two carefully controlled alternatives to subjects in order to determine which is preferred or has better results. A marketing experiment may compare two sizes of packages to see if one size results in more sales than the other. A study could determine the effect of offering a 50-cent coupon to grocery shoppers on their choice of cereal brands.

NET KNOWLEDGE

The U.S. Census Bureau provides very detailed data that helps businesses make marketing strategy decisions. Access the www.census.gov website. Click on the American FactFinder or search for the link and locate census information on your community. Study the data and locate (1) the number of people who are 15–19 years old and the number of people who are 20–24 years old and (2) the number of renter-occupied and owner-occupied homes in your community. How might businesses use that information?

CHECKPOINT ✓
List the steps in a marketing research study.

Applied Skills

Writing Across the Curriculum Assign students to prepare a paragraph that shows the connection between the process used to obtain marketing research to the research process used in another class, such as a science class.

LO 10.2.2

PRODUCT PLANNING

Each part of the marketing mix is important when you decide to buy a product. The product must be available through effective distribution and must have an affordable and fair price. You must be aware of the product through effective promotion and know how it will meet your needs better than other choices. However, one mix element is more critical than the other three. If the product itself is not what you want, the effectiveness of the other mix elements does not matter. A business must carefully plan each of its products to make sure it meets the needs of the target market better than similar products offered by competitors.

Parts of a Product

A **product** is everything a business offers to satisfy a customer's needs. A product is made up of several components. It starts with the *basic product*, which is the simplest form of a product. The basic product is not unique and is usually available from several companies. Additions and improvements to the basic product are known as *product features*. Most smartphones offer built-in digital cameras, wireless access, and GPS as features. When customers are offered choices of features, the choices are known as *options*. When buying an automobile, customers can choose options such as color, engine size, and manual or automatic transmission.

A *brand name* provides a unique identification for a company's products. Companies try to develop a memorable brand name with an appealing image.

Packaging is a part of many products. *Packaging* provides protection and security for the product before it is used. It also may make product storage and use easier. A new container for ground coffee is created with indentations that allow customers to pick it up easily with one hand. Some customers struggled with handling the original round container. The package is a convenient way to provide information to customers that helps them make a purchase decision or explains how to use the product.

A way to build customer confidence in a company's products is by offering a *guarantee* or *warranty*. If the product breaks or does not meet customer expectations, the company will repair it, replace it, or provide a refund.

Product Planning

New product planning is a costly and time-consuming process. It is not unusual for a company to invest several million dollars and spend years to develop a new product. Many people are involved in creating the product idea, determining how it will be produced and marketed, analyzing costs, and predicting sales. When that much money is at stake, companies need a procedure that results in products customers want and that can make a profit for the company for several years. The planning process involves multiple stages.

Idea Development Generating new product ideas is a creative process. Ideas come from the work of scientists, from the suggestions of salespeople and other employees, and from consumer surveys and focus

wavebreakmedia/Shutterstock.com

What risks do businesses take if they do not follow a careful product planning procedure?

TEACH

Bring a product to show the class that illustrates the components of a product described in the lesson. As you discuss each of the components, ask students to identify them on the example product.

THINK CRITICALLY THROUGH VISUALS

If businesses do not follow a product planning procedure, they risk developing a product that consumers do not want or will not be willing to pay for or developing one that will cost too much to produce and market properly. They will waste the company's money and time.

Applied Skills

Word Processing/Office Technology Ask students to use statistics similar to the information gathered in the Net Knowledge feature to create a graph or chart that illustrates the characteristics of people in your community. For example, they might make a chart using all the age ranges presented in the Fact Finder for a particular community.

TEACH

Write the steps in the product planning procedure in large print on poster board. Cut out each step and lay them on a table. Instruct students to stand around the table and study the individual steps. Ask them to agree on the correct order for the product planning procedure. Compare the order developed by the students with the order provided in the lesson.

Work as a TEAM

Ask students whether they believe that maintaining the quality of a product would be easier or more difficult than maintaining the quality of a service.

ONGOING ASSESSMENT

CHECKPOINT ✓ANSWER

Products are everything businesses offer to customers and are composed of the basic product, product features, its brand name and packaging, and sometimes a guarantee or warranty.

TEACH

List the four characteristics of services that make them different from products. Ask students to identify several well-known services. For each service, students should describe each of the four characteristics as it applies to that service.

groups. Most ideas are for improvements to existing products.

Idea Screening Companies encourage the development of a large number of new product ideas. Then they evaluate the ideas to determine which have the best chance to be successful. Ideas are screened to determine if a demand exists for the new product. Do other companies offer similar products? Can the product be produced at a reasonable cost? Is the product legal and safe?

Strategy Development If a product idea appears to be workable, the next step is to develop a full marketing strategy. The target market for the product is studied carefully. There must be a strong need for the new product. Alternative marketing mixes are developed and tested with potential customers. The costs of the alternatives are compared to determine which provide the greatest value.

Production and Financial Planning Next, the company develops a production procedure and identifies the facilities, equipment, and people that will be needed to produce the product. The costs of production and marketing are determined and a financial plan is developed to be sure the product will make a profit.

Limited Production and Test Marketing If a new product idea makes its way through the planning process, a company may produce a limited quantity of the product and test it in a small part of the market. This step allows the company to make sure the product can be produced and marketed as planned before a large investment is made for full production.

Full-Scale Production If each of the preceding steps is completed successfully, the new product will move into full-scale production and marketing. The company will continue to gather information on production and sales to be sure financial projections are being met. Competitors will also be watched because they will likely introduce competitive products if the new product is successful. Few unsuccessful products should make it through. Products that are fully screened have a much greater chance of being successful than new products that do not go through a planning procedure.

CHECKPOINT ✓

What are the components of a product?

LO 10.2.3

SERVICES

Products are tangible items you can see and examine, such as books, boats, and hamburgers. Marketing is used for both products and services, but services are more difficult to market. **Services** are activities that are consumed at the same time they are produced.

Services are **intangible**, meaning that they have no physical form. Because services are intangible, it is more difficult to examine a service and determine if it will meet your needs. Marketers must find ways to clearly describe the service to prospective customers.

Effective service marketing is done in much the same way as product marketing. Using the two-step marketing strategy, service marketers first identify target markets for services. They then develop a marketing mix that appeals to the market. In addition to the service itself, the market mix includes distribution, pricing, and promotion of the service. The nature of services compared to the nature of products requires a change in the way they are marketed.

Work as a TEAM

The employees of a company that provides a service to consumers are responsible for the quality of the service. If your team owned a pet-sitting business, what would you do to make sure the employees provided high-quality service for each customer?

Different Learning Abilities

At-Risk Assign students to use the Internet or library resources to gather information on careers in product planning. Ask them to describe the jobs and what would be interesting about that career area.

Applied Skills

Performing Arts Assign students to work in groups to write, produce, direct, and perform a short skit related to ethical marketing. Arrange for groups to perform their skits in front of the class.

Creatista/Shutterstock.com

How can a server affect your perception of a restaurant?

Services are **inseparable**, meaning that they are consumed at the same time they are produced. The person or technology producing the service must be available when and where the customer needs it. Marketers must determine where and when consumers want a service and must be able to provide it at that location and time.

Services are **perishable**, meaning that the availability of a service must match the demand for that service at a specific time. A service cannot be stored for later consumption like many products. If all seats at a concert are filled, no more people will be able to hear that performance. If a hair stylist does not have a client, the service goes unused.

Services are **heterogeneous**, meaning that there will be differences in the type and quality of service provided. Because people usually provide services at the time they are consumed, there is less control over quality than is possible with products. The skill, training, and motivation of the service provider affect service quality.

CHECKPOINT ✓

In what ways are services different from products?

10.2 ASSESSMENT

Key Concepts

Determine the best answer.

1. True or False. Most new products introduced by companies are not totally new, but are improvements on existing products.
2. True or False. The first step in marketing research is to develop a data collection procedure.
3. The availability of a service must match the demand for that service at a specific time because it is:
   a. heterogeneous
   b. perishable
   c. inseparable
   d. intangible

Make Academic Connections

4. **Critical Thinking** Use the Internet to locate an article describing a new product that failed. Review the information to determine the possible reasons for failure. Write a short memo to the company describing how using the new product planning process may have reduced the likelihood of failure for the product.
5. **Research** Identify a product that many of your classmates use regularly. Prepare a five-question survey to determine their feelings about the strengths and weaknesses of the product and possible ways the product could be improved. Give the survey to at least 10 students. Present the results in a short report including at least one table, graph, or chart.

THINK CRITICALLY THROUGH VISUALS

A server in a restaurant can make the experience pleasant and ensure repeat customers by being attentive and providing good service.

ONGOING ASSESSMENT

CHECKPOINT ✓ANSWER

Products are tangible and may be nonperishable; it is generally easier to control the quality and marketability of these items. Services, however, are intangible, more difficult to market, and perishable.

ASSESS

Key Concepts *Answers*

1. True
2. False. The first step in marketing research is to define the marketing problem.
3. b. perishable

Make Academic Connections *Answers*

4. Letters regarding a product that failed will vary.
5. Results will vary.

CLOSE Ask students to list ways that companies can increase customer satisfaction with their products and services.

RETEACH Ask one group of students to list and summarize the steps in the marketing research process and another group to list and summarize the steps in the product development process.

ENRICH Instruct students to use the Internet to locate information on the top-rated brand names in several product and service categories based on customer satisfaction.

Focus on REAL LIFE

Ask students to think about problems they have experienced with the purchase of products. Then ask them to provide examples that are related to distribution, such as damaged products, products not available, or delivery of the wrong product. Remind them that people responsible for distribution activities are very important to the success of marketing.

TEACH

Ask students how they determine whether the price on a product is a good value or not. When are they willing to pay a higher price than they expected, and when will they decide not to buy because the price is too high?

Instruct students to cut an arrow out of a sheet of paper. As you list each of the pricing factors in the lesson, ask each student to hold their arrow pointing up or down to reflect whether they believe the factor causes a product's price to go up or down.

10.3 Price and Distribute Products

Learning Outcomes

10.3.1 Discuss how the selling price of a product is calculated.

10.3.2 Differentiate between a direct and an indirect channel of distribution.

Key Terms

- price 245
- distribution 246
- channel of distribution 246
- channel members 247
- retailers 247

Focus on REAL LIFE

Max was beginning his summer employment at a shipper's local terminal. His new boss, John, explained his duties. "We help many companies fill orders for products purchased online. If a product isn't delivered when and where customers want it, if it is damaged in shipment, or if the costs of shipping are higher than customers want to pay, these companies can lose future sales."

Max said, "When I buy products online, I can track the shipment."

John replied, "We track everything. We have benchmarks that include how long a product stays in storage, how many times it is handled, the percentage of items damaged during distribution, and many other measures of performance. We are judged on these benchmarks."

LO 10.3.1

VALUE AND PRICE

When you decide to purchase a product, how do you determine what to pay? Do you always pay the price that is marked on the product by the seller? Do you compare prices of several businesses to find the lowest price? Do you consider how much money you have available to spend in determining what price to pay? Are you concerned whether the seller is making a profit and whether that profit is low or high? Buyers usually want to pay the lowest price possible and sellers want to charge the highest price possible. Determining the best price for a product is a difficult marketing challenge.

Pricing Factors

Many factors go into a decision about a fair price. What you might consider an appropriate price may be different from the decision of other customers. It probably is very different from the price the seller believes is appropriate. There are both general and specific factors that influence the price paid for a product.

Supply and Demand A product that has a ready supply will have a lower price than a product with a very limited supply. If demand for a product is high, prices will increase. Products with low levels of demand will have comparatively low prices.

Uniqueness When a product has few close competitors because it is unique, the price will be higher than products that are very similar to others.

Age When products are first introduced to the market, prices will be quite high. As products age, the price gradually decreases.

Season Many products are used at a particular time of the year. Winter apparel, air conditioners, and holiday decorations have high levels of sales for a

Different Learning Abilities

Hearing Impaired As you describe each of the pricing factors, speak slowly and make sure to face the student. Write each of the terms on the board as they are introduced.

short time and then almost no sales for the rest of the year. Prices will be highest just before and at the beginning of the season. Prices will be lower during other times of the year.

Complexity Highly complex and technical products have higher prices than simple products. Products with many features and options will also command higher prices.

Convenience People pay for convenience. If a product is easily available and the seller provides a high level of customer service, prices will go up. Customers expect to pay low prices if they shop at a large warehouse store that is not as conveniently located and offers little service.

Price a Product

Price is the money a customer must pay for a product or service. The price of a product changes as it moves from producer to consumer. The manufacturer sets a price that is paid by other businesses that will sell the product to the final customer. The price is set by the business by adding together the product costs, operating expenses, and profit. The formula for calculating the selling price is shown in Figure 10-4.

Selling price is the price paid by the customer for the product.

Product costs are the costs to the manufacturer of producing the product or the price paid by other businesses to buy the product.

Operating expenses are all expenses of operating the business that are associated with the product. They can include salaries, storage and display equipment, facilities, utilities, taxes, and many others.

Profit is the amount of money available to the business after all costs and expenses have been paid.

Gross margin is an important factor in product pricing. The *gross margin* is the difference between the selling price and the product costs. It represents the amount of money on hand to pay for operating expenses and provide a profit.

SELLING PRICE FORMULA
Product costs + Operating expenses + Profit = Selling price

FIGURE 10-4
What is the selling price for a rocking chair if the company buys the chair from the supplier for $65, has operating expenses of $17, and makes a profit of $48?

Markup A pricing concept related to gross margin is markup. A *markup* is the amount added to the cost of a product to set the selling price. The markup is equal to the expected gross margin. A markup is stated as a percentage of the product's cost or as a percentage of the product's selling price. If a product costs $15 and has a 100 percent markup on cost, the markup is $15 and the selling price is $30. That $30 product would have a markup on selling price of 50 percent. The formulas for calculating markup on cost and markup on selling are shown in Figure 10-5.

Markdown Businesses are not always able to sell products at the original price they set. If customer demand is not as high as projected, if the selling season is ending, or if there is a flaw in the product, the business may have to take a markdown. A *markdown* is a reduction from the original selling price.

MARKUP FORMULAS
Markup on Cost
Product cost × Percent markup = Markup on cost
Markup on Selling Price
Gross margin ÷ Selling price = Percent markup on selling price

FIGURE 10-5
What is the relationship between markup and the expected gross margin?

TEACH

Write each of the components of price on a separate sheet of paper. Tape each one on the board as you describe its meaning. Once all of the components are taped on the board, ask students to identify the math functions that need to be added in order to calculate selling price. Then instruct students to rearrange the items to develop formulas for calculating each of the other components.

▶ **Figure 10-4** ***ANSWER***
The selling price is $130.

▶ **Figure 10-5** ***ANSWER***
The markup is equal to the expected gross margin.

Applied Skills

Mathematics Give students several examples of the amounts of the components for a product price, but leave out the amount of a different component each time. Instruct students to use the pricing formula to calculate the missing figure for each of the examples.

TEACH

Ask students: "Why should a markdown be considered a pricing mistake?" If a company consistently has to take large markdowns, what does it say about how customers view the company's products?

ONGOING ASSESSMENT

CHECKPOINT ✓ANSWER

Selling price = Product cost + Operating expenses + Profit.

TEACH

List three local businesses—a manufacturer, a retailer, and a service business. Ask students to identify the two parts of distribution for each of the businesses—the location and a method used to make the product or service available to the target market.

THINK CRITICALLY THROUGH VISUALS

Parcel delivery services have made it possible for small online businesses to exist without handling their own distribution function.

A markdown should be thought of as a pricing mistake because it reduces the amount of money the business has to cover operating expenses and profits. However, the original selling price can be set high because the product is new and there is higher demand. Small markdowns result in most of the remaining products being sold while still making a profit. The leftover products may need to be sold at large markdowns that still provide some money to cover the product cost and expenses.

> **CHECKPOINT ✓**
> What is the formula for calculating the selling price of a product?

LO 10.3.2

CHANNELS OF DISTRIBUTION

Do you own any products that were produced in India or New Zealand? If so, the process of getting the products from those countries to a store in your area was probably difficult and time consuming. In contrast, have you shopped at a farmers' market? Here, local producers sell fruits, vegetables, and other homegrown products. The products have to be transported only a short distance and may be harvested the same morning they are sold. Each situation describes a distribution process.

Distribution involves determining the best methods and procedures to use so customers can find, obtain, and use a product or service. As a marketing mix element, **distribution** is the locations and methods used to make a product or service available to the target market. The route a product follows and the businesses involved in moving a product from the producer to the final consumer are known as a **channel of distribution**.

Dmitry Kalinovsky/Shutterstock.com

How have parcel delivery services influenced the success of many online businesses?

Need for Distribution Channels

In the earliest economic exchanges, people often bartered to exchange goods and services. If two people each had something the other person wanted, they would agree on how much of each product would be exchanged and the trade would be made. For example, a bushel of apples might be traded for a yard of fabric. The distribution process was relatively simple. In complex economies, exchanges are much more difficult due to several differences that exist between producers and consumers.

- **Differences in Quantity** Businesses produce or sell large amounts of each product to many customers. Each consumer needs only a very small number of products at a given time.
- **Differences in Assortment** Businesses typically specialize in producing a specific type of product while consumers want to purchase a variety of products.
- **Differences in Location** In today's global economy, thousands of miles often separate producers and consumers. Businesses may need to distribute their products to customers in many countries.

Different Learning Styles

Visual Learner Ask students to create a drawing or other visual depicting an example of a channel of distribution for agricultural products as they move from a farm to the final consumers. Invite students to display their work.

- **Differences in Timing** Businesses gain efficiency by producing large amounts of a product at one time. Some agricultural products can only be produced at a specific time of the year. Consumers may want to buy products at different times than when they are produced.

Distribution channels develop to make adjustments in these differences. An effective channel of distribution takes the large quantities produced and breaks them into quantities customers want to buy. The channel gathers products from many producers to offer customers the array of products they need in convenient locations. It moves products efficiently from where they are produced to where they can be sold. Distribution channels store products from the time they are produced until customers want to buy them.

Channels and Channel Members

The businesses that take part in a channel of distribution are known as **channel members**. All marketing functions and activities are performed by a channel member or by the consumer. Businesses join a channel of distribution when either the producer or consumer does not want to perform one or more marketing activities or when the business can perform the activities better or at a lower cost.

Channels are either direct or indirect. In a *direct channel of distribution*, products move from the producer straight to the consumer with no other organizations participating. An *indirect channel of distribution* includes one or more other businesses between the producer and consumer. These other businesses provide one or more of the marketing functions.

Work as a TEAM

A musical instrument store in your community is concerned that it is losing business to online companies that deliver products directly to customers' homes. The prices of the competitors are lower and people seem to like the convenience. Brainstorm suggestions for ways the musical instrument store can compete against the online stores.

Indirect distribution channels can include *wholesalers*. Wholesalers are intermediaries between manufacturers and retailers. They create an assortment by breaking larger bulks of producer's products into smaller units then repacking and redistributing products into smaller lots for retailers and other industrial buyers. Wholesalers who take *title*, or ownership of goods, are called merchant wholesalers. Other types of wholesalers who don't take title include agents and brokers.

Retailing Retailers are a well-known and important part of distribution channels for consumer products. **Retailers** are the final business organization in an indirect

Monkey Business Images/Shutterstock.com

Name several ways a distribution center improves the exchange process between businesses and consumers.

Work as a TEAM

Invite students to discuss the advantages and disadvantages that a retail store has compared to an online business that doesn't have a local facility in which consumers can shop.

TEACH

As you introduce each of the differences between producers and consumers that must be resolved in a channel of distribution, ask students to list examples of products that fit each type and how a channel of distribution helps solve the problem.

Explain to students that there are many different types of specialist businesses that offer specific services in a channel of distribution. Students should list any distribution specialists they are familiar with. Then, instruct students to use business directories and the Internet to find other examples of distribution specialists.

THINK CRITICALLY THROUGH VISUALS

A distribution center can provide products in quantities consumers want, in convenient locations, and at the time the products are wanted.

Applied Skills

Communication Assign students to write a four-paragraph essay titled, "Why distribution is important to producers and consumers." Remind students that an essay reflects the perspective of the author.

TEACH

Students will have considerable experience with retailers. Assign students to develop a table categorizing retailers by the type of services they offer. Discounters are likely to have few services while department stores will offer more. Specialty retailers, such as technology stores, are likely to have deeper levels of expertise.

THINK CRITICALLY THROUGH VISUALS

A knowledgeable salesperson provides the information the consumer needs to make an informed purchase decision.

ONGOING ASSESSMENT

CHECKPOINT ✓ANSWER

In a direct channel of distribution, products move directly from the producer to the consumer. In an indirect channel, others may participate in the movement of products from the producer to the consumer, such as transportation services and retailers.

ASSESS

Key Concepts *Answers*

1. b. a large quantity of available products
2. c. assortment

Make Academic Connections *Answers*

3. Spreadsheets will vary depending on the five products selected.
4. Answers will vary depending on the businesses selected.

CandyBox Images/Shutterstock.com

How can a knowledgeable salesperson increase customer confidence in their decision to purchase a product?

channel of distribution for consumer products. Retailers offer a range of products at convenient locations for consumers. They help consumers to select the best products. They can provide financing and delivery services. They may even offer repairs and other customer services. Retailers assist manufacturers by storing, displaying, and advertising the products and often paying the manufacturer well before final consumers buy the products.

CHECKPOINT ✓

What is the difference between a direct and an indirect channel of distribution?

10.3 ASSESSMENT

Key Concepts

Determine the best answer.

1. Which of the following conditions will result in a lower rather than a higher price?
   a. a high customer demand
   b. a large quantity of available products
   c. a product that has very few similar competing products
   d. All would result in lower prices.
2. When businesses specialize in producing a specific type of product, a channel of distribution will be needed to adjust differences in
   a. timing
   b. location
   c. assortment
   d. quantity

Make Academic Connections

3. **Math** Visit a department store or the online catalog of an Internet business. Identify five products that have been marked down and for which the original price and sale price are listed. Prepare a spreadsheet on which you list the product, the original price, and the sale price. Calculate the amount of the markdown and the markdown percentage. Determine the amount you would pay if you purchased all five items at the original price and if you purchased them at the sale price. What is the total savings in dollars and as a percentage of the original prices?
4. **Research** List the seven marketing functions. Use a business directory or the Internet to locate a business that specializes in the first function on your list. Choose a business that is part of an indirect channel of distribution. Do this for each function on your list.

CLOSE Ask students to define and compare the advantages and disadvantages of a direct and indirect channel of distribution.

RETEACH Ask students to review the lesson and develop two multiple-choice questions from the lesson information. Students should take turns asking questions to the class and then identifying the correct answer.

ENRICH Instruct students to use the Internet to learn how technology is being used to improve the quality and speed of distribution activities.

10.4 Plan Promotion

Learning Outcomes

10.4.1 Justify the importance of communication in marketing.

10.4.2 Identify and describe the common types of promotion.

Key Terms

promotion 249
effective communication 250
personal selling 251
advertising 252
merchandising 253

Focus on REAL LIFE

As an account representative for an advertising agency, Melody is trying to sell the agency's services to a new customer—Calista Whitford.

"The most powerful marketing tool influencing consumer behavior is promotion," Melody says.

"Really?" Calista asks.

"Yes, it can attract attention and remind customers of their needs. Advertising can tap their emotions and encourage them to buy."

"How does advertising influence emotions?" asks Calista.

"Advertising can create an image with a picture or other graphic, the language we use, even the colors of the headline, text, picture, or background. All of these things can establish feelings of pleasure, happiness, fear, or sadness," explains Melody. "We can create an advertisement that leaves your customers with a positive feeling toward your products."

LO 10.4.1

COMMUNICATION AND PROMOTION

Promotional messages from businesses, organizations, government agencies, and political candidates bombard you on a regular basis. Each day, newspapers, television and radio programs, and mailboxes are filled with advertisements. Sides of buses, tops of taxis, even posters in public restrooms contain promotional messages asking you to buy something, support a cause, or change an opinion. Every time you access the Internet, you are exposed to a variety of virtual promotions. It is apparent that businesses and organizations believe in the power of promotion, but is it always effective? What determines whether promotion is compelling or not?

Promotion is any form of communication used to inform, persuade, or remind. Businesses, organizations, groups, or individuals use promotion. It is used to influence knowledge, beliefs, and actions about products, services, or ideas. To plan effective promotion, marketers must first understand the communication process. They then must apply effective communication to interact with consumers in a way that results in information, understanding, and action.

The Communication Process

Most of you have played the game where one person starts a message by whispering in the ear of a second person. That person

Life-Span Plan

How easily are you able to communicate with other people? Explain how an ability to communicate with other people can affect the life-span goals you set and your ability to achieve them.

Focus on REAL LIFE

Ask students why promotion is considered the most powerful marketing tool. Lead a discussion about businesses' effective and ineffective uses of promotion.

TEACH

Challenge students to generate a list of all of the different types of promotion they can imagine. Remind them to consider non-business promotions as well as those provided by businesses.

Life-Span Plan Answer

Answers will vary. Students should describe their communication abilities and explain how these abilities may affect their life-span goals.

TEACH

Remind students that they should always proofread ads for effectiveness. Additionally, they may consider gathering a focus group of the intended audience to evaluate the communication in order to ensure that the proper message is being received.

Different Learning Abilities

Specific Learning Disability (SLD) Ask students to describe or find an example of a promotion they believe is effective and one they believe is not effective. Students should describe what makes the promotion effective or ineffective in their opinion.

TEACH

Ask students to describe differences between effective communication and effective promotion. Ask them if a promotion by a business has to result in the sale of a product or service in order to be considered successful.

▶ Figure 10-6 *ANSWER*

Communication begins when the sender prepares information (encodes) before using a specific channel to reach the receiver. The receiver interprets (decodes) the information and provides feedback to the sender. If the receiver responds in a way the sender expected, communication was effective. If the receiver does not respond as expected, communication failed.

TEACH

Point out Figure 10-6. Assign students to work in groups and ask them to describe several business communications and how they move through the components of the model.

Discuss with students why a company that has identified a specific target market will be able to develop better promotions and have more effective communications than companies that try to appeal to a mass market.

Work as a TEAM

Students should discuss each of the components of effective communication as shown in Figure 10-6 as they make their decisions.

Components of Effective Communication

FIGURE 10-6

Describe the communication process.

whispers to the next and so on until several people have heard the message. When the last person states what he or she heard, it is seldom the same as the initial message. The game makes the point that effective communication is not easy. **Effective communication** is the exchange of information so there is common understanding by all participants. Effective communication is illustrated in Figure 10-6.

Communication begins with a person or organization (*sender*) that has information to communicate to another person or organization (*receiver*). The sender chooses the way (*communication channel*) the information will be transmitted to the receiver. Before sending the message, the sender decides the form in which the information will be sent—text, spoken words, pictures. Preparing the information to be communicated is called *encoding*. The receiver obtains the information from the channel and interprets it for understanding (*decoding*). To be sure that the communication achieved the desired result, the sender needs to have a response from the receiver (*feedback*). If feedback shows that the receiver understood the information in a way the sender intended, then communication was effective. If the receiver does not receive or misinterprets the message, communication failed.

Communicating Through Promotion

Promotion is an important form of communication. A business needs to provide information to consumers in order to persuade them to make a purchase. As the sender, the business decides what information to provide. The consumer is the receiver. The information is encoded in the form of a promotional message such as an advertisement. The business chooses an information channel. Common promotional channels include advertising media, salespeople, and the Internet. If the customer sees or hears the message, it is decoded. The response of the customer gives feedback to the business about the effectiveness of the promotion.

Choosing target markets and studying their needs and decision-making processes can make promotion more effective. When the focus of a business is a target market, communication can be very specific to the needs of that group, using media that are familiar to and trusted by those consumers. The business will understand where the customers are in the decision-making process. It will tailor promotional messages at that stage. Businesses will often gather a focus group of members of the intended audience to evaluate the communication

Work as a TEAM

Choose a newspaper, television, or magazine advertisement for a product that is familiar to each person. Using that advertisement, identify each of the components of the communication channel. Discuss whether the advertiser seems to be demonstrating effective or ineffective communication.

Applied Skills

Writing Across the Curriculum Assign students to write a paragraph that demonstrates how the communication process applies in another class they are currently taking. Invite students to share their ideas with the class.

to ensure that the proper message is being received. Early messages get attention and give simple information about the product or service and the needs it satisfies. Later promotions can compare the product to competing brands. They may point out advantages that are important to the target market. When customers purchase the product, promotions can switch to providing reinforcement of their decision and offering after-sale services.

CHECKPOINT
How does identifying a target market improve promotion communications?

LO 10.4.2

TYPES OF PROMOTION

An inventor asks you for advice on how to promote a new type of smartphone that provides satellite TV reception. What types of promotion would you recommend? Would it be a glitzy television campaign or direct mail to cellular service subscribers? Maybe you would suggest text messages delivered to potential buyers. What about salespeople ready to demonstrate the new product to customers who visit shopping mall kiosks? There are many choices for promotional communications. The types of promotion are divided into personalized promotion and mass promotion. *Personalized promotion* communicates directly with each customer using information tailored to that person. *Mass promotion* communicates with many people at the same time with a common message.

Personalized Promotion

Personalized promotion is the most effective form of marketing communication. It is also the most expensive. The most well-known type of personalized promotion is personal selling. **Personal selling** is direct, individualized communication with prospective customers to assess their needs and assist them in satisfying those needs with appropriate products and services. Personal selling usually is done face to face with each customer. The customer visits the business to meet with a salesperson, or the salesperson goes to the home or business of the customer. Personal selling also can be completed using telephone calls or live audio and video Internet connections. Because personal selling is often used for complex and expensive products and services, it may require several contacts between the salesperson and the customer to complete the sale.

To prepare for a sale, salespeople gather information on the prospective customer they will visit. They study

FYI Brick and mortar businesses are using visual merchandising to compete with online retailers. Traditional stores are adding interactive technology, customizable displays, and frequent display changes to engage customers. The number of touchscreens in stores is expected to grow from three to twelve million over the next few years.

Photodisc/Getty Images

What questions would help a salesperson determine the best clothing and jewelry to recommend for a particular consumer?

ONGOING ASSESSMENT

CHECKPOINT ANSWER

Communication can be developed and directed more specifically if a target market is identified.

FYI

Ask students to discuss any innovative displays they have seen on recent trips to retailers.

TEACH

As a class, students should develop a list of the characteristics they believe are important to an effective salesperson. Ask them if they believe most salespeople are concerned about making sure their customers are really satisfied with their purchases. Ask students to explain their answers.

THINK CRITICALLY THROUGH VISUALS

Answers will vary. Students should realize that a salesperson would want to determine who would be wearing the clothing or jewelry, when the items will be worn, and how much the consumer is willing to spend. Examples of questions include: Are you buying these items for work or casual use? Do you want the clothes and jewelry to match or do you want more versatility? Do you have items at home you want to match with these as well? What is your budget for this purchase?

Different Learning Styles

Tactile Learner Give students a familiar consumer product such as a calculator, camera, smartphone, or video game console. Assign students to develop a short sales presentation that emphasizes three important product features and the benefits of each feature for the consumer. Invite volunteers to give their presentations to other students acting as consumers.

TEACH

Instruct students to use library resources or the Internet to locate a recent listing of top-rated television commercials. Ask students to discuss the commercials on the list that they are familiar with and decide whether they agree that they deserve the top rating or not.

Assign students to prepare a table to compare the three types of mass promotion described: publicity, public relations, and sales promotion. Suggest the following table headings: Uses, Strengths, Weaknesses.

A Question of Ethics

Ask students whether they believe companies can be so successful that they cause problems for themselves because other businesses find it difficult to compete. Explain that Microsoft finds itself in that position. The feature asks students to consider what actions are ethical and unethical in reducing the amount of competition a company faces.

Think Critically *Answers*

1. Answers will vary. Students may cite antitrust laws, or they may side with Google or Microsoft on the grounds of free enterprise.
2. Competition generally benefits consumers in that it decreases prices while increasing quality and assortment.
3. Findings will vary depending on when the assignment is completed. Provide direction for how students are to report their findings.

product information. They need to be able to make the best match of products to customer needs. When a customer is qualified, meaning they appear to have the need for and resources to buy a product, the salesperson schedules a meeting with the customer. During the meeting, the salesperson asks questions, provides information, and demonstrates the product for the customer. If the salesperson can demonstrate that the product meets the customer's needs, the salesperson helps the customer make a decision to purchase. The salesperson may also arrange payment or financing as well as product delivery and any services the customer requires. After the customer has used the product, the salesperson contacts the customer to answer additional questions and determine that the customer is satisfied.

Mass Promotion

Mass promotion is directed to many people at the same time. If the people are from the same target market, it is likely they will have similar needs. Because the promotional message is aimed at many people, it cannot be as individualized and specific as personalized promotion. However, reaching many people with the same message through mass media is much less expensive. While a large company may spend hundreds of thousands of dollars on a television advertisement, it reaches more than a million people. Therefore the cost of the message for each customer is quite low.

Advertising is the most known and used type of mass promotion. **Advertising** is any paid form of communication through mass media directed at identified consumers to provide information and

A QUESTION OF ETHICS

The Price of Success

Should a successful company be penalized because it has developed a successful product? An important principle of private enterprise is that businesses and consumers benefit from competition. The belief is that competition increases the choices and quality of products and reduces prices for consumers. European courts recently stepped in to fine Google for trying to reduce competition by favoring its products and services over competition in search results.

Google provides more than 90 percent of search results in Europe. Google also has over 70 percent of the mobile operating system share in Europe. Smartphones with Google's Android operating system and computers with Google's Chrome browser dominate online searches in Europe. When someone searches for price or product comparisons through Google, Google's shopping service results provide click-throughs to retailers where Google can receive a click-through fee.

Google is not the only U.S. business to face anticompetitive action in Europe. Microsoft was accused of monopolizing the European market by forcing computer manufacturers to include its products and reject the similar products of competitors. Microsoft includes many features that are automatically added to its operating system. These include an Internet browser, e-mail and productivity programs, and a media player. All of the added programs are owned and sold by Microsoft. It is not easy for consumers to uninstall the programs once they buy a computer. Microsoft's competitors have difficulty getting computer manufacturers and consumers to purchase and use their programs because Microsoft has already included them in the system.

Think Critically

1. Should courts step in to prevent Google and Microsoft from dominating their industries?
2. Do you believe competition among businesses usually benefits consumers? Why or why not?
3. Use the Internet to gather the latest information on legal actions taken by governments and competitors against Google and Microsoft with the aim of encouraging greater competition.

Applied Skills

Communication Assign students to choose a popular consumer product and create a print advertisement for the product. Make sure they identify a target market that serves as a focus for the advertisement.

influence their actions. The most common advertising media are television, radio, newspapers, magazines, mass mailings, outdoor displays, and the Internet.

Consumers are exposed to hundreds of communications—including promotional communications—in the media each day. These messages are not developed for or delivered directly to individuals. For this reason, the advertisements must be designed to attract attention and focus the consumer on a small amount of specific information. Most advertisements do not result in an immediate sale. Rather, they attempt to influence prospects to take additional action such as visit a store, gather more information, or test the product.

Advertising campaigns direct communication efforts for both institutional advertising for the entire business and product advertising for the individual product. Advertising campaigns and individual ads should be analyzed for effectiveness. Individual ads are often tested before they are placed by using focus groups. Campaigns are evaluated during and after they are completed to see if the desired communication has been received.

Other types of mass promotion are publicity, sales promotion, and public relations. *Publicity* is non-paid promotional communication presented by the media rather than by the business or organization that is being promoted. *Public relations* is an ongoing program of non-paid and paid communications. It is planned to favorably influence public opinion about an organization, marketing effort, idea, or issue. *Sales promotion* includes activities and materials designed to reinforce a company's brand and image. It is also a direct incentive to take an action likely to immediately increase sales of a product or service. Sales promotion includes contests and games as well as the many products companies give away to consumers or sell at a low cost that highlight a brand name or product.

iStockphoto.com/ARSELA

How can stores communicate effectively with customers through merchandising and displays?

Merchandising

Retailers often attempt to induce action from their customers by engaging in merchandising. **Merchandising** includes a set of promotional activities designed to generate sales in the retail setting. There are a number of retail merchandising strategies. *Visual merchandising* uses visual signals to communicate in a retail setting. These include the use of shelf labels, signs, or displays. Visual merchandising allows a retailer to use visual signals to replace a salesperson for information.

Retailers will also set up a *display* to exhibit a product at the point of sale. For example, retailers will place product displays at the front of stores to entice customers into the store. Sale items may be displayed at the back of the store to bring customers past other merchandise to increase impulse purchasing.

Retailers should develop merchandising plans that identify strategies for price markdowns or markups, visual displays,

TEACH

Ask students to offer examples of how local retailers merchandise and display their products. Get the conversation started by asking students to describe where merchandise and displays are located in stores that they visit regularly. Students should think about what merchandising and display techniques are found in different parts of the stores.

Assign students to prepare a table to evaluate the techniques and quality of merchandising and display strategies used by national store chains versus locally owned retail stores.

THINK CRITICALLY THROUGH VISUALS

Answers will vary. Students should describe how stores use visual merchandising through visual signals such as using displays of merchandise, signs, or labels. Students should point out that stores use merchandising strategies such as price markdowns or markups, visual displays, and special events such as seasonal sales.

Portfolio Activity

Assign the Portfolio Activity for Chapter 10.
COLLECT Encourage students to be creative as they look for an example.
CREATE Remind students that their flowchart needs to show the connection between the item collected and the completion of an exchange within a channel of distribution.
CONNECT Point out that students need to connect their flowchart to something already in their portfolio or to a concept from another class.

TEACH

Ask students: Why is the Internet so effective for mass personalization promotion?

ONGOING ASSESSMENT

CHECKPOINT ✓ANSWER

Personalized promotion allows the provider to meet customers and identify customer needs. It is, however, the most expensive type of promotion. Mass promotion reaches a larger target market and is much less expensive. It does not, however, provide for individualized service, and sales (results) are often not immediate.

ASSESS

Key Concepts *Answers*

1. c. the advertisement
2. a. personal selling

Make Academic Connections *Answers*

3. Illustrations will vary depending on the examples.
4. Answers will vary depending on the products or services identified. Provide students with suggestions for how to communicate their answers. For example, they might prepare a short report, a bulleted list, a display, or a short presentation.

and special events such as seasonal sales. For example, many stores start their holiday displays as early as Thanksgiving. The entire holiday season may require a specific merchandising plan. The merchandising plan may come from a corporate headquarters with specific instructions for each store in a chain. Stores that do not have a corporate merchandising staff need to develop their own merchandising plans.

Mass Personalization

Businesses can combine the advantages of personalized and mass promotion by using mass personalization promotion. Mass personalization begins with promotion through mass media such as newspapers, mass mailings, or the Internet. Prospective customers see the advertisement and become interested in the product or service. The company then provides an easy-to-use method for the consumer to gather more personalized information.

A customer who views an Internet advertisement or uses a search engine to gather information can be encouraged to complete an online survey. The questions provide the business with more specific information about the consumer, including their interests and needs. When the survey is submitted, the consumer is taken to a more specific website tailored to their profile or they are sent specific information via e-mail. They can even contact an online customer service representative who can answer detailed questions. A simpler form of mass personalization on the Internet is a set of links that take customers with specific questions to other web pages. The links can help them choose a specific product and complete an online purchase.

CHECKPOINT ✓

Describe the advantages and disadvantages of the major types of promotion.

10.4 ASSESSMENT

Key Concepts

Determine the best answer.

1. Which of the following is not a part of effective communication?
   - **a.** the sender
   - **b.** the receiver
   - **c.** the advertisement
   - **d.** information
2. The most expensive but also most effective type of promotion is
   - **a.** personal selling
   - **b.** advertising
   - **c.** publicity
   - **d.** public relations

Make Academic Connections

3. **Critical Thinking** Use Figure 10-6 to illustrate three different examples of business communications: a business-to-business communication, a business-to-final consumer communication, and a consumer-to-business communication.
4. **Research** Identify three different products or services you would consider buying. For each product, identify the information you need to help you make a purchase decision and what media or information source you would choose to gather the information. Describe how a business could use promotion to influence your decision.

CLOSE Ask students: "What should a business do to make sure its promotion is effective?"

RETEACH Ask students to use Figure 10-6 to discuss how businesses can plan to use each of the promotional methods described in the chapter.

ENRICH Ask students to describe ways that promotion can be used to increase the effectiveness of each of the other three marketing mix elements.

LIFE/WORK SKILLS

FLEXIBILITY AND ADAPTABILITY

Resolve Conflict

Conflict can be defined as competing differences between two or more people. These differences are often caused by struggles over goals, motives, values, ideas, and resources. Believe it or not, conflict can be both good and bad, depending upon the results of the conflict. The costs of negative, unresolved conflict include decreased productivity, low employee morale, and heightened workplace tensions. These all have the potential to damage the success of a business. But conflict of the right nature can be beneficial to business. For example, friendly conflict can encourage competition, diverse thinking, creativity, and a wider variety of solutions to business problems. Prevention is the solution to many problems, including workplace conflict. Some tips for preventing negative conflict in the workplace include the following:

- Be open to others' ideas. Listen before making up your mind.
- Avoid stereotyping your co-workers and superiors.
- Do not use language or expressions that may be offensive or demeaning to others.
- Disagree constructively. Offer alternative suggestions or solutions rather than simply rejecting others' ideas.
- Above all, treat your co-workers and superiors with the respect you want them to show you.

Unfortunately, conflict cannot always be avoided. All types of conflict can arise, from personality clashes to conflict over business ideas. The following strategies can be helpful in managing conflict with co-workers.

- **Intervention** Ask a co-worker or supervisor to provide a setting for conflict resolution between you and those with whom you are in conflict. A supervisor also might speak on your behalf to the co-worker with whom you are in conflict.
- **Confrontation** Approach the co-worker with whom you are having trouble. Both of you must recognize the problem and then work together toward a solution.
- **Compromise** If the conflict involves a disagreement over a particular business issue, you might work out a compromise solution. For example, you may agree to your co-worker's idea in exchange for similar treatment during the next conflict.
- **Avoidance** The avoidance technique should be your last solution, but in some situations it may be best. If you simply cannot solve a personality conflict, deal with the individual when you need to, but otherwise steer clear.

Conflict between a worker and a superior is acceptable, and in some cases even beneficial, if it leads to increased mutual respect. Conflict with superiors must be handled with care and should not be seen as a challenge to the superior's authority. Conflict with superiors should be kept professional and private.

Think Critically

1. What is conflict?
2. What are the consequences of negative conflict?

Golden Pixels LLC/Shutterstock.com

How are the people in this photo demonstrating respect for each other?

LIFE/WORK SKILLS

Unresolved conflicts in business, even if they involve only minor issues, can ripen into serious problems for the people involved and even for the company. Employees and managers need to recognize when conflicts are developing into problems and work to resolve them in positive ways. Having the ability to resolve conflicts is a skill valued by employers.

THINK CRITICALLY THROUGH VISUALS

The people in the photo are facing the speaker and appear to be paying attention. They all have body language that shows they are listening.

Think Critically *Answers*

1. Answers may vary. The article defines conflict as competing differences between two or more people.

2. Answers may vary. The article lists decreased productivity, low employee morale, heightened workplace tensions, and, ultimately, loss of business success.

Teaching Strategies

Collaborative Learning Divide students into small work teams. Ask each team to identify a common conflict that could occur in business. Each team should prepare a skit that shows how the conflict develops and how it can be resolved effectively. Teams should then take turns performing their skits for the class.

Think Critically About Business *Answers*

1. Answers will vary. Students are to identify businesses from their community as being marketing businesses or not marketing businesses.

2. Answers will vary. Students are to find local businesses whose work relates to each of the marketing functions.

3. A business consumer for this product could be an office supply chain, and a final consumer could be a salesperson who is frequently on the road. Both consumers would be interested in a good price. The business consumer would want to know how the printer could be sold with other products, while the final consumer would want to hear about its convenience and reliability.

Chapter 10 Assessment

Review Business Concepts

10.1 Marketing Basics

- Marketing is the activity, set of institutions, and processes for creating, communicating, delivering, and exchanging offerings that have value for customers, clients, partners, and society at large. The seven marketing functions are product and service management, distribution, selling, marketing-information management, financial analysis, pricing, and promotion.
- A marketing strategy is a two-step process used to plan and market products. The first step is to identify a target market and the second step is to develop a marketing mix.
- The steps in the consumer decision-making process are: recognize a need, gather information, select and evaluate alternatives, make a purchase decision, and determine the effectiveness of the decision.

10.2 Develop Effective Products and Services

- The steps in a marketing research study are: define the marketing problem, study the situation, develop a data collection procedure, gather and analyze information, and propose a solution.
- The components of a product are the basic product, product features, options, brand name, packaging, and a guarantee or warranty.
- Products are tangible items that you can see and examine. Services are intangible activities that are consumed at the same time they are produced.

10.3 Price and Distribute Products

- Businesses use the following formula for setting the price of a product: Selling price = Product costs + Operating expenses + Profit.
- A direct channel of distribution moves products from the producer directly to the consumer with no other organizations participating. An indirect channel of distribution includes one or more other businesses between the producer and consumer. These other businesses provide one or more of the marketing functions.

10.4 Plan Promotion

- When the focus of a business is a target market, communication can be very specific to the needs of that group using media that are familiar to and trusted by those consumers.
- There are two major types of promotion. Personalized promotion communicates directly with each customer using information tailored to that person. Mass promotion communicates with many people at the same time with a common message.

Think Critically About Business

1. Most companies are not marketing businesses, but complete marketing activities as a part of their business operations. Other businesses are marketing businesses because their primary activities are to complete marketing activities. Identify three businesses from your community that are not marketing businesses and three that are marketing businesses. Justify your choices.
2. Use the Yellow Pages or search the Internet for your town or city. For each of the seven marketing functions, locate a business whose primary work relates to that function. Identify the work of the business to show how it relates to the marketing function.
3. You are planning the marketing strategy for a new portable printer that weighs less than two pounds and can fit in a backpack or briefcase. Identify one target market for the printer that is a business consumer and one that is a final consumer. Describe how the marketing mix would be similar and different for each target market.

4. Often it is believed that people will purchase the lowest-priced product available, but experience shows people will pay more for a product if they believe the higher-priced product is better than the lowest-priced products. Think of several products you purchase for which you know there are less-expensive alternatives. List the features of the products that cause you to pay a higher price. After you have developed the list, classify the reasons according to the four elements of the marketing mix: product, distribution, price, promotion.

5. The price charged for a product is affected by a number of factors. For each of the following situations, identify whether you believe it will result in a higher or lower price. Write one or two sentences to justify each answer.
   a. One customer purchases a very large quantity of a product.
   b. A business provides a high level of customer service.
   c. The product is very fragile and requires special handling.
   d. The product moves through many businesses in the channel of distribution before it reaches customers.

6. Internet services have the same traits as those provided by bricks and mortar businesses. Locate an Internet service business. Review the company's website and find information that describes how the service is intangible, inseparable, perishable, and heterogeneous.

Develop Your Business Language

Match the terms listed with the definitions.

7. Any paid form of communication through mass media directed at identified consumers to provide information and influence their actions.
8. The exchange of information so there is common understanding by all participants.
9. A specific group of consumers that have similar wants and needs.
10. The specific sequence of steps consumers follow to make a purchase.
11. The locations and methods used to make a product or service available to the target market.
12. The blending of the marketing elements.
13. Intangible activities that are consumed at the same time they are produced.
14. The activity, set of institutions, and processes for creating, communicating, delivering, and exchanging offerings that have value for customers, clients, partners, and society at large.
15. The route a product follows and the businesses involved in moving a product from the producer to the final consumer.
16. Finding solutions to problems through carefully designed studies involving consumers.
17. A company's plan that identifies how it will use marketing to achieve its goals.
18. The reasons consumers decide what products and services to purchase.
19. Direct individualized communication with prospective customers to assess their needs and assist them in satisfying those needs with appropriate products and services.
20. Any form of communication used to inform, persuade, or remind.
21. The money a customer must pay for a product or service.
22. The final business organization in an indirect channel of distribution for consumer products.
23. A set of promotional activities designed to obtain sales in the retail setting.

Key Terms

a. advertising
b. buying motives
c. channel of distribution
d. consumer decision-making process
e. distribution
f. effective communication
g. marketing
h. marketing mix
i. marketing research
j. marketing strategy
k. merchandising
l. personal selling
m. price
n. promotion
o. retailer
p. services
q. target market

4. Answers will vary. Students are to come to some conclusions about why they (and people in general) are sometimes willing to pay more for a product than necessary.

5a. Buying in quantity generally results in a lower price.

5b. High levels of personalized customer service often result in a higher price.

5c. A product that requires special handling often has a higher price.

5d. A product that passes through many businesses generally has a higher price because each business must make its profit.

6. Answers will vary. Students are to find an Internet service business and analyze how its service is intangible, inseparable, perishable, and heterogeneous.

Develop Your Business Language *Answers*

7. a. advertising
8. f. effective communication
9. q. target market
10. d. consumer decision-making process
11. e. distribution
12. h. marketing mix
13. p. services
14. g. marketing
15. c. channel of distribution
16. i. marketing research
17. j. marketing strategy
18. b. buying motives
19. l. personal selling
20. n. promotion
21. m. price
22. o. retailer
23. k. merchandising

Make Academic Connections

24. **Math** The use of intermediaries reduces the number of exchanges needed to distribute products from producers. Consider a situation where three manufacturers produce products that are purchased by 1,000 customers. Use the following information to determine the number of exchanges needed for each customer to purchase one product from each manufacturer.
    a. How many exchanges will be needed if each manufacturer sells one product to each of the 1,000 customers?
    b. How many exchanges will be needed if each manufacturer sells its products to 10 retailers and each of the retailers sells all three products to 100 customers?

25. **Research** Use the Internet, business magazines, or newspapers to locate a report on a marketing research study. Review the research and prepare a two-page analysis. The report should include the purpose of the research, the characteristics of the people studied, the data collection method, important findings, and the sponsor of the research. Describe how a business could use the research to improve its marketing strategy.

26. **Communication** Promotion is used for three purposes: to inform, to persuade, and to remind. Select a product or service with which you are familiar. Write three short radio advertisements for the product. Direct each advertisement at one of the three purposes of promotion.

27. **Math** Calculate the missing amounts in the table below for each product.

Product	Product Cost	Markup Percent	Markup Amount	Selling Price	Total Cost	Net Profit
A	$30	40	$12			$2
B		50	$50			$25
C	$60			$84	$72	

Make Your Case

DeeLites is a popular bakery in a small Iowa town. The bakery produces a variety of fresh pastries, cakes, pies, and other specialty desserts that have reduced calories. Loyal customers say that the low-calorie baked goods are better tasting than similar higher-calorie products they can purchase elsewhere. Customers have encouraged the owner of DeeLites to allow ordering over the Internet so their friends and relatives from other cities and states can purchase the products. The owner would like to increase sales, but is concerned whether the Internet is a good way to expand.

28. What would be the advantages of using the Internet to expand sales?

29. What changes in the marketing mix would have to be made to sell products using the Internet?

Interactions and Connections

30. Interview three people from your community to learn more about the consumer decision-making process. One person should be approximately your age or younger, another at least 10 years older than you, and the third at least 20 years older than you. Ask each to identify a product they recently purchased. Then ask them questions about how they decided they needed to make the purchase, how they gathered information about choices, and how they made the decision, as well as their satisfaction following the decision. Ask them if they believe they made an effective decision or not and why. When you have completed all of the interviews, compare the procedures they followed with the steps of the consumer decision-making process.

Make Academic Connections *Answers*

24a. 3 manufacturers × 1,000 customers = 3,000 exchanges

24b. 3 manufacturers × 10 retailers = 30 exchanges; 10 retailers × 100 customers = 1,000 exchanges; 30 + 1,000 = 1,030 exchanges

25. Findings will vary.

26. Advertisements will vary. Encourage interested students to work with classmates to produce their ads using live or recorded performances.

27. Product A: selling price, $42; total cost, $40. Product B: product cost, $100; selling price, $150; total cost, $125. Product C: markup percent, 40%; markup amount, $24; net profit, $12.

Make Your Case *Answers*

28. Using the Internet would allow DeeLites to expand its market. It would also allow DeeLites to increase awareness of its products and communicate quickly with customers.

29. By carefully designing its website, DeeLites could maintain its concept of a sweet shop, but it would become a virtual shop. Pricing may have to be adjusted to include shipping and any additional expenses involved. Promotions would have to include keyword use on the website to attract hits, and DeeLites would want to advertise the website to existing customers. Distribution would include new shipping methods. The goods probably would not change unless there were adjustments needed to ensure freshness and stability in shipping, and services would have to increase to include personnel to handle incoming orders. Services would also have to shift to include phone or e-mail communication.

Interactions and Connections

30. Students are to talk to several people of different ages about the consumer decision-making process, then compare how they made buying decisions and whether there were differences based on age.

31. The Internet is a very strong tool for marketing research. Companies can place surveys online, run online focus groups, and deliver alternative web page content to see what is most effective. Harris Interactive, part of the global Nielsen marketing research company, has 6 million members from more than 80 different countries in its Harris Poll Online Panel.

Visit the Harris Interactive website. Evaluate the benefits that this research service offers customers. Read an article that appears under the "News" tab. Describe how the information that Harris has collected could help a business.

Browse through the Harris site and list the strategic marketing solutions where Harris provides marketing research services.

List three of the omnibus groups that Harris uses to collect information for companies. Why would companies be interested in these market segments?

Advertising Campaign

Successful businesses develop effective advertising campaigns that outline the schedule of all planned advertising and all sales promotion activities.

For this event, the advertising campaign may be completed by individuals or teams consisting of two or three members. Participants in the event must demonstrate critical-thinking skills to develop an advertising campaign for an existing business. The advertising campaign must outline all planned advertising and sales promotion activities for an entire year. The advertising campaign should also include a budget for all activities.

The advertising campaign document must follow guidelines provided by DECA. Participants will have 10 minutes to present the advertising campaign to the judge or class. Visual aids and a copy of the advertising campaign may be used during the presentation. Five minutes are scheduled following the presentation for the judge or class to ask questions.

Performance Indicators Evaluated

- Conduct research to determine the most effective advertising strategies.
- Analyze facts about existing advertising campaigns to make the best choices.
- Demonstrate critical-thinking and problem-solving skills.
- Work effectively as a team.
- Prioritize tasks and practice time management.
- Demonstrate oral and written communication skills.

You will be evaluated for:

- Quality of research findings and conclusions
- Credibility of the proposed advertising campaign
- Ability to present information in a convincing manner with factual information

For more detailed information about performance indicators, go to the DECA website.

Think Critically

1. Why must a business outline an advertising campaign for an entire year?
2. Why is it important to research the competition when developing an advertising campaign?
3. Why is the budget an important element of the advertising campaign?
4. How could a consumer panel's input strengthen the advertising campaign?

www.deca.org

WINNING EDGE

Advertising Campaign

Think Critically *Answers*

1. Companies create advertising campaigns for a full year to determine how much money must be budgeted. Promotional events and advertising take time to develop. An ad campaign is prepared for an entire year to allow enough time to successfully carry out the proposed promotional activities and plan for the needed resources.

2. Research will allow the team to determine effective advertising and promotional strategies for successful companies and incorporate the strategies into their advertising campaigns.

3. Advertising and promotional activities require money. The budget will be the guide for advertising and promotional activities.

4. Businesses that seek the input of target markets are more likely to develop successful advertising campaigns that will result in greater sales.

31. Students should find research related to marketing strategy, product and service innovation, brand communication, stakeholder relationships, performance measurement, and corporate reputation. A sample of specialty Omnibus panels include Global, Youth, Parent, Influencers, Affluent, and Boomer. Companies are interested in these market segments because each represents a viable market segment for business.

CHAPTER OVERVIEW

In this chapter, students will obtain a basic knowledge of the use of computer systems and technology in various business settings.

11.1 Computer Systems

In this lesson, an overview of computer systems, along with various software applications, is presented.

11.2 Business Applications of Technology

Management information systems and other uses of technology, including e-commerce, are discussed in this lesson.

11.3 Other Technology Issues

This lesson considers some of the workplace and personal applications of technology, along with various social concerns.

Chapter 11 Business and Technology

Reuters/Landov

Instructor Resources

- Activities and Study Guide IE
- Chapter and Unit Tests IE
- Lesson Plans
- PowerPoint Presentation
- Cognero Test, Ch. 11

Student Resources

Activities and Study Guide
www.cengage.com/swep/pob9e
- Portfolio Activity

PLANNING A CAREER IN . . .

INFORMATION TECHNOLOGY

Almost every job in business is touched by technology. Technology supports core business functions such as communication through phones and e-mail, information storage and processing by computers, and reporting through printing, presentations, and conferencing.

Related Job Titles

- **Information Systems Manager**
- **Computer Programmer**
- **Software Engineer**
- **Computer Support Specialist**
- **Network Administrator**
- **Systems Analyst**
- **Computer Scientist**
- **Database Administrator**

Information technology workers use a variety of skills and educational backgrounds to help businesses function. These skills can be used to support hardware, such as computer or communication networks. Technology workers can also support software usage by installing, programming, or training others to use computer programs.

Most high schools offer a number of computer classes. Instruction is also available at computer training centers. Some employers will pay for employees to take computer courses. Self-paced and online programs are also available. Information technology training may be achieved through a specialized vocational program or a college degree program. Knowledge of computer systems, computer languages, application software, and other technology is required for specialized positions.

Analyze Career Opportunities in . . .

INFORMATION TECHNOLOGY

Use library and Internet resources to learn more about careers in information technology. Choose one of the job titles listed in the box and answer the following questions.

1. Identify the minimum educational requirements for job. Explain other training or education that might be needed for advancement.
2. Is this a career that interests you? Describe a few things you could do to learn more about this career.

What it's like to work as a . . . Web Developer

"Should we use a Flash intro? Will a banner heading be most appropriate? What functions are required to serve the needs of this new customer?" Kellye, a web developer, is in a morning brainstorming session with her team. The team plans to have some ideas ready in time for a meeting with the customer tomorrow.

Around the world, more than three billion people access the Internet for information, entertainment, and business activities. Websites are the basic element of the Internet. Web developers analyze, plan, design, implement, and support the websites of their organizations. Many businesses use outside vendors like Kellye's company to create and maintain their websites.

Knowledge of multimedia software is a key requirement for web developers. Graphics, digital imagery, audio, and video are vital to the appeal and effectiveness of a website. Web developers are often involved with creating websites for online selling and other activities.

What about you? In what ways do you use computers and technology each day that might be the basis for a future career?

PLANNING A CAREER IN . . .

INFORMATION TECHNOLOGY

Computers and technology influence nearly every job in our society. This feature provides a focused look at employment positions directly related to information technology.

Ask students to describe some work duties for the job titles listed. Also discuss the types of skills and experiences needed for these positions. Be sure to emphasize both technology skills and other career competencies.

After reading the Career feature, ask students what they think about the position described. Do they know anyone who holds a similar job? At the conclusion of the discussion, direct students to answer the What About You question that follows the feature.

What About You?
Answer

Answers will vary. Students may not realize that their daily use of computers and technology could be preparing them for future careers.

Analyze Career Opportunities *Answers*
Student answers will vary depending on when the assignment is completed and individual interests.

Additional Career Information

Encourage students to investigate careers they find interesting and explore unfamiliar careers. Two resources for additional career information are the *Occupational Outlook Handbook*, an online publication (www.bls.gov) of the U.S. Bureau of Labor Statistics, and the O*NET Resource Center (www.onetcenter.org) developed by the U.S. Department of Labor. Information about specific careers and jobs can be used to demonstrate the relevance of skills learned in this course.

Focus on REAL LIFE

This opening situation can help to show the influence of technology in various settings in our society.

TEACH

Ask students to elaborate on the statement, "Computers are everywhere." Ask them to provide examples of where they see computers. Challenge them to identify situations where they don't actually see the computer, but they know a computer is being used. For example, they might not see a computer, but they know that a standardized test is being scored by a computer.

THINK CRITICALLY THROUGH VISUALS

Computerized records management uses electronic folders and files instead of paper files. Computers access and search records much more quickly than people could. Computers can pull information from a vast number of records and quickly prepare reports. Computers also make it easier to share file information with people in other offices.

11.1 Computer Systems

Learning Outcomes

11.1.1 Identify the main elements of a computer system.

11.1.2 Describe input devices and processing activities.

11.1.3 Explain computer storage media and output types.

Key Terms

- computer system 263
- hardware 263
- software 263
- computer network 263
- central processing unit (CPU) 265
- program 265
- computer language 265
- operating system software 265
- application software 265

Focus on REAL LIFE

Ms. Jenkins announced to her class, "The French Club will meet today during sixth period. The topic for discussion will be computers and new technology."

Fran looked at Brenda and said, "That doesn't make sense! What do computers have to do with the French Club?"

"Recently our club decided to use a database program to keep track of our membership records," said Brenda. "In addition," she went on, "the club is using e-mail to talk to students in France. Then, we are planning a video conference with other French clubs around the United States. We will also use our computer network to. . ."

"Wait a minute!" Fran exclaimed. "OK. OK. Computers do have a lot to do with the French Club."

"Well then, I guess you'll be coming to the meeting today after school," responded Brenda.

LO 11.1.1

COMPUTERS IN SOCIETY

Computers are everywhere. They are vital to businesses, prevalent in our homes, and key to many individuals' social lives.

Andrey_Popov/Shutterstock.com

How have computers changed records management in business?

Computers in business are used to store, process, and report information. Computers are also used to design factories, control traffic patterns, and measure medical test results.

With billions of business transactions processed each day, business needs quick, efficient processing to control its operating costs, manage resources, and stay competitive. As managers plan and implement computerized activities, they must decide how best to use technology to serve the production and distribution needs of the organization.

Smartphones have revolutionized consumer and business use of computers. Managers can access their e-mail and company applications anywhere in the world. Individuals use smartphone apps to access shopping, social media sites, and entertainment.

Different Learning Abilities

Specific Learning Disability (SLD) Motivate passive students and those lacking confidence by asking them to name some uses of computers they have observed. Encourage them to discuss some of the business applications of computers in our society.

Elements of a Computer System

Video games, smartphones, and automated highway toll collection systems all have four basic components:

1. Input device
2. Processing unit
3. Memory and storage
4. Output device

These four basic components make up what is called a **computer system**. The physical elements of a computer system are called the **hardware**. Examples of computer hardware include keyboards, cameras, microphones, speakers, monitors (or screens), chips, and printers.

Hardware is constantly changing and expanding. For example, today most computers can handle sound, graphics, animation, and video. These features are being offered on faster and more compact computers as well as other devices. Most smartphones offer some computer functions.

In contrast to hardware, **software** refers to the instructions that run the computer system. Businesses commonly use several types of software. These include word processing, spreadsheet, database, presentation, and communications programs.

> **Life-Span Plan**
>
> Do you think that you are *computer literate*—able to understand and use computers efficiently? Are you comfortable using computers? Describe how the computerization of our society and economy may affect your ability to achieve your life-span goals.

Computer Networks

Computers in businesses and schools are commonly linked together in a **computer network**. Organizations link computers together so users can share hardware, software, and data.

The Internet is the largest and best-known computer network in the world. The Internet is most often used for two activities: exchanging e-mail and accessing the World Wide Web.

The World Wide Web (WWW) is also called the Web. It allows computer users to access information on almost every topic. The Web uses text, images, hyperlinks, graphics, frames, animation, video, and audio. It is an extensive information source. This global computer network

iStockphoto.com/VvoeVale

What are the components of a computer system?

TEACH

Explain each element of a computer system. Ask students to name examples of items in each element of a computer system.

Contrast the difference between hardware and software. Ask students to describe the main purposes of hardware and software.

Provide a basic explanation of computer networks. Point out the various types of computer networks that students may have experienced in school, at home, and in stores.

Life-Span Plan Answer

Answers will vary. Students should explain why computer skills are important for achieving life-span goals.

THINK CRITICALLY THROUGH VISUALS

Desktops, laptops, and smartphones have the same components. These include a processing unit and input devices such as a keyboard, touchscreen, voice, mouse, and camera. Memory and storage devices include hard drives and memory chips. Output devices include monitors, printers, and speakers.

Different Learning Styles

Visual Learner Encourage visual learners to discuss each of the main elements of a computer system. Ask them to use drawings or photos to create a display that represents the main elements of a computer system.

Auditory Learner Encourage auditory learners to repeat the various terms in this lesson. Ask students to then describe the use of each item in a school or business setting.

TEACH

Explain the difference between the Internet and an intranet. Ask students to try to describe situations when each might be used.

Ask students to suggest possible uses of local computer networks in businesses and other organizations.

THINK CRITICALLY THROUGH VISUALS

Student answers will vary and will hopefully be quite creative. So many once-unimaginable devices have already been invented that this might be a difficult question. Shown here, an attendee at the 2015 Consumer Electronics Show (CES) in Las Vegas, Nevada, converses via Beam, a remote presence system manufactured by Suitable Technologies Inc.

ONGOING ASSESSMENT

CHECKPOINT ✓ ANSWER

The four main elements of a computer system are the input device(s), processing unit, memory and storage, and output device(s).

TEACH

Explain the various types of input devices.

Ask students to describe input devices they have used.

Bloomberg/Getty Images

What do you think the next innovative, popular computer-related device might be?

provides access to information, facilitates online commerce, and allows millions of people around the world to make connections. The World Wide Web is also an important source for handling business transactions.

A local computer network, sometimes called an *intranet*, is an organization's private computer network. It is based on the same communication standards as the Internet. An intranet is a smaller version of the Internet. Only members or employees can utilize an intranet. An intranet's website looks and functions just like a typical website, but it is private and only accessible to authorized users.

Like the Internet, an intranet is primarily used to share information. An intranet is an effective tool for saving time and money for companies. It can bring many benefits to an organization.

CHECKPOINT ✓
List the four main elements of a computer system.

LO 11.1.2

INPUT AND PROCESSING

Computer systems start with the entering of data or other input items. Operation of the system continues with the processing of the data.

Input: Getting Started

The first major component of a computer system is known as *input*. While people are mostly concerned with the results of computer operations, there has to be a starting point. Data is entered into a computer system with an input device.

The keyboard, either as a separate device or a touch screen, is a common input device. Keyboards are generally used to enter text and numbers. Another common input device is the mouse, a hand-controlled device used to point to commands or images on the computer screen.

Other input devices are often used for specific activities. The list in the next page includes some common examples.

Different Learning Abilities

English Language Learners (ELL) Obtain translations of the four components of a computer system, as well as other key terms in the lesson, to reinforce these concepts in both English and other dominant languages used by students. Use visuals and ask students to name the items in both English and other languages.

- Touchpads built into smartphones, tablets, and laptop computers allow the user to type and select items on the screen.
- Controllers and motion trackers for video games allow players to direct the actions of game characters.
- Touch-sensitive screens allow users to apply finger contact to enter data, give commands, and make selections.
- Laser devices use light to read bar codes to track sales, inventory, and shipping.
- Webcams allow for video conferencing anywhere in the world.
- Scanners translate words and images into computer-readable formats.
- Voice-activated systems allow words spoken into a microphone to be entered as data or translated into instructions or commands.
- Microphones and cameras allow input of audio and video.

Processing: Making Things Happen

How does data become meaningful information to be used by organizations and individuals? *Processing* is the second major component of a computer system. This activity takes place in the **central processing unit (CPU)**, which is the control center of the computer.

The CPU is the "brain" of a computer system. In a personal computer, the CPU consists of tiny chips. These chips carry instructions and data using electronic pulses.

The most common way to give instructions to a computer is with a program. A **program** is a series of detailed, step-by-step instructions that tell the computer what functions to complete.

Most powerful computer programs are in formats that are difficult to understand. The format of a computer program is a computer language. A **computer language** is a system of letters, words, numbers, and symbols used to communicate with a computer.

FYI Biometric input devices are used to recognize fingerprints, facial features, voices, and eye patterns. These personal characteristics are scanned and processed to allow access to buildings, offices, and other secured areas. They are also used to authorize access to computers, files, and specific transactions, including purchases.

The two main types of computer programs are operating system software and application software. **Operating system software** translates commands and allows application programs to interact with the computer's hardware. The most commonly used operating system for businesses is Windows®.

Application software refers to programs that perform specific tasks such as word processing, database management, or accounting. Commonly used application software includes word processing, desktop publishing, database, spreadsheet, and presentation software.

Word Processing An organization's reports, correspondence, and other information are created with word processing software. This type of program allows the

iStockphoto.com/AdamRadosavljevic

What types of smartphone apps have you found most useful in your daily life?

FYI Ask students to share any experiences they may have had with biometric input devices.

TEACH

Explain the main purpose of the *processing* phase of a computer system.

Provide an overview of various application software that students may use in school or on the job.

THINK CRITICALLY THROUGH VISUALS

Answers will vary depending on what apps students use frequently. They will probably report using smartphone apps for e-mail and instant messaging, Internet browsing, playing games, listening to music or watching videos, banking, bidding on items through eBay, or even buying concert tickets.

Portfolio Activity

Assign the Portfolio Activity for Chapter 11, available on the website for this textbook.

COLLECT Encourage students to look for information about computers and technology used in a variety of business settings.

CREATE Remind students their flowchart needs to communicate a process that uses computers in a business situation or home activity.

CONNECT Point out students need to connect their flowchart to something in their portfolio.

TEACH

Point out how desktop publishing might be used by students or in business situations.

Ask students to name various lists used by companies. Explain that these lists are usually maintained using database software.

Explain the various functions of spreadsheet software. Ask students to describe the value of these functions for businesses and other organizations.

▸ Figure 11-1 *ANSWER*

Spreadsheet software can make numerous and complex computations that are free of human error. If one figure must be changed in a spreadsheet, the entire page can be recalculated instantly. If the error were corrected manually, the entire spreadsheet would have to be copied by hand or rekeyed, providing an opportunity to introduce additional errors.

user to enter, store, revise, and print text for letters, memos, reports, or standard business forms.

Desktop Publishing Word processing activities may be expanded to produce newsletters, brochures, and other publications. Desktop publishing usually includes graphics software to prepare charts, graphs, and other visual elements. Today, computer graphics are commonly used in television commercials, movies, training materials, and in other settings with a need for visuals.

Database Software "Create a list of employees who speak a language used in Asia." This type of request would involve the use of *database software*. A *database* is an organized collection of information with data items related to one another in some way.

In recent years, *database marketing* has become a standard process. Software is used to maintain, analyze, and combine customer information files. The information about customers is then used to increase sales by better serving customer needs. For example, a household with young children might receive advertising about educational software. Using a database increases the chance of reaching potential customers who are likely to buy the product.

Spreadsheet In the past, accountants used worksheet paper with many rows and columns. Such a worksheet is an example of a manually prepared spreadsheet. *Spreadsheet software* is a program that formats data in columns and rows in order to do calculations.

The location where a column and row intersect is called a *cell*. A spreadsheet is created with specific information, words, numbers, or formulas entered into the cells. Spreadsheets are used to prepare payroll records, financial statements, budgets, and other financial documents. An example of a spreadsheet screen appears in Figure 11-1.

	A B C D E F	G	H	I	J	K	L
1		PROFIT & LOSS - ACTUAL VS. BUDGET					
2							
3		Actual		Budget		$ Over/(Under) Budget	
4							
5	Income						
6	Product Sales	432,144		450,000		(17,856)	
7	Service Sales	471,866		500,000		(28,134)	
8	Total Income	904,010		950,000		(45,990)	
9	Cost of Goods Sold						
10	Payroll-Direct Labor	186,433		200,000		(13,567)	
11	Subcontractors	201,074		172,500		28,574	
12	Other Cost of Goods Sold	34,975		42,500		(7,525)	
13	Total Cost of Goods Sold	422,482		415,000		7,482	
14	Gross Profit	481,528		535,000		(53,472)	
15	Overhead Expenses						
16	Advertising	742		500		242	
17	Bad Debt	1,050		0		1,050	
18	Depreciation	17,433		17,500		(67)	
19	Employee Benefits	32,876		35,000		(2,124)	
20	Insurance	32,777		33,500		(723)	
21	Office Expenses	2,192		2,000		192	
22	Payroll-Administrative	153,044		175,000		(21,956)	
23	Professional Fees	12,125		11,750		375	
24	Rent	67,200		67,200		0	
25	Taxes-Business	16,433		17,000		(567)	
26	Taxes-Payroll	34,362		38,000		(3,638)	
27	Travel Expenses	15,273		12,200		3,073	
28	Utilities	8,924		9,475		(551)	
29	Total Expenses	394,431		419,125		(24,694)	
30							

FIGURE 11-1
How can spreadsheet software improve accuracy?

Applied Skills

Office Technology Ask students to describe experiences with various software application programs. Instruct them to prepare a brief demonstration of the software or to show a sample of output from these various applications.

Spreadsheet software may also be used to do a *what-if* analysis of a situation. For example, a manager may want to see the effect of different prices on profit. The spreadsheet automatically recalculates for each price.

Presentation Software Creating slide shows for educational and business seminars has become very common. The use of *presentation software* allows a speaker to show text, data, photos, and other visuals. These images may be accompanied by sound effects, music, or other audio. The use of multimedia elements adds to the value and enjoyment of presentations.

CHECKPOINT ✓
What are common input devices?

Work as a TEAM

Your school experiences are continually changing because of technology. Create a list of ways in which you have used computers and other technology in school settings and when doing homework. Discuss ways in which technology might be used to enhance the school learning environment.

LO 11.1.3

MEMORY AND OUTPUT

Various programs must be stored for use in the computer system. Memory is also used for data processing activities.

Memory and Storage: Saving for Later

The third major component of a computer system is the *memory*. When in use, a program is stored in the computer's memory. This memory within the computer is also called *internal* (or *primary*) *storage*. During processing, both the program and any data entered with an input device are stored in memory.

As shown in Figure 11-2, memory capacity is measured using units such as *bit*, *nibble*, *byte*, and *kilobyte* (*K*). To give you an idea of a computer's internal storage capacity, it would take at least a 1K computer to store the information on an average page in this book.

Primary storage is accessed by the CPU for data and software processing. Primary storage cannot hold all of the data and programs needed by users, so *external* (or *auxiliary*) *storage* is accessed for most programs and data.

Data can be held on a hard disk drive, CD, DVD, memory card, or flash memory stick. For large systems, magnetic tapes may be used. Computing devices on the Internet can access the *Cloud*, or storage systems that use multiple memory devices in multiple locations to hold data for retrieval.

Output: Obtaining Results

The final component of a computer system is known as *output*. This element is of greatest interest to most people. Your score on a video game, the results of a test, or the sales for a new product are important outcomes of data processing activities.

Output devices present data in a form that can be retrieved later or may be

MEMORY CAPACITY	
Bit	smallest unit
Nibble	4 bits; a ½ byte
Byte	8 bits
Kilobyte	1,024 bytes
Megabyte	a million bytes
Gigabyte	a billion bytes
Terabyte	a thousand gigabytes

FIGURE 11-2
Why is it important to know the number of bytes of memory capacity in a computer? How many kilobytes of memory are in a computer with 3 gigabytes of memory?

TEACH

Ask students to describe situations, other than a talk or lecture, in which presentation software might be used.

ONGOING ASSESSMENT

CHECKPOINT ✓ANSWER

Common input devices include keyboard, mouse, game controller, joystick, touch-sensitive screen, scanner, voice-activated system, microphone, and camera.

Work as a TEAM

Encourage students to think of new ways to use technology in schools.

TEACH

Explain the importance of the memory component of a computer system.

Ask students to name various output devices. Discuss the benefits of various output devices.

▸ Figure 11-2 *ANSWER*

It is important to know the number of bytes of memory capacity in a computer to determine whether there is room on the system for files or programs you wish to add.

A computer with 3 gigabytes of memory has 2,929,687.5 kilobytes of memory. A gigabyte is one million bytes and a kilobyte is 1,024 bytes.

To calculate the number of kilobytes in a computer with 3 gigabytes of memory, divide 3 billion by 1,024. (3,000,000,000 ÷ 1,024 = 2,929,687.5)

Different Learning Abilities

Visually Impaired Make arrangements for students to touch and hold samples of various output devices and media to allow students to better understand these elements of a computer system.

TEACH

Provide explanations of the major output items listed on this page.

THINK CRITICALLY THROUGH VISUALS

A business's website can provide text, graphics, audio, and video output. Other examples are printed letters, forms, receipts, reports, mass mailings, and medical or school records.

ONGOING ASSESSMENT

CHECKPOINT ✓ANSWER

Internal memory is inside the computer and holds a fixed amount of data. External memory is not stored within the computer and it is highly portable.

ASSESS

Key Concepts *Answers*

1. a. input

2. d. database

3. b. DVD

Make Academic Connections *Answers*

4. If your class has the equipment and software, presentations can be created using software such as Microsoft PowerPoint.

5. After an initial investment, computer technology should help businesses run more efficiently with fewer people, so operating costs should decrease and profit should increase. Highly skilled computer workers might see an increase in their earnings. However, computer technology might decrease the need for unskilled labor.

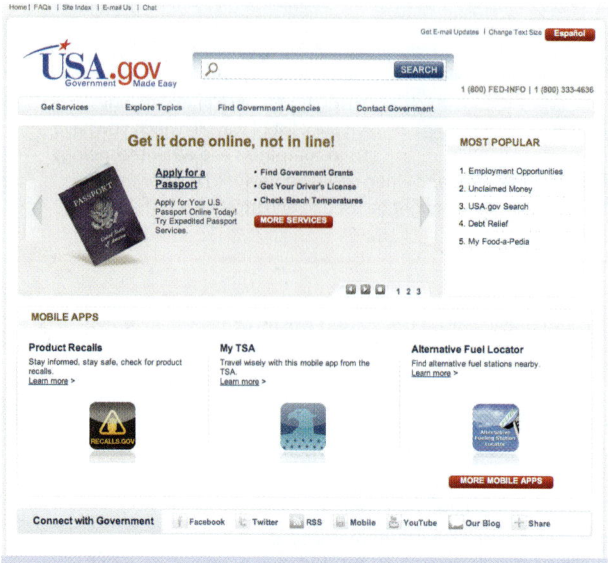

www.usa.gov

What types of data output do you expect to see on a business's website? What types of data output are used routinely in the workplace? Give some examples.

communicated immediately. There are four common types of output:

1. Text output, which includes processing results displayed on a computer screen (monitor) or in a printed report
2. Graphics output, which might include company logos, photos, drawings, scrolling messages, and animated graphics
3. Audio output, which involves music and broadcast clips as well as presentations for training seminars
4. Video output, which may be in the form of a training film, television commercial, or news report

Quite often, a single output source, such as a website, includes more than one of these categories.

CHECKPOINT ✓

How do internal and external memory differ?

11.1 ASSESSMENT

Key Concepts

Determine the best answer.

1. A computer's camera is a device in the ________ component of a computer system.
   - **a.** input
   - **b.** output
   - **c.** memory
   - **d.** processing
2. A list of potential customers for your new product would be created using ________ software.
   - **a.** desktop publishing
   - **b.** word processing
   - **c.** accounting
   - **d.** database
3. Which of the following is an example of auxiliary storage?
   - **a.** CPU
   - **b.** DVD
   - **c.** monitor
   - **d.** software

Make Academic Connections

4. **Technology** Prepare a visual presentation of a computer system and explain how each part works in the system.
5. **Economics** Describe how technology might affect the operating costs and profits of a company. What are possible effects of technology on the wages of workers?

RETEACH Divide the class into four groups, each representing one component of the computer system. Ask each group to describe various activities associated with this element.

ENRICH Ask students to develop a computer system for a local business or a company of their choice.

CLOSE Ask students to compare computer systems that might be used in different business settings.

DOING BUSINESS IN. . . EGYPT

Protected by deserts on both sides, Egypt has a tradition of architecture and culture. Today, the country is dependent on the fertile land along the Nile River. Cotton, fruits, and vegetables are some of the country's main exports. The Suez Canal provides a vital trade route between the Atlantic Ocean and the Indian Ocean.

As you enter a meeting in Egypt, several greetings may be used. The handshake is most common. Expect to see some traditional clothing, but foreign businesspeople should wear business suits. Clothing styles should always be modest and conservative. Even though the weather can be extremely hot, most of the body must remain covered. Even shirt collars are expected to be buttoned. You may be expected to take off your shoes, but only after following the lead of your host.

The workweek in Egypt runs from Saturday to Wednesday. Friday is the Muslim holy day, and most people also take off Thursday. In your negotiations, the pace will start slowly. Do not rush the situation. Because Egyptians must get to know you and like you before doing business, the decision process will take time. Also, be ready to compromise in your negotiations.

While the main language of Egypt is Arabic, many business discussions may be carried out in English or French. Business cards will be better received if one side is English and the other side is Arabic. Language meaning will not always be direct. A "yes" may in fact mean "possibly."

Be cautious of body language. The left hand is considered unclean in the Arab world. Always use your right hand unless both are needed, such as for lifting a heavy object. While Egyptians may gesture with their hands when speaking, pointing is considered very rude. The "thumbs up" sign is offensive.

Your conversations may include talk of soccer, basketball, and boxing. Avoid talking about political issues. In regard to food, many of the most popular Egyptian recipes are thousands of years old. Wheat and barley are the basis for many breads, pastries, and cakes. Peas, beans, lettuce, cucumbers, leeks, and other vegetables are often served with oil and vinegar dressing. Figs, dates, pomegranates, and grapes are important parts of the Egyptian diet, as are fish, poultry, lamb, and beef.

Think Critically

1. How does doing business in Egypt differ from business activities with which you are familiar?
2. What common mistakes might a person make when doing business in Egypt?
3. Conduct library or Internet research to find additional information about business and economic activities in Egypt.

How do climate and geography impact doing business in Egypt?

EPA/Landov

Applied Skills

Geography Provide students with maps or tell them to locate maps online. Ask students to identify the location of Egypt and surrounding countries. Based on information derived from the map, students should suggest some types of business that might be common in this region.

Doing Business in... EGYPT

While geographically located on the continent of Africa, Egypt is culturally linked to the Middle East. Remind students that most international business mistakes are the result of cultural differences.

THINK CRITICALLY THROUGH VISUALS

Egypt uses the Nile to produce fruits and vegetables for domestic consumption and export.

Think Critically *Answers*

1. Student answers will vary, but they will probably comment on the workweek running from Saturday through Thursday instead of from Monday through Friday, having a long getting-to-know-you phase before beginning negotiations instead of the Western "let's get right down to business" approach, and the fact that "yes" can mean "possibly."
2. Because the left hand is considered unclean, a two-handed handshake, considered warm in the West, would be offensive. The cheerful thumbs up sign would be considered rude. Discussing hot political issues, which Americans do freely, would also be a mistake. Scheduling business meetings on Thursday or Friday or wearing short sleeves or shorts on a hot day would also send negative messages.
3. Students will find varied information about Egypt depending on what sources they locate during their library or Internet research. Consider asking each student to share his or her most interesting findings.

Focus on REAL LIFE

This scenario provides an overview of business uses of computers. Ask students to describe situations in which they have seen computers and other technology in work situations.

TEACH

Ask students to explain why information is important for making decisions in business and other settings.

Explain the purpose of a management information system (MIS).

THINK CRITICALLY THROUGH VISUALS

Computer systems and software are essential parts of an MIS because they organize, process, and store an organization's vital information.

11.2 Business Applications of Technology

Learning Outcomes

11.2.1 Describe the components of a management information system (MIS).

11.2.2 Identify computer applications in service industries.

11.2.3 Discuss e-commerce activities.

Key Terms

management information system (MIS) 270
computer-assisted instruction (CAI) 272
e-commerce 274

Focus on REAL LIFE

Josh Aki arrived on the first day of his new part-time job at NBI Distributors. This retailing company sells an array of products by mail, telephone orders, and the Internet.

During orientation, Josh met the sales manager and learned that some of the firm's products were doing well and others were just sitting in the warehouse. After he got settled at his desk, Josh's supervisor said, "Josh, please outline a report with the sales results of the new products we have introduced over the past six months. Alicia will help you get started."

After some initial pleasantries, Alicia showed Josh how to check the database for sales results. She suggested that he summarize the data on the spreadsheet program and prepare his report with word processing software.

"Thanks, will you be around if I need more help?" Josh asked.

Alicia smiled and said, "Sure, Josh. Welcome to the NBI team."

LO 11.2.1

MANAGEMENT INFORMATION SYSTEMS

Managers need information to make business decisions. A **management information system (MIS)** is a coordinated system of processing and reporting information in an organization. Computer systems and software are essential parts of management information systems.

A company may need a departmental budget that provides information on expected income and expenses for the next three months. Using an accounting program, past company data and future projections can be processed to create this budget. Budgets help with day-to-day decisions and planning for the future.

Digital Vision/Getty Images

Why are computer systems and software essential parts of an MIS?

Components of an MIS

As shown in Figure 11-3 on the next page, the four main components of an MIS are gathering data, analyzing data, storing data, and reporting results. These activities allow an organization to obtain needed information in four main categories—financial, production and inventory, marketing and sales, and human resources.

Applied Skills

Technology Ask students to explain why information needs vary for different types of industries. Help start the discussion by asking students to think about the information needs of a particular business, such as a local manufacturing company or grocery store.

Main Components of Management Information Systems

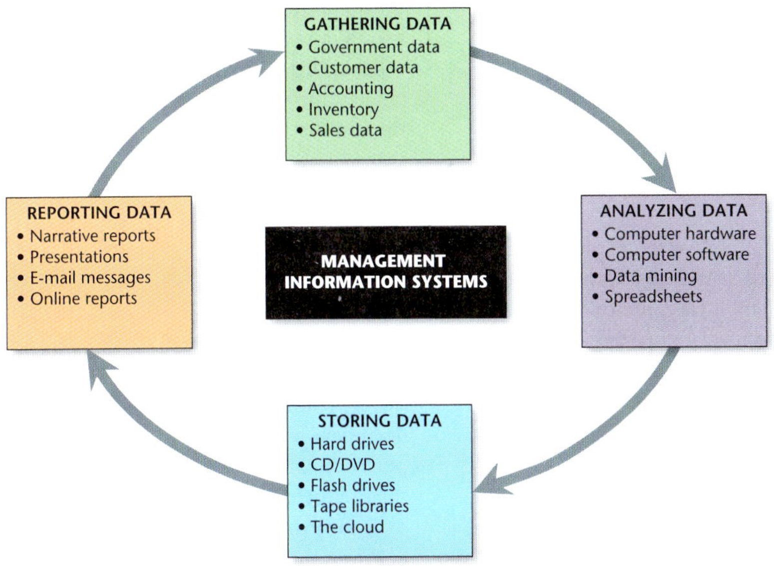

FIGURE 11-3
Explain why these functions are important for decision making and how they are interconnected.

1. *Financial information*, including budgets, sales reports, and financial statements
2. *Production and inventory information*, including production summaries, lists of tools and supplies, and finished goods reports
3. *Marketing and sales information*, including data on customer needs, current economic conditions, and actions of competitors
4. *Human resources information*, including salaries, employee benefit data, and employee evaluations

Data Sources

The information for an MIS comes from several sources. *External data sources* are outside an organization. Financial institutions, government agencies, and customers are examples of external data sources.

In contrast, *internal data sources* provide input from within the organization. Internal data includes accounting records, inventory information, and company sales figures. While gathering raw data may be an easy task, changing these facts and figures into meaningful information is the major goal of an MIS.

The MIS in Action

What activities are involved in a management information system? How is needed information communicated to managers? The operation of the MIS involves the following steps:

1. Identify the information needs of the organization.
2. Obtain facts, figures, and other data.
3. Process, analyze, and organize data in a useful manner.
4. Distribute information reports to those who make decisions.
5. Update data files as needed.

TEACH

Use Figure 11-3 to provide an overview of elements of a management information system (MIS).

Explain the four types of information most commonly used by businesses.

Contrast the difference between external and internal data sources. Ask students to name examples of each.

Describe the five steps of a management information system (MIS).

▸ **Figure 11-3** ***ANSWER***

Students should respond that information is often collected from multiple sources. Information must then be analyzed and stored so it can be accessed for developing reports. Provide examples of how information is used to make decisions in business, schools, government, and other organizations.

Different Learning Styles

Kinesthetic Learner Instruct students to use Figure 11-3 and the steps involved in the operation of an MIS to create a poster, tabletop display, or slide presentation. Provide an opportunity for students to display their work.

Work as a TEAM

This activity can help expand student awareness of both technology and global business activities.

ONGOING ASSESSMENT

CHECKPOINT ✓ANSWER

The four components are gathering data, analyzing data, storing data, and reporting results.

TEACH

Ask students to name types of service companies. Ask how information needs might differ among various types of service businesses.

Point out some of the uses of technology by government agencies.

Explain various types of computer-assisted instruction.

THINK CRITICALLY THROUGH VISUALS

Students may not realize how much computers have changed the educational environment because they have grown up with computers in the classroom. Today, even very young students can use interactive programs. Teachers use computers to calculate grades, communicate by e-mail with parents and colleagues, and create teaching presentations. Students use computers to take tests, conduct research, and receive enrichment or remedial instruction. With computer-assisted instruction (CAI), students can learn at home on a computer connected to a training location.

Work as a TEAM

Websites for international business must be adapted to cultural factors in other countries. Design a website for doing business in another country. Consider the language, format, design, colors, graphics, and other factors.

Computer networks are often used in an MIS to distribute information to managers, employees, and others. These networks connect computers, printers, and other equipment within a company or around the world.

Worldwide networks are set up through telephone lines, satellites, and other communication technology. Also important for communicating information is e-mail. E-mail gives users the ability to send data quickly through a computer system. After an employee prepares a letter or report, the document is sent electronically to another computer on the local or worldwide network.

CHECKPOINT ✓

What are the four components of a management information system?

LO 11.2.2

TECHNOLOGY IN SERVICE INDUSTRIES

Almost 80 percent of workers in the United States are employed in service industries. The use of computers in these organizations is extensive.

Public Service

Government agencies use computers to keep records. For example, the federal government keeps social security records for all past and present workers in the United States and military records for people who have served in the armed forces.

Agencies are always expanding their use of computers. Medical information can be found within seconds; this can save lives. Police records can be sent to other locations minutes after a crime has occurred, helping to solve the crime. Schools and other agencies can transfer records easily when someone moves to another area of the country.

Education

Computers have become vital teaching devices. Computers make it possible to train and test workers in a range of professions. Office workers use word processing software in their daily tasks. The software helps them with the proper use of grammar, spelling, punctuation, capitalization, and document formats. Airline pilots use computerized simulators to learn and improve skills needed for flying new types of aircraft.

Computer-assisted instruction (CAI) is the use of computers to help people learn or improve skills at their own pace. With CAI, students work at a speed that best serves their needs. The

iStockphoto.com/sjlocke

How have computers changed the classroom in recent years?

Applied Skills

Writing Across the Curriculum Assign students to write a short report that describes the use of technology in settings other than business, education, government, or health care. For example, they could focus on science, agriculture, music, or art.

student does not have to go to a school building for instruction. The student can learn at home on a computer network system connected to a central training location.

The demand for computer and *information technology* (IT) training in the workplace continues to grow. With the proper computer skills, you will be able to compete for some of the best-paying jobs in the business world.

Health Care

Computers are widely used in hospitals and other medical facilities. Uses range from keeping patient records to monitoring medications during surgery.

Medical professionals are also able to see to the healthcare needs of people in rural areas without leaving the city. The use of *telemedicine* with video-conferencing equipment allows diagnosis by a doctor in a different location, followed by treatment provided by a local healthcare professional. Technology of this type helps to expand the availability of health care in remote areas of less-developed economies.

Financial Services

Paying bills online, checking your credit report, and selling stocks and bonds are just a few examples of computerized financial activities. Electronic banking and other financial services have enabled consumers to do business beyond usual banking hours. Each day, computers transfer billions of dollars. Payments to workers, businesses, and government flow through local and global computer networks.

Most people are familiar with credit cards and cash cards. You may not be aware of the existence of *smart cards*. These plastic cards with a silicon chip are used to store information. The chip within the card stores such data as your current account balance and credit history. It may even store medical information for emergencies.

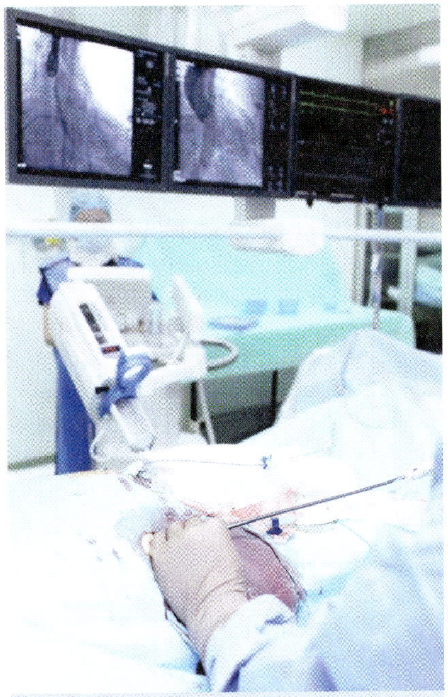

sfam_photo/Shutterstock.com

What are some of the benefits of computers in science?

Such cards can serve as personal record keepers for travel and other expenses. In addition, a smart card can be used to prove you paid for merchandise you want to exchange, to gain admittance to your place of work, or to unlock and start your car without keys.

CHECKPOINT ✓
What service industries make extensive use of computers?

FYI The use of mobile phones and other wireless technology is sometimes called "m-commerce" (m for mobile). Various handheld devices are expanding and enhancing e-commerce activities. Instant messaging, stock trading, banking, online shopping, music, and sports video clips are most common. Close to 75 percent of the world's population will use wireless technology in the near future.

TEACH

Explain the importance of information technology (IT) departments in every type of organization.

Describe uses of computer systems for banking, insurance, and other financial services.

THINK CRITICALLY THROUGH VISUALS

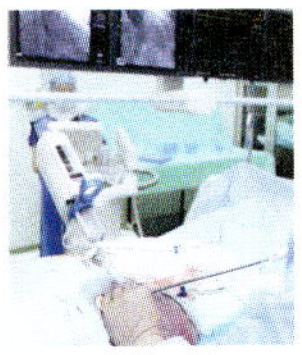

Computers allow scientists to work with large and complex calculations and vast amounts of data so they can quickly and accurately draw conclusions from experiments and extrapolate their findings to solve challenging problems.

ONGOING ASSESSMENT

CHECKPOINT ✓ ANSWER

Service industries that make extensive use of computers include public service organizations such as government, military, and police agencies; educational institutions such as local school districts, community colleges, and universities; healthcare facilities, such as hospitals and doctors' offices; and financial services industries, such as banks and insurance companies.

FYI

Point out the expanded use of wireless technology in various business settings. Challenge students to think of new business applications for mobile technology.

Different Learning Abilities

Gifted Ask students to research and report findings on new developments related to wireless technology uses for various business, school, and government situations.

TEACH

Explain the basics of e-commerce. Remind students that e-commerce involves more than buying and selling online. Point out the e-commerce activities listed on this page.

Describe examples of B2C and B2B transactions—the most common e-commerce patterns.

THINK CRITICALLY THROUGH VISUALS

Many students may assert that e-commerce provides more opportunities for entrepreneurs of all ages because it allows for easy entry into markets at low costs. It also opens up the entire world as a possible market.

▶ Figure 11-4 *ANSWER*

Answers will vary. Students should discuss how the Internet allows buyers and sellers to communicate, exchange information about products and prices, and facilitate purchases.

LO 11.2.3

E-COMMERCE

You are walking through the mall. As you pass a clothing store, a message appears on your smartphone screen. "Now on special for spring, waterproof jackets, $34.95." This targeted promotion is just one example of the fast, powerful capabilities of e-commerce and wireless technology.

E-commerce (e for *electronic*) refers to conducting business transactions using the Internet or other technology. These online business activities come in a range of forms. Almost every function of a company has been adapted to e-commerce. The most common e-commerce activities include:

- Providing product information
- Promoting a company
- Selling online
- Conducting market research
- Making payments
- Obtaining parts and supplies
- Tracking shipments

Types of E-Commerce

E-commerce opens up opportunities to companies previously limited by geographic, financial, or political restrictions. These online economic activities involve four basic models with two selling and buying parties: businesses (B) and consumers (C). See Figure 11-4.

E-Commerce Matrix

	Business Seller	Consumer Seller
Business Buyer	B2B	C2B
Consumer Buyer	B2C	C2C

FIGURE 11-4
How does the Internet help each of these e-commerce models operate efficiently?

Do you think e-commerce provides more opportunities for an entrepreneur?

The first and most familiar model is Business-to-Consumer, or B2C. Most large retailers have looked to B2C for sales growth. Amazon is an online-only retailer. Most other retailers have their own website. Walmart.com, target.com, and bestbuy.com are examples.

The second e-commerce model is Business-to-Business, or B2B. These online exchanges are the largest and fastest-growing segment of e-commerce. More than $500 billion in B2B commerce is transacted each year in the United States. For instance, Ford and General Motors buy many parts online from their suppliers.

Consumer-to-Business (C2B) is the third e-commerce model. In C2B, consumers originate online transactions through price offers to businesses. The online company Priceline was one of the first companies in this category. Priceline allows shoppers to make bids for products and services such as airline tickets and hotels. The airline and hotel companies then decide whether to accept the offers. Although C2B activity is not presently as prevalent as the first two models, it could expand with new technologies and consumer initiatives.

Finally, Consumer-to-Consumer (C2C) is the fourth e-commerce model. In the long

Applied Skills

Technology Encourage students to investigate the use of blogs on various topics. What are the benefits and drawbacks of this communication activity?

economic tradition of bartering and auctions, buying and selling among consumers is growing in cyberspace. The ease and speed of transactions among online parties is encouraging more C2C exchanges. An example is the online company eBay.

Global E-Commerce

Internet-based computer systems, along with software that translates information from one language to another, make it possible to do business around the world without leaving your computer. Instant transmission of data with the use of satellites makes even the farthest point on earth as close as a button on your computer. Increased global business can have an important impact on world trade and international relations.

Importing and exporting can be facilitated by a computer system. Goods are shipped from the closest location to save time and money. For example, you may order an item from a company in Italy using your computer. When the Italian marketers receive your order on their computer, they check a database and find there are five such items in stock in Canada. They instruct the Canadian importers through the Internet to ship one of the items to you. You receive it the next day.

You pay the Italian company. Later, the Italian and Canadian companies settle their accounts through the computerized banking system.

Another way of bringing people together to do business is *video conferencing*. This system allows people in different geographic locations to meet "face-to-face" by satellite. It is used for sales presentations, training sessions, and other types of meetings. A sales staff in Peru can make a presentation to potential customers in Spain, South Africa, Pakistan, and the United States without leaving their offices in Lima.

Life-Span Plan

Have you purchased products online? Conducted searches for product information online? Do you have ideas for products you would like to sell online? Explain how you believe the growth of e-commerce will affect the life-span goals you set or your ability to achieve them.

CHECKPOINT

What do the notations B2C and B2B mean?

11.2 ASSESSMENT

Key Concepts

Determine the best answer.

1. An example of external data would be
   a. a company sales report
   b. a list of employee qualifications
   c. a government economic forecast
   d. payroll records
2. CAI refers to
   a. paying bills online
   b. electronic inventory control
   c. providing health care to remote areas
   d. individualized instruction
3. When a packaged food producer sells items to a restaurant, this is considered to be a ________ e-commerce transaction.
   a. B2C
   b. B2B
   c. C2B
   d. C2C

Make Academic Connections

4. **Visual Art** Create a visual presentation of a management information system for a specific information flow for a company of your choice.
5. **Culture** Research other cultures to determine how people in these societies might react to various aspects of e-commerce.

Life-Span Plan Answer

Answers will vary. Students should describe how the growth of e-commerce has changed the life-span goals they might set for themselves.

TEACH

Ask students to consider the benefits and limitations of global e-commerce.

Then ask them to list the types of businesses that would best be served by global e-commerce.

ONGOING ASSESSMENT

CHECKPOINT ANSWER

The notation B2C refers to the Business-to-Consumer e-commerce model, while B2B means the Business-to-Business e-commerce model.

ASSESS

Key Concepts Answers

1. c. a government economic forecast
2. d. individualized instruction
3. b. B2B

Make Academic Connections Answers

4. Presentations will vary depending on which companies' management information systems students choose to illustrate.
5. Findings will vary. For example, potential buyers in Middle Eastern and African cultures who value face-to-face negotiation before closing a business deal might resist the impersonal nature of e-commerce.

CLOSE Ask students to describe the uses of technology by various businesses in your community.

RETEACH Ask students to discuss the purpose and elements of a management information system (MIS).

ENRICH Challenge students to design a product that might be sold online to consumers around the world. Invite interested students to plan a website to accommodate e-commerce for this product.

Focus on REAL LIFE

Use this segment to point out some of the ways technology influences the way people live, work, and play. Be sure to include both the positive and the negative changes that technology has delivered.

TEACH

Explain the benefits of robotics in various work settings.

Describe situations in which artificial intelligence and expert systems are commonly used.

11.3 Other Technology Issues

Learning Outcomes

11.3.1 Explain workplace uses of technology.

11.3.2 Identify home and personal applications of technology.

11.3.3 Discuss social concerns related to technology.

Key Terms

- robotics 276
- artificial intelligence (AI) 276
- expert systems 277
- computer-aided design (CAD) 277
- telecommuting 277
- piracy 280
- computer virus 280

Focus on REAL LIFE

Herb Cunningham is a talented worker, but he has seen demand for his skills as a bookkeeper declining. More and more, computerized accounting systems are keeping track of sales and expenses in companies.

"I guess it's time to upgrade my technology skills," Herb commented to his son, Joe. "I'm going to enroll in an online training class for accounting software."

"That's a good idea, but it might not be enough, Dad," responded Joe. "You should learn how to use spreadsheets, work with tax software, and learn about computer-based accounting systems."

"I'm not sure I'll be able to learn how to do all of those things," was Herb's reply.

"But, Dad, I'll be here to help you," said Joe. "We are learning how to use this type of software in school. My teacher has also told us that the local college is using computer-assisted instruction to teach modern bookkeeping practices."

LO 11.3.1

WORKPLACE TECHNOLOGY

Computers are present in almost every business situation. They help improve efficiency and productivity. Computers can be found in oil fields, warehouses, retail stores, hospitals, offices, and factories.

Robotics

Most of you have seen robots and other computer systems in science fiction movies set in outer space and in the future. Currently, **robotics** involves mechanical devices programmed to do routine tasks, such as those in many factories. Robots are often used for assembly line work that requires repetitive tasks.

Early robots did only simple tasks, such as tightening a bolt on an automobile. Today, robots exist that can see, hear, smell, and feel. These computerized workers can perform in such dangerous settings as outer space, underwater, or underground. Newer robots are being developed that can roll, walk, run, and communicate with people. As technology advances, robots will handle more complex tasks.

Expert Systems

Have you ever wanted a quick answer to a question without having to find a book or person who knew the answer? **Artificial intelligence (AI)** is software that enables computers to reason, learn, and make decisions. It uses logical methods similar to the methods humans use. IBM developed an artificial intelligence system called Watson. Watson played the television quiz game *Jeopardy!* and defeated the best human opponents. This required Watson to interpret a statement such as, "This person

Different Learning Abilities

Dyslexia Prepare some short assignments requiring answers with a few words to help students understand robotics and expert systems. For example, ask students to make a list of specific uses of robotics. Encourage all students to participate.

could not tell a lie," and then respond with a question, "Who is George Washington?"

Computer programs such as Watson that help people solve technical problems are called **expert systems**. They are now available for medical services, financial planning, and legal matters. Expert systems are based on the knowledge of human experts in many specialized areas. These systems provide intelligent answers as effectively as human experts in those subject matters. For example, employees of the Internal Revenue Service use an expert system to quickly answer questions from taxpayers.

Computer-Aided Design

Computers created many of the products you use each day. **Computer-aided design (CAD)** refers to the use of technology to create product styles and designs. CAD allows businesses to try different sizes, shapes, and materials for a new machine, automobile, or food package. This process can be used to experiment with many variations before spending time and money building a model or going into production.

CAD systems are used in conjunction with 3D printers to create models and final products. 3D printers act mechanically like an inkjet printer, but instead of ink they spray melted plastic or metal compounds. A combination of CAD systems and 3D printers has lowered the cost of customized manufacturing and the development of prototypes.

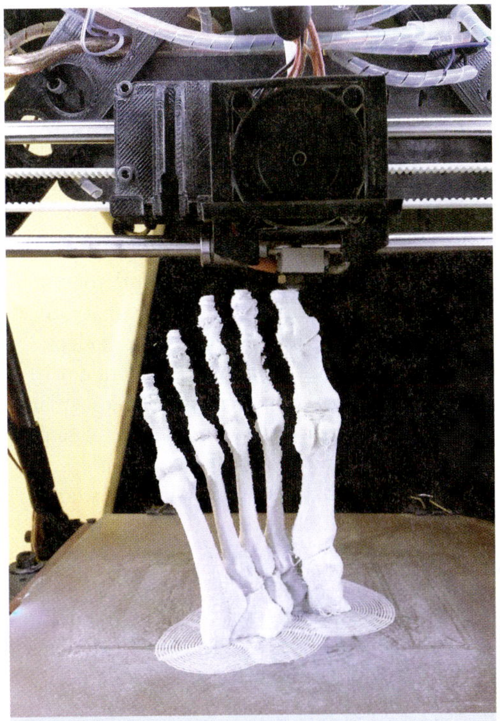

Dario Sabljak/Shutterstock.com

What types of businesses might use computer-aided design?

Telecommuting

Each morning, more than 3 million Americans travel to their offices—in another room of their homes! These people do all or part of their work at home. **Telecommuting** involves the activities of a worker using a computer at home to do a job. Telecommuting saves travel time and costs. It results in less traffic along with reduced noise and air pollution.

Each year more people become telecommuters. This working arrangement is especially attractive to people who have a hard time leaving their home to go to work. These include workers who are disabled or parents who want to be with their young children. A work-at-home arrangement is most common among workers such as writers and editors, researchers, accounting clerks, sales representatives, computer programmers, and website designers.

These workers can easily send their reports, documents, and ideas to their employers by computer. Telecommuting is made possible with computers and other technology. E-mail and faxes allow an employee to communicate with the company's main office.

CHECKPOINT ✓
How is computer-aided design (CAD) used by businesses?

TEACH

Ask students to name situations in which expert systems might be used.

Explain the uses of computer-aided design (CAD) in various settings.

Ask students to describe work situations that would be appropriate for telecommuting.

THINK CRITICALLY THROUGH VISUALS

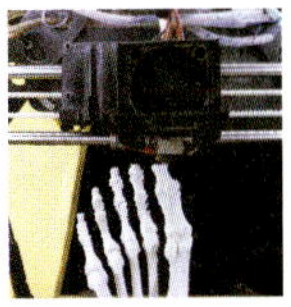

Computer-aided design (CAD) is a wonderful tool for businesses such as medicine or medical research, architects, engineering firms, packaging designers, manufacturers, and any business that needs to create a three-dimensional object.

ONGOING ASSESSMENT

CHECKPOINT ✓ANSWER

Businesses use CAD to experiment with many variations of different sizes, shapes, and materials before spending time and money on building prototypes or starting actual production.

Applied Skills

Science Encourage students to research the use of computer-aided design (CAD) and 3D printing in various laboratory and production settings.

Teaching Strategies

Expand Beyond the Classroom Invite a local business professional to speak to students about robotics, expert systems, computer-aided design, or telecommuting.

TEACH

Explain common uses of computers and technology in home settings.

Ask students to describe their observations of computer use in homes.

NET KNOWLEDGE

Students should use a search engine to visit the Apple free app page. Suggested categories include social networking, games, entertainment, research, and large company apps. Creative ideas will vary. Students should take their creative ideas and input those terms along with "app" in a search engine to see if such an app already exists.

THINK CRITICALLY THROUGH VISUALS

The highest percentage of use for Facebook is information posting. Twitter is used most often for messaging. These are followed by Instagram for photo sharing, Pinterest for sharing ideas, and Tumblr for blogging.

ONGOING ASSESSMENT

CHECKPOINT ✓ANSWER

Available tools include word processing software for preparing written assignments, Internet browsers for conducting research, online dictionaries and encyclopedias, and presentation software for creating slide shows.

LO 11.3.2

HOME AND PERSONAL TECHNOLOGY

Computers not only change the way you work, but technology also affects almost all aspects of life.

School and Homework

Computers are a key homework tool for students. Census reports show that more than 90 percent of high school students' homes have computers. In addition to traditional computers, students use smartphones to access the Internet for research, homework, and collaboration with peers. One problem is that low-income students have less technology access at home.

In 2011, a tornado destroyed the high school in Joplin, Missouri. When the school was rebuilt it became "paperless." The school received laptops for students as a gift from United Arab Emirates. There are no paper textbooks for students or books in the library. Everything is accessed through computers.

Home Robotics

Robots are no longer just found in factories and businesses. Computerized systems now exist for repetitive chores such as vacuuming and mowing the lawn. Toys and other electronic devices for children can both entertain and educate. In the future, you can expect home robots to monitor household appliances, roll trash cans to the street, and assist the elderly with lifting heavy items.

Monkey Business Images/Shutterstock.com

What are the most common uses for the major social networks?

Social Networking

The Pew Research Center has found that almost 75 percent of Americans engage in some type of social networking. The highest percentage use is for Facebook for information posting and Twitter for messaging. These are followed by Instagram for photo sharing, Pinterest for sharing ideas, and Tumblr for blogging.

LinkedIn is a professional social networking site used by more than 300 million people worldwide. Professionals can post information about their career skills and be endorsed by other professionals. In the hiring process, many businesses use LinkedIn to review potential employees' skills instead of traditional résumés.

Pew has found that individuals who use social networking sites are less socially isolated, have more close relationships, and get more support from their friends. Social networks are easily accessed on smartphones.

NET KNOWLEDGE

Apps seem to be everywhere. Apple's App Store reached 20,000 new apps a month with 20 billion downloads in one year. Individuals around the world are developing apps for iOS, Android, and Windows operating systems.

The ability to develop apps requires both programing skills and the development of creative ideas. Use a search engine to visit Apple's free app page at the iTunes website. Develop a category list of the different types of apps available. Of the apps listed, choose the one that you find most useful and explain why.

CHECKPOINT ✓

What types of technology tools are available to students?

Applied Skills

Mathematics Instruct students to survey friends and relatives to obtain data on the types of software most commonly used in homes. Assign students to work in small groups to combine their data and create a graph reporting the results of their surveys.

LO 11.3.3

SOCIAL CONCERNS OF TECHNOLOGY

New technology will continue to expand the potential uses of computers in business. New software will eliminate some jobs while increasing job growth in others. It will also continue to change the way work is done.

Expanded computer use has resulted in concerns about health and safety, criminal activities, and privacy. While computers are beneficial to society, the wise person will not place complete faith in the reliability or safety of computer systems.

Employment Trends

Many people think computers are taking away their jobs. What is actually occurring is a shift in the job duties and skills needed to work in business and industry. When computers replace workers, companies need to retrain the workers with skills in programming, operating, or repairing computer systems.

Displaced workers are workers who are unemployed because of changing job conditions. They must adapt to the changing job market in order to have continued employment. What actions can companies and workers take to be ready for the new jobs of the future?

Computers and other technology are becoming more important in our lives each day. The ability to use this technology is vital to each person's economic survival. *Computer literacy* is the ability to use computers to process information or solve problems. You do not have to understand how to program a computer in order to use it. You do need to know how to enter, store, process, and retrieve information.

Health Concerns

Various products and substances can be dangerous. While little danger exists from using computers and other technology, some people have encountered discomfort resulting from on-the-job activities. For example, eyestrain and vision problems have been linked with prolonged work at computer screens. Muscle tension and nerve damage can occur from too many hours at a keyboard. These and other concerns have resulted in guidelines from labor organizations and government agencies for safe computer operation.

Computer Crime

Widespread use of computers has led to an increase in white-collar crime. *White-collar crime* is illegal acts carried out by office or professional workers while at work. Workers may steal money, information, or computer time through improper use of databases or illegal access to computer systems.

While the typical bank robbery results in a loss of $5,000, computer crimes involving banks can be much more costly. In one case, more than $1 billion was stolen from a series of banks outside of the United States. Theft of a physical item is obvious. Theft of computer time or information from a database is usually harder to detect.

Piracy is stealing or illegally copying software packages or information. It can be a significant problem. In some countries,

Yuri Arcurs/Shutterstock.com

What concerns have resulted from the use of computer technology?

TEACH

Ask students to name some concerns that could result from technology.

Point out the need for continuing education related to technology.

Explain potential health concerns related to technology.

Ask students to explain the costs to society that result from criminal activity using computers.

THINK CRITICALLY THROUGH VISUALS

The use of computer technology has brought benefits but also concerns. Repetitious motions in non-ergonomic computer work environments have led to carpal tunnel syndrome, possible eyestrain, and other health problems. Some workers will be displaced by new computer technology. Technology provides new opportunities for white-collar computer crime, identity theft, piracy of computer software and other copyrighted materials, identity theft and other privacy concerns, and the ravages of computer hackers and virus creators.

Different Learning Styles

Print Learner Use the headings on this page and the next to emphasize the main social concerns associated with computers and technology. In addition, encourage students to use library and Internet resources to read more about these topics.

Work as a TEAM

Use this activity to encourage students to better understand the need for continued learning throughout their lives.

TEACH

Explain concerns associated with piracy, computer viruses, and privacy violations. Take this opportunity to review school policies regarding these issues.

ONGOING ASSESSMENT

CHECKPOINT ✓ANSWER

Software piracy robs the creators of software of their legal profits. It is very expensive to develop new software, often requiring teams of hundreds of workers for a single program. Because of software piracy, companies have fewer dollars available to spend on creating new software.

ASSESS

Key Concepts *Answers*

1. b. working at home by computer
2. c. a virus
3. d. white-collar crime

Make Academic Connections *Answers*

4. Memos will vary.
5. Answer will vary. In this exercise, students may learn that music that would reduce stress in an office setting might vary depending on the age of the workers. Classical or instrumental music might prove the most calming without causing a distraction among most workers.

Work as a TEAM

The workplace is constantly changing because of technology. Some jobs are eliminated, while others are created. Describe various career skills and activities that will be needed to work with technology in the future.

between one-third and one-half of all software used is obtained illegally. Companies that develop software may lose more than half of their profits to information pirates who violate the law. Copyright laws apply to software as well as books and music.

Destructive efforts are also a concern to computer users. A **computer virus** is program code hidden in a system that can later do damage to software or stored data. The virus may be programmed to become active on a certain date or when certain data is accessed. Some computer viruses are harmless, only showing up as a funny message. Others have been known to destroy critical government records.

Cybercrimes are not just conducted by individuals. Criminal gangs and governments also engage in computer crime. Cybercrime and espionage costs businesses around the world more than $445 billion annually.

Privacy Concerns

One of the greatest challenges facing computer users is the need to guarantee privacy. Some dishonest people have learned how to illegally access computer databases. While some laws exist to protect your privacy, many concerned people believe these regulations are not strong enough. Some businesses are becoming stricter about who can access and use company information. Tighter security systems are being developed. Some organizations change the password needed to access information several times a day to protect their databases.

In recent years, *identity theft* has become a major concern for consumers and companies. Thieves obtain information online about a person. They apply for a credit card in the person's name or access their bank account. More than 13 million people have their identities stolen in the United States each year. Con artists illegally obtain millions of dollars each year through identity theft.

CHECKPOINT ✓

How are software developers impacted by software piracy?

11.3 ASSESSMENT

Key Concepts

Determine the best answer.

1. Telecommuting refers to
   a. the use of computers to design products
   b. working at home by computer
   c. difficulties from overusing computers
   d. illegal acts of office workers
2. Hidden software code that can damage computer operations is
   a. piracy
   b. a virus
   c. a displaced worker
   d. computer literacy
3. Illegal acts carried out by office or professional workers while at work are referred to as
   a. computer crime
   b. piracy
   c. identity theft
   d. white-collar crime

Make Academic Connections

4. **Communication** Prepare a memo that sets out the benefits of telecommuting for an organization. In your memo, present specific details of a job that would be appropriate for telecommuting.
5. **Music** Select three different types of music. Discuss how each might be appropriate or inappropriate for an office setting to reduce stress associated with working on computers.

RETEACH Ask students to name the major uses of computers and technology in homes.

ENRICH Ask students to explain technology's role in improving the quality of life in developing economies.

CLOSE Ask students to describe actions that might be taken to address various concerns associated with technology.

BUSINESS IMPROVING SOCIETY

GREEN AMERICA

Every time you spend or invest a dollar, it goes to work in the world.
–Green America website

Green America is an organization with a vision. The vision includes a world where:

- All people have enough.
- All communities are healthy and safe.
- The bounty of the earth is preserved for generations to come.

iStockphoto.com/vishureddy

How is a farmer in a developing country helped when you purchase a fair trade cotton shirt?

The organization was founded on the belief that your purchases can support businesses that create jobs, care about their communities, engage in fair trade, and protect the environment. The mission is "to harness economic power—the strength of consumers, businesses and the marketplace—to create a socially just and environmentally sustainable society." Green America was started in 1982 under the name Co-op America to provide practical tools to address today's social and environmental problems. While many environmental organizations fight political and legal battles, Green America educates people and businesses about making improvements through the economic system. Descriptions of some of their programs are shown below.

- **Climate Action Campaign** Encourages consumers and businesses to minimize their carbon footprint and offers strategies for pressuring corporate polluters to take climate change seriously.
- **Green Business** Provides resources for businesses interested in being socially and environmentally responsible.
- **Fair Trade** Helps to ensure that developing world farmers and artisans receive a fair price and that environmental standards and labor rights are met.
- **Responsible Shopper** Profiles hundreds of companies and offers guidance for shopping decisions that promote corporate responsibility.
- **Social Investing** Suggests strategies for making socially and environmentally responsible investment decisions.

Green America publishes a variety of materials. The organization's National Green Pages is a directory of America's leading socially and environmentally responsible businesses.

Green America has 100,000 individual members and 4,000 member businesses that work together to achieve the goals of the organization. In addition, Green America manages the Social Investment Forum, a trade organization for socially responsible investing professionals.

Each day, Green America encourages consumers to rethink their buying habits. You should purchase from companies that are trying to become more socially and environmentally responsible. Investors are encouraged to support socially responsible companies. Most importantly, Green America wants consumers, investors, and businesses to demand change.

Think Critically

1. How does Green America serve consumers and businesses in our society?
2. What aspect of Green America do you believe is most valuable for people in your state or community?
3. Go to the website of Green America to obtain additional details about the activities of this organization.

BUSINESS IMPROVING SOCIETY

Explain the benefits of knowing where your money goes when you buy a product. Describe the information a consumer might like to know about a product before making a purchase.

THINK CRITICALLY THROUGH VISUALS

Fair trade allows the farmer to receive a fair price for the cotton that was used to produce the shirt.

Think Critically *Answers*

1. Green America serves consumers and businesses in our society by helping them make informed decisions so that they can "vote" for environmentally and socially responsible companies through their purchases.
2. Answers will vary depending on the state in which you live and student perspectives.
3. Students visit the Green America website to gain additional information about this innovative service. Consider encouraging students to search the site for information about companies and activities in your state.

Think Critically About Business *Answers*

1a. monitor—hardware

1b. word processing program—software

1c. chips—hardware

1d. keyboard—hardware

1e. operating system program—software

1f. disk drive—hardware

1g. mouse—hardware

1h. printer—hardware

2. Examples include bank tellers, cashiers, order takers, and teachers.

3a. spreadsheet software

3b. database software

3c. word processing software

3d. graphics software or any program containing a chart feature

3e. spreadsheet software

3f. database software

3g. word processing software (could merge data from database software)

4. External data would include government reports and information provided by customers and financial institutions. Internal data could include a company's own accounting records, inventory information, employee records, and sales figures.

5. Schools could benefit because each teacher could reach more students. Schools would not have to provide facilities. Students could benefit because they could continue their education while employed, save time and money by not commuting, and learn at their own pace.

Chapter 11 Assessment

Review Business Notes

11.1 Computer Systems

- Computer systems consist of four main components: the input device, the processing unit, the memory and storage facilities, and an output device.
- Commonly used input devices include the keyboard, mouse, video game controllers, touch-sensitive screens, scanners, and voice-activated mechanisms.
- The main types of storage devices are the internal memory in a computer and external memory such as disks, CDs, DVDs, magnetic tape, flash memory sticks and Cloud storage. Data processing results are reported as text output, graphics output, audio output, or video output.

11.2 Business Applications of Technology

- The four main components of a management information system (MIS) are gathering data, analyzing data, storing data, and reporting results. The goal of an MIS is to change raw data (facts and figures) into information that can be used by managers.
- Service industries that make extensive use of computers and technology include public service organizations, educational institutions, healthcare facilities, and financial service organizations.
- E-commerce involves the conducting of business transactions over the Internet or through other electronic technology.

11.3 Other Technology Issues

- Robotics, expert systems, computer-aided design (CAD), and telecommuting are used in a variety of business situations to help improve efficiency and productivity.
- Personal technology applications include schoolwork, home robotics, and social networking.
- Expanded technology and computer use can result in concerns about job loss, health and safety, criminal activities, privacy, and identity theft.

Think Critically About Business

1. Identify each of the following items as either *hardware* or *software.*
   - **a.** monitor (screen)
   - **b.** word processing program
   - **c.** chips
   - **d.** keyboard
   - **e.** operating system program
   - **f.** disk drive
   - **g.** mouse
   - **h.** printer
2. What are possible business activities currently performed by people that might be performed in the future using a computer system?
3. Identify whether word processing software, database software, spreadsheet software, or graphics software would be used to perform the following computer applications.
   - **a.** Preparing a report of new equipment purchased for each office of a company
   - **b.** Preparing a list of employees that is sorted by ZIP code
   - **c.** Creating a form letter to distribute to new customers of a mail-order business
   - **d.** Creating a pie chart showing the portion of sales of each product
   - **e.** Preparing a document listing the total sales for each geographic area of the country
   - **f.** Listing the employees who have not missed a day of work in five years
   - **g.** Sending a letter to each employee who has not missed a day of work in five years
4. List examples of (a) external data and (b) internal data used by most companies.
5. Who would benefit from schools that would allow students to take classes at home by computer?

6. Workers benefit because they save time and money by not having to commute. They also gain flexibility in their schedules. Employers benefit because they do not have to provide resources for employees who are not in the office. They also gain employee loyalty. Society benefits because more workers are able to adjust their schedules to care for family. Companies operate more efficiently, possibly leading to lower prices. Also, home-based workers do not commute, taking some pressure off of city rush hours and the environment.

6. Describe the benefits to workers, employers, and society when an organization allows some of its employees to do all or part of their work at home.
7. How has e-commerce expanded global business in countries that previously had limited economic activity?
8. How is it possible for the increased use of computers to create more jobs than are lost?
9. How might expert systems be used in the future to help people solve medical, legal, financial, and other technical problems?
10. What are potential benefits from the use of smart cards in handling everyday transactions?
11. What actions could be taken by organizations to prevent computer crime?

Develop Your Business Language

Match the terms listed with the definitions.

12. Several computers linked into a single system.
13. Computer programs that perform specific tasks such as word processing, database management, or accounting.
14. Instructions that run a computer system.
15. The control center of the computer.
16. The combination of an input device, a processing unit, memory and storage facilities, and an output device.
17. Conducting business transactions over the Internet or using other technology.
18. Software that translates a computer user's commands and allows application programs to interact with the computer's hardware.
19. A system of letters, words, numbers, and symbols used to communicate with a computer.
20. The components or equipment of a computer system.
21. A series of detailed step-by-step instructions that tell the computer what functions to complete and when to complete them.
22. The use of computers to help people learn or improve skills at their own pace.
23. A term used to describe the activities of a worker using a computer at home to perform a job.
24. Mechanical devices programmed to do routine tasks.
25. Technological assistance used to create product styles and designs.
26. Stealing or illegally copying software packages or information.
27. Programs that assist people in solving technical problems.
28. An organized system of processing and reporting information in an organization.
29. A program code hidden in a system that can later do damage to software or stored data.
30. Programs that enable computers to reason, learn, and make decisions using logical methods similar to the methods humans use.

Key Terms

- **a.** application software
- **b.** artificial intelligence (AI)
- **c.** central processing unit (CPU)
- **d.** computer language
- **e.** computer network
- **f.** computer system
- **g.** computer virus
- **h.** computer-aided design (CAD)
- **i.** computer-assisted instruction (CAI)
- **j.** e-commerce
- **k.** expert systems
- **l.** hardware
- **m.** management information system (MIS)
- **n.** operating system software
- **o.** piracy
- **p.** program
- **q.** robotics
- **r.** software
- **s.** telecommuting

7. E-commerce has expanded global business by providing a lower-cost way to enter the business world. E-commerce allows a business owner to serve customers anywhere that packages can be delivered, lessening the disadvantage of a remote location.

8. It creates new jobs in programming, computer systems analysis, and operating and repairing computers.

9. Expert systems might help solve medical problems by logically deducing the best possible courses of treatment and could also help scientists draw conclusions from medical research. Expert systems could research volumes of case law to help lawyers prepare cases for their clients.

Expert systems could connect potential borrowers with the best lenders for their needs or help investors choose the most promising investments.

10. One benefit of using smart cards for everyday transactions is improved personal record keeping. The smart card could replace your car keys and open the door for you at work. It could alert you when your checking account is low and streamline the process of applying for a loan.

11. Organizations can have employees use passwords to log on to their computers, monitor employee e-mail, and encrypt sensitive data when it is sent over the Internet.

Develop Your Business Language *Answers*

12. e. computer network
13. a. application software
14. r. software
15. c. central processing unit
16. f. computer system
17. j. e-commerce
18. n. operating system software
19. d. computer language
20. l. hardware
21. p. program
22. i. computer-assisted instruction
23. s. telecommuting
24. q. robotics
25. h. computer-aided design
26. o. piracy
27. k. expert systems
28. m. management information system
29. g. computer virus
30. b. artificial intelligence

Make Academic Connections *Answers*

31. Findings will vary.

32. Tables will vary.

33. Lists will vary. For example, smart cards can be used to store bank account information, credit history, and employment data. They can also be used to gain entry to a workplace or dormitory, verify class attendance, and make purchases.

34. Findings will vary. Students should understand that telemedicine is the use of telecommunication to provide medical information and services. Telesurgery allows a surgeon to operate from a distance using video, robotics, and sensory devices.

35. The Barkley Corporation is spending $1,596 a month on conventional mail. Switching to e-mail will save $346 per month, or about 22 percent. Before making the change to e-mail, the company will need to investigate the cost of upgrading to the new system. Barkley Corporation should also do some market research to determine how the e-mail will be received and what percentage of individuals have e-mail access.

36. Discuss challenges the countries might have experienced in installing and maintaining reliable phone service lines.

37. Reports will vary. Discuss ways to protect computers from viruses and what to do if a virus is found.

38. Lists will vary.

39. Answers will vary depending on the article selected. Provide guidance for the citation format you want students to use.

Make Academic Connections

31. **Technology** Research types of input, output, and memory devices that have recently been developed for use by businesses and individuals. Find an example of each type of device and write a paragraph about each one.

32. **Communication** Talk to people who make online purchases. What types of products do they buy most frequently? What do they like best about shopping online? What concerns do they have about buying online? Prepare a table with a summary of your findings.

33. **Technology** Prepare a list of daily activities and information items that might be included in the processing and storage capabilities of a smart card. Using information from your list, provide an example of a situation where a smart card might be used.

34. **Science** Investigate various uses of telemedicine and telesurgery in the United States and in other areas of the world.

35. **Math** The Barkley Corporation usually sends about 3,800 pieces of mail per month at $0.42 each. If the firm switches to e-mail service at a cost of $1,250 per month, how much money would it save or lose? What other factors should the company consider before making this change?

36. **Geography** Many nations around the world do not have reliable telephone service. As a result, mobile and wireless communication has grown at a fast pace in these countries. Conduct research and prepare a map reporting the countries with a significant usage rate of wireless communication.

37. **Technology** Research recent computer viruses. What types of damage do various viruses do to computer systems? How can you protect your computer against virus attacks?

38. **Law** Conduct an Internet search to obtain information about avoiding identity theft. Make a list of 10 ways to protect your identity. Write a short explanation of how each of the protection strategies helps protect your identity.

39. **Read** Find a news article that relates to e-commerce. Read the article and outline the major concepts presented in the article using bullet points. Include a properly formatted citation for your source. Possible sources include printed and online versions of newspapers or magazines. You should also consider independent online sources that produce original content.

Make Your Case

The Kendall Manufacturing Company assembles electronic devices used in offices and homes. They employ about 600 people in various office, factory, and warehouse positions. Currently, all factory and warehouse jobs are performed manually.

Managers at Kendall are considering replacing 150 assembly line workers with a computerized system. The company can save $135,000 a year in operating costs by using this new technology.

40. What factors should the company consider before using the computerized assembly line system?

41. If the company uses this new system, what should the company do to help workers who are displaced by this technology?

Interactions and Connections

42. Talk with a few members of your community about the computers and technology they use on the job. Ask them to describe technology changes they have seen in their jobs during the last year and during the last three years. Also ask them to identify the computer skills they think are important for career success. Prepare a one-minute presentation that summarizes your findings.

43. The number and popularity of social networking sites on the Internet continue to grow. Social networking websites allow multiple users to communicate through an individual's website. There are a wide variety of social networking sites with many users. Facebook alone has more than 1.4 billion users worldwide. The enjoyment and convenience of a social networking site is tempered by concerns about illegal and unethical behavior. All users need to take precautions when using these sites.

Make Your Case *Answers*

40. The company may want to phase in the new system one assembly line at a time. They will want to be sure they have employees who are trained to operate the new system.

41. Employees with technical aptitude could be retrained and transferred to new jobs. To maintain as much goodwill as possible, Kendall will want to provide employees who cannot be switched to other jobs with training and severance pay.

Make a list of the activities that people participate in while using social networking sites.
Then, make a list of problems that might arise when using social networking sites.

Use the Internet or library resources to identify recommendations for safe social networking practices. Create a one-page flyer of tips for social network users.

Professional Selling Event

The Professional Selling and Consulting Event provides an opportunity for participants to demonstrate skills needed for a career in sales and/or consulting. Participants will organize and deliver a sales presentation for one or more products and/or services.

Wearable sensors have become a mainstay of the fitness world. There are numerous benefits to wearing one. With just a little training, these sensors will help you understand your behaviors and could lead to an improved and healthier lifestyle.

You will assume the role of a sales representative of a major electronics company. A large school district with more than 2,500 educators and support staff wants to improve the overall wellness of its employees. Improved wellness will reduce the cost of health care and potentially the number of sick days. The school district is searching for wearable technology to purchase for every employee and to improve wellness across the school district. You have a meeting scheduled with the district's human resources manager to pitch your company's products and price points.

The participant will organize appropriate information and present a sales presentation. The participant may use visual aids during the sales presentation. The oral presentation may be a maximum of 20 minutes in length. The first 15 minutes will include a sales presentation and will be followed by 5 minutes for the judges' questions.

Performance Indicators Evaluated

- The opening is effective and engaging.
- Establish relationship with customer/client.
- Communicate understanding of customer/client needs.
- Recommend specific products, services, or actions.
- Acquire product knowledge to communicate product benefits and to ensure appropriateness of product for the customer.
- Presentation is well-organized using professional grammar and vocabulary. Voice conveys proper volume, enthusiasm, and pronunciation.

You will be evaluated for:

- Overall quality of the presentation.
- Effectiveness of public speaking and presentation skills.
- Ability to respond to questions.

For more detailed information about performance indicators, go to the DECA website.

Think Critically

1. How will you determine if the wearable technology was useful in keeping employees healthy?
2. What types of incentives or challenges will be introduced to encourage the employees to wear the technology?
3. How would you promote this technology to your employees?

www.deca.org

Interactions and Connections

42. Presentations will vary. Consider making a class list of all technologies reported to have changed and the computer skills recommended for career success.

Invite students to work in small groups to develop strategies for learning computer skills and keeping up with computer skills in the future.

43. Lists and flyers will vary. Students should recognize the potential dangers of sharing personal information with strangers. Flyers should focus on safe social networking practices and offer specific tips.

WINNING EDGE

Professional Selling Event

Think Critically *Answers*

1. Students should mention data tracking. How many people initially wore the product and how many persist in doing so? How frequently do they log into the website to track their progress and compare it to their peers?

2. Proposals will vary. Challenges to be the most active might be issued to individuals or departments for various intervals of time. The use of teams encourages employees to motivate one another. Students might consider issuing prizes to winners.

3. Students might remind employees that the technology is an investment in them. Employees could be allowed to customize the devices' colors and the text printed on them. Devices may be passed out to everyone at once in a ceremony that emphasizes full participation and inclusion.

CHAPTER OVERVIEW

The chapter presents information on financial planning and decision-making procedures used in business.

12.1 Financial Planning

This lesson examines the financial questions faced by businesses and how to prepare and use business budgets.

12.2 Financial Records and Financial Statements

This lesson describes financial records needed by businesses and explains the differences between an income statement and a balance sheet.

12.3 Payroll Management

This lesson describes the components of a payroll system and the information that is included in payroll records and paychecks.

12.4 Financial Decision Making

This lesson discusses the financial information that managers use when making decisions and the steps they follow to make financial decisions in their businesses.

Chapter 12 Financial Management

wavebreakmedia/Shutterstock.com

Instructor Resources

- Activities and Study Guide IE
- Chapter and Unit Tests IE
- Lesson Plans
- PowerPoint Presentation
- Cognero Test, Ch. 12

Student Resources

Activities and Study Guide

www.cengage.com/swep/pob9e

- Portfolio Activity

PLANNING A CAREER IN . . .
ACCOUNTING

Managing the financial records and decisions is one of the most important responsibilities in a business. All income and expenses must be accurately identified and recorded. Financial records must be kept up to date and financial statements must be prepared. When managers request financial information, the necessary records must be retrieved, the information needs to be summarized, and reports must be quickly and accurately prepared. All financial records, reports, and decisions need to comply with federal and state laws as well as ethical standards. Accountants and other financial personnel are responsible for all of these activities.

Public accountants perform accounting, auditing, tax, and consulting activities for their clients. Management accountants are employed by companies and complete the day-to-day financial activities of business. They advise executives and other managers to help them make good business decisions. A unique and growing career area is forensic accounting. Forensic accountants investigate possible criminal activity such as securities fraud, embezzlement, and money laundering. They often serve as expert witnesses in criminal and civil cases.

Related Job Titles

- **Auditor**
- **Budget Analyst**
- **Chief Financial Officer**
- **Payroll Accountant**
- **Regulation and Control Manager**
- **Credit Manager**
- **Compliance Manager**

Analyze Career Opportunities in . . .
ACCOUNTING

Use library and Internet resources to learn more about careers in accounting. Choose one of the job titles listed in the box above or another one of interest to you and answer the following questions.

1. What is the employment outlook for careers in this field?
2. Why does this career interest you? Explain how careers in this field match up with your goals and interests.

What it's like to work as an . . . Accountant

After graduating from a community college, Ali worked as an accounting technician. She enjoyed her job, but wanted to grow and advance. Ali enrolled in a 4-year college and earned a bachelor's degree in Accounting. A public accounting firm hired Ali as a junior staff accountant. She was assigned to work on several auditing projects of large companies. Her auditing team would usually spend several weeks at the offices of a client reviewing financial records and preparing audit reports. After several years, Ali wanted a new challenge. She completed the rigorous requirements to become a Certified Public Accountant (CPA).

Today, Ali is employed as a managerial accountant for a communications company. She is a part of a 15-person department that oversees all company accounting and financial planning activities. Most days, Ali spends her time assigning work and reviewing the reports and records generated by her staff. She meets with company managers as they prepare forecasts and budgets and also to present and explain financial reports.

What about you? What aspects of a career as an account do you think you would you find interesting?

PLANNING A CAREER IN . . .
ACCOUNTING

One of the most popular and challenging career areas in business is accounting. It combines mathematics skills with business understanding to prepare and maintain the financial records of a business and help business managers make effective financial decisions. Accounting and finance professionals must be knowledgeable about state and federal laws and regulations related to producing and maintaining financial records. Technology has effected an important impact on accounting practice, so accounting and finance personnel must be able to use a variety of business computer software.

What About You?
Answers

Answers regarding careers in accounting will vary. Some students will be attracted to the challenge and independence of a public accounting firm or even starting their own public accounting business, while others might want to apply their skills in a specific industry by developing a financial career in a corporation.

Analyze Career Opportunities *Answers*
Student answers will vary depending on when the assignment is completed and individual interests.

Additional Career Information

Encourage students to investigate careers they find interesting and explore unfamiliar careers. Two resources for additional career information are the *Occupational Outlook Handbook*, an online publication (www.bls.gov/oco) of the U.S. Bureau of Labor Statistics, and the O*NET Resource Center (www.onetcenter.org) developed by the U.S. Department of Labor. Information about specific careers and jobs can be used to demonstrate the relevance of skills learned in this course.

Focus on REAL LIFE

Tell students that today all businesspeople must understand and use basic financial information and reports. Tell them that the mathematics skills required to understand and use financial reports are not as complicated as many people believe.

TEACH

Ask students to individually generate a question that new business owners might need to consider that involves finance. Guide them by identifying key areas of business operations such as the need for capital and equipment, personnel, supplies, marketing, technology, and so forth.

THINK CRITICALLY THROUGH VISUALS

The monthly lease payment is an expense. A building lease may be one of the largest regular expenses of the new business.

12.1 Financial Planning

Learning Outcomes

12.1.1 Recognize important financial questions a business must answer and explain the basic financial equation.

12.1.2 List the steps in budget preparation.

12.1.3 Describe three types of business budgets.

Key Terms

revenue 289	start-up budget 292
expenses 289	operating budget 293
budget 290	cash budget 293

Focus on REAL LIFE

Ernest enjoys everything about his job as a sales manager—including the thing many of his colleagues do not—studying and understanding financial information. Each week he receives a number of financial reports. Some describe the financial condition of the entire business and some are specific to his department. He sees the payroll expenses for his employees, the changing costs of materials and supplies, as well as all other expenses of his department. The reports show whether he is over or under budget for every expenditure and whether sales are meeting the goals he set.

At first, Ernest wasn't always sure what he should do with the information. But he was comfortable asking questions of other managers and the company's accountants. He knows that the financial decisions he makes are among the most important to the success of his department and his career. He is constantly seeking ways to improve his financial management skills.

LO 12.1.1

FINANCIAL PLANNING

Picture yourself as a business owner. You will continually face the pressure to maintain adequate financial resources to operate the business. Each day you will need to make decisions about how to use the financial resources of your business most effectively. Financial questions never go away. Even the most successful businesses are continually active in financial planning.

Beginning a Business

The moment you decide to start a business, financial planning begins. How much money will be needed to start the business? Where will that financing come from? How will adequate funds be obtained to operate the business for the months or years until the business becomes profitable? What will be the best sources of sales and other income? What will be the major expenses? When must they be paid?

Many new businesses fail due to poor financial planning. Every new business owner should consult with experts in business finance. Those experts recognize the importance of financial planning and will help the new owner develop needed financial management skills.

istockphoto.com/IDFK303

Why is the cost of leasing a building or office space important to financial planning for a new business?

Teaching Strategies

Expand Beyond the Classroom Assign students to interview a successful business owner about the importance of financing and financial decision making. Ask students to share their findings.

Ongoing Operations

Finances are a key part of the operations of all businesses. Every business activity has a cost. Without careful planning and management, those costs can grow to a level where the business will be unable to meet them. All income that a business receives over a period of time is called **revenue**. Businesses also have expenses. **Expenses** are the costs of operating a business. Planning and decisions are guided by the basic financial equation: revenue minus expenses equals profit or loss. The equation is illustrated in Figure 12-1.

The difference between revenue and expenses determines whether a business makes a profit or loss. If revenue is greater than expenses, the business will make a *profit*. If expenses exceed revenue, the business will suffer a *loss*.

Managers are responsible for the costs of the part of the business they manage. Each employee should also be concerned about those costs. The profitability of a business is directly linked to the number of employees and the type of work they do.

While the costs of employee wages and benefits are some of the highest expenses for most businesses, reducing those costs by employing fewer people or paying them less will not usually result in higher profits. Employees are needed to do the work of the business. Employees that are well trained, motivated, and efficient will be more productive than those that are not. A business that tries to save money by hiring fewer people, paying lower wages, or reducing the amount of training may find that costs increase due to waste, inefficiency, or poor-quality products.

Managers and employees should find ways to reduce waste and control expenses. They can also help determine ways to increase sales and income through better products and services.

Ongoing operations require that employees be paid, supplies and materials ordered, and buildings maintained. Equipment must be repaired and technology updated.

BASIC FINANCIAL EQUATION
Revenue − Expenses = Profit or Loss
Revenue > Expenses = Profit
Revenue < Expenses = Loss

FIGURE 12-1

If a business has annual revenue of $5 million and expenses of $4.5 million, did the business make a profit or suffer a loss?

Each decision related to ongoing operations requires careful attention to costs.

Business Expansion

Over time, successful businesses expand to serve more customers, enter new markets, and introduce new products. That expansion costs money. The goal is that the income generated by the expansion will be far greater than the cost and a more profitable business will result.

Business expansion requires research to develop new and improved products and identify new markets. New factories and equipment may be needed to produce the products. Additional employees must be hired and trained. Employees may need to be retrained or new employees may need to be hired. Marketing activities will be planned and implemented to distribute and promote the products. Expansion plans can take months and years and cost many thousands or even millions of dollars. Each time business expansion is anticipated, careful financial planning must be completed. The planning must anticipate the costs associated with the expansion, the source of the funds to pay for the expansion, and the expected income that will result from the new plans. If the planning is not correct and the expansion results in substantial losses rather than profits, the previously successful business may fail.

CHECKPOINT
What is the basic financial equation for businesses?

TEACH

List the following areas of a business and ask students how managers and employees working in each of those areas can help to control costs: production, transportation, sales, accounting, information management, and customer service.

▸ Figure 12-1 *ANSWER*

The business made a profit of $500,000. Provide additional scenarios and ask students to use the figures to help determine if the businesses make profits or sustain losses.

ONGOING ASSESSMENT

CHECKPOINT ✓ *ANSWER*

The basic financial equation for businesses is revenue minus expenses equals profit or loss. If revenue exceeds expenses, profit results. If expenses exceed revenue, the result is loss.

Applied Skills

Technology Instruct students to use a spreadsheet program to build a model that demonstrates the basic financial equation. The model should include cells for revenue, expenses, and profit/loss with a formula in the profit/loss cell.

Communication Assign students to use a computer software program to prepare a slide presentation that compares the three types of business budgets. Organize students into small groups and ask them to share their presentations within the groups.

TEACH

List the two main purposes of a business budget on the board. Lead a discussion about why each of the purposes is important to a business and what happens if a business is not able to accomplish one or both of the purposes.

Business Insight

Individuals and businesses must keep careful track of income and expenditures in order to maintain their financial health. Financial records do not always present a current picture of what a person or company owns and owes. Businesses need to determine the method they will use for their financial records and what the records say about the company's current financial condition.

Think Critically *Answers*

1. The business owner may be used to the cash method when keeping personal financial records. The owner may or may not be aware of the accrual method or its benefits. It may be less risky because the business has fewer financial transactions and the owner can more easily remember large sales or purchases and the amount of cash on hand.

2. Answers may vary. Two common situations that require accrual accounting are businesses that operate as public corporations and most businesses with more than $5 million in sales.

LO 12.1.2

DEVELOPING BUSINESS BUDGETS

A **budget** provides detailed plans for the financial needs of individuals, families, and businesses. A *business budget* has two main purposes:

1. Anticipate sources and amounts of income for a business.
2. Predict the types and amounts of expenses for a specific business activity or the entire business.

The business must be able to identify and predict the amount of each source of income and each type of expense. In addition, the business will need to determine when each expense must be paid and when income will be received. For the business to succeed, enough revenue must be available to pay all expenses as they are due.

Sources of Budget Information

To develop an effective budget, information to predict income and expenses is needed. If a business has operated for several years, identifying sources of income and types of expenses will not be difficult. The main source of that information is the financial records of the business. Budgeting is much

Business Insight

Cash or Accrual?

When you pay for something with cash you know you no longer have that amount of money to spend. But what about a credit card purchase? You may not receive a statement until several weeks after you made the purchase and then still have several weeks to pay the bill. When do you recognize that you no longer have the money you spent for that purchase?

Businesses face a similar issue when maintaining their financial records. When do they identify the income and expenses? Many small businesses use a *cash method* where income and expenses are recorded when money is actually received or a payment is made. Even though the business has billed a customer for a purchase, the associated income is not recognized until the customer actually pays. In the same way, if the business purchases inventory from a supplier and owes money for the purchase, the amount of the purchase is not recognized in the financial records until a check has been issued.

Most businesses do not use the cash method; they use an *accrual method*. Accruals recognize income and expenses when they actually occur rather than when the associated payment is made or received. If a product is sold to a customer, the amount of the sale is recorded in the financial records of the seller at the time of sale rather than waiting for cash to be received. At the time a company makes a purchase, whether payment is made immediately or not, the financial records identify the expense.

Keeping track of what you actually owe and the income you have really earned gives you a much more accurate picture of your financial situation than waiting until the money exchanges hands. Businesses make many financial transactions each day amounting to thousands of dollars. They might soon find themselves in financial difficulty if they only recorded cash receipts and expenditures.

Think Critically

1. Why might many small businesses use a cash rather than accrual method to maintain their financial records? Why are they at less risk than larger businesses when using the cash method?
2. Accounting rules and laws require many businesses to use the accrual method in their financial record keeping. Use the Internet to determine two situations where accrual accounting is required.

Different Learning Abilities

Dyslexia Ask students to review the lesson and prepare a short outline that lists financial planning decisions for a business for each of the following situations: beginning a business, ongoing operation, and business expansion.

harder for a new business. No financial records exist to serve as a guide. Other sources of information must be used.

The Small Business Administration (SBA) provides many planning tools for new businesses. Among those tools are guides to developing a budget and financial information to help new business owners predict income and expenses. Another source of information is private businesses that collect and publish financial information on similar businesses and industries. Examples of those companies are Dun and Bradstreet, Value Line, and Standard and Poor's. Some information is also available from business magazines, websites, and newspapers including *Fortune*, *Forbes*, *Inc. Magazine*, *Bloomberg Businessweek*, *Black Enterprise*, *Latin Business Today*, and *The Wall Street Journal*.

Professional associations, such as the National Federation of Independent Business and the Retail Merchants Association, offer resources to help with financial planning. A new franchise will typically receive assistance with financial planning from the franchisor. This help might include a complete beginning budget. A bank or other financial institution where a new business has established accounts is another source of financial planning. Franchisors and financial institutions want to see businesses succeed, so they typically require careful financial planning.

Budget Preparation

The important first step in financial planning is developing a budget. You can compare the use of a budget to the use of a GPS app when you are traveling to an unfamiliar location. Without directions, you will have little idea where you are going while you travel. If you take a wrong turn, you will have difficulty knowing your mistake. It will be hard to get back to the correct road without the app. In the same way, a budget identifies where a business is going. It allows the owner to determine if the business is making progress toward its financial destination. By regularly comparing the business's financial performance to the budget, the owner can determine if the budget goals are being met. If not, the owner can make corrections before serious financial problems occur.

FYI In 2013, U.S. businesses spent more than $1.48 trillion dollars on investments in buildings, equipment, and technology. The industry with the greatest level of spending was manufacturing. Most spending by manufacturing in recent years was for equipment and technology rather than buildings.

A business budget has the same basic goals as a personal or family budget developed to manage the household finances. The goals are to determine the sources and amounts of income, to identify the types of expenses and predict their costs, to determine how income will be distributed to cover those expenses, and to reward investors if there is a profit.

istockphoto.com/Susan Chiang

What do you think are important personal and family budget categories for most people? How might they be similar to or different from categories in a business budget?

FYI

Tell students that often "You have to spend money to make money." Students may be surprised at the amount businesses spend each year on buildings, equipment, and technology. The expenditures are necessary in order to produce goods and services needed by consumers.

TEACH

Tell students that personal characteristics of many entrepreneurs make them unwilling to ask for help and advice. That often leads to problems with financial planning and decision making. All businesspeople should be willing to gather information and ask for help and advice, especially in the important area of business financing.

THINK CRITICALLY THROUGH VISUALS

Answers will vary as to which budget categories are most important. Categories for both businesses and individuals would include sources of income, utilities, taxes, insurance, and investments. Businesses would have categories for employee-related expenses and capital investments such as technology, operating equipment, and buildings, while individuals might have housing, transportation, education, and child care expenses.

Different Learning Styles

Tactile Learner Instruct students to visit a library or bookstore with an extensive business collection and locate books and magazines that provide useful financial information for new business owners. Ask students to develop a bibliography of the resources they located.

Work as a TEAM

Before the teams begin, discuss the types of work done by large landscaping businesses to help determine categories of income and expenses. Also discuss what factors can result in higher or lower monthly amounts in various income and expense categories.

TEACH

Review the skills that are needed by people responsible for preparing a budget. Ask students to identify ways these skills could be developed.

ONGOING ASSESSMENT

CHECKPOINT ✓ ANSWER

The four steps are (1) preparing a list of each type of income and expense that will be a part of the budget, (2) gathering accurate information from business records and other information sources for each type of income and expense, (3) creating the budget by calculating each type of income, expense, and the amount of net income or loss, and (4) explaining the budget to people who need financial information.

TEACH

Ask students to list the three types of budgets. As each is discussed, students should write the definition of each and note the differences among the budgets.

THINK CRITICALLY THROUGH VISUALS

Budget items that need to be considered include sales tax, title and license fees, insurance, maintenance and repairs, fuel, and wages for delivery personnel.

Work as a TEAM

Your team is developing a budget for a large landscaping business that has operated for five years. As a group, agree on three categories of income and five categories of expenses that will be a part of the budget. For each category, brainstorm several ways the business could accurately estimate the monthly amount of income or expense to include in the budget.

The budgeting process involves four fundamental steps.

1. Prepare a list of each type of income and expense that will be a part of the budget.
2. Gather accurate information from business records and other information sources for each type of income and expense.
3. Create the budget by calculating each type of income, expense, and the amount of net income or loss.
4. Explain the budget to people who need financial information to make decisions.

The people responsible for preparing business budgets need several skills. Budgeting requires an understanding of financial information, computer skills, mathematical abilities, and effective communications skills. New small business owners often seek the help of an accountant or banker when preparing a budget for the first time. Small and medium-sized businesses may hire an accounting firm to maintain financial records and to help with budget development. Larger businesses employ accountants and other financial planning experts to maintain the business's financial records. They also help with budgeting and using budget information.

CHECKPOINT ✓
What are the four steps in preparing a business budget?

LO 12.1.3

TYPES OF BUDGETS

A large business will have many specialized budgets. Each manager will be responsible for one or more budgets in his or her area of operations. For every business, three particular budgets are essential. They are the start-up budget, the operating budget, and the cash budget. The **start-up budget** plans income and expenses from the beginning of a new business or a major business expansion until it becomes profitable. Most start-ups require expenditures of thousands or even hundreds of thousands of dollars in order to open. Buildings and equipment must be purchased or leased. Inventory, supplies, and materials are needed. New employees will be hired or existing employees retrained. Expenses for utilities, licenses, advertising, and transportation will be incurred before the company can sell its new products and services. Sources of financing for these expenditures must be identified either from inside the company or from outside financial sources.

istockphoto.com/nullplus

In addition to price, what other budget information would the owners of a company need to consider when buying a delivery van?

Portfolio Activity

Assign the Portfolio Activity for Chapter 12, available on the product website.

COLLECT Offer suggestions to help students locate the financial planning process and tools used in business.

CREATE Remind students that a flowchart needs to show the direction of the flow of information.

CONNECT Point out that students need to connect visuals to something already in their portfolio or to a concept from another class.

The amount of start-up expenses must be predicted correctly so that ample start-up financing is available until the new activities produce adequate income.

The **operating budget** describes the financial plan for ongoing operations of the business for a specific period. The operating budget is usually planned for three months, six months, or a year. An operating budget is typically prepared for the entire business. Each department and division of a large business will also develop and follow its own operating budget.

When planning an operating budget, income and expenses from prior budgets are reviewed. Planners look for possible changes that could increase or decrease income and expenses. Then the budget for the next period is prepared. It is used to manage the operations of the company for the period covered by the budget.

A **cash budget** is an estimate of the actual money received and paid out for a specific period. A cash budget anticipates that cash will come into a business and cash will be paid out during each week or month of operation. Even though a new business might not be making a profit, it still must have adequate cash on hand to pay current expenses. Even profitable businesses may have times when adequate cash is not available due to high expenses or a delay in receiving payments from customers.

A cash budget will determine if a business has adequate financial resources on hand to pay bills as they become due or if they will need to borrow money. It will also show when there is so much cash on hand that some of it can be invested. Investing cash on hand provides another source of business income.

CHECKPOINT ✓
Identify and describe the three types of budgets needed by all businesses.

12.1 ASSESSMENT

Key Concepts

Determine the best answer.

1. True or False. Financial planning is needed by a small business only until it begins to make a profit.
2. The basic financial equation is
   a. revenue − profit = loss
   b. expenses + revenue = profit or loss
   c. profit − loss = revenue and expenses
   d. revenue − expenses = profit or loss
3. True or False. A cash budget is an estimate of the actual money received and paid out for a specific period.

Make Academic Connections

4. **Math** Use the basic financial equation to determine the profit or loss for each of the following:
   a. revenue $85,695; expenses $72,624
   b. revenue $1,824,300; expenses $2,183,680
   c. revenue $729,655; expenses $499,220
5. **Technology** Use the Internet to locate a sample business budget. Enter the entire budget into a spreadsheet program. Develop a new budget by adjusting each of the income and expense items in the budget with a 3 percent increase. Then develop another budget by adjusting the original income and expense items with a 1.5 percent decrease.
6. **Economics** Locate a newspaper or magazine article that describes an anticipated change in the economy that might result in higher or lower income or expenses for businesses. Write two paragraphs discussing how financial planners should use the information when developing an operating budget.

RETEACH Ask students how budgets help businesses plan for items in the basic financial equation.

CLOSE Ask each student to identify a way that a budget can help businesspeople make better decisions.

ENRICH Tell students to search the Internet to locate computer software programs that can help small business owners with financial planning and budgeting.

TEACH

Ask students why a business has a problem when it does not have enough cash on hand, even if it is making a profit. Remind them that they may be late with payments, making their suppliers unhappy, or they will have to borrow money, thus adding to the business expenses.

ONGOING ASSESSMENT

CHECKPOINT ✓ANSWER

Businesses use a start-up budget, which plans income and expenses from the beginning of a new business or a major business expansion until it becomes profitable; the operating budget, which describes the financial plan for ongoing operations for a specific period; and the cash budget, which is an estimate of the actual money received and paid out for a specific period.

ASSESS

Key Concepts *Answers*

1. False. It is important for a new business to have a budget to guide its financial decisions from the very beginning.
2. d. revenue – expenses = profit or loss
3. True

Make Academic Connections *Answers*

4. a. Profit: $85,695 – $72,624 = $13,071
   b. Loss: $1,824,300 – $2,183,680 = –$359,380
   c. Profit: $729,655 – $499,220 = $230,435
5. Answers will vary depending on the business budget used.
6. Answers will vary depending on the articles selected.

Focus on REAL LIFE

Ask students to read the feature and then discuss why Paulette's accountant would be concerned about the loan payment if Paulette was currently not behind in her payments. How should Paulette deal with important customers who do not pay their bills on time?

TEACH

Tell students that many people are not in the habit of keeping financial records for their personal lives. Therefore, it is difficult to get in the habit of record keeping when starting a new business. If you develop and use records for your personal finances, you will gain experience that will be helpful in your business career.

Write the names of each of the types of records in random order. Then, as you read the definition of each type of record from the lesson, ask students to match the definition with the correct record name.

Work as a TEAM

Instruct students to list the estimated financial value of each of the items on their lists. Then ask them to total the amounts in each of the table columns and determine which column has the greater value.

12.2 Financial Records and Financial Statements

Learning Outcomes

12.2.1 Identify several types of financial records needed by businesses.

12.2.2 Describe the differences between an income statement and a balance sheet.

Key Terms

financial records 294
assets 296
liabilities 296
owner's equity 296
balance sheet 296
income statement 297

Focus on REAL LIFE

Paulette was locking the door of her bakery for the night when her accountant called.

"I was reviewing your accounts and wanted to alert you that you currently don't have enough cash to pay the quarterly loan payment that will be due in three weeks. I don't want to alarm you, but I think you need a plan so you can keep your loan current and still have money to cover other expenses."

Pauline responded, "I appreciate your call. I try to make my loan payments on time but sometimes it's hard to have enough cash at the right time. I delivered two large orders for restaurant customers but I haven't yet been paid. They're big customers but they're slow payers. I hate to be too pushy about payment because I don't want them to take their business elsewhere."

Her accountant responded, "I know it's hard to always meet your cash needs and I know your bank appreciates how timely you have been in the past on your payments. Let's meet to talk about ways you might make sure you are building up a good cash balance in advance of your next loan payment."

LO 12.2.1

FINANCIAL RECORDS

Budgets reflect the financial plans of businesses. To determine if those plans have resulted in success, financial records are needed. **Financial records** are used to record and analyze the financial performance of a business. Several types of records are maintained. They provide detailed information about the financial activities of the company. Local, state, and federal governments require some records. Other records provide information needed by owners and managers to aid their decision making.

Work as a TEAM

Create a table with two headings: Things I Own and Things I Owe. Have each member of your team in turn add items to the list representing their personal assets and liabilities. After the lists are complete, review each list and divide them into current and long-term assets and liabilities.

Types of Records

The following records are commonly maintained to document the performance of a business.

- *Asset records* identify the buildings and equipment owned by the business, their original and current value, and the amount owed if money was borrowed to purchase the assets.
- *Depreciation records* identify the amount assets have decreased in value due to their age and use.
- *Inventory records* identify the type and quantity of resources and products on

Different Learning Styles

Auditory Learner Provide students with the opportunity to read each of the types of records and their definitions aloud to help them distinguish among the types. Consider allowing students to work in pairs or small groups.

hand along with the current value of each. Accurate records are crucial to determine if adequate resources are available to meet operating and production needs as well as customer demand.

- *Records of accounts* identify all purchases and sales made using credit. An *accounts payable record* identifies the companies from which credit purchases were made and the amounts purchased, paid, and owed. An *accounts receivable record* identifies customers that made purchases using credit and the status of each account.
- *Cash records* list all cash received and spent by the business.
- *Payroll records* contain information on all employees of the company, their compensation, and benefits.
- *Tax records* show all taxes collected, owed, and paid. As a part of payroll, employers must withhold a percentage of employees' salaries and wages for income taxes, Social Security and Medicare taxes, and, in some cases, unemployment compensation insurance. In addition to the taxes withheld from employees, businesses must pay the employer's share of Social Security and Medicare taxes, and other taxes that are calculated as a percentage of payroll. Depending on the type of business and the location, a company may have to collect and pay state and local sales taxes. Businesses may have to pay several types of taxes on their income and value of their assets. Adequate records must be maintained to accurately calculate any taxes owed and to file the necessary tax forms.

Maintaining Financial Records

Business records have to be accurate and should be kept up to date. In the past, the preparation and maintenance of financial records was an expensive and time-consuming process. It was often done manually using paper documents that had to be carefully completed, saved, and protected. Then those documents were sent to the people responsible for preparing the company's financial records.

Technology has changed the way financial information is collected in many businesses. Much of the information is now collected using point-of-production and point-of-sale technology such as scanners, touchscreens, wireless tablets, and card readers. Data files are often transferred instantly and securely from where they are stored to the computers of the people who prepare the financial records. Technology is also changing the way financial records are prepared and maintained. Businesses use computerized financial systems that have templates for each financial record. The software completes the necessary mathematical calculations. It updates records and compares those records with budgets. The software can even complete what-if

Life-Span Plan

Describe ways in which the financial planning activities of a business are similar to the financial planning that must be done by people to achieve their life-span goals. Evaluate the status of your own financial planning. How will you know what financial resources you will need to achieve your life-span goals?

istockphoto.com/Patrick Heagney

What are the differences between keeping records manually and on a computer?

Life-Span Plan Answer

Answers will vary. Students should describe similarities between business financial planning and life-span planning.

TEACH

Ask students to describe how the use of computers can increase the accuracy of financial records.
Can students think of any instances where the use of computers to manage financial records might result in inaccuracies?

THINK CRITICALLY THROUGH VISUALS

Keeping financial records manually is an expensive and time-consuming process. With computer technology, financial data can often be automatically entered and calculated. If a change is made, all the calculations involving that change can be updated automatically.

Different Learning Abilities

At-Risk Instruct students to visit a local business and identify several uses of technology that can aid in maintaining financial records. Suggest that students ask the manager about the use of technology in record keeping.

ONGOING ASSESSMENT

CHECKPOINT ✓ANSWER

Asset records, depreciation records, inventory records, records of accounts, cash records, payroll records, and tax records are all examples of records businesses must keep.

TEACH

Instruct students to write each of the financial terms on a separate note card. Then, as you introduce each of the two financial statements, ask students to hold up the cards of the financial terms that are reported on that statement.

Students should study the balance sheet in Figure 12-2 to identify the types of items that are current and long-term assets and current and long-term liabilities. Discuss the differences in the items that make them appropriate for each category.

▸ Figure 12-2 ANSWER

Students should be able to study this balance sheet and determine that the business is financially successful because total assets are greater than total liabilities.

comparisons to help managers determine the impact of changes in budgets and financial performance.

CHECKPOINT

What are some types of financial records that businesses must keep?

LO 12.2.2

FINANCIAL STATEMENTS

The three most important elements of a company's financial strength are its assets, liabilities, and owner's equity. In simple terms, **assets** are what a company owns, **liabilities** are what a company owes, and **owner's equity** is the value of the owner's investment in the business.

Reports that sum up the financial performance of a business are *financial statements*. A company reports its assets, liabilities, and owner's equity on the *balance sheet*.

Three other key financial elements for a business are the amounts of *sales*, *expenses*, and *profits*. Sales, expenses, and profits (or losses) for a specific time period are reported on the company's *income statement*.

The Balance Sheet

The assets, liabilities, and owner's equity for a specific date are listed on the **balance sheet**. The balance sheet is usually prepared monthly or quarterly. It must be prepared at least once each year. Figure 12-2 shows a balance sheet.

The left side of the balance sheet lists all assets. *Assets* are anything of value owned by the business. There are two common divisions of assets. *Current assets* include cash and those items that can be readily converted to cash such as inventory and accounts receivable. *Long-term assets* (also known as *fixed assets*) are the assets with a life span of more than a year. Common fixed assets are land, buildings, equipment, and expensive technology.

The right side of the balance sheet is divided into two categories. *Liabilities* are amounts owed by the business to others. As with assets, there are two types

The Co-Operate Company
Balance Sheet
June 30, 20xx

Assets			***Liabilities***		
Current Assets			***Current Liabilities***		
Cash	$22,225		Accounts payable	$18,250	
Accounts receivable	42,200		Payroll taxes payable	1,900	
Inventory	98,200		Wages payable	23,525	
Prepaid expenses	5,340		Short-term bank loan payable	5,700	
Total Current Assets		$167,965	***Total Current Liabilities***		$49,375
Long-Term Assets			***Long-Term Liabilities***		
Vehicles	68,500		Long-term notes payable	85,200	
Furniture and fixtures	21,450		Mortgage payable	120,600	
Equipment	33,000		***Total Long-Term Liabilities***		$205,800
Buildings	320,000				
Land	82,500		**Total Liabilities**		$255,175
Total Long-Term Assets		$525,450			
			Owner's Equity		$438,240
Total Assets		$693,415	**Total Liabilities and Owner's Equity**		$693,415

FIGURE 12-2

What can you tell about the success of this business based on this balance sheet?

Applied Skills

Mathematics Instruct students to modify Figure 12-2 by decreasing each of the assets by 5 percent and increasing each of the liabilities by 3 percent. Using the new amounts, students should calculate the totals for each of the categories of assets, liabilities, and owner's equity.

of liabilities. *Current liabilities* are those that will be paid within a year. *Long-term liabilities* are debts that will continue for longer than a year. Current liabilities include payments owed to banks and other financial institutions for short-term loans. Also included are payments due to suppliers for inventory purchases, supplies, and inexpensive equipment. Long-term liabilities are debts owed for land, buildings, and expensive equipment.

Finally, *owner's equity* is the value of the business after liabilities are subtracted from assets. It shows how much the business is worth on the date the balance sheet is prepared. Another way of thinking about owner's equity is that it represents the value of the investments owners have made in the business.

SW Productions/Photodisc/Getty Images

What must you consider when establishing a sales price for your product?

The Income Statement

To report the revenue, expenses, and net income or loss from operations for a specific period, a business prepares an **income statement**. An income statement usually covers three or six months but may also encompass a shorter time period. An annual income statement is always prepared. Figure 12-3 shows a sample income statement.

The Netinc Company
Income Statement
For the 6-month Period Ending December 31, 20xx

Revenue			
Sales	$1,289,650		
Sales returns and allowances	–20,200		
Net sales		$1,269,450	
Cost of goods sold		–325,650	
Interest earned		80,263	
Total Revenue			$1,024,063
Expenses			
Selling expense		$32,050	
Marketing expense		282,954	
Administrative expense		52,445	
Rent expense		38,220	
Utilities expense		22,900	
Payroll expense		184,908	
Total Expenses			$613,477
Income taxes			–68,250
Net Income			$342,336

FIGURE 12-3
What can you tell about the success of this business during this time period based on this income statement?

THINK CRITICALLY THROUGH VISUALS

Anticipated expenses and projected revenue must be considered when establishing a sales price for a product so that the seller can recoup all operating expenses and make a profit on the sales.

TEACH

Ask students to compare Figures 12-2 and 12-3. Ask them to point out the differences. What can they learn about a business from an income statement that they cannot learn from a balance sheet?

▸ Figure 12-3 ***ANSWER***

Students should be able to study this income statement and determine that the business was financially successful for the identified time period because revenue was greater than expenses, resulting in a profit.

Applied Skills

Mathematics Ask students to use the income statement in Figure 12-3 to demonstrate what happens if sales decrease by 5 percent, while all expenses increase by 10 percent. Invite students to set up a spreadsheet with the data shown in Figure 12-3 and demonstrate the impact of changing the figures for sales and expenses.

ONGOING ASSESSMENT

CHECKPOINT ✓ANSWER

A balance sheet reports assets, liabilities, and owner's equity as of a specific date. An income statement reports revenues, expenses, and net profit or loss for a specified time period.

ASSESS

Key Concepts *Answers*

1. b. asset records
2. False. Assets, liabilities, and owner's equity are reported on the balance sheet. An income statement reports revenue, expenses, and net income or loss.
3. c. one year
4. b. balance sheet

Make Academic Connections *Answers*

5. Tables will vary.
6. Personal balance sheets and income statements will vary.

CLOSE Ask students to complete the following sentences: "The purpose of a balance sheet is. . . ." "The purpose of an income statement is. . . ."

Revenue is all income received by the business during the period. Sources of income include the sale of products and services, plus interest earned from investments. *Expenses* are all of the costs of operating the business during the period. Expenses include things such as rent, supplies, inventory, payroll, and utilities. The business has a *net income* when revenue is greater than expenses. A *net loss* occurs when expenses are greater than income.

Business managers and owners review financial statements carefully to determine how their businesses are performing. Because the statements summarize financial performance for a specific time, the performance of the current period can be compared with the performance of last month or last year. If the value of assets is increasing in relation to liabilities, the business is in a better financial position. That may allow additional investment in new products, buildings, and equipment. A rapid rise in liabilities or decline in owner's equity should be carefully evaluated to determine what is causing the change. If net income is increasing, that performance should be maintained or improved. On the other hand, if expenses are increasing but revenue is not, the reasons for the problem must be identified and corrected.

In addition to comparing financial performance from one time period to another, financial statements allow comparisons with other businesses. A business that is less profitable than similar businesses, or with lower sales or higher expenses, may have difficulty competing.

CHECKPOINT ✓
What is the difference between a balance sheet and an income statement?

12.2 ASSESSMENT

Key Concepts

Determine the best answer.

1. The value of the buildings and equipment owned by a business can be determined in the
   a. inventory records
   b. asset records
   c. records of accounts
   d. tax records
2. True or False. A company reports its assets, liabilities, and owner's equity on the income statement.
3. Current liabilities are amounts owed that will be paid in less than
   a. one month
   b. six months
   c. one year
   d. five years
4. The current value of investments made by the owners of a business can be found in the
   a. income statement
   b. balance sheet
   c. tax records
   d. record of accounts

Make Academic Connections

5. **Government** A business is required to collect taxes and make payments to local, state, and federal governments for its employees. Use the Internet to gather information on payroll taxes (local, state, and federal) that must be collected by a business in your community. Prepare a table that identifies each type of payroll tax, how the amount of tax to be collected is determined, and when and to whom the payments must be made.
6. **Accounting** Using the examples in Figures 12-2 and 12-3, any records, and your best memory, create a personal balance sheet and income statement. The balance sheet should reflect your personal financial status as of the current date. The income statement should represent your income and expenditures for the past three months.

RETEACH Display Figures 12-2 and 12-3. Ask students to offer definitions of each of the major headings on the two financial statements and describe how each statement helps in understanding the financial condition of the business.

ENRICH Instruct students to enter the financial statements shown in Figures 12-2 and 12-3 into a spreadsheet program and insert the formulas to make the necessary calculations. Then ask them to demonstrate how the spreadsheet can be used to update each financial statement after six months.

12.3 Payroll Management

Learning Outcomes

12.3.1 Describe the components of a business payroll system.

12.3.2 Identify key information included in payroll records and paychecks.

Key Terms

payroll 299

payroll records 301

direct deposit 302

Focus on REAL LIFE

Zena picked up her paycheck from the human resources office on her way to the parking lot. She had finished a hard week of work and was looking forward to a meal and a movie with friends. She would stop by her bank on the way to the restaurant to deposit her paycheck in her savings account and get some cash for the weekend.

Zena ripped open the envelope and looked at her check and the earnings report. First she looked at the amount of the check to make sure she got paid for the overtime hours she had worked. Then she looked to see how many vacation days and sick days she had earned. She had nine vacation days—more than enough to cover the week of camping she had planned for the end of the month.

She continued to look at the earnings report and noticed that the cost of all of her benefits, including health and dental insurance, reduced her take-home pay by $62 each pay period. She also saw that the required withholding and other payments to federal and state governments totaled $143. Halfway through the year, Zena's deductions and withholding already had topped $3,500.

LO 12.3.1

PAYROLL SYSTEMS

One of the most important ongoing financial duties of a business is maintaining a payroll. A **payroll** is the financial record of employee compensation, deductions, and net pay. A *payroll system* maintains information on each employee in order to calculate the company's payroll and make the necessary payments to each employee, as well as any required payments to government.

Most businesses pay every employee on a weekly, bi-weekly, or monthly basis. A majority of employees in most businesses receive an hourly wage, but the wage rate may be different for each employee. Some employees work part time and others work full time. Some may earn overtime compensation. The rest of the employees, especially managers and others in professional positions, receive a weekly or monthly salary. Again, the amount of salary for each person may be different. Some may earn additional payments in the form of commissions, bonuses, and profit sharing.

As a part of the compensation system, most businesses provide employees a range of benefits. Benefits include such

istockphoto.com/manley099

What are other types of income that employees might earn besides wages and salaries?

Focus on REAL LIFE

Ask students why it is important for businesses to provide employees with detailed information about the type and cost of benefits and deductions as a part of the payroll process. Discuss what a business should do to make sure employees understand each of the items listed on the earnings report.

TEACH

Before beginning a discussion of payroll, show students Figure 12-4. Instruct them to study the figure carefully and identify all of the information that is included in the payroll record. Ask them why each of the types of information in the record is needed by the business and the employee.

THINK CRITICALLY THROUGH VISUALS

Other sources of income students may suggest in addition to the typical standard paycheck are tips for waitstaff positions, royalties for creative works, dividend income from investments in stocks and bonds, payment for freelance work, fares and tips for taxi drivers, bonuses for outstanding performance or end-of-year holidays, profit sharing and pension payments, sales commissions, and signing bonuses when sought-after new employees are hired.

Different Learning Abilities

Specific Learning Disability (SLD) Assign students several math problems that involve an hourly wage rate and the number of hours an employee works each week. Ask students to calculate the amount that would be earned in one week for each example. Provide a calculator for students if needed.

FYI

Instruct students to use the Internet to determine the current withholding rates that employees, employers, and self-employed persons pay for Medicare and Social Security.

A Question of Ethics

Explain to students that confidentiality is important in business. Employees and managers need to be very careful not to disclose personal and confidential information about other employees, customers, and the business. Confidentiality is both a legal issue and a matter of ethical behavior.

Think Critically *Answers*

1. Answers will vary. Some will probably feel the probationary employee deserved more feedback about the co-workers' opinions and an opportunity to tell her side of the story. Others will feel that it is the employer's right to hire or fire employees as he or she thinks best.

2. The supervisor could have asked the complaining employees to provide specific examples of their concerns and shared those concerns with the new employee. Specific examples of negative behavior should have been documented. The decision to fire should not have been made based on general, vague feelings. The new employee should have asked for candid feedback from her supervisor throughout the probationary period.

FYI In addition to income taxes, people who are employed by companies and people who are self-employed all pay taxes for Medicare and Social Security. Employers pay half of the required payment for each employee. The other half is deducted from the employee's paycheck. Proprietors must pay self-employment taxes, which cover their contributions to Medicare and Social Security. Because they are self-employed they pay the full amount.

things as insurance options, paid or unpaid vacation, sick leave and personal time off, retirement plans, and education assistance. A business must keep records of employee benefits earned and used. The direct cost of benefits to the business and each employee is usually a part of the company's payroll system.

The final part of the payroll system is tax records and payments. Businesses are responsible for making required federal and state payments for each employee. These taxes consist of income taxes, Social Security, Medicare, and unemployment taxes and are commonly referred to as *payroll taxes.*

Income Taxes The federal government, most states, and some local governments require employers to withhold income tax from their employees' pay. The amount withheld is based on the wages or salary paid and the number of employee dependents.

Social Security and Medicare These payments are often referred to as FICA (Federal Insurance Contributions Act). The government requires employers to withhold and deposit these contributions from employees' paychecks along with matching contributions by the employer.

Unemployment Taxes As required by the Federal Unemployment Tax Act (FUTA), many employers must contribute to the

A QUESTION OF ETHICS

Disclosing Employee Performance Information

Following a three-month probationary period, a new employee was fired. The supervisor had heard from several employees that the new worker was hard to get along with and was not carrying her full share of the work. While two work evaluations completed by the supervisor rated her performance as above average, her performance was not outstanding, so the decision was made to terminate her employment. When the employee was notified of the decision, she was shocked and asked why she was being fired. Not wanting to create problems for the current employees who had complained or to disclose that the evaluations had not shown serious problems, the supervisor declined to provide reasons. Should the employee have a right to know why she was fired?

There are federal and state laws that regulate an employee's right to information. An employee generally can examine information in his or her personnel file that relates to work performance. That includes any written notes and formal performance evaluations. An employer should be careful about making judgments that are heavily influenced by the opinions of others without direct evidence. Also, providing regular feedback on evaluations and discussing any issues or concerns before they become major problems are important management responsibilities.

Think Critically

1. Do you believe the supervisor was right in not disclosing the information gathered from the new employee's co-workers? Why or why not? Do you feel the same way about the results of the work evaluations?
2. What recommendations would you make to the supervisor to prevent the type of situation from occurring again? As a new employee, what would you do to make sure you have adequate feedback on how you are doing?

Applied Skills

Writing Across the Curriculum Assign students to write a paragraph that explores how the concept of acting ethically with respect to confidential information is applicable to material in another class in which they are enrolled.

unemployment insurance system. The amount owed is based on the business's total employee wages. Many states also have their own unemployment taxes. Unemployment taxes are collected to compensate employees who lose their jobs through no fault of their own.

Employers withhold taxes from employee wages and salaries as well as make their own required contributions. Businesses must prepare and maintain tax records and then send quarterly or annual required payments to the federal and state governments.

Most payroll systems are part of a larger personnel records system. That system is a central location for all information the company maintains on all employees from the time they are hired until well after they no longer work for the business. Personnel records include personal information, employment history, performance evaluations, compensation records, and other information needed by the company. Most information in personnel files is confidential. Because of this, businesses must carefully and securely maintain these records.

Ruth Peterkin/Shutterstock.com

How do payroll records reflect an employee's vacation time?

CHECKPOINT
What is the purpose of the payroll system?

LO 12.3.2
PREPARING A PAYROLL

Maintaining payroll records and preparing paychecks is an ongoing and often time-consuming task for businesses. In the past, employees completed and submitted a time card. Payroll clerks entered the information into each employee's payroll record. When paychecks were to be issued at the end of each pay period, employee compensation and deductions had to be calculated, withholding and benefits records completed, and paychecks prepared. Today, computerized personnel records systems make the payroll process much more efficient and accurate. Software is available to manage simple or very complex payroll systems. Technology is used to collect employee time and production records each work period. When paychecks need to be prepared, information on benefits and deductions is determined and each employee's pay is calculated. All payroll records are updated and paychecks are printed, or electronic deposits are transmitted to employees' bank accounts.

Payroll Records

Payroll records are the documentation used to process earnings payments and record each employee's pay history. While a few small companies still maintain records in paper form, most now use computerized systems to maintain payroll records electronically.

The payroll records for each employee contain all the information an employer needs in order to pay the worker. This includes detailed personal information for each employee. An individual payroll record also has salary and wage rate data

THINK CRITICALLY THROUGH VISUALS

Most businesses use their payroll system to keep track of the vacation time each employee has earned and used. Some employees may receive paid vacation while others may get time off without pay. Either scenario must be reflected in each employee's record.

ONGOING ASSESSMENT

CHECKPOINT ANSWER

The purpose of the payroll system is to maintain information on each employee in order to calculate the company's payroll and make the necessary payments to each employee, taking the proper reductions for the costs of benefits, as well as state and federal deductions from each paycheck.

TEACH

Invite a manager who is responsible for overseeing the preparation of a company payroll to speak to the class. Ask the person to describe the procedures that are completed, the technology used, and the amount of time it takes to process the entire company payroll each time.

Different Learning Abilities

English Language Learners (ELL) Ask students to review the lesson and write any terms related to payroll and payroll records that they have difficulty pronouncing or understanding on a sheet of paper. Review each of the words with the student to help with comprehension.

Work as a TEAM

Assign students to work together to role-play the discussion with an employee. After watching several scenarios, ask students which method seemed to be most effective at answering the employee's questions.

TEACH

Remind students about the benefits of using direct deposit of an employee's paycheck to the employee, the business, and the bank. Ask whether students see any disadvantages of using direct deposit for any of the three.

THINK CRITICALLY THROUGH VISUALS

The employee should review the earnings report for accuracy and to check the current status of benefits. The amount of the direct deposit should be recorded in the employee's personal financial records, such as a check register, to maintain an accurate and up-to-date balance.

ONGOING ASSESSMENT

CHECKPOINT ✓ANSWER

A payroll record is documentation used to process earnings payments and record each employee's pay history. An earnings report contains an employee's earnings and deductions information for the current pay period as well as the cumulative amounts for the year.

Work as a TEAM

Review the information in the Focus on Real Life at the beginning of the lesson. Imagine you are a human resources manager. Discuss with your team what you could say to employees concerned with the amount of money taken from their paycheck each pay period to pay for benefits and taxes.

along with information about vacation and sick days earned. The tax filing status for the employee is included in order to calculate withholding for federal, state, and local taxes. Additional information is required for payroll deductions. This information includes health insurance payments and retirement plan contributions.

Each employee's pay history is maintained in the payroll records. This includes the amount of gross pay, withholding and deductions, net pay for each pay period, and a year-to-date balance for each item. Each time payroll is processed, each payroll record is updated.

istockphoto.com/laflor

What should an employee do with each earnings report and notification of direct deposit?

Preparing Paychecks

The information maintained in the payroll records is used to process payroll. For each pay period, the amounts for gross pay, withholding, deductions, and net pay are calculated and a paycheck is prepared for each person. The actual paycheck shows only the net pay amount—it is the amount of the check.

Employees want to know how the amount of pay they receive is determined and the type and amount of deductions made. Most businesses print an *earnings report* that is included with the employee's paycheck. It usually provides information for the current pay period as well as the cumulative amounts for the year. The earnings report is often attached to the paycheck and is sometimes called a *pay stub*.

Many businesses offer a direct deposit service for employees. With **direct deposit**, the employer transfers net pay electronically into the employee's bank account. The employee does not receive a printed paycheck but is given a printed or e-mailed notification of the funds transfer. In addition to the notification, sometimes called *advice of deposit*, the employee also receives an earnings report.

The earnings report may be posted to a secure area on the company's website where the employee can view it, save it electronically, or print a copy. An example of an employee earnings report and direct deposit notice is shown in Figure 12-4.

CHECKPOINT ✓
What is the difference between a payroll record and an earnings report?

Applied Skills

Communication Assign students to create a communication designed to encourage employees to choose direct deposit for their paychecks. Offer suggestions for the medium that students might consider for communicating their message. For example, they might prepare an insert for pay envelopes, a poster, a bulletin board, or a feature article for the employee website or newsletter.

Sample Earnings Report and Direct Deposit Notification

Employee Earnings Report

Marquese Co.	**Taylor Carson**	Date	05/21/20xx
525 Liberty Street	**2346 Transport Dr.**	Document number	18925
Anchora, IN 46200	**Tollboard, IN 46299**	**Net pay**	**375.00**

SSN XXX-XX-XXXX				
Employee ID	83-221		Pay period start	05/10/20xx
Federal filing status	S	1	Pay period end	05/16/20xx
State filing status	S	1	Pay frequency	Weekly

EARNINGS

Pay Type	Hours	Rate	Current	YTD
Regular Pay	40.00	12.00	480.00	8928.00
Overtime Pay	2.00	18.00	36.00	72.00
Holiday Pay	0.00			192.00
Vacation Pay	0.00			480.00
Sick Pay	0.00			
Total Hours	42.00			

SUMMARY

	Gross	Taxes	Deductions	Net Pay
Current	516.00	97.70	43.30	375.00
YTD	9672.00	1790.20	833.60	7048.20

DEDUCTIONS

Deduction	Current	YTD
401k (5.00%)	25.80	483.60
Health Insurance	17.50	350.00

TAXES

Tax Type	Current	YTD
Federal Income	41.34	734.46
Medicare	7.48	140.24
Social Security	31.99	599.66
IN State Income	16.89	315.84

NET PAY DISTRIBUTION

Account	Type	Amount
XXXX2077	Checking	355.00
XXXX1129	Savings	20.00
Check amount		0.00
Total net pay		375.00

FIGURE 12-4

How is the employee's net pay determined?

12.3 ASSESSMENT

Key Concepts

Determine the best answer.

1. The financial record of employee compensation, deductions, and net pay is known as
   a. compensation
   b. payroll
   c. earnings report
   d. paycheck
2. True or False. Businesses are responsible for making required federal and state payments for each employee.
3. The electronic transfer of net pay into an employee's bank account is known as
   a. tax withholding
   b. FICA
   c. direct deposit
   d. an automated payroll system
4. True or False. Payroll records need to be maintained for all full-time employees, but not for part-time employees.

Make Academic Connections

5. **Math** Calculate the amount of employee withholding for Social Security (6.2%) and Medicare (1.45%) for each of the following employee's wages.
   Marjorie Elder: $865.00
   Antoine Fresher: $726.40
   Amelda Francois: $1,480.90
6. **Art** Create a poster or flowchart that illustrates the steps in the payroll process from the point that employees complete their work until their paychecks are issued and required government tax payments are made.

▶ **Figure 12-4** ***ANSWER***

The employee's net pay is determined by subtracting all deductions from the gross pay.

ASSESS

Key Concepts *Answers*

1. b. payroll

2. True

3 c. direct deposit

4. False. Payroll records need to be maintained for all employees.

Make Academic Connections *Answers*

5. Marjorie Elder: $53.63, Social Security; $12.54, Medicare.

Antoine Fresher: $45.04, Social Security; $10.53, Medicare.

Amelda Francois: $91.82, Social Security; $21.47, Medicare.

6. Posters and flowcharts should clearly illustrate the steps. Consider allowing students to work in pairs.

CLOSE Ask students to identify one important fact about payroll that they have learned as a result of the lesson.

RETEACH Assign students to review the lesson and write one true/false question related to each of the lesson objectives. Organize the students into two teams. Teams should alternate asking the other team a question. Record the number of correct answers for each team.

ENRICH Some businesses issue paychecks to employees weekly, some bi-weekly, and some monthly. Lead a discussion about why a business might choose a longer time period than weekly to calculate payroll and issue paychecks.

LIFE/WORK SKILLS

Emphasize that productivity and accountability are essential skills for both managers and employees at all levels in a business. Discuss why those skills are important to business success and how the skills can be developed and demonstrated in classes, clubs, and extracurricular and non school activities.

THINK CRITICALLY THROUGH VISUALS

A team can draw on the individual skills and interests of team members to plan and complete a project. At the same time, team members will need to collaborate and cooperate to successfully manage the project and produce results.

Think Critically *Answers*

1. Successful project management is needed to produce intended results. A poor plan or poor work habits may result in wasted time and resources.

2. Examples will vary but should relate to one of the bullet points listed under the heading Being Accountable. For example, asking for help with a school assignment rather than giving up or continuing to struggle on your own makes you accountable for your own learning.

LIFE/WORK SKILLS

PRODUCTIVITY AND ACCOUNTABILITY

Success in the workplace requires the ability to function in complex and competitive environments. You need to be able to manage projects and produce results.

Managing Projects

Most people have some experience managing projects. Getting your chores finished in time to go out with friends, preparing a family meal, or writing a term paper are all examples of projects that need to be managed. The ability to manage projects, big and small, complex and simple, is critical to success in today's workplace. In order to manage a project you must be able to:

- Set realistic goals
- Allocate resources including money, time, and energy
- Chart progress
- Overcome obstacles
- Meet goals

Producing Results

Producing results involves more than finishing the project on schedule and within budget. Although time and money are often the focus of attention, the quality of the results, the efficiency of the process, and a sense of satisfaction for all participants are also important.

In addition to managing a project to achieve the intended result, you need to demonstrate attributes that are associated with producing high-quality products and services. These attributes are based on respect—respect for yourself and respect for others. Examples include:

- Positive attitude
- Ethical behavior
- Active participation
- Professional appearance
- Proper etiquette

Being Accountable

Accountability means being able to explain your actions and accept responsibility for the outcome. Employees and managers are paid to produce goods and services. A baker is expected to produce baked goods such as bread and cookies. An auto mechanic is expected to provide automotive services such as oil changes and engine tune-ups. In addition to producing goods and services, employees are expected to be accountable for the quantity and quality of their work, their personal behavior, and their interactions with colleagues, customers, and vendors. You can demonstrate accountability by:

- Collaborating and cooperating with others
- Respecting and appreciating diversity
- Being punctual and reliable
- Being honest
- Owning up to mistakes
- Asking for help when needed
- Working to improve skills

Think Critically

1. How does the ability to effectively manage a project relate to productivity?
2. Provide a specific example of how you can demonstrate accountability at school, home, and another situation.

istockphoto.com/MorePixels

How is team management of a project different from individual project management?

12.4 Financial Decision Making

Learning Outcomes

12.4.1 Recognize important financial information managers use to make decisions.

12.4.2 Identify the steps in making financial decisions in business.

Key Terms

financial performance ratios 305

discrepancies 308

Focus on REAL LIFE

John sat with his business partner, Anna, for their monthly meeting to review the company's financial statements.

"Once again our sales are up dramatically but our profit margins continue to hold steady or decline slightly," John noted. "We need to deal with this before it becomes a major problem."

"Well, we can see that the raw materials costs of our two top-selling products have gone up steadily over the past year and we are paying a lot more for utilities for our buildings and fuel for our vehicles," Anna responded.

"Yes, those two products are no longer really contributing much to profit even though they are by far our best sellers. Is it possible to reduce other expenses related to them or should we find ways to sell more of our currently profitable products?" John questioned.

Anna and John had a lot more work to do before making important decisions that would affect their company's future. They would need to study the financial reports in great detail to determine what needed to be done.

LO 12.4.1

USING FINANCIAL INFORMATION

Financial statements are important management tools for business owners and managers. Financial statements present summaries of the financial activities of a business. Managers who understand the information in financial statements will be better able to make decisions that result in the wise use of the company's money.

Important Financial Information

Three very important elements of a company's financial strength are its assets, liabilities, and owner's equity. Three other key elements are the amount of sales, expenses, and profits. A company reports its assets, liabilities, and owner's equity on the balance sheet. Sales, expenses, and profits for a specific period are reported on the company's income statement.

Understanding Financial Performance Ratios

Managers use the financial elements found on the financial statements to calculate financial performance ratios. **Financial performance ratios** are comparisons of a company's financial elements that indicate how well the business is performing. Some important financial performance ratios

Life-Span Plan

Explain why making good financial decisions is no less important to individuals than it is to businesses. How do you currently make important financial decisions? In what ways can you improve the process to help you achieve your life-span goals?

Focus on REAL LIFE

Tell students that just like John and Anna, business owners and managers rely on financial information to aid them in making important decisions about a company's future direction. Tell them that detailed financial information can help identify the types of issues Anna and John are facing before they damage a company.

TEACH

Before beginning the discussion, ask students to review the previous lessons in the chapter and identify the types of financial information they believe managers need to make good decisions about the use of the company's money. Compare their lists with the information presented in this lesson.

Life-Span Plan Answer

Answers will vary. Students should recognize the value of preparing a budget, using the budget, and making adjustments.

Different Learning Styles

Tactile Learner Print copies of Figures 12-2 and 12-3. Instruct students to review the copies to remind themselves how the important financial information is organized and presented in the two main financial statements.

TEACH

Financial performance ratios are an advanced topic and may be difficult for some students to immediately understand. As some students demonstrate their understanding of the ratios, use peer learning to pair those students with other students who have not yet grasped the concept to help with explanation and understanding.

▶ **Figure 12-5** ***ANSWER***

A debt to equity ratio higher than 2:1 indicates that a business might have too much debt. This puts a business at risk because it may have trouble meeting its obligations to its lenders.

ONGOING ASSESSMENT

CHECKPOINT ✓*ANSWER*

Four important financial performance ratios used by managers to determine how well a business is performing are (1) current ratio, (2) debt to equity ratio, (3) return on equity ratio, and (4) net income ratio.

THINK CRITICALLY THROUGH VISUALS

If your company's net income ratio increases from one year to the next, it shows that current-year sales have been more effective in adding to the company's profit than those in the past year.

Financial Performance Ratios

$$\text{Current Ratio} = \frac{\text{Current Assets}}{\text{Current Liabilities}}$$

$$\text{Debt to Equity Ratio} = \frac{\text{Total Liabilities}}{\text{Owner's Equity}}$$

$$\text{Return on Equity Ratio} = \frac{\text{Net Profit}}{\text{Owner's Equity}}$$

$$\text{Net Income Ratio} = \frac{\text{Total Sales}}{\text{Net Income}}$$

FIGURE 12-5

Why do banks want to see a debt to equity ratio no higher than 2:1 when they offer a business loan?

are the current ratio, debt to equity ratio, return on equity ratio, and net income ratio. Figure 12-5 shows the formulas used to calculate each ratio.

Current Ratio The *current ratio* compares the value of current assets with the amount of current liabilities. Current assets are those that the business could convert to cash within one year. Current liabilities are all payments owed to creditors that must be made within one year. The current ratio tells you if the business can pay its debts as they become due. The current ratio should be at least 1:1 for a healthy business. A 1:1 ratio means that there are at least as many current assets as current liabilities.

Debt to Equity Ratio The company's liabilities divided by the owner's equity is the *debt to equity ratio*. This ratio tells you how much the business is relying on money borrowed from others that will have to be paid back rather than money provided by the owners. Most banks want to see a debt to equity ratio of about 1:1 but no higher than 2:1. Too little debt means a company may not be using all of its resources effectively while too much debt puts a business at risk in meeting its obligations to lenders.

Return on Equity Ratio The net profit of the business compared to the amount of owner's equity is the *return on equity ratio*. The return on equity ratio shows the rate of return the owners are getting on the money they invested in the company. It should be compared to the return they could receive if they used their money in other ways such as savings, investing in other companies, or purchasing stocks and bonds.

Net Income Ratio The total sales compared to the net income for a period such as six months or a year is the *net income ratio*. The net income ratio shows how much profit is being made by each dollar of sales for the period being analyzed. The net income ratio can be compared to past periods and with similar companies. The ratio will show if additional sales are as effective in adding to the company's profit as those in the past.

CHECKPOINT ✓

Identify four important financial performance ratios used by managers to determine how well the business is performing.

Steve Cole/Digital Vision/Getty Images

What does it mean if your company's net income ratio increases from one year to the next?

Teaching Strategies

Collaborative Learning Organize students into learning teams and have each team answer the following question: How can a business experience increases in both sales and assets and still have financial problems? Use the financial performance ratios to answer the question.

LO 12.4.2

MAKING FINANCIAL DECISIONS

Managers are responsible for the financial health of their company and for the specific areas of the company under their control. If adequate finances are not available, the work that is required will not be done as well or as quickly as needed. On the other hand, if too much money is spent on certain operations, there may not be enough for other parts of the company.

The first step in financial decision making is preparing a budget. The budget identifies the amount of money needed for all parts of the business to complete planned activities. It also projects what types and amounts of income will be earned from the sale of the company's products, services, and other investments.

Once a budget is developed and approved, managers use the budget as a guide to operate the business. They

NET KNOWLEDGE

Managers use financial ratios to measure the general and specific financial performance of their businesses. Go online and find a site that identifies several additional financial ratios for business that aren't listed in this text. Select three ratios that strike you as important for business. Prepare a digital image for each ratio that shows the name of the ratio and the mathematical formula used for the calculation, as well as an explanation of what the ratio reveals about a company's performance.

Business Insight

How Much Is Enough?

In 2014, the average compensation of the top executives of the largest 100 U.S. companies was $10.5 million. That was an increase of 16 percent from the previous year. Most American workers had received almost no pay increases for several years. In recent years, executive compensation has grown at an exponential rate to that of employee pay. In 1968, the average corporate CEO made 20 times more than the average worker. Today the ratio is nearly 300 to 1. As many companies have reduced the number of employees and made cutbacks in wages and benefit packages, many people are questioning the appropriateness of big paydays for executives. They are asking, "How much is enough?"

Corporate boards set executive compensation levels. Some critics, including shareholders, accuse board members of having close relationships with executives that result in the higher pay levels. Board members respond that managing a large corporation is extremely difficult and requires huge personal sacrifices. The compensation levels reflect those demands. They point out that total compensation for executives is a tiny percentage of overall company revenues and that successful management increases profits and financial returns to shareholders.

In response to concern about excessive executive compensation, regulations have been enacted that require more disclosure about compensation packages. The 2010 Dodd–Frank Wall Street Reform and Consumer Protection Act requires public companies to submit executive pay plans to a non-binding shareholder vote to give them a "say on pay" in their companies.

Think Critically

1. If a company has annual revenues of tens or even hundreds of billions of dollars, is it appropriate for the CEO to make $10 million or more in a year? Why or why not?
2. Do you believe there should be a relationship between compensation of a company's CEO and average employees' wages? Justify your answer.

NET KNOWLEDGE

Ask students to share the slides they develop with the class. Students should discuss each ratio separately to determine how managers can benefit from the information it provides.

TEACH

Explain that financial conditions can change rapidly, and managers can be more prepared to deal with problems or take advantage of opportunities if they have the most current financial information.

Business Insight

The issue of executive compensation is likely to be a divisive one among students. Provide a forum where every student's voice can be heard.

Think Critically
Answers

1. Answers will vary. Discuss ethical issues that arise when some members of an organization are extremely well-compensated while the vast majority must rely on public assistance to make ends meet.
2. Answers will vary. Discuss methods for determining the success of corporate executives and the contributions of employees to that success.

Applied skills

Language Arts Ask students to complete the sentence: I believe the most important financial information needed by managers is ____ because ____.

Work as a TEAM

The performance ratios are:
Current ratio: 3.4 (167,965 ÷ 49,375)
Debt to equity ratio: 0.58 (255,175 ÷ 438,240)
Net income ratio: 3.77 (1,289,650 ÷ 342,336)

ONGOING ASSESSMENT

CHECKPOINT ✓ *ANSWER*

The three steps are (1) preparing a budget, (2) using the budget as a guide to the operation of the business, and (3) making needed adjustments to bring performance in line with the budget.

ASSESS

Key Concepts *Answers*

1. c. payroll
2. True
3. False. Managers are responsible for the financial health of a company.
4. d. discrepancies

Make Academic Connections *Answers*

5. Share several students' presentations with the class to reinforce the concept.
6. Answers will vary. Perhaps a new product was introduced later than expected, unanticipated overtime was needed to meet production quotas, or a product defect resulted in a number or returned and cancelled orders.
7. Debt to equity ratio 2.40:1 ($786,050/$326,927) Return on equity ratio 0.08:1 ($27,293/$326,927)

CLOSE Ask students to offer specific comparisons of the management of their personal finances to the management of a company's finances.

Work as a TEAM

Use the information from Figures 12-2 and 12-3 to calculate three of the financial performance ratios described in this lesson: current ratio, debt to equity ratio, and net income ratio. Use decimals to express your answers. Discuss what the results mean for the businesses.

regularly check to see if income and expenses are meeting budgeted amounts. Income should be as high as or higher than planned. Expenses should not exceed the budgeted amount. Managers receive regular financial reports and examine them carefully, looking for discrepancies. **Discrepancies** are differences between actual and budgeted performance.

Discrepancies let managers identify problems before they become serious enough to harm the business. They might also see areas where financial performance is better than what was budgeted.

The final step is to make needed adjustments. If income and expenses are similar to the budget, the manager will not need to take action. If there are financial problems, managers will take corrective action to try to bring performance back in line with the budget. That might include finding ways to improve revenue as well as seeking ways to cut expenses. In some cases, performance cannot be improved or factors outside the managers' control are responsible for the poor performance. The managers may have to adjust the budget. This should be done as a last resort because the budget was carefully planned.

At the end of the period covered by the budget, the business will prepare new financial statements. It will use the results to determine the financial success of the operations. The company will also use the results to prepare new budgets and improve the budgeting process in the future.

CHECKPOINT ✓
List the three steps in financial decision making.

12.4 ASSESSMENT

Key Concepts

Determine the best answer.

1. Which of the following is not one of the three important elements of a company's financial strength?
   a. assets
   b. owner's equity
   c. payroll
   d. liabilities
2. True or False. Sales and profits for a specific period are reported in a company's income statement.
3. True or False. Employees—rather than managers—are responsible for the financial health of a company.
4. Differences between actual and expected performance are
   a. ratios
   b. budgets
   c. profit or loss
   d. discrepancies

Make Academic Connections

5. **Communication** You are responsible for helping a new manager understand financial statements. Prepare and present a short presentation explaining the importance of the balance sheet and income statement. Use a computer and presentation software to develop several slides for your presentation.
6. **Critical Thinking** In comparing current operating costs with the budget, you see that payroll expenses are much higher than budgeted, but income has not increased. How would you attempt to identify the problem? What might be some reasons for the discrepancy?
7. **Math** At the end of the year, the financial statements of a small business showed total liabilities of $786,050; net profit of $27,293, and owner's equity of $326,927. Calculate the debt to equity and return on equity ratios for the company. Round your results to the nearest hundredth.

ENRICH Ask students to identify how they believe employees can help to improve the financial performance of an organization. Ask for examples in the areas of revenues, expenses, and profits. Discuss why employees should be concerned about the financial performance of the company they work for.

RETEACH List the three steps in financial decision making on the board. Lead a class discussion about how managers should complete each step and how the step contributes to the financial health of the business.

DOING BUSINESS IN... SPAIN

Spain's economic and cultural history reveals several dramatic shifts in fortune. As one of the leading European empires from the 1500s through the 1800s, Spain extended its economic and political reach throughout the Western Hemisphere. With their expansive navy, Spanish conquistadors exerted ruthless control over people and land from South to North America, the Caribbean, Africa, and into Asia. The cost of maintaining the empire combined with a series of weak and inept monarchs led to the demise of the empire. While much of Europe was experiencing a social and economic awakening, Spain languished. The dictator Francisco Franco seized control of the country in 1936 and maintained it until his death in 1975. Spain now is a parliamentary monarchy, effectively a democracy, with King Felipe VI as the head of state and a prime minister leading the country's government.

Spain was one of 12 countries that signed the first Treaty on European Union in 1992. As a European Union (EU) member, Spain quickly became an economic leader in Europe, establishing itself as the fourth-largest European economy. Its historic and recent success has been propelled by its location on the Iberian Peninsula. Bordered on three sides by large bodies of water and sitting as the physical gateway to Europe, Africa, and the Middle East, Spain attracted foreign investment and tourism that resulted in a construction and real estate boom in the early part of this century. Recently, however, Spain's economy has experienced a sharp downturn. This is due to the global recession and real estate slump, as well as poor government planning and control of financial, education, and investment strategies. The economy is only now starting to recover and still suffers from both high unemployment and public debt as well as a poor education system.

Despite this, Spain has been effective in attracting foreign investment to build its economy. Many Spanish companies have multinational operations. Spain has historically been the second-largest investor in Latin America after the United States. It is home to the world's largest renewable energy company, Iberdrola, and the second-largest construction company in the world, Grupo ACS.

Although some business in Spain might be conducted in English, business documents and materials are generally printed in Spanish. The hours businesses can operate are regulated by the government. Professional businesses and shops are generally closed from 2 to 4 P.M. for the traditional lunch and rest time. Spain is made up of 17 regions, each with its own culture and customs. There are even language and dialect differences between regions. Nearly 2.5 million small shops and businesses in cities and villages contribute to the Spanish economy.

Think Critically

1. Why has Spain's geographic location been important to its historic world power as well as its economic development as an EU member?
2. What advantages might Spain's large multinational businesses provide to Spain's economy?
3. Conduct library or Internet research to learn more about business and economic activities in Spain. Prepare a short report on your findings.

How does this photograph of a pedestrian bridge in Bilbao suggest that Spain has worked to attract tourism and foreign businesses?

Doing Business in . . . SPAIN

Use a map to help students focus on Spain's location and size.

THINK CRITICALLY THROUGH VISUALS

Answers will vary. Students might point out that the bridge appears to be new and has a modern design which might make them think Spain is working on ways to make cities appealing and inviting places to live, work, and visit.

Think Critically *Answers*

1. Spain's location allows it easy access to the rest of Europe, Africa, and the Middle East. It is a great tourist destination.
2. Renewable energy and construction are both important areas for economic growth worldwide. They provide employment and profits for the Spanish economy, can complete major energy and construction projects in the country, and participate in the economic development of other countries.
3. Students should summarize and report the results of their research.

Think Critically About Business *Answers*

1. Expenses for the start-up could be building rental, furniture, equipment, inventory, hiring and training personnel, or state and local licenses and permits. Expenses for ongoing operations might include sales, marketing and distribution costs, operating and production expenses, raw materials and inventory replacement, or personnel costs. Expansion phase expenses could be similar to start-up expenses to pay for opening branch locations, additional advertising and distribution expenses, or costs of moving production to another location.

2. A budget is a future projection based on financial history and current trends. A financial record is an accounting of the actual financial performance of a company.

Budgets chart the future; financial records keep companies on track to meet performance goals.

3. A business needs an accurate cash budget to determine how much money will be received and paid out for a specified period so it has enough money on hand to pay bills. It will also show when a business may have excess cash on hand. A business needs access to cash so that it can pay current expenses. Even profitable businesses need access to cash for unexpected expenses or when they experience a delay in receiving payments.

4. A balance sheet contains information about assets, liabilities, and owner's equity as of a specific date. The income statement focuses on profitability from sales and expenses for a specific time period.

Chapter 12 Assessment

Review Business Concepts

12.1 Financial Planning

- The financial questions that must be answered in a business include: How much money is needed to start the business? From where will the financing come? How will funds be obtained to run the business for the months or years until it becomes profitable? What will be the best sources of sales and other income? What will be the expenses? When must they be paid?
- The four main steps in budget preparation are: prepare a list of the income and expenses that will be a part of the budget; gather accurate information for each income and expense; create the budget by calculating each type of income, expense, and amount of net income or loss; and show and explain the budget to people who need financial information to make decisions.
- There are three types of business budgets. The start-up budget plans income and expenses from the beginning of a new business or a major expansion until it becomes profitable. The operating budget describes the financial plan for ongoing operations of the business for a specific period. A cash budget is an estimate of the actual money received and paid out for a specific period.

12.2 Financial Records and Financial Statements

- Financial records are used to record and analyze the financial performance of a business. The types of records maintained include asset, depreciation, inventory, account, cash, payroll, and tax records.
- The two most common and important financial statements for businesses are the income statement and balance sheet. The business's assets, liabilities, and owner's equity for a specific date are listed on the balance sheet. An income statement reports the revenue, expenses, and net income or loss from operations for a specific period.

12.3 Payroll Management

- A payroll is the financial record of employee compensation, deductions, and net pay. A payroll system maintains information on each employee in order to calculate the company's payroll and to make the necessary payments to each employee.
- Payroll records are the documentation used to process earnings payments and record each employee's pay history. An individual payroll record contains the employee's name, some personal information, individual tax information, and a record of all benefits received. After all payroll records have been completed and pay amounts have been calculated, a paycheck is prepared for each person. An earnings report lists the employee's current and cumulative pay amounts and the type and amount of deductions.

12.4 Financial Decision Making

- Three important elements of a company's financial strength are assets, liabilities, and owner's equity. Two other key elements for a business are the amount of sales and profits. Managers use those financial elements to calculate financial performance ratios to make decisions that result in the wise use of the company's money.
- The first step in financial decision making is preparing a budget. Second, managers use the budget as a guide to the operations of the business. The final step is to make any needed adjustments.

Think Critically About Business

1. Identify several unique business expenses for three important times in a business's life: start-up, ongoing operations, and expansion.
2. What is the difference between a budget and a financial record? Why are both needed in a business?
3. Why is it important to maintain an accurate cash budget for a business? What happens to a business if it does not have access to cash even though it has other assets worth a lot of money?
4. What information is contained in a balance sheet that is not in an income statement?

5. Answers will vary. Payroll managers could have employees sign confidentiality agreements. Both computer and paper files should be maintained securely with well-controlled access.

6. Direct deposit cons: People like receiving a paycheck, want the freedom to deposit it in varying banks, fear it will be more difficult to resolve problems with inaccuracies, or do not like or trust change. Pros: Increased security, reduced costs, and time savings when employees don't have to handle the paycheck.

5. Confidentiality of the personal information of employees is very important in businesses and other organizations. If you were the payroll manager of a large company and had several employees who had access to personnel and payroll records, what would you do to protect the confidentiality of the information that they could access as a part of their work?

6. The use of direct deposit for employee paychecks saves businesses and banks a large amount of time and money. Some employees are still reluctant to use it. What are some reasons people may not want to use this system? How might you convince a reluctant employee to use direct deposit?

7. Why are the assets, liabilities, and owner's equity more important to the financial strength of a business than the amount of profit they earned in a particular period?

8. If you were a stockholder in a business, which of the four financial performance ratios would be most important to you? Why? If you were a banker considering loaning money to a business, which ratios would be most important to you? Why?

9. Do you believe the financial performance of a business is a more important measure of a manager's effectiveness than other factors, such as customer satisfaction or employee satisfaction or turnover? Justify your answer.

Develop Your Business Language

Match the terms listed with the definitions.

10. Reports the revenue, expenses, and net income or loss from business operations for a specific period.
11. Provides detailed plans for the financial needs of individuals, families, and businesses.
12. The employer electronically transfers net pay into the employee's bank account.
13. Plans income and expenses from the beginning of a new business or a major business expansion until it becomes profitable.
14. Used to record and analyze the financial performance of a business.
15. All income that a business receives over a period of time.
16. Lists the business's assets, liabilities, and owner's equity for a specific date.
17. Differences between actual and budgeted performance.
18. Describes the financial plan for ongoing operations of the business for a specific period.
19. What a company owns.
20. The costs of operating a business.
21. An estimate of the actual money received and paid out for a specific period.
22. The documentation used to process earnings payments and record each employee's pay history.
23. Comparisons of a company's financial elements that indicate how well the business is performing.
24. The financial records of employee compensation, deductions, and net pay.
25. The value of the owners' investment in the business.
26. What a company owes.

Key Terms

a. assets
b. balance sheet
c. budget
d. cash budget
e. direct deposit
f. discrepancies
g. expenses
h. financial performance ratios
i. financial records
j. income statement
k. liabilities
l. operating budget
m. payroll
n. payroll records
o. owner's equity
p. revenue
q. start-up budget

7. Profits are determined for a specific shorter period of time. The balance sheet shows the overall financial health of a company in terms of its major assets, liabilities, and equity.

8. A stockholder would be most interested in a company's return on equity ratio as it would show whether this investment is as profitable as other available investment options. A banker would be most interested in the debt to equity ratio to be sure the business does not already have too much debt.

9. Answers will vary. Most students will probably agree that financial performance is the most important measure of a manager's effectiveness, but financial success often results from the other factors as well.

Develop Your Business Language *Answers*

10. j. income statement
11. c. budget
12. e. direct deposit
13. q. start-up budget
14. i. financial records
15. p. revenue
16. b. balance sheet
17. f. discrepancies
18. l. operating budget
19. a. assets
20. g. expenses
21. d. cash budget
22. n. payroll records
23. h. financial performance ratios
24. m. payroll
25. o. owner's equity
26. k. liabilities

Make Academic Connections *Answers*

27a. Last year, Mr. Chan earned $78,250 in sales; this year, he earned $80,725 in sales.

27b. His total cost of doing business last year was $71,880; this year, it was $69,055.

27c. Last year, Mr. Chan had a profit of $6,370; this year, he had a profit of $11,670. His profit was $5,300 greater this year than last, an increase of about 45%.

28. Answers will vary.

29. Note cards will vary.

30. Answers will vary depending on the article selected. Provide guidance for the citation format you want students to use.

Make Your Case *Answers*

31. Positive findings: ability to pay himself some salary, increase in the value of company assets, decrease in long-term liabilities, positive sales growth, increased cash on hand, declining losses.

Negative findings: continued need for his part-time job, lack of funds to hire another employee, increase in total liabilities, no change in the value of the owner's equity, increasing cost of inventory, and increased operating expenses.

32. Dominic's business is successful in the sense that it is improving and moving in the right direction. However, the business is at the three-year mark where it should begin to show a profit. He might want to re-evaluate the company's financial situation at the end of the third year to determine whether the business just needs a little more time or whether his investment and energies could be better spent elsewhere.

Interactions and Connections

33. Town and cities will usually prepare an annual balance sheet. They may not have an income statement but will have a similar form often called the *statement of revenues, expenditures and changes in funds balances.*

The balance sheet will list assets and liabilities but will not have owner's equity since the government relies on tax revenues rather than ownership investments. The revenue and expenditures statement lists revenues rather than income, including taxes and other revenues. It lists expenses of operating the town, similar to business expenses. There will be no net income but the statement will show whether revenues exceeded expenses or not.

Other important statements include asset records, statements of cash flows, and any special assessments or revenue or operating funds.

Make Academic Connections

27. Math Lee Chan has owned a computer repair business for three years. The first year, Mr. Chan barely earned a profit. The next year's profit was more substantial. As shown in the table, he has just received the financial results from the third year and wants to compare them to those of the second year of operations.

a. How much money did Mr. Chan earn from sales each year?
b. What was his total cost of doing business each year?
c. What profit or loss did Mr. Chan earn this year? What is the dollar amount and percentage difference in the profit or loss from last year?

	LAST YEAR	THIS YEAR
Rent	$28,000	$28,000
Sales	78,250	80,725
Inventory	15,000	13,750
Payroll	17,850	18,210
Utilities	10,010	7,075
Supplies	1,020	2,020

28. Technology Use the Internet to identify two software programs that can be used by a small business to manage payroll. Evaluate the two programs and prepare a table that compares the features of the two programs. Prepare a written recommendation to a business owner on the software you believe would be the best choice. Include reasons for your decision.

29. Economics The budgets of a business are affected by events and changes outside the business, including the actions of competitors and the strength and weakness of the local, national, and global economies. Review recent newspapers and business magazines. Find several articles that report on the economy and competition that could have a positive or negative effect on businesses in your community. Prepare a note card for each article on which you summarize the key points of the article and describe how the information could affect the financial decisions made by business managers.

30. Reading Comprehension Find a news article that relates to financial decision making. Read the article and write a one-paragraph summary of the main idea. Include a properly formatted citation for your source. Possible sources include printed and online versions of newspapers and magazines. You should also consider independent online sources that produce original content.

Make Your Case

Dominic sat at his office computer reviewing the financial statements for his three-year-old business. He had yet to make a profit. He was able to pay himself a small salary, but he still had to hold a part-time job to maintain his family's lifestyle. He had added a part-time employee and needed another, but didn't have the money to pay another person right now. Dominic studied the balance sheets and income statements side by side. The balance sheets showed that the value of assets was increasing. Liabilities had increased as well due to the need to continue to borrow money to purchase inventory as his sales increased. He had been able to make regular payments on his building and equipment loans, so long-term liabilities were decreasing. There had been no change in the value of the owner's equity, so his investment was not paying off. When he shifted his attention to the income statement, he could see that sales were up sharply, but so were the costs of his inventory and operating expenses. He did notice that he had more cash on hand to pay bills as they came due and that the losses were getting smaller and smaller.

31. Based on Dominic's review, which findings are positive? Which findings are negative?

32. Based on the financial information provided, do you believe Dominic's business is successful or not? Justify your answer.

Interactions and Connections

33. Locate copies of the most recent year's financial statements for your local town or city. You should be able to find them on the government website or by visiting the administrative offices. Review the list of documents and identify those that are the same or similar as the balance sheet and income statement discussed in Lesson 12.2. Study each of those forms reflecting the financial condition of your town or city. What major similarities and differences do you notice between the two financial statements of your town or city and those shown in Figures 12-2 and 12-3? What other financial statements published by your town or city would be important in helping citizens understand its financial health?

34. Visit the website of the United States Internal Revenue Service. Locate information about the following tax forms related to business payroll:

Form W-2
Form W-4
Form 940
Form 941
Form 944

a. Prepare a brief description of the purpose of each form. Include answers to the following questions: Who is responsible for completing the form? When must it be completed? Where is it sent or distributed?

b. Other than sending checks, how can businesses make payroll tax payments to the federal government?

Entrepreneurship Event

In order to avoid the high failure rate experienced by many new businesses, successful entrepreneurs must conduct research, secure financing, and convince consumers to purchase the goods and services they offer. Developing a business plan is a good way to organize these activities.

For this event you must develop a business plan for a new restaurant to be located near a university campus that has 30,000 students during the regular school year. Your business plan must demonstrate how you will maintain favorable sales for the restaurant throughout the entire year. Currently the country is experiencing an economic recession.

Your business plan must include the products and services to be provided, market analysis, customer profile, competition, short-range operational goals, financial analysis (income statement, balance sheet, cash flow statement, and other analyses), and supporting research documents. The business plan must not exceed 10 single-spaced pages.

You will orally present your business plan to the judges or class members for 10 minutes. Following your presentation, they will have up to five minutes to ask questions about your business plan.

Performance Indicators Evaluated

- Develop a written business plan for a start-up business during a recession.
- Identify the customer base, including consumer and organizational markets, highlighting demographics.
- Analyze financial data.
- Demonstrate successful price selection methods.
- Identify and use internal and external resources.

You will be evaluated for your

- Knowledge and understanding of entrepreneurship
- Communication of research in a clear and concise manner both orally and in writing
- Demonstration of effective persuasive and informative communication and presentation skills

For more detailed information about performance indicators, go to the BPA website.

Think Critically

1. What is an apparent risk associated with opening a restaurant near a large university?
2. What are the strengths, weaknesses, opportunities, and threats with this business proposal?
3. What is the most effective means to advertise your business?
4. Who are the best external sources to finance your business? How will you convince these sources to invest in the business?
5. When do you plan on first making a profit with this business venture? How will the business survive until it makes its first profit?

www.bpa.org

WINNING EDGE

Entrepreneurship Event

The Entrepreneurship Event challenges students to conduct research and learn the steps for starting a new business. Students must understand the importance of a thorough business plan that can be used to persuade investors.

Think Critically *Answers*

1. The number of people on and around a university campus is usually higher during the school year. The restaurant must have a marketing plan to maintain business during the summer months.

2. Answers will vary. A possible strength is a product for which there is high demand. The bad economy is a possible weakness. There is an opportunity to offer a demanded product, but there is a threat that consumers will not spend money during a recession.

3. The advertising campaign should emphasize media preferred by students, including local radio stations, campus newspapers, Internet, billboards, and special promotions on and around campus.

4. Financial sources include banks, venture capitalists, family investment, a franchise, and incorporating with a few shareholders.

5. Answers will vary. Most businesses take up to three years to make a profit. The entrepreneur must plan to accumulate enough money to fund the first three years of operation.

34a. Employees complete form W-4 and give it to their employer. Employers complete and file all other forms with the IRS. Forms 940 and 941 are used by employers to file quarterly payments of Social Security, Medicare, and unemployment taxes. Form 944 can be used by small businesses to make annual rather than quarterly payroll tax payments.

34b. Payroll tax payments can be made by check or direct wire transfer from a bank account, a business credit or debit card, or using the Electronic Federal Tax Payment System of the U.S. Treasury Department.

CHAPTER OVERVIEW

Chapter 13 describes how production occurs in businesses and how businesses organize and manage their operations.

13.1 Types of Production

This lesson addresses the role of producers and production in the economy and the various methods used to manufacture products.

13.2 Production Planning

Major production activities and how manufacturing procedures are organized are the focus of this lesson.

13.3 Planning and Managing Business Operations

This lesson helps students understand the importance of effective business operations and tools used to manage those operations.

Chapter 13 Production and Business Operations

Photo by Karen Caldwell

Instructor Resources

- Activities and Study Guide IE
- Chapter and Unit Tests IE
- Lesson Plans
- PowerPoint Presentation
- Cognero Test, Ch. 13

Student Resources

Activities and Study Guide
www.cengage.com/swep/pob9e
- Portfolio Activity

Science, Technology, Engineering & Mathematics

PLANNING A CAREER IN . . .
INDUSTRIAL ENGINEERING

Industrial engineers work to improve the ways that businesses use the factors of production to develop products and services needed by businesses and consumers. They are involved in designing new products and improving the quality and usability of existing products. They help to improve the operations of businesses by introducing new technology, reorganizing work, and promoting the health and safety of workers.

Related Job Titles

- **Project Engineer**
- **Operations Analyst**
- **Quality Engineer**
- **Ergonomist**
- **Standards Engineer**
- **Systems Analyst**
- **Business Process Manager**
- **Supply Chain Engineer**
- **Industrial Engineering Leader**

Industrial engineers are highly educated scientists. They conduct research and apply mathematical and statistical models to problems. They work with managers and other experts in businesses to solve problems, reduce costs, and improve operations.

Even though the number of manufacturing companies and jobs is declining, the demand for industrial engineers is stable. Most industrial engineers work in manufacturing industries, but some work in health care, government, and higher education.

Analyze Career Opportunities in . . .
INDUSTRIAL ENGINEERING

Use library and internet resources to learn more about careers in industrial engineering. Choose one of the job titles listed in the box and answer the following questions.

1. How would you describe the earning potential for this field?
2. Is this a career that interests you? Describe how you might use your talents, abilities, and skills in this career.

What it's like to work as an . . . Industrial Engineer

Four industrial engineers and old friends were gathered at the national conference of the Institute for Industrial Engineering. They had all graduated from the same engineering school 10 years ago and were discussing their recent projects.

Eva had just redesigned a work process in her company's metals recycling plant that resulted in safer working conditions. Nia was developing a prototype for a miniaturized GPS unit for use in search and rescue operations. Jacob had spent the last three years redesigning the emergency room layout, equipment, and procedures for a hospital in London. Frank had just began a new job where he would develop and test new materials to be used in high-speed rail systems.

As they talked about their work, they realized that they were in an exciting, rapidly changing professional area. They were making important contributions to their organizations and to society. Everyone agreed to meet again in a few years and see where their careers had taken them.

What about you? Why do you think industrial engineers are able to work in such varied types of businesses?

PLANNING A CAREER IN . . .
INDUSTRIAL ENGINEERING

Engineering is one of the most important career areas in manufacturing and production. In addition to helping design new products, engineers plan the production processes and design the equipment and tools needed. They also test products and check procedures to improve the quality of products and efficiency of production.

What About You?
Answer

Student answers will vary. Industrial engineers are able to work in varied fields because almost every business enterprise needs to design new products that meet important needs of individuals and society. They also develop efficient manufacturing and production methods, as well as improve the performance of existing operations and manufacturing processes.

Analyze Career Opportunities *Answers*
Student answers will vary depending on when the assignment is completed and individual interests.

Additional Career Information

Encourage students to investigate careers they find interesting and explore unfamiliar careers. Two resources for additional career information are the *Occupational Outlook Handbook*, an online publication (www.bis.gov/oco) of the U.S. Bureau of Labor Statistics, and the O*NET Resource Center (www.onetcenter.org) developed by the U.S. Department of Labor. Information about specific careers and jobs can be used to demonstrate the relevance of skills learned in this course.

Focus on REAL LIFE

The production of most products we use today is very complex. It often involves several companies that may be located in different parts of the world. They must work together to plan and produce all of the parts and pieces of a complicated product and bring them all together for assembly. Ask students to consider a familiar product. Challenge them to try to determine all of the components that need to be produced and assembled to form the final product.

TEACH

Write this statement on the board: "The economy begins with production." Instruct students to write a paragraph that describes what the statement means to them based on the understanding of economics they developed in previous chapters.

List the three categories of products on the board: natural resources, agricultural products, and processed goods. Solicit student suggestions of products produced in your state that fit within each of the categories.

13.1 Types of Production

Learning Outcomes

13.1.1 Describe the role of producers in the economy and the forms of production.

13.1.2 Differentiate among the various types of manufacturing.

Key Terms

extraction and cultivation 317
processing 317
manufacturing 317
mass production 319
custom manufacturing 319
materials processing 319

Focus on REAL LIFE

Lucy closed her web browser and turned to her mother. "I think I found the answer to the question you had while we were shopping the other day. Remember the jeans with the *Assembled in the USA* tag? We were wondering whether they were an American-made product or not."

"I've seen lots of labels that seem to identify the country where a product is manufactured such as *Made in China* or *Made in Mexico*," her mom responded. "But, I'm not sure how *assembled* and *made* are different."

"According to the Federal Trade Commission," Lucy said, "for a product to be labeled *Made in the USA*, virtually all of the parts and materials used to produce it must come from the United States. Also, it must be assembled in the United States. Jeans have denim, thread, zippers, buttons, and other materials. Only a small percentage of these things could be produced elsewhere for the jeans to carry a *Made in the USA* label."

"So that means much of the materials used in the jeans we saw must have come from other countries to a U.S. plant for final assembly. With all of the parts that go into many products, I can see why it is more and more difficult to find any that are completely made in just one country."

LO 13.1.1

PRODUCTION AS AN ECONOMIC ACTIVITY

The economy begins with production. Consumers need products and services to satisfy their needs and wants. Businesses also need products and services. They incorporate products and services into the products they produce and use them in operations. They also resell them to their customers.

Role of Producers

The role of producers can be described by the categories of products produced and the types of businesses that make products. The three categories of products used by businesses and consumers are natural resources, agricultural products, and processed goods. *Natural resources* are raw materials supplied by nature. *Agricultural products* are crops and animals raised by farmers. *Processed goods* are products that have been changed in form to increase their value and usefulness.

There are four types of businesses that are responsible for production: producers, extractors, farmers, and manufacturers. *Producers* develop products to sell to other businesses or consumers. *Extractors* obtain natural resources, such as water, oil, coal, and timber, from the earth for processing and use. *Farmers* tend land and other resources to grow crops and livestock that are later sold and processed. *Manufacturers* obtain materials from other producers and convert them into products for sale to consumers and other businesses.

Applied Skills

Building Study Skills Before students begin their study of the chapter, tell them to scan the chapter and develop an outline in their notebooks by copying the major headings and subheadings. Then, as they study the chapter, students should complete the outline by organizing key information under the appropriate heading. They can then use the outline for reviewing the chapter.

Forms of Production

The forms of production are extraction and cultivation, processing, and manufacturing. In **extraction and cultivation**, products are obtained from nature or grown using natural resources. Extraction and cultivation ensure that there is an available supply of natural resources and the crops, livestock, fish, and other agricultural products needed. This is the most basic form of production.

B Brown/Shutterstock.com

Describe a process that farmers or other producers might use to turn a crop into a product ready for sale.

Processing involves changing and improving the form of another product. Few products are used exactly as they are found in nature or grown on farms. Most are processed in some way before they are used. Water must be filtered and treated before it can be consumed or used in the production of other products. Timber is cut and formed into lumber or processed into paper or other materials. Oil is pumped from deep in the earth. The oil is then sent to refineries to be converted into gasoline, heating oil, and petroleum-based products. Processed products are then used in the production of other products such as plastics, cosmetics, medicines, and food. The crops and livestock raised by farmers are sent to processing plants. They are inspected, packed, and shipped to supermarkets or processed and combined with other products. This gives you access to the variety of foods you enjoy at home and in restaurants.

Manufacturing combines raw materials and processed goods into finished products. Other businesses and final consumers use these finished products. Manufacturing can be as simple as a cabinetmaker using tools and materials to build an entertainment center for a home media room. It also can be as complex as designing a microprocessor for a robotized surgical tool used in a hospital's operating room or building a high-speed rail system.

Each of these forms of production is needed to make all of the goods and services demanded by businesses and consumers. Each requires specialized tools and equipment, in addition to well-trained and often highly skilled personnel. The requirements to locate and pump oil from miles below the ocean floor or the ability to plan and build a small spacecraft that can be piloted from the Earth's atmosphere into space and back are hard to comprehend. But they are no more important to your quality of life than the expertise of the production team on an assembly line installing airbags into automobiles or the capability of the person inspecting the prescription drugs as they are processed and packed for distribution to hospitals and pharmacies.

CHECKPOINT ✓
What are the three forms of production?

TEACH

Organize the class into three teams—extraction and cultivation, processing, and manufacturing. Assign each team to plan and draw a mural that illustrates their form of production so that the finished mural provides an accurate view of production.

THINK CRITICALLY THROUGH VISUALS

Answers will vary depending on students' knowledge of agriculture. Students should recognize that few crops go directly from the farm to the consumer. For example, after a farmer harvests soybeans, the beans are dried to the proper moisture content in bins and then carried by large trucks to a grain elevator, where the soybeans are inspected and shipped via train or river barge to processing plants. From there, the soybeans are sold to companies with factories that use them in a wide variety of food products.

ONGOING ASSESSMENT

CHECKPOINT ✓ANSWER

The three forms of production are (1) extraction and cultivation, (2) processing, and (3) manufacturing.

Different Learning Abilities

At-Risk Ask students to list the three forms of production. Then tell them to use the *Occupational Outlook Handbook* to locate one job or career area that interests them for each of the forms of production. Ask them to write a short statement that explains why each job interests them.

Work as a TEAM

Ask students to review their completed lists and identify what differentiates the products in each column from those in other columns and requires the use of specific manufacturing procedures.

TEACH

Tell students that manufacturing processes today are very different compared to those followed many years ago. Due to pressures on companies to produce more products at lower costs, most manufacturing now uses fewer but more highly skilled employees and very sophisticated equipment that is often controlled by computers.

THINK CRITICALLY THROUGH VISUALS

An assembly line is a more efficient method of manufacturing because it uses mass production techniques to assemble a large quantity at a low cost. Assembly line jobs require employees to complete very specific skills that result in lower costs to train, but higher quality.

Work as a TEAM

In your team, create a table with three columns. Label each column with one of the types of manufacturing procedures. Agree on five products that would be manufactured using each procedure and list them in the column under the correct heading.

LO 13.1.2

MANUFACTURING

Manufacturers get products or raw materials from other businesses. They combine and change them into a form that their customers can use. One manufacturer might use hardwoods, carbon fiber, titanium, and other materials to make many parts into products such as skis or snowboards for winter sports. Another may purchase meat, vegetables, and fruit from farms to create frozen entrees you can heat in your microwave. A third may take timber from a forest and process it into lumber and plywood. A construction company might then purchase those building materials to build the houses for a new neighborhood.

A Manufacturing Process

Usually, several manufacturers are a part of the total activity needed to produce goods that are purchased by consumers or other businesses. Think about the jeans described in Focus on Real Life. The manufacturing process begins when a textile mill in Brazil buys cotton grown on a ranch in Paraguay. It spins the cotton into yarn which is sent to a fabric company in Canada. That company weaves, dyes, and processes many types of fabric, including the denim used in jeans. A New York City apparel manufacturer buys the denim as well as other materials needed. The fabric is finished and cut, and sewers assemble the jeans before they are shipped to retailers.

While that entire process could have been completed by U.S. firms, increasingly manufacturing involves businesses from all over the world. Raw materials and processed goods often move long distances as they are produced, processed, and prepared for sale. Working together, producers each add unique processes that change the form of raw materials into products that fulfill consumers' needs.

Types of Manufacturing Procedures

Manufacturing businesses organize production in several ways to make their products. The number of products needed and the characteristics of the products will determine the type of manufacturing procedures.

Mass Production An assembly process that makes a large number of identical products using a continuous, efficient

iStockphoto.com/gerenme

What makes an assembly line a more efficient way of manufacturing?

Different Learning Styles

Visual Learner Instruct students to locate pictures of manufacturing activities and facilities to illustrate how manufacturing has changed over the last 100 years. Ask students to point out the differences and similarities in equipment and procedures from the past to the present.

procedure is **mass production**. Mass production is sometimes called repetitive production. Automobile assemblies or beverage bottling plants often use this type of production. Mass production allows a business to assemble standardized products in very large quantities at a low cost.

With mass production, employees usually complete a small number of very precise tasks. They use specialized tools and equipment as they work on product assembly. That allows training costs to be lower while maintaining quality. It can also result in monotonous work and worker boredom. Companies have been implementing ways to improve the work environment by rotating work tasks and using teams to complete complex procedures. Computers and mechanized equipment now assist with or perform many of the repetitive assembly line procedures.

Custom Manufacturing Building a specific and unique product to meet the needs of each customer is done with **custom manufacturing**. Custom manufacturers make products ranging from specially designed motorcycles to a new stadium for a professional football team to meet particular design standards. When each customer has quite different needs or someone is building the product for a specific use, it may require custom manufacturing.

A business using custom manufacturing works closely with the customer to plan and design the product. The job may call for unique materials or a special assembly process. With products such as buildings, bridges, or landscaping, the construction takes place at a new site each time. In other situations, such as the design of a unique tool for repairing the International Space Station or a special running shoe for a Paralympic athlete, the design and assembly of the unique product will occur at the manufacturer's site. Sometimes, a small team of designers, toolmakers, and assemblers take part in highly specialized custom manufacturing. This team works closely with one another and the customer to create a particularly unique product such as a new theme park attraction or a submersible vessel for scientific exploration of the ocean floor.

Comstock/Stockbyte/Getty Images

What kinds of everyday products are often custom made?

Materials Processing Changing the form of raw materials so they can be consumed or used to make other products is **materials processing**. Oil companies refine crude oil to produce gasoline and other petroleum products. Mills process grain into flour, cereal, and feed for animals. Digital editors convert a variety of audio and image files into films, music videos, and other multimedia presentations.

There are two types of materials processing. With *continuous processing*, the raw materials constantly move through

FYI The U.S. manufacturing economy is the world's second largest, trailing only China, according to the National Association of Manufacturers. Nearly 18 million people work in U.S. manufacturing jobs and U.S. worker productivity remains the highest in the world. Manufacturing contributes more than $2.5 trillion to the U.S. economy annually.

TEACH

Ask students to make a list of products that are produced using custom manufacturing. Challenge them to identify the characteristics of the products and the needs of consumers that require customization. Discuss why customization results in higher costs and the reasons consumers are willing to pay those higher costs.

THINK CRITICALLY THROUGH VISUALS

Student answers will vary. Dentures, prescription eye glasses, artwork, individual pieces of jewelry, floral arrangements, landscape designs for homes, cakes for special events, and many other common products are a few of the things that can be custom made.

FYI

Suggest to students that while service jobs vastly outnumber manufacturing jobs, the manufacturing sector is still very important to the US economy. Instruct students to use the Internet to identify other facts about the size and importance of manufacturing in the U.S.

Applied Skills

Communication Instruct students to use computer software to prepare a visual presentation that compares the three major types of manufacturing procedures.

TEACH

Ask students why continuous processing is more efficient than intermittent processing. Why do businesses use intermittent processing if it is slower and more expensive?

THINK CRITICALLY THROUGH VISUALS

Materials used include flour, water, milk, eggs, oil, salt, and yeast. Some commercial bakeries may add supplements and preservatives.

ONGOING ASSESSMENT

CHECKPOINT ✓ANSWER

Custom manufacturing is building a unique product to meet the needs of one customer. Materials processing is changing the form of raw materials so they can be used to make other products. Custom manufacturing involves a smaller amount of materials; materials processing involves larger quantities.

ASSESS

Key Concepts *Answers*

1. d. All of the answers are correct.

2. False. Extraction and cultivation is the most basic form of production.

3. d. custom manufacturing

4. c. textbooks

Make Academic Connections *Answers*

5. Reports will vary.

6. Results will vary depending on the item selected. Product labels provide much of the information on the materials used.

specially designed equipment. This changes them into a specific product useable for consumption or for further manufacturing. Raw milk is sprayed into huge drying machines to produce powdered milk. Hydroelectric generators convert the power of rapidly moving water into a continuous supply of electricity.

Intermittent processing uses short production runs to produce a precise amount of a variation of a product. The machinery or materials are reconfigured each time to provide the required variation. A printer uses intermittent processing to complete a special order of stationary or to print and assemble a uniquely designed brochure. A baker resets the equipment to blend and bake wheat bread after making a batch of pumpernickel loaves.

Ikonoklast Fotografie/Shutterstock.com

What raw materials are used when making bread?

CHECKPOINT ✓

What is the difference between custom manufacturing and materials processing?

13.1 ASSESSMENT

Key Concepts

Determine the best answer.

1. Which of the following is not one of the categories of products used by consumers and businesses?
   - **a.** natural resources
   - **b.** agricultural production
   - **c.** processed goods
   - **d.** All of the answers are correct.

2. True or False. The most basic form of production is manufacturing.

3. Building a specific and unique product to meet the needs of one customer is known as
   - **a.** materials processing
   - **b.** mass production
   - **c.** extraction
   - **d.** custom manufacturing

4. Intermittent processing would most likely be used in the production of
   - **a.** automobiles
   - **b.** customized houses
   - **c.** textbooks
   - **d.** televisions

Make Academic Connections

5. **Writing** Conduct research on how automation has changed manufacturing procedures in an industry that interests you. Prepare a two-page report with a bibliography.

6. **Geography** Select an article of clothing or a popular food item. Conduct research to determine the major raw materials and natural resources that are used in the production of the product. Identify the country or countries that are the major sources of the production or supply of those materials.

RETEACH Organize students into teams to review the lesson and create a study tool.

ENRICH Encourage students to write a short story communicating their ideas about the future of manufacturing.

CLOSE Remind students that production and manufacturing are still at the heart of business. Without them, many consumer needs would go unsatisfied.

13.2 Production Planning

Learning Outcomes

13.2.1 Identify the activities involved in production planning.

13.2.2 Describe how manufacturing is organized.

Key Terms

applied research 321
pure research 321
production process 322
continuous process improvement 325
benchmarks 326

Focus on REAL LIFE

Yori sat with his partner, Ted, reviewing the latest production report. They were proud of their five-year-old business that produced beach shoes from recycled plastic.

"Our sales continue to grow at over 10 percent a year, but profits are not keeping pace," said Yori. "I've noticed that as we have added new shoe designs our production errors have increased. Also, customer orders are not shipping as fast, resulting in more complaints."

Ted responded, "I'm not sure we should be using the same procedures we were using before we added five new products and 35 employees. Maybe there is more efficient technology we can use."

"It's clearly time we get help with our production planning," suggested Yori. "Improving our quality now will surely keep us from facing even greater problems in the future."

LO 13.2.1

PRODUCTION ACTIVITIES

Production and manufacturing processes are very complex. They involve a number of activities and resources that businesses must carefully plan and coordinate. Before a company can manufacture a product, it must have the facilities and equipment needed to carry out the production activities. The company must obtain the materials needed for production. It must hire enough people with the required skills. It must check finished products for quality and store them until sold. The business must then distribute them to customers when and where they are needed.

Product Development

Before any production planning occurs, a company decides what products it will produce. A business cannot rely on selling the same products year after year. As customer needs and competition change, new products will have to be developed. Product planning involves two steps—product research and product design.

Product Research Companies devote a large amount of their resources to discovering new product ideas. For example, U.S. businesses, universities, and government agencies spent more than $307 billion for research in 2014. Many scientists and engineers devote all of their work time to research and development activities. Their goals are to develop new products that will meet the needs of customers and improve upon the current products offered by the company and its competitors.

Companies carry out two types of research to discover new product ideas. **Applied research** studies existing products to develop design improvements or new product uses. Engineers working for an automobile manufacturer will study the current designs to improve the efficiency and durability of engines or increase passenger safety. **Pure research** is research

Focus on REAL LIFE

Tell students that almost all businesses and organizations today are concerned about quality improvement. Service businesses, government agencies, and even schools now have quality teams and apply quality principles to their work.

Quality improvement can occur through carefully designed procedures and well-trained employees. But it requires a commitment from all managers and employees to eliminate errors and poor artisanship.

TEACH

Encourage students to brainstorm activities that must be completed in order to produce a product and move it to customers. As each activity is named, write it on the board. When students have named as many activities as possible, ask them to review the list and try to put the activities in order from the first thing that needs to be done to the last.

Different Learning Styles

Kinesthetic Learner As you introduce and discuss the major production activities, instruct students to use flowchart symbols to prepare a visual depiction of the sequence of activities in the production process.

Work as a TEAM

Ask students how the idea of target marketing relates to their discussion of differences in people's views of products. How could a company use the results of the discussion to plan and market its products?

TEACH

Ask students to compare the process used by an inventor to create a new product and the process used by scientists and researchers. Is one of the processes more or less likely to result in new product ideas with high potential for success and profitability?

THINK CRITICALLY THROUGH VISUALS

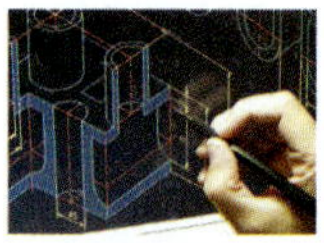

Making a model of a product allows testing of the idea so that the product is as well designed as possible. It helps in determining what materials will be needed and the steps required to produce the final product. Moving ahead without a model could result in unanticipated costs and production mistakes.

TEACH

Ask students to identify three different problems that could occur in managing an inventory for manufacturing. Examples could be late delivery, incorrect quantities, damaged inventory, or poor record keeping. As a class, discuss how each problem would affect the manufacturing process and ways to avoid the problem.

Work as a TEAM

Make a list of several new products that some members of your team like and some do not. Discuss the differences among the products and determine what makes some products appealing and others unappealing.

done without a specific product in mind with the goal of discovering new solutions to problems. For example, scientists working for drug manufacturers study diseases and immune systems of the body. Their goal is to uncover treatments and cures.

Product Design When scientists develop a new product idea, businesses must turn that idea into a product that they can make and sell profitably. Design engineers create models and test them to come up with the best possible design. They select materials that make the product useable and durable.

After engineers build and test a model, the business determines all of the materials and parts needed for the final product. Financial experts calculate the cost of making the product. They will use information from customers and competitors to decide the price at which they can sell the new product. By comparing cost and pricing information, the business can determine whether the product can be made and sold profitably.

Fernando Blanco Calzada/Shutterstock.com

What are the benefits of making a model of a new product first?

Production Planning

If a company develops and tests a new product idea and concludes that it can sell the product at a profit, the company then develops plans to produce the product. Production planning includes three activities. First, the company develops a production process. Next, it obtains production resources. Finally, the company selects and prepares production personnel.

Production Process The activities, equipment, and resources needed to manufacture a product are part of the **production process**. If the business will make the product using mass production, it must organize the assembly line. Customized manufacturing requires that the company identify the changes in materials and assembly procedures that will be required for customizing each product.

Production Resources Next, the business orders or builds the machines, tools, and other equipment required for each step of the production process. Often, new products will call for customized equipment. The business must locate and organize adequate space to perform the needed production activities. This allows employees to complete work efficiently and safely. In some cases, a business will have to buy or construct a new building. In other situations, it can remodel current facilities from the production of older products that are being discontinued.

Another planning step is to determine the sources of the raw materials, parts, and supplies needed to make the product. Often the manufacturing company will not have all the needed resources. It will have to identify suppliers and negotiate agreements so an adequate and timely supply is available at an appropriate price. The company may decide it can produce some of the parts and materials needed.

Portfolio Activity

Assign the Portfolio Activity for Chapter 13, available on the website for this textbook.

COLLECT Offer suggestions to help students locate information about a product that is produced or manufactured in your community.

CREATE Remind students to create a visual to illustrate the steps in the production process.

CONNECT Point out that students need to connect visuals to something already in their portfolio or to a concept from another class.

Personnel Finally, the company focuses on personnel planning. It estimates the number of employees needed to complete all production activities. It determines the skills required of each employee. The company will check to see if there are enough employees in the company and if they have the needed abilities. If not, it must hire and train new employees. Another option is to find a separate company with the capability and employees needed to complete some or all of the production activities rather than using its own employees and facilities.

Life-Span Plan

Identify and describe similarities between production planning and life-span planning. Describe steps you could take to produce success in achieving your life-span goals.

Inventory Management

Inventory is a detailed account of a company's materials, supplies, and finished products. *Inventory management* maintains the supply of all resources needed for production and the products produced. Inventory management is a vital manufacturing activity. Most products are assembled using many different parts and supplies. Each of the items needed to make a product must be available at the time and place needed for assembly. If an item is not on hand, the assembly process must be stopped.

Business Insight

Philips HomeLab

Can your home sense that you are too hot or cold and automatically adjust the temperature? As you get ready for school in the morning can you call up your favorite TV program as a digital image in your bathroom mirror? That is the vision guiding research in the Royal Philips electronics company. Their scientists created a laboratory called HomeLab in Eindhoven, The Netherlands. HomeLab is an actual house occupied by real consumers selected for the research. Their interactions with prototypes of products the company is designing are recorded with small digital cameras and microphones.

Philips calls the technology *ambient intelligence*. They believe that, in the home of the future, people won't control products with knobs and switches. Instead technology will respond to the movements, sounds, gestures, and physical characteristics of the residents. They believe the unique research will result in innovative lighting, appliances, entertainment products, and even clothing that can interpret and respond to individual requests and actions.

While the HomeLab is a very expensive research investment, the company believes it provides an ideal setting to conceive, test, and improve new products in an environment that reflects the way consumers live. It speeds new product development because the products are tested at the same time they are being developed. According to Philips' Chief Technology Officer, "Our innovation is centered around what consumers want. By observing them using our technology in their natural habitat—the home—we can better adapt that technology into real-world products."

Think Critically

1. What problems might the researchers encounter when observing people who know they are being observed? How might they overcome these problems?
2. Other than those listed, what types of products do you believe could benefit from study in this type of research laboratory?

Teaching Strategies

Collaborative Learning Group students into learning teams. Instruct teams to locate a website of a product that can be customized using online tools. Ask each team to identify two different customers that might purchase the product and then develop a customized product fitting the needs of each customer.

Life-Span Plan Answer

Answers will vary. Students should explain that people create life-span plans to use resources in the best way possible to produce results that satisfy their life-span goals.

Business Insight

Many consumer-products manufacturers are creating "living laboratories" where consumers can test new products the company is developing. Philips HomeLab is an example. While it is expensive, the company believes the type of research they can do in the home provides important benefits in new product development.

Think Critically *Answers*

1. People who know they are being observed may behave differently, perhaps reacting more favorably to products in a subconscious effort to "please" the company. This can be overcome by making the observations as noninvasively as possible and by conducting the observations over a long period of time so that the research participants will let down their guard and interact naturally with the products.
2. Answers will vary. Most consumer products could be tested in a research facility where consumers have the opportunity to examine and use the product in a realistic setting. New product designs could particularly benefit from this research because consumers have not seen or used them before.

NET KNOWLEDGE

Students are to visit the Baldrige Award website and review information on recent recipients. Ask students to discuss why businesses would choose to apply for the award. Suggest that the reason may transcend the recognition for winning. Efforts taken to qualify for the award should result in improving quality in the businesses that apply.

ONGOING ASSESSMENT

CHECKPOINT ✓ANSWER

The three activities that are a part of production planning are (1) developing a production process, (2) obtaining production resources, and (3) identifying and preparing production personnel.

TEACH

Write two headings on the board: "Working Alone" and "Working as a Team." Lead a discussion about the advantages and disadvantages of each method for organizing work on an assembly line. After the discussion, students should determine which method they would personally prefer and which method they believe would result in the most effective manufacturing.

NET KNOWLEDGE

The Malcolm Baldrige National Quality Award is presented each year to businesses and organizations demonstrating outstanding quality processes, commitment to customer satisfaction, and continuing improvement to their operating procedures. Use an Internet search tool to locate the most recent year of Baldrige Award recipients. Review the profile of each company or organization, including the highlights of their quality performance efforts.

If a supply of any of the items is larger than the business can use in a short time, inventory and storage costs will be higher than necessary.

Inventory managers keep records of the supply and cost of all resources used in production. They work to ensure that suppliers deliver orders on time and in the correct quantities and prices. The business maintains adequate storage space for parts and materials. In addition to being secure, the space needs to be organized so that parts and materials can be quickly and safely moved to production areas.

After the business completes product assembly and inspection, it moves the products into storage or immediately delivers them to customers. Accurate, complete inventory records help sales and production departments coordinate their efforts so all customer orders can be filled when promised. Although a business needs to have enough inventory to meet demand, it does not want to have too much inventory. Storing excess inventory can be costly and products might grow outdated and go unsold.

CHECKPOINT ✓

Describe the three activities that are a part of production planning.

LO 13.2.2

MANUFACTURING PROCEDURES

One of the biggest changes in manufacturing businesses is the production procedures used. Old factories used long assembly lines with employees located at work stations along the line. Each employee was surrounded by tools and a supply of any parts they needed to complete one specific part of the assembly. As products were assembled, they moved slowly along the line. There were frequent delays if additional time was needed to complete a procedure, correct a problem, or resupply a work station.

Today's procedures are quite different. Employees often work in teams, completing a complex assembly procedure. Each employee is trained to be able to perform several assembly tasks. Supplies and parts moving on conveyor belts, chains high above the work areas, or robot-driven carts arrive just as needed. Managers, team leaders, and employees study computer screens that monitor the assembly process and provide production information. Specialists can quickly step in when needed to repair equipment or solve problems. Products move rapidly through the assembly process. Monitoring equipment checks products for quality at several points. The assembly process can be customized to meet specific customer requirements as products are assembled. When assembly is completed, the products are packaged, labeled, and moved to a distribution area for immediate shipment to sales outlets or customers.

Organizing the Work Area

The type of product and production process will determine how the work area is organized. Mass production usually requires a large building. There must be space for the assembly line, equipment, tools, and employee work areas, as well as storage for the materials and parts needed for assembly and finished products. If the

Different Learning Abilities

Specific Learning Disability (SLD) When assigning the Net Bookmark activity, ask another student to work with each SLD student to locate the Internet site, review information on each award recipient, and discuss the quality procedures of each company.

company completes customized production of products such as framed artwork, a designer dress, or a unique furniture piece, there will often be a larger work space for the full assembly of the product by individual employees or teams. They will have easy access to the variety of parts and materials needed for each product assembly. Often, as production of each customized product is planned, one employee will be assigned to collect the materials needed for an order. With the order in hand, the employee will wheel a cart through the room that stores parts and quickly select those needed. Then the employee will move the cart to the work area of other employees who will complete the product assembly.

Building or assembling a product at the customer's location provides different challenges. Some examples are home construction, landscaping, and installing a business telecommunications system. In these activities, employees, equipment, and supplies must be moved to the customer's location. Transportation, storage, and security become important issues. Managers at the assembly site must be able to communicate with supplier companies, inventory managers, and the people who are transporting the supplies and materials. Usually companies identify a project manager who may work in the company's office and has responsibility for many activities that are a part of the overall project. These activities may occur at several work sites. Assistant managers are located where the construction or assembly work is being done. They are responsible for the site work and are in regular communication with the project manager.

Improving Manufacturing

Manufacturers face challenges today as they cope with rising costs, greater competition in the global marketplace, and growing customer demands. The challenges include the need for faster production, increased quality, and reduced costs. Companies are responding with improved manufacturing procedures, better employee training, and more attention to quality.

Manufacturing is made up of a series of processes. One process follows another until production is complete. In the past, if there was a problem within a process, managers and employees would try to identify the problem and attempt to correct it. This was time-consuming and it affected all of the processes that followed. Improvements were made only after problems were discovered.

Manufacturers have now adopted continuous process improvement, detailed in Figure 13-1, as a way to make sure manufacturing processes are completed as effectively and efficiently as possible. **Continuous process improvement (CPI)** increases the quality of work by reducing errors, inefficiencies, and waste. Rather than waiting for a problem to occur, processes are continuously reviewed with the goal of finding ways to improve them and reduce defects and production errors.

CPI is designed to help an organization achieve its goals by improving

Continuous Process Improvement

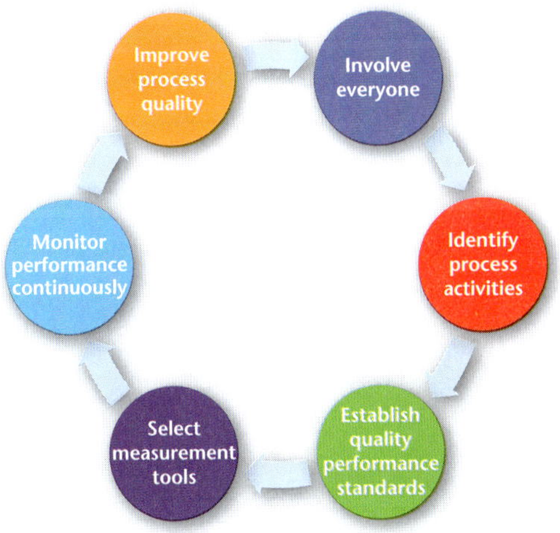

FIGURE 13-1
How should continuous process improvement affect the prices that consumers pay for products?

TEACH

Develop a simple assembly procedure for student teams to complete in class, such as constructing a paper chain or collating and stapling a five-page handout. Give each team the necessary supplies, assembly instructions, and a work space. Ask each team to organize the work space to make the assembly as efficient as possible. Each team should demonstrate the assembly and describe the reasons for their organizing decisions.

▸ **Figure 13-1** ***ANSWER***

In a competitive business environment, continuous process improvement should control increases in consumer prices that result from inefficiency and waste. While there will be costs associated with implementing CPI, the company should reduce costly production errors and delays while increasing customer satisfaction as a result of higher product quality.

Different Learning Abilities

Visually Impaired Enlarge the copy of Figure 13-1 to aid students in viewing the information. Ask a sighted student or an aide to read the description of each part of the process to visually impaired students.

TEACH

Ask students why it would benefit an organization to involve everyone in CPI activities rather than just the managers.

THINK CRITICALLY THROUGH VISUALS

Answers will vary. Consumer products of all kinds have been recalled by the manufacturer or government.

ONGOING ASSESSMENT

CHECKPOINT ✓ANSWER

Manufacturers have implemented CPI because it can help meet the need for faster production, increased quality, and reduced costs. CPI increases the quality of work by reducing errors, inefficiencies, and waste.

ASSESS

Key Concepts *Answers*

1. False. As customer needs and competition change, new products must be developed.

2. True

3. c. production resources and finished products

4. b. benchmarks

Make Academic Connections *Answers*

5. Answers will vary.

6a. January: 0.92%; February: 0.90%; March: 0.72%

6b. Average production: 3,821. Average number of defects: 32.3. Average defect rate: 0.85%.

6c. Graphs and charts should accurately illustrate the data.

the quality of work. CPI should involve everyone linked to work processes. That includes employees, managers, other businesses involved in the process, and even customers. It begins by listing all of the activities involved in the process. Standards for quality performance are developed. Often the standards are based on **benchmarks**, or the best practices used by competitors. Measurement tools are chosen and measurements are taken to determine if activities are meeting the standards that have been set. Based on those results, the people involved look for ways to improve each procedure to meet and exceed the standards. They also consider ways to improve the overall process by changes in activities, equipment, and resources.

Photodisc/Getty Images

Some children's car seats have been recalled because they did not meet safety standards. Can you think of any other products that have recently been recalled?

CHECKPOINT ✓

Why have manufacturers implemented continuous process improvement (CPI)?

13.2 ASSESSMENT

Key Concepts

Determine the best answer.

1. True or False. Once a company has developed successful products, it should be able to continue to sell them year after year.
2. True or False. Pure research is done without a specific product in mind.
3. Inventory managers keep records of
   a. personnel
   b. customers
   c. production resources and finished products
   d. All of the answers are correct.
4. The best practices among all competitors are
   a. standards
   b. benchmarks
   c. CPI
   d. quality measures

Make Academic Connections

5. **Art** Choose a small household product that you or your family uses regularly. Evaluate the product and determine a design improvement for the product. Sketch a new design that illustrates the improvement. Show your sketch to other students and explain the product design.
6. **Math** A company keeps track of the number of defective products as part of its CPI program. For three months, the number of products and defects were

   January: 3,358 products, 31 defects
   February: 4,210 products, 38 defects
   March: 3,895 products, 28 defects

   a. Calculate the percent of defects for each month.
   b. Calculate the average production and defect rates for all three months.
   c. Create a graph or chart that illustrates and compares the three months of data.

RETEACH Tell students to read each of the lesson checkpoints and prepare written answers for each.

ENRICH Instruct students to use the Internet to gather information on a company or organization that has adopted CPI. Assign students to report on the company, the CPI tools and procedures used, and the benefits reported by the company.

CLOSE Remind students that manufacturers are constantly looking for ways to control costs and improve quality to remain competitive.

13.3 Planning and Managing Business Operations

Learning Outcomes

13.3.1 Discuss the importance of effective business operations.

13.3.2 Describe tools used to manage business operations.

Key Terms

logistics 328	schedule 332
just-in-time 329	standard 333
operational plan 332	

Focus on REAL LIFE

Alton was clearly frustrated when his friend Kim picked him up in her car. "I can't believe the new digital media player I bought to stream TV shows won't connect to our TV. Now I have to go back to the store and buy an expensive adapter."

"I had a similar problem with the digital camera I bought last month," said Kim. "It takes a different type of media card. Not only did I need a new card, but I didn't have any way of viewing the pictures on my old card."

"Why does this happen?" asked Alton. "Why can't manufacturers get together and agree on standard designs, connections, and formats for their products?"

LO 13.3.1

THE IMPORTANCE OF BUSINESS OPERATIONS

The day-to-day operations of a business often determine its success or failure. A company may have products that meet customer needs. They may have competitive prices. Still, several things can go wrong in daily operations that result in problems. Work procedures may not be efficient. Security issues may result in product thefts or damage to buildings and equipment. Lack of maintenance can lead to costly repairs or safety hazards for employees and customers. A poor work environment can result in dissatisfied employees who are less productive than they could otherwise be. Businesspeople need to plan business operations as carefully as they work to satisfy their customers or plan for new products.

Types of Business Operations

Some business operations are specific to the type of business. The production activities of a manufacturer are different from the merchandise display and promotion activities of a retailer. They are certainly different from the patient care activities of a hospital. However, even among those very different types of businesses, there are some common types of business operations. They are facilities management, logistics, scheduling, and safety and security.

Photodisc/Getty Images

What are some jobs where worker safety is a concern?

Focus on REAL LIFE

Ask students to discuss their experiences with the products from several manufacturers that are not compatible with each other such as video games, computer software, or smartphones. Ask them to consider why manufacturers may believe they benefit from that situation even though it is frustrating to consumers.

TEACH

Ask students to identify the day-to-day operating problems that many businesses face that are listed in the lesson. Challenge them to suggest ways that managers and employees can attempt to prevent each of the problems.

THINK CRITICALLY THROUGH VISUALS

Students should have no trouble thinking of jobs in which safety is a concern: firefighter, electrical worker, hazardous materials cleanup, construction worker, police officer, farmer, and coal miner are just a few examples. Point out that any job can be unsafe if safety precautions are not taken.

Different Learning Styles

Visual Learner Ask students to look around the school, businesses, and their homes to locate examples of safety warnings, labels, posters, and the like. Instruct them to make a list of the types of safety issues that are identified by the warnings.

TEACH

Ask students to start an outline in their notes using the common types of business operations as the major headings. Then, instruct them to add a description of each to their notes during discussion, plus descriptions of the important activities that need to be completed for each type.

THINK CRITICALLY THROUGH VISUALS

Students should suggest improvements businesses could make to their facilities in order to attract more customers. Some examples are additional parking, improved seating in a restaurant or theater, better lighting, fresh paint, indoor plants, landscaping, new flooring, and updated signage.

Facilities Management Buildings are one of the largest investments of a business. Buildings house the work and employees. They provide space for all of the business operations as well as storage of materials, supplies, and products. Facilities management protects the company's investment of thousands or even millions of dollars.

Facilities management begins with making economic decisions about the buildings needed. Some companies buy existing facilities. Others build new buildings to house their operations. It may be more cost-effective to rent some or all of the facilities. Facilities managers continually study the long-term plans of the company. They must determine if the current buildings are adequate, if more space is needed, or if some facilities are no longer needed or are out of date. It may be necessary to buy additional buildings or expand existing facilities. The expansion may require that expensive land be purchased. Some companies purchase land at a low price many years in advance in anticipation of expansion.

Building maintenance and repair is another vital task of facilities management. A regular schedule is developed and followed. From time to time, walls must be painted, floor coverings cleaned or replaced, and equipment updated. Exterior maintenance, including access roads, parking lots and landscaping, is another ongoing task. A business must maintain a professional appearance for visitors and employees. It must also make repairs to facilities and equipment immediately so the problems don't affect operations. Failure to complete needed maintenance and improvements on a regular schedule will result in operating problems and higher costs in the future.

Give an example of an improvement a business could make to its facility in order to attract more customers.

Another key area of facilities management is energy and environmental management. Energy costs are a rapidly growing expense. Companies need a ready supply of resources such as electricity, fuel, natural gas, and water. Yet they need to control utilities costs. Facilities managers study ways to conserve energy resources. They also monitor the quality of air, building temperature, and other environmental factors to maintain a healthy and productive workforce. Many businesses are actively involved in implementing green management practices. *Green management* is concerned with protecting the environment through conservation of natural resources, wise energy use, and reduction of emissions, waste, and pollution.

Logistics Large quantities of products and materials move in, around, and out of a business on a daily basis. **Logistics** is managing the acquisition, movement, and storage of supplies, materials, and finished products in a business. Logistics has become a very important part of business operations. A newer term for managing

Different Learning Abilities

Attention Deficit Disorder Ask students to look around the classroom and identify two things that require regular maintenance and two things that require repair.

logistics is supply chain management. A *supply chain* is all of the businesses involved from the time raw materials are obtained until finished products are sold and delivered.

The major activities that make up logistics are locating sources of supplies, purchasing, transportation, and sales. In addition to the physical movement of resources, logistics is responsible for effective communication and information among all participants in the supply chain. One important logistics process is using just-in-time. With **just-in-time**, goods arrive when needed (just in time) for production, use, or sale rather than sitting in storage. Just-in-time logistics requires careful planning and coordination among supply chain members. It also requires an effective information system.

Brand X Pictures/Getty Images

What are some complications that might occur when scheduling transportation of goods?

Scheduling Even in small businesses, many activities occur at the same time. Scheduling involves determining the activities that need to be completed, the people who will perform the work, the resources needed, and the amount of time required for the task. Consider a factory that produces a number of products to fill hundreds of customer orders. The factory must maintain the right inventory of products to fill each order. If customers have to wait too long, they may cancel their order. If too much time is spent producing one type of product, supplies of others may run low. If raw materials needed to produce a particular product arrive late, production of that product must be halted. Retail and service businesses find the same types of scheduling problems as they make sure they can match their resources with customer demand.

An important part of logistics planning is employee scheduling. Companies have a workforce made up of full-time, part-time, permanent, and temporary employees. The company assigns each employee to a work area. Each employee has a specific set of skills to meet job requirements. The company depends on having the right number of people available at any time to complete the scheduled work. The human resources department is responsible for making sure enough employees are available with the skills needed. They balance the workforce by determining the number of each type of employee needed. They may need to hire more employees at certain times or reduce the number of employees at other times. A key human resource activity is training. Training ensures employees have the skills needed for their job assignments.

Managers, supervisors, and team leaders are responsible for the weekly and daily work schedules. They determine the work that is required. They also prepare the work schedule. If a heavier than usual workload is expected, employees may be scheduled to work more hours. The schedule must anticipate employee vacations and the possibility that employees will be absent or leave the company. Most managers have a specific wage and salary

TEACH

Locate an illustration of a chain or draw a simple diagram of a chain on the board. Tell students that supply chain is a relatively new term to describe all of the businesses that must work together to supply a customer's needs. Ask them why the image of a chain is appropriate to describe the relationships among the businesses. Ideas include the strength of each link, many links are required, the order of the links, and how the links are independent yet connected.

THINK CRITICALLY THROUGH VISUALS

Complications in scheduling transportation of goods could include finding the proper amount of space on carriers (air, truck, train, or ship), negotiating contracts, packaging products for shipment, producing products on time, loading and unloading equipment and personnel, and arranging insurance on products being shipped.

TEACH

Ask students to consider the advantages and disadvantages to a business and its supplier of using a just-in-time system to deliver products from the supplier to the business rather than carrying large inventories of the products.

Different Learning Abilities

English Language Learners (ELL) Instruct students to use a language translation dictionary to determine the word in their primary language that has a similar meaning to logistics. Ask them to look up the full definition of logistics in a dictionary and then write the meaning of the term in their own words.

FYI

Tell students to locate loss statistics for recent years and compare them with the data provided. Discuss the increase or decrease, sources of losses, and what the data mean to businesses and consumers.

TEACH

Remind students that, based on the growing amount and types of security in the United States and worldwide, companies are focusing even more attention on safety and security. Companies need to protect employees, facilities, equipment, customers, and products. Companies spend large amounts of money and time and hire additional personnel to increase security and safety.

THINK CRITICALLY THROUGH VISUALS

Retailers can recover losses suffered from shoplifting by charging customers higher prices. Alternatively, they can try to reduce operating expenses. Retailers invest in employee training, electronic security tags, locked displays, video cameras, and undercover security personnel in an attempt to reduce shoplifting losses.

FYI The National Retail Security Survey reports that retailers lost more than $44 billion of their inventories in a recent year. The sources and proportion of those losses are

- Employee theft: 41%
- Shoplifting and organized retail crime (ORC): 33%
- Administrative errors: 15%
- Vendor fraud: 6%
- Unknown sources: 5%

budget they are expected to meet. They must schedule carefully so as not to exceed the budget while still getting the work accomplished.

Safety and Security Companies are responsible for protecting people and property. Many events and circumstances can result in injury to people or damage to property. Companies devote a great deal of effort and expense to providing security and safety.

Security procedures and personnel protect both people and property. Damage and injury can occur because of crime, unintentional actions, or natural causes, such as tornados, floods, hurricanes, and earthquakes. Security personnel study the resources and activities of a business to identify potential security problems. They then prepare security plans and procedures to prevent problems whenever possible. The plans also identify ways to provide protection and minimize the losses if a security problem occurs.

Safety is another main business concern. The business wants to prevent accidents and injuries to employees and customers. Businesses work to maintain safe work areas and work procedures. They provide safety training and enforce rules and regulations designed to reduce accidents. Many businesses place safety posters around the workplace. They recognize and reward work units that have a record of no accidents or injuries for a period of time.

Information Management

Effective business operations require the coordination of many activities, resources, and people throughout the business. It usually involves the activities of other businesses as well. For a growing number of businesses, operations in many locations and even in other countries need to be coordinated. *Information management* uses technology to access and use needed information to complete the work of an organization. Information management has four goals.

1. To collect, organize, and securely maintain all needed information.
2. To provide instantaneous access to information required to perform work and make decisions.
3. To prevent access to information by those unauthorized to use it.
4. To use technology to improve communication and information sharing.

Jupiterimages/Polka Dot/Getty Images Plus/Getty Images

What can retailers do to recover losses suffered from shoplifting?

Applied Skills

Technology Instruct students to gather information on innovative products in development that aim to help solve safety and security concerns of businesses, government, and other organizations. Ask students to provide a picture or illustration of the technology and a description of its potential use.

LDprod/Shutterstock.com

Can you think of ways that technology has made communication in business easier and more effective?

There are many types of information used in businesses. They include text, data, graphics, pictures, and video. Businesses exchange information in a number of ways. Oral communications include telephone, voice mail, face-to-face meetings, and voice-over-Internet. Written communications take the form of letters, memos, reports, brochures, product manuals, e-mail, text and instant messages, and many others.

Information managers are responsible for designing, purchasing, installing, and maintaining the many types of technology used in the business. They must develop procedures for collecting, storing, and using information. They make sure the information is accessible yet secure. They provide training and policies for all employees on the use of technology as well as on effective communications skills.

The Internet has become an important resource for communication and information management. Because most areas of the world are now connected through the Internet, businesses are able to provide continuous access to information by employees, customers, and business partners. Internet technology allows worldwide instantaneous voice, video, text and graphics communications. Businesses can replace many face-to-face meetings with Internet conferences, saving time and travel budgets. Digital communications are usually less expensive to produce, send, and store.

Those same technologies also present challenges. Information managers must deal with viruses, hackers, software glitches, and hardware failures. Digital records must be protected and stored securely. Upgrading to the latest, most secure technology can be expensive. Businesses are working hard to find ways to meet these challenges.

CHECKPOINT ✓
Identify four important types of business operations.

TEACH

Tell students to read the four goals of information management. Ask them to consider how the development of many new Internet technologies has made it easier to accomplish each goal. Then ask them to identify problems the Internet has created for businesses related to each of the goals.

THINK CRITICALLY THROUGH VISUALS

Technology has made communication easier by making it faster and more convenient. Instant messaging allows employees to communicate in real time. Documents can be shared quickly by e-mail, dropbox, or cloud computing. Voice-over-Internet offers an alternative to traditional telephone systems. Web cameras and video-conferencing technologies allow both face-to-face and oral communication through group conferencing or apps on individual smartphones and tablets.

ONGOING ASSESSMENT

CHECKPOINT ✓**ANSWER**

Four important types of business operations are (1) facilities management, (2) logistics, (3) scheduling, and (4) safety and security.

Different Learning Styles

Print Learner Ask students to reread the definition and four goals of information management. To reinforce the lesson, suggest that students locate and read an article about information management and write a one-paragraph summary.

TEACH

Remind students that, just as employees have tools and equipment to perform their jobs, so do managers. However, the most important management tools are often plans, procedures, and standards. Ask students to compare the types of management tools listed with the tools and equipment used by employees working on an assembly line. Students should compare how these tools help both managers and employees to complete their work.

THINK CRITICALLY THROUGH VISUALS

An ATM can affect a bank's work schedule by reducing the number of tellers needed to serve customers. Also, an ATM might allow the bank's lobby hours to be shortened. However, the ATM will require maintenance and service personnel to be available at any time during the day or evening.

LO 13.3.2

TOOLS FOR BUSINESS OPERATIONS

Several tools help people manage the day-to-day operations of a business. They include management tools and technology tools.

Management Tools

Operations activities require continuous management attention. The activities must be carefully planned, implemented, and controlled. Operations activities are the work completed to help a business achieve its goals. Operational plans are developed in each area of a business to identify necessary activities. An **operational plan** identifies how work will be done, who will do it, and what resources will be needed. An operational plan for the production area of a factory determines when each product will be produced. It assigns production activities and determines the number of employees needed. It also schedules adequate supplies of resources. In a marketing department, the operational plan will match salespeople to customer groups, outline the sales plan, and schedule promotional activities. The operational plan for marketing must be coordinated with the production operational plan. Together the plans must ensure that enough products are produced to meet customer demand and all inventory is sold.

How can an ATM affect work schedules for a bank?

OPIS Zagreb/Shutterstock.com

Several management tools support the operational plans. An *operating budget* is a detailed financial plan for a specific area of the business. An operating budget is prepared for the production unit, the marketing department, and every other area of the business. The budgets help managers determine the amount of money needed for planned operations as well as how and when the money will be spent. The budgets will anticipate all types of operating expenses and areas of income, if any, for the specific area of the business.

A **schedule** is a time plan for completing activities. Schedules match people with resources to make sure activities are finished on time. A supervisor develops a weekly work schedule for employees. An inventory manager prepares a schedule of suppliers' deliveries of raw materials. An advertising manager makes up a schedule that coordinates television and newspaper advertising.

Applied Skills

Word Processing/Office Technology Instruct students to use a word processing program to create a template on which to build a personal schedule. The template should be a table with seven columns, one for each day of the week, and 24 rows, one for each hour of the day. Students should use the template to develop a complete personal schedule for the next week, identifying planned use of time for school, work, study, activities, personal and social time, sleep, and any other activities.

A *procedure* is a list of steps to be followed for performing a particular work activity. To maintain the quality of an activity and make sure it is completed as quickly as possible, a company may set up operating procedures. Employees are trained to follow those procedures. Following procedures and schedules helps employees coordinate their work with others.

A **standard** is a specific measurement against which an activity or result is judged. Businesses set standards for key activities to make sure appropriate levels of performance and quality are maintained. The standard may state the number of products that should be finished on an assembly line. It may set the number of customers that should be served in a fast-food restaurant in a stated time period. It may also establish an acceptable number of product defects or customer complaints for those operations. Standards must be clear and realistic. By establishing standards and using them to measure performance, employees will know what is expected of them and the quality of operations should remain high.

Work as a TEAM

Work with your team to agree on the procedure that should be used to make a cash withdrawal at an ATM. Record the procedure by listing the steps on a sheet of paper. Share the procedure with another team and see if they agree with the steps.

Using Technology to Manage Operations

Using technology correctly to help manage operations will make planning and decision making more accurate, rapid, and timely. It also makes it easier to access, analyze, and exchange information. The exchange may occur within a company, with other business partners, or with customers. Some of the most important software used in businesses to manage operations is described in Figure 13-2.

Various types of software are now available to assist with supply chain

COMMON TYPES OF OPERATIONS SOFTWARE	
Project Management	Keeps track of project calendars, tasks, to-do lists, work assignments, and project resources.
Budgeting	Automates budget planning, compares budgets from one time period to another, and coordinates budgets among departments.
Scheduling	Manages employee, facility, resources, and production scheduling. Allows easy review of schedules by all participants as well as quick updating.
Inventory	Helps the management of sales, purchases, and payments; tracks production, usage, and sales levels; and prints bar codes.
Computer Security	Provides access and restrictions, usage data, privacy, and virus protection for computers and networks.
Document and Management	Controls the production, storage, management, and distribution of electronic documents.
Manufacturing Automation	Monitors and often controls manufacturing machines, checks for errors and defects, and reports on production levels.

FIGURE 13-2
What are the advantages of each of the types of software in the operation of a business?

TEACH

Ask students to list jobs in which the standard must be perfection and no errors are acceptable, such as an air traffic controller. Then ask them to list jobs in which there are required standards, but perfection is not required, such as the delivery time for pizzas. Discuss how the company would determine an acceptable standard for those jobs in which perfection is not required.

Use Figure 13-2 to introduce common types of operations software. Point out that you could use a common spreadsheet to prepare operational plans for all parts of a business, but it might prove insufficient. Specific-purpose software is designed by experts for the particular tasks it supports and is tested to make sure it is effective for the designed purpose.

Work as a TEAM

Tell students that individuals may develop slightly different ways to complete procedures. The procedures may also differ based on the type of ATM being used. Variations in procedures may be acceptable to a business if the activity is completed successfully. Variations may be unacceptable if they take too much time or result in errors.

▸ Figure 13-2 *ANSWER*

Each type of software is specifically designed for an important operating area of businesses. The software provides a template or an organized procedure to help managers complete tasks, analyze information, make decisions, and evaluate results.

Applied Skills

Communication Assign students to create an advertisement for a company that is selling a computerized inventory management system. The advertisement must show how use of the product will improve businesses' inventory management procedures.

THINK CRITICALLY THROUGH VISUALS

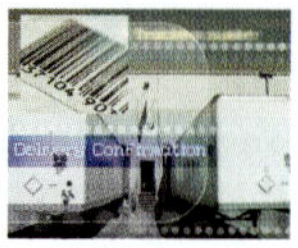

Technologies allow companies in a supply chain to instantaneously exchange information with each other and to track products and activities as they move from location to location.

ONGOING ASSESSMENT

CHECKPOINT ✓ANSWER

Technology makes planning and decision making more accurate, rapid, and timely. It also makes it easier to access, analyze, and exchange information.

ASSESS

Key Concepts *Answers*

1. c. energy and environmental management

2. b. schedule

3. False. This software controls the production, storage, management, and distribution of electronic documents.

Make Academic Connections *Answers*

4. Losses in each category: employee theft, $18.9 billion; shoplifting and ORC, $15.2 billion; administrative errors, $6.9 billion; vendor fraud, $2.8 billion; unknown sources, $2.3 billion. (Amounts have been rounded.)

5. Answers will vary. A major concern is protecting personal customer information and payment security.

---

management and support virtual collaboration of team members. *Supply chain management software* allows cooperating companies to share ordering, production, and shipping information, track products, and exchange customer data. *Collaboration software* (also called *groupware*) provides real-time communications capabilities by voice, text, and video. It also allows team members working at their own computers or mobile devices from anywhere in the world to develop, view, and edit the same documents on their computer screens while they work on them as a team or independently. Companies are replacing software on individual computers with *cloud computing*. Needed software, resources, and work files are maintained on a network of servers and accessed by employees where and when needed.

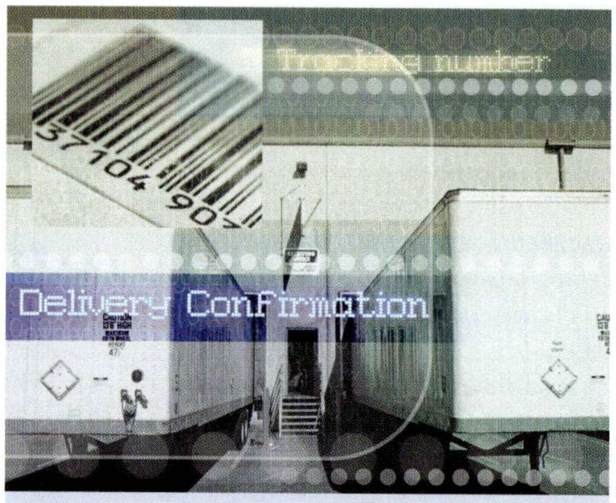

Chad Baker/Ryan McVay/Getty Images

How have advances in technology changed the coordination of supply chain activities?

CHECKPOINT ✓
What are the benefits of using technology to help manage business operations?

13.3 ASSESSMENT

Key Concepts

Determine the best answer.

1. Which of the following is a part of facilities management?
   - **a.** personnel scheduling
   - **b.** logistics
   - **c.** energy and environmental management
   - **d.** information management
2. A(n) ________ is a time plan for completing activities.
   - **a.** budget
   - **b.** schedule
   - **c.** operating plan
   - **d.** standard
3. True or False. Document management software keeps track of project calendars, tasks, to-do lists, work assignments, and project resources.

Make Academic Connections

4. **Math** Assume that the total U.S. retail sales losses for last year were $46.2 billion. Use the information that appears in the FYI feature on page 330 to calculate the amount lost in each of the following categories: employee theft, shoplifting and organized retail crime, administrative errors, vendor fraud, and unknown sources.
5. **Writing** A small business owner has been using the Internet to provide basic information about the business and its products as well as to communicate with customers and suppliers. The company will soon add a catalog to its website with purchasing capabilities. Write a one-page memo to the owner that discusses security issues that the business may encounter. Make three recommendations of ways to protect the business and customers.

RETEACH Divide students into study teams and assign each team one of the major headings in the lesson. Each team should study the information for their heading and prepare a summary of the information.

ENRICH Invite the facilities manager for a large business to visit the class to discuss operations activities.

CLOSE Instruct students to list the various types of operations that businesses must manage.

BUSINESS IMPROVING SOCIETY

DESIGNS FOR DISASTERS

When natural disasters strike, people's lives are devastated. They are often left without food, water, or shelter. All of their possessions may have been swept away. Medical assistance and supplies, as well as emergency food and water, can usually be rushed to the area within a few days, but victims of disasters are often left without lodging. It may take months to rebuild lost homes and regain normalcy. Even temporary shelters are costly and time consuming to build. Supplies and relief workers are frequently unavailable or very costly. The number of housing units needed in large disasters outstrips the available resources.

Several companies and organizations are working to develop innovative, low-cost solutions. Some treat the task as a pure business venture, aiming for a profit. Other, nonprofit organizations work to find a solution (and the funding) to quickly deliver housing and other relief as soon as a disaster strikes.

One of the first to deliver a portable housing alternative was ShelterBox, sponsored by Rotary International. Beginning in 2002, Rotarians in the United Kingdom searched for ways to help with disasters occurring around the world. They developed a compact kit containing important survival tools to allow families to get through the first few weeks until more help could come. Called a ShelterBox, it can be tailored to a specific disaster but typically contains a family tent, thermal blankets, water purification equipment, solar lamps, cooking utensils, a basic tool kit, mosquito nets, and a children's activity pack. Today, ShelterBox is sponsored by Rotarians around the world and has aided survivors of more than 100 disasters in over 70 countries.

IKEA, through its IKEA Foundation, worked with the United Nations High Commissioner for Refugees to develop the Flatpack Refugee Shelter. The 188-square-foot structure, made of lightweight polymer panels, can house up to five people. Four people can assemble it in a few hours with no additional tools. It comes with a solar panel for lighting and is safer and more durable than a traditional tent. Each Flatpack costs less than $1,000; with IKEA's experience in packing and shipping, they can be delivered quickly and inexpensively around the world.

As Michael McDaniel watched the neighborhoods of New Orleans disappear under the floodwaters of Hurricane Katrina, he wondered why immediate assistance in the form of emergency housing was not available. Looking at the simplicity of an inverted Styrofoam cup, he worked on a design that resulted in the EXO Rapid Deployment Module. The 80-square-foot, $5,000 unit has two parts—a floor and an upper composite aluminum shell making up the walls and roof. Units can be quickly delivered in large numbers with trucks or cargo planes and assembled in less than two minutes by latching the two parts together. In the eight years it has taken for planning and production, funding has been obtained through a crowd-sourcing site, Indiegogo, as well as from venture capitalists. EXO units were first deployed to house refugee families in Syria and Haiti.

istockphoto.com/michaelbwatkins

What kinds of businesses might be involved in helping people rebuild their lives and communities after a disaster?

Think Critically

1. Use the Internet to locate information about other companies or organizations that are working on innovative solutions for helping people affected by natural disasters. Write three paragraphs describing one of the projects you reviewed.
2. Discuss why it is important that for-profit businesses, nonprofit organizations and government agencies all focus their efforts on providing new ways to offer aid when natural disasters strike.

BUSINESS IMPROVING SOCIETY

Businesses, organizations, and individuals can help develop innovative solutions that help to solve important problems. Natural disasters often take almost everything away from the people in their path. A service organization, an international business, and an individual each has been involved in developing solutions to the emergency housing needs faced by victims of disasters.

THINK CRITICALLY THROUGH VISUALS

Students can provide many answers. A very large number of manufacturing and service businesses as well as nonprofit organizations and government agencies will be needed immediately and for years after the disaster to repair, rebuild, and help people with the many problems they will face.

Think Critically *Answers*

1. Students will search for additional information on innovative businesses and organizations on the Internet and then prepare a short report on one.

2. Because of the wide scope and cost of many natural disasters, all types of businesses, organization, and government agencies will need to be involved. Products, services, the labor of many people, and financial resources will be needed to help those affected.

Think Critically About Business *Answers*

1. Natural resources—examples: coal, iron, water, forests, natural gas, silver, gold, tin, salt; consumer uses: heat, light; business uses: heat, light, energy. Agricultural products—examples: corn, wheat, farm-raised fish, cotton, soy beans, vegetables, lumber, apples, silk worms, poultry; consumer uses: food, apparel; business uses: to create processed foods or goods; Processed goods—examples: flour, cars, paper, computers, appliances, clothing, watches, furniture; consumer uses: homes, restaurant foods, books, dishwashers, cars; business uses: office equipment and supplies, buildings, packaging.

2. A processing business changes and improves the form of another product, while a manufacturing business combines raw materials and processed goods into finished products. Both businesses change the form of the materials they use. Processing businesses use agricultural and natural resources; manufacturing businesses use raw materials and processed materials.

3. Each manufacturer can specialize in one aspect of the production, using its unique combination of resources and expertise.

4. Scientists conducting pure research study problems, looking for all possible solutions. Scientists involved in applied research study existing products, seeking to discover improvements or new product uses. A company might use the results of pure research to develop brand new product ideas or choose applied research in order to improve the quality or features of its products.

Chapter 13 Assessment

Review Business Concepts

13.1 Types of Production

- Producers are businesses that develop products to be sold to other businesses or consumers. Consumers need products and services to satisfy their needs and wants. Businesses also need products and services to be incorporated into the products they produce, to be used in operations, and for resale to their customers. The three forms of production are extraction and cultivation, processing, and manufacturing.
- Manufacturing businesses can organize production in several ways to produce products. The types of manufacturing procedures are mass production, custom manufacturing, and materials processing.

13.2 Production Planning

- Production and manufacturing processes are very complex. They need to be carefully planned and coordinated. Product planning involves two steps—new product research and product design. Production planning includes three activities: a production process is developed, production resources are obtained, and production personnel are identified and prepared. Inventory management maintains the supply of all of the resources needed for production and the products produced.
- The type of product and production process will determine how the work area is organized. Manufacturers face many challenges including the need for faster production, increased quality, and reduced costs.

13.3 Planning and Managing Business Operations

- The day-to-day operations of a business often determine its success or failure. Businesspeople need to plan business operations as carefully as they work to satisfy their customers or plan for new products. Common types of business operations are facilities management, logistics, scheduling, and safety and security.
- Several tools help people manage the day-to-day operations of a business. They include management tools and technology tools.

Think Critically About Business

1. Provide two examples for each of the three categories of products. For each example, identify one consumer use and one business use of the product.
2. What are the major differences between a processing business and a manufacturing business? What, if any, are the similarities between the two types of producers?
3. Why are several manufacturers usually a part of the total activity needed to produce a product? Why do you believe most manufacturers do not want to or are unable to complete the entire manufacturing process for a product?
4. How does the approach scientists use for pure research differ from the approach used for applied research? Why would a company choose to use one type of research over the other?
5. Identify three new products that appear to have been developed using applied research. Then identify three products that appear to have been developed based on results from pure research. What differences, if any, do you see in the types of products that result from each type of research?
6. What are the advantages for a company and for employees in using an employee team to assemble a product rather than the traditional assembly line where each employee completes a specific task?
7. Why should business partners and customers be involved in a continuous improvement process? What can they offer that managers and employees cannot?

5. Answers will vary. In general, products that result from applied research will be variations on existing products, while those resulting from pure research will be completely new products that meet consumer needs in an innovative way.

6. The total production process does not have to wait as each task is completed. Several tasks can be completed at the same time. Employees combine their skills to improve the process and to solve problems.

8. For each of the following types of businesses, identify a business operation that would be unique to that business and not to the others.
   a. Hospital
   b. Law firm
   c. Dairy farm
   d. Internet service provider
   e. Taxi service

9. Make recommendations to a retail business that would help reduce losses from each of the following sources: employee theft, shoplifting, administrative errors, vendor fraud.

10. In what ways has the Internet improved communications within a business and among businesses? What issues and problems have developed because of the use of the Internet for business communications?

Develop Your Business Language

Match the terms listed with the definitions.

11. The best practices used by competitors.
12. Managing the acquisition, movement, and storage of supplies, materials, and finished products in a business.
13. Changes the form of raw materials so they can be consumed or used to manufacture other products.
14. Studies existing products to develop design improvements or new product uses.
15. Products are obtained from nature or grown using natural resources.
16. Combines raw materials and processed goods into finished products.
17. Increases the quality of work by reducing errors, inefficiencies, and waste.
18. An assembly process that produces a large number of identical products using a continuous, efficient procedure.
19. A specific measurement against which an activity or result is judged.
20. Identifies how work will be done, who will do it, and what resources will be needed.
21. Goods arrive when needed for production, use, or sale rather than sitting in storage.
22. Changing and improving the form of another product.
23. Building a specific and unique product to meet the needs of each customer.
24. The activities, equipment, and resources needed to manufacture a product.
25. Time plans for completing activities.
26. Done without a specific product in mind with the goal of discovering new solutions to problems.

Key Terms

a. applied research
b. benchmarks
c. continuous process improvement (CPI)
d. custom manufacturing
e. extraction and cultivation
f. just-in-time
g. logistics
h. manufacturing
i. mass production
j. materials processing
k. operational plan
l. processing
m. production process
n. pure research
o. schedule
p. standard

7. Business partners and customers should be involved in CPI because they can help identify problems with the quality or delivery of a company's products. The company can then use CPI to solve those problems.

8. Answers will vary.

9. Employee theft—bonuses for low theft rate, employee discounts, surveillance camera

Shoplifting—surveillance cameras, electronic anti-theft tags, undercover personnel, dressing room attendants

Administrative errors—using up-to-date computer software, giving employees training on all software, giving bonuses for error-free performance

Vendor fraud—closely monitoring invoices to be sure they match goods received, dealing with established vendors

10. The Internet has made business communication faster, more accurate, and global, saving time and reducing the need for business travel. However, use of the Internet presents some security challenges. As businesses become dependent on Internet communication, they are vulnerable to attacks by hackers and computer viruses, equipment and software failures, and abuse by employees who spend time surfing the Internet or chatting with online friends while on the job.

Develop Your Business Language *Answers*

11. b. benchmarks
12. g. logistics
13. j. materials processing
14. a. applied research
15. e. extraction and cultivation
16. h. manufacturing
17. c. continuous process improvement (CPI)
18. i. mass production
19. p. standard
20. k. operational plan
21. f. just-in-time
22. l. processing
23. d. custom manufacturing
24. m. production process
25. o. schedule
26. n. pure research

Make Academic Connections *Answers*

27. Answers will vary depending on the state.

28. Answers will vary depending on the manufacturers and products identified.

29. Timelines will vary.

30. Reports will vary.

31a. The total sales for all five companies was $1,091,541,000,000. The combined net profit was $70,230,000,000.

31b. Exxon Mobil, 8.0%; Chevron, 9.7%; Phillips 66, 2.3%; General Motors, 3.4%; Ford Motor, 4.9%

Make Your Case *Answers*

32. Answers will vary. Advantages to Option A include simple business operations including the use of unskilled labor, routine scheduling, uncomplicated production, lower costs, and a product with mass appeal. Disadvantages include possible quality issues, additional administrative work related to volume, and the need to sell more houses to achieve higher profit.

Advantages to Option B include less administrative work, prestige, better product, and the opportunity to command premium prices. Disadvantages include need for skilled employees, expense of custom materials, and more complicated schedules.

33. Answers will vary depending on personal preferences.

Make Academic Connections

27. Science Identify several natural resources that are extracted and processed in your state. Using the Internet, print a map of your state. Mark and label the primary sources of those resources on the state map. List one company that is involved in the extraction or processing of each of the natural resources.

28. Geography Some manufacturers locate their businesses very close to the sources of supply for the materials they need for production. Others locate closer to their main customers. Identify three manufacturers that fit each of those categories. Based on the types of products produced by the companies in each category, suggest reasons for the location decisions.

29. History Research the history of manufacturing in the United States from the early 1900s to the present. Prepare a visual timeline that identifies 15 events, products, and people that had a significant influence on manufacturing procedures during that time. To add perspective to the timeline, include 10 historical events such as presidential elections.

30. Reading Comprehension Pure and applied research is an ongoing activity of businesses, universities, and government agencies. Use the Internet to locate a news report of a current research project that holds promise for a new product or product improvement. Based on your reading, write a short sidebar article that could be posted online describing the research and the potential future benefits of the research to consumers.

31. Math In 2014, *Fortune* magazine identified the top five U.S. manufacturers and processors. The companies and their 2013 sales and profits are shown in the table below.

COMPANY	TOTAL SALES (in millions)	PROFIT (in millions)
Exxon Mobil	$407,666	$32,580
Chevron	220,356	21,423
Phillips 66	161,175	3,726
General Motors	155,427	5,346
Ford Motor	146,917	7,155

a. Determine the total sales and net profit earned by all five companies combined.

b. What percentage of each company's sales is represented by its net profit?

Make Your Case

Eric Elongue has worked in construction his entire life. He worked part-time with a small contractor while completing his bachelor's degree in Construction Management at Eastern State University. Since then, he has been employed full-time for the past 15 years in positions of increasing responsibility with a national homebuilder. He now wants to start his own home construction business. He is deciding between two options for his business.

OPTION A: Use a mass-production process in which he builds four models of homes. Customers can choose one of the four models, but cannot customize them. With this business model, Eric can build 20 homes a year. His work crews will not need to be as skilled. Materials and operating costs will be 10 percent lower than the industry average.

OPTION B: Build custom houses in which each home is specifically designed for the homebuyer. Eric's company will only be able to build 12 custom homes a year. It will require workers with much higher construction skills, and his costs will be 15 percent higher than the industry average. If he is able to maintain quality, he will be able to command premium prices for the custom homes.

32. What are the advantages and disadvantages of each option from the viewpoint of (a) managing business operations and (b) controlling quality and costs?

33. What option would you recommend to Eric? Why?

Interactions and Connections

34. Safety and security is an increasingly important issue for families, communities, and businesses. Interview several people representing different parts of your community. Identify and discuss their concerns about personal and community safety and security. Prepare a list of recommendations that address the safety and security concerns you heard. For each recommendation, identify who should be responsible for implementing the recommendation and the procedures that need to be followed.

Interactions and Connections

34. Answers will vary. Recommendations can be made for personal, neighborhood, or community safety. Whether answers are simple or complex, they should describe responsibilities and procedures.

35. Businesses and organizations are "going green" to protect the environment and reduce energy use and waste. Use the Internet to locate descriptions of green practices businesses have adopted. Look for specific examples related to building design, energy, the environment, and product design.

a. Develop a table that summarizes the green business practices you found using the following headings: Building Design, Energy and the Environment, Product Design.

b. Using the information from the table, prepare a poster that illustrates several important green business practices.

Buying and Merchandising Team Decision-Making Event

Teams consisting of two students will participate in this event. Each team will have 30 minutes to develop their plan of action based on the scenario presented. Teams have 10 minutes to present a detailed strategy to the owners (judge or class).

Martin Furniture is a high-volume furniture store located in a large city in the United States. Last year the company developed a website and now sells merchandise throughout the country. The company offers free delivery to locations within a 50-mile radius of the store. Fees for delivery to points further away are determined by the distance between the store and the destination.

The Martin Furniture warehouse employs more than 200 workers to receive, prepare, and deliver furniture. The owners of the company count on a smooth, accident-free operation. Employees are expected to understand how to prevent damage to furniture and use safe procedures to avoid accidents and injuries.

The owners receive regular, detailed reports about the company's warehouse operation. The reports include quantity of damaged furniture, number of accidents in the warehouse, and missing furniture. Recent reports indicate a noticeable increase in warehouse accidents since Martin Furniture expanded delivery service throughout the country. These accidents have resulted in injuries to employees and damage to merchandise. The amount of damaged furniture has increased by 30 percent. When damaged, the furniture must be repaired and then resold at a 40 percent discount. The reports also indicate a 10 percent jump in the amount of merchandise that has disappeared. The owners are particularly concerned about this information because they believe that employee theft may be responsible for most of the missing furniture.

The owners of Martin Furniture have asked your operations and loss prevention team to develop a strategy that will reduce the amount of damaged furniture, injuries to warehouse employees, and missing furniture.

Performance Indicators Evaluated

- Recommend a plan to maintain a safe work environment.
- Develop a plan that will help enforce safety precautions.
- Analyze business systems and procedures.
- Explain how employees have a responsibility for the company's profitability.
- Explain security monitoring systems in a warehouse setting.
- Describe company strategies to strengthen employee commitment and honesty.
- Establish policies/procedures for preventing internal theft.

For more detailed information about performance indicators, go to the DECA website.

Think Critically

1. Why does business expansion sometimes result in operations problems and financial losses?
2. How can Martin Furniture monitor activity in the warehouse?
3. Why must all employees be involved with saving money for the business operation?
4. How can a company develop and maintain a workforce that demonstrates honesty and dependability?

www.deca.org

WINNING EDGE

Buying and Merchandising Team Decision-Making Event

This event encourages students to work effectively as a team. It emphasizes communication skills, analytical skills, critical thinking and problem-solving skills, teamwork, and time management skills.

Think Critically *Answers*

1. Growth of a business may require new procedures and more work for employees. They may try to work faster and be less careful, resulting in more errors and accidents.

2. The furniture store can implement strict operating procedures and use cameras, inventory tags, and other security devices to monitor activity in the warehouse.

3. Higher profits for a company could affect bonus plans and salary budgets. Conserving resources and controlling financial expenses are ways that employees can help a business make a higher profit.

4. Honesty and dependability in the workplace start with respect between management and employees. Companies should treat employees fairly, involve them in decisions, and provide effective training to build loyalty.

35a. Tables will summarize the green practices from the articles.

35b. Posters should illustrate several important green business practices.

CHAPTER OVERVIEW

Chapter 14 discusses the risks faced by businesses and identifies ways to deal with insurable and uninsurable risks.

14.1 Overview of Risk Management

After studying this lesson, students will be able to identify important business risks and learn how businesses deal with these risks.

14.2 Insurable Risks

In this lesson, students will study important insurance concepts and the primary types of business insurance.

14.3 Uninsurable Risks

This lesson describes risks businesses face that cannot be insured and strategies businesses can employ to reduce risks in national and international activities.

Chapter 14 Risk Management

Reuters/Landov

Instructor Resources

- Activities and Study Guide IE
- Chapter and Unit Tests IE
- Lesson Plans
- PowerPoint Presentation
- Cognero Test, Ch. 14

Student Resources

Activities and Study Guide
www.cengage.com/swep/pob9e
- Portfolio Activity

PLANNING A CAREER IN . . .

RISK ANALYSIS

Consumers and businesses buy insurance for protection against risks. When people who have insurance are injured, need health care, or suffer property damage, insurance companies pay for some or all of the costs. Insurance companies rely on actuaries to determine the premiums needed to cover the costs. Actuaries determine the amount of risk insurance companies face and set the rates charged. They also evaluate investments to maximize the company's return.

Although actuaries work in all parts of the economy, many work in financial services businesses. Many actuaries work for insurance companies and consulting firms. Corporations and state and federal governments also employ actuaries. In order to demonstrate knowledge and skill to employers, colleagues, and clients, actuaries complete a series of professional exams. Since 1988, the *Jobs Rated Almanac* has rated the job of actuary as one of the five best jobs in the United States.

Related Job Titles

- **Actuarial Assistant**
- **Pension Analyst**
- **Chief of Analytics**
- **Senior Actuary**
- **Chief Risk Officer**
- **Actuarial Consultant**
- **Risk Modeler**
- **Health Actuary**

Analyze Career Opportunities in . . .

RISK ANALYSIS

Use library and Internet resources to learn more about careers in risk analysis. Choose one of the job titles listed in the box and answer the following questions.

1. How would you describe the nature of the work? Include examples of things that might happen in a typical work day.
2. Is this a career that interests you? What can you do now to help prepare yourself for this career?

What it's like to work as an . . . Actuary

After Janine graduated from college, she obtained her first job working for a large health insurance company as an actuarial assistant. During the first year, she worked on a project that will help employers reduce medical claims by emphasizing employee wellness and fitness. She worked with a team to develop a questionnaire to gather cost information from employers.

Janine was happy to learn her company encourages its actuaries to prepare for and pass the series of professional exams. New employees met twice a month with experienced actuaries for study sessions. Janine completed the first exam while in college. Since she started working, she has passed another exam and is preparing for the next one.

While her work is hectic, she enjoys the variety of the projects. "No day is like any other day," Janine stated. "You have to like pressure and tight deadlines." Eventually, she hopes to move into a management position and then maybe into consulting, with the goal of owning her own business.

What about you? What would you find interesting and rewarding about the work Janine is doing for her employer? Are there things you wouldn't like about being an actuary?

PLANNING A CAREER IN . . .

RISK ANALYSIS

Most people are aware of the career of insurance salesperson, but many are not aware of the variety of other insurance careers. One of the most important insurance career areas is in risk analysis. Insurance companies rely on expert risk analysts, known as actuaries, to determine the potential costs of damages the company will have to pay to the individuals and organizations it insures. If the analysis is not accurate, the insurance company can lose a great deal of money.

What About You? ***Answers***

Answers will vary. Some students might say that they would enjoy working with data and being part of a team. They might also express interest in a job that is fast-paced and includes variety. Some students might indicate that they are not interested in a career that requires studying and taking exams. The idea of working in an office and working with tight deadlines might also be a deterrent for some students.

Analyze Career Opportunities *Answers*

Student answers will vary depending on when the assignment is completed and individual interests.

Additional Career Information

Encourage students to investigate careers they find interesting and explore unfamiliar careers. Two resources for additional career information are the *Occupational Outlook Handbook*, an online publication (www.bls.gov/oco) of the U.S. Bureau of Labor Statistics, and the O*NET Resource Center (www.onetcenter.org) developed by the U.S. Department of Labor. Information about specific careers and jobs can be used to demonstrate the relevance of skills learned in this course.

Focus on REAL LIFE

Ask students how often they think about the risks associated with the decisions they are about to make. Point out that almost every decision involves some amount of risk. Some risks are financial, while others may involve risks to their health or future. Planning for risks means understanding their options and the possible results of those options.

TEACH

Start the discussion by asking students, "What are you risking if. . ." and give them several scenarios such as . . . you don't wear your seat belt when driving? . . . you don't study for an important test? . . . you skip work and don't tell your boss? Students should analyze what might happen in each scenario as a way to begin to think about risk.

THINK CRITICALLY THROUGH VISUALS

Consumers may be concerned that an expensive purchase may be damaged, lost, or stolen. By purchasing a product warranty, they get assurance the product will be repaired or replaced.

14.1 Overview of Risk Management

Learning Outcomes

14.1.1 Identify the types of risks facing businesses.

14.1.2 Describe ways that businesses can deal with risks.

Key Terms

risk 342
economic risk 343
personal risk 343
property risk 343
liability risk 343
pure risk 343
controllable risk 343
insurance 343

Focus on REAL LIFE

As Jamie walked away from the mobile kiosk, he was facing two important decisions. He had found a smartphone with all of the features he wanted. It was a bit more expensive than he anticipated, but he had enough money. The monthly plan was affordable and offered the services he wanted. The salesperson told Jamie he could save $300 on the price of the phone if he would sign a two-year contract with the wireless service provider. Yet if he cancelled the service during that time, he would have to pay the company up to $400. The service provider was not one with which Jamie was familar. Jamie was worried he might not like the service or the phone enough to risk a two-year commitment.

In addition, the salesperson offered Jamie a protection plan for an additional $6.95 a month that would provide a replacement if Jamie's phone is damaged or lost. Jamie had never lost his phone but knew of several friends who had. He knew he could not afford to replace the phone.

As Jamie walked away, he was thinking about the contract and the protection plan. He would have to think about the costs versus the risks before making a final decision.

LO 14.1.1

IDENTIFYING RISKS

Every day you face risks. **Risk** is the possibility of incurring a loss. You face many types of risks and possible losses. Some are very important to you and can have long-term effects. The risk of a serious illness or an accident that results in an injury would have a major impact on your life. A hurricane, tornado, or fire can leave homes, businesses, and even entire communities damaged or ruined.

Other risks are inconvenient but have little lasting effect. If you are caught in traffic, you risk being late for an appointment. When you buy a new product, you risk that it might go on sale in two weeks. Even if you are very careful, you cannot avoid all risks and losses. Still, individuals and businesses need to be aware of risks and try to reduce possible losses, especially for

Minerva Studio/Shutterstock.com

Can you think of reasons for buying an extended warranty on a product you just purchased?

Different Learning Abilities

Attention Deficit Disorder Ask students to write the term *risk* and its definition. Then ask them to identify three risks they currently face and three they may face in the future. Assign students to work in pairs or small groups to discuss possible consequences of the risks they have identified.

those risks that may result in physical or financial harm.

Types of Risks

There are many ways of viewing risks. Being able to identify the type of risk helps to determine how to plan for the risk. Planning for a risk may reduce the chance that it will occur or reduce its impact if it does occur.

Economic and Noneconomic Risks

An **economic risk** can result in financial loss. There are three categories of economic risks. A **personal risk** can result in personal losses to one's health and personal well-being. A **property risk** can lead to loss of personal or business property including money, vehicles, and buildings. A **liability risk** relates to harm or injury to other people or their property because of your actions.

Noneconomic risks may result in inconvenience or discomfort but do not have a financial impact. A traffic accident is an economic risk. It can result in expenses such as medical care, automobile repairs, and higher insurance rates. Deciding with your friends to perform at the school talent show is a noneconomic risk. You may be uncomfortable or embarrassed if the performance does not go well, but you won't suffer financially.

Jack Dagley Photography, 2010/Used under license from Shutterstock.com

What unexpected economic and noneconomic issues may result from a traffic accident?

Pure and Speculative Risks A **pure risk** presents the chance of loss but no opportunity for gain. Severe weather is an example of a pure risk. The storm may pass with no harm to a business. A heavy snowstorm that causes the business to close for a day or two will reduce sales. Wind and rain damage to a building will add to expenses because of the cost of repairs.

A *speculative risk* offers the chance either to gain or to lose. Suppose you invest your money in a new business. If it is successful, you can make a nice profit. On the other hand, if it fails, you can lose all of the money you invested.

Controllable and Uncontrollable Risks

A **controllable risk** can be reduced or eliminated by actions you take. To prevent loss from theft, businesses install security systems, hire guards, and train employees to be alert for possible problems. An *uncontrollable risk* cannot be reduced by your actions. A sudden hailstorm or prolonged drought can affect a farmer's crops and little can be done to reduce the losses suffered.

Insurable and Uninsurable Risks People look for ways to protect themselves from the negative effects of risks. A common form of protection is insurance. **Insurance** exchanges the uncertainty of a possible large financial loss for a certain smaller payment. If a large number of people face a given risk and the cost of possible losses can be predicted, it is an *insurable risk*. If a risk is not common or if it is impossible to predict the amount of loss that could be suffered, it is an *uninsurable risk*.

CHECKPOINT ✓
What is risk?

TEACH

Assign students to prepare an outline of the terms related to the types of risks discussed in the lesson. Ask them to record each of the major types of risks and the categories for each of the types. Students should list the examples from the lesson under each category and then identify one additional example of each.

THINK CRITICALLY THROUGH VISUALS

Unexpected economic issues that may result from a traffic accident include: the cost of repairing the vehicles and other damage; the cost of medical care for anyone who was injured; time away from work to get estimates and have repairs made; the cost of replacement transportation while the vehicle is in the shop; fines and court costs; and higher insurance rates. Noneconomic issues could include pain and mobility problems if an injury occurred, and possibly frustration and anger.

ONGOING ASSESSMENT

CHECKPOINT ✓ANSWER

Risk is the possibility of incurring a loss.

Different Learning Styles

Visual Learner Assign students to create a poster that visually identifies each of the types and categories of risks described in the lesson. Instruct students to locate a picture or illustration that represents each risk and add it to the poster.

FYI

Before students read the data, ask them to predict the number of catastrophes and disasters and the amount of losses that occur in one year. Discuss why the insured losses may have been significantly less in 2014. Then, instruct them to use the Internet to learn more about the Swiss Re studies.

TEACH

Ask students to read the example of the simple insurance system organized by the golfers. Lead a discussion about the advantages and disadvantages of the system. What would happen if two of the friends were golfing and both sets of clubs were stolen while the golfers were taking a break in the clubhouse? The cost to each member would double to $120.

▶ Figure 14-1 ***ANSWER***

Student answers will vary, depending on their individual levels of risk tolerance and their confidence in being able to protect their golf clubs.

FYI According to Swiss Re, a large international reinsurance company, 189 natural catastrophes and 147 man-made disasters resulted in nearly $110 billion of losses worldwide in 2014. Only $35 billion of the losses were insured, well below the $64 billion average for the previous 10 years.

LO 14.1.2

DEALING WITH RISKS

Suppose you and nine of your friends each have a new set of golf clubs. Each set is worth about $600. You all decide to form the GolFriends Association (GFA). The purpose of GFA is to reduce the risk of a large financial loss should one member's clubs get stolen. To provide protection, each member agrees to share the cost of replacing a set of stolen clubs. You all agree on a replacement cost of $600. Therefore each member contributes $60 to a golf club replacement insurance fund. If you are not a member of the GFA and your clubs were stolen, you would have to pay the total cost of new clubs—$600. As a member, replacing your stolen clubs costs you only $60. Figure 14-1 illustrates the costs for members and non-members.

By contributing to the insurance fund, each member suffers only a comparatively small economic loss. In that way, the members help one another by sharing the risk of economic loss.

Everyone faces risks. Many of these risks will result in financial damage or possible disaster if the loss is severe. Individuals and businesses must determine how they will deal with the risks and possible losses they face. Figure 14-2 shows that there are four possible ways to deal with risks: avoid, transfer, insure, and assume.

COST TO REPLACE ONE SET OF STOLEN GOLF CLUBS	
Total Cost ÷ Number of People = Cost Per Person	
GFA members	$600 ÷ 10 = $60
Non-members	$600 ÷ 1 = $600

FIGURE 14-1

Would you want to pay for someone else's clubs if you believed you could take care of your own clubs to make sure they were not stolen?

Avoid the Risk

With thought and planning, you might be able to avoid some risks. If you don't believe you have enough experience or skill to start your own business, you can decide not to become an entrepreneur. If a snowstorm is in the forecast, you can choose not to drive your car to avoid a possible accident. If market research suggests there may not be enough demand for a new product to cover the costs, a business can choose not to make that product.

In order to avoid risks, decision makers need to be aware of risks that can threaten a decision. They must determine the costs and possible rewards of their decisions. They must estimate the size of losses if anticipated problems occur. If the likelihood of risk or the amount of loss is too great, they may make the decision to avoid the action. This ensures that there will be no loss.

Transfer the Risk

Sometimes an activity must occur even though there is a risk that can have serious financial consequences. If a business is not in a position to assume the risk, it may choose to transfer it. When a business transfers a risk, someone else assumes the risk. A company may not be able to afford losses that it could suffer if the company offers customer credit and several credit customers do not pay their bills. In that situation, the company may transfer the risk of offering credit to a bank or credit card company. These businesses already have a credit operation. They are able to manage credit customers more effectively. They are also in a position to handle larger credit losses. The bank or credit card company will be willing to accept the risk of

Applied Skills

Mathematics An insurance company insures eight businesses for fire loss in one city. Each business has insured property valued at an average of $340,000. The insurance company estimates that there will be fire losses of 12 percent of the total insured value in any year, but they budget 110 percent of the estimated losses each year in case losses are higher than average. How much should the insurance company budget to cover the fire losses of the eight businesses each year?
Answer: $8 \times \$340{,}000 \times 0.12 \times 1.1 = \$359{,}040$

credit sales with the likelihood that they can make a profit on fees paid by the company on credit sales and interest paid by credit customers.

A company can transfer the risk of product damage by using other channel members to store and distribute products. A manufacturer can transfer the risk of a costly or unsuccessful research process by forming a joint venture with an experienced research firm. The cost of the research will be shared with the other company that already employs experienced researchers. If the research is successful, the manufacturer will produce and sell the product. It will then share the profits with the research partner.

Insure the Risk

If a business faces the same type of risk also faced by others and the size of losses can be reasonably predicted, it is possible to purchase insurance. In the case of the

michaeljung/Shutterstock.com

How might a business traveler deal with the possibility of having his or her personal computer stolen?

FOUR POSSIBLE WAYS TO DEAL WITH RISK

METHOD	ACTIVITY
Avoid	Choose not to complete the risky activity
Transfer	Find another business to complete the activity
Insure	Purchase insurance to pay for any losses
Assume	Complete the activity with full responsibility

FIGURE 14-2
What method would you use to avoid the risk of your smartphone being lost, damaged, or stolen?

GolFriends Association described earlier, each club owner insured the risk of stolen clubs by paying a small amount to the Association. In the same way, businesses that face the risk of fire damage to their buildings, equipment, and inventories can pool those risks with other businesses by purchasing fire insurance.

It is possible that a few businesses will have losses from fires during a specific period. Based on the history of fires in businesses, experts can reasonably estimate the total amount of fire damage among a number of businesses for that amount of time. Each business will pay a small amount for insurance that will cover the losses of the businesses that suffer a loss from fire.

Assume the Risk

Some companies decide that they are willing to assume certain risks. That means that if they suffer a loss, they will deal with the result. Typically, if a business decides to assume a risk, it means that the result of damage will not have serious negative consequences for the business. The company believes available funds can cover any financial loss.

A very large business may choose to set aside a small amount of money each month instead of purchasing insurance. They

Applied Skills

Language Arts Ask students to write a paragraph explaining why it is important for businesses to identify the risks they face and how they should plan to deal with those risks. Invite several students to read their paragraphs aloud.

TEACH

Ask students why one company would want to assume risks faced by another company. In almost all cases, it is because they can manage the risk better and believe they can make a profit or obtain another benefit for their business.

▶ Figure 14-2 ***ANSWER***

Students could choose the avoid method by simply not owning a smartphone. They might be able to choose the insure method by paying a monthly fee to insure the phone against loss, damage, or theft. Or they may assume the risk, use the smartphone as carefully as possible, and hope nothing happens to it. They might even be able to transfer the risk by renting or borrowing a phone.

THINK CRITICALLY THROUGH VISUALS

Risks include losing the importance and value of the personal computer as well as the programs and information (personal and business-related) that are stored on the computer's hard drive. Computer owners should plan in advance the best ways to avoid, transfer, insure, or assume all of the risks involved.

TEACH

Ask students to think of possible risks faced by individuals and businesses. For each of the identified risks, students should try to identify an example of how to avoid, transfer, insure, and assume the risk.

Work as a TEAM

After teams have completed their work, invite a school administrator who is familiar with the types of insurance carried by the school or school district to meet with the class and discuss how the school identifies its insurance needs.

ONGOING ASSESSMENT

CHECKPOINT ✓ANSWER

Business can deal with risk by (1) avoiding the risk, (2) transferring the risk, (3) insuring the risk, or (4) assuming the risk.

ASSESS

Key Concepts *Answers*

1. False. The loss may not occur. Speculative risks even offer the chance to gain.
2. d. All are economic risks.
3. c. transferring
4. True

Make Academic Connections *Answers*

5. Tables will vary depending on when the assignment is completed.
6. Student answers will vary depending on the 10 risks they choose for their lists.

CLOSE Ask students to explain why understanding risks and how to deal with them are very important to businesses.

Work as a TEAM

Work with your team to recognize several risks that could affect your school, students, staff, and visitors. Identify one or more risks that fit each of the following types: economic, noneconomic, controllable, and uncontrollable. Discuss how the identified risks could be reduced.

believe that if a financial loss occurs because of a risk, there will be enough money saved to cover the amount of the loss.

In other situations, it may not be possible to avoid, transfer, or insure a risk. If that is the case, the business will need to assume the risk. Once a business produces or purchases products for resale, it must be able to sell the products at a reasonable price in order to cover its costs. If the sales goals are not met, the business suffers a loss. It assumes the risk of being able to sell its inventory at a profit.

Some risks are so unlikely that the company decides to do nothing. It assumes a problem will not occur. The company may be forced to take emergency actions if it is wrong. A company hires enough employees to operate the business. Company managers know a few extra employees are needed because at any time a certain number will be on vacation, sick, or absent for other reasons. If the company is suddenly hit with a major flu epidemic, there may not be enough employees available to run the business for a few days. Managers will have to decide whether to hire temporary employees, reduce some operations, or even close the business until employees recover.

CHECKPOINT ✓

Identify four ways that a business can deal with risks.

14.1 ASSESSMENT

Key Concepts

Determine the best answer.

1. True or False. Every risk you face results in a loss.
2. Which of the following is not a type of economic risk?
   - **a.** personal risk
   - **b.** property risk
   - **c.** liability risk
   - **d.** All are economic risks.
3. Using another business to complete a risky activity is known as ________ the risk.
   - **a.** assuming
   - **b.** avoiding
   - **c.** transferring
   - **d.** insuring
4. True or False. For a risk to be insurable, it must be shared by a large number of businesses or individuals.

Make Academic Connections

5. **Geography** Storms, earthquakes, and other natural disasters are often very costly to individuals, businesses, and communities. Millions of dollars in damages are suffered. It takes months and even years to recover. Use the Internet to identify the most costly natural disasters that have occurred in recent years. Identify the type of disaster, the country or region affected, and the estimated financial costs of each. Prepare a table to report your findings.
6. **Critical Thinking** Think carefully about the types of risks you and other family members face as a part of your daily lives. Make a list of 10 such risks. Classify each risk as controllable or uncontrollable and justify each of your classification decisions. For each of the controllable risks, describe actions you and your family members can take to reduce the risk or the possible damage that could occur.

RETEACH Ask students to write each of the key terms in their notebooks, then locate the definition of the term and record it beside the term. Then students should write a sentence that demonstrates their understanding of each term.

ENRICH Instruct students to use the Internet to find examples of unusual items that have been insured.

LIFE/WORK SKILLS

INITIATIVE AND SELF-DIRECTION

The decisions people make about lifestyles are by far the most important factors influencing their health. The U.S. Centers for Disease Control and Prevention report that several key factors influence a person's well-being.

- Quality of medical care, 10%
- Heredity, 18%
- Living and working environment, 19%
- Lifestyle choices, 53%

People want to live long, healthy, and happy lives. Even so, the day-to-day choices you make can result in poor physical and emotional health, accidents, and relationship problems. Your lifestyle reflects your activities, values, beliefs, and behaviors. Day-to-day choices also have an impact on your long-term health and happiness. Making risky choices or failing to be concerned about your physical and emotional health can have negative consequences. These consequences may be hard to overcome or even life-threatening.

istockphoto.com/PeopleImages

How can interpersonal relationships affect your emotional health?

Making positive lifestyle choices now and throughout your lifetime is key to reducing personal risks.

Nutrition Eat a balanced diet that includes a variety of foods. Select foods that promote energy and health. Don't overeat or eat too little. Avoid excessive snacking or foods and beverages filled with empty calories.

Physical Activity Maintain an active schedule involving enjoyable physical activities. Take part in activities that exercise your heart, strengthen muscles, and build flexibility. Develop skills in physical activities you can enjoy all of your life.

Medical Care Schedule regular visits with your doctor, dentist, and eye-care specialist. Actively participate in your medical care by providing accurate and complete information, asking questions, and following the advice of your healthcare providers.

Emotional Health Stay active mentally and emotionally. Develop friendships, but also take time for yourself. Engage in creative activities. Develop positive emotional energy. Don't be afraid to discuss your feelings or seek help from counselors and mentors.

Interpersonal Relationships Spend time with family and friends. Avoid using negative communications that others can easily misinterpret. Be open to people with different backgrounds and experiences. Resolve conflicts before they create problems or affect long-term relationships.

Personal Development Set personal, academic, and career goals and make plans to achieve them. Commit to lifelong learning.

Personal Safety Think about the short- and long-term consequences of your decisions and actions. Reject risky behaviors such as using tobacco, alcohol, and drugs. Drive safely, wear your seat belt, don't use your phone while behind the wheel, and avoid other distractions while driving. Think before participating in activities that can lead to accidents or injuries to you or others.

Think Critically

1. How can decisions made today affect your lifestyle in the future?
2. What additional recommendations can you make for a healthy and happy lifestyle?

LIFE/WORK SKILLS

Point out that people often don't think about risks until it is too late. Then they suffer the consequences of those risks. By anticipating risks and thinking about their consequences, people might decide to do things differently so that negative results are greatly reduced or even eliminated.

THINK CRITICALLY THROUGH VISUALS

Relationships that are positive and supportive improve your emotional health. Interpersonal conflicts, distrust, or negative relationships create stress and anxiety.

Think Critically *Answers*

1. Many lifestyle choices may not immediately seem risky but can have negative effects on health and well-being in the future.

2. Student answers will vary. This should make for a lively discussion. Students should be able to supply specific reasons for their suggestions.

Applied Skills

Writing Across the Curriculum Assign students to write a paragraph that shows a connection between the information in the Life/Work Skills feature and course material in one or more classes they have taken in the past or in which they are currently enrolled.

Focus on REAL LIFE

Explain that even minor mishaps can cause financial setbacks for businesses and individuals that may be hard to overcome. Until a loss is suffered, the full financial impact is difficult to anticipate.

TEACH

Remind students that a common way of reducing the amount of possible financial loss from a risk is to purchase insurance. Insurance is available to individuals and to businesses. The same basic principles and features apply to both types of insurance. Consumers and businesspeople need to understand the basics of insurance to make wise decisions about the type, amount, source, and cost of insurance.

Life-Span Plan Answers

Answers will vary. Students should describe significant losses that could prevent them from achieving their life-span goals. Examples include sickness, accidents, and loss of income.

14.2 Insurable Risks

Learning Outcomes

14.2.1 Recognize important insurance concepts.

14.2.2 Describe several types of business insurance.

Key Terms

insurer 348
insured 348
policyholder 348
insurance policy 348
premium 348
claim 348

Focus on REAL LIFE

Samuel looked on as the fire trucks pulled out of the parking lot of his wholesale produce business. As he watched, his insurance agent, Jake, walked up.

"I'm really sorry about the fire, Samuel," Jake said. "Luckily it looks like they were able to prevent extensive damage to the building."

"Yes, the fire marshal talked to me," replied Samuel. "Even though most of the damage is from smoke and water, all the inventory will have to be replaced, and some of the equipment needs to be repaired. It will probably take several weeks to get back in business."

"We'll get to work immediately getting your insurance claims filed." Jake vowed. "I know you will need cash and we should have your first insurance check tomorrow."

"I'm certainly glad you convinced me to spend a bit more on extended coverage, Jake. I should be able to continue to pay my employees and pay for other operating expenses while we recover."

LO 14.2.1

PURCHASING INSURANCE

Most people and businesses cannot afford to pay for large economic losses. However, they can buy insurance to provide the financial protection they need in the event they suffer a financial loss. Insurance enables them to share the risk with other individuals or businesses. While insurance has a cost, it brings peace of mind. In the event of an accident, injury, or other loss, people and organizations can concentrate on recovery rather than how to pay for losses.

Life-Span Plan

Describe several examples of losses you might suffer that would prevent you from achieving your life-span goals. Explain why taking measures to reduce risks, including buying adequate insurance, is an important part of every person's life-span plan.

Insurance Basics

Insurance companies provide planned protection against economic losses. The company, called an **insurer**, agrees to take on certain economic risks and to pay for losses if they occur. The person or business for which the insurer assumes the risk is the **insured**. To show that it has taken on the risk, the company issues a written contract, or insurance policy. The person or company buying the policy is the **policyholder**. An **insurance policy** states the conditions to which the insurance company and the policyholder have agreed. The amount the policyholder must pay for insurance coverage is a **premium**. The policyholder makes regular payments, usually every six months or once a year. A **claim** is a policyholder's request for payment for a loss that the insurance policy covers.

Different Learning Abilities

English Language Learners (ELL) Ask students to study each of the insurance terms and their definitions. Then ask them to pronounce each term to you and describe their understanding of the meaning of each term. Clarify any misunderstandings.

At-Risk Encourage students to discuss the idea of insurance with family members. Suggest that they talk about the types of risks the family faces and whether those risks are insurable or not.

Insurance Companies

In addition to offering financial protection for policyholders, insurance companies are also investment companies. The premiums collected from the policyholders make up the funds from which the insurance company pays for claims. The company invests these premiums. The premiums collected and the amount earned from investments is used to cover the cost of claims and provide a profit for the insurance company.

Insurance protection can be obtained in several ways. Individuals can buy insurance directly from an insurance company. Employers may provide insurance as an employee benefit. Professional organizations and other groups may offer insurance coverage to members. Businesses often offer insurance for customers to provide protection for related risks. Credit insurance is available when customers borrow large sums of money. Shippers may offer transportation insurance. Data management companies purchase insurance for hacking and cyber attacks.

Many people purchase insurance from an insurance agent. An *insurance agent* represents the insurance company and sells insurance policies to individuals and businesses. A key part of an insurance agent's job is to help each client choose the proper kind and amount of protection from possible economic losses. The agent uses the client's choices to submit information to the insurance company that will prepare the policy.

There are two basic types of insurance agents. One works for a large insurance company and sells only policies written by that company. The other is an independent agent who may sell many kinds of policies from a number of different companies. You can also purchase insurance directly from an insurance company or through an agent using the Internet.

Most people are concerned about the type and cost of insurance when choosing an insurance company. Any time you purchase insurance, the offerings of several companies should be compared for features and prices. Another key factor is the service provided by the company if a loss occurs. When a loss is suffered, policyholders want to be able to rely on the insurance company to act quickly in providing help. It should be easy to contact the company. Their response should be prompt. The process used to file a claim needs to be

Work as a TEAM

Instruct team members to locate the websites of several insurance agents in your community. Identify the insurance company or companies that the agent represents and the types of insurance sold by each for consumers and for businesses. The team should prepare a spreadsheet classifying the insurance products of each agent.

Andersen Ross/Stockbyte/Getty Images

What other types of insurance might an employer purchase on an employee's behalf besides health insurance?

TEACH

Ask students to consider the impact of the Internet on the role of local insurance agents. Encourage students to discuss the advantages of having access to a local agent when making a decision to purchase insurance or when a loss is suffered.

Work as a TEAM

Ask students to use the information they gathered to classify the insurance agents as independent agents or employees of an insurance company. Does the classification seem to be different based on the types of insurance sold?

THINK CRITICALLY THROUGH VISUALS

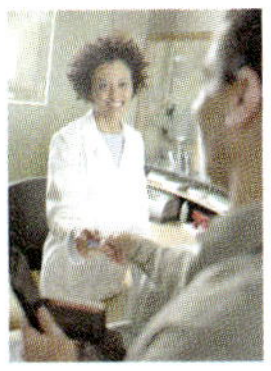

An employer might purchase dental, vision, unemployment, life, or disability insurance for an employee.

Portfolio Activity

Assign the Portfolio Activity for Chapter 14, located on the product website.

COLLECT Offer suggestions to help students locate information about events from the news that describe important risks faced by businesses.

CREATE Remind students that their illustration needs to include steps to reduce risks businesses face.

CONNECT Point out that students need to use their illustration to prepare a one-minute presentation on how businesses deal with risks.

ONGOING ASSESSMENT

CHECKPOINT ✓ANSWER

When selecting an insurance company, consider the type and cost of insurance and the quality of service provided by the company if a loss occurs.

TEACH

Before beginning the discussion, tell students that businesses normally carry insurance to protect against risks to their major assets. Ask students to identify what they believe the major assets of most businesses are that would need to be insured.

Explain that the per-person cost of health insurance for a large group of employees is usually lower than the cost of comparable individual coverage. With group insurance, the risks are spread across a large number of people, so the chances of a loss for any one group member is less.

▶ Figure 14-3 ANSWER

Answers will vary. Most examples will be financial losses resulting from increased expenses or reduced revenues in each of the categories. Costs related to personnel include reduced productivity, medical expenses, and liabilities from lawsuits. Property expenses could increase due to the need to rebuild or repair equipment and buildings. Losses in the operations category may be attributable to lower sales due to the inability to operate the business or the cost of liability claims against the company.

easy and understandable. Full reimbursement for losses covered by the policy should be processed as quickly as possible. Most insurance companies provide online resources and mobile apps to make documenting, filing, and tracking claims rapid and easy for policyholders.

Insured Losses

Both consumers and businesses can buy insurance to cover almost any kind of economic loss. Violinists can insure their fingers. Professional athletes can insure against injuries. Writers may insure their manuscripts. Businesses can insure against the loss of property damaged by fire, injury to consumers resulting from the use of the company's product, or theft by employees.

The kinds of insurance protection that will be important to most consumers are vehicle, property, health, and life insurance. Businesses also insure their vehicles and property. They may provide health and life insurance for some or all employees. They also need liability insurance. *Liability insurance* protects against losses from injury to people or property resulting from the products, services, or actions of a business.

BUSINESS INSURANCE	
MAIN CATEGORIES	**EXAMPLES**
Personnel	• Health insurance • Group insurance • Disability insurance • Workers' compensation • Life insurance
Property	• Commercial property insurance • Vehicle insurance
Business Operations	• Business interruption insurance • Liability insurance • Information security and privacy liability insurance

FIGURE 14-3
What types of losses might a business face if each of these categories is not properly insured?

CHECKPOINT ✓
What information should be considered when selecting an insurance company?

LO 14.2.2
BUSINESS INSURANCE

A company uses its financial resources to invest in land, buildings, operating equipment, inventory, and people. If the business suffers a significant loss of any of these resources, the business may have trouble replacing the resources and continuing to operate. Businesses buy many types of insurance to obtain financial protection for their assets. Figure 14-3 illustrates the three major business insurance categories of personnel, property, and business operations.

Insuring Personnel

The health and well-being of managers and employees are important to a business. If workers are sick or injured, they will not be able to work. The costs of medical care are high. Costs will need to be paid by either the employee or the company. If an accident occurs on the job, the business will often be responsible for the cost of medical care and lost wages while the employee recovers. Businesses can purchase or allow employees to buy several types of insurance to provide protection for the costs of those risks.

Health Insurance Many businesses offer *health insurance*, which provides assistance with the high costs of individual health care. Health insurance provides payments for routine costs of medical care as well as costs for hospitalization or other needed medical treatments. Businesses often offer group health insurance. With *group insurance*, the employees of a

Applied Skills

Building Study Skills As students study and discuss each of the major categories of business insurance, ask them to prepare a written summary that describes each category.

business and their dependents can be covered under one policy. A group insurance policy covers a large number of people, and premiums are paid for all members of the group. As risk is spread among many people, insurance rates decrease. Per person, it is far cheaper to insure many people than one person. Some companies pay for the entire cost of employee health insurance. Most pay a percentage of the cost and employees pay the remainder of the premium, as well as some of the costs of medical treatments.

Disability Insurance *Disability insurance* provides payments to employees who are not able to work for an extended period due to serious illness or injury. The amount of payment is usually 50 to 70 percent of the employee's income. There is usually a maximum amount of money or time period for payments. A special type of disability insurance is known as workers' compensation. *Workers' compensation* is a system of insurance set up by state law that pays employees who are injured on the job. Each business makes payments to the insurance fund based on the number of employees.

Life Insurance Many businesses also offer *life insurance*, which pays the amount of the insurance policy upon the death of the insured. The payment is made to people named in the policy as beneficiaries. Beneficiaries are usually family members of the insured. Partnerships often purchase a life insurance policy on each partner with the company named as beneficiary. This provides money that will be used to maintain the business operations that the deceased partner performed. Corporations often insure the lives of key executives or employees because of their importance to the company's success. Businesses may offer a small amount of life insurance for each employee or allow employees to purchase low-cost life insurance as a benefit.

NET KNOWLEDGE

A small business owner needs to be knowledgeable about a variety of types of insurance in order to have adequate protection from the risks the business faces. Use the Internet to locate the websites of insurance companies offering insurance for small businesses. Select one company and make a list of the types of insurance it provides for businesses. Write a short sentence for each type of insurance describing the risks covered.

Insuring Property

Businesses buy various types of insurance policies to protect company assets from losses that may result from a variety of risks. Businesses want to protect buildings and the inventory and operating equipment within them. Businesses owning automobiles and other vehicles want to insure those assets as well.

Commercial Property Insurance Many businesses own one or more buildings that would be expensive to replace. In addition, the buildings contain company assets such as equipment, supplies, raw materials, component parts, and finished goods. *Commercial property insurance* covers property losses resulting from fire, storms, accidents, theft, and vandalism. Special policies are available to provide coverage for hazards unique to a location or the type of business.

Vehicle Insurance Businesses own and operate all types of commercial vehicles including cars, vans, light- and heavy-duty trucks, trailers, and other business vehicles. By purchasing commercial *vehicle insurance*, damages to the vehicles and occupants resulting from accidents are covered. Vehicle insurance also pays the costs of damage to the property of others as well as medical costs for those injured if people driving a company vehicle cause an accident.

Insuring Business Operations

A business may suffer financial losses resulting from the actions of employees or business operations. Those actions

NET KNOWLEDGE

Ask students to compare their lists of the types of business insurance recommended by the insurance companies they studied. To help them learn more about the major types of business insurance, introduce students to the website insureuonline.org. Ask them to choose the link to InsureU for Small Business and click on the picture of the chalkboard. They can review each of the six types of business insurance listed in the Get Smart section and then take the Small Business Insurance Quiz. When they pass the quiz they will be awarded a certificate from the National Association of Insurance Commissioners.

TEACH

Explain that, even if a business insures many types of property with one insurance company, the insurer will need to determine the risk of loss on each type of property and usually will write a specific policy for each type. Some policies cover a number of related risks to a property type. For example, a commercial package policy allows businesses to combine a number of types of property insurance coverage along with liability coverage in one policy.

Different Learning Abilities

Visually Impaired Provide students with an audio recording of the lesson information. After students listen to the lesson, discuss the information to clarify any misunderstandings. Make the audio recording available to all interested students.

THINK CRITICALLY THROUGH VISUALS

A business might file claims for property damage through its property insurance policy. Its business interruption insurance might provide compensation for ongoing business expenses. If anyone was hurt, the business will file liability insurance claims. If employees are injured or die in the fire, it might make claims through its employee health insurer, disability insurer, or life insurance company.

ONGOING ASSESSMENT

CHECKPOINT ✓ANSWER

(1) personnel, (2) property, and (3) business operations.

ASSESS

Key Concepts *Answers*

1. b. provide financial protection
2. False. The policyholder is the person or business that buys the insurance policy.
3. True
4. d. liability insurance

Make Academic Connections *Answers*

5. Paragraphs will vary.

6a. \$380 + \$425 = \$805. \$805 × 12 months = \$9,660 annually. \$586.50 × 12 months = \$7,038 annually. The group policy reduces the annual total premium cost by \$2,622.

6b. The employer contribution is \$636 annually (\$265 × 0.2 × 12 = \$636) and the employee cost is \$6,402 (\$586.50 × 12 − 636 = \$6,402). The employee savings will be \$3,258 per year compared to the previous policy.

or operations may result in accidents, injuries, property damage, or other types of losses. Insurance can be purchased to protect against those losses. Two common types of insurance for business operations are business interruption insurance and liability insurance.

Business Interruption Insurance Most businesses cannot afford to shut down for a few days or weeks without sustaining an economic loss. *Business interruption insurance* provides compensation for ongoing business expenses that occur if a business has a temporary shutdown due to a covered hazard.

Liability Insurance Many businesses purchase *liability insurance* to cover claims by others based on damages suffered because of business operations, employees, or products. A customer may be injured while visiting the business. The use of a product may result in injury, illness, or death. An employee may be dishonest or engage in actions that are harmful to the business. An increasingly important type of liability insurance is information security and privacy insurance. It offers protection for claims resulting from theft, loss, or misuse of private customer information held by the company.

Photodisc/Getty Images

Which types of business insurance policies might cover damage related to a fire?

CHECKPOINT ✓
What are the three major areas that can be covered by business insurance?

14.2 ASSESSMENT

Key Concepts

Determine the best answer.

1. The reason businesses and individuals purchase insurance is to
   a. make a profit
   b. provide financial protection
   c. reduce taxes
   d. increase sales
2. True or False. Another term for an insurance company is the policyholder.
3. True or False. An insurance agent can work for only one insurance company or may represent several.
4. Insurance that provides coverage for claims by others based on damages suffered as a result of business operations, employees, or products is
   a. health insurance
   b. property insurance
   c. vehicle insurance
   d. liability insurance

Make Academic Connections

5. **Debate** Prepare a paragraph to support the following statement: The maximum amount of damages that a company should have to pay to one individual for any liability claim should be \$1 million. Write a second paragraph in opposition.
6. **Math** Before being hired, a new employee had an individual health insurance policy that costs \$380 per month plus \$425 per month for his spouse and two children. The company offers a group policy that costs \$265 a month for an individual or \$586.50 for the entire family. The company contributes 20 percent of the cost of the individual policy toward either choice.
   a. By how much does the group policy reduce the annual cost of health insurance premiums for the entire family without the company's contribution?
   b. What is the annual employer contribution to employee health insurance costs? What will the employee pay for family health insurance premiums for an entire year? What is the annual savings compared to the previous individually purchased policy?

RETEACH Assign teams of students one of the categories of business insurance in Figure 14-3. Ask the group to review the lesson information and develop a presentation to be delivered to the other teams.

ENRICH Invite an insurance agent to speak about the impact of technology on his or her work.

CLOSE Discuss ways that businesses can reduce the cost of insurance while still protecting against risks.

14.3 Uninsurable Risks

Learning Outcomes

14.3.1 Describe why some business risks are uninsurable.

14.3.2 List the strategies a company can use to reduce the risks of doing business internationally.

Key Terms

property rights 357
counterfeiting 358

Focus on REAL LIFE

Sophia looked up from her computer when Josh asked what she was doing.

"Reading about software piracy. It says here that Microsoft products dominate the Chinese market but the company is not happy. Most of their software has been pirated. That means Microsoft doesn't get paid for those products."

"I know people who have tried to make copies of computer software here in the United States," said Josh, "but our laws are strict. The penalties are severe if people are caught."

"According to this article, more than 75 percent of software used in China has been pirated, resulting in losses of nearly $9 billion to the legitimate owners. By comparison, the U.S. piracy rate is less than 20 percent" Sophia reported. "However, since the United States has so many more computers than China, the actual dollar loss to businesses is higher, nearly $10 billion."

"I guess some people don't worry about big companies like Microsoft, but billions of dollars lost each year means all of us pay more for our legal copies."

LO 14.3.1

IDENTIFYING AND MANAGING RISKS

Businesses cannot insure many of the risks they face. To be insurable, the risk and amount of loss must be predictable. If the chance that a risk will occur cannot be reasonably predicted or the possible financial loss to the business cannot be calculated, it is not likely that an insurance company will provide coverage. The costs of some risks are so high that a business cannot afford the cost of insurance protection. In these cases, the business must determine other ways to deal with those uninsurable risks.

Uninsurable Risk Factors

Several factors can lead to business risks that may be very costly to a company. The factors are economic conditions, consumer demand, competitors' actions, technology changes, local factors, and business operations.

iStockphoto.com/pixdeluxe

What are the economic results of illegally downloading digital music and video files from the Internet?

Focus on REAL LIFE

This scenario can be used to spark discussion about software piracy and property rights. Ask students to think about what happens each time an individual makes an illegal copy of software or a digital music file. Software developers, music producers, and artists want to make their products available to prospective customers, but they also want to be compensated for their work.

TEACH

Ask students: "What would happen to a business if it tried to purchase insurance for every risk it faces?" Students should recognize that the cost would be very high and that they probably could not find companies to insure every risk even if they were willing to pay.

THINK CRITICALLY THROUGH VISUALS

When music and video files are pirated, the media company that hired the artists, the programmers, and others who worked on the project do not receive any compensation and the media company will have to charge its paying customers more in order to make a profit. If they cannot raise the price, they will have to stop producing the merchandise. Artists do not receive royalties from the pirated copies. The businesses that sell authentic CDs and digital files may have to close retail locations or websites. Also, companies will have less money to develop new entertainment media.

Applied Skills

Communication Assign students to create an Internet advertisement that discourages people from pirating software. Encourage students to use available resources to produce a storyboard or multimedia presentation for their ad. Consider allowing students to work in pairs.

FYI

Explain that online crime now costs large businesses, on average, more than $1.5 million each year. Instruct students to use the Internet to locate and report additional statistics on the cost and effects of online crime on businesses and consumers.

TEACH

For each of the categories of uninsurable factors, ask students to describe why the risks are uninsurable and what companies can do to try to reduce or manage the risk.

THINK CRITICALLY THROUGH VISUALS

Brick and mortar stores can compete with Internet retailers by offering better customer service, incentives for loyal customers, convenient return policies, updated and attractive interiors and product displays, knowledgeable and helpful salespeople, and an atmosphere that makes people want to come into the store. They may need to begin offering alternative shopping services that allow customers more purchasing and delivery convenience than typically offered by traditional retail stores.

FYI A growing risk facing businesses is Internet security. Worldwide business losses from Internet fraud and cyber attacks now are estimated to exceed $500 billion a year and are increasing. Major risks are information theft, viruses, equipment failure, denial of service attacks, and online fraud.

Economic Conditions When the economy is strong, consumers and business customers are more willing to spend money. Sales are brisk and profits are high. A downturn in the economy can quickly reduce sales and profits. If a company does not cut production and expenses, it can experience real problems. Managers need to study the economy carefully. They must be prepared to respond to improvements or declines in economic conditions.

Consumer Demand Companies produce products that they think will meet consumer demand. They study customer needs and preferences. If they can predict a change in demand, they may be able to take advantage of the change with new products. If consumer tastes change, an unprepared company may end up with inventory that they are unable to sell at a profit.

Competitors' Actions Businesses function in a competitive environment. The actions of competitors can affect the success of a business. If a competitor starts a unique promotion or decides to reduce prices, a business will have to decide whether it needs to respond or not. The wrong decision can result in lost sales and profits or additional unneeded expenses. A new competitor may enter the market or a current competitor may introduce a new service. If a company is not prepared for these types of competitive actions, its share of the market can quickly decline.

Technology Changes What happened to traditional businesses when other companies started to use the Internet? If a company is not prepared to accept debit cards as a form of payment, will customers take their business elsewhere? Now that consumers can easily and inexpensively download music and movies from websites, what has happened to brick-and-mortar music and video stores? Changes in technology may require changes in business practices. The cost of putting new technology in place may be high, but if a business

istockphoto.com/RomanBabakin

What can brick and mortar stores do to retain traditional customers who have turned to the Internet for shopping?

Applied Skills

Technology Ask students to visit the websites of online merchants and identify ways that businesses are attempting to reduce risks they and their customers face when they engage in online shopping. Ask students to discuss their findings.

doesn't adopt the technology customers prefer, it may lose sales.

Local Factors The highway that runs in front of a fast-food business closes for a month for repair. The utility company serving the city has a 5 percent rate increase for the cost of electricity. The county zoning board rejects a business's request to expand its production facilities. The laws, regulations, taxes, and infrastructure of a local community can influence the operations and finances of a business. Some businesses decide to relocate from one state or country to another to secure conditions that are more favorable. Businesses work with government officials and community organizations to maintain a positive environment for business.

Business Operations The day-to-day operations of a business can have a major impact on its success or failure. A poorly run business will have higher costs, low

Business Insight

Businesses Respond to a Disaster

When Hurricane Katrina hit New Orleans and the gulf coast of the United States in 2005, federal, state, and local governments struggled to respond to the devastation. Faced with a growing crisis, businesses sprang into action with the same efficiency and effectiveness they use in their day-to-day operations to respond to emergencies in communities affected by the storm and its aftermath. Thousands of businesses, large and small, demonstrated their commitment to aiding people in need with donations of money, equipment, materials, and employee time.

Before Katrina made landfall, Wal-Mart prepared 45 trucks loaded with supplies at its Brookhaven, Mississippi, distribution center, ready for delivery. With 34,000 of its own employees affected by the storm, Wal-Mart immediately promised and delivered $20 million in cash donations, 1,500 truckloads of free merchandise, and food for 100,000 meals.

Two home improvement giants, Home Depot and Lowe's, suffered extensive damage to many of their stores. All along the storm's path, managers and dedicated employees opened less-damaged stores within hours to provide generators and emergency supplies for their neighbors. In addition, Home Depot pledged more than $11 million and worked with volunteer organizations to rebuild more than 100 playgrounds and athletic fields. Lowe's teamed with designer Marianne Cusato to develop plans and materials for small, permanent homes called Katrina Cottages. They served as affordable alternatives to FEMA trailers for displaced residents and emergency workers.

Marriott Corporation committed to help its 2,800 employees who worked at 15 New Orleans hotels as they faced the loss of their jobs and, in some cases, their homes. Many employees were bused to Houston where they were housed and fed in the ballroom of the Houston Airport Marriott while the company helped them find temporary housing and jobs.

Hurricane Katrina remains the most expensive natural disaster in U.S. history, costing $150 billion and 2,000 lives. However, the immediate and long-term efforts of businesses coordinated with government, organizations, and individual volunteers demonstrate that recovery from even the worst disasters is possible. The Katrina response illustrates ways businesses respond to disasters and how their efforts can help communities and individuals recover.

Think Critically

1. Why are businesses willing to commit resources to help deal with emergencies that affect other areas as well as their own communities?
2. How might the expertise of businesses be used by government agencies to improve responses to future disasters and emergencies?

Different Learning Styles

Kinesthetic Learner Assign students to use the newspaper or Internet to locate information on road work and street repairs planned for their community or area of the state. Using an online map program, students can locate businesses that may be affected by the work and suggest how those businesses might be affected.

TEACH

Ask students to collect examples from local newspapers of activities by government agencies that may have negative effects on businesses. Discuss how and why businesses are affected, why the government is taking the action, and what businesses are doing to try to reduce the impact.

Business Insight

When communities, states, and countries are hit by huge natural disasters, there are usually losses in property, jobs, and even lives. While insurance provides some protection, many of the losses are either too large or are not covered by insurance. Individuals, community organizations, and businesses are usually quick to jump in to offer a variety of types of help to those affected.

Think Critically *Answers*

1. Businesses have a financial incentive to help deal with emergencies. Recovery will mean customers can once again spend money. In addition, when a disaster strikes, businesses in the community want to help their employees and neighbors because they are all part of the same community.

2. Governments may ask businesses to share expertise and help with training to be better prepared for disasters. They also can coordinate their efforts with businesses during the recovery to speed up their response and increase the available resources.

TEACH

Ask students to study the section "Managing Risks" and develop an outline of the main ways businesses and their employees can identify, manage, and reduce risks.

THINK CRITICALLY THROUGH VISUALS

Stores deter theft by employing security personnel, prosecuting shoplifters, installing security cameras and alarms, and using electronic security tags on merchandise. They maintain rigorous inventory control to deter employee theft.

ONGOING ASSESSMENT

CHECKPOINT ✓ANSWER

The factors include economic conditions, consumer demand, competitors' actions, technology changes, local factors, and business operations.

Andre Kudyusov/Photodisc/Getty Images

What security measures are put in place by retail stores to deter theft?

morale, increased turnover, and a poor customer image. A lack of employee training and poor management can lead to production errors, safety problems that result in accidents and injuries, poorly maintained equipment and facilities, and labor relations problems. If managers and employees are not committed to the success of the company, they will miss opportunities to improve operations, increase customer satisfaction, and control expenses.

Managing Risks

Each of the situations just described poses a risk to businesses. Alone, any of the risks can cause serious financial problems. If several occur at the same time, the business may not be able to survive. Uninsurable risks present important challenges to managers and employees. Businesses that understand the importance of recognizing and managing risks will be much better prepared to anticipate situations that can cause problems and to manage problems in a way that reduces the financial impact on the company.

Everyone in a business needs to be aware that there are many uninsurable risks. Employees should be informed about all potential risks related to their work, how to identify any problems that are developing, and what actions they should take when a situation occurs.

Every business needs a written risk management plan in place. The plan includes procedures to gather and analyze information for all possible risk areas. Customer information should be collected and analyzed. This data includes problems, requests, and complaints. Product sales should be monitored to identify sales trends. All operating costs should be analyzed to ensure they remain in line with budgeted amounts.

Businesses should inspect facilities and equipment routinely to make sure they are well-maintained and free of safety hazards. Careful employee selection and ongoing training will improve the efficiency of operations and reduce the chances of accidents and injuries. Security measures should be established to prevent theft and vandalism and to protect employees and customers. Company records should be accurately maintained and protected from all forms of possible damage. Copies should be prepared and stored in secure locations.

Businesses should be active and involved in their communities and maintain a positive image. They should build relationships with community organizations, consumer and business groups, and government officials. Businesses should monitor proposed laws and regulations changes and work with government to draft legislation that benefits everyone. Careful study and planning followed by positive actions will have the greatest effect on managing business risks.

CHECKPOINT ✓

What are several major factors affecting business that often present uninsurable risks?

Different Learning Abilities

Hearing Impaired Prepare computer-generated slides or printed handouts containing key points and discussion details and provide them to the students in advance of the discussion. Give the students ample opportunities to ask questions or seek clarification for the information provided.

LO 14.3.2

RISKS IN INTERNATIONAL BUSINESS

As an international business manager, would you be willing to ship products to a customer in another country before receiving payment? Would you agree to accept another country's currency for payment instead of U.S. dollars? These are examples of risks faced by every organization involved in international business.

Strategies for Reducing Risk

The following strategies will help reduce international business risk. First, work with customers from several countries. This approach reduces the risk faced when doing business in only one country or region. If problems develop in one nation, causing lost sales and profits, the global company is shielded with profits from other markets.

Next, offer a range of products. When an organization broadens its product line, reduced sales of one item will not mean complete failure for the company. Successful global organizations continually create new products, seek new uses for existing products, and look for new markets for their products.

Third, involve local business partners in business decisions and activities. Joint ventures with local companies help to reduce political and social risks. An agreement between a global company and a local business can help both organizations. In addition, the citizens and government of the host nation should be more welcoming to a foreign business if a company they are familiar with is involved.

Finally, employ local people in key management positions. Executives and other managers who are native to a country or region usually have a better understanding of the cultural and social norms and the political environment. This knowledge can help the international company adapt its products and operations to the needs of the market being served.

International Property Rights

Each year the FIFA World Cup is played, replica jerseys of the top players are illegally manufactured and sold around the world. In many countries, copies of popular movies, music videos, and computer software are illegally duplicated and sold by street vendors. These are examples of violations of property rights.

Property rights are the exclusive rights to possess and use property and its profits. This excludes everyone else from interfering with the production, sale, or use of the item. *Intellectual property* refers to technical knowledge or creative work. It includes software, clothing designs, music, books, and movies. A *patent* is the exclusive right of an inventor to make, sell, and use a product or process. An inventor may obtain a patent on a computer component, a new package design, or a prescription drug. Patents are designed to encourage innovation and progress.

A *trademark* is a distinctive name, symbol, word, picture, or combination of these that a company uses to identify products or services. Common trademarks known around the world include the McDonald's golden arches and Target's red circles. A *copyright* protects the original works of authors, composers, playwrights, artists, and publishers. In the United States, a new copyright gives originators sole rights to publish and exhibit their creative works for their lifetime plus 70 years.

Work as a TEAM

Work with your team members to describe a possible joint venture between companies in two different countries. Explain why the businesses might want to work together. What are possible benefits for each organization? How might the venture reduce risks facing each company?

TEACH

Tell students that companies that participate in international business face different risks as well as more of the same types of risks they face in their home countries. If businesspeople are not aware of these new risks and do not prepare for them, the international business activities have a greater chance of failing.

List the major types of property rights on the board. As each is introduced, ask students to list examples of products or services that illustrate each type of property right and discuss how the property right could be violated.

Explain that property rights are a particularly challenging issue in international business. Countries do not all have the same laws dealing with property rights, and it is more difficult to enforce property rights laws in some countries. Also, it is difficult to monitor intellectual property all over the world in order to recognize when property rights are being violated.

Work as a TEAM

Ask students if they believe forming a joint venture with a company in another country reduces or increases the number of risks faced by each company alone. Students should provide reasons for their decision.

Different Learning Abilities

Gifted Assign students to use library or Internet resources to locate information on a court case where a U.S. company tried to enforce its intellectual property rights in another country. Ask students to provide an oral summary of the case to the other class members.

THINK CRITICALLY THROUGH VISUALS

The creators of the original goods and businesses that stock them are hurt due to lost sales and the possible loss of image and prestige if numerous counterfeit items are sold. Customers who purchase the legitimate brands are hurt due to the availability of cheaper counterfeit merchandise diminishing the value of the brand.

ONGOING ASSESSMENT

CHECKPOINT ✓ANSWER

Companies can make sure they do business in numerous countries to diffuse the risk. They can offer a variety of products so they are not reliant on any one to succeed. Companies can also pair with local companies and hire local people for important roles.

ASSESS

Key Concepts *Answers*

1. False. Some risks are too expensive or uncommon to insure.
2. b. technology change
3. True
4. c. patent

Make Academic Connections *Answers*

5. Reports will vary.
6. Tables will vary.

CLOSE Ask students: "Do you believe insurable risks or uninsurable risks present a greater challenge to businesses?" Challenge them to defend their answers.

For both individuals and businesses, their intellectual properties are valuable assets that generate sales and profits. The exclusive rights provide a competitive advantage. Most other countries have similar laws offering protections for property rights. There may be differences in the definitions and type of protection. However, some countries do little to enforce property rights laws, especially when the products of a foreign company are involved. **Counterfeiting** refers to illegal uses of intellectual property, patents, trademarks, and copyrights. For example, a company may make slight changes to a well-known product and sell it in other countries. They are illegally copying the product so they don't have to pay the development costs of their own products or pay the original company for the right to sell the product. By using the actual product name or trademark illegally, they are profiting from the reputation of the established company. When property rights laws are not enforced, companies lose sales and profits.

Who is hurt by the sale of counterfeit goods such as handbags and watches?

CHECKPOINT ✓

What actions can U.S. companies take to minimize the risk of doing business in foreign markets?

14.3 ASSESSMENT

Key Concepts

Determine the best answer.

1. True or False. Every risk a business faces can be insured.
2. The ever-expanding use of the Internet as a business tool is an example of what type of business risk?
   a. economic conditions
   b. technology change
   c. consumer demand
   d. competitors' actions.
3. True or False. To reduce the risks of international business, a company should conduct business in many countries.
4. The exclusive right of an inventor to make, sell, and use a product or process is a
   a. trademark
   b. copyright
   c. patent
   d. None of the above is correct.

Make Academic Connections

5. **Economics** Use the business section of newspapers and business magazines to gather information on predictions for changes in the economy for the next 6 to 12 months. Based on this information, prepare a two-page written report for small business owners in your community identifying how the changes might affect their businesses in positive or negative ways.
6. **Business Law** Use the Internet to gather information on the fraudulent use of the intellectual property of U.S. businesses in other countries. Develop a table that identifies the U.S. company, the product that has been misused, the country or countries in which the fraud has occurred, and any action taken by the company to protect its property rights. Present the information in your table to other class members. Discuss the effect of the fraud on businesses and consumers.

RETEACH Instruct students to review the lesson and prepare one quiz question for each of the major headings for the lesson. Organize the class into small learning teams of four or five students. Students should ask each other the questions and discuss the correct answers.

ENRICH Assign students to use the Internet to find examples of small businesses that have been successful in international markets. Ask students to identify ways the small businesses were able to reduce some of the risks they faced in those markets.

DOING BUSINESS IN… COSTA RICA

With more than 130 protected parks, refuges, and reserves, the natural beauty of Costa Rica is the foundation of this country's pride and its main tourist attraction. People come from all over the globe to enjoy Costa Rica's jungles, mountains, oceans, wildlife, and exotic birds. A growing part of the tourism industry is ecotourism—enjoying natural areas, but minimizing your impact on the environment.

Costa Rica is an independent democratic republic with a representative government made up of three branches: executive, legislative, and judiciary. Costa Rica elects its president. It is one of the most peaceful and stable democracies in Latin America and the world.

The stable political and economic environment of Costa Rica makes it an attractive Latin American location for foreign business investment. Unlike many countries, full ownership of real estate and businesses by foreigners is allowed. The 4.8 million inhabitants of Costa Rica value education. Its 93 percent literacy rate makes it the most literate country in Central America. The high educational standards make it appealing to international companies. High-tech businesses including microchip and medical products producers are adding to the economic base of the country. Even as technology exports increase, traditional agricultural products, including coffee, bananas, sugar, and beef, continue to contribute to the country's total trade.

The open foreign trade policies of Costa Rica enable 50 percent of its GDP to be earned from exports. While the economy has slowed recently due to economic problems throughout the world, it has grown at an annual rate of nearly 5 percent since 1990. The growing economy has allowed the country to focus on reducing the poverty rate among its citizens from 40 percent to under 20 percent.

Because of the number of U.S. high-tech companies that have invested in the country, Costa Rica has been called "the Silicon Valley of Latin America." Companies establishing major operations in the country include Microsoft, IBM, Procter & Gamble, General Electric, Abbott Laboratories, and Intel. Western Union established its Latin American regional operations center in the capital city, San José. Over 250 multinational corporations currently operate in Costa Rica.

Costa Rica is easily accessible for both tourism and trade. Major airports are served by 20 international passenger airlines and 8 cargo airlines. Major ports on both the Atlantic and Pacific coasts allow cargo shipments in and out of the country. Cruise ships regularly dock at the ports, bringing tourists to explore the tropical environments, beaches, cities, and villages.

Relationships are formal unless business associates are well known to each other. Handshakes are more common than hugs, which are reserved for family and close friends. Punctuality is important for business meetings, but less so for post-business social events and dinners.

Think Critically

1. What are some of the factors that have made Costa Rica an attractive location for foreign investment?
2. What elements of the Costa Rican political and social environment help to enhance the country's economic development?
3. Conduct library or Internet research to find additional information about business and economic activities in Costa Rica.

How does the growth of ecotourism contribute to Costa Rica's image as a popular tourist destination?

Applied Skills

Geography Ask students to find an example, other than Costa Rica, of a location that might be an ecotourism destination. Assign students to work in small groups to produce a brochure, slide show, video, multimedia presentation, or table-top display featuring a specific location and the concept of ecotourism. Ask students to include continent and country maps as well as multiple photographs of the location.

Doing Business in… COSTA RICA

Every country provides unique business opportunities for international trade, including markets for exporting the products and services of the country. Costa Rica is a small country in terms of both geography and population. However, due to its close proximity, agricultural production, and positive view of foreign investment, it has become an important trading partner for the United States.

THINK CRITICALLY THROUGH VISUALS

Many tourists are looking for locations where they can visit unspoiled natural environments. Costa Rica offers many different ecosystems, ranging from jungles, mountains, and oceans to beaches and rainforests. They provide a variety of tourism experiences.

Think Critically *Answers*

1. It is a Central American country with easy access by both air and water. It has a moderate climate and a variety of natural resources. Costa Rica has a high literacy rate with an educated labor force.
2. Costa Rica has a long history of political stability, a belief in education that translates to a high literacy rate, and declining poverty rates.
3. Student answers will vary depending on what additional information they locate about business and economic activities in Costa Rica.

Think Critically About Business *Answers*

1. Answers will vary. You might ask whether students found similarities between risks faced by individuals and businesses.

2. Answers will vary. Students should be able to identify controllable and uncontrollable risks and explain the difference between the two.

3. Risks can be avoided, transferred, insured, or assumed. Avoiding risk results in no loss, but there is no opportunity for profit. Transferring risk means that someone with more expertise is managing the risk, but the transfer has a cost. Insuring risk allows it to be pooled with others so the cost is affordable, but premiums have costs. Assuming risk involves no immediate costs, but the disadvantage is the full cost of any losses.

4. Answers will vary. Generally, students will consider buying insurance to protect themselves against very large losses. Some insurable risks that students may choose not to protect against might be covered by life, health, or disability insurance.

5. Answers will vary, but could include finding out how claims are processed, the types and number of customer complaints, how the company's financial strength is rated, whether the company allows larger deductibles to lower premium costs, payment options, and how much the insurance will cost for various coverage options.

Chapter 14 Assessment

Review Business Concepts

14.1 Overview of Risk Management

- There are many types of risks and possible losses. The main types of risks are economic and noneconomic, pure and speculative, controllable and uncontrollable, and insurable and uninsurable. Individuals and businesses need to be aware of risks and attempt to reduce possible losses, especially those that may result in physical or financial harm.
- Individuals and businesses must determine how they will deal with the risks and possible losses they face. There are four possible ways to deal with risks: avoid the risk, transfer the risk, insure the risk, or assume the risk.

14.2 Insurable Risks

- Most individuals and businesses are unable to pay for large economic losses, so they share the risk with other individuals or businesses. They purchase insurance to provide the needed financial protection in the event they suffer a financial loss.
- Businesses purchase a variety of types of insurance to obtain financial protection for their assets. Business insurance can be categorized within three major areas: personnel, property, and business operations.

14.3 Uninsurable Risks

- If the chance that a risk will occur cannot be reasonably predicted or the possible financial loss to the business calculated, it will be unlikely that an insurance company will provide coverage. The costs of some risks are so high that a business cannot afford the cost of insurance protection.
- To reduce international business risks, companies should conduct business in many countries, offer a variety of products, involve local business partners, and employ local personnel in key management positions.

Think Critically About Business

1. Identify one personal, property, and liability risk faced by a family. Identify one of each that is faced by a business. Now identify a noneconomic risk for an individual and for a business.
2. What are several controllable risks you and your friends might face? What are some uncontrollable risks you and your friends might face? What makes the risks you identified controllable or uncontrollable?
3. People and businesses can deal with risks in four ways. Identify the four ways and describe the advantages and disadvantages of each.
4. Under what circumstances should you consider buying insurance? Are there circumstances where you are facing an insurable risk and you would choose not to buy insurance? Why would you make that decision?
5. List several questions you would want answered about an insurance company before you decided to purchase insurance from the company.
6. Use the Internet to find information on buying flood insurance for homeowners and business owners. How is purchasing flood insurance different from purchasing other forms of property insurance? Who is required to purchase flood insurance?
7. Visit the website of a large employer in your community or region. Locate information about the insurance benefits that the company offers its employees. Determine the types of insurance offered, who is eligible for the insurance benefits, and whether the company pays some or all of the costs for the insurance premiums.
8. Identify a type of business you would consider owning or managing. What are some specific risks the business could face that would be uninsurable because the chance of the risk or the amount of loss cannot be easily predicted? What are some risks facing the business that could be very expensive to insure?

6. The National Flood Insurance Program is a federal insurance program administered by FEMA but sold by private insurance companies. Homes and buildings in high-risk flood areas with mortgages from federally regulated or insured lenders are required to have flood insurance.

7. Answers will vary, depending on the business chosen. Students may find that some companies offer different levels of insurance benefits depending on the classification of employment. Options for coverage and cost may be available to employees to meet their individual and family needs and budgets.

9. What information sources are available that could be used by businesspeople to keep track of changes in economic conditions that could affect their companies? What are some current economic conditions that could have a positive or negative effect on U.S. businesses?

10. Suggest several ways that a retail business can improve security to prevent theft of merchandise by customers and employees. In what ways can operations be changed or improved to reduce the chances of theft?

11. You own a small business that produces computer games. You are considering selling the games in several foreign countries. What risks might you face as you branch out into international trade that you didn't face in the United States? Which of the risks are controllable and which are uncontrollable? Identify several steps you could take to reduce these risks.

Develop Your Business Language

Match the terms listed with the definitions.

12. Agrees to take on certain economic risks and to pay for losses if they occur.
13. Those that can be reduced or eliminated by actions you take.
14. Illegal uses of intellectual property, patents, trademarks, and copyrights.
15. The amount the policyholder must pay for insurance coverage.
16. The person or business for which the risk is assumed.
17. Those that can result in financial loss.
18. The possibility of incurring a loss.
19. A policyholder's request for payment for a loss that is covered by the insurance policy.
20. The person or company purchasing the policy.
21. Presents the chance of loss but no opportunity for gain.
22. The exclusive rights to possess and use property and its profits.
23. States the conditions to which the insurance company and the policyholder have agreed.
24. Exchanges the uncertainty of a possible large financial loss for a certain smaller payment.
25. Can result in losses, such as health and personal well-being.
26. Can lead to a loss of personal or business items such as money, vehicles, and buildings.
27. Related to harm or injury to other people or their property because of your actions.

Key Terms

a. claim
b. controllable risk
c. counterfeiting
d. economic risk
e. insurance
f. insurance policy
g. insured
h. insurer
i. liability risks
j. personal risks
k. policyholder
l. premium
m. property rights
n. property risks
o. pure risk
p. risk

8. Answers will vary, depending on the types of businesses students choose. They should demonstrate that they understand the types of risks businesses face and that companies cannot insure themselves against all risks.

9. Sources of information that businesspeople could use are newspapers and financial magazines; online news services and business blogs; trade publications specific to a particular industry; conferences, seminars and trade shows; government reports; and organizations' annual reports. Student answers will vary based on current economic conditions.

10. Answers will vary. Students should suggest various ways retailers can curb theft, such as hiring security personnel, using electronic tags on merchandise, using computer software to maintain tight control of inventory, and installing video surveillance cameras and other security technology.

11. Risks would include currency exchange fluctuations; financing difficulties; the prospect of having the games pirated and the host country not enforcing property rights laws; the product not being designed to match the interests, culture, or language of each country; and national political and economic conditions. Students are to list whether the risks they identify are controllable or uncontrollable and several steps they could take to reduce the risks.

Develop Your Business Language *Answers*

12. h. insurer
13. b. controllable risk
14. c. counterfeiting
15. l. premium
16. g. insured
17. d. economic risk
18. p. risk
19. a. claim
20. k. policyholder
21. o. pure risk
22. m. property rights
23. f. insurance policy
24. e. insurance
25. j. personal risks
26. n. property risks
27. i. liability risks

Make Academic Connections

28. **Economics** Speculative risks offer the chance to gain or to lose. People invest their money hoping to get a good return on the investment. Still, most investments have some risk, which means the money can be lost. Common investments are savings accounts, stocks, and real estate. Identify two additional investments. Prepare a table that describes and compares each of the investments in terms of their risk and possible gain or loss.

29. **Writing** You have been asked by a business owner to give advice on how to deal with a risk the business is facing. During the winter after an ice storm, the parking lot and sidewalks are often very slippery. There is a risk that employees and visitors may slip on the ice and be injured. Prepare a memo to the business owner describing some ways the business might deal with the risk. Recommend the actions that should be taken and reasons for your recommendations.

30. **Technology** Identify five insurance agents that sell business insurance in your area. Use a computer to create a database of information about the agents. Include the agent's name, agency name, address, telephone number, e-mail address, insurance company represented, and types of business insurance sold.

31. **Reading** Healthcare practitioners face many risks. Malpractice insurance provides protection if there is a lawsuit for problems resulting from a medical procedure. However, the cost of malpractice insurance is affecting the cost and availability of many medical services. Locate an article in a magazine, newspaper, or on the Internet that addresses the effect of the cost of malpractice insurance on health care. Use a computer presentation program to outline the major concepts presented in the article using bullet points.

32. **Art** Businesses try to reduce the number of accidents and injuries in their buildings by continually reminding employees of the importance of safety. Prepare a poster with an attention-getting message about safety and accident prevention that is appropriate for display in a business setting.

33. **Business Research** Identify a business in your community that has recently closed. Gather information about the business by reviewing newspaper articles and Internet information sources. Identify factors that contributed to the business failure. Write a one-page report on the major risks the business faced and why each contributed to the business failure.

34. **International Business** Several unique types of insurance are available for companies that participate in international commerce. Use the Internet to identify five types of insurance a company buying or selling products in another country might need. Prepare a table that identifies each type of insurance, its purpose, and a company or organization that offers the insurance for sale.

Make Your Case

The Chrismann Company is a manufacturer of lawn equipment. It sells its products through garden centers in a 10-state region of the upper Midwest. To distribute its products, it maintains a fleet of 25 delivery vans. It also has 18 cars driven by its salespeople. The company recently finished a review of its vehicle insurance costs. Records show that the average cost to insure each van is $1,960 a year. Cars cost an average of $1,525 to insure. Insurance claims filed for the past eight years averaged $61,200 a year. The company's executives are considering canceling their vehicle insurance. They want to set up a fund using the money they currently pay to the insurance company. This fund would be used to pay costs of repairs and injuries resulting from any vehicle accidents.

35. If the average costs related to repairs and injuries continue for the next five years, how much will the company save using their new plan?

36. Develop reasons for and against the new plan. If you were an executive, would you be in favor of or opposed to the plan?

Interactions and Connections

37. Read, watch, and listen to local news reports and identify the types of risks that are currently affecting the quality of life in your community. Make a list of the risks you identify and determine if they are mainly controllable or uncontrollable, insurable or uninsurable. Determine what plans are being made by community leaders, including government, business, social service organizations, and others, to deal with the risks and reduce their potential impact on the citizens and visitors.

Make Academic Connections *Answers*

28. Tables will vary depending on the investments chosen.

29. Memos will vary. Students might suggest that in addition to purchasing adequate liability insurance, the business owner should hire employees or contract with a service to plow and shovel snow from the parking lot and to apply products to sidewalks that will aid melting and help people avoid slipping.

30. Databases will vary.

31. Presentations will vary.

32. Posters will vary.

33. Information in the report will vary based on the business selected and information gathered.

34. Tables will vary. Some common types are transit and cargo insurance, medical travel insurance, export credit insurance, and political risk insurance.

Make Your Case *Answers*

35. If average costs continue for the next five years, the company will save $76,250 over the five-year period (present cost to insure the trucks and cars for five years is $382,250; under the new plan they would allocate $306,000 to pay for repairs and injuries).

36. Answers will vary. One reason to adopt the new plan is for the potential cost savings. When claims are low, the savings will be even greater. Even if costs go up, the insurance rates are likely to increase as well. The major reason not to self-insure is that, in the event of a much higher accident rate, or a catastrophic loss, such as a major accident involving bodily injuries, the costs to the company could be much higher than the premiums.

Interactions and Connections

37. The risks students identify will vary. For example, they might mention risks related to the weather, the economy, public health, and personal safety.

Insurance companies benefit when their policyholders work to reduce the risks that are covered by insurance policies. Many nonprofit organizations and government agencies also try to help individuals and businesses reduce the risks they face. Use an Internet search engine to identify websites that offer information on how to reduce a specific risk facing individuals or businesses.

38. Locate websites that provide information on reducing risks. Select one website for each of these categories: (a) insurance company, (b) government agency, and (c) nonprofit organization.

39. Prepare a table that identifies the sponsor of the website; the type of risk discussed; whether it is a risk facing individuals, businesses, or both; and whether it is an economic or noneconomic risk.

40. For each website selected, write one paragraph explaining why the business, agency, or organization is interested in reducing the particular risk or risks. What are their goals or how do they benefit if individuals or businesses follow their advice?

Retail Merchandising Series Event Role Play

In 2009, retail crimes such as shoplifting, employee theft, and supply chain fraud equaled 1.48% of sales in the United States, or $42.3 billion. Employee theft accounted for more than 40 percent of these losses. Some cases involve taking merchandise without paying for it, but employees are also involved in other kinds of thefts. They facilitate shoplifting by friends and family members, they abuse their employee discount, and their actions cause retailers to charge higher prices for merchandise to cover the losses.

The manager of a retail store is upset with reports indicating that 12 percent, or $120,000, of the store's merchandise was stolen or shoplifted. The manager has determined that much of the stolen merchandise is related to employee activity. For this event, you must develop a strategy for reducing the losses related to theft and shoplifting. Your role-playing scenario must address the following issues: loss of merchandise, basic insurance needs for the business, and stronger security systems.

Individual participants have 10 minutes to study the business situation described above and develop a plan of action for the role-playing scenario. Participants are allowed to take notes regarding their response to the situation. Individual participants then have 10 minutes to present their scenario to the judge or class. Five additional minutes are scheduled for the judge and class to ask questions.

Performance Indicators Evaluated

- Define business risk.
- Describe employee ethics with regard to shoplifting and employee theft.
- Describe strategies to reduce business risk and associated losses.
- Explain the purpose of purchasing insurance to cover losses due to employee theft and shoplifting.
- Describe a work environment that requires and rewards positive ethical behavior.

For more detailed information about performance indicators, go to the DECA website.

Think Critically

1. Why do many businesses purchase insurance to cover losses due to employee theft and shoplifting?
2. Why is it important to monitor employee behavior in retail businesses?
3. What are three specific strategies that can be used to deter theft and shoplifting?
4. How might shoplifting or employee theft present an ethical dilemma for a retail employee?
5. How does shoplifting affect prices charged for merchandise at a retail establishment?

www.deca.org

38. Answers will vary based on websites chosen.

39. Tables will vary.

40. Paragraphs will vary depending on the organizations selected.

WINNING EDGE

Retail Merchandising Series Event Role Play

Participants are challenged to design security systems and management strategies to decrease the loss of merchandise from theft and shoplifting. Students must understand that these losses result in higher prices so lost revenue and the cost of insurance can be covered.

Think Critically *Answers*

1. Insurance is purchased because employee theft and shoplifting account for billions of dollars in lost revenue.

2. Management must monitor the activities of employees in retail businesses because statistics indicate that the largest loss of merchandise and revenue can be attributed to employee theft.

3. Answers will vary. Strategies include the use of theft prevention devices, tamper-proof price tags, and security personnel. Store design, display strategies, and security cameras can be used to reduce losses. Providing training and maintaining open communication between employees and management are also effective.

4. Answers will vary. Examples might include an employee having to make a decision about reporting a co-worker who is stealing merchandise, using employee discounts for a friend's purchase, or using merchandise without paying for it.

5. Retailers must raise prices to help compensate for lost revenue and for the costs of security.

UNIT 4
Personal Financial Management

In this unit, students will learn about personal business skills such as consumer buying, money management, banking, consumer credit, saving and investing, and insurance.

Chapter 15 Consumers in the Global Economy This chapter covers the basics of buying as well as consumer rights and responsibilities.

Chapter 16 Money Management and Financial Planning The basics of budgeting and personal financial planning are addressed in this chapter.

Chapter 17 Banking and Financial Services Savings, payment, and other banking services are covered in this chapter.

Chapter 18 Consumer Credit The types of credit and the wise use of credit are the main focus of this chapter.

Chapter 19 Savings and Investment Strategies Savings plans, stocks, bonds, mutual funds, real estate, and other investment alternatives are the basis for this chapter.

Chapter 20 Insurance Motor vehicle, home, life, and health insurance coverages are the major topics of this chapter.

UNIT 4

Personal Financial Management

Unit 4 Global Business Project

Suggest that students read the chapter and lesson titles for this unit to get acquainted with personal finance management. Introduce the Global Business Project for this unit: **Manage International Business Operations**.

Ask students to read the project assignment and plan to work on it as they progress through the unit. The project can be found on the website: www.cengage.com/swep/pob9e

Business Vision

Financial planning activities are the foundation of business and personal decisions. Each year, poor money management in our society results in millions of personal bankruptcies. Billions of dollars are lost yearly to fraud.

In this unit, you will study the components of personal financial management. It pays to be a wise consumer. Your financial options are dictated by your daily money-management skills. These include budgeting and the careful use of credit. Your ability to select and use banking services is another skill that will help you achieve your financial goals. Finally, your knowledge of savings, investment, and insurance alternatives will help to provide for long-term financial security.

Financial Services Around the World

To conduct your banking activities, you might visit an ATM. A person in India might do their banking at the post office. Someone in Cameroon might go to a village lending group for their banking needs. Around the world, people obtain financial services in varied settings.

Today, in the United States and other industrialized countries, people use credit cards more than checks. The use of electronic banking services through cash machines, home computers, and smartphones continues to expand.

In India, the postal service is a major provider of banking and other financial services. Since 1854, using the brand name "India Post," this government-operated enterprise offers savings accounts, money transfers, money orders, life insurance, and mutual funds through more than 155,000 offices. More recently, India Post allows customers to electronically transfer funds to pay bills at any postal service office.

People in developing economies lack access to formal financial institutions. As a result, rotating savings and credit associations (RoSCAs) operate in many developing countries to help people obtain loans. These community-based groups allow people to save or obtain credit to pay for household expenses or run a business. RoSCA members periodically pool their funds and take turns utilizing the combined resources.

At the RoSCA meetings, usually held weekly or monthly, group members make small payments. The full amount collected at each meeting goes to one person. Then, at the next meeting, another person obtains the funds, until each person has a turn. RoSCAs have various names. In Cameroon and other French-speaking countries, they are *tontines*. In India, they are *chitty*, *tandas* in Mexico, and *osusu* in Nigeria.

Think Critically

What factors might influence the types of financial services offered in different countries?

Business Vision

Encourage students to read the introduction to Unit 4. Suggest that students read the chapter and lesson titles for this unit to get acquainted with personal financial management.

Point out that financial planning activities are the foundation of business and personal decisions. Each year, poor money management in our society results in millions of personal bankruptcies and the loss of billions of dollars from various frauds.

Financial Services Around the World

After reading the feature, ask students why formal banks do not exist in many parts of the world. Explain that as a result, many informal financial services have developed to facilitate local business activities.

Think Critically *Answer*
Financial services can be influenced by history (the British influence in India), culture (village lending groups), politics (banking regulations), or technology.

Portfolio Activity

Portfolio work samples validate skill level and a student's ability to accomplish tasks frequently performed on the job. The most important reason for including samples in a portfolio is to demonstrate a student's abilities and skills. In selecting work samples for each unit, students should always have a choice of which activities to include. Students might be encouraged to include samples from the end-of-chapter activities, particularly Think Critically About Business, Make Your Case, Make Academic Connections, and Interactions and Connections.

CHAPTER OVERVIEW

Suggestions for wise buying activities and protecting consumer rights are the main focus of this chapter.

15.1 Consumer Buying Decisions

Consumer information sources, wise buying actions, and shopping locations are the basis of this lesson.

15.2 Consumer Rights and Responsibilities

This lesson covers the various rights and corresponding responsibilities of consumers.

15.3 Consumer Protection Actions

Various actions to resolve consumer problems along with legal alternatives are the focus of this lesson.

Chapter 15

Consumers in the Global Economy

Niki Love/Shutterstock.com

Instructor Resources

- Activities and Study Guide IE
- Chapter and Unit Tests IE
- Lesson Plans
- PowerPoint Presentation
- Cognero Test, Ch. 15

Student Resources

Activities and Study Guide
www.cengage.com/swep/pob9e
- Portfolio Activity

PLANNING A CAREER IN . . .
CUSTOMER SERVICE

Marketing, Sales & Service

Related Job Titles

- Customer Service Representative
- Bank Teller
- Catalog Sales Agent
- Computer Support Specialist
- Customer Assistance Coordinator
- Customer Service Specialist
- Financial Service Representative
- Internet Customer Service Representative
- Hotel Desk Clerk
- Receptionist
- Retail Sales Clerk

Each day, millions of customers seek all kinds of services. For example, they might want to purchase a computer, return a defective toaster, exchange a gift, schedule a delivery, complain about poor service, request information, apply for a loan, or pay a parking ticket. Employment opportunities in customer service include careers in business, in government, or with a nonprofit organization. Customer service employees work directly with customers in places such as banks, hospitals, and retail stores. They also work in offices and call centers. The specific focus of customer service positions varies widely. For example, there are customer service professionals who help people check into hotels, buy products, make insurance claims, and register for social services. They even offer suggestions for how to cook a turkey.

Analyze Career Opportunities in . . .
CUSTOMER SERVICE

Use library and Internet resources to learn more about careers in customer service. Choose one of the job titles listed in the box and answer the following questions.

1. How would you describe the physical work environment for jobs in this field?
2. Is this a career that interests you? Describe a few things you could do to learn more about this career.

What it's like to work as a . . .Customer Service Specialist

Before he even takes off his coat, Brian starts his day by checking his e-mail. Today, several messages request information about identity theft. Yesterday, it was complaints about online auctions. Tomorrow, it could be comments about a proposed consumer protection law.

As a customer service specialist with the state consumer protection office, Brian must be ready for a variety of activities. Research, responding to requests, and report preparation are just a few of his daily responsibilities. Recently, Brian has been collecting information to help the state attorney general develop policies that will expand consumer protections.

When talking to people about his job, Brian always mentions the satisfaction he gets from helping others. He also mentions how much he likes having variety in his day. He never knows what he will find in his inbox.

What about you? Would working in the field of customer service be of interest to you?

PLANNING A CAREER IN . . .
CUSTOMER SERVICE

The complexity of the U.S. economy and business activities can result in many consumer concerns. A wide range of job opportunities are available to inform and assist consumers when planning and making buying decisions.

What About You? ***Answers***

Some students would find the job's high level of human contact stimulating and the ability to do something to help people rewarding. Others might see this job as merely dealing with other people's problems. Encourage students to share their experiences with customer service professionals. Refer them to the related job titles that appear on this page to get the conversation started. Ask which aspects of the jobs they think they would enjoy and which they would dislike.

Analyze Career Opportunities ***Answers***

Student answers will vary depending on when the assignment is completed and individual interests.

Additional Career Information

Encourage students to investigate careers they find interesting and explore unfamiliar careers. Two resources for additional career information are the *Occupational Outlook Handbook*, an online publication (www.bls.gov/) of the U.S. Bureau of Labor Statistics, and the O*NET Resource Center (www.onetcenter.org) developed by the U.S. Department of Labor. Information about specific careers and jobs can be used to demonstrate the relevance of skills learned in this course.

Focus on REAL LIFE

This scenario can serve as a launching point for a discussion about the various factors to consider when making a consumer purchase.

TEACH

Ask students to name various information sources they might consider when making consumer buying decisions. Explain the activities of product testing organizations, such as AHAM and Consumers Union.

15.1 Consumer Buying Decisions

Learning Outcomes

15.1.1 Identify major sources of consumer information.

15.1.2 Explain wise buying actions.

15.1.3 Describe the main types of shopping locations.

Key Terms

unit price 372

brand 373

impulse buying 374

Focus on REAL LIFE

"I am going on a wilderness retreat with a community service group and I have to buy a sleeping bag," Kristen said to Joshua. "I don't know much about sleeping bags, but I want to get the best one for my trip. I stopped by the sporting goods store and they had many varieties and prices. I was confused. Can you help?"

"I don't know much either, but I expect your choice depends on where you will use the bag," said Joshua. "Did you gather information before you began looking? There are consumer groups that test products. If you want, I can help you look online, or we can go to the library to find magazine articles."

"That sounds like a good idea," Kristen replied. "A salesperson at the store might be able to help, but researching in advance should help me ask the right questions."

LO 15.1.1

CONSUMER INFORMATION SOURCES

Consumers have the power to decide to buy or not to buy. Businesses must serve the needs of consumers. Without satisfied consumers, businesses would not make sales, earn profits, or remain in business. Several information sources are available to help consumers with their buying decisions.

Product Testing Organizations

Product testing organizations test products and services for the benefit of consumers and business. Manufacturers pay these organizations to perform safety tests on products. Underwriters Laboratories tests electrical components of products from all over the world for fire and electrical safety. The UL symbol indicates that the product has been tested and judged safe for normal use.

The Association of Home Appliance Manufacturers (AHAM) develops and maintains performance standards for appliances such as refrigerators, air conditioners, and freezers. The AHAM seal indicates that a product has met performance standards. The Carpet and Rug Institute and the Motorist Assurance Program issue other seals of quality.

Consumers Union reports scientific, technical, and educational information about products and services. This non-profit organization performs independent tests on consumer goods. It publishes articles in a monthly magazine called *Consumer Reports.*

Media Sources

Each day, you have access to a range of media sources offering consumer information. Most media exist in both traditional and online formats.

Print-Based Media Many magazines and newspapers offer various types of consumer assistance. General interest magazines such as *Consumers Digest*, *Good Housekeeping*,

Different Learning Abilities

Visually Impaired Prepare or obtain enlarged versions of various consumer information materials to assist students in this lesson and when making purchases.

and *Parents* provide articles and product information. For money management, financial planning, and investment advice, you could read *Money* or *Kiplinger's Personal Finance Magazine*.

Specialty magazines and newspapers also provide information about specific types of products or services. These publications cover topics such as motor vehicles, computers, boats, electronic equipment, travel, and education. Readers can obtain a better understanding of the technical aspects of these products and services.

Internet-Only Media Websites with or without affiliation to print or broadcast media have become a valuable resource for consumers. The use of a search engine allows you to obtain specific answers for your consumer questions.

Broadcast-Based Media Radio and television programs are valuable sources of up-to-date consumer information. Many stations carry programs or archive information on their websites to inform you about product safety, care and use of products, and shopping tips.

Government Agencies

Federal, state, and local governments also inform consumers. The Federal Trade Commission (FTC) has a Consumer Information website which serves as a portal for consumer information. The FTC also allows consumers to submit complaints to the Consumer Sentinel Network, which provides information to civil and criminal law enforcement agencies.

The United States Department of Agriculture (USDA) offers information about food buying, meal planning, and nutrition on its website. The USDA also inspects and grades meat and other foods. It makes that information available to consumers.

Other federal government agencies that provide consumer information include the Food and Drug Administration (FDA), Consumer Product Safety Commission (CPSC), National Highway Traffic Safety Administration (NHTSA), Department of Housing and Urban Development (HUD), Environmental Protection Agency (EPA), and Consumer Financial Protection Bureau (CFPB).

Every state has consumer protection agencies. These agencies have websites to provide information and handle consumer questions. State departments of banking

NET KNOWLEDGE

Through the Federal Trade Commission's Consumer Information website, the U.S. federal government maintains one of the most comprehensive sites for consumer information. Access the FTC Consumer Information website. Select a specific consumer category. What types of information are available on this topic? What other federal agencies provide this information? Describe some specific suggestions for consumers related to this topic.

A and N photography/Shutterstock.com

Name some ways in which you are protected on a daily basis by the activities of a government agency.

NET KNOWLEDGE

Students explore the FTC's Consumer Information resources. Ask whether students were surprised at the amount of information available on their chosen consumer category. Was it more or less information than they expected?

TEACH

Ask students to name various magazines and newspapers that could be valuable to consumers.

Point out the value of various radio and television programs when planning a consumer purchase.

Explain how each of the government agencies listed may be valuable to consumers.

THINK CRITICALLY THROUGH VISUALS

Student answers will vary. For example, government agencies protect consumers by setting and enforcing safety standards for products, assuring the safety of food and drugs, providing police and fire protection in local communities, safeguarding our economy by watching the activities of those who invest in securities, protecting U.S. interests at home and abroad, enforcing workplace health and safety laws, and enacting and enforcing environmental laws.

Different Learning Styles

Auditory Learner Ask auditory learners to repeat the names of the main consumer information sources discussed in this lesson. Encourage students to verbalize examples of materials from various consumer information sources.

TEACH

Explain the value of various business sources for consumer information.

Ask students to describe experiences of obtaining consumer information from friends or relatives.

THINK CRITICALLY THROUGH VISUALS

A product label is a more reliable source of information than advertising because it contains factual, specific information. Advertising, on the other hand, may simply appeal to emotions and will attempt to encourage you to buy the product.

ONGOING ASSESSMENT

CHECKPOINT ✓ANSWER

The main sources of consumer information are product testing organizations, media sources, government agencies, business sources, and personal contacts.

and insurance are available to assist with those areas. Large cities and counties also have consumer assistance offices.

Business Sources

As a public service and in an effort to sell goods and services, businesses make consumer information available.

Advertising Advertising is widely available. It is a popular source of consumer information. The main purpose of an advertisement is to encourage you to buy. Because of this, you should carefully evaluate this information source.

Advertising can be helpful. Useful advertisements tell you what a product is, how it is made, and what it will do. Advertisements give facts that you can use to compare products with other competing products. Beware of advertising claims that are not substantial. If an advertisement states that a product is better, ask yourself, "Better than what?"

Product Labels A label, attached to or printed on a product, provides useful information. A label will report the nature or content of a product. The label will also likely tell you what the product is made of, its size, how to care for it, and when and where it was made. Clothing labels must tell you what the product is made of and must give instructions for washing or cleaning.

Customer Service Departments Many businesses have special departments focused on customer service. Some firms provide customers with booklets on a range of consumer topics. For example, banks and insurance companies publish booklets to help consumers manage their money. Some large retail firms provide printed materials to help consumers with their buying problems.

Better Business Bureau The Better Business Bureau (BBB) can provide helpful information. If you plan to buy a used car from a particular dealer, you could call the BBB to find out what experiences others have had with that dealer. If consumers have reported problems with the firm, you could find out about these complaints. BBBs give facts only. They do not recommend products or firms.

Customer Feedback

An often-used information source is "word of mouth." This includes information received from other people. Consumers often trust information provided by others who have bought and used a product. Many websites have rating systems where customers provide both a star rating and comments on products or services. Star ratings with very few responses may not be as reliable as ones with a large number of consumer responses.

Minerva Studio/Shutterstock.com

Would you find more reliable information in an advertisement or on a product label? How do you know?

CHECKPOINT ✓
What are the main sources of consumer information?

Teaching Strategies

Expand Beyond the Classroom Ask students to obtain examples of various product labels (food, clothing, appliances, and other items). Instruct them to report on what they believe to be the most useful information presented on these labels.

LO 15.1.2

WISE BUYING STRATEGIES

Whenever you plan to buy something, consider several key questions. Do you really need the item now or can you wait? Which stores should you consider? What quality do you want? What price are you willing to pay? Should you pay cash or use credit? If you make the purchase, what other important item may you have to do without?

Use Decision-Making Steps

As a consumer, you should follow the decision-making steps when making a purchase.

1. *Identify your needs or wants.* Be able to state clearly why you intend to buy something.
2. *Know the choices available.* These choices include price, quality, location, variety, reputation, and other factors.
3. *Determine your desired satisfaction.* You should develop answers to questions such as, "How much am I willing to pay?" "What quality level do I want?" and "How long am I willing to wait for the item?"
4. *Evaluate alternatives.* At this stage, you will shop for the products and services that could satisfy your needs. You will compare them in terms of the criteria you have identified.
5. *Make the decision.* Decide whether to buy or not. Determine what product or service is most satisfying. Decide from which business you will make the purchase.

Business Insight

Customer Online Reviews

You are looking to buy a new technology product. Which brand should you buy and what store should you patronize? Answers to these questions often start with personal contacts. According to a Nielsen online survey, 84 percent of global respondents stated that word-of-mouth recommendations from friends and family are the most influential source of information. Nielsen also found that consumer opinions posted online are now the second-most important source of information.

Currently, over 60 percent of customers read online reviews before making a purchase decision. Studies have shown that positive online reviews influence consumers to buy products or services and negative online reviews cause consumers to refrain from buying them.

A number of customer review and rating sites now operate online. These businesses offer consumer ratings and links to purchase products or services. Some of these rating sites are industry-specific; Zagat, OpenTable, Zomato, and Yelp focus on restaurants while TripAdvisor, Hotels.com, and Room Key concentrate on hotels and travel.

As the consumer online review process evolves, online reviews are increasingly linked to social networks. This allows you to see reviews written by your friends and family.

Think Critically

1. How do online reviews benefit consumers?
2. How should a business react to the online review process?

TEACH

Ask students to name some actions that might be considered as wise buying actions.

Describe consumer actions related to each decision-making step.

Students should provide examples for each of the decision-making steps listed.

Business Insight

Emphasize to students that peer opinion has a strong influence on consumers' buying decisions.

Think Critically *Answers*

1. Students should link online reviews to consumers' willingness to purchase or not purchase products. Instruct students to visit an online review website. Students should be able to identify what type of information would influence a consumers' decision about a product or service.

2. Businesses have an opportunity to track customers' opinions of their products or services. This can allow them to make adjustments to improve performance. At the same time, businesses should not rely solely upon online reviews. All businesses should consider multiple sources of information before they take strategic actions.

Applied Skills

Communication Ask students to create a poster or other visual presentation that illustrates the decision-making steps a consumer should use when making a purchase. Instruct students to include a specific example showing how to use the decision-making steps. Consider allowing students to work in pairs. Make arrangements to display students' work.

TEACH

Explain the process for calculating unit prices.

Ask students to share some of their experiences related to differences in quality for various types of purchases.

Describe differences in services offered by various businesses.

Point out differences between promotional sales and clearance sales.

THINK CRITICALLY THROUGH VISUALS

Student answers will vary depending on how they comparison shopped. Did most students in your class use the same methods, or did they employ a wide variety of comparison shopping strategies?

Good buying skills will make you a better consumer. You can get greater value for your money each time you make a purchase.

Comparison Shopping

Smart consumers are comparison shoppers. They compare price, quality, services, and brands.

Compare Prices A **unit price** is a price per unit of measure. Most stores help consumers compare among various brands and sizes of the same product. Shelf labels show both the total price and the price of one standard measure, or unit, of the product.

petrunjela/Shutterstock.com

Name an instance when you spent time comparing prices, quality, and service on an item before making a purchase. How did you determine which item was the best choice?

If you need to calculate a unit price, divide the price of the item by the number of units per measure. For instance, in the supermarket, you see that a 16-ounce bag of Golden Frozen Corn costs $1.26. An 8-ounce box of Yellow Perfection Corn sells for $0.69 per box. Which is the better buy for the dollar?

If you compare the total prices only, it is not easy to decide. Because stores usually post the cost per ounce, the unit price, you could quickly compare the two package sizes. In this case, the 16-ounce bag would show a unit price of 7.9 cents an ounce ($1.26 ÷ 16). The 8-ounce box would be 8.6 cents per ounce ($0.69 ÷ 8). Unit pricing would quickly tell you that the 16-ounce bag is a better buy per ounce for the dollar.

Prices of products can vary greatly. The cost of the same item often differs from store to store and in different geographic regions. For example, an identical camera may be available with prices ranging from $25 to more than $40. These price differences emphasize the need for comparison shopping.

Compare Quality High-quality products and services often cost more. Buying lower-quality items can sometimes turn out to be more expensive than buying higher-quality items. For example, if you buy a lower-quality pair of shoes, they may wear out in a short time. You will have to replace the lower-quality shoes sooner. You may end up buying two pairs of low-quality shoes in a short span of time.

Compare Services Most businesses try to provide good service, but types of services can differ. Some businesses sell for cash only. Others offer credit. Some businesses provide free delivery. Other services offered may include layaways, repairs, and special orders. Service is important, but be careful not to pay for more service than you need.

Compare Sales The word "sale" is perhaps the most overused and least trusted word in marketing. You have probably seen sale signs a thousand times. When an item is really on sale, it is offered at a price lower than its normal selling price. Some "sales" may not really be sales at all.

Applied Skills

Mathematics Ask students to calculate the unit price for several brands and several package sizes for a product. The results may be presented in a graph along with comments about which might be the wisest consumer choice.

Promotional sales are used to promote the selling of regular merchandise with short-term price reductions. This type of sale may be used when a new store opens or when new products are introduced. Retailers may use promotional sales in hopes that customers will buy the sale items as well as other products not on sale.

A *clearance sale* is used to clear merchandise that stores no longer wish to carry. This may be end-of-season items, odd sizes and models, or discontinued merchandise. Clearance sales usually offer some bargains. Be sure that you need a sale item before you buy it.

Compare Brands A **brand** is a name given to a product or service to distinguish it from other similar and competitive items. The company that makes the product or service usually creates a *brand name*. Brand names are designed to help build customer loyalty.

National brands are advertised all over the country. They are sold in almost every community. Among these goods are items such as food, clothing, shoes, tools, and cosmetics. Manufacturers of such goods often place brand names on the items they make. Well-known brand names include Kellogg's, JELL-O, Colgate, Gap, and L'Oreal. Recognizing national brand names allows you to expect uniform quality. Brand-name goods are especially preferential when it is hard to inspect for quality, such as with packaged products.

Some stores have their own brand names, called *store brands* or *private label brands*. For example, Craftsman has long been one of the brand names on tools sold by Sears. Store brands are usually sold at a lower cost than national brands. Buying store brands may save you money and offer good quality at the same time.

Stores may also carry unbranded items at reduced prices, called *generic products*. Generic products are less expensive because they do not require advertising and fancy packaging. These lower costs result in lower prices. Differences in quality between generic and branded products may be small, making these items a good value.

Life-Span Plan

Explain why an ability to make wise buying decisions is important for achieving your life-span goals. Do you believe buying skills contribute to your ability to reach your life-span goals? What could you do to improve your buying skills?

Wise Buying: A Summary

Skillful consumers are efficient in their shopping activities. They save time, energy, and money by planning.

Take Your Time "I just don't have the time" is something many people say. Spending time planning purchases usually results in savings. Taking your time will allow you to look for the best values. As a good shopper, you should refuse to be hurried. Then, you can avoid buying things that you really do not want or need.

Time Your Purchases For some items, prices are lowest at predictable times.

Noel Hendrickson/Digital Vision/Getty Images

Compare different brands of similar items. Name similarities and differences. Is one better than the other? Why?

Life-Span Plan Answer

Answers will vary. Students should explain that funds wasted through bad buying decisions are funds that cannot be used to help them achieve their life-span goals.

TEACH

Provide an overview of the types of brands (national, store brands, generic). Ask students about their experiences and preferences for various brands.

Highlight the key points in the wise buying summary.

THINK CRITICALLY THROUGH VISUALS

Those who say the store brand items are just as good may argue that if the ingredients are the same the products are the same. Others will contend that the brand-name products have gone through extensive consumer testing and are made with better formulas and processes. These students may have also found brand-name items to be of more consistent quality. Other students will be willing to give store brand products a chance, having found that they are often just as good.

Portfolio Activity

Assign the Portfolio Activity for Chapter 15, available on the website for this textbook.

COLLECT Remind students that they need to select a specific product.

CREATE Encourage students to format their tables to make the information easy to use.

CONNECT Point out that students need to summarize their findings and their experience.

TEACH

Create a few hypothetical situations in which consumers might consider the timing of purchases.

Ask students for some of the factors that influence Impulse buying.

ONGOING ASSESSMENT

CHECKPOINT ANSWER

Decision-making steps that should be taken when making a purchase are (1) identifying your needs or wants, (2) knowing the choices available, (3) determining your desired satisfaction, (4) evaluating alternatives, and (5) making the decision.

Work as a TEAM

This activity will help students develop a better awareness of shopping locations.

TEACH

Describe product lines and services of traditional retailers.

Ask students to describe their experiences with contemporary retailers.

Recall the earlier discussion of supply and demand. Certain seasons and conditions favor goods and services being sold at reduced prices. Some examples include:

- Fresh fruits are usually lower in price during the local growing season.
- Winter clothing is often on sale in January.
- Firewood often costs less in the summer.

Consumer information sources, including advertisements, can help you identify good times to make certain kinds of purchases.

Avoid Being Impulsive The opposite of spending time and effort to make the right purchase is buying too quickly. This is called **impulse buying**. Impulse buying should be avoided. It often happens when an item is nicely displayed where customers are likely to see it, such as near the checkout counter.

Some impulse buying is harmless when the cost is small and the item is worth the price. Be aware that buying more expensive items on impulse can be costly. One of the best ways to avoid impulse buying is to use a shopping list. You can save money with a list, whether it is for groceries, hardware, or clothing.

CHECKPOINT

What decision-making steps should be taken when making a purchase?

Work as a TEAM

Today, consumers have more ways to buy than ever before. Using the three main categories of buying locations (traditional retailers, contemporary retailers, and non-store shopping), create a list of businesses in your community. Then, discuss the advantages and disadvantages of using each of the three categories.

LO 15.1.3

SHOPPING LOCATIONS

When deciding where to buy, you have many choices, including traditional stores and online options. In many cases, retails adopt both a physical and online presence.

Traditional Retailers

Traditional retailers are also called "brick and mortar" stores because of their physical structure. *Department stores* have an extensive product line and emphasize service. They may offer personal shoppers, make deliveries, and wrap gifts.

Discount stores emphasize lower prices on their products. Most discount stores base their success on a high volume of sales and low prices. If service is not important to you, this may be where you should shop.

Specialty stores have a special line of products for sale. They carry a wide variety of products in a narrow line. Sporting goods, jewelry, or women's footwear stores are examples. Some specialty stores may also be discount stores.

In food retailing, a *supermarket* is the large, full-service store that carries many brands. *Convenience stores* are small stores that emphasize the sale of food items, an accessible location, and long operating hours. These stores usually stock popular items at higher prices.

Contemporary Retailers

Today, *specialty superstores* offer low prices and a wide variety of a limited product line. These include retailers such as Office Depot, Home Depot, and Best Buy.

Discount stores have expanded to include a wide array of food products. These *superstores* may also include other retail services such as bakeries, restaurants, pharmacies, health clinics, or banks.

Different Learning Abilities

English Language Learners (ELL) Obtain translations of wise buying activities to reinforce these concepts in both English and other dominant languages used by students. Also use ads, labels, packages, and other visuals in their native language as examples.

Specific Learning Disability (SLD) Encourage students to locate and bring to class examples of various types of brands that are available to consumers. Ask them to explain possible differences of quality and price among the brands.

The *warehouse club* is a no-frills outlet focusing on the sale of large quantities at reasonable prices. Products are displayed in simple settings resembling a warehouse. These stores target small business owners who are looking to buy various supplies and equipment.

Factory outlets have a reputation for selling high-quality merchandise at low prices. Products arrive directly from the factory and sometimes have minor flaws.

Non-Store Shopping

Shopping at home started with door-to-door sales. Then, *mail order catalogs* allowed products to be ordered and delivered to one's home. Today, online shopping is the preferred way to shop at home. Consumers can use computers, smartphones, or their televisions to purchase products for home delivery.

Non-store shopping also includes *vending machines*. Vending machines at different locations may sell different sorts of things. In Japan, a person can buy everything from eggs and toys to flowers and toilet paper from a vending machine.

Monkey Business Images/Shutterstock.com

What are some advantages to shopping in a store rather than using a catalog or shopping online?

CHECKPOINT
What are the main categories of shopping locations?

15.1 ASSESSMENT

Key Concepts

Determine the best answer.

1. The most reliable consumer information source will usually be
   a. advertising
   b. comments from salespeople
   c. comments from other consumers
   d. reports from consumer testing organizations
2. The first step in the buying decision-making process is to
   a. identify product alternatives
   b. evaluate the services at different stores
   c. decide whether to use cash or credit
   d. identify your needs
3. Which of the following is an example of a non-store shopping location?
   a. club warehouse
   b. vending machine
   c. factory outlet
   d. supermarket

Make Academic Connections

4. **Math** A 12-ounce package of cereal is priced at \$3.20. A larger container of the cereal costs \$5.20 for 1½ pounds. What is the unit price for each item?
5. **Communication** Select several advertisements. Develop a list of questions to ask when evaluating advertising. Use these guidelines to evaluate the ads you selected. Prepare a one-page summary of your findings.

TEACH

Ask students to explain potential benefits of non-store shopping.

THINK CRITICALLY THROUGH VISUALS

Some advantages of shopping in a store include obtaining the product right away, being able to touch and see the actual product, being able to ask questions of a salesperson and perhaps even negotiate a lower price for large-ticket items, and not having to pay shipping costs.

ONGOING ASSESSMENT

CHECKPOINT ANSWER

The main categories of shopping locations are traditional retail stores, contemporary retail stores, and non-store shopping.

ASSESS

Key Concepts *Answers*

1. d. reports from consumer testing organizations
2. d. identify your needs
3. b. vending machine

Make Academic Connections *Answers*

4. The 12-ounce package costs \$0.27 per ounce. The larger container is 24 ounces and it costs \$0.22 per ounce.
5. Students will evaluate several advertisements. You may ask students to share their list of questions. Were their questions similar?

RETEACH Provide examples of comparison shopping activities.

CLOSE Ask students to name the most important consumer buying actions.

ENRICH Encourage students to create a comparison chart showing product lines and services commonly offered by different types of retailers.

Focus on REAL LIFE

Ask students to comment on this scenario and to provide their own experiences in various shopping situations.

TEACH

Ask students to name common concerns of consumers. Explain how actions in the consumer movement have helped address these concerns.

▶ **Figure 15-1** ***ANSWER***

Examples will vary. Students might mention nutrition labels as an example of their right to be informed. You may want to discuss times when they have been denied these rights, perhaps by stores that refuse to let students enter without an adult or limit the number of students they allow in the store at one time. If time allows, you may want to ask whether there are limits on these rights and, if so, what those limits are.

15.2 Consumer Rights and Responsibilities

Learning Outcomes

15.2.1 Explain the consumer movement.

15.2.2 Explain the eight consumer rights.

15.2.3 Describe consumer responsibilities.

Key Terms

consumer movement 376
fraud 377
guarantee 379
express warranty 379
implied warranty 379

Focus on REAL LIFE

Juan met Michelle after school. "Hi, Michelle. Have you decided which computer to buy?"

"I don't know," replied Michelle. "I looked at the computers at Bayside Computer Store and they have the lowest price. But I got the impression they didn't take me seriously because of my age."

Young people often comment that businesses do not respect them as customers or treat them as well as adults. Successful businesses recognize that teens are an important consumer group with significant purchasing power. They not only choose where they want to spend their money, but they also often influence the buying decisions of family and friends.

Businesses that ignore or disrespect younger customers jeopardize sales. They may also lose long-term customers who don't feel comfortable when shopping in these stores. You can be sure that businesses that are aware of consumer rights and buying power will welcome teen customers.

LO 15.2.1

THE CONSUMER MOVEMENT

In the past, some businesses took advantage of consumers. False claims were sometimes made about products. Prices were often too high. Some products were unsafe. To fight against unfair business practices, consumers united to demand fair treatment from businesses, giving rise to what is known as the **consumer movement**.

Because of this movement, public and private agencies, policies, laws, and regulations were developed to protect consumer interests. In 1962, President John F. Kennedy presented his Consumer Bill of Rights and declared that every consumer has the first four rights shown in Figure 15-1. In 1969, President Richard M. Nixon added the fifth right to the list. In 1975, President Gerald R. Ford added the sixth. In 1994, President William J. Clinton added the seventh. In 2012, President Barack Obama proposed the eighth.

CONSUMER BILL OR RIGHTS	
1.	The right to be informed.
2.	The right to safety.
3.	The right to choose.
4.	The right to be heard.
5.	The right to a remedy.
6.	The right to consumer education.
7.	The right to service.
8.	The right to privacy of personal information.

FIGURE 15-1
Give examples of how your rights as a consumer are respected.

Applied Skills

Writing Across the Curriculum Write a paragraph that demonstrates the connection between various concerns faced by consumers in the past and the development of the Consumer Bill of Rights. Suggest that interested students create a timeline to put things in historical perspective.

CHECKPOINT
What conditions inspired the consumer movement?

LO 15.2.2
YOUR CONSUMER RIGHTS

As a consumer, you have the right to expect honesty and fair treatment from businesses. Few businesses are intentionally dishonest. Being a skilled consumer means that you know the Consumer Bill of Rights and how to exercise these rights.

The Right to Be Informed

Most products and services are described in advertisements, on labels, or by a salesperson. You have a right to know what the product or service is and what it will do for you.

Fraud occurs when consumers are given false information in an effort to make a sale. If a salesperson knows a car's odometer has been tampered with and sells it to you under false pretenses, fraud has occurred.

Not all product information you receive can be expected to be perfectly accurate. Suppose you were looking for a used car for transportation to and from school. If a salesperson told you she thought the car would get about 20 miles to the gallon but it only got 18, you were not deceived. The salesperson may not have been accurate in estimating gas mileage, but no guarantee was made.

When a salesperson exaggerates the good qualities of a product and says, "It's the best" or "It's a great buy," there is no fraud. On the other hand, if the salesperson tells you a car has new brakes and it does not, this is fraud.

The Right to Safety

Consumers have a right to be safe from harm associated with using products or services. Several agencies work to assure the safety of consumers. The Consumer Product Safety Commission has the authority to set safety standards, ban hazardous products, and recall dangerous products from the market.

The Food and Drug Administration (FDA) makes certain that food, drug, and cosmetic products are not harmful to consumers. This federal agency enforces laws and regulations that prevent the distribution of unsafe or misbranded foods, drugs, and cosmetics.

The FDA also works to ensure that product labels do not mislead consumers. The United States Department of Agriculture (USDA) helps ensure consumer safety by setting quality standards for farm products. The USDA also controls the processing, inspection, and labeling of meat products.

The Right to Choose

The right of consumers to choose from a variety of goods and services has become well established. In fact, one of the main activities of the Federal Trade Commission (FTC) is to prevent one firm from using unfair practices to force competing firms out of business. When a business has no competitors and controls the market for a product or service, it is said to have a *monopoly*. Competing firms encourage customers to buy from them by

iStockphoto.com/zeljkosantrac

Why is it important for consumers to have choices?

ONGOING ASSESSMENT

CHECKPOINT *ANSWER*

Some businesses exploited consumers with false claims, high prices, and dangerous products.

TEACH

Explain situations that can occur when consumers do not use their right to be informed.

Describe various frauds that consumers may encounter.

Point out how monopolies reduce consumer choice and hurt activities in the economy.

THINK CRITICALLY THROUGH VISUALS

If consumers do not have choices, that means there is no competition among companies to meet their needs. Competition drives innovation and keeps prices low, while monopolies lead to fewer choices and higher prices.

Different Learning Abilities

Hearing Impaired Create a visual to identify and illustrate the eight consumer rights presented in this lesson. Ask all interested students to develop a memory device for remembering the rights. Invite students to share their ideas.

Work as a TEAM

This activity will help to reinforce the use of consumer rights. Encourage teams to share their results with the entire class.

TEACH

Explain various elements of the right to be heard. Point out the importance of these activities.

A Question of Ethics

Many students do not realize how certain actions affect business costs and consumer prices. This feature provides examples of various irresponsible actions by consumers.

Think Critically *Answers*

1. Students may be able to think of additional examples of consumer fraud, which can result in higher prices. For example, consumers may shoplift, may lie about children's ages to receive discounts on restaurant meals or entertainment, may damage merchandise by careless handling, or may not report an accidental undercharging for a purchase.

2. Answers will vary. Electronic tags, alert salespeople, and undercover security personnel can lessen shoplifting and customer carelessness with merchandise. Cash registers that compute the amount of change due can help cashiers make fewer mistakes.

Work as a TEAM

Your consumer rights are commonly taken for granted. As a team, create a table with three columns and eight rows. List the eight consumer rights in the left column. In the center column, describe situations in which each consumer right is involved. In the right column, describe actions that people can take to more effectively use each consumer right.

offering a choice of products and services at a range of prices. By driving away this competition, monopolies limit the right to choose.

The Right to Be Heard

Most large businesses have a customer service department to hear the concerns or complaints of customers. Some smaller businesses have a specific person assigned to that duty. Businesses are usually happy to take care of problems you have with their products or services.

Several federal government agencies, such as the FTC, also assure your right to be heard. As a consumer, you can complain directly to the FTC if you believe that your consumer rights have been violated. The FTC regulates advertising and encourages informative and truthful advertising.

State government agencies, such as the Office of the Attorney General or the Department of Consumer Affairs, have responsibility for protecting the rights of consumers. They can prosecute businesses for breaking state consumer protection laws. These offices also inspect advertising practices. They handle consumer problems related to automobile repairs, credit, and door-to-door sales practices.

Privately funded groups also help to make certain you are heard. Various national and local groups inform and protect consumers in a variety of purchasing areas. Some groups specialize in auto

A QUESTION OF ETHICS

Frauds by Consumers

Most people are familiar with bait-and-switch tactics, work-at-home schemes, and "lose weight fast" scams. These frauds against consumers result in lost money for consumers and are usually illegal. Various actions by consumers can also cause higher prices. People who would not consider shoplifting may be dishonest in other ways. Deceptive actions by consumers include the following.

- Eating items in a store without paying for them
- Buying a book, reading it, and returning it for a full refund
- Copying a DVD and giving it to friends so they can watch a movie without paying
- Making photocopies of sheet music and passing them out to all the members of your chorus
- Buying clothing, wearing the item, and then returning it
- Asking for a cup for water and using it to take a soft drink from a self-serve dispenser
- Switching price tags from lower-priced items and putting them on more expensive items

While most of these actions are illegal, all affect the operating costs of businesses. Each of these "frauds by consumers" results in higher prices. Many of these practices have become more difficult with technology.

While new electronic devices have improved store security, this equipment has also added to business costs and higher prices. Assume a business has one product stolen that costs $10 and sells for $12. The business needs to sell 5 more products, or $60 worth of product, to make up for that one stolen item.

Think Critically

1. What other actions by consumers can result in higher prices for the things you buy?
2. Describe how businesses and individual consumers might help reduce these actions that result in higher prices for everyone.

Different Learning Styles

Tactile Learner Use props and visuals to communicate each of the consumer rights. For example, use a scale to weigh a five-pound bag of sugar to demonstrate the right to be informed.

safety or consumer credit. Others will assist with any consumer problem.

The Better Business Bureau is concerned with problems arising from false advertising or misrepresented products and services. Dues paid by member businesses support BBBs. They work to maintain ethical practices and combat consumer fraud. If you believe your consumer rights have been violated, you can get help from one of 120 Better Business Bureaus around the country. After reporting your concern, the bureau will try to persuade the business to fix the problem. Most businesses willingly carry out BBB requests.

ALLESALLTAG BILDAGENTUR/AGE Fotostock

Discuss a time when you had difficulty returning an item. How many people did you speak with? Were you successful, or did you give up? Why?

The Right to a Remedy

The Fair Packaging and Labeling Act, National Traffic and Motor Vehicle Safety Act, Truth in Labeling Act, and Fair Debt Collection Practices Act all protect consumers. These and other laws are designed to provide assurances that consumers can seek a legal remedy when a problem occurs.

Consumers may also be granted protection through a guarantee. With some purchases, a consumer can expect a guarantee or a warranty. A **guarantee** is a promise by the manufacturer or dealer, usually in writing, that a product is of a certain quality. A guarantee may apply to the entire item or only to some parts of it. It may promise that defective parts will be replaced only if a problem occurs during a specified period. No guarantee covers damages caused by misuse.

When making a purchase, a skillful consumer asks about a guarantee. A guarantee may appear in the form of statements such as these: "The working parts of this watch are guaranteed for one year." "This sweater will not shrink more than 3 percent." These kinds of guarantees are sometimes called express warranties. An **express warranty** is made orally or in writing and promises a specific quality of performance.

You should review the guarantee before buying an item. You can also require a business to put in writing any other guarantees that have been offered orally. Written guarantees are useful if you need to return a faulty product. Read the guarantee carefully to find out exactly what is covered and for what period.

Some guarantees are not written. They are called implied warranties. An **implied warranty** is imposed by law and is understood to apply even though it has not been stated. In general, the law requires certain standards to be met. For example, it is implied that healthcare products purchased over the counter at a pharmacy will not harm you when used according to the directions.

The Right to Consumer Education

Although individual buying decisions are important, educated consumers need to understand how their choices affect the economy. Consumer education should take into account how buying actions create an interaction between consumers and producers. Educated consumers are aware

FYI Teenage consumers spend more than $250 billion each year. The main categories of their spending are food and snacks, clothing, entertainment, school items, and automobile expenses.

TEACH

Explain the various types of guarantees and warranties. Contrast the difference between an express warranty and an implied warranty.

THINK CRITICALLY THROUGH VISUALS

Student answers will vary. Invite a few volunteers to share details of their experiences when attempting to return unsatisfactory items they had purchased.

FYI

Emphasize the buying influence that young consumers have in our economy. Ask students to name actions that young consumers might take to make wiser use of their consumer rights.

Applied Skills

Building Study Skills Instruct students to create review questions for this lesson. Ask each student to contribute one question for each of the main ideas related to consumer rights and responsibilities. Use the questions as the basis for an in-class competition.

TEACH

Ask students to name some of the topics and activities that might be used in a consumer education class.

THINK CRITICALLY THROUGH VISUALS

The company that sells you a smartphone should provide you with convenience, courtesy, and responsiveness to any problems you might have with the device.

ONGOING ASSESSMENT

CHECKPOINT ✓ANSWER

The eight rights of consumers are (1) the right to be informed, (2) the right to safety, (3) the right to choose, (4) the right to be heard, (5) the right to a remedy, (6) the right to consumer education, (7) the right to service, and (8) the right to privacy of personal information.

TEACH

Provide an overview of the main consumer responsibilities. Ask students to explain why these actions are important to society.

that their decisions not only affect their personal situation, but also have economic and social implications.

The Right to Service

This right suggests consumers can expect convenience, courtesy, and responsiveness to consumer problems and needs. The right to service encourages businesses to take steps necessary to ensure that products and services meet the quality and performance levels claimed for those products and services.

The Right to Privacy

The Consumer Privacy Bill of Rights gives guidance on what customers should expect from those who handle their personal information and sets expectations for companies that use personal data. There are four major areas. These include proposals that would require companies to inform customers when their private information is stolen before fraudulent charges appear on their account. Banks and other organizations are encouraged to offer free credit checks so customers can see if fraud is occurring. Individuals should have the right to decide what personal information gets collected and how it gets used. Children should not have their personal information used for targeted advertising.

istockphoto.com/AdamGregor

What kind of service should you expect from the company that sells you a smartphone?

CHECKPOINT ✓

What are the eight rights of consumers?

LO 15.2.3

YOUR CONSUMER RESPONSIBILITIES

Just as some businesses have not met their responsibilities to consumers, some consumers try to take advantage of businesses. Even consumers who are not unethical or dishonest may have expectations that businesses cannot meet. Consumers also have responsibilities in business relationships.

Be Honest

Most people are honest, but those who are not cause others to pay higher prices. Shoplifting losses are estimated to be in the billions of dollars each year. Businesses make up for losses from shoplifting by charging higher prices.

As a responsible consumer, you must be as honest with a business as you want it to be with you. You should be as quick to tell the cashier that you received too much change at the checkout counter as you are to say that you received too little.

Be Reasonable

As a buyer, you are usually responsible for what you buy if the business has been honest. If you are dissatisfied and wish to complain, you should complain in a reasonable way.

You should first be sure that you have a cause for complaint. Be sure that you have followed the directions for using the product. After you have confirmed the details of your complaint, calmly explain the problem to an employee of the business from which you bought the item. In most cases, the business will be glad to correct the problem because it does not want to lose you as a customer.

Different Learning Abilities

Dyslexia Prepare a matching exercise to help students learn and remember each of the consumer rights and responsibilities. Prepare two cards for each of the eight rights: one card for the name of the right and one for a brief description. Do the same for the responsibilities. Ask students to pair the appropriate cards.

Be Active

As a responsible consumer, you should report unethical business practices to prevent other consumers from becoming victims. By reporting the matter to a consumer agency, you might be able to get the shop to keep its word both to you and to future customers.

Be Informed

The most important responsibility you have as a consumer is to be informed. Just having the right to be informed will not make you an informed consumer. You must find and use the information available to you.

You should also keep informed about your rights as a consumer. Learn about the laws and agencies that protect your rights and how to report a violation of your rights. Being an informed consumer is hard work, but the extra effort spent in making your dollars go as far as possible will be worth it.

Be Involved

In the United States, involvement is an important consumer activity. As a citizen, you have a responsibility to participate in government, which starts by being an informed voter.

As a consumer, you also have responsibilities. When the opportunity arises, make your concerns known to government officials or consumer agencies. Only when you become involved as a consumer can agencies do their jobs and legislative bodies pass appropriate laws.

You have an obligation to society to be a wise and efficient consumer. The world has only a limited supply of natural resources such as petroleum, metals, clean air, and clean water. Sometimes, uninformed consumers unnecessarily waste these resources and contribute to damaging the environment.

CHECKPOINT
What actions can be taken to be an involved consumer?

15.2 ASSESSMENT

Key Concepts

Determine the best answer.

1. True or False. The U.S. Consumer Product Safety Commission is responsible for regulating the safety of food.
2. True or False. An implied warranty is usually printed in the owner's manual of a product.
3. A person who compares product information on labels is using the consumer right to
   a. service **b.** be informed
   c. be heard **d.** a remedy
4. If a person returns an item as new for a refund after using it, this violates the consumer responsibility to be
   a. honest **b.** involved
   c. informed **d.** active

Make Academic Connections

5. **Research** Go to the website of your state's office of consumer protection. What services does this government agency provide? How do you and other consumers benefit from the actions of this agency?
6. **Law** The Truth in Labeling Act requires that certain information be presented on food labels. Using a label from a food product in your home, identify some of these required items. How would you make food labels more informative for consumers?

ONGOING ASSESSMENT

CHECKPOINT ✓ANSWER

To be an involved consumer, you should be honest, reasonable, active, informed, and involved.

ASSESS

Key Concepts *Answers*

1. False. The Consumer Product Safety Commission regulates the safety of products. (The Food and Drug Administration regulates the safety of food.)
2. False. An implied warranty is understood to apply even though it is not written.
3. b. be informed
4. a. honest

Make Academic Connections *Answers*

5. Answers will vary.
6. Answers will vary. Suggestions for making food labels more informative might include inclusion of information about country of origin, genetically modified ingredients, and use of antibiotics and pesticides.

CLOSE Ask students to explain or dramatize actions that represent irresponsible consumer behavior.

RETEACH Form 13 small groups. Ask each group to prepare a summary for one of the rights or responsibilities addressed in this lesson.

ENRICH Ask students to create a list of government agencies that might be contacted for various consumer concerns.

BUSINESS IMPROVING SOCIETY

Consumers Union provides information that is considered by many to be some of the most objective available to consumers. The organization accepts no advertising for its magazine to avoid business influence on its testing and reporting activities.

THINK CRITICALLY THROUGH VISUALS

Answers will vary. Learning about the results of the test will allow consumers to make informed decisions. Consumers will have a better idea of which washers will provide the best value.

Think Critically *Answers*

1. Consumers Union assists consumers by providing information on products and services, sorting out low-quality and unsafe products from those that offer solid value. It publishes a monthly magazine, *Consumer Reports,* and a number of websites where consumers can read the results of extensive testing of all kinds of consumer products and services. Consumers Union also advocates for improved consumer protection laws. The advocacy arm of Consumers Union conducts research, offers educational programs on consumer topics, publishes reports, organizes conferences, and testifies at government hearings.
2. Answers will vary depending on what issues are currently being investigated by Consumers Union.

BUSINESS IMPROVING SOCIETY

CONSUMERS UNION

Imagine 24 different washing machines all operating in the same room. Envision 32 cameras being used by a small group of people. These are scenes you might encounter in one of the 50 testing laboratories of Consumers Union in Yonkers, New York.

Consumers Union was created in 1936 to provide information on products and services to help buyers get the most for their money. Today, Consumers Union continues to sort out low-quality and unsafe products from those items that will give you the best value. Each month, the results of these consumer tests are reported in *Consumer Reports* magazine and its associated website.

Digital Vision/Getty Images

Why would consumers be interested in the results of lab tests conducted on 24 different washing machines before making a purchase?

Consumers Union also conducts extensive testing on motor vehicles. Each year, the organization buys the vehicles the same way you would buy a car. That is, Consumers Union has shoppers bargain with dealers for the best price. After an inspection of the vehicle's features, road testing occurs on a 195-mile course. Engineers record various performance data. Finally, crash tests are conducted to assess safety and the possibility of a rollover. All of these findings are then published to help consumers make wiser car-buying choices.

In recent years, as consumers spend more of their income on services, Consumers Union has expanded its activities. Every month in the magazine, consumers are provided with information about banking services, health care, insurance, lawyers, and other personal and financial services.

Consumers Union is involved with protecting consumers in other ways. Offices in Washington, DC, California, and Texas promote improved consumer protection laws. The Washington office works to build support for laws related to telecommunications, product safety, food safety, financial services, healthcare policy, energy, international trade, and other consumer issues.

The advocacy arm of Consumers Union conducts research and offers educational programs on consumer topics. This group also publishes reports, organizes conferences, and testifies at government hearings.

Think Critically

1. How do the activities of Consumers Union assist consumers?
2. Conduct research to create a list of current consumer issues that are of concern to Consumers Union.

Applied Skills

Science A variety of scientific methods are used when testing consumer products. Ask students to describe how various products might be analyzed based on the ingredients of these items.

15.3 Consumer Protection Actions

Learning Outcomes

15.3.1 List common consumer concerns.

15.3.2 Describe the steps of the consumer complaint process.

15.3.3 Explain legal actions available to assist consumers.

Key Terms

mediation 386

arbitration 386

class action suit 386

small claims court 387

Focus on REAL LIFE

Monica was annoyed as she walked into the store, but she knew that getting upset or angry was not a good idea. She took a deep breath, walked up to the counter, and spoke to the sales associate.

"Hi, I bought this about six weeks ago," Monica said calmly as she took an expensive leather purse out of a shopping bag. "I really like the bag, but the zipper broke."

The salesperson smiled warmly, picked up the handbag, and asked, "Do you have your receipt?"

"Here it is," Monica said as she got the receipt out of the bag.

"This will be easy," the salesperson said as she looked at the receipt. "With a receipt you have a choice of a replacement, a store credit, or a refund."

"Oh, a replacement would be terrific, but I didn't see this one on display." Monica said.

"Let me check our inventory. Even if we don't have that exact bag, I know I can help you find something you will enjoy. We just got some new things this morning that are still in the stockroom."

"Thanks, you're right—this is easy."

LO 15.3.1

COMMON CONSUMER PROBLEMS

Consumers hope that their purchases will always result in a satisfactory transaction. Still, problems sometimes arise. The item may have been damaged in transit. The wrong size sweater may have been shipped. These types of consumer problems are usually resolved quite easily.

Sometimes, problems that are more serious might occur. Your credit card payment may not be properly recorded to your account. A product you purchased might stop working after just a few days of use.

Sources of Complaints

State attorneys general have the primary responsibility for the enforcement of their state's consumer protection laws.

Figure 15-2 shows the top 10 consumer complaints compiled by the National Association of Attorneys General (NAAG).

TOP 10 LIST OF CONSUMER COMPLAINTS	
1.	Automotive Complaints
2.	Debt Collection
3.	Home Repair and Construction
4.	Telemarketing and Do-Not-Call
5.	Predatory Lending and Mortgages
6.	Telecommunications, Slamming, and Cramming
7.	Retail Sales
8.	Mortgage Foreclosure Rescue
9.	Landlord–tenant and Mobile Homes
10.	Internet Goods and Services

Source: National Association of Attorneys General Association

FIGURE 15-2
What are some examples of specific problems that might cause consumers to complain?

Focus on REAL LIFE

Use this feature to point out common problems faced by consumers.

Point out that this consumer problem had a pleasant ending. Explain that most businesses are eager to solve problems that consumers have. They want happy, satisfied customers who will return.

Emphasize that solving consumer problems is usually a matter of practicing good two-way communication. Customers need to let the business know what they want. The job of the business is to tell customers what to expect. If both consumer and business are honest and fair, the problem can be solved.

TEACH

Ask students to name various problems commonly encountered by consumers. Describe examples of consumer problems related to the categories listed on this page.

▸ **Figure 15-2** *ANSWER*

Examples will vary. Students might mention some of the following: phone calls from aggressive debt collectors, cars that turn out to be lemons, shabby home repairs or constructions, increases in credit card interest rates, online purchases that lack quality, confusing loan documents, telephone calls during dinner, auto repair shops using inferior parts, car warranties that do not provide expected coverage, and unexpected charges to telephone bills.

Applied Skills

Technology Instruct students to locate a blog with information about various consumer problems or complaints. What information is presented that might be useful?

FYI

Remind students that they should only give their personal information to trusted entities.

TEACH

Explain various types of deceptive business practices. Point out how these situations affect business activities and consumer trust.

Highlight some of the main consumer protection tools available for shoppers.

ONGOING ASSESSMENT

CHECKPOINT ✓ANSWER

Sources of common consumer complaints include debt collection, auto sales, home repair and construction, credit cards, Internet goods and services, predatory lending and mortgages, telemarketing and do-not-call, auto repair, auto warranties, and telecom, slamming, and cramming.

THINK CRITICALLY THROUGH VISUALS

Student answers will vary. They may suggest "phishing" as a common Internet scam. In this case, consumers could be tipped off that they are not receiving legitimate communications because reputable companies do not request financial and account information through e-mail links. Chain letters, whether through the mail or e-mail, sweepstakes, and pyramid schemes are other scams your students may mention.

FYI "Phishing" is a high-tech scam that uses spam or pop-up messages to deceive you into revealing your credit card number, bank account information, Social Security number, passwords, or other sensitive information. The Federal Trade Commission warns consumers never to disclose personal data online to a questionable source.

Deceptive Business Activities

Consumer fraud can be discovered in media ads, in the mail, or even on a city street corner. Various scams, cons, and swindles have been around for a long time. When a deal seems like it's too good to be true, it probably is! Each year, federal government agencies report consumers losing billions of dollars on phony investments and other deceptive offers.

The Internet has become the number one source of fraudulent offers. Consumers may not know the identity or location of all online merchants. This makes it difficult to track down the con artist after you have already lost your money.

The most common online scams involve sales of Internet services and general merchandise. Online auctions, non-delivery of products, credit/debit card scams, and work-at-home offers are also common sources of fraud.

Internet scams can also take the form of prizes, sweepstakes, and credit card offers. The average loss to a consumer who is the victim of Internet fraud exceeds $6,000. Be cautious when making online purchases.

Protection for Shoppers

With the increasing popularity of e-commerce comes the concern for consumer rights. Federal laws that protect Internet and TV shoppers are the same as those that govern purchases made by telephone. The seller must send you the item within 30 days or within another period specifically stated by the company. If there is a delay, the seller must notify you. You then have the right to cancel your order.

If an unreceived or returned item is billed to your credit card, you have 60 days to dispute it. The credit card company then has 30 days to respond. Within 90 days of your letter, the credit card company must investigate the matter and explain why the bill is correct or incorrect.

You do not have to pay the part of your credit card bill under dispute until the matter is resolved. To avoid finance charges, you must pay the rest of your bill on time.

CHECKPOINT ✓
What are sources of common consumer complaints?

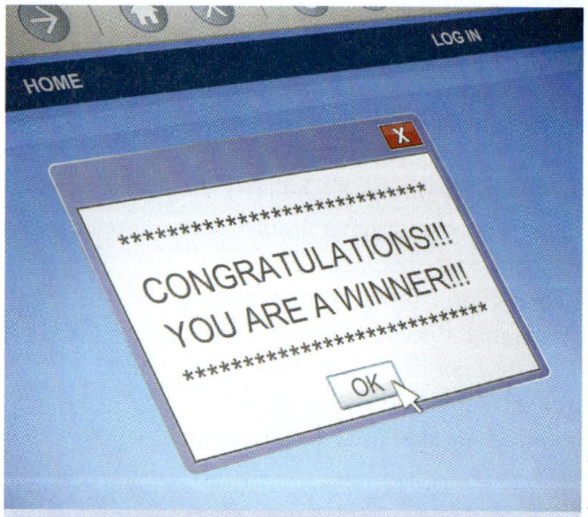

Sam72/Shutterstock.com

Describe some Internet scams or other suspicious schemes. How do you know that they are probably not legitimate offers?

Different Learning Abilities

At-Risk Connect various topics (consumer complaints, deceptive business practices) to student experiences. Point out the importance of understanding these potential problem areas.

LO 15.3.2

THE COMPLAINT PROCESS

While no one wants consumer problems, they do occur. When problems happen, you should be prepared. Consumer protection experts suggest four steps when trying to resolve a purchasing problem.

Step 1 Contact the Place of Purchase

Most consumer complaints are settled by returning to the place of purchase. Calmly explain the situation. Provide evidence of your purchase and the problem. A receipt or other dated documents will help you convince the store to take action in your favor.

Step 2 Contact the Company Headquarters

If communicating with the place of purchase does not bring satisfaction, you should move up in the organization. Contact the customer service department or other office within the company. The address, phone, and e-mail of most organizations can be obtained on the package or through a search.

When contacting the company, once again provide facts about the situation. Tell what happened in a brief letter or e-mail. Include copies of any documents that back up your story. Be specific about what action you would like them to take.

Step 3 Involve a Consumer Agency

If communication with the business fails to satisfy your demands, consider using the services of a consumer agency or public interest organization. Contacting a local, state, or federal government agency can encourage the business to take action.

Some agencies and organizations specialize in specific consumer topics such as consumer credit, health care, motor vehicles, or telecommunications. Other groups, such as state consumer protection offices, will help you with almost any consumer concern.

Step 4 Take Legal Action

When the first three steps do not work, more extreme actions may be required. Several legal actions are available to consumers. These include the use of a third party for dispute resolution, class action suits, small claims court, and hiring a lawyer.

CHECKPOINT
List the steps of the consumer complaint.

istockphoto.com/TommL

Why might someone decide not to pursue a lawsuit against a company even when the company has acted fraudulently?

TEACH

Ask students to describe the actions they would take to solve a consumer problem.

Provide an overview of the complaint process.

Point out methods that students could use to obtain company contact info, such as package information, toll-free telephone numbers, Web search, or company website.

ONGOING ASSESSMENT

CHECKPOINT ANSWER

Steps of the consumer complaint process are (1) contact the place of purchase, (2) contact the company headquarters, (3) involve a consumer agency, and (4) take legal action.

THINK CRITICALLY THROUGH VISUALS

Not every consumer problem is worth pursuing to the fourth step of taking legal action against the fraudulent company. If the amount of money involved is small, the consumer might not consider it worth the time and expense of using the legal system to attain satisfaction.

Applied Skills

Office Technology Instruct students to use word processing software to create a complaint letter to a company based on an actual or potential consumer problem. Be sure students clearly describe the situation and explain the action they would like the company to take.

Work as a TEAM

This activity will help expand student awareness of consumer problem-solving activities.

TEACH

Contrast the difference between mediation and arbitration.

Describe situations in which a class action suit might be appropriate.

THINK CRITICALLY THROUGH VISUALS

Joining a class action suit is a practical way for a consumer to get satisfaction for a small injustice by banding together with many other consumers. The participant in a class action suit does not have to hire a lawyer or be present at lengthy court proceedings.

Work as a TEAM

Each day, many consumers encounter consumer difficulties. Based on your experiences and observations, prepare an individual list of consumer problems of which you are aware. Then, compare your list with others on your team. How did most people become aware of various consumer problems? What actions were taken to resolve some of these concerns?

LO 15.3.3

LEGAL ACTIONS FOR CONSUMERS

If contacting the business or a consumer agency does not resolve the problem, various legal actions may be considered.

Third-Party Settlements

A third party may be used to settle consumer differences. **Mediation** involves the use of a third party who tries to resolve the complaint between the consumer and the business. A mediator suggests a compromise between the two parties. This process helps the parties work out their own mutually agreeable solution to the dispute.

If the parties agree to it in advance, another third-party action may be used. **Arbitration** results in a decision that is legally binding. After hearing both sides and considering evidence, the arbitrator makes a decision. Both the consumer and business must abide by the arbitrator's verdict.

Class Action Suits

What would you do if you are overcharged a couple of dollars? You may not be concerned enough to take action, but what if this same injustice occurred to thousands of consumers?

A **class action** suit is a legal action by one party on behalf of a group of people who all have the same grievance. In this type of lawsuit, one person or a small group represents the interests of many others (the *class*). The settlement may result in a refund to all consumers involved. If they cannot all be identified, the funds are sometimes given to public education programs or schools.

Photodisc/Getty Images

Name some benefits of joining a class action suit rather than trying to win a case alone.

Teaching Strategies

Expand Beyond the Classroom Ask students to talk to a person with some legal knowledge related to consumer problems. Alternatively, invite a speaker visit your class to talk about various consumer problems and legal actions available to resolve these situations.

Small Claims Court

In every state, a court system exists to resolve cases involving small amounts. These courts are called **small claims court**. In these courts, disputes are resolved quickly and inexpensively.

The rules are simple and informal, and the dispute must involve less than a set amount. The limits for cases heard in small claims court vary by state. The amount ranges from less than $1,000 in some states to $10,000 in others.

Most often, lawyers are not involved. Individuals present the facts of the situation and provide written and other evidence. Witnesses may also be used.

istockphoto.com/Deborah Cheramie

Name some types of cases that would be appropriate for small claims court.

Using a Lawyer

If all else fails, a final step might be to hire a lawyer. When a situation involves larger amounts of money or severe injuries from a product, the use of an attorney may be appropriate. Information about potential lawyers may be obtained from advertisements or referrals from other people.

Before using the services of a lawyer, you should ask various questions. Is the lawyer experienced in this type of case? Will you be charged a flat fee or an hourly rate? When will you be required to make payment for services?

CHECKPOINT
How does mediation differ from arbitration?

15.3 ASSESSMENT

Key Concepts

Determine the best answer.

1. Most consumer complaints are resolved by
   a. taking legal action
   b. using arbitration
   c. hiring a lawyer with consumer protection experience
   d. returning to the place of purchase
2. A company refused to refund $10 to more than 4,000 customers. This situation might result in the use of
   a. mediation
   b. arbitration
   c. a class action suit
   d. small claims court

Make Academic Connections

3. **Visual Communication** Create a poster or other visual that communicates the four steps in the consumer complaint process. Use a specific consumer problem as the basis for your visual presentation.
4. **Research** Use library materials or an Internet search to determine the small claims court limit amount in your state. Also, obtain information about filing a case in small claims court.

TEACH

Explain situations in which small claims court and using a lawyer would be appropriate.

THINK CRITICALLY THROUGH VISUALS

Answers will vary. Types of cases that might be heard in small claims court could include landlord/tenant disputes, automobile accident issues, property damage, collection of personal debts, and consumer complaints.

ONGOING ASSESSMENT

CHECKPOINT ANSWER

Mediation involves the use of a third party who tries to resolve the complaint, while arbitration results in a decision that is legally binding on both parties in a dispute.

ASSESS

Key Concepts *Answers*

1. d. returning to the place of purchase
2. c. a class action suit

Make Academic Connections *Answers*

3. Students create a visual to illustrate the four steps in the consumer complaint process for a specific consumer problem.
4. Students use the library or the Internet to learn the small claims court monetary limit and filing procedures in your state.

RETEACH Provide examples of comparison shopping activities.

ENRICH Ask students to describe situations that might be appropriate for mediation or arbitration.

CLOSE Emphasize steps that might be taken to resolve consumer problems.

Think Critically About Business *Answers*

1. Because well-informed consumers have realistic expectations and understand their own responsibilities, the transaction is usually pleasant and satisfying. Well-informed consumers will likely become return customers when they have a satisfying experience.

2. Answers will vary. Students will probably admit that they sometimes skip one or more steps when comparison shopping to save time or to purchase an item they desperately want.

3. Answers will vary. Students should list factors such as the reliability, independence, and timeliness of the consumer information source.

4. Answers will vary but could include a product testing organization's rating, recommendation of friends and family who have purchased smartphones, and a salesperson's advice.

5. Carrie could contact the Better Business Bureau to see if the company is a member or has any complaints against it. She could check the company's credentials with an industry trade group to learn if they are a member in good standing or a member at all. She should proceed very cautiously because it is unusual for reputable service companies to solicit door-to-door offering to perform immediate work.

6. An impulse purchase could be a harmless activity if the cost is very low and the item is not an important, long-term acquisition.

Chapter 15 Assessment

Review Business Concepts

15.1 Consumer Buying Decisions

- The main sources of consumer information are product-testing organizations; media sources such as print publishers, broadcast organizations, and the Internet; government agencies; business sources such as product labels, customer service departments, and Better Business Bureaus; and personal contacts.
- Comparison shoppers will evaluate price, quality, service, sales, and brands when making a purchase. Wise consumers take their time when making purchases, buy when prices are lowest, and avoid impulse buying with shopping lists.
- The main shopping locations used by consumers can be divided into three categories. Traditional retailers include department stores, discount stores, specialty stores, supermarkets, and convenience stores. Contemporary retailers include specialty superstores, warehouse clubs, and factory outlets. Non-store shopping options include door-to-door, mail order, phone, online, and vending machines.

15.2 Consumer Rights and Responsibilities

- The consumer movement emerged to fight unfair business practices. Because of this movement, public and private agencies, policies, laws, and regulations were developed to protect consumer interests.
- The Consumer Bill of Rights declares that every consumer has the right to be informed, to safety, to choose, to be heard, to a remedy, to consumer education, to service, and to information privacy. Being a skilled consumer means that you know the Consumer Bill of Rights and how to exercise these rights.
- Consumers also have responsibilities in business relationships. The five basic responsibilities of consumers are to be honest, to be reasonable, to report unethical practices, to be informed, and to be involved.

15.3 Consumer Protection Actions

- The main consumer complaints are related to auto complaints; debt collection; home repair and construction; telemarketing and do-not-call; predatory lending and mortgages; telecom, slamming, and cramming; retail sales; mortgage foreclosure rescue; landlord–tenant and mobile homes; and Internet goods and services.
- Four steps are suggested when encountering a consumer problem: (1) contact the place of purchase, (2) contact the company headquarters, (3) involve a consumer agency, and (4) take legal action.
- Various legal actions are available to help consumers. Mediation and arbitration involve the use of a third party to resolve a consumer complaint. Class action suits allow a small group of consumers to act on behalf of many. Small claims court allows a person to take legal action without the use of a lawyer.

Think Critically About Business

1. Why do you think most businesspeople like to have well-informed customers?
2. Do you go through all of the steps of comparison shopping on every purchase you make? Explain.
3. List factors you might consider when evaluating the usefulness of a consumer information source.
4. If you were planning to buy a smartphone, what information sources might be most valuable?
5. One autumn day, a woman and a man appear at Carrie Franklin's door. They introduce themselves as chimney sweeps who would like to clean her chimney before she begins to use her fireplace. The man says it will be inexpensive and make her home safer, reducing the chances of a chimney fire. Carrie sees the name "Chim Chim Chimney Sweeps" on their truck. What can Carrie do to protect herself from a scam?

7. Answers will vary. Factors that influence where to shop could include location, product line, prices, reputation, and safety.

8. Answers will vary, but it is likely that students will have used many of the consumer rights.

9. Consumer fraud still exists because disreputable companies see an opportunity for financial gain by cheating customers. Many consumers are uneducated about their rights and possible methods of recourse if a purchase results in a problem, and

6. When would you consider an impulse purchase a harmless activity?

7. What are some factors you might consider when deciding where to shop?

8. Which of the consumer rights have you recently used?

9. Why, with all of the laws and organizations to protect consumers, do you continue to hear of examples of consumer fraud?

10. Which of the following situations would be considered fraud? Why?

    a. A salesperson says the sound system you are looking at is the best on the market. After you buy it, you find it rated in a consumer magazine as second best.

    b. An advertisement for a bookcase cabinet claims it is made of solid walnut. Upon close inspection after buying the bookcase, you see that it is only walnut veneer glued over less expensive plywood.

    c. The person who sells an electric corn popper says it is completely washable. Before using it, you put it into a sink filled with water to wash it. The first time you try to make popcorn, there is a flash and the popper's electrical unit catches fire. When you return the popper to the store, the salesperson tells you that she did not mean the popper could be put under water. She says you should have known that electrical appliances should not be put in water. She refuses to give you either a refund or an exchange.

11. Describe situations in which a person might use (a) a class action suit and (b) small claims court.

12. When might you use a lawyer to resolve a consumer dispute? What are some of the pros and cons of using a lawyer as opposed to other dispute resolution methods?

Develop Your Business Language

Match the terms listed with the definitions.

13. Use of a third party who attempts to resolve the complaint between a consumer and business.

14. Buying too rapidly without much thought.

15. A name given to a product or service to distinguish it from other similar products or services.

16. A legal system for resolving cases involving small monetary amounts.

17. The price per unit of measure of a product.

18. When false information is given to a customer in an effort to make a sale.

19. A lawsuit brought by one party on behalf of a group with the same grievance.

20. A guarantee made orally or in writing that promises a specific quality of performance.

21. Third-party settlement resulting in a decision that is legally binding.

22. A promise by the manufacturer or dealer, usually in writing, that a product is of a certain quality.

23. A guarantee imposed by law that is not stated orally or in writing and that requires certain standards to be met.

24. Banding together of consumers to demand fair treatment from businesses.

Key Terms

a. arbitration
b. brand
c. class action suit
d. consumer movement
e. express warranty
f. fraud
g. guarantee
h. implied warranty
i. impulse buying
j. mediation
k. small claims court
l. unit price

some companies hope to take advantage of this ignorance.

10a. This would not be considered fraud because the salesperson may have genuinely believed the sound system to be the best on the market and could claim he or she was unaware of the magazine's rating.

10b. This would be fraud because a specific written description of the item was substantially inaccurate.

10c. This would not be considered fraud. However, the store may nurture customer loyalty by giving the consumer a new corn popper to restore good will and avoid possible fraud accusations.

11. Answers will vary. Class action suits are useful when the amount of the fraud is small for each individual member of the class but large when the class is considered as a whole. Small claims court is useful in resolving complaints involving relatively small amounts of money or damage.

12. A lawyer could be used to resolve a consumer dispute that involves a large purchase or when significant harm was done because of the purchase. A lawyer has the legal expertise to understand the consumer's legal rights and how best to present the case in court. Sometimes simply receiving a letter from a lawyer will cause a company that has broken the law to make restitution. The disadvantage of using a lawyer is the cost and time.

Develop Your Business Language *Answers*

13. j. mediation
14. i. impulse buying
15. b. brand
16. k. small claims court
17. l. unit price
18. f. fraud
19. c. class action suit
20. e. express warranty
21. a. arbitration
22. g. guarantee
23. h. implied warranty
24. d. consumer movement

Make Academic Connections *Answers*

25. Answers will vary.

26. Answers will vary

27. Answers will vary.

28. Labels will vary.

29a. With the discount, the new phone would cost \$93.10 (\$98 × 0.05 = \$4.90; \$98 – \$4.90 = \$93.10).

29b. The reconditioned smartphone is 77 percent of the price of a new phone (75 ÷ 98 = 0.765; 0.77 × 100 = 77 percent).

29c. Berri would save \$18.10 by purchasing the reconditioned phone. (\$93.10 – \$75 = \$18.10)

30. Answers will vary.

31a. 48.3 kilometers × 0.62 = 29.95, rounded to 30 miles per gallon.

31b. Because 10.5 liters converts to 2.77 gallons, the car got 32.5 miles per gallon, which is better than the warranty claimed. (Note: Students can use Appendix D to convert from metric to U.S. measures.)

32. Answers will vary. You may want students to share with the class any unexpected differences and similarities between shopping habits then and now.

Make Your Case *Answers*

33. Pierre could include independent reports from product testing organizations, in-store displays of various cameras, talking to knowledgeable friends and family, and the Internet.

Make Academic Connections

25. **Law** Prepare a summary of various federal consumer agencies and laws designed to protect consumers with regards to product safety, motor vehicles, food, medical products, and consumer credit.

26. **Visual Communications** Select a magazine advertisement. Create a poster describing various elements of the ad. Highlight the sections of the ad that would be useful or deceptive to consumers.

27. **Research** Collect examples of advertisements with the word "sale" included. Group the ads into categories based on the type of sale being displayed. What types of sales are most common?

28. **Art** Design a label for a food product with your own brand, product name, graphics, nutritional information, and other features.

29. **Math** Berri purchased a new smartphone that stopped working one month after the warranty expired. When she returned to the store, she was offered the choice of purchasing a new phone for 5 percent off the list price of \$98 or a reconditioned phone that carried the same warranty as a new phone for \$75.

a. What would be the price of the new phone with the discount?
b. What percent of the price of a new telephone is the price of the reconditioned phone?
c. How much money would Berri save by purchasing the reconditioned phone?

30. **Technology** Conduct an online search of Internet frauds. What types are most common? How can a person avoid these deceptive online business practices?

31. **Math** The Jones family ordered a new car from Germany. The express warranty said the average driver would travel 48.3 kilometers for every 3.85 liters of gasoline used.

a. How many miles per gallon is this?
b. If they traveled 90 miles and used 10.5 liters of gas, did the car perform better or worse than the warranty claimed?

32. **History** Conduct research on the way that people shopped from the 1800s to mid-1900s. Comment on some of the cultural, geographic, economic, and social factors that contributed to these customs.

Make Your Case

Pierre needs a new digital camera to take on his trip to Mexico as an exchange student. He is not a photography expert, but he has taken some pictures for the school newspaper. He intends to use the camera to take indoor and outdoor pictures of people as well as scenery.

Pierre has about \$150 to spend on the camera. He wants the camera to be sturdy, easy to use, and to take good-quality pictures.

33. What sources of information could Pierre use to find out what cameras are in his price range?

34. What two sources of information do you believe are best? Why?

Interactions and Connections

35. Talk to people in your community about the types of consumer problems they have encountered. What was the nature of the situation? What actions did they take to resolve the problem? What suggestions do they have for other consumers? Prepare a short written or oral summary of your findings.

34. Answers will vary. Students may consider product testing organizations and experiences of family and friends to be reliable sources.

Interactions and Connections

35. Summaries will vary. Allow an opportunity for students to share their findings with classmates.

36. For years, the Consumer Union has provided product comparison information in its *Consumer Reports* magazine. Today, many websites provide direct side-by-side comparison of products. These sites allow consumers to evaluate features, prices, and even customer reviews. Consumers can then click to an online retailer to purchase the product. This can be helpful when a consumer is researching or planning to purchase a product or service.

a. Identify two different websites that provide product comparisons, reviews, and ratings to help others with their purchase. Write a brief description of the sites and how their systems work.

b. Explain how the comparison information provided might influence consumer purchasing decisions.

Global Marketing Team Event

American farmers are interested in selling beef, pork, wheat, and corn to international markets. Your team has been hired by your state's agricultural department to market American agricultural products in Japan.

Your team of two will develop an international marketing plan for the agricultural products mentioned above. The marketing plan must not exceed 10 single-spaced pages. Team members will present before a panel of judges (class members) and a timekeeper. The length of the presentation will be no more than 10 minutes.

The completed plan should include the following components:

Title page and table of contents
Synopsis or mini-plan
Company goals
Description of customers and their needs
Description of pricing strategy
Competition
Price selection methods

Performance Indicators Evaluated

- Develop an international marketing plan.
- Identify a customer base, including consumer and organizational markets.
- Illustrate fundamentals of consumer behavior in different cultures.

You will be evaluated for your

- Knowledge of demographics in the international market
- Understanding of the marketing mix
- Understanding of economic, social, legal, and technological trends
- Use of appropriate research and accompanying documentation
- Description of timeline for business success

For more detailed information about performance indicators, go to the BPA website.

Think Critically

1. Why is Japan a good prospective market for American farm products?
2. Why must the culture of Japan be researched before developing the marketing campaign?
3. How do politics affect international business?
4. What demographic and cultural issues must be considered when marketing these products?
5. What characteristics of American products should be emphasized for international trade?

www.bpa.org

36a. Descriptions will vary depending on the sites selected. Students might select technology products, appliances, or software.

36b. Answers will vary. Students might suggest that easy access to this type of information may lead customers to engage in a more systematic evaluation of alternatives process before they purchase.

WINNING EDGE

Global Marketing Team Event

This event encourages students to work effectively as a team. It emphasizes communication skills, analytical skills, critical thinking and problem-solving skills, teamwork, and time management skills.

Think Critically

Answers

1. Japanese demand for farm products such as beef, wheat, and corn makes Japan a good prospective market for American farm products. Japan does not have the space or the climate to grow corn and wheat. In addition, dense population permits limited space for raising livestock. Beef, wheat, and corn can be produced more efficiently in the United States because the United States has the capacity for large-scale farming and ranching operations.

2. Successful international trade depends upon understanding the culture of the potential trade partner. Businesses must conduct research to learn about the culture of potential international trade partners.

3. Politics have a major impact on international trade. Trade is affected when governments impose trade sanctions based upon political concerns.

4. Answers will vary. Students should conduct research on the demographics and culture of Japan.

5. High-quality, wholesome food that meets strict Japanese government standards should be emphasized.

CHAPTER OVERVIEW

This chapter provides students with the information needed to better understand money management activities, budgeting strategies, and future financial decisions.

16.1 Personal Financial Statements

This lesson provides information about money management basics and the reports used to measure financial progress.

16.2 Budgeting Techniques

This lesson introduces budgeting activities along with an explanation of personal financial statements.

16.3 Taxes in Your Life

This lesson provides information on types of taxes along with actions necessary for filing a federal tax return.

16.4 Your Financial Future

A discussion of financial planning is the focus for this lesson.

Chapter 16 Money Management and Financial Planning

iStockphoto.com/Pamela Moore

Instructor Resources

- Activities and Study Guide IE
- Chapter and Unit Tests IE
- Lesson Plans
- PowerPoint Presentation
- Cognero Test, Ch. 16

Student Resources

Activities and Study Guide
www.cengage.com/swep/pob9e
- Portfolio Activity

PLANNING A CAREER IN . . .
FINANCIAL PLANNING

Most people have questions about their finances such as: *How much should I save for retirement? What is the best type of life insurance for my family situation? How can I get out of debt?*

These and many other questions are answered by people who work in personal financial planning. Employment in this field has a wide range of opportunities. If you choose a career in financial planning your work may involve providing financial planning services through a large financial services corporation, a small consulting firm, or a community-based bank. You will likely have a diverse group of clients. Some clients may have little knowledge about financial planning and others might be well-informed and eager to learn even more. In addition, the income and personal wealth of your clients will likely vary.

Related Job Titles

- **Credit Counselor**
- **Certified Financial Planner**
- **Personal Financial Advisor**
- **Family Money Management Counselor**
- **Tax Preparer**
- **Chartered Financial Analyst**
- **Insurance Agent**
- **Stock Broker**

As an alternative, you might work for a social service agency or consumer advocacy organization. In these environments you will help people deal with financial difficulties and develop a plan for avoiding future problems.

Analyze Career Opportunities in . . .
FINANCIAL PLANNING

Use library and Internet resources to learn more about careers in personal financial planning. Choose one of the job titles listed in the box and answer the following questions.

1. Identify the minimum educational requirements for this job. Explain other training or education that might be needed for advancement.
2. Is this a career that interests you? Explain how careers in this field match up with your goals and interests.

What it's like to work as a . . . Financial Planner

As the sun comes up, Carl leaves his kitchen and heads for work. His office is only seconds away. Carl runs a personal financial planning business out of his home. This morning he is reviewing the files of several clients before advising them about various personal financial decisions. Then it's time to get on the road. At 10 A.M., Carl is scheduled to meet with a client who just retired but does not have enough income to cover current living expenses. At noon, he meets with several small business owners who want to create a retirement fund for their employees.

The afternoon is open for Carl to relax or take care of personal business. In the evening, things get busy. Right after dinner, Carl meets with a family who wants to create a savings and investment program to set aside funds for their children's college education. His day ends with a phone call from a client who has a question about recent tax law changes.

What about you? What personal financial situations might result in a need for hiring someone trained as a financial planner or budget counselor?

PLANNING A CAREER IN . . .
FINANCIAL PLANNING

Financial planning and money management activities affect every person in our society. Consumer demand for expert advice provides many employment opportunities.

What About You?
Answers

Answers will vary. Personal financial situations that might result in a need for hiring someone like Carl could include starting a business, beginning a career after college and needing to pay student loans, getting married, buying a house, planning for retirement, expecting a child, or saving for college for a child.

Analyze Career Opportunities *Answers*
Student answers will vary depending on when the assignment is completed and individual interests.

Additional Career Information

Encourage students to investigate careers they find interesting and explore unfamiliar careers. Two resources for additional career information are the *Occupational Outlook Handbook*, an online publication (www.bis.gov/oco) of the U.S. Bureau of Labor Statistics, and the O*NET Resource Center (www.onetcenter.org) developed by the U.S. Department of Labor. Information about specific careers and jobs can be used to demonstrate the relevance of skills learned in this course.

Focus on REAL LIFE

This situation can help students better understand the importance of money management activities.

TEACH

Ask students to name common activities and decisions associated with managing money.

THINK CRITICALLY THROUGH VISUALS

Answers will vary depending on the individual situations of students. Some students might say they do not keep track. Others might report they keep track in their heads. Still others might keep track of the spending by using their bank statements or check registers. A few students might report that they use computer software to track their spending.

16.1 Personal Financial Statements

Learning Outcomes

16.1.1 Explain the basics of money management.

16.1.2 Create a personal balance sheet.

16.1.3 Develop a personal cash flow statement.

Key Terms

money management 394

personal assets 395

net worth 396

cash flow statement 396

Focus on REAL LIFE

"My financial situation is just fine—or it is a disaster! It all depends on what day of the week it is."

"Tell me; what's the problem, Yung-su?" asks his neighbor.

"Mr. Liang, I can't seem to get a grip on my finances. I work 10 hours a week and make about $10 per hour. That seems like a lot of money for a part-time job while going to school. But I always seem to run out of money before I get paid."

"I suppose that also means you are not saving any money, but rather spending everything you make. My advice is to get some lessons in money management. I'd be glad to help."

The one thing most people have in common is a desire to use money wisely so that needs, wants, and goals will be satisfied. While no individual, family, or organization is likely to have every desire met, several money management techniques can help you use your financial resources wisely.

LO 16.1.1

MONEY MANAGEMENT BASICS

Right now $1,000, or maybe $100, seems like a lot of money to you. Once you graduate from high school, and perhaps college, and have a full-time job, your thinking about what is a large amount of money will change. You will probably earn nearly two million dollars, or more, in your lifetime. As a college graduate, you will likely make even more.

While this may seem like a lot of money, remember that you will be responsible for many living expenses. You will have to pay for food, housing, clothing, and transportation as well as other goods and services you need and want. Upon beginning a career and living on your own, you will face the same problem you face now—having a limited amount of money to pay for all the goods and services you want and need.

Money management refers to the day-to-day financial activities associated

istockphoto.com/fizkes

Do you keep track of how you spend your money? What method do you use?

Applied Skills

Writing Across the Curriculum Assign students to prepare a paragraph demonstrating a connection between money management activities and other classes in their curriculum.

with using limited income to satisfy your unlimited needs and wants. Money management involves getting the most for your money through careful planning, saving, and spending. It involves making and using a plan for spending.

Some people have the wrong idea about money management. They think it means never spending, doing without things, and not having any fun. If you learn to manage your money well, you will be able to buy what you really want. Planning ahead and deciding what is important will help you have money for things you enjoy. If you set goals, make wise decisions, buy wisely, and live within your income, you will be a successful money manager.

The process of good money management should start with knowing your current financial status. When watching a baseball or soccer game, most people want to know the score. In the money management game, score is kept with the use of two financial statements: the balance sheet and the cash flow statement.

CHECKPOINT ✓
What are some characteristics of a wise money manager?

FYI According to the Bureau of the Census, the main assets of U.S. households are motor vehicles, homes, checking and savings accounts, U.S. savings bonds, certificates of deposit, mutual funds, stocks, corporate bonds, and retirement accounts

LO 16.1.2

PERSONAL BALANCE SHEET

"How much money do you have?" might be the first question many people would ask when measuring your financial situation.

The answer to that question would not reveal the entire picture because most people have other items of value besides money. A *balance sheet* is a record of assets and liabilities at a point in time. It reports what a person or family owns as well as owes. The main parts of a balance sheet are displayed in Figure 16-1.

Assets

Items of value are **personal assets**. Assets include such things as money in bank accounts, investments, furniture, clothing, automobiles, jewelry, and rare coins. The current value of all assets of an individual or family is the first thing stated on a balance sheet.

PERSONAL BALANCE SHEET			
Assets		***Liabilities***	
Home	$97,000	Home mortgage	$45,000
Automobile	4,600	Education loan	1,800
Household items and furniture	6,200	Credit card balance	230
Personal computer	1,600	*Total liabilities*	$47,030
Jewelry	1,100		
Savings account	2,300		
Checking account	450	***Owner's Equity (Net Worth)***	
Total assets	$113,250	Total assets – Total liabilities	$66,220

FIGURE 16-1
What accounts for the bulk of this family's assets, liabilities, and equity?

FYI
Point out that anything of value that a student owns is an asset. Ask students to list various assets they possess.

TEACH

Describe various actions that might be considered wise money management.

ONGOING ASSESSMENT

CHECKPOINT ✓ ***ANSWER***
Wise money managers get the most from their limited incomes through careful planning, saving, and spending. They set goals, make wise decisions, buy wisely, and live within their incomes.

TEACH

Provide an overview of the elements of a personal balance sheet—assets, liabilities, and equity.

Ask students to name various assets that might be listed on a personal balance sheet.

▸ **Figure 16-1** ***ANSWER***
The largest of this family's assets is its house. Its greatest liability is its home mortgage. The percentage of the home already paid for constitutes most of the family's equity.

Different Learning Styles

Visual Learner Ask students to focus their attention on Figure 16-1 as you review the information that appears under the heading Personal Balance Sheet. Also suggest that students review the illustration of a business balance sheet that appears in Figure 12-2 on page 296.

Work as a TEAM

This activity will help students understand actions that might be taken to reduce spending or increase income.

TEACH

Explain that liabilities are amounts currently owed and not amounts owed in the future, such as next month's rent.

Describe the process of determining net worth (equity) on a personal balance sheet. Point out that this amount is not money, but that it represents the value of the assets that can be claimed by the person after deducting what would be paid to others (liabilities).

ONGOING ASSESSMENT

CHECKPOINT ✓ ANSWER

The three main categories of the personal balance sheet are (1) assets, (2) liabilities, and (3) net worth or owner's equity.

TEACH

Explain the purpose of a personal cash flow statement.

Ask students to name the major sources of cash inflows for most households.

THINK CRITICALLY THROUGH VISUALS

Answers will vary. Some ways to increase one's cash inflows are to invest savings in higher-yielding investments, attain a promotion or a higher-paying job, take an additional job, or sell personal property.

Work as a TEAM

Some people may have more cash outflows than inflows, resulting in financial difficulties. As a team, create a list of actions that a person or household might take to make sure cash outflows are less than cash inflows.

Liabilities

Amounts owed to others are *liabilities*. These debts may include credit card balances, car loans, home mortgages, or personal loans. A listing of your liabilities is the second item on a balance sheet.

Net Worth

The difference between a person's assets and liabilities is their **net worth**. This difference represents the amount of money that could be claimed if all assets were sold for cash and all debts were paid off. For example, if a family has $189,000 in assets (including the value of a home) and has $87,000 in debts (mainly their home mortgage), the family has a net worth of $102,000. Net worth is also referred to as *owner's equity*.

A balance sheet is a helpful way to measure financial strength. Businesses commonly prepare a balance sheet either once a month or quarterly to determine the financial condition of the business. In the same way, a balance sheet can help in measuring financial progress.

CHECKPOINT ✓

What are three main categories of a personal balance sheet?

LO 16.1.3

PERSONAL CASH FLOW STATEMENT

A balance sheet reports assets, liabilities, and net worth on a given date. Almost every day, business transactions occur that change these balance sheet items. For example, when you make a loan payment, your liabilities decrease. If you save part of your earnings, your assets and net worth increase by the amount of the savings.

To examine changes in a person's net worth, another financial statement can be helpful. A **cash flow statement** reports net wages and other income along with spending for a period, such as for a month. Figure 16-2 on the next page includes typical items found in a cash flow statement.

Cash Inflows

The first part of a cash flow statement reports cash inflows, or your income. *Cash inflows* is the money you have available to spend as a result of working or from other income, such as interest earned on your savings.

When preparing a cash flow statement, first report your *net pay* or *take-home pay*, which is the amount of a paycheck after taxes and other payroll deductions. These deductions may include retirement contributions, charges for health benefits, and other things, as well as local, state, and federal taxes. Your take-home pay is the amount you actually have available

istockphoto.com/Daisy-Daisy

Make a list of ways to increase your current cash inflows.

Applied Skills

Mathematics Instruct students to create a list of personal assets and liabilities. Ask them to total each and determine the net worth. Ask students to explain how their personal balance sheet might change in the future.

to spend. Be sure to include any other income, such as interest earned.

Cash Outflows

The second part of a cash flow statement reports your *cash outflows*, or your expenditures. Amounts spent for food, clothing, transportation, and other living costs are cash outflows. Keeping track of how much is spent for various living expenses will help you plan and control your spending. Your personal cash flow statement can be used to develop a budget, which can help you avoid cash flow problems.

Compare Inflows and Outflows

The final step in preparing the cash flow statement is to subtract the cash outflows (total spending) from the cash inflows (total income). If you spent less than you earned, the difference represents an increase in your net worth. Most likely, this amount will be kept in savings for future needs or wants. If you spent more than you had in income, you either had to use some of your savings or had to use credit to pay these additional expenses.

PERSONAL CASH FLOW STATEMENT		
Cash Inflows (Income)		
Net income (take-home pay)	$1,300	
Other income (interest)	10	
Total Income		$1,310
Cash Outflows (Expenditures)		
Rent	$300	
Food	400	
Clothing	50	
Utilities	60	
Telephone	30	
Transportation	120	
Personal care	30	
Recreation/entertainment	75	
Total Spending		$1,065
Net Cash Flow		$245

FIGURE 16-2

What percentage of total income did this person spend on basic needs?

CHECKPOINT ✓

What do cash outflows represent?

16.1 ASSESSMENT

Key Concepts

Determine the best answer.

1. Savings accounts and a home are examples of
   - **a.** liabilities
   - **b.** assets
   - **c.** net worth
   - **d.** cash outflows
2. A payment for rent represents
   - **a.** a cash inflow
   - **b.** a cash outflow
   - **c.** a liability
   - **d.** an asset

Make Academic Connections

3. **Math** Calculate the missing amount.

a.	Assets	$7,000
	Liabilities	$1,800
	Net worth	______
b.	Assets	$26,000
	Liabilities	______
	Net worth	$19,000
c.	Assets	______
	Liabilities	$5,600
	Net worth	$67,800

4. **Research** What types of liabilities are commonly listed on the personal balance sheets of households in the United States?

TEACH

Describe common cash outflows for an individual or household.

Ask students to describe what actions a person might take after comparing cash inflows and outflows.

▸ **Figure 16-2 *ANSWER***

The person depicted in this cash flow statement spent about 76% of his or her total income on basic needs ($990 ÷ $1,310 = 0.7557; 0.76 × 100 = 76%).

ONGOING ASSESSMENT

CHECKPOINT ✓*ANSWER*

Cash outflows represent amounts spent for food, clothing, transportation, and other living expenses.

ASSESS

Key Concepts *Answers*

1. b. assets
2. b. a cash outflow

Make Academic Connections *Answers*

3a. $5,200 ($7,000 – $1,800 = $5,200)

3b. $7,000 ($26,000 – $19,000 = $7,000)

3c. $73,400 ($67,800 + $5,600 = $73,400)

4. Answers will vary. Students might mention credit card balances, automobile loans, home mortgages, student loans, and personal loans.

CLOSE Ask students to explain the importance of a cash flow statement when planning money management activities.

RETEACH Explain the difference between a personal balance sheet and personal cash flow statement.

ENRICH Ask students to list various items that might appear on a personal balance sheet and a personal cash flow statement.

Doing Business in . . . NIGERIA

Learning about U.S. trading partners helps students understand the interdependence of the global economy.

Think Critically *Answers*

1. Important business is conducted in face-to-face meetings where business attire or traditional dress might be worn. Formal titles, respect for older persons, and lengthy greetings are important in business dealings. The conversation at the beginning of negotiations may be more personal than in other cultures. Use of the left hand is offensive and should be avoided in situations such as handshakes or passing food dishes. The underground economy may impact business transactions.

2. Benefits of informal economic activities include employment and the availability of needed goods and services. Concerns related to informal economic activities include the government's inability to collect taxes, regulate businesses, and protect consumers and workers.

3. Answers will vary.

THINK CRITICALLY THROUGH VISUALS

Oil production can result in greater economic benefits such as increased exports, higher worker incomes, and greater tax revenues for government.

DOING BUSINESS IN . . . NIGERIA

Imagine trying to do business in a country that has more than 250 languages and ethnic groups. In Nigeria, the most populous country in Africa, you are likely to encounter a variety of business situations.

When in Nigeria, you will conduct important business in face-to-face meetings. In these settings, you may see Nigerian businessmen wearing a suit and tie. Or, they might wear traditional clothing such as a buba, a loose-fitting shirt that extends to the knees.

As you greet business associates in Nigeria, remember that formal titles are very important. Be ready to address someone as "Chief," "Prince," or "Alhaji." Respect for older persons is vital. It is offensive in Nigerian society to pass an elderly person without a greeting. Handshakes are the most appropriate greeting.

At the first meeting with a business contact, be patient and expect many ongoing greetings. At first the conversation might seem overly personal, because Nigerians like to know the people with whom they are doing business.

If you are having lunch with a business acquaintance, make sure you always use your right hand (or both hands) to pass and accept dishes. The left hand is taboo and is rarely used for interpersonal transactions. Left-handers are especially advised to practice the use of their right hand. Foods that you will likely encounter include yams, cassava (a starchy root), and rice. Meats you are offered might include beef, chicken, turkey, goat, goose, and fish.

Nigeria is one of the world's largest oil producers. Due to political turmoil and unstable financial conditions, the country has continually faced economic difficulties. The informal economy (also called the underground economy) accounts for more than half of the business activities in Nigeria. Large numbers of workers make their living in unregulated settings. The items they produce and sell create income not reported to the government.

Think Critically

1. How does doing business in Nigeria differ from doing business in other countries?
2. What are the benefits and concerns related to informal economic activities?
3. Conduct library or Internet research to obtain additional information about business and economic activities in Nigeria. Write a paragraph summarizing your findings.

What benefits might result from the oil production in Nigeria?

Andrew Holt/Photographer's Choice RF/Getty Images

398 **Chapter 16** | Money Management and Financial Planning

Applied Skills

Geography Instruct students to use the Internet or library resources to locate a map of Nigeria and its neighboring countries. Ask students to make a list of the countries that border Nigeria. Lists should include Benin, Cameroon, Chad, and Niger.

16.2 Budgeting Techniques

Learning Outcomes

16.2.1 Identify purposes of a budget.

16.2.2 Describe steps for preparing a budget.

16.2.3 Describe characteristics of successful budgeting.

Key Terms

fixed expenses 400

variable expenses 400

allowance 401

budget variance 402

Focus on REAL LIFE

Brandon Zeng has been practicing his Chinese through written communication with relatives in Hong Kong and conversations with his parents. He also has taken several business courses in high school. Brandon aspires to a career in international business working in the Pacific Rim countries.

"I can't wait to go to Asia next summer, but the trip is going to cost me a fortune! The air transportation, housing, food, and other living expenses will cost more than $6,000. My parents have agreed to pay half. Fortunately for me, I developed a plan to save money for this trip. By the end of the year I will have the $3,000 I need. It's going to be a great experience. Hey Josh, why don't you go with me?"

"Are you kidding? I'm not as disciplined as you! I would never be able to save enough money. You are a pro at managing money. Maybe you can give me a few tips."

LO 16.2.1

BUDGET ACTIVITIES

A *budget* allows you to meet your personal goals with a system of saving and wise spending. Having a plan for saving will help you

- Live within your income.
- Make wise buying decisions.
- Avoid credit problems.
- Plan for financial emergencies.
- Develop money management skills.
- Achieve your financial goals.

istockphoto.com/InspiredFootage

Make a list of items you buy regularly. How might you start spending less on these items?

Having a written budget is a key part of successful money management. Your budget may be a simple record of how much you make, how much you plan to spend, and how much you want to save. On the other hand, your budget may be a more detailed record with specific amounts to be spent in categories such as food, clothing, and transportation. With a budget, you will be in control of your life. Without a budget, others will be in control, such as those to whom you owe money. Use a budget to control where your money goes. Don't overspend and let debt control your life. A good budget can be created quickly and will provide needed information on your spending and savings plans.

CHECKPOINT

What are the main purposes of a budget?

Focus on REAL LIFE

Use this situation to encourage students to think about better planning for spending and saving their money.

TEACH

Ask students to describe situations that might occur as a result of poor budgeting activities.

Highlight and explain the purposes of a budget that are listed on this page.

THINK CRITICALLY THROUGH VISUALS

Answers will vary. Most students should be able to discover ways to spend less on the items they buy through planned spending, careful comparison shopping, postponing purchases, or eliminating unnecessary purchases.

ONGOING ASSESSMENT

CHECKPOINT ✓ANSWER

The main purposes of a budget are to help people live within their incomes, achieve financial goals, buy wisely, avoid credit problems, plan for financial emergencies, and develop good money management skills.

Different Learning Styles

Tactile Learner Use sample items or objects to represent the purposes of a budget. Ask students to identify these purposes based on the tangible items they are given.

Life-Span Plan Answer

Answers will vary. Students should point out that people who learn to create and use a budget when they are young are often better able to manage their funds when they are adults.

TEACH

Provide an overview of the four steps of the budgeting process.

Ask students to give examples of fixed and variable expenses.

▶ **Figure 16-3** ***ANSWER***

The SMART approach helps you focus on exactly what you want to achieve including goals that can be measured. It also helps you identify the actions you need to take to achieve the goals. This approach requires you to determine if the goals are realistic and how long it will take to reach the goals.

THINK CRITICALLY THROUGH VISUALS

Answers will vary depending on the personal short- and long-term goals of students. Actions to achieve goals can include savings, budgeting, buying insurance, and reducing credit use.

TEACH

Encourage students to keep a "daily spending diary" with a record of all spending. This may seem tedious, but it helps people understand where their money goes. This information can be the foundation for better budgeting and wise money management. Several apps for monitoring spending are also available, such as Spending Tracker, Mint, Level Money, and Spendee.

Life-Span Plan

Explain why it is important for people to create and use a budget when they are young even if they have only small amounts of income and few expenditures. How can a budget process help you achieve your life-span goals?

LO 16.2.2

THE BUDGET PROCESS

The process of creating and using a budget involves four main steps.

1. Set financial goals.
2. Plan budget categories.
3. Maintain financial records.
4. Evaluate your budget.

Any individual, family, or organization can use these steps to maximize the power of their available financial resources.

Set Financial Goals

Setting financial goals is the first step for any financial action. Goals identify results you want to achieve. Your financial goals should take a SMART approach—specific, measurable, action-oriented, realistic, and time-based. Figure 16-3 provides more details about the SMART approach.

Writing down short-term and long-term goals will help you decide how to spend and save your money. If your goals include going to college, your budget will require more for savings. If you are working at a job that requires you to spend a large amount for transportation, you will likely budget more for this item.

Photodisc/Getty Images

Make a list of short-term and long-term financial goals. What steps do you need to take to reach these goals?

Plan Budget Categories

Most financial advisers recommend that an amount be set aside for savings as the first part of a budget. If savings are not considered first, other expenses may use all available income.

After savings, two types of living expenses must be considered: fixed and variable expenses. **Fixed expenses** are costs that occur on a regular basis and are for the same amount each time. Examples of fixed expenses are rent, mortgage payments, and insurance premiums.

Variable expenses involve living costs that differ each time and may not be as easy to estimate. These types of expenses include food, clothing, and utilities. Some variable expenses, such as medical and dental costs, occur less often and may be large when they do occur. Such expenses must be accounted for in the budget.

SMART APPROACH TO SETTING FINANCIAL GOALS

S	Specific	Make the goals specific so you know exactly what you want to achieve.
M	Measurable	Make the goals measurable so that you know the specific amount to save.
A	Action-oriented	Make the goals action-oriented so that you know what actions you need to take.
R	Realistic	Make the goals realistic based on your income.
T	Time-based	Make the goals time-based so that you have a time frame for achieving them.

FIGURE 16-3

What are some of the advantages to the SMART approach?

Different Learning Abilities

Attention Deficit Disorder Provide clear directions to students, asking them to write down two financial goals they have for the future. Ask them to explain actions that might be taken to achieve those goals.

The amount budgeted for savings and other expenditures is referred to as an allowance. An **allowance** is the amount of money you plan to use for a certain budget category. Although budget categories can vary for different situations, eight main divisions are commonly used.

1. **Savings** Savings accounts, government bonds, stocks, and other investments
2. **Food** Food eaten at home and meals eaten away from home
3. **Clothing** Clothing, shoes, dry cleaning, and repairs
4. **Household** Rent, mortgage, property taxes, insurance, utilities, furnishings, household supplies, and repairs
5. **Transportation** Auto payments, insurance, operating costs, maintenance, repairs, and public transportation
6. **Health and Personal Care** Medical and dental expenses, medications, eyeglasses, health insurance, and personal care costs
7. **Recreation and Education** Books and other reading materials, theater tickets, concerts, vacations, school expenses, hobbies, and club dues
8. **Gifts and Contributions** Charitable contributions and personal gifts

FYI

A once-popular system for family budgeting used envelopes marked with labels for different expenses such as "Food," "Housing," and "Automobile." Each envelope contained the budgeted amount of money, and expenses were paid from the money in the envelopes. This system allows a person to see where the money is going. Unfortunately, a danger exists with keeping large amounts of cash at home.

At this point, ask yourself, "How much should I set aside for each category?" Planned spending for various budget categories will depend on income, family size, ages of children, cost of living in your area, and work-related expenses. It will also depend on personal values, needs, and goals. A cash flow statement, similar to Figure 16-2, can help you develop budget categories.

Other help for developing a budget can come from government reports on family spending or from articles in magazines, such as *Kiplinger's Personal Finance* and *Money*. An example of a family budget for one month is shown in Figure 16-4.

Family Budget for One Month

CHUNG HOUSEHOLD				
Monthly Budget				
January, 20xx				
ESTIMATED INCOME			ESTIMATED EXPENSE	
Manuel's net income	$4,225		Savings	$2,225
Lydia's net income	4,350		Food	1,100
			Clothing	475
			Household	1,825
			Transportation	1,275
			Health & personal care	450
			Recreation & education	800
			Gifts & contributions	425
Total Income	$8,575		Total Expenses	$8,575

FIGURE 16-4
What percentage of income have the Chungs budgeted for savings? How do people decide how much to save?

FYI

Explain to students how the envelope system can be replicated in a safer fashion with the use of technology.

TEACH

Explain the eight main categories that could be used for a budget. Ask students to describe spending items for each category.

▸ **Figure 16-4** ***ANSWER***

The Chungs have budgeted approximately 26 percent of their income for savings. This is a fairly large amount, which may not be possible for most people. However, the Chungs may be saving for a down payment to buy a house or to pay for returning to school for an advanced degree. Deciding how much to save is a personal decision based on short- and long-term goals.

Different Learning Abilities

Visually Impaired Create enlarged visuals showing the eight categories commonly used for a budget: (1) Savings, (2) Food, (3) Clothing, (4) Household, (5) Transportation, (6) Health and Personal Care, (7) Recreation and Education, and (8) Gifts and Contributions that appear on pages 400 and 401. Use the visuals to explain these budget categories. These visuals also can be used for review.

TEACH

Ask students to suggest methods that might be used for personal financial record keeping.

Explain how a budget variance is calculated. Describe actions that might be taken when a budget variance occurs.

ONGOING ASSESSMENT

CHECKPOINT ✓ *ANSWER*

Eight commonly used budget categories are (1) savings, (2) food, (3) clothing, (4) household, (5) transportation, (6) health and personal care, (7) recreation and education, and (8) gifts and contributions.

THINK CRITICALLY THROUGH VISUALS

Answers will vary depending on the current situation of students. Reduced spending for certain items, reduced use of credit, and increased income sources are common answers.

TEACH

Point out the main characteristics of an effective budget listed on this page.

Ask students to describe budgeting activities they have experienced or observed.

Maintain Financial Records

After planning a budget, individuals and families should record their income and expenses to find out if the plan is working. An example is shown in Figure 16-5. The first line shows the monthly income available to the family ($8,575 after taxes and other paycheck deductions) and the budget allowances for each category.

During the month, entries for expenditures were recorded. Because the family pays most bills by check, a checkbook is a reference for the information needed to prepare the income and expense summary.

Evaluate Your Budget

All columns are totaled at the end of the month. Actual spending is compared with the budgeted amounts. Any difference between these amounts is a **budget variance.**

If actual spending is greater than planned spending, such as for the "Household" category, it is referred to as a *deficit.* When actual spending is less than the budgeted amount, as with the "Food" category, a *surplus* occurs.

A category-by-category comparison allows you to find areas where changes in the budget may be appropriate. A variance in the actual amount spent and the budgeted amount does not always mean a change in your spending plan is necessary.

Your budgeted amount may still be appropriate with a slight deficit or surplus occurring every few months in some categories. If you expect necessary higher or lower spending in a certain category, a change in your budget is probably needed.

CHECKPOINT ✓
What are eight commonly used budget categories?

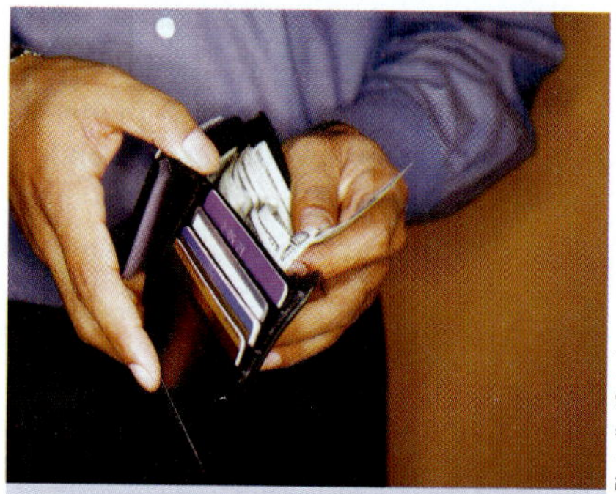

Photodisc/Getty Images

What kinds of adjustments would you have to make to live within a budget?

LO 16.2.3

SUCCESSFUL BUDGETING

Effective budgeting will be an ongoing learning process for you.

Characteristics of an Effective Budget

The following are common characteristics of a successful budget.

- *Must be realistic.* It should reflect current income and planned spending.
- *Should be flexible.* When unexpected expenses arise, your spending plan should be able to adapt for these living costs.
- *Should be evaluated regularly.* Every few months, evaluate the budget to determine whether it still is appropriate.
- *Must be well planned and clearly communicated.* All family members should discuss financial goals, wants and needs, and plans for spending.
- *Should have a simple format.* If it is too detailed and difficult to understand, family members may not be willing to use the spending plan.

Budgeting Formats

A good budgeting system allows the user to develop a budget, track expenses, and pay bills. Some people prefer to use the latest technology for their budget and others prefer to work with traditional

Applied Skills

Mathematics Ask students to create situations in which a budget *deficit* or a *surplus* is present. Students should calculate the amount of the deficit or surplus. Invite interested students to set up a budget worksheet using spreadsheet software.

Family Income and Expense Record

Chung Household												
Income and Expense Record												
Date	TT	Explanation	Totals		Distribution of Savings and Expenditures							
			Receipts	Payments	Savings	Food	Clothing	Household	Transport.	Health/ Per.	Rec./Edu.	Gifts & Con.
		Budget	$8,575.00		$2,225.00	$1,100.00	$475.00	$1,825.00	$1,275.00	$450.00	$800.00	$425.00
January	1	**Balance**	1,300.00									
		Manuel's net income	2,112.50									
		Lydia's net income	2,175.00									
	2			2,225.00	2,225.00							
	7			1,075.00		210.00	140.00	100.00	100.00	150.00	225.00	150.00
	14			950.00		230.00	90.00	200.00	145.00	125.00	90.00	70.00
	15	Manuel's net income	2,112.50									
		Lydia's net income	2,175.00									
	17	Mortgage payment		1,200.00				1,200.00				
	21	Car payment		850.00					850.00			
	22			925.00		200.00	150.00	190.00	75.00		160.00	150.00
	29			1,055.00		300.00	95.00	220.00	50.00	200.00	90.00	100.00
	31	**Totals**	$9,875.00	$8,280.00	$2,225.00	$940.00	$475.00	$1,910.00	$1,220.00	475.00	$565.00	$470.00
February	1	**Balance***	$1,595.00									

*Balance = January's total receipts – total payments = $9,875.00 – $8,280.00

FIGURE 16-5
In which categories did the Chung's expenditures exceed the amount they had budgeted? In which were they less than the amount budgeted?

TEACH

Use Figure 16-5 to highlight the various activities in the budgeting process.

Ask students to evaluate the Chung's budgeting process. What are the benefits and drawbacks of the system they use?

▸ Figure 16-5 *ANSWER*

The Chung's expenditures exceeded the amounts they had budgeted in the household, health and personal care, and gifts and contributions categories. Their expenditures were less than budgeted in the food, transportation, and recreation and education categories. Expenses were equal to the budgeted amounts in the remaining categories.

Different Learning Abilities

Gifted Instruct students to conduct online research regarding money management activities and budgeting procedures. The findings may be reported in a written format or oral presentation to the class.

Work as a TEAM

Encourage students to think of situations that could affect budgeting activities. Ask representatives from the various teams to report to the class.

TEACH

Explain each of the budgeting formats discussed on the page. Ask students to point out the benefits and drawbacks of each one.

ONGOING ASSESSMENT

CHECKPOINT ✓ ANSWER

Five characteristics of an effective budget are that it is (1) realistic, (2) flexible, (3) evaluated regularly, (4) well planned and clearly communicated, and (5) in a simple format.

ASSESS

Key Concepts *Answers*

1. False. Retirement planning is usually considered a long-term goal.

2. b. achieve financial goals

3. a. estimating variable expenses

Make Academic Connections *Answers*

4a. The total amount spent for food was $331.

4b. Mary and Fred had a budget surplus of $9.

5. Posters and presentations will vary.

Work as a TEAM

For a budget to be successful, it must be followed. Work as a team to identify some situations in which a person or household may not be able to stay within their budget. Then explain actions that might be taken to resolve the situation.

handwritten documents. There are also people who try to keep their budgets in their heads. There are advantages and disadvantages to each format.

Money management software, smartphone apps, and financial websites offer budgeting tools. Although there are wide variations among the tools available, they are generally easy to use, provide guidance and organization, and utilize built-in calculators.

Handwritten budgets have the advantage of being inexpensive. They require nothing more than pencil and paper, although some people use a calculator or spreadsheet to help with calculations. For people with a single source of income and few expenses, a handwritten budget might be a good choice.

Some people choose to use their checkbook register and bank statements as a substitute for a budget. These documents allow the user to pay bills and monitor deposits and balances, but there is no mechanism for financial planning.

The idea of keeping a budget in your head is appealing to some people because of its simplicity. However the possibility of mistakes is greatly reduced when budget information is documented on paper or in an electronic file.

Your decision for a budgeting system will depend on your personal situation and your personal preferences. Most important is choosing a method that provides accurate and timely information for helping you achieve your financial goals.

CHECKPOINT ✓

What are five characteristics of an effective budget?

16.2 ASSESSMENT

Key Concepts

Determine the best answer.

1. True or False. Retirement planning is usually considered a short-term goal.
2. A major purpose of a budget is to
   - **a.** assist with comparison shopping
   - **b.** achieve financial goals
   - **c.** reduce a person's enjoyment of life
   - **d.** gather data for using credit cards
3. The most uncertain aspect of the budgeting process involves
   - **a.** estimating variable expenses
   - **b.** determining net worth
   - **c.** estimating fixed expenses
   - **d.** setting financial goals

Make Academic Connections

4. **Math** Mary and Fred James budgeted $340 a month for groceries. During the month, they spent $87, $93, $38, $61, and $52 at the supermarket.
   - **a.** What was the total amount spent for food?
   - **b.** Did Mary and Fred have a budget deficit or surplus? What was the amount?
5. **Visual Art** Talk to several people about various short-term and long-term goals they have had in their lives. Prepare a poster or computerized presentation summarizing various types of goals, both financial and personal.

CLOSE Highlight the purposes and process of creating and implementing a budget.

RETEACH Ask students to name examples of fixed and variable expenses.

ENRICH Assign students to create a budget for their current income or for an assumed amount in the future.

16.3 Taxes in Your Life

Learning Outcomes

16.3.1 Identify the types of taxes paid by consumers.

16.3.2 Describe the steps when filing a federal income tax return.

16.3.3 Explain tax assistance sources.

16.3.4 Identify common tax-planning strategies.

Key Terms

tax 405
earned income 407
investment income 407
tax deduction 407
exemption 408
taxable income 408
tax credit 408

Focus on REAL LIFE

"I just got my first paycheck and was I ever surprised," commented Nick. "I earned more than $200, but my check was for less than $160. What's the deal with that?"

"I guess you didn't pay attention in business class when we discussed income taxes and Social Security taxes," suggested Margie.

"Well, I do know that some of my pay has to go for roads, parks, and protecting our country," responded Nick. "And that I must file a tax return to get my refund or to pay an additional amount. Also, my tax return must be filed each year by…"

"OK—it sounds like you did learn a few things about taxes in our business class," acknowledged Margie.

LO 16.3.1

TYPES OF TAXES

Each day, without thinking about it, people pay taxes. Many people pay taxes through paycheck deductions. Depending where you live and shop, you might pay taxes when you make purchases. Wise tax planning starts with knowing the types of taxes you pay.

A **tax** is a charge imposed by a government to finance public services. Federal, state, and local governments levy taxes. Most people pay taxes in four major categories: purchases, property, wealth, and earnings. Common taxes on purchases are sales tax and excise tax. Real estate property tax and personal property taxes are examples of taxes on property. Taxes on wealth include estate tax, inheritance tax, and gift tax. Social Security tax and income tax are examples of taxes on earnings. Examples of common taxes are described in Figure 16-6.

Not everyone pays every kind of tax. The types of taxes you pay and how much you pay is related to where you live, how much money you earn, and how you spend and save your money.

When and Where You Pay Taxes

Some taxes are paid as part of everyday living. Other taxes are due on specific dates. And some taxes, such as estate taxes, are triggered by an event—the death of a person.

Sales tax is collected at the time of purchase. If you buy a jacket for $80 you might pay more than $80. If your state has a 5 percent sales tax and you are shopping in a county with a 1 percent sales tax, you will pay the $84.80 for the jacket. The seller will pay $4 to the state and $0.80 to the county. In recent years, five states did not have a state sales tax: Alaska, Delaware, Montana, New Hampshire, and Oregon.

In addition to paying sales tax at the cash register, you also pay taxes at the pump. The state price of gasoline includes various taxes. The tax may be hidden, but you still pay it.

Focus on REAL LIFE

Use this situation to determine how much students know about the taxes they pay.

TEACH

Ask students to name taxes that they pay.

Use Figure 16-6 (on page 406) to highlight the main types of taxes paid by people in our society.

Applied Skills

Writing Across the Curriculum Assign students to prepare a paragraph explaining why some states do not have sales tax or state income tax. Be sure the discussion addresses other revenue sources.

▸ **Figure 16-6 *ANSWER***

While student answers will vary, likely answers include sales, excise, income, and property taxes as well as others listed in Figure 16-6.

TEACH

Explain how sales tax is calculated on purchases.

Ask students to describe how taxes are sometimes included in the price of an item.

Ask students if they have ever received a paycheck with income taxes deducted.

ONGOING ASSESSMENT

CHECKPOINT ✓ *ANSWER*

The four main categories of taxes are: taxes on purchases, taxes on property, taxes on wealth, and taxes on earnings.

COMMON TAXES		
CATEGORIES	**EXAMPLES**	**DESCRIPTION**
Taxes on purchases	Sales tax	A sales tax is a state or local tax on goods and services that is collected by the seller. Food and prescription drugs are often exempt.
	Excise tax	An excise tax is imposed on specific goods and services. For example, all states impose an excise tax on gasoline.
Taxes on property	Real estate property tax	This tax is based on the value of land and buildings. Most property tax revenue is used to pay for schools and local government services.
	Personal property tax	This tax is based on the value of personal property such as boats, cars, and trucks.
Taxes on wealth	Estate tax	This tax is based on the value of a person's property at death.
	Inheritance tax	This tax is based on the value of items received from a deceased person.
	Gift tax	This tax applies to gifts of any kind of property, including money, when the value of the gift exceeds a certain dollar amount. Generally the donor is responsible for the gift tax.
Taxes on earnings	Social Security tax	This tax is based on earnings and is used to finance retirement and disability benefits.
	Income tax	This tax is based on earnings and other sources of income and is a source of revenue for governments.

FIGURE 16-6
What are some taxes that you and your family pay?

Real estate taxes are usually due once or twice a year. Some property owners choose to pay the bill when it is due. Others choose to add money to their mortgage payments and ask the financial institution that holds the mortgage to set the money aside until it is time to pay the property tax. The financial institution then pays the bill when it is due.

Income Tax Payments

People make payments for federal, state, and local income taxes in two ways: withholding and estimated payments. Withholding is a "pay-as-you-go system" in which an employer deducts income tax from the earnings of workers each pay period. In January, workers receive a W-2 from each employer. A W-2 is a summary of a worker's earnings for the previous year and includes the amounts deducted for taxes.

Some people are required to make estimated payments for income taxes. Examples of income that may require estimated payments include significant income from savings and investments, income from royalties and pensions, and income from self-employment or working as an independent contractor. Estimated payments are made directly to the government and are due quarterly. Estimated payments for federal income tax are due on April 15, June 15, September 15, and January 15 of the next year.

Most states also have an income tax to fund the cost of highways, state parks, and other public services. In recent years, these states did not have a state income tax: Alaska, Florida, Nevada, South Dakota, Texas, Washington, and Wyoming. These states fund services with other types of taxes and fees.

CHECKPOINT ✓
What are the four main categories of taxes?

Different Learning Styles

Auditory Learner Encourage students to read aloud the names of the different taxes listed in Figure 16-6.

Kinesthetic Learner Encourage students to make flip cards using the information presented in Figure 16-6.

LO 16.3.2

PREPARING THE FEDERAL INCOME TAX RETURN

The Internal Revenue Service (IRS) is part of the U.S. Treasury. The IRS is the agency responsible for collecting federal income tax. In order to make sure that people pay the taxes they owe, the IRS requires taxpayers to file, or submit, a federal income tax return each year. With some exceptions, the filing deadline is April 15 of the next year.

The main purpose of preparing a federal income tax return is to determine the amount of tax a taxpayer is required to pay for a particular year. Because most people make tax payments throughout the year, the form is also used to determine whether you have paid all that you owe, you need to pay more, or you are entitled to a refund or credit. The seven main steps in the preparation of a federal income tax return are presented in Figure 16-7.

Step 1: Determine Gross Income The two main types of income for most people are earned income and investment income. **Earned income** results from wages, salary, commission, fees, tips, and bonuses. **Investment income** is the result of earnings from dividends, interest, and rent. Federal income tax must also be paid on other types of income such as alimony, awards, lottery winnings, and prizes. For example, cash and prizes won on television game shows are subject to both federal and states taxes.

Tax-exempt income is income not subject to tax. Interest earned on most state and city bonds, for example, is exempt from federal income tax. In contrast, *tax-deferred income* will be taxed at a later date.

Step 2: Calculate Adjusted Gross Income Certain items, called *adjustments to income*, are subtracted from gross income to obtain adjusted gross income (AGI). These reductions include deposits in retirement accounts and alimony payments.

Step 3: Subtract Deductions A **tax deduction** is an amount that reduces taxable income. All taxpayers are eligible for a standard deduction, an amount on which no taxes are paid. As an alternative, a taxpayer may choose to itemize deductions. The rules regarding what can be included in itemized deductions are very specific and change to reflect tax policies and laws.

Examples of items that might be included in itemized deductions include:

- Certain medical and dental expenses
- Taxes paid for state and local income tax and property taxes
- Interest paid on a home mortgage or home equity loan
- Contributions to charitable organizations
- Casualty and theft losses
- Moving expenses when a new job is more than 50 miles away
- Certain job-related expenses such as union dues, required continuing education, work clothes, and tax preparation fees

The decision to use the standard deduction or to itemize your deductions

FEDERAL INCOME TAX RETURN PREPARATION	
Step 1	Determine gross income
Step 2	Calculate adjusted gross income
Step 3	Subtract deductions
Step 4	Determine exemptions
Step 5	Compute taxable income
Step 6	Calculate tax owed
Step 7	Make tax payments or ask for a refund or credit

FIGURE 16-7
What are some ways that tax money is used by the federal government?

TEACH

Use Figure 16-7 to provide an overview of the steps for preparing a federal income tax return.

▶ Figure 16-7 *ANSWER*

The money paid for federal income taxes is used for the costs of the military, national parks, regulating food and other products, assisting people in need, and other federal government services.

TEACH

Explain the difference between earned income and investment income.

Point out how tax-exempt income and tax-deferred income affects a person's taxes.

Describe examples of common tax deductions.

Different Learning Styles

Visual Learner Organize students into small groups and ask them to suggest items or pictures that might be used to represent the steps involved in preparing a federal income tax return. (See Figure 16-7.) Ask students to present one or more of the steps to the class.

TEACH

Explain the criteria for exemptions.

Compare the difference between a tax deduction and a tax credit.

FYI

Point out how saving during the year might be a wiser financial decision than getting a large refund.

THINK CRITICALLY THROUGH VISUALS

Necessary documents include the appropriate tax forms and instructions, income information, and receipts for tax deductions.

FYI Each year, Americans receive more than $250 billion in tax refunds. This figure represents several billion in lost earning from savings and investing. By having less withheld and obtaining a smaller refund, you can save and invest these funds for your own benefit. Another $1 billion of tax refunds goes unclaimed each year.

depends on your income and your expenses for the year. In some cases it is worthwhile to calculate your tax liability both ways and choose the one that is more advantageous.

Step 4: Determine Exemptions An **exemption** is a tax deduction for the taxpayer, a spouse, and each dependent. For each exemption, taxable income is reduced by a set amount. Therefore, the more dependents a taxpayer can claim, the greater the reduction in taxable income.

In most cases dependents are minor children, but specific criteria must be met. For a person to qualify as a dependent, all three of the following conditions are necessary:

1. The person must not earn more than a certain amount unless he or she is under age 19 or is a full-time student under age 24.
2. The taxpayer must provide more than half of the dependent's support.
3. The dependent must live with the taxpayer or be a relative.

Step 5: Compute Taxable Income **Taxable income** is the amount on which taxes are calculated. This amount results from subtracting adjustments to income, deductions, and exemptions from gross income.

Step 6: Taxes Owed Tax rates are the percentages used to compute the amount owed for taxes. In recent years, the federal income tax rates have ranged from 10 to 39.6 percent, depending on the level of taxable income.

A person's taxes can be reduced by a **tax credit**, an amount subtracted directly from taxes owed. Tax credits may be obtained for child- and dependent-care expenses. Low-income workers may qualify for the earned-income credit (EIC).

Remember that a tax credit differs from a deduction in that a tax credit lowers taxes by the full dollar amount. In contrast, a deduction reduces the amount on which the taxes are calculated.

Step 7: Make Tax Payments or Ask for a Refund or Credit The final step in preparing a tax return is to compare the amount paid with the amount owed for taxes. You may owe an additional amount, or you may receive a refund or credit if you paid more than you owe for taxes. Many people like receiving a refund. However, it is important to remember that your money was being held by the government and you were not able to use it or earn interest on it.

micro10x/Shutterstock.com

What documents would you need to complete your federal tax return?

Applied Skills

Geography Ask students to create a single map illustrating states that have state income tax and states that have state sales tax. Instruct students to include the percentage of the sales tax for each state. Point out that they can use color and graphics to help illustrate the map.

Completing the Federal Income Tax Return

The process of completing the federal income tax return requires taxpayers to determine their filing status and which tax form is appropriate for their situation. It is important to provide complete and accurate information and avoid common filing errors. The completed tax return must be filed with the IRS by mailing it to an IRS processing center or submitting it electronically.

Filing Status All U.S. citizens and residents are required to file a federal income tax return if their income exceeds a certain amount. Marital status and the number of dependents determine a taxpayer's filing status. The five options for filing status are explained in Figure 16-8.

Tax Forms Taxpayers use one of three forms to file their federal income tax return. Form 1040 is the basic form and Form 1040A and Form 1040EZ are shorter, less complicated versions.

Form 1040EZ allows a person with a simple tax situation to easily file a federal income tax return. While a little more complicated than the EZ, Form 1040A may be used by people who have less than $100,000 in taxable income from wages, salaries, tips, unemployment compensation, interest, or dividends and use the standard deduction. The most detailed of the three forms, Form 1040, has sections for all types of income. A person must use this form if income is over $100,000 or if claimed as a dependent by a parent while having interest or dividends over a certain amount. Form 1040 is also used when itemizing deductions. The decision regarding which tax form to use depends on your income level, the amount of your deductions, and other complexities of your tax situation.

Pierre Yu/Shutterstock.com

How are Forms 1040A and 1040EZ related to Form 1040?

INCOME TAX FILING STATUS	
Single	Refers to individuals who are unmarried, divorced, or legally separated with no dependents.
Married filing jointly	Refers to a married couple filing a joint return.
Married filing separately	Is an option available to a married couple when each spouse takes responsibility for his or her own tax return.
Head of household	Refers to an unmarried individual or a surviving spouse who maintains a household (paying for more than half of the costs) for a child or a dependent relative.
Qualifying widow or widower	Refers to an individual whose spouse died within the past two years and who has a qualifying dependent child.

FIGURE 16-8

Why might people who are married choose the filing status *married filing separately*?

TEACH

Explain the factors that affect a person's filing status.

Ask students to describe situations that could affect a person's use of Form 1040, Form 1040A, and Form 1040EZ.

Describe the common filing errors that taxpayers make.

Point out the benefits of filing your taxes online.

▸ Figure 16-8 *ANSWER*

Married people might prefer to file separately to reduce the total amount of tax they owe.

THINK CRITICALLY THROUGH VISUALS

Forms 1040A and 1040EZ are shorter, less complicated versions of Form 1040.

Applied Skills

Communication Instruct students to create an advertisement to promote actions by students to learn more about the tax preparation process. Encourage students to communicate the benefits of being a wise taxpayer. Consider allowing students to work in pairs or small groups.

ONGOING ASSESSMENT

CHECKPOINT ✓ANSWER

(1) Determine gross income. (2) Calculate adjusted gross income. (3) Subtract deductions. (4) Determine exemptions. (5) Compute taxable income. (6) Calculate tax owed. (7) Make tax payments or ask for a refund or credit.

TEACH

Explain why some people prepare their own tax returns while others use a professional tax service.

Ask students to name possible sources for tax information and assistance.

Work as a TEAM

This activity will help students understand actions that might be taken to reduce errors when preparing an income tax return.

Avoiding Common Filing Errors Filing errors can cost time and money. An error might delay a refund or result in paying more tax than you really owe. Errors can also result in penalty and interest charges for not filing on time or underpayment of taxes. When preparing a federal tax return, mistakes can be avoided by

- Creating a filing system for tax documents, receipts, and tax forms.
- Following instructions carefully.
- Using the proper tax form, tax table, and correct filing status.
- Checking—and rechecking—calculations carefully.
- Including all required documents, such as a copy of your W-2 form.
- Signing the tax return.
- Making your check payable to the U.S. Treasury.
- Writing your Social Security number and the tax year on your check.
- Filing online or mailing your return before the deadline.
- Using the proper amount of postage if mailing your return.
- Keeping a copy of the tax return.

Filing Taxes Online The use of tax preparation software can save many hours of time. These computer programs allow taxpayers to prepare their federal and state tax forms by answering a series of questions or entering requested information. The tax forms can be printed for filing by mail, or filed online.

The Internal Revenue Service, state departments of revenue, and tax software makes online filing easy at low or no cost. The Free File Alliance provides online tax preparation and e-filing free to millions of taxpayers. This program is a partnership between the IRS and the tax software industry.

Work as a TEAM

Many people make mistakes when preparing their tax return, resulting in delays in processing and penalties. As a team, create a list of specific actions that a person might take to avoid common errors when filing an income tax return.

CHECKPOINT ✓

What are the seven steps for preparing a federal income tax return?

LO 16.3.3

TAX PREPARATION ASSISTANCE

Many taxpayers prepare their own federal income tax returns by hand or with tax preparation software. Other taxpayers use the services of a tax professional to prepare their returns. While some people like the convenience, others choose a professional because they are not comfortable completing their own tax return. Many resources are available to help taxpayers with the preparation of their federal tax return and tax planning.

IRS Services Tax information and assistance is available directly from the Internal Revenue Service. The IRS website allows you to access needed tax forms and instructions. The IRS also offers

- Tax forms online or requested by telephone
- Answers to specific tax questions by calling a toll-free hotline
- Walk-in tax assistance at local IRS offices around the country

Another IRS service is the Volunteer Income Tax Assistance (VITA), which offers free tax help to low- and moderate-income taxpayers who cannot prepare their own tax returns.

Tax Publications Commercial tax guides are available to assist taxpayers.

Different Learning Abilities

Visually Impaired Create a large print poster with the list of common filing errors listed in the text to help students understand the mistakes to avoid when filing their federal income tax return.

This activity will help students understand actions that might be taken to reduce errors when preparing an income tax return.

These guides cover a wide range of topics. Some are intended for specific groups, such as small businesses, and are updated annually.

Online Sources Many websites focus on tax information. These may be located using an online search.

Tax Preparation Software Many taxpayers use tax preparation software to prepare tax returns. These products allow users to print returns for filing or to file online. Data entry is quick and easy. Options allow for updating information from last year's return and accessing income data from employers and financial institutions.

Tax preparation software also has features to help taxpayers organize records, avoid common mistakes, and take advantage of appropriate deductions and credits. Tax planning features offer strategies for making financial decisions.

Tax Preparation Services Many taxpayers pay for professional tax preparation service. Some might pay as little as $35 and others pay thousands of dollars for these services. The fee varies based on the complexity of the tax return and the level of training of the tax preparer. Professional tax preparation services include:

- Tax services ranging from local, one-person organizations to national companies with hundreds of offices
- Enrolled agents who are government-approved tax preparers with specific training
- Certified public accountants (CPA) with specific tax training to assist with tax planning and preparation of tax returns

In the past, some businesses offered *refund anticipation loans*. The credit terms on this loan often had an annual interest rate of more than 100 percent. Today, these high-cost loans have been replaced by *refund anticipation checks*. Taxpayers are charged a fee of $30 or more to receive

NotarYES/Shutterstock.com

What factors might a person consider when selecting a professional tax service?

TEACH

Describe the benefits of tax preparation software.

Explain the services provided by various tax professionals.

THINK CRITICALLY THROUGH VISUALS

Factors a person might consider include location, reputation, experience, cost, and references of others.

Applied Skills

Technology Ask students to visit the IRS website to find the mailing or online filing instructions for

1. Sending Form 1040EZ with no payment because you are getting a refund.
2. Sending Form 1040 with a payment for the amount you owe.
3. Sending Form 1040-ES along with an estimated tax payment.

ONGOING ASSESSMENT

CHECKPOINT ✓ ANSWER

Tax assistance is available from the IRS, tax services, enrolled agents, accountants, and lawyers.

TEACH

Ask students to describe possible actions people might take to reduce the taxes they owe.

Explain how owning a home can reduce a person's taxes.

Describe examples of tax-exempt and tax-deferred investments that might be used to reduce taxes.

ONGOING ASSESSMENT

CHECKPOINT ✓ ANSWER

No federal income tax is ever paid on tax-exempt investments.

ASSESS

Key Concepts *Answers*

1. c. income
2. b. a refund of $24

Make Academic Connections *Answers*

3. Answers will vary. Students should find information about the value-added tax (VAT) used in Europe, Japan, and elsewhere.
4. Students should clearly communicate the various features and information available on this website.

their refunds sooner. Refunds may also be obtained on a prepaid debit card, which usually has various fees.

CHECKPOINT ✓
Name the professionals from whom a person can obtain tax assistance.

LO 16.3.4

EFFECTIVE TAX STRATEGIES

Tax laws and tax forms change frequently. Using online resources, attending classes, and consulting with financial professionals are ways of staying informed about taxes. Being knowledgeable can help you develop strategies and make decisions that limit the amount of taxes you are required to pay. It is also important to understand that your personal and financial situation will change over time and you will need to be aware of how these changes relate to taxes.

Three common ways to reduce the amount of income tax you owe are home ownership, tax-exempt investments, and tax-deferred investments.

Home Ownership Home ownership may reduce taxable income if the taxpayer itemizes deductions. Amounts paid for real estate taxes and mortgage interest are itemized deductions that reduce taxable income. Interest on a home-equity loan of up to $100,000 is also an itemized deduction.

Tax-Exempt Investments Interest income from municipal bonds, issued by state and local governments, and other tax-exempt investments is not subject to federal income tax.

Tax-Deferred Investments Income from tax-deferred investments has the advantage of lowering current taxes. A common tax strategy for working people is the use of tax-deferred retirement plans to reduce their current taxes.

CHECKPOINT ✓
What is the main difference between tax-exempt investments and tax-deferred investments?

16.3 ASSESSMENT

Key Concepts

Determine the best answer.

1. A tax on earnings would be an ________ tax.
   a. inheritance
   b. estate
   c. income
   d. excise
2. Cami Bartosz calculated that she owed taxes of $254 and had $278 withheld from her pay during the year. This would result in
   a. a refund of $278.
   b. a refund of $24.
   c. additional taxes owed of $254.
   d. additional taxes owed of $24.

Make Academic Connections

3. **Culture** Different types of taxes exist in other countries based on government policies and other factors. Conduct library or online research to determine the taxes people might encounter in European or Asian countries. Prepare a brief written summary of your findings.
4. **Technology** Locate a website that people might use to prepare their federal income tax return. Prepare a poster or computer presentation that illustrates the web address, features of the website, cost of the services, and other information available to taxpayers.

CLOSE Emphasize the role of taxes for society and for personal financial planning.

RETEACH Review the steps in preparing a federal tax return.

ENRICH Ask students to list various actions they might take to learn more about how taxes affect a person's financial decisions.

16.4 Your Financial Future

Learning Outcomes

16.4.1 Describe the financial planning process.

16.4.2 Explain actions for implementing a financial plan.

16.4.3 Identify actions for reviewing a financial plan.

Key Terms

financial plan 413

individual retirement account (IRA) 416

estate planning 418

Focus on REAL LIFE

"Gloria, are you going to the business speakers luncheon program on Friday?"

"I really hadn't given it much thought, Maria. Are you?"

"Yes! The speaker is from the local college and is supposed to be very dynamic and informative. The topic is financial planning, and if I am going to go to college, I need some help in planning right now! Why don't you meet me there?"

"Great idea, Maria. I always thought of financial planning as something for people out of college. But it certainly makes sense to start now! I guess if I start planning early, I can get a head start on my future!"

LO 16.4.1

DEVELOPING A FINANCIAL PLAN

To successfully reach financial goals, you must have a plan. Successful coaches have a game plan. Travel agents refer to vacation plans. Builders must have house plans. Successful consumers and businesspeople must have a financial plan. A **financial plan** is a report that summarizes your current financial condition, acknowledges your financial needs, and sets a direction for your future financial activities.

Financial planning includes evaluating one's financial position, setting financial goals, and guiding activities and resources toward reaching those goals. Everyone should have a carefully developed financial plan.

Your financial plan should include all that you know about good money management. This plan should be developed carefully. It should be evaluated and updated frequently. A well-developed financial plan can make your financial life more satisfying.

Financial planning offers several specific advantages.

- Your financial uncertainties will be reduced.
- You will gain more control of your financial activities.
- Your family and household members will know more about your financial situation in case they need to assume control of your finances.
- Earning, spending, protecting, and saving your resources will be more systematic.

Life-Span Plan

Describe the role of financial planning in the creation of a person's life-span plan. Do you have a financial plan? Explain why people who fail to create and follow a financial plan often fail to achieve their life-span goals.

Focus on REAL LIFE

Encourage students to consider the impact their present financial decisions have on their financial future.

TEACH

Explain that financial planning, while similar to budgeting, is more comprehensive and involves a long-term perspective.

Ask students to name financial planning activities. Also, ask them to list items that might be included in a financial plan.

Life-Span Plan Answer

Answers will vary. Students should point out that most life-span goals require a significant allocation of funds that can only be accumulated through careful financial planning over time.

Different Learning Abilities

English Language Learners (ELL) Obtain translations for various key terms in this chapter to reinforce these concepts in both English and other dominant languages used by students.

TEACH

Explain the advantages of financial planning listed on this page. Highlight the steps in the financial planning process.

Ask students to name items that might be included in a financial inventory.

Name some of the financial documents that students will encounter now and in the future.

Point out differences in financial activities in various stages of a person's life cycle.

▸ Figure 16-9 *ANSWER*

Computers have made financial record keeping more efficient by calculating personal income and expenses quickly and accurately. Computers can prepare detailed reports of all income and expense categories and simplify record keeping for budgeting and tax purposes.

Financial Planning Process

Financial planning experts recommend the following steps.

1. *Analyze your current financial condition.* You should create a balance sheet and cash flow statement.
2. *Develop financial goals that are responsive to your vision.* What short-term and long-term objectives do you have? How much money will you need, and when?
3. *Create your financial plan.* This activity will require that you plan various actions for your saving and spending goals. This step may require help from a financial planner or other financial specialists.
4. *Implement the plan.* This may involve buying or selling property or investments, moving bank accounts, acquiring insurance, or any number of financial activities.
5. *Revise your financial plan.* As time goes on, you will frequently evaluate and revise your financial plan.

Financial Inventory

Think of a financial inventory as a financial checkup. When you get a medical checkup, the physician assesses your health. A financial inventory is a careful assessment of your finances.

A financial inventory will usually include the creation of a personal balance sheet and cash flow statement. This process will provide information about your current financial position in terms of income, savings, investments, property, living expenses, insurance, and money owed.

Personal Financial Filing System

To keep your financial inventory and other records in order, you should create a personal financial filing system. Well-organized files are key to financial planning. These files should contain all of the documents and records related to such things as contracts, bills, receipts, bank balances, and legal papers. The files will be an invaluable resource to you as you progress with your financial planning. Using a paper filing system, computer folders, or online storage can help you organize these records in categories as shown in Figure 16-9.

A FILING SYSTEM FOR PERSONAL FINANCIAL RECORDS	
Personal records • Birth certificate • Social Security card • Current résumé	**Housing records** • Lease • Mortgage papers • Property tax records
Money management records • Current budget • Personal balance sheet • Cash flow statement	**Insurance records** • Insurance policies • Medical information • Claim reports
Financial services and credit records • Bank statements • Certificates of deposit • Monthly credit card statements	**Consumer purchase records** • Warranties • Receipts for major purchases • Motor vehicle registration
Tax records • Play stub, W-2 forms • Receipts for tax deductions • Income tax forms	**Investment, retirement, and estate records** • Investment account statements • Pension plan information • Will, trust information

FIGURE 16-9

Name some ways computers have made financial record keeping more efficient.

Applied Skills

Building Study Skills Ask students to prepare three multiple choice questions from the lesson to help other students review the material. Encourage students to meet in small groups to discuss the lesson and quiz amongst themselves.

Financial Life Cycle

Most people's lives follow a predictable pattern called a *life cycle*. Each stage of life is distinguished by unique characteristics, requirements, and expectations. For example, during the teen years, people are exploring career options, developing plans for independence, and evaluating future financial needs. In your twenties, you will likely train for a career, set up a household, and perhaps marry and have children.

Later in life, you may decide to obtain additional career training or make plans for paying for children's education. Then retirement plans, investing, and estate planning will likely become a priority.

Each life stage has financial matters that need attention. That attention can be provided through the development of a good financial plan. Remember, a good plan is one that is flexible and useful throughout several life stages.

Using a Financial Planner

Creating a financial plan is not a simple task. Doing your own financial planning requires time, information, and patience. Financial planners are professionals who can help you. Qualified financial planners must study and pass examinations on various topics, including investments, insurance, taxes, real estate, and estate planning.

Questions you might ask when choosing a financial planner include the following:

- What experience and training do you have?
- Are you willing to supply references from past clients?
- How are your fees determined?

Work as a TEAM

Having an organized system of financial records is important for financial planning success. As a team, (1) develop a list of financial records in addition to those in Figure 16-9, (2) discuss where you might keep various documents in addition to a home file, (3) decide how long various documents should be kept.

CHECKPOINT

List five recommended steps for financial planning.

LO 16.4.2

IMPLEMENT A FINANCIAL PLAN

Implementing your plan may involve a wide variety of actions. You may need to move your savings to an account in which you will earn a higher interest rate. You may buy a bond. Maybe you will begin to work more hours at your part-time job to earn more money.

The list of financial planning actions can seem almost endless. For your plan to

Monkey Business Images/Shutterstock.com

Talk with an older person who started saving when he or she was your age. What can you learn from this person's financial successes or mistakes?

TEACH

Relate the categories of documents in Figure 16-9 to various financial planning activities in different stages of a person's life.

Describe actions that might be taken when deciding whether to use the services of a financial planner.

Work as a TEAM

This activity can help students become more aware of the various financial documents and records they will use throughout their lives.

ONGOING ASSESSMENT

CHECKPOINT ANSWER

Five recommended steps for financial planning are (1) analyze your current financial condition, (2) develop financial goals that are responsive to your vision, (3) create your financial plan, (4) implement the plan, and (5) revise your financial plan.

THINK CRITICALLY THROUGH VISUALS

Answers will vary. Students might report that saving regularly helped someone achieve financial goals. They also might report that not having a plan has resulted in disappointment.

Different Learning Styles

Kinesthetic Learner Ask students to draw samples for two or three of the documents listed in Figure 16-9. Students should explain the information included in the document they created.

Auditory Learner Assign students to work in pairs to review this lesson. Encourage them to take turns reading the headings aloud and explaining the content.

NET KNOWLEDGE

Students select a financial planning topic and research it. Survey the class to learn whether many of them picked the same topics or whether they picked a wide variety of topics.

TEACH

Highlight some of the major actions that might be taken when implementing a financial plan.

Explain disability income insurance and unemployment insurance.

Ask students to name various sources of retirement income.

NET KNOWLEDGE

An extensive amount of financial planning information is available on the Internet. Locate a website that specializes in personal financial planning, and select a specific financial planning topic. Why is this area of financial planning of interest to you? What information did you learn about this topic? What additional answers do you need about this topic?

lead to achieving your financial goals, several common areas should be considered.

Insure Current Income

Protecting your income so that it contributes to your goals is a key financial planning action. Insurance is available that will provide an income in the event of the two most common causes of loss of income: disability and unemployment.

Disability Income Insurance To replace income that is lost when you cannot work because of an illness or injury, you can purchase *disability income insurance.* Many different disability income policies are available. Most disability income insurance will pay 60 to 70 percent of your salary while you are disabled. Before the benefits begin, there is usually a waiting period from one week to 90 days after you are disabled. Many employers provide this type of insurance.

Unemployment Insurance Unemployment is another hazard to a financial plan. To reduce the financial hardship of unemployment, most states have an *unemployment insurance* program, administered in cooperation with the federal government. This coverage provides cash payments for a limited time to people who are out of work for a reason other than illness. A local unemployment office will provide guidance to help find a new job. If no suitable job is found, you may qualify for payments to replace part of your lost wages.

Plan for Future Income

The success of any financial plan also calls for a stream of future income. Once people retire, their salaries stop, but they continue to need money to cover living expenses. Workers can ensure that they will have enough income during their retirement years through Social Security, pensions, individual retirement accounts, and annuities.

Social Security A key form of income protection comes through the federal government's Social Security system called *retirement, survivors, and disability insurance.* This part of Social Security provides pensions to retired workers and their families, death benefits to dependents of workers who die, and benefits to disabled workers and their families.

Social Security benefits are funded by payroll taxes from both workers and employers. The taxes are deducted from employees' paychecks. Employers match the amounts paid by their employees. Self-employed people, such as farmers and small business owners, pay the entire tax themselves.

When a worker retires, becomes disabled, or dies, monthly payments are made from the trust fund. The amount of benefits received depends on how long a worker was employed and how much a worker earned while employed.

Pensions A *pension* is a series of regular payments made to a retired worker under an organized plan. Some employers offer plans that provide monthly payments to retired workers. Unions often establish similar plans. To qualify under most pension plans, you must work for the same organization for a minimum number of years.

Retirement Accounts People can also develop their own retirement income plans. The most popular of these plans is the **individual retirement account (IRA)**. An IRA is a tax-sheltered retirement plan in which people can annually

Applied Skills

Communication Assign students to prepare a short written report about one of the following topics: disability income insurance, unemployment insurance, Social Security, pensions, retirement accounts, or annuities. Encourage students to use Internet and library resources to obtain additional information on their topic. Invite interested students to share one or two things they discovered about their topics.

invest earnings up to a certain amount. Contributions to traditional IRAs are tax-deductible. The investment gains are tax-deferred and the funds are taxed when they are withdrawn after age 59½. Contributions to a Roth IRA are not tax-deductible. However, all funds, including any investment gains, are tax-free when withdrawn after age 59½.

Other types of retirement accounts for self-employed workers and people who run their own businesses include the 401(k), Keogh, SIMPLE, and SEP plans. Each of these involves tax-deferred retirement income. *Tax-deferred* means the investment earnings will be taxed later, after retirement. The type of retirement plan for which you qualify will depend on your employment situation and income level.

Annuities An amount of money an insurance company pays to a person who has previously deposited money with the company is called an *annuity*. This financial agreement is an investment plan for retirement income. You pay the insurance company a certain amount of money either in a lump sum or in a series of payments. In return, the company agrees to pay you a regular income beginning at a certain age and continuing for life or for a specified number of years.

istockphoto.com/Susan Chiang

How much money per month will you need to live comfortably when you retire? Where will this money come from?

CHECKPOINT
What are common sources of income during retirement?

LO 16.4.3

REVIEW YOUR FINANCIAL PLAN

A financial plan must be flexible. View your financial plan as a changeable document. Your plan should be evaluated and adjusted on a regular basis to produce the outcomes you desire.

Revise Financial Goals

Once you have an understanding of changes in your financial or personal situation, you should consider changes in your financial goals. These goals may be short-term or long-term. They are usually stated in dollar amounts. An example of a short-term goal is "saving $1,000 in one year." This goal is simple, straightforward, and fairly short-term.

By contrast, long-term financial goals are often more complex and involve a

TEACH

Explain the process and benefits of pensions and retirement accounts.

Ask students why many people do not have adequate income when they reach retirement age.

ONGOING ASSESSMENT

CHECKPOINT ✓ANSWER

Common sources of income during retirement are Social Security, pensions, individual retirement accounts, Roth IRAs, 401(k) plans, Keogh plans, and annuities.

TEACH

Point out the importance of reviewing a financial plan on a periodic basis.

Ask students to describe situations that might create a need for a person to revise financial goals.

THINK CRITICALLY THROUGH VISUALS

Answers will vary and will depend on the income they plan to achieve and the lifestyle they hope to maintain in retirement. Students may not have thought about possible sources for this money—sources that depend in large part on their choices of employment and consistency in saving.

Portfolio Activity

Assign the Portfolio Activity for Chapter 16, available on the website for this textbook.

COLLECT Suggest that students collect their examples of financial goals and financial planning activities over a period of several days.

CREATE Remind students that their financial plan should include short-term and long-term goals.

CONNECT Point out that students need to connect visuals to something already in their portfolio or to a concept from another class.

TEACH

Point out the importance of a periodic review of a person's financial planning activities.

Explain the concept of "estate planning." Ask students to describe reasons why people share their financial resources with others through donations and charitable contributions.

ONGOING ASSESSMENT

CHECKPOINT ✓ *ANSWER*

When reviewing a financial plan, one should revise short- and long-term financial goals on a regular basis, make changes in spending and saving habits as needed, and engage in estate planning to build assets and arrange to distribute property after death.

ASSESS

Key Concepts *Answers*

1. c. pensions

2. c. using the services of a financial planner

Make Academic Connections *Answers*

3. Answers will vary, but should reflect the changing life realities and financial planning needs of persons in their 20s, 30s, 40s, 50s, 60s, and older.

4. Interviews and suggestions will vary.

longer period. These might include "owning a home by age 30."

Often, short-term goals may need to be sacrificed in order to achieve long-term ones. For example, you may have to forgo buying a bicycle in order to save for an automobile.

Review Financial Activities

Changes in your goals will require changes in spending and saving habits. Although retirement may be years away, preparing for it is a vital part of financial planning. Chances are very good that you will spend many happy and healthy years in retirement. Those years will be happier and healthier if you have an adequate supply of money.

Estate planning involves the accumulation and management of property during one's lifetime and the distribution of one's property at death. During your life you build your estate through savings, investments, and insurance. You also decide how your estate will be transferred when you die.

Remember to Save and Share

Money management and financial planning are ongoing activities. Every decision you make will affect both current spending and long-term financial security. The only way to have money in the future is to spend less than you receive. The overuse of credit and other poor spending habits are the basis for long-term financial disaster. Your budget and spending activities should also involve sharing some resources. This may involve religious donations or contributions to local and global organizations that provide food, housing, and other necessities to people in need.

CHECKPOINT ✓

What activities are involved when reviewing a financial plan?

16.4 ASSESSMENT

Key Concepts

Determine the best answer.

1. A common source of retirement income is
   - **a.** disability income insurance
   - **b.** a mortgage
   - **c.** pensions
   - **d.** unemployment insurance
2. A long-term financial goal usually involves
   - **a.** less than two years
   - **b.** buying with a credit card
   - **c.** using the services of a financial planner
   - **d.** saving over many years

Make Academic Connections

3. **Research** Use library or online research to determine common financial planning activities for different stages of life. Prepare a poster to summarize your findings for people in their 20s, 30s, 40s, 50s, 60s, and older.
4. **Oral Communication** Conduct an interview with another student. Ask that person about her or his financial goals. Suggest actions to help the person achieve those goals.

CLOSE Emphasize the importance of saving for successful money management and financial planning.

RETEACH Use Figure 16-9 to emphasize the various categories and documents of financial planning.

ENRICH Ask students to prepare a list of actions that might be considered when engaging in estate planning.

LIFE/WORK SKILLS

SOCIAL AND CROSS CULTURAL SKILLS

Effective Interviewing

As a job applicant, you will be interviewed. You will be asked questions to determine your experiences and knowledge. In contrast, your ability to interview others can be of value in several ways. Someday you may interview potential employees for a company. Or, you may interview people for information for class assignments or in work situations.

When conducting an interview to make a business decision or to obtain information, follow these guidelines.

1. Create four or five open-ended questions related to the topic to get the person talking.
2. Develop questions that cannot be answered with one or two words.
3. The best interview questions start with *why*, *what*, *when*, *where*, *how*, and *describe*.
4. Listen for major themes or key ideas. Give the respondent time to answer. Don't interrupt.
5. Use follow-up questions to obtain additional information.
6. Do not ask leading questions—ones that suggest an answer for which you are looking.

Probing and Clarifying

Two valuable interviewing techniques are probing and clarifying. Probing is a technique to obtain additional information from a respondent. Probing starts with careful questioning by the interviewer. Probing can be achieved with repeating a question. Probing phrases include:

- Anything else?
- Please tell me more.
- What do you mean by that?
- Why do you feel that way?

Clarifying is a process to get an explanation about an answer that has already been given. You want to know specifically what is meant by an answer. One clarifying technique is to ask, "What do you mean by. . ." and then repeat the respondent's exact words. Another way to clarify is to ask the respondent to provide additional information about some response that has already been given.

Professional Behavior

Whether you are the person being interviewed or you are the person conducting the interview, the situation requires a professional appearance and demeanor. Being well-groomed, dressed appropriately, and punctual are all signs of respect. It is also important to demonstrate the kinds of social skills that will be needed on the job. Shaking hands, maintaining eye contact, sitting up straight, speaking clearly, and not interrupting others are all examples.

An effective interview provides an opportunity for both parties to gain knowledge that relates to the business situation. When an interview is going well it is easy to slip into a personal conversation and provide too much information or say something inappropriate. While you want to be friendly and open, your goal should be to conduct the interview in a professional manner.

Think Critically

1. What are situations in which your ability to interview others would be useful?
2. What actions could you take to improve your interview skills?
3. Conduct an interview to obtain information about a career, company, or country. Write an essay about your experience.

Phillip Jarrell/Photodisc/Getty Images

What are some of the social skills you need to demonstrate when participating in an interview?

LIFE/WORK SKILLS

Point out the importance of developing effective interviewing skills. Explain that interviewing skills can be used to gain information in a wide variety of situations.

THINK CRITICALLY THROUGH VISUALS

Answers will vary. Students might mention punctuality, good grooming, open body language, courtesy, and politeness.

Think Critically *Answers*

1. Situations in which an ability to interview others would be useful include hiring employees; reporting stories for a newsletter, magazine, or journal; and gathering information for class assignments or work challenges.

2. To improve interviewing skills, practice interviewing people of varying ages and backgrounds. When interviewing people you know fairly well, try to discover facts about that person that you didn't know.

3. Essays will vary depending on the person interviewed and the topic selected.

Think Critically About Business *Answers*

1a. Money owed to the dentist is a liability.

1b. An automobile is an asset.

1c. Clothing is an asset.

1d. A savings account is an asset.

1e. A credit card balance is a liability.

1f. An amount due for a personal loan is a liability.

1g. 100 shares of stock are assets.

2. Answers will vary. Planning ahead and deciding what is important will help you have money for things you enjoy.

3. Answers will vary. Short-term goals are goals for the near future, such as paying back a $200 debt in six months. Long-term goals look farther into the future; for example, paying off a mortgage in 15 instead of 30 years.

4. Answers will vary, but could include things such as increasing income by finding a better paying job, getting a roommate, or foregoing nonessential expenses.

5. Chris is not following good money management because he does not have a plan for how much he spends or saves.

6a. Answers will vary. Fixed expenses could include rent, insurance, utilities, or savings.

6b. Answers will vary. Variable expenses could include food, clothing, and recreation.

6c. Answers will vary. Families with younger children might have child care expenses. Families with no children would have lower expenses in many categories, such as food and clothing.

Chapter 16 Assessment

Review Business Concepts

16.1 Personal Financial Statements

- You can manage your money wisely by planning carefully, using information to help you better understand and take action on your money matters, comparing products and prices, and making wise decisions.
- A balance sheet is a record of assets and liabilities at a point in time. Assets are items of value. Liabilities are amounts owed to others. Net worth is the difference between assets and liabilities.
- A cash flow statement is a record of cash inflows (income) and cash outflows (payments for living expenses) for a given period, such as a month.

16.2 Budgeting Techniques

- The main purposes of a budget are to help you live within your income, achieve your financial goals, buy wisely, avoid credit problems, plan for financial emergencies, and develop good money management skills. Having a written budget is an important phase of successful money management.
- Creating and using a budget involves setting financial goals, planning budget categories, maintaining financial records, and evaluating your budget.
- A successful budget will be realistic, flexible, evaluated regularly, well planned, clearly communicated to those involved, and formatted simply.

16.3 Taxes in Your Life

- The main taxes are sales, excise, real estate property, personal property, estate, inheritance, gift, Social Security, and income.
- The steps for filing a federal tax return are: (1) determine gross income, (2) calculate adjusted gross income, (3) subtract deductions, (4) determine exemptions, (5) compute taxable income, (6) calculate tax owed, and (7) make tax payments or ask for a refund or credit.
- The main sources of tax information and assistance are the IRS, online sources, printed materials, tax preparation software, and tax professionals.
- Common strategies to reduce income tax liability are home ownership, tax-exempt investments, and tax-deferred investments.

16.4 Your Financial Future

- The steps in the financial planning process are: (1) analyze your current financial condition, (2) develop financial goals, (3) create a financial plan, (4) implement the plan, and (5) evaluate and revise the plan.
- Two key areas to consider when implementing a financial plan are protecting current income and providing for future income. Current income can be protected by disability income insurance and unemployment insurance. Sources of future income during retirement include Social Security, pensions, individual retirement accounts, and annuities.
- When reviewing your financial plan, view it as a fluid, changeable document that will accommodate opportunity. You should revise financial goals as your financial or personal situation changes. Changes in your goals will require changes in spending and saving habits. Most importantly, remember to save.

Think Critically About Business

1. Identify each of the following items as an asset or a liability:
   a. Money owed to the dentist
   b. An automobile
   c. Clothing
   d. Savings account
   e. Credit card balance
   f. Amount due for a personal loan
   g. 100 shares of stock
2. "Money management means never spending, doing without things, and not having any fun." Do you agree with this statement? Explain your answer.
3. Describe the difference between short-term and long-term goals. Give two examples of each type.
4. What two actions could you take if your expenditures were consistently greater than your income?

7. A knowledge of tax laws will allow you to file your taxes correctly, without penalty. In addition, you can make financial decisions that will reduce your taxes.

8. Assuming one has an income, doing nothing about financial planning is in effect doing something, possibly spending unwisely and neglecting to save for the future.

5. Every week, Chris Thorson puts any amount he has not spent during the week into a savings account. If he needs more money than he has during a week, he withdraws it from his savings. Is Chris following a good money management plan? Explain.

6. Consider a family of four people: mother, a supermarket manager; father, a department store salesperson; and two children, ages 14 and 11.
   a. List four fixed expenses that this family would likely have each month.
   b. What are some variable expenses that they are likely to have?
   c. How are the family's expenses different from those of other families with younger children or no children?

7. Why might a person want to better understand income tax laws?

8. One financial planner has said, "Doing nothing about financial planning is equivalent to making a decision about financial planning." What do you think she meant by this?

9. How does a budget differ from a financial plan?

10. Give examples of activities that might be involved in implementing a financial plan.

11. Some people claim that living by a budget is too structured and restrictive. That is, they do not like to live such a planned and strict economic life. What would you say to those individuals who have that point of view in order to convince them that budgets can be helpful to everyone?

12. Tell in your own words how people's financial goals change throughout their life cycle.

13. List some items that might be a want for one person but a need for someone else.

Develop Your Business Language

Match the terms listed with the definitions.

14. The amount of money you plan to use for a certain budget category.
15. A tax deduction for the taxpayer, a spouse, and each dependent.
16. Living costs involving differing amounts each time.
17. The financial statement that reports net wages and other income along with spending for a given period.
18. The amount on which taxes are calculated.
19. Accumulation and management of property during one's lifetime and the distribution of one's property at death.
20. Costs that occur regularly and are for the same amount each time.
21. An amount subtracted directly from taxes owed.
22. Items of value.
23. Earnings from dividends, interest, and rent.
24. A tax-sheltered retirement plan in which people can annually invest earnings up to a certain amount. The earnings contributed and interest earned are tax-free until the funds are withdrawn.
25. The day-to-day financial activities associated with using limited income to satisfy your unlimited needs and wants.
26. The difference between a person's or family's assets and liabilities.
27. An amount that reduces taxable income.
28. Money from wages, salary, commission, fees, tips, and bonuses.
29. A difference between actual spending and planned spending.
30. A report that summarizes your current financial condition, acknowledges your financial needs, and sets a direction for your future financial activities.
31. A charge imposed by a government to finance public services.

KEY TERMS

a. allowance
b. budget variance
c. cash flow statement
d. earned income
e. estate planning
f. exemption
g. financial plan
h. fixed expenses
i. individual retirement account (IRA)
j. investment income
k. money management
l. net worth
m. personal assets
n. tax
o. tax credit
p. tax deduction
q. taxable income
r. variable expenses

9. A budget is a plan for saving and spending income that will help a person or family live within its income and achieve financial goals. A financial plan summarizes one's current financial condition, acknowledges financial needs, and sets a direction for future financial activities. A budget helps manage day-to-day decisions, while a financial plan guides an individual into the future.

10. Examples include meeting with a financial planner, insuring current income, planning for future income, moving money into accounts that will better meet financial goals, and making employment and education decisions.

11. Students might explain that reckless spending and sporadic saving will make people less financially secure and less able to purchase the things they want.

12. Students should be able to describe how financial goals might change throughout a person's lifetime, from saving for college, to purchasing a home, to supporting a family, to saving for retirement.

13. Answers will vary. An example of something that is a want for one person and a need for another would be a professional athlete's jersey that is a need for the athlete, but a want for a fan. A high-powered computer is a necessity for a graphic design business, but a luxury item for a teenager who wants to play video games.

Develop Your Business Language *Answers*

14. a. allowance
15. f. exemption
16. r. variable expenses
17. c. cash flow statement
18. q. taxable income
19. e. estate planning
20. h. fixed expenses
21. o. tax credit
22. m. personal assets
23. j. investment income
24. i. individual retirement account (IRA)
25. k. money management
26. l. net worth
27. p. tax deduction
28. d. earned income
29. b. budget variance
30. g. financial plan
31. n. tax

Make Academic Connections *Answers*

32. Local real estate websites with home descriptions and prices in your area and the Kelley Blue Book website are possible resources.

33. Findings will vary depending on sources used.

34. The Gage family's owner's equity is $102,100. They could increase their net worth by paying down their debt on mortgages and other loans or by increasing their income or savings.

35. Findings will vary.

36. Summaries will vary.

37. Flowcharts will vary.

38. Tables will vary.

39. Summaries will vary.

40. Summaries will vary.

41. Tables will vary.

42. Spreadsheets will vary depending on when the assignment is completed.

43. Tables will vary.

Make Your Case *Answers*

44. Answers will vary. Students might suggest that Joan should begin a consistent savings plan to accumulate a down payment on a house. She should invest her savings wisely so that her future down payment fund grows steadily. She should pay her car loan and college loan on time in order to establish a good credit rating.

45. When Joan finally goes to the bank seeking a mortgage loan, she might want to prepare a personal balance sheet and cash flow statement to demonstrate her financial health. She will also need to be able to provide the potential lender with any financial records needed to process the loan application, such as payroll stubs or copies of past tax returns.

46. Summaries will vary, but should reflect an understanding of basic money management principles.

Make Academic Connections

32. Economics Use print ads and online research to determine the current value of various assets such as homes, motor vehicles, jewelry, antiques, and rare coins.

33. Culture Conduct research using personal interviews and other sources to determine the main assets (possessions) of typical households in other countries.

34. Math The Gage family's assets total $268,400. Their total liabilities are $166,300. What is the amount of their owner's equity? What actions could they take to increase their net worth?

35. Technology Conduct an online search for budget guidelines suggested for various categories of spending such as food, housing, transportation, clothing, health care, and others.

36. Research Locate online information about available money management apps. Prepare a brief written summary comparing the features of different apps.

37. Visual Art Create a flowchart to communicate the five steps of the financial planning process.

38. Research Conduct research to identify various professionals who might help you with your financial planning in the future. Prepare a summary table reporting the name, title, training and background, area of specialization, and cost of services for various financial planners.

39. Law Obtain information about recent changes in Social Security taxes and benefits. Prepare a two- to three-paragraph summary.

40. Research Locate a copy of a budget or financial report for your school, church, city government, or a public company from at least five years ago, as well as a copy of the current budget for the same entity. Compare the two budgets. Prepare a brief summary comparing assets, liabilities, and net income. Discuss what factors may have caused these differences.

41. Economics Interview fellow students, your parents, or other adults who are employed. Gather information about the deductions that are taken from their paychecks. Prepare a table listing the various deductions. Indicate which deductions are required and which are optional.

42. Personal Finance Assume you have been given a three-year-old car as a gift. Research the monthly costs associated with owning a car. Include items such as insurance, license, local annual use taxes, cost of gasoline based on 10,000 miles per year, and regular maintenance costs. Use a spreadsheet to present your findings.

43. Culture Select one city each in North America, South America, Europe, and Australia. Conduct online research to determine the per-person cost of an afternoon out with your friends in each city. Use the current exchange rate to convert the costs to U.S. dollars. Include items such as transportation, lunch, a movie, and a music download. Present your findings in a table.

Make Your Case

Joan Leitzel just graduated from college and got her first job as a speech therapist. Joan wants to make sure she manages her income wisely so that she can be independent and eventually buy a house on her own. She lives with her parents now, so her only expenses are payments on a college loan and an auto loan.

44. What advice would you give Joan if she wants to buy a house in the future?

45. When she eventually goes to the bank for a loan, how should Joan organize her financial information?

46. Write a short summary of your suggested actions for Joan. Also discuss what information she might need when facing new financial decisions in the future.

Interactions and Connections

Talk with friends, family members, or others in your community about their money management activities. What are their main budgeting concerns? How do they cope with these? What actions do they take to save money for the future? What types of investments do they recommend?

Presentation Management—Team Event

This event will assess your use of current desktop technologies and software to prepare and deliver an effective multimedia presentation.

You will design a computer-generated multimedia presentation. You have 15 minutes for preparation and setup. The presentation will last a minimum of seven minutes and a maximum of 10 minutes. Up to five minutes will be allowed for questions from the judges. The participants must make effective use of current multimedia technology in the presentation. In preparation for the presentation, participants should use space, color, and text as design factors. No VCR or laserdisc may be used in the presentation. Charts and other graphics should be used in the presentation. Participants are responsible for securing a release form from any individual whose name, photograph, or other information is included in the presentation.

You will prepare a presentation for middle school students that encourages saving money for future purchases. Your presentation should include interactive activities with your middle school audience. The following concepts must be addressed:

- The Rule of 72 and the advantages of saving over using credit for major purchases
- Savings options with different rates of return
- The role of government agencies that insure financial institutions
- The relationship between risk and financial return or reward
- Time commitment for different types of savings and liquidity

Performance Indicators Evaluated

- Demonstrate knowledge of multimedia software and components.
- Demonstrate effective oral communication skills.
- Apply technical skills to create a multimedia presentation that enhances the oral presentation.

You will be evaluated for your

- Knowledge of the topic
- Organized presentation of the topic
- Confidence, quality of voice, and eye contact
- Relationship of the topic to business strategy

For more detailed information about performance indicators, go to the BPA website.

Think Critically

1. What does liquidity of an investment mean?
2. Which investments involve greater risk?
3. Why should middle school students start saving now?
4. How does the Rule of 72 work?

www.bpa.org

Interactions and Connections

Answers will vary. Offer suggestions for how students should report their findings.

WINNING EDGE

Presentation Management—Team Event

This activity offers students an opportunity to use technology to develop a visual presentation. Encourage students to carefully integrate visuals that effectively enhance the content of their presentation. High school students have the opportunity to teach the financial concept of savings to middle school students—a great learning experience for both groups.

Think Critically *Answers*

1. Liquidity means how readily the investment can be exchanged for cash.

2. Futures and collectibles involve greater risk. Any investment that is not insured involves greater risk.

3. Middle school students need savings for college, automobiles, and other large future purchases.

4. The Rule of 72 determines how long it takes an investment to double by dividing 72 by the interest rate. An investment earning 8 percent would double in value in 9 years.

CHAPTER OVERVIEW

This chapter introduces and explains various financial institutions and banking services commonly used by consumers.

17.1 Banks and Other Financial Institutions

The banking system and discussion of financial institutions are the focus of this lesson.

17.2 Financial Services and Electronic Banking

Savings, payments, loans, and other financial services are presented in this lesson.

17.3 Checks and Payment Methods

This lesson covers transferring funds using checks and other payment systems.

Chapter 17 Banking and Financial Services

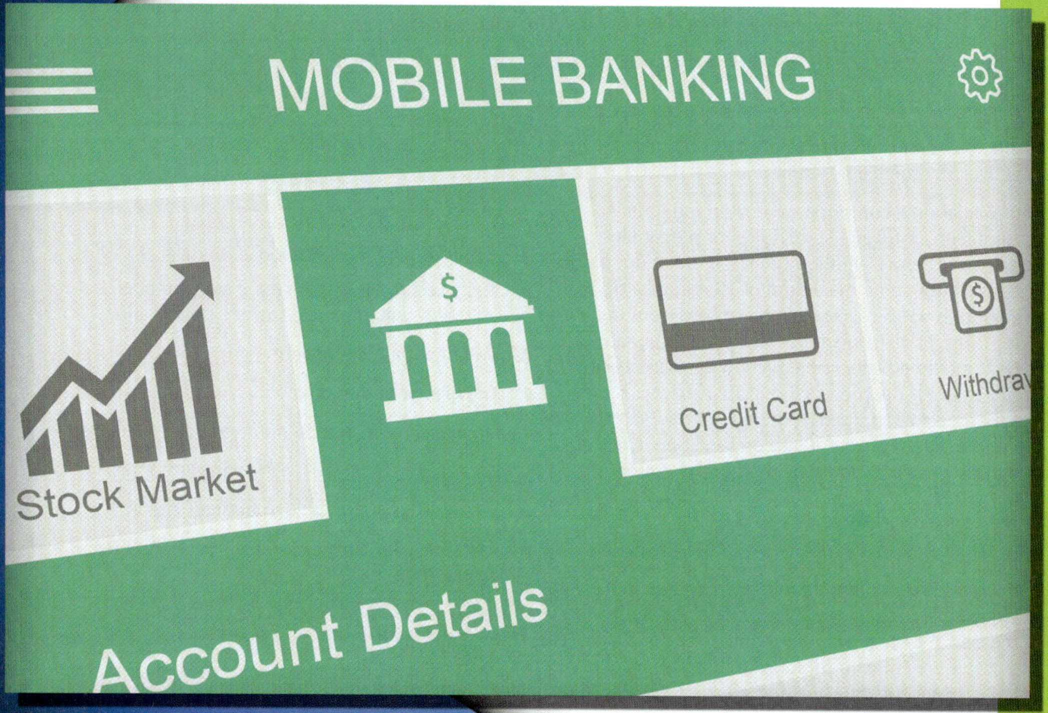

iStockphoto.com/alexsl

17.1 Banks and Other Financial Institutions

17.2 Financial Services and Electronic Banking

17.3 Checks and Payment Methods

424 **Chapter 17** | Banking and Financial Services

Instructor Resources

- Activities and Study Guide IE
- Chapter and Unit Tests IE
- Lesson Plans
- PowerPoint Presentation
- Cognero Test, Ch. 17

Student Resources

Activities and Study Guide
www.cengage.com/swep/pob9e
- Portfolio Activity

PLANNING A CAREER IN . . .
BANKING

The banking and financial services industry offers many career opportunities. Numerous financial workers are employed in commercial banks, specialized banks, savings and loan associations, credit unions, and finance companies. Work activities in the financial services industry range from serving customers and researching economic trends to planning marketing activities for financial institutions.

Related Job Titles

- **Branch Manager**
- **Teller**
- **Loan Officer**
- **Customer Service Representative**
- **Financial Services Sales Agent**
- **Financial Manager**
- **Information Processing Manager**
- **Economist**

When working in the banking industry, you will encounter various tasks, depending on your position. Tellers process daily customer transactions, receiving deposits or loan payments. Bank officers, such as loan department managers, meet with people applying for credit. These interactions with borrowers can involve auto loans, education loans, or small business loans.

The marketing department of a bank communicates services available and attempts to expand the customer base. Advertising, personal selling, and other promotional activities are used to maintain and enhance customer satisfaction. When working with various target markets or in international banking, you will likely use your foreign language skills.

Analyze Career Opportunities in . . .
BANKING

Use library and Internet resources to learn more about careers in banking. Choose one of the job titles listed in the box above and answer the following questions.

1. What is the employment outlook for careers in this field?
2. Is this a career that interests you? Describe how you might use your talents, abilities, and skills in this career.

What it's like to work as a . . . Bank Economist

Each morning, Ken Li goes online to see how various economic factors are affecting interest rates. He knows that when money is more expensive, borrowing by businesses and consumers declines. But if interest rates are lower, the use of credit will likely increase. This additional borrowing can result in higher earnings for banks and economic expansion.

Changing interest rates are just one area of research for Ken, who works for a bank with offices in 23 states. Today, he must also investigate current trends for employment, consumer spending, and retail sales. These economic indicators provide managers with information to better plan strategies for their banking organizations.

Since starting in the banking industry, Ken has observed two important trends. First, technology has improved many aspects of the business. Today, he is able to obtain better and faster data. Second, banks continually encounter changing government regulations.

What about you? What aspects of Ken's job sound interesting to you?

PLANNING A CAREER IN . . .
BANKING AND FINANCIALS SERVICES

Competition and technology are affecting the banking industry. Many large banks have taken over smaller competitors. In addition, computers and other automation systems are affecting needed skills and employment opportunities in this industry.

What About You?
Answer

Answers will vary. Some students will express interest in doing research and working as part of a team.

Analyze Career Opportunities *Answers*
Student answers will vary depending on when the assignment is completed and individual interests.

Additional Career Information

Encourage students to investigate careers they find interesting and explore unfamiliar careers. Two resources for additional career information are the *Occupational Outlook Handbook,* an online publication (www.bls.gov/oco) of the U.S. Bureau of Labor Statistics, and the O*NET Resource Center (www.onetcenter.org) developed by the U.S. Department of Labor. Information about specific careers and jobs can be used to demonstrate the relevance of skills learned in this course.

Focus on REAL LIFE

This situation can be the foundation for a basic discussion of banks and financial services.

TEACH

Ask students what is meant by "the banking system."

Explain the basic role of the Federal Reserve System in our economy.

THINK CRITICALLY THROUGH VISUALS

The Federal Reserve System supervises and regulates member banks and helps banks serve the public efficiently.

Life-Span Plan Answers

Answers will vary. Students should point out that people need a reliable banking system as a place to store their savings and obtain credit when necessary.

17.1 Banks and Other Financial Institutions

Learning Outcomes

17.1.1 Explain the purpose of the Federal Reserve System.

17.1.2 List the types of financial institutions.

17.1.3 Discuss factors for selecting a financial institution.

Key Terms

Federal Reserve System (Fed) 427

commercial bank 428

credit union 429

Federal Deposit Insurance Corporation (FDIC) 430

Focus on REAL LIFE

"I finally got a job for the summer," Gerri told Mike. "I can save money and go on that trip."

"Where are you going to save your money?" asked Mike.

"At home, of course," responded Gerri.

"Are you kidding?" Mike went on to say. "That's dangerous! Your money can get lost, or you might spend it before summer comes."

"Well, what should I do with my money?" asked Gerri.

"Deposit it in a bank," answered Mike.

"Will my money be safer in a bank?" asked Gerri.

"For sure," said Mike. "Banks and other financial institutions provide safety and growth for your money. Plus they help their customers in many ways with other financial matters."

"You're kidding! I guess it's time I learn about banking," Gerri responded.

LO 17.1.1

THE BANKING SYSTEM

Some people do not think of a bank as a business. However, banks operate in much the same way as stores, factories, and other companies. As a business, a bank sells services such as checking and payment accounts, savings accounts, loans, and investments.

Banks are regulated more strictly than most other businesses. If a business fails, some people lose money. If a bank fails, thousands of people are affected.

Dgrilla/Shutterstock.com

What is the purpose of the Federal Reserve?

Life-Span Plan

Do you believe that people need a safe and reliable banking system to achieve their life-span goals? Describe how you expect to use banks and other financial institutions to reach the goals you set in your life-span plan.

Different Learning Styles

Specific Learning Disability (SLD) Motivate students to learn more about banking, money, and financial activities by pointing out the connection between the Federal Reserve System and the money they use every day.

The Federal Reserve System

Most banks attempt to attract the deposits of customers. However, as an individual, you cannot open an account in a Federal Reserve Bank because it is a *bank for banks*.

The federal government set up the **Federal Reserve System (Fed)** to supervise and regulate member banks and to help banks serve the public efficiently. All national banks are required to join the Federal Reserve System, and state banks may join. Banks that join the system are known as *member banks*. The United States is divided into 12 Federal Reserve districts, with a central Federal Reserve Bank in each district, as shown in Figure 17-1.

Federal Reserve Activities

A Federal Reserve Bank serves member banks and the economy in several ways. One service provided by the Fed is the holding of *reserves*. Banks cannot lend all of the money they receive from customers. They are required to keep a part of the money deposited by customers on deposit with the Federal Reserve System. The Fed holds these deposits in case the banks need additional funds to meet daily customer demand.

As a result, a bank will lend only a certain percentage of deposited funds. It keeps the rest in reserve. This regulation is designed to help the banking system and the economy operate efficiently and to protect deposits.

For example, suppose a customer deposits $1,000 and the bank is required to hold 15 percent of all deposits in reserve. This means the bank can lend $850, which is 85 percent of the new deposit (85% × $1,000 = $850).

Work as a TEAM

Banks are considered one of the most important types of businesses in any economy. Prepare a list of ways in which the banking system affects (1) businesses, (2) consumers, and (3) workers.

Federal Reserve Districts

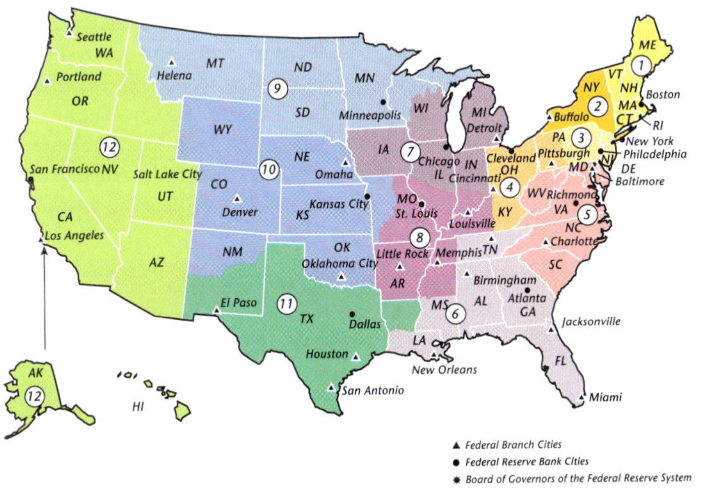

Source: Federal Reserve System

FIGURE 17-1
Which Federal Reserve Regional Bank serves banks in your community?

Work as a TEAM

This activity can help students better understand the role of banking and financial services in an economy.

TEACH

Explain how reserves create additional funds in the economy.

Describe the importance of the clearing process for checks and other payments.

▸ **Figure 17-1** ***ANSWER***

Answers will vary depending on where your school is located.

Applied Skills

Geography Explain that the Federal Reserve district identification appears to the left of Washington's image on the face of the one-dollar Federal Reserve note. Use several one-dollar bills from different Federal Reserve Banks to demonstrate that money from several districts is likely to be in circulation in your area.

TEACH

Highlight the banking activities that can promote economic growth.

ONGOING ASSESSMENT

CHECKPOINT ✓ANSWER

The Federal Reserve System was created by the federal government to supervise and regulate member banks and to help banks serve the public efficiently by holding reserves and clearing checks.

TEACH

Use Figure 17-2 to provide an overview of the main categories and types of financial institutions.

Describe the major services provided by a commercial bank.

▸ Figure 17-2 ANSWER

Answers will vary depending on which institutions students have done business with in the past.

Another service of the Federal Reserve System is electronic transfer of funds for checks and other payments. *Clearing* refers to the process of making payments among different banks. The Fed electronically processes millions of payments each day, making sure that the correct amounts are added to and subtracted from the appropriate accounts.

Banking and the Economy

The actions of the banking system affect you in many ways. Several million people work in banks, savings and loan associations, credit unions, and other financial institutions. The following activities are just some of the ways that individuals, businesses, and governments use banking services.

- Borrow money to build roads
- Borrow money to buy seeds for crops
- Deposit cash from business operations
- Finance a college education
- Invest for retirement
- Obtain a mortgage
- Process credit card transactions
- Save for a vacation

The savings you and others deposit make banking services possible. Deposits do not remain idle in bank vaults. They are put to work. When you and others deposit money in a bank, you are helping to create jobs and economic growth that benefit your community and your society.

CHECKPOINT ✓

What is the main purpose of the Federal Reserve System?

LO 17.1.2

TYPES OF FINANCIAL INSTITUTIONS

When someone says, "I'm going to the bank," the person might actually mean a credit union or a cash machine. There are many types of financial institutions that provide a wide range of products and services. Figure 17-2 shows how financial institutions are classified.

Deposit Institutions

Deposit institutions, also called *depository intermediaries*, accept deposits from people and businesses and use them to finance their business.

Commercial Banks The most common way for a bank to be organized is as a **commercial bank**. Commercial banks are often called *full-service banks* because they offer a wide range of financial services. Commercial banks offer checking accounts, provide savings accounts, make loans to individuals and to businesses, and offer other services. In large banks, different departments may handle these services. There may be a loan department, a trust department, a real estate department, and an investment department. Many banks

FINANCIAL INSTITUTIONS	
DEPOSIT INSTITUTIONS	**NON-DEPOSIT INSTITUTIONS**
• Commercial banks • Savings and loan associations • Mutual savings banks • Credit unions	• Life insurance companies • Investment companies • Consumer finance companies • Mortgage companies • Check cashing outlets • Pawnshops

FIGURE 17-2

Which of these types of institutions have you done business with?

Different Learning Styles

Print Learner After students read the information about banking and the economy, ask them to use their own words to explain how banking services contribute to the economy of a country. Encourage discussion and ask for other examples of the ways that individuals, businesses, and governments use banking services.

have full-service branch offices in shopping centers and grocery stores.

Savings and Loan Associations Traditionally, a savings and loan association (S&L) specialized in savings accounts and making loans for home mortgages. More recently, these institutions have expanded their services. They have become more like banks. Today, many S&Ls use the words *savings bank* in their names.

Mutual Savings Banks A *mutual savings bank* is a savings bank that is owned by, and operated for the benefit of, its depositors. The profits are distributed in proportion to the amount of business each participant does with the company. While a mutual savings bank provides a variety of services, it is organized mainly for savings and home loans. Mutual savings banks are located mainly in the northeastern United States.

Credit Unions A user-owned, not-for-profit, cooperative financial institution is called a **credit union**. People in the same company, government agency, labor union, or profession often form credit unions. Serving members only, credit unions accept savings deposits and make loans for a variety of purposes. When people deposit money in a credit union, they become members because deposits are considered partial ownership in the credit union. Today, credit unions also offer a wide range of financial services. The National Credit Union Administration (NCUA), a federal agency, regulates these financial institutions.

iStockphoto.com/YinYang

What is unique about a credit union?

Non-Deposit Financial Institutions

The other major category of financial institutions is *non-deposit institutions* or *non-depository intermediaries*. They do not take or hold deposits. They earn their money selling specific services or policies.

Life Insurance Companies People commonly buy life insurance to provide financial security for their dependents. Besides protection, many life insurance companies also offer financial services such as investments. Through careful investing in new and existing companies, life insurance companies help to expand business in the economy.

Investment Companies People can choose investment opportunities for long-term growth of their money through investment companies. Many investors own shares of one of the more than 60,000 mutual funds worldwide. Investment companies make these mutual funds available.

Consumer Finance Companies A business that specializes in making loans for long-lasting or durable goods, such as cars and refrigerators, and for financial emergencies is a consumer finance company. Because consumer finance companies make loans, they are a part of the financial services industry. Unlike banks and other financial institutions, consumer finance companies do not accept savings deposits.

TEACH

Describe the services provided by savings and loan associations, mutual savings banks, and credit unions. Ask students to describe their experiences with various financial institutions.

Explain how non-deposit financial institutions differ from deposit institutions.

Contrast the services offered by life insurance companies, investment companies, and consumer finance companies.

THINK CRITICALLY THROUGH VISUALS

Unlike banks, credit unions are user-owned, not-for-profit, cooperative financial institutions that serve members only.

Applied Skills

Communication Assign students to create a poster or computer presentation to communicate the various types of financial institutions used by consumers. Consider allowing students to work in pairs.

TEACH

Caution students about using check-cashing outlets and pawnshops. Also warn students about the high costs of payday loan companies and rent-to-own businesses.

ONGOING ASSESSMENT

CHECKPOINT ✓ANSWER

Examples of non-deposit financial institutions include life insurance companies, investment companies, consumer finance companies, mortgage companies, check-cashing outlets, and pawnshops.

THINK CRITICALLY THROUGH VISUALS

Banks are safe places for valuables because their well-guarded vaults provide more security than a home. Most bank deposits are insured up to $250,000 by the Federal Deposit Insurance Corporation (FDIC).

TEACH

Provide an overview of the factors to consider when selecting a financial institution.

Explain the major services offered by various financial institutions.

Point out the main function of the Federal Deposit Insurance Corporation.

Mortgage Companies Buying a home is an important activity in society. Mortgage companies, along with other financial institutions, provide loans for buying a home or other real estate.

Check-Cashing Outlets People who do not have bank accounts may use check-cashing outlets (CCOs) to cash paychecks and to obtain other financial services. CCOs offer many services such as electronic tax filing, prepaid debit cards, money orders, private postal boxes, utility bill payment, and the sale of transit cards. The services provided at a CCO are usually more expensive than those at other financial institutions.

Pawnshops Pawnshops make loans based on the value of some tangible object, such as jewelry or other valuable items. Pawnshops commonly charge higher fees than other financial institutions and should usually be avoided.

iStockphoto.com/Depo881

Why is a bank a safe place for your valuables? Are there any risks?

CHECKPOINT ✓
What are some examples of non-deposit financial institutions?

LO 17.1.3

SELECTING A FINANCIAL INSTITUTION

To obtain the best value for your financial services dollar, comparison shop. You should think about the services offered, safety, convenience, fees and charges, and restrictions.

Services Offered

As financial institutions offer additional financial services, your choices may become confusing. There are four basic types of banking services you will use.

1. Savings accounts
2. Checking and payment accounts
3. Loans and other credit plans
4. Other services, such as safe deposit boxes and investment advice

As you work through the marketplace maze, it is important for you to determine which banking services meet your needs. Do not be attracted by fancy financial product names or flashy services that you might never need or use.

Safety

The federal agency that helps to regulate banks and other financial institutions is the **Federal Deposit Insurance Corporation (FDIC)**. It protects depositors' money in case of the failure of a bank or financial institution that it regulates. The FDIC insures all accounts in the same name at each bank up to an amount of $250,000. Although the FDIC is a government agency, banks provide money for its operation. Almost 99 percent of all banks are FDIC members.

The National Credit Union Administration (NCUA) regulates credit unions.

Different Learning Abilities

English Language Learners (ELL) Obtain translations for the list of financial services presented on this page. Use these translations to reinforce these concepts in both English and other dominant languages used by students. Some banks provide brochures about services in several languages, and many banks offer a Spanish-language version of their website.

NCUA insures a depositor's funds, through its National Credit Union Share Insurance Fund. Some state-chartered credit unions use a private insurance program.

Although most banks and financial institutions have federal deposit insurance, do not assume that this is the case at every financial institution. Make sure the institution where you keep your savings is insured.

Convenience

Do you want online banking services? Do you want branch offices near your home or work? These are some of the factors you will need to think about as you decide about convenience. In the past, more convenience would usually mean higher costs. Today, however, online banking has resulted in lower costs for many consumers.

Fees and Charges

Financial services have costs. Compare your needs with the price you pay. Remember, seemingly low fees for using an ATM or maintaining a checking account can add up to hundreds of dollars in a short time.

Restrictions

Costs are not always measured in dollars. If you must keep $500 on deposit to get "free" checking you may be losing the chance to earn interest on those funds in a savings account.

If you must keep money on deposit for two years to earn a higher rate, you are restricted from using those funds for some unplanned purpose. Always balance your needs with the conditions imposed upon you. When you are not satisfied, shop around to compare the services and costs of other financial institutions.

CHECKPOINT ✓
What factors should be considered when selecting a financial institution?

17.1 ASSESSMENT

Key Concepts

Determine the best answer.

1. The financial institution most likely to charge the highest rate for a loan would be a
   a. bank
   b. pawnshop
   c. credit union
   d. mortgage company
2. If deposit insurance is most important to you when selecting a financial institution, you are most concerned with
   a. safety
   b. convenience
   c. services
   d. fees

Make Academic Connections

3. **Research** Conduct library and online research about the Federal Reserve System. When and why did it start? What are the main responsibilities of the Fed?
4. **Technology** Visit the website of the Federal Deposit Insurance Corporation to obtain current information on deposit insurance. What other information on the FDIC website would be valuable to consumers?
5. **Math** A person is required to keep a $300 balance for a free checking account. What would be the amount of lost interest over five years if the person could earn 4 percent on savings in another type of account?

TEACH

Describe the insurance coverage available for savings accounts through the FDIC and the NCUA.

Ask students to name actions that might be taken to reduce the fees paid for various financial services.

ONGOING ASSESSMENT

CHECKPOINT ✓ANSWER

Factors to consider when selecting a financial institution include the services offered, safety, convenience, fees and charges, and restrictions.

ASSESS

Key Concepts *Answers*

1. b. pawnshop
2. a. safety

Make Academic Connections *Answers*

3. The Federal Reserve System was created in 1913 to provide a safer, more flexible, and more stable monetary and financial system. The main responsibilities of the Fed are to conduct monetary policy, supervise and regulate the banking industry, and provide financial services to depository institutions.
4. Findings will vary. The FDIC website includes information, alerts, and advice for consumers. The site has information about specific topics such as identity theft and privacy.
5. Lost interest over five years is $60 ($300 × 0.04 × 5).

RETEACH Review the main functions of the Federal Reserve System.

CLOSE Ask students to name the main types of financial institutions.

ENRICH Ask students to describe situations when a person might use various non-deposit financial institutions.

Focus on REAL LIFE

This feature can help students become more aware of expensive banking fees.

TEACH

Ask students to name various financial services that they or family members use.

Provide an overview of the purpose of savings and payment services.

THINK CRITICALLY THROUGH VISUALS

To reduce or eliminate bank fees, shop for banks with the lowest fees, use only ATMs affiliated with your bank that charge no fees or, if this is not possible, use ATMs only in emergencies.

17.2 Financial Services and Electronic Banking

Learning Outcomes

17.2.1 Identify the financial services used by consumers.

17.2.2 Explain types of checking accounts.

17.2.3 Describe electronic banking activities.

Key Terms

safe deposit box 434

service charge 434

debit card 436

Focus on REAL LIFE

"Sixteen dollars for ATM fees!" exclaimed Hans George as he opened his bank statement. "I guess the cost of those cash withdrawals adds up fast!"

Hans George has a routine of using his cash card at an automatic teller machine several times a week. He really likes the convenience of obtaining cash.

Hans also finds that when getting cash is easy, he easily overspends. While automatic teller machines are convenient and easy to use, you must also consider fees and the potential for impulse buying. In recent years, ATM fees have risen from nothing to $2 or $3 per withdrawal.

How much can cash machine transaction fees cost? If you pay two $2 transaction fees a week, you will pay $208 in fees over the course of a year.

LO 17.2.1

TYPES OF FINANCIAL SERVICES

Financial institutions provide services for various personal and business activities. The services you use depend on your needs.

Savings Services

Safe storage of funds for future use is a common need. One of the main services that financial institutions offer is accepting money from customers for safekeeping. A range of savings plans are available for this purpose.

Payment Services

The ability to transfer money to others is necessary for daily business activities. Types of payment services include checking accounts, debit cards, online payments, automatic withdrawals, and peer-to-peer (P2P) payments.

Thinkstock/Stockbyte/Getty Images

What can you do to reduce or eliminate bank fees?

Different Learning Styles

Auditory Learner Encourage students to review the types of financial services discussed in this lesson by listening to a partner reading aloud. Suggest that students listen without taking notes.

Lending Services

Most people, businesses, and governments borrow money at some time. A business may want to borrow money to build a new warehouse or buy products to resell. Individuals may borrow to buy a car or pay college tuition. Banks make most of their income from the interest they charge on loans.

Banks offer many types of lending services. These include auto loans, business loans, and mortgages. Credit cards allow individuals to buy items without immediately paying the cash. When paying with a credit card, you are borrowing money from the bank.

Work as a TEAM

Banking services continually change as a result of technology. As a team, create a written description of recently developed and possible new methods that banks might use to offer savings, loans, and other financial services.

Electronic Banking

Electronic funds transfer (EFT) refers to the use of computers and other technology for banking activities. Electronic banking services include the use of automatic teller machines (ATMs), point-of-sale transactions, direct deposit, and automatic bill payment. Online banking

Business Insight

Emerging Technology for Banking Services

Technology is creating new and expanded financial services to enhance service opportunities, convenience, and security for bank customers.

Banking Apps Most financial institutions allow access to services through smartphone apps. Some app customers may authorize a person from their phone contacts to obtain money. The recipient is sent a *cash code* for withdrawal of an approved amount. Some banks also offer a credit card "lock and limit" app for improved security. This feature can block overseas transactions where the card isn't present.

Prepaid Debit Cards Prepaid debit cards are increasing in popularity. They allow *loading* (adding funds) by cash, check, direct deposit, online transfer, smartphone check photo, or credit card cash advance. These cards are replacing traditional banking services for some consumers. However, many costly fees are associated with prepaid debit cards, such as an activation fee, a monthly fee, a transaction fee, a cash-withdrawal (ATM) fee, a balance-inquiry fee, a deposit fee, a dormancy fee, and others. The use of prepaid cards may result in reduced debt since the debit card can help control spending and reduce buying on credit.

Peer-to-Peer Payments Direct transfer of funds from person to person is more popular than ever. Instead of requiring a debit card, credit card, or bank account information, peer-to-peer (P2P) payments utilize e-mail or a secure website. The fee for a P2P payment may range from less than a dollar to a percentage of the transaction amount.

Biometric Banking Security Biometry, the analysis of biological data, is now being used for banking safety. Fingerprint verification can authorize a payment when the customer places a finger on a scanner. With iris scanning, the unique features of a person's eyeball are used as a bank account "password." With a voice-activated system, customers may obtain an account balance or transfer money. Face recognition compares two images of a face to authorize bank transactions.

Think Critically

1. What concerns might be associated with these emerging banking activities?
2. Conduct an online search to obtain additional information on new technology being used for banking transactions. Choose one technology and write a short report.

Work as a TEAM

Encourage students to think of ways to use existing and future technology for delivering additional types of online banking services.

TEACH

Ask students to name reasons that individuals, businesses, and governments use lending services.

Provide an overview of the main electronic banking services.

Business Insight

This feature discusses several recent technological innovations and trends in the banking industry.

Think Critically
Answers

1. Answers will vary. Privacy, personal information, and potential computer crime issues may be mentioned.
2. Reports will vary. Encourage students to find additional information about the items in this feature.

Portfolio Activity

Assign the Portfolio Activity for Chapter 17, located on the website for this textbook.

COLLECT Offer suggestions to help students locate information and images related to electronic banking services.

CREATE Remind students the flowchart needs to communicate the flow of electronic funds.

CONNECT Point out that students need to connect visuals to something already in their portfolio or to a concept from another class.

TEACH

Describe items that might be kept in a safe deposit box.

Ask students to describe situations when investment advice and trust management services might be used.

ONGOING ASSESSMENT

CHECKPOINT ✓ANSWER

The main financial services used by consumers are savings services, payment services, lending services, electronic banking, storage of valuables, investment advice, and management of trusts.

TEACH

Provide an overview of the main types of checking accounts.

THINK CRITICALLY THROUGH VISUALS

Online banking makes managing personal finances more convenient because it can be done at any time of the day or night from the safety of one's own home. Records of financial transactions can be printed out and balances can be checked whenever desired.

and mobile apps have expanded customer access to financial services.

Storage of Valuables

Banks offer **safe deposit boxes** for storage of valuables. Because these safe deposit boxes are in secure areas, they are very safe places to keep jewelry, rare coins, investment certificates, birth records, a list of insurance policies, and other valuable documents.

Only you or someone to whom you have given the right to open the box may open it. Not even a bank has the right to open your safe deposit box unless it is ordered to do so by a court. Safe deposit boxes are available for rental and come in a variety of sizes.

Investment Advice

Many financial institutions help customers by offering financial advice and investment services. Banks can assist customers with decisions about buying a home, offer tips on money management, and help customers exchange U.S. funds for foreign currency.

Most banks offer advice on investments. This involves savings that are put to work to earn more money. Types of investments include government bonds, stocks, and mutual funds.

Management of Trusts

Many banks manage investments on behalf of customers. When they do this, the money or other property that is turned over for the bank to manage is said to be held in *trust*. This service can be offered through a trust company or through trust departments in banks.

Trusts are used by people of all ages. They are especially useful for very young people and for some elderly people. A young person who inherits money may not have the skill and experience to manage it wisely. Elderly people who are ill may ask the trust department of a bank to manage their money. The bank makes investments and keeps the customers informed about what is happening to their money.

CHECKPOINT ✓

What are the main financial services used by consumers?

LO 17.2.2

TYPES OF CHECKING ACCOUNTS

While fewer checks are written each year, a checking account is usually required for other banking services such as a debit card. Three types of checking accounts are most common.

Regular Checking Accounts

If you write a lot of checks each month, consider a regular checking account. A **service charge** is a fee a bank charges for handling a checking account. With most banks, there is no service charge for a regular checking account as long as you maintain a certain minimum balance. This amount varies and is often $300 or higher.

racorn/Shutterstock.com

How does online banking make managing your checking account and paying bills more convenient?

Applied Skills

Building Study Skills Instruct students to develop a summary outline and multiple choice questions to use as a review of the main types of financial services.

Technology Assign students to create a flowchart to explain various components and movement of funds for several electronic banking services. Ask a group of volunteers to share their findings with the class.

A checking account at a credit union may be called a *share draft account* because the members are called *shareholders*.

Interest-Earning Checking Accounts

Many financial institutions offer checking accounts that earn interest. These accounts may require a higher monthly balance than regular checking accounts. If the account falls below the required amount, the bank usually pays no interest and may add a service charge.

The rates of interest that banks pay their customers also vary. Usually, a bank will offer a higher rate of interest when a higher balance is kept in the account. Very often, interest rates on checking accounts are quite low. When you are depositing larger amounts of money, consider other savings alternatives.

Special Checking Accounts

If you only have a few transactions each month, consider a *special checking account.* Also called an *activity account*, banks charge customers about 10 to 20 cents for each check written. A monthly service charge may also be added.

Comparing Checking Accounts

When selecting a checking account, evaluate the following items.

- Minimum balance
- Interest rate earned, if any
- Monthly service charge
- Fees for other services, such as printing checks and stop payment orders
- Other restrictions

When choosing a checking account, be careful. A bank may attract you with a low minimum balance, but fees can result in a higher total cost.

CHECKPOINT ✓
What are three main types of checking accounts?

LO 17.2.3

ONLINE AND MOBILE BANKING

Each day, more and more people are using electronic banking services. ATMs, personal computers, cell phones, and other electronic devices are processing most bank transactions.

Electronic Banking Activities

Over the years, banks have expanded their hours of operation to meet the demands of their customers. Traditional "banker's hours" of 9 A.M. to 3 P.M. are a thing of the past. Banks have expanded their hours and locations, while ATMs and online banking are available 24 hours a day. Figure 17-3 lists various mobile and online banking services.

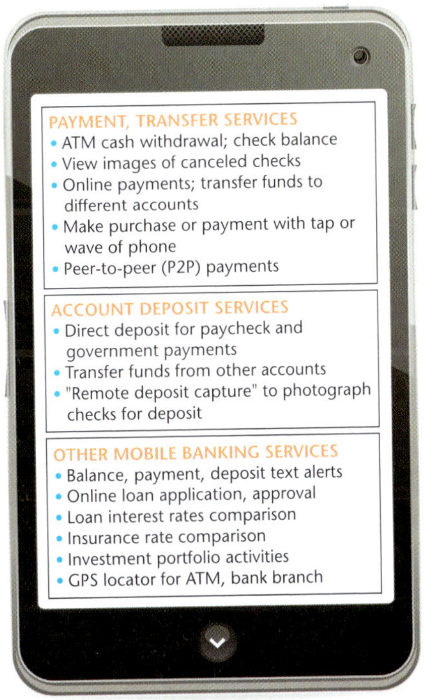

M.Stasy/Shutterstock.com

FIGURE 17-3
Mobile Banking Activities

TEACH

Explain the features of interest-earning and special checking accounts.

Provide an overview of the main factors to consider when comparing checking accounts.

ONGOING ASSESSMENT

CHECKPOINT ✓ANSWER

Three main types of checking accounts are (1) regular checking accounts, (2) interest-earning checking accounts, and (3) special checking accounts.

TEACH

Use Figure 17-3 to provide an overview of electronic banking services.

▶ **Figure 17-3 *ANSWER***

Answers will vary. Students might mention the convenience of getting cash from an ATM or checking account balances online. Some students might report that they like having paychecks and tax refunds deposited directly to their accounts.

Different Learning Styles

Kinesthetic Learner Assign students to work in pairs to demonstrate electronic banking services described in this lesson. Encourage them to create scenarios to explain how and why a person would use these services.

NET KNOWLEDGE

Students will access information that can help consumers when selecting and using a checking or savings account.

TEACH

Explain the various components of electronic banking: ATMs, point-of-sale payments, direct deposit, and automatic bill payments.

Ask students whether people are writing fewer checks than a few years ago. Point out that debit card transactions and online payments are being used instead of checks in many situations.

NET KNOWLEDGE

Many different banking services are available from various types of financial institutions. Conduct an online search to locate a website that helps consumers compare different types of checking and savings accounts. What information is available to help consumers select and use these financial services? How might this information be useful to you?

Automatic Teller Machines Commonly called a *cash machine*, an *automatic teller machine (ATM)* offers many banking services. The most common use of an ATM is withdrawing cash from a bank account or getting a cash advance from a credit card. Bank customers also can use ATMs to check account balances, make deposits, or transfer funds from one account to another.

A **debit card**, or *cash card*, is used for ATM transactions. A debit card is different from a *credit card*. With a debit card issued by your bank, you are using money that is in your account. With a credit card, you are borrowing from the bank to pay later.

A lost or stolen debit card can be expensive. If you notify the financial institution within two days of the lost card, your liability for unauthorized use is $50. After that, you can be liable for up to $500 of unauthorized use for up to 60 days.

ATM services have expanded to provide other types of transactions. You can often use these machines to buy bus passes, postage stamps, and gift cards.

Be aware that many banks charge fees for ATM usage. To minimize ATM fees, compare rates at several financial institutions. Use your bank's ATMs to avoid surcharges. Withdraw larger amounts to avoid fees on several small transactions.

Payments at the Point-of-Sale In a *point-of-sale transaction*, a merchant accepts a debit card to pay for purchases. Most gas stations, stores, and restaurants accept this type of payment. Vending machines that accept debit cards are also becoming more common.

Direct Deposit A major portion of society uses *direct deposit* of paychecks and government payments. Funds are deposited electronically and available automatically for your use.

Automatic Bill Payments Each month, many people pay their rent, mortgage, loans, utilities, and other bills without doing anything. *Automatic bill payment* requires a bank customer to authorize preset amounts of monthly expenses. The bank deducts the payments from your account and transfers them to the appropriate companies. With automatic bill payments, be sure to check each month that the correct amounts have been deducted.

Electronic Payment Options

The use of cash, checks, and credit cards is declining. These payment methods are being replaced by newer electronic alternatives.

Debit Card Transactions Most stores, restaurants, and other businesses accept debit cards issued by Visa and MasterCard. You may also know these cards as *check cards*. When the debit card transaction is processed, the amount of the purchase is deducted from your checking account.

Online Payments Various Internet-based companies, as well as banks, now provide online bill payment services between buyers and sellers. When using these services, be sure to think about the monthly charge as well as online security and customer service availability.

Different Learning Abilities

Gifted Encourage students to obtain additional information about technology and government regulations for electronic banking. Invite interested students to prepare a display or presentation based on their research.

Some online payment services give you a choice of using a credit or a bank account, while others require one or the other. Disputed transactions are more likely to be resolved in the consumer's favor if a credit card, rather than a bank account, is used.

Stored-Value Cards The gift card your aunt sent you for your birthday is a stored-value card. Prepaid cards for phone service, transit fares, highway tolls, and school lunches are common. Some stored-value cards are disposable. Others can be reloaded with additional funds. Some employers use prepaid cards instead of paper paychecks to help employees avoid check-cashing fees. Employees can use the cards to make purchases and to withdraw cash at ATMs.

Smart Cards These "electronic wallets" are similar to ATM cards. *Smart cards* feature embedded microchips that store prepaid amounts as well as account balances, transaction records, insurance information, and medical history.

Banking in the Future

Smartphone and tablet apps for banking will only continue to expand. Text banking provides account information and conducts transactions by text message. Mobile banking involves online access to a financial institution's website. Many banking apps are available to perform various financial transactions.

A system called *near-field communications (NFC)* technology stores credit card and bank account information for consumer use. Instead of using a debit or credit card, a tap or wave of your phone at an in-store sensor completes the purchase. In the future, these mobile transactions may bypass banks and appear directly on your phone bill.

FYI Banking apps for your phone allow you to check your account balances, make payments and transfer funds, locate ATMs, and obtain information and assistance with various banking services. These smartphone apps, which range in price from free to a few dollars, are available from banks, financial institutions, and other sources. Banking apps are becoming a "virtual wallet" for many people.

CHECKPOINT
What are common electronic banking services?

17.2 ASSESSMENT

Key Concepts

Determine the best answer.

1. True or False. Using a debit card is similar to writing a check.
2. True or False. Automatic payments are made through automatic teller machines.
3. True or False. If you write only a few checks each month you should consider a regular checking account.

Make Academic Connections

4. **Visual Communication** Conduct a survey of 20 students to determine the types of financial services they use. Create a table or graph to report your findings.
5. **Technology** Locate examples of online payment services and online lenders. What services are provided? What concerns might be associated with these services?

TEACH

Discuss the features and benefits associated with online payments, stored-value cards, and smart cards.

FYI
Use the FYI feature to discuss the many ways people use smartphones to help them handle their finances. Discuss the pros and cons of the "virtual wallet."

ONGOING ASSESSMENT

CHECKPOINT ✓ANSWER
Common electronic banking services include automatic teller machines (ATMs), point-of-sale payments, direct deposit, and automatic bill payments. Some other electronic payment options are debit card transactions, online payments, stored-value cards, and smart cards.

ASSESS

Key Concepts *Answers*

1. True
2. False. A bank deducts an automatic payment from a customer's account and transfers the money to the appropriate company to pay the customer's bill.
3. False. If you write many checks each month you should consider a regular checking account.

Make Academic Connections *Answers*

4. Tables and graphs will vary.
5. Answers will vary. Services mentioned may include sending money, paying for goods and services, and collecting payments from buyers. Concerns may include identity theft, fraud, and phishing.

RETEACH List the major services provided by financial institutions.

ENRICH Ask students to describe situations that illustrate how consumers use various banking services.

CLOSE Explain actions that might be taken to reduce the fees and charges for various financial services.

BUSINESS IMPROVING SOCIETY

While many attempts have been made to improve economic development in poor countries, few have been successful. The use of microlending has been effective in various settings.

THINK CRITICALLY THROUGH VISUALS

Loans help women start and operate businesses which generate income to support the women and their families. Income from these businesses is also used to repay the loans.

Think Critically *Answers*

1. Microfinance programs allow low-income people who have no access to formal financial institutions to generate enough income to provide for life's necessities and family needs. By providing affordable loans, microfinance programs improve the economy of rural areas. Some microfinance programs have expanded to provide other financial services, such as savings accounts and insurance coverage, thus helping borrowers build assets and protect against risks.

2. These loan programs may not be available to extremely poor people. Unscrupulous operators of microfinance programs may cheat poverty-stricken clients. Loans made for business are sometimes used for personal needs and household expenses.

3. Students will search the Internet for more examples of microfinance programs around the world.

BUSINESS IMPROVING SOCIETY

MICROFINANCE

How could a loan of $50 result in a life-changing experience? In countries such as Bangladesh, Nepal, the Philippines, and Zimbabwe, microfinance has helped improve the economy and society.

Microfinance, also called microlending and microcredit, involves programs of small loans to people for self-employment projects. The resulting business activities generate enough income to provide for life necessities and family needs. Most microcredit program are funded by nonprofit organizations that hope to help communities become self-sufficient.

Danita Delimont/Gallo Images/Getty Images

How do loans from BRAC change the lives of women in Bangladesh?

Microfinance clients usually have minimal income and no access to formal financial institutions. They are usually self-employed, household-based entrepreneurs. In rural areas, clients are small farmers or food-processing workers. In urban areas, microfinance clients include shopkeepers, service providers, artisans, and street vendors.

In southeastern Bangladesh, one of the poorest regions in the world, BRAC (formerly the Bangladesh Rural Advancement Committee) helps women obtain loans. Loans help them farm fish, keep cows for milk production, grow vegetables, raise poultry, buy rickshaws, and sew clothing. The women pay 15 percent simple interest on loans, which is much less than they would have to pay to loan sharks. The banking is done in the village through an agent of the microfinance institution. Loans are not secured through collateral. Repayment is made in 52 weekly installments in a year's time, and simple interest is used rather than compound interest.

BRAC also works to improve the health of women and children. More than 30,000 volunteers have been trained by BRAC to recognize and treat 10 common illnesses such as anemia, diarrhea, ringworm, and scabies.

The success of microfinance is not limited to Bangladesh. Organizations around the world provide affordable financing to improve the economy in many poor countries. Using a model similar to the one used by BRAC, an organization offers a small inexpensive loan to help an entrepreneur start or grow a small business. Income generated by the business is then used to cover living expenses, operate the business, and repay the loan.

Most microfinance organizations have expanded their services to include a L-I-S-T approach. In addition to loans (L), clients have access to insurance (I), savings accounts (S), and transfer of funds (T), often through mobile banking. These services help borrowers build assets and protect against risks.

Think Critically

1. What are the main benefits of microfinance programs?
2. What are some concerns that might arise when using microfinance?
3. Conduct an online search to locate other examples of microfinance activities around the world.

Applied Skills

Culture Encourage students to talk to people who have lived in or visited other countries. How do people's attitudes and behaviors differ regarding the use of banking services?

17.3 Checks and Payment Methods

Learning Outcomes

17.3.1 Describe three main types of endorsements.

17.3.2 Describe proper check-writing procedures.

17.3.3 Explain the bank reconciliation process.

17.3.4 Identify other payment methods.

Key Terms

endorsement 440	bank statement 443
check register 441	bank reconciliation 445
stop payment order 443	outstanding checks 445

Focus on REAL LIFE

Alicia Garcia made her first deposit in her new checking account. Her friend Joni asked her, "If I write you a check, could you give me the cash? You can deposit my check in your account later."

"How do I know your check is good?" Alicia asked.

"What? We've been friends for more than 10 years," Joni responded. "Don't you trust me?"

"Of course I trust you," said Alicia. "Just remember that if a check isn't good, it can result in some expensive service fees."

The next day, Joni approached Alicia and said, "I can't wait to order this sweater online, and I'd like to pay for it with my checking account. How does that work?"

"Let me show you the routing number and account number on your checks," responded Alicia.

LO 17.3.1

OPENING A CHECKING ACCOUNT

While fewer checks are being written each year, a checking account is usually the foundation for a debit card as well as online and mobile banking activities.

Traditionally, checks provide convenience, ease, and safety for making payments, while also being used as proof of payment and a record of spending. These benefits of a checking account continue.

The First Deposit

Opening a checking account starts with providing personal data and a sample of your signature. In the past, a *signature card* was used. This document usually required your legal name, address, phone number, Social Security number, driver's license number, and e-mail address. Today, signature cards might not be actual cards. Most financial institutions enter your personal data online and use an electronic capture device to obtain your signature sample. The electronic image of your signature is then available to bank employees.

These methods are used to verify your signature. The bank compares the signature on checks to the one on record when the account was opened. Signatures will likely be verified when you are cashing a large check at your bank, or when the bank suspects that a forged check is being presented for payment.

iStockphoto.com/Slobo

How does recording your signature when you open a checking account protect you and the bank?

17.3 Checks and Payment Methods | **439**

Focus on REAL LIFE

This situation can be used to discuss some of the activities involved with checking accounts.

TEACH

Explain the main benefits of checking accounts. Use Figure 17-4 to point out the actions required to open a checking account.

THINK CRITICALLY THROUGH VISUALS

Recording a signature protects account holders and the bank by allowing the bank to verify that checks are signed by the account holders and not by imposters.

Different Learning Abilities

At-Risk Explain the importance of understanding checking accounts and other financial services. Ask students to name situations in which these services would be needed.

TEACH

Provide an explanation of the main types of endorsements using Figure 17-4.

▶ **Figure 17-4 *ANSWER***

A special (or full) endorsement allows an individual to transfer a check to another person. A restrictive endorsement limits the use of the check to the purpose given in the endorsement. An endorsement with two signatures is used when the name on the check differs from the official signature on the checking account so that the bank can be sure it is depositing the check to the correct account.

Sometimes two or more people have an account together called a *joint account.* Each person who will write checks on the account must provide a sample signature. Any signer for a joint account can write checks on the account as if he or she were the only owner.

When you deposit money in a checking account, you fill out a *deposit slip*. This form lists all items you are depositing—currency, coins, or checks. The deposit slip shows your name, account number, the date, the items deposited, and the total amount of the deposit.

Types of Endorsements

Before depositing a check, it must be endorsed. This involves writing your name on the back of the left end of the check. An **endorsement** is written evidence that you received payment or that you transferred your right to receive payment to someone else.

When you endorse a check, your responsibilities are almost as great as if you had written the check yourself. As an endorser, you are actually making this promise: "If this check is not paid by the bank, I will pay it."

Your endorsement must be made in the 1½-inch space on the left side of the check. If you write outside this limit, the bank may return the check. Different endorsements have different purposes. Figure 17-4 shows some examples.

Blank Endorsement An endorsement that consists of only the endorser's name is a *blank endorsement.* To endorse a check, sign your name in ink exactly as it is written on the face of the check. If the name on the check is different from your official signature, you will need to endorse the check twice. First, use the name as given on the check. Then, write your name as it appears on the account.

A blank endorsement makes a check payable to anyone who has the check. While you can use this endorsement to transfer any check, sometimes another type of endorsement is better.

Full Endorsement The use of a *full endorsement,* also called a *special endorsement,* allows you to transfer a check to another person. You write the words "Pay to the order of..." followed by the name of the person or business to which the check is being transferred. This is followed by your signature. This phrasing results in only the specified person being able to sign and cash the check.

Restrictive Endorsement A *restrictive endorsement* limits the use of the check to the purpose given in the endorsement. For example, you may have several checks that you want to mail to the bank. You could write *For deposit only* above your signature, followed by your account number. This endorsement restricts use of the check so it can only be deposited to your account. Often, organizations that receive many

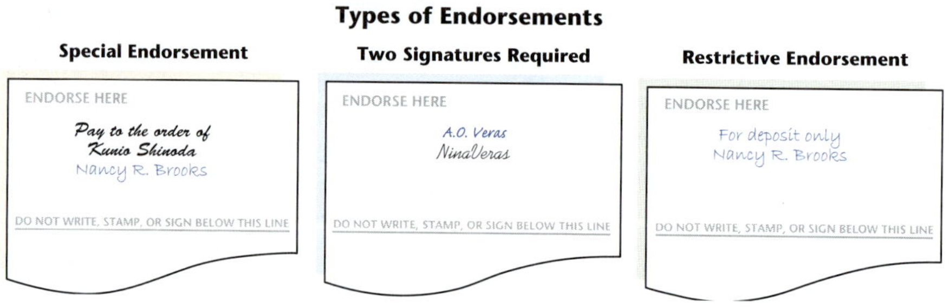

FIGURE 17-4
Describe the benefits of each type of endorsement.

Different Learning Styles

Kinesthetic Learner Instruct students to write out sample endorsements for various types of situations. Explain the situation and ask students to select which endorsement to use.

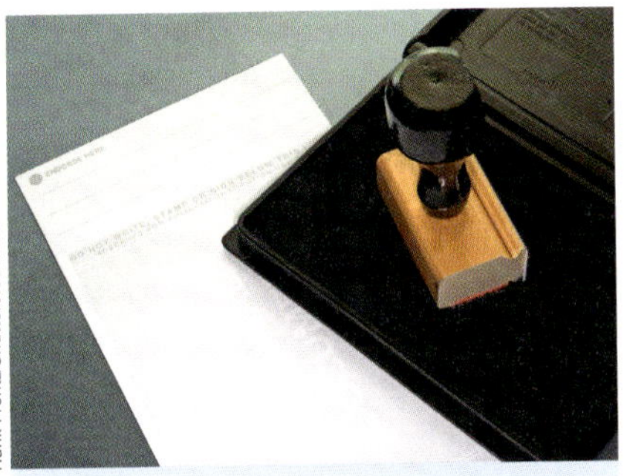

Hank Frentz/Shutterstock.com

Why do some businesses use a stamp to endorse checks?

checks use a rubber stamp with the words *For Deposit Only* followed by the company name and its account number.

CHECKPOINT
What are the three types of endorsements?

LO 17.3.2

USING A CHECKING ACCOUNT

To use a checking account correctly, you must understand certain information and follow some specific procedures.

Check-Writing Procedures

Some checks are light blue or green in color. Others have a picture of a forest, a sports team logo, or an inspirational quote. No matter what they look like, all checks contain the same information.

Elements of a Check Figure 17-5 shows some terms that are used to identify the parts of a check. Three parties are shown on each check.

- The *drawer* is the owner of the account who signs the check.
- The *payee* is the person to whom the check is written.
- The *drawee* is the bank or other financial institution that pays the check.

The Check Register Your checkbook will provide one of three formats for recording account activities. The *check stub* is a form attached to the check by a perforated line. A **check register** is a separate book, usually the same size as the checkbook, that allows you to maintain a record of the checks written. A *duplicate copy* of the check may also be automatically created when you write the check.

Parts of a Check

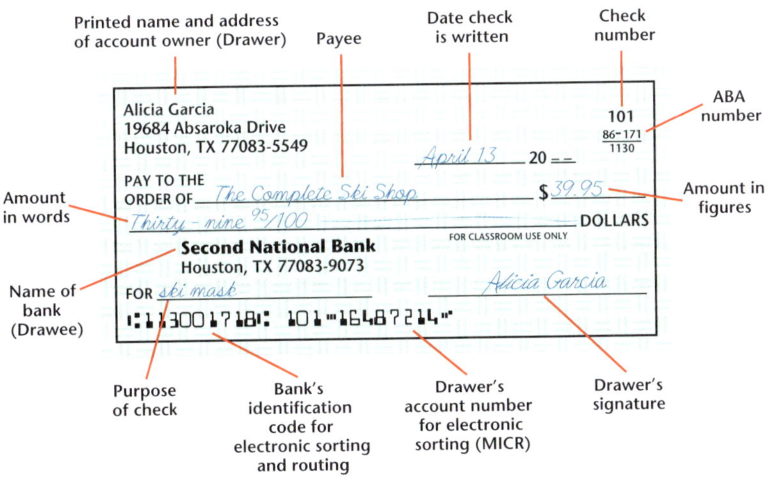

FIGURE 17-5
Why is the amount of this check written twice?

TEACH

Explain situations in which full and restrictive and endorsements may be used.

THINK CRITICALLY THROUGH VISUALS

Using a stamp to endorse checks allows businesses to process checks quickly.

ONGOING ASSESSMENT

CHECKPOINT ✓*ANSWER*

The three types of endorsements are the (1) blank endorsement, (2) full endorsement, and (3) restrictive endorsement.

TEACH

Use Figure 17-5 to explain the main elements of a check and the check-writing process.

▶ **Figure 17-5** *ANSWER*

The amount of the check is written twice to reduce the possibility of error.

Different Learning Styles

Tactile Learner Use samples of checks to allow students to practice proper check writing for various payment situations. Students should practice endorsing the backs of the sample checks.

Work as a TEAM

Use this activity to highlight common errors made when writing checks.

TEACH

Explain the importance of a check register. Describe how a check stub and duplicate check copy serve a similar purpose.

Highlight the steps for writing a check. Emphasize the importance of properly filling out a check. Remind students that accuracy is required for the bank to correctly process the payment. Ask students to name various errors that might be made when writing a check.

Point out that while checks continue to be used, many other payment methods are now common. This includes debit cards, online payments, and stored-value cards.

Work as a TEAM

Many people carelessly write checks, making it easy for others to alter the checks. Review the steps for proper check writing and discuss the importance of each item. Write a list of common errors of check writing and what problems might occur.

Always fill out the stub or register first. If you write the check first, you may forget to record the information before you transfer the check. Your check register should also be used for maintaining a record of debit card payments and cash withdrawals.

Writing a Check Fill out the check completely and carefully using the following seven steps.

1. Write checks in order by number so you know which checks have been paid.
2. Write the date in the proper space.
3. Write the payee's name on the line following *Pay to the Order of.*
4. Write the amount of the check in numerals after the printed dollar sign. Write the amount close to the dollar sign to prevent someone from altering your check. Write the cents figures close to the dollar figures so that additional numbers cannot be inserted.
5. Write the dollar amount in words on the line below the payee's name. Write the cents in figures as a fraction of a dollar. Begin writing at the far left end of the line. Draw a line from the fraction to the printed word *Dollars* to fill all unused space.
6. Write the purpose of the payment on the line at the bottom of the check.
7. Sign checks with the same signature you wrote on your signature card.

Proper Check Writing Poor check writing can cause problems and financial difficulties. Follow these tips to avoid trouble.

1. *Write checks only on the forms provided by your bank.* Checks can be written on just about anything—even a paper bag—but sorting and processing can be delayed when you do not use the proper form.
2. *Write checks in ink.* This prevents someone from altering the amount.
3. *Only write checks if money is available.* Writing a check for more than is in your account can result in an *overdrawn account.* The bank may not pay the check and you will most likely be charged a fee.
4. *Use the current date.* A *postdated check* is one that is dated later than the date on which it is written. This business practice is unwise and can result in additional service charges.
5. *Avoid making checks payable to "Cash" or to "Bearer."* Such a check can be cashed by anyone. Instead, make the check out to yourself or to the bank as payee.
6. *Always fill in the amount.* If you leave it blank, you may be held responsible for amounts filled in by others.
7. *Void checks on which you make errors.* Do not try to erase or retrace your writing. Write "Void" across the check. Make note of the voided check in the check register.
8. *Record every payment from your checking account, whether the payment is by check, debit card, or automatic payment.* Some people carry a few blank checks. When you write a check, make a note of it and record it in the register. Also, promptly record all transactions made at an ATM.

Stopping Payment

In certain situations, you may not want your bank to pay a check that you have

Different Learning Styles

Visual Learner Encourage visual learners to close their eyes and mentally picture the process of writing a check. Then instruct them to write a check using a blank sheet of paper.

written. To do so, you will fill out a **stop payment order**, a written notice that tells the bank not to pay a certain check. Because banks charge a high fee for stopping payment on a check, use this process only for good reason. You may learn, for example, that a check you have written to pay a bill was lost in the mail. A check you have written may have been stolen. Before you write a new check, you should stop payment on the one that was lost or stolen.

CHECKPOINT
What is the purpose of a check register?

LO 17.3.3

THE RECONCILIATION PROCESS

As a depositor, you will need to review the record of your account that the bank keeps. At regular intervals, usually monthly, the bank will send you a report on the status of your account known as a **bank statement**.

Bank Statement Information

While bank statement formats vary, most present the following information.

- The balance at the beginning of the month.
- The deposits made during the month.
- The checks paid by the bank during the month.
- Any automatic teller transactions made during the month.
- Any electronic fund transfers (EFT) or special payments the bank has made.
- Service charges for the month, including charges for services such as stopping payment on a check.
- Any interest earned on the account.
- The balance at the end of the month.

Examples of some of these items appear on the bank statement shown in Figure 17-6 on page 444.

Determine Checks Paid

When your bank statement arrives, compare the checks you wrote to those that have been paid by your bank. Banks might not return actual *canceled checks* that have been paid. Instead, banks can use a *substitute check*, which is a digital reproduction of the original paper check. In some cases banks do not return checks or provide substitute checks unless the customer requests them.

There are times when you need to show proof of a payment. In most cases, information on the statement will be sufficient to prove payment. If the check showing the endorsement is needed, a substitute check is considered a legal equivalent of the original check.

iStockphoto.com/sjlocke

How can a computer program help with reconciling your checkbook?

TEACH

Describe the steps for proper check writing.

Explain the purpose of a stop payment order.

ONGOING ASSESSMENT

CHECKPOINT ANSWER

The purpose of a check register is to record all account activities so that the account holder will always know the account balance. The check register is also used for reconciling a checkbook with a bank's monthly statement.

TEACH

Explain the purpose of a bank statement.

THINK CRITICALLY THROUGH VISUALS

A computer program can help with reconciling a checkbook by providing accurate, detailed records of all account activity.

Teaching Strategies

Expand Beyond the Classroom Contact a local bank or credit union to obtain samples of some of the documents (checks, signature card, stop payment order) that are discussed in this lesson.

TEACH

Use Figure 17-6 to highlight the various items reported on a bank statement. Ask students to share observations from their own bank statements.

Explain how a person might use a bank statement to serve as a proof of payment.

▶ **Figure 17-6** ***ANSWER***

Twelve checks were paid by the bank and posted to Alicia's account.

Monthly Account Statement

Second National Bank
Checking Account Statement
Account Number: 1648-7214
Alicia Garcia
19684 Absaroka Drive
Houston, TX 77083-5549

Page: 1 of 2
Date: 5/1/20xx

Checking Account Summary

Balance Summary					Transaction Summary	
Beginning balance	Deposits and other additions	Checks and other deductions	Charges and fees	Ending balance	Withdrawals	Deposits
0.00	926.95	533.89	3.00	390.06	14	4

Activity Detail

Deposits and Other Additions

Date	Description	Amount	Date	Description	Amount
4/10/20xx	Deposit	331.85	4/24/20xx	Deposit	175.00
4/16/20xx	Deposit	150.00	4/29/20xx	Direct Deposit	270.10

Checks and Substitute Checks

Date paid	Check number	Amount	Date paid	Check number	Amount
4/13/20xx	101	39.95	4/26/20xx	*109	65.33
4/15/20xx	102	50.00	4/27/20xx	110	33.46
4/22/20xx	103	32.97	4/27/20xx	111	24.33
4/22/20xx	104	100.87	4/27/20xx	112	5.80
4/24/20xx	*106	16.30	4/27/20xx	113	12.85
4/24/20xx	107	25.78	4/30/20xx	114	4.25

Banking/Check Card Withdrawals and Purchases

Date	Description	Amount	Detail
4/23/20xx	ATM-W	50.00	ATM withdrawal 3970 Waverly Ave

Online and Electronic Banking Deductions

Date	Description	Amount	Detail
4/30/20xx	AP	72.00	TexPower automatic payment

Other Deductions

Date	Description	Amount	
4/30/20xx	SC	3.00	Service charge for checking

* Indicates a missing check number; the checks that cleared for this statement were not consecutive.

FIGURE 17-6
How many checks were paid by the bank and posted to Alicia's account?

Different Learning Abilities

Visually Impaired Create an enlarged version of a bank statement to allow students to see the details. Consider contacting a local bank to inquire about services they offer for customers with visual impairments.

Find Differences

You keep your own record of your checking account, usually in a check register. The bank statement is the bank's record of your account.

The document created to show how the two balances were brought into agreement is called the **bank reconciliation**. Bringing the balances into agreement is known as *reconciling the bank balance*. The bank often prints forms for reconciling on the backs of bank statements. Figure 17-7 shows an example of a bank reconciliation.

The balances shown on your records and the bank statement may be different. Some of the most common reasons for differences are

- Some of the checks you wrote may not have *cleared* (been paid). These checks, which have not been deducted from the bank statement balance, are called **outstanding checks**.
- You may have forgotten to record a transaction in your register, such as an ATM deposit or automatic bill payment.
- A service charge may appear on the bank statement.
- You may have mailed a deposit to the bank that has not yet been received.
- Interest earned may have been added.
- You may have recorded the amount of a check incorrectly in the check register. You may have added or subtracted incorrectly.

Sample Bank Reconciliation Form

BANK RECONCILIATION

Directions: You can easily balance your checkbook by following the procedure outlined on this form. Fill in below amounts from your checkbook and bank statement.

BALANCE SHOWN ON BANK STATEMENT $ 390.06

ADD DEPOSITS NOT ON STATEMENT $

A

TOTAL $ 390.06

SUBTRACT CHECKS ISSUED BUT NOT ON STATEMENT

B

108	$ 10.00
115	21.00
116	17.50

E TOTAL $ 48.50

BALANCE $ 341.56

BALANCE SHOWN ON YOUR CHECKBOOK $ 416.56

ADD ANY DEPOSITS NOT ALREADY ENTERED IN CHECKBOOK $

C

TOTAL $ 416.56

D SUBTRACT SERVICE CHARGES AND OTHER BANK CHARGES NOT IN CHECKBOOK

$ 3.00

Tax Power 72.00

E TOTAL $ 75.00

BALANCE $ 341.56

These totals represent the correct amount of money you have in the bank and should agree. Differences, if any, should be reported to the bank within ten days after the receipt of your statement.

A You recorded these deposits in your check register, but the bank has not posted them to your account.

B You recorded these checks in your check register when you wrote them, but they have not cleared.

C The bank recorded these deposits when they were received, but you have not recorded them in your check register.

D The bank recorded these withdrawals when they occurred, but you have not recorded them in your check register.

E Both the revised bank statement balance and the revised checkbook balance should be equal.

FIGURE 17-7
What does the $341.56 balance represent? Is it always less than the balance shown on the statement? Explain your answer.

TEACH

Ask students to describe reasons why a person's checkbook balance might differ from the bank statement. Explain the items listed on this page and the next that could cause a difference between the checkbook balance and the bank statement.

▶ Figure 17-7 *ANSWER*

The $341.56 balance represents the actual amount of cash available at this point in time, after taking into account all checks that have been written, bank fees and charges, and any errors. The balance shown at the bottom of the bank reconciliation form can be more or less than the balance shown on the statement. It would be more if there were a deposit in transit.

Applied Skills

Office Technology Explain how spreadsheet software might be used to prepare a bank reconciliation. Invite interested students to set up a spreadsheet using the numbers from the figure on this page.

THINK CRITICALLY THROUGH VISUALS

Bank statements typically include the balance at the beginning and end of the month, the deposits made and checks paid by the bank during the month, ATM transactions, EFT transfers, service charges, and any interest earned.

TEACH

Explain the calculation for completing the bank reconciliation process. Describe the actions to take if the adjusted checkbook balance and the adjusted bank balance do not agree.

ONGOING ASSESSMENT

CHECKPOINT ✓ANSWER

Most differences between the bank statement balance and a person's check register are attributable to checks that have not cleared, transactions that may not have been recorded in the check register, service charges, deposits mailed to the bank that may not have arrived by the time the statement was issued, interest earned, or transactions whose amounts were not recorded correctly.

TEACH

Describe situations in which a person might use a certified check, a cashier's check, or traveler's checks.

Monkey Business Images/Shutterstock.com

What information is included on your bank statement?

Calculate Adjusted Balance

To determine the true balance in your account, take the following steps.

1. Subtract the total of the outstanding checks from the bank statement balance.
2. Add any *deposits in transit* to the balance statement balance.
3. Subtract service charges, fees, and automatic payments from your checkbook balance.
4. Add any interest earned to your check register balance.

At this point, if the balances do not agree, either you or your bank has made an error. You should check each of the steps again. Then, carefully go over the calculations in your check register. If you do not find an error in your calculations, contact your bank.

After you have reconciled your bank statement, correct any errors that you made on your register. The new balance now agrees with the bank statement. With your account updated, you can write checks on the new balance.

CHECKPOINT ✓

What are some reasons for differences between the bank statement balance and a person's check register?

LO 17.3.4

OTHER TYPES OF PAYMENTS

Often, you might need to make a payment in a situation when a personal check is not acceptable. Several payment alternatives are available.

Certified Checks

A *certified check* is a personal check for which a bank has guaranteed payment. The certification is stamped on the face of the check and is signed or initialed by a bank officer.

Cashier's Checks

A bank usually keeps funds in an account of its own on which it writes its own checks. A *cashier's check* is a check that a bank draws on its own funds. A cashier's check costs the amount of the check plus a service fee. These banker's checks are more acceptable than the personal checks of an individual whom the payee may not know.

Traveler's Checks

There is a service that allows travelers to pay easily throughout the world while avoiding the dangers that come along with carrying large amounts of cash. *Traveler's checks* are special forms designed for making payments when away from home. You can buy them at banks, credit unions, and travel bureaus. Traveler's checks are sold in various denominations. In addition to the value of the checks, a fee may be charged. In recent years, the use of this payment form has declined. Prepaid debit cards are often used instead.

Different Learning Styles

Kinesthetic Learner Invite students to create a short presentation about certified checks, cashier's checks, traveler's checks or money orders. Encourage students to include examples of situations where the payment method might be used. Consider allowing students to work in pairs.

Traveler's checks require your signature in two places. First, you sign each one when they are bought. Then, when you cash a check or pay for a purchase with it, you sign it again in the presence of the person accepting it. Businesses throughout the world commonly accept traveler's checks.

Money Orders

A person who does not have a checking account and wants to send a payment through the mail may purchase a money order. A *money order* is a form of payment that orders the issuing agency to pay the amount printed on the form to another party.

Several types of organizations commonly sell money orders.

- A bank money order is sold by a bank. It states that money is to be paid to a specific person or business.
- A *postal money order* purchased from the U.S. Post Office can be sent safely through the mail. It can be cashed only after the payee signs it.
- An *express money order* is issued by various organizations, including traveler's check companies, travel agencies, and many supermarkets, pharmacies, and convenience stores.
- A *telegraphic money order* allows the quick transfer of funds at a telegraph office to a person or business at another telegraph office.

If a money order is lost or stolen, the receipt copy that you receive may be used to make a claim.

FYI In recent years, several states required banks to offer basic checking accounts for low-income consumers. These lifeline accounts provide checking services for a minimal fee; they also limit the number of transactions each month.

CHECKPOINT ✓
How does a certified check differ from a cashier's check?

17.3 ASSESSMENT

Key Concepts

Determine the best answer.

1. The first document that must be completed when opening a checking account is the
   - **a.** deposit slip
   - **b.** reconciliation statement
   - **c.** check register
   - **d.** signature card
2. A personal check with guaranteed payment is a
   - **a.** cashier's check
   - **b.** money order
   - **c.** certified check
   - **d.** traveler's check

Make Academic Connections

3. **Math** Service charges for Tom Harding's regular checking account at Second National Bank are based on the bank's rate schedule:

Minimum Balance	Charge
0–$199	$6
$200–$399	$4
$400 and over	no charge

During a recent six-month period, Tom's balances were: April, $148.00; May, $201.97; June, $101.61; July, $418.53; August, $248.29; and September, $154.36.
   - **a.** How much was Tom's service charge for each month?
   - **b.** What was the total service charge for the six-month period?

FYI
Instruct students to conduct research to determine whether their state requires banks to offer lifeline accounts.

ONGOING ASSESSMENT

CHECKPOINT ✓ANSWER
A certified check is a personal check for which a bank has guaranteed payment. A cashier's check is a check that a bank draws on its own funds.

ASSESS

Key Concepts *Answers*

1. d. signature card

2. c. certified check

Make Academic Connections *Answers*

3a. Tom's service charges were April, $6; May, $4; June, $6; July, no charge; August, $4; and September, $6.

3b. Tom's total service charge for the six-month period was $26.

CLOSE Highlight the main points to remember when writing checks.

RETEACH Explain the process of reconciling a bank statement.

ENRICH Ask students to design a format for a bank statement that might be more informative to consumers.

Think Critically About Business *Answers*

1. Answers will vary. Arguments for more government controls on banks could focus on making the banking system safer, free from corruption, and less likely to take advantage of poor or uneducated consumers. Arguments against increased government regulation are that banks are freer to offer innovative new services and can pay higher interest rates without additional restrictions.

2. A major factor is the location and availability in your community. Other factors would be comparing fees, services, and interest rates offered by both credit unions and banks.

3a. A person planning to open a fitness center – checking account, small business loan

3b. A musical group – checking account, savings account, small business loan, safe deposit boxes to store important records while the group is on the road

3c. A wealthy senior citizen – checking account, savings account, safe deposit box, investment advice, trust.

3d. A buyer of a van – automobile loan, checking and savings accounts

3e. A high school recycling club – checking account

4. Jake will need to ask himself whether he plans to make many withdrawals or payments to others using the money in the account. If so, he needs a checking account. If the $1,000 is his savings and he does not foresee many withdrawals, he will want a savings account that pays interest.

Chapter 17 Assessment

Review Business Concepts

17.1 Banks and Other Financial Institutions

- The Federal Reserve System serves member banks by accepting their deposits, lending them money, clearing transfers of funds, and providing other services.
- The main deposit-type institutions are commercial banks, savings and loan associations, mutual savings banks, and credit unions. Non-deposit financial institutions include life insurance companies, investment companies, consumer finance companies, mortgage companies, check-cashing outlets, and pawnshops.
- To obtain the best value for your financial services dollar, compare services offered, safety, convenience, fees and charges, and restrictions.

17.2 Financial Services and Electronic Banking

- The most common services offered by financial institutions are accepting deposits, transferring funds, lending money, electronic banking, storing valuables, providing financial advice, and managing trusts.
- The main types of checking accounts are regular checking accounts, interest-earning checking accounts, and special checking accounts.
- Electronic banking services include the use of automatic teller machines (ATM), point-of-sale transactions, direct deposit, automatic bill payment, online payments, stored-value cards and smart cards.

17.3 Checks and Payment Methods

- The purpose of an endorsement is to allow the recipient of the check to cash, deposit, or transfer it to someone else. A blank endorsement consists of only the endorser's name. A full endorsement, also called the special endorsement, allows you to transfer a check to another person. A restrictive endorsement limits the use of the check to the purpose given in the endorsement.
- Checks should be written carefully so they are free of errors and difficult to alter. A stop payment order may be used to prevent a bank from cashing a check that a customer has written.
- Reconciling a checking account involves finding the differences between the balance on the bank statement and the balance in your checkbook.
- Other types of payment methods include certified checks, cashier's checks, traveler's checks, and money orders.

Think Critically About Business

1. Some people believe that banks need more regulations and control by the government. Others would like fewer regulations for banks. What are some arguments for each point of view?
2. What factors might affect whether you use a commercial bank or a credit union for your banking activities?
3. List the type of banking service each consumer would be most likely to use. Explain your answer.
   a. A person planning to open a fitness center
   b. A musical group
   c. A wealthy senior citizen
   d. A buyer of a van
   e. A high school recycling club
4. Jake Olsen has decided to put $1,000 in the bank. List several questions Jake might want to ask before choosing whether to put the money in a checking or a savings account.
5. Cher Alonso often makes deposits and withdrawals at the ATM that she passes on her way to work. She frequently forgets to record these banking activities in her check register and never seems to know how much money she has in the bank. In addition, she has overdrawn her account twice and has had to pay a fee each time. Can you suggest a plan for Cher to follow that would allow her to use the automatic teller services and still maintain an accurate record?

5. Answers will vary. One suggestion for Cher is to always use the ATM's option to print a receipt for each transaction. She could place the receipt in her check register and remove it only when she has recorded the transaction. An even better plan would be to record the transaction in her check register before leaving home and visiting the ATM.

6. Answers will vary, but could include important papers such as birth, marriage, and death certificates; Social Security cards; important financial documents, such as insurance policies and stock certificates; valuable jewelry; and rare coins.

6. Name items that a person might keep in a safe deposit box.

7. While using a debit card increases the speed and efficiency of business transactions, what effect can this have on a person's money management skills?

8. Isaac Ahlred has received his bank statement for the month of May. The bank statement shows a balance of $401.19, but his check register shows a balance of only $364.52.
   a. What is the most likely reason that the bank's balance is larger than Isaac's?
   b. What steps should Isaac take to bring his balances into agreement?

9. While on a trip, the Mendoza family decided to buy a painting which cost $500. The art dealer would not accept a personal check or credit cards. What method could be used to pay for the painting?

10. "You should shop for the best place to open a checking account as carefully as you shop for the best buy in any product or service." Give two reasons to support this statement.

11. Matt Huffman believes that it is a waste of time to record information each time he uses his debit card or writes a check. "The bank sends me a statement each month. That's all I need," he says. How could you convince Matt that he should keep records?

Develop Your Business Language

Match the terms listed with the definitions.

12. A bank that offers a full range of financial services.

13. A nationwide banking plan set up by the federal government to supervise and regulate member banks.

14. A written notice telling the bank not to pay a certain check.

15. A separate form on which the depositor keeps a record of deposits and checks.

16. A device used for cash machine transactions.

17. A container in a secured area in a bank vault for storing valuables.

18. Written evidence that you received payment or that you transferred your right of receiving payment to someone else.

19. A report sent by the bank to a depositor showing the status of his or her account.

20. A federal agency that protects deposited money in case of the failure of a bank or financial institution that it regulates.

21. A fee a bank charges for handling a checking account.

22. Checks that have not been deducted from the bank statement balance.

23. A user-owned, not-for-profit cooperative financial institution.

24. A statement showing how the checkbook balance and the bank statement were brought into agreement.

Key Terms

a. bank reconciliation
b. bank statement
c. commercial bank
d. check register
e. credit union
f. debit card
g. endorsement
h. Federal Deposit Insurance Corporation (FDIC)
i. Federal Reserve System
j. outstanding checks
k. safe deposit box
l. service charge
m. stop payment order

Develop Your Business Language *Answers*

12. c. commercial bank
13. i. Federal Reserve System
14. m. stop payment order
15. d. check register
16. f. debit card
17. k. safe deposit box
18. g. endorsement
19. b. bank statement
20. h. Federal Deposit Insurance Corporation (FDIC)
21. l. service charge
22. j. outstanding checks
23. e. credit union
24. a. bank reconciliation

7. Answers will vary. Debit cards do make it easier to forget to properly record transactions in the check register, increasing the possibility of an overdraft.

8a. The most likely reason the bank's balance is larger than Isaac's is that his account has some outstanding checks.

8b. Isaac should deduct the amount of all outstanding checks in his check register from the bank's balance. Also, he should determine whether there are any fees he needs to deduct or any interest earned he needs to add.

9. If the Mendoza family's ATM agreement allowed a large withdrawal, they could electronically withdraw that much cash to pay for the painting. They could use a debit card, if accepted by the dealer, or obtain a cashier's check at a local bank that would accept their check or credit card. Traveler's checks or a money order are other possibilities.

10. One reason for carefully shopping for the best checking account is because even small monthly fees will add up. Conversely, even slightly higher interest rates on interest-bearing checking accounts will add to savings over the months and years. Good service and convenient hours also will have a large impact on the account holder's daily life.

11. Without a record, Matt may spend more than he has available. Errors can also occur. Some checks can be lost or the amounts altered. If he does not balance his checkbook, he will never be aware of such problems. Balancing a checkbook also allows Matt to know his spending trends to help him better manage his finances.

Make Academic Connections *Answers*

25. Answers will vary depending on the bills students examine. The seal is located to the left of George Washington's portrait.

26. Answers will vary.

27. Posters will vary.

28. Answers will vary depending on the credit unions in your area.

29. Answers will vary depending on the state in which your students live.

30. Answers will vary depending on the economic measures students select.

31. $\$520 = \$2 \times 52 \times 5$

32. Role-play situations will vary.

33. Subtract the outstanding checks ($7.16 + $15.10 + $9.95) from the bank balance: $378.65 – $32.21 = $346.44. Then, subtract the $3 service charge from his checkbook balance ($349.44 – $3.00 = $346.44) to equal the bank's balance.

34. Answers will vary depending on the information selected. Provide guidance for the citation format you want students to use. Encourage students to be creative in the illustration that they use to communicate their key findings.

Make Your Case *Answers*

35. The Hamiltons will want to consider the services offered, the convenience of each institution's locations and hours, any fees and charges, the quality of service, and any restrictions on accounts.

Make Academic Connections

25. **Geography** Look at several U.S. one dollar bills. Which Federal Reserve Banks are noted on the seal of these banknotes?

26. **Culture** Research financial services and payment methods commonly used in various countries around the world.

27. **Communication** Collect advertisements, promotions, and online information from several financial institutions. Analyze these materials to determine information that is useful for consumers. Create a poster to highlight and report your findings.

28. **History** Investigate the availability of credit unions in your community. Who may join? What services are offered?

29. **Law** Check-cashing outlets, pawnshops, and payday loan companies frequently charge fees and rates much higher than other financial institutions. Research laws that regulate these financial institutions. Prepare a one-page summary of your findings.

30. **Economics** Select various economic measurements of the economy, such as interest rates and consumer prices. Describe how changes in these economic factors might affect the use of financial services.

31. **Math** If a person pays $2 in ATM fees each week for 5 years, what would be the total cost of that service?

32. **Communication** Work with a partner to act out situations in which you might use a certified check, a cashier's check, traveler's checks, and a money order.

33. **Math** In October, Tom Jarez received his bank statement that showed a balance of $378.65. The service charge was $3. In examining his statement, he found that the following checks were outstanding: No. 31, $7.16; No. 34, $15.10; and No. 35, $9.95. His checkbook balance at the end of the month was $349.44. Reconcile his bank statement.

34. **Read** Find an online article that relates to the use of location-based services for banking. Read the information and create an illustration that displays a concept, idea, or process discussed in the article. Include a properly formatted citation for your source.

Make Your Case

Fran and Bill Hamilton recently moved to a new community. They are having trouble deciding whether to use a financial institution near their workplaces or near their home. The Hamiltons have the opportunity to do business with a credit union, a national bank with many branches, a local bank with strong personal service, or a savings and loan association.

35. What factors should the Hamiltons consider when selecting a financial institution?

36. How could Fran and Bill obtain information about the financial institution that would best serve their needs?

37. Locate the website of a large bank that offers financial services for several types of customers. Prepare a brief written summary of the features of the bank's website that might be of value to the Hamiltons.

38. Based on the bank's website, make a list of the loans and other financial services that are only offered to commercial customers.

Interactions and Connections

Information about financial services is available from many sources. Talk to people in your community about the financial institutions and financial services they use. Which of these have you learned about in this chapter? Are there other financial services that you need to learn about? Create a two-paragraph summary of your findings.

36. Fran and Bill could ask questions over the phone. They could visit the establishments and ask about accounts and services. The Hamiltons could visit websites, read brochures, and talk to neighbors.

37. Summaries will vary depending on the bank chosen.

38. Lists will vary depending on available services.

Interactions and Connections

Summary paragraphs will vary.

Presentation Management Individual Event

This event will assess your ability to use current technology to prepare and deliver an effective multimedia presentation. You will research the assigned topic and design a presentation to deliver your findings. On the day of the event, you will have 15 minutes to set up your presentation. The actual presentation must last a minimum of 7 minutes and a maximum of 10 minutes. Up to 5 minutes will be allowed for questions from the judges.

Effective multimedia presentations use audio and visual elements to complement and enhance the content of the presentation. You will need to decide how to use images, color, text, white space, and other design elements to make your presentation interesting without overwhelming your audience. Selecting the appropriate music, sounds, audio clips, and narration is also part of the process. You will need to secure a signed release from any individual whose name, photograph, and other information is included in the presentation.

For this event you must prepare an electronic multimedia presentation that thoroughly explains debit cards. You must conduct research to learn about the purpose and uses of debit cards and describe the pros and cons associated with using debit cards when making purchases and reservations. The presentation must be objective and cannot emphasize one side of the issue.

Performance Indicators Evaluated

- Demonstrate knowledge of multimedia software and components.
- Demonstrate effective multiple communication skills.
- Apply technical skills to create a multimedia presentation that enhances the oral presentation.

You will be evaluated for your

- Knowledge of the topic
- Organized presentation of the topic
- Confidence, quality of voice, and eye contact

For more detailed information about performance indicators, go to the BPA website.

Think Critically

1. What are some advantages of debit cards? List two specific examples.
2. What are some disadvantages of debit cards? List two specific examples.
3. Why should the record keeping for a debit card be the same as record keeping for a checking account?

www.bpa.org

WINNING EDGE

Presentation Management Individual Event

This activity provides students with an opportunity to make a presentation in a simulated business setting. Encourage students to research the topic, prepare a professional presentation, and practice their presentations.

Think Critically *Answers*

1. Answers may vary. Debit cards increase payment options for consumers. They allow individuals the convenience of making purchases without carrying cash. They also allow users to make purchases at various locations without the aid of a cashier. Debit cards can also be used to make online purchases and to hold reservations.

2. Answers may vary. The use of debit cards may result in additional transaction fees. There is also a possibility of account funds being frozen when used for hotel and automobile rental reservations until the debit transactions clear.

3. Consumers should accurately record transactions involving their bank account whether they write checks, use debit cards, or both. An accurate record of each transaction allows the account holder to see how money is being spent, track the account balance, and avoid overdrafts, card rejections, and bounced checks.

CHAPTER OVERVIEW

This chapter presents coverage of types of consumer credit accounts along with information on the wise use of credit.

18.1 Credit Fundamentals

This lesson explains the types of consumer credit along with the advantages and disadvantages of using credit.

18.2 Cost of Credit

Calculating interest and finance charges is the main focus of this lesson.

18.3 Credit Application and Documents

Credit applications, loan contracts, monthly statements, and other credit documents are covered in this lesson.

18.4 Protection of Credit Rights

Various regulations protecting credit users and problems of using credit are the basis of this lesson.

Chapter 18 Consumer Credit

iStockphoto.com/andresrl

18.1 Credit Fundamentals

18.2 Cost of Credit

18.3 Credit Application and Documents

18.4 Protection of Credit Rights

Instructor Resources

- Activities and Study Guide IE
- Chapter and Unit Tests IE
- Lesson Plans
- PowerPoint Presentation
- Cognero Test, Ch. 18

Student Resources

Activities and Study Guide
www.cengage.com/swep/pob9e
- Portfolio Activity

PLANNING A CAREER IN . . .
CONSUMER CREDIT

Credit is important in most economies. Many individuals and businesses use credit for various purchases. Consumer credit involves loans for housing, motor vehicles, and college expenses. Business loans are vital for companies to start operations, purchase inventory, and buy equipment. As a result, many workers employed by banks and credit card companies are involved in approving, processing, servicing, and collecting credit transactions.

People do not always make wise credit and buying choices. Workers in consumer credit also find jobs in credit counseling, helping people regain control of their finances and plan for their financial future.

Workers in consumer credit must combine knowledge of finance and economics with excellent communication skills for interaction with customers. They also must have strong computer and math skills.

Related Job Titles

- Bill and Account Collector
- Credit Clerk
- Loan Officer
- Credit Analyst
- Loan Counselor
- Information and Record Clerk
- Credit Counselor
- Credit Administrator
- Credit and Collections Manager
- Commercial Credit Analyst

Analyze Career Opportunities in . . .
CONSUMER CREDIT

Use library and Internet resources to learn more about careers in consumer credit. Choose one of the job titles listed in the box and answer the following questions.

1. How would you describe the earnings potential for this field?
2. Is this a career that interests you? What can you do now to help prepare yourself for this career?

What it's like to work as a . . . Credit Counselor

"We're not sure where our money goes each month. We just know we owe more than $8,000 in credit card bills," explained Joan Salvatore.

Joan and her husband, Hank, have a monthly income of $3,750, but their expenses are more than $4,400. That's why they came to the community credit counseling service. Joan and Hank were assigned to Bev Gonzalez. Bev worked for a consumer loan company for more than 15 years. Today, instead of granting credit to people, she helps them with credit problems.

Bev recommends that the Salvatores set up a budget to help them plan purchases and reduce spending. For example, Joan and Hank can eat at home more often and make occasional restaurant meals a treat. The extra money the Salvatores will have as a result of following a budget can be used to pay off their debt. In addition to offering a strategy for getting out of debt, Bev will help Joan and Hank learn how to manage their money in the future. No more arguing about money and no more calls about late bill payments.

What about you? What work activities in the consumer credit field appeal to you? What will you have to do to achieve success in this career field?

PLANNING A CAREER IN . . .
CONSUMER CREDIT

The many borrowing opportunities available to consumers create a variety of career opportunities.

What About You?
Answers

Answers will vary. To achieve success in the consumer credit career field, a student will need an understanding of finance and economics, proficiency with spreadsheet and database application programs, and good interpersonal skills.

Analyze Career Opportunities *Answers*
Student answers will vary depending on when the assignment is completed and individual interests.

Additional Career Information

Encourage students to investigate careers they find interesting and explore unfamiliar careers. Two resources for additional career information are the *Occupational Outlook Handbook,* an online publication (www.bls.gov/oco) of the U.S. Bureau of Labor Statistics, and the O*NET Resource Center (www.onetcenter.org) developed by the U.S. Department of Labor. Information about specific careers and jobs can be used to demonstrate the relevance of skills learned in this course.

Focus on REAL LIFE

This feature provides an opportunity to point out that credit is used by individuals, businesses, and governments.

TEACH

Ask students to name the best thing about using credit. Then ask them about the major concerns. Provide an overview of the use of credit by explaining the terms *debtor* and *creditor*.

Explain the difference between trade credit and consumer credit.

Explain the *installments* of loan credit.

18.1 Credit Fundamentals

Learning Outcomes

18.1.1 Identify the types of consumer credit.

18.1.2 Describe the benefits of using credit.

18.1.3 Explain some disadvantages of using credit.

Key Terms

credit 454	promissory note 458
finance charge 455	collateral 458
down payment 458	cosigner 458
installment loan 458	credit rating 459

Focus on REAL LIFE

In most economies, consumers, businesses, and governments use credit. For example, a person buys gas with an oil company credit card. A student applies for and receives a government loan to help with college expenses. A business receives a $2 million loan to build a new store. Another company borrows $150,000 to finance the purchase of additional inventory. The state of Louisiana may borrow $35 million through a bond issue to build new college buildings. A county board might borrow $250,000 to make emergency road repairs.

What do these people, businesses, and governmental institutions have in common? They all have wants, but lack the money to satisfy those wants. If they borrow money to satisfy their wants, they will be using credit.

LO 18.1.1

USING CREDIT

Credit is the privilege of using someone else's money for a period of time. That privilege is based on the belief that the person receiving credit will honor a promise to repay the amount owed at a future date. Two parties are involved in a credit transaction. Anyone who buys on credit or receives a loan is a *debtor*. The one who sells on credit or makes a loan is the *creditor*.

Although the credit system uses forms and legal documents, it also depends on trust between the debtor and creditor. This trust means that the creditor believes that the debtor will honor the promise to pay. Without that trust, the credit system could not operate.

Types of Credit

Businesses use trade credit. *Trade credit* occurs when a company receives goods from a supplier and pays for them later. Businesses may secure long-term loans for land, equipment, and buildings. They may also borrow money for shorter periods, usually for 30 to 90 days, to meet short-term needs for cash.

Local, state, and federal governments often use credit to provide goods and services that benefit the public. Governments may use credit to buy items such as cars, aircraft, and police uniforms. They may also borrow funds to build highways, parks, and airports.

Most consumers use credit. You may use credit to buy expensive products that will last a long time. You may also use credit for convenience in making smaller purchases.

If you borrow money to use for some special purpose, you are using *loan credit*. Loans are available from several kinds of financial institutions. Loan credit usually involves a written contract. The borrower agrees to repay the loan in specified amounts, called *installments*, over a period of time.

Different Learning Abilities

At-Risk Describe careers and personal finance activities related to consumer credit. Emphasize the importance of knowing and understanding the various topics in this lesson.

If you charge a purchase at the time you buy the good or service, you are using *sales credit*. Most businesses offer sales credit. Sales credit involves the use of charge accounts and credit cards by consumers.

FYI Trade credit terms are often stated "2/10, n/30." This means that the business can take a 2 percent discount if the bill is paid within 10 days from the billing date. The full or net amount must be paid within 30 days.

Charge Accounts

A charge account represents a contract between the firm offering the account and the customer. Three types of charge accounts are generally available: regular, budget, and revolving.

Regular Accounts A regular charge account requires the buyer to make full payment within a stated period—usually 25 to 30 days. The seller may set a limit on the total amount that may be charged during that time. People use regular accounts for everyday needs and small purchases. Service providers, such as doctors, dentists, lawyers, and plumbers, commonly offer this type of credit.

Budget Accounts Some stores and utility companies offer *budget charge accounts*. This credit agreement requires that a customer make payments of a fixed amount over several months. One budget plan that businesses offer is the 90-day, three-payment plan. Under this plan, you pay for your purchase over a 90-day period, usually in three equal monthly payments.

With a utility company budget plan, the company makes an estimate for gas or electricity charges during a certain period, such as a year. You then agree to pay a certain amount each month to cover those charges. This plan avoids large payments during some times of the year. You pay the same amount each month.

Revolving Accounts The most popular form of sales credit is the *revolving account*. You may charge purchases at any time, but only part of the debt must be paid each month. Features of revolving credit include the following.

- A maximum amount may be owed at one time, called a *credit limit*.
- A payment is required once a month, but the total amount owed need not be paid at one time.
- A finance charge is added if the total amount owed is not paid. A **finance charge** is the total dollar cost of credit, including interest and all other charges. You must pay this additional amount for the convenience of using credit.

Revolving charge accounts are convenient, but they can make overspending easy. The finance charges on unpaid balances can be quite high, sometimes 1½ percent

Racheal Grazias/Shutterstock.com

What are some reasons that a business would borrow funds?

FYI
Explain to students that when speaking, "2/10, n/30" is read as "two ten, net thirty."

TEACH

Contrast the difference between regular charge accounts and budget accounts. Explain the features of a revolving charge account.

THINK CRITICALLY THROUGH VISUALS

Businesses might borrow funds to pay for goods they will resell at a profit or for new equipment, building projects, and facility upgrades that will make them more profitable in the long run. Businesses also sometimes borrow money for short periods to meet short-term cash needs.

Different Learning Styles

Tactile Learner Use various objects to represent the use of credit among individuals, businesses, and governments. Ask students to describe the use of credit based on the object they are holding.

Life-Span Plan Answers

Answers will vary. Students should identify major expenditures, such as buying a house or paying for higher education, that few people could afford without credit.

TEACH

Ask students to name various types of credit cards. Explain how the cost of using a credit card is passed on to consumers.

Explain situations in which consumers might use charge cards and retail store credit cards.

THINK CRITICALLY THROUGH VISUALS

The different types of credit cards include bank cards, charge cards, affinity cards, and retail store cards.

Life-Span Plan

What life-span goals might you set that would require you to use credit? Make a list of specific reasons you might consider borrowing funds in the next 10 years. Describe steps you can take in the next few years to create a credit history that will help you borrow funds in the future.

per month (18 percent per year) or higher. There is rarely a finance charge if balances are paid in full within a specified period, such as within 25 days.

Credit Cards

Charging purchases with credit cards is common. Most credit cards issued today are multipurpose cards. Consumers can use them at thousands of stores, restaurants, and other businesses, as well as to pay for goods and services online.

Bank Cards Bank credit cards have become very popular all over the world. MasterCard and Visa are two of the best known. Sometimes an annual fee must be paid for the privilege of using these cards.

While banks and various merchants may issue credit cards, most credit card processing is done through *Independent Sales Organizations (ISOs)*. When you use your bank credit card, electronic terminals typically send the transaction data to an ISO, which then authorizes payment. The transaction data can be processed in real time or sent in a batch file at the end of the day. Real-time processing can be used to evaluate a transaction for fraud by using the bank's credit card purchase database. If you have a credit card and someone used your credit card information to purchase something that you do not normally buy, the bank's database system may ask for further identification or may call you to ask whether you made the purchase. A gas station pump may send information in a batch file. The card is verified by matching the billing address to a zip code entered at the pump.

dean bertoncelj/Shutterstock.com

What are the different types of credit cards that a person can apply for?

The bank pays the business for the sales amount minus a service fee. This fee covers the bank's expenses of processing the sales receipts and collecting amounts owed from customers. The bank is doing the work that the business's own credit departments would do.

Business owners like bank credit cards because the bank takes on the liability and expense of granting credit. Customers like bank charge cards because they are accepted by many businesses all over the world.

Charge Cards American Express and Diners Club, once called travel and entertainment cards, are widely used charge cards. Subscribers pay a yearly membership fee that is usually higher than the fee for bank cards. Cardholders are not given a spending limit. They are usually expected to pay the full balance each month. Business travelers like to use charge cards because the detailed records they receive are useful for business and tax record keeping. They offer proof of travel expenses.

Affinity Cards Some organizations allow their names to be affiliated with a credit card. These affinity cards are *co-branded* with an issuing bank. They allow an organization, such as a charity, sports team, or

Different Learning Abilities

English Language Learners (ELL) Obtain translations of the key terms in this chapter to reinforce these concepts in both English and other dominant languages used by students.

oil company, to receive a small percentage of credit sales.

Retail Store Cards Many retail stores offer their own credit cards to customers. These cards show the name of the store that issues them. Customers can only use these cards at the issuing stores.

Installment Credit

You may want to purchase a new $600 flat screen TV or $500 laptop computer. For these purchases you may use a different type of credit. *Installment sales credit* is a contract issued by the seller that requires periodic payments at specified times. The seller adds finance charges to the cost of the items purchased. The credit agreement shows the total amount to be paid. Consumers often purchase furniture and household appliances with installment sales credit.

Unlike credit cards, installment sales credit is a contractual agreement directly between the buyer and the seller. The following are some features of installment credit.

- Signing a sales contract that shows the terms of the purchase.
- Receiving the purchased item at the time of the sale. Be aware that the seller has the right to *repossess*, or take back, an item if payments are not made on time.

Business Insight

Switching to a Smart Credit Card

Credit card fraud is a concern in the United States. While credit card fraud losses account for only a little over 5 cents per $100, the total annual losses exceed $11 billion in the United States alone. Credit card fraud hurts individuals and banks, but the worst impact is often felt by the business making the sale.

Thieves use a variety of methods to obtain credit card information. A service person could copy a credit card's information by taking a picture of the card's front and back. Some thieves use card readers that can be placed in card swipe terminal slots. Other thieves use computer hacking to steal credit card information. In 2008, information from over 135 million accounts was stolen from Heartland Payment Systems, a payment processor.

Banks in the United States are changing to a more secure credit card design currently used in most of the world. The EMV credit card design, which stands for Europay, MasterCard, and Visa, is a global standard for cards that are equipped with computer chips used to authenticate chip-card transactions. These cards generate a unique transaction code that is sent through the processing system so that information cannot be used to make another purchase. The card is dipped into a slot at the transaction terminal or touched to a wireless terminal. There may or may not be a PIN number associated with the card.

The change to EMV credit cards and debit cards started in 2015, but with over 1 billion cards to change, and over 15 million terminals in need of upgrades, the change will take years. Businesses that do not switch to EMV terminals could become liable for all future credit card fraud. One huge concern about EMV cards is the security of online purchases. EMV chips' security systems work at terminals, but not for online transactions.

Think Critically

1. Why are banks switching to EMV cards? Do you think EMV cards will reduce credit card fraud?
2. Use Internet and library resources to learn what you can do to avoid becoming a victim of credit card fraud.

TEACH

Describe the features of installment credit.

Explain the purpose of a down payment.

Ask students to name reasons why a person might apply for a loan.

Contrast the difference between an installment loan and a single-payment loan.

Business Insight

The credit card industry tries to minimize its losses to fraud by using a variety of techniques, including tracking customer purchases, requiring PIN numbers for cash withdrawals, and adopting the EMV smart chip credit card to ensure secure transactions.

Think Critically *Answers*

1. Answers will vary. Credit card fraud is a multibillion dollar problem in the United States. The EMV card has been successfully used in Europe and other parts of the world to reduce credit card fraud. This may not be a permanent solution; thieves have proven themselves to be resourceful. EMV chips work at terminals, but not for online transactions.

2. Answers will vary. Students can use the Federal Trade Commission's *Protecting Against Credit Card Fraud* site, a bank's credit card fraud protections site, or many other sources of information.

Different Learning Styles

Auditory Learner Encourage auditory learners to work with a partner to learn about the types of credit cards presented in this lesson. Suggest that students use rhymes or rhythms to help them remember material.

TEACH

Ask students to name items that could serve as *collateral* for a loan.

Work as a TEAM

This feature will require students to think about various positive and negative aspects of a business offering credit.

ONGOING ASSESSMENT

CHECKPOINT ✓ANSWER

The major types of consumer credit are loan credit and sales credit.

TEACH

Highlight the main benefits of using credit.

Ask students to name actions that could affect a person's credit rating.

- Making a **down payment**, which is a payment of part of the purchase price. It is usually made at the time of the purchase.
- Paying a finance charge on the amount owed.
- Making regular payments at stated times, usually weekly or monthly. For example, if a total of $120 is to be repaid in 12 monthly installments, $10 is paid each month.

In some cases, the seller charges a penalty if a payment is received after the due date. In others, all remaining payments may become due at once if only one payment is missed.

Consumer Loans

A loan is an alternative to charge account buying or installment sales credit. Terms of loans and requirements for securing loans differ.

An **installment loan** is one in which you agree to make monthly payments in specific amounts over a period of time. The payments are installments. The total amount you repay includes the amount you borrowed plus the finance charge on your loan.

Another kind of loan is a *single-payment loan*. With this type of credit, you do not pay anything until the end of the loan period, possibly 60 or 90 days. At that time, you repay the full amount you borrowed plus the finance charge.

A lender needs some assurance that each loan will be repaid. If you are a good credit risk, you may be able to sign a promissory note. A **promissory note** is a written promise to repay based on a debtor's excellent credit history. The amount borrowed, usually with some interest, is due on a certain date. Promissory notes should include the following components:

- **Principal** The amount that is promised to be paid
- **Time** The days or months from the date of the note until it should be paid
- **Date of maturity** The date on which the note is due
- **Payee** The one to whom the note is payable
- **Interest rate** The rate paid for the use of the money
- **Maker** The one who promises to make payment

In some cases, the lender may ask you to offer some property you own, such as a car, a house, or jewelry, as *security*. Property that is used as security is called **collateral**. You give the lender the right to sell this property to get back the amount of the loan if you do not repay it. This type of loan is a *secured loan*.

What if you do not have an established credit history or any property to offer as security? You may be able to get a relative or friend who has property or a good credit history to sign your note. They become the legal **cosigner**. The cosigner of a note is responsible for payment of the note if you do not pay as promised.

Work as a TEAM

Most businesses sell on credit. Create a list of situations in which a company may not offer credit to customers. What would be benefits and drawbacks of this action?

CHECKPOINT ✓

What are the major types of consumer credit?

LO 18.1.2

BENEFITS OF CREDIT

Both businesses and consumers can benefit from credit use. The main advantages of credit for consumers include the following:

- **Convenience** Credit can make it easy for you to buy. You can shop without carrying much cash.
- **Immediate Possession** Credit allows you to have the item now. A family can buy

Applied Skills

Writing Across the Curriculum Instruct students to prepare a paragraph that connects the benefits of consumer credit to other business topics or to another class they are taking.

a dishwasher on credit and begin using it at once.

- **Savings** Sometimes credit allows you to buy an item on sale at a good price. Some stores, especially department and furniture stores, send notices of special sales to credit customers.
- **Credit Rating** A person's reputation for paying bills on time is known as a **credit rating**. If you buy on credit and pay your bills on time, you gain a reputation for being dependable. In that way, you establish a favorable credit rating. A credit rating is valuable when you need to borrow money or when you want to make a major purchase.
- **Useful for Emergencies** Access to credit can help in unexpected situations. Sometimes you may not have enough cash and have an urgent need for something. For example, your car might need repairs.

CHECKPOINT ✓
What are the main advantages of consumer credit?

LO 18.1.3

CREDIT CONCERNS

Buying on credit is convenient and can be beneficial. There are also some disadvantages if you are not careful.

- **Overbuying** A common spending hazard of credit involves buying something that is more expensive than you can afford. Attractive store displays and advertisements invite you to make purchases.

Business Insight

Databases, Personal Privacy, and Identity Theft

Information about you is readily available to many people. Businesses and governments all over the world use computer databases and electronic networks to store and exchange this information about you.

How is this information obtained? Most databases are created from information given voluntarily. For instance, you offer information when you apply for credit, obtain telephone service, apply for a driver's license, obtain insurance, and answer survey questions.

Privacy is a basic right to have information about you kept confidential. Like most consumers, you are probably concerned about your privacy. While there is some reason to be concerned about databases and personal privacy, protections exist. Decisions about granting credit or obtaining insurance are most often based on accurate, up-to-date information. The information gathered is used for legitimate business reasons.

Various state and federal privacy laws continue to evolve. Government officials must decide what information is private and when consumers should be asked to give permission before credit or medical reports are released to others. In recent years, stronger privacy protection laws have been enacted.

Identity theft is the fastest-growing financial crime. That's the bad news. The good news is that the technology that is used to steal a person's identity can also be used to protect it. Each year, credit card companies, retail stores, and online businesses improve their security systems. These efforts help to ensure that your personal information and financial data will not be viewed or used by unauthorized individuals or companies.

Think Critically

1. What dangers are involved with having private information easily accessible to others?
2. Conduct a web search to determine actions you can take to protect your privacy.

ONGOING ASSESSMENT

CHECKPOINT ✓ANSWER

The main advantages of consumer credit are convenience (shopping without carrying cash), immediate possession of items bought on credit, savings (when stores offer special prices to credit customers), the chance to build a favorable credit rating, and for emergencies.

TEACH

Explain the main concerns associated with using credit.

Business Insight

Privacy breaches and identity theft are major concerns. Use this feature to expand student awareness of these issues.

Think Critically *Answers*

1. Private information that is easily accessible to others could be misused. For example, a criminal could steal a person's identity or stalk an individual whose personal information is easy to get.

2. Answers will vary. Their research should help students create lists of practical measures they can take to protect their privacy. Ask what actions they plan to take and whether any of the measures seem too extreme or impractical for the privacy benefit gained.

Different Learning Abilities

Gifted Assign students to conduct research about identity theft. Encourage students to explore the methods used to commit the crime, how stolen identities are used, and the impact on individual victims, businesses, and society. Their findings may be reported in a paper or an oral presentation to the class.

TEACH

Solicit student opinions about the questions to ask before using credit. Which of these questions are most important?

THINK CRITICALLY THROUGH VISUALS

Stores offer discounts to attract customers who may buy on credit. While the store may not earn much on the sale, selling on credit can result in earnings from interest.

ONGOING ASSESSMENT

CHECKPOINT ✓ *ANSWER*

Potential drawbacks of buying on credit include overbuying, careless buying, paying higher prices, and overuse of credit.

ASSESS

Key Concepts *Answers*

1. b. installment credit
2. c. a loan
3. b. convenience

Make Academic Connections *Answers*

4. Findings will vary.
5. Tables will vary. The benefits of credit include convenience, immediate possession, savings, credit rating, and usefulness in emergencies. Credit concerns include overbuying, careless buying, higher prices, and overuse of credit.

- **Careless Buying** If you become impatient or distracted in your shopping, you may not shop carefully. You may fail to make comparisons, causing you to buy at the wrong time or the wrong place. Credit can tempt you not to wait for a better price on an item you want now.
- **Higher Prices** Stores that only accept cash may sell items at lower prices than stores that offer credit. Extending credit is expensive for stores. When customers do not pay as agreed, there are collection costs. Sometimes businesses must write off consumer debts as uncollectible. These increased costs often result in higher prices.
- **Overuse of Credit** Buying now and paying later may sound like a good idea. If too many payments need to be made later, the total amount due can become a problem. Consumers must keep records of the total amount owed so that they do not have monthly payments that exceed their ability to pay.

Questions to Ask

Before making a final decision about whether to buy on credit, think about these important questions.

Stephen Coburn/Shutterstock.com

Why do you think stores offer discounts to consumers?

- How will you benefit from this use of credit?
- Is this the best buy you can make or should you shop around?
- What will be the total cost of your purchase, including the finance charges?
- What would you save if you paid cash?
- Will the payments be too high for your income?

Answering these questions will help you make wise credit decisions.

CHECKPOINT ✓

What are potential drawbacks of buying on credit?

18.1 ASSESSMENT

Key Concepts

Determine the best answer.

1. Large purchases (such as motorcycles and automobiles) are commonly bought using
   - **a.** a bank credit card
   - **b.** installment credit
   - **c.** a charge account
   - **d.** trade credit
2. Signing a promissory note occurs when using
   - **a.** a credit card
   - **b.** a charge account
   - **c.** a loan
   - **d.** trade credit
3. Which of the following is an advantage of using credit?
   - **a.** overbuying
   - **b.** convenience
   - **c.** higher prices
   - **d.** lower credit rating

Make Academic Connections

4. **Marketing** Collect advertisements from newspapers, magazines, and websites for companies that offer credit. What types of credit are offered? Is the company selling credit as its primary product or using credit to promote the sale of other goods and services?
5. **Economics** Create a table showing the benefits of credit and credit concerns. For each benefit and each concern, describe the effect consumer credit has on individuals and businesses.

RETEACH Ask students to name the benefits and concerns of consumer credit.

ENRICH Describe uses of credit by your local government.

CLOSE Ask students to name the major types of consumer credit.

18.2 Cost of Credit

Learning Outcomes

18.2.1 Calculate interest in consumer credit situations.

18.2.2 Explain finance charges when using credit.

Key Terms

interest 461

annual percentage rate (APR) 464

Focus on REAL LIFE

"Dad, I think I need a credit card," Peter said.

"Really? What are you planning to buy and how are you going to pay the bill?" asked Peter's father.

"Dad, it is almost impossible to buy anything online without a credit card. I want to be able to download music and maybe buy movie tickets. Plus, it would be nice to pay at the pump when I put gas in the car. I have money from my allowance and my job. I'm not planning a big shopping spree, but I think having a credit card would be a good idea," responded Peter.

"I think you're right. Let's look at our bank's website and see what kinds of cards they offer. They might have a credit card with a low credit limit or something else designed for someone your age. Then we can shop around for the best terms—credit is not free."

LO 18.2.1

FINDING INTEREST

Borrowing money has a cost. **Interest**, *I*, is the cost of using someone else's money. The amount of interest paid on a loan or charge account should be clearly understood. To determine this amount, you need to know the following.

1. **Principal, *P*** Amount of the loan.
2. **Interest Rate, *R*** Percent of interest charged or earned. Remember that a percent can also be expressed as a decimal or a fraction. The symbol for percent is %.
3. **Time, *T*** Length of time for which interest will be charged, usually expressed in years or parts of a year.

Simple Interest

On single-payment loans, interest is usually *simple interest*. The formula for computing simple interest is shown below.

$$\text{Interest} = \text{Prinicipal} \times \text{Rate} \times \text{Time}$$
$$I = P \times R \times T$$

A simple interest rate of 12 percent per year means you are paying 12 cents for each dollar you borrow for a year. At this rate, if you borrow \$1, you pay 12 cents in interest. If you borrow \$2, you pay 24 cents. If you borrow \$10, you pay \$1.20, and so on.

Business Wire/Handout/Getty Images

How does time affect the amount of interest that you pay?

Focus on REAL LIFE

Point out that the financial cost of credit should be a major factor when planning and selecting among borrowing alternatives.

TEACH

Explain the three elements that are used to calculate interest. Show sample calculations for interest.

THINK CRITICALLY THROUGH VISUALS

The longer it takes to pay back borrowed money, the more interest the borrower will pay. Time increases the amount of interest owed.

Different Learning Abilities

Visually Impaired Prepare enlarged materials with the main components and formula to explain interest calculations. Consider asking all students to participate in preparing tapes or audio files that can be used for review.

TEACH

Present the different interest calculations to point out how various factors are used in this process.

Explain the maturity date. Use the example presented to clarify the process of determining the maturity date.

THINK CRITICALLY THROUGH VISUALS

Making the payments for too much debt can limit your ability to pay for current needs. This can lead to late payments and poor credit ratings.

▶ **Figure 18-1** ***ANSWER***

The due date would be May 3.

Suppose you borrow \$100 (P) at 12 percent (R) for one year (T). To calculate the amount of interest, first change 12 percent to a decimal, 0.12. Using the formula, the interest is \$12.

$$I = P \times R \times T$$

$$I = \$100 \times 0.12 \times 1 = \$12$$

If you borrow \$100 at 12 percent for two years, you pay twice as much interest, or \$24.

$$I = \$100 \times 0.12 \times 2 = \$24$$

If you borrow the money for three years, you pay \$36, and so on.

Time in Months Your loan may be for one month instead of one year. How is simple interest calculated for less than a year? The amount of interest is based on the portion of the year. There are 12 months in a year, so one month is one-twelfth of a year, regardless of the number of days in the particular month.

If you borrow \$100 at 12 percent for one month, the interest is

$$I = P \times R \times T$$

$$I = \$100 \times 0.12 \times \frac{1}{12} = \$1$$

Time in Days A loan may be for a certain number of days such as 30, 60, or 90 days. To make the computation easy, a year is often considered as 360 days. The interest on a loan of \$100 at 12 percent for 60 days is \$2.

$$I = P \times R \times T$$

$$I = \$100 \times 0.12 \times \frac{60}{360} = \$2$$

Maturity Dates

The date on which a loan must be repaid is the *maturity date*. When the time of the loan is stated in months, the date of maturity is the same day of the month as the date on which the loan was made. A one-month loan made on January 15 will be due February 15. A two-month loan will be due March 15, and so on.

When the time is in days, you must count the exact number of days to find the date of maturity. First, determine the number of days remaining in the month when the loan was made. For example, if the loan was made on January 10, there would be 21 days counted in January, because there are 31 days in January. Then add the days in the following months until the total equals the required number of days.

Suppose you want to find the date of maturity of a 90-day loan made on March 4. First find the number of days remaining in March. Then add the days in the following months until you reach 90 days. In this case, the due date is June 2. Figure 18-1 illustrates the process.

iStockphoto.com/killerb10

What happens when you use credit to take on too much debt?

FINDING MATURITY DATE	
March	27 days (31-4)
April	30 days
May	31 days
June	2 days
Total	90 days

FIGURE 18-1

What would the due date be for a 60-day loan made on March 4?

Applied Skills

Mathematics Based on the example in this lesson and your own experience, develop several scenarios that require interest calculations. Be sure to use different rates, amounts, and time periods. Students should calculate interest amounts for various situations.

Installment Interest

When you borrow money, you usually make several partial payments instead of one large single payment. A loan that you repay in partial payments is an installment loan (or consumer loan). Each payment is an *installment*.

Banks, credit unions, and consumer finance companies all offer installment loans. With an installment loan, the bank gives the borrower a schedule of payments. It shows how much the borrower must pay each month.

With some loans, the lender adds the amount of the interest to the amount you borrow. You sign a *promissory note* for the total amount. You then repay the note in equal monthly installments.

Suppose you borrow $100, sign a note for $110, and agree to repay the loan in 12 monthly installments of $9.17 each. If you had borrowed $100 for one year and paid $110 at maturity, the interest rate would be 10 percent ($10 ÷ $100 = 0.10).

However, you paid off just part of the loan each month. You had the use of the entire $100 for one month and a smaller amount each succeeding month as you repaid the loan. In this case, the true interest rate amounts to 18.5 percent.

Amortization Schedules On some installment loans, interest is calculated on the amount that is unpaid at the end of each month. The payment table of principal and interest over time is called an *amortization schedule*.

Suppose that a person obtained a loan for $1,000 and agreed to repay $100 per month. The lender applies the payment to principal and interest. The borrower makes payments each month on a level payment schedule. Figure 18-2, on page 464, shows this amortization schedule.

Life-Span Plan

Think about how the use of credit can help people achieve their life-span goals. Explain why the excessive use of credit can prevent people from achieving their goals. What are some things you should consider when trying to decide whether or not to borrow funds?

Amortization schedules show that when loans are first taken, a larger percentage of the payments go to interest. At the end of

mangostock/Shutterstock.com

What large purchases often require an individual to apply for an installment loan?

TEACH

Ask students to explain why it is important to know the amount of interest you will pay on a loan.

It is important to know the amount of interest that will be paid on a loan to help in making wise purchasing decisions (the purchase may not be worth it if the total costs are too high) and to shop for loans with the best interest rates.

Life-Span Plan Answers

Answers will vary. Students should point out that excessive use of credit might prevent them from saving funds they need to achieve their life-span goals. The cost of credit should be considered when deciding whether or not to borrow funds.

THINK CRITICALLY THROUGH VISUALS

Large purchases that often require individuals to apply for installment loans include vehicles; large appliances, such as washing machines and refrigerators; major home improvements; a college education; and luxuries, such as boats and vacations.

Applied Skills

Technology Ask students to work in pairs to investigate the use of spreadsheet software to calculate installment payments for a loan. Invite students to share their findings with the class.

NET KNOWLEDGE

Answers will vary depending on the topics selected.

TEACH

Use Figure 18-2 to explain how a constant payment is often used to pay off a loan plus the interest.

ONGOING ASSESSMENT

CHECKPOINT ✓ANSWER

To calculate interest, one must know the principal (amount of the loan), the interest rate, and the length of time for which interest will be charged.

▶ **Figure 18-2 ANSWER**

A level loan payment schedule is most often used for very large loans paid back over a number of years.

TEACH

Explain the importance of knowing and using the annual percentage rate.

Point out other fees and costs that may be associated with a loan.

NET KNOWLEDGE

Consumers need to stay informed about using credit wisely. The federal government has developed a MyMoney website to help strengthen the financial capability and increase access to financial services for all Americans. Access the MyMoney website, or another site using the search terms "using credit wisely." Select two topics that are presented and prepare a summary of the main ideas. Explain how this information might be valuable to consumers who use credit.

the schedule, more goes to principal. For example, the second payment includes more than $9 in interest and the tenth payment includes only $1.57 in interest. Only $90.90 from the second loan payment is applied to the principal. The tenth payment includes more than $98 in principal.

CHECKPOINT

What three things are necessary to calculate interest?

LO 18.2.2

FINANCE CHARGES

Before you borrow money or charge a purchase, you should know the exact cost of using credit. Three things to consider are the annual percentage rate, the total dollar charges, and the alternative sources of credit.

Annual Percentage Rate

The **annual percentage rate (APR)** is a disclosure required by law. It states the percentage cost of credit on a yearly basis. All credit agreements, whether for sales credit or loan credit, require disclosure of the APR.

In addition to interest, the APR includes other charges that may be made. *Service fees* involve the time and money it takes a creditor to investigate your credit history, process your loan or charge account application, and keep records of your payments and balances.

The costs of collecting from those who do not pay their accounts may also be passed on to other borrowers. *Uncollectible*

AMORTIZATION SCHEDULE
$1,000 loan, 12% Interest rate, monthly payments are $100

PAYMENT	INTEREST	APPLIED TO PRINCIPAL	LOAN BALANCE
			$1,000.00
$1000.00	$10.00	$90.00	910.00
100.00	9.10	90.90	819.10
100.00	8.19	91.81	727.29
100.00	7.28	92.72	634.57
100.00	6.35	93.65	540.92
100.00	5.41	94.59	446.33
100.00	4.46	95.54	350.79
100.00	3.51	96.49	254.30
100.00	2.54	97.46	156.84
100.00	1.57	98.43	58.41
58.99	0.58	58.41	------

FIGURE 18-2

Which kind of loan schedule would be best for very large loans paid back over a number of years?

Different Learning Styles

Visual Learner Use Figure 18-2 to highlight the payment amounts, interest, amount applied to principal, and loan balance for the situation presented. Ask students to point out and explain trends they see when they look at the amortization schedule.

accounts are frequently referred to as *bad debts* or *doubtful accounts*.

Lenders may also add an amount to cover the cost of credit insurance. This coverage repays the balance of the amount owed if the borrower dies or becomes disabled.

Total Dollar Charges

To make you aware of the total cost of credit, federal law requires that the lender must tell you the finance charge. The *finance charge* is the total dollar cost of credit, including interest and all other charges. Either your contract or your charge account statement must state this finance charge.

Compare Credit Costs

If you have to borrow money or buy on credit, be sure to compare the total cost of credit among alternative sources. Check with several lenders and compare the APRs.

If you make a purchase with a credit card, know which card has the lowest APR. If an installment sales contract is required, think about whether an installment loan from a financial institution may be cheaper for you.

Work as a TEAM

Various factors affect interest rates. Create two lists: (1) What economic factors can affect interest rates? (2) What personal factors can affect the rate a lender charges a borrower?

When getting a loan, shop around just as carefully as you would for any major purchase. Borrowing money is costly, so make sure that you get the best loan. Some of the things you should check include the annual percentage rate, the amount of the monthly payments, and the finance charge.

Always remember that when you use credit, you are spending future income. If you decide to use credit, the benefits of making the purchase now should outweigh the costs of using credit. Effectively used, credit can help you have more and enjoy more. Misused, credit can result in too much debt, loss of reputation, and even bankruptcy.

CHECKPOINT ✓

What does APR represent?

18.2 ASSESSMENT

Key Concepts

Determine the best answer.

1. True or False. The principal of a loan is the total amount of interest that will be paid.
2. True or False. Interest rates are stated on the basis of one year even if a loan is for several years.
3. The most valuable number to consider when comparing credit among various borrowing sources is the
   a. total finance charge
   b. maturity date
   c. annual percentage rate
   d. principal

Make Academic Connections

4. **Math** Calculate the amount of interest for each of the following loans.
   a. $6,000 borrowed for 1 year at 7% APR
   b. $2,000 borrowed for 4 months at 8% APR
   c. $1,100 borrowed for 2½ years at 6% APR
5. **Economics** Several types of interest rates exist in every economy. Use library materials or an Internet search to determine common reported interest rates. Which of these rates are related to consumer credit?

Work as a TEAM

This activity can help students understand that both economic and personal factors can affect the interest rate for a loan or other credit.

TEACH

Point out that the "finance charge" is the total *dollar* value of using credit as opposed to the rate communicated with the APR.

Emphasize the importance of comparing the cost of credit at various lenders.

ONGOING ASSESSMENT

CHECKPOINT ✓ ANSWER

APR represents the annual percentage rate, which is the percentage cost of credit on a yearly basis. This disclosure is required by law.

ASSESS

Key Concepts *Answers*

1. False. The principal of a loan is the total amount borrowed.
2. True
3. c. annual percentage rate

Make Academic Connections *Answers*

4a. The interest is $420 ($6,000 × 0.07% × 1).

4b. The interest is $53.33 ($2,000 × 0.08% × 1/3).

4c. The interest is $165 ($1,100 × 0.06% × 2.5).

5. Answers will vary depending on when the assignment is completed.

RETEACH Explain APR and total finance charges.

CLOSE Ask students to name the three factors needed to calculate interest.

ENRICH Ask students to list factors that can affect interest rates for a loan.

Focus on REAL LIFE

This situation will help students better understand the process of establishing credit. It is an opportunity to encourage students to begin taking some of the necessary steps toward establishing their own credit.

TEACH

Ask students to name factors that might be considered when applying for credit.

Describe each of the 3 Cs of credit. Ask students to name items that might be included in each category.

Explain the purpose of a credit application.

18.3 Credit Application and Documents

Learning Outcomes

18.3.1 Explain the credit application process.

18.3.2 Describe the activities of a credit bureau.

18.3.3 Discuss commonly used credit documents.

Key Terms

credit application 466

credit bureau 469

statement of account 470

Focus on REAL LIFE

"I don't get it. How do you get credit if you never had it? It seems like you have to have a good credit history before you even have credit."

When Amy Compton mentioned her concerns during her business class, a few students said they were already working on establishing good credit. Some students said they had credit union or bank accounts in their own names. Others reported that they had part-time jobs.

Everyone agreed that the first step toward getting credit was opening a bank account and demonstrating your ability to repay a debt.

LO 18.3.1

CREDIT APPLICATION PROCESS

To obtain a loan or credit card, you must prove that you are a good credit risk. Not everyone who wants credit will receive it. Lenders need certain information in order to make a decision about granting credit. They want to be assured of two things: your ability to repay a debt and your willingness to do so.

The Three Cs of Credit

In deciding whether to grant you credit, businesses consider three main factors, known as the three Cs—character, capacity, and capital.

Character refers to your honesty and willingness to pay a debt when it is due. If you have a history of paying bills on time, creditors believe that you are a good credit risk.

Capacity refers to a person's ability to pay a debt when it is due. The lender or seller must decide if you have enough income to pay your bills. If your income is too small or unsteady, granting you credit may not be wise. In contrast, your income may be high, but if you have other debts, you may not be able to handle more payments.

Capital is the value of the borrower's possessions. Capital includes the money and property you own. Your capital may include a car that is paid for and a house on which a large amount has been paid. A checking account and savings also add to your capital. The amount of capital gives the lender some assurance that you will be able to meet your credit obligations.

Credit Applications

When you apply for credit or a loan, the lender will ask you to fill out an application. A **credit application** is a form on which you provide information needed by a lender to make a decision about granting credit. Figure 18-3 shows an example of a store charge card application. In addition to printed applications, many companies take credit card applications online.

One of the most important parts of a credit application is your *credit references*—businesses or individuals who are able and willing to provide information about your

Portfolio Activity

Assign the Portfolio Activity for Chapter 18, located on the product website.

COLLECT Encourage students to look for interesting visuals that represent the three Cs of credit.

CREATE Help students create a presentation that provides an overview of the three Cs of credit.

CONNECT Ask students to explain how consumer credit is related to other topics they have studied.

FAMILY STORES CHARGE CARD APPLICATION FAMILY STORES

Important: Fill in all information requested below.

1. Information About Yourself *(Name of person in whose name card will be issued)*

☐ Mr. ☐ Mrs. ☐ Miss ☐ Ms. First Name | Middle | Last Name | E-mail

(Courtesy titles are optional)

Home Address | Apt. | City | State | ZIP Code | How Long? Years ___ Mos. ___

Previous Address (if less than 2 years at present address) | Apt. | City | State | ZIP Code

Home Telephone ( ) | Business Telephone ( ) | Social Security Number | Date of Birth / / | No. of Dependents (Exclude Yourself)

Are You a U.S. Citizen? ☐ Yes ☐ No | If No, Explain Immigration Status | Are You a Permanent Resident? ☐ Yes ☐ No | Do You: ☐ Own ☐ Rent ☐ Other | Monthly Rent or Mortgage $

2. Employment Information *(Your total yearly income from all sources)*

Employer | Address | City | State | ZIP Code

How Long? Years ___ Mos. ___ | Occupation | Yearly Gross Salary $ | Other Income* | Source

Former Employer (if less than 1 year with present employer) | How Long? Years ___ Mos. ___ | **Note: Alimony, child support or separate maintenance income need not be disclosed if you do not wish to have it considered as a basis for paying this obligation.*

Nearest Relative Not Living with You | Address | City | State | Relation | Telephone

3. Other Credit

Major Credit Cards (Visa, MasterCard, etc....) | Account Number

Other Credit Cards (Dept. Stores, etc....) | Account Number

Other Credit | Account Number

4. Banking Information

☐ Checking | Name of Bank | City | Account Number

☐ Savings | Name of Bank (if different from above) | City | Account Number

☐ Other (Check here if you have any of the following:) IRA CD | Money Market Account Stocks/Bonds | Investments Cash Management Account

5. References

Name | Address

Telephone ( ) | E-mail

6. Additional Cards *(Complete this section if you want cards issued to additional buyers on your account.)*

1. Spouse First Name | Middle | Last Name

2. Other First Name | Middle | Last Name

7. Signatures

I authorize the Second National BankCorp to check my credit record and to verify my credit, employment, and income references.
I have read the important information on the reverse side.

X ______________ Applicant's Signature | X ______________ Joint Applicant's Signature

I understand that Second National BankCorp may amend the account terms and charges specified in the Cardmember Agreement in the future.

FIGURE 18-3
Why is it important to fill in all the blanks and to do so accurately?

TEACH

Ask students to explain why certain information is requested on the credit application. Describe how information on the credit application is used by providers of credit.

▸ Figure 18-3 *ANSWER*

It is important to accurately fill in all the blanks on a credit card application so that the lender can make the best possible decision about whether to extend credit. If you do not sign the application, the potential creditor cannot contact your credit references. You are building a credit history, and your credit cannot be reported accurately to credit bureaus if you do not supply the lender with correct information. Finally, supplying false information on a credit application is illegal.

Different Learning Abilities

Hearing Impaired Prepare a visual aid that includes a written description of the various sections of a credit application. Encourage students to ask questions about the form.

Think Critically Through Visuals

A landlord wants to rent to tenants with good credit histories because they are more likely to pay their rent on time and in full. Anyone who is considering loaning you money—car dealers, credit card companies, and so forth—and even employers may request a copy of your credit report.

TEACH

Explain the process used to verify various items reported on a credit application.

Ask students to suggest some actions that might be taken to establish credit by a person who has never had credit. Highlight commonly suggested actions that might be taken to establish credit.

ONGOING ASSESSMENT

CHECKPOINT ✓ ANSWER

The three Cs of credit are (1) character, (2) capacity, and (3) capital.

iStockphoto.com/Vesna Andjic

Why is good credit important to a landlord? Who else might request a copy of your credit report?

creditworthiness. Your signature on the application gives a lender permission to contact your credit references to inquire about your credit record.

Your signature also indicates that you understand the type of credit and that the information you have provided is true. You need to fill out the credit application completely, accurately, and honestly. You should only sign it when you understand it and have provided the requested information.

Documenting Credit Data

Information provided on credit applications must be verified to assure its accuracy. Present and former employers can verify employment dates and salary figures. Banks and other financial institutions can report whether the applicants have the accounts they listed. Landlords can indicate how long tenants have been renting and if they pay their rent on time. Other creditors can report how an applicant makes payments on accounts.

You may list a personal reference because you do not have sufficient business credit references. The person you list can indicate how he or she feels you conduct your personal business activities. In each case, the reference helps the credit manager to get a better picture of you as a credit risk. The credit manager can then make an accurate appraisal of your creditworthiness.

Actions to Establish Credit

Building a good record of creditworthiness can be important. You can begin while you are still in school. Trust and reliability are important in matters of credit. You can help to establish yourself by having a good record of grades and attendance. Both employers and lenders know that school behavior patterns tend to carry on later in life.

In addition, start a checking and savings account. If you keep a balance in each account, a lender can see that you can handle money. Making regular deposits to your savings account also suggests that you will be a good credit risk.

Some people establish credit records by charging small purchases. You may buy a sweater on credit and make the payments according to the agreement. This action is an important step toward proving you are a good credit risk. You may want to pay off your account within 30 days and avoid an interest charge. Either way, you will be building a good credit record.

Having a good part-time or full-time employment record also helps establish a favorable credit record. Changing jobs often does not look good. Being on a job for two or more years is a positive part of a good credit record.

Other information that lenders will want to know relates to your finances. You will need to report how much you earn, what kinds of savings and investments you have, and whether you have any other sources of income. A lender may also want to know about your reliability. In other words, they will want to know your occupation, how long you have been with your present employer, how long you have lived at the same address, and whether you own or rent your home.

CHECKPOINT ✓
What are the three Cs of credit?

Different Learning Styles

Kinesthetic Learner Instruct students to create a credit application. Ask students to explain why certain items are requested on the form they develop.

LO 18.3.2

CREDIT BUREAU

In addition to checking with your credit references, a lender will usually check with a credit bureau. A **credit bureau**, or credit reporting agency, is a company that gathers information on credit users. It sells this information to businesses offering credit. Banks, finance companies, and retail stores are among the customers of credit bureaus.

Credit bureaus keep debt records of consumers. They can record only information that is officially reported to them. For example, mortgage lenders and credit card companies report information about their customers. The information shows if payments are up to date or overdue and if any action has been taken to collect overdue bills. Credit information from other sources such as utility companies, collection agencies, and courts may be added to create a month-by-month credit history for the consumer accounts.

National and local credit bureaus cooperate with each other and share information. If you are new to an area, the local credit bureau can obtain information from the bureau in your previous community.

FYI The three major companies that store data on consumers and provide information to lenders are Experian, Equifax, and TransUnion. Equifax maintains more than 190 million credit files on U.S. consumers.

Credit Report

A credit bureau uses your debt records to grade you as a credit risk. Your *credit report* shows the debts you owe, how often you use credit, whether you pay your debts on time, and other credit data. All of this information is of interest to credit grantors. Credit bureaus do not make value judgments about any individual. The bureau simply gathers facts as reported to them.

The formats used by credit bureaus vary, but credit reports all contain similar information. Reports are usually divided into six parts: personal information, public records, accounts in good standing, adverse accounts, credit history requests, and personal statement. Figure 18-4 lists the main components of a credit report along with descriptions and examples for each component.

MAIN COMPONENTS OF A CREDIT REPORT		
COMPONENT	**DESCRIPTION**	**EXAMPLES**
Personal Information	Information that helps identify or locate the consumer	Names, aliases, current and former addresses, Social Security number, and telephone numbers
Public Records	Information from public records that might be viewed negatively by the creditors	Information about bankruptcy, liens, judgments, and garnishments
Adverse Accounts	Information about accounts that might be viewed negatively by creditors	Accounts that are past due or in dispute as well as accounts that have missed or late payments
Accounts in Good Standing	Information about accounts that have a positive status	Accounts that are current or that have been paid off on time
Credit History Requests	Information about creditors who have requested credit history information	Businesses and lenders where the consumer has applied for a mortgage, loan, credit card, or charge card
Personal Statement	Optional statement provided by the consumer	Information about identity theft, unemployment, and disputed charges

FIGURE 18-4

What kind of information would be on your credit report?

FYI

Remind students of the importance of periodically checking their credit scores. Point out that credit reports might vary depending on the issuer. Explain that this is because bureaus might not have access to the same information or different bureaus may treat the same information differently.

TEACH

Describe the functions of a credit bureau.

Use Figure 18-4 to point out the information commonly contained in a credit report. Locate a sample of a credit report and share it with students. Samples can be found on the Internet by searching *sample credit report*.

▶ **Figure 18-4** ***ANSWER***

Answers will vary depending on their employment and credit histories. Some students may have no credit reports at this time in their lives.

Applied Skills

Communication Ask students to create a public service announcement with suggested actions to take when establishing credit. Encourage students to use scripts and storyboards for planning.

Technology Ask students to describe how a credit bureau might use database software to process various information items on a credit report.

Work as a TEAM

This activity will help students better understand the elements of a credit contract.

ONGOING ASSESSMENT

CHECKPOINT ✓ANSWER

The main purpose of a credit bureau is to gather information on credit users and report the facts in credit reports that it sells to businesses that offer credit.

TEACH

Ask students to describe problems that could arise with credit contracts.

Explain the questions that should be considered before signing a contract.

THINK CRITICALLY THROUGH VISUALS

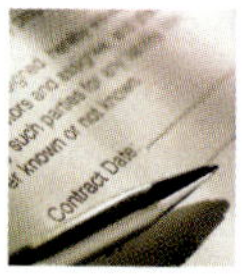

It is important to read and understand credit documents before signing them because, after they are signed, they are legally binding contracts.

Work as a TEAM

Create a contract that might be used in a consumer credit situation. What information should be included in the contract? How should the information be worded so consumers better understand what they are signing?

Your credit record is confidential. That is, only you or those who have a legitimate reason for examining it can obtain it. For example, when you fill out an application to rent an apartment, you might be asked to give the landlord or leasing agent permission to check your credit. The same is true when you apply for a loan or a credit card.

CHECKPOINT ✓

What is the main purpose of a credit bureau?

LO 18.3.3

CREDIT DOCUMENTS

Credit is important in many ways. Millions of consumers and businesses enjoy this privilege. No matter what kind of credit is involved, both parties have legal responsibilities.

You can help maintain a good credit record by keeping track of your purchases and payments. When you buy on credit, you should keep a copy of the sales slip, credit card receipt, or other documents. As you make payments by check, keep track of the date and check number.

Photodisc/Getty Images

Why is it important to read and understand credit documents before signing them?

Credit Contracts

"KWYS" are four letters to keep in mind when signing any legal form. These letters stand for "know what you're signing." This principle applies to all credit contracts. An installment contract is one of the most important forms you may sign. Before signing one, consider the following questions.

- How much are the finance charges? Are they clearly shown on the contract?
- Does the contract include the cost of services you may need, such as repairs to a television or a washing machine?
- Does the contract have an add-on feature so that you can later buy other items?
- If you pay the contract in full before the ending date, will the finance charge be reduced?
- Is the contract completely filled in before you sign? Be sure to draw a line through any blank space before signing.
- Will you be given a copy of the contract?
- Under what conditions can the seller repossess the merchandise if you do not pay on time?

Statement of Account

As a credit card or charge account customer, you will receive a monthly summary of your account. The **statement of account**, or simply the *statement*, is a record of the transactions completed during the billing period. Most statements report the following information:

- The balance that was due when the last statement was mailed
- The amounts charged during the month
- The amounts credited to your account for payments or for returned items
- The current balance, which is the old balance + finance charges + purchases − payments
- The minimum amount of your next payment and when it is due

Figure 18-5 shows a sample of part of a monthly credit card statement.

Teaching Strategies

Expand Beyond the Classroom Contact a lawyer or law advisor to talk to the class about various aspects of contracts and other credit documents. Alternatively, ask students to talk to people they know about credit contracts.

Second National Bank Credit Card Account Statement
Account Number Ending in 9999
February 21, 20xx to March 22, 20xx

Summary of Account Activity	
Previous Balance	$535.07
Payments	−$450.00
Other Credits	−$13.45
Purchases	+$529.57
Balance Transfers	+$785.00
Cash Advances	+$318.00
Past Due Amount	+$0.00
Fees Charged	**+$69.45**
Interest Charged	**+$10.89**
New Balance	$1,784.53
Credit limit	$2,000.00
Available credit	$215.47
Statement closing date	3/22/20xx
Days in billing cycle	30

QUESTIONS?

Call Customer Service	1-832-555-0000
Lost or Stolen Credit Card	1-832-555-0000

Please send billing inquiries and correspondence to: PO Box 9073999, Houston, TX, 77083

Payment Information	
New Balance	$1,784.53
Minimum Payment Due	$48.00
Payment Due Date	4/20/20xx

Late Payment Warning: If we do not receive your minimum payment by the date listed above, you may have to pay a $35 late fee and your APR may be increased up to the Penalty APR of 28.99%.

Minimum Payment Warning: If you make only the minimum payment each period, you will pay more in interest and it will take you longer to pay off your balance. For example:

If you make no additional charges using this card and each month you pay …	You will pay off the balance shown on this statement in about …	And you will end up paying an estimated total of …
Only the minimum payment	10 years	$3,284
$62	3 years	$2,232 (Savings = $1,052)

If you would like information about credit counseling services, call 1-800-555-0000.

Transactions

Reference Number	Trans Date	Post Date	Description of Transaction or Credit	Amount
			Payments and Other Credits	
854338203FS8OO0Z5	2/25	2/25	PAYMENT THANK YOU	$450.00–
045148714518979874	3/4	3/5	BIG BOX CENTRAL 412 HOUSTON TX	$13.45–
			Purchases	
5884186PS0388W6YM	2/22	2/23	FOOD COURT 0006 HOUSTON TX	$2.05
55541860705RDYD0X	2/24	2/25	FOOD COURT 0006 HOUSTON TX	$4.63
554328608008W90M0	2/24	2/25	WESTSIDE STORE HOUSTON TX	$114.95
841517877845AKOJIO	2/25	2/26	ONLINE BOOKSELLER ST LOUIS MO 63101	$40.35
895848561561894KOH	2/26	2/27	FIVE STAR DINER KATY TX	$27.68
1871556189456SAMKL	2/26	2/27	BIG BOX CENTRAL 412 HOUSTON TX	$124.76
2564894185189LKDFID	2/27	2/28	CORNER GASOLINE BAYSIDE TX	$32.87

(transactions continued on next page)

Sources: United States Treasury and Federal Reserve Board

FIGURE 18-5
Why would it be better to pay more than the minimum payment on a credit card?

TEACH

Ask students to name information that would be included on a statement of account for a credit card or charge account. Use Figure 18-5 to explain the various elements of a monthly credit statement.

▶ Figure 18-5 *ANSWER*

Paying the minimum could take many years and cost much more money over time. In this example, the minimum could take 10 years and cost over a thousand dollars more with fees and interest charges.

TEACH

Tell students that many banks and credit card companies are trying to "go paperless." These companies don't send a physical statement. They allow the cardholder to obtain their account statements online.

There are additional advantages to online access to your credit card account. You can check your open credit balance, look for unauthorized charges, and learn more about the terms of your account.

Different Learning Abilities

Dyslexia Prepare a series of short assignments requesting students to locate various information items on the credit statement presented in Figure 18-5.

TEACH

Emphasize the importance of keeping accurate records of credit purchases and statements.

Ask students to suggest possible frauds that might occur with credit cards.

THINK CRITICALLY THROUGH VISUALS

Safety precautions include encrypted web pages for entering credit card information and the use of card expiration dates and security numbers printed on the card.

ONGOING ASSESSMENT

CHECKPOINT ✓ANSWER

The main items reported are the balance due, the amounts charged during the month, the amounts credited for payments or returns, the current balance, and the minimum amount due.

ASSESS

Key Concepts *Answers*

1. c. character
2. d. report information on the use of credit by consumers

Make Academic Connections *Answers*

3. Don's beginning balance from the previous month was $201. Use the formula: Current balance = old balance + finance charges + purchases − payments ($\$178 = x + \$2 + 45 - \$70$, $\$178 = x - \$23$, $x = \$201$).
4. Answers will vary depending on which agency students choose.
5. Reviews will vary.

Accuracy of Records

Accurate record keeping is a good personal business practice. Keeping accurate records will help you avoid credit problems.

Many errors are simply honest mistakes. Whatever the source of the error, you need to contact the business, explain the problem, and request a correction. Your creditworthiness may be at stake. Businesses are usually as eager to correct errors as you are. Bad publicity could hurt the reputation of the business if errors are not corrected.

Avoiding Fraud

The Federal Trade Commission reports that credit card fraud is a major problem. To avoid loss due to fraud, you should check your credit card account statements very carefully for errors.

Each month, you should check the accuracy of your statement by comparing it with your copies of credit card receipts. This includes the receipts you get from merchants and documents you print or save when you make online purchases. Verify payments and other credits, such as amounts subtracted when merchandise is returned. If you discover an error on a statement, you should notify the business as well as the credit card company. Keep checking new statements to ensure the problem is resolved.

In some cases, your credit card company may contact you if fraud is suspected. This happens when charges being made on a card do not match the pattern of past purchases. Unusual product purchases or charges made in new locations often trigger fraud alerts.

To help prevent Internet fraud, online credit card transactions require account numbers, expiration dates, and printed security numbers. The data transfer is also encrypted.

iStockphoto.com/alexsl

What safety precautions are in place on the Internet to prevent credit card fraud?

CHECKPOINT ✓
What are the main items reported on a statement of account?

18.3 ASSESSMENT

Key Concepts

Determine the best answer.

1. A reputation for paying bills on time relates to a person's
   a. capacity
   b. collateral
   c. character
   d. capital
2. The main activity of a credit bureau is to
   a. calculate the cost of credit for lenders and borrowers
   b. determine when a person is overusing credit
   c. contact a government agency when lenders overcharge for credit
   d. report information on the use of credit by consumers

Make Academic Connections

3. **Math** Don Ghonski received his credit card statement. This report showed $45 in new purchases, a current balance of $178, a payment of $70, and finance charges of $2. What was the amount of Don's beginning balance from the previous month?
4. **Technology** Go to the website of one of the major credit reporting agencies. What services does the agency provide for businesses? What information is available to assist consumers?
5. **Read** Find an online news article that relates to credit card debt. Read the article and write a 140-character review for your classmates that includes the URL and your suggestion to read, skim, or ignore the article.

RETEACH Highlight various items that appear on a credit report.

CLOSE Ask students to describe actions that could be taken to establish credit.

ENRICH Instruct students to prepare a short report to summarize actions that should be taken before signing a credit contract.

DOING BUSINESS IN . . . MEXICO

Mexico and the United States share a long history and a long border—more than three thousand kilometers long. Much of the southwest United States once belonged to Mexico and is still strongly influenced by Mexican culture and the Spanish language. The connection continues today; trade between the two countries is valued at more than $534 billion. Mexico is the third-largest U.S. trade partner after Canada and China.

Mexico's main exports are manufactured goods, oil and oil products, silver, and agricultural products such as fruits, vegetables, coffee, and cotton. Imports include metalworking machines, steel mill products, agricultural machinery, electrical equipment, and car and truck parts for assembly and repair.

In Mexico, business meetings are normally conducted in Spanish, the official language. It is likely that business executives will be able to speak English, but to show respect, it is important to learn some Spanish. Any printed information should be in Spanish.

Mexican work days usually start around 8 A.M. and end at 6 P.M. Your business meeting could include lunch, the main meal of the day, which can last for several hours. Business lunches are a time to socialize, not a time to present formal business information. In Mexico, relationships are developed first, and business follows.

Mexican business meetings are formal and you should dress conservatively. A dark suit is appropriate. Status is important and individuals should be addressed by their titles. Top executives will want to meet with individuals of similar rank. Always shake hands when you meet and when you leave. Personal contact is important. Negotiations should start with small talk and family is a common topic. When you move on to business, the discussions are likely to be unstructured and not follow a specific agenda.

In Mexico, time is flexible. The concept of *mañana*, or an indefinite time in the future, is the rule. So, don't be surprised if your contact is late. You, however, should arrive on time and ready to work.

Think Critically

1. What cultural factors would you need to take into consideration when doing business in Mexico?
2. Describe how you could develop a relationship with your Mexican business partner.
3. Conduct library or Internet research to find additional information about business activities and economic conditions in Mexico.

Why would an Oregon berry farm be interested in doing business with a raspberry farm in Mexico? How could the raspberry farm benefit from this relationship?

MCT /Landov

Applied Skills

Communication Ask a small group of students to role-play a business meeting of Mexican and U.S. business representatives taking place in Mexico. Instruct other students to watch the performance and identify the aspects that are related to the content of the feature about doing business in Mexico.

Doing Business in . . . MEXICO

While Mexico is geographically linked to the United States, Mexican culture is considerably different from U.S. culture. Remind students that most international business mistakes are the result of cultural differences.

THINK CRITICALLY THROUGH VISUALS

A relationship with a Mexican farm would give the Oregon farm the opportunity to supply raspberries to customers beyond the typical U.S. growing season. Doing business with a farm in the United States could provide a large market for Mexican raspberries.

Think Critically *Answers*

1. Student answers will vary, but they will probably comment on the long lunch periods and the formality of the business culture. There is also a strong relationship development period before getting down to business and a casual attitude about time.
2. Answers will vary, but students should recommend that the meeting start with handshakes. A long lunch should be used to develop relationships. Discussions should start by focusing on families. Students should not be upset if their business partner shows up late for the meeting.
3. Students will find varied information about Mexico depending on what sources they use. Encourage students to share their most interesting findings.

Focus on REAL LIFE

This scenario provides an overview of various problems that can occur when using credit.

TEACH

Ask students to name some deceptions that might occur when using credit.

Explain how the Truth-in-Lending Act and the CARD Act of 2009 protect consumers.

18.4 Protection of Credit Rights

Learning Outcomes

18.4.1 Identify credit application regulations.

18.4.2 Explain credit use regulations.

18.4.3 Discuss credit problems and available assistance.

Key Terms

credit counselor 477

bankruptcy 478

Focus on REAL LIFE

Ben Khan mistakenly left a credit card lying on a counter at a store. After asking at the store and waiting a few weeks, he realized the card would not be returned. On his next statement, he noticed that more than $200 worth of merchandise was charged by someone else.

Julie Roma checked her charge account statement and found several errors on it. One charge is for a purchase she did not make, and this is the third month in a row that this charge has shown up on the statement.

Monique and Gary Buckman had their loan application turned down. The loan officer explained that their credit bureau report was not good. Monique and Gary were shocked. They always pay their bills on time, with only a few minor exceptions. They needed this loan for home improvements.

These credit problems can happen to anyone. If consumers know about credit laws and regulations, they can take actions to avoid and correct problems.

LO 18.4.1

CREDIT APPLICATION REGULATIONS

Most businesses are honest in their business dealings. Unfortunately, some are not. Because of this, it became necessary for federal and state governments to pass laws to protect credit consumers.

Truth-in-Lending Act

The *Truth-in-Lending Act of 1968* was the first of a series of credit protection laws. Truth-in-Lending requires that you be told the cost of credit before signing an agreement. The lender must clearly state the annual percentage rate (APR) and total finance charge.

The Truth-in-Lending Act also protects consumers against unauthorized use of credit cards. The law limits your liability to $50 for unauthorized credit card purchases made prior to notifying the card issuer. You are not liable for any fraudulent charges made after you have notified the credit card company. You can notify the company by telephone, but you should also put your notification in writing.

Credit Card Act of 2009

The *Credit Card Accountability Responsibility and Disclosure Act of 2009* was designed to establish fair and transparent credit card practices. Among its provisions, the CARD Act keeps credit card companies from changing fees and interest rates without cardholder approval. Cardholders must be notified of changes and they then have the right of refusal. Cardholders can also request a lower credit limit.

The CARD Act requires a credit card statement to show how long it would take to pay off the balance if the cardholder pays only the minimum due. The act also protects people under 21, college students, and other vulnerable consumers.

Different Learning Abilities

Specific Learning Disability (SLD) Encourage students to name the purpose of Truth-in-Lending and other consumer laws in this lesson. Ask students how these laws impact their lives.

Equal Credit Opportunity Act

The *Equal Credit Opportunity Act* prohibits creditors from denying a person credit because of age, race, sex, or marital status. Young people who may have just entered the labor market cannot be denied credit based only on age. Older, possibly retired people also have special protection under this act.

Married women who previously found it difficult to establish credit in their own names now have a legal right to do so. Under this law, a woman has a right to her own credit if she proves to be creditworthy.

Unless your state still requires a person to be at least 21 to enter into a contract, a creditor cannot deny you credit based on your age alone. A creditor must look into your creditworthiness. Upon request, a creditor must give any person who is denied credit a written statement of the reasons for denial.

CHECKPOINT ✓
How does the Truth-in-Lending Act assist consumers?

LO 18.4.2

CREDIT USE REGULATIONS

Several laws have been created to protect your rights when using credit.

Fair Credit Billing Act

The *Fair Credit Billing Act* requires prompt correction of billing mistakes. To get a correction of an error, you must notify the creditor in writing within 60 days after your statement was mailed. A good rule is to report errors as soon as you discover them. After you report an error, remember the following points.

- While waiting for an answer, you are not required to pay any amount in question.
- The creditor must acknowledge your complaint within 30 days unless your statement is corrected before that time.
- You do not pay finance charges on any amount in error.
- If no error is found, the creditor must bill you again. The bill may include finance charges that have accumulated plus any minimum payments that were missed while the statement was being questioned.

Blend Images/Shutterstock.com

Why is the Equal Credit Opportunity Act so important?

TEACH

Ask students to describe factors that might result in a person being discriminated against when applying for credit.

ONGOING ASSESSMENT

CHECKPOINT ✓ANSWER

The Truth-in-Lending Act assists consumers by requiring that they be fully informed of all of the costs of credit before signing an agreement. Borrowers must be informed of the annual percentage rate and total finance charge. The law also limits consumers' liability for unauthorized use of credit cards to $50 for unauthorized purchases made prior to notifying the card issuer, and cardholders are not liable for any purchases made after notifying the credit card company.

THINK CRITICALLY THROUGH VISUALS

The Equal Credit Opportunity Act is important because it prohibits creditors from denying a person credit because of age, race, sex, or marital status. A creditor must investigate an applicant's creditworthiness and, upon request, give any person who is denied credit a written statement of the reasons for the denial.

TEACH

Explain the features of the Fair Credit Billing Act.

Different Learning Styles

Print Learner Suggest that students focus their attention on the list of provisions of the Fair Credit Billing Act on this page. Ask them to develop a scenario that illustrates all four points.

TEACH

Explain various situations in which consumers would be protected by the Fair Credit Reporting Act.

A Question of Ethics

A variety of deceptive credit businesses exist in our society. Use this feature to caution students about these various credit swindles.

Think Critically *Answers*

1. People are attracted to these credit situations when they do not have a relationship with a bank or have poor credit histories that prevent them from obtaining credit more inexpensively. Low-income people are especially likely to use these types of credit services, although payday loan companies are becoming more common in middle-class areas, perhaps due to an increase in poor money management practices.

2. Reports will vary.

The Fair Credit Billing Act also provides that you may withhold payment of any balance due on defective merchandise or services purchased with a credit card. Your first step should be to contact the business and try to resolve the problem. You can correct many situations if your complaint is made in a courteous but firm manner. The law protects you if you have made this "good faith" effort to work with the business.

Fair Credit Reporting Act

The *Fair Credit Reporting Act* is the law that gives consumers the right to know what information credit bureaus are giving to potential creditors, employers, and insurers. This law provides that if credit is denied based on information in a credit report, the applicant must be given the name, address, and phone number of the credit bureau that provided the information.
In addition, credit records for both a husband and wife are kept if both are responsible for the debt. This allows a credit history to be developed for each spouse.

Prior to the passage of this law, many consumers were unaware that potential lenders had access to reports on their bill-paying habits. This act makes those reports available to the consumer. It provides ways in which consumers can access and correct information.

The Fair Credit Reporting Act also requires that credit bureaus must delete any information dealing with a personal bankruptcy that is more than 10 years old. The credit bureau must also delete any other adverse information if it is more than seven years old.

Consumer Credit Reporting Reform Act

An unfavorable credit report can cause you to be denied for a loan or pay a higher interest rate. *The Consumer Credit Reporting Reform Act* places the burden of proof

A QUESTION OF ETHICS

Pawnshops, Payday Loans, and Credit Repair

Consumer credit is an area where unfair and deceitful business credit practices thrive. Pawnshops lend money based on the value of property, such as jewelry. These small loans are usually repaid in a month or two, but typically at a high interest rate. Some states allow pawnshops to charge 3 percent a month—that's 36 percent a year.

People in need of a small amount of money for a short time may use a *payday loan*. Nearly 20,000 of these companies now operate in the United States. The interest rate for this cash advance can be more than 600 percent. With a payday loan, a consumer may write a personal check for $230 to borrow $200 for 14 days. The lender agrees to hold the check until the next payday. This $30 finance charge for the 14 days translates into an APR of nearly 400 percent. Often, a customer continues to borrow without paying anything back. Within a few weeks, the finance charge can exceed the amount borrowed.

"Credit Repair—Are you in trouble with past due payments? Is your credit record being ruined? We can fix all problems quickly—come in today." Every day, credit repair companies offer to help consumers with poor credit histories. They promise to improve your credit rating, for a fee. Too often, after paying hundreds of dollars, consumers get nothing. Companies disappear with your money. To protect consumers, the Credit Repair Organizations Act requires that credit repair companies cannot collect their fee until completing the promised services.

Think Critically

1. Why are people attracted to these credit situations?
2. Conduct research to obtain additional information about pawnshops, payday loans, and credit repair companies. Compile your findings into a short report.

Applied Skills

Building Study Skills Allow students to work as a class to develop a summary table reporting the purpose of the consumer credit laws discussed in this lesson. Ask students to create a large version of the table for classroom display and a smaller version that can be used as a study tool.

for accurate credit information on the credit reporting agency rather than on you. Under this law, the creditor must certify that disputed data is accurate. If a creditor or the credit bureau verifies incorrect data, you can sue for damages. The federal government and state attorneys general can also sue creditors for civil damages.

Fair Debt Collection Practices Act

A *debt collection agency* attempts to obtain money that is past due. The agency may contact people who are overdue with credit payments.

To prevent threats and other inappropriate actions, the *Fair Debt Collection Practices Act* requires that debt collectors treat you fairly. It bans various debt collection actions. This law does not take away the debts that are owed.

A debt collector may contact you in person, by mail, telephone, telegram, or fax. A debt collector may not contact you at inconvenient times or places, such as before 8 A.M. or after 9 P.M. They also may not contact you at work if your employer prohibits such contact.

CHECKPOINT ✓
What is the purpose of the Fair Credit Reporting Act?

LO 18.4.3

CREDIT PROBLEMS AND ASSISTANCE

A person who cannot pay his or her bills when they are due might take these four steps.

1. Contact creditors and explain the situation.
2. Make a realistic proposal for when and what you can pay. Don't just say, "I can't pay."
3. Keep any promises you make.
4. Make a written copy of your agreement to avoid problems later.

Work as a TEAM

Many people have financial problems that result from the use of credit. Describe three situations in which people have credit problems. As a team, discuss the actions that might be taken to address these situations.

You may be able to work out a *debt repayment plan*. A creditor and a debtor develop this agreement to reduce payments to a more manageable level and still pay off the debt. This is good for both the creditor and the debtor.

One thing to avoid is being misled by advertisements that tell you, "Erase bad credit! 100% guaranteed." Claims such as these are fraudulent. No one can unconditionally correct a bad credit record—it does not work that way. If you need help with a credit problem, contact a reputable credit counseling organization.

Credit Counseling

Different kinds of help are available to people with credit problems. A **credit counselor** discusses and suggests actions to take to reduce spending and eliminate credit difficulties.

Various nonprofit counseling services are available around the country. The National Foundation of Consumer Credit can direct you to a local credit assistance program. This nonprofit organization has hundreds of member agencies that operate local offices around the country. Many of the member agencies are known as Consumer Credit Counseling Services (CCCS). Consumers are warned to be cautious of for-profit credit counseling services.

Free Credit Reports

Once a year, individuals can get free copies of their credit report from each of the big three consumer reporting agencies. These reports can be obtained online.

Applied Skills

Communication Assign students to prepare a poster or brochure to report the steps to take when facing credit problems. Encourage the use of photos and graphics.

Work as a TEAM

This activity can help students become more aware of various problems associated with using credit.

TEACH

Describe the purpose of the Consumer Credit Reporting Reform Act.

Ask students to describe situations in which a debt collector uses inappropriate behavior or tactics.

Explain the provisions of the Fair Debt Collections Act.

Highlight the suggested actions to take when a person is facing credit problems.

ONGOING ASSESSMENT

CHECKPOINT ✓ANSWER

The purpose of the Fair Credit Reporting Act is to give consumers the right to know what information credit bureaus are giving to potential creditors, employers, and insurers. The Act requires credit bureaus to keep records for both a husband and wife if both are responsible for the debt so that each spouse can develop a credit history. It also requires credit bureaus to delete information dealing with a personal bankruptcy that is more than 10 years old and any other adverse information that is more than 7 years old.

TEACH

Warn students about companies that claim to easily solve your credit problems. Describe credit counseling services available to consumers.

Explain situations when bankruptcy may be appropriate. Emphasize the drawbacks of bankruptcy for both consumers and society.

Mel Yates/DigitalVision/Getty Images

What can a credit counselor do for people with credit problems?

The federally authorized website is the Annual Credit Report site. Many companies advertise a "free" credit report, but may charge for additional services. Checking your credit report each year helps to ensure accurate records.

Bankruptcy

Consumers may take one additional step when facing credit problems. They should use this final option only for extreme situations. **Bankruptcy** is the legal process of reducing or eliminating an amount owed. This process is costly and requires legal assistance. Consumers can usually avoid bankruptcy by using credit wisely and practicing sensible money management.

CHECKPOINT
What actions can a person take when facing credit problems?

18.4 ASSESSMENT

Key Concepts

Determine the best answer.

1. A person may be denied credit on the basis of his or her
   - **a.** gender
   - **b.** marriage status
   - **c.** income
   - **d.** type of job
2. The federal law that provides protection when an error occurs on a monthly statement is the
   - **a.** Truth-in-Lending Law
   - **b.** Fair Credit Reporting Act
   - **c.** Fair Credit Billing Act
   - **d.** Equal Credit Opportunity Act
3. The legal process of reducing or eliminating an amount owed is
   - **a.** credit
   - **b.** credit reporting
   - **c.** bankruptcy
   - **d.** financing

Make Academic Connections

4. **Statistics** Obtain current data about the number of people who have declared personal bankruptcy in recent years. Prepare a chart to show the trend of these data. Give an explanation as to why the trend occurred. What are the costs of bankruptcy to a society?
5. **Communication** Create a role-playing situation in which you are denied credit. One person should explain how he or she encountered credit problems. The other person should suggest actions to eliminate the credit problems.

THINK CRITICALLY THROUGH VISUALS

A reputable credit counselor can help individuals assess their credit problems and suggest actions to take to reduce spending and eliminate credit difficulties.

ONGOING ASSESSMENT

CHECKPOINT ANSWER

When facing credit problems, a person can contact creditors and explain the situation, make a realistic proposal for when and what he or she can pay, keep any promises made, and make a written copy of agreements to avoid later misunderstandings. A person with credit problems may be able to work out a debt repayment plan. He or she could also contact a credit counselor for advice. Bankruptcy is a final option for extreme debt situations.

ASSESS

Key Concepts *Answers*

1. c. income
2. c. Fair Credit Billing Act
3. c. bankruptcy

Make Academic Connections *Answers*

4. Charts will vary depending on when the assignment is completed. Answers should indicate that students understand that the societal costs of bankruptcy include financial loss to businesses and the individual's loss of creditworthiness.
5. Students role-play to explore credit problems and solutions.

RETEACH Highlight the main provisions of the credit protection laws discussed in this lesson.

ENRICH Instruct students to prepare a list of questions that a credit counselor might ask a client.

CLOSE Ask students to describe the major causes of credit problems.

LIFE/WORK SKILLS

LEADERSHIP AND RESPONSIBILITY

Time Management—A Leadership Skill

Effective leaders know how to manage their time. They spend time planning how they will use their time to achieve their goals.

Plan and Use Your Time

You need a way to plan your day, your week, your month, and more. There are plenty of tools to help you, but it all starts with a calendar. It might be in your computer, in your pocket, on the wall, or on your phone.

Spend a few minutes at the beginning of the day checking your calendar to see what you will be doing that day and the rest of the week. Spend a few minutes at the end of the day looking at your calendar to ensure that you will be ready for tomorrow.

Your calendar should reflect the time you have committed to others and yourself. It should include meetings, appointments, social engagements, and other activities. For example, if you have a part-time job, you should block out the times you work as soon as you get your schedule. If you are supposed to be somewhere doing something, it should be on your calendar.

What about your other time commitments? It is easy to record the due date for a project on your calendar, but you also need to carve out time to work on the project. Depending on your current situation, you might need to schedule time to work on projects, read assignments, study for tests, pay bills, balance your checkbook, or practice your jump shot.

Respect Other People's Time

Part of planning and monitoring your own time is learning to respect other people's time. You need to be on time for work, appointments, and meetings. When you are late, you send a message that you do not value other people's time. It makes you appear self-absorbed and disrespectful.

Meetings should start and end on time. Waiting for latecomers to arrive is unfair to those who arrived on time. Allowing a meeting to drag on past the planned end time interferes with other plans and puts people in the uncomfortable position of having to decide if they should stay or leave.

Respect Your Own Time

Effective leaders learn how to balance their work with their personal life. Scheduling time for exercise, relaxation, and personal interests are good habits. It is also important to establish routines that allow you to eat well and get adequate sleep. According to the National Sleep Foundation, adults need 7 to 9 hours of sleep each night and teens require 8.5 to 9.25 hours. Adequate sleep helps you pay attention and remember new information.

Knowing when to say "no" is another component of time management. People who demonstrate leadership skills are recognized for their accomplishments and sought after for assignments and committees at work and in the community. Effective leaders learn to work to their capacity without overextending themselves. They also learn to identify the strengths of others and help develop and inspire new leaders.

Think Critically

1. How does being late distract from your ability to lead others?
2. What are some things that you can do right now to improve your time management skills?

Andrey_Popov/Shutterstock.com

What are some advantages to using an electronic calendar? What are some disadvantages?

LIFE/WORK SKILLS

Point out that time management skills are important to success in all types of work and are also used in everyday life. Ask students to provide some examples of how they use time management skills now and how they could improve their skills. Encourage students to share tips and strategies that they use for managing their time.

Ask students to discuss how the need for good time management skills might change after high school.

THICK CRITICALLY THROUGH VISUALS

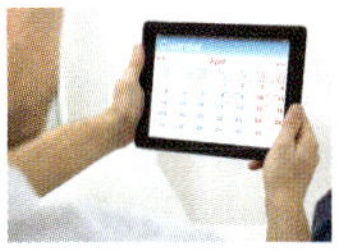

Answers will vary. An electronic calendar allows you to see items conveniently. Such calendars provide details and a day, week, or month view at a glance. They can be effective tools for project planning. Others can post events in your electronic calendar.

Think Critically *Answers*

1. Being late is disrespectful and most people would prefer to follow a leader they respect.
2. Answers will vary. Things that students can do now to improve their time management skills include reviewing calendars at the beginning and end of each day, recording all commitments, striving to be punctual, and scheduling personal time.

Think Critically About Business *Answers*

1a. Students will probably say Debbie's plan is safer.

1b. Answers will vary. Students might suggest that Edward not spend more than he earns. They might suggest that Debbie use credit cards wisely to take advantage of special sales on products she needs and to avoid carrying large amounts of cash while shopping.

2. Extending credit could help Gerry's business because customers will be more likely to make large purchases. Her business could be hurt if customers do not pay their debts. She could offer credit card options to her customers; even though she will have to pay the credit card company a small percentage of her sales, she will not risk a loss if a customer does not pay.

3a. Most students will agree that this can be a convenience as long as the credit user does not accumulate too much debt.

3b. Most students will agree that this is a wise approach, but may not always be possible.

3c. Although this is true, sometimes there are valid reasons for postponing paying for a purchase when the borrower has a plan for paying off the debt.

3d. Some students may agree; however, they may not realize that even a small finance charge may represent a very high interest rate.

Chapter 18 Assessment

Review Business Concepts

18.1 Credit Fundamentals

- Credit is the privilege of using someone else's money with the obligation to repay it at a future time. The major types of consumer credit are charge accounts, credit cards, installment credit, and consumer loans.
- Credit used wisely makes some buying more convenient, gives the purchaser immediate possession rather than waiting until later, allows buyers to take advantage of special sales, and establishes a person's credit rating.
- Credit is misused if it results in overbuying, careless buying, paying higher prices in stores that grant credit, or incurring excessive debt.

18.2 Cost of Credit

- The amount of interest expense is calculated by multiplying the interest rate times the principal times the number of days or months.
- The annual percentage rate (APR) states the percentage cost of credit on a yearly basis. Costs of credit in addition to interest include service fees, the cost of collecting bad debts, and credit insurance. The finance charge is the total dollar cost of credit, including interest and all other charges.
- The cost of credit varies among lenders. You can save money by shopping around to compare the APR, amount of monthly payments, and total finance charge.

18.3 Credit Application and Documents

- A credit application is a document on which you provide information needed by a lender. A business considers a person's character (honesty and willingness to pay debts), capacity (the ability to pay debts), and capital (the value of the person's possessions) in reviewing an applicant for credit.
- A credit bureau gathers information on credit users. A credit record documents your credit history. You can maintain a good credit history by paying your bills on time.
- Two commonly used credit documents are the installment contract and the statement of account. Before signing an installment contract, consider the finance charges and other features of the loan. Credit statements should be checked carefully and errors reported as soon as they are discovered.

18.4 Protection of Credit Rights

- The Truth-in-Lending Law, the CARD Act, and the Equal Credit Opportunity Act provide information and protection when applying for credit.
- The Fair Credit Billing Act, the Fair Credit Reporting Act, the Consumer Credit Reporting Act, and the Fair Debt Collections Act protect consumers when using credit.
- Assistance with credit problems is available from counselors, debt consolidation, and, as a last option, bankruptcy.

Think Critically About Business

1. Edward Adiska buys everything he possibly can on credit. If he does not have enough money to cover his monthly payments when they are due, he borrows money to pay them. His sister, Debbie, likes to buy things only after she has saved enough money to pay cash for them.
   a. Whose plan do you think is better? Why?
   b. What suggestions about the use of credit might you make to Edward and Debbie?
2. Gerry Shadle owns and operates a flower shop. She is considering expanding her shop to include home decorating items. At present, the flower shop only accepts cash. How might extending credit help or hurt her business?
3. Read the following statements and explain why you agree or disagree.
   a. "A credit card is nice to have. If I'm out of cash, I can still buy what I want."
   b. "I don't believe in using credit for most purchases. I pay cash for everyday items and use credit only for expensive items, such as a new refrigerator."

c. "If I can't pay cash, I can't afford it. I won't buy anything unless I can pay cash."
d. "I often don't pay the full amount of my charge account when it is due; the finance charges are quite reasonable."

4. Les Heddle needs to borrow $15,000 to do some remodeling in his store and has three options:

OPTION 1: The Thrifty Loan Company offered him an APR of 16 percent for a three-year loan. Monthly payments, including finance charges, would be $555.

OPTION 2: The Greenback Bank offered him a five-year loan at 15 percent APR with a total monthly payment of $375.

OPTION 3: The Silk Purse Finance Lending Shop did not quote an APR figure but said, "We have a 'no frills' loan policy, and you can have a four-year loan with monthly payments at the amazingly low figure of $496 per month."

Construct a loan comparison chart showing the lender, APR, loan length, monthly payment, total payment, and cost of credit. Then decide which loan would be the best for Les Heddle. Give reasons for your decision.

5. Suzanne Winters does not believe in buying anything on credit. She says too many people get into trouble with credit and many errors are made in credit transactions. Explain to Suzanne ways in which laws protect consumers who engage in credit transactions and tell her about some of the help that is available for consumers who have credit problems.

Develop Your Business Language

Match the terms listed with the definitions.

6. Your reputation for paying your bills on time.
7. Someone who becomes responsible for payment of a note if you do not pay as promised.
8. The privilege of using someone else's money for a period of time.
9. A loan in which you agree to make monthly payments in specific amounts over a period of time.
10. The legal process of reducing or eliminating an amount owed.
11. A person who suggests actions to reduce spending and eliminate credit difficulties.
12. A payment of part of the purchase price that is made as part of a credit agreement.
13. A written promise to repay based on the debtor's excellent credit rating.
14. Property that is offered as security for some loan agreements.
15. The total dollar cost of credit, including interest and all other charges.
16. The percentage cost of credit on a yearly basis.
17. A company that gathers information on credit users and sells that information in the form of credit reports to credit grantors.
18. A record of the transactions that you have completed with a business during a billing period.
19. A form in which you provide information needed by a lender to make a decision about granting credit.
20. The cost of using someone else's money.

Key Terms

a. annual percentage rate (APR)
b. bankruptcy
c. collateral
d. cosigner
e. credit
f. credit application
g. credit bureau
h. credit counselor
i. credit rating
j. down payment
k. finance charge
l. installment loan
m. interest
n. promissory note
o. statement of account

4. The loan comparison chart appears at the bottom of this page.

This exercise should convince students that it is worth the time it takes to shop for credit. The Thrifty loan has the lowest cost, but the Greenback loan could be paid back with the lowest monthly payments.

5. Suzanne should be told about consumer credit protection laws, consumer credit counseling services, and debt-repayment plans.

Develop Your Business Language *Answers*

6. i. credit rating
7. d. cosigner
8. e. credit
9. l. installment loan
10. b. bankruptcy
11. h. credit counselor
12. j. down payment
13. n. promissory note
14. c. collateral
15. k. finance charge
16. a. annual percentage rate (APR)
17. g. credit bureau
18. o. statement of account
19. f. credit application
20. m. interest

4. The completed loan comparison chart appears below.

Lender	APR	Loan Length	Monthly Payment	Total Payment	Cost of Credit
Thrifty	16%	3 yrs.	$555	$19,980	$4,980
Greenback	15%	5 yrs.	$375	$22,500	$7,500
Silk Purse	?	4 yrs.	$496	$23,808	$8,808

Make Academic Connections

21. **History** Research the use of credit throughout history. When was credit first used in various civilizations? How has credit been used to influence the development of retailing and other business activities in the United States?

22. **Culture** People in different countries have different attitudes toward credit. Based on web searches, library research, and talking with people who know about other countries, prepare a summary of how credit is used around the world.

23. **Research** Collect credit applications, advertisements, and online offers. Create a table to compare the different APRs reported in the various credit information sources.

24. **Communication** Prepare a one-minute oral summary of the activities of a credit bureau. Explain how credit bureaus serve both consumers and businesses.

25. **Math** Find the date of maturity for each of these loans:

DATE OF LOAN	TIME OF LOAN
March 15	4 months
May 26	3 months
July 31	5 months
April 30	30 days
October 5	45 days

26. **Research** Some credit contracts include the "Rule of 78." This condition results in a "prepayment penalty" if a loan is paid off early. Conduct a web search to obtain a basic understanding of the Rule of 78.

27. **Technology** Conduct a web search to locate a sample of a credit contract. What features of the contract provide consumers with clear information about the cost of credit and other terms of the loan agreement?

28. **Law** Several federal agencies, including the Federal Trade Commission and the Federal Reserve Board, administer consumer credit protection laws. Conduct research on the laws discussed in the chapter. Prepare a table with a summary of which agency to contact when your rights are violated.

29. **Math** Before borrowing $200, Laura Demetry visited a small loan company and the loan department of a bank. At the loan company, she found that she could borrow the $200 if she signed a note agreeing to repay the balance in six equal monthly installments of $36.50. At the bank, she could borrow the money by signing a promissory note for $215 and repaying the balance in six equal monthly payments.

   a. What would be the cost of the loan at the small loan company?
   b. What would be the cost of the loan at the bank?

Make Your Case

Samantha Mae has been out of school for three years and has held four different jobs with different employers. She has been on her present job for two months. Her monthly take-home pay is $1,362. She shares an apartment with two friends to keep expenses down, but she is always in debt. Each month, she is short of the money she needs to pay all of her charge accounts. Her checking account is frequently overdrawn. Samantha has decided it would be better to live by herself. She blames her roommates for her credit spending sprees. She has come to you for a loan of $2,000. Her new apartment will cost $400 a month, and she wants to pay off some of her bills that are past due. She assures you that she will pay you at least $50 each month.

30. What are some criteria you would use to determine whether a personal loan for Samantha would be a good idea? What additional information might you want?

31. Would you loan the money to Samantha? Why or why not?

Interactions and Connections

32. Obtain information on the responsibilities involved with cosigning a loan. Talk to people in your community. What do they know about being a cosigner? What precautions should be taken when cosigning? Talk with a credit counselor to obtain information about problems associated with cosigning a loan.

Make Academic Connections *Answers*

21. Answers will vary.

22. Summaries will vary.

23. Tables will vary.

24. Oral summaries will vary.

25. The date of maturity of each loan is as follows: July 15; August 26; December 31; May 30; November 19.

26. The "Rule of 78" results in higher interest payments when loans are paid off early because the lender received 75 percent of the interest payments in the first half of the loan payment schedule.

27. Answers will vary.

28. Students prepare a table summarizing the credit protection provided by the various laws presented in this chapter and indicate which agency to contact when rights protected by the laws are violated. Laws discussed in this chapter include the FDIC's Truth-in-Lending Act of 1968, and the FTC's Equal Credit Opportunity Act, the Fair Credit Billing Act, the Fair Credit Reporting Act, the Credit Repair Organizations Act, the Consumer Credit Reporting Reform Act, and the Fair Debt Collection Practices Act.

29a. The cost of the loan at the small loan company would be $19 for a total loan repayment of $219.

29b. The cost of the loan at the bank would be $15 for a total loan repayment of $215.

Make Your Case *Answers*

30. When considering making a loan, one should evaluate the potential borrower's ability to pay. Samantha has a good job and her new apartment would cost less than one-fourth of her income, but she has not demonstrated fiscal restraint in her present lifestyle. Additional information that might be helpful would be the reasons for the frequent job changes and the stability of her current job.

31. Answers will vary. Most students will probably say they would not loan Samantha the money.

Interactions and Connections

32. Students talk to people they know about the risks and precautions that should be taken when cosigning a loan. They then talk to a credit counselor to discuss problems with cosigning a loan.

33. Individuals should give considerable thought to choosing a credit card and not react to free offers, temporary low interest rates, or pre-approved cards. Individuals should choose a credit card offer that meets their needs. Use the Internet to identify a wide variety of card types. Evaluate different card offerings using at least three different credit card sources such as a bank, a credit card company, or other businesses that offer reward cards (airlines, hotels, etc.). Develop a table to evaluate at least three different cards. Choose from this list a card you would like to use and justify your choice.

Then, identify cards that are directed toward students. Compare interest rates for cards directed toward students versus cards for individuals with good credit ratings. Explain why there are differences.

Impromptu Speaking Event

Leaders have the special skill to express their thoughts without prior preparation. Poise, self-confidence, and organization of facts are three valuable skills that are beneficial for articulate leaders.

Participants will draw a current event and will be given 10 minutes to organize their speech. One 4″ by 6″ index card will be given to the participant and may be used during the preparation and performance of the impromptu speech. Information may be written on both sides of the note card. Your speech should be four minutes in length, and no reference materials may be brought to or used during the preparation or presentation. No microphone will be used for your speech. Participants will receive a five-point deduction for any time under 3:31 or over 4:29 minutes. Some impromptu topics:

- Importance of Credit
- Minding Your Cs of Credit
- Credit Protection and Rights
- Avoiding Credit Disasters

Performance Indicators Evaluated

- Understand the three Cs of credit.
- Differentiate the pros and cons of credit.
- Define the role of credit in the market economy.
- Explain credit concepts in a clear, concise manner.

For more detailed information about performance indicators, go to the FBLA website.

Think Critically

1. List two advantages and two disadvantages of credit.
2. What are the three Cs of credit? How can individuals protect their credit rating?
3. Do you believe that consumers are addicted to credit in a negative way? Explain your answer.

www.fbla-pbl.org

WINNING EDGE

Impromptu Speaking Event

An ability to speak with little or no preparation is a very important skill. Encourage students to gain confidence with the use of this activity.

Think Critically *Answers*

1. Advantages of credit: buy now and pay later, good for big purchase items. Disadvantages of credit: overextension of credit, high interest costs.

2. The three Cs of credit are character, capacity, and capital. Individuals must use credit wisely and not get carried away with excessive purchases.

3. Answers will vary. There is a large amount of consumer debt in America and consumers may be tempted to overspend.

33. Answers will vary. Students should identify considerable differences between targeted markets and card offerings. Students should find that interest rates for student cards are higher than for those individuals with good credit. This is due to a lack of credit history for most students.

CHAPTER OVERVIEW

Information for identifying and analyzing investment alternatives is presented in this chapter.

19.1 Saving and Investment Planning
Types of investments and factors to consider when selecting an investment are the main topics in this lesson.

19.2 Stock Investments
Type of stock, investing in stock, and stock values are the focus of this lesson.

19.3 Bonds and Mutual Funds
This lesson provides explanations of government bonds, corporate bonds, and mutual funds.

19.4 Real Estate Investments
Various housing options, along with discussion of home-buying activities, are covered in this lesson.

19.5 Other Investments
This lesson explains investing in commodities and collectibles.

Chapter 19 Savings and Investment Strategies

iStockphoto.com/baramee2554

Instructor Resources

- Activities and Study Guide IE
- Chapter and Unit Tests IE
- Lesson Plans
- PowerPoint Presentation
- Cognero Test, Ch. 19

Student Resources

Activities and Study Guide
www.cengage.com/swep/pob9e
- Portfolio Activity

PLANNING A CAREER IN . . .
INVESTMENTS

People and organizations save and invest money in many ways. Some careers in the investment industry involve working with individual investors, while others revolve around institutional investors, such as banks and pension funds.

Career opportunities exist for workers who want to work directly with clients and those who prefer to work behind the scenes. Positions are located in diverse settings such as retail outlets, call centers, and corporate headquarters. Although some positions are located in major financial centers, career opportunities exist around the country and around the world.

Related Job Titles

- Brokerage Account Executive
- Brokerage Clerk
- Economist
- Financial Analyst
- Fund Manager
- Investment Banker
- Real Estate Appraiser
- Real Estate Agent
- Securities Research Analyst
- Securities and Commodities Sales Agent
- Stockbroker

New and different investment products continue to be created. These investment alternatives result in employment opportunities for those interested in helping others plan their financial futures. Changing interest rates, foreign currency fluctuations, and global economic conditions influence these emerging investment vehicles.

Analyze Career Opportunities in . . .
INVESTMENTS

Use library and Internet resources to learn more about careers in investments. Choose one of the job titles listed in the box and answer the following questions.

1. How would you describe the nature of the work? Include examples of things that might happen in a typical work day.
2. Is this a career that interests you? Describe a few things you could do to learn more about this career.

What it's like to work as an . . . Investment Broker

"Do you think I should sell my healthcare stocks? Or will they be a good investment for my future? How will changing interest rates affect my investments? Will I have to pay a fee to sell my stocks? How much will it be?"

These questions are commonly asked of Roberto Jiminez, an investment broker. He has found that an understanding of economic conditions and business trends is the foundation of success in this field.

Each day, financial markets around the world process millions of transactions to buy and sell investments. Stocks, bonds, mutual funds, real estate, currencies, commodities, gold, and silver are bought and sold by investors. The people who research, sell, and record these transactions are employed by a variety of investment companies and other financial businesses.

What about you? How could economic conditions affect the demand for investment jobs? What training and knowledge would be important for success in investment careers?

PLANNING A CAREER IN . . .
INVESTMENTS

Global business activities, technology, and other factors have generated increased interest in personal investing. Many career opportunities have been created by this trend.

What About You? *Answers*

When the economy is strong, many people will be looking for ways to invest their money and the demand for investment jobs will increase. Training and knowledge that are important for success in investment careers include a thorough understanding of economics and how business systems work. Fluency with investment terms and a grasp of the legal aspects of investing are also essential.

Analyze Career Opportunities *Answers*

Student answers will vary depending on when the assignment is completed and individual interests.

Additional Career Information

Encourage students to investigate careers they find interesting and explore unfamiliar careers. Two resources for additional career information are the *Occupational Outlook Handbook,* an online publication (www.bls.gov/oco) of the U.S. Bureau of Labor Statistics, and the O*NET Resource Center (www.onetcenter.org) developed by the U.S. Department of Labor. Information about specific careers and jobs can be used to demonstrate the relevance of skills learned in this course.

Focus on REAL LIFE

This feature provides a starting point for students to think about saving and investing. Invite students to share any personal experiences they have with saving and investing.

TEACH

Ask students to name reasons why saving and investing for the future is important. Describe the economic benefits of saving and investing for individuals, businesses, and society.

Explain the differences between *saving* and *investing*.

19.1 Saving and Investment Planning

Learning Outcomes

19.1.1 Explain the basics of saving and investing.

19.1.2 Identify types of savings and investments.

19.1.3 Discuss factors to consider when evaluating savings and investment alternatives.

Key Terms

saving 486
investing 486
yield 489
liquidity 491

Focus on REAL LIFE

"I'd sure like to buy a new smartphone," said Mel. "I found one that has all the features I want. But it costs about $150. I can't afford it."

"Try saving your money," Hank said in an encouraging voice. "Maybe if you cut back on some of your other spending, you could save enough money to buy it."

"That would take forever," sighed Mel.

"It's easier than you think," responded Hank. "If you put aside just a dollar a day, within six months you'd have more than $150. If you save even more each day, you could buy the phone fairly soon."

"You're kidding!" exclaimed Mel.

"Really," said Hank. "Most people don't realize that saving small amounts of money on a regular basis can result in large amounts in the future, and that doesn't even include the interest you can earn."

LO 19.1.1

SAVING AND INVESTMENT BASICS

Creating a personal saving and investing strategy is vital for every financial plan. Putting money aside in a systematic way is necessary to achieve financial goals.

When savings are invested and used, the economy benefits. Individuals, businesses, and governments borrow money from financial institutions. People commonly borrow the savings of others to pay for homes, motor vehicles, and college. When this money is spent, demand for goods and services increases. This results in more jobs and creates more spending by workers.

Businesses borrow funds to operate or expand their operations. Building a new factory, replacing old equipment, or selling a new product are common reasons for business borrowing. These actions create jobs and expand economic activity.

Governments may borrow for highways, schools, or other public services. An economy would be significantly weakened without savings and investments.

Savings and Investment Activities

Saving is the storage of money for future use. How much you save, where you put your savings, and what you save for are important decisions. People save different amounts of money for different reasons and in different ways.

Some people save for years and then use those funds for a down payment to buy a home. Saving is also important in order to have money available for emergencies. Financial planning experts encourage people to deposit 10 percent of their income into a savings account or other investment each month.

After building up some savings, most people want to earn more. **Investing**

Different Learning Abilities

At-Risk Emphasize to students the importance of saving and investment knowledge for various aspects of their lives. Ask students to explain how investing might benefit them in the future. Ask students to focus their attention on the next year and the next five years.

means using your savings to earn more money. While a savings plan is a simple type of investing, many other investment choices are available.

Determine Investment Goals

Every saver and investor has one of two major financial goals: income or growth. People who want income for current living expenses desire *current income.* Various types of savings plans and investments provide current income.

In contrast, *long-term growth* is the other main investment goal. This goal is for those who desire financial security in the future. Investors who desire long-term growth choose investments that they hope will increase in value over time.

The Growth of Savings

In addition to putting money aside as savings, you should make those savings work for you. *Interest* is money you receive for letting others use your money.

If you save $50 a month, in a year, the savings will amount to $600. Suppose you deposit this money in a savings program that earns 6 percent simple interest, paid quarterly. You will earn $9 every three months. You will earn $36 each year. The interest may not be added to your account, but instead paid directly to you. At the end of 10 years, you will still have $600 in the account but will have earned $360 in interest.

Compound Interest Earning interest on previously earned interest results in faster growth of savings. *Compound interest* is computed on the amount saved plus the interest previously earned. For example, simple annual interest of 10 percent on $1,000 is $100.

If the interest is compounded, then the interest computed at the end of the next year is based on $1,100 ($1,000 + $100 first-year interest). The 10 percent interest earned in the second year is $110.

Interest the third year is based on $1,210 ($1,100 + $110 second-year interest) and is $121. When interest is compounded, the amount of interest paid increases each time it is calculated. Without compounding, the interest paid would be only $100 each year.

Interest can be compounded daily, monthly, quarterly, semiannually, or annually. The more frequent the compounding, the greater the growth in your savings. Figure 19-1 shows how quickly monthly savings of different amounts increase when interest is compounded quarterly at 6 percent.

Life-Span Plan

Explain why people who have created life-span plans are often more successful in saving than those who have not. Include some specific examples. How might your life-span plan help you save?

CHECKPOINT

How does saving influence economic activity?

COMPOUND INTEREST (QUARTERLY)					
MONTHLY SAVINGS	END OF FIRST YEAR	END OF SECOND YEAR	END OF THIRD YEAR	END OF FOURTH YEAR	END OF FIFTH YEAR
$ 5.00	$ 61.98	$ 127.76	$ 197.76	$ 271.68	$ 350.32
10.00	123.95	255.52	395.15	543.35	700.47
25.00	309.89	638.79	987.87	1,358.38	1,751.62
30.00	371.86	766.55	1,185.45	1,630.05	2,101.94
35.00	433.84	894.30	1,383.02	1,901.73	2,452.26
50.00	619.77	1,277.58	1,975.74	2,716.75	3,503.24

FIGURE 19-1

What would be the effect if the interest was compounded monthly or weekly?

TEACH

Emphasize the importance of investing for economic growth.

Explain the two main goals of investing: current income and long-term growth. Ask students to describe situations for each of these two types of goals.

Use Figure 19-1 to illustrate the potential growth of savings.

Life-Span Plan *Answers*

Answers will vary. Students should point out that most people are better able to work and save when they have a clear idea of what they want to achieve.

ONGOING ASSESSMENT

CHECKPOINT *ANSWER*

Saving benefits the economy by making more money available for borrowing by individuals, businesses, and governments. When this money is spent, demand for goods and services increases, resulting in more jobs and more spending by workers.

▸ Figure 19-1 *ANSWER*

This savings account would grow more quickly if the interest were compounded more frequently.

Applied Skills

Mathematics Explain the difference between simple and compound interest for a person's savings and investments. Use visuals to show the faster growth of money with compounding interest. Invite interested students to construct tables similar to Figure 19-1 for interest compounded weekly and monthly.

Work as a Team

Use this activity to help students understand how investment needs change for different life situations.

TEACH

Provide an overview of the main categories of savings plans. Ask students to describe situations in which different savings plans would be appropriate.

Instruct students to create a list of various types of investments.

THINK CRITICALLY THROUGH VISUALS

In addition to the classic piggy bank shown here, many banking institutions allow young people to open savings accounts. Some families buy a small amount of inexpensive stock for their children and then teach the children how to follow the stock's progress.

Work as a TEAM

Identify different investments for different life situations. Prepare descriptions of four people of varied ages and different household situations. Suggest investments that might be appropriate for each person.

LO 19.1.2

SAVING AND INVESTMENT CHOICES

Many choices are available for your saving and investing dollars. The choices range from very safe savings accounts to rather risky investments.

Savings Plans

Banks, credit unions, and other financial institutions offer a choice of savings plans. Regular savings accounts, certificates of deposit, and money market accounts all provide a safe location for storage of your money.

Anna Hoychuk/Shutterstock.com

What savings options are available to young people?

Savings Account A savings plan with a low balance is a regular savings account. Usually, you may deposit and withdraw money as needed. These accounts pay interest while keeping money safe.

Certificate of Deposit A *certificate of deposit* (also called a CD) allows you to earn a higher interest rate than a regular savings account. This savings instrument usually requires a minimum deposit of $100 to $1,000 or more. You must leave the money on deposit for a specified period, from a few days to several years. Penalties, in addition to loss of interest, may be assessed if the money is withdrawn early.

Money Market Account A *money market account* pays a variable interest rate based on various government and corporate securities. Interest paid on money market accounts reflects the current rates of interest being paid in the money markets.

In general, money market accounts do not require long-term deposits. They may require a large minimum balance. The earnings on money market accounts are usually higher than regular savings accounts but less than long-term certificates of deposit.

Securities

Investments in securities include stocks, bonds, and mutual funds. Corporations and governments sell these securities to raise money.

Stock Investments When you buy a share of stock, you become part owner of a company. A stock purchase, made directly or indirectly through mutual funds, is a very common way of investing. If a stock increases in value and is then sold for more than its original cost, a *capital gain* results. When an investment is sold for less than its original cost, a *capital loss* is the result.

Bond Investments Lending money for use by businesses and governments is another common investment. *Bonds*

Different Learning Styles

Visual Learner Use the main headings in this lesson to present and reinforce the main types of saving plans and investments. Ask students to write the terms and definitions on flash cards.

represent debt. When you purchase a bond, you are lending funds to a company or government agency to use for their business activities.

Mutual Funds Instead of buying individual stocks and bonds, people can buy shares in a mutual fund managed by an investment company. Money from many investors is used to invest in a variety of securities. Mutual funds allow investors to spread out their risk among many investments.

Alternative Investments

Other investment choices include real estate, commodities, and collectibles. These choices often carry greater risk than savings or securities choices. As with all investments, you should carefully review your situation and options before investing in these areas.

Real Estate People invest in real estate for numerous reasons. Many people purchase their own home for the sense of security and stability. Some purchase property for rental income. Others buy vacant property in hopes that its value will increase. Housing, farmland, apartment buildings, and shopping malls are some examples of real estate investments.

Commodities Grain, livestock, precious metals, currency, and financial instruments are all commodities. Investors purchase commodity contracts in anticipation of higher market prices for the commodity in the near future. Commodity investing is considered very risky.

Collectibles Old coins, works of art, antique furniture, and other rare items are often bought with the hopes that their value will increase.

CHECKPOINT ✓
What are the nine main categories of saving and investment alternatives?

FYI To determine how many years it will take your savings to double, use the "Rule of 72." To use this rule, divide 72 by the interest rate on your investment. The result is the number of years it will take you to double your money. For example, if your investment is earning 6 percent interest, you divide 72 by 6. At an interest rate of 6 percent, your money will double in 12 years.

LO 19.1.3

EVALUATING SAVINGS AND INVESTMENTS

As you decide which investments are best for you, four main factors should be considered: safety, return, liquidity, and taxes.

Safety and Risk

Today, savings accounts at most financial institutions are insured up to $250,000 by the federal government. This insurance is a promise that your money will be available when you need it. *Safety* is assurance that the money you have invested will be returned to you.

Suppose you lend $100 to someone who promises to pay it back with 10 percent interest at the end of one year. If the loan is paid back, you will receive $110 ($100 + $10 interest). If the borrower has no money at the end of the year, you may get nothing back. You may lose both the $100 you loaned and the $10 interest you should have earned.

Not all investors require the same degree of safety. Someone may have enough money to make 20 different investments. If one of them loses value, the investor still has the other 19. Another person may only have a small amount of money and can make only one investment. One loss would be serious. Most people want to make investments that are relatively safe.

Potential Return

A good savings plan or investment should earn a reasonable return. The **yield** is the percentage of money earned on your

FYI

Consider providing students with example interest rates and asking them to use the Rule of 72 to calculate the number of years it will take an investment to double at these rates.

TEACH

Explain the main categories of securities and other investment alternatives.

ONGOING ASSESSMENT

CHECKPOINT ✓ANSWER

The nine main categories of saving and investment alternatives are (1) savings accounts, (2) certificates of deposit, (3) money market accounts, (4) stock investments, (5) bond investments, (6) mutual funds, (7) real estate, (8) commodities, and (9) collectibles.

TEACH

Provide an overview of the factors that can be used to evaluate investments.

Explain the meaning of *yield*.

Use Figure 19-2 on page 490 to demonstrate the impact of the interest rate on the yield.

Different Learning Styles

English Language Learners (ELL) Obtain translations for the names of savings plans and investments to reinforce these concepts in both English and other dominant languages used by students. Also consider using visuals to communicate these ideas.

▶ **Figure 19-2 *ANSWER***

The trade-off of investing in high-yielding securities is that, as the opportunity for return goes up, so does the risk.

TEACH

Point out the value of the Truth in Savings Act (TISA) to consumers.

Use Figure 19-3 to help students understand risk levels for various types of investments.

▶ **Figure 19-3 *ANSWER***

A person might invest in a high-risk investment if he or she perceives an opportunity for a high return on the investment. People with more assets are better suited to take such risks.

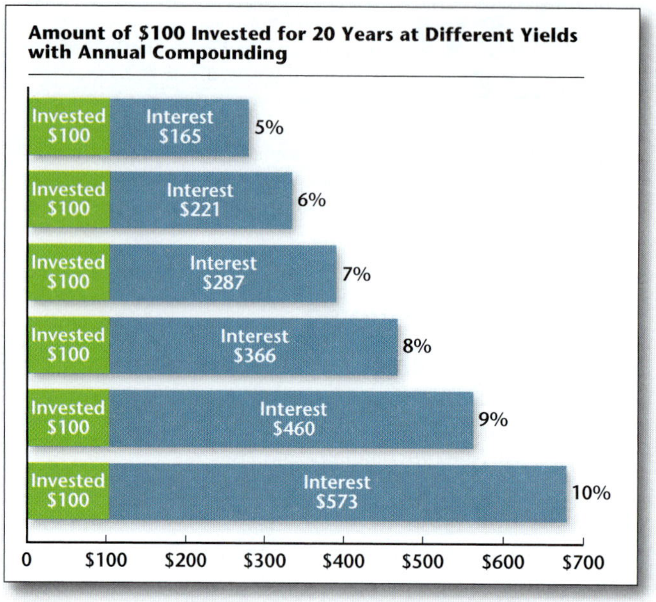

FIGURE 19-2
What is the trade-off of investing in higher-yielding securities?

savings or investment over a year. Other common names for yield are the *rate of return* or the *annual yield*. Figure 19-2 shows the value of an investment of $100 after 20 years at several different yields.

Usually, higher yields and greater risk of loss go together. Investments you make with the federal government are the safest. When you invest money with individuals or businesses, it usually earns higher interest than that paid by the government because there is less safety. For example, the government may pay 3 percent interest on an investment. At the same time, one business may pay 5 percent while a business with even greater risk may have to pay 10 percent.

Most investors will not accept higher risk unless the potential yield is greater. However, a low rate of return on an investment does not guarantee safety. Similarly, high rates of interest do not mean that a loss will occur. Higher yields mean that investors believe the situation involves a higher risk. Figure 19-3 shows the risk level for various investments.

The Truth in Savings Act (TISA) requires that financial institutions give consumers information to compare savings accounts. The law defines the *annual percentage yield* (APY) as the percentage rate equal to the total amount of interest that a $100 deposit would earn based on a 365-day period. APY helps eliminate confusion caused by different interest calculation methods. Some financial institutions previously used 360- or 366-day years to calculate interest.

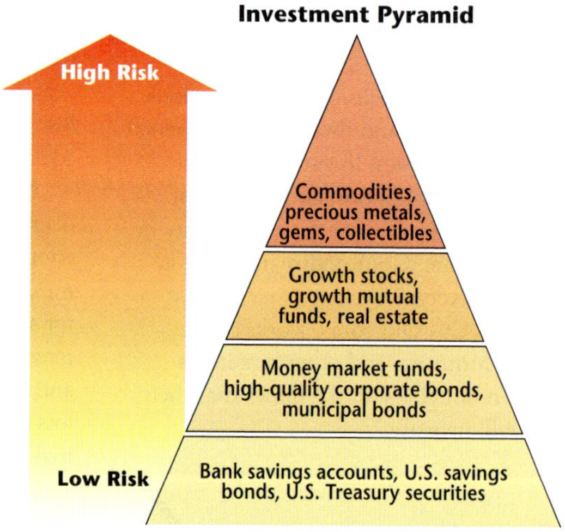

FIGURE 19-3
Why would a person make a high-risk investment?

Applied Skills

Communication Assign students to create a visual presentation to communicate the major factors to consider when evaluating savings and investing alternatives. Encourage them to use photos and other graphics to enhance their presentation.

Liquidity

Sometimes cash is needed quickly to pay unexpected bills. Investments that can be turned into money quickly are called *liquid*. **Liquidity** is the ease with which an investment can be changed into cash without losing its value.

Suppose you have $5,000 on deposit in a bank. If you need money right away, you usually can go to your bank and withdraw it. On the other hand, suppose you own a piece of land that you bought for $5,000. The land may be a safe investment. However, if you need money immediately, you may find it difficult to sell the land right away. You might even have to sell it for less than $5,000 if you cannot wait for a buyer who is willing to pay your price.

If you have several investments, not all of them need high liquidity. The amount of liquid investments you should have will depend on your expected need for cash in the near future.

Taxes

Earnings from most savings and investments are taxed. Taxes reduce your rate of return. For example, if you earn $100 in interest but 20 percent is taken in taxes, you have only earned $80, $100 − ($100 × 0.20). Some investments have *tax-exempt earnings*, meaning you don't have to pay taxes on that income. These investments are attractive because the tax-free yield may actually be higher than a comparable taxable investment.

CHECKPOINT
What are four factors to consider when selecting an investment?

19.1 ASSESSMENT

Key Concepts

Determine the best answer.

1. Which of the following is investing for current income?
   a. retired person who needs to pay living expenses
   b. business manager planning for retirement
   c. student putting away money for college
   d. family that wants to buy a vacation home
2. The most liquid investment listed here is
   a. rare coins
   b. real estate
   c. a savings account
   d. a house
3. A person who desires high income from an investment would be most concerned with
   a. safety
   b. return
   c. liquidity
   d. risk

Make Academic Connections

4. **Math** To determine the annual yield (rate of return) on an investment, divide the income from the investment for the year by the original amount invested. Look at the example. Then, calculate the annual yield for the other investments.

INVESTMENT	ANNUAL INCOME	AMOUNT INVESTED	ANNUAL YIELD
Example	$80	$800	10%
Savings account	$4	$200	
Bond	$85	$1,000	
Real estate	$6,400	$40,000	

5. **Economics** Prepare a list of benefits of saving and investing for (a) consumers, (b) business, and (c) government.

TEACH

Ask students to name savings and investments that are easy to convert to cash.

Explain the meaning of *liquidity*. Provide examples of items with different degrees of liquidity.

Describe how savings and investment income that is taxable reduces a person's rate of return.

Explain how tax-exempt investments benefit people.

ONGOING ASSESSMENT

CHECKPOINT ✓ANSWER

Four factors to consider when selecting an investment are (1) safety, (2) return, (3) liquidity, and (4) taxes.

ASSESS

Key Concepts *Answers*

1. a. retired person who needs to pay living expenses
2. c. a savings account
3. b. return

Make Academic Connections *Answers*

4. Savings account, 2%; Bond, 8.5%; Real estate, 16%
5. Answers will vary. Consumers benefit by earning money and having a larger amount in the future. Businesses and government have funds available to borrow for expansion and providing public services.

CLOSE Ask students to describe the main two investment goals.

RETEACH Use Figure 19-3 to review the main types of saving and investments discussed in this lesson.

ENRICH Instruct students to create a list of savings plans and investments. Ask students to put them in order from most liquid to least liquid.

Focus on REAL LIFE

Use this feature to encourage students to start thinking about the role of stocks in their investment plans.

TEACH

Ask students to name some of the reasons a person might buy stock in a company.

Explain the differences between preferred and common stock.

Explain the process that might be used to determine the dividends for stockholders.

Life-Span Plan Answers

Answers will vary. Students should explain that having a clear idea of life-span goals they want to achieve could cause them to make investment choices that involve different levels of risk.

19.2 Stock Investments

Learning Outcomes

19.2.1 Compare the two major types of stock.

19.2.2 Describe the activities involved with buying or selling stock.

19.2.3 Identify factors that affect the value of a stock.

Key Terms

preferred stock 492
common stock 493
stockbroker 493
stock exchange 493
market value 494

Focus on REAL LIFE

Josie's older brother buys stock with part of his wages. He is planning for his retirement years. One day, Josie asked her brother about the benefits of investing in stock.

"You have the opportunity for big growth of your money over the years," he responded, "if you pick the right stocks."

"That's for me," Josie said. "I'm putting all my savings I have earned from babysitting in stock!"

"Wait a minute," warned her brother, "it's not that easy! You have to determine which companies have stocks with the most growth potential. Then you have to contact a broker or open an online account. Next you should..."

"That's enough," was Josie's response. "I'm really not interested in something that complicated."

"Don't give up," encouraged her brother. "While investing in stock may not be best for you right now, it is a topic that you should start learning about."

LO 19.2.1

TYPES OF STOCK

When you buy shares of ownership in a corporation, you become a *stockholder*. If a business is profitable, it may pay out part of the profits in cash to the stockholders. These payments are *dividends*. The opportunity to earn a high rate of return attracts people to invest in stocks. Keep in mind that the risk of losing money on a stock investment also exists.

Before it can pay any dividends to stockholders, a corporation must pay bondholders the rate of interest promised to them. Sometimes there is not enough money left to pay dividends. If the corporation decides to put the money it earns toward future growth, stockholders may receive no dividends. If a corporation goes out of business, stockholders may get little or nothing back from their investment.

> **Life-Span Plan**
> Describe how a life-span plan can influence the types of investment choices a person makes. How much risk are you willing to take? How may your willingness to accept risk affect the life-span goals you set for yourself?

Preferred Stock

The two main classes of stock issued by corporations are preferred stock and common stock. **Preferred stock** has priority over common stock in the payment of dividends. The dividends paid to preferred stockholders are usually limited to a set rate. Investing in preferred stock is less risky than common stock, but preferred stockholders generally have no voting rights.

Different Learning Styles

Gifted Assign students to conduct research to obtain additional information about preferred and common stock. The findings may be reported in a written format or in a presentation to the class.

Common Stock

The second main class of stock is common stock. **Common stock** represents general ownership in a corporation and a right to share in its profits. Common stock has no stated dividend rate. As part owners of the corporation, common stockholders are invited to the annual meeting of the corporation. They are entitled to one vote per share of common stock owned.

Common stockholders receive dividends only after preferred stockholders are paid their dividends. Yet, if the profits of a company are large, the common stockholders may receive higher dividends than preferred stockholders. Suppose that a company has issued \$100,000 worth of common stock and \$100,000 worth of preferred stock with a dividend rate of 6 percent. The company earns a profit of \$20,000 and pays all the profit out as dividends. Preferred stockholders would be paid \$6,000 in dividends, $\$100,000 \times 0.06$. The remaining \$14,000 $(\$20,000 - \$6,000)$ would be available to pay dividends to the common stockholders. The common stockholders would earn a return of 14 percent.

CHECKPOINT
How does preferred stock differ from common stock?

LO 19.2.2

STOCK TRANSACTIONS

Each day, people buy and sell billions of shares of stock. Buying a stock that is right for you is an important decision.

Using a Stockbroker

A licensed specialist in the buying and selling of stocks and bonds is a **stockbroker**. Through brokers, stockholders state the price at which they are willing to sell their shares. Interested buyers tell brokers what they would be willing to pay for those shares. The brokers then work out a price that is acceptable to both buyers and sellers. For their services, brokers charge a fee called a *commission*.

Two types of brokers are common. A *full-service broker* provides information about securities you may want to buy. Full-service brokers work for brokerage houses with large research staffs.

In contrast, a *discount broker* just places orders and offers limited research and other services. They charge lower commissions than full-service brokers. Investors who do their own research can save money by using a discount broker.

NET KNOWLEDGE

There are many online information sources to help investors. Select a type of investment discussed in the chapter. Locate two online articles related to this investment. What are the main suggestions offered to investors regarding this type of investment?

Online Investing

Every broker provides online services. These services allow investors to access account information as well as buy and sell securities. When investing online, you are serving as your own financial planner.

These transactions are usually less expensive and more convenient than using a financial planner or broker. There are also disadvantages to investing online. Inexperience in making investment trading decisions can result in a large financial loss. Many online investors buy or sell stocks too quickly because making trades is only a click away.

Stock Exchanges

Brokers work through a **stock exchange**, which is a business organization that accommodates the buying and selling of securities. The best-known stock exchange is the New York Stock Exchange in New York City. The American Stock Exchange is also in New York City. Regional stock exchanges operate in Boston, Chicago,

ONGOING ASSESSMENT

CHECKPOINT ANSWER

Preferred stock has priority over common stock in the payment of dividends. Investing in preferred stock is less risky than common stock, but preferred stockholders generally have no voting rights within the corporation. Common stock, on the other hand, represents general ownership in a corporation and a right to share in its profits. Common stockholders are entitled to one vote per share of common stock owned. Although preferred stockholders are paid first, their dividends usually are limited to a set rate. If the profits of a company are large, the common stockholders may receive higher dividends than preferred stockholders.

TEACH

Describe the services provided by a stockbroker. Explain the differences between a full-service broker and a discount broker.

Point out some of the benefits and limitations of online investing.

Ask students to describe the purpose of a stock exchange.

NET KNOWLEDGE

Answers will vary depending on the types of investments students select for this exercise.

Applied Skills

Technology Instruct students to locate information on the services provided by online brokers. Ask them to determine the benefits and costs of the services provided.

TEACH

Discuss the various stock exchanges in the United States and throughout the world.

Explain the purpose of an *over-the-counter (OTC) market*.

Ask students to name factors that might affect the value of a stock.

Use Figure 19-4 to explain how stock prices are reported.

▸ **Figure 19-4** ***ANSWER***

A wide range of factors affect the value of a company's stock. These can include current economic conditions, such as consumer spending, inflation, and interest rates. In addition, company actions that influence profitability, such as new products, the use of debt, and cost-cutting decisions, will affect whether investors buy or sell its stock.

ONGOING ASSESSMENT

CHECKPOINT ✓***ANSWER***

The purpose of a stock exchange is to accommodate the buying and selling of securities.

Philadelphia, and San Francisco. More than 100 stock exchanges operate around the world.

Usually, stocks of smaller companies are not traded on a stock exchange. The *over-the-counter (OTC) market* is a network where securities transactions occur using telephones and computers rather than on an exchange. The OTC market in the United States is the NASDAQ, which stands for the National Association of Security Dealers Automated Quotations. Today, the NASDAQ includes many large companies.

Changing Stock Values

The **market value** of a stock is the price at which a share of stock can be bought and sold in the stock market. The market value indicates the current value of a share of stock.

The prices at which stocks are being bought and sold are available through stock market listings in online reports. Figure 19-4 shows a stock market price report.

The market value can change rapidly. If the business is doing well, the market value is likely to go up. If the business has a poor record, the market value usually goes down. The market value also may be affected by current economic conditions as well as national and global politics.

Another measurement of investment values is a *stock index*. These indicators of stock values are commonly reported on websites, television, radio, and in newspapers. The Dow Jones Industrial Average (DJIA) includes 30 of the largest U.S. companies. Another commonly reported stock index is the Standard & Poor's (S&P) 500, which is based on stock values of 500 major companies.

CHECKPOINT ✓
What is the purpose of a stock exchange?

Stock Market Price Report

1	2	3	4	5	6	7	8	9	10	11	12
52-Week					Yld.		Vol.				Net
Hi	Lo	Stock	Sym.	Div.	%	PE	100s	Hi	Lo	Close	Chg.
64.99	40.28	Deere	DE	1.20	1.9	28	46125	60.14	59.23	60.02	−0.42
97.75	63.46	FedExCp	FDX	0.48	0.6	22	72259	83.64	82.00	83.39	+2.43
56.00	45.58	Kellogg	K	1.50	2.9	15	27920	51.51	50.67	51.34	−0.24
24.60	17.08	Mattel	MAT	0.75	3.5	13	42107	21.82	21.08	21.79	+0.55
78.55	51.43	Nike	NKE	1.08	1.5	19	37279	73.95	72.48	73.22	+0.48

1 – Highest price paid for stock during past 52 weeks
2 – Lowest price paid for stock during the past 52 weeks
3 – Abbreviated company name
4 – Symbol used to report company
5 – Current dividend per share (in dollars)
6 – Dividend yield based on current selling price
7 – Price-earnings ratio
8 – Number of shares traded, expressed in hundreds, on the trading day
9 – Highest price for a share on the trading day
10 – Lowest price for a share on the trading day
11 – Closing price for the day
12 – Change in closing price compared to previous trading day

FIGURE 19-4
What factors might affect the daily changes in the market value of a company's stock?

Applied Skills

Geography Assign students to research a stock exchange in another region of the world (South America, Asia, Africa, Europe, the Middle East). Ask them to prepare a report on the activities of the stock exchange and the companies that use it.

LO 19.2.3

STOCK SELECTION

Buying stocks can involve a process similar to the one shown in Figure 19-5. By viewing various economic and social trends in the United States and around the world, you may be able to determine what types of companies will benefit from those trends. For example, as people live longer, they require increased health care. Companies involved in healthcare products may be a wise investment.

Stock Information Sources

When choosing stocks, you should learn about the company. Several online sources and printed reports are available to assist you. Sources commonly used by investors include *Marketwatch.com*, *Google Finance*, *Value Line*, and *Yahoo Finance*. Publications and websites like these provide data about net worth, debt, sales revenue, profits, dividend history, and the future prospects of companies.

The U.S. Securities and Exchange Commission (SEC) oversees the financial markets. It requires all companies that issue publicly traded securities to electronically file detailed reports. You can access these reports on the SEC website.

Work as a TEAM

Discuss various business and economic trends. Prepare a list of stocks that your team believes would be good investments. Explain what factors influenced the selection of these companies.

Economic Factors

Many economic conditions affect stock prices. Awareness of these factors will help you make better choices about stock investments. You should consider the following economic factors.

- **Inflation** Higher prices can result in lower spending by consumers, reducing company profits.
- **Interest rates** As the cost of money changes, company profits may increase or decline.
- **Consumer spending** Profits of companies that sell products and services to households are directly affected by buying habits.

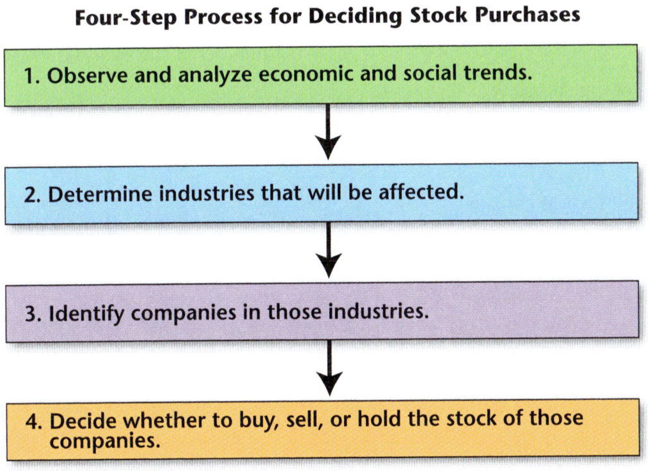

FIGURE 19-5
Name a company or industry that has profited from a trend in recent months.

TEACH

Use Figure 19-5 to describe the process that might be used when planning to buy stock. Provide an overview of the main stock information sources.

Ensure that students understand how economic factors affect stock prices.

Work as a TEAM

This activity can help students better understand the connection between current world developments and stock prices. Consider discussing the merits and drawbacks of each team's selections with the entire class.

▶ **Figure 19-5** ***ANSWER***

Answers will vary depending on the companies students name and current economic and social trends.

Teaching Strategies

Expand Beyond the Classroom Assign students to select a company and chart the stock value of the organization over several weeks. Ask students to describe situations that may have caused changes in the value of the company's stock.

TEACH

Ask students why the company factors questions might be important when evaluating a stock.

Explain the process for calculating the dividend yield.

Describe how the price earnings (P/E) ratio might be used by investors.

ONGOING ASSESSMENT

CHECKPOINT ✓ANSWER

Inflation affects stock prices by causing lower spending by consumers, reducing company profits out of which dividends are paid. Falling or rising interest rates can also increase or decrease company profits as the cost of money changes. The employment rate also affects stock prices; when more people are employed, they spend more money on a company's products and stock prices rise.

ASSESS

Key Concepts *Answers*

1. b. first priority for receiving dividends

2. a. electronics

Make Academic Connections *Answers*

3a. 4,612,500 shares of Deere were traded.

3b. The highest price of a share of Kellogg paid during the past year was $56.

3c. The closing price of Mattel on the previous trading day was $21.24 ($21.79 – $0.55 = $21.24).

4. Survey results, tables, and analyses will vary.

- **Employment** As people obtain or lose jobs, the amount of money they have for spending will affect company profits.

Company Factors

If you are considering investing in a company, ask the following questions.

- Has the company been profitable during the past several years?
- Have the company's managers made good business decisions?
- Does the company have growth potential in coming years?
- Does the company have an unusually large amount of debt?
- How does the company compare with others in its industry?

Other information about a company should also be considered. The *yield* of a stock is important if your goal is to earn a good return from your investment.

Suppose a company is paying a quarterly dividend of $0.60 a share. The total dividend for the year would be $2.40. If the stock were selling for $40 a share, the current yield (return) would be calculated as

$$\frac{\text{Dividend per share}}{\text{Market price per share}} = \text{Dividend Yield}$$

$$\frac{\$2.40}{\$40} = 0.06 \text{ or } 6\%$$

The price of a stock should also be considered. Many investors look at the stock's *price-earnings (P/E) ratio*, which is the relationship between a stock's selling price and its earnings per share. The P/E ratio gives you an indication of whether the stock is priced high or low in relation to its earnings per share.

CHECKPOINT ✓
How do various economic factors affect stock prices?

19.2 ASSESSMENT

Key Concepts

Determine the best answer.

1. Which of these statements best describes preferred stock?
   a. vote at the annual meeting of the company
   b. first priority for receiving dividends
   c. low priority for receiving dividends
   d. no stated dividend rate
2. Higher spending for recreation and entertainment in the economy would most benefit the stock prices for companies in the ________ industry.
   a. electronics
   b. health care
   c. office equipment
   d. financial services

Make Academic Connections

3. **Math** Based on Figure 19-4, answer the following questions:
   a. What number of shares was traded for Deere on this day?
   b. What is the highest price of a share of Kellogg's stock during the past year?
   c. What was the closing price of Mattel on the previous trading day?
4. **Communication** Gather a sample of people and conduct a survey about what they believe are the most important factors to consider when selecting a stock. Prepare a summary data table and written analysis of your findings.

RETEACH Provide a review of the process to use when selecting a stock investment.

ENRICH Encourage students to research a stock and explain whether they believe it might be a good investment or not.

CLOSE Ask students to explain the benefits and risks of investing in stock.

19.3 Bonds and Mutual Funds

Learning Outcomes

19.3.1 List types of government bonds.

19.3.2 Describe features of corporate bonds.

19.3.3 Describe various types of mutual funds.

Key Terms

municipal bonds 497

corporate bonds 499

mutual fund 499

Focus on REAL LIFE

Barbara Malcolm has decided to invest in bonds. She believes that bonds provide greater security for her investment funds. However, after looking into buying bonds, the process seemed very complicated.

"I'm not sure what to do," Barbara commented to her friend. "I'd like to invest in bonds, but you have to be an expert to pick the right ones."

"Instead, how about investing in a mutual fund?" responded Barbara's friend Mandy.

"What's a mutual fund?" asked Barbara.

Mandy explained, "A mutual fund takes money from many people and buys several investments. This action allows an expert to manage your investment funds."

"That sounds like something I should consider," said Barbara. "Tell me more."

LO 19.3.1

GOVERNMENT BONDS

To raise money for current operations or future expansion, most governments and corporations sell bonds. A *bond* is a certificate representing a promise to pay a definite amount of money at a stated interest rate on a specified due date. The due date is also called the *maturity date*. Bonds are similar to promissory notes issued by individual borrowers. When you buy a bond, you are lending money to the organization selling the bond. You become a *creditor* of the organization. Governments issue bonds to raise money for funding public services. The federal, state, and local governments issue a variety of bonds.

Why do state and local governments issue bonds?

Donovan Reese/Photodisc/Getty Images

Municipal Bonds

A city may want to build a new park or new school. A state may need funds to build or repair highways and bridges. Bonds issued by local and state governments are called **municipal bonds**, or *munis*.

Focus on REAL LIFE

This feature will introduce students to some of the issues associated with investing in bonds and mutual funds.

TEACH

Ask students to explain why governments often borrow money.

Explain the features of a municipal bond.

THINK CRITICALLY THROUGH VISUALS

State and local governments can raise money for public service projects by issuing municipal bonds.

Different Learning Abilities

Dyslexia Prepare some short fill-in assignments focused on the various types of bonds. Clearly present the material and encourage students to provide the correct answer.

TEACH

Explain the features of U.S. savings bonds.

Ask students to describe situations in which savings bonds might be appropriate for an individual or family.

Contrast the difference between a Treasury bill and a Treasury note.

THINK CRITICALLY THROUGH VISUALS

Investors can check the prices of individual stocks in the daily stock listings that are published in newspapers and online. For a general idea of how their portfolios are faring, investors can check a daily stock index, such as the Dow Jones Industrial Average or the Standard & Poor's 500.

ONGOING ASSESSMENT

CHECKPOINT ✓ANSWER

The types of U.S. savings bonds issued by the federal government are savings bonds (Series EE bonds and I bonds), treasury bills, treasury notes, and treasury bonds.

iStockphoto.com/MerveKarahan

How do investors keep track of their changing investment values?

Municipal bonds often have an advantage over bonds issued by companies. Usually, interest earned on municipal bonds is exempt from federal and most state income taxes. In order to avoid taxes, people buy municipal bonds even though the interest rates usually are not as high as the rates offered on corporate bonds. In general, most municipal bonds are considered safer investments than corporate bonds.

U.S. Savings Bonds

For people with small amounts of money to invest, U.S. savings bonds are a safe investment. Series EE savings bonds come in denominations ranging from $50 to $10,000.

A Series EE bond is bought at half its face value. A $50 bond costs $25. At the end of its full term, it pays at least $50. The difference between the purchase price and the redemption value is the interest earned. The length of time the bond is held determines the amount of interest. The time it takes for a savings bond to mature will vary depending on the current interest rate being paid.

In addition to paying interest, Series EE bonds have tax advantages. Interest is exempt from state and local taxes, and you do not pay federal income tax on the earnings until the bonds are redeemed. Funds from Series EE bonds may be exempt from federal income tax if the funds are used to pay tuition and fees at a college, university, or qualified technical school. This benefit is designed to assist low- and middle-income households. People with incomes above a certain amount do not qualify.

Another type of savings bond is the *I bond*. These investments pay an interest rate that changes with inflation. I bonds are purchased at face value, a $50 bond costs $50.

Other Federal Securities

The federal government also borrows using Treasury bills and notes. The difference between these debt securities is the length of time to maturity. *Treasury bills*, or *T-bills*, involve short-term borrowing with maturities from 91 days to one year. *Treasury notes*, or *T-notes*, have maturities from 1 to 10 years.

The U.S. government also issues *treasury bonds*, called *T-bonds*. These involve long-term borrowing, with a maturity of up to 30 years.

CHECKPOINT ✓

List the types of bonds issued by the federal government of the United States.

LO 19.3.2

CORPORATE BONDS

Investing in the bonds of a company is quite different from investing in stock. When you invest in stock, you become an owner. When you buy a bond, you are lending

Different Learning Styles

Auditory Learner Encourage auditory learners to repeat the names of the types of bonds discussed under the heading Government Bonds. Ask them to explain each type of bond.

money to the company. Bonds issued by corporations are **corporate bonds**.

Bond Components

Each bond has a *face value*, also called the *maturity value*. This is the amount being borrowed by the corporation issuing the bond. Corporate bonds are issued for $1,000 and $25,000, and sometimes higher amounts.

Interest is paid to the investor periodically (usually twice a year) based on the face value and the stated interest rate. On the bond's maturity date, the face value is repaid to the investor.

Bond Values

Bonds are bought and sold in the bond market. The market value of a bond varies based on changing interest rates and the credit rating of the borrowing organization.

Make a list of long-term investment options. What are the pros and cons for each type?

Bond values are reported similarly to the way stocks are reported. Corporate bond prices are stated in 100s, but the bonds are sold in $1,000 denominations (10 times the listed amount). For example, a bond reported at 100 is selling at its face value—$1,000. A bond selling at 105 has a market value of $1,050.

The price investors are willing to pay for a bond depends upon the *stated interest rate*. If the bond's stated rate is lower than interest rates on similar bonds, investors will want to buy the bond for less than its face value. If the bond's stated interest rate is higher than interest rates on similar bonds, the seller of the bond will want to receive more than its face value.

CHECKPOINT
What affects the value of a bond?

LO 19.3.3

MUTUAL FUNDS

Many people who are interested in investing do not have the time or knowledge needed to make wise investment decisions. A **mutual fund** is an investment fund set up and managed by a company that receives money from many investors. The mutual fund is managed by a professional who uses the investors' money to buy and sell a wide variety of stocks or bonds. The value and income of the investments made determine the value of the mutual fund shares.

Types of Mutual Funds

More than 75,000 different mutual funds are available to investors around the world. These funds have many different objectives. For instance, some emphasize investing in growth stocks, some emphasize stocks that pay high dividends, and some emphasize international stocks. The following list includes some of the main types of mutual funds.

TEACH

Describe the purpose of corporate bonds. Explain how bond values change as a result of changing interest rates.

ONGOING ASSESSMENT

CHECKPOINT ANSWER

The value of a bond is affected by changing interest rates. If the bond's stated rate is lower than interest rates on similar bonds, investors will want to buy the bond for less than its face value. If the bond's stated interest rate is higher than interest rates on similar bonds, the seller of the bond will want to receive more than its face value.

THINK CRITICALLY THROUGH VISUALS

Long-term investment options are certificates of deposit, mutual funds, individual retirement accounts, stocks, 401(k) and other retirement plans, T-bills and T-notes, T-bonds, and corporate bonds. These all have the advantage of being vehicles to grow savings over time. The disadvantage of all these instruments is lack of liquidity.

TEACH

Ask students to explain the purpose of a mutual fund. Describe the purpose of different types of mutual funds.

Applied Skills

Office Technology Assign students to create a presentation to communicate information about different types of mutual funds. Encourage students to use photos and other graphics in their presentation.

Work as a TEAM

This activity will help students better understand the various types of mutual funds.

TEACH

Provide an overview of the main types of mutual funds. Explain how the value of a mutual fund changes.

ONGOING ASSESSMENT

CHECKPOINT ✓ANSWER

The main types of mutual funds are aggressive-growth stock funds, income funds, international funds, sector funds, bond funds, and balanced funds.

ASSESS

Key Concepts *Answers*

1. d. state and local governments
2. b. the value of investments
3. False. A bondholder is a creditor of the bond issuer. A stockholder is part owner of a company.
4. True. Interest rates in an economy will make a bond more or less valuable than its face value, depending on whether the bond's stated interest rate is higher or lower than the rates available elsewhere.

Make Academic Connections *Answers*

5. Students visit the website for U.S. savings bonds to learn more about this savings alternative.
6. Students locate information that can help them evaluate the myriad mutual fund choices in today's market.

Work as a TEAM

Review the list of types of mutual funds. Describe situations in which each type might be appropriate for a particular individual or family. Explain how this type of mutual fund could meet various investment goals.

- Aggressive-growth stock funds seek quick growth, but also have higher risk.
- Income funds specialize in stocks that pay regular dividends.
- International funds invest in stock of companies from around the world.
- Sector funds buy stocks of companies in the same industry such as health care, energy, or telecommunications.
- Bond funds specialize in corporate bonds.
- Balanced funds invest in both stock and bonds.

When selecting a mutual fund in which to invest, match your personal investment goals to the type of mutual fund.

Mutual Fund Values

Mutual fund investors own shares of the mutual fund. The value of each share is based on the total value of all investments made by the mutual fund company. For example, if the investments were worth $400,000 and 80,000 shares existed, each share would be worth $5, $400,000 ÷ 80,000 = $5. This amount is called the *net asset value (NAV)* of a mutual fund.

A part of the dividends and interest received from the fund's investments is used to pay operating expenses of the fund. The major portion of earnings is distributed to the mutual fund shareholders or reinvested in the fund.

CHECKPOINT ✓

What are the main types of mutual funds?

19.3 ASSESSMENT

Key Concepts

Determine the best answer.

1. Municipal bonds are issued by
   - **a.** corporations
   - **b.** the federal government
   - **c.** international companies
   - **d.** state and local governments
2. The price of a mutual fund share is most affected by
   - **a.** current tax rates
   - **b.** the value of investments
   - **c.** current foreign rates
   - **d.** the value of housing
3. True or False. A bondholder is part owner of a company.
4. True or False. Interest rates in an economy affect the value of a bond.

Make Academic Connections

5. **Technology** Go to the website for U.S. savings bonds to obtain information about how to buy savings bonds online. What features are available online to calculate the current value of savings bonds?
6. **Research** With thousands of mutual funds available to investors, how could a person evaluate them? Locate library and online information that could provide assistance when deciding in which mutual funds to invest.

RETEACH Explain how bond values are affected by changing interest rates.

CLOSE Ask students to explain the difference between a bond and a mutual fund.

ENRICH Encourage students to write a goal that might be achieved by investing in each type of mutual fund mentioned on this page.

19.4 Real Estate Investments

Learning Outcomes

19.4.1 Describe housing alternatives

19.4.2 Explain the benefits of home ownership.

19.4.3 Discuss the costs of home ownership.

Key Terms

real estate 501

mortgage 502

equity 503

assessed value 505

Focus on REAL LIFE

Driving home from their honeymoon, Joshua Moskowitz addressed his bride Carrie. "You know, we have some money that we received as wedding gifts," said Joshua. "We should buy some stocks for our long-term financial future. I have heard of a lot of people who made fortunes with stocks."

"How much do you know about stocks? Are you sure we won't lose our money?" asked Carrie.

"Well, it's true, I don't know much about stocks," responded Joshua. "But I do know baseball cards! Let's invest our money in baseball cards."

"That's kind of risky, isn't it?" was Carrie's next question.

"OK...OK. Then let's buy gold bars. Gold can be a solid investment," replied Joshua. "You can't go wrong with gold."

"Hold on. We both want what's best for our future, but don't you think that first we'd better find a place to live?" responded Carrie.

LO 19.4.1

SELECTING HOUSING

Real estate—land and anything that is attached to it—is one investment that many people eventually acquire. Getting started with real estate usually means finding a place in which to live.

Renting Your Residence

Most people start by renting an apartment. As a renter, you are freed from much of the work and expense of property maintenance. Renting also makes it easier for you to move when needed. As a tenant, you must take some responsibility for the care of the rented property, but you are not able to call the apartment your own.

Many people want to own a house and yard that they can maintain and fix up just the way they want. To realize this goal, they must save money for a down payment on a house.

Kzenon/Shutterstock.com

What are the pros and cons of renting compared to buying your residence?

Focus on REAL LIFE

This situation can encourage students to start thinking about various future financial decisions, including their housing.

TEACH

Ask students to describe real estate decisions they might make in the future.

Students should name some benefits and potential drawbacks of renting a place of residence.

THINK CRITICALLY THROUGH VISUALS

Renters are liberated from the work and expense of property maintenance and are freer to move whenever they desire. Renters also do not have to come up with a large down payment, as when purchasing a house, and rent payments are typically lower than mortgage payments. However, rent payments do not purchase anything tangible, but simply allow the renter to live in the property for a specified amount of time. Many people prefer to buy a house as an investment. Part of the money spent on a home mortgage payment goes to pay for the house, which is usually increasing in value. Homeowners often prefer to do their own home maintenance, gardening, and decorating so that things can be done according to their personal specifications.

Applied Skills

Law Provide students with a copy of an apartment lease or rental agreement. Ask them to describe the information that is presented in this legal document. Encourage discussion about the obligations spelled out in the document.

THINK CRITICALLY THROUGH VISUALS

Advantages of owning a mobile home are the lower initial purchase cost compared to a traditional home and the option to move the home to a new location if needed. The disadvantages are that mobile homes do not increase in value as conventional homes do and they may be less safe than traditional homes in the event of storms with very high winds.

TEACH

Explain potential benefits of a mobile home. Ask students to name some actions that would need to be taken when buying a home.

Describe the purpose of a mortgage. Contrast the difference between a fixed-rate mortgage and an adjustable-rate mortgage.

Life-Span Plan Answers

Answers will vary. Students should point out that a home is different from other investments because it provides a current benefit instead of only the hope of a future return.

Digital Vision/Photodisc/Getty Images

What are the advantages and disadvantages of owning a mobile home?

Owning a Mobile Home

To become a real estate owner, some people purchase a mobile home. This financial decision provides the opportunity for home ownership. An advantage of owning a mobile home is having a place to call your own. As time passes, a person might consider other types of real estate purchases.

Buying a Home

Unless you have thousands of dollars available, you will need to borrow to buy a house. A **mortgage** is a legal document giving the lender a claim against the property if the principal, interest, or both are not paid as agreed.

Mortgages are long-term loans—for 15, 20, or 30 years—that require monthly payments. These payments are usually higher than rent. A mortgage payment includes a portion of the principal and interest charges. In addition, it often includes money to be used to pay property taxes and insurance. Money used for a down payment reduces the amount of the loan needed with the mortgage.

Interest rates on mortgages may be set for the term of the loan. This type of mortgage is called a *fixed-rate mortgage*. Market interest rates generally increase or decrease during the life of a mortgage depending on economic conditions. Therefore, lenders also offer an *adjustable-rate mortgage (ARM)*. The interest rate of an ARM is raised or lowered from time to time depending upon the current interest rate being charged by lenders. Monthly payments for ARMs may be lower, especially in the early years of the mortgage, compared with fixed-rate mortgages.

Life-Span Plan

Is home ownership one of your life-span goals? Describe how different family and household situations might affect the housing choice you make. Explain how buying a home is different from other types of investments you may make.

Different Learning Abilities

Hearing Impaired Communicate the main types of housing choices available to a person using a variety of visuals. Consider using photographs, illustrations, and floor plans. Make copies of the visuals available to all interested students.

Visually Impaired Prepare or obtain enlarged materials to communicate the benefits and costs of home ownership. Ask students to explain the various items with additional information or an example.

Services of Real Estate Agents

Buying a house is not a simple matter. Most homebuyers use a real estate agent. This person is trained and licensed to help with the buying and selling of real estate. Someone who wants to buy a house contacts a real estate agent. The agent helps the person decide what they want in a house. The agent will also arrange for the prospective buyer to view homes offered for sale.

Sellers of real estate may also use the services of a real estate agent. Someone who wants to sell a house contacts an agent. The real estate professional helps to set the selling price and promotes that the house is for sale.

Other Real Estate Professionals

Legal matters are also a part of the real estate purchase process. A lawyer, working with the real estate agent, will help you with the transaction. A lawyer assures that your property has no claims against it, such as back taxes. Having a lawyer represent you in the transaction can help to avoid legal problems.

When buying a house, an appraiser's report on the home's value is also important. An *appraiser* is someone trained to estimate the value of property and who can give an official report on the value. Factors such as the quality of construction, the location, and the price of similar houses are considered when doing the appraisal.

Buying a Condominium

In some areas, *condominiums*, or *condos*, are popular. This is an individually owned housing unit in an apartment-like complex. The maintenance and yard work are normally taken care of with a service fee paid by condo owners.

What real estate professionals might you need when purchasing real estate?

CHECKPOINT ✓

What are four available housing alternatives?

LO 19.4.2

BENEFITS OF HOME OWNERSHIP

The advantages of home ownership include tax benefits, increased equity, and pride of ownership.

Tax Benefits

Although you may pay both mortgage loan interest and property taxes on real estate you own, these costs can be to your benefit. Reduced income taxes result when the interest paid on a mortgage is included as a deductible expense. Real estate property taxes are usually also deductible when computing your federal income taxes.

Increased Equity

From an investment standpoint, the potential increase in home value is an important aspect of ownership. **Equity** is the difference between the price at which

TEACH

Point out some of the services provided by a real estate agent.

Ask students to explain the benefits of using a lawyer and an appraiser when buying a home.

Explain the benefits of owning a condominium.

THINK CRITICALLY THROUGH VISUALS

In addition to a real estate agent, you may need the services of a real estate appraiser, a home inspector, a lawyer, an insurance agent, and a loan officer when purchasing a house.

ONGOING ASSESSMENT

CHECKPOINT ✓ *ANSWER*

Four housing alternatives are (1) renting, (2) owning a mobile home, (3) buying a traditional home, and (4) buying a condominium.

TEACH

Ask students to name some benefits of home ownership. Explain how mortgage interest and property taxes reduce a person's income taxes.

Describe the benefits of equity to a homeowner. Explain how equity in a home is calculated.

Teaching Strategies

Expand Beyond the Classroom Arrange for a class speaker who is a real estate agent, lawyer, insurance agent, or home inspector. Ask that person to explain information needed when buying or owning a home.

ONGOING ASSESSMENT

CHECKPOINT ✓ANSWER

The main benefits of home ownership are tax benefits, increased equity, and pride of ownership.

As in all types of business transactions, computerized activities are being used when buying a home.

Think Critically *Answers*

1. Benefits are the reduced paperwork and processing time and the ability to easily compare mortgage rates. Concerns are that a consumer might not be as aware of important details or negotiate as skillfully as a real estate professional.

2. Reports will vary.

you could currently sell your house and the amount owed on the mortgage. Equity builds up over the years. It increases rapidly in the last few years of a mortgage.

Because of *appreciation*, a general increase in the value of property that occurs over time, homes increase in value. During the 10 years that one family had lived in their home, its market value had increased to $244,000 and their debt decreased to $165,000. Therefore, their equity was $79,000.

Many factors affect the value of a home. Most important is location. In addition, the quality of schools, maintenance of the property, and home features increase home values. Features that can add to the value of a home include an updated kitchen, remodeled bathrooms, a master bedroom suite, a finished basement, and a large garage.

Pride of Ownership

Another advantage of owning real estate is pride of ownership. Many people feel a sense of accomplishment when they buy a home. Having a home to use and decorate as desired is a strong motivation for many home buyers.

CHECKPOINT ✓
What are the main benefits of home ownership?

LO 19.4.3
COSTS OF HOME OWNERSHIP

While there are benefits to owning your own property, various costs also exist. Home ownership has costs such as property taxes, interest payments, property insurance, and maintenance.

Buying a Home Online: Mistakes to Avoid

Online home buying is faster and easier than the traditional method. Researching available homes, negotiating a price, obtaining financing, and closing the transaction are completed through websites and electronic communication. The time needed to process paper-based documents for a home purchase may take 45 days; the online process can be completed in a few hours.

However, despite this convenience, homebuyers need to be aware of potential concerns:

1. Avoid too narrow of a search. Many people fail to seek out "for sale by owner" homes. Use a variety of information sources, real estate blogs, and different search engines.
2. Be cautious with your time. Don't spend time viewing properties you cannot afford. Use an online home buying calculator to estimate the price range for homes for which you qualify. The websites of local real estate agents can help you focus your search.
3. Don't do it all by yourself. Consider obtaining assistance and guidance from a real estate agent. Use a lawyer and other professionals to prepare and process necessary documents.
4. Watch out for fraudulent listings. Scam artists may attempt to obtain personal information or money from unsuspecting homebuyers.

Think Critically

1. What benefits and concerns are associated with buying a home online?
2. Conduct an online search to obtain additional information about online home buying. Prepare a report about your findings.

Portfolio Activity

Assign the Portfolio Activity for Chapter 19, located on the companion website.

COLLECT Offer suggestion for where students might look for images that represent investments.

CREATE Suggest that students review the investment pyramid shown in Figure 19–3 on page 490.

CONNECT Remind students to connect their visuals with a short summary explaining how various factors affect the risk and value of investments.

Property Taxes

Property taxes vary greatly from state to state and community to community. Generally, real estate taxes range from 2 to 4 percent of the market value of the property. Taxes are based on the **assessed value**, which is the amount that your local government determines your property to be worth for tax purposes. Assessed values normally are lower than the market value; often the assessed value is only about half.

A home with a market value of $180,000 may be assessed at $90,000. If the tax rate is $60 per $1,000 of assessed value, the annual taxes are $5,400.

$$\$90,000 \div 1,000 \times \$60 = \times \$5,400$$

The tax rate is 6 percent of the assessed value, but only 3 percent of the market value.

Interest Payments

Interest payments add to the cost of the house. A 30-year mortgage for $100,000 at 8 percent interest would result in more than $164,000 in interest paid over the life of the loan.

Property Insurance

Property insurance is an essential home ownership cost. The value of the house, the construction material, the location in respect to other buildings, and the availability of fire protection are some factors that affect the cost of homeowners insurance. Typical annual home insurance costs are less than 1 percent of the market value of the house. Property insurance provides protection from fire, theft, accident, or other losses of your home or property.

Work as a TEAM

Various factors affect the value of a home. Prepare two lists with your team: (1) situations and actions that could increase the value of a home, and (2) factors that might decrease a home's value.

Maintenance

The cost of *upkeep*—maintaining your property in good condition—is important in home ownership. Annual upkeep costs average about 2 percent of the property's value. Postponing repairs or not taking good care of the house and yard through regular maintenance can be very costly in the long run.

CHECKPOINT

What are common costs of home ownership?

19.4 ASSESSMENT

Key Concepts

Determine the best answer.

1. The person who reports on the value of a home is a(n)
   - **a.** lawyer
   - **b.** real estate agent
   - **c.** appraiser
   - **d.** mortgage broker
2. A common financial benefit of home ownership is
   - **a.** low property insurance costs
   - **b.** tax deduction for your down payment
   - **c.** increased property value
   - **d.** low maintenance costs

Make Academic Connections

3. **Finance** Find the asking price for three different homes that are currently for sale in your community. Use an online mortgage calculator to calculate the monthly payments for each home for a 30-year fixed rate mortgage with a 10 percent down payment and with a 20 percent down payment. Report your findings in a table.
4. **Math** A home worth $123,000 with a mortgage of $72,400 would have equity of $________. A home with an assessed value of $178,000 and a tax rate of $52 per $1,000 would have a property tax bill of $________.

TEACH

Provide an overview of home ownership costs.

Explain how the assessed value is used to calculate property taxes.

Explain the example for calculating property taxes.

Point out that when a mortgage is paid off faster than scheduled, a home-buyer can save thousands of dollars of interest.

Emphasize the importance of property insurance for both homeowners and renters.

Work as a TEAM

This activity can help students better understand the factors that affect home values.

ONGOING ASSESSMENT

CHECKPOINT *ANSWER*

Common costs of home ownership are property taxes, interest payments, property insurance, and maintenance.

ASSESS

Key Concepts *Answers*

1. c. appraiser
2. c. increased property value

Make Academic Connections *Answers*

3. Tables will vary.
4. A home worth $123,000 with a mortgage of $72,400 would have equity of $50,600 (value of home − amount still owed = equity). A home with an assessed value of $178,000 with a tax rate of $52 per $1,000 would have a property tax bill of $9,256 ($178,000 ÷ $1,000 × $52 = $9,256).

RETEACH Compare situations when renting and buying would be most appropriate.

ENRICH Ask students to name actions that they might take today to prepare to buy a home in the future.

CLOSE Ask students to name common benefits and costs of home ownership.

Doing Business in... THAILAND

Asia is a very diverse region with regard to culture, religion, foods, and other factors. Encourage students to talk to people who have lived in or visited this region of the world to obtain a better understanding of the people and business environment.

THINK CRITICALLY THROUGH VISUALS

Answers will vary. Businesses involved in fashion and home furnishings might be interested in hand-woven textiles.

Think Critically *Answers*

1. In Thailand, expect to spend up to two hours at a business lunch. Use the time to develop business relationships. Sports are a good topic of conversation. With English the second most common language after Thai, language should not be a major problem.

2. When negotiating in Thailand, maintain a sense of humor and a pleasant attitude, and remember that Thais will never say "no." Greet others with a *wai* to communicate respect. Never touch another person's head as the head is considered sacred. Avoid pointing one's feet toward others; remove shoes before entering a home. Don't speak loudly or show anger in public. Avoid confrontation.

3. Answers will vary depending on what students uncover in their research on business and economic activities in Thailand.

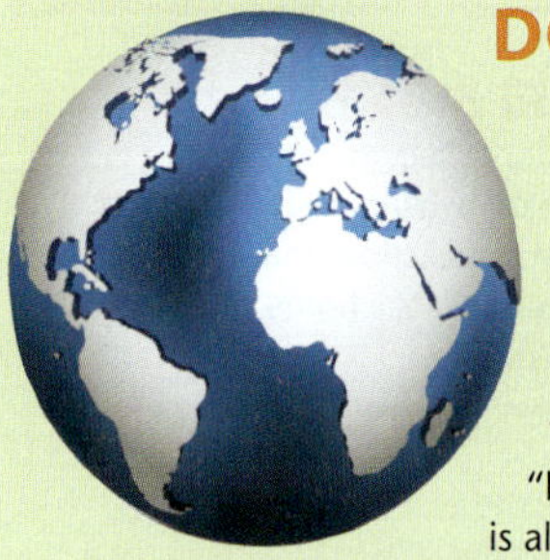

DOING BUSINESS IN... THAILAND

Known as Siam until 1939, Thailand is the only nation in Southeast Asia that was never colonized. The country's name means "land of the free." Thailand is also known as the "Land of Smiles." A sense of humor, laughter, and a pleasant attitude are highly regarded.

While Thailand guarantees freedom of religion (and many religions have a presence there), 95 percent of the population is Buddhist. Traditionally, all young men are expected to become monks for at least three months to study Buddhist principles.

Monks in Thailand are highly respected. The first rows of the theater are reserved for them and for high-ranking officials. People are also expected to give up their seats on a bus or train to a monk who is standing.

Men should greet others in Thailand with a *wai* (pronounced *why*), in which you place the palms of your hands together at chest level, fingers extended, and bow slightly. A wai communicates respect. Women should curtsy.

The head is considered very sacred in Thailand. Never touch another person's head or pass an object over it. In contrast, the bottoms of the feet are least sacred. Avoid pointing your feet toward others. Stamping your feet is considered very improper. Removing your shoes is customary when entering a Buddhist temple or private home.

A business lunch may last two hours, from 1 to 3 P.M. The time is used to develop relationships with business associates. You may discuss sports such as soccer, table tennis, badminton, volleyball, and basketball, all of which are popular in Thailand.

Dinner may extend from 7 to 10 P.M. with an eight- or nine-course meal. Rice is served with nearly every meal. In addition, you will likely be treated to spicy dishes consisting of meat, vegetables, fish, eggs, and fruit.

English is the second most common language after Thai. Remember that speaking loudly or showing anger in public is offensive. During negotiations, Thais will never say "no." Avoiding confrontation is a high priority.

Think Critically

1. What actions might be necessary when doing business in Thailand?
2. How might a person negotiate with business associates in Thailand?
3. Conduct library or Internet research to find additional information about business and economic activities in Thailand.

What type of businesses might be interested in doing business with women who use traditional looms to weave textiles?

Gautier Willaume/Shutterstock.com

Different Learning Styles

Kinesthetic Learner Instruct students to draw a flowchart, map, or other visual that communicates the trade relations of Thailand with other countries in its region or around the world. Ask students to explain what factors might affect the creation and success of a trade route.

19.5 Other Investments

Learning Outcomes

19.5.1 Discuss types of commodity investments.

19.5.2 Explain the use of collectibles as an investment.

Key Terms

commodities 507

futures contract 507

collectibles 509

Focus on REAL LIFE

"Take a look at this one! It must be more than 100 years old," said Colin. "Now that's a great investment."

"But how do we know these coins are genuine and whether they will increase in value?" asked Paul.

"Well, we could check online or get another opinion," responded Colin.

"But that's a lot of money to invest in something with that much risk," cautioned Paul. "I'm not sure that's how I want to invest my college savings."

"Come on," urged Colin. "You have to take a risk to make big bucks."

"But I could also lose big bucks!" noted Paul.

"OK, that's enough. I guess you need to consider other types of investments that match your risk level and investment goals," Colin said.

LO 19.5.1

COMMODITIES AND FUTURES

Another type of investment considered by experienced investors is commodities. **Commodities** include grain, livestock, and precious metals. Generally, commodity investing is considered to be speculative. A *speculative investment* is one with an unusually high risk.

Commodity investors buy and sell futures contracts. An agreement to buy or sell an amount of a commodity at a specified price in the future is a **futures contract**. Futures contracts also involve the buying and selling of currencies and financial instruments.

Commodity Exchanges

Commodities are bought and sold on exchanges similar to stock exchanges. Buyers and sellers are represented by traders on the exchanges.

One of the best known commodities exchanges is the Chicago Board of Trade (CBOT). Established in 1848 to provide a market for agricultural products, CBOT helps to avoid the huge price variances for these products. Today, the CBOT is affiliated with the Chicago Mercantile Exchange and called the CME Group.

Other commodity exchanges around the world include the Kansas City Board of Trade, Brazilian Futures Exchange, the African Mercantile Exchange, and the London Metal Exchange.

Agricultural Commodities

Agricultural products, such as corn, soybeans, and wheat, are some of the items traded on commodity exchanges. Agricultural producers sell their crops in advance of a harvest at what they believe is a good price. Farmers will then know in advance how much they will receive for a crop.

Focus on REAL LIFE

This feature can help students to become aware of other types of investments.

TEACH

Ask students to name products they use each day that include various agricultural products.

Point out that investing in commodity futures is very risky. Explain the purpose of a commodity exchange.

Applied Skills

Writing Across the Curriculum Prepare a paragraph that shows the connection of agricultural commodities to various business topics or to another class such as math, history, science, or foreign language.

FYI

Consider obtaining different denominations of euros for students to compare with U.S. dollars. Ask students to find current exchange rates.

TEACH

Describe how food companies use agricultural futures contracts to protect themselves from extreme price changes.

Explain the value of investing in precious metals. Explain that the spot market refers to the current value of an item, in contrast to the value in a futures contract.

Point out how foreign currencies and other financial items are used as investments.

ONGOING ASSESSMENT

CHECKPOINT ✓ANSWER

Types of commodities commonly used with futures contracts are agricultural commodities, such as grain and livestock, and precious metals.

THINK CRITICALLY THROUGH VISUALS

Answers will vary. Students should have no trouble thinking of collectibles that have increased in value such as stamps, coins, sports cards, dolls, antiques, and fine art paintings.

FYI People often confuse the euro and a Eurodollar. The euro is the official currency of the European Union. A Eurodollar is a U.S. dollar deposited in a bank outside the United States. It was originally called the Eurodollar because most of those deposits occurred in Europe. Today, the U.S. dollar is used in all regions of the world.

The futures contract buyers hope the price of the crop will go up when harvested so that they can earn a profit. Conditions that affect agricultural commodity prices include weather, international trade agreements, and worldwide demand and supply.

Gold, Silver, and Precious Metals

Precious metals have worldwide importance. Investors have traded gold and silver on commodity markets for centuries. Gold has the longest history as a monetary commodity, going back to gold coins that were circulated as early as 500 BC. Gold is highly prized for both ornamental and industrial reasons. More recently, other metals, such as copper and platinum, have also become valuable commodities.

Prices of these metals are affected by economic conditions as well as supply and demand. Since 1979, the price of an ounce of gold has ranged from more than $1,900 to less than $300. These changing values usually provide investors with protection against inflation.

Precious metals are quoted as *spot prices* per one troy ounce. This is the current price quoted for precious metals in the world markets. You can find the spot price for gold in London and New York in newspapers and online.

Money invested in precious metals does not earn interest. If you hold gold, silver, or platinum, you might profit by selling them later at a price higher than what you paid. Gold and other precious metals have another advantage—many view them as protection against currency becoming worthless. Gold could be used for buying goods and services when paper money might not be accepted.

Currency and Financial Instruments

Currencies, such as the U.S. dollar, euro, and Japanese yen, and financial instruments, such as Treasury bills and notes, are traded on the futures markets. The price of currency and financial instruments is affected by a country's economic outlook and current interest rates. Again, investors buy currency or financial instruments expecting the prices to increase in the future so that they can sell them to others at a profit.

CHECKPOINT ✓
What types of commodities are commonly used with futures contracts?

Ppictures/Shutterstock.com

Can you think of some collectibles that may be worth more now than when they were acquired? Provide some examples.

Applied Skills

Science Instruct students to research the use of gold, silver, and other precious metals in various products. Ask students to explain what features of these metals create long-term value.

LO 19.5.2

COLLECTIBLES

Another form of investment that is popular with many people is collectibles. **Collectibles** are items of personal interest to collectors that can increase in value in the future.

An advantage of collectibles is the personal pleasure of buying, collecting, storing, arranging, and displaying what is collected. Often, collectors even form organizations. For example, stamp clubs around the country bring together stamp collectors who buy, sell, trade, display, and discuss their stamps. Baseball and other sports card trading takes place at scheduled events in huge arenas as well as over kitchen tables. Antique dealers and collectors gather for major events at which they buy and sell their items.

Types of Collectibles

A wide variety of collectible items may serve as investments. Commonly obtained items are stamps, coins, sports trading cards, and antiques. In addition, unusual items purchased as investments include autographs and letters of famous people, Chinese ceramics, movie posters, glassware, rare books, and toys.

Work as a TEAM

On paper, create three columns. In the first column, list various collectibles that might be used as an investment. In the second column, describe people who might buy these items as investments. Finally, in the third column, describe factors that could affect the value of the collectibles.

Collectible Values

The possibility of the average buyer of collectibles making a large profit is uncertain. Only rare stamps, coins, art, and antiques—which may cost hundreds or thousands of dollars—tend to be items on which the investor can make a considerable profit. The wise investor in collectibles studies the market, knows the product well, and analyzes the potential risk.

CHECKPOINT

What are some common types of collectibles?

19.5 ASSESSMENT

Key Concepts

Determine the best answer.

1. The spot price for gold or silver refers to the
   a. interest for borrowing to buy the precious metal.
   b. current market price of the precious metal.
   c. future market price of the precious metal.
   d. global price for the metal set by the World Bank.
2. The value of collectibles is most influenced by
   a. the current tax rate on investments.
   b. government regulations of the market.
   c. the futures market for commodities.
   d. interested buyers and potential sellers.

Make Academic Connections

3. **Research** Go to the website of a commodity exchange. Prepare a summary of the commodities and financial instruments traded on this exchange.
4. **Art** Identify paintings and other works of art that would be considered valuable investments.
5. **Read** Find a news article about the cost of agricultural commodities. Read the article and illustrate the effect of changing farm prices on consumers. Include a properly formatted citation for your source. Possible sources include printed and online versions of newspapers and magazines. You should also consider online sources that produce original content.

CLOSE Ask students to name groups that might benefit by investing in commodity futures.

RETEACH Emphasize the risks associated with commodity futures and collectibles.

ENRICH Ask students to describe how economic conditions might affect the value of commodities and collectibles.

TEACH

Ask students to explain why certain items might be valued as collectibles. Point out factors that could affect the value of collectibles.

Work as a TEAM

This activity can help students better understand common collectibles, who collects, and the value of collectibles.

ONGOING ASSESSMENT

CHECKPOINT ✓ANSWER

Common types of collectibles include stamps, coins, sport trading cards, and antiques, as well as unusual items purchased as investments.

ASSESS

Key Concepts *Answers*

1. b. current market price of the precious metal.
2. d. interested buyers and potential sellers.

Make Academic Connections *Answers*

3. Summaries will vary.
4. Answers will vary depending on the paintings and other works of art that students identify as valuable investments.
5. Answers will vary. Examples might include higher wheat prices affecting the cost of bread or cereal products. Or, lower dairy costs resulting in lower milk or cheese prices.

Think Critically About Business *Answers*

1. Answers will vary. Employers could offer to deduct money from each paycheck to deposit into savings and possibly match a portion of that deduction. Government could provide tax breaks for savings.

2. Inflation increases the risk that an investment will not keep pace with the higher prices in the economy, causing consumers to lose buying power of their savings.

3. The investment may make sense for Ella because it represents a small portion of her total savings. However, $5,000 represents a large portion of Frank's net worth, so it might be a poor choice for him to risk investing in a newly formed company.

Chapter 19 Assessment

Review Business Concepts

19.1 Saving and Investment Planning

- Savings plans help buy needed goods and services as well as prepare for future expenses and emergencies. Savings help the economy by making funds available to individuals, businesses, and governments for borrowing. The main investment goals are current income and long-term growth.
- The major categories of savings and investments are savings accounts, certificates of deposit, money market accounts, stocks, bonds, mutual funds, real estate, commodities, and collectibles.
- When evaluating savings and investments, consider safety, yield, liquidity, and taxes.

19.2 Stock Investments

- Stock is equity and represents ownership. Preferred stock has priority over common stock in the payment of dividends. Preferred stockholders receive dividends paid at a set rate. Common stock represents general ownership in a corporation and a right to share in its profits. Common stockholders vote to elect the officers of the corporation.
- Stockbrokers work through stock exchanges to buy and sell shares of stock for investors.
- When selecting stock investments, consider a company's profitability, debt, growth potential, yield, and price-earnings ratio (P/E). Also consider economic factors such as inflation, interest rates, consumer spending, and employment.

19.3 Bonds and Mutual Funds

- A bond represents a debt owed by an organization. Government and companies sell bonds to raise funds to finance current operations or future expansion. Local and state governments sell municipal bonds. The federal government sells savings bonds, Treasury bills, and Treasury notes.
- Companies issue corporate bonds to raise funds. Investors are paid interest for lending money to the company.
- Mutual funds allow people to combine their funds to buy a variety of securities, which reduces risk and increases potential returns. Types of mutual funds include aggressive-growth stock funds, income funds, international funds, sector funds, bond funds, and balanced funds.

19.4 Real Estate Investments

- A person can get started in real estate by renting a place to live or buying a mobile home. When buying a home, you may need to obtain a mortgage and use the services of a real estate agent and lawyer.
- The advantages of home ownership are tax benefits, increased equity, and pride of ownership.
- The major costs associated with owning a house include property taxes, interest payments, property insurance, and maintenance.

19.5 Other Investments

- Commodities commonly used as investments include corn, soybeans, wheat, gold, silver, copper, platinum, foreign currencies, and Treasury debt instruments.
- Collectibles can combine a hobby with an investment that may increase in value.

Think Critically About Business

1. What actions could employers and government take to encourage saving in society?
2. How does inflation increase the risk of an investment?
3. Ella Chapman, a wealthy businessperson, invests $5,000 in a newly organized company. Frank Brokaw earns a moderate salary and has $5,000 in a savings account. Because Ella has a reputation for being a good investor, Frank decides to also invest

in that company. Does the fact that the investment may be a good one for Ella mean that it is also a good investment for Frank? Explain your answer.

4. What are some reasons people buy stocks even though they are not as safe as other types of investments?

5. Why do municipal bonds usually pay a lower rate of interest than corporate bonds?

6. Susan Haugen bought $5,000 of gold mining stocks a few years ago. Last week, she received a letter saying that the company went out of business. It could not operate profitably, so it closed down. How much of her investment might Susan lose?

7. People who buy and sell land and houses commonly say that the three most important factors to consider when buying real estate are "location, location, and location!" Why do you think this is their belief?

8. Blair Vazquez owns a house that has a value of $180,000. For the past three years, the upkeep has averaged less than $800 a year. Can Blair assume that his expenses will be only $800 in future years?

Develop Your Business Language

Match the terms listed with the definitions.

9. The amount that your local government determines your property to be worth for tax purposes.

10. Licensed specialist in the buying and selling of stocks and bonds.

11. Land and anything that is attached to it.

12. Represents general ownership in a corporation and a right to share in its profits.

13. An investment set up and managed by a company that receives money from many investors.

14. A legal document giving the lender a claim against real estate property.

15. Items of personal interest to collectors that can increase in value in the future.

16. Using your savings to earn more money.

17. The percentage of money earned on your savings or investment over a year, also called the rate of return.

18. Bonds issued by local and state governments.

19. Storage of money for future use.

20. The difference between the price at which you could currently sell your house and the amount owed on the mortgage.

21. A business organization that accommodates the buying and selling of securities.

22. Bonds issued by corporations.

23. An agreement to buy or sell an amount of a commodity at a specified price in the future.

24. The price at which a share of stock can be bought and sold in the stock market.

25. Grain, livestock, and precious metals.

26. Stock that has first priority in the payment of dividends.

27. The ease with which an investment can be changed into cash without losing its value.

Key Terms

- **a.** assessed value
- **b.** collectibles
- **c.** commodities
- **d.** common stock
- **e.** corporate bonds
- **f.** equity
- **g.** futures contract
- **h.** investing
- **i.** liquidity
- **j.** market value
- **k.** mortgage
- **l.** municipal bonds
- **m.** mutual fund
- **n.** preferred stock
- **o.** real estate
- **p.** saving
- **q.** stock exchange
- **r.** stockbroker
- **s.** yield

4. People buy stocks because, even though they do not have a guaranteed rate of return, they have the possibility of earning a much higher return than safer investment choices.

5. Municipal bonds are considered safer investments than corporate bonds, and interest on municipal bonds is tax exempt from federal and most state income taxes.

6. Susan could lose all of her $5,000 investment.

7. People will buy a less-than-perfect home in a desirable area, but they will not buy a home in an undesirable area with poor schools, poor public services, or lack of convenient access to jobs and shopping.

8. No, Blair may have to pay much more than $800 in some future year if his home needs a major repair, such as replacing the roof or the heating and air conditioning system, which could cost thousands of dollars.

Develop Your Business Language *Answers*

9. a. assessed value
10. r. stockbroker
11. o. real estate
12. d. common stock
13. m. mutual fund
14. k. mortgage
15. b. collectibles
16. h. investing
17. s. yield
18. l. municipal bonds
19. p. saving
20. f. equity
21. q. stock exchange
22. e. corporate bonds
23. g. futures contract
24. j. market value
25. c. commodities
26. n preferred stock
27. i. liquidity

Make Academic Connections *Answers*

28. Students conduct online research about the Truth in Savings Act (TISA).

29a. Charles Jason: $73 (365 × $0.20 = $73)

29b. Carla Spivak: $49.40 (52 × $0.95 = $49.40)

29c. Alice Farney: $260 (26 × $10 = $260)

29d. Nolan Robinson: $240 (12 × $20 = $240)

30. Findings will vary.

31a. earnings per share: $1.50 ($150,000 ÷ 100,000 = $1.50)

31b. the company's P/E ratio: 20 ($30 ÷ $1.50 = 20)

32. Maps will vary.

33. Tables and descriptions will vary.

34. Answers will vary.

35. Answers will vary.

36. Findings will vary.

37. Findings will vary.

Make Your Case *Answers*

38. Jennie might want to invest at least a portion of her money in investments that are slightly less safe but could provide a much higher rate of return. Because she does not plan to spend the money in the next few years, she does not need a highly liquid investment. She will likely realize a higher return by giving up some safety and liquidity.

39. Jennie should first determine her current and future financial goals. She might want to use the services of a full-services stock broker. Or, she can learn about the companies by using various library materials or online resources to obtain data about the companies' net worth, debt, sales revenue, profits, dividend history, and future prospects. Many websites provide detailed information and analyses on companies for prospective investors.

40. Descriptions of typical postings will vary. Validity of blog information can be determined by checking other sources.

Interactions and Connections

Students interview people about the types of investments they own and their recommendations for people of various ages. They should visually summarize their findings.

Make Academic Connections

28. Law The Truth in Savings Act was created to provide consumers with clear, accurate information on the earnings of savings accounts. Conduct an online search to obtain additional information about this law.

29. Math Small amounts add up to large sums in a short time. How much will each person below save in one year (365 days) if he or she saves the following amounts without interest being added?

- **a.** Charles Jason: 20 cents a day
- **b.** Carla Spivak: 95 cents a week
- **c.** Alice Farney: $10 every two weeks
- **d.** Nolan Robinson: $20 a month

30. Technology Buying investments online is convenient and reduces commission costs. Locate a website that allows you to buy and sell stock and other investments online. What services are provided by this broker? What costs are involved?

31. Math The price-earnings (P/E) ratio is calculated by dividing the price per share by the earnings per share. If a company has 100,000 shares of stock and earns a net profit of $150,000, (a) what is the earnings per share? (b) If the company's stock is selling for $30 per share, what is the P/E?

32. Geography Research the location of stock exchanges around the world. Identify one in Europe, one in Asia, one in Africa, and one in Latin America. Prepare a map showing the locations of these stock exchanges.

33. Economics Select a company and research its stock price for one day a week for the past eight weeks. Prepare a table showing the changing market value of the stock. Describe situations that may have affected the market value of this stock.

34. Communications Talk to a person who is a member of an investment club. What is the purpose of an investment club? How do these groups help investors earn money while learning about stocks and bonds?

35. Economics Locate current bond prices in the newspaper or online. Select a bond for a company. Identify the following: (a) company name, (b) stated rate of the bond, (c) bond maturity date, (d) current yield, and (e) current market value of the bond. What economic and company trends are likely affecting the current market value of the bond?

36. Research Junk bonds are investments with high risk but also potential for a high return. Conduct library or online research to obtain information about these risky bonds.

37. Business Commodity trading is governed by the Commodity Futures Trading Commission (CFTC) and the National Futures Association (NFA). Conduct library and online research to obtain additional information on these agencies.

Make Your Case

Jennie Wolfe has inherited $18,000. She graduated from high school three years ago, has an accounting job, is renting a small apartment, and saves regularly.

Jennie understands the need to evaluate stock and bond investments based on safety, liquidity, and rate of return. In addition, she realizes that the investments she selects must be guided by her personal financial needs and goals. Jennie also believes that she will not need any large amounts of cash for the next several years.

38. Jennie wants to invest in stocks that will be very safe, highly liquid, and earn a fair return. Is there anything wrong with this investment goal?

39. What advice would you give Jennie to help her study the companies from which she is considering buying bonds and stocks?

40. Investment blogs provide information based on experiences of various investors. Locate a blog that discusses investments. Describe several typical postings. What actions might Jennie take to make sure the information presented on this blog is valid?

Interactions and Connections

Talk to people you know about their investments. What types of investments do they own? (Do not ask the value of the investments.) Why did they select these investments? What types of investments do they recommend for people of various ages? Prepare a visual summary (photos, graphs, tables, company labels) of your findings.

Presentation Management—Team Event

This event will assess your use of current desktop technologies and software to prepare and deliver an effective multimedia presentation.

You will design a computer-generated multimedia presentation. You have 15 minutes for preparation and setup. The presentation will last a minimum of seven minutes and a maximum of 10 minutes. Up to five minutes will be allowed for questions from the judges. Contestants must make effective use of current multimedia technology in the presentation. In preparation for the presentation, contestants should use space, color, and text as design factors. Charts and other graphics should be used in the presentation. Contestants are responsible for securing a release form from any individual whose name, photograph, or other information is included in the presentation.

The topic for this team event is introduction to investing. The presentation should help audience members understand investment options based on the amount of money available to invest, risk factors, and rate of return. Your presentation must cover stocks, bonds, real estate, futures, commodities, and collectibles. You must discuss the safety, liquidity, and possible rate of return for each investment.

Performance Indicators Evaluated

- Demonstrate knowledge of multimedia software and components.
- Demonstrate effective oral communication skills.
- Apply technical skills to create a multimedia presentation that enhances the oral presentation.

You will be evaluated for your

- Knowledge of the topic
- Organized presentation of the topic
- Confidence, quality of voice, and eye contact

For more detailed information about performance indicators, go to the BPA website.

Think Critically

1. What does liquidity of an investment mean?
2. Which investments involve greater risk?
3. What is the advantage of investing in real estate?
4. Why are futures markets and collectibles classified as riskier investments?

www.bpa.org

WINNING EDGE

Presentation Management—Team Event

This activity offers students an opportunity to use technology to develop a visual presentation. Encourage students to carefully integrate visuals that effectively enhance the content of their presentation.

Think Critically *Answers*

1. Liquidity means how readily the investment can be exchanged for cash.

2. Futures and collectibles involve greater risk. Any investment that is not insured involves greater risk.

3. Real estate usually goes up in value.

4. Futures markets and collectibles depend on possible demand or desire for the items. They are both risky investments.

CHAPTER OVERVIEW

This chapter describes the types of insurance that consumers should consider based on their personal circumstances and resources.

20.1 Vehicle Insurance

Students will learn the types of risks they face as automobile owners and the insurance coverage related to each risk.

20.2 Property Insurance

This lesson discusses the various types of coverage available through property insurance and the factors that affect the cost of that insurance.

20.3 Life Insurance

Students will study life insurance principles and learn the process used to buy insurance.

20.4 Health Insurance

The lesson offers information on health, disability, and long-term care insurance as well as the providers of health insurance.

Chapter 20 Insurance

iStockphoto.com/Steve Debenport

Instructor Resources

- Activities and Study Guide IE
- Chapter and Unit Tests IE
- Lesson Plans
- PowerPoint Presentation
- Cognero Test, Ch. 20

Student Resources

Activities and Study Guide
www.cengage.com/swep/pob9e
- Portfolio Activity

PLANNING A CAREER IN . . .
INSURANCE

In the United States, more than 2.5 million people work in the insurance industry. The main focus of their work is to determine and satisfy the insurance needs of consumers and business organizations.

Related Job Titles

- **Insurance Sales Agent**
- **Actuary**
- **Insurance Broker**
- **Insurance Underwriter**
- **Claims Examiner**
- **Auto Damage Appraiser**
- **Insurance Policy Processing Clerk**
- **Customer Service Representative**
- **Insurance Fraud Investigator**

Insurance employment opportunities involve diverse positions including sales, management, and technical work, such as underwriting. Your work setting can range from a large office in a major city to a one-person sales agency in a rural area.

Varied types of personal and business insurance create a need for varied training to work in this industry. Assessing and managing risk requires a diverse knowledge of geographic, economic, political, and social situations.

Working in the insurance business will often require specialized training and continuing professional education. These upgraded skills, obtained through courses offered by insurance organizations, provide workers with an ability to identify and plan for the changing insurance needs of households and companies.

Analyze Career Opportunities in . . .
INSURANCE

Use library and Internet resources to learn more about careers in insurance. Choose one of the job titles listed in the box and answer the following questions.

1. How would you describe the physical work environment for jobs in this field?
2. Is this a career that interests you? Explain how careers in this field match up with your goals and interests.

What it's like to work as an . . . Insurance Agent

"Now that we have your life, car, and home insured, how about considering a portfolio of mutual funds for your retirement plan?" asked Valerie Esposito.

"Wait a minute, I thought you were an insurance agent, not an investment broker," responded Jane Conley.

"Well, we now do a lot more than just sell insurance," responded Valerie. "My company offers all types of insurance for businesses and individuals. In addition, we can help you with various financial services and investment products. We also make car loans and mortgages, and we issue credit cards."

"That's nice to know," commented Jane. "I'll be able to get assistance from you about my insurance needs, but I will also be able to borrow and invest through your company. How convenient!"

What about you? What aspects of the insurance business might interest you for a future career?

PLANNING A CAREER IN . . .
INSURANCE

The insurance industry is very large and is growing larger. It encompasses a variety of career opportunities. Many types of insurance coverages are available to consumers, and each type needs to be carefully planned, sold, and managed. From beginning jobs to highly technical careers, students can find interesting opportunities that match their interests and abilities.

What About You? ***Answer***

Answers will vary depending on students' career interests. Encourage students to match their specific interests and educational plans with possible insurance careers.

Analyze Career Opportunities *Answers*

Student answers will vary depending on when the assignment is completed and individual interests.

Additional Career Information

Encourage students to investigate careers they find interesting and explore unfamiliar careers. Two resources for additional career information are the *Occupational Outlook Handbook,* an online publication (www.bls.gov/oco) of the U.S. Bureau of Labor Statistics, and the O*NET Resource Center (www.onetcenter.org) developed by the U.S. Department of Labor. Information about specific careers and jobs can be used to demonstrate the relevance of skills learned in this course.

Focus on REAL LIFE

Ask students to identify expenses associated with owning or driving a car or truck. Ask them which of the expenses are the highest. If insurance is near the top, discuss why the cost is so high for teenagers.

TEACH

Plan and print the map for a 100-mile trip from your city following a variety of types of roads. Show the map to students and ask them to identify the possible risks and hazards they might face if they had to drive a car over the route.

THINK CRITICALLY THROUGH VISUALS

Automobile insurance can protect a policyholder from the economic risk of expensive car repairs and perhaps medical intervention in the event of an accident.

20.1 Vehicle Insurance

Learning Outcomes

20.1.1 Discuss motor vehicle risks.

20.1.2 Explain auto insurance coverage.

20.1.3 Identify factors that affect auto insurance costs.

Key Terms

- bodily injury liability 517
- medical payments coverage 518
- uninsured motorist coverage 518
- property damage liability 518
- collision coverage 518
- deductible 518
- comprehensive coverage 519

Focus on REAL LIFE

"Chris! What a great-looking car! How did you ever afford it?"

"It's not easy, Roberto, to afford a car and still be in school. Not only do I have to make car payments, but I also have to pay for insurance. It's been quite a shock! I did save enough money from a part-time job last summer to put a down payment on the car, but I didn't plan on the high cost of insurance. I'm looking for a job right now so I can afford to keep the car."

Purchasing car insurance can be expensive, but not everyone has to pay high premiums. Drivers who insurance companies view as low risks pay significantly less than those in the high-risk category.

LO 20.1.1

MOTOR VEHICLE RISKS

Owning a vehicle puts you in a position of high economic risk. You might have an accident and injure yourself or other people. You might damage your vehicle or the property of others. Your vehicle might be vandalized or stolen. Someone could sue you because of an accident.

Paying for treatment of injured people and for repair or replacement of damaged property resulting from an automobile accident can take all of the assets of a person who does not have insurance. The amount of money paid to injured people and to owners of damaged property has increased dramatically in recent years. Vehicle insurance provides protection from the financial risks involved with owning and driving a car.

Sometimes you cannot avoid an accident. No one may be directly blamed for it. However, in most cases someone is at fault. The person who is legally at fault is liable for damages and financial losses that result from the accident. Although you may think you are faultless, you can be sued. If you are insured, your insurance company will provide legal defense for the suit. If the court decides that you are legally liable for injuries or damage to property, your insurance company will pay up to the limits stated in your insurance policy.

Individual states regulate laws related to vehicle insurance. Most of these laws benefit responsible drivers. Owners of vehicles should know about financial responsibility laws and compulsory insurance laws.

In what ways can automobile insurance protect you?

Different Learning Abilities

Specific Learning Disability (SLD) Ask students to list one risk they could face in each of the situations: (1) as the driver of a car, (2) as the passenger in a car, (3) as a pedestrian crossing a street, and (4) as a vehicle owner who loans a vehicle to another driver.

Financial Responsibility

All states have some type of *financial responsibility law*. These laws protect the public from financial loss caused by drivers. If you cause an accident and cannot pay for damages or injuries through insurance, the legal system may take other action. Your savings or property may be taken. Your driver's license will also likely be suspended or taken away. Financial responsibility laws make you legally responsible for any injuries you cause to people. You are also responsible for damage to the property of others.

Compulsory Insurance

Most states require drivers to carry certain types of automobile insurance before they can get a license for their car. In these states, it is compulsory that an automobile owner have insurance for personal injury and property damage. Compulsory insurance laws may not allow a driver to register a car or get a driver's license without proof of the required insurance coverage.

CHECKPOINT
What are financial responsibility laws?

LO 20.1.2

AUTOMOBILE INSURANCE COVERAGE

Insurance companies offer several types of auto insurance protection. The two main categories are personal injury coverage and property damage coverage. Figure 20-1 summarizes the types of automobile insurance coverage.

Personal Injury Coverage

Personal injury coverage includes bodily injury liability, medical payments, and uninsured motorist protection. These three types of coverage are the main source of money paid in claims by automobile insurance companies.

Bodily Injury Liability Protection

Insurance that protects a driver from claims resulting from injuries or deaths for which the insured is at fault is **bodily injury liability** coverage. This type of insurance covers people in other cars, passengers riding with the insured, and pedestrians. The insured and, in most cases, the insured's immediate family are not covered.

Dollar amounts of bodily injury coverage are generally expressed as two numbers, such as 100/300. The first number refers to the limit in thousands of dollars

Automobile Insurance Coverage

TYPES OF COVERAGE	COVERAGE ON	
PERSONAL INJURY COVERAGE	**POLICYHOLDER**	**OTHERS**
Bodily injury liability	No	Yes
Medical payments	Yes	Yes
Uninsured/Underinsured motorist protection	Yes	Yes
PROPERTY DAMAGE COVERAGE	**POLICYHOLDER'S AUTOMOBILE**	**PROPERTY OF OTHERS**
Property damage liability	No	Yes
Collision insurance	Yes	No
Comprehensive physical damage	Yes	No

FIGURE 20-1
Which types of auto insurance coverage do you think might be the most important? Why?

ONGOING ASSESSMENT

CHECKPOINT ANSWER

Financial responsibility laws exist in some form in every state. These laws protect the public from the financial loss caused by uninsured drivers by making drivers legally responsible for any injuries or property damage they cause.

TEACH

Obtain a brochure from an automobile insurance agent or the Internet that lists and describes the types of automobile insurance coverage offered by the company. Encourage students to compare those listed with the types described in the lesson.

Figure 20-1 ANSWER

Answers will vary. Some students might suggest liability coverages are the most important because not having liability coverages can result in the highest potential financial loss.

Teaching Strategies

Expand Beyond the Classroom Instruct students to use library resources or the Internet to determine what the state's financial responsibility and compulsory insurance requirements are for automobile ownership and how they are enforced.

FYI

Highlight actions that can help reduce auto accidents. Ask students for their comments about monitoring devices.

TEACH

Tell students that there are many types of auto insurance coverage, but that those types of coverage in total can be quite expensive. Ask students to rank the types of coverage in terms of which they believe are most important if they didn't have enough money to buy all coverage. What financial issues might await someone who doesn't carry some of the coverage?

FYI To reduce accidents among younger drivers, some vehicles have an in-car monitoring device that records seat belt use, engine speed, and tire traction. This system also beeps when preset limits for speed, braking, or sharp turns are violated.

that the insurance company will pay for injuries to any one person in an accident. For example, with 100/300 bodily injury liability coverage, the insurance company would pay up to $100,000 for injuries to one person.

The second number, 300, is the maximum amount that the company would pay for injuries to multiple people because of the accident. If more than three people were injured, each person may not receive the full $100,000. The insurance company is only liable for $300,000 in this case. You may obtain larger amounts of bodily injury protection for a slight increase in your premium.

Medical Payments Protection Policyholders and family members are covered if they are injured while riding in their car or another car through **medical payments coverage**. This protection may also cover them if they are walking and are hit by a car. In addition, the policy protects guests in the insured car.

Medical payments insurance covers the costs of medical, dental, ambulance, hospital, nursing, and funeral services. Payment, up to the limit stated in the policy, is made no matter who is at fault. Car owners usually purchase medical payments insurance along with bodily injury liability coverage.

Uninsured Motorist Protection In some cases, injuries are caused by hit-and-run drivers or by drivers without insurance or money to pay claims. To protect against these drivers, insurance companies offer **uninsured motorist coverage**.

This coverage is available only to those people who carry bodily injury liability insurance. Uninsured motorist protection covers the policyholder and family members. It also covers guests in the policyholder's car. Uninsured motorist protection covers the insured person only if the uninsured motorist is at fault. This is different from medical payments coverage, which pays regardless of who is at fault.

Insurance companies also offer *underinsured motorist coverage*. This insures you for losses caused by another driver whose coverage is insufficient.

Property Damage Coverage

Three types of automobile insurance protect you from economic loss as a result of property damage. The three types of coverage are property damage liability, collision, and comprehensive damage.

Property Damage Liability Insurance that protects a driver against claims if the insured's car damages someone else's property and the insured is at fault is **property damage liability** coverage. The damaged property is often another car, but it may also be property such as telephone poles, fire hydrants, or buildings. Property damage liability insurance does not cover damage to the insured's car.

Collision Insurance Insurance that protects a car owner against financial loss resulting from a collision or rollover is **collision coverage**. This insurance does not cover injuries to people or damage to the property of others.

Collision coverage is usually written with a **deductible** clause. You must pay this amount before the insurance company pays a claim. For example, suppose your car suffers $2,500 damage in an accident and your deductible amount is $500. You would pay $500 and the insurance company would pay a $2,000 claim ($2,500 damages − $500 deductible = $2,000). Deductible amounts are often $200, $500, or more. Deductibles reduce the premium cost.

Applied Skills

Office Technology Instruct students to use a word processing program to recreate the table shown in Figure 20-1. Ask them to add an additional column on the right side of the table and add a brief description of each type of coverage in that column.

Darren Brode/Shutterstock.com

Why might insurance rates be higher on vehicles such as a Porsche?

Collision coverage does not provide for payment of damages greater than the car's value. Suppose the insured's car incurs $6,500 in damages in a collision with another vehicle. If the car has a value of only $6,100, the collision coverage would pay only $6,100, not $6,500.

Collision coverage may not be worthwhile on a car that has little value. In some situations, the cost of repairing the car may be more than the car is worth.

Comprehensive Coverage Your car can be damaged or destroyed in other ways. Common causes of loss include theft or damage from fire, tornado, flood, vandalism, or falling objects. **Comprehensive coverage** protects the insured against almost all damage losses except those caused from a collision or rollover.

If the insured's car is stolen or destroyed, the amount paid by insurance is not necessarily equal to the amount paid for the car. Rather, it is equal to the car's estimated value at the time of the loss.

Suppose the insured's car cost $15,000. It is stolen soon after it is purchased. The insurance company will probably pay almost as much as the car cost—perhaps $14,500. If the car is stolen two years after it is purchased, the insurance company may pay only $10,500. The car is older and its value has decreased.

No-Fault Insurance Laws

In an effort to reduce insurance costs and speed up claim settlements, *no-fault insurance* has been adopted by some states. Under this program, people injured in an automobile accident collect for their financial losses from their own insurance companies no matter who is at fault. These losses include their medical bills, loss of wages, and other related expenses.

CHECKPOINT ✓
What are the two main categories of automobile insurance coverage?

THINK CRITICALLY THROUGH VISUALS

Insurance rates might be higher on vehicles that are more expensive to repair, that are more likely to be driven at high speeds, or that perform poorly in crash safety tests.

TEACH

Ask students to debate the advantages and disadvantages of carrying a very high deductible amount, such as $1,000, to get a substantial savings in the auto insurance premium.

ONGOING ASSESSMENT

CHECKPOINT ✓ ANSWER

The two main categories of automobile insurance coverage are (1) personal injury coverage and (2) property damage coverage.

Applied Skills

Building Study Skills Encourage students to discuss automobile insurance coverage. Ask them to develop a study outline that lists each coverage and provides an outline of what protection it offers.

TEACH

As each of the factors used to determine insurance rates is identified, ask students to suggest why the factor can lead to higher or lower rates.

THINK CRITICALLY THROUGH VISUALS

Actions drivers can take to increase their driving safety include using both hands on the steering wheel, obeying all traffic laws, observing posted speed limits, wearing safety belts, and lessening in-car distractions, such as digital devices, items hanging from the rearview mirror, and rowdy passengers.

LO 20.1.3

AUTOMOBILE INSURANCE COSTS

Automobile insurance is expensive. When purchasing it, you should spend your money wisely and carefully. It is important to understand how to get the most protection for your insurance dollar.

What are some actions you can take to increase your driving safety?

Insurance Rates

Insurance companies use several factors to determine automobile insurance costs. Examples of these factors include:

- Your age and other characteristics such as accident record, marital status, academic standing, and credit rating
- Purpose for which you use your car
- Number of miles you drive each year
- Value and type of your car
- Community in which you live
- Amount of coverage and deductibles

Because some drivers are more likely to have accidents than others, they pay higher premiums. To determine premium rates, drivers are classified according to age, marital status, driving record, and scholastic achievement.

The lowest rates are reserved for the best risks—those least likely to have an accident. When a driver in the family is under age 25, the cost of insurance is usually higher than if all drivers are over age 25.

The purpose for which a car is driven and the number of miles it is driven in a year also affect insurance rates. Cars used for business purposes are generally driven more miles in a year than are cars driven for pleasure. This increases the chances of an accident.

The value of your car has an important effect on the cost of insurance. Premiums for collision coverage and comprehensive physical damage coverage are higher for a car worth $18,000 than for a car worth only $11,000. The insurance company runs the risk of paying out much more to the insured if the $18,000 car is destroyed or stolen. The type of car also affects the rate. Drivers of luxury cars or sports cars will pay higher rates.

Rates for automobile insurance vary from state to state. They vary from city to city within a state. The population in a particular area and the number of accidents that occur in the area also affect insurance rates. Insurance companies gather statistics on the amount of claims paid for in an area. They base their rates on this information.

The cost of your automobile insurance will vary according to the coverage you have and the deductibles you choose. The more coverage you carry, the higher the cost.

Reducing Auto Insurance Costs

By planning your automobile insurance purchase carefully, you can save money. For example, insurance companies often decrease the extra amount charged for young drivers if they complete a driver education course. Companies in most states also offer young people a good student discount.

Selecting a Company

Automobile insurance premiums also vary from company to company. Be sure to compare rates. Companies may offer lower rates if the family insures more than one

Different Learning Abilities

Gifted Encourage students to visit an insurance company website that allows rate comparisons. Ask them to make a list of several types of coverage they would need to insure an automobile. They should then compare the cost of the same coverage for several different automobile models and several different ages of the same model.

car or if the insured buys other types of insurance from the same company. Also, paying premiums on a monthly basis is usually more expensive than paying a premium for six months or one year.

Assigned-Risk Plans

Usually as a result of a poor driving record, some drivers are unable to buy automobile insurance in the normal fashion. Because of this, every state has an *assigned-risk plan*. Every automobile insurance company in the state is assigned a certain number of high-risk drivers, based on the amount of insurance each company sells. Each company has to insure a fair proportion of high-risk drivers. Drivers in high-risk categories pay much higher premiums.

Insurance for Other Vehicles

Insurance on motorcycles, recreational vehicles, and snowmobiles is similar to automobile insurance. Bodily injury liability, property damage liability, collision, and comprehensive physical damage insurance are the most important types of coverage. The engine size and value of the vehicle are the key factors in determining the cost. Generally, the larger and more expensive the vehicle, the higher the insurance cost.

Work as a TEAM

Automobile insurance can be very expensive, but it is necessary. As a team, prepare a list of actions that a person can take to lower automobile insurance costs. Suggest promotional activities that insurance companies might take to inform drivers of ways to lower their rates.

CHECKPOINT

What factors affect the cost of automobile insurance?

20.1 ASSESSMENT

Key Concepts

Determine the best answer.

1. Healthcare costs for a person you hit while driving would be covered by
   - **a.** collision
   - **b.** medical payments
   - **c.** bodily injury liability
   - **d.** uninsured motorist
2. While driving, you damage a fence. The repair costs would be covered by
   - **a.** collision
   - **b.** property damage liability
   - **c.** comprehensive
   - **d.** no-fault insurance

Make Academic Connections

3. **Math** Joan Nordland is a college student who took a driver education course in high school. She has a B + average in her college work. She qualifies for a driver education discount of 20 percent and a good student discount of 15 percent off the premium for her automobile insurance. If the standard premium for her policy is $850 per year, how much will Joan save?
4. **Communication** Research automobile accident rates for various age groups. Create a graph to communicate the data.

Work as a TEAM

Ask students to discuss which of the actions would be easiest and most difficult to take, and then review the list to determine which actions would result in the greatest reduction in insurance costs.

ONGOING ASSESSMENT

CHECKPOINT ✓ANSWER

Factors include the driver's age, accident record, marital status, academic standing, and credit rating; the purpose for which the car is driven; the number of miles driven each year; value and type of car; the community in which the driver lives; and the amount of coverage and deductibles.

ASSESS

Key Concepts *Answers*

1. c. bodily injury liability
2. b. property damage liability

Make Academic Connections *Answers*

3. With her two discounts, Joan will save $297.50, dropping her annual premium from $850 to $552.50. ($850 × 0.20 = $170 plus $850 × 0.15 = $127.50)
4. Graphs will vary depending on when the assignment is completed and the source material used.

CLOSE Encourage students to list the things they can do to reduce the cost of automobile insurance.

RETEACH Assign teams of students each of the types of coverage for automobile insurance. Instruct each team to review the information on that coverage and provide an oral summary to the other teams.

ENRICH Ask students to use the Internet to identify areas of the country that have very high automobile insurance rates and other areas that have very low rates. Ask them to describe the characteristics of the areas that they believe contribute to those rate differences.

Focus on REAL LIFE

Many renters do not buy insurance. They assume nothing bad will happen to their belongings or that the building owner's insurance policy will cover their belongings in the event of loss. Renters may suffer losses that they don't expect and cannot afford because of their lack of knowledge.

TEACH

Instruct students to work together to list the major types of property they might own. For each type of property, ask them to make a list of the types of damage that could occur resulting in a financial loss for the owner.

THINK CRITICALLY THROUGH VISUALS

Answers will vary depending on where students live and could include tornados, earthquakes, hurricanes, floods, fire, mudslides, or hail.

20.2 Property Insurance

Learning Outcomes

20.2.1 Describe property insurance coverage.

20.2.2 Explain property insurance policies.

20.2.3 Identify factors that affect property insurance costs.

Key Terms

personal liability coverage 523

homeowners policy 523

depreciation 525

Focus on REAL LIFE

"I love our new apartment! We spent a lot of money getting it ready to move into when school starts, but now I'm broke! Are you sure we really need renters insurance?"

"Trust me, Susan, with three college girls sharing an apartment, we need insurance. If our belongings were stolen or destroyed in a fire, we would be out a lot of money. I couldn't afford to replace all my personal items if they were stolen or destroyed. And with three of us sharing the insurance expense, it really won't cost us that much money."

"I guess you're right, Ashley. I know I couldn't replace all my personal belongings either. Go ahead and call your mom's insurance agent and find out what we need to do to get the process started."

LO 20.2.1

PROPERTY INSURANCE COVERAGE

Insurance that protects you from the financial loss you would incur if some of your property were lost or destroyed due to fire, theft, vandalism, flood, or other hazard is *property insurance*. Property owners also are at risk of being sued by other people who are injured on their property. Because the risks of loss in these situations can often be high, most people decide to purchase property insurance.

Home and property insurance protect you against three kinds of economic loss.

1. Damage to your home or property
2. Expenses you must pay to live somewhere else if your home is damaged and must be repaired or rebuilt
3. Liability losses related to your property

Damage to Home or Property

You should insure your home and other expensive property for damage from fire, vandalism, unavoidable accidents, and natural disasters such as lightning, wind, and hail. If your property is damaged and you are insured, the insurance company will pay all or a portion of the cost of repair or replacement.

Don Farrall/Photodisc/Getty Images

What kinds of weather might cause property damage in your area?

Different Learning Styles

Visual Learner Instruct students to prepare a drawing or other type of visual that illustrates a major type of risk that might affect property owners in your area.

Additional Living Expenses

If a fire or other disaster strikes your home, one of the first shocks you will experience is that you do not have a place to live. You may have to move into a hotel, motel, or furnished apartment while your home is being repaired.

Property insurance often includes coverage for *additional living expenses*. This insurance feature helps to pay for the living costs you would incur if something happened to your home.

Liability Losses

The third kind of loss, liability loss, is protected by personal liability insurance. **Personal liability coverage** covers claims from injuries to people or damage to property caused by you, your family, or even your pets. Suppose a neighbor slips on your icy sidewalk and it is proven you are at fault. Personal liability coverage will pay for any medical and legal costs up to a stated limit. What if a child damages a car in an adjacent driveway with a tricycle? Claims will be paid through the policy of the child's family. Specifically, the provisions that cover liability for physical damage to the property of others will be used to determine the claim amount.

These kinds of events may seem remote and rather petty. Yet court awards to those who suffer the damage or injury often are neither remote nor petty. In fact, these awards (and therefore premiums) are increasing so quickly that the insurance industry often refers to it as the insurance liability crisis. Awards to injured people for millions of dollars are not uncommon. Everyone should have some form of liability protection from economic loss.

CHECKPOINT
What are the three main types of property insurance coverage?

LO 20.2.2

PROPERTY INSURANCE POLICIES

When purchasing property insurance, you must first decide what you should insure. You must also decide the perils from which you should insure your property. *Perils* are the causes of loss such as fire, wind, or theft.

Property permanently attached to land, such as a house or garage, is *real property*. Property not attached to land, such as furniture or clothing, is known as *personal property*. You may insure real and personal property with a homeowners policy.

Homeowners Policies

The most common form of home and property insurance policy sold today is a **homeowners policy**. This coverage provides a very convenient package-type insurance policy designed to insure homes and property. Homeowners policies come in several forms.

istockphoto.com/Daniel Cardiff

What different kinds of perils should a home be insured against?

ONGOING ASSESSMENT

CHECKPOINT ANSWER
The three main types of property insurance coverage are coverage for (1) damage to home or property, (2) additional living expenses, and (3) liability protection.

TEACH

Ask students why renters need to purchase insurance coverage for personal property, but not real property. Use their answers to make sure they understand the differences between the two types of property insurance.

THINK CRITICALLY THROUGH VISUALS

Homes should be insured against perils such as wind, fire, or theft. Floods and earthquakes are perils not usually included in typical policies, but homeowners can purchase special policies to cover these threats.

Applied Skills

Communication Ask students to create a magazine advertisement that encourages first-time renters to consider purchasing personal property insurance.

▶ Figure 20-2 *ANSWER*

Answers will vary depending on students' homes and where they are located. Fire or lightning, windstorm or hail, theft, and vandalism are likely to be cited most often.

TEACH

Ask students to consider why an insurance company combines many types of coverage into one homeowners policy rather than selling several individual policies. Tell them it usually results in collecting more premiums, but is still a cost savings for the homeowner. It reduces administrative costs, but may result in a larger claim if there is substantial damage to the property.

Home and Property Insurance

Common Perils Related to Home Ownership		
• Fire, lightning • Windstorm, hail • Explosion • Riot or civil commotion • Aircraft • Vehicles • Discharge of water	• Freezing • Smoke • Vandalism or malicious mischief • Theft • Glass breakage • Volcanic eruption	• Falling objects • Tearing apart of heating system or appliance • Weight of ice, snow, or sleet • Accidental damage from steam or electrical current

Homeowners Insurance Policies		
Several types of home insurance policies are available. Each covers the perils listed above, as well as other items noted for each policy type:		
HO-3	**Special Form (All risk)**	Covers all above perils, plus any other perils except exclusions, such as flood, war, earthquake, and nuclear accidents
HO-4	**Tenants Form**	Covers personal belongings of renters against the perils listed above.
HO-5	**Comprehensive Form**	Expands HO-3 to include replacement cost coverage for home contents and buildings.
HO-6	**Condominium Form**	Covers personal belongings for condominium owners.
HO-7	**Country Home Form**	Provides coverage for agricultural buildings and equipment for non-farm business rural residents.
Other major coverages for each policy type usually include: personal liability, medical payments for visitors and guests on your property, and additional living expenses when you are required to live elsewhere due to a home insurance claim.		

Note: In the past, insurance companies also offered HO-1 (Basic Form), HO-2 (Broad Form), and HO-8 (Modified Coverage Form for older homes with a high replacement value); these policies are no longer offered by most companies.

FIGURE 20-2
Which kinds of perils pose the greatest risk of causing damage to your home?

All forms of homeowners policies cover the perils listed at the top of Figure 20-2. The *special form* and *comprehensive form* policies have become the most common types of home insurance. These policies insure against most perils except those excluded by the policy. Other home insurance policies are designed for special situations such as condominium owners and renters.

Personal liability coverage is included with all forms of the homeowners policy. With a homeowners policy, you are as protected as you would be if you bought several separate policies.

Renters Policies

Many people rent homes, condominiums, or apartments. Their dwellings are filled with personal property. Renters have many of the same property and liability insurance needs as homeowners. A *renters policy* is a property and liability policy suitable for renters.

This policy covers household goods and personal belongings. This coverage provides protection against the same kinds of perils covered by homeowners policies. A renters policy may include personal liability coverage, but it doesn't protect the actual dwelling. The dwelling should be covered under the owner's policy.

Other Coverage

You can purchase policies for damage caused by flood in a flood-prone area. You can also obtain insurance to protect against economic losses caused by earthquakes.

Different Learning Abilities

English Language Learners (ELL) Arrange for students to work with a bilingual student or aide to review the types of perils listed in Figure 20-2. The partner can make sure ELL students understand each of the types.

Neither of these two perils is typically covered in other policies.

Making a Claim

If you have to make a claim for a property loss, you will want to be well prepared. You should keep a list, called an *inventory*, of personal property that you have insured. The list should include the following information.

1. The brand name and description of each item
2. The purchase price
3. The date and place of the purchase

In addition to an up-to-date personal property inventory, insurance agents suggest keeping receipts for purchases. Taking photographs or making videos of your furniture and other property can also help to support claims.

Inventory records along with photographs or videos should be stored in a location that cannot be damaged by fire, water, or smoke. If the records are lost or damaged, it will be hard to provide the insurance company with the information it needs to make a payment for your claim. A safe deposit box in a bank or other safe location away from your home is a good storage area for property records.

The age of a personal property item is quite important. Most property becomes old, gradually wears out, and decreases in value. This decrease in value is **depreciation**. It may affect the amount an insurance company will pay if the property is destroyed.

For example, a sofa costing \$700 that is expected to last 10 years would depreciate \$70 each year (\$700 cost ÷ 10 years = \$70 depreciation per year). Its value after six years would be \$280 (depreciation per year \$70 × 6 years = total depreciation \$420); (original cost \$700 − total depreciation \$420= \$280).

FYI While more than nine of ten homeowners have property insurance, only about three of ten renters have coverage for property damage and personal liability risks. Many renters mistakenly believe that the insurance of the building owner covers the personal property of tenants.

In recent years, homeowners have begun to purchase *replacement insurance*. With this method, the insurance company actually replaces an item that has been destroyed. No depreciation is deducted. Instead, the item is actually replaced no matter what the current cost may be. A replacement cost policy would pay whatever it costs to replace your property.

CHECKPOINT ✓
How does a renters policy differ from homeowners insurance?

iStockphoto.com/ligonography

How much are homes worth in your neighborhood? How does this affect insurance rates in your area?

FYI
Remind students about the importance of renters policies. Ask them whether they could afford to replace several of their more expensive possessions without it.

ONGOING ASSESSMENT

CHECKPOINT ✓ANSWER

A renters policy may include personal liability coverage, but unlike homeowners insurance, it doesn't protect the actual dwelling, which should be covered under the owner's policy.

THINK CRITICALLY THROUGH VISUALS

Answers will vary depending on the value of homes in the communities where students live. Generally, the more expensive the home is, the more costly the insurance protection. However, high crime can cause higher rates even in a neighborhood of less expensive homes.

Applied Skills

Technology Instruct students to conduct an Internet search to locate a website that features forms that can be used to create a personal property inventory. Forms are often available on the websites of insurance or moving companies. Ask students to begin the process of completing a personal inventory for themselves or their family by adding information for several items they own.

Life-Span Plan Answers

Answers will vary. Students should point out that losses of a person's personal property or harm they cause others can prevent them from achieving their life-span goals unless they are appropriately insured.

TEACH

Ask students to discuss the difference between insuring property for its current value and its replacement cost. Ask them which type of insurance would cost more and why.

THINK CRITICALLY THROUGH VISUALS

A detailed household inventory can help a homeowner remember every covered item in the event of a claim.

Why is the purchase of property and liability insurance important to all life-span plans? What amounts and types of insurance should you plan to buy in the next few years? What resources might be valuable as you look for information about insurance coverages?

LO 20.2.3

PROPERTY INSURANCE COSTS

As with any insurance purchase, a wise consumer should seek the proper property protection at the lowest cost. This process involves making sure that you insure the property for the correct amount. You should also carefully consider the factors affecting property insurance costs. The value of a home and furnishings represents the largest investment that many people make. The purchase of a carefully selected insurance plan to protect these items makes good sense.

Coverage Selection

Suppose a family had a house built in 2004 for $180,000. They insured it for that amount. If today's cost of building a similar house is $220,000, the current replacement value of the house is $220,000. Yet if the house is destroyed by fire, the insurance company may pay the family only $180,000.

Some insurance companies provide for automatic increases in property coverage as the property value increases. Others will pay the current replacement value if the property is insured for at least 80 percent of that replacement value.

Building costs and property values increase almost every year. Property owners should review the value of their homes and insurance coverage on a regular basis. They should determine the cost of replacing their property. They must make sure that their insurance policies provide enough protection.

Special care should be taken to correctly estimate the value of personal property. Because personal property includes many items, some may be overlooked. Most homeowners policies provide personal property coverage at 50 to 70 percent of policy value. For example, if your home is insured for $100,000, your personal property is insured for 60 percent

Rob Melnychuk/Photodisc/Getty Images

Why is a detailed household inventory helpful if you need to submit an insurance claim?

Applied Skills

Mathematics Provide the following scenario and questions to students. A home was valued at $165,000 when it was purchased. If the value of the home has increased by 8 percent, what is the current value of the home? ($165,000 × 1.08 = $178,200) If the home must be insured for at least 80 percent of the replacement value, what is the amount of insurance coverage required at the time of purchase and today? ($165,000 × 0.8 = $132,000; $178,200 × 0.8 = $142,560) of this, or $60,000. The value of personal property that you obtain over the years is often high. In many cases, a homeowner's personal property is worth a great deal more than the coverage provided. Additional coverage is available for a slightly higher premium.

Insurance Premiums

Premiums paid for homeowners insurance have increased over the years. Several factors determine the price that you pay for insurance on a home and furnishings. The most important factor is the estimated danger of loss based on the insurance company's past experiences. In addition to the loss experiences, an insurance company considers the following factors in determining homeowners' insurance premiums.

- Value of the property insured
- Construction of the building: whether it is made of brick, wood, or concrete, and the construction of the roof
- Number of claims on the property
- Type of policy
- Distance to the nearest fire department and water supply
- Amount of deductible (the higher the deductible, the lower the premium)
- Credit rating of the insured

You should consider these variables before purchasing or building a home. You should also keep them in mind when you are shopping for insurance on a home you already own. In addition, homeowners insurance discounts are often available for policyholders who are nonsmokers, for installing smoke detectors and burglar alarms, and for buying multiple policies, such as life and auto insurance, from the same company.

Work as a TEAM

When items are stolen or damaged, insurance companies require that you prove the value of the item. Prepare a list of possessions that are commonly found in a home. Describe actions that might be taken to prove the value of these items.

CHECKPOINT

What factors affect the cost of home insurance?

20.2 ASSESSMENT

Key Concepts

Determine the best answer.

1. True or False. Most property insurance policies will pay for the policyholder to live somewhere else while a damaged home is being repaired.
2. True or False. A garage is an example of personal property.
3. The most coverage is provided by the ________ form of homeowners insurance.
   a. tenants
   b. special
   c. comprehensive
   d. condominium
4. Renters would not be covered for
   a. living expenses
   b. personal liability
   c. personal property
   d. real property

Make Academic Connections

5. **Visual Art** Use photos, drawings, and other visual images to create a display that communicates the various perils covered by property insurance.
6. **Research** Contact a local insurance agent to obtain information on the costs of renters insurance in your community.

Work as a TEAM

Teams should list recommendations they would make to property owners to ensure they have adequate information for filing a claim with an insurance company.

ONGOING ASSESSMENT

CHECKPOINT ANSWER

Factors include the estimated danger of loss based on the insurance company's past experiences, the value of property insured, construction of the building, number of claims on the property, type of policy, distance to the nearest fire department and water supply, amount of deductible, and credit rating of the insured. Sometimes discounts are available for policyholders who are nonsmokers, who have installed smoke detectors and burglar alarms, and who buy multiple policies from the same company.

ASSESS

Key Concepts *Answers*

1. True
2. False. A garage is real property because it is attached to land.
3. c. comprehensive
4. d. real property

Make Academic Connections *Answers*

5. Displays will vary. The various perils covered by property insurance should be represented.
6. Findings will vary.

RETEACH Divide students into learning teams of three or four students. Instruct each team to review the lesson and create a study outline of the important information about property insurance.

ENRICH Encourage students to compare the similarities and differences between automobile insurance and property insurance.

CLOSE Ask students to describe three reasons why property owners should purchase insurance.

LIFE/WORK SKILLS

Ask students to identify five different ways that visual information can be presented and compare the advantages and disadvantages of each in terms of ease of use and effectiveness of communication.

THINK CRITICALLY THROUGH VISUALS

Answers will vary. Students might suggest using props or a computer presentation.

Think Critically *Answers*

1. Visuals can enhance the effectiveness of a presentation by communicating data more effectively than mere written information. The audience will grasp the information more clearly and quickly and will recall it longer when visuals are used.

2. Visual presentations will vary. They should reflect the guidelines outlined in this feature.

LIFE/WORK SKILLS

CREATIVITY AND INNOVATION

An audience benefits from the visual presentation of data, ideas, and concepts through improved clarity and stronger recall. A graph can illustrate the importance of sales figures. A map can help participants understand the geographic context of a talk. An interesting graphic can capture people's attention.

Create Effective Visuals

Commonly used visuals include slides, posters, videos, models, photographs, flip charts, computer images, dry erase boards, maps, and demonstrations. To create effective visuals, be sure to use the following guidelines.

- Keep the design simple. Include only one major idea per visual.
- Limit how many visuals you use.
- Be concise and accurate. Proofread text and check calculations.
- Choose the visual that is most appropriate for the information or data you are presenting.
- Make sure that data are represented accurately.
- Make visuals large enough to be seen by the entire audience.
- Position yourself so the audience can clearly see the visuals.

Charts and graphs can enhance a presentation by creating a visual representation of data. They are particularly helpful in demonstrating relationships and trends. Commonly used charts and graphs include pie charts, organization charts, bar graphs, flow charts, line graphs, and pictographs.

Stockbyte/Getty Images

What are some alternatives to the visual shown in this photo?

Use Presentation Software

Presentation software such as PowerPoint® or Keynote® can enhance an oral report. Templates and designs should be selected carefully to create audience appeal and limit distraction. When creating a presentation using software, consider these guidelines.

- Limit the text quantity to six lines per slide and approximately six words per line.
- Choose text and background colors that contrast for easy reading.
- Use a consistent font style with a size that can be read.
- Add images, such as photos, maps, graphs, and illustrations, to emphasize key ideas.
- Avoid distracting transitions, animation, and sound effects.

When presenting, do not read from the screen or your notes. Talk to your audience with enthusiasm, expression, and voice projection.

Think Critically

1. How can visuals enhance the effectiveness of a presentation?
2. Create a visual that could be used with a presentation for a class or other situation.

Applied Skills

Writing Across the Curriculum Assign students to write a paragraph that illustrates how they could use the information contained in the "Life/Work Skills" feature to create an effective presentation for another class.

20.3 Life Insurance

Learning Outcomes

20.3.1 Discuss the principles of life insurance.

20.3.2 Explain the types of life insurance.

20.3.3 Describe the process of buying life insurance.

Key Terms

beneficiary 529

term life insurance 530

permanent life insurance 530

Focus on REAL LIFE

"I was shocked when I heard that one of my fraternity brothers died. He was only 30 and he had young children—just like me. Now, I can't stop worrying about my own family. What would they do if something happened to me?"

"Rafael, I know this is upsetting, but I'm sure you have life insurance. Maybe you need to check to make sure you have enough coverage," replied Steve.

"You probably won't believe this, Steve, but I don't have any life insurance. I have other kinds of insurance, but I thought I was too young to worry about life insurance."

"Everyone needs life insurance to protect their family against economic loss. Julie and I just met with our insurance agent to make sure we had the right kind of coverage. She talked to us about some policies that combine insurance and investments. Do you want her name and phone number?"

This seems like a good time for Rafael to consider purchasing life insurance. He will need to decide what kind of life insurance to buy, how much to buy, and where to buy it.

LO 20.3.1

LIFE INSURANCE PRINCIPLES

Life insurance protects survivors against financial loss associated with death. Specifically, it is designed to replace a loss of income for family members who are financially dependent upon another person. Life insurance can also be regarded as a means of saving or investing, but its primary purpose is always protection against financial loss.

The Life Insurance Policy

A life insurance policy is a contract between the insurance company and the person buying the insurance, called the *insured*. The following are the major elements of a life insurance policy.

- Name of the insured
- Amount of coverage, also called the face value or death benefit of the policy
- Cost of the insurance, called the premium amount
- Name of the beneficiary

Beneficiary Selection

When you buy life insurance, you must name a beneficiary. A **beneficiary** is the person named in the policy to receive the insurance benefits. Beneficiaries are most often spouses, children, or other dependents. You may insure not only your own life, but also the life of any person in whom you have an insurable interest. To have an *insurable interest* in the life of another person, you must receive some kind of financial benefit from that person's continued life.

Focus on REAL LIFE

Ask students what they believe is the appropriate age for someone to consider purchasing life insurance. Are there factors more important than a person's age that could determine whether life insurance is needed or not?

TEACH

Ask students: Why should life insurance be viewed as a way to provide financial protection for survivors first rather than as a method of investment? Tell them there are many other options for investing that provide a greater return, but insurance offers immediate financial protection for survivors no matter how many premiums have been paid.

Different Learning Styles

Print Learner Instruct students to prepare written definitions for each of the following insurance terms: face value, premium amount, and beneficiary.

ONGOING ASSESSMENT

CHECKPOINT ✓ANSWER

An insurable interest in the life of another person means receiving some kind of financial benefit from that person's continued life.

TEACH

Write the names of the two basic types of life insurance on the board: term and permanent. Ask students to read the descriptions of each in the lesson and then discuss the similarities and differences between them.

THINK CRITICALLY THROUGH VISUALS

Dependents who might be protected by life insurance could include a person's children and spouse, elderly parents, or business partners.

You have, for example, an insurable interest in the lives of your parents. You do not have an insurable interest in a stranger's life. A partner in a business has an insurable interest in the lives of other partners.

> **CHECKPOINT ✓**
> What is an insurable interest?

LO 20.3.2

TYPES OF LIFE INSURANCE

Insurance companies offer a variety of life insurance plans that meet different needs. The two basic types of life insurance policies are term life and permanent (or cash value) life.

Term Life Insurance

Insurance that provides financial protection from losses resulting from a death during a definite period, or term, is **term life insurance**. This coverage is the least expensive form of life insurance. Term insurance is also the *only* form of life insurance that is purely life insurance. All other forms of insurance also have savings or investment features.

Term policies may run for a period of 1 to 20 years or more. If the insured dies during the period for which the insurance was purchased, the amount of the policy is paid to the beneficiary. If the insured does not die during the period for which the policy was purchased, the insurance company is not required to pay anything. Protection ends when the term expires.

By paying a slightly higher premium, a person can buy *renewable term insurance*. This type of policy allows the policyholder to continue term insurance for one or more terms without taking another physical examination.

Term insurance policies may be level term or decreasing term. With *level term insurance*, the amount of protection and the premiums remain the same while the insurance is in effect. With *decreasing term insurance*, the amount of protection gradually becomes smaller, but premiums remain the same during the term. This is often appropriate because the need for insurance normally declines as children become independent and other savings and investments grow.

Permanent Life Insurance

The common characteristics of **permanent life insurance** are that it has cash value and an investment feature. Part of the premium you pay for permanent life insurance is used for insurance that provides protection. This feature is just like term insurance. The insurance company invests the remaining part of the premium that is not needed to pay for the coverage. This adds to the cash value of the insurance policy.

Digital Vision/Photodisc/Getty Images

Name some of the various types of dependents who might be protected by life insurance.

Different Learning Abilities

At-Risk Encourage students to ask a parent or adult friend if they have life insurance coverage and how they made the decision to buy or not to buy the insurance.

Attention Deficit Disorder Instruct students to describe the main difference between an ordinary life policy and a limited payment policy in terms of the payment of premiums.

Cash value refers to the amount of money that the insurance company will pay if the policyholder decides the insurance is no longer needed. The cash value is much less than the death benefit that would be paid to beneficiaries. As long as permanent policies are kept in force, they accumulate cash value in addition to providing life insurance.

The longer you keep your permanent life insurance policy, the higher its cash value will be. If you give up or surrender your policy, you receive the amount of the cash value. If you need money but do not want to cancel your policy, you can borrow an amount up to the cash value from the insurance company. If you should die before the loan is repaid, the insurance company will withhold the unpaid amount from the face value of the policy when it pays your survivors. *Face value* is the amount of insurance coverage that was originally purchased and that will be paid upon the death of the insured.

The cash value of permanent life insurance can be seen as a savings plan. Usually, the return on your money in the cash value portion of permanent life insurance is not large. Nevertheless, permanent insurance plans have a built-in savings feature that encourages people to save for the future. Permanent life insurance comes in the form of whole life, variable life, and universal life policies. Each type builds up cash value.

Whole Life Insurance Permanent insurance that extends over the lifetime, or whole life, of the insured is *whole life insurance*. One type of whole life insurance is an *ordinary life policy*. Premiums for ordinary life insurance remain the same each year as long as the policyholder lives.

Some whole life insurance policies are meant to be paid in full in a certain number of years. *Limited-payment policies* may be designated by the number of years the policyholder agrees to pay on them, such as 20-payment life policies. They are like ordinary life policies except that premiums are paid for a limited number of years or until a person reaches a certain age. Limited-payment policies free the insured from paying premiums during retirement when income may be lower.

> **Life-Span Plan**
> Many life-span plans are created to serve a family. Explain why these plans should include life insurance for all adult members. When do you expect to purchase life insurance? How much and what type will you buy?

Variable Life Insurance An insurance plan that resembles an investment portfolio is *variable life insurance*. This plan lets the policyholder choose among a broad range of investments. These investments include stocks, bonds, and mutual funds. The death benefits and cash values of variable life policies vary according to the yield on the investments that the policyholder selects.

Monkey Business Images/Shutterstock.com

Why do people's insurance needs change at different times in their lives?

Portfolio Activity

Assign the Portfolio Activity for Chapter 20, located on the companion website.

COLLECT Students may use the photos in this chapter as images that communicate potential financial losses.

CREATE Suggest that students work in small groups where each person can focus on a specific type of insurance coverage.

CONNECT Students should to think of ways to relate their visuals to concepts from other classes.

TEACH

Tell students that borrowing against the cash value of an insurance policy should be done only after a great deal of thought. If the money is borrowed and not repaid, the beneficiaries will not receive the full value of the insurance policy. If money is borrowed, plans should be made to repay the loan as quickly as possible.

Life-Span Plan Answers

Answers will vary. Students should point out that life insurance protects a family from financial losses resulting from the death of a family member. At least some life insurance should be purchased when people are first married.

THINK CRITICALLY THROUGH VISUALS

People tend to need more life insurance when they are younger because they are more likely to have dependent children and large debts, such as mortgages. Older individuals may need less life insurance because they do not have dependents, they own their homes, and their investments and savings have grown.

▸ **Figure 20-3 *ANSWER***

Term insurance is the least expensive type of insurance for a given amount of death benefit, although the protection expires when the policy's term ends.

TEACH

Ask students to use the information in Figure 20-3 to discuss reasons why they would or would not purchase each of the types of insurance policies listed.

The insurance company first designates an amount of the variable life premiums to cover the cost of insurance. It places the remaining amount in an investment account. Both the death benefit and the cash value rise and fall with the success of the investment account.

A variable life policy might guarantee a minimum death benefit. There is no guaranteed cash value. The minimum death benefit, in relation to premiums paid, is well below other types of life insurance. On the positive side, a strong rate of return on the investment account can increase the cash value and the death benefit.

Universal Life Insurance *Universal life insurance* provides both insurance protection and a substantial savings plan. The premium that you pay for universal life insurance is split in three ways. One portion of it pays for insurance protection. The insurance company takes a second portion for its expenses. The third portion goes into interest-earning investments for the policyholder.

The most important feature of universal life insurance is that the investment portion of the policy earns a variable rate of return. This rate is usually higher than is paid on other types of cash value life insurance. This yield on the investment portion tends to rise or fall based on changing economic conditions. Figure 20-3 compares the features of the different types of life insurance.

Types of Life Insurance Policies

		PERMANENT LIFE INSURANCE			
		Whole Life Insurance			
POLICY FEATURES	TERM LIFE INSURANCE	Ordinary Life Insurance	Limited Life Insurance	Variable Life Insurance	Universal Life Insurance
Premium	Begins low but increases gradually	High, but usually stays constant	Higher than ordinary life insurance but constant	Fixed and regular	Varies at the discretion of the policyholder
Payment Period	Specified number of years—normally 5, 10, or 15 years	Life of the insured	Specified number of years—normally 20 to 30 years	Specified period	Specified period
Cash Value	None	Some cash value	More cash value than ordinary life but less than variable life	Varies with the rise or fall in the value of the investment account	Varies with the interest rate paid on the cash value
Death Benefit	Fixed	Fixed	Fixed	Death benefit always exceeds cash value	Can vary at the discretion of the policyholder
Purposes	Protection for a specified period of time	Protection for life, some cash value for policyholder	Protection for life, some cash value for policyholder	Life insurance plus an opportunity to select different cash value investment options	Life insurance with a fairly high rate of return on cash value

FIGURE 20-3

Which kind of insurance is least expensive for a given amount of death benefit?

Different Learning Abilities

Visually Impaired Enlarge Figure 20-3 so that it is visible for students. For students who cannot read the enlarged figure, ask them to work with another student who can read and explain the information.

Group Life Insurance

Some individuals are fortunate to have an employer or some other group offer the opportunity to buy group life insurance. An insurance policy that covers a group of people is called *group life insurance*. The group acts as a single unit in buying the insurance.

The cost of group life insurance is less than the cost of a similar individual policy. These savings result from the insurance company covering many people in one policy.

Most group life insurance plans offer term rather than permanent insurance. The insurance company works with an employer or other organization, such as a union, to develop the insurance plan. Then, each employee or member of the organization may purchase individual life insurance coverage.

CHECKPOINT ✓

What is the difference between term and permanent life insurance?

Lawrence Wee/Shutterstock.com

Why do people working in dangerous occupations cost more to insure?

LO 20.3.3

BUYING LIFE INSURANCE

Many people need the protection offered by life insurance. Without insurance, few people have the financial resources needed to pay for a funeral and other related expenses when someone close to them dies. For a life insurance program to be effective, it must fit your needs and those of your family.

Coverage Amount

Anyone with dependents should consider life insurance. A *dependent* is a person who must rely on another for financial support. In the future, you will need to ask the question, "What would happen to the people who are financially dependent on me if I die tomorrow?" If they could not live financially in the way in which they lived before your death, you most likely need life insurance.

The following questions will help to determine your need for life insurance.

- How much money is required for your dependents' financial stability if your income is lost?

NET KNOWLEDGE

Insurance can be confusing, but many valuable online information sources are available. Select one of the types of insurance discussed in this chapter. Locate a website with insurance information. Explain how this information might be used in your life now or in the future.

ONGOING ASSESSMENT

CHECKPOINT ✓ANSWER

Term insurance is less expensive. It is pure life insurance without any savings or investment features. Term insurance expires at the end of the term. If the insured does not die during the term, he or she must renew the policy to continue the coverage. Permanent life insurance has a cash value that increases the longer the policyholder maintains the policy. A policyholder can cash in a permanent life insurance policy for its cash value and can also borrow money up to the amount of the policy's cash value.

TEACH

Ask students: Why does covering many people under one group life insurance policy usually result in cost savings? They can identify the lower administrative costs, a mix of older and younger people, and other factors.

THINK CRITICALLY THROUGH VISUALS

People in dangerous occupations pay more for life insurance because they are at greater risk of death than the general population.

NET KNOWLEDGE

Students should be able to explain how information they find might be useful now or in the future.

Different Learning Styles

Tactile Learner Instruct students to create a bulletin board, poster, or tabletop display that illustrates the differences between term and permanent life insurance. Consider allowing students to work in pairs or small groups.

Work as a TEAM

Explain that the phrase "insurance poor" describes people who buy much more insurance than they really need or can afford.

TEACH

Ask students to discuss why the premium paid for a whole life policy stays the same, while the cost for a term policy gets higher as the purchaser ages.

ONGOING ASSESSMENT

CHECKPOINT ✓ANSWER

Factors include the number of dependents who rely on the person, the amount of savings the person has to leave to those dependents, and the amount of the person's debts.

ASSESS

Key Concepts *Answers*

1. c. Term

2. c. receives money when the insured dies

Make Academic Connections *Answers*

3. Findings will vary. Encourage students to discuss their findings and compare the answers they found for common questions.

4. The cash value of the investment portion will be $18,784.50 at the end of the year ($17,643 × 0.0647 = $1,141.50; add that amount to the original cash value: $17,643 + $1,141.50 = $18,784.50).

CLOSE Ask students to list reasons why a person would or would not decide to purchase life insurance.

Work as a TEAM

Life insurance needs vary, and determining how much life insurance you need requires careful consideration. As a team, prepare a list of factors that a person might consider when determining the amount of life insurance to obtain.

- How much income will you need when you retire and what will be the sources of your income?
- What can you afford to pay for your life insurance needs?

Answers to these questions will help you purchase the best life insurance program for you.

Life Insurance Application

To buy individual life insurance coverage, you need to complete a life insurance application. You apply for this coverage through an insurance agent representing an insurance company.

You may be required to take a physical exam to assess your health. If you have no serious health problems, you then pay a premium and receive your life insurance policy.

If you are in poor health or work in a dangerous job, you may be considered a poor risk. Even so, you likely will be able to obtain life insurance. You will probably pay higher premiums than people who are in good health or are employed in less hazardous jobs.

Premium Payments

In addition to the health and occupation of the insured, the type of policy affects the cost of life insurance. The age of the person being insured also affects premiums. In purchasing a whole life policy, for example, the premiums for ordinary life insurance are higher than those for term insurance, but the annual premium stays the same throughout the insured's life. The premiums on limited-payment life insurance are higher than those for ordinary life insurance, but they are payable for only a limited number of years.

CHECKPOINT ✓

What factors affect the need for life insurance?

20.3 ASSESSMENT

Key Concepts

Determine the best answer.

1. ________ life insurance is considered temporary coverage.
   a. Whole
   b. Universal
   c. Term
   d. Variable
2. The beneficiary of a life insurance policy
   a. is the cost of insurance
   b. makes the premium payments
   c. receives money when the insured dies
   d. is the period for which the policy is in effect

Make Academic Connections

3. **Technology** Use the Internet to find an insurance company website that includes frequently asked questions about life insurance. Find three questions that interest you. Copy the questions and their answers along with the name of the company and the URL.
4. **Math** The rate of return on the investment portion of a life insurance policy is 6.47 percent for a given year. If the investment portion (cash value) was $17,643 at the beginning of the year, what will it be worth at the end of the year? Round to the nearest cent.

RETEACH Instruct students to review the information in Figure 20-3 and clarify any questions they have about the different types of life insurance policies.

ENRICH Ask students to prepare a description of the type and amount of life insurance they believe they should have at age 20, 35, and 65. Students should justify their decisions.

20.4 Health Insurance

Learning Outcomes

20.4.1 Describe health insurance coverage.

20.4.2 Discuss health insurance providers.

20.4.3 Explain disability and long-term care insurance.

Key Terms

hospital insurance 535
surgical insurance 535
regular medical insurance 536
major medical insurance 536
coinsurance 536
comprehensive medical policy 537
disability income insurance 541

Focus on REAL LIFE

"Carlotta! Welcome back to school! We really missed you. How is your arm?"

"Kendra, my arm is doing great. Thanks for asking. I can't believe that a simple fall put me in the hospital and I had to have surgery," responded Carlotta. "I'm almost feeling normal again, and we were very fortunate that the insurance company paid nearly all of my bills. My mother has very good health insurance at her job. Without that coverage, we would have had to pay more than $40,000."

"Wow! I'm glad you were covered by your mother's insurance. Now, Carlotta, how soon before you can throw again?" asked Kendra.

"Sooner than I would be able to pay my medical bills if I didn't have health insurance!"

20.4.1 HEALTH INSURANCE COVERAGE

Several types of health-related insurance are available to provide different kinds of coverage. One type of health insurance is *medical insurance*. It can be classified as (1) hospital insurance, (2) surgical insurance, (3) regular medical insurance, (4) major medical insurance, and (5) a comprehensive medical policy. Insurance companies also offer combination policies.

Hospital Insurance

An illness or injury may require you to be hospitalized. In this situation, **hospital insurance** usually pays most or all of the charges. These include expenses for your room, food, and medical items such as use of an operating room, anesthesia, X-rays, laboratory tests, and medications. Because of the high cost of hospitalization, people purchase hospital insurance more than any other kind of health insurance.

You can buy hospital insurance from insurance companies or from nonprofit corporations, such as Blue Cross. If expenses are more than the amount covered by the hospital insurance plan, the patient must pay the difference.

Surgical Insurance

Surgery is a major reason for hospitalization. It can be very expensive. **Surgical insurance** covers all or part of the surgeon's fees for an operation. The typical surgical policy lists the types of operations that it covers and the amount allowed for each. Some policies allow larger amounts for operations than others. This, of course, requires that a higher premium be paid. Surgical insurance is often bought in combination with hospital insurance.

Again, you can buy surgical insurance from insurance companies or from nonprofit organizations. Surgical plans cover mainly medical and surgical treatment

Focus on REAL LIFE

Tell students that insurance companies and companies that provide health insurance for employers are working to reduce the costs of health insurance. Ask students to describe things people can do to reduce the costs of their medical care.

TEACH

Ask volunteers to share things that have happened to them that have required a trip to a physician or hospital. Get the discussion going by asking if anyone has broken a bone or had a tonsillectomy. As the types of insurance coverage are introduced, match the student experiences to the correct type of health insurance coverage.

Different Learning Styles

Kinesthetic Learner Instruct students to use a variety of resources to locate advertisements for health insurance companies. Students should match the types of insurance offered by each company with the coverage descriptions from the lesson.

THINK CRITICALLY THROUGH VISUALS

Hospital insurance is expensive because the cost of medical procedures keeps rising as new treatments are discovered. The escalating cost of malpractice insurance also plays a role. With today's high-tech medical care, hospital stays can easily cost tens of thousands or even hundreds of thousands of dollars.

TEACH

Explain to students that coinsurance is sometimes called a "copayment" or "copay." Some insurance policies require policyholders to pay a small copay of 10 to 25 dollars for each visit to a doctor and each prescription. Instruct students to discuss why the use of that small copay might reduce the costs of health care by causing the policyholders to think carefully about whether a trip to a doctor is needed or not.

rather than hospital care. These plans list the maximum amounts that they will pay for different types of surgery. They also cover the doctor's charges for care in the hospital. Some plans pay the doctor's charges for office or home care. The coverage generally does not provide for preexisting conditions or for illnesses or injuries that are covered by other insurance.

Regular Medical Insurance

Sometimes normal care provided by a physician can be quite expensive. **Regular medical insurance** covers fees for nonsurgical care given in the doctor's office, the patient's home, or a hospital. The policy states the amount payable for each visit or call. It also lists the maximum number of visits covered. Some plans provide payments for diagnostic and laboratory expenses.

Regular medical insurance is usually combined in one policy with hospital and surgical insurance. The protection provided by regular medical, hospital, and surgical insurance is often referred to as *basic health coverage*.

Major Medical Insurance

Long illnesses and serious injuries can be very expensive. Bills of $50,000 to $100,000 and higher are not unusual. **Major medical insurance** provides protection against the high costs of serious illnesses or injuries. This coverage complements the other forms of medical insurance.

Major medical insurance helps pay for most kinds of extended and specialized health care prescribed by a doctor. It covers the cost of treatment in and out of the hospital, special nursing care, X-rays, psychiatric care, medicine, and many other healthcare needs. Maximum benefits may be limited, but usually extend to a high amount, such as $500,000 or $1,000,000.

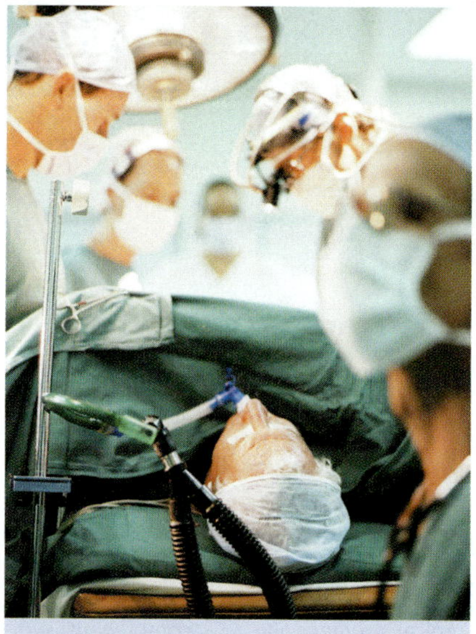

Hoby Finn/Photodisc/Getty Images

Why is hospital insurance so expensive?

All major medical policies have a *deductible* clause. The clause is similar to the one found in automobile collision insurance. With this clause, the policyholder agrees to pay the first part of the expense resulting from sickness or injury. The deductible may be $500 or more.

Major medical policies usually contain a *coinsurance* clause. **Coinsurance** is the sharing of expenses by the policyholder and the insurance company. The policyholder typically pays a deductible and then shares the remaining cost with the insurance company.

For example, the insurance company may pay 80 percent of the cost for medical treatment after the deductible is paid. The policyholder will then pay the remaining 20 percent. The policyholder's share is limited to a specific dollar amount stated in the policy. Once the deductible and the coinsurance amounts are met, the insurance company reimburses 100 percent of the cost up to the policy's coverage limits.

Applied Skills

Mathematics Provide the following scenario and question to students. A consumer has an insurance policy with a $500 deductible and coinsurance of 20 percent of the costs above the deductible. If the total bill is $5,300, how much must the consumer pay? (The consumer pays $1,460. Subtract the deductible from the total bill, $5,300 – $500 = $4,800. Multiply the difference by 20 percent, $4,800 × 0.2 = $960. The consumer pays $960 plus the $500 deductible.)

The deductible clause discourages the filing of minor claims. The coinsurance clause encourages the policyholder to keep medical expenses as reasonable as possible. Thus, both clauses help to lower premiums because they help to reduce payments of insurance claims.

Comprehensive Medical Policy

Insurance providers have developed a **comprehensive medical policy** that combines the features of hospital, surgical, regular, and major medical insurance. This coverage retains the features of each separate coverage, such as amounts-payable limits. The policy has only one deductible. A combination of coverages will likely be less expensive than the total of the separate coverage.

Dental Insurance

As dental expenses have increased over the years, insurance companies now offer coverage to help pay for normal dental care. Dental insurance usually includes examinations, X-rays, cleaning, and fillings. It may cover part or all of complicated dental work such as crowns or bridges. This policy also covers dental injuries resulting from accidents.

Most dental plans contain deductible and coinsurance provisions to reduce the cost of premiums. Dental insurance is offered mainly through group plans. It continues to grow in popularity.

Vision Care Insurance

In anticipation of eye care expenses, many individual consumers and groups purchase vision care insurance. These policies cover eye examinations, prescription lenses, frames, and contact lenses. Some vision care plans now cover the cost of laser eye surgery, which can eliminate the need for glasses. New medical developments may result in additional vision care coverage.

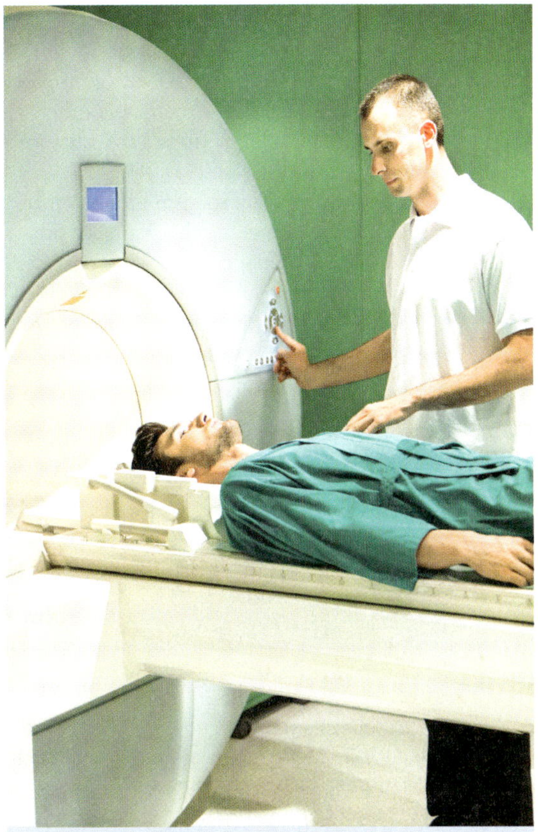

iStockphoto.com/fotostorm

Why do most people need some kind of health insurance?

CHECKPOINT ✓

What four types of health insurance would be included in a comprehensive medical policy?

LO 20.4.2

HEALTH INSURANCE PROVIDERS

Health insurance is available from several sources. These options include group health insurance, individual health insurance, health maintenance organizations, preferred provider organizations, and government programs.

THINK CRITICALLY THROUGH VISUALS

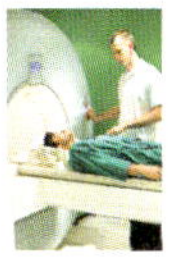

Most people need some kind of health insurance because they do not have enough assets to pay for the costs of today's high-tech medical care. Even a relatively routine hospital stay could cause financial ruin for many people.

TEACH

Ask students if they believe that purchasing medical, dental, and vision care insurance results in people taking better care of themselves or not. Some will suggest that, because they are spending money for the insurance, they will try to take better care of themselves. Others will suggest that those who don't have insurance will be more careful because they know they don't have insurance protection.

ONGOING ASSESSMENT

CHECKPOINT ✓ ANSWER

A comprehensive medical policy would include the following four types of health insurance: (1) hospital, (2) surgical, (3) regular, and (4) major medical insurance.

Different Learning Styles

Visual Learner Instruct students to visit the employment section of the websites of three different companies that describe the healthcare benefits provided to employees of the company. Ask them to develop a chart or table that compares the healthcare policies of the companies.

TEACH

Instruct students to use the Internet to identify organizations that are not employers and not government agencies that offer group health insurance policies for their members. Ask students why they believe each organization offers that benefit.

Business Insight

Point out that telemedicine is not a medical specialty and does not always involve the direct delivery of clinical services. Invite students to share their ideas about how telemedicine might touch their own lives.

Think Critically *Answers*

1. Answers will vary. Students should recognize that some telemedicine services might cost less than a traditional service. The use of some telemedicine services for monitoring and prevention may help reduce overall healthcare costs. Telemedicine might also drive up healthcare costs by making expensive procedures more widely available.

2. Summaries will vary. Students are likely to find examples of telemedicine being used in a variety of settings. For example, large medical centers offer services to rural populations, the reading of X-rays is routinely outsourced to physicians in other countries, the use of electronic medical records is on the rise, and a successful demonstration of telesurgery using robotics has been documented.

Group Health Insurance

The most popular way to buy health insurance is through a group. As with group life insurance, employers, unions, and other organizations offer group health insurance policies.

Companies that sponsor group policies often pay part or all of the insurance premiums for their employees. They provide this as an employment benefit. Employees can usually buy coverage for family members as well.

The cost of group health insurance is lower per insured than the cost of a comparable individual policy. The costs are lower because insurance companies can manage group plans more economically.

Individual Health Insurance

Some people are not eligible for group health insurance. They may be self-employed and have no employer to help buy health insurance. One alternative is to buy individual health insurance. These policies are available to individuals and are adapted to individual needs. Individual health insurance policies are usually rather expensive. They may require a

Business Insight

Telemedicine

A physician in a rural hospital learns new surgery techniques by viewing live images of a procedure being performed by a surgeon halfway around the world. A nurse in an emergency room prepares for the arrival of a heart attack patient while receiving real-time data from diagnostic equipment being used by paramedics in the field. While sitting at a home computer, a teenager with cancer participates in a support group with young people from around the globe.

These are examples of *telemedicine*, which refers to a wide range of activities involving medicine, communication technology, and distance.

Specialist referral services usually involve specialists helping other physicians diagnose a patient's condition. For example, a radiologist, a physician who specializes in the interpretation of diagnostic images, can read a chest X-ray from a remote location across town or in a different country.

Patient consultations are direct interactions between a patient and a healthcare provider. A common situation may involve a patient in a rural clinic communicating with a physician in another location such as a private medical office or a hospital.

Remote patient monitoring relies on devices to collect data from a patient and transmit it to another location for interpretation. Home health agencies use this technology to monitor chronic conditions such as diabetes and congestive heart failure.

Medical education provides continuing education and special training to healthcare professionals. Telemedicine is a convenient and cost-effective way to participate in classes, seminars, workshops, and demonstrations.

Consumer medical and health information offers online medical and health resources for the general public as well as specialized service for specific patients or groups. Examples include online chats with midwives, web-based food diaries for nutritional counseling, blogs focused on issues family caregivers face, and e-mail follow-up after an office visit.

The use of telemedicine is growing and changing with the introduction of new technologies and innovations. While concerns exist about cost-effectiveness, insurance coverage, and privacy, it is likely that many telemedicine services will become routine.

Think Critically

1. How might the availability of telemedicine services impact the cost of health care?
2. Use library or online resources to find three examples of telemedicine being used in different settings. Write a short summary of your findings.

Applied Skills

Technology Encourage students to investigate the use of telemedicine in your community. Ask students to focus their attention on business activities related to telemedicine. For example, they might learn more about a company that manufactures equipment that facilitates telemedicine, a medical practice or hospital that markets telemedicine services, or an insurance company that covers telemedicine services.

physical exam and impose a waiting period before the policy takes effect.

Managed Care Plans

Various alternative health insurance plans have grown in popularity. Known as *managed health care* or *managed care*, these programs cover more than two-thirds of Americans who have insurance through their employer. These plans often provide lower-cost, comprehensive health care through networks of medical professionals.

Managed care plans usually have higher monthly premiums. Yet the overall cost of health care may be lower for the consumer because of low or no deductibles, low copayments, and little or no paperwork. A potential drawback is that patients have less control and limited choices of healthcare providers. Managed care plans have various names, such as HMOs (health maintenance organizations) and PPOs (preferred provider organizations).

The growth of managed care is a result of large companies' attempts to control the rising cost of providing healthcare coverage for employees. Today, many managed care plans are run by insurance companies.

Health Maintenance Organization (HMO) One managed care choice is a health maintenance organization. A *health maintenance organization (HMO)* commonly consists of a staffed medical clinic to serve members. You join an HMO for a fixed monthly fee. As a member, you are entitled to a wide range of prepaid healthcare services, including hospitalization. HMOs emphasize preventive health care. Early detection and treatment of illnesses help reduce hospital visits and keep costs down. Generally, HMOs do not cover treatment or care that is not authorized by a physician or procedures that are above the average cost for the area.

Preferred Provider Organization (PPO) A popular alternative is the *preferred provider organization (PPO)*. This system involves several healthcare providers, such as a group of physicians, a clinic, or a hospital. These medical professionals contract with an insurance company to provide services to members. These providers agree to charge set fees for services.

Members are encouraged, but not required, to use the PPO services through financial incentives. Members are able to get medical treatment through the PPO at a significant discount. They may seek medical treatment elsewhere. However, expenses for treatment outside the PPO may be only partially reimbursed.

Work as a TEAM

Everyone is affected by rising healthcare costs. As a team, prepare a list of actions that might be taken by (a) individuals, (b) businesses, and (c) government to (1) improve the health of people in society and (2) reduce costs for medical services.

State Government Assistance

An important health insurance program administered by state governments is *workers' compensation*. This insurance plan provides medical and survivor benefits for people injured, disabled, or killed on the job. Accidents can occur on almost any job. Employees may suffer injuries or develop illness because of working conditions. Workers' compensation laws provide medical benefits to employees who are injured on the job or become ill as a direct result of their working conditions. Under these laws, most employers are required to provide and pay for this insurance for their employees.

State governments also administer a form of medical aid to some low-income individuals and families known as *Medicaid*. The federal government and state governments share the cost of providing health benefits to eligible individuals and families. Services covered by Medicaid include hospital care, doctor services, X-rays, lab tests,

Work as a TEAM

Ask students to discuss the effects on individuals and businesses of rapidly rising healthcare and health insurance costs.

TEACH

Write "HMO" and "PPO" on the board. Instruct students to list the similarities and differences between the two types of managed care. Ask them to decide which of the two they would personally prefer and why.

Teaching Strategies

Expand Beyond the Classroom Assign a team of students to act as an investigative news group and prepare a report on measures companies take to improve the health of their employees. The group should prepare a video "news report" and play the video for the other class members.

TEACH

Instruct students to identify the differences between Medicare and Medicaid.

THINK CRITICALLY THROUGH VISUALS

Health insurance costs can be reduced by carefully buying only the coverage needed, by following a healthful lifestyle and using medical benefits only when necessary, and by getting a second opinion for major medical decisions. Health insurance costs can also be lowered through coinsurance and deductibles and using outpatient surgery whenever possible.

ONGOING ASSESSMENT

CHECKPOINT ✓ANSWER

The main providers of health insurance are group health insurance, individual health insurance, health maintenance organizations, preferred provider organizations, and government programs.

nursing home care, and home health care services. States may also offer health insurance programs for people who have trouble obtaining coverage. Past health conditions can result in a person being turned down by most health insurance providers.

Federal Government Assistance

The nation's Social Security laws provide a national program of health insurance known as *Medicare*. This insurance helps people aged 65 and older and some people with disabilities pay for health care. Medicare has two basic parts: hospital insurance and medical insurance.

The hospital insurance plan includes coverage for hospital care, service in an approved nursing home, and home health care up to a certain number of visits. No premium payments are required for the hospital insurance. Almost everyone 65 years old and older may qualify.

The medical insurance portion of Medicare is often called supplementary or voluntary medical insurance. The services covered under this plan include doctor services, medical services, supplies, and home health services. The medical insurance requires a monthly premium. The federal government pays an equal amount to help cover the cost of the medical insurance.

The Health Insurance Marketplace can assist those under age 65 without health insurance. Also called the Health Insurance Exchange, this online resource provides information on health insurance along with options for buying health coverages. Some states have their own health insurance marketplaces, which can be accessed through the federal government website. Consumers with lower incomes can determine their eligibility for assistance with paying health insurance premiums.

Cost Reduction Actions

Healthcare costs have consistently increased faster than the overall cost of living. The cost of health insurance is determined by

Photodisc/Getty Images

What can you do to reduce your health insurance costs?

four main factors: extent of coverage, number of claims filed, age of the policyholder, and number of dependents. You have no control over your age and little control over the number of people who depend on you. However, you can make sure you buy only the kind and amount of insurance you need. You can also take care of yourself and not use medical benefits unnecessarily.

Insurance companies encourage policyholders to play an active role in *cost containment*, or keeping costs down. The most common methods are coinsurance and deductibles.

Another cost-containment strategy is the use of outpatient services for some surgical procedures. In the past, people undergoing some procedures might have been admitted to the hospital for one or two days. Now, the person comes to the hospital or an outpatient center in the morning. After the surgery, the patient returns home the same day.

CHECKPOINT ✓

Who are the main providers of health insurance?

LO 20.4.3

DISABILITY AND LONG-TERM CARE INSURANCE

The need for health insurance goes beyond various medical expenses. Disability income and long-term care insurance

Different Learning Styles

Print Learner Ask students to look through recent newspapers and magazines to find articles on efforts undertaken by consumer groups, government, businesses, and the healthcare industry to contain healthcare costs. Encourage them to clip or copy the articles and organize them for others to read.

programs protect people in other types of situations.

Disability Income Insurance

For most people, income from employment is their single most important economic resource. Protecting your income is very important. One form of health insurance provides periodic payments if the policyholder becomes disabled. **Disability income insurance** protects you against the loss of income caused by a long illness or an accident. The insured receives weekly or monthly payments until they are able to return to work.

Disability income policies often include a waiting period. This requires the policyholder to wait a specified time after the disability occurs before payment begins. Monthly payments under disability insurance plans are usually much smaller than the income people earn from their jobs. The amount may be 40–60 percent of the normal income, but many disability payments are not subject to income taxes.

Long-Term Care Insurance

With people living longer, *long-term care insurance* is the fastest-growing type of protection. This coverage provides *long-term care*, which is daily assistance needed because of a long-term illness or disability. This assistance may involve a stay in a nursing home. It may cover help that is provided at home for daily activities such as dressing, bathing, and doing household chores.

iStockphoto.com/lisafx

What effect does the increasing average lifespan have on the health insurance industry?

CHECKPOINT

What is the purpose of disability income insurance?

20.4 ASSESSMENT

Key Concepts

Determine the best answer.

1. ________ insurance provides coverage for a long illness.
   a. Hospital
   b. Surgical
   c. Regular medical
   d. Major medical

2. If you are injured on the job, you are likely to be covered by
   a. Medicare
   b. Medicaid
   c. workers' compensation
   d. an HMO

Make Academic Connections

3. **Government** Investigate health insurance resources provided by your state government. Write a short report about your findings.

4. **Visual Communication** Create a poster or video that addresses one of the concepts presented in this lesson.

5. **Read** Find a recent article about changes in health insurance. Read the article and create an outline of the main points that are presented. Include a properly formatted citation for your source. Possible sources include printed and online versions of newspapers, magazines, or a website that produces original content.

RETEACH Divide the class into study teams and assign each team one type of insurance discussed in the chapter. Ask teams to review the information and develop a written study outline of the important information. Teams should distribute their outlines and discuss them with other teams.

ENRICH Ask each student to prepare a personal health insurance plan identifying the type of insurance coverage needed and the reason for each type of insurance. If the student chooses not to carry a type of insurance, ask the student to explain that decision.

TEACH

Ask students to compare benefits provided by health insurance, disability income insurance, and long-term care insurance. Why should a person consider purchasing all three types of insurance?

THINK CRITICALLY THROUGH VISUALS

Longer lifespan means people are using medical insurance longer. Also, older persons usually require more medical intervention to remain healthy than younger persons.

ONGOING ASSESSMENT

CHECKPOINT ANSWER

The purpose of disability income insurance is to provide periodic payments if the policyholder becomes disabled and loses his or her income.

ASSESS

Key Concepts *Answers*

1. d. Major medical
2. c. workers' compensation

Make Academic Connections *Answers*

3. Findings will vary.
4. Posters will vary.
5. Answers will vary depending on the article selected. Provide guidance for the citation format you want students to use.

CLOSE Ask students: Why is the cost of health care and health insurance such an important issue in the United States today? What can businesses and consumers do to reduce those costs?

Think Critically About Business *Answers*

1a. Personal injury coverage (bodily injury liability)

1b. Personal injury coverage covers the family member (bodily injury liability) and property damage coverage covers the parked car (property damage liability)

1c. Property damage coverage (property damage liability)

1d. Property damage coverage (comprehensive coverage)

2. The coverage was enough for all but $5,000 of the total $105,000 in bodily injury costs. The 50/100 coverage means the insurance company will pay up to $50,000 per bodily injury and up to $100,000 in total bodily injury costs when more than one person is injured in an accident.

3. Collision coverage does not pay for damages greater than the car's current value. The 10-year-old car probably has a low current value so that, even if the insurance company paid the policyholder the entire amount, it might not be enough to make a needed car repair. If the 10-year-old car is very valuable, however, its owner may still want to pay for collision coverage.

Chapter 20 Assessment

Review Business Concepts

20.1 Vehicle Insurance

- Motor vehicle risks include having an accident, having your vehicle stolen, injuring yourself or another person, or damaging another's property.
- Personal injury insurance covers bodily injury liability, medical payments, and uninsured motorist protection. Property damage liability protects you against claims if you damage another person's property.
- Automobile insurance rates are affected by age, accidents, marital status, academics, credit rating, car use, number of miles driven a year, value of car, and where you live.

20.2 Property Insurance

- Home and property insurance protect against three economic losses: (1) damage to home or property, (2) expenses to live somewhere else if your home is badly damaged, and (3) liability losses.
- A homeowners insurance policy provides coverage for various perils. Renters insurance is available for those who rent.
- Wise consumers select the most appropriate protection at the lowest cost.

20.3 Life Insurance

- Life insurance protects survivors against the financial loss associated with dying. It replaces a loss of income for a family who is financially dependent upon another person.
- Term life insurance provides financial protection from loss of life during a definite period. Permanent insurance has both cash value and an investment feature.
- To buy individual life insurance coverage, a person applies to an insurance agent. A physical exam may be required to assess the person's health. Life insurance premiums depend on the type of policy and the age and health of the person being insured.

20.4 Health Insurance

- Five common types of medical insurance are hospital insurance, surgical insurance, regular medical insurance, major medical insurance, and a comprehensive policy. Dental and vision care insurance provide specific coverage for these medical needs.
- Health insurance providers include group health insurance, individual health insurance, health maintenance organizations, preferred provider organizations, and government programs.
- Disability income insurance protects against income loss due to illness or accident. The insured receives payments until able to return to work. Long-term care insurance provides daily assistance needed because of a long-term illness or disability.

Think Critically About Business

1. Which type of automobile insurance would cover the following situations?
   a. A pedestrian is injured by a driver.
   b. A family member is injured when you run into a parked car.
   c. You, in an attempt to avoid hitting a dog in the street, run into a parked car.
   d. Winds cause a tree branch to break your windshield and dent the hood.
2. A driver was at fault when three passengers were badly hurt. The court awarded two of the people $30,000 each and $45,000 to the third person. The driver had bodily injury liability coverage of 50/100. Was this enough coverage for financial loss? Why or why not?
3. Why is collision coverage on a 10-year-old car less important than on a three-year-old car? Why may a person still want to have collision coverage on a 10-year-old car?

4a. damage to home or property insurance coverage

4b. additional living expenses coverage

4c. personal liability coverage

5. Typical homeowners policies do not include flood insurance, so the homeowners in the Iowa valley probably did suffer a significant financial loss unless they had purchased special flood insurance policies.

4. What type of property insurance would cover these situations?
   a. Damage to furniture because of a fire
   b. The cost of staying at a hotel after your home was damaged by fire
   c. Injury to a repairperson on your property
5. Recently, homes in an Iowa valley were destroyed when heavy rains caused the Mississippi River to rise above flood level. Do you think those Iowa residents who had homeowners policies suffered any financial losses? Why or why not?
6. What type of life insurance policy would you recommend for these people?
   a. Carlos Medina, age 27, wants a policy with premiums as low as possible for the next 10 years.
   b. Julie Hovel, age 45, wants a policy with no premium payments after she retires.
7. Why is a physical examination not usually required when buying group life insurance coverage?

Develop Your Business Language

Match the terms listed with the definitions.

8. Health insurance that covers all or part of surgeon's fees.
9. The person named in the life insurance policy to receive the benefits.
10. Covers claims for injuries or damage to property caused by you or your family.
11. The amount the insured pays before the insurance company pays a claim.
12. Coverage that provides protection against the high costs of serious illnesses or injuries.
13. Coverage for claims resulting from injuries or deaths for which the insured is at fault.
14. Health coverage for your room, food, and other hospital expenses.
15. The decrease in value of property.
16. Insurance coverage for medical expenses of a policyholder and family members if they are injured while riding in a car.
17. Coverage for injuries caused by hit-and-run drivers or by drivers without insurance.
18. Protection against the loss of income caused by a long illness or an accident.
19. Life insurance coverage with a cash value and an investment feature.
20. Coverage that protects a driver against claims if the insured's car damages someone else's property.
21. Health insurance for non-surgical care in a doctor's office, patient's home, or hospital.
22. A package-type insurance policy designed to insure homes and property.
23. Auto coverage for a loss resulting from a collision with another car or object.
24. A health policy combining hospital, surgical, regular, and major medical insurance.
25. Auto coverage for almost all damage losses except those caused from a collision.
26. Life insurance that provides financial protection during a set period.
27. The sharing of expenses by the policyholder and the insurance company.

Key Terms

a. beneficiary
b. bodily injury liability
c. coinsurance
d. collision coverage
e. comprehensive coverage
f. comprehensive medical policy
g. deductible
h. depreciation
i. disability income insurance
j. homeowners policy
k. hospital insurance
l. major medical insurance
m. medical payments coverage
n. permanent life insurance
o. personal liability coverage
p. property damage liability
q. regular medical insurance
r. surgical insurance
s. term life insurance
t. uninsured motorist coverage

6a. Carlos should investigate term insurance options because term insurance has the lowest premiums and can be purchased in terms of 10 years.

6b. Julie Hovel should purchase a limited-payment whole life insurance policy.

7. The rates for group life insurance are based on the life expectancies of a large group of people instead of an individual person's health status.

Develop Your Business Language *Answers*

8. r. surgical insurance
9. a. beneficiary
10. o. personal liability coverage
11. g. deductible
12. l. major medical insurance
13. b. bodily injury liability
14. k. hospital insurance
15. h. depreciation
16. m. medical payments coverage
17. t. uninsured motorist coverage
18. i. disability income insurance
19. n. permanent life insurance
20. p. property damage liability
21. q. regular medical insurance
22. j. homeowners policy
23. d. collision coverage
24. f. comprehensive medical policy
25. e. comprehensive coverage
26. s. term life insurance
27. c. coinsurance

Make Academic Connections *Answers*

28. Findings about financial responsibility and automobile insurance requirements will vary by state.

29. Findings about costs of automobile insurance for young drivers will vary.

30. Orien will be required to pay $1,129.80 ($3,228 × 0.35). The other driver will pay $2,098.20 ($3,228 − $1,129.80).

31. Answers will vary as students explain various liability situations.

32. Students may notice that the value of certain items depreciates quickly (such as automobiles), while houses usually appreciate (increase in value).

33. Ellen should be insured for $78,400 ($98,000 × 0.80).

34. Scripts and skits will vary.

35. Findings will vary.

36. Posters will vary.

37a. The total cost of the medical exam was $665.

37b. Fran paid $98 ($15 + $44 + $20 + $10 + $9).

37c. The insurance company paid $567, or 85 percent, of the total cost ($567 ÷ $665 = 0.85).

Make Your Case *Answers*

38. Jane could destroy or damage her car and other cars, as well as property her car could run into, should she lose control of her vehicle. Worst of all, her reckless driving risks liability of the most severe sort should she cause bodily injury to herself, her passengers, persons in other cars, or pedestrians.

39. Jane's auto insurance premiums will rise substantially due to the two claims for fender bender accidents and the two speeding tickets she has received in such a short period of time.

40. Jane should immediately assume responsibility for improving her driving habits. She should stop speeding and focus on the task of driving safely. She will have to pay a higher premium for a while, but if she maintains a clean driving record, her premium will go down after a few years.

41. Student response will vary. Encourage students to locate information not covered in class.

Make Academic Connections

28. **Law** Obtain information on the financial responsibility and automobile insurance requirements in your state.

29. **Research** Contact a local insurance agent to obtain information on the costs of automobile insurance for young drivers.

30. **Math** Orien was involved in an automobile accident. The total damage to both vehicles was $3,228. The state in which Orien lives assigns a percentage of fault to each driver involved in an accident. Each driver must pay the percentage of damages based on the percentage of fault assigned. If Orien was assigned 35 percent of the fault in the accident, how much of the damages will he be required to pay? How much must the other driver pay?

31. **Law** Describe in writing or present in class various liability situations that would be covered by a person's homeowners or renters insurance policy.

32. **Accounting** The value of personal property declines due to time and use. Using advertisements and online sources, compare the value of various new and used items. What observations can you make about depreciation?

33. **Math** If Ellen Williams owned a home worth $98,000 and wanted to be certain it was insured for 80 percent of its value, for how much should it be insured?

34. **Communication** Working with other students, write a script and present a short skit that communicates the need for life insurance in various family situations. Consider using simple props and costumes to help communicate your message.

35. **Research** Conduct library or online research about actions that might be taken to reduce the costs of health care.

36. **Visual Arts** Create a poster to educate and remind classmates about financial and social responsibilities that come with owning or driving a car or truck. Consider including concepts related to insurance, safety, and the environment.

37. **Math** Fran Markowitz had her annual medical examination. According to her insurance plan, she paid a portion of the costs of the services. The total costs and her share of each were as shown in the table.

SERVICE	TOTAL COST	PATIENT SHARE
Doctor visit	$80	$15 deductible
Lab work	$220	20% copay
Prescriptions	$120	$20 copay
Vision exam	$65	$10 deductible
New lenses	$180	5%

a. What was the total cost of the medical examination?
b. How much of the total cost did Fran pay?
c. What percent of the total cost did the insurance company pay?

Make Your Case

Jane sometimes drives carelessly. She is a 17-year-old with a late-model compact car that looks sporty and is equipped for speed. Jane loves to drive fast and has a poor traffic record. In only one year, she has had two "fender bender" accidents and received two speeding tickets. Those who care about Jane have suggested that her reckless driving habits are putting her and others at risk.

38. What potential property and liability risks are associated with Jane's driving habits?

39. How is Jane's driving affecting her auto insurance premiums?

40. What suggestions do you have for Jane about her driving?

41. Search online for information about safe driving and how it relates to automobile insurance savings. What did you find that may be helpful to Jane?

Interactions and Connections

Talk to two of three people in your community about the types of insurance they have. Has any of the coverage been obtained through group policies? What actions do they recommend when buying various types of insurance?

Entrepreneurship Case Study

This event is composed of two parts: a written objective test and a decision-making problem, also known as a case study. Teams consisting of three participants will present and defend their solution to a business challenge.

Once you receive your business topic, you have 30 minutes to prepare your presentation and argument. Each participant will be given two index cards that may be used during the preparation and presentation to the judges. No reference materials or visual aids may be used during the preparation or performance.

Your team has 10 minutes to present the case and your solutions. One member should introduce the team and describe the case. All team members must participate in the presentation. Note cards may be used to explain decisions and rationales to the judges. After the presentation, five minutes are allowed for questions and answers.

Your case involves the rising cost of insurance. Health insurance is an important fringe benefit that you provide your employees. The cost of health insurance is rising at a rapid rate, and now your company is faced with determining strategies to continue to offer employee health insurance. Why is health insurance so important? How much can the company afford? How much should employees be asked to contribute? What are the alternatives to keeping the current coverage? Which fringe benefits are most important to the company and the employees?

Performance Indicators Evaluated

- Understand the importance of health insurance for employees.
- Prepare a concise plan for funding the rising costs of health insurance.
- Explain the sacrifices that must be made to fund health insurance.
- Explain the importance of shopping around for health insurance.

For more detailed information about performance indicators, go to the FBLA website.

Think Critically

1. Why is health insurance such an important fringe benefit?
2. What can a company do to encourage employees to live healthy lifestyles?
3. What kinds of communication might be used to introduce changes in health insurance benefits to employees?

www.fbla-pbl.org

Interactions and Connections

Answers will vary. Encourage students to share the suggestions they heard about buying various types of insurance.

WINNING EDGE Entrepreneurship Case Study

All businesses, but especially new small businesses, must pay very careful attention to areas of rising costs. Health insurance is one area that provides problems for entrepreneurs because of the high cost. Large businesses may be able to attract the good employees of a small business by offering better coverage or requiring smaller employee contributions for insurance.

Think Critically *Answers*

1. Healthcare costs and health insurance are expensive. Individuals should understand the importance of health insurance coverage.
2. To encourage healthy lifestyles, companies can provide memberships to health clubs, incentives for healthy lifestyles, and lower insurance rates for healthy employees.
3. Answers will vary. Students might mention some of the following: employee meetings, brochures, e-mail messages, letters, videos, company website, and information booths.

APPENDIX A Using a Calculator and Computer Keypad

TYPES OF CALCULATORS

Many different models of calculators, both desktop and handheld, are available. All calculators have their own features and particular placement of operation keys. Therefore, it is necessary to refer to the user's manual for specific instructions and locations of the operating keys for the calculator being used.

HANDHELD CALCULATORS

There are many different kinds of handheld or pocket calculators. They come in all shapes and sizes with a variety of keys and functions. All calculators have number keys (0 to 9), operation keys (+, −, ×, ÷), and clear keys (C or CE). Most calculators have a percent key (%). Many handheld calculators come with a memory for storing numbers and calculation results. These are shown as M+, M−, and MR. Others, such as scientific calculators, have many more keys including x^2, 1/x, and √.

It is important to read the user's manual to learn how your particular calculator works. Be sure to keep the manual in a safe place so you can refer to it for help in solving various mathematical problems.

DESKTOP CALCULATORS

Several operating switches on a desktop calculator must be engaged before it will produce the desired results.

The *decimal selector* sets the appropriate decimal places for numbers that will be entered. For example, if the decimal selector is set at 2, both the numbers entered and the answer will be displayed with two decimal places. If the decimal selector is set at F, the calculator automatically sets the needed decimal places. The F setting allows the answer to be unrounded and carried out to the maximum number of decimal places possible.

The *decimal rounding selector* rounds the answers. The down arrow position will drop any digits beyond the last digit desired. The up arrow position will drop any digits beyond the last digit desired and round the last digit up. In the 5/4 position, the calculator rounds the last desired digit up only when the following digit is 5 or greater. If the following digit is less than 5, the last desired digit remains unchanged.

The *GT* or *grand total switch* in the on position accumulates totals.

Ten-Key Touch System

Striking the numbers 0 to 9 on a desktop calculator or numeric keypad on a computer without looking at the keyboard is called the *touch system*. Using the touch system develops both speed and accuracy.

The 4, 5, and 6 keys are called the *home row*. If the right hand is used for the keyboard, the index finger is placed on the 4 key, the middle finger on the 5 key, and the ring finger on the 6 key. If the left hand is used, the ring finger is placed on the 4 key, the middle finger on the 5 key, and the index finger on the 6 key.

Place the fingers on the home row keys. Curve the fingers and keep the wrist straight. These keys may feel slightly concave or the 5 key may have a raised dot or bar. The differences in the home row allow the user to recognize the home row by touch rather than by sight.

Maintain the position of the fingers on the home row. The finger used to strike the 4 key will also strike the 7 key and the 1 key. Stretch the finger up to reach the 7 and stretch the finger down to reach the 1 key. Visualize the position of these keys.

Again, place the fingers on the home row. Stretch the finger that strikes the 5 key up to reach the 8 key and down to reach the 2 key. Likewise, stretch the finger that strikes the 6 key up to strike the 9 key and down to strike the 3 key. This same finger will stretch down again to hit the decimal point.

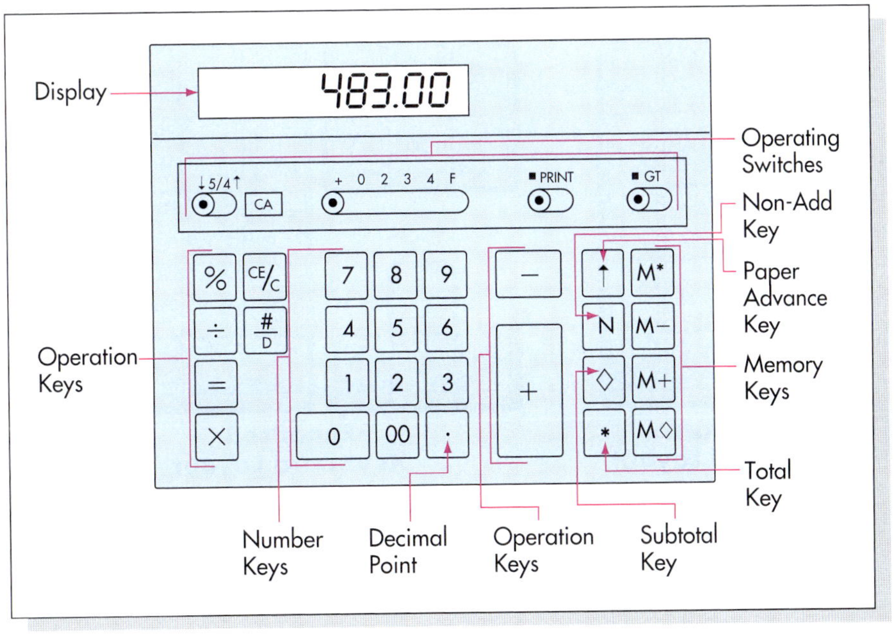

If the right hand is used, the thumb will be used to strike the 0 and 00 keys and the little finger to strike the addition key. If the left hand is used, the little finger will be used to strike the 0 and 00 keys and the thumb to strike the addition key.

Performing Mathematical Operations on Desktop Calculators

Calculators allow mathematical operations to be performed quickly and efficiently. The basic operations of addition, subtraction, multiplication, and division are used frequently on a calculator. Here is how these operations are completed on a typical desktop calculator.

Addition Each number to be added is called an *addend*. The answer to an addition problem is called the *sum*.

Addition is performed by entering an addend and striking the addition key (+). All numbers are entered on a calculator in the exact order they are given. To enter the number 4,375.68, strike the 4, 3, 7, 5, decimal, 6, and 8 keys in that order, and then strike the addition key. Commas are not entered. Continue in this manner until all addends have been entered. To obtain the sum, strike the total key on the calculator.

Subtraction The top number or first number of a subtraction problem is called the *minuend*. The number to be subtracted from the minuend is called the *subtrahend*. The answer to a subtraction problem is called the *difference*.

Subtraction is performed by first entering the minuend and striking the addition key (+). The subtrahend is then entered, followed by the minus key (−), followed by the total key.

Multiplication The numbers being multiplied together are called *factors*. The answer to a multiplication problem is called the *product*.

Multiplication is performed by entering one factor, striking the multiplication key (×), entering the other factor, and then striking the equals key (=). The calculator will automatically multiply and give the product.

Division The number to be divided is called the *dividend*. The number the dividend will be divided by is called the *divisor*. The answer to a division problem is called the *quotient*.

Division is performed by entering the dividend and striking the division key (÷). The divisor is then entered, following by the equals key (=). The calculator will automatically divide and give the quotient.

Correcting Errors If an error is made while using a calculator, several methods of correction may be used. If an incorrect number has been entered and the addition key or equals key has not yet been struck, strike the clear entry (CE) key one time. This key will clear only the last number that was entered. However, if the clear entry key is depressed more than one time, the entire problem will be cleared on some calculators. If an incorrect number has been entered and the addition key has been struck, strike the minus key one time only. This will automatically subtract the last number added, thus removing it from the total.

COMPUTER KEYPADS

Most computers have a keypad on the right side of the keyboard called the *numeric keypad*. Even though there are several styles of computer keyboards, there are two basic layouts for the numeric keypad, as shown in the illustration on this page.

The *Num Lock* key, located above the 7 key, is an important feature of the numeric keypad. When the Num Lock key is turned on, numbers are entered when the keys on the keypad are pressed. Most keyboards have a small light that indicates when the Num Lock key is on. When Num Lock is not on, the arrow, Home, Page Up, Page Down, End, Insert, and Delete keys can be used. Enhanced keyboards allow you to keep the Num Lock key activated at all times.

The asterisk (*) on the computer is used for multiplication. The slash key (/) is used for division.

Performing Mathematical Operations on Computers

Calculations with a computer keypad are performed in much the same way as on a desktop calculator. However, after the + key is depressed, the display usually shows the accumulated total. Therefore, the total key is not found on the computer keypad. Some computer programs will not calculate the total until the Enter key is pressed.

Subtraction is performed differently on many computer keypads. The minuend is entered, followed by the minus (−) key. Then the subtrahend is entered. Pressing either the + key, the = key, or the Enter key will display the difference.

Multiplication and division are performed the same way as on a desktop calculator. Keep in mind that computers use the * for multiplication and / for division.

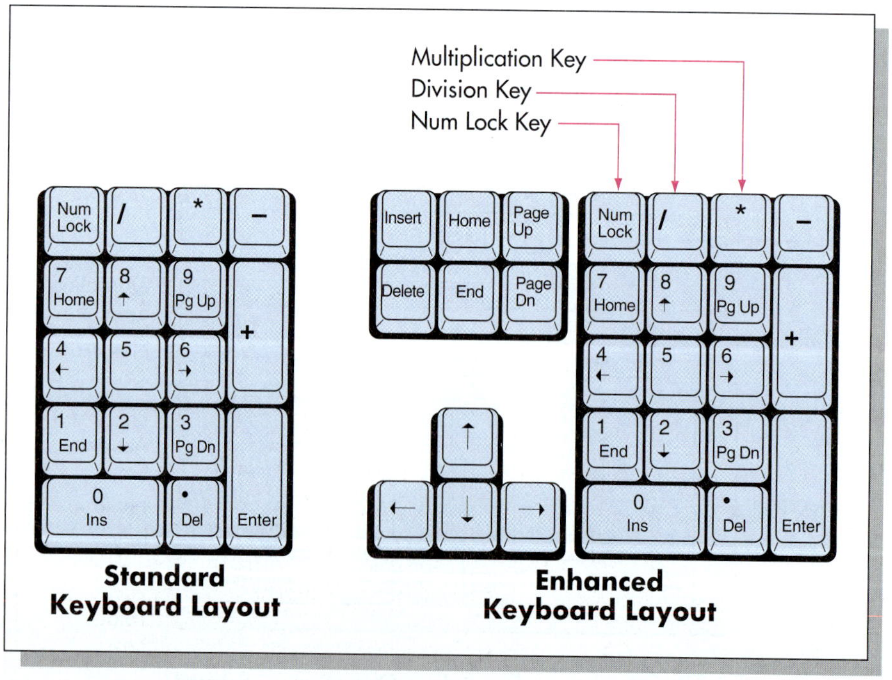

APPENDIX B

Math Review

This arithmetic review will help you solve many of the end-of-chapter problems in this text as well as common arithmetic problems you may encounter in business.

ESTIMATING SUMS AND DIFFERENCES

In some situations, an **estimate** may be useful. Sometimes an exact answer is not needed, so you can estimate. Other times, estimation can be used to check mathematical calculations, especially when using a calculator.

Most people estimate by **rounding** numbers. Rounded numbers are easier to work with. Rounded numbers usually contain one or two nonzero digits followed by all zeros.

Examples

The U.S. Bureau of the Census estimated the 2014 population of Texas at 26,956,958.

- Round 26,956,958 to the nearest ten million.

  26,956,958 ⟶ 30,000,000

  Because 6 is greater than 5, round up to 30,000,000.

- Round 26,956,958 to the nearest million.

  26,956,958 ⟶ 27,000,000

  Because 9 is larger than 5, round up to 27,000,000.

One new car has a list price of $27,209.50.

- Round $25,209.50 to the nearest thousand dollars.

  $25,209.50 ⟶ $25,000

  Because 2 is less than 5, round down to $25,000.

- Round $25,209.50 to the nearest dollar.

  $25,209.50 ⟶ $25,210

  Because 5 is greater than or equal to 5, round up to $25,210.

Examples

- Estimate the answer to 24,432 + 15,000.

	Option 1: Round to the nearest ten thousand.	Option 2: Round to the nearest ten thousand.
24,432	20,000	24,000
+15,000	+20,000	+15,000
	40,000	39,000

- Estimate the answer to $32.23 − $17.54.

	Option 1: Round to the nearest ten dollars.	Option 2: Round to the nearest ten dollar.
$32.23	$30.00	$32.00
−17.54	−20.00	−18.00
	$10.00	$14.00

- Estimate how much change you should get if you give the clerk $20 to pay for a bill of $6.98.

	Round to the nearest dollars.
$20.00	$20.00
−6.98	−7.00
	$13.00

MULTIPLYING NUMBERS ENDING IN ZEROS

When you multiply numbers that have *final zeros*, you can use this shortcut:

> Multiply the numbers by using only the digits that are not final zeros. Then write as many final zeros in the product as there are final zeros in the numbers being multiplied.

Examples

$200 \times 7 = 1{,}400$

2 zeros $2 \times 7 = 14$ 2 zeros

$40 \times 5{,}000 = 200{,}000$

1 zero   3 zeros $4 \times 5 = 20$ 4 zeros

When multiplying larger numbers, use an imaginary line to separate zeros from the rest of the digits.

$36 \times 2{,}500$

```
    36 |
 × 25  | 00   ← 2 zeros
   180 |
   72  |
   900 | 00   ← 2 zeros     90,000 Answer
```

$3{,}600 \times 25{,}000$

```
    36 | 00      ← 2 zeros
 × 25  | 000     ← 3 zeros
   180 |           2 + 3 = 5 zeros
   72  |
   900 | 00000   ← 5 zeros
      90,000,000  Answer
```

ESTIMATING PRODUCTS

There are various ways to estimate the answer to a multiplication problem.

- Option 1: Round both numbers **up**. Estimate will be greater than the actual product.
- Option 2: Round both numbers **down**. Estimate will be less than the actual product.
- Option 3: Round each number to the nearest unit with one nonzero digit. The estimate will be close to the actual product.

Examples

Estimate $82{,}543 \times 653$.

Option 1: $90{,}000 \times 700 = 63{,}000{,}000$

Option 2: $80{,}000 \times 600 = 48{,}000{,}000$

Option 3: $80{,}000 \times 700 = 56{,}000{,}000$

DIVIDING WHOLE NUMBERS

Division is the opposite of multiplication. Division is shown in several ways. To show that 18 divided by 3 is 6, you may use any of these forms:

$$18 \div 3 = 6 \qquad \frac{18}{3} = 6 \qquad 3\overline{)18}^{\,6}$$

In each case, 18 is the dividend, 3 is the divisor, and 6 is the quotient.

$$\text{dividend} \div \text{divisor} = \text{quotient}$$

$$\frac{\text{dividend}}{\text{divisor}} = \text{quotient} \qquad \text{divisor}\overline{)\text{dividend}}^{\,\text{quotient}}$$

DIVIDING NUMBERS ENDING IN ZEROS

When you divide multiples of 10, there are several shortcuts you can use. Try either of the shortcuts discussed below:

- Write the numbers as a fraction. Cross out the same number of zeros in both the numerator and denominator of the fraction.
- Move the decimal point in the dividend to the left the same number of places as there are zeros in the divisor.

Examples

- $1{,}000{,}000{,}000 \div 10{,}000 = \dfrac{1{,}000{,}000{,}000}{10{,}000}$
- $1{,}000{,}000{,}000 \div 10{,}000$

  $= 100000.0000. \div 1.0000. = 100{,}000$

ESTIMATING QUOTIENTS

One way to estimate the answer to a division problem is to start by rounding the divisor to a number with one nonzero number followed by all zeros. Then round the dividend to a multiple of that rounded divisor.

Examples

- Estimate $609 \div 19$.

  Round 19 to 20 and 609 to 600.

  $600 \div 20 = 30$

- Estimate $19{,}876{,}548 \div 650$.

  650 rounds up to 700.

  Multiples of 7 are 7, 14, 21, 28, 35, and so on. Use the closest multiple, 21.

  $$21{,}000{,}000 \div 700 = \frac{21000000}{700}$$

  $$= \frac{210000}{7} = 30{,}000$$

ADDING AND SUBTRACTING DECIMALS

When adding and subtracting decimals, align the decimal points. Then add or subtract as for whole numbers. Place the decimal point in the answer directly below where it is located in the computation. A number like 532 can also be written as 532. or 532.0. When writing decimals less than one, a zero is placed before the decimal point to show that there are no ones.

Examples

- Find the sum of 33.67, 72.84, 0.75, and 43.34.

$$\begin{array}{r} 33.67 \\ 72.84 \\ 0.75 \\ +43.34 \\ \hline 150.60 \end{array}$$

- Find the sum of 320.5471, 1.4, and 82.352.

$$\begin{array}{r} 320.5471 \\ 1.4 \\ +82.352 \\ \hline 404.2991 \end{array}$$

- Find the difference between 952.1 and 34.2517.

$$\begin{array}{r} 952.1 \\ -34.2517 \\ \hline \end{array} \quad \rightarrow \quad \begin{array}{r} 952.1\mathbf{000} \\ -34.2517 \\ \hline 917.8483 \end{array}$$

Add 0s to the **right** after the decimal point.

MULTIPLYING DECIMALS

When multiplying decimals, align the numbers at the right. Multiply as if you are multiplying whole numbers. To locate the decimal point in the answer, count all digits to the right of the decimal point in each number being multiplied and place the decimal point so there are that many digits after the decimal point in the answer.

Remember: Estimation can be used to check that your answer is reasonable and that you have correctly located the decimal point in the answer.

Examples

- Multiply 7.46 by 3.2.

$$\begin{array}{rl} 7.46 & \leftarrow \text{2 decimal places} \\ \times\ 3.2 & \leftarrow \text{1 decimal place} \\ \hline 1492 & \quad 2 + 1 = 3 \\ 2238 & \\ \hline 23.872 & \leftarrow \text{3 decimal places} \end{array}$$

- Multiply 0.193 by 0.2.

$$\begin{array}{rr} 0.193 \leftarrow & \text{3 decimal places} \\ \times\ 0.2 \leftarrow & +\text{1 decimal place} \\ \hline 0.\mathbf{0}386 \leftarrow & \text{4 decimal places} \end{array}$$

If needed to get enough decimal places, add a zero before the numeric answer but after the decimal point.

Remember that the zero before the decimal point shows that there are no ones in the product. The answer is less than one.

Estimate to check your answer.

$0.2 \times 0.2 = 0.04$

0.04 is close to 0.0386, so the answer is reasonable.

MULTIPLYING BY POWERS OF 10

Numbers like 100,000,000, 10,000, 100, 0.1, 0.01, and 0.00001 are powers of 10. To multiply by these, simply move the decimal point in the number being multiplied.

When multiplying by a power of 10 greater than one, move the decimal point to the right. The answer is larger than the number you started with.

When multiplying by a power of 10 less than one, move the decimal point to the left. The answer is smaller than the number you started with.

Examples

- Multiply 25,397 by ten thousand.

  25,397 × 10,000 = 253,970,000

  Think: 25397.0000.
- Multiply 0.078 by one hundred.

  0.078 × 100 = 7.8

  Think: = 0.07.8
- Multiply 192,536 by one ten-thousandth.

  192,536 × 0.0001 = 19.2536

  Think: 19.2536.
- Multiply 0.293 by one hundredth.

  0.293 × 0.01 = 0.00293

  Think: 0.00.293

SHORTCUTS WHEN MULTIPLYING WITH MONEY

Businesses price items at amounts such as 49¢, $5.98, or $99.95. A price of $99.95 seems less to the buyer than an even $100. When finding the cost of several such items, you can use a mathematical shortcut.

Examples

- Find the cost of 27 items at 98¢ each.

  normal multiplication

  $$\begin{array}{r} \$0.98 \\ \times\ 27 \\ \hline 686 \\ 196 \\ \hline \$26.46 \end{array}$$

  Shortcut: Think: 98¢ = $1 − 2¢

  (27 × $1) −(27 × 2¢) = $27 − 54¢

  54¢ = $0.54

  $$\begin{array}{r} \$27.00 \\ -0.54 \\ \hline \$26.46 \end{array}$$
- Find the cost of 32 items at $6.95 each.

  Shortcut: Think $6.95 = $7 − $0.05

  (32 × $7) − (32 × $0.05)

  =$224 − $1.60 = $222.40
- Find the cost of 101 items at $9.99 each.

  Shortcut: Think $9.99 = $10 − $0.01

  (101 × $10) − (101 × $0.01)

  = $1,010 − $1.01 = $1,008.99

  Alternate Shortcut:

  Think: 101 = 100 + 1

  (100 × $9.99) + (1 × $9.99) =

  $999 + $9.99 = $1,008.99

MULTIPLYING A WHOLE NUMBER BY A FRACTION

To multiply a whole number by a fraction, multiply the whole number by the numerator (top number) and then divide that answer by the denominator (bottom number).

Examples

- $180 \times \frac{2}{3} = \frac{180 \times 2}{3} = \frac{360}{3} = 120$
- $500 \times \frac{3}{4} = \frac{500 \times 3}{4} = \frac{1500}{4} = 375$
- $768 \times \frac{1}{8} = \frac{768 \times 1}{8} = \frac{768}{8} = 96$
- $90 \times \frac{4}{5} = \frac{90 \times 4}{5} = \frac{360}{5} = 72$

Simplifying Fractions

When working with fractions, you can simplify the fractions by dividing the numerator and the denominator by a common factor (a number that will divide into both numbers evenly). Division by such common factors is called **canceling** or **cancellation**.

Examples

- Simplify $\frac{10}{12}$.

Think: 2 is a factor of both 10 and 12.

$$\frac{\overset{5}{\cancel{10}}}{\underset{6}{\cancel{12}}} = \frac{5}{6}$$

$10 \div 2 = 5$

$12 \div 2 = 6$

- Simplify $\frac{75}{100}$.

Think: Use 25 as a common factor.

$$\frac{\overset{3}{\cancel{75}}}{\underset{4}{\cancel{100}}} = \frac{3}{4}$$

$75 \div 25 = 3$

$100 \div 25 = 4$

- Simplify $\frac{280}{60}$.

Think: Use 20 as a common factor.

$$\frac{\overset{14}{\cancel{280}}}{\underset{3}{\cancel{60}}} = \frac{14}{3}$$

$280 \div 20 = 14$

$60 \div 20 = 3$

Using Fractional Parts of $1.00 in Multiplying Mentally

While goods and services may be priced at any amount, prices are frequently expressed in fractional parts of $1, $10, or $100. For instance, 2 items for $1 is the same as $\frac{1}{2}$ of 100¢, or 50¢ per item, and 3 items for $10 is the same as $\frac{1}{3}$ of $10, or $\$3.33\frac{1}{3}$ per item.

You can also use fractional parts of $1.00 to find the cost of multiple items mentally.

24 items selling for $1.00 would cost $24.00

24 items at 50¢ each = $\frac{1}{2}$ of $24 or $12.00

24 items at 25¢ each = $\frac{1}{4}$ of $24 or $6.00

24 items at $33\frac{1}{3}$¢ each = $\frac{1}{3}$ of $24 or $8

Many similar calculations can be made mentally. While there are many fractional parts of $1.00, a chart of those most commonly used follows.

FRACTION	PART OF $1.00
$\frac{1}{8}$	$\$0.12\frac{1}{2}$
$\frac{1}{6}$	$\$0.16\frac{2}{3}$
$\frac{1}{5}$	$0.20
$\frac{1}{4}$	$0.25
$\frac{1}{3}$	$\$0.33\frac{1}{3}$
$\frac{3}{8}$	$\$0.37\frac{1}{2}$
$\frac{2}{5}$	$0.40
$\frac{1}{2}$	$0.50
$\frac{3}{5}$	$0.60
$\frac{5}{8}$	$\$0.62\frac{1}{2}$
$\frac{2}{3}$	$\$0.66\frac{2}{3}$
$\frac{3}{4}$	$0.75
$\frac{4}{5}$	$0.80
$\frac{5}{6}$	$\$0.83\frac{1}{3}$
$\frac{7}{8}$	$\$0.87\frac{1}{2}$

Examples

- Find the cost of 16 items at $12\frac{1}{2}$¢ each.

Think: $12\frac{1}{2}$¢ = $\frac{1}{8}$ of $1

$16 \times \frac{1}{8} = 2$

16 items at $12\frac{1}{2}$¢ each will cost $2.

- Find the cost of 33 items at 25¢ each.

Think: 25¢ = $\frac{1}{4}$ of $1

$33 \times \frac{1}{4} = \frac{33}{4}$, or $8\frac{1}{4}$

33 items at 25¢ each will cost $\$8\frac{1}{4}$, or $8.25.

- Find the cost of 48 items at 75¢ each.

Think: $75¢ = \frac{3}{4}$ of \$1

$$48 \times \frac{3}{4} = \frac{\overset{12}{\cancel{48}} \times 3}{\underset{1}{\cancel{4}}} = \frac{12 \times 3}{1} = \frac{36}{1} = 36$$

48 items at 75¢ each is \$36.

- Find the cost of 34 items at $62\frac{1}{2}$¢ each.

Think: $62\frac{1}{2}¢ = \frac{5}{8}$ of \$1

$$34 \times \frac{5}{8} = \frac{\overset{17}{\cancel{34}} \times 5}{\underset{4}{\cancel{8}}} = \frac{17 \times 5}{4} = \frac{85}{4} = 21\frac{1}{4}$$

34 items at $62\frac{1}{2}$¢ each is \$$21\frac{1}{4}$, or \$21.25.

Fractional Parts of Other Amounts

You can use the table on the previous page to find fractional parts of multiples of 10.

Examples

- Find $\frac{5}{6}$ of \$1,000.

$$\frac{5}{6} \text{ of } \$1{,}000 = 1000 \times \frac{5}{6} \text{ of } \$1$$
$$= 1000 \times \$0.83\frac{1}{3}$$
$$= \$833.33\frac{1}{3}$$

So, $\frac{5}{6}$ of \$1,000 is \$833.33.

($\frac{1}{3}$ dollar = \$$0.33\frac{1}{3}$, which is \$0.33 when rounded to the nearest cent.)

- Find $\frac{3}{4}$ of \$100.

$$\frac{3}{4} \text{ of } \$100 = 100 \times \frac{3}{4} \text{ of } \$1$$
$$= 100 \times \$0.75$$
$$= \$75$$

So, $\frac{3}{4}$ of \$100 is \$75.

- Find $\frac{7}{8}$ of \$10.

$$\frac{7}{8} \text{ of } \$10 = 10 \times \frac{7}{8} \text{ of } \$1$$
$$= 10 \times \$0.875$$
$$= \$8.75$$

So, $\frac{7}{8}$ of \$10 is \$8.75.

Dividing Decimals

Division involving decimals is completed like division of whole numbers, except for dealing with the decimal point. When you divide a decimal by a whole number, you divide as for whole numbers and place the decimal point directly above the location of the decimal point in the dividend.

Examples

- Divide 12.944 by 8.

$$\begin{array}{r} 1.618 \\ 8\overline{)12.944} \\ \underline{8} \\ 49 \\ \underline{48} \\ 14 \\ \underline{8} \\ 64 \\ \underline{64} \\ 0 \end{array}$$

To check division, multiply your quotient by the divisor. The result should be the dividend.

$$\begin{array}{r} 1.618 \\ \times \quad 8 \\ \hline 12.944 \end{array} \checkmark$$

- Divide 37 by 4.

$$\begin{array}{r} 9.25 \\ 4\overline{)37.00} \\ \underline{36} \\ 10 \\ \underline{8} \\ 20 \\ \underline{20} \\ 0 \end{array}$$

Add zeros as needed.

Check:
$$\begin{array}{r} 9.25 \\ \times \quad 4 \\ \hline 37.00 \end{array} \checkmark$$

To divide by a decimal, move the decimal point to the right the same number of places in both the divisor and the dividend so you are dividing by a whole number.

Examples

- Divide 12.944 by 0.8.

  Think: 0.8 has one decimal place, move the decimal points in the divisor and the dividend right one place.

```
          16.18
0.8.)12.9.44
      8
      49
      48
       14
        8
        64
        64
         0
```

- Divide 37 by 0.004.

```
           9 250.
0.004.)37.000.        Add zeros as needed.
       36
        1 0
          8
          20
          20
           0
```

Remember: Estimation can be used to check that your answer is reasonable and that you have correctly located the decimal point in the answer.

APPENDIX C

Determining Percentages and Interest in Business

Two frequently used mathematical functions in business are determining percentages and calculating simple interest. If you are preparing for a business career you need to be comfortable with these calculations. Using a calculator simplifies the work but you also need to understand how the calculations are completed to check the accuracy of answers.

MEANING OF PERCENT

Percent is derived from two Latin words, "per centum," meaning "by the hundred." You can express a percent as a common fraction or a decimal fraction. When the percent involves a fraction, such as $7\frac{1}{4}\%$, change the mixed number to a decimal and move the decimal point two places to the left.

$$7\frac{1}{4}\% = 7.25\% = 0.725$$

Examples

- Write 19% as a fraction and a decimal.

  Percent means *per one hundred*, so write it as a fraction with a denominator of 100.

  $$19\% = \frac{19}{100} = 0.19$$

- Write 0.98 as a fraction and a percent.

  $$0.98 = \frac{98}{100} = 98\%$$

- Write $\frac{3}{100}$ as a decimal and a percent.

  $$\frac{3}{100} = 0.03 = 3\%$$

- Write $8\frac{1}{2}\%$ as a decimal and a fraction.

  $$8\frac{1}{2}\% = 8.5\% = 0.085 = \frac{85}{1000}$$

  Notice that 0.085 is 85 *thousandths*, so the fraction has a denominator of 1000.

FINDING A PERCENT OF A NUMBER

To find the percent of a number, change the percent to a fraction or decimal and multiply.

Examples

- Find 18% of 117,334.

  With fractions:

  $$117{,}334 \times \frac{18}{100} = \frac{117334 \times 18}{100} = \frac{2112012}{100} = 21{,}120.12$$

- Find 18% of 117,334.

  With decimals:

  $$\begin{array}{r} 117{,}334 \\ \times \quad 0.18 \\ \hline 938672 \\ 117334 \\ \hline 21{,}120.12 \end{array}$$

- Find 10% of 359.

  $$359 \times 0.10 = 35.9$$

CALCULATING SIMPLE INTEREST

Interest is the fee paid to a lender for the use of borrowed money. Interest is always expressed as a percent. The *principal* is the amount of money borrowed. Simple interest (I) is calculated by multiplying the principal (P) times the annual interest rate (R) times the length of time in years (T). The formula is written as:

$$I = P \times R \times T$$

Examples

- Find the amount of simple interest due on \$400 borrowed for 2 years at 8%.

  $I = \$400 \times 0.08 \times 2 = \$64$

- Find the amount of simple interest due on \$600 borrowed for 1 month at 18%.

  Think: 1 month is $\frac{1}{12}$ of a year.

  $I = \$600 \times 0.18 \times \frac{1}{12} = \$9$

- Find the amount of simple interest due on \$3,000 borrowed for 6 months at $9\frac{3}{4}$%.

  $I = \$3{,}000 \times 0.0975 \times \frac{6}{12} = \$146.25$

COMPOUND INTEREST

Compound interest is used more frequently than simple interest. Compound interest calculates interest not only on the amount borrowed but on the interest accumulated in prior periods. For example, a credit card may say that it charges 1.5% interest per month. It then seems that you are paying 12 × 1.5%, or 18% interest per year. However, in reality you are charged more than 18% interest per year because you are paying interest on the interest accumulated each month.

Example

Suppose that you owe \$100 on your credit card and do not make any payments for one year. Assuming there are no late fees, your balance at the end of each month would be the amount shown in the last column of the following table. When the interest is calculated, all amounts are rounded up to the next cent. For example, the ending balance for May is \$107.74225, which has been round up to \$107.75.

FINDING WHAT PERCENT A NUMBER IS OF ANOTHER

To find what percent a number is of another, divide the one number (the part) by the other number (the whole). Then show the result as a percent.

Example

- 50 is what percent of 200?

  Divide 50 by 200.

$$\begin{array}{r} 0.25 \\ 200\overline{)50.00} \\ \underline{40\ 0} \\ 10\ 00 \\ 10\ 00 \end{array}$$

0.25 = 25%

50 is 25% of 200.

MONTH	BEGINNING BALANCE	INTEREST (1.5% PER MONTH)	ENDING BALANCE
Jan.	\$100.00	\$1.50	\$101.50
Feb.	\$101.50	\$1.53	\$103.03
Mar.	\$103.03	\$1.55	\$104.58
Apr.	\$104.58	\$1.57	\$106.15
May	\$106.15	\$1.60	\$107.75
June	\$107.75	\$1.62	\$109.37
July	\$109.37	\$1.65	\$111.02
Aug.	\$111.02	\$1.67	\$112.69
Sept.	\$112.69	\$1.70	\$114.39
Oct.	\$114.39	\$1.72	\$116.11
Nov.	\$116.11	\$1.75	\$117.86
Dec.	\$117.86	\$1.77	\$119.63

After 12 months you must pay \$19.63 in interest on \$100. This means that the interest rate is really 19.63%, not 18%.

APPENDIX D

Using Measurements in Business

The metric system of measurement is used in business by most nations in the world. Because of extensive trade with other countries, the United States has taken some steps toward conversion to the metric system. Most U.S. companies have already made the change, so you should be familiar with the metric system.

There are some things about the metric system that may already be familiar to you. For example, if you have been to a track meet or swimming meet or have seen one on television, you know that distances can be measured in meters, not just in feet, yards, or miles. Food is often labeled to show amounts in grams as well as pounds or ounces. Meters, kilometers, and grams are examples of metric units of measurement.

BASIC METRIC UNITS

The basic metric units are the meter (length), the liter (capacity), and the gram (mass or weight). All measurements can be expressed in terms of these three basic units. However, prefixes are used with the basic units to avoid dealing with very large and very small numbers. The most common prefixes used in the metric system are:

kilo- ⟶ one thousand times
centi- ⟶ one one-hundredth of
milli- ⟶ one one-thousandth of

Look at the chart in this page. The same prefixes are used for length, capacity, and mass or weight.

LENGTH
1 kilometer = 1000 meters
1 meter = 100 centimeters
1 meter = 1000 millimeters
1 centimeter = 10 millimeters
1 centimeter = 0.01 meter
1 millimeter = 0.001 meter
CAPACITY
1 kiloliter = 1000 liters
1 liter = 100 centiliters
1 liter = 1000 milliliters
1 centiliter = 10 milliliters
1 centiliter = 0.01 liter
1 milliliter = 0.001 liter
MASS (WEIGHT)
1 kilogram = 1000 grams
1 gram = 100 centigrams
1 gram = 1000 milligrams
1 centigram = 10 milligrams
1 centigram = 0.01 gram
1 milligram = 0.001 gram

The abbreviations, or symbols, for metric measurements are also uniform, changing only to show whether you are measuring length, capacity, or mass. This is illustrated in the chart at the top of the next page.

LENGTH	
kilometer	km
meter	m
centimeter	cm
millimeter	mm
CAPACITY	
kiloliter	kL
liter	L
centiliter	cL
milliliter	mL
MASS (WEIGHT)	
kilogram	kg
gram	g
centigram	cg
milligram	mg

CONVERTING UNITS WITHIN THE METRIC SYSTEM

Using the tables above, you can see that one kilometer is 1000 times as long as a meter and that one millimeter is one-thousandth of a meter. Because the relationships between the prefixes are multiples of 10, you can change from one unit to another by multiplying by a power of ten, which can be done by moving the decimal point.

Examples

- Change 0.36 meters to centimeters.

  Think: 1 meter = 100 centimeters

  To get from 1 to 100, move the decimal point to the right 2 spaces. 0.36.

  So 0.36 meters = 36 centimeters

- Change 5000 grams to kilograms.

  Think: 1000 grams = 1 kilogram

  To get from 1000 to 1, move the decimal point to the left 3 spaces. 5.000.

  So 5000 grams = 5 kilograms

- Change 4.5 liters to milliliters.

  Think: 1 liter = 1000 milliliters

  To get from 1 to 1000, move the decimal point to the right 3 spaces.

  4.500. Notice how zeros are added so the decimal can be moved the needed number of spaces to the right.

  So 4.5 liters = 4500 milliliters

- Change 0.86 millimeters to centimeters.

  Think: 10 millimeters = 1 centimeter

  To get from 10 to 1, move the decimal point to the left 1 space.

  0.0.86 Notice that a zero is added so the decimal can be moved the needed number of spaces to the left.

  So 0.86 millimeters = 0.086 centimeters

CUSTOMARY MEASUREMENT

In the United States feet, pounds, and gallons are still common units of measure. Below is a list of common customary measurements and their equivalents.

LENGTH
1 foot = 12 inches
1 yard = 3 feet
1,760 yards = 1 mile
5,280 feet = 1 mile
CAPACITY
1 pint = 2 cups
1 quart = 2 pints
1 gallon = 4 quarts
WEIGHT
1 pound = 16 ounces
1 ton = 2,000 pounds

MEASURING TEMPERATURE

Thermometers that measure temperature are marked in degrees Celsius (°C) or in degrees Fahrenheit (°F). The Celsius scale is a metric scale. The Fahrenheit scale is nonmetric.

CELSIUS	EVENT	FAHRENHEIT
100°C	Water boils	212°F
37°C	Normal body temperature	98.6°F
0°C	Water freezes	32°F

CONVERTING BETWEEN SYSTEMS

Once in a while it may be necessary to convert from the metric system to the customary system or vice versa. You can use the charts on this page when you need to change metric measurements to customary or vice versa.

Examples

- You are in a 440-yard race. How many meters long is the race?

  To change from yards to meters, multiply by 0.91.

  $440 \times 0.91 = 400.4$

  The race is 400.4 meters long.

- A store shelf has a weight limit of 250 kilograms. What is that limit in pounds?

  To change kilograms to pounds, multiply by 2.20.

  $250 \times 2.20 = 550$

  The weight limit is 550 pounds.

- It is 10°C outside. What is the temperature in degrees Fahrenheit?

  To change from °C to °F, multiply by 9, divide by 5, then add 32.

  $10 \times 9 = 90;\ 90 \div 5 = 18;\ 18 + 32 = 50$

  The temperature is 50°F.

- It is 95°F outside. What is the temperature in degrees Celsius?

  To change from °F to °C, subtract 32, multiply by 5, then divide by 9.

  $95 - 32 = 63;\ 63 \times 5 = 315;\ 315 \div 9 = 35$

  The temperature is 35°C.

LENGTH/DISTANCE

When you know:	You can find:	If you multiply by:
inches	millimeters	25.40
inches	centimeters	2.54
feet	meters	0.305
yards	meters	0.91
miles	kilometers	1.61
millimeters	inches	0.04
centimeters	inches	0.39
meters	inches	39.37
meters	feet	3.28
meters	yards	1.09
kilometers	miles	0.62

WEIGHT/MASS

When you know:	You can find:	If you multiply by:
ounces	grams	28.35
pounds	kilograms	0.45
grams	ounces	0.035
kilograms	pounds	2.20

CAPACITY/VOLUME

When you know:	You can find:	If you multiply by:
pints	liters	0.47
quarts	liters	0.95
gallons	liters	3.78
liters	pints	2.11
liters	quarts	1.06
liters	gallons	0.26

TEMPERATURE

When you know:	You can find:	If you:
°F (degrees Fahrenheit)	°C (degrees Celsius)	subtract 32, multiply by 5, then divide by 9
°C (degrees Celsius)	°F (degrees Fahrenheit)	multiply by 9, divide by 5, then add 32

GLOSSARY

A

Ability the quality of being able to perform a mental or physical task.

Absolute advantage a situation where a country can produce a good or service at a lower cost than other countries.

Accountability taking responsibility for the results achieved.

Accounts payable record a financial document that identifies the companies from which credit purchases were made and the amount purchased, paid, and owed.

Accounts receivable record a financial document that identifies customers that made purchases using credit and the status of each account.

Adjustable-rate mortgage (ARM) a mortgage in which the interest rate is raised or lowered from time to time depending on the current interest rate being charged by lenders.

Advertising any paid form of communication through mass media directed at identified consumers to provide information and influence their actions.

Agricultural products crops and animals raised by farmers.

AI See **Artificial intelligence**

Allowance the amount of money you plan to use for a certain budget category.

All-risk policy See **Special form**

Annual percentage rate (APR) the percentage cost of credit on a yearly basis.

Annual percentage yield (APY) the percentage rate equal to the total amount of interest that a $100 deposit would earn based on a 365-day period.

Annuity an amount of money an insurance company pays (usually monthly) to a person who has previously deposited money with the company.

Antitrust laws laws that prevent monopolies and promote competition and fairness.

Application form a document used by employers that asks for information related to employment. It gives the employer standard information about each job applicant.

Application software computer programs that perform specific tasks such as word processing, database management, or accounting.

Applied research marketing research that studies existing products to develop design improvements or new product uses.

Appraiser someone trained to estimate the value of property and who can give an official report on the value.

Appreciation a general increase in the value of property that occurs over time.

APR See **Annual percentage rate**

APY See **Annual percentage yield**

Arbitration a third-party action resulting in a decision that is legally binding.

ARM See **Adjustable-rate mortgage**

Articles of incorporation a written legal document that defines ownership and operating procedures and conditions for the business.

Artificial intelligence (AI) software that enables computers to reason, learn, and make decisions using logical methods similar to the methods humans use.

Assessed value the amount that your local government determines your property to be worth for tax purposes.

Asset records financial documents that name the buildings and equipment owned by the business, their original and current value, and the amount owed if money was borrowed to purchase the assets.

Assets what a company owns; anything of value owned by a business.

Assigned risk plan a plan in which every automobile insurance company in the state is assigned a certain number of high-risk drivers based on the amount of insurance each company sells.

Authority the right to make decisions about how responsibilities should be accomplished.

Automatic bill payment a service by which a bank deducts a payment from your account and transfers the funds to the appropriate companies. This service requires a bank customer to authorize preset amounts of monthly expenses.

Automatic teller machine a computerized device that allows customers to make bank transactions including withdrawing cash.

B

Baby boomers people born between 1946 and 1964.

Balance of payments the difference between the amount of money that comes into a country and the amount that goes out of a country.

Balance of trade the difference between a country's total exports and total imports.

Balance sheet a report that lists a company's assets, liabilities, and owner's equity at a specific point in time.

Bank money order a form sold by a bank stating that money is to be paid to a specific person or business.

Bank reconciliation the document created to show how your own record of your checking account and the bank's record of your account were brought into agreement.

Bankruptcy the legal process of reducing or eliminating an amount owed.

Bank statement a report on the status of a bank account.

Base plus incentive a compensation system which combines a wage or salary with an additional amount based on the employee's performance.

Basic economic problem the mismatch of unlimited wants and needs and limited economic resources.

Basic health coverage protection provided by regular medical, hospital, and surgical insurance.

Basic product the simplest form of a product. It is not unique and is usually available from several companies.

Behavioral interviewing an interview that evaluates an applicant's on-the-job potential. Questions typically begin with "describe" or "tell me about."

Benchmarks the best practices among all competitors.

Beneficiary the person named in an insurance policy to receive the insurance benefits.

Benefits compensation in forms other than direct payment.

Blank endorsement an endorsement of a check that consists of only the endorser's name.

Blue-collar workers workers who are involved in physical work, including the operation of machinery and equipment or other production activities.

Board of directors the people who make the major policy and financial decisions for the business.

Bodily injury liability insurance that protects a driver from claims resulting from injuries or deaths for which the insured is at fault.

Bond a certificate representing a promise to pay a definite amount of money at a stated interest rate on a specified due date.

Brand a name given to a product or service to distinguish it from other similar and competitive items.

Brand name a unique identification for a company's products.

Budget detailed plans for the financial needs of individuals, families, and businesses.

Budget charge accounts credit agreements that require customers to make payments of a fixed amount over several months.

Budget deficit a financial situation that occurs when a government spends more than it takes in.

Budget surplus a financial situation that occurs when a government spends less than it takes in.

Budget variance any difference between actual spending and budgeted amounts.

Business consumers persons, companies, and organizations that buy products for the operation of a business, for incorporation into other products and services, or for resale to their customers.

Business cycle the movement of the economy from one condition to another and back again. The four phases are prosperity, recession, depression, and recovery.

Business ethics rules about how businesses and their employees ought to behave.

Business interruption insurance compensation for ongoing business expenses that occur if a business has a temporary shutdown due to a fire, flood, or other major problem.

Business plan a written description of the business idea and how it will be carried out, including all major business activities.

Buying motives the reasons consumers decide what products and services to purchase.

C

CAD See **Computer-aided design**

Cafeteria plan an employee benefit program that allocates a certain amount of money to each employee that can be spent on benefits.

CAI See **Computer-assisted instruction**

Capacity a person's ability to pay a debt when it is due.

Capital the value of the borrower's possessions, including money and the property owned.

Capital gain the result of a stock increasing in value and then being sold for more than its original cost.

Capitalism the private ownership of economic resources by individuals rather than by the government.

Capital loss the result of an investment being sold for less than its original cost.

Capital projects spending by businesses for items such as land, buildings, equipment, and new products.

Capital resources products and money used to produce goods and services.

Capital spending money spent by a business for an item that will be used over a long period.

Career a goal for work that is fulfilled through an occupation or series of occupations.

Career planning the process of studying careers, assessing yourself in terms of careers, and making decisions about a future career.

Career portfolio tangible evidence of your ability and skills.

Cash budget an estimate of the actual money received and paid out for a specific period of time.

Cash card See **Debit card**

Cash flow statement a financial statement that reports net wages and other income along with spending for a period, such as for a month.

Cashier's check a check that a bank draws on its own funds.

Cash inflows money you have available to spend as a result of working or from other income, such as interest earned on your savings.

Cash machine See **Automatic teller machine**

Cash outflows your expenditures including amounts spent for food, clothing, transportation, and other living costs.

Cash record a financial document that lists all cash received and spent by the business.

Cash value the amount of money that the insurance company will pay if the policyholder decides the insurance is no longer needed.

Cell the location where a column and row intersect.

Central processing unit (CPU) the control center of the computer.

Certificate of deposit a savings instrument that requires a minimum deposit for a specified period of time.

Certificate of deposit rate the rate for six-month time deposits at savings institutions.

Certified check a personal check for which a bank has guaranteed payment.

Channel members businesses that take part in a channel of distribution.

Channel of distribution the route a product follows and the businesses involved in moving a product from the producer to the final consumer.

Character a person's honesty and willingness to pay a debt when it is due.

Check card See **Debit card**

Check register a separate book form on which the depositor keeps a record of checking account activities.

Check stub a form attached to the check by a perforated line.

Civil case a legal action in which a plaintiff asks the court to take action against a defendant.

Claim a policyholder's request for payment for a loss that the insurance policy covers.

Class action suit a legal action by one party on behalf of a group of people who all have the same grievance.

Clearance sale sale used to clear merchandise that stores no longer wish to carry.

Clearing paying of checks among different banks in different cities.

Cloud computing using software, resources, and work files that are maintained on a common server.

Co-branded credit card a company credit card that is affiliated with a bank card company.

Code of ethics a set of rules for guiding the action of employees or members of an organization.

Coinsurance the sharing of expenses by the policyholder and the insurance company.

Collaboration software (groupware) software that provides real-time communications capabilities by voice, text, and video.

Collateral property that is offered as security for some loan agreements.

Collectibles items of personal interest to collectors that can increase in value in the future.

Collective bargaining formal negotiation between members of unions and management to resolve issues.

Collision coverage insurance that protects a car owner against financial loss resulting from a collision with another car or object.

Command economy an economy in which resources are owned and controlled by the government.

Commercial bank a bank that offers a full range of financial services.

Commercial property insurance coverage of property losses resulting from fire, storms, accidents, theft, and vandalism.

Commission the amount of money an employee is paid based on a percentage of sales for which he or she is responsible; the fee stockbrokers charge for their services.

Commodities grain, livestock, and precious metals.

Common market (economic community) a market in which members do away with duties and other trade barriers.

Common stock stock that represents general ownership in a corporation and a right to share in its profits.

Communication channel the way the information being communicated from a sender is being transmitted to the receiver.

Comparative advantage a situation in which a country specializes in the production of a good or service at which it is relatively more efficient.

Compensation the amount of money paid to an employee for work performed, including salary and wages.

Compensation and benefits the human resource activity involving planning and managing payroll, personnel records, and benefits programs.

Competition the rivalry among businesses to sell their goods and services.

Competitors businesses offering very similar products to the same customers.

Compound interest the interest computed on the amount saved plus the interest previously earned.

Comprehensive coverage insurance that protects the insured against almost all damage losses except those caused from a collision or rollover.

Comprehensive form homeowners insurance that expands special form policy to include replacement cost coverage for home contents and buildings.

Comprehensive medical policy a policy that combines the features of hospital, surgical, regular, and major medical insurance.

Computer-aided design (CAD) the use of technology to create product styles and designs.

Computer-assisted instruction (CAI) the use of computers to help people learn or improve skills at their own pace.

Computer language a system of letters, words, numbers, and symbols used to communicate with a computer.

Computer literacy the ability to use computers to process information or solve problems.

Computer network a group of computers such as those in businesses and schools that are linked together so users can share hardware, software, and data.

Computer system all functional components of a computer, including an input device, processing unit, memory and storage, and an output device.

Computer virus a program code hidden in a system that can later do damage to software or stored data.

Conditions of work clauses related to employee well-being while on the job that are often included in labor contracts and company policy manuals.

Condominium (condo) an individually owned housing unit in an apartment-like complex.

Conflict of interest a situation in which an action by a company or individual results in an unfair benefit.

Conservation saving scarce natural resources.

Consumer a person who buys and uses goods and services.

Consumer decision-making process the specific sequence of steps consumers follow to make a purchase.

Consumer movement consumers united to demand fair treatment from businesses and to fight against unfair business practices.

Contingent worker one who has no explicit or implicit contract for long-term employment.

Continuous process improvement (CPI) a way to increase the quality of work by reducing errors, inefficiencies, and waste. Rather than waiting for a problem to occur, processes are continuously reviewed with the goal of finding ways to improve them.

Continuous processing changing the form of raw materials into a specific product useable for consumption or for further manufacturing by constantly moving the materials through specially designed equipment.

Contract an agreement to exchange goods or services for something of value, usually money.

Controllable risk a risk that you can reduce or eliminate by actions you take.

Controlling determines to what extent the business is accomplishing the goals it set out to reach in the planning stage.

Convenience stores small stores that emphasize the sale of food items, an accessible location, and long operating hours.

Cooperative a business formed to market products produced by members or to purchase products needed by the members. It is owned by members, serves their needs, and is managed in their interest.

Copyright the protection of the creative work of authors, composers, and artists.

Core values the important principles that guide decisions and actions in the company.

Corporate bond rate the cost of borrowing for large U.S. corporations.

Corporate bonds bonds issued by corporations.

Corporate bylaws the operating procedures for the corporation.

Corporation a separate legal entity formed by documents filed with a state. It is owned by one or more shareholders and managed by a board of directors.

Cosigner the party responsible for payment of a note if the borrower does not pay as promised.

Cost containment keeping costs down.

Counterfeiting illegal uses of intellectual property, patents, trademarks, and copyrights.

Cover letter a letter expressing your interest in a specific job.

Credit the privilege of using someone else's money for a period of time.

Credit application a form on which you provide information needed by a lender to make a decision about granting credit.

Credit bureau a company that gathers information on credit users and sells that information in the form of credit reports to businesses offering credit.

Credit counselor a person who suggests actions to reduce spending and eliminate credit difficulties.

Credit limit a maximum amount that may be owed at one time.

Creditor one who sells on credit or makes a loan; the purchaser of a corporate or government bond.

Credit rating a person's reputation for paying bills on time.

Credit references businesses or individuals who are able and willing to provide information about your creditworthiness.

Credit report a document that shows the debts a person owes, how often credit is used, and whether he or she pays debts on time.

Credit union a user-owned, not-for-profit, cooperative financial institution.

Criminal case a legal action brought for violations of criminal laws.

Culture the accepted behaviors, customs, and values of a society.

Current assets cash and those items that can be readily converted to cash such as inventory and accounts receivable.

Current income income for current living expenses.

Current liabilities amounts owed by the business that will be paid within a year.

Current ratio current assets compared to the current liabilities.

Custom manufacturing building a specific and unique product to meet the needs of one customer.

D

Database an organized collection of information with data items related to one another in some way.

Database marketing using information about customers to increase sales.

Database software software that allows you to maintain, analyze, and combine a collection of information.

Debit card (cash card) a bank-issued card used for ATM transactions.

Debt money owed to others.

Debt collection agency a company that attempts to obtain money that is past due.

Debtor anyone who buys on credit or receives a loan.

Debt repayment plan an agreement between a creditor and a debtor to reduce payments to a more manageable level and still pay off the debt.

Debt to equity ratio the company's liabilities divided by the owners' equity.

Decoding interpreting information for understanding.

Decreasing term insurance the amount of protection gradually becomes smaller, but premiums remain the same while the insurance is in effect.

Deductible the amount the insured must pay before the insurance company pays a claim.

Deficit a financial situation in which actual spending is greater than planned spending.

Deflation a decrease in the general level of prices.

Demand the quantity of a good or service that consumers are willing and able to buy.

Demand curve the graphic view of the demand for a product or service. The demand curve for a product, for example, illustrates the relationship between the price of the product and the quantity demanded by consumers.

Department stores stores that have an extensive product line and emphasize service.

Dependent a person who must rely on another for financial support.

Deposit institutions financial institutions that accept deposits from individuals and businesses and use the money to finance their businesses.

Depreciation the decrease in value of a property as it becomes old and gradually wears out.

Depreciation records financial documents that identify the amount assets have decreased in value due to their age and use.

Depression the phase of the business cycle that is marked by a prolonged period of high unemployment, weak consumer sales, and business failures.

Direct channel of distribution a channel in which products move from the producer straight to the consumer with no other organizations participating.

Direct deposit the process by which funds are deposited electronically and available automatically for your use.

Disability income insurance insurance that replaces income that is lost when the insured cannot work because of an illness or injury.

Discharge a type of termination that ends employment due to inappropriate work behavior.

Discount broker a stockbroker who places orders and offers limited research and other services.

Discount rate the rate financial institutions are charged to borrow funds from the Federal Reserve banks.

Discount stores stores that emphasize lower prices on their products.

Discrepancies differences between actual and budgeted performance.

Displaced workers workers who are unemployed because of changing job conditions.

Display a device used by retailers to exhibit a product at the point of sale.

Distribution the locations and methods used to make a product or service available to the target market; determining the best ways for customers to locate, obtain, and use the products and services of an organization.

Diversity the comprehensive inclusion of people with differences in personal characteristics and attributes.

Dividends payments of profits in cash to stockholders.

Division of labor a strategy where workers are assigned specific elements of a manufacturing process to improve efficiency and productivity.

Domestic business the making, buying, and selling of goods and services within a country.

Down payment a payment of part of the purchase price that is made as part of a credit agreement.

Downsizing a planned reduction in the number of employees needed in a firm in order to reduce costs and make the business more efficient.

Drawee the bank or other financial institution that pays the check.

Drawer the owner of the account who signs the check.

E

Earned income money from wages, salary, commission, fees, tips, and bonuses.

Earnings report a report, usually included with the employee's paycheck, which includes information for the current pay period as well as the cumulative amounts for the year.

E-commerce conducting business transactions using the Internet or other technology.

Economic community See **Common market**

Economic decision-making the process of choosing which needs and wants will be satisfied.

Economic resources things available to be used to produce goods and services.

Economic risk a risk that can result in financial loss, including personal risk, property risk, and liability risk.

Economic system the method a country uses to answer the three economic questions.

Effective communication the exchange of information so there is common understanding by all participants.

EFT See **Electronic funds transfer**

Electronic funds transfer (EFT) the use of computers and other technology for banking activities, including the use of automatic teller machines (ATM), point-of-sale transactions, direct deposit, and automatic bill payment.

Embargo an action imposed by the government to stop the export or import of a product completely.

Emerging markets places where consumer incomes and buying power are increasing because of economic expansion.

Emotional buying motives reasons consumers decide what products and services to purchase based on feelings, beliefs, and attitudes.

Employee benefits compensation in forms other than direct payment such as vacation time, insurance coverage, and retirement programs.

Employee relations responsible for maintaining a safe, healthy, and productive work environment for all employees.

Employment interview a two-way conversation in which the interviewer learns about you and you learn about the job and the company.

Encoding preparing the information to be communicated.

Endorsement written evidence that a person received payment or transferred the right to receive payment to someone else.

Entrepreneur someone who takes a risk in starting a business to earn a profit.

Entrepreneurship the process of starting, organizing, managing, and assuming the responsibility for a business.

Equity stock ownership; the difference between the price at which you could currently sell your house and the amount owed on the mortgage.

Estate planning planning for the accumulation and management of property during one's lifetime and the distribution of one's property at death.

Ethical business practices practices that ensure the appropriate standards of conduct are observed in a company's relationships with everyone who is a part of the business or affected by the business' activities.

Ethics principles of morality or rules of conduct.

Exchange rate the value of a currency in one country compared with the value in another.

Executives top-level managers with responsibilities for the direction and success of the entire business.

Exemption a tax deduction for the taxpayer, a spouse, and each dependent.

Exit interview an interview in which your employer asks questions about your work upon your leaving the company.

Expenses costs of operating a business.

Experienced-based résumé a résumé in which experiences are listed in order of work history.

Experiment a method of marketing research which presents two carefully controlled alternatives to subjects in order to determine which is preferred or has better results.

Expert influence influence that arises when group members recognize that the leader has special expertise in the area.

Expert systems computer programs that help people solve technical problems.

Exports goods and services sold to other countries.

Express money order a form issued by various organizations including traveler's check companies, travel agencies, and many supermarkets, pharmacies, and convenience stores.

Express warranty a warranty that is made orally or in writing and promises a specific quality of performance.

External communication communication that occurs between those inside the organization and outsiders such as customers, suppliers, and other businesses.

External data sources input provided to the management information system from outside an organization, such as financial institutions, government agencies, and customers.

Extraction and cultivation a form of production in which products are obtained from nature or grown using natural resources.

Extractors businesses that take resources from nature for direct consumption or for use in developing other products.

F

Face value the amount of insurance coverage that was originally purchased and that will be paid upon the death of the insured.

Factors of production economic resources, including natural resources, human resources, and capital resources.

Factory outlets stores that sell merchandise that arrives directly from the factory.

Family leave policy a policy that allows employees to take a leave of absence for the birth or adoption of a child, to care for a sick family member, or for other personal emergencies.

Farmers people who cultivate land and use other natural resources to grow crops and raise livestock for consumption.

Federal Deposit Insurance Corporation (FDIC) the federal agency that helps to regulate banks and other financial institutions.

Federal Reserve System (Fed) a system set up by the federal government to supervise and regulate member banks and to help banks serve the public efficiently. All national banks are required to join the Federal Reserve System, and state banks may join.

Feedback a response to the sender from the receiver.

Final consumers persons who buy products and services mostly for their own use.

Finance charge the total dollar cost of credit including interest and all other charges.

Financial analysis budgeting for marketing activities, obtaining the necessary funds needed for operations, and providing financial assistance to customers so they can purchase the business's products and services.

Financial performance ratios comparisons of a company's financial elements that indicate how well the business is performing.

Financial plan a report that summarizes your current financial condition, acknowledges your financial needs, and sets a direction for your future financial activities.

Financial records financial documents that are used to record and analyze the financial performance of a business.

Financial responsibility law a law that protects the public from financial loss caused by drivers.

Financial statements reports that sum up the financial performance of a business.

Fixed expenses costs that occur on a regular basis and are for the same amount each time.

Fixed-rate mortgage interest rates on mortgages that are set for the term of the loan.

Flexplace a program that allows some employees to complete part or all of their work away from the business site.

Flextime a program that allows employees some choice in how their work days and work hours are arranged.

Focus group a marketing research study that gathers the ideas, experiences, and opinions from a small number of consumers who take part in a group discussion.

Foreign debt the amount a country owes to other countries.

Foreign exchange market banks that buy and sell different currencies.

Foreign trade See **International business**

Formal communications communication methods that have been established and approved by the organization.

Formal influence power based on a leader's position within the formal structure.

Franchise a written contract granting permission to operate a business to sell products and services in a set way.

Franchisee the company purchasing the rights to run the business.

Franchiser the company that owns the product or service and grants the rights to another business.

Fraud deception of consumers by providing false information in an effort to make a sale.

Freedom of choice the freedom to make decisions independently while accepting the consequences of those decisions.

Free-trade agreement an agreement between member countries to remove duties and trade barriers on products traded among them.

Free-trade zone a selected area where products can be imported duty-free and then stored, assembled, and/or used in manufacturing.

Full endorsement (special endorsement) an endorsement that allows you to transfer a check to another person.

Full-service broker a broker who provides information about securities you may want to buy. They work for brokerage houses with large research staffs.

Full-time employee one who regularly works a schedule of 30 hours or more a week.

Functional organizational structure work is arranged within main business functions such as production, operations, marketing, and human resources.

Futures contract agreement to buy or sell an amount of a commodity at a specified price in the future; contract involving the buying and selling of currencies and financial instruments.

G

GDP See **Gross domestic product**

GDP per capita the output per person, calculated by dividing gross domestic product (GDP) by the total production.

Generic products unbranded items at reduced prices because they do not require advertising and fancy packaging.

Glass ceiling an artificial limit placed on minority groups moving into positions of authority and decision making.

Global strategy a strategy that uses the same product and marketing strategy worldwide.

Goal a precise statement of results the business expects to achieve.

Goods things you can see and touch; they are products you can purchase to meet your wants and needs.

Goods-producing industries businesses that produce or manufacture products used by other businesses or purchased by final consumers.

Green management facilities management using the practice of protecting the environment through conservation of natural resources, wise energy use, and reduction of emissions, waste, and pollution.

Gross domestic product (GDP) the total value of all final goods and services produced in a country during one year.

Gross margin the difference between the selling price and the product costs.

Group insurance health insurance coverage offered to a large number of employees and their family members.

Group life insurance an insurance policy that covers a group of people. The group acts as single unit in buying the insurance.

Guarantee a promise by the manufacturer or dealer, usually in writing, that a product is of a certain quality.

H

Hardware the physical elements of a computer system.

Health insurance protection against the high costs of individual health care. It covers routine costs of medical care and may also cover costs of hospitalization or other needed medical treatments.

Health maintenance organization (HMO) a managed care plan whose members are entitled to a wide range of prepaid healthcare services, including hospitalization.

Heterogeneous characterized by the differences in the type and quality of service provided.

HMO See **Health maintenance organization**

Homeowners policy a package-type insurance policy designed to insure homes and property.

Horizontal communications communications that move across the organization at the same level—employee to employee or manager to manager.

Hospital insurance insurance that usually pays most or all hospital charges if an illness or injury requires the insured to be hospitalized.

Host country the country in which the multinational company (MNC) places business activities.

Human relations the way people get along with each other.

Human resources people producing goods and services; people who work for a business.

I

I bond bond that pays an interest rate that is lower than the rate of other savings bonds, but it is a variable rate that increases with inflation.

Identity influence influence that stems from the personal trust and respect members have for the leader.

Identity theft stealing information about a person from online sources to obtain money.

Implementing a manager's effort to direct and lead people to accomplish the planned work of the organization.

Implied warranty a guarantee imposed by law and understood to apply even though it has not been written or stated.

Imports goods and services bought from other countries.

Improvement a designed change that increases the usefulness of a product, service, or process.

Impulse buying buying quickly without much thought.

Incentive systems compensation systems connected to the quality or quantity of an employee's performance.

Income statement a report of revenue, expenses, and net income or loss from operations for a specific period.

Income taxes taxes levied on the income of individuals.

Indirect channel of distribution a channel in which products move from the producer to the consumer through one or more other businesses.

Individual retirement account (IRA) a tax-sheltered retirement plan in which people can annually invest earnings up to a certain amount.

Inflation an increase in the general level of prices.

Influence power enabling a person to affect the actions of others.

Informal communications common but unofficial ways that information moves in an organization.

Informal influence power resulting from the personal characteristics of a leader rather than the formal structure of an organization.

Informational interview a planned discussion with a worker who is willing to help you find out about the work that person does, the preparation needed for that career, and the person's feelings about the career.

Information management using technology to access and exchange information to complete the work of an organization.

Infrastructure a factor that supports international trade in industrialized countries, including a nation's transportation, communication, and utility systems.

Innovation an invention or creation that is brand new.

Inseparable something that is consumed at the same time it is produced.

Installment the specified amount a borrower agrees to repay on a loan for a given interval of time.

Installment loan a loan in which you agree to make monthly payments in specific amounts over a period of time.

Installment sales credit a type of credit contract issued by the seller that requires periodic payments at specified times. The seller adds finance charges to the cost of the items purchased.

Insurable interest a financial benefit from an insured person's continued life.

Insurable risk when a large number of people face a given risk and the cost of the possible losses can be predicted.

Insurance a form of risk protection that exchanges the uncertainty of a possible large financial loss for a certain smaller payment.

Insurance agent an agent who represents the insurance company and sells insurance policies to individuals and businesses.

Insurance policy a policy stating the conditions to which the insurance company and the policyholder have agreed.

Insured the person or business for which the insurer assumes the risk.

Insurer a company that agrees to take on certain economic risks and to pay for losses if they occur.

Intangible something that has no physical form.

Intellectual property technical knowledge or creative work. It includes software, clothing designs, music, books, and movies.

Interest the money you receive for letting others use your money; the money you pay for using someone else's money.

Interest rates the cost of using someone else's money.

Interests activities that give you satisfaction and that can provide a basis for your employment goals and possible career paths.

Intermediaries businesses involved in selling the goods and services of producers to consumers and other businesses.

Intermittent processing using short production runs to produce a precise amount of a variation of a product.

Internal communications communications that occur between managers, employees, and work groups.

Internal data sources input provided to the management information system from within the organization, such as accounting records, inventory information, and company sales figures.

International business business activities needed for creating, shipping, and selling goods and services across national borders.

Internship work experience in an organization while learning about a career field.

Interstate commerce business dealings involving companies in more than one state.

Intranet a local computer network based on the same communication standards as the Internet. It looks like and functions just like a typical website, but it is private and only accessible to authorized users.

Intrastate commerce business dealings involving companies that do business in only one state.

Inventory a detailed account of a company's materials, supplies, and finished products.

Inventory management maintains the supply of all resources needed for production and the products produced.

Inventory records financial documents that identify the type and number of products on hand for sale.

Investing using your savings to earn more money.

Investment income earnings from dividends, interest, and rent.

IRA See **Individual retirement account**

J

Job analysis a specific study of a job to identify in detail the job duties and skill requirements.

Job shadow a person who spends time with a worker for a day or a week to learn about that person's occupation.

Job sharing an arrangement in which one job is offered to two people. Each person works a part-time schedule. They share the work space and duties of the job.

Joint account when two or more people have an account together.

Joint venture a unique business organized by two or more other businesses to operate for a limited time and for a specific project. It is a type of partnership.

Just-in-time a logistics process in which goods arrive when needed for production, use, or sale rather than sitting in storage.

L

Labor force all people above age 16 who are actively working or seeking work.

Labor union an organized group of employees who negotiate with employers about issues, such as wages and working conditions.

Layoff a type of termination which is a temporary or permanent reduction in the number of employees due to changing business conditions.

Leadership the ability to motivate individuals and groups to accomplish important goals.

Level term insurance the amount of protection and the premiums remain the same while the insurance is in effect.

Liabilities what a company owes.

Liability insurance protection against losses from injury to people or property resulting from the products, services, or actions of a business.

Liability risk a risk that relates to harm or injury to other people or their property because of your actions.

Licensing selling the right to use some intangible property (production process, trademark, or brand name) for a fee or royalty.

Life cycle predictable pattern of life stages that are distinguished by unique characteristics, requirements, and expectations.

Life insurance insurance that pays the amount of the insurance policy upon the death of the insured. The payment is made to people named in the policy known as beneficiaries.

Limited liability company (LLC) form of business ownership that provides liability protection for owners. It has a simpler set of organizing and operating requirements than a corporation. No articles of incorporation or bylaws are needed. A simple document much like a partnership agreement must be developed.

Limited liability partnership (LLP) a partnership that identifies some investors who cannot lose more than the amount of their investment, but they are not allowed to participate in the day-to-day management of the business.

Limited-payment policies a whole life insurance policy that is designated by the number of years the policyholder agrees to pay on it, such as a 20-payment life policy.

Liquidity the ease with which an investment can be changed into cash without losing its value.

Loan credit borrowed money for special use. It usually involves a written contract.

Locational unemployment unemployment that occurs when jobs are available in one place but go unfilled because those who are qualified to fill those jobs live elsewhere and are not willing to relocate.

Logistics managing the acquisition, movement, and storage of supplies, materials, and finished products in a business.

Long-term assets (fixed assets) the assets with a lifespan of more than a year, such as land, buildings, equipment, and expensive technology.

Long-term care insurance insurance that provides long-term care including daily assistance needed because of a long-term illness or disability.

Long-term financing money needed for the main resources of a business (such as land, buildings, and equipment) that will last for many years.

Long-term liabilities business debts that will continue for longer than a year.

M

Mail order catalogs catalogs whereby customers can shop and send in their orders by mail and by telephone.

Major medical insurance protection against the high costs of serious illness or injuries. It complements other forms of medical insurance.

Management the process of accomplishing the goals of an organization through the effective use of people and other resources.

Management information system (MIS) a coordinated system of processing and reporting information in an organization.

Management style the way a manager treats and involves employees.

Manufacturers businesses that get supplies from other producers and convert them into products. They sell their products to consumers and other businesses.

Manufacturing combining raw materials and processed goods into finished products.

Markdown a reduction from the original selling price.

Market economy an economy in which the resources are owned and controlled by the people of the country.

Marketing The activity, set of institutions, and processes for creating, communicating, delivering, and exchanging offerings that have value for customers, clients, partners, and society at large.

Marketing-information management obtaining, managing, and using market information to improve business decision-making and the performance of marketing activities.

Marketing mix the blending of four marketing elements—products, distribution, price, and promotion.

Marketing orientation an approach that considers the needs of customers when developing a marketing mix.

Marketing research finding solutions to problems through carefully designed studies involving customers.

Marketing strategy a company's plan that identifies how it will use marketing to achieve its goals.

Marketplace anywhere that goods and services are exchanged.

Market price the point where supply and demand are equal.

Market value the price at which a share of stock can be bought and sold in the stock market.

Markup the amount added to the cost of a product to set the selling price.

Mass production an assembly process that makes a large number of identical products using a continuous efficient procedure.

Mass promotion communication to many people at the same time with a common message.

Materials processing changing the form of raw materials so they can be consumed or used to make other products.

Matrix organizational structure work is structured around specific projects, products, or consumers.

Maturity date the date on which a loan must be repaid.

Maturity value (face value) the amount being borrowed by the corporation issuing the bond.

Mediation use of a third party who tries to resolve the complaint between the consumer and the business.

Medicaid a form of medical aid to low-income individuals and families administered by state governments. The federal government shares the cost of providing health benefits to eligible individuals and families.

Medical payments coverage insurance that covers policyholders and family members if they are injured while riding in their car or another car.

Medicare a national health insurance program for people aged 65 and older and some disabled people.

Memory a component of a computer system that stores a computer program.

Mentor an experienced employee who serves as counselor to a person with less experience.

Merchandising a set of promotional activities designed to obtain sales in the retail setting.

Middle managers specialists with responsibilities for specific parts of a company's operations.

MIS See **Management information system**

Mission statement short, specific written statement of the reason a business exists and what it wants to achieve.

Mixed economy an economy that combines elements of the command and market economies.

Mixed management the combined use of tactical and strategic management styles.

MNC See **Multinational company**

Mobility the willingness and ability of a person to move to where jobs are located.

Money management the day-to-day financial activities associated with using limited income to satisfy your unlimited needs and wants.

Money market account an account that pays a variable interest rate based on various government and corporate securities.

Money order a form of payment that orders the issuing agency to pay the amount printed on the form to another party.

Monopoly when a business has control of the market for a product or service.

Mortgage a legal document giving the lender a claim against the property if the principal, interest, or both are not paid as agreed.

Mortgage rate the amount individuals pay to borrow for the purchase of a home.

Multinational company (MNC) an organization that does business in several countries. It usually consists of a home country and divisions or separate companies in one or more host countries.

Multinational strategy a strategy that treats each country market differently. Firms develop products and marketing strategies that adapt to the customs, tastes, and buying habits of a distinct national market.

Municipal bonds bonds issued by local and state governments.

Mutual fund an investment fund set up and managed by companies that receive money from many investors.

Mutual savings bank a savings bank that is owned by, and operated for the benefit of, its depositors.

N

National brands brands that are advertised all over the country.

National debt the total amount owed by the federal government.

Natural resources raw materials supplied by nature.

Near-field communications a system that stores credit card and bank account information for consumer use.

Needs things that are required in order to live.

Negative or unfavorable balance of payments the result of a country sending more money out than it brings in.

Net asset value (NAV) the market share price of a mutual fund based on the total current worth of all stocks and bonds owned by the investment company.

Net income the result of revenue being greater than expenses.

Net income ratio the total sales compared to the net income for a period such as six months or a year.

Net loss the result of expenses being greater than income.

Net pay the amount of a paycheck after taxes and other payroll deductions; take-home pay.

Networking the process of talking to other people about their jobs.

Net worth the difference between a person's assets and liabilities.

No-fault insurance insurance allowing people who are injured in an automobile accident to collect for their financial losses from their own insurance companies no matter who is at fault. Those losses include their medical bills, loss of wages, and other related expenses.

Non-deposit institutions a category of financial institutions that does not take or hold deposits. They earn their money selling specific services or policies.

Non-economic risks may result in inconvenience or discomfort but do not have a financial impact.

Nonprofit corporation a group of people who join to do some activity that benefits the public.

Nonrenewable resource a natural resource that cannot be replaced when used up.

O

Observation a method of marketing research that collects information by recording the actions of consumers rather than asking them questions.

Occupation a task or series of tasks that is performed to provide a good or service.

Operating budget describes the financial plan for ongoing operations of the business for a specific period of time.

Operating expenses all of the expenses of operating the business that are associated with the product.

Operating system software a computer program that translates commands and allows application programs to interact with the computer's hardware.

Operational plan identifies how work will be done, who will do it, and what resources will be needed.

Opportunity cost the value of the next-best alternative that you were not able to choose.

Options choices of product features.

Oral communications communications that are spoken.

Ordinary life policy a type of whole life insurance in which premiums remain the same each year as long as the policyholder lives.

Organizational culture the environment in which people work, made up of the atmosphere, behaviors, beliefs, and relationships.

Organization chart a diagram that shows the structure of an organization, classifications of work and jobs, and the relationships among those classifications.

Organizing the function of a manager involving identifying and arranging the work and resources needed to achieve the goals that have been set.

Output a component of a computer system that presents data in a form that can be retrieved later or may be communicated immediately.

Outsourcing removing work from one company and sending it to another company that can complete it at a lower cost.

Outstanding checks checks that have not been deducted from the bank statement balance.

Over-the-counter (OTC) market a network where securities transactions occur using telephones and computers rather than on an exchange.

Owner's equity the value of the business after liabilities are subtracted from assets; the value of the owner's investment in the business.

P

Packaging protection and security for the product before it is used.

Partnership a business owned and controlled by two or more people who have entered into a written agreement.

Partnership agreement a written agreement among all owners detailing the rules and procedures that guide ownership and operations.

Part-time employee one who works a schedule with either fewer hours each day or fewer than 30 hours each week.

Patent the exclusive right of an inventor to make, sell, and use a product or process.

Payee the person to whom the check is written.

Payroll the financial record of employee compensation, deductions, and net pay.

Payroll records documentation used to process earnings payments and record each employee's pay history.

Payroll system maintains information on each employee in order to calculate the company's payroll and to make the necessary payments to each employee.

Payroll taxes required federal and state payments for each employee, consisting of income taxes, Social Security, Medicare, and unemployment taxes.

Pension a series of regular payments made to a retired worker under an organized plan.

Performance management evaluating the work of employees and improving performance through training and development.

Perils the causes of loss, such as fire, wind, or theft.

Perishable the availability of a service to match the demand for that service at a specific time.

Permanent employee one to whom the company makes a long-term commitment. It is expected that the employee will work for the business as long as the business is profitable and the employee's performance is satisfactory.

Permanent life insurance life insurance that has cash value and an investment feature.

Personal assets items of value.

Personal data sheet a summary of your important job-related information.

Personal income salaries and wages as well as investment income and government payments to individuals.

Personalized promotion communication directly with each customer using information tailored to that person.

Personal liability coverage insurance that covers claims for injuries to people or damage to property caused by you or your family.

Personal property property not attached to the land, such as furniture or clothing.

Personal risk a risk that can result in personal losses such as loss of health or personal well-being.

Personal selling direct, individualized communication with prospective customers to assess their needs and assist them in satisfying those needs with appropriate products and services.

Personal time a few hours each month that can be scheduled for non-job activities.

Piece rate a pay-for-performance plan in which an employee receives a specific amount for each unit of work produced.

Piracy stealing or illegally copying software packages or information.

Planning the function of a manager that involves analyzing information, setting goals, and making decisions about what needs to be done.

Planning and staffing activities activities directed at identifying and filling all of the jobs in the company with qualified people.

Point-of-sale transaction a transaction in which a merchant accepts debit cards to pay for purchases.

Policies guidelines used in making consistent decisions.

Policyholder the person or company buying the policy.

Pollution occurs when the environment is tainted with the by-products of human actions.

Position influence the ability to get others to accomplish tasks because of the position the leader holds.

Positive or favorable balance of payments occurs when a nation receives more money in a year than it pays out.

Postal money order a form of payment purchased from the U.S. Post Office that can be sent safely through the mail.

Postdated check a check that is dated later than the date on which it is written.

Preferred provider organization (PPO) a managed care plan that involves several healthcare providers, such as a group of physicians, a clinic, or a hospital.

Preferred stock stock that has priority over common stock in the payment of dividends.

Premium the amount a policyholder must pay for insurance coverage.

Presentation software a program that allows a speaker to show text, data, photos, and other visuals. The images may be accompanied by sound effects, music, or other audio.

Price money customer must pay for a product or service.

Price-earnings (P/E) ratio the relationship between a stock's selling price and its earnings per share.

Price index a number that compares prices in one year with some earlier base year.

Pricing setting and communicating the value of products and services.

Primary research studies carried out to gather new information specifically directed at a current problem.

Prime rate the rate banks make available to their best business customers, such as large corporations.

Procedure a list of steps to be followed for performing a particular work activity; a description of the way work is to be done.

Processed goods products that have been changed in form to increase their value and usefulness.

Processing changing and improving the form of another product.

Producers individuals and organizations that determine what products and services will be available for sale.

Product everything a business offers to satisfy a customer's needs.

Product and service management designing, developing, maintaining, improving, and acquiring products and services that meet consumer needs.

Product costs costs to the manufacturer of producing the product or the price paid by other businesses to buy the product.

Product features additions and improvements to the basic product.

Production process the activities, equipment, and resources needed to manufacture a product.

Productivity the production output in relation to a unit of input, such as a worker.

Profit the amount of money available to the business after all costs and expenses have been paid.

Program a series of detailed, step-by-step instructions that tell the computer what functions to complete.

Promissory note a written promise to repay based on a debtor's excellent credit history.

Promotion any form of communication used to inform, persuade, or remind; communicating information about products and services to potential customers; the advancement of an employee to a position with greater responsibility.

Promotional sales sales used to promote the selling of regular merchandise with short-term price reductions.

Property damage liability insurance that protects a driver against claims if the insured's car damages someone else's property and the insured is at fault.

Property insurance insurance that protects you from the financial loss you would incur if some of your property were lost or destroyed due to fire, theft, vandalism, flood, or other hazard.

Property rights the exclusive rights to possess and use property and its profits.

Property risk a risk that can lead to loss of personal or business property including money, vehicles, and buildings.

Property tax a major source of revenue for local governments based on the value of land and buildings.

Proprietorship a business owned and run by just one person.

Prosperity the peak of the business cycle, it is a period in which most people who want to work are working, businesses produce goods and services in record numbers, wages are good, and the rate of gross domestic product (GDP) growth increases.

Publicity non-paid promotional communication presented by the media rather than by the business or organization that is being promoted.

Public relations an ongoing program of non-paid and paid communications intended to favorably influence public opinion about an organization, marketing effort, idea, or issue.

Public utility an organization that supplies a service or product vital to all people including companies that provide local telephone service, water, and electricity.

Pure research research done without a specific product in mind with the goal of discovering new solutions to problems.

Pure risk a risk that presents the chance of loss but no opportunity for gain.

Q

Qualifications-based résumé a résumé in which your abilities and experiences related to the job for which you are applying are highlighted.

Quota a government-set limit on the quantity of a product that may be imported or exported within a given period.

R

Rational buying motives reasons consumers decide what products and services to purchase based on facts and logic.

Real estate land and anything that is attached to it.

Real property property permanently attached to land, such as a house or garage.

Receiver a person or organization that is being communicated to by another person or organization.

Recession the phase of the business cycle in which demand begins to decrease, businesses lower production, unemployment begins to rise, and gross domestic product (GDP) growth slows for two or more quarters of the calendar year.

Records of account financial documents that identify all purchases and sales made using credit.

Recovery the phase in the business cycle in which unemployment begins to decrease, demand for goods and services increases, and gross domestic product (GDP) begins to rise again.

References people who can give a report about your character, education, and work habits. These individuals may be teachers, previous employers, supervisors, or coworkers.

Refund anticipation checks business-issued checks offered to taxpayers who want their tax refunds quickly. The business typically charges a flat fee and may load the refund onto a debit card that charges other fees.

Refund anticipation loans short-term loans based on the expected amount of a tax refund. They were largely outlawed in 2013.

Regular medical insurance insurance that covers fees for nonsurgical care given in the doctor's office, the patient's home, or a hospital. The policy states the amount payable for each visit or call. It also lists the maximum number of visits covered.

Renewable term insurance an insurance policy that allows the policyholder to continue term insurance for one or more terms without taking another physical examination.

Renters policy a property and liability insurance policy suitable for renters. It covers household goods and personal belongings and protects against the same kinds of perils covered by homeowners policies.

Replacement insurance insurance in which the insurance company actually replaces an item that has been destroyed. No depreciation is deducted.

Responsibility the obligation to complete specific work.

Restrictive endorsement an endorsement that limits the use of the check to the purpose given in the endorsement.

Résumé a tool that provides information about you to a potential employer.

Retailers the final business organizations in an indirect channel of distribution for consumer products.

Retail sales the sales of durable and nondurable goods bought by consumers.

Return on equity ratio the net profit of the business compared to the amount of owners' equity.

Revenue all income that a business receives over a period of time; government income.

Revolving account allows account holder to charge purchases at any time, but only part of the debt must be paid each month.

Reward influence influence that results from a leader's ability to give or withhold rewards.

Risk the possibility of incurring a loss.

Robotics mechanical devices programmed to do routine tasks, such as those in many factories.

S

Safe deposit box a container for storage of valuables offered by banks.

Salary and wages direct payment of money to an employee for work completed.

Sales credit involves the use of charge accounts and credit cards by consumers purchasing goods and services.

Sales promotion activities and materials designed to reinforce a company's brand and image. It is also a direct incentive to take an action likely to immediately increase sales of a product or service.

Sales tax a state or local tax on goods and services that is collected by the seller.

Saving the storage of money for future use.

Savings rate the percentage of total income that is saved.

SBA See **Small Business Administration**

Scarcity not having enough resources to satisfy every need.

Schedule a time plan for completing activities. It matches people with resources to make sure activities are finished on time.

S corporation a corporate form of business that offers the limited liability of a corporation.

Secondary research analyzing existing information gathered for another purpose but used to solve a current problem.

Secured loan a loan in which you must put up property or collateral as security for repayment.

Selling communicating directly with potential customers to determine and satisfy their needs.

Selling price the price paid by the customer for the product.

Sender a person or organization that has information to communicate to another person or organization.

Service business a business that carries out activities that are consumed by its customers.

Service charge the fee a bank charges for handling a checking account.

Service fees charges for the time and money it takes a creditor to investigate your credit history, process your loan or charge account application, and keep records of your payments and balances.

Service-providing industries businesses that perform services that satisfy the needs of other businesses and consumers.

Services activities provided for the satisfaction of others that are consumed at the same time they are produced.

Share draft account a checking account at a credit union.

Shareholders members of credit unions.

Short-term financing the money needed to pay for the current operating activities of a business.

Signature card a document used to verify your signature.

Simple interest the interest on single-payment loans.

Single-payment loan a loan in which you do not pay anything until the end of the loan period, possibly 60 or 90 days. At that time, you pay the full amount you borrowed plus the finance charge.

Small business an independent business with fewer than 500 employees.

Small Business Administration (SBA) a government agency that helps small business owners develop business plans and obtain financing and other support for their companies.

Small claims court a court system in every state that exists to resolve cases involving small amounts.

Smart cards plastic cards with silicon chips that are used to store information. The chip within the card stores such data as a cardholder's current account balance, credit history, or medical information.

Social responsibility the duty of a business to contribute to the well-being of a community.

Software the instructions that run the computer system.

Span of control the number of employees who are assigned to a particular work task and manager.

Special checking account checking accounts for people who only write a few checks each month. Banks charge customers about 10 to 20 cents for each check written.

Special form a form of a homeowners policy that insures property against all perils except earthquakes, flood, war, nuclear accidents, and certain others.

Specialization of labor the training of workers to do a specific task.

Specialty stores stores that have a special line of products for sale.

Specialty superstores stores that offer low prices and a wide variety of a limited product line.

Speculative risk the chance either to gain or to lose.

Spreadsheet software a program that formats data in columns and rows in order to do calculations.

Staffing the function of a manager including all of the activities involved in obtaining, preparing, and compensating the employees of a business.

Standard a specific measurement against which an activity or result is judged.

Start-up budget a budget that plans income and expenses from the beginning of a new business or a major business expansion until it becomes profitable.

Start-up financing the amount of money needed to open the business.

Statement of account a record of the transactions completed during the billing period.

Stock ownership in a corporation.

Stockbroker a licensed specialist in the buying and selling of stocks and bonds.

Stock exchange a business organization that accommodates the buying and selling of securities.

Stockholder someone who owns stock in a corporation.

Stock index a measurement of investment values.

Stop payment order a written notice that tells the bank not to pay a certain check.

Store brands (private label brands) brands owned by stores. For example, Craftsman is one of the brand names on tools sold by Sears.

Straight salary a specific amount of money paid to an employee for each week or month worked.

Strategic management a style in which managers are less directive and involve employees in decision making.

Substitute check a digital reproduction of the original paper check.

Supermarket in food retailing, it is the large, full-service store that carries name brands.

Superstores discount stores that have expanded to include a wide variety of food products. They may also include other retail services such as a bakery, restaurant, pharmacy, video rentals, and banking.

Supervisors the first level of management in a business, responsible for the work of a group of employees and some non-management duties.

Supply the quantity of a good or service that businesses are willing and able to provide.

Supply chain all businesses involved with a product from the time raw materials are obtained until the finished product is sold.

Supply chain management See **Logistics**

Supply chain management software software that allows cooperating companies to share ordering, production, and shipping information.

Supply curve the graphic view of the supply for a product or service. The supply curve for a product, for example, illustrates the relationship between the price of the product and the quantity businesses will supply.

Surgical insurance insurance that covers all or part of the surgeon's fees for an operation.

Surplus a financial situation in which actual spending is less than the budgeted amount.

Surveys a marketing research study that gathers information from people using a carefully planned set of questions.

T

Tactical management a style in which the manager is directive and controlling.

Take-home pay See **Net pay**

Talent a natural, inborn aptitude to do certain things.

Targeted application letter a letter that provides a quick summary of your ability to meet the needs of an organization. It usually includes a list of major skills and competencies.

Target market a specific group of customers that have similar wants and needs.

Tariff a tax that a government places on certain imported products.

Tax a charge imposed by a government to finance public services.

Taxable income the amount on which taxes are calculated.

Tax credit an amount subtracted directly from taxes owed.

Tax deduction an amount that reduces taxable income.

Tax-deferred income income will be taxed at a later date.

Tax-exempt earnings earnings on which the recipient is not required to pay taxes.

Tax-exempt income income not subject to tax. Interest earned on most state and city bonds, for example, is exempt from federal income tax.

Tax records financial documents that show all taxes collected, owed, and paid.

T-bill rate the yield on short-term (13-week) U.S. government debt obligations.

T-bills See **Treasury bills**

T-bonds See **Treasury bonds**

Technology the use of automatic machines, electronic equipment, and integrated computer systems to help increase the efficiency of producing goods and services.

Telecommuting allows employees who primarily use personal computers and other technology to work from home. They communicate with managers, coworkers, and customers using the Internet, telephone, and fax machines.

Telemedicine the use of technology to provide remote medical care.

Temporary employee one hired for a specific time or to complete a specific assignment.

Tentative career decision a decision that is subject to change as new information is received.

Termination the end of an employment relationship between a company and an employee.

Term life insurance insurance that provides financial protection from losses resulting from a death during a definite period or term.

Time wage a specific amount of money paid to an employee for each hour worked.

Title ownership of goods.

T-notes See **Treasury notes**

Trade barriers restrictions to free trade.

Trade credit occurs when a company receives goods from a supplier and pays for them later.

Trade deficit a situation in which a country imports (buys) more than it exports (sells).

Trademark a distinctive name, symbol, word, picture, or combination of these that a company uses to identify products or services.

Trade-off what you make when you give something up to have something else.

Trade surplus a situation in which a country exports (sells) more than it imports (buys).

Traditional economy an economy in which goods and services are produced the way they have always been produced. It is used in countries that are less developed and are not yet participating in the global economy.

Transfer the assignment of an employee to another job in the company with a similar level of responsibility.

Traveler's checks special forms designed for making payments when away from home.

Treasury bills (T-bills) bills that involve short-term borrowing with maturities from 91 days to one year.

Treasury bond rate the yield on long-term (20-year) U.S. government debt obligations.

Treasury bonds (T-bonds) bonds that involve long-term borrowing, with maturities ranging from 10 to 30 years.

Treasury notes (T-notes) notes that involve borrowing with maturities from 1 to 10 years.

U

Uncollectible accounts bad debts or doubtful accounts.

Uncontrollable risk a risk that cannot be reduced by your actions.

Under-insured motorist coverage insurance that protects you from losses caused by another driver whose coverage is insufficient.

Unemployment insurance insurance to reduce financial hardship of unemployment.

Unemployment rate the portion of people in the labor force who are not working.

Uninsurable risk when a risk is not common or if it is impossible to predict the amount of loss that could be suffered.

Uninsured motorist coverage protection against hit-and-run drivers or drivers without insurance money to pay claims.

Unit price a price per unit of measure.

Unity of command a clear reporting relationship for all staff of a business.

Universal life insurance insurance that provides both insurance protection and a substantial savings plan.

Upkeep maintaining your property in good condition.

V

Values things that are important to you.

Variable expenses living costs that differ each time and may not be as easy to estimate.

Variable life insurance an insurance plan that resembles an investment portfolio. It lets the policyholder choose among a broad range of investments.

Vehicle insurance coverage of automobiles, trucks, and other business vehicles.

Vending machines non-store shopping where customers can shop for items by putting money into machines.

Venture capital money provided by large investors to finance new products and new businesses that have a good chance to be very profitable.

Vertical communications communications that move up or down in an organization between management and employees.

Video conferencing allows people in different geographic locations to meet "face-to-face" by satellite.

Visual merchandising visual signals used to communicate information in a retail setting.

W

Wants things that add comfort and pleasure to your life.

Warehouse club a no-frills outlet focusing on the sale of large quantities at reasonable prices.

White-collar crime illegal acts carried out by office or professional workers while at work.

White-collar worker one whose work is more mental than physical and involves the handling and processing of information.

Whole life insurance permanent insurance that extends over the lifetime, or whole life, of the insured.

Wholesalers intermediaries between manufacturers and retailers.

Work environment the physical conditions and the psychological atmosphere in which employees work.

Workers' compensation an insurance plan that provides medical and survivor benefits for people injured, disabled, or killed on the job.

Workforce all of the people 16 years or older who are employed or who are looking for a job.

World trade See **International business**

Written communication communication that includes notes, letters, reports, and e-mail messages.

Y

Yield the percentage of money earned on savings or investment over a year.

INDEX

A

B

D

E

G

M

Q

R

S

T

U

V

W